D1561191

Microeconomic Theories of Imperfect Competition

The International Library of Critical Writings in Economics

Series Editor: Mark Blaug

Professor Emeritus, University of London
Professor Emeritus, University of Buckingham
Visting Professor, University of Exeter

This series is an essential reference source for students, researchers and lecturers in economics. It presents by theme a selection of the most important articles across the entire spectrum of economics. Each volume has been prepared by a leading specialist who has written an authoritative introduction to the literature included.

A full list of published and future titles in this series is printed at the end of this volume.

For a list of all Edward Elgar published titles visit our site on the World Wide Web at
http://www.e-elgar.co.uk

Microeconomic Theories of Imperfect Competition
Old Problems and New Perspectives

Edited by

Jean J. Gabszewicz

Professor of Economics,
CORE,
Université Catholique de Louvain,
Belgium

and

Jacques-François Thisse

Professor of Economics,
CORE,
Université Catholique de Louvain,
Belgium

THE INTERNATIONAL LIBRARY OF CRITICAL WRITINGS IN ECONOMICS

An Elgar Reference Collection
Cheltenham, UK • Northampton, MA, USA

Published by
Edward Elgar Publishing Ltd
Glensanda House
Montpellier Parade
Cheltenham
Glos GL50 1UA
UK

Edward Elgar Publishing, Inc.
6 Market Street
Northampton
Massachusetts 01060
USA

A catalogue record for this book is available from the British Library.

Library of Congress Cataloging in Publication Data

Microeconomic theories of imperfect competition—old problems and new
   perspectives / edited by Jean J. Gabszewicz and Jacques-François Thisse.
      (The international library of critical writings in economics : 102)
      A collection of journal articles published by various scholars
   between 1925–1988.
      Includes bibliographical references.
      1. Competition, Imperfect. 2. Microeconomics. I. Gabszewicz,
Jean Jaskold. II. Thisse, Jacques-François. III. Series.
IV. Series: An Elgar reference collection.
HB238.M53   1999
338.6'048—dc21   98–46608
                                                              CIP

ISBN 1 85898 146 8
Printed and bound in Great Britain by
MPG Books Ltd, Bodmin, Cornwall

Contents

Acknowledgements

The editors and publishers wish to thank the authors and the following publishers who have kindly given permission for the use of copyright material.

Academic Press, Inc. for articles: Peter A. Diamond (1971), 'A Model of Price Adjustment', *Journal of Economic Theory*, **3**, 156–68; Darius W. Gaskins, Jr. (1971), 'Dynamic Limit Pricing: Optimal Pricing under Threat of Entry', *Journal of Economic Theory*, **3**, 306–22; Jean Jaskold Gabszewicz and Jean-Philippe Vial (1972), 'Oligopoly "A la Cournot" in a General Equilibrium Analysis', *Journal of Economic Theory*, **4**, 381–400; J. Jaskold Gabszewicz and J.-F. Thisse (1980), 'Entry (and Exit) in a Differentiated Industry', *Journal of Economic Theory*, **22**, 327–38; David M. Kreps and Robert Wilson (1982), 'Reputation and Imperfect Information', *Journal of Economic Theory*, **27**, 253–79; Xavier Vives (1984), 'Duopoly Information Equilibrium: Cournot and Bertrand', *Journal of Economic Theory*, **34**, 71–94.

American Economic Association for articles: Jesse W. Markham (1951), 'The Nature and Significance of Price Leadership', *American Economic Review*, **XLI**, 891–905; D.K. Osborne (1976), 'Cartel Problems', *American Economic Review*, **66** (5), December, 835–44; Avinash K. Dixit and Joseph E. Stiglitz (1977), 'Monopolistic Competition and Optimum Product Diversity', *American Economic Review*, **67** (3), June, 297–308; William J. Baumol (1982), 'Contestable Markets: An Uprising in the Theory of Industry Structure', *American Economic Review*, **72** (1), March, 1–15; Drew Fudenberg and Jean Tirole (1984), 'The Fat-Cat Effect, The Puppy-Dog Ploy, and the Lean and Hungry Look', *American Economic Review Papers and Proceedings*, **74** (2), May, 361–6.

Blackwell Publishers Ltd for articles: Harold Hotelling (1929), 'Stability in Competition', *Economic Journal*, **XXXIX**, March, 41–57; Nicholas Kaldor (1935), 'Market Imperfection and Excess Capacity', *Economica* (N.S.), **II** (5–8), February, 33–50; M. McManus (1962), 'Numbers and Size in Cournot Oligopoly', *Yorkshire Bulletin of Economic and Social Research*, **14**, 14–22; Avinash Dixit (1980), 'The Role of Investment in Entry-Deterrence', *Economic Journal*, **90**, March, 95–106; Jean-Pascal Benassy (1988), 'The Objective Demand Curve in General Equilibrium with Price Makers', *Economic Journal*, **98** (390), 37–49.

Econometric Society for articles: Jean Jaskold Gabszewicz and Jean-François Mertens (1971), 'An Equivalence Theorem for the Core of an Economy whose Atoms are not "too" big', *Econometrica*, **39** (5), September, 713–21; Benyamin Shitovitz (1973), 'Oligopoly in Markets with a Continuum of Traders', *Econometrica*, **41** (3), May, 467–501; Paul Milgrom and John Roberts (1982), 'Limit Pricing and Entry under Incomplete Information: An Equilibrium Analysis', *Econometrica*, **50** (2), March, 443–59; Avner Shaked and John Sutton

(1983), 'Natural Oligopolies', *Econometrica*, **51** (5), September, 1469–83; Edward J. Green and Robert H. Porter (1984), 'Noncooperative Collusion under Imperfect Price Information', *Econometrica*, **52** (1), January, 87–100; A. de Palma, V. Ginsburgh, Y.Y. Papageorgiou and J.-F. Thisse (1985), 'The Principle of Minimum Differentiation Holds under Sufficient Heterogeneity', *Econometrica*, **53** (4), July, 767–81; Eric Maskin and Jean Tirole (1988), 'A Theory of Dynamic Oligopoly, II: Price Competition, Kinked Demand Curves, and Edgeworth Cycles', *Econometrica*, **56** (3), May, 571–99.

Elsevier Science BV for excerpt: Jean-Pascal Benassy (1986), 'On the Existence of Bertrand–Edgeworth Equilibria with Differentiated Commodities', in Werner Hildenbrand and Andreu Mas-Colell (eds), *Contributions to Mathematical Economics. In Honor of Gérard Debreu*, Chapter 4, 57–78.

Harvard University Press for excerpts: E.H. Chamberlin (1933), 'Group Equilibrium', *The Theory of Monopolistic Competition*, Section V.3, 81–100; Joe S. Bain (1956/1965), 'The Importance of the Condition of Entry', *Barriers to New Competition: Their Character and Consequences in Manufacturing Industries*, Chapter 1, 1–41.

Institute of Management Sciences (currently INFORMS) for article: Jean-Pierre Ponssard (1979), 'The Strategic Role of Information on the Demand Function in an Oligopolistic Market', *Management Science*, **25** (3), March, 243–50.

Kluwer Academic Publishers for article: Reinhard Selten (1978), 'The Chain Store Paradox', *Theory and Decision*, **9** (2), April, 127–59.

Macmillan Press Ltd for excerpt: F.Y. Edgeworth (1925), 'The Pure Theory of Monopoly', *Papers Relating to Political Economy*, Volume I, Section II, 111–42.

MIT Press Journals for article: Edward H. Chamberlin (1953), 'The product as an economic variable', *Quarterly Journal of Economics*, **LXVII** (1), February, 1–29.

RAND for articles: Edward C. Prescott and Michael Visscher (1977), 'Sequential location among firms with foresight', *Bell Journal of Economics*, **8** (2), Autumn, 378–93; B. Curtis Eaton and Richard G. Lipsey (1980), 'Exit barriers are entry barriers: the durability of capital as a barrier to entry', *Bell Journal of Economics*, **11** (2), Autumn, 721–9; David M. Kreps and José A. Scheinkman (1983), 'Quantity precommitment and Bertrand competition yield Cournot outcomes', *Bell Journal of Economics*, **14** (2), Autumn, 326–37.

Regional Science Association International for article: Martin J. Beckmann (1972), 'Spatial Cournot Oligopoly', *Regional Science Association Papers*, **28**, 37–47.

Review of Economic Studies Ltd for articles: Takashi Negishi (1961), 'Monopolistic Competition and General Equilibrium', *Review of Economic Studies*, **XXVIII** (75, 76 & 77), 196–201; Charles R. Frank, Jr. (1965), 'Entry in a Cournot Market', *Review of Economic Studies*, **XXXII**, 245–50; James W. Friedman (1971), 'A Non-cooperative Equilibrium for

Supergames', *Review of Economic Studies*, **XXXVIII**, 1–12; Steven Salop and Joseph Stiglitz (1977), 'Bargains and Ripoffs: A Model of Monopolistically Competitive Price Dispersion', *Review of Economic Studies*, **XLIV**, 493–510; Oliver D. Hart (1979), 'Monopolistic Competition in a Large Economy with Differentiated Commodities', *Review of Economic Studies*, **XLVI**, 1–30; William Novshek (1980), 'Cournot Equilibrium with Free Entry', *Review of Economic Studies*, **XLVII**, 473–86.

Springer-Verlag for excerpt: J.W. Friedman (1979), 'On Entry Preventing Behavior and Limit Price Models of Entry', in S.J. Brams, A. Schotter and G. Schwödiauer (eds), *Applied Game Theory*, 236–53.

University of Chicago Press for articles: Franco Modigliani (1958), 'New Developments on the Oligopoly Front', *Journal of Political Economy*, **LXVI** (3), June, 215–32; George J. Stigler (1964), 'A Theory of Oligopoly', *Journal of Political Economy*, **LXXII** (1), February, 44–61.

Every effort has been made to trace all the copyright holders but if any have been inadvertently overlooked the publishers will be pleased to make the necessary arrangment at the first opportunity.

In addition the publishers wish to thank the Library of the London School of Economics and Political Science, the Marshall Library of Economics, Cambridge University, and B & N Microfilm for their assistance in obtaining these articles.

Introduction*

Jean J. Gabszewicz and Jacques-François Thisse

1.   A *perfectly competitive market* must satisfy four assumptions. First, the number of sellers and buyers operating in the market is so *large* that no agent expects to affect the market price by his or her own action. In other words, both firms and consumers are price takers. Second, there are no entry and exit *barriers*, which means that any agent can enter or exit the market as a buyer or seller whenever he or she finds it profitable to do so. The condition of free entry allows the number of sellers and buyers to increase up to the point where it is no longer advantageous for more agents to be active in this market. Third, the product sold on the market is *homogeneous*. Hence transactions involve perfectly substitutable goods so that traders do not have to pay attention to whom they buy from, provided that prices are identical and known to them. When products are differentiated, consumers must distinguish among sellers and find the price/product combination that fits them both. Fourth, and last, all agents have *perfect information* about the market price. This implies that the price prevailing in a market is unique. Otherwise consumers would buy from the firm offering the lowest price, thus inducing other firms to drop their own prices. In summary, *in perfectly competitive markets, prices summarize all the information agents need to make their production or consumption decisions.*[1]

How to define imperfect competition? We say that *imperfect competition arises when (at least) one of the above four assumptions does not hold.* Clearly, such situations are so many and diverse that analysis in this area may look like a patchwork of unrelated investigations. Hence, it would be futile, at least at the present stage of research, to expect imperfect competition to constitute an integrated body that would be as elegant as the Arrow and Debreu (1954) formulation of the competitive model. In order to find some paths in the geography of the field, it is useful to narrow the subject matter by restricting ourselves to market situations involving *conscious interaction* among agents. This is also the approach taken by Malinvaud (1970, p. 144) for whom the basic ingredient of imperfect competition is to be found in the fact that: 'when deciding on his own actions, each agent must form some precise idea of the decisions of each of the other agents taken individually'.

This additional restriction leads us to put aside the monopoly case since it is sufficient for a monopolist to know the aggregate demand for his or her product without knowing the individual motivations lying behind this demand. Furthermore, and despite the context of interactive decision making it involves, we have chosen not to deal with R&D competition either. In our opinion, R&D competition has more to do with the microeconomic underpinnings of economic growth (as exemplified by the work of Aghion and Howitt, 1998)

* In preparing this essay, we have benefited from the comments and suggestions made by several colleagues and students. We wish to thank Ilhem Baghdadli, Isabel Grilo, Gianmarco Ottaviano, Alessandro Turrini, Xavier Wauthy and, especially, James Friedman.

than with imperfect competition *per se*. This is why technological competition is not considered either in this essay or in this collection of readings, even though we acknowledge that market structure influences the pace of technological progress (see, for example, Kamien and Schwartz, 1983) and that process-innovations affect the cost side of an industry and, therefore, the resulting market structure. Recent contributions in industrial organization, such as vertical restraints, network externalities, or regulation under asymmetric information, have been purposely excluded from this collection. Nor do we deal with noncooperative bargaining which governs strategic price making in some markets. It should be clear, however, that this does not reflect a prejudice on our part against this kind of work (quite the reverse). Instead we have chosen to concentrate on classical problems of imperfect competition only to provide a more focused collection of readings.[2]

In the selection of papers, we have followed the description of perfect competition given above and organized them into four categories, depending on the assumption of perfect competition which is assumed not to hold any more. In so doing, we have chosen to follow some methodological principles rather than chronological order. We have also retained a combination of papers tackling long-lasting problems (*old problems*) or suggesting new and powerful methods (*new perspectives*) according to our own predilections and interests, being aware that our choice of menu may alienate some of those who are among the main contributors in the field. The selected papers are given with the reference date together with their chapter number in the collection. We have also chosen to include papers published more than 10 years ago to avoid fads.

Before proceeding, the following remarks are in order. First, scale economies makes the price-taking hypothesis problematic. The introduction of increasing returns to scale into the general equilibrium model has generated much interest in recent years. Without denying that these attempts are interesting, they remain unsatisfactory, largely because they do not answer the question posed by Sraffa (1926): *to what extent is price-taking compatible with increasing returns to scale?* Suppose the firm size that minimizes average production cost is 'large' relative to the size of the market. A price-taking equilibrium could not have 'many' firms, each operating at inefficiently small scale, because each such firm would have a profit incentive to increase its output. Hence the market can only accommodate a 'few' firms of efficient size. But with only a few firms, how does one justify the hypothesis that firms treat prices as given, since firms must realize that their size permits them to influence prices to their own advantage?

Second, besides permitting a better understanding of actual markets, models of imperfect competition serve more and more to revisit standard economic theories like international trade (Helpman and Krugman, 1985), growth and development (Grossman and Helpman, 1991) or issues in public finance (where contributions are more dispersed). Even in macroeconomics, imperfectly competitive markets are now used frequently because the policy prescriptions drawn from models based on perfect competition may vastly differ from those derived from models resting on imperfectly competitive products (Matsuyama, 1995; Silvestre, 1993; Hahn and Solow, 1995). It is our contention that many recommendations developed within the competitive paradigm could well be reconsidered once it is recognized that firms act on markets characterized by imperfect competition.

2.   First, we wish to clarify some conceptual and historical issues in the hope of putting them

into perspective. We hope thereby to avoid some standard misunderstandings which have emerged from long-standing, but fuzzy, debates. It is generally recognized that the first contribution to imperfect competition is due to Cournot (1838, ch. 7, Chapter 1). He proposed a theory of oligopoly based on quantity competition between a few firms selling a homogeneous good. Having understood monopoly and perfect competition (Cournot, 1838, chs 5 and 8), Cournot turned to intermediate situations, and his desire to understand them has driven his discovery of the oligopolistic structure. To this end, he developed what was going to be one of the most powerful analytical tools in economics: *simultaneous causality*, thus laying down the foundations of modern equilibrium theory. In his review of Cournot's book, Bertrand (1883) raised the *objection péremptoire* that price choice might well be a more suitable strategy than quantity choice. He then argued that the equilibrium arising under quantity competition would not be robust against this change of strategy. This was the beginning of a long-standing debate among economists.

Cournot also left another legacy by raising the following fundamental question: does the market structure get close to the competitive outcome when the number of sellers facing a demand function becomes large? Edgeworth (1881) considered a similar question but from a different perspective. He first argued that the outcome of an exchange process involving two agents should be situated on a locus he called the *contract curve*; this corresponds to the game-theoretic concept of *core*. When the number of agents becomes arbitrarily large, the contract curve shrinks to the set of competitive outcomes. So, it is fair to say that Edgeworth, as well as Cournot, has seen perfect competition as the emerging outcome as the number of agents becomes arbitrarily large. As observed by Schumpeter (1954, p. 973): 'The advantage of this approach is that it emphasizes the fact that pure competition *results* from certain conditions: this is much better than to posit it as an institutional datum'.

Finally, Launhardt (1885, ch. 29) questioned the validity of the price-taking assumption by observing that firms dispersed over space have some market power over the customers situated in their vicinity, thus allowing them to manipulate their prices to their own advantage.[3] Being unaware of Cournot's work, Launhardt introduced the concept of a price equilibrium in a differentiated oligopoly:

> In this battle, there exists a basis for peace on which each of the producers regulates the quantity of production and the prices of goods in such a way that the opponent cannot increase its total profit either by way of a simultaneous increase in production and reduction of price to obtain sales, nor by way of reduced production and the increased prices. (p. 154)

Regarding the impact of the spatial setting on market structure, Hotelling (1929, Chapter 27) was even more explicit. He made it clear that his purpose was to introduce heterogeneity among consumers' demands in order to smooth firms' demand functions and subvert the extreme conclusions that follow from Bertrand-style price competition. Hotelling did this by distributing consumers in space so they have different transportation costs to firms. In other words, the assumption of a continuum of agents was made in order to restore continuity in the aggregate. More importantly, Hotelling also provided a framework allowing for a precise analysis of product selection by oligopolistic firms (see Section III).

Despite its empirical relevance and some brilliant early contributors, imperfect competition has languished for a long time without attracting widespread attention among economists. Notwithstanding a few exceptions, like Fellner (1949) and Shubik (1959a), it is fair to say that the state of the art in the early 1970s was not really different from the situation described by Cournot as he saw it in 1838:

> Every one has a vague idea of the effects of competition. Theory should have attempted to render this idea more precise; and yet, for lack of regarding the question from the proper point of view, and for want of resources to symbols (of which the use in this connection becomes indispensable), economic writers have not in the least improved on popular notions in this respect. These notions have remained as ill-defined and ill-applied in their works, as in popular language. (p. 79)

In particular, the equilibrium concept introduced by Cournot has long been misunderstood by economists interested in oligopolistic markets. They did miss the strategic interdependence encapsulated in Cournot's concept and brought up instead a naive – not to say wrong – interpretation of the equilibrium. A suggestive description of such repeated mistakes is provided by Johansen (1982) and is well illustrated by the following quotation from Chamberlin (1933, pp. 31–2):

> One of the conditions of the problem must be the complete interdependence of the two sellers, for obviously, if they combine, there is monopoly. The interdependence must, however, be interepreted with care, for, in the nature of the case, when they are two or a few sellers, their *fortunes* are not independent. ... Each is forced by the situation itself to take into account the policy of his rival in determining his one.

So far so good. However, in the name of common sense, Chamberlin keeps going and writes:

> If a seller determines upon his policy under the assumption that his rivals are unaffected by what he does, we may say that he takes into account only the direct influence which he has upon the price. Since the problem of duopoly has usually been conceived of in this way, we shall examine first the results under such an assumption. Following this, it will be argued that the only solution fully consistent with the central hypothesis that each seller seeks his maximum profit is one in which he does take into account the effects of his policy on his rival (and hence upon himself again). In this latter case we may say that he considers his *total* influence upon the price, indirect as well as direct.

In other words, Chamberlin mixed the equilibrium of a static model with dynamic considerations. As noticed by Friedman in various publications, Chamberlin and others hope to capture some dynamic aspects of competition, but they do not seem to be aware that such considerations are beyond the reach of the models they use. One should not allow dynamics to enter 'by the back door' through the use of an inappropriate game and/or solution concept.

The idea of using game theory to model imperfect competition is not new. In this respect, the book *Oligopoly and the Theory of Games* by Friedman (1977) clearly shows that oligopolistic markets are best modelled as *noncooperative games*. This book was the most reliable and rigorous synthesis available until the New Industrial Economics burst on to the scene. In fact, it is only recently that imperfect competition became a popular field, mainly because of the rapid developments of game theory, but also because it has been applied successfully to other fields of economics, as mentioned in the foregoing. Game theory has permitted the unification of different strands of literature on imperfect competition, as well as raising new and fundamental questions about the working of actual markets. On the other hand, using *cooperative game theory* to model collusion and the formation of coalitions in markets had already been studied since the pioneering work of Shubik (1959b), a field that reached a real state of maturity in the 1970s. We shall return to this approach in Section V.

I. Industry Size: Quantity and Price Competition

1.   Cournot is the first author who has addressed in a rigorous manner the question of equilibrium when competition takes place among the few. The equilibrium being defined as the solution to a simultaneous system of equations given by the first-order conditions for profit maximization, Cournot ignored the usual second-order conditions. However, as observed by McManus (1962, Chapter 2), for the existence of an equilibrium to be ascertained, 'even the complete calculus conditions do not go far enough, because they are conditions for purely local optimization' (p. 19).

   This difficulty has been overlooked by many economists. One must wait for the work of Nash (1951) to get a full proof of the existence of noncooperative equilibrium in a game with a finite number of pure strategies. Nikaido and Isoda (1955) showed later the existence of an equilibrium for games with a continuum of pure strategies.

   Although some scholars who worked or studied in Princeton in the 1950s were probably aware of how to prove the existence of a Cournot equilibrium,[4] McManus (1962, Chapter 2) seems to be the first who provided a written proof of the existence of such an equilibrium. This author (1964), and independently J. Roberts and Sonnenschein (1976), have also shown the existence of a Cournot equilibrium for general downward-sloping (inverse) demand functions when firms have identical convex technologies. This result is obtained by using the Intermediate Value Theorem. When firms are heterogeneous in technologies, this no longer applies; existence rests on fixed point theorems such as Brouwer's. More precisely, when demand is concave in total output and technologies are convex, profits are concave so that a standard existence theorem from noncooperative game theory can be applied. Novshek (1985) has improved upon this result by showing existence under weaker assumptions: (i) demand is such that the marginal revenue is decreasing in the aggregate output of the competitors (a condition less restrictive than concavity) and (ii) costs are lower semi-continuous (thus allowing for set-up costs). In the same vein, Amir (1997) has obtained an alternative result by proving that a log-concave demand and lower semi-continuous costs are sufficient to guarantee the existence of an equilibrium in Cournot games.[5]

   As said above, Cournot also maintained that as the number of firms rises, total output increases, price decreases, and the share of each firm decreases. In the limit perfect competition obtains. This corresponds to the widespread opinion that (i) entry is always desirable from the social point of view (whence the needs of antitrust policy) and (ii) perfect competition is approximated when firms are small relative to the market. The second claim, called by Novshek the 'Folk Theorem of Competitive Markets', is important to the extent that it would provide a rationale for approximating the working of actual markets by the competitive paradigm in large economies. Frank (1965, Chapter 3) constitutes one of the first rigorous attempts made to identify conditions for such a theorem to hold (see also Ruffin, 1971). However, the conditions he used are fairly restrictive. It is only in the eighties that Novshek (1980, Chapter 4) has been able to demonstrate convergence when technologies exhibit Marshallian U-shaped average costs similar to those described in economics textbooks. In the spirit of methods used in modern general equilibrium theory (see Section V), Novshek chooses to make firms small relative to the market by replicating the demand side a sufficient number of times. For a sufficiently large number of replications, this author shows that the equilibrium is nearly competitive.

This is not the end of the story, however. Indeed, McManus (1962, Chapter 2) has shown an example where the increase in the number of firms from two to three leads to a reduction in total output for what he calls 'a perfectly ordinary looking demand curve' (that is, downward sloping). In this example, the number of firms is 'small'. Consequently, and not very surprisingly, restrictions on costs and demand are necessary for the convergence to the competitive outcome to hold for any number of firms. And, indeed, Demange (1986) has demonstrated that, without strong assumptions regarding demand (such as concavity), several 'perverse phenomena' may arise when the number of firms increases. In particular, the entry of one more firm may well lead to a decrease in total output and to an increase in market price. This is because in so doing one may conduct a comparative statics experiment on equilibria which are unstable. Hence, if economists can safely assume perfect competition when firms selling a homogeneous product are small relative to the market size, they do not know if entry is always socially beneficial because the market solutions do not necessarily show monotonicity. This becomes even more problematic when markets are differentiated. We shall return to this issue in Sections III and V.

Another problem which has generated a long controversy deals with the possibility of viewing a Cournot equilibrium as the outcome of interaction among players over time. Cournot suggested an adjustment process in which each firm chooses today the best reply against the strategy selected yesterday by its rival and identified conditions on demand for which the stability of this process holds. McManus (1962, Chapter 2) made the important observation that, in studying stability, 'everything depends upon what dynamics assumptions are made' (p. 19). In other words, an equilibrium is not stable *per se*, but stable with respect to some explicit dynamics. Deschamps (1975) has proposed a more general process (borrowed from game theory) which has more intuitive appeal, namely fictitious play. Instead of reacting against him or her opponent's last choice, each duopolist is supposed to select a quantity which maximizes his or her expected profit against the frequency distribution of his or her opponent's past choices. Assuming concave revenue and nondecreasing marginal costs, Deschamps showed that *fictitious play converges towards the Cournot equilibrium.*[6] In fact, fictitious play can be viewed as an improvement upon the Cournot process which is completely myopic; it does not, however, account for the whole strategic interaction that underlines the Cournot model. In this perspective, Moulin (1984) has suggested a third adjustment process based on the successive elimination of dominated strategies. Here players' behaviour is *sophisticated*. Yet, Moulin shows that this process has strong connections with Cournot's in that the Nash equilibrium of a Cournot duopoly is stable for one process if and only if it is stable for the other. For more general settings, dominance-stability implies Cournot-stability.

2.   As observed by Bertrand (1883), *Cournot's equilibrium is not robust to a change in the specification of strategies.* When firms compete in prices instead of quantities, each one is able to capture the whole market by slightly undercutting its rival's price. Consequently, if at

least two firms with equal and constant marginal costs compete in prices, the only pure strategy Nash equilibrium is marginal cost pricing, that is, the competitive outcome. In other words, two would be enough for perfect competition. At the other extreme of the spectrum, one can say that any arbitrarily small but positive entry cost would be sufficient for an incumbent firm to monopolize the market if competition ensuing entry is in prices.

Although formally correct, these results strike us (and others) as being implausible. Indeed, it seems hard to find markets with a few firms selling at marginal cost. Several proposals have been made to resolve the so-called 'Bertrand paradox'. Perhaps the most convincing solutions are to appeal to product differentiation (as discussed in Section III) or to price coordination (as discussed below in Section I.4). Other solutions have been proposed by Edgeworth (1897, Chapter 5) and Sweezy (1939). According to Edgeworth, firms undercut each other to increase demand until prices become so low that the lowest-pricing firm is unable to serve market demand (or because the price cut turns out to be too costly). It then becomes profitable for the firms to raise their prices up to the monopoly level where they find it again profitable to start a price war. As will be seen below, some consumers are rationed in that they cannot buy the product from the firm charging the lowest price. This points to a major difference between quantity and price competition. In the former case, the residual demand is always Walrasian whereas, in the latter, it depends crucially on the specifics of the rationing scheme.

Sweezy's approach is quite different in that he seems to assume a 'focal' price around which firms would implicitly agree for the following reasons. If a firm cuts its price, it expects its competitors to follow suit, thus making such a deviation unprofitable unless total demand strongly expands; if a firm raises its price, it expects its competitors not to follow, so that the deviating firm finds itself with a large drop in demand. Unlike Edgeworth who seems to plead for price instability, Sweezy wants to support the idea of price rigidity around the focal price.

The standard game-theoretic solution to the problem of nonexistence of an equilibrium in Edgeworth's capacity constrained duopoly is to appeal to *mixed strategies*. Using mixed strategies often allows for the 'convexification' of problems which are nonconvex in pure strategies. Ignoring the behavioural difficulties raised by the recourse to mixed strategies,[7] the theoretical problem is far from being trivial, however. First, one must be careful in specifying the rationing rule to be used, that is, which consumers buy from the high-priced firm once the low-priced firm is constrained by its capacity. For instance, one may suppose that the low-priced firm serves the high-price part of the demand curve or, to put it differently, that consumers are served by decreasing order of their reservation price. In this case, the residual demand to the high-priced firm is obtained as if consumers were able to resell the goods among themselves at no costs. It is therefore the total demand at the high price minus the capacity of the low-priced firm (Levitan and Shubik, 1972). Another rule, used by Beckmann (1965), consists in drawing at random from all consumers willing to buy at the lower price those who will be served. This implies that the residual demand is now a fraction of total demand at the higher price (those who have not been served). As observed by Levitan and Shubik, the actual shape of the residual demand can hardly be justified on pure reasoning since it is likely to depend upon the details of firms' marketing policy. This shows how the market outcome may change with the rationing rule selected. Second, Edgeworth's duopoly exhibits discontinuous profit functions in prices while existence theorems of mixed strategy equilibria typically assume that payoffs are continuous with respect to pure strategies. We had to wait for the work of Dagsputa and Maskin (1986a,b) to obtain general existence theorems applicable to capacity constrained oligopolies with various rationing rules.

A different line of research has been explored by Maskin and Tirole (1988a; 1988b, Chapter 6) who show that price cycles may arise as the long-run equilibrium of a dynamic game where each firm reacts to the current actions of the others. More precisely, they consider two firms maximizing the discounted sum of single-period profits and choosing their price alternately in discrete time. If the discount factor is close to 1 and if profits are concave, there exists a symmetric Markov perfect equilibrium[8] involving two prices $p' > p''$ such that firms gradually decrease their prices from p' to p'' over time and, thereafter, price either at marginal cost with a positive probability or at a level slightly above p' with the complementary probability. Such a price cycle corresponds to an ergodic state of the Markov chain generated by the choice of prices during the transitory periods. Average profits along a cycle are shown to be bounded away from the competitive outcome. To be complete, note that the same authors also show the existence of another ergodic state containing the sole monopoly price which would correspond to the 'kink' of the perceived demand proposed by Sweezy.[9]

Finally, Dastidar (1995) argues that *undercutting is no longer necessarily profitable when firms have increasing marginal costs* because of the rise in the cost of serving additional consumers. Assuming that firms do not ration consumers, this author shows that a price equilibrium always exists and that all firms with positive sales charge the same price. In the case of identical technologies, there is a whole range of equilibria: the lowest equilibrium price equals the average production cost (so profits are zero as in Bertrand) whereas the highest one equals the marginal production cost (so the equilibrium is competitive as in Bertrand). These results are nice but are obtained under the questionable assumption that firms must serve any demand, even though such a behaviour contradicts profit maximization.

3.   We now turn to one of the most debatable issues of oligopolistic competition: the choice of *price* versus *quantity* in modelling firms' decision making. In the monopoly case, it is well known that the market solution is independent of the variable chosen. On the contrary, we have seen that the two market outcomes differ vastly in the oligopoly case: a quantity game is very different from a price game. This difference is sometimes considered by the economics profession as a 'major flaw' of oligopoly theory. Taking a pragmatic view, Fudenberg and Tirole (1984, Chapter 20) consider price competition and quantity competition as 'two different reduced forms for the determination of both prices and outputs' (p. 365). But then, the choice of one variable instead of the other is made more by decree than by analysis. At the opposite side of the spectrum, Singh and Vives (1984) propose to endogenize the choice between prices and quantities according to strategic considerations. This does not strike us as a meaningful approach. First, Jéhiel and Walliser (1995) have shown that such a strategic approach may also lead to the emergence of other configurations in which some firms would choose quantities and other prices. In other words, the predictive power of the approach turns out to be weak. Second, to the extent that quantity and price competition correspond to different institutional rules in price determination, it is hard to see how both rules can be applied to the same market. Third, it seems to us (and to others) that firms do choose *both* variables in the real world.

In this perspective, for the cases when prices are more flexible than quantities, Kreps and Scheinkman (1983, Chapter 7) use a two-stage model in which firms choose first quantities and then prices. Once the volumes of output have been selected, they are interpreted as the committed choices of production capacities, so that price competition arises in a setting identical to that considered by Edgeworth (1897). Using the rationing rule under which the low-priced firm serves the high-price part of the demand curve, Kreps and Scheinkman then show that *the market outcome is identical to the Cournot equilibrium.*[10] Hence as Tirole (1988, p. 217) puts it, 'firms ... avoid accumulating capacities in order to soften price competition'. This seems to provide a reconciliation between the two models. However, Davidson and Deneckere (1986) have demonstrated that the choice of the rationing rule is critical for this reconciliation. Given what we said above about the choice of such a rule, it appears that the answer provided by Kreps and Scheinkman is only partial. This is not really surprising, however, since the rationing rule they use is precisely that implicitly employed in Walrasian models and, hence, in Cournot too.

A more general approach has been explored independently by Bénassy (1986, Chapter 8) and Friedman (1988). We know that firms may not be willing to serve all demands addressed to them at any price because of their technological constraints. In such cases, *they must account for both prices and quantities selected by their rivals.* Assuming that products are differentiated in order to smooth out firms' demands, the main lessons of those two papers are as follows.

1. When prices and quantities are chosen simultaneously, no (pure strategy) equilibrium exists.
2. When prices are chosen first and a (subgame perfect) equilibrium exists, the corresponding prices are the same as those arising in the price competition model only.
3. When quantities are chosen first (as in Kreps and Scheinkman (1983, Chapter 7)) and a (subgame perfect) equilibrium exists, the corresponding quantities are identical to those obtained in the quantity model only.

In the case where firms post prices, wait for orders from consumers and then produce to order, Bénassy (1989) shows that an equilibrium exists under standard assumptions of concavity when firms have enough 'unused' capacities.

However, it also seems reasonable to think of a single-variable approach, at least as a first-order approximation. What strategic variable is really important is then likely to depend on the specifics of the market (Friedman, 1983a, ch. 2). For example, in some markets; prices (or quantities) may be changed almost instantaneously; in others they may be highly inflexible. Hence the problem would become an empirical one: for some markets quantity competition would provide the best approximation; for others price competition would be preferable. In this perspective, Vives (1986) has developed a theoretical approach showing that both Cournot and Bertrand equilibria may emerge as possible outcomes of a game in which firms have access to technologies exhibiting different degrees of flexibility. In this model, firms choose simultaneously their capacity levels while price is determined competitively. However, firms may want to produce more than their capacities. When there is no penalty in expanding capacities (flexible technologies), the market outcome is identical to the Bertrand equilibrium. On the other hand, when the penalty is prohibitive, the market solution is given by the Cournot equilibrium (inflexible technologies). Thus the market equilibrium is here determined by the properties of the technologies.

We have seen that a price choice model can be viewed as a shorthand for a model in which both price and quantity are chosen, but price is chosen first, while a quantity choice model can be interpreted as a shorthand for a model in which quantity is chosen first. An alternative way to look at the debate between Cournot and Bertrand is as follows. With price-setting firms, each consumer just elects the firm that offers him or her the best deal. By contrast, with quantity-setting firms, the institutional arrangement which determines the market price corresponding to the total output supplied is not specified although it is implicitly assumed to be known by the firms. The work of d'Aspremont, Dos Santos Ferreira and Gérard-Varet (1991) sheds more light on this issue. These authors show that Cournot and Bertrand equilibria can be viewed as the two extreme cases of a system in which firms obey pricing schemes (corresponding to institutional rules to be specified) associating a market price with a vector of announced prices. Then, *Cournot equilibrium requires some coordination between firms* (organized maybe by the Walrasian auctioneer) under the form of combinations between the announced prices. By contrast, *Bertrand equilibria coincides with the complete absence of coordination* since the price scheme always picks the lowest announced price.[11]

4. By restricting the effective number of agents, collusion affects the organization of markets. As observed by von Neumann and Morgenstern (1944, p. 98):

> it is clear that, if certain great groups of participants – for any reason whatsoever – act together, then the great number of participants may not become effective, the decisive exchange may take place directly between large 'coalitions' (such as trade unions, consumers' co-operatives ...), and not between individuals, many in number, acting indepenently.

This does not mean that collusion is necessarily desirable for the agents involved in the agreement. Indeed, the following fundamental question suggests itself: is it in the interest of the economic agents to substitute a (binding) agreement for their individual freedom?[12]

Both Bertrand and Chamberlin vehemently rejected the solution put forward by Cournot because of its lack of 'realism', and saw collusion as the 'natural' market outcome when competition involves a small number of firms. For example, Chamberlin (1933, p. 48) claimed that:

> If each seller seeks his maximum profits rationally and intelligently, he will realize that when there are only two or a few sellers, his own move has a considerable effect upon his competitors, and that this makes it idle to suppose that they will accept without retaliation the losses he forces upon them. Since the result of a cut by any one is inevitably to decrease his own profits, no one will cut, and although the sellers are entirely independent, the equilibrium result is the same as though there were a monopolistic agreement between them.

However, Chamberlin did not provide any formal justification for his view. In fact, collusion is complex to implement because firms will disagree about the appropriate collusive solution (the sharing problem) and because each firm has incentives to cheat secretly by choosing an action different from that prescribed in the agreement (the cheating problem). For a long time, the conventional wisdom was rather that cartels were inherently unstable because of the sharing and detecting problems. Yet, colluding seems to become simpler once it is recognized that the play is repeated so that firms are able to punish the deviator, thus making deviation less attractive to him or her (a setting that seems to fit better the economic environment Chamberlin had in mind). It is only recently that all these intuitive arguments have been made clear in the economic literature, thanks to progress made in game theory.

The first point to address is the stability of a collusive agreement. To be sure, by maximizing joint profit, firms earn more in the aggregate. Nevertheless, this argument simply overlooks the fact that a cartel faces four *internal* problems: (i) to locate the profit possibility frontier, which requires full information about demand and costs; (ii) to select a point on this frontier; (iii) to detect and (iv) to deter cheating. Putting aside the first problem, it appears that participants in the cartel have incentives to cheat because of the positive marginal profit they make at the output quota. As noticed by Osborne (1976, Chapter 9), 'To resolve that dilemma the cartel must assign each member a quota *rule*, an operating rule incorporating a deterrent to cheating; and the deterrent must take the form of a credible threat of retaliation' (p. 838, italics in original).

No cartel member is tempted to cheat when he or she expects other members to follow the rule (unless he or she can escape detection by the others) when firms set in a dynamic context (this is implict in Osborne). But how to design such a rule? Osborne proposed an ingenious one based on market share that could do the job. At the time, however, Friedman (1971, Chapter 10) had already shown that, when the same game is played repeatedly and firms are interested in their long-run profits, the door is open to scenarios involving *threat* and *punishment* that enable firms to sustain collusion. In other words, outcomes that require cooperation (that is, binding agreements) in a one-shot game can emerge as noncooperative Nash equilibria of the repeated oligopolistic game.

This idea goes back to early work in game theory due to Aumann (1960) – see Friedman (1997) for a historical and topical overview of the Folk Theorem of Game Theory. However, the proposed solution failed to deal with the idea of credible threats by using standard Nash equilibria. Instead, Friedman (1971, Chapter 10) used what is called today a refinement of the Nash equilibrium. Specifically, he employed a *trigger strategy*: when each firm selects its cooperative action in all previous periods, then each of them selects the same action in the current period; if one firm has deviated in the previous period, then each firm chooses for ever the action associated with the one-shot Nash equilibrium that players all have in mind when someone defects. This solution is a subgame perfect Nash equilibrium, a concept developed independently by Selten (1965, 1975), if and only if the discount rate is not too large. Indeed, if a firm does not place much value on the present, it never pays to deviate from the collusive solution since the present value of the loss incurred by shifting to the one-shot equilibrium is larger than the extra profit earned today by deviating from the cooperative outcome. The punishment considered here is to return to the one-shot equilibrium. Such a punishment is credible because the one-shot equilibrium is also subgame perfect.

In fact, there exist many outcomes that can be sustained by a trigger strategy. In other words, *if repetition enables cooperation, it does not force it*. In this sense, the Folk Theorem has a poor predictive power since almost any outcome of the one-shot game can be an equilibrium of the infinitely repeated game (Fudenberg and Maskin, 1986). Formal game theory does not provide any reason to choose one equilibrium instead of another.[13] It took a while for the economics profession to evaluate the implications of the Folk Theorem. Nowadays, they are widely known and applications of repeated games to oligopoly are many. In particular, alternative, less extreme strategies have been proposed to replace trigger strategies (see, for example, the survey provided by Friedman, 1997). In any case, the story remains basically the same: all sorts of tacit agreements can be sustained as refined Nash equilibria of the repeated game.

For such agreements to be enforceable in a noncooperative setting, the game must be played indefinitely (or, to put it differently, the end of the game must be undetermined).[14] If there is a last time the firms will interact, they fail to achieve the benefits of cooperation when they approach the end of the relationship. In addition, many things must be observable to all firms. For example, locating the profit possibility frontier may become problematic when firms have incomplete information about their rivals' costs.[15] Similarly, when demand is uncertain, a fall in profits may be due to a sudden drop in demand as well as to a secret output expansion by another participant in the agreement. As usual, Stigler (1964, Chapter 11) cuts to the heart of the matter when he claimed more than thirty years ago: 'the problem of policing a collusive agreement ... proves to be a problem in the theory of information' (p. 44).

One had to wait for the recent developments in the economics of information in order to be able to tackle this difficult problem that will be further discussed in Section IV.[16]

Besides the four internal problems described in the foregoing, a cartel also faces an *external* problem: how to predict the production by non-members? The simplest case arises when a single cartel forms while the remaining firms act on an individual basis. This is akin to the industry structure considered by Markham (1951, Chapter 12) and known as the *price leadership model*. One firm (or group of firms) is said to be a *dominant firm* when the other firms in the industry recognize and accept the price set up by this firm and behave competitively at that price. The dominant firm selects the price that best serves its own interest, taking into account the supply reactions of the fringe firms. It remains to explain how such a market arrangement emerges. One possible explanation is to view the source of the power of the dominant firm in the formation of a cartel of market participants who have succeeded in combining together, and act in unison when choosing price in order to maximize the profit per firm in the cartel. The firms which are not cartel members then remain in the 'competitive fringe' and accept the price set by the collusive price leadership cartel.

The stability of this collusive process has been examined by d'Aspremont et al. (1983a) who define stability as follows. A cartel is stable when it is the subgame perfect Nash equilibrium of the following two-stage game. In the first stage, each firm chooses to belong to the cartel or to act independently; in the second, the membership decisions of firms are revealed and payoffs are determined according to the above model of the dominant firm. These authors then show that there always exists a stable price leadership cartel when all firms acting in the market are identical.

The foregoing discussion clearly shows that *a collusive agreement is inherently complex* to analyse in that cartels are not necessarily unstable or stable *per se*. As accurately observed by Osborne (1976, Chapter 9), 'Though it [the cartel] can solve its problems in principle, it might nevertheless fail to solve them in practice. But to recognize that a cartel might collapse because it cannot control ... cheating is quite different from believing that all are necessary doomed' (p. 843).

II. Entry Barriers

1.   The theory of competitive markets typically assumes that entry of new firms is easy. As observed by Bain (1956, ch. 1, Chapter 13), for entry to be easy, three conditions must be fulfilled: (i) established firms have no cost advantages over potential entrants such as those generated by learning economies; (ii) the optimal scale of any (existing or potential) firm is a small fraction of the total industry output; and (iii) established firms have no product differentiation advantages, such as reputation and goodwill, over potential entrants. Bain viewed these conditions are necessary and sufficient for easy entry to arise. Consequently, easy entry will not be observed when one departs from one of these conditions.

In the standard competitive paradigm, one neglects the possibility for the established firms to have advantage over their potential competitors that allow them to earn pure profits. These advantages may result from given technological and market conditions such as large-scale economies. They may also be built by the incumbents each time that erecting entry barriers turns out to be profitable for them, although such actions would not be undertaken in the absence of entry threat. In other words, *there is some interdependence* not only among established sellers but *between established sellers and potential entrants*. This implies that potential competition is able to affect the behaviour of incumbents even when entry does not effectively take place.

The aim of the theory of *contestable markets* is precisely to show how potential competition can discipline market behaviour when only a few firms are established because of nonconvex technologies. The key assumption is that of *free exit*, which means here that any firm can leave the market at any time and recoup any cost incurred during the entry process. Although the bulk of the theory was addressed to the case of a multiproduct natural monopoly (more or less in the sense of Bain), we focus here on the body dealing with oligopoly. According to Baumol (1982, Chapter 14), when entry and exit are completely free, incumbent oligopolists will choose to price at average cost, thus offering consumers the benefit of Marshallian long-run perfect competition. Indeed any unilateral deviation would make them vulnerable to hit-and-run entry or would lead them to make losses. Although the analysis offered by Baumol, Panzar and Willig (1982) is appealing and ingenious as well as applicable, probably, to some particular industries, the story seems to be too good to be true. Stated differently, it is hard to believe that the Invisible Hand may govern most oligopolistic markets.

A very much related idea has been precisely tackled by Demange and Henriet (1991). In our opinion, these authors have obtained some of the most interesting results in this strand of literature. Assuming that consumers have single-peaked preferences about differentiated products, Demange and Henriet show, under fairly weak assumptions regarding technologies, that a vector of offers (each defined as the characteristics and price of a product) by firms and a partition of consumers both exist such that no customer can be better off, no firm makes a loss and no firm (active or inactive) can make an alternative offer that would give it a strictly higher profit (so there is free entry but entry is no longer profitable). Such a configuration, called a *sustainable oligopoly*, is also optimal in that no other configuration with firms making nonnegative profits can be found at which consumers are strictly better off.

However, it is easy to see how entry may be blockaded when producing involves *sunk costs*, that is, costs that cannot be recovered upon exit or for which the corresponding investment is product-specific. Consider a market for a homogeneous product where the technology entails a positive fixed cost and a constant marginal cost. There is one incumbent and one potential entrant. When post-entry competition is in price, we know from Section I.2 that both firms will sell at the common marginal cost if entry were to occur. Anticipating this outcome, the potential entrant will choose to stay out. This is understood by the incumbent who can therefore safely charge the monopoly price, irrespective of the level of sunk costs. Although very extreme, this example is sufficient to show that free exit is crucial for the idea of contestability to be operational. Furthermore, it remains unclear how sustainable configurations may actually be reached.

The work of Maskin and Tirole (1988a) offers a possible answer by deriving a zero-profit configuration as a long-run equilibrium in a setting similar to their price model discussed in Section I.2, but in which firms now compete in quantities under large fixed costs. When the discount factor is close to one, these authors show that a single firm operates, its output level being such that its current profits are approximately zero (when fixed costs are large, this is the best solution one may obtain on a free market). What yields this result is that each firm is committed to its output during a certain time period. Since firms value future profits almost as much as current profits, any firm then wishes to preempt the whole market by selling the output for which its profits are zero.

2.   Returning to Bain (1956, ch. 1, Chapter 13), one must also give him credit for his detailed and insightful discussion of the 'typical circumstances' that give to established firms a cost or product differentiation advantage over potential entrants, or that lead to significant scale economies discouraging entry. In particular, Bain highlights the possible pricing strategies that can be followed by a (single) established firm *vis-à-vis* its potential competitors. Four possible situations may arise: (i) entry is *easy* so that price in the long-run cannot exceed the competitive level; (ii) the incumbent could raise his or her price above the competitive level without inviting new firms, but it would be better off if entry is *accommodated*; (iii) entry is *deterred* in that, at the best entry-forestalling price, the incumbent's profits are greater than those earned if entry were accommodated; and (iv) entry is *blockaded* at the monopoly price.

At the same time, Sylos-Labini (1957) put forward some theoretical developments whose purpose is to show that 'fewness' is the result of purely economic forces, that were further investigated by Modigliani (1958, Chapter 15). This author accurately observed that the price that is relevant to the potential entrant is the price prevailing after entry, so that assumptions must be made about the attitudes of the incumbents after entry has taken place. In order to find a solution to this problem, Modigliani then followed Sylos-Labini and rephrased his basic assumption as follows: 'potential entrants behave as though they expected existing firms to adopt the policy most unfavorable to them, namely, the policy of maintaining output while reducing the price (or accepting reductions) to the extent required to enforce such an output policy' (p 217).

Let $D(p)$ be the market demand function for a homogeneous product and p_b the price before entry. Then, under the above assumption, the demand faced by the entrant is not perfectly elastic as in Bertrand; it is now given by the segment of the sloped demand to the right of p_b. If p_b is such that the resulting demand is everywhere below the average cost of the potential competitor, then entry is not profitable. In the words of Bain, p_b is therefore an entry-forestalling price. What became known as the *limit price* is then given by the highest entry-forestalling price. This leads Modigliani (1958, Chapter 15) to conclude that, under

Sylos-Labini's assumption, 'there is a well-defined, maximum premium that the oligopolists can command over the competitive price, and this premium tends to increase with the importance of economies of scale and to decrease with the size of market and the elasticity of demand' (p. 220).

The work of Bain, Sylos-Labini and Modigliani has had a lasting influence on economists. Yet, these authors fail to explain and describe what is the optimal pricing strategy of a monopolist over time, *given the threat of entry*. By casting the problem within the framework of optimal control theory, Gaskins (1971, Chapter 16) was able to overcome this difficulty for the special case of the dominant firm (see Section I.4). Defining the state variable as the size of the competitive fringe, he assumed that the flow of entry is proportional to the discrepancy between the current price and the limit price. When the dominant firm maximizes its long-run profits, it can be shown that the firm sacrifices market share by initially pricing substantially above the limit price and gradually lowering its price to the limit price. The long-run market share of the dominant firm is an increasing function of the cost advantage it enjoys.

In the same vein, Kamien and Schwartz (1971) suppose that entry is now probabilistic and that the risk of entry rises with the current price selected by the dominant firm. Once a firm has entered, it is supposed that profits are constant. Kamien and Schwartz then show that the dominant firm sets a price which is constant until the first entry. Depending on the risk of entry, three cases are possible: (i) when the non-price barriers to entry are high enough, entry is blocked and the optimal price is the monopoly price; (ii) the optimal price is the limit price so that entry is effectively impeded; and (iii) the optimal price is such that entry is accepted.[17]

3.   In a stimulating paper, Friedman (1979, Chapter 17) has questioned the validity of the limit price model in a very neat way:

> an entrant has no direct interest in an established firm's pre-entry price policy. What matters to him is the price pattern which would emerge after he were to come in. That is, he wants to know what equilibrium behavior in the market would be if he were in, and he wants to know what profits he would have under such an equilibrium.
>
>   Now, after entry occurs, the established firm and the entrant are in a two person game whose structure and form are entirely independent of the pre-entry price policy of the established firm; hence, whose equilibria are independent of the pre-entry price policy of the established firm. If both participants are fully informed at the outset concerning the profit functions which would prevail after entry, then it is difficult to see the relevance of pre-entry prices to the plans of the entrant. (p. 237)

Hence it is unrealistic to assume that the monopolist's pre-entry and post-entry prices will remain the same. *The incumbent's threat to stick at his or her pre-entry price (or output) is not credible because it is often profitable for it to deviate if entry had to happen.* This does not imply, however, that limit pricing never will be observed. An incumbent will choose a limit price in the following precise circumstances. Let $\prod^M$ denote the monopoly profits, $\prod^L$ the largest profits attainable under the constraint that the established firm blockades entry, and $\prod^D$ the profits it would have if entry were to occur. If $\prod^M = \prod^L$, then entry is blocked at the monopoly price. If $\prod^D \geq \prod^L$, limit pricing is never optimal since accommodating entry gives the incumbent higher profits. Consequently, limit pricing is a possible outcome only in the case where $\prod^M > \prod^L > \prod^D$. Let now α be the firm's discounting factor. Assuming that entry would occur in period t, prevention is optimal if and only if sacrificing some short-run profits is more than balanced by the gains obtained in the future from forestalling entry:

$$\frac{1}{1-\alpha} \Pi^{L} > \frac{1-\alpha^{t}}{1-\alpha} \Pi^{M} + \frac{\alpha^{t}}{1-\alpha} \Pi^{D}.$$

In the 1980s, the focus of entry deterrence has shifted to investment (in physical capital, goodwill, or knowledge) as a strategic variable. As observed by Friedman (1979, Chapter 17), 'The crucial difference between price and investment is, of course, that today's investment decision makes an inevitable change in the future circumstances one will face, but today's price decisions only affect today' (p. 237).

Unlike price and output, *capital levels* (interpreted in a number of ways) *have a commitment value* because they are irreversible. In other words, the threat to use a large capital stock after the entry of a rival is credible because this capital *does* exist. More precisely, the work of Friedman (1979, Chapter 17; 1981) and Dixit (1980, Chapter 18) on the choice of capacity levels shows how large-scale entry is moulded by strategic considerations on the part of the installed producer by focusing on the fundamental distinction between pre- and post-entry considerations. The analysis is essentially dynamic since the competitive environment is changed as a result of the investment decisions made by firms. The basic idea lying in this new strand of literature is well summarized by Dixit (1980, Chapter 18): 'The established firm's pre-entry decisions can influence the prospective entrant's view of what will happen if he enters, and the established firm will try to exploit this possibility to its own advantage' (p. 95).

For example, suppose that the incumbent first chooses a pre-entry capacity level which may subsequently be increased only at a higher adjustment cost. Then, the initial capacity choice affects the marginal cost of the established firm, which in turn affects his or her reaction function in the post-entry subgame. Once this choice is made, both the incumbent and the potential entrant may anticipate the outcome of the post-entry duopoly subgame, and the latter decides whether or not to enter on the basis of his or her anticipated profits. Bearing this in mind, the former chooses his or her capacity in order to maximize his or her intertemporal profits., So, the following question suggests itself: does it pay for the incumbent to overinvest in capacity in order to deter entry?

Putting aside the obvious situation where the monopoly output is sufficient to deter entry (the fourth case in Bain's analysis), *the incumbent* then faces the following tradeoff: he or she *must bear the cost of a capacity larger than the monopoly one in order to be able to expand his or her output if entry were to occur.* As shown by Dixit and Friedman, the solution depends on the values of the cost parameters. The following two situations may arise: (i) it is better for the established firm to allow for entry so that a duopoly emerges in the second period, and (ii) the established firm finds it profitable to install a *limit-capacity* and be the only firm in the market.[18] Note, however, that Dixit shows that the incumbent never builds a capacity that would remain idle in the pre-entry phase. In other words, one would not observe excess capacity in (subgame perfect) equilibrium.

As argued by Eaton and Lipsey (1980, Chapter 19), besides its size, the durability of capital may also affect its effectiveness as an entry barrier. The point that these authors want to make is that it is not the existence of large-scale economies *per se* which allows them to create entry barriers. Rather, it is the intertemporal commitment of specific capital to a market, together with scale economies, which allow the incumbent to deter entry. More precisely, they show that a deterring-entry monopolist may choose to replace his or her capital before it is economically obsolete or, alternately, may choose a capital more durable than the cost-minimizing one. This result suggests the existence of a *limit durability* comparable to the limit capacity.[19]

When overinvestment by the incumbent reduces the profitability of the entrant, we have just seen with Friedman, Dixit, Eaton and Lipsey that such a strategy may well be selected by the installed firm. However, overinvestment may not be the reasonable strategy because it may reduce the incentive of the incumbent to be aggressive in the post-entry subgame. In this case, *underinvestment may be more desirable from the incumbent's point of view*. Those ideas have been summarized by Fudenberg and Tirole (1984, Chapter 20) who show how the incumbent's strategic incentive to accommodate/deter entry depends on the way the entrant's reaction function changes with his or her pre-entry action.

To illustrate, consider the case where the reaction curves of the post-entry subgame are upward sloping, an assumption common to several models of price competition with differentiated products. In the first-stage game, the incumbent may choose between an entry-accommodating strategy or an entry-deterring one. Furthermore, he or she may play soft or tough in the post-entry subgame (in a way which has been made precise by Bulow et al., 1985). This gives rise to four possible market outcomes. When an entry-accommodating strategy is elected, the incumbent may overinvest by becoming a *fat cat*; he or she can then play soft with the entrant. Alternatively, he or she may underinvest and choose to be a *puppy dog*; he or she then turns him- or herself into a small firm which will be nonaggressive when competing with a tough entrant. On the contrary, when an entry-deterring strategy is chosen, the incumbent may decide to overinvest and to be a *top dog*, presenting him- or herself as an aggressive player if entry were to arise. Instead, he or she may underinvest and take a *lean and hungry look* to deter entry because he or she is now inclined to match the entrant's price. Specific behaviours are likely to be associated with some market features. For example, the fat-cat effect typically arises in a market characterized by brand loyalty and switching costs (Schmalensee, 1982; Klemperer, 1987; Gabszewicz, Pepall and Thisse, 1992).

4.   Commitments may allow the established firms to build pure profits even under free entry. This possibility is especially well illustrated in a market with differentiated products. Anticipating the discussion provided in Section III, we now use the spatial model of product differentiation to show how firms can guarantee to themselves supranormal profits by choosing their products strategically. The argument runs as follows. Given the (probable) high value of relocation costs, it is reasonable to assume that firms locate once and for all. In such a context, as noticed by Eaton and Lipsey (1978), *a free entry equilibrium may exist in which incumbents make positive pure profits*. For that, it is sufficient that the anticipated demand curve of a potential entrant lies everywhere below the average cost curve, so that no entry takes place, while the demand curves for the established firms lie above the average cost corresponding to the equilibrium price, thus guaranteeing positive pure profits. In other words, since an entrant must fit between incumbents it expects to make substantially lower profits, thus leaving the established firms with unassailable rents. This result provides a clear illustration of an early observation made by Schelling (1960) about the strategic value of

commitment. Although incumbents seem to be at a disadvantage *vis-à-vis* the potential entrants as they are stuck to their locations, it appears that this commitment deters further entry and leads them to earn supranormal profits.

Furthermore, Prescott and Visscher (1977, Chapter 21) observe that entry is unlikely to occur simultaneously but rather sequentially. At each stage of the entry process, the entrant considers as given the locations of firms entered at earlier stages but treats the location of firms entering at later stages as conditional upon his or her own choice. In other words, the entrant is a *follower* in the sense of Stackelberg with respect to the incumbents, and a *leader* with respect to future competition. The location chosen by each entrant is then obtained by backward induction, from the optimal solution of the location problem faced by the ultimate entrant, to the entrant him- or herself. While it may be reasonable to assume that products are selected sequentially and once and for all, it may be better to assume that prices can costlessly be readjusted by the established firms after a new entry. Clearly, the long-run market outcome depends on the sequence of decisions made by the firms or, to put it succinctly, *history matters* (Eaton and Lipsey, 1977), thus making the geography of the industry much more intricate than in standard models.

When history matters, the freedom of the new entrants is constrained by the decision made earlier. However, the first entrants should also be aware that competition will ensue. This leads Prescott and Visscher (1977, Chapter 21) to raise the following fundamental question:

> since firms move sequentially, why does the first firm to enter not locate at all positions in the equilibrium industry structure and obtain all potential profits in the market rather than be content with only the first location and less profit? In other words, why should the first firm not be a monopoly? (p. 391)

Prescott and Visscher appeal to imperfections in capital markets as well as to the inability of agents to foresee the extent of the market as possible explanations. According to Schmalensee (1978), it would rather seem that the established firms want to follow such a 'proliferation' strategy by expanding their product lines with the aim of making the entry of a new firm unprofitable. Entry deterrence could then be achieved by crowding the brand space. Judd (1985) shows that the story is not that simple. For the incumbent to be able to preempt the market, he or she must be able to commit to all brands in his or her product line. This is possible only if the exit of existing brands is prohibitively costly, a condition which does not seem to be very common. Hence preemption is not an easy strategy to implement, but it seems to us alternative aspects are still to be explored.

In particular, a related issue, often neglected by economists, has been investigated in marketing where it is known as *cannibalization*. Specifically, *when a firm offers several varieties, it competes with itself because of the consumer self-selection constraints imposed by its joint supply.* As a result, the firm may find it optimal not to provide the whole array of potential varieties. In such cases, besides cost considerations and entry threat, the monopolist finds it optimal to bunch segments of consumers on the same variety and, therefore, to supply only a small array of varieties (Gabszewicz, 1983). This is sufficient to show that brand proliferation is not necessarily an optimal strategy. Cannibalization and market preemption creates opposite incentives to brand proliferation and the study of the balance between these forces remains a major task for the future.[20]

III. Product Differentiation

1. Product selection is one of the firms' major decision variables. This was made clear by Chamberlin in several publications, especially in his 1953 paper, already available in 1936 as a mimeo. As Chamberlin (1953, Chapter 22) said: 'it seems difficult to understand how the economist can pretend to explain (or to prescribe for) the economic system and leave products out of the picture. Why not leave price out? And why is one more important than the other?' (p. 27).

However, an appropriate framework to analyse rigorously the selection of products was missing. Despite the early contribution of Hotelling, economists waited for the work of Lancaster (1966) to define precisely when products are differentiated, that is, when they all have the *same* characteristics but not in the same amounts. Products are then identified by their position in a given space of characteristics. The relative positions of two products can be expressed in two different ways, thus leading to two different types of differentiation (Lancaster, 1979). Two products are said to be *horizontally differentiated* when the level of some characteristics is augmented while it is lowered for some others, as in the case of the different versions of a car. Two products are *vertically differentiated* when the level of all characteristics is augmented or lowered, as in the case of cars in different series. Or, using consumers' indirect utility, two products are horizontally differentiated when, offered at the same price, they both obtain a positive market share; they are vertically differentiated when one product gets the entire set of consumers. In the latter case, it is then allowable to describe products by their *quality*.

Despite the pathbreaking work of Hotelling (Laundhart was ignored until recently in the non-German-speaking scientific community) and the repeated efforts of Chamberlin over the period 1933–53, product differentiation remained at the periphery of mainstream economics. Only with progress in the new industrial economics have economists moved to a world where product differentiation became a basic ingredient of competition. It is now clear that product differentiation drastically affects the process of competition. This should already be apparent from our discussion of product differentiation when used by firms as a weapon to deter entry. More fundamentally, as noticed early by Laundhart (1885) and Hotelling (1929, Chapter 27), but often forgotten by economists, product differentiation relaxes price competition because firms have market power over the consumers who like their products best. Put in a slightly different way, firms are able to get out of the zero profit equilibrium trap and to earn positive markups when they sell differentiated products. In this sense, it is fair to say that product differentiation provides a solution to the Bertrand paradox discussed in I.2. In introducing consumer taste heterogeneity, Hotelling's aim was to show that the discontinuities of the Bertrand and Edgeworth models are not inherent to price competition. According to Hotelling (1929, Chapter 27), it should be clear that

> a discontinuity, like a vacuum, is abhorred by nature. More typical of real situations is the case in which the quantity sold by each merchant is a continuous function of two variables, his own price and his competitor's. Quite commonly, a tiny increase in price by one seller will send only a few customers to the other. (p. 44)

In addition, product differentiation may help in proving the existence of a (pure strategy) price equilibrium in market environments plagued by nonexistence of an equilibrium. For example, the work of Canoy (1996) and Wauthy (1996) shows that a pure strategy equilibrium in the Edgeworth oligopoly does exist when products are differentiated enough. Finally, observe that product differentiation also appends new dimensions to the welfare analysis of imperfectly competitive markets. Indeed, pricing above marginal cost might well not be the main source of inefficiency in differentiated markets. There are two other potential sources of inefficiency: the number of products supplied by the market and the specification of the products made available to the consumers. This observation leads Spence (1976a, p. 408) to conjecture that: 'a significant fraction of the cost of imperfect competition may be due to the currently unmeasured cost of having too many, too few, or the wrong products'.

In what follows, we first discuss Chamberlinian models of monopolistic competition. We then turn to the 'spatial' criticism raised by Kaldor and others for whom product symmetry is not an acceptable assumption, thus changing drastically the nature of the competition. These two families of models have often been considered as two exclusive approaches to the process of competition with differentiated products (see, for example, Archibald, Eaton and Lipsey, 1986) and we will see exactly why and how they differ. Moreover, in these two families of models, the specification of products is given a priori. It then remains to analyse the problem of product selection under horizontal and vertical differentiation. Surprisingly enough, it will be shown that the latter difference is more fundamental for the formation of market structure than the standard opposition between models *à la* Chamberlin and models *à la* Hotelling–Kaldor.

2.   Despite his multifaceted contributions to the economics of product differentiation, Chamberlin (1933, Chapter 23; 1951) is mainly remembered for his symmetric model of monopolistic competition in which a large number of firms selling differentiated variants each face a downward-sloping demand curve (like a monopolist) whose position depends on the policy elected by all other firms in the market (as in perfect competition). Hence, like Cournot, Chamberlin aimed at erecting a bridge between monopoly and perfect competition.[21] However, his model fails to do so because it lacks the coherence that has permitted the Cournot model to capture intermediate situations. In a sense, this difficulty is reflected by the somewhat awkward expression coined by Chamberlin himself, that is, 'monopolistic competition'.

In Chamberlin's monopolistic competition the effect of a price change by one firm is spread out (more or less) equally across all other firms so that the price change has only a negligible impact on each competitor's demand. At first order, this impact may therefore be neglected. This idea is nicely formulated in the following quotation from Chamberlin (1933, p. 74):

> Theory may well disregard the interdependence between markets whenever business men do, in fact, ignore it. This is true ... in a multitude of cases where the effects of a price change inaugurated by any one seller are spread over such a large number of competitors that they are negligible for each.

Thus, the conscious interaction stressed in the above is absent from Chamberlinian models of competition. However, given their widespread use in economics, we believe that it is not possible to ignore these models.

It is only recently that Chamberlin's ideas have been formally cast into a precise framework, developed by Spence (1976b) and Dixit and Stiglitz (1977, Chapter 24). These authors view monopolistic competition as a market structure determined by consumers' preference for variety and firms' fixed requirements for limited productive resources. Each firm produces one variety and, with freedom of entry, profits will be just sufficient to cover average costs as in Marshallian long-run equilibrium. A representative consumer who has a preference for variety (*varietas delectat*) allows one to capture the fact that the market demands reflect the different and mutually exclusive choices made by consumers having heterogeneous tastes,[22] as well as the tendency for firms to supply differentiated products. When all variants are equally priced, the representative consumer then buys a positive (presumably small) amount of each variant. To express such a behaviour, a CES utility function whose variants are equally weighted is used.

In addition, Dixit and Stiglitz formalize the process of monopolistic competition in a way that makes it really different from other approaches and that seems to be in Chamberlin's spirit of large group competition. They assume that *each firm is negligible in the sense that it can ignore its impact on, and hence reactions from, other firms, but retains enough market power for pricing above marginal cost regardless of the total number of firms*. Recall that the CES-demand to a firm is given by a ratio; the numerator depends only upon the firm's price whereas the denominator can be interpreted as the price index of the corresponding industry (up to a power transformation). A small price change by a firm affects the numerator of its demand in a standard way. However, since each firm has a negligible impact on the market, the firm's price change does not affect the level of the price index that comprises the denominator. Consequently, each firm faces an iso-elastic downward-sloping demand whose elasticity equals the elasticity of substitution between variants. Since variants are equally weighted in the utility function, the equilibrium price is the same across firms and equal to the common marginal production cost times a positive markup.

As suggested by the nonstrategic assumption made above, the equilibrium price is equal to the limit of the Nash equilibrium prices when the number of firms is arbitrarily large (Anderson et al., 1992, ch. 7). The monopolistic competition price is, therefore, lower than the oligopolistic competition price. The markup itself increases with the elasticity of substitution between variants. In other words, *when products are more differentiated, firms charge higher prices*. On the other hand, the equilibrium price falls as the number of variants rises. Note that this effect is not due to price competition since competition is nonstrategic in the Dixit–Stiglitz model. Instead, it is due to the preference for variety which leads the representative consumer to spread his or her demand over all existing variants. This intensifies product competition which in turn yields a downward shift of demand and, therefore, to a price fall. Similarly, each entrant chooses to offer a variant different from the existing ones because he or she thus obtains a higher share of the market than by replicating the variant of an existing firm. It is worth mentioning that these effects are similar to those derived under strategic price competition (as discussed in Section III.3, below) but are obtained through a different market process.

The emphasis of the enquiry has usually been on the number of firms (variants) in equilibrium and the optimum number in the case where firms faced fixed production costs. Does the market provide the 'right' number or is there excess/insufficient product diversity? This is the question studied by the First Theorem of Welfare Economics but within a very different framework since firms act on a monopolistically competitive market. The nature of the forces at work has been elucidated by Spence (1976b), On the one hand, revenues may not be high enough to cover costs even when the social value of an additional variant is positive. Thus some variants that ought to be produced are not offered in the market. On the other hand, when a new variant is introduced, it affects other firms adversely but a firm's entry decision does not account for that impact. This tends to generate too many variants. Hence it is a priori difficult to predict the welfare properties of the market equilibrium and the analysis conducted by Dixit and Stiglitz suggests that the answer is ambiguous. This is because the market price is assumed to be low, a fact that discourages entry. Nevertheless, when strategic interaction is explicitly taken into account in price competition, Anderson, de Palma and Nesterov (1995) have been able to show that the market never underprovides product variety by more than one variety; in addition, *excess variety is the most standard result.*

Finally, it has been shown that, under the CES, the Folk Theorem of Competitive Markets does not hold: *when fixed costs become arbitrarily small, the equilibrium price does not (necessarily) converge towards marginal cost.* Or, to put it differently, the demand for each variant does not approach a perfectly elastic demand so that the markup remains bounded away from zero, regardless of the size of firms relative to the market. This establishes that monopolistic competition is indeed a real market structure, despite the arguments raised against it by Joan Robinson and others. In other words , while each firm has a negligible impact on the others, it still maintains significant market power. The nonconvergence towards the competitive outcome is not easy to understand. It is due to the fact that the degree of substitutability between variants is bounded from below. One possible explanation is that the distribution of consumer tastes does not decrease rapidly enough for a large matching value, thus allowing firms to find enough consumers in the distribution tail to maintain some market power. On the other hand, when the support of consumer tastes is compact, or when the distribution of tastes converges fast enough towards zero, Perloff and Salop (1985) show that a new entrant always finds a sufficiently close variety, thus inducing fierce competition between the corresponding producers. In such cases, the Folk Theorem of Competitive Markets holds in a differentiated industry. We shall see that convergence also arises in spatial models of monopolistic competition.[23]

3.   In his criticism of Chamberlin, Kaldor (1935, Chapter 25), but also Lösch (1940) in the space-economy, argued that product locations in characteristics space mould the nature of competition in a very specific way.[24] Whatever the number of firms participating in the aggregate, competition is *localized*: each firm competes more vigorously with its immediate neighbours than with more distant neighbours. To see this, we anticipate our discussion of Hotelling's work and suppose that n firms are distributed equidistantly along a circle. Firm i has two direct competitors, firms $i - 1$ and $i + 1$. The market situated between firms $i - 1$ and $i + 1$ is segmented according to the following principle: each consumer patronizes the firm with the lowest 'full price' defined as the posted price plus the transportation cost to the corresponding firm. Following Hotelling's suggestion, transportation costs may be interpreted as the utility loss incurred by a consumer from not consuming his or her ideal product. Hence, for a vector of prices, there are three groups of consumers in this local market: those who buy from firm $i - 1$, from firm $i + 1$ and from firm i. Firm i has two market boundaries. The boundary between the two firms' markets is given by the location of the consumer indifferent between the two firms; it is called the marginal consumer. The location of this consumer is endogenous since it depends on the prices set by firms. Hence, a unilateral

price cut by firm i will extend its own market only at the expense of firms $i - 1$ and $i + 1$, while the other firms are not directly affected. This market structure is by nature oligopolistic in that each firm is only concerned directly with a small number of competitors, whatever the total number of firms in the industry. In this sense it differs fundamentally from the symmetric model of Chamberlin (1933) in which a firm that cuts its price will attract customers from all the other firms.[25] In the words of Kaldor (1935, Chapter 25):

> the different producers' products will never possess the same substitutability in relation to any particular product. Any particular producer will always be faced with rivals who are nearer to him, and others who are "farther off". In fact, he should be able to class his rivals, *from his own point of view*, in a certain order, according to the influence of their prices upon his demand. (p. 38, italic in original)

And indeed, as shown by Eaton and Wooders (1985), the impact of a price cut by a firm on non-neighbouring firms strongly declines with the distance to it. This does not imply, however, that the industry is formed by independent clusters of sellers. Since a chain connects any two firms, all of them are interrelated within a complex network of interactions. The equilibrium price is the same across firms but is now equal to the common marginal production cost augmented by a positive markup; this one increases with the transport cost parameter, showing once more that more product differentiation yields higher prices. As space gets crowded by more and more variants (maybe because fixed costs fall relative to the market size), the distance between two neighbouring variants becomes arbitrarily small and available products get closer and closer substitutes. As a result, the sequence of equilibrium prices converges towards the common marginal cost.

Consider now the efficient configuration. How many firms should be in the market and where should they be located? In the setting considered by Hotelling, the optimal number and locations of firms minimize the firms' fixed production costs plus consumers' total transport costs. As shown by Beckmann (1972, Chapter 26) in the case of a linear space, and later on by Lancaster (1975) and Salop (1979) in the case of a circular space, there is a fundamental tradeoff in a differentiated industry in that increasing the number of firms, hence fixed costs, reduces the aggregate transport costs and vice versa. Firms consider a similar tradeoff when deciding whether or not to enter. A firm will only enter if it can locate sufficiently far from other firms so that it can serve enough consumers, and charge a high enough price, to cover its fixed costs. In addition, Beckmann shows that, for the same configuration of parameters, the equilibrium price is lower when firms compete in two-dimensional characteristics spaces than in one-dimensional spaces. Anticipating somewhat our discussions below, we can say that this is because each firm has six competitors (located at the vertices of a hexagon) instead of two.

In general the equilibrium number of firms is larger than the optimal number, a result that points to the same direction as Anderson et al. (1995). Numbers are not the same, however. This can be explained as follows. In Chamberlinian models, each firm competes directly with every other one, thus making competition especially fierce. On the contrary, in the unidimensional spatial model, *a firm competes only with its two neighbours*. Therefore, price competition should be more intense in the former models than in the latter. Lower profits for the incumbents would then invite less entry and would explain the observed difference in results (see also Deneckere and Rothschild, 1992).

Observe, finally, that contrary to general belief the Dixit–Stiglitz model may be reconciled with spatial models *à la* Kaldor under particular conditions. Indeed, Anderson et al. (1989; 1992, ch. 4) have shown that the Dixit–Stiglitz model (as well as other similar models) is formally equivalent to a spatial model in which the dimension of the characteristics space is at least equal to the number of variants minus one. In this way, each market space intersects any other one and, thereby, each firm competes directly with all others. As a result, the reasons for the differences observed between the Dixit–Stiglitz model and the spatial model are to be found in (i) *the respective dimensions of the characteristics space* and (ii) *the nature of price competition among firms* (recall that the equilibrium price in the Dixit–Stiglitz model is not a Nash equilibrium).

4.   All the above models assume that variants are given and, therefore, ignore the process of product specification by firms. The prototype of product selection in an oligopolistic setting is due to Hotelling (1929, Chapter 27). To this end, he used a spatial metaphor, by assuming a market where the consumers live at locations continuously and uniformly distributed along a line segment – Main Street – and where duopolists sell an identical good at different locations. As observed by Hotelling (1929, Chapter 27), it is easy to reinterpret this framework in terms of ideal products:

> distance, as we have used it for illustration, is only a figurative term for a great congeries of qualities. Instead of sellers an identical commodity separated geographically we might have considered two competing cider merchants side by side, one selling a sweeter liquid than the other. If the consumers of cider be thought of as varying by infinitesimal degrees in the sourness they desire, we have much the same situation as before. The measure of sourness now replaces distance, while instead of transportation costs there are the degrees of disutility resulting from a consumer getting cider more or less different from what he wants. (p. 54)

For each pair of prices, each consumer purchases one unit from the firm which, for him or her, has the lower full price. The consumers are thus divided into two segments, with each firm's aggregate demand represented by the consumers in one segment. As said above, the location of the marginal consumer depends on the prices set by both firms. Because of the continuous dispersion of consumers, a marginal variation in price changes the boundary, and changes each firm's demand by the same order.[26] Unlike the Bertrand case, heterogeneity in consumer tastes, introduced through transportation costs, ensures here that each firm's demand is continuous, while permitting consumers to react discontinuously at the individual level (nonconvex preferences). Specifically, individual discontinuities are distributed such that they are not noticeable to the firms, thus smoothing price competition (formally, the consumer distribution is supposed to be absolutely continuous).

Hotelling considers a two-stage decision process where firms first simultaneously choose their location and afterwards their price. This decoupling of decisions captures the idea that firms select their location in anticipation of later competing on price. For each location pair, Hotelling determines what he thinks will be the price in a noncooperative equilibrium of the corresponding price subgame. He includes these prices, which are functions of firms' locations, in the profit functions which then depend only upon locations. These new profit functions are used to study the game of choosing locations. Hotelling finds an equilibrium where the two firms locate at the centre of the market, a result which had to be known as the Principle of Minimum Differentiation.

The idea to formulate a game on price and locations according to a two-stage procedure was extremely ingenious and original (it precedes by many years the work of Selten on subgame perfect equilibrium). Unfortunately Hotelling's analysis was incorrect. When the two firms are sufficiently close, there does not exist an equilibrium in pure strategies for the corresponding price subgame. The study of the location game is accordingly incomplete. However, as established by d'Aspremont, Gabszewicz and Thisse (1979), if transport costs are quadratic rather than linear, a unique price equilibrium will exist for any pair of locations. Reconstructing Hotelling's analysis, these authors then show that the two firms wish to place themselves at the two ends of the market segment. Among other things, this result sheds light on another dimension of the welfare problem. Even though the equilibrium and optimum numbers of firms would be the same, the firms in equilibrium might not locate efficiently. For example, if the optimal and equilibrium number of firms is two, the optimal locations on the interval from zero to one are at the first and third quartiles, whereas the equilibrium locations will be at the endpoints. Hence there is a loss of efficiency generated by the choice of products made by firms.

The tendency to product differentiation is robust to alternative specifications of the demand side (Gabszewicz and Thisse, 1992). However, when there are several characteristics, firms may want to differentiate along one dimension only and to standardize along the others (Irmen and Thisse, 1998), a result which does not necessarily imply that the market provides insufficient differentiation since the answer depends on the number of characteristics. Even though the debate is not closed, yet one may say that the so-called Principle of Minimum Differentiation is to be replaced by the Principle of Differentiation: *firms always have incentives to differentiate their products in order to soften price competition* (d'Aspremont, Gabszewicz and Thisse, 1983).

This conclusion is based on the extreme price-sensitivity of consumers. In Hotelling-like models, each consumer has a threshold price difference below which he or she will not switch firms, and above which he or she switches with probability one. Such an extreme behaviour seems unwarranted, and psychologists have suggested an alternative model of consumer choice which softens it. This model imputes a random term to utility and makes the consumer's decision whether to switch firms probabilistically. This changes the outcome of competition in the Hotelling model as follows. The observer, for example, the firm, assigns a probability between zero and one to whether a particular consumer on a particular date will respond to a price difference by switching firms; this probability reflects the lack of information of firms about consumer preferences at the very moment of their purchase. Probabilistic behaviour can be modelled by assuming that consumers maximize a random utility rather than a deterministic utility.[27] This means that firms implicitly sell heterogeneous products while the random term in the consumer's utility establishes his or her ranking of firms at the time of purchase (Anderson et al., 1989; 1992, chs 3–4). A possible interpretation, reminiscent of the Spence–Dixit–Stiglitz approach, is that each consumer likes product variety so that, even if prices do not vary, he or she does not always purchase from the same firm. Another is to assume consumer heterogeneity as to the value they place on the characteristics of the products supplied by firms which, in turn, know only the distribution of these valuations across the population of consumers.

In the Hotelling model, if two firms are located side by side along the observable characteristic (Main Street) with identical prices, a small price reduction of one firm will attract all the customers. If consumers' switching behaviour is probabilistic, the aggregate response to a price cut will not be so abrupt. This modification to the Hotelling model, which has been developed by de Palma et al. (1985, Chapter 28), has two major implications. First, if consumers' purchasing behaviour becomes sufficiently dispersed, firms' demand functions are smoothed sufficiently when they are located close together so that a price equilibrium in pure strategies exists.[28] Second, under the same condition, firms tend to agglomerate at the market centre instead of selecting distant locations. Price competition is relaxed because of the implicit differentiation among vendors associated with their random behaviour, which gives them market power even when they are agglomerated along the observable characteristic.

It is worth noting here that this model allows for a partial reconciliation between models *à la* Spence–Dixit–Stiglitz and localized models of product differentiation. Indeed, under standard random utility models, each consumer has a positive probability of buying from each firm. However, these probabilities are not equal: consumers have a high probability of patronizing cheap products and a low probability of purchasing expensive products. In this way, firms compete all together but retain more market power over their adjacent consumers. This line of research has been developed recently by Anderson and de Palma (1996).

5.   Vertical differentiation and horizontal differentiation seem a priori to be very similar since they both correspond to particular forms of localized competition (products compete directly with their neighbours on the quality axis). Yet, the two types of models turn out to lead to quite different market outcomes. To the best of our knowledge, Gabszewicz and Thisse (1979) have been the first to tackle the problem of oligopolistic competition when firms sell products with distinct qualities. The difference in quality leads each consumer to have a different willingness-to-pay for the various products. Consequently, the high-quality firm chooses to specialize on the segment of consumers who have a high willingness-to-pay, typically those with high incomes. As a result, the consumers who have a low willingness-to-pay fall back on the low-quality product. In other words, we see that *market segmentation mirrors income dispersion.*

Starting with a duopoly and a population of consumers with a highly dispersed income distribution, Gabszewicz and Thisse (1979) show that the equilibrium prices are such that the entire market is not served. As the high-quality firm offers its product at quite a high price, the low-quality firm finds it profitable to supply the middle-class consumers only by selecting a price which remains too high for the poor consumers to buy its product. When the income span shrinks, price competition is intensified because the high-quality firm has an incentive to reduce its price. As a result, the whole market is now supplied. An interesting and new result occurs when the income range shrinks further: only the high-quality firm is active in the market. This does not mean that it behaves like a monopolist. Instead it charges a price below the monopoly level, which rises with the quality gap. In this case, the potential competition exercised by the low-quality firm forces the high-quality one to lower its price to a level that just reflects the difference in quality. This result has a strong contestability flavour in that the price differential decreases as the quality gap narrows down.

The analysis of the oligopoly case reveals that the natural monopoly structure uncovered in the above discussion extends to that of *natural oligopoly* (Gabszewicz and Thisse, 1980, Chapter 29). However small the entry costs are and regardless of the number of potential entrants, the price equilibrium is such that only a certain number of firms are active in the market; the number depends positively on the size of the income range. When marginal production costs are positive and increasing with quality. Shaked and Sutton (1983, Chapter 30) have demonstrated that the finiteness property still holds if products are ranked unanimously by consumers when priced at marginal cost. The reason for the natural oligopoly lies in the fact that low-quality products must be low enough to compensate consumers for the loss of quality. For some of these products, this implies pricing below marginal cost, in which case the corresponding firms choose to be out of business in equilibrium. Looking at this market structure from the entry standpoint, we can say that, when the industry has reached its maximum size, *the entry of firms with a higher quality/cost ratio induces the exit of those with a lower ratio.* Therefore, the model of vertical differentiation captures some aspects of the Schumpeterian process of creative destruction, mentioned in the introduction, through the entry and exit of firms embodying product/process innovations.

IV. Incomplete Information

1. There are many ways to introduce incomplete information in imperfect market models. In this section, we consider only three types of problems which are representative of the main trends in this new field of economics.[29] In the first one, consumers are imperfectly informed about the prices set and/or the characteristics of the products sold by firms. This is one of the very first issues addressed in the economics of information (Stigler, 1961) which has also been shown to lead firms to depart from marginal cost pricing. We then move to the reverse case where firms have incomplete information about market demand and/or competitors' types. When uncertainty is about the payoffs or about the 'nature' of competitors, it directly affects the premises of competition. Last, an additional dimension arises once it is recognized that firms (players) may use information strategically. We do not consider, however, the recent contributions devoted to experimentation and learning by firms about market fundamentals, because most of the existing contributions deal with the monopoly case (see, however, Fishman and Rob, 1998) for a recent exception).

2. Historically, the first studies of markets with incomplete information considered situations where consumers are poorly informed about firms' prices. The standard assumption is that consumers know the distribution of prices but do not know which firm quotes which price. When gathering information is costly, each consumer must then compare the cost of an additional bit of information with the expected gain in terms of expected surplus. In such a context, firms set prices and each firm faces downward-sloping demand because a price cut will induce more customers to visit the firm by increasing the expected surplus of an additional search. Since these demands also depend on prices charged by the other firms, competition has a strategic dimension.[30]

In a market where identical firms supply a homogeneous good at a constant, identical marginal cost and where consumers bear the same search cost, Diamond (1971, Chapter 31) shows that *all firms choose to price at the monopoly price level.* Furthermore, at equilibrium, consumers do not undertake any search because each consumer buys from the first firm he or she visits. This work can be viewed as a model of imperfect competition where firms face downward-sloping demands caused by the advantage given to the firm's product once a consumer visits that firm and observes the firm's price. *Hence, as do product differentiation and capacity constraints, uncertainty about firms' prices leads to a substantial departure from the competitive level on the firms' part.* Salop and Stiglitz (1977, Chapter 32) provide the intuitive rationale for this:

> The central implication of costly information-gathering is that the equilibrium will not occur at the perfectly competitive price. ... Suppose every firm did charge the perfectly competitive price. Then some firm(s) could raise price slightly without losing any consumers. Consumers would be unwilling to gather the extra information needed to switch stores or brands. Clearly there is a limit on the price increases at one store that consumers will tolerate without leaving. However, since the *relative* store prices determine the gains from a search, then as every store raises price slightly, the cycle of price rises by a few stores may occur again. Hence prices throughout the market continue to rise. (p. 493, italics in original)

In the same way as Bertrand has prompted much new research, the 'Diamond paradox' has been at the source of many developments in the modern analysis of markets under imperfect information. We shall restrict ourselves to a few contributions which are typical of the research triggered by the work of Diamond.

First, within a very different setting, Gabszewicz and Garella (1986) obtain results fairly similar to those of Diamond. Using the Hotelling framework of Section III.4 with the two firms located at the endpoints of the market, these authors assume that each consumer knows the price of the nearer store but has beliefs about the price set by the more distant store. The cost to be incurred to know this price increases with the distance between the consumer and the corresponding firm (as is the case when the consumer has to drive to the store) so that search costs are different across consumers. For any given belief about the more distant firm's price, every consumer is characterized by a willingness to buy at the nearer store's price without visiting the farther firm, which decreases with the distance to that firm. The Nash price equilibrium (if any) is then such that both firms charge the same price which equals the highest price that the half-way consumer is willing to afford. Thus, at equilibrium, *firms manipulate prices in such a way that no consumer engages in a search* and choose the highest price compatible with the absence of search.

Second, when some consumers decide to become perfectly informed at some specific costs, Salop and Stiglitz (1977, Chapter 32) come to the conclusion that *the presence of informed consumers is sufficient to induce some degree of competition among firms, resulting in an average price lower than the monopoly price.* More precisely, they consider a setting in which firms may induce information-gathering by consumers who know the distribution of prices across firms but not which firm charges which price. The high-information-cost consumers *choose* to remain uninformed and purchase randomly from the first store visited; the low-information-cost consumers choose to become informed and purchase from a lowest-price store. At a free entry Nash equilibrium (which may not exist), two prices emerge, that is, marginal cost pricing and monopoly pricing. The informed consumers buy from the 'competitive' firms at their very first visit. On the other hand, uninformed consumers may buy from either type of firm.

Third, assuming that consumers sample sequentially from a known continuous distribution of prices and maximize expected utility, Reinganum (1979) shows that the law of the single price in Diamond's model leaves room for an equilibrium with *continuous price dispersion* once firms have different marginal costs and consumers have elastic demands. As usual, prices are not driven down to the competitive level because of search costs but not all prices jump to the monopoly level because consumers now buy different amounts of the product at different prices.

Last, Diamond's result holds regardless of the number of firms operating in the market and whatever the (positive) value of the search cost. Such a result is surprising since one would expect the competitive outcome to approximately hold when the number of firms is large and the search cost low (see our discussion above about the Folk Theorem of Competitive Markets). *The 'Diamond paradox' therefore suggests an immense discontinuity between the Bertrand and the Diamond cases as search costs go from zero to some arbitrarily low level.* This seems very implausible. Once again, introducing product differentiation might well smooth out equilibrium pricing and yield less dramatic results. As observed by Wolinsky (1986), *consumers not only search for the best price but also for the best variant once the market is differentiated.* To study such a situation, Wolinsky grafts a search model on to a discrete choice model of competition such as that of Perloff and Salop (1985). Since consumers are heterogeneous, they search over more than one firm when the corresponding costs are not too high. In this case, firms will always choose a price above marginal cost, even though the number of firms is large. This is because it is never optimal for consumers to search over too many firms, thus limiting the degree of substitutability among variants. Nevertheless, when the search cost tends to become very low while the market gets close to a homogeneous one, the equilibrium price approaches the competitive level. This result is more in accordance with intuition and suggests, once more, that using product differentiation as a starting assumption might well be more appropriate than the standard approach focusing on homogeneous markets.

3.   We now switch to the stability of collusion when firms do not observe demand with certainty. As seen in Section I.4, Osborne (1976, Chapter 9) and Friedman (1971, Chapter 10) have shown how a collusive agreement may be sustained as a noncooperative equilibrium once it is recognized that firms operate in a dynamic setting. Green and Porter (1984, Chapter 33) observe that 'incentives in these equilibria are so perfect that the deterrent mechanisms are never observed' (p. 88). And this is so because of the certainty world in which these models are formulated. In marked contrast, *when demand fluctuations are not directly observable by firms, they might well revert to vigorous competition for some periods of time simply because of low demand, even though no firm is cheating.* Specifically, firms act monopolistically as long as prices remain high but revert to the one-shot equilibrium for some fixed amount of time when prices fall below a level they initially agreed upon. If not, each firm would have an incentive to supply a bit more than what is called for in agreement and to blame the demand shock for the resulting lower equilibrium price. This makes the story quite different from what it is under certainty, as discussed in II.2.

To illustrate how this works, Green and Porter (1984, Chapter 33) consider a Cournot oligopoly with a homogeneous good as in Friedman (1971, Chapter 10) except that demand is subject to random shocks and that past and present outputs are private information, all other variables and parameters being public information. Collusion under uncertainty about demand is then defined by a Nash equilibrium where a strategy is now a sequence formed by rules specifying the firm's output as a function of past prices (recall that firms do not observe rivals' outputs directly). In this way, an equilibrium accounts for the fact that each firm must balance the marginal revenue resulting from an increase of its output against the marginal increase in the probability of suffering loss during a 'reversionary' period.[31] However, if each firm expects the others not to cheat, the following question suggests itself: if a low price at some particular time has been observed, why do firms not disregard it? The answer is that firms understand the nature of the incentive contained in the definition of an equilibrium. *If firms were not to revert to the one-shot equilibrium in reaction to low prices, monopolistic behaviour would cease to be individually rational.* In other words, the threat of punishing deviators must remain credible. In the likely case where there is uncertainty about demand, the conventional wisdom that price wars are evidence of the fragility of collusion may therefore be erroneous.

Thus price wars are consistent with equilibrium behaviour by industry participants who operate in interactive decision making under incomplete information. Similarly, *aggressive behaviour* may be rationalized under incomplete information in situations which otherwise would never display such a behaviour. For example, predatory pricing (entry generates severe price cuts) has long been a mystery for economists in that it does not seem to be consistent with rational behaviour (McGee, 1980). And indeed, great sophistication is needed to show how predation may occur. Assume that potential entrants have complete information. If they know that predation is unprofitable (profitable) for the incumbent, they enter (will not enter) and, in either case, no predation will be observed. It is essential, therefore, that the entrants have some *doubts* about the incumbent's reaction and are not sure that predation will (or will not) occur. But for that, history must matter. However, in repeated games, 'history matters only because firms threaten to make it matter' (Kreps and Spence, 1985, p. 360).

In a celebrated paper, Selten (1978, Chapter 34) provided an illustrative example showing that predation is not consistent with rational behaviour (defined here as subgame perfection). A chain store operates in 20 identical towns and the game is played over a sequence of 20 periods. In each town k a small firm, called player k, decides whether or not to enter. The incumbent (that is the chain store) may react in two ways in each local market: he or she may choose to accommodate entry and to earn 2, or to be aggressive and to earn 0. As for the entrant, he or she is better off when entry is accompanied (his or her payoff is 2) while entry turns out not to be profitable when the incumbent is aggressive (his or her payoff is 0). When player k stays out, he or she earns 1. The payoff matrix of a subgame is displayed in Table 1.

Table 1   The chain store's current payoffs and player k's payoffs

Chain store / Player k	Enter		Stay out	
Accommodating behaviour	2	2	5	1
Aggressive behaviour	0	0	5	1

This is a game of perfect information in which the chain store aims at maximizing the sum of its profits over the 20 periods. Using a backward induction argument shows that this game has a unique subgame perfect Nash equilibrium in which *the chain store will choose to accommodate entry in each town.* Indeed, it is in the interest of the incumbent to accommodate entry in the last period since the corresponding profit is 2 instead of 0, and so regardless of the actions chosen in the previous periods. Now, consider period 19. We already know that the decision made during this period has no influence on what will be decided in period 20. Therefore, everything works as if period 19 were the last one so that the incumbent will choose again to accommodate entry in town 19. And so on up to period 1 where entry is accommodate in town 1. Since the game is of perfect information, being aggressive in one period does not imply any change in the prospects for the subsequent period.

Yet, it is intuitively plausible that the chain store should rather fight against potential entrants during the initial periods in order to build a reputation that would deter the entry of subsequent players and to accommodate entry when the game comes close to its end. This is precisely why Selten called his game the 'chain store paradox'. This implies that one would like to find a game in which *the incumbent is able to build a reputation which acts as an entry-deterrent for some subsequent periods*. In repeated games, as the one considered by Selten, 'firms do not look backward in order to learn from the past', although 'previous experiences explain more of which outcomes merge than any other feature of the competition' (Kreps and Spence, 1985, pp. 359–60). This prevents the building of a reputation by the incumbent. Hence another innovation from game theory was required to tackle such situations.

Since the purpose is to find formal models in which firms learn from the past behaviour of their rivals, one needs to introduce something about which firms are uncertain. The flow of events may help them to resolve this uncertainty. This can be achieved by appealing to games of incomplete information.[32] To this end, suppose that *potential entrants are unsure about the incumbent's payoffs*, perhaps because they are unsure about the incumbent's costs or because there may be nonmonetary gains that the incumbent enjoys by being tough. More precisely, for the entrants the payoff structure is either as described in Table 1 or as in Table 2.

Table 2   The chain store's current payoffs and player k's payoffs when the incumbent is 'tough'

Chain store / Player k	Enter		Stay out	
Accommodating behaviour	2	2	5	1
Aggressive behaviour	3	0	5	1

In this second table, it appears that the chain store chooses to be aggressive when player k enters, thus making entry undesirable. In other words, the entrants entertain some uncertainty about the chain store's payoff. As time passes, the history of the game prior to period k enables the corresponding entrant to revise its priors about the relative likelihood of the incumbent's two possible payoffs. The incumbent, by being aggressive at any early entry, might then use this behaviour to convince latter opponents that he or she will always fight, thus deterring later entries. What makes such an outcome possible is that the potential entrants believe that the incumbent entrants believe that the incumbent does not necessarily choose to accommodate entry because of the positive prior they assess to Table 2. In game-theoretic words, this means that (i) 'nature' initially determines the incumbent's payoff structure, (ii) nature's move is observed by the incumbent but not by the potential entrants, and (iii) each player finds a strategy which is optimal for him- or herself, *given the private information he or she received before the beginning of the game as well as the new information collected over time.*

Because of the reputation he or she has established over the initial periods, the chain store will not face entry for several periods. It is very likely that, at the last period, player 20 will enter in town 20. This same might hold for a few periods preceding the last one. But the reputation built by the chain store will allow it to enjoy a monopoly during several periods. Alternative formulations have been proposed by Kreps and Wilson (1982, Chapter 35) and by Milgrom and Roberts (1982a) to describe such situations. The basic principles underlying such solutions have been formulated in a neat way by Kreps and Spence (1985, p. 365):

> if potential entrants are initially uncertain about whether predation really is costly to the monopolist in the short run, then even if the chances that it is costly are close to one, the monopolist will engage in predation, in an attempt to gain a reputation for being tough. In other words, the monopolist, realizing that potential entrants will look at his/her 'track record' in previous encounters, can effectively threaten to abuse any entrant for demonstration purposes. Even if it is costly to abuse entrants in the short run, the long-run gain accruing from forestalling subsequent entry is more than worth it.

Hence games of incomplete information allow one to rationalize predation which is to be observed along the equilibrium path. The most surprising (and somewhat irritating) result of all this analysis is probably that 'a small amount of uncertainty about what each player knows about the others can be very destructive of easy conclusions arrived at by assuming that no such uncertainty exists' (Kreps, 1990, p. 82). This is confirmed by the limit pricing model. We have seen in Section II.2 that an entrant has no interest in the incumbent's pre-entry price when there is complete information (Friedman, 1979, Chapter 17). As shown by Milgrom and Roberts (1982b, Chapter 36) and Friedman (1983b), the story changes dramatically when the entrant is unsure about the profit function of the incumbent. Milgrom and Roberts consider the case where the entrant does not know whether the incumbent has a 'low' or a 'high' marginal production cost. Under complete information, the entrant does not learn anything from the observation of the incumbent's price. This is no longer true when incomplete information prevails since *the pre-entry price may convey information about the price that will prevail after entry.* More precisely, a low (high) pre-entry price may signal a low (high) cost, thus providing the potential entrant with information regarding the market conditions that should prevail after entry.

To keep matters simple, suppose that the entrant would like to enter if the incumbent's marginal cost is higher than some critical value c^* but would prefer to stay out otherwise. Assume that the incumbent maximizes its short-run profits and that the entrant believes it does so. Then, the pre-entry price becomes a *signal* concerning the incumbent's cost and thus concerning the price to be expected after entry. In other words, through the pre-entry market price, the entrant is able to make inferences about what the incumbent's cost is and, therefore, to decide whether or not to enter. *Past decisions therefore influence present decisions.* This is not the end of the story, however. If the incumbent believes that the entrant follows such a simple rule, the monopolist has incentives to 'bluff'. For example, if his or her cost is slightly larger than c^*, he or she might choose a price slightly below the monopoly price in the hope of hiding its actual cost and to convince the entrant that he or she has a cost lower than what it really is. In other words, he or she tries to signal a cost lower than its actual cost. In such a context of behavioural uncertainty, Milgrom and Roberts show that very different equilibria may emerge. In particular, there are situations where the incumbent will deter entry that would have taken place under complete information, but there are others where entry occurs but would have been avoided under complete information.

It is fair to say, therefore, that combining asymmetric information and strategic considerations has provided new and important insights about some fundamental issues regarding the working of actual markets (see Milgrom and Roberts, 1987), for a very competent and lucid analysis of the strengths and weaknesses of such games). Yet it would be hard to deny that asymmetric information games often suffer from the plague of yielding too large a set of posssible outcomes. As in the case of the Folk Theorem (see Section I.4), this makes the predictive power of this type of work weaker than initially expected. As acknowledged by Milgrom and Roberts themselves (1987, p. 191), in asymmetric information games 'it is typically the case that the set of optimal actions varies widely as we alter the players' beliefs about how play has proceeded and what information the others may have'.

4. Recognizing that information is incomplete opens the door to very specific considerations such as the strategic value of information. If the value of information has been the heart of the literature devoted to search, the use of information in a strategic manner by firms is a very different issue which has gained interest only recently. To the best of our knowledge, Ponssard (1979, Chapter 37) has been the first who addressed that important issue in a very simple setting. Consider a homogeneous oligopolistic market with linear demand $S - ap$ and n Cournotian firms with constant marginal costs. The demand intercept S, defined as the market size, is a random variable whose distribution function is known to all firms. If firms are risk-neutral, this game is equivalent to a game of incomplete information in which each firm maximizes profits, S being replaced by its expected value.

What happens now when $k < n$ firms decide to acquire (individually) information about the market size while the others do not. Such a situation can be modelled as a game of incomplete information in which 'nature' moves first; the exact value of the market size is then revealed to the firms that choose to acquire information but not to the others. The equilibrium strategies are such that the informed firms maximize profits conditional on the market size while the uninformed firms maximize expected profits. Ponssard shows that the profits of the informed firms are increased by $\text{Var } S / a(k + 1)^2$ while the expected profits of the uninformed are unaffected. Accordingly, *there is an incentive for firms to acquire private information*; however this incentive decreases as the number of firms acquiring information rises so that *informed firms have an incentive not to share information*. This means that the acquisition of information is similar to the entry of new firms. Since acquiring information is costly (think of a fixed cost as in consumer search models), all firms will acquire information, but only a few of them will do so if collecting information turns out to be very expensive.

These results quite naturally led to the investigation of a new set of questions: (i) How does information sharing affect the intensity of competition? (ii) When does information sharing arise as an equilibrium? (iii) Does information sharing improve efficiency? These various questions have been addressed within a more general framework, described by Vives (1984, Chapter 38), in which each firm receives a noisy (and costless) signal about the market unknown.[33] Thus firms correlate their error terms when they pool their private information because information sharing allows them to reduce, but not to annihilate, uncertainty; where information is not pooled, the error terms are independent. To achieve this goal, Vives considers a two-stage game in which each firm commits either to reveal its information or to keep it private. Information is collected by an agency, such as a trade association. In the second stage, the agency sends the pooled information to the firms which then take an action (price or quantity). In this game, a strategy is a function that specifies an action for each possible signal the firm may receive.

The basic forces underlying the incentives for a firm to share information are well summarized by Vives (1990b, p. 413): 'the increased precision of the information for a firm has a positive effect on its expected profit, while the increased precision of the rivals and the increased strategy correlation have different impact, depending on the nature of competition and uncertainty'.

This means that a change in the strategic variable (price or quantity), in the source of uncertainty (demand or cost), or in the type of uncertainty (common value or private value) yields completely different results. Not surprisingly, therefore, the questions raised above have 'too many answers'. In addition, it is supposed that profits are quadratic whereas signals are drawn from a normal distribution, in order to get closed-form expressions permitting the solution of first-stage game. The main trend seems to be that *information sharing is an equilibrium with common value of uncertainty about demand under price competition but not under quantity competition.* Once more, the distinction between strategic complements and substitutes turns out to be crucial.

V.   General Equilibrium with Imperfect Competition

1.   The theories presented so far have been formulated in a partial equilibrium context.[34] Note that product differentiation or monopolistic competition models lie at a higher level of complexity since they allow for substitution between goods, but only within the range of goods belonging to the same industry. However, it remains that, even in such cases, the need for a more general formulation was felt a long time ago by Triffin (1940, p. 89): 'the new wine of monopolistic competition should not be poured into the old goatskins of partial equilibrium methodology'.

There are good reasons for economists not be content with a partial equilibrium approach to imperfect competition. First of all, modern economies are characterized by the existence of large firms operating simultaneously on several markets. The interplay of their strategies can hardly be analysed without taking into account the full complexity of the economic system. Second, the partial equilibrium approach allows us to capture in isolation some effects of economic agents' market power on the allocation of resources, thus permitting the analysis of local market distortions it may create in a particular industry. However this method does not account for the overall impact of imperfectly competitive behaviour on the whole economy: the general equilibrium methodology is needed to capture all the corresponding implications. Finally, a general equilibrium synthesis of the partial equilibrium theories presented in the foregoing is required with the aim of checking their robustness in a broader setting as well as their mutual consistency.

Although the problem of extending partial equilibrium theories of imperfect competition to a general equilibrium framework was already posed by Triffin as early as 1940, it is only in the 1970s that it has received deeper attention. Contributions have developed along two directions, differing from each other by the game-theoretic concepts used in the description of market equilibria, namely the cooperative concept of the core and the noncooperative Nash equilibrium.

2.   The first approach, organized around the concept of core, was formulated within the framework of an exchange economy with a continuum of traders. The *core* of an exchange economy is defined as follows. A *coalition* is any subset of agents. A coalition is said to *improve upon* an allocation when it can distribute to each of its members a commodity bundle which is preferred by each of them to the bundle received at that allocation, using only the aggregate initial endowments of the members of the coalition. The *core* is the set of allocations which cannot be improved upon by any coalition. This concept is interesting for the study of imperfectly competitive markets because it allows for the formation of coalitions which are a priori excluded from the competitive paradigm while retaining the general interdependence between markets (Gabszewicz, 1970).

In a pathbreaking paper published in 1964, Aumann proved that in a pure exchange economy consisting of an atomless set of traders, the core of the economy must coincide with the set of its competitive allocations.[35] The assumption of atomless economies was made to formalize the standard idea of perfect competition that the influence of any economic agent is negligible *per se*: formally, each agent is represented by a point inside of a continuum. In other words, the central feature of perfect competition is 'built into the model' (Aumann, 1964, p. 39), whence it is not surprising that the competitive equilibria are the only possible outcomes of the group decision-making underlying the concept of core.[36] This result may be viewed as the cooperative counterpart of the Folk Theorem of Competitive Markets within the context of an exchange economy (Mas-Colell, 1984): *although agents can collude by forming any kinds of coalitions, only the competitive outcomes emerge.*

Of course, the atomless representation of an economy precludes the possibility of considering market situations in which some particular agents have market power, either because they have a corner on some commodity, or because these agents correspond to large groups of participants acting together with a view to influencing to their advantage the collective decision process which consists in choosing an allocation of goods. These are precisely situations most commonly encountered in the context of imperfect competition. Accordingly, the atomless model is not appropriate to deal with such situations and must be amended to handle the imperfect competitive market ingredients so far. As observed by Gabszewicz and Shitovitz (1992, p. 461):

> To the extent that the economy under consideration embodies, in particular, a very large number of participants with negligible influence, the continuous model is still the most natural one to represent this 'oceanic sector' of the economy. As for the non-negligible market participants – monopolists, oligopolists, cartels, syndicates or other institutional forms of collusive agreements – their formal counterpart in the model *cannot* be simply points with null measure in the continuum; such a formal representation would entail per se that the actions of these participants *are* mathematically negligible when clearly they are not.

Accordingly, it was proposed in the 1970s to consider a variant of Aumann's model, the *mixed* model, consisting both of an atomless part, representing the perfectly competitive sector of the economy, and of *atoms*, where an atom is a set of strictly positive measure which includes no proper subset of strictly positive measure, representing non-negligible participants (the oligopolists). In this model, one should not expect the equivalence between the core and the set of competitive equilibria to hold. And indeed, the presence of atoms may preclude the possibility of forming some coalitions which would be necessary to improve upon a particular allocation which is in the core but not competitive. Yet, the following question suggests itself: despite the existence of atoms, can the above equivalence principle be extended to market economies in which some traders are 'large'? There are at least two interesting cases in which the answer turns out to be positive. The first one corresponds to exchange economies in which large traders are similar to each other in the sense that they have the same preferences and the same initial endowment without necessarily having the same measure (Shitovitz, 1973, Chapter 39). In the second case, the exchange economy is such that each large trader is associated with a set of small traders (belonging to the oceanic sector) which are similar to him or her in the sense that they have the same preferences and initial endowments (Gabszewicz and Mertens, 1971, Chapter 40). Such results suggest that the presence of small competitors similar to large traders may well imply a full dilution of their market power. In a way, this is reminiscent of Bertrand competition since the large agents cannot guarantee to themselves more than their competitive share when they have similar (possibly smaller) competitors in the economy.

In atomless economies, Aumann's equivalence result also implies that all core allocations can be decentralized through the competitive price mechanism. This property is no longer guaranteed when there are atoms. Does this mean that core allocations cannot be characterized via *some* price mechanism? A major result obtained in the mixed model is that any core allocation can still be characterized by a price system which, although not carrying all the properties of a competitive price system, shares with it some interesting features. In particular, at this price system, no small agent can, with the value of his or her initial endowment, afford a commodity bundle that he or she strictly prefers to the bundle he or she received at the core allocation. However this property does not apply to atoms. Consequently, *small traders are 'budgetarily exploited' at the prices sustaining a core allocation* (Shitovitz, 1973, Chapter 39).

An interesting economic interpretation of atoms can be provided in terms of a collusive agreement made among traders in an atomless economy. Suppose, indeed, that some subset of traders decide, for any reason whatsoever, to act only in unison, for instance by delegating to a single decision unit the task of representing their economic interests in the exchange process. Whenever effective, this binding agreement definitely prevents the formation of any coalition of traders including a proper subset of participants to the agreement; although such coalitions were allowed before the collusive agreement, they are now forbidden. The resulting *syndicate* of traders constitutes an atom in the economy which was initially atomless, and the decisions made by the syndicate are no longer negligible in the process of exchange. The stability of particular 'syndicate structures' with respect to the core allocations has been examined by Gabszewicz and Dréze (1971). Unexpectedly, Aumann (1973) has shown the existence of 'disadvantageous' syndicates, by giving examples of exchange economies for which the core includes only allocations giving to all syndicate members a commodity bundle which is strictly less preferred than the bundle they would receive at any competitive allocation.

3.   The second body of contributions dealing with imperfect competition at a general

equilibrium level has developed around the concept of noncooperative (Nash) equilibrium. The fundamental goal of this approach is to cast, in general equilibrium terms, the stories proposed by Cournot and Bertrand when analysing strategic interactions among a few sellers in a homogeneous industry. The first contribution along this line was that of Negishi (1960–61, Chapter 41). This author considers a private ownership economy *à la* Arrow–Debreu in which some firms have monopolistic power on one or several markets. Furthermore, Negishi assumes that, given a state of the market, each monopolistic firm has, for each good for which it is a monopolist, a *conjecture* concerning the price it could charge for any level of output it would sell in the corresponding market. These conjectures are restricted to be self-fulfilling at any state of the market, with a linear decreasing graph. An equilibrium is then defined as a state of the market where demand equals supply in each market at the corresponding price system, while every consumer maximizes utility on his or her budget line, every competitive firm maximizes its profit as a price taker, and *every monopolist makes a production decision which, on the basis of the state of the market and its conjecture, maximizes its profit.* Assuming that the production set of every firm is convex and contains the origin, which precludes the existence of increasing returns to scale, Negishi was able to prove the existence of such an equilibrium.

This approach can be criticized on the basis that there is an element of arbitrariness in the conjectures of monopolistic firms. As Hart (1985b, p. 107) states:

> The problem is that the very generality of the model gives it very little predictive power. Given particular subjective demand functions ... the model will of course generate a small number of equilibria (possibly only one). However the model does not tell us how these conjectures are formed. To an outside observer who is asked to predict the market outcome but who does not know what conjectures are, almost anything could be an equilibrium.

And indeed, Gary-Bobo (1989) has proved that every feasible allocation in which each firm has positive production yielding nonnegative profits is an equilibrium in the sense of Negishi, that is, there exist conjectures for which this allocation is an equilibrium (see also Hart, 1982).

To avoid this type of arbitrariness referred to above, Gabszewicz and Vial (1972, Chapter 42) have proposed a general equilibrium *à la* Cournot based on the 'true' or 'objective' demand functions faced by the firms endowed with market power, instead of conjectural or subjective demands. These objective demand functions are derived from consumers' demand in the exchange economy resulting from earlier productive activities (Gabszewicz and Vial, 1972, Chapter 42):

> The institutional organisation of this economy can be described as follows. The consumers provide firms with labor and other nonconsumable resources, like primary factors. With these resources, the firms choose production plans which consist only of bundles of consumption goods. The various forms of labor and other primary factors are not 'marketable'; rather, the firms distribute 'real wages' to the consumers – who have provided them with these factors and labor – in terms of preassigned shares of their output. At the end of the production process, each consumer is thus endowed with the sum of his shares in the various firms, namely, with some bundle of consumption goods. Exchange markets are then organized, where the consumers aim at improving their consumption through trade. The institutional rule of exchange consists in using a price mechanism. The prices on the exchange markets then serve as an information for the firms, to adjust eventually their production plans according to some preassigned rule. (pp. 381–82)

A *Cournot-Walrus equilibrium* is then defined as a set of production plans such that, given the production plans selected by its rivals, each firm maximizes its profit with respect to any unilateral deviation from its equilibrium production plan, taking into account the price variations in the exchange economy which result from the corresponding deviation. This concept of equilibrium constitutes the exact counterpart, in general equilibrium analysis, of the Cournot equilibrium defined in partial equilibrium analysis. There are, however, several drawbacks with this approach. First, given the production plans selected by oligopolistic firms, there may exist several competitive equilibria in the exchange economy obtained by using these production plans as endowments. This gives rise to an indeterminacy in the prices to be taken into account in the evaluation of the profits earned by the oligopolists at the corresponding production plans. This problem may be solved by using a selection rule (which may itself be part of the definition of an extended equilibrium concept).

Second, a specification of a normalization rule on prices is required in view of going from relative prices to absolute prices. Gabszewicz and Vial (1972, Chapter 42) provide an example showing that, contrary to a well-known property of the competitive equilibrium, the Cournot–Walras equilibrium is not invariant to the normalization rule selected. In other words, *the choice of the numeraire matters for the Cournot-Walrus equilibrium*. This turns out to be a major problem in general equilibrium analysis of oligopolistic competition which is due to the fact that changing the price normalization amounts to altering the objective functions of the firms in that profit functions based on different price normalizations are generally not related to each other by monotone tranformations.[37] Third, and again contrary to another well-known property of the competitive model, *profit maximization by an oligopolistic firm does not necessarily entail welfare maximization of its owners*. This is due to the difficulty of aggregating owners' preference for goods when the firms can manipulate their relative prices. Last, it is extremely difficult to tackle the problem of existence of a Cournot–Walras equilibrium without resorting to several *ad hoc* assumptions, such as assuming the quasi-concavity of profit functions. In this respect, J. Roberts and Sonnenschein (1977) have constructed examples satisfying all standard assumptions for which the resulting objective demand functions do not generate quasi-concave profits for oligopolistic firms, a feature that may prevent the existence of any equilibrium. Worse: H. Dierker and Grodal (1986) have provided a counterexample to existence even when oligopolists are allowed to use mixed strategies for certain normalization rules and selections. However, pure strategy Nash equilibria exist for some other normalization rules and selections.

These various difficulties have motivated several investigations. For instance, it was shown by Gabszewicz and Michel (1997) that neither the price normalization nor the owners' welfare maximization problems arise when the analysis is transposed to an exchange model in which oligopolists have a corner on some commodities and maximize their individual utility at equilibrium. Recently, E. Dierker and Grodal (1996) have shown how the maximization of *shareholders' real wealth*, which takes shareholders' aggregate demand explicitly into account, allows for circumventing the normalization problem when firms use prices as strategic variables. The theoretical and practical implications of implementing such an objective are still to be investigated. Observe, finally, that one of the most positive results in this strand of the literature has been provided by K. Roberts. (1980) who has established that, for almost all economies, *competitive equilibria are the limit of a sequence of Cournot-*

Walrus equilibria, thus showing how perfect competition can emerge as an asymptotic version of a Cournot setting.

A similar problem has been considered by Novshek and Sonnenschein in a series of papers (see their survey published in 1987) that extend Novshek (1980, Chapter 4) to a general equilibrium framework. They consider a broader framework containing two distinct theories of perfect competition: Marshall and Arrow–Debreu. The differences between the two include:

1. Marshallian theory allows for a variable number of firms while the number of firms is fixed in Arrow–Debreu theory;
2. Marshallian theory is based on the U-shaped average cost curve, while Arrow and Debreu consider only convex technologies;
3. in Marshallian theory, firms are price-taking only if their efficient scale is small relative to the market, while firms in Arrow–Debreu theory are price-takers in all circumstances;
4. Marshallian theory abstracts from interdependencies across markets while Arrow–Debreu theory is explicitly general equilibrium;
5. Marshallian analysis of equilibria is dynamic in the sense that firms enter and/or exit until equilibrium is achieved, while Arrow–Debreu theory does not allow explicitly for such a process.

The key to the synthesis of these theories is the arbitrary small size of firms relative to the market achieved at a free-entry Cournot equilibrium. This reconciles the Arrow–Debreu assumptions of perfect competition among a given number of firms with the Marshallian approach since, at sufficiently small scale, no single firm's change in quantity can affect the market price. This reconciliation, however, is true asymptotically and does not deal with 'large' firms. Novshek and Sonnenschein (1987) have been able to go one step further by showing the existence of such sequences of Cournot–Walras equilibria provided that firms are small relative to the market.

In the above framework, oligopolists are supposed to use output levels as strategic variables and prices are assumed to be determined by the law of supply and demand. Several authors have instead followed another approach, by assuming that firms' strategies are prices rather than output levels (Marschak and Selten, 1974; Bénassy, 1988, Chapter 43). The last author considers the price counterpart of Gabszewicz and Vial. His approach requires that all firms set prices subject to their objective demand (unlike Negishi) which embeds all the effects that their prices exert on other agents' supply and demand decisions. Firms are owned by individuals who are price makers as producers, but price takers as consumers. *This makes the price model much more involved than in partial equilibrium since demands are very different from those used in oligopoly theory; in particular, they need not be downward sloping in own price.* The difference with the competitive paradigm is here transparent since prices no longer convey all information required to make decisions: firms must also account for the other agents' decisions through their demands. By using a general technology, Bénassy shows that an imperfect competitor may not want to serve his or her whole demand, that is, may want to ration consumers. This allows him or her to set up links between imperfect competition and fix-price theories of market disequilibrium (Bénassy, 1982).

Before concluding, it remains to discuss what we have learned in general equilibrium analysis with differentiated products. The main contribution is due to Hart (1979, Chapter 44). In fact, what Hart does in that paper is to study the Folk theorem of Competitive Markets in a general equilibrium framework with differentiated products. Like Novshek and Sonneschein (1987), he wants to show that 'when firms are small relative to the aggregate economy, a monopolistically competitive equilibrium is approximately Pareto optimal' (p. 2). Hence market imperfections and efficiency losses associated with product differentiation would disappear when the economy is large enough. But Hart also assumes that the set of potential products is compact. Although he does not stress the role of this assumption, this makes his work the general equilibrium counterpart of what Perloff and Salop (1985) had to show explicitly in a partial equilibrium setting (see Section III.3). Later on, Hart (1985a) qualified his position and it seems fair to say that the idea that negligible firms are not necessarily firms without market power is now widely accepted.[38]

Concluding Comments

The foregoing sections have illustrated some of the answers provided by economists to the problems arising when the competitive paradigm is abandoned, and replaced by more realistic assumptions. As said in the introduction, these answers look like a highly coloured patchwork of often unrelated investigations, which mirror the incredible complexity of real market phenomena.

Beyond the problem of a theoretical fragmentation into a myriad of particular models, the analysis of imperfect competition suffers from another deep drawback: it has not been able so far to link in a satisfactory way market power and increasing returns to scale. In most theoretical investigations devoted to imperfect competition, strategic interaction among economic agents finds its origin in the demand conditions they face: rivalry arises because few firms sell their product to the same pool of buyers, and struggle to obtain the largest share of it. It seems to us, however, that another major source of market power comes from the technological conditions under which firms operate. Most likely, these conditions determine both the number of firms which can survive at equilibrium, and the kind of market arrangement at which they may arrive, given the aggregate demand existing for the products in the industry. A more complete integration of the technological conditions into the theory of imperfect competition seems to us the most challenging aspect for further research in the field surveyed in this essay.

Notes

1. The reader is referred to Stigler (1957) for a historical analysis of the idea of perfect competition. What makes this paper especially interesting for our purpose is that the analysis is developed at the light of the 'imperfect competition revolution' of the 1930s. A broader view of 'what is competition' in the economic literature is provided by Blaug (1997).
2. In order to avoid too many duplications, we have not included in this collection some papers that have been republished in other volumes belonging to the same series (Thisse and Norman, 1994; Levine and Lippman, 1995). They are discussed, however, in our introductory notes.
3. For a modern presentation of the Launhardt model and some related developments, see Dos Santos Ferreira and Thisse (1996).

4. See, for example, Mayberry, Nash and Shubik (1953).
5. More recently, an alternative approach, based on Tarski's fixed point theorem for lattices, allows one to show existence and ordered structure of Nash equilibria when payoffs satisfy some monotonicity properties but need not be quasi-concave (Topkis, 1978; Milgrom and Roberts, 1990; Vives, 1990a).
6. This property does not hold in general for non zero sum games.
7. See the debate in the January 1992 issue of *Rationality and Society*.
8. This means that the history of the game relevant at any period *t* for one firm is summarized in the action taken by the rival during the previous period which gives the approach a Cournotian flavour. In other words, a firm reacts only to the immediate action chosen by its competitor and not to the whole history of the game. Although still consistent with subgame perfection, the concept of a Markov equilibrium deals with reactions which are different from credible threats used in supergames.
9. See Friedman (1992) for a modern overview of these early contributions.
10. For those who knew the work of Levitan and Shubik (1972), this result is not totally surprising since these authors noticed that the Cournot outcome may correspond to the price equilibrium arising under some capacity constraints.
11. Bulow, Geanakoplos and Klemperer (1985) suggest another approach to the dilemma Cournot/ Bertrand: 'It has long been suspected that any result in oligopoly theory, or its converse, can be generated by an appropriate choice of assumptions. Strategic substitutes and complements help explain this basic ambiguity and so focus on a critical distinction. When thinking about oligopoly markets the crucial question may not be, Do these markets exhibit price competition or quantity competition or competition using some other strategic variable? but rather, Do competitors think of the products as strategic substitutes or as strategic complements?' (p. 510).
12. The study of collusion in the context of cooperative game theory is postponed to Section V.2.
13. The idea of Schelling (1960) concerning a focal point is one possibility (when there are plenty of equilibria, find one which has some distinctive feature) but seems difficult to formalize.
14. At least when the single shot Nash is unique. If it is not unique, then all the folk/trigger stuff can go through in a finite horizon game; see Benoît and Krishna (1985) and Friedman (1985). See also Radner (1980) for a different approach.
15. Or when there is entry. Many would probably agree that the implicit collusion story no longer works when there is free entry. And indeed, some discontinuity may arise in the limit. Using a symmetric Cournot setting, Lambson (1984) shows that the Folk Theorem may fail to hold when the number of firms becomes arbitrarily large.
16. We do not discuss here the case of semicollusion in which some decisions are made in a noncollusive way but with the understanding that product market collusion will follow. Friedman and Thisse (1993) show that semicollusive outcomes do not necessarily fall in between collusive and noncollusive solutions. See also Phlips (1995, Section III) as well as Friedman, Jehiel and Thisse (1995) for further developments.
17. See Jacquemin and Thisse (1972) for an overview of the main applications of optimal control theory to industrial organization.
18. The issue becomes more difficult when several firms are already in the markets. In this case, entry-prevention has the nature of a public good. Thus each firm could free-ride on the entry-preventing actions of their competitors. Surprisingly, Gilbert and Vives (1986) show that this does not necessarily arise in a Cournot competition model: overinvestment may occur because each incumbent wants to be the preventer.
19. A different persepctive is taken by Gelman and Salop (1983) who focus instead on the entrant's strategy. They show that the entrant may induce the established firm to accommodate entry by choosing a nonaggressive policy in terms of capacity. If the new firm enters the market with a small capacity, it never pays for the incumbent to deter entry.
20. In the same vein, it would be worthwhile revisiting the approach taken by Schwartz and Thompson (1986) which suggests that divisionalization, that is, the creation of new independent divisions inside a given firm that are able to exploit scope economies and to economize overhead costs. This could be a profitable strategy in implementing brand proliferation when incumbent firms face the

threat of entry. By the same token, this should lead to an interesting connection between industrial economics and organization theory.

21. In fact, Chamberlin built two bridges: the large numbers case which was his main thrust, and the small numbers case to which he did not devote much attention. The latter is a sort of intermediate case.

22. And indeed, Anderson, de Palma and Thisse (1980; 1992, chs 3–4) have shown that there exist distributions of consumer tastes such that each consumer purchases a single variant while aggregate demands equal those obtained from maximizing a CES utility under an aggregate budget constraint.

23. Note that Hart (1985a) has argued that the limiting result obtained in the Dixit–Stiglitz model is due to some irregular limiting behaviour. He then presents a model in which each consumer is interested only in a small number of brands, so that substitution between brands is limited. This is reasonable in spatial models of product differentiation where consumers likely discard variants which are too far from their most preferred product, but seems less acceptable in the context of the large group symmetric model. However, a rationale for such a restriction may be provided when consumers have to search for the best-price-product mix in a market with incomplete information (see Section IV.1).

24. It is fair to say that Chamberlin does have this 'chain market' notion which captures precisely this (see p. 104 of this book). However, he did not really explore the implications of this approach as Kaldor did. See also Eaton and Lipsey (1977) and Gabszewicz and Thisse (1986).

25. It is worth pointing out that Vickrey (1964, ch. 8) has anticipated several developments of the spatial model of product differentiation that took place later on. The excerpt is to be republished in the *International Journal of Industrial Organization*.

26. D'Aspremont, Gabszewicz and Thisse (1979) have shown that the hypotheses made by Hotelling do not guarantee continuity at the global level. For that it is necessary to replace the assumption of linear transport costs by one in which transport costs are increasing and strictly convex in distance.

27. See Anderson et al. (1992, ch. 2) for a survey of this literature whose use in economics has been pioneered by McFadden (1981).

28. This result is suggestive of what seems to be a general principle in economic modelling: *competition tends to stabilize when agents are heterogeneous enough* (see, for example, Kirman, 1992).

29. A detailed analysis of the impact of incomplete information for the product market may be found in Stiglitz (1989) whereas McMillan and Rothschild (1994) provided a detailed overview of search models and of their main implications. The economics of information in itself is fairly new and has attracted considerable attention during the last two decades. The reader is referred to Macho-Stadler and Pérez-Castrillo (1997) for a modern overview of this field.

30. This is somewhat reminiscent of the Bertrand–Edgeworth problem in that not all consumers have access to the lowest price, thus generating a captive demand which serves as a basis for a strategic behaviour. However, the two mechanisms are different.

31. This additional incentive constraint implies that it may not be possible to sustain the monopoly output (Porter, 1983).

32. According to Harsanyi (1967–68), a game of incomplete information allows for the modelling of situations where players are unsure about certain things their rivals know. In Harsanyi's formulation, each player knows the others up to a parameter, referred to as the player's type, which itself is known up to a (finite) probability distribution. The type of a player includes everything which is relevant to the player's decision making. Each player knows his or her own type but not the actual type of the other players.

33. In Ponssard (1979, Chapter 37), the informed firms receive a signal with a zero variance whereas the uninformed firms receive a signal with an infinite variance.

34. A noticeable, but particular, exception is provided by the Dixit–Stiglitz model of monopolistic competition.

35. An asymptotic version of Aumann's result was provided earlier by Debreu and Scarf (1963).

36. As seen in the introduction, the idea of using a continuum of agents in order to restore continuity

at the aggregate level had already been put forward by Hotelling (1929, Chapter 27).

37. The same holds in partial equilibrium models. For example, in the standard Cournot model, when the profit of a function is written as $\prod_i = [p(Q) - c_i]q_i$, it is implicitly assumed that the numeraire is an outside good. If the good produced in the industry under consideration were chosen as the numeraire, firm i's profit would become $[p(Q) - c_i]q_i / p(Q)$ and the equilibrium (if any) would be different from the previous one.

38. This turns out to be a critical element in the success of the Dixit–Stiglitz model in applications where a large number of firms is assumed. Indeed, a positive profit margin is needed to finance R&D expenses in growth models. The same idea is applied to models of economic geography.

References

Aghion, P. and P. Howitt (1998), *Endogenous Growth Theory*, Cambridge, MA: MIT Press.

Amir, R. (1997) 'Cournot oligopoly and the theory of supermodular games', *Games and Economic Behaviour*, **15**, 132–48.

Anderson, S.P. and A. de Palma (1996) 'From local to global competition', CEPR Discussion Paper No. 1328, *European Economic Review*, forthcoming.

Anderson, S.P., A. de Palma and Y. Nesterov (1995) 'Oligopolistic competition and the optimal provision of products', *Econometrica*, **63**, 1281–301.

Anderson, S.P., A. de Palma and J.-F. Thisse (1989), 'Demand for differentiated products, discrete choice models, and the characteristics approach', *Review of Economic Studies*, **56**, 21–35.

Anderson, S.P., A. de Palma and J.-F. Thisse (1992), *Discrete Choice Theory of Product Differentiation*, Cambridge, MA: MIT Press.

Archibald, G.C. and B.C. Eaton and R.G. Lipsey (1986), 'Address models of value theory', in J.E. Stiglitz and G.F. Mathewson (eds), *New Developments in the Analysis of Market Structure*, Cambridge, MA: MIT Press, 3–47.

Arrow, K. and G. Debreu (1954), 'Existence of an equilibrium for a competitive economy', *Econometrica*, **22**, 265–90.

Aumann, R.J. (1960), 'Acceptable points in games of perfect information', *Pacific Journal of Mathematics*, **10**, 381–417.

Aumann, R.J. (1964), 'Markets with a continuum of traders', *Econometrica*, **32**, 39–50.

Aumann, R.J. (1973), 'Disadvantageous monopolies', *Journal of Economic Theory*, **6**, 1–11.

Bain, J. (1956), *Barriers to New Competition*, Cambridge, MA: Harvard University Press.

Baumol, W.J. (1982), 'Contestable markets: an uprising in the theory of industry structure', *American Economic Review*, **72**, 1–15.

Baumol, W.J., J.C. Panzar and R.D. Willig (1982), *Contestable Markets and the Theory of Industry Structure*, Orlando, FL: Harcourt Brace Jovanovich.

Beckmann, M.J. (1965), 'Edgeworth–Bertrand duopoly revisited', in R. Henn (ed.), *Operations Research Verfahren, III*, Meisenheim: Sonderdruck Verlag Anton Hein, 55–68.

Beckmann, M.J. (1972), 'Spatial Cournot oligopoly', *Papers and Proceedings of the Regional Science Association*, **28**, 37–47.

Bénassy, J.-P. (1982), *The Economics of Market Disequilibrium*, New York: Academic Press.

Bénassy, J.-P. (1986), 'On the existence of Bertrand–Edgeworth equilibria with differentiated commodities', in W. Hildenbrand and A. Mas-Colell (eds), *Contributions to Mathematical Economics in Honor of Gérard Debreu*, Amsterdam: North-Holland, 57–78.

Bénassy, J.-P. (1988), 'The objective demand curve in general equilibrium with price makers', *Economic Journal*, **98** (suppl.), 37–49.

Bénassy, J.-P. (1989), 'Market size and substitutability in imperfect competition: a Bertrand–Edgeworth–Chamberlin model', *Review of Economic Studies*, **56**, 217–34.

Benoît, J.-P. and V. Krishna (1985), 'Finitely reported games', *Econometrica*, **53**, 509–22.

Bertrand, J. (1983), 'Book review of *Théorie mathématique de la richesse sociale et notital. Recherches sur les principes mathématiques de la richesse*', *Journal des Savants*, 890–904.

Blaug, M. (1997), 'Competition as an end-state and competition as a process', in Eaton B. Curtis and R.G. Harris (eds), *Trade, Technology and Economics. Essays in Honor of Richard G. Lipsey*, Cheltenham: Edward Elgar, 241–62.

Bulow, J.I., J.D. Geanakoplos and P.D. Klemperer (1985), 'Multimarket oligopoly: strategic substitutes and complements', *Journal of Political Economy*, **93**, 488–511.

Canoy, M. (1996), 'Product differentiation in a Bertrand–Edgeworth duopoly', *Journal of Economic Theory*, **70**, 158–79.

Chamberlin, E.H. (1933), *The Theory of Monopolistic Competition*, Cambridge, MA: Harvard University Press.

Chamberlin, E.H. (1951), 'Monopolistic competition revisited', *Economica*, **18**, 343–62.

Chamberlin, E.H. (1953), 'The product as an economic variable', *Quarterly Journal of Economics*, **67**, 1–29.

Cournot, A.A. (1838), *Recherches sur les principes mathématiques de la théorie des richesses*, Paris: Hachette. English translation: *Researches into the Mathematical Principles of the Theory of Wealth*, New York: Macmillan, 1897.

Dasgupta, P. and E. Maskin (1986a), 'The existence of equilibrium in discontinuous economic games: I: theory', *Review of Economic Studies*, **53**, 1–26.

Dasgupta, P. and E. Maskin (1986b), 'The existence of equilibrium in discontinuous economic games, II: applications', *Review of Economic Studies*, **53**, 27–41.

d'Aspremont, C., R. Dos Santos Ferreira and L.-A. Gérard-Varet (1991), 'Pricing schemes and Cournotion equilibria', *American Economic Review*, **81**, 666–73.

d'Aspremont, C., J.J. Gabszewicz, A. Jacquemin and J.A. Weymark (1983a), 'On the stability of collusive price leadership', *Canadian Journal of Economics*, **14**, 17–25.

d'Aspremont, C., J.J. Gabszewicz, and J.-F. Thisse (1979)', 'On Hotelling's "Stability of competition"', *Econometrica*, **47**, 1045–50.

d'Aspremont, C., J.J. Gabszewicz, and J.-F. Thisse (1983b)', 'Product differences and prices', *Economics Letters*, **11**, 19–23.

Dastidar, K.G. (1995), 'On the existence of pure strategy Bertrand equilibria', *Economic Theory*, **5**, 19–32.

Davidson, C. and R. Deneckere (1986), 'Long-run competition in capacity, short-run competition in price, and the Cournot model', *Rand Journal of Economics*, **17**, 404–15.

Debreu, G. and H. Scarf (1963), 'A limit theorem on the core of an economy', *International Economic Review*, **4**, 235–46.

Demange, G. (1986), 'Free entry and stability in a Cournot model', *Journal of Economic Theory*, **40**, 283–303.

Demange, G. and D. Henriet (1991), 'Sustainable oligopolies', *Journal of Economic Theory*, **54**, 417–28.

Deneckere, R. and M. Rothschild (1992), 'Monopolistic competition and preference diversity', *Review of Economic Studies*, **59**, 361–73.

de Palma, A., V. Ginsburgh, Y. Papageorgiou and J.-F. Thisse (1985), 'The principle of minimum differentiation holds under sufficient heterogeneity', *Econometrica*, **53**, 767–81.

Deschamps, R. (1975), 'An algorithm of game theory applied to the duopoly problem', *European Economic Review*, **6**, 187–94.

Diamond, P.A. (1971), 'A model of price adjustment', *Journal of Economic Theory*, **3**, 156–68.

Dierker, E. and B. Grodal (1996), 'The price normalization problem in imperfect competition and the objective of the firm', University of Vienna, Department of Economics, Working Paper No. 9616.

Dierker, E. and B. Grodal (1986), 'Non existence of Cournot–Walras equilibrium in a general equilibrium model with two oligopolists', in W. Hildenbrand and A. Mas-Colell (eds), *Contribution to Mathematical Economics*, Amsterdam: North-Holland, 167–85.

Dixit, A.K. (1980), 'The role of investment in entry-deterrence', *Economic Journal*, **90**, 95–106.

Dixit, A.K. and J.E. Stiglitz (1977), 'Monopolistic competition and optimum product diversity', *American Economic Review*, **67**, 297–308.

Dos Santos Ferreira, R. and J.-F. Thisse (1996), 'Horizontal and vertical differentiation: the Launhardt Model', *International Journal of Industrial Organization*, **14**, 485–506.

Eaton, B.C. and R.G. Lipsey (1977), 'The introduction of space into the neoclassical model of value theory', in M. Artis and A. Nobay (eds), *Studies in Modern Economics*, Oxford: Basil Blackwell, 59–96.

Eaton, B.C. and R.G. Lipsey (1978), Freedom of entry and the existence of pure profits', *Economic Journal*, **88**, 455–69.

Eaton, B.C. and R.G. Lipsey (1980), 'Exit barriers are entry barriers: the durability of capital as a barrier to entry', *Bell Journal of Economics*, **11**, 721–9.

Eaton, B.C. and M.H. Wooders (1985), 'Sophisticated entry in a model of spatial competition', *Rand Journal of Economics*, **16**, 282–97.

Edgeworth, F. (1881), *Mathematical Psychics*, London: Kegan.

Edgeworth, F. (1897), 'La teoria pura del monopolio', *Giornale degli Economisti*, **40**, 13–31. English translation: Edgeworth, F., 'The pure theory of monopoly', *Papers Relating to Political Economy*, London: Macmillan, 1925, 111–42.

Fellner, W.J. (1949), *Competition Among the Few*, New York: Knopf.

Fishman, A and Rob (1998), 'Experimentation and competition', *Journal of Economic Theory*, **78**, 299–328.

Frank, C.R. (1965), 'Entry in a Cournot market', *Review of Economic Studies*, **32**, 245–50.

Friedman, J.W. (1971), 'A non-cooperative equilibrium for supergames', *Review of Economic Studies*, **38**, 1–12.

Friedman, J.W. (1977), *Oligopoly and the Theory of Games*, Amsterdam: North-Holland.

Friedman, J.W. (1979), 'On entry preventing behaviour and limit price models of entry', in S.J. Brams, A. Schotter and G. Schwödiauer (eds), *Applied Game Theory*, Würzburg: Physica-Verlag, 236–53.

Friedman, J.W. (1981), 'Limit pricing and entry', *Journal of Economic Dynamics and Control*, **3**, 319–23.

Friedman, J.W. (1983a), *Oligopoly Theory*, Cambridge: Cambridge University Press.

Friedman, J.W. (1983b), 'Limit price entry prevention when complete information is lacking', *Journal of Economic Dynamics and Control*, **5**, 187–99.

Friedman, J.W. (1985), 'Cooperative equilibria in finite horizon noncooperative supergames', *Journal of Economic Theory*, **35**, 390–98.

Friedman, J.W. (1988), 'On the strategic importance of prices versus quantities', *Rand Journal of Economics*, **19**, 607–22.

Friedman, J.W. (1992), 'The interaction between game theory and theoretical industrial economics', *Scottish Journal of Political Economy*, **39**, 353–73.

Friedman, J.W. (1997), 'A guided tour to the Folk Theorem', mimeo, University of North Carolina.

Friedman, J.W., Ph. Jehiel and J.-F. Thisse (1995), 'Collusion and antitrust detection', *Japanese Economic Review*, **46**, 226–46.

Friedman, J.W and J.-F. Thisse (1993), 'Partial collusion fosters minimum product differentiation', *Rand Journal of Economics*, **24**, 631–45.

Fudenberg, D. and E. Maskin (1986), 'The folk theorem in repeated games with discounting and with incomplete information', *Econometrica*, **54**, 533–54.

Fudenberg, D. and J. Tirole (1984), 'The fat-cat effect, the puppy-dog ploy, and the lean and hungry look', *Papers and Proceedings of the American Economic Association*, **74**, 361–6.

Gabszewicz, J.J. (1970), 'Théorie du noyau et concurrence imparfaite', *Recherches Economiques de Louvain*, **36**, 21–37.

Gabszewicz, J.J. (1983), 'Blue and red cars, or red cars only. A note on product variety', *Economica*, **50**, 203–6.

Gabszewicz, J.J. and J. Drèze (1971), 'Syndicates of traders in an exchange economy', in G. Szegö (ed), *Differential Games and Related Topics*, Amsterdam: North-Holland, 399–414.

Gabszewicz, J.J. and P. Garella (1986), 'Subjective price search and price competition', *International Journal of Industrial Organization*, **4**, 306–15.

Gabszewicz, J.J. and J.-F. Mertens (1971), 'An equivalence theorem for the core of an economy whose atoms are not "too" big', *Econometrica*, **39**, 713–21.

Gabszewicz, J.J. and P. Michel (1997), 'Oligopoly equilibrium in exchange economics', in B. Eaton Curtis and R.G. Harris (eds), *Trade, Technology and Economics. Essays in Honour of Richard G.*

Lipsey, Cheltenham: Edward Elgar, 217–40.

Gabszewicz, J.J., L. Pepall and J.-F. Thisse (1992), 'Sequential entry with brand loyalty caused by consumer earning-by-using' *Journal of Industrial Economics*, **40**, 397–416.

Gabszewicz, J.J. and B. Shitovitz (1992), 'The core in imperfectly competitive economies', in R. Aumann and S. Hart (eds), *Handbook of Game Theory, Volume I*, Amsterdam: North-Holland, 460–83.

Gabszewicz, J.J. and J.-F. Thisse (1979), 'Price competition, quality and income disparities', *Journal of Economic Theory*, **20**, 340–59.

Gabszewicz, J.J. and J.-F. Thisse (1980), 'Entry (and exit) in a differentiated industry', *Journal of Economic Theory*, **22**, 327–38.

Gabszewicz, J.J. and J.-F. Thisse (1986), 'Spatial competition and the location of firms', in J.J. Gabszewicz, J.-F. Thisse, M. Fujita and U. Schweizer, *Location Theory*, Chur: Harwood Academic Publishers, 1–71. (*Fundamentals of Pure and Applied Economics*, 5.)

Gabszewicz, J.J. and J.-F. Thisse (1992), 'Location', in R. Aumann and S. Hart (eds), *Handbook of Game Theory, Volume I*, Amsterdam: North-Holland, 281–304.

Gabszewicz, J.J. and J.-P. Vial (1972), 'Oligopoly "à la Cournot" in general equilibrium analysis', *Journal of Economic Theory*, **4**, 381–400.

Gary-Bobo, R. (1989), 'Cournot–Walras and locally consistent equilibria', *Journal of Economic Theory*, **49**, 10–32.

Gaskins, D. (1971), 'Dynamic limit pricing: optimal pricing under threat of entry', *Journal of Economic Theory*, **3**, 306–22.

Gelman, J. and S. Salop (1983), 'Judo economics: capacity limitations and coupon competition', *Bell Journal of Economics*, **14**, 315–25.

Gilbert, R. and X. Vives (1986), 'Entry deterrence and the free-rider problem', *Review of Economic Studies*, **53**, 71–83.

Green, E. and R. Porter (1984), 'Non-cooperative collusion under imperfect price information', *Econometrica*, **52**, 87–100.

Grossman, G.M. and E. Helpman (1991), *Innovation and Growth in the Global Economy*, Cambridge, MA: MIT Press.

Hahn, F. and R. Solow (1995), *A Critical Essay on Modern Macroeconomic Theory*, Cambridge, MA: MIT Press.

Harsanyi, J.C. (1967–68), 'Games with incomplete information played by Bayesian players', *Management Science*, **14**, 159–82, 320–34, 486–502.

Hart, O. (1979), 'Monopolistic competition in a large economy with differentiated commodities', *Review of Economic Studies*, **46**, 1–30.

Hart, O. (1982), 'Reasonable conjectures', London School of Economics, International Centre for Economics and Related Disciplines.

Hart, O. (1985a), 'Monopolistic competition in the spirit of Chamberlin: special results', *Economic Journal*, **95**, 889–908.

Hart, O. (1985b), 'Imperfect competition in general equilibrium: an overview of recent work', in K. Arrow and S. Honkapohja (eds), *Frontiers in Economics*, Oxford: Basil Blackwell, 100–149.

Helpman, E. and P.R. Krugman (1985), *Market Structure and Foreign Trade*, Cambridge, MA: MIT Press.

Hotelling, H. (1929), 'Stability in competition', *Economic Journal*, **39**, 41–57.

Irmen, A. and J.-F. Thisse (1998), 'Competition in multi-characteristics spaces: Hotelling was almost right', *Journal of Economic Theory*, **78**, 76–102.

Jacquemin, A. and J.-F. Thisse (1972), 'Strategy of the firm and market structure: an application of optimal control theory', in K. Cowling (ed.), *Market Structure and Corporate Behaviour*, London: Gray-Mills Publ., 61–84.

Jéhiel, Ph. and B. Walliser (1995), 'How to select a dual Nash equilibrium', *Games and Economic Behaviour*, **10**, 333–54.

Johansen, L. (1982), 'On the status of the Nash type of noncooperative equilibrium in economic theory', *Scandinavian Journal of Economics*, **84**, 421–41.

Judd, K.L. (1985), 'Credible spatial preemption', *Rand Journal of Economics*, **16**, 153–66.

Kaldor, N. (1935), 'Market imperfection and excess capacity', *Economica* (N.S.), **2**, 35–50.

Kamien, M.I. and N.L. Schwartz (1971), 'Limit pricing and uncertain entry', *Econometrica*, **39**, 441–54.

Kamien, M.I. and N.L. Schwartz (1983), *Market Structure and Innovation*, Cambridge: Cambridge University Press.

Kirman, A.P. (1992), 'Whom or what does the representative individual represent?', *Journal of Economic Perspectives*, **6**, 117–36.

Klemperer, P. (1987), 'Markets with consumer switching costs', *Quarterly Journal of Economics*, **102**, 375–94.

Kreps, D.M. (1990), *Game Theory and Economic Modelling*, Clarendon Press.

Kreps, D.M. and J.A. Scheinkman (1983), 'Quantity precommitment and Bertrand competition yield Cournot outcomes', *Bell Journal of Economics*, **14**, 326–37.

Kreps, D.M. and A.M. Spence (1985), 'Modelling the role of history in industrial organization and competition', in G.R. Feiwel (ed.), *Issues in Contemporary Microeconomics and Welfare*, London: Macmillan, 340–78.

Kreps, D.M. and R. Wilson (1982), 'Reputation and imperfect information', *Journal of Economic Theory*, **27**, 253–79.

Lambson, V.E. (1984), 'Self-enforcing collusion in large dynamic markets', *Journal of Economic Theory*, **34**, 282–91.

Lancaster, K.J. (1966), 'A new approach to consumer theory', *Journal of Political Economy*, **74**, 132–57.

Lancaster, K. (1975), 'Socially optimal product differentiation', *American Economic Review*, **65**, 567–85.

Lancaster, K. (1979), *Variety, Equity and Efficiency*, Oxford: Basil Blackwell.

Launhardt, W. (1885), *Mathematische Begründung der Volkwirtschafslehre*, Leipzig: B.G. Teubner. English translation: *Mathematical Principles of Economics*, Aldershot: Edward Elgar, 1993.

Levine, D.K. and S.A. Lippman (eds) (1995), *The Economics of Information*, Aldershot: Edward Elgar, Classics in Economics.

Levitan, R. and M. Shubik (1972), 'Price duopoly and capacity constraints', *International Economic Review*, **13**, 111–22.

Lösch, A. (1940), *Die Räumliche Ordnung der Wirtschaft*, Jena: Gustav Fischer. English translation: *The Economics of Location*, New Haven, CT: Yale University Press, 1954.

Macho-Stadler, I. and D. Pérez-Castrillo (1997), *An Introduction to the Theory of Information*, Oxford: Oxford University Press.

Malinvaud, E. (1968), *Leçons de théorie microéconomique*, Paris: Dunod. English translation: *Lessons in Microeconomic Theory*, Amsterdam: North-Holland, 1970.

Markham, J.W. (1951), 'The nature and significance of price leadership', *American Economic Review*, **41**, 891–905.

Marschak, T. and R. Selten (1974), *General Equilibrium with Price-making Firms*, Berlin: Springer-Verlag.

Mas-Colell, A. (1984), 'On the theory of perfect competition', 1984–Nancy L. Schwartz Memorial Lecture, J.L. Kellog Graduate School of Management, Northwestern University.

Maskin, E. and J. Tirole (1988a), 'A theory of dynamic oligopoly, I: overview and quantity competition with large fixed costs', *Econometrica*, **56**, 549–69.

Maskin, E. and J. Tirole (1988b), 'A theory of dynamic oligopoly, II: price competition, kinked demand curves, and Edgeworth cycles', *Econometrica*, **56**, 571–99.

Matsuyama, K. (1995), 'Complementarities and cumulative process in models of monopolistic competition', *Journal of Economic Literature*, **33**, 701–29.

Mayberry, J.P., J.F. Nash and M. Shubik (1953), 'A comparison of treatments of a duopoly situation', *Econometrica*, **21**, 131–54.

McGee, J. (1980), 'Predatory pricing revisited', *Journal of Law and Economics*, **23**, 289–330.

McFadden, D. (1981), 'Econometric models of probabilistic choice', in C.F. Manski and D. McFadden (eds), *Structural Analysis of Discrete Data with Econometric Applications*, Cambridge, MA: MIT Press, 198–272.

McManus, M. (1962), 'Numbers and size in Cournot oligopoly', *Yorkshire Bulletin of Social and Economic Research*, **14**, 14–22.

McManus, M. (1964), 'Equilibrium, Numbers and Sizes in Cournot oligopoly', *Yorkshire Bulletin of Social and Economic Research*, **16**, 68–75.

McMillan, J. and M. Rothschild (1994), 'Search', in R. Aumann and S. Hart (eds), *Handbook of Game Theory, Volume II*, Amsterdam: North-Holland, 905–27.

Milgrom, P. and J. Roberts (1982a), 'Predation, reputation and entry deterrence', *Journal of Economic Theory*, **27**, 280–312.

Milgrom, P. and J. Roberts (1982b), 'Limit pricing and entry under incomplete information: an equilibrium analysis', *Econometrica*, **50**, 443–59.

Milgrom, P. and J. Roberts (1987), 'Informational asymmetries, strategic behavior, and industrial organization', *Papers and Proceedings of the American Economic Association*, **77**, 184–93.

Milgrom, P. and J. Roberts (1990), 'Rationalizability, learning and equilibrium in games with strategic complementarities', *Econometrica*, **58**, 1255–77.

Modigliani, F. (1958), 'New developments on the oligopoly front', *Journal of Political Economy*, **66**, 215–32.

Moulin, H. (1984), 'Dominance solvability and Cournot equilibrium', *Mathematical Social Sciences*, **7**, 83–102.

Nash, J. (1951), 'Noncooperative games', *Annals of Mathematics*, **45**, 286–95.

Negishi, T. (1960–61), 'Monopolistic competition and general equilibrium', *Review of Economic Studies*, **28**, 196–201.

Nikaido, H. (1975), *Monopolistic Competition and Effective Demand*, Princeton: Princeton University Press.

Nikaido, H. and K. Isoda (1955), 'Notes on non-cooperative games', *Pacific Journal of Mathematics*, **5**, 807–15.

Novshek, W. (1980), 'Cournot equilibrium with free entry', *Review of Economic Studies*, **47**, 473–86.

Novshek, W. (1985), 'On the existence of a Cournot equilibrium', *Review of Economic Studies*, **52**, 85–98.

Novshek, W. and H. Sonnenschein (1987), 'General equilibrium with free entry: a synthetic approach to the theory of perfect competition', *Journal of Economic Literature*, **25**, 1281–306.

Osborne, D.K. (1976), 'Cartel problems', *American Economic Review*, **66**, 835–44.

Perloff, J.M. and S.C. Salop (1985), 'Equilibrium with product differentiation', *Review of Economic Studies*, **52**, 107–20.

Phlips, L. (1995), *Competition Policy: A Game-theoretic Perspective*, Cambridge: Cambridge University Press.

Ponssard, J.-P. (1979), 'The strategic role of information on the demand function in an oligopolistic market', *Management Science*, **25**, 243–50.

Porter, R. (1983), 'Optimal cartel trigger-price strategies', *Journal of Economic Theory*, **29**, 313–38.

Prescott, E.C. and M. Visscher (1977), 'Sequential location among firms with foresight', *Bell Journal of Economics*, **8**, 378–93.

Radner, R. (1980), 'Collusive behavior in noncooperative epsilon-equilibria of oligopolies with long but finite lives', *Journal of Economic Theory*, **22**, 136–54.

Rationality and Society (1992), Special issue devoted to 'The Use of Game Theory in the Social Sciences', **4**, 1992.

Reinganum, J.F. (1979), 'A simple model of price dispersion', *Journal of Political Economy*, **87**, 851–8

Roberts, J. and H. Sonnenschein (1976), 'On the existence of Cournot equilibrium without concave profit functions', *Journal of Economic Theory*, **13**, 112–17.

Roberts, J. and H. Sonnenschein (1977), 'On the foundations of the theory of monopolistic competition', *Econometrica*, **45**, 101–14.

Roberts, K. (1980), 'The limit points of monopolistic competition', *Journal of Economic Theory*, **22**, 256–78.

Ruffin, R. (1971), 'Cournot oligopoly and competitive behavior', *Review of Economic Studies*, **38**, 493–502.

Salop, S.C. (1979), 'Monopolistic competition with outside goods', *Bell Journal of Economics*, **10**, 141–56.

Salop, S.C. and J.E. Stiglitz (1977), 'Bargains and ripoffs: a model of monopolistically competitive price dispersion', *Review of Economic Studies*, **44**, 493–510.

Schelling, T. (1960), *The Strategy of Conflict*, Cambridge, MA: Harvard University Press.

Schmalensee, R. (1978), 'Entry deterrence in the ready-to-eat breakfast cereal industry', *Bell Journal of Economics*, **9**, 305–27.

Schmalensee, R. (1982), 'Product differentiation advantages of pioneering brands', *American Economic Review*, **72**, 349–65.

Schwartz, M. and E.A. Thompson (1986), 'Divisionalization and entry deterrence', *Journal of Economics*, **101**, 307–21.

Schumpeter, J. (1954), *History of Economic Analysis*, London: Allen & Unwin.

Selten, R. (1965), 'Spieltheoretische Behandlung eines Oligopolmodells mit Nachfrageträgheit', *Zeitschrift für die Gesamte Staatswissenschaft*, **121**, 301–24, 667–89.

Selten, R. (1975), 'Reexamination of the perfectness concept for equilibrium points in extensive form games', *International Journal of Game Theory*, **4**, 25–55.

Selten, R. (1978), 'The chain-store paradox', *Theory and Decision*, **9**, 127–59.

Shaked, A. and J. Sutton (1983), 'Natural Oligopolies', *Econometrica*, **51**, 1469–83.

Shitovitz, B. (1973), 'Oligopoly in markets with a continuum of traders', *Econometrica*, **41**, 467–501.

Shubik, M. (1959a), *Strategy and Market Structure*, New York: Wiley.

Shubik, M. (1959b), 'Edgeworth market games', *Contributions to the Theory of Games IV. Annals of Mathematical Studies*, 267–78.

Silvestre, J. (1993), 'The market-power foundations of macroeconomic policy', *Journal of Economic Literature*, **31**, 105–41.

Singh, N. and X. Vives (1984), 'Price and quantity competition in a differentiated duopoly', *Rand Journal of Economics*, **15**, 546–54.

Spence, A.M. (1976a), 'Product differentiation and welfare', *Papers and Proceedings of the American Economic Association*, **66**, 407–14.

Spence, A.M. (1976b), 'Product selection, fixed costs and monopolistic competition', *Review of Economic Studies*, **43**, 217–36.

Sraffa, P. (1926), 'The laws of return under competitive conditions', *Economic Journal*, **36**, 535–50.

Stigler, G.J. (1957), 'Perfect competition, historically contemplated', *Journal of Political Economy*, **65**, 1–17.

Stigler, G.J. (1961), 'The economics of information', *Journal of Political Economy*, **69**, 213–25.

Stigler, G.J. (1964), 'A theory of oligopoly', *Journal of Political Economy*, **72**, 44–61.

Stiglitz, J.E. (1989), 'Imperfect information in the product market', in R. Schmalensee and R. Willig (eds), *Handbook of Industrial Organization*, Amsterdam: North-Holland, 769–847.

Sweezy, P. (1939), 'Demand under conditions of oligopoly', *Journal of Political Economy*, **47**, 568–73.

Sylos-Labini, P. (1957), *Oligopolio e progreso tecnico*, Milano: Guiffrè. English translation: *Oligopoly and Technological Progress*, Cambridge, MA: Harvard University Press, 1962.

Thisse, J.-F. and G. Norman (eds) (1994), *The Economics of Product Differentiation*, Aldershot: Edward Elgar, Classics in Economics.

Tirole, J. (1988), *The Theory of Industrial Organization*, Cambridge, MA: MIT Press.

Topkis, D.M. (1978), 'Equilibrium points in non-zero-sum *n*-person submodular games', *SIAM Journal of Control and Optimization*, **17**, 773–87.

Triffin, R. (1940), *Monopolistic Competition and General Equilibrium Theory*, Cambridge, MA: Harvard University Press.

Vickrey, W.S. (1964), *Microstatics*, New York: Harcourt, Brace & World.

Vives, X. (1984), 'Duopoly information equilibrium: Cournot and Bertrand', *Journal of Economic Theory*, **34**, 71–94.

Vives, X. (1986), 'Commitment, flexibility and market outcomes', *International Journal of Industrial Organization*, **4**, 217–29.

Vives, X. (1990a), 'Nash equilibrium with strategic complementarity', *Journal of Mathematical Economics*, **19**, 305–21.

Vives, X. (1990b), 'Trade association disclosure rules, incentives to share information, and welfare', *Rand Journal of Economics*, **21**, 409–30.

von Neumann, J. and O. Morgenstern (1944), *Theory of Games and Economic Behavior*, Princeton: Princeton University Press.

Wauthy, X. (1996), 'Capacity constraints may restore the existence of an equilibrium in the Hotelling model', *Journal of Economics*, **64**, 315–24.

Wolinsky, A. (1986), 'True monopolistic competition as a result of imperfect information', *Quarterly Journal of Economics*, **101**, 493–511.

Part I
Industry Size: Quantity and Price Competition

[1]

OF THE COMPETITION OF PRODUCERS

43. Every one has a vague idea of the effects of competition. Theory should have attempted to render this idea more precise; and yet, for lack of regarding the question from the proper point of view, and for want of recourse to symbols (of which the use in this connection becomes indispensable), economic writers have not in the least improved on popular notions in this respect. These notions have remained as ill-defined and ill-applied in their works, as in popular language.

To make the abstract idea of monopoly comprehensible, we imagined one spring and one proprietor. Let us now imagine two proprietors and two springs of which the qualities are identical, and which, on account of their similar positions, supply the same market in competition. In this case the price is necessarily the same for each proprietor. If p is this price, $D = F(p)$ the total sales, D_1 the sales from the spring (1) and D_2 the sales from the spring (2), then $D_1 + D_2 = D$. If, to begin with, we neglect the cost of production, the respective incomes of the proprietors will be pD_1 and pD_2; and *each of them independently* will seek to make this income as large as possible.

We say *each independently*, and this restriction is very

80   *THE MATHEMATICAL PRINCIPLES*

essential, as will soon appear; for if they should come to an agreement so as to obtain for each the greatest possible income, the results would be entirely different, and would not differ, so far as consumers are concerned, from those obtained in treating of a monopoly.

Instead of adopting $D = F(p)$ as before, in this case it will be convenient to adopt the inverse notation $p = f(D)$; and then the profits of proprietors (1) and (2) will be respectively expressed by

$$D_1 \times f(D_1 + D_2), \text{ and } D_2 \times f(D_1 + D_2),$$

i.e. by functions into each of which enter two variables, D_1 and D_2.

Proprietor (1) can have no direct influence on the determination of D_2: all that he can do, when D_2 has been determined by proprietor (2), is to choose for D_1 the value which is best for him. This he will be able to accomplish, by properly adjusting his price, except as proprietor (2), who, seeing himself forced to accept this price and this value of D_1, may adopt a new value for D_2, more favourable to his interests than the preceding one.

Analytically this is equivalent to saying that D_1 will be determined in terms of D_2 by the condition

$$\frac{d[D_1 f(D_1 + D_2)]}{dD_1} = 0,$$

and that D_2 will be determined in terms of D_1 by the analogous condition

$$\frac{d[D_2 f(D_1 + D_2)]}{dD_2} = 0,$$

OF THE THEORY OF WEALTH   81

whence it follows that the final values of D_1 and D_2, and consequently of D and of p, will be determined by the system of equations

(1) $$f(D_1 + D_2) + D_1 f'(D_1 + D_2) = 0,$$
(2) $$f(D_1 + D_2) + D_2 f'(D_1 + D_2) = 0.$$

Let us suppose the curve $m_1 n_1$ (Fig. 2) to be the plot of equation (1), and the curve $m_2 n_2$ that of equation (2), the variables D_1 and D_2 being represented by rectangular coordinates. If proprietor (1) should adopt for D_1 a value represented by ox_1, proprietor (2) would adopt for D_2 the value oy_1, which, for the supposed value of D_1, would give him the greatest profit. But then, for the same reason, producer (1) ought to adopt for D_1 the value ox_{11}, which gives the maximum profit when D_2 has the value oy_1. This would bring producer (2) to the value oy_{11} for D_2, and so forth; from which it is evident that an equilibrium can only be established where the coordinates ox and oy of the point of intersection i represent the values of D_1 and D_2. The same construction repeated on a point of the figure on the other side of the point i leads to symmetrical results.

The state of equilibrium corresponding to the system of values ox and oy is therefore *stable*; *i.e.* if either of the producers, misled as to his true interest, leaves it temporarily, he will be brought back to it by a series of reactions, constantly declining in amplitude, and of which the dotted lines of the figure give a representation by their arrangement in steps.

The preceding construction assumes that $om_1 > om_2$ and $on_1 < on_2$: the results would be diametrically opposite if these inequalities should change sign, and if the curves m_1n_1 and m_2n_2 should assume the disposition represented by Fig. 3. The coördinates of the point i, where the two curves intersect, would then cease to correspond to a state of stable equilibrium. But it is easy to prove that such a disposition of the curves is inadmissible. In fact, if $D_1 = 0$, equations (1) and (2) reduce, the first to

$$f(D_2) = 0,$$

and the second to

$$f(D_2) + D_2 f'(D_2) = 0.$$

The value of D_2 derived from the first would correspond to $p = 0$; the value of D_2 derived from the second corresponds to a value of p which would make the product pD_2 a maximum. Therefore the first root is necessarily greater than the second, or $om_1 > om_2$, and for the same reason $on_2 > on_1$.

44. From equations (1) and (2) we derive first $D_1 = D_2$ (which ought to be the case, as the springs are supposed to be similar and similarly situated), and then by addition:

$$2f(D) + Df'(D) = 0,$$

an equation which can be transformed into

(3) $$D + 2p\frac{dD}{dp} = 0,$$

whereas, if the two springs had belonged to the same property, or if the two proprietors *had come to an understanding*, the value of p would have been determined by the equation

(4) $$D + p\frac{dD}{dp} = 0,$$

and would have rendered the total income Dp a *maximum*, and consequently would have assigned to each of the producers a greater income than what they can obtain with the value of p derived from equation (3).

Why is it then that, for want of an understanding, the producers do not stop, as in the case of a monopoly or of an association, at the value of p derived from equation (4), which would really give them the greatest income?

The reason is that, producer (1) having fixed his production at what it should be according to equation (4) and the condition $D_1 = D_2$, the other will be able to fix his own production at a higher or lower rate with a *temporary benefit*. To be sure, he will soon be punished for his mistake, because he will force the first producer to adopt a new scale of production which will react unfavourably on producer (2) himself. But these successive reactions, far from bringing both producers nearer to the original condition [of monopoly], will separate them further and further from it. In other words, this condition is not one of stable equilibrium ; and, although the most favourable for both producers, it can only be maintained by means of a formal engagement ; for in the moral sphere men cannot be supposed to be free from error and lack of forethought any more than in the physical world bodies can be considered perfectly rigid, or supports perfectly solid, etc.

45. The root of equation (3) is graphically determined by the intersection of the line $y = 2x$ with the curve $y = -\dfrac{F(x)}{F'(x)}$; while that of equation (4) is graphically shown by the intersection of the same curve with the line $y = x$.

84   *THE MATHEMATICAL PRINCIPLES*

But, if it is possible to assign a real and positive value to the function $y = - \dfrac{F(x)}{F'(x)}$ for every real and positive value of x, then the abscissa x of the first point of intersection will be smaller than that of the second, as is sufficiently proved simply by the plot of Fig. 4. It is easily proved also that the condition for this result is always realized by the very nature of the law of demand. In consequence the root of equation (3) is always smaller than that of equation (4); or (as every one believes without any analysis) the result of competition is to reduce prices.

46. If there were 3, 4, . . ., n producers in competition, all their conditions being the same, equation (3) would be successively replaced by the following:

$$D + 3p\frac{dD}{dp} = 0, \ D + 4p\frac{dD}{dp} = 0, \ \cdots \ D + np\frac{dD}{dp} = 0;$$

and the value of p which results would diminish indefinitely with the indefinite increase of the number n.

In all the preceding, the supposition has been that natural limitation of their productive powers has not prevented producers from choosing each of the most advantageous rate of production. Let us now admit, besides the n producers, who are in this condition, that there are others who reach the limit of their productive capacity, and that the total production of this class is Λ; we shall continue to have the n equations

$$(5) \quad \begin{cases} f(D) + D_1 f'(D) = 0, \\ f(D) + D_2 f'(D) = 0, \\ \quad \cdot \quad \cdot \quad \cdot \quad \cdot \quad \cdot \quad \cdot \quad \cdot \\ f(D) + D_n f'(D) = 0, \end{cases}$$

which will give $D_1 = D_2 = \cdots = D_n$, and by addition,

$$nf(D) + nD_1 f'(D) = 0,$$

But $D = nD_1 + \Delta$, whence

$$nf(D) + (D - \Delta)f'(D) = 0,$$

or
$$D - \Delta + np\,\frac{dD}{dp} = 0.$$

This last equation will now replace equation (3) and determine the value of p and consequently of D.

47. Each producer being subject to a cost of production expressed by the functions $\phi_1(D_1)$, $\phi_2(D_2)$, $\cdots$, $\phi_n(D_n)$, the equations of (5) will become

$$(6) \quad \begin{cases} f(D) + D_1 f'(D) - \phi_1'(D_1) = 0, \\ f(D) + D_2 f'(D) - \phi_2'(D_2) = 0, \\ \cdot \quad \cdot \quad \cdot \quad \cdot \quad \cdot \quad \cdot \quad \cdot \quad \cdot \quad \cdot \quad \cdot \quad \cdot \\ f(D) + D_n f'(D) - \phi_n'(D_n) = 0. \end{cases}$$

If any two of these equations are combined by subtraction, for instance if the second is subtracted from the first, we shall obtain

$$\begin{aligned} D_1 - D_2 &= \frac{1}{f'(D)}\,[\phi_1'(D_1) - \phi_2'(D_2)] \\ &= \frac{dD}{dp}\,[\phi_1'(D_1) - \phi_2'(D)]. \end{aligned}$$

As $\dfrac{dD}{dp}$ is essentially negative, we shall therefore have at the same time

$$D_1 \gtrless D_2, \text{ and } \phi_1'(D_1) \lessgtr \phi_2'(D_2).$$

86   *THE MATHEMATICAL PRINCIPLES*

Thus the production of plant *A* will be greater than that of plant *B*, whenever it will require greater expense to increase the production of *B* than to increase the production of *A* by the same amount.

For a concrete example, let us imagine the case of a number of coal mines supplying the same market in competition one with another, and that, in a state of stable equilibrium, mine *A* markets annually 20,000 hectoliters and mine *B*, 15,000. We can be sure that a greater addition to the cost would be necessary to produce and bring to market from mine *B* an additional 1000 hectoliters than to produce the same increase of 1000 hectoliters in the yield of mine *A*.

This does not make it impossible that the costs at mine *A* should exceed those at mine *B* at a lower limit of production. For instance, if the production of each were reduced to 10,000 hectoliters, the costs of production at *B* might be smaller than at *A*.

48. By addition of equations (6), we obtain

$$nf(D) + Df'(D) - \Sigma\phi_n'(D_n) = 0,$$

or (7) $$D + \frac{dD}{dp}[np - \Sigma\phi_n'(D_n)] = 0.$$

If we compare this equation with the one which would determine the value of *p* in case all the plants were dependent on a monopolist, viz.

(8) $$D + \frac{dD}{dp}[p - \phi'(D)] = 0,$$

we shall recognize that on the one hand substitution of the

OF THE THEORY OF WEALTH 87

term np for the term p tends to diminish the value of p; but on the other hand substitution of the term $\sum\phi_n'(D_n)$ for the term $\phi'(D)$ tends to increase it, for the reason that we shall always have

$$\sum\phi_n'(D_n) > \phi'(D);$$

and, in fact, not only is the sum of the terms $\phi_n'(D_n)$ greater than $\phi'(D)$, but even the average of these terms is greater than $\phi'(D)$, *i.e.* we shall have the inequality

$$\frac{\sum\phi_n'(D_n)}{n} > \phi'(D).$$

To satisfy one's self of this, it is only necessary to consider that any capitalist, holding a monopoly of productive property, would operate by preference the plants of which the operation is the least costly, leaving the others idle if necessary; while the least favoured competitor will not make up his mind to close his works so long as he can obtain any profit from them, however modest. Consequently, for a given value of p, or of the same total production, the costs will always be greater for competing producers than they would be under a monopoly.

It now remains to be proved that the value of p derived from equation (8) is always greater than the value of p derived from equation (7).

For this we can see at once that if in the expression $\phi'(D)$ we substitute the value $D = F(p)$, we can change $\phi'(D)$ into a function $\psi(p)$; and each of the terms which enter into the summational expression $\sum\phi_n'(D_n)$, can also be regarded as an implicit function of p, in virtue of the relation $D = F(p)$ and of the system of equations (6). In consequence the root of equation (7) will be the abscissa of the point of intersection of the curve

$$(a) \qquad\qquad y = -\frac{F(x)}{F'(x)},$$

with the curve

$$(b) \qquad y = nx - [\psi_1(x) + \psi_2(x) + \cdots + \psi_n(x)] ;$$

while the root of equation (8) will be the abscissa of the point of intersection of the curve (a) with one which has for its equation

$$(b') \qquad\qquad y = x - \psi(x).$$

As has been already noted, equation (a) is represented by the curve MN (Fig. 5), of which the ordinates are always real and positive ; we can represent equation (b) by the curve PQ, and equation (b') by the curve $P'Q'$. In consequence of the relation just proved, viz.,

$$\Sigma \, \psi_n(x) > \psi(x),$$

we find for the value $x = 0$, $OP > OP'$. It remains to be proved that the curve $P'Q'$ cuts the curve PQ at a point I situated below MN, so that the abscissa of the point Q' will be greater than that of the point Q.

This amounts to proving that at the points Q and Q', the ordinate of the curve (b) is greater than the ordinate of the curve (b') corresponding to the same abscissa.

Suppose that it were not so, and that we should have

$$x - \psi(x) > nx - [\psi_1(x) + \psi_2(x) + \cdots + \psi_n(x)],$$

or $\quad (n-1)x < \psi_1(x) + \psi_2(x) + \cdots + \psi_n(x) - \psi(x).$

$\psi(x)$ is an intermediate quantity between the greatest and smallest of the terms $\psi_1(x)$, $\psi_2(x)$, $\cdots$, $\psi_{n-1}(x)$, $\psi_n(x)$; if we suppose that $\psi_n(x)$ denotes the smallest term of this series, the preceding inequality will involve the following inequality :

$$(n - 1)\, x < \psi_1(x) + \psi_2(x) + \cdots + \psi_{n-1}(x).$$

Therefore x will be smaller than the average of the $n - 1$ terms of which the sum forms the second member of the inequality ; and among these terms there will be some which are greater than x. But this is impossible, because producer (k), for instance, will stop producing as soon as p becomes less than $\phi_k'(D_k)$ or $\psi_k(p)$.

49. Therefore if it should happen that the value of p derived from equations (6), combined with the relations

(9) $\quad D_1 + D_2 + \cdots + D_n = D$, and $D = F(p)$,

should involve the inequality

$$p - \phi_k'(D_k) < 0,$$

it would be necessary to remove the equation

$$f(D) + D_k f'(D) - \phi_k'(D_k) = 0$$

from the list of equations (6), and to substitute for it

$$p - \phi_k'(D_k) = 0,$$

which would determine D_k as a function of p. The remaining equations of (6), combined with equations (9), will determine all the other unknown quantities of the problem.

Figures

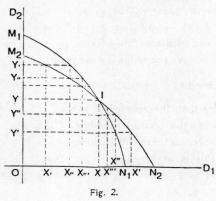

Fig. 2.

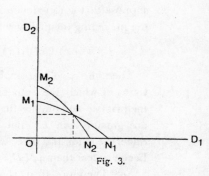

Fig. 3.

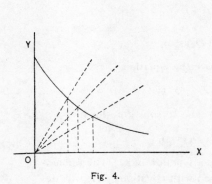

Fig. 4.

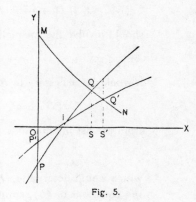

Fig. 5.

[2]

NUMBERS AND SIZE IN COURNOT OLIGOPOLY [1]

I. Cournot [2] stated that total industry equilibrium output increases with the number of oligopolists if they behave according to his assumptions. This proposition is rejected by Professor Baumol [3]. Although Baumol's rejection is right, his argument is not. In this paper, an actual counter-example to Cournot's assertion is produced, a general result along similar lines to the assertion is proved, and Cournot's and Baumol's analyses are briefly criticized. It is a pity that the new result is of less positive significance than Cournot's, and is proved only for the special case of zero costs, but the detailed study is justified on the grounds that the subject is of great historical, though not practical, importance, and that the methods developed may prove useful in tackling other problems.

II. In Cournot oligopoly, each firm tries to maximize its own profits while working on the assumption that the other firms' outputs are fixed. It is assumed that each firm produces the same product and that this is subject to a market demand curve which is known to each firm. The simplest case is that in which costs of production are zero, so that profit is the same as revenue.

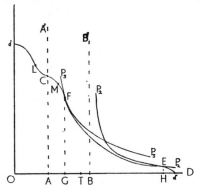

Figure 1.

The equilibrium position can be ascertained diagrammatically as in Fig. 1. The industry demand curve is dd'. Suppose that the outputs of all firms except one total OA. Then on Cournot's assumptions the remaining firm's demand curve is Cd', with its output measured from A instead of from O. Its iso-profit

[1] The author alone is responsible for the contents, but is grateful for useful correspondence with Mr. J. Black on the subject, and for valuable comments by Professor W. M. Gorman.

[2] A. Augustin Cournot, *Researches into the Mathematical Principles of the Theory of Wealth*, New York: Macmillan, 1897 (original French edition 1838), p. 84.

[3] W. J. Baumol, *Business Behavior, Value and Growth*, New York: Macmillan, 1959, pp. 25–6.

(iso-revenue) curves are rectangular hyperbolae with AA' and AD as asymptotes. One of these, P_3, touches the demand curve at F and does not lie below it anywhere, so that this firm's optimal output under these conditions is AG. The curves are drawn so that this output is one half of OA, the combined output of the other firms. This situation is therefore an equilibrium one for three Cournot oligopolists, since each firm in turn can be considered to be the third, and the picture is the same in each case.

In precisely the same way, it may be verified that E is an equilibrium duopoly position, with each firm producing OB or BH, the 'second' firm's optimal iso-revenue curve being P_2 with BB' and OD as asymptotes. Thus the perfectly ordinary looking demand curve in Fig. 1 provides a counter-example to Cournot's proposition, since it shows a duopoly equilibrium total output larger than an equilibrium industry output for three Cournot oligopolists.

III. Three simple properties of the model are now established.

The elasticity of an iso-revenue curve with respect to its asymptotes is unity so that the (undrawn) tangent to P_3 at F in Fig. 1 cuts OD at a point, T, such that $GT = AG$. Therefore, the elasticity of market demand at F is

$$\frac{GT}{OG} = \frac{AG}{OG} = \frac{AG}{3AG} = \tfrac{1}{3}.$$

Similarly, the elasticity of demand at duopoly equilibrium point E is $1/2$, and, in general, $1/n$ is the value of the elasticity of market demand at a Cournot no-cost equilibrium with n firms [1].

The equilibria described above are 'symmetric' in that each firm produces the same output. This is the only possibility as long as the demand curve is smooth. To see this, let some point on the demand curve be an equilibrium position. Then the demand curve must be tangential to an iso-revenue curve for *any* one firm, given the others' outputs. But there is only one rectangular hyperbola that can be drawn with a given slope through a given point with OD as one asymptote. Hence the situation must look the same to each firm.

On the other hand, the same geometric considerations show that a whole continuum of equilibria may exist for a given total output if the industry demand curve is kinked or is discontinuous at this output. The symmetric solution, however, is always one of the possibilities.

Finally, there may be more than one position on the demand curve which is an equilibrium for a given number of firms. For instance, a little visual imagination will show that there is another duopoly equilibrium in Fig. 1 a little to the left of F and another equilibrium for three firms a little to the right of E. In fact, if the elasticity of industry demand remains constant at $1/n$ for a stretch, each point of the stretch may be an equilibrium for n firms.

IV. The propositions now to be proved are that, for an 'ordinary' industry demand curve, at least one Cournot equilibrium exists for each number of firms, and a sequence of equilibria may be so chosen that industry output does not decrease as the number of firms is increased.

An 'ordinary' demand curve means here that demand can be choked off completely at a finite price, that price cannot be infinitely high for any positive demand, that demand is always finite, even if the good is free, that there is some positive demand at some positive price, and that the demand curve is

---

[1] Cournot, loc. cit. p. 84, derived an equivalent condition mathematically.

'closed'.[1] However, kinks, discontinuities, 'forward-rising' stretches or 'backward-bending' ones are allowed.

Attention is first concentrated on any one particular firm. Given the combined output of the remaining firms, iso-revenue curves for this one can be drawn. The assumptions about the demand curve ensure that there is at least one finite optimum for the one firm for each stipulated combined output of the rest.[2] Thus in Fig. 2, for each value of D_r, the combined output of the rest, from zero to D_m, the maximum permitted by the demand curve, there is at least one corresponding total output for all firms, D_t. The result will be called the 'cumulative reaction' graph.[3] When D_r is zero, D_t takes on the monopoly value, which is definitely positive on the present assumptions. Possible positions are A and A' in Fig. 2. At the other extreme, there is no market left for the firm singled out if the rest produce D_m, so that D_t equals D_r, yielding point B. It must be stressed that D_r takes on arbitrarily selected values in order to determine this graph; nothing is said about the number of participating firms, nor about them being in or out of equilibrium.

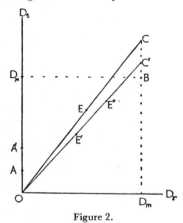

Figure 2.

The crucial property of the cumulative reaction graph is that it is completely monotonically non-decreasing, that is, no value of D_t corresponding to a particular value of D_r can be less than any value of D_t corresponding to a lower value of D_r. To see this, first consider any one situation which is optimal for the last firm, say position F in Fig. 1 for D_r equal to OA. Now consider a slightly larger value for D_r. The last firm now has a new map of iso-revenue curves, obtained by shifting the old map to the right by the amount of increase in D_r. One iso-revenue curve on the new map must pass through F. This curve corresponds to one of the lower curves on the old map. Since iso-revenue curves are radial projections of each other and are convex to the origin, they

---

[1] This means that the curve cannot approach a given point arbitrarily closely and yet not include that point.

[2] See the Appendix.

[3] This is an awkward name, but is reasonably descriptive. What is usually called a reaction curve is a plot of the one firm's optimal output, $D_s = D_t - D_r$, against arbitrary values of D_r. The cumulative reaction graph is obtainable from it by adding a 45° line to it vertically. The more usual graph less convenient in the present analysis.

become steeper for horizontal movements to the left on a given map. Thus when the lower curve is shifted to the right to meet the higher curve at F, it has a greater slope at F than has P_3, and it lies definitely above (below) P_3 all to the left (right) of F.

By assumption, the demand curve does not rise above P_3 for any output, and so the new iso-revenue curve through F lies definitely above the demand curve for all total outputs less than OG.[1] This shows that any output for the last firm which brings the total for the industry up to less than OG is less profitable for it than is that output which makes total output equal to OG. Hence the position which is optimal for the last firm in the new circumstances cannot lie to the left of the old position, and in fact lies somewhere to the right of it if the demand curve is smooth there.[2] Since this argument applies to *any* position which is optimal for the last firm for *any* given total of the others' outputs, the monotonicity property is established.[3]

Given the number of firms, a ray with slope $nD_r/n—1$ can be drawn through the origin of Fig. 2. Since n is a positive integer and is larger than $n—1$, the ray passes through a point C which lies directly above B. Although the cumulative reaction graph may not be continuous in any sense, it is visually apparent that at least one point, say E, along OC belongs to the graph, because the graph starts at a point or points like A and/or A', never falls, and finishes at B.[4]

Now the value of D_t at any point like E is a Cournot equilibrium, because the last firm is producing $1/n^{th}$ of the total output, so that if each firm produces this same amount industry output is precisely this total and each firm is in equilibrium. This proves that a Cournot equilibrium always exists under the assumed conditions, a fact which is far from being obvious.

The final step is to choose a larger value of n. This yields a new ray passing through a point like C', lying between B and C. Again some point, say E', of this ray must also belong to the cumulative reaction graph, and it represents a Cournot equilibrium for the larger number of firms. As the example of Fig. 1 suggests, it is quite possible for E' to lie below E, as drawn in Fig. 2. But since the cumulative reaction graph cannot fall after E and must finish at B, it must also meet OC' at some Cournot point, E'', further on than E, that is, at a higher level of industry output. Similarly, since the cumulative reaction graph starts above the origin and is monotonically increasing, there must be another Cournot point on OC to the left and below E'. It follows that industry equilibrium output if anything increases with the number of firms if the largest (smallest) equilibrium output for each number of firms is considered. The propositions are thus proved.

V. Two interesting special cases are now described. One is that in which only one equilibrium total output is possible for each number of firms, since the result then reduces to Cournot's proposition, at any rate for an ordinary demand curve. Necessary conditions for this case to hold are not obvious. but reasonably weak sufficient conditions can be established fairly easily. Since the elasticity of market demand is $1/n$ at an equilibrium position on a smooth part of the demand curve, it suffices to postulate that the elasticity does not assume this value more than once for each number n for a smooth ordinary

---

[1] Total outputs less than the assumed D_r are not feasible.
[2] It is total industry output that expands; the last firm's output may well fall.
[3] An algebraic proof is given in the Appendix.
[4] See the Appendix for a proof.

demand curve which does not 'rise forward' anywhere though it may 'bend backwards.' The reason is that the elasticity of such a demand curve is infinitely high when demand is zero, is zero when the price is zero, and is continuous (where this property includes continuity at infinity).[1] Thus the values 1, 1/2, 1/3, ... must occur at increasing sizes of demand if they are attained only once each. These output levels are precisely all the Cournot equilibria, because they are the only positions which could be equilibria, and each is the equilibrium for the appropriate number of firms, since at least one equilibrium exists for each number of firms. A downward-sloping straight line demand curve provides a simple case, for the elasticity in this case continuously falls from infinity to zero.

Another corollary compares monopoly output with duopoly or higher order oligopoly. There may be several possible monopoly positions, but it is clear from the shifting iso-revenue curve technique, and is strikingly apparent from Fig. 2, that in the no-cost case any Cournot oligopoly industry output must exceed any monopoly output. In fact, this statement holds regardless of conditions on the demand curve, though it may happen then that some positions cannot be compared because they do not exist.

VI. Cournot's and Baumol's arguments are now judged in the light of the above results.

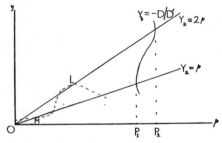

Figure 3.

Fig. 3 reproduces Baumol's Fig. 3:4 with some alterations and additions, and this is to be compared with Cournot's Fig. 4. If D' is the slope of the demand curve with respect to the price axis, the equilibrium condition $e = 1/n$ can be written as $np = -D/D'$. Hence at a Cournot equilibrium the graphs of $-D/D'$ and of np in Fig. 3 meet. Cournot draws the $-D/D'$ graph as a downward-sloping curve, so that there is only one intersection with each ray, and this at successively higher values of p (lower values of D) as n decreases. By drawing the solid $-D/D'$ curve as shown, however, Baumol contends that duopoly price (output) may be higher (lower) than monopoly price (output). Fig. 1 shows that Cournot's result is wrong, but the second corollary mentioned in the last section shows that Baumol is also wrong.

Cournot gives no reason for the shape of his $-D/D'$ curve. He assumes that the demand curve is downward-sloping, and (loc. cit. p. 55) thinks it likely that the total revenue curve is unimodal, that is, that it has only one

---

[1] See the Appendix. To take into account the possibility of kinks, it should be postulated instead that the value l/n does not lie between the 'left hand' and 'right hand' elasticity values for more than one point for each value of n.

turning point, or that demand has unit elasticity in only one situation. But even this assumption, unwarranted as it is, does not guarantee a downward-sloping $-D/D'$ curve. For example, the demand curve in Fig. 1 can be made to satisfy the unimodality assumption by straightening out the stretch between d and M. Such a change does not affect equilibria F and E, and the associated $-D/D'$ curve has a slope greater than 3 for some prices between GF and HE.

Thus Baumol is correct in thinking that the $-D/D'$ curve need not slope downwards all the way, but on the other hand it cannot have the shape he gives it. His continuous curve is undoubtedly thought of as the result of having a smooth demand curve. The curve shows several different values of $-D/D'$ for certain prices. Yet a smooth downward-sloping demand curve yields a single valued $-D/D'$ curve, a smooth demand curve which is forward rising in parts yields a $-D/D'$ curve which is multi-valued by spiralling around the price axis, and one which starts bending backwards at some price yields a $-D/D'$ curve which switches from plus to minus infinity at that price.

Charles E. Ferguson has pointed out in an unpublished paper that the usual calculus second-order conditions, ignored by Cournot and Baumol alike, make it impossible for the $-D/D'$ curve to be steeper than the monopoly ray at a monopoly point as Baumol wishes it to be. However, it is also true that the second-order conditions do not prevent the $-D/D'$ curve cutting the np rays from below for $n > 1$, so Baumol's argument would have been free from this criticism had he compared duopoly with higher order oligopoly.[1]

In any case, even the complete calculus conditions do not go far enough, because they are conditions for purely local optimization. For example, there is a true unique monopoly equilibrium in Fig. 1 at M, where output is larger than at L, at which point the first-order and second-order conditions for duopoly equilibrium are satisfied. A situation like this can give rise to a $-D/D'$ curve like the dotted curve in Fig. 3, with monopoly point, M, and an apparent duopoly equilibrium point, L, lying to its right. In actual fact, such a point does not refer to a duopoly equilibrium at all, except perhaps for myopic duopolists. The Cournot-Baumol graphical method is logically incapable of either proving or refuting Cournot's proposition, since there is no way of knowing which of the points of intersection are relevant, except by conducting a global analysis, such as that in sections IV and V, which, however, gives an answer directly. Thus Fig. 3 is completely otiose.

Dynamics have been ignored in the present analysis. Cournot (loc. cit. p. 81) argued that his duopoly equilibrium is stable according to a simple dynamic scheme. But R. D. Theocharis[2] shows that this is not so for higher order oligopoly. In any case, everything depends upon what dynamic assumptions are made.[3] Thus the results must be interpreted carefully. The proposition of section IV states that there are equilibria which are in the desired order; it does not state that any such sequence would actually result by introducing new firms, or by existing ones dropping out or being absorbed, since some of these equilibria may be unstable according to some accepted dynamic theory.[4]

---

[1] See the Appendix.

[2] "On the Stability of the Cournot Solution on the Oligopoly Problem," *Review of Economic Studies*, Vol. XXVII (2), No. 73, Feb. 1960, pp. 133–4.

[3] See M. McManus and Richard E. Quandt, "Comments on the Stability of the Cournot Oligopoly Model", *Review of Economic Studies*, Vol. XXVIII (2), No. 76, Feb. 1961, pp. 136–9.

[4] On the importance of the 'Correspondence Principle,' see P. A. Samuelson, *Foundations of Economic Analysis*, Cambridge: Harvard U.P., 1947, chapters IX and X.

Finally, Cournot (loc. cit. pp. 85–9) purports to derive the same result even when the firms have costs, but the above criticisms still apply. This more general case is more difficult to analyse, and it is hoped to treat it in a future article.

M. McMANUS

University of Birmingham

APPENDIX

There are several lemmas in the preceding argument for which the fastidious reader might require detailed proof.

The first concerns the existence of an optimum for a single firm for a given combined output of the rest of the industry. Now, by assumption, the set of points which is the demand curve is closed. Hence the set of values for industry total revenue is closed. This implies that the set of values for total revenue for a single firm, given the outputs of the other firms, is closed. The assumptions of finite corresponding prices and demands ensures that the firm's revenue is bounded. From these closedness and boundedness properties, it follows that a maximal revenue for the firm exists for any given total output of the remaining firms. Some weaker or economically more relevant assumptions may suffice instead, but the point is not pursued here.

The second major step is to prove that increasing D_r increases D_t when the last firm is maximizing its revenue. Let $D_t = D_t^0$ and $p = p^0$ when $D_r = D_r^0 < < D_m > 0$. If $D_t^0 = D_r^0$, an increase in D_r certainly increases D_t, since $D_t \geqq D_r$. Now suppose that $D_t^0 > D_r^0$, and consider any D_r^1 satisfying $D_r^0 < D_r^1 < D_t^0$. Let $D_t = D_t^1$ and $p = p^1$ for this D_r. Then, by definition of a maximum,

$$(1) \quad p^0(D_t^0 - D_r^0) \geqq p^1(D_t^1 - D_r^0),$$

$$(2) \quad p^1(D_t^1 - D_r^1) \geqq p^0(D_t^0 - D_r^1).$$

Adding these, cancelling where possible, and collecting terms yields

$$(3) \quad (p^1 - p^0)(D_r^1 - D_r^0) \leqq 0.$$

Since $D_r^1 > D_r^0$, $p^1 \leqq p^0$. Since p^0, p^1, and the brackets in (2) are non-negative, $p^1 \leqq p^0$ implies that $(D_t^1 - D_r^1) \geqq (D_t^0 - D_r^1)$, which implies that $D_t^1 \geqq D_t^0$, as was to be proved.

A third difficulty is to prove that maximizing revenue of the last firm ensures that $D_t = nD_r/n - 1$ for some $D_r > 0$ when $n > 1$. The previous results give D_t as a multi-valued function of D_r, $D_t = T(D_r)$, such that $T(0) > 0$, $T(D_r^1) \geqq T(D_r^0)$ for $D_r^1 > D_r^0$, and $T(D_m) = D_m$. Now $D_t > nD_r/n - 1$ for $D_r = 0$, and $D_t < nD_r/n - 1$ for $D_r = D_m$, so consider $D_r = D_m/2$. If $T(D_m/2) = nD_m/2(n - 1)$, the proposition is proved. If $T(D_m/2)$ is too small, test $T(D_m/4)$ instead. If $T(D_m/2)$ is too large, test $T(3D_m/4)$. If $T(D_m/4)$ is appropriate and exceeds $nD_m/4(n - 1)$, go on to test $T(3D_m/8)$. If $T(D_m/4)$ is appropriate but too small, go on to test $T(D_m/8)$. If, however, $T(3D_m/4)$ is appropriate, next test $T(5D_m/8)$ or $T(7D_m/8)$ according to whether $T(3D_m/4)$ is too small or too large. This halving process proceeds, and defines a sequence of nested intervals of D_r such that in the ith interval the lower end value of

D_r, D_r^i, gives a value of D_t which is too large, and the upper end value, D_r^I, gives a value of D_t which is too small. Either the process ends after a finite number of steps at a value of D_r satisfying the desired condition, or else the infinite sequence of nested intervals closes down on a point of accumulation, D_r^a. Since D_r^a is contained in every interval, the defining characteristics of the intervals and the monotonicity of $T(D_r)$ imply that

$$(4) \quad \frac{nD_r^i}{n-1} < T(D_r^i) \leqq T(D_r^a) \leqq T(D_r^1) < \frac{nD_r^1}{n-1}$$

for all i. But D_r^i and D_r^1 have the common limit D_r^a, so that the first, third and fifth terms of (4) imply that

$$(5) \quad \frac{nD_r^a}{n-1} = \lim \frac{nD_r^i}{n-1} \leqq T(D_r^a) \leqq \lim \frac{nD_r^1}{n-1} = \frac{nD_r^a}{n-1},$$

which is impossible except by having the equalities hold. Hence D_r^a satisfies the desired condition.

Section V makes use of the proposition that the elasticity of a smooth ordinary demand curve is zero when the price is zero, and infinitely high or low [1] when demand is zero.

First consider $p = 0$. If D' is finite at this price, $e(p) = -pD'/D = 0$, as required. Now suppose instead that $D'(0) = -\infty$. By the assumed continuity of $D(p)$ and $D'(p)$, it is possible to choose a small neighbourhood of $p = 0$, N, such that, for all $p \, \varepsilon \, N$, $0 < D(p) < D(0)$ and $0 > D'(p) > -\infty$, so that $0 < e(p) < \infty$. By continuity, therefore,

$$(6) \quad 0 \leqq e(0) \leqq \infty.$$

The objective is to show that the first equality holds, so provisionally assume that it does not. This implies that it is possible to choose a number δ and a neighbourhood of $p = 0$, $M(\delta) \subset N$, such that

$$(7) \quad 0 < \delta < e(p) < \infty, \qquad p \, \varepsilon \, M(\delta).$$

Now choose any member of M, p_0 and consider the function,

$$(8) \quad p^\theta q = p_0^\theta D(p_0),$$

for positive θ. Since $p_0 > 0 < D(p_0)$, there is a positive p for each positive q. The graph of the function in the non-negative quadrant approaches the q-axis asymptotically. The elasticity of this curve is constant at θ. Choose θ so that $\theta < \delta < e(p_0)$. Then $0 < -q'(p_0) < -D'(p_0)$ since $q(p_0) = D(p_0)$, and so $D(p) > q(p)$ for some $p = p_1$ satisfying $0 < p_1 < p_0$. Now $D(p)$ is continuous and $D(0) < \infty$, whereas $q(p)$ is continuous and $q(0) = \infty$, so that there is a set of prices, P, such that $0 < p_2 < p_1$ and $q(p_2) = D(p_2)$ for $p_2 \, \varepsilon \, P$. Moreover, $-q'(p_{2m}) \geqq -D'(p_{2m})$ for the smallest of these prices, p_{2m}. Hence

$$(9) \quad e(p_{2m}) = -p_{2m} D'(p_{2m})/D(p_{2m})$$
$$\leqq -p_{2m}q'(p_{2m})/q(p_{2m})$$
$$= \theta < \delta,$$

which contradicts (7), since $p_{2m} \, \varepsilon \, M(\delta)$. Hence $e(0) = 0$ by (6).

---

[1] High in the case considered in the text, low if the demand curve starts rising at zero demand.

To prove that $e(0) = 0$ if $D'(0) = +\infty$, the same general method can be used with modifications that are fairly obvious and are left to the reader. The trick in this case is to choose θ small and negative in (8). To complete the proof, an analogous procedure can be used to prove that $e = \pm \infty$ at $D = 0$.

Finally, it can be proved that the $-D/D'$ curve may be steeper than an np ray, even at an equilibrium point, except when $n = 1$.

The ith firm tries to maximize its profit, pD^i, assuming that other outputs are constant. The second-order conditions are $2p' + D^i p'' \leq 0$, where a prime denotes one operation of differentiation. Summed over firms, this becomes $2np' + Dp'' \leq 0$. Since $p' = 1/D'$ and $p'' = -D''/D'^3$, the condition reduces to

$$(10) \quad \frac{DD''}{D'^2} \leq 2n.$$

On the other hand, it is easily seen that the $-D/D'$ curve is steeper than the np ray if and only if

$$(11) \quad n + 1 < \frac{DD''}{D'^2}.$$

Clearly (10) does not preclude (11), except when $n = 1$.

[3]
Entry in a Cournot Market *

Augustin Cournot in his classic work, *Recherches sur les Principes de la Théorie des Richesses*, developed his theory of the firm as a general theory with monopoly and perfect competition as special limiting cases. He maintained that as the number of firms in an industry increases, industry output rises, price falls, the output of any one firm becomes a smaller proportion of industry output, and in the limit perfect competition (" unlimited competition" in Cournot's terminology) results.[1] If Cournot is right, then to the extent that actual markets follow a Cournot pattern, the public policy implication is that the number of sellers in a market is a reasonable criterion with which to judge the social desirability of the structure of an industry. In this paper we shall prove that certain conditions which depend on the slopes of the demand and cost curves are sufficient for the Cournot propositions to hold.[2] Cognizance is taken of the fact that some variables are subject to inequalities, namely the output of any firm cannot be negative, and firms producing zero output are permissible. The theorems are stated in terms of finite changes in the parameters rather than in terms of infinitesimal variations.

Consider the following definitions:

D.1. x_i is the output of the ith firm.

D.2.   There are n firms. Total or industry output is $Q = \sum_{i=1}^{n} x_i$.

D.3.   Price $p = f(Q)$ is a function of industry output.

D.4.   The total cost $C_i(x_i)$ is a function of its output.

D.5.   The total output of all firms exclusive of the ith firm is $Q_i = \sum_{i \neq j} x_j$.

D.6.   The profit π_i of the ith firm is price times output (revenue) less cost, or

$$\pi_i = x_i \cdot f(Q) - C_i(x_i) \text{ or}$$
(1)
$$\pi_i(x_i, Q_i) = x_i \cdot f(Q_i + x_i) - C_i(x_i).$$

D.7. x_i is an equilibrium output for the ith firm with respect to Q_i if x_i maximizes profit $\pi_i(x_i, Q_i)$ with Q_i held constant.

D.8.   A Cournot equilibrium is a set of outputs x_i^* for $i = 1, \ldots,$ such that each x_i^* is an equilibrium output with respect to $Q_i^* = \sum_{j \neq i} x_j^*$.

D.9.   A competitive equilibrium output $\bar{Q} = \bar{Q}_i + \bar{x}_i$ one for which the following set of inequalities is satisfied:

(2)
$$f(\bar{x}_i + \bar{Q}_i) - \partial C_i / \partial x_i \leq 0 \qquad \text{for } i = 1, \ldots, n.$$

* The author would like to thank Richard E. Quandt of Princeton University for his helpful criticism of an earlier draft and the participants of the Princeton Economics Department " Research in Progress Seminar " in which a draft of this paper was discussed.

[1] See Augustin Cournot [1]. Since Cournot other authors have stated these same propositions in various ways. For example, E. H. Chamberlin [2] states that " as the number of sellers increases from one to infinity, the price is continually lowered from what it would be under monopoly conditions to what it would be under purely competitive conditions ". A. M. Henderson and R. E. Quandt [3] write: " As the number of sellers is increased, the output of each represents a progressively smaller proportion of industry total, and the effects of an individual's actions upon his rivals becomes less and less noticeable. In the limit the Cournot solution approaches the perfectly competitive result."

[2] C. R. Frank and R. E Quandt [4] give an example in which the demand and cost curves do not satisfy these conditions and output in fact decreases and price rises as the number of sellers increases.

A Cournot equilibrium is attained when if any one producer changes his output, given the total output of all other producers, his profit will remain the same or be lowered. Thus no one producer alone has an incentive to change his output unless others do also. A competitive equilibrium is one where price is not greater than marginal cost.

We make the following assumptions throughout:

A.1. $x_i \geqq 0$ for all i. Negative outputs are not permitted.

A.2. $p = f(Q)$ is twice differentiable.

A.3. $C_i(x_i)$ is monotonically increasing (total cost rises with increases in output) and is twice differentiable.

A.4. For all $Q > M$ where M is sufficiently large, $p = f(Q) = 0$. If total output is very large, the good in question is a free good.

A.5. Each profit function π_i is strictly concave. For all values of Q_i and x_i, the second derivative of the profit function is negative, or

$$\frac{\partial^2 \pi_i}{\partial x_i^2} = x_i \frac{\partial^2 f}{\partial x_i^2} + 2\frac{\partial f}{\partial x_i} - \frac{\partial^2 C_i}{\partial x_i^2} < 0. \tag{3}$$

The assumption of strict concavity means one of three things: (a) marginal revenue is falling and marginal cost is rising; (b) marginal revenue is rising, but marginal cost is rising faster; or (c) marginal revenue is falling faster than marginal cost is falling.

The above assumptions are sufficient to show the existence of a Cournot equilibrium.[1] In order that profit be maximized at equilibrium the following condition [2] is necessary:

$$\frac{\partial \pi_i(x_i^*, Q_i^*)}{\partial x_i} = \frac{x_i^* \, \partial f(x_i^*, Q_i^*)}{\partial x_i} + f(x_i^*, Q_i^*) - \frac{\partial C_i(x_i^*)}{\partial x_i} \leqq 0, \tag{4}$$

and if $x_i > 0$, then

$$\frac{\partial_i(x_i^*, Q_i^*)}{\partial x_i} = 0.$$

The condition (4) above merely asserts that at equilibrium for each firm marginal revenue is less than or equal to marginal cost, and if the output of any firm is positive, then marginal revenue is equal to marginal cost.

Effect of Entry on Output and Price

Before proceeding to the main results we shall prove two lemmas, one of which depends on (5) below and other on (6) below.

$$x_i \frac{\partial^2 f}{\partial x_i^2} + \frac{\partial f}{\partial x_i} < 0 \text{ for all } x_i \text{ and } Q_i \quad (i = 1, \ldots, n), \tag{5}$$

$$\frac{\partial f}{\partial x_i} - \frac{\partial^2 C_i}{\partial x_i^2} < 0 \text{ for all } x_i \text{ and } Q_i \quad (i = 1, \ldots, n). \tag{6}$$

[1] See C. R. Frank and R. E. Quandt [4]. This paper contains a proof of the existence of a Cournot equilibrium under less restrictive assumptions than the above.

[2] This is a statement of the non-linear programming condition in the simplest case. See Kuhn and Tucker [5].

OPTIMUM ACCUMULATION AND INTERNATIONAL TRADE   247

Using the chain rule for derivatives, one may show that (5) is equivalent to

(7) $$\frac{\partial^2 \pi_i}{\partial x_i \partial Q_i} = x_i \frac{\partial^2 f}{\partial x_i \partial Q_i} + \frac{\partial f}{\partial Q_i} < 0 \text{ for all } x_i \text{ and } Q_i \quad (i = 1, \ldots, n),$$

(5) is always satisfied if marginal revenue is falling at a rate steeper than the slope of the demand curve. (6) is satisfied if the demand curve is not positively sloped and marginal cost increases with the output of the ith firm. Note that either (5) or (6) must be true. Otherwise assumption A.5 is not satisfied.

Suppose there is some exogenous change which does not affect the demand curve or the cost curve of the ith firm. Such an exogenous change could result from a shift in the cost curves of other firms or from the entry of a new firm into the industry. Let Q_i^{**} be the new equilibrium output of all firms except the ith firm. The lemma below asserts that the equilibrium output of the ith firm does not increase if the equilibrium total output of all other firms increases.

Lemma 1. If (5) is satisfied and if $Q_i^{**} > Q_i^*$ ($<Q_i^*$), then $x_i^{**} \leqq x_i^*$ ($\geqq x_i^*$).

Proof. The proof for the case where $Q_i^{**} > Q_i^*$ is similar to the proof for $Q_i^{**} < Q_i^*$. We shall give a proof only for the former case. By assumptions A.2 and A.3, the first derivative of the profit function is a continuous and differentiable function of x_i and Q_i. Thus the Mean Value Theorem is applicable. This theorem asserts that

(8) $$\frac{\dfrac{\partial \pi_i(x_i^*, Q_i^{**})}{\partial x_i} - \dfrac{\partial \pi_i(x_i^*, Q_i^*)}{\partial x_i}}{Q_i^{**} - Q_i^*} = \frac{\partial^2 \pi_i(x_i^*, Q_i^0)}{\partial x_i \partial Q_i}$$

where $Q_i^{**} > Q_i^0 > Q_i^*$. From (4), (7), and (8) one obtains the inequality

(9) $$\frac{\partial \pi_i(x_i^*, Q_i^{**})}{\partial x_i} < 0.$$

Now suppose the lemma is not true and $x_i^{**} > x_i^*$. Again we may apply the Mean Value Theorem to get the result:

(10) $$\frac{\dfrac{\partial \pi_i(x_i^{**}, Q_i^{**})}{\partial x_i} - \dfrac{\partial \pi_i(x_i^*, Q_i^{**})}{\partial x_i}}{x_i^{**} - x_i^*} = \frac{\partial^2 \pi_i(x_i^0, Q_i^{**})}{\partial x_i^2}$$

where $x_i^{**} > x_i^0 > x_i^*$. According to (4), (5), and (10), the following inequality holds:

(11) $$\frac{\partial \pi_i(x_i^*, Q_i^{**})}{\partial x_i} > 0.$$

Now (11) and (9) contradict each other and thus the lemma must be true. Q.E.D.

Lemma 2 below asserts that if the equilibrium outputs of all firms exclusive of the ith firm increase, the equilibrium output of the ith firm decreases but not by as much as the increase in the equilibrium output of all other firms together.

Lemma 2. If (6) holds and if $Q_i^{**} \neq Q_i^*$, then

$$\frac{x_i^{**} - x_i^*}{Q_i^{**} - Q_i^*} > -1.$$

Proof. Again there are two cases to consider, one where $Q_i^{**} > Q_i^*$ and one where $Q_i^{**} < Q_i^*$. We shall prove only the former as the proof of the latter is similar.

If $x_i^{**} \geq x_i^*$, then the proof is trivial; so let us turn to the case where $x_i^{**} < x_i^*$. Now we may apply the Mean Value Theorem as in (8) and (10), and then divide equation (8) by equation (10). Division is permissible since (10) is non-zero according to (3). We get

$$(12) \quad \left[\frac{\dfrac{\partial \pi_i(x_i^*, Q_i^{**})}{\partial x_i} - \dfrac{\partial \pi_i(x_i^*, Q_i^*)}{\partial x_i}}{\dfrac{\partial \pi_i(x_i^{**}, Q_i^{**})}{\partial x_i} - \dfrac{\partial \pi_i(x_i^*, Q_i^{**})}{\partial x_i}} \right] \frac{x_i^{**} - x_i^*}{Q_i^{**} - Q_i^*} = \frac{\dfrac{\partial^2 \pi_i(x_i^*, Q_i^0)}{\partial x_i \partial Q_i}}{\dfrac{\partial^2 \pi_i(x^0, Q_i^{**})}{\partial x_i^2}}$$

where $x_i^* > x_i^0 > x_i^{**}$ and $Q_i^{**} > Q_i^0 > Q_i^*$. Since $x_i^{**} \geq 0$, certainly $x_i^* > 0$, and from (4), we have

$$(13) \quad \frac{\partial \pi_i(x_i^*, Q_i^*)}{\partial x_i} = 0.$$

Substituting (13) in (12) and dividing both sides of (12) by the term in brackets on the left-hand side of (12), (division is permissible since by (9) the numerator in the brackets is non-zero), we obtain

$$(14) \quad \frac{x_i^{**} - x_i^*}{Q_i^{**} - Q_i^*} = \frac{\dfrac{\partial^2 \pi_i(x_i^*, Q_i^0)}{\partial x_i \partial Q_i}}{\dfrac{\partial^2 \pi_i(x_i^0, Q_i^{**})}{\partial x_i^2}} \left[-1 + \frac{\dfrac{\partial \pi_i(x_i^{**}, Q_i^{**})}{\partial x_i}}{\dfrac{\partial \pi_i(x_i^*, Q_i^{**})}{\partial x_i}} \right]$$

According to (3) and (7), the term outside the brackets on the right-hand side of (14) is positive. According to (4) and (9), the second term in the brackets on the right-hand side of (14) is non-negative. Thus the following inequality must hold:

$$(15) \quad \frac{x_i^{**} - x_i^*}{Q_i^{**} - Q^*} \geq -\frac{\dfrac{\partial^2 \pi_i}{\partial x_i \partial Q_i}}{\dfrac{\partial^2 \pi_i}{\partial x_i^2}} = \frac{-\left(x_i \dfrac{\partial^2 f}{\partial x_i^2} + \dfrac{\partial f}{\partial x_i} \right)}{x_i \dfrac{\partial^2 f}{\partial x_i^2} + 2 \dfrac{\partial f}{\partial x_i} - \dfrac{\partial^2 C_i}{\partial x_i^2}}$$

From (3), (5), (6), and (7), one may deduce that the right-hand side of the inequality (15) is greater than -1, and hence so is the left-hand side. Q.E.D.

We are now ready to prove the main results.

Theorem 1. *If (5) and (6) are satisfied, then an increase in the number of firms from n to $n + 1$, where the $n + 1$st firm produces a positive equilibrium output $x_{n+1}^{**} > 0$, results in a new equilibrium total output Q^{**} which is greater than Q^*, the old equilibrium total output.*

Proof. Suppose the following is true:

$$(16) \quad Q_i^{**} \leq Q_i^* \text{ for } i = 1, \ldots, n.$$

Assumption A.5 of strict concavity implies that there is a unique profit maximizing output for the ith firm. Thus if $Q_i^{**} = Q_i^*$, then $x_i^{**} = x_i^*$. If $Q_i^{**} < Q_i^*$, according to Lemma 1, $x_i^{**} \geq x_i^*$. Thus if (16) holds, $x_i^{**} \geq x_i^*$ for $i = 1, \ldots, n$, and since x_{n+1}^{**} is positive, we have

$$(17) \quad Q^{**} = \sum_{}^{n} x_i^{**} + x_{n+1}^* > Q^* = \sum_{}^{n} x_i^*.$$

On the other hand, if $Q_i^{**} = Q_i^*$, since the profit maximizing output of the ith firm is unique $x_i^{**} - x_i^* = Q_i^* - Q_i^{**} = 0$. According to Lemma 2, if $Q_i^{**} < Q_i^*$, then $x_i^{**} - x_i^* < Q_i^* - Q_i^{**}$. Thus $x_i^{**} - x_i^* \leq Q_i^* - Q_i^{**}$, or

$$(18) \quad Q^{**} = x_i^{**} + Q_i^* \leq Q^* = Q_i^* + x_i^*.$$

Now (18) contradicts (17), and hence (16) cannot be true. Thus $Q_i^{**} > Q_i^*$ for at least one i. According to Lemma 2, $x_i^{**} - x_i^* > Q_i^* - Q_i^{**}$, or $Q^{**} = Q_i^{**} + x_i^{**} > Q^* = Q_i^* + x_i^*$. Q.E.D.

Theorem 2. If the premises of Theorem 1 are satisfied, then

$$\frac{x_i^{**}}{Q^{**}} < \frac{x_i^*}{Q^*} \quad \text{for } i = 1, \ldots, n.$$

The entry of a new firm results in a reduction of the proportion of total industry output produced by each of the old firms.

Proof. In the proof of Theorem 1 we demonstrated that $Q_i^{**} > Q_i^*$ for at least one i. Furthermore, $Q_i^{**} > Q_i^*$ for all i. Otherwise Lemma 2 implies both $Q^{**} > Q^*$ and $Q^* > Q^{**}$ which is a contradiction. From Lemma 1, $x_i^{**} \leq x_i^*$ for $i = 1, \ldots, n$,

and from Theorem 1 $Q^{**} > Q^*$. Thus $\frac{x_i^{**}}{Q^{**}} < \frac{x_i^*}{Q^*}$ for $i = 1, \ldots, n$. Q.E.D.

Theorem 3. If the premises of Theorem 1 are satisfied and if $\frac{dp}{dQ} = \frac{df(Q)}{dQ} < 0$, then

$p^{**} < p^*$. The entry of a new firm lowers price if the demand curve is negatively sloped.

Proof. The proof is a simple application of the Mean Value Theorem. Q.E.D.

Convergence to Perfect Competition
In order to show the convergence of total output to a perfectly competitive output, we require an additional assumption.

A.6. There are N different types of cost functions. The set I_j is the set of all firms having a cost function of type j, and the number of firms in the set I_j is n_j for $j = 1, \ldots, N$. Then

$$C_i(x_i) = C^j(x_i) \quad \text{for all } i \text{ contained in } I_j.$$

Theorem 4. Let $n_j \to \infty$ for $j = 1, \ldots, N$. If the premises of Theorem 1 are satisfied, then $\lim_{n \to \infty} Q^* = \bar{Q}$. As the number of firms in each category becomes larger and larger, total industry output approaches a perfectly competitive output.

Proof. The equilibrium outputs of any two firms having identical cost functions is identical. To prove this, suppose the contrary, i.e. $x_{i'}^* > x_{i''}^*$ where i' and i'' both belong to I_j. Applying the Mean Value Theorem, we have from (6)

$$\frac{\frac{\delta \pi_i(x_{i'}^*)}{\delta x_i} - \frac{\delta \pi_i(x_{i''}^*)}{\delta x_i}}{x_{i'}^* - x_{i''}^*} = \frac{\delta f(x_i^0)}{\delta x_i} - \frac{\delta^2 C(x_i^0)}{\delta x_i} < 0.$$

Since $x_{i'}^* > x_{i''}^*$ and $x_{i'}^* > 0$, it follows from (4) that

$$\frac{\delta \pi_i(x_{i''}^*)}{\delta x_i} > 0.$$

This contradicts (4), however, and thus $x_{i''}^* = x_{i'}^*$. Furthermore, if Q^j is the sum of the equilibrium outputs of all firms having a type j cost function, then $x_{i''}^* = x_{i'}^* = \frac{1}{n_j} \cdot Q^j$.

Now Q^* is bounded. This follows immediately Assumption A.4 that for sufficiently large Q, $p = f(Q) = 0$ and from the assumption of a monotonically increasing cost function for each firm. Since Q^* is monotonically increasing (Theorem 1), Q^* as well as $Q^* \cdot \delta f(Q^*)/\delta x_i$ converge to some finite value, call it M. Now (4) must be satisfied at equilibrium but (4) and (2) are equivalent as $n_j \to \infty$ for every j since

$$\lim_{n_j \to \infty} x_i \frac{\delta f(Q^*)}{\delta x_i} = \lim \frac{1}{n_j} \cdot Q^j \frac{\delta f(Q^*)}{\delta x_i} = \lim \frac{1}{n_j} \cdot M = 0. \quad \text{Q.E.D.}$$

East African Institute of Social Research and Makerere University College.

CHARLES R. FRANK, JR.

REFERENCES

[1] Cournot, Augustin. *Mathematical Principles of the Theory of Wealth*, English translation by Nathaniel O. Bacon, New York. The Macmillan Company, 1927, Chapter VIII.

[2] Chamberlin, E. H. *The Theory of Monopolistic Competition*. 7th edition, Cambridge, Harvard University Press, 1956, p. 34.

[3] Henderson, A. M. and Quandt, R. E. *Microeconomic Theory: A Mathematical Approach*. New York, McGraw-Hill, 1958, p. 179.

[4] Frank, Jr., C. R. and Quandt, R. E. " On the Existence of Cournot Equilibrium ", *International Economic Review*, Vol. 4, No. 1 (January, 1963), pp. 92-96.

[5] Kuhn, H. W. and Tucker, A. " Non-linear Programming ", *Proceedings of the Second Berkeley Symposium on Mathematical Statistics and Probability*. Berkeley, University of California Press, 1951, pp. 481-492.

[4]

Review of Economic Studies (1980) XLVII, 473–486
© 1980 The Society for Economic Analysis Limited

0034-6527/80/00280473$02.00

Cournot Equilibrium with Free Entry

WILLIAM NOVSHEK

Stanford University

Despite the fact that the assumptions underlying perfect competition never actually hold, the use of the competitive model, as an idealization, is justified if the predictions of the model approximate the outcomes of situations it is used to represent. In partial equilibrium analysis, this justification is embodied in the " Folk Theorem " which states that if firms are small relative to the market, then the market outcome is approximately competitive. This paper provides a precise statement and proof of the " Folk Theorem " for competitive markets with a single homogeneous good, and free entry and exit. It is shown that if firms are small relative to the market then there is a Cournot equilibrium with free entry; furthermore, any Cournot equilibrium with free entry is approximately competitive. More specifically, if we consider an appropriate sequence of markets in which firms become arbitrarily small relative to the market, then there is a Cournot equilibrium with free entry for all markets in the tail of the sequence, and aggregate equilibrium output converges to perfectly competitive output. If firms have strictly U-shaped average cost curves, then individual firm behaviour converges to competitive behaviour. The treatment of free entry distinguishes this paper from other papers dealing with the " Folk Theorem ", where either the number of firms is exogenous, ruling out free entry, or free entry is treated as being equivalent to a zero profit condition, ignoring the integer problem that arises when the number of firms is finite but unspecified.

Firms may become small relative to the market in two ways: through changes in technology, absolute firm size (the smallest output at which minimum average cost is attained) may become small, or, through shifts in demand, the absolute size of the market (the market demand at competitive price) may become large. We allow both types of changes here, though shifts in demand, especially in the form of replication of the consumer sector, may be more familiar. In his conclusion, Ruffin (1971) presents a verbal argument for the " Folk Theorem " which is based on replication of demand and entry. Hart (1979), though not concerned with existence, shows that in a general equilibrium model with differentiated products and free entry, equilibria are approximately competitive (Pareto optimal) when consumers have been replicated a sufficient number of times.

The paper is organized as follows: Section 1 contains the perfectly competitive model and its assumptions, Section 2 contains the assumptions and definitions for the imperfectly competitive model, Section 3 contains an example contrasting the usual treatment of the " Folk Theorem " and the present approach, Section 4 contains the proofs of the main results, and Section 5 contains remarks on the results and indicates how some of the assumptions that are used can be weakened.

SECTION 1

The classical long run perfectly competitive model of a market for a single homogeneous good, where factor prices are constant, can be found in most textbooks which survey microeconomics at any level. All firms have identical technology, and in the long run firms can choose plant size, and enter or leave the market. The long run perfectly competitive market result is aggregate output X^* and price $F(X^*)$ (F is inverse demand) such that $F(X^*) = $ minimum long run average cost $= LRAC(y^*)$, with each active firm operating the optimally efficient size plant at output y^*, and earning zero profit. With constant input factor prices, long run supply is a horizontal line at price $= LRAC(y^*)$.

There are two reasons why firms must be infinitesimal in the perfectly competitive model: first, if firms produce significant output then they have an effect on price; second, if y^* is significant, then long run supply at price $= LRAC(y^*)$ is the discrete set of points which are integer multiples of y^*, not a horizontal line, so if X^* is not an integer multiple of y^*, long run perfectly competitive equilibrium does not exist. Both of these problems vanish when firms are infinitesimal.

The assumptions used in the long run perfectly competitive model are:

(1) long run average cost is strictly U-shaped with minimum attained at $y^* \neq 0$ (non-zero in the scale of the firm);

(2) there exists $X^* \in (0, \infty)$ such that inverse demand $F(X) \gtreqless LRAC(y^*)$ as $X \lesseqgtr X^*$;

(3) (a) firms are identical and infinitesimal with respect to X^*,

  (b) firms maximize profit by choosing quantity viewing price as fixed,

and

  (c) firms are free to enter and leave the market.

Since firms are infinitesimal they have no effect on price. Thus viewing price as fixed is equivalent to viewing the aggregate output of other firms as fixed.

The long run average cost and inverse demand functions are also commonly assumed to satisfy differentiability conditions.

The long run perfectly competitive equilibrium is characterized by:

(4) each active firm's output is a profit maximizing response to price (and hence to the aggregate output of all other firms);

(5) each active firm has non-negative profit;

(6) no potential entrant can earn strictly positive profit by entry, assuming price (and hence the aggregate output of all other firms) is fixed.

SECTION 2

When firms are small but not infinitesimal (y^* is small but significant) they have an effect on price, and we assume they recognize this effect, but no other substantial changes are made in the assumptions or the equilibrium properties. In this context, the "Folk Theorem" says that if y^* is significant but small relative to X^*, then market equilibrium output exists and is approximately X^*. Henceforth, we deal exclusively with non-infinitesimal firms, and the terms "perfectly competitive price" and "perfectly competitive output" refer to minimum average cost and demand at price equal to minimum average cost respectively.

Let AC and C be long run average cost and long run cost functions respectively, and let F be the inverse demand function. The first two assumptions for imperfectly competitive markets correspond to Assumptions (1) and (2) for the perfectly competitive model, with the addition of suitable differentiability conditions.

(C1) AC is twice continuously differentiable on $(0, \infty)$ and strictly U-shaped, with minimum attained at $y^* \in (0, \infty)$ ($AC(y^*) \in (0, \infty)$). Also, $AC''(y^*) > 0$ and $C(0) = 0$.

(F1) There exists $X^* \in (0, \infty)$ such that $F(X) \gtreqless AC(y^*)$ as $X \lesseqgtr X^*$. F is twice continuously differentiable on $(0, \infty)$ and downward sloping (i.e. $F'(X) < 0$ if $F(X) > 0$).

NOVSHEK   COURNOT EQUILIBRIUM   475

These assumptions are much stronger than necessary (see Section 5.4) but their use greatly simplifies the basic proofs of the theorems. The condition $C(0) = 0$ implies that firms can freely exit from the market by producing zero. Note that C need not be continuous at 0, so " set up " costs are allowed.

The measure of firm size is a natural one that is based on technology: the smallest output at which minimum average cost is attained, minimum efficient scale, *MES*. In our partial equilibrium framework, each firm is completely described by its average cost function, so for convenience we identify the firm with its average cost function, and speak of the firm, *AC*.

Definition 1. Let *AC* be an average cost function. Then the size of a firm, *AC*, is

$$MES(AC): = \inf \{y \in (0, \infty) \mid AC(y) \leq AC(z), \quad \forall z \in (0, \infty)\}.$$

If *AC* satisfies (C1) then $MES(AC) = y^* > 0$.

In order to generate a family of average cost functions (indexed by α), a transformation which changes the scale of measurement of output is used. (More general families could be allowed. See Section 5.4.)

Definition 2. Let *AC* be an average cost function satisfying (C1). For each $\alpha \in (0, \infty)$, the α-size firm corresponding to *AC* is the firm AC_α defined by $AC_\alpha(y): = AC(y/\alpha)$.

This transformation changes the scale of measurement of output by a factor of α

$$(AC(y) = AC_\alpha(\alpha y)).$$

With this transformation, we can assume that any basic average cost function under consideration has minimum efficient scale equal to one, and use α to generate the other average cost functions with different minimum efficient scales. This assumption that minimum efficient scale equals one for basic cost functions entails no loss of generality.

(C2) $MES(AC) = 1$.

If *AC* satisfies (C1) and (C2), then an α-size firm relative to *AC* has $MES(AC_\alpha) = \alpha$, and the use of size in Definitions 1 and 2 is consistent. Denote the cost function corresponding to AC_α by C_α, so $C_\alpha(y) = \alpha C(y/\alpha)$.

The measure of market size is also natural: " perfectly competitive demand ", D (which of course depends on the " perfectly competitive price " as well as the inverse demand function).

Definition 3. Let F be an inverse demand function and $p \in (0, \infty)$. Then the size of a market with inverse demand F and " perfectly competitive price " p is

$$D(F, p): = \sup \{X \in (0, \infty) \mid F(X) \geq p\}.$$

If *AC* satisfies (C1) and F satisfies (F1), then the " perfectly competitive price " is $AC(y^*)$ and $D(F, AC(y^*)) = X^*$.

In order to generate a family of inverse demand functions, (indexed by β), a transformation which changes the scale of measurement of output is used. (More general families could be allowed. See Section 5.4.)

Definition 4. Let F be an inverse demand function satisfying (F1). For each $\beta \in (0, \infty)$, the β-size market corresponding to F is the market with inverse demand function F_β defined by $F_\beta(X): = F(X/\beta)$.

For β an integer, F_β corresponds to a β-times replication of the demand sector corresponding to F. Without loss of generality, we assume the basic inverse demand function has competitive demand one and use β to generate other inverse demand functions.

(F2) $D(F, AC(y^*)) = 1$.

If AC satisfies (C1) and F satisfies (F1) and (F2), then $D(F_\beta, AC(y^*)) = \beta$, the " perfectly competitive demand ", and the use of size in Definitions 3 and 4 is consistent.

The market under consideration is completely described by α, C, β, and F, so we denote the market by (α, C, β, F). Note that in any (α, C, β, F) market all firms, including potential entrants, have the same cost function C_α.

The equilibrium concept used here has properties similar to those listed for the long run perfectly competitive equilibrium:

    (i) The outputs of the active firms yield a Cournot equilibrium (without free entry), i.e. a Nash equilibrium with quantity as the strategic variable,

    (ii) all firms make non-negative profit,

and

    (iii) there is no profit incentive for additional firms to enter the market.

Definition 5. Given a cost function C, an inverse demand function F, and α, $\beta \in (0, \infty)$, an (α, C, β, F) market equilibrium with free entry is an integer n and a set $\{y_1, ..., y_n\}$ of positive outputs such that, for

$$X_{)i(} := \textstyle\sum_{j=1, j \neq i}^n y_j \text{ and } X_T := \sum_{i=1}^n y_i,$$

(a) $F_\beta(X_{)i(} + y_i)y_i - C_\alpha(y_i) \geq F_\beta(X_{)i(} + y)y - C_\alpha(y) \ \forall y \in [0, \infty), \forall i \in \{1, 2, ..., n\}$;

and

(b) $F_\beta(X_T + y)y - C_\alpha(y) \leq 0 \ \ \forall y \in [0, \infty]$.

The set of all (α, C, β, F) market equilibria with free entry is denoted by $E(\alpha, C, \beta, F)$.

Condition (a) is the Nash condition for producing firms. When firms are infinitesimal, y is infinitesimal with respect to (the integral) $X_{)i(}$, so $F(X_{)i(} + y)$ is a fixed price and (a) becomes the profit maximizing condition for a competitive firm. If $C(0) = 0$, condition (a) implies that all firms make non-negative profit since $C_\alpha(0) = 0$. Condition (b), the free entry condition, requires that no potential entrant, acting alone, can achieve positive profit by entry. When firms are infinitesimal, this reduces to the competitive entry condition. Notice that the n used in the definition is endogenous, not prespecified, and given α, C, β, and F, $E(\alpha, C, \beta, F)$ may contain several equilibria, with different values of n.

The main results of the paper are Theorems 1 and 2.

Theorem 1. *Given a cost function satisfying* (C1) *and* (C2), *an inverse demand function F satisfying* (F1) *and* (F2), *and α, $\beta \in (0, \infty)$, if n, $\{y_1, ..., y_n\}$ is an element of $E(\alpha, C, \beta, F)$ then $X_T := \sum_{i=1}^n y_i \in [\beta - \alpha, \beta]$.*

Hence, if α is small relative to β, then any equilibrium in $E(\alpha, C, \beta, F)$ (if one exists) yields a market output which is approximately the perfectly competitive output, β.

Theorem 2. *Given a cost function C satisfying* (C1), (C2), *and an inverse demand function F satisfying* (F1) *and* (F2), *there exists $\kappa > 0$ such that for all α, $\beta \in (0, \infty)$, with $\alpha/\beta \leq \kappa$, $E(\alpha, C, \beta, F) \neq \emptyset$.*

Theorems 1 and 2 provide a precise statement and proof of the " Folk Theorem ": if firms are small relative to the market then there is a market equilibrium and the market output is approximately competitive.

SECTION 3

In this section, for a simple example with U-shaped average cost, we contrast the usual treatment of the " Folk Theorem " with the approach adopted in Section 2. The usual treatment fixes cost and demand functions, fixes the number of firms, n, and finds an n-firm Cournot equilibrium. Then n is exogenously increased, so each firm's output (the measure of size) becomes arbitrarily small. In this context, the " Folk Theorem " is valid if and only if the aggregate output of the n-firm Cournot equilibrium converges to perfectly competitive output as n becomes arbitrarily large. When average cost is U-shaped, if each n-firm equilibrium is viable (all n firms producing positive output earn non-negative profit) then the " Folk Theorem " must invariably fail, since price converges to $AC(0+)$—the limit of average cost as output converges to zero—in order to maintain non-negative profit for the firms whose output is becoming arbitrarily small. Treatment of the convergence of n-firm Cournot output to competitive output can be found in Frank (1965), Ruffin (1971) and Okuguchi (1973). Ruffin and Okuguchi recognize the importance of minimum average cost $= C'(0+)$ $(= AC(0+)$ for C Continuous at 0 with $C(0) = 0)$ for the validity of the " Folk Theorem " in this context.

Several extremely strong assumptions on the demand and cost functions are commonly made in order to ensure the existence of equilibrium for each n. The assumption that profit functions are concave for all outputs of the individual firms, for all aggregate outputs of the other firms, is almost universal. Roberts and Sonnenschein (1977) have shown how unreasonably restrictive this assumption is.

In Example A, n-firm Cournot equilibrium fails to exist for all n greater than 1.

Example A.

$$C(y) = \begin{cases} 0 & \text{if } y = 0 \\ 10+y & \text{if } y \in (0, 1] \\ \infty & \text{if } y \in (1, \infty) \end{cases} \quad \text{and} \quad F(X) = \begin{cases} 60 & \text{if } X \in [0, \tfrac{1}{4}] \\ 14-2X & \text{if } X \in (\tfrac{1}{4}, 7] \\ 0 & \text{if } X \in (7, \infty). \end{cases}$$

The only Cournot equilibrium occurs when n equals 1.[1] However, if entry is allowed, a second firm, assuming the output of the first firm is fixed, has profit incentive for entry. The discontinuity of F, the fact that F' is not negative initially, the discontinuity of C at zero and the fact that output is bounded are not essential to the results, and the approach of Section 2 works for this example.

In contrast to the n-firm Cournot technique, the approach of Section 2 measures firm size by technology and treats the number of firms as an endogenous variable. In this context, the " Folk Theorem " is valid under very general assumptions.

Example B shows the failure of the " Folk Theorem " using the n-firm Cournot technique. Example B', using the same basic cost and demand functions, demonstrates the validity of the " Folk Theorem " using the approach of Section 2. For both examples, the non-differentiability of the cost function serves to simplify the reaction correspondences, and does not affect the nature of the results.

Example B. The cost function is

$$C(y) = \begin{cases} \tfrac{3}{2}y-\tfrac{1}{2}y^2 & \text{if } y \in [0, 1] \\ \tfrac{1}{2}y+\tfrac{1}{2}y^2 & \text{if } y \in [1, \infty) \end{cases}$$

and the inverse demand function is $F(X) = 3-2X$. Let $\{y_1, ..., y_n\}$ be an n-firm Cournot equilibrium, and let $X_{)i(} := \sum_{j=1, j \neq i}^{n} y_j$ for each i. The reaction function for each firm is

$$y_i(X_{)i(}) = \begin{cases} \tfrac{2}{3}(\tfrac{3}{4}-X_{)i(}) & \text{if } X_{)i(} \in [0, \tfrac{3}{4}] \\ 0 & \text{if } X_{)i(} \in (\tfrac{3}{4}, \infty) \end{cases}$$

so summing over i, recognizing that $\sum_{i=1}^{n} X_{)i(} = (n-1)\sum_{i=1}^{n} y_i$, and rearranging, we get

$$\sum_{i=1}^{n} y_i = \tfrac{3}{4}\left(\frac{n}{n+\tfrac{1}{2}}\right) < \tfrac{3}{4}.$$

Then $X_{)i(} < \tfrac{3}{4}$ so $y_i > 0$ for all i, and

$$y_i = \tfrac{3}{4}\left(\frac{1}{n+\tfrac{1}{2}}\right) \quad \text{for all } i = 1, ..., n$$

is an equilibrium, and it is the only n-firm equilibrium (to see that $y_i = y_j$ for all i, j, fix the output of any $n-2$ firms and notice that the only equilibrium for the two remaining firms, facing the residual demand as a Cournot duopoly, is $y_i = y_j$). As n is exogenously increased, the output of each individual firm converges to 0, while aggregate output converges to $\frac{3}{4}$, not to competitive output 1. Price converges to $\frac{3}{2} = AC(0+) = C'(0+)$. Notice that for any finite n, price is greater than $\frac{3}{2}$, so if entry is allowed, it will take place; i.e. by producing an output sufficiently close to zero the entrant can maintain price above its average cost. Also, as n increases the behaviour of the firms does not converge to price taking behaviour (the second order condition for a price taking profit maximizer is violated at y_i, and the price taking response to

$$X_{)H(} = \tfrac{3}{4}\left(\frac{n-1}{n+\frac{1}{2}}\right)$$

is always greater than 1, while y_i converges to 0).

Example B'. The basic inverse demand and cost functions are the same as in Example B. For α, $\beta \in (0, \infty)$,

$$C_a(y) = \begin{cases} \frac{3}{2}y - \dfrac{1}{2\alpha}\,y^2 & \text{if } y \in [0, \alpha] \\[2mm] \frac{1}{2}y + \dfrac{1}{2\alpha}\,y^2 & \text{if } y \in (\alpha, \infty) \end{cases} , \qquad F_\beta(X) = 3 - 2X/\beta.$$

We show that for $\alpha/\beta \in (0, \frac{1}{4})$, $E(\alpha, C, \beta, F) \neq \varnothing$. In fact, $E(\alpha, C, \beta, F) \neq \varnothing$ for all $\alpha/\beta \in (0, \frac{1}{2}]$, but for $\alpha/\beta \in [\frac{1}{4}, \frac{1}{2}]$ the properties of the reaction correspondence are different. This example is to serve as a preview to the proof of Theorem 2, so the proof for $\alpha \in [\frac{1}{4}, \frac{1}{2}]$ is extraneous. For $\alpha/\beta \in (\frac{1}{2}, \infty)$, $E(\alpha, C, \beta, F) = \varnothing$ since, as in example B, the free entry condition is not satisfied for any finite number of firms. Fix α, β with $\alpha/\beta < \frac{1}{4}$. The reaction correspondence of a firm with cost function C_a, reacting to output X by other firms, when inverse demand is F_β, is

$$y(X \mid \alpha, \beta) = \begin{cases} \left(\dfrac{\alpha\beta}{4\alpha+\beta}\right)(\frac{5}{2}-2X/\beta) & \text{if } X \in \left[0, \dfrac{3\beta}{4}-2\alpha\right) \\[2mm] \alpha & \text{if } X \in \left[\dfrac{3\beta}{4}-2\alpha, \beta-\alpha\right) \\[2mm] \{0, \alpha\} & \text{if } X = \beta-\alpha, \\[1mm] 0 & \text{if } X \in (\beta-\alpha, \infty). \end{cases}$$

The reaction correspondence is shown in Figure 1. There is a symmetric n-firm Cournot equilibrium (without free entry) if and only if the line

$$L(n): = \{(X, y) \mid (n-1)y = X\}$$

intersects the graph of the reaction correspondence. When n is greater than β/α, $L(n)$ goes through the jump at $X = \beta-\alpha$ and does not intersect the graph of the reaction correspondence. Let $n(\alpha, \beta): = [\beta/\alpha]$, the greatest integer less than or equal to β/α. For all integers $n \leq n(\alpha, \beta)$, there is a symmetric n-firm Cournot equilibrium (without free entry), and in fact it is easy to show that all Cournot equilibria are symmetric.

It remains to show that at least one of these equilibria has aggregate output greater than or equal to $\beta-\alpha$, so that it is a Cournot equilibrium with free entry (from the reaction correspondence we see that if aggregate output is at least $\beta-\alpha$, then an optimal response for a potential entrant is to maintain zero output). In the $n(\alpha, \beta)$ firm equilibrium all firms produce α, so aggregate output is $\alpha n(\alpha, \beta) > \alpha((\beta/\alpha)-1) = \beta-\alpha$ where the inequality

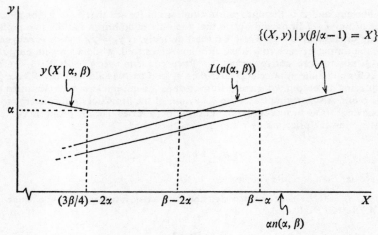

FIGURE 1

follows from the definition of $n(\alpha, \beta)$. Thus, $n(\alpha, \beta)$, $\{\alpha, \alpha, ..., \alpha\} \in E(\alpha, C, \beta, F)$. Notice that

(i) when α/β is small the aggregate output is near the perfectly competitive output β,

(ii) in equilibrium, each active firm's action is approximately equal to the action of a price taking firm faced with the same aggregate output by other firms,

(iii) all active firms earn strictly positive profit except when β/α is an integer. However, in that case, there is also another equilibrium with free entry, $(\beta/\alpha)-1$, $\{\alpha, \alpha, ..., \alpha\}$ in which all active firms earn strictly positive profit.

SECTION 4

The results of Example B' are generalized in Theorems 1 and 2, the first of which shows that if α is small relative to β, then every element of $E(\alpha, C, \beta, F)$ yields a market output which is approximately the perfectly competitive output.

Theorem 1. *Given a cost function* C *satisfying* (C1) *and* (C2), *an inverse demand function* F *satisfying* (F1) *and* (F2), *and* α, $\beta \in (0, \infty)$, *if* n, $\{y_1, ..., y_n\}$ *is an element of* $E(\alpha, C, \beta, F)$ *then* $X_T := \sum_{i=1}^{n} y_i \in [\beta - \alpha, \beta]$.

Proof. If $X_T > \beta$ then $y_i > 0$ for some i, and market price $F(X_T)$ is less than minimum average cost, so the firm producing $y_i > 0$ has strictly negative profit, contrary to the Nash condition and $C_\alpha(0) = 0$.

If $X_T < \beta - \alpha$, by producing α, an entrant changes price to $F_\beta(X_T + \alpha) > AC_\alpha(\alpha)$ since $X_T + \alpha < \beta$, and earns profit $(F_\beta(X_T + \alpha) - AC_\alpha(\alpha))\alpha > 0$, contrary to the free entry condition. ‖

In order for this result to be meaningful, $E(\alpha, C, \beta, F)$ must be non-empty for α small relative to β. There are two ways in which $E(\alpha, C, \beta, F)$ can be empty. First, as in Example B' for $\alpha/\beta \in (\frac{1}{2}, \infty)$, no finite number of firms may be enough to remove the incentive for additional firms to enter, while n-firm Cournot equilibria without free entry exist for all n. Second, n-firm Cournot equilibrium may not exist for all but a finite number of n values, with the free entry condition failing at those Cournot equilibria that do exist.

The second way in which $E(\alpha, C, \beta, F)$ may be empty illustrates the integer problem that arises when free entry is allowed with non-infinitesimal firms. Most of the time, free entry has been treated as equivalent to a zero profit condition, and when firms are non-infinitesimal, the number of firms is treated as a continuous variable in order to get zero profit, after which some statement is made about rounding off the number of firms to an integer. Using that approach, equilibrium with free entry may fail to exist when the number of firms is rounded to an integer. In Example A of Section 3 the zero profit condition is satisfied with $n = \frac{3}{2}$, but equilibrium with free entry does not exist for any n, including $n = 1$ and $n = 2$.

Theorem 2 shows that if α is small enough relative to β, then both types of non-existence are overcome, and $E(\alpha, C, \beta, F)$ is not empty.

Theorem 2. *Given a cost function C satisfying* (C1), (C2), *and an inverse demand function F satisfying* (F1) *and* (F2), *there exists $\kappa > 0$ such that for all α, $\beta \in (0, \infty)$, with $\alpha/\beta \leq \kappa$, $E(\alpha, C, \beta, F) \neq \varnothing$.*

In order to prove the Theorem, we show that for α/β sufficiently small, the reaction correspondence is similar to that of Example B', at least in the interval $[\beta - 2\alpha, \beta]$. In particular, we show that for all α, $\beta \in (0, \infty)$ with α/β sufficiently small, there exists a unique $X(\alpha, \beta) \in [\beta - \alpha, \beta)$ such that, for $y(X \mid \alpha, \beta)$ the reaction correspondence for a firm of size α in a market of size β when the aggregate action of other firms is X,

(i) $y(X \mid \alpha, \beta) = \{0\}$ for all $X > X(\alpha, \beta)$,

(ii) $y(X(\alpha, \beta) \mid \alpha, \beta) = \{0, y(\alpha, \beta)\}$ where $y(\alpha, \beta)$ (which is defined by this condition) is non-zero and approximately equal to α,

(iii) $y(X \mid \alpha, \beta)$ is single valued, greater than or equal to $y(\alpha, \beta)$, and non-increasing in X for $X \in [\beta - 2\alpha, X(\alpha, \beta))$. Thus $X(\alpha, \beta)$ and $y(\alpha, \beta)$ correspond to $\beta - \alpha$ and α respectively in Example B', where for $\alpha/\beta < \frac{1}{4}$,

$$y(X \mid \alpha, \beta) = \begin{cases} \{0\} & X > \beta - \alpha \\ \{0, \alpha\} & X = \beta - \alpha \\ \{\alpha\} & X \in [\beta - 2\alpha, \beta - \alpha). \end{cases}$$

We then show that if the number of active firms, $n(\alpha, \beta)$, is chosen in the same manner as in Example B' (i.e. as the greatest integer less than or equal to $\{X(\alpha, \beta) + y(\alpha, \beta)\}/y(\alpha, \beta)$) then there is an $n(\alpha, \beta)$ firm equilibrium with free entry in $E(\alpha, C, \beta, F)$.

Proof of Theorem 2.

Let $y(X \mid \alpha, \beta)$ be the reaction correspondence and define $X(\alpha, \beta)$ to be the largest X with a non-zero optimal response by the firm, and $y(\alpha, \beta)$ to be the largest optimal response to $X(\alpha, \beta)$:

$$X(\alpha, \beta): = \sup \{X \mid y(X \mid \alpha, \beta) \neq \{0\}\},$$

$$y(\alpha, \beta): = \sup \{y \mid y \in y(X(\alpha, \beta) \mid \alpha, \beta)\}.$$

A firm can just break even in response to $X(\alpha, \beta)$. It is clear from the proof of Theorem 1 that $X(\alpha, \beta) \in [\beta - \alpha, \beta)$. When α/β is small, AC_α is sharply U-shaped relative to the slope of F_β near β, and if we consider a residual demand diagram as in Figure 2, we see that $X(\alpha, \beta)$ and $y(\alpha, \beta)$ are well defined and $y(\alpha, \beta)$ is non-zero and approximately α.[2]

By (C1) and (C2), for all α

$$C_\alpha''(\alpha) = (1/\alpha)(2AC'(1) + AC''(1)) = (1/\alpha)AC''(1) > 0,$$

so we can choose a $\delta \in (0, 1]$ such that marginal cost is increasing ($C_\alpha''(y) > 0$) for all $y \in [\alpha(1 - \delta), \alpha(1 + \delta)]$. Picking such a δ, and a $Z \in (0, 1)$ such that

$$AC(1) < F(Z) < \min \{AC(1 - \delta), AC(1 + \delta)\}, \quad \text{for any } \alpha,$$

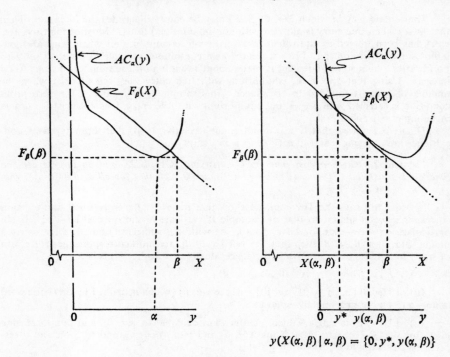

$$y(X(\alpha, \beta) \mid \alpha, \beta) = \{0, y^*, y(\alpha, \beta)\}$$

FIGURE 2

all optimal responses to any $X \geqq \beta Z$ when inverse demand is F_β are either zero or in the interval $(\alpha(1-\delta), \alpha(1+\delta)) \cap [0, \beta - X]$. (If y is greater than $\beta - X$ then

$$F_\beta(X+y) < AC(1) \leqq AC_\alpha(y),$$

while if $0 \neq y \notin (\alpha(1-\delta), \alpha(1+\delta))$ then

$$AC_\alpha(y) > F_\beta(\beta Z) > F_\beta(X+y)$$

by downward sloping inverse demand and U-shaped average cost. In either case, y cannot be an optimal response since zero profit is available for zero output.) For $\alpha/\beta < (1-Z)/2$, βZ is less than $\beta - 2\alpha$, and $X(\alpha, \beta)$ and $y(\alpha, \beta)$ are well defined. Clearly, by downward sloping inverse demand, zero is an optimal response to X if and only if $X \geqq X(\alpha, \beta)$, and zero is the unique optimal response if $X > X(\alpha, \beta)$. We are interested in the non-zero optimal responses when $X \in [\beta - 2\alpha, X(\alpha, \beta)]$, and we have just seen that if $\alpha/\beta < (1-Z)/2$ and $X \in [\beta Z, X(\alpha, \beta)](\supset [\beta - 2\alpha, X(\alpha, \beta)])$ then non-zero optimal responses exist and lie in an interval, $(\alpha(1-\delta), \alpha(1+\delta)) \cap [0, \beta - X]$, of increasing marginal cost.

We now show that when α/β is sufficiently small, marginal revenue is decreasing in both individual firm output, y, and aggregate output of other firms, X, when $X \in [\beta - 2\alpha, \beta]$ and $y \in [0, \beta - X]$. Then, by the last paragraph, for each $X \in [\beta - 2\alpha, X(\alpha, \beta)]$ there is a unique non-zero optimal response for which marginal revenue is equal to marginal cost.

Let

$$\kappa := (\tfrac{1}{4}) \min \left\{ \min_{X \in [Z, 1]} \left\{ \frac{-F'(X)}{\max\{0, F''(X)\}} \right\}, 1 - Z \right\} > 0,$$

and let

$$MR(y, X, \beta): = F_\beta(X+y) + yF'_\beta(X+y),$$

the marginal revenue function. For $\alpha/\beta \leq \kappa$,

$$X \in [\beta(1-2\kappa), \beta] \quad \text{and} \quad y \in [0, \beta - X] \subset [0, 2\beta\kappa]$$

so

$$X+y \in [\beta(1-2\kappa), \beta]), \quad \partial MR/\partial y = 2F'_\beta(X+y) + yF''_\beta(X+y)$$

$$\text{and} \quad \partial MR/\partial X = F'_\beta(X+y) + yF''_\beta(X+y).$$

Inverse demand is downward sloping so $\partial MR/\partial y \leq \partial MR/\partial X$, and if $F''_\beta(X+y) \leq 0$, then marginal revenue is decreasing in both y and X. However, if $F''_\beta(X+y) > 0$,

$$\partial MR/\partial X = F'_\beta(X+y) + yF''_\beta(X+y) \leq F'_\beta(X+y) + 2\beta\kappa F''_\beta(X+y)$$

$$= -F''_\beta(X+y) \left\{ \frac{-F'_\beta(X+y)}{F''_\beta(X+y)} - 2\beta\kappa \right\}$$

$$= -F''_\beta(X+y) \left\{ \frac{-(1/\beta)F'((X+y)/\beta)}{(1/\beta^2)F''((X+y)/\beta)} - 2\beta\kappa \right\}$$

$$= -\beta F''_\beta(X+y) \left\{ \frac{-F'((X+y)/\beta)}{F''((X+y)/\beta)} - 2\kappa \right\}$$

$$< 0,$$

since $F''_\beta(X+y) > 0$ by hypothesis and $(X+y)/\beta \in [1-2\kappa, 1] \subset [Z, 1]$ so the term in brackets is strictly positive by the choice of κ. Hence marginal revenue is decreasing in both y and X for $\alpha/\beta \leq \kappa$, $X \in [\beta(1-2\kappa), \beta]$ and $y \in [0, \beta - X]$. Note that these X, y values include all those we are interested in since $\beta(1-2\kappa) \leq \beta - 2\alpha$, $\kappa < (1-Z)/2$, and $y \in [0, \beta - X]$ for all optimal y. Marginal revenue is decreasing and marginal cost is increasing in the relevant regions, so for $\alpha/\beta \leq \kappa$, for each $X \in [\beta - 2\alpha, X(\alpha, \beta)]$ there is a unique non-zero optimal response, and that response satisfies the first order condition: marginal revenue equals marginal cost.

In order to show that the non-zero optimal response is non-increasing in X for $X \in [\beta - 2\alpha, X(\alpha, \beta))$, we can either use implicit differentiation of the first order condition to get

$$\frac{\partial y(X \mid \alpha, \beta)}{\partial X} = - \left\{ \frac{F'_\beta(X+y) + yF''_\beta(X+y)}{2F'_\beta(X+y) + yF''_\beta(X+y) - C''_\alpha(y)} \right\} \in (-1, 0),$$

or we can notice that whenever marginal revenue is decreasing in both y and X, if $X_1 < X_2$ then the largest optimal response to X_2 is no larger than the smallest optimal response to X_1, regardless of the cost function.

To complete the proof of Theorem 2, let $n(\alpha, \beta): = [\{X(\alpha, \beta) + y(\alpha, \beta)\}/y(\alpha, \beta)]$, the greatest integer less than or equal to $\{X(\alpha, \beta) + y(\alpha, \beta)\}/y(\alpha, \beta)$. (Because of the transformations used to define AC_α and F_β, $X(\alpha, \beta) = \beta X(\alpha/\beta, 1)$ and $y(\alpha, \beta) = \beta y(\alpha/\beta, 1)$, so $n(\alpha, \beta)$ depends only on the ratio of α to β, as in Example B'.) We now show that with κ defined as above, if $\alpha/\beta \leq \kappa$, then there is an $n(\alpha, \beta)$ firm symmetric equilibrium in $E(\alpha, C, \beta, F)$. This is easy to see from Figure 3. First

$$X(\alpha, \beta) \geq \beta - \alpha \quad \text{and} \quad y(\alpha, \beta) \leq \beta - X(\alpha, \beta) \leq \alpha$$

so $X(\alpha, \beta) - y(\alpha, \beta) \geq \beta - 2\alpha$. By definition of $n(\alpha, \beta)$,

$$X(\alpha, \beta) - y(\alpha, \beta) < (n(\alpha, \beta) - 1)y(\alpha, \beta) \leq X(\alpha, \beta)$$

so by the properties of the reaction correspondence for $X \in [\beta - 2\alpha, X(\alpha, \beta)]$, the line $\{(X, y) \mid (n(\alpha, \beta) - 1)y = X\}$ must intersect the graph of the reaction correspondence at a

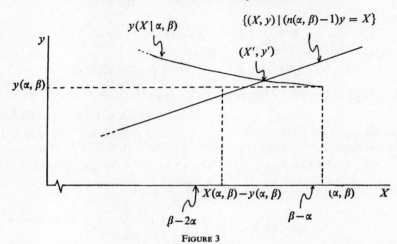

FIGURE 3

point (X', y') with $X' \in (X(\alpha, \beta) - y(\alpha, \beta), X(\alpha, \beta)]$ and $y' \geq y(\alpha, \beta)$. Thus there is an $n(\alpha, \beta)$ firm equilibrium without free entry. The entry condition is also satisfied since $X' + y' > X(\alpha, \beta) - y(\alpha, \beta) + y(\alpha, \beta) = X(\alpha, \beta)$ and the only optimal response for a potential entrant is to maintain zero output. Hence $n(\alpha, \beta), \{y', y', \ldots, y'\} \in E(\alpha, C, \beta, F)$.   ‖

SECTION 5

5.1. It has been assumed throughout the paper that firms act non-cooperatively. Ignoring the possibility of threat strategies, any cartel must practice limit pricing because of the possibility of entry so the total industry gains from collusion are small, and converge to zero as α converges to zero. Because of the problems and costs involved with collusion among a large number of firms, when α is small, the gains from collusion will not justify the formation of large cartels. If a small coalition of firms acts collusively, other producing firms will generally be even better off than the coalition members, so with a large pool of producing firms, a " free rider problem " works against the formation of small coalitions. Finally, for α sufficiently small, at an equilibrium, it is generally not profitable for a producing firm to act collusively with an entering firm. On the other hand, if threat strategies are allowed, cartel threats are only credible if the average cartel member has greater financial assets than an entrant, since the entrant can do at least as well as any active cartel member when the threat is carried out. Thus, the assumption of non-cooperative behaviour seems justified when α is small relative to β.

5.2. If $(\alpha_j/\beta_j)_{j=1}^{\infty}$ is a sequence converging to 0 and $n^j, \{y_1^j, \ldots, y_{n_j}^j\} \in E(\alpha_j, C, \beta_j, F)$ for all j, then n_j converges to ∞ and $\max_{1 \leq i \leq n_j} \{y_i^j/\beta_j\}$ converges to 0. This follows from the optimality of each firm's response and the fact that aggregate output $X_T^j \in [\beta_j - \alpha_j, \beta_j]$ for all j. As the firms become technologically small with respect to the market, the endogenously determined number of operating firms becomes large, each firm's actions converge to price taking actions, aggregate output " converges " to perfectly competitive output and price converges to perfectly competitive price. Compared to the n-firm Cournot technique, where the number of firms is exogenously increased and the output of each firm becomes small, the method used in this paper offers a much more natural interpretation of the " Folk Theorem ", and can be used to prove the " Folk Theorem " when average cost curves are U-shaped and n-firm Cournot equilibrium invariably fails to converge to the perfectly competitive equilibrium as n is increased.

Notice that in general firm profit is strictly positive at equilibrium even with free entry, because only integral numbers of firms can operate. All the equilibria constructed in the proof have strictly positive profit except in the case where

$$n(\alpha, \beta) = \{X(\alpha, \beta) + y(\alpha, \beta)\}/y(\alpha, \beta)$$

(i.e. when it is not necessary to " round off " to obtain an integer), but even in that case there is another equilibrium with $n(\alpha/\beta) - 1$ firms and positive profit for each firm.

5.3. It is clear that Cournot equilibrium with entry may exist for some large α/β. For example, if $AC(0+) > F(0+)$ then for all α/β sufficiently large, the average cost curve will always lie strictly above the inverse demand function, so no firm can profitably operate, and $0, \varnothing \in E(\alpha, C, \beta, F)$. Also, for a sequence of α/β values, the Chamberlinian type tangency will correspond to a Cournot equilibrium with entry with an integral number of firms and zero profit for each firm. This occurs when there is a non-zero

$$y \in y(X(\alpha, \beta) \mid \alpha, \beta)$$

such that $X(\alpha, \beta)/y$ is an integer, $n-1$. Then

$$n, \{y, y, ..., y\} \in E(\alpha, C, \beta, F)$$

(and $n, \{sy, sy, ..., sy\} \in E(s\alpha, C, s\beta, F)$ for all $s > 0$).

5.4. The assumptions used are stronger than necessary in some obvious ways: differentiability is only needed locally near $F(1)$ and $AC(1)$; non-differentiable kinks as in Example B′ could be introduced; and capacity constraints on firm production could be allowed. If we define $AC(0): = \lim \inf_{y \to 0+} AC(y)$ then we need not require that average cost be strictly U-shaped but only that $AC(1) \leq AC(y)$ for all $y \in [0, \infty)$, with strict inequality for $0 \leq y < 1$. This allows flat bottomed average cost curves and multiple distinct minima (an extra step is necessary in the proof for certain of these cases). In (C1) we assumed $AC''(1) > 0$, though for the method of proof used we need only assume that $AC''(y)$ is non-negative for all y in some neighbourhood of one, which is violated only by non-economic curiosa.

It should also be noted that Theorem 2 is true even when average cost is always decreasing, so long as marginal cost is non-decreasing for all sufficiently large outputs (e.g. with a fixed cost plus constant marginal cost). Assumption (C2) must be dropped, and Theorem 1 must be modified to be of interest in this case since minimum average cost is not attained at any finite output.

Finally, it should be clear from the proofs that the families of average cost and inverse demand functions need not be formed in the manner used in Definitions 2 and 4. If we restrict our attention to $\alpha \leq 1$ and $\beta \geq 1$ then the results will hold as long as each individual function (AC_α for each α, F_β for each β) satisfies the appropriate properties, and there are " standardized limit functions " (such as AC^* and F^* where $AC^*(y): = \lim_{\alpha \to 0} AC_\alpha(\alpha y)$ and $F^*(X): = \lim_{\beta \to \infty} F_\beta(\beta X)$) which also satisfy the appropriate properties.

5.5. When several cost functions are simultaneously available, results similar to Theorems 1 and 2 still hold. Given m cost functions $C^1, C^2, ..., C^m$ each of which satisfies (C1), with $MES(AC^i) = y_i^*$ and $AC^i(y_i^*) = p_i$, assume there is free entry for cost functions $1, 2, ..., j$, but an upper bound $n_i^* < \infty$ on the number of possible firms using cost function C^i for $j < i \leq m$ (by (C1) free exit applies to all cost functions). Also assume, without loss of generality, that cost functions are labelled and output is normalized so that $p_1 \leq p_i, i = 2, 3, ..., j$ and $1 = y_1^* \leq y_i^*$ for all $i \in \{2, 3, ..., j\}$ with $p_i = p_1$. Note that for $i > j$ (the cost functions with restricted entry) $p_i < p_1$ and $y_i^* < y_1^*$ are possible.

With the obvious definitions of the market

$$(\alpha, C^1, C^2, ..., C^j, C^{j+1}, n_{j+1}^*, ..., C^m, n_m^*, \beta, F)$$

and Cournot equilibrium with free entry (the entry condition only applies to cost function $i>j$ if $n_i<n_i^*$), if $X^* = F^{-1}(\min_{1 \leq i \leq m} p_i)$ and $X^{**} = F^{-1}(p_1)$ then we obtain an analogue of Theorem 1: for all α/β, aggregate output in any Cournot equilibrium with free entry lies in $[\beta X^{**} - \alpha, \beta X^*]$, and for α/β sufficiently small, the aggregate output lies in $[\beta X^{**} - \alpha, \beta X^{**}]$. When p_1 is the lowest minimum average cost, $\beta X^{**} = \beta X^*$ and we have convergence to the " perfectly competitive output ", βX^*. When p_1 is not the lowest minimum average cost then $\beta X^{**} < \beta X^*$, and the restriction on entry for the most efficient technologies prevents convergence to the " perfectly competitive output ", βX^*, as α/β becomes arbitrarily small.

If we assume $C^{i''}(y) \geq 0$ whenever $AC^i(y) < p_1$ (i.e. whenever the restricted entry technologies have average cost less than the lowest minimum average cost of the free entry technologies, the restricted technologies have non-decreasing marginal cost) then we obtain an existence theorem similar to Theorem 2. The equilibrium is constructed so that the only free entry technology used is C^1, and for $i>j$ all n_i^* available firms are used if $p_i < p_1$ or, $p_i = p_1$ and $y_i^* < y_1^*$ (otherwise no firms of type i are used). A bit of computation shows that when α/β is sufficiently small, a Cournot equilibrium with free entry can be found, avoiding all the discontinuities in the various reaction correspondences.

6. CONCLUSION

In the partial equilibrium analysis of a market for a single homogeneous good, with constant factor prices, the " Folk Theorem " is valid under quite general assumptions. With firm size measured by technology, market size measured by perfectly competitive demand, and the number of firms endogenous, if firms are small relative to the market then Cournot equilibrium with free entry does exist, and the aggregate output is approximately perfectly competitive. The treatment of free entry recognizes that free entry is not equivalent to a zero profit condition when firms are significant and handles the integer problem that does arise with free entry.

Theorems 1 and 2 show that it is not necessary to mix the significant and infinitesimal cases in the discussion of a single perfectly competitive market in the long run. When firms are significant but small, they can be assumed to recognize their effect on price, and a Cournot equilibrium with free entry still exists. The market outcome in this equilibrium is approximately perfectly competitive, with aggregate output, price and individual firm output near perfectly competitive demand, perfectly competitive price, and efficient output respectively. This provides a justification for use of the long run perfectly competitive model, with infinitesimal firms, as an idealization of markets with free entry where firms are technologically small relative to the market.

First version received October 1977; final version accepted May 1979 (Eds.).

Conversations with Wayne Shafer led to the use of the long run perfectly competitive model in the presentation of the results, and also raised the question of possible incentives for collusion. Questions concerning the properties of equilibrium with free entry evolved out of conversations with Hugo Sonnenschein, whose comments on earlier drafts, along with the comments of Peter Hammond and a referee, greatly improved the presentation. Of course, all errors remain my own.

NOTES

1. The optimal responses are $\frac{1}{4} - X$ for $X \in [0, 15/228]$, 1 for $X \in [15/228, \frac{1}{2}]$, and 0 for $X \in [\frac{1}{2}, \infty)$.
2. The double tangency shown in Figure 2 is a special case. Later in the proof we show that when α/β is sufficiently small there is a unique tangency point as claimed in (ii).

REFERENCES

FRANK, C. R. (1965), " Entry in a Cournot Market ", *Review of Economic Studies*, **32**, 245–250.
HART, O. D. (1979), " Monopolistic Competition in a Large Economy with Differentiated Commodities ", *Review of Economic Studies*, **46**, 1–30.

486   REVIEW OF ECONOMIC STUDIES

OKUGUCHI, K. (1973), " Quasi-Competitiveness and Cournot Oligopoly ", *Review of Economic Studies*, **40**, 145–148.

ROBERTS, J. and SONNENSCHEIN, H. (1977), " On the Foundations of the Theory of Monopolistic Competition ", *Econometrica*, **45**, 101–113.

RUFFIN, R. J. (1971), " Cournot Oligopoly and Competitive Behavior ", *Review of Economic Studies*, **38**, 493–502.

[5]

THE PURE THEORY OF MONOPOLY

[THIS is a translation of *Teoria Pura del Monopolio* published the *Giornale degli Economisti*, 1897; itself a translation from an English original which has been lost. Much of the contents might with equal propriety have appeared in the Sections dealing with Taxation and Mathematical Economics. But it has not seemed advisable to break up the article. The theory of monopoly in the ordinary sense of the term is connected with the theory of two-sided monopoly or "duopoly." Cournot had represented the transactions between two parties to be determinate in the same sense as competitive prices. But heavy blows had been dealt on this part of his system by Bertrand in the *Journal des Savants*, 1883, and by Marshall, in an early edition of his *Principles of Economics*. Still in 1897 much of Cournot's construction remained standing; the large part which is based on the supposition that the monopolist's expenses of production obey the law of diminishing returns. Now the demolition of Cournot's theory is generally accepted. Professor Amoroso is singular in his fidelity to Cournot (*cp.* ECONOMIC JOURNAL, September 1922).]

CONTENTS

111

112   THEORY OF MONOPOLY

single monopolist dealing with groups of competitors—cases of correlation in respect of production or consumption.

SECTION IV.—Summary in simple language of the theses maintained in the preceding sections.

SECTION I.—*On the effects of a tax in the simple case of a single monopolist dealing with a group (or groups) of individuals competing against each other.*

Cournot has fully discussed the typical case in which a commodity of uniform quality is offered at one and the same price by a monopolist producer to consumers who compete against each other. The price is determined by the condition that the net gain of the monopolist should be a maximum. The quantity which is to be maximised may be represented by the expression

$$pD - \varphi(D), \text{ where } D = F(p);$$

if p is the price, $F(p)$ the quantity of the article which is demanded at the price p, and $\varphi(D)$ the cost of producing the quantity D. This formula remains applicable if we suppose that $\varphi(D)$ indicates not merely the money cost, the expenses of the monopolist, but the measure of "real cost," [1] the pecuniary equivalent of the efforts and sacrifices incurred by him in the production. Thus interpreted the formula may be extended, by simply changing the signs, to a monopolist consumer who deals with producers competing against each other. In this case $F(p)$ expresses the quantity of an article offered by competitive producers at the price p; and $\varphi(D)$ represents the total utility for the monopolist of the quantity (D).[2]

The effects on the price and on the quantity of an article which are caused by a tax are represented by the same expression in both the cases. If V is the total net utility of the monopolist, whether he is producer or consumer, then for the increment of price consequent on a small tax, for instance, u per unit of product, we have in both cases

$$uF'(p) \div \frac{d^2V}{dp^2}; \text{ [3]}$$

which expression is necessarily positive. To investigate the effect

---

[1] *Cp.* Marshall, *Principles of Economics, sub voce* " Real Cost."

[2] The total utility *simpliciter*, if the monopoly is enjoyed by an individual; but if the part of monopolist is played by a combination—for instance, a co-operative buyers' association—there should be understood the sum of the total utilities obtained by each member from the portion of commodity assigned to him ; a conception which is not necessarily identical with the *Gemeinnutzen* of Auspitz and Lieben, relating to a regime of Competition.

[3] Cournot, *Recherches*, Art. 38.

THE PURE THEORY OF MONOPOLY   113

of the tax on the quantity of the commodity taken at the price, it is convenient to consider the price as a function of the quantity; say $p = f(x)$.[1] * Then, if the monopolist is the producer, we have

$$V = xf(x) - \varphi(x),$$

and for the increment of x

$$\Delta x = u \div \frac{d^2 V}{dx^2};$$

which expression is necessarily negative. If the monopolist is the buyer, the signs in the expression for V are changed; while the equation for Δx remains the same.

As the tax may very well be imposed not on the monopolist but on the competitive group, especially when the latter act as producers, it may be well to observe that in general it makes no difference theoretically on which of the two parties the tax is imposed.[2]

Analogous propositions may be proved for an *ad valorem* tax which is not regressive by inserting in the expression for the tax, instead of u, x as just now, any function of x (or of p) which increases (or diminishes) with the increase (or decrease) of x.[3]

I hasten to pass on to less beaten ground.

An interesting variety of the case in which the monopolist is the buyer occurs when the quantity of the commodity that is on sale is absolutely limited; for instance, when it consists of land offered by competing owners. Here $F'(p)$ is zero, and accordingly

$$dV, = d(\varphi \zeta F(p)) - pF(p), = - F(p)dp.$$

Whence, as the price is continually reduced, the net profit of the monopolist continually increases up to the point at which the sellers are beaten down to nothing—theoretically nothing, practically next to nothing.

In a case of this kind a tax on rent would not fall on the competing landlords at all, but altogether on the monopolist tenant. There occurs in this case what is erroneously supposed to occur in general, that in the phrase of Mill " the price cannot be further raised to compensate for the tax, and it must be paid from the monopoly profits." [4] †

---

[1] *Op. cit.* Art. 43, p. 89.

* x has been substituted for Cournot's D here and in the sequel.

[2] *Op. cit.* Art. 37.

[3] Cournot, *op. cit.* Art. 41. Marshall, *Principles*, 3rd ed., p. 433, note.

[4] Mill, *Political Economy*, Book V. ch. iv. § 6. He is followed by some eminent writers, but naturally not by any of the mathematical school. See Cournot, *Recherches*, ch. vi., and Marshall, *Principles*, Book V. ch. xiii. ed. 3.

† It may be recalled, however, that, though the monopolist has an interest

It may now be asked : Will the case be materially altered if, between the monopolist buyer and the group that is under the necessity of selling without a reserved price, there is interposed a third party, namely, another competitive group with an ordinary degree of " elasticity." Where there are two groups each consisting of individuals competing against each other the introduction of a third group completely changes the incidence of a tax. Thus a tax on the ground rent of cultivable land will in general fall entirely on the owner; a tax on agricultural produce will not in general fall entirely on the owner. Does there exist a similar distinction in the case of monopoly ?

It will be well to begin with the case in which all the individuals in each group are competitors; as the classical writers have hardly discussed this case in all its generality, having limited it by the special supposition that the commodity of which the supply is fixed is not all of the same quality.[1] Let us start with the supposition of three islands, A, B, C, which carry on an international trade of the following description. A buys from B goods, say b, for the production of which B must buy from C certain materials or " agents of production," say c; which are periodically supplied to C in constant quantities not capable of being increased by human effort—for instance, seaweed deposited on the shores of C. Let p_1 be the price of b, and p_2 that of c. Considering any particular producer in B, let us denote by z_t the quantity of finished goods offered by him to inhabitants of A; and by ζ_t the quantity of raw material or agent of production demanded by him from inhabitants of C. Then the net advantage of this individual, say u_t, increases with the net profit $z_t p_1 - \zeta_t p_2$; *ceteris paribus*, and abstraction being made of the efforts and sacrifices involved in the increase of production. Likewise the advantage diminishes with the increase of z_t and increases with the increase of ζ_t (the increase of material facilitating production) in virtue of these efforts and sacrifices; abstraction being made of the satisfaction resulting from increased gain. These relations may be thus expressed :—

$$u_t = F_t(+ (z_t p_1 - \zeta_t p_2), - z_t, + \zeta_t).$$

As z_t and ζ_t are both controlled by the individual, he will vary

---

in reducing the tax, it is not a very great interest, for a reason pointed out below. [*Cp.* ECONOMIC JOURNAL, 1922, p. 439.]

    [1] Ricardo in his discussion of taxes on raw material introduces at the beginning a phrase applicable to the general case, " that capital which pays no rent " (*Political Economy*, ch. ix. par. 1). But he immediately proceeds to suppose land of different qualities. Cp. Mill, *Political Economy*, Book V. ch. iv. § 3.

them up to the point at which u_t is a maximum. We have thus the two equations :—

$$(a)\ \frac{du_t}{dz_t} = 0 \quad (b)\ \frac{du_t}{d\zeta_t} = 0.$$

Eliminating ζ_t from the equations (a) and (b), we might obtain an equation of the form $z_t = \varphi_t(p_1,\ p_2)$, representing the offer of b by the individual No. t in B (at the prices p_1 and p_2). Summing the offers of all the producers in B, we have

$$Sz = S\varphi(p_1,\ p_2) = \text{say } \Phi(p_1,\ p_2).$$

This offer ought to be equal to the demand in A for b at the price p_1; say (1) $\Phi(p_1,\ p_2) = F(p_1)$. Again, eliminating z_t from the equations (a) and (b) we might obtain an equation of the form $\zeta_t = \psi(p_1,\ p_2)$. Whence as the sum of the ζ's is constant we have an equation of the form

$$(2)\ \Psi(p_1\ p_2) = K;\ \text{where } K \text{ is a constant.}$$

To investigate the effect of a tax, say of u per unit of seaweed, or use of land or other limited commodity obtained from C, it is proper to put $(p_2 + u)$ for p_2 in the equations (1) and (2) from which the two prices are determined. It is evident that the value of p_1 which is obtained by eliminating the other variable is not altered by the change; the tax falls entirely on the inhabitants of C.

To study the effect of a like tax on the produce of B we ought to substitute for p_1, $(p_1 + u)$ in the left-hand member of the equation (1), or $(p_1 - u)$ in the right-hand member. In general the offer of b expressed by Φ will fall; and consequently the demand for c expressed by Ψ. The quantity of c being fixed, the fall on the demand for it is attended with a fall in its price. There is a limiting case in which the price of c is not altered, and the entire tax falls upon A. This occurs when the demand on the part of A for b is perfectly inelastic. Then $F(p_1 + u) = F(p_1)$. And so the price paid to the producers in B and their demand for c remain unaltered. Everything goes on as before, except that the inhabitants of A pay the tax in addition to the price of b.[1]

We have now to consider how these relations are modified when it is supposed that b is bought by a monopolist. Equation (2) remains as before; but for equation (1) we ought to

[1] *Cp.* II. 134.

substitute the condition that V, the net advantage of the monopolist, should be a maximum; and V is of the form

$$\Theta[\Phi(p_1, p_2)] - p_1\Phi(p_1, p_2).$$

Whence it follows that we ought to equate to zero the differential coefficient of the expression $V - \lambda(\Psi - K)$ (where λ is the undetermined multiplier proper to problems of relative maximum) —the complete differential, not simply the partial differential with respect to the variable which is directly under the control of the monopolist, viz. p_1. For why should the monopolist stop at the value of p_1 which is given by the equation $\left(\dfrac{dV}{dp_1}\right) = 0$; p_2 not varying. He will go on making p_1 to vary directly and p_2 in virtue of equation (2), indirectly up to the point at which V cannot be increased by any variation of p_1 consistent with equation (2).

It appears from this analysis that, as before, a tax on c will fall entirely on C. With respect to a tax on b, the case of monopoly agrees with that of competition in this respect, that in general the price of c will be somewhat reduced.

Suppose now that either of the groups B or C becomes solidified as a monopolist. Presumably each monopolist will fix the price which is directly under his control at that figure which he thinks likely to afford him the greatest net advantage, account being had of the price which will probably be fixed by the other monopolist for the article under his control. It is thus that the stroke of a fencer is influenced by his prevision of what his adversary's parry will be. The economic fencing-match may continue till one of the fencers is ruined. Pure theory does not seem to assign any stage at which they must stop.

This is a particular case of the general proposition that, when more than one monopolist takes part in a system of bargains, value is indeterminate. The proof of this proposition presents a difficulty which must be overcome before we can proceed to the more complicated cases of value in a regime of monopoly.

SECTION II.—*Proof of the proposition that when two or more monopolists are dealing with competitive groups, economic equilibrium is indeterminate.*

To establish this proposition it will suffice to consider the typical cases formed by two monopolists, each of whom, acting independently, offers to a competitive group one of two articles that are either (A) *rival* or (B) *complementary* as objects of demand.[1]

A. The simplest case under this head is that in which the rival articles are not merely substitutes for each other, but actually identical. This case is treated by Cournot [2] as the first step in the transition from monopoly to perfect competition. He concludes that a determinate proposition of equilibrium defined by certain quantities of the articles will be reached. Cournot's conclusion has been shown to be erroneous by Bertrand [3] for the

---

[1] I define these terms as follows. I assume, notwithstanding the objections raised by some distinguished economists, in particular Prof. V. Pareto in the *Giornale degli Economisti* [*cp. Manuel*], and Prof. Irving Fisher in his *Mathematical Investigations*, p. 89, that for every system of quantities assigned to the two articles, that is, for every pair of x and y (at any rate for values above a certain minimum of these commodities—*cp.* Marshall, *Principles*, Appendix, Note vi, and passage there referred to), there is for each individual a money measure of the total utility which he derives from the consumption of assigned quantities (x and y), a measure represented by a function of those quantities (see Dupuit, article " Utility," *Journal des Economistes*, 1853).

If x and y are the quantities sold at the prices ξ and η, we have $\xi = \dfrac{dF_r}{dx_r}$, $\eta = \dfrac{dF_r}{dy_r}$ for each individual; x_r and y_r being the quantities purchased by the individual numbered r. Whence, if $F(x, y)$ is put for $\Sigma\ F_r(x_r,\ y_r)$—corresponding to the " Gesammtnützlichkeit " of Messrs. Auspitz and Lieben— $\xi = \dfrac{dF}{dx}, \ \eta = \dfrac{dF}{dy}$.

Well then, the articles are rival or complementary objects of demand according as $\dfrac{d^2F}{dxdy}$ is negative or positive. We shall have the first case when $\dfrac{d^2F_r}{dx_r dy_r}$ is negative for every individual (or at least on an average); the second case when that expression is positive.

From the last two paragraphs we deduce that $\dfrac{d\xi}{dy} = \dfrac{d\eta}{dx}$ is negative for rival and positive for complementary articles. Also, if x and y are considered as functions of ξ and η which may be obtained from the above given values of ξ and η in terms of x and y, it will be found that $\dfrac{dx}{d\eta}$ and $\dfrac{dy}{d\xi}$ are positive for rival and negative for complementary articles. The proof of this proposition involves the condition

$$\left(\frac{d\xi}{dx}\right)\left(\frac{d\eta}{dy}\right) - \left(\frac{d\xi}{dy}\right)\left(\frac{d\eta}{dx}\right) > 0.$$

This condition follows from the condition that in equilibrium the total utility of each individual ought to be a maximum because otherwise he will continue to buy at the prices ξ and η. Whence it is deducible that the total utility $F(xy)$ ought to be a maximum. Whence

$$\left(\frac{d^2F}{dx^2}\right)\left(\frac{d^2F}{dy^2}\right) - \left(\frac{d^2F}{dx,\ dy}\right)^2 > 0,$$

which is identical with the said condition (*cp.* below, Sect. III.).

[2] *Op. cit.* ch. vii.

[3] *Journal des Savants*, 1883.

case in which there is no cost of production; by Professor Marshall [1] for the case in which the cost follows the law of increasing returns; and by the present writer [2] for the case in which the cost follows the law of diminishing returns.

In the last case there will be an indeterminate tract through which the index of value will oscillate, or rather will vibrate irregularly for an indefinite length of time. There will never be reached that determinate position of equilibrium which is characteristic of perfect competition defined by the condition that no individual in any group, whether of buyers or sellers, can make a new contract with individuals in other groups, such that all the re-contracting parties should be better off than they were under the preceding system of contracts.

The theory may be illustrated by the extreme case of decreasing returns,* the case in which there is a fixed limit to the amount that can be produced. Suppose, for instance, that there are two monopolists, each owning a spring of mineral water (Cournot's " source minérale "), the output of which per day is limited to a certain quantity, the same for both springs. To further simplify the example, suppose that the delivery of the commodity is not attended with any expense. Further, let the demand-curve be the same for every consumer; and that the simplest possible, namely, a right line. Thus let $x_r = 1 - p$ where p is the price and x_r is the amount of the commodity demanded at that price by any individual. Accordingly, if x is the collective demand of a set of customers numbering n,

$$x = n(1 - p).$$

In Fig. 1 let us represent x by a horizontal abscissa, and p by a vertical ordinate, in accordance with Marshall's well-known construction. We may begin with the supposition that each monopolist deals with only half the total number of potential customers; which is, say, $2N$. The collective demand-curve for one of the

[1] *Principles of Economics*, first ed., note to p. 485.

[2] *Mathematical Psychics*. The competition of the two monopolists will reduce the price below the point Q in the figure on p. 114 (*op. cit.*) to within the tract between Q and T. *Cp.* note to p. 116, where the statement that " the system will reach a final settlement at some intermediate point " is inaccurate. Suppose that there are two B's dealing with an indefinite number of A's, as in the case now under consideration. The B's will force each other below the point Q; and between that point and T the position of (temporary) equilibrium will continue to vary; since it will always be the interest of one or more of the A's to re-contract with one or both of the B's; getting on to the partial or " supplementary contract curves " which are indicated at p. 37 (*op. cit.*), but not represented in the figure on p. 114.

* For an example not thus limited see ECONOMIC JOURNAL, September 1922.

markets thus constituted may be represented by the right line
RC, making an angle of forty-five degrees with each of the
co-ordinates, if the units pertaining to the co-ordinates are
properly taken.   Let *OR* be the unit of price.   Let *OA* represent
the quantity of commodity which is demanded at the price
$OP \ (= \frac{1}{2}), = \frac{1}{2}c$ (units of commodity).   Let $OB, = \frac{3}{4}c$, be the
amount to which the daily output of the monopolist is limited.
Let *RC'* likewise represent the demand-curve of the *N* customers
who are supposed initially to be dealing with the other monopolist; with similar conventions as to the abscissa *OA', OB', OC'*
(= *OA, OB, OC* respectively).

Now if each monopolist were dealing independently of the
other with half of the customers he would fix the price at *OP*,
since his net profit $Np(1 - p)$ is a maximum.   When $p = \frac{1}{2}$ the

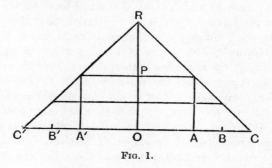

FIG. 1.

corresponding quantity would be $\frac{1}{2}c$.   Let us start from this
position.   If the commodities were quite uncorrelated we would
stop there.   But as things are, it will be the interest of one of
the monopolists to lower his price by a little, say δp, so as to
attract his rival's customers.   Throwing his whole stock on the
market, he would realise a greater profit than before, namely,
$\frac{3}{4}c(\frac{1}{2} - \delta p)$.   He would not indeed be able with his limited supply
to satisfy the entire demand, namely $c(\frac{1}{2} - \delta p)$, evoked by the
lowered price.   But he would have deprived his rival of a great
part of his initial custom.   However, the rival will now follow
suit with a still lower price.   So by successive steps, by variations
of price which may be supposed to occur from day to day, the
price may be lowered to $OQ, = \frac{1}{4}$, which is just sufficient to take
off the whole supply of one monopolist offered to half the market,
consisting of *N* customers.   At this point it might seem that
equilibrium would have been reached.   Certainly it is not the
interest of either monopolist to lower the price still further.

But it is the interest of each to raise it. At the price $\frac{1}{4}$ set by one of the monopolists he is able to serve only N customers (say the first N on a queue) out of the total number $2N$. The remaining N will be glad to be served at any price (short of unity, $= OR$). The other monopolist may therefore serve this remainder at the price most advantageous to himself, namely $\frac{1}{2}$. He need not fear the competition of his rival, since that rival has already done his worst by putting his whole supply on the market. The best that the rival can now do in his own interest is to follow the example set him and raise his price to $\frac{1}{2}$. And so we return to the position from which we started and are ready to begin a new

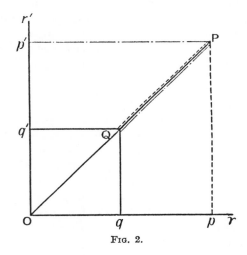

Fɪɢ. 2.

cycle. This need not have exactly the same path as that which we have described. For at every stage in the fall of price, and before it has reached its limiting value $\frac{1}{4}$, it is competent to each monopolist to deliberate whether it will pay him better to lower the price against his rival as already described, or rather to raise it to a higher, perhaps the initial, level for that remainder of customers of which he cannot be deprived by his rival (owing to the latter's limitation of supply). Long before the lowest point has been reached, that alternative will have become more advantageous than the course first described.

The matter may be put in a clearer light by taking ξ and η as co-ordinates representing the prices of the articles which are in the limiting case now considered identical, but in general only rival. The *dotted* lines in Fig. 2 represent the locus of maximum profit for the monopolist owning the commodity x, of which the price is ξ—the *watershed*, so to speak, of the utility surface for that monopolist (or more exactly the locus of that price of x which for any assigned price of η affords maximum profit to the owner of x).* The corresponding locus for the second monopolist is represented by the *broken* lines. Corresponding to the data above defined, put $Op = Op' = \frac{1}{2}$; $Oq = Oq' = \frac{1}{4}$.

If we start from a price Or, above Op, the same for both, it will be the interest of one monopolist to lower his price to Op. The other monopolist from a similar motive, and faced with the loss of custom, follows suit. So we come to the point P, the position of equilibrium if the two markets were separate, or if the two monopolists were in combination. Now it is the interest of the seller of x to lower his price by a little and so (the price of y remaining the same) to move to the point where the dotted line parallel to PQ intersects the broken line Pp'. The seller of y then lowers his price η to a point on the broken line which hugs the diagonal on the right. And so the system may dance down to the point which corresponds to the price Oq ($= Oq'$), below which there is no tendency for the price to be lowered. But before this limit has been reached, the first price may have jumped back to the border-line Pp. The second will then presumably jump on to the line Pp'; and so *perpetual motion* is set up.

It will readily be understood that the extent of indeterminateness diminishes with the diminution of the degree of correlation between the articles. The illustration above given may be adapted to exhibit this incident.†

In the limiting case of no correlation between the commodities the locus of maximum advantage for each monopolist becomes a line parallel to one of the axes. For instance, if Oa in Fig. 3 is the value of ξ which affords maximum profit to the owner of x when η, the price of y, is zero, Oa continues to do so when η varies; aQ is the locus of maximum advantage for the owner of x.

B. The case of complementary demand may be illustrated by

* In general the maximum value of ξ would depend not only on the assigned value of η, but also on the value of y.

† The figure is adapted only to cases which are adjacent to the one discussed in the text : suppose two sources of just distinguishable mineral waters which are supplied by two competing monopolists without cost of production. Some notion of the complications which arise when these simplifying suppositions are removed may be obtained from the example considered in the ECONOMIC JOURNAL, 1922; where it should be remarked that the quantities supplied, not as here the prices, are taken as the variables.

supposing $2N$ homogeneous customers whose laws of demand are for the first article :—

$$x = 2N(1 - \xi - \alpha\eta),$$

and for the second article :—

$$y = 2N(1 - \beta\xi - \eta).$$

To begin with, α and β may be supposed very small and equal. Then the loci of maximum profit are for the respective monopolists :—

$$1 - 2\xi - \alpha\eta = 0;$$
$$1 - \alpha\xi - 2\eta = 0.$$

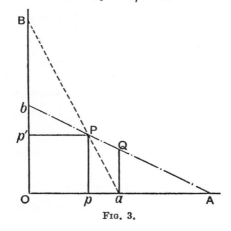

FIG. 3.

They may be imagined (they are not shown) as passing respectively through A and a in Fig. 3; the first almost vertical, the second almost horizontal.

The limiting case in which the two articles are perfectly complementary may be represented by putting α equal to 1. This is the case considered by Cournot when he supposes that each commodity has only one use; namely, to enter in a fixed proportion into the composition of a certain article for which there is a demand.[1] There are then given two monopolists who

---

[1] *Recherches*, ch. ix. It may excite surprise that when Cournot treats of two monopolists dealing in two perfectly rival articles, he supposes the steps towards equilibrium to be made by varying one *quantity* while the other remains constant (ch. vii.); whereas when he treats of two monopolists dealing in two articles perfectly complementary, he supposes that the steps are made by varying one of the *prices* while the other remains constant. An explanation may be found in the term " perfectly." If the articles are perfectly rival (that is, identical) there cannot well be supposed two prices; and if the articles are perfectly complementary (as in the case to which this note refers) there cannot be supposed two (independent variations of the) quantities.

offer in a market of competitive purchasers two complementary articles which enter in definite proportions $m_1 : m_2$ into the composition of an article for which the demand is $F(p)$, or $F(m_1p_1 + m_2p_2)$, where p_1 and p_2 are the prices of the complementary articles.* Abstracting cost of production we have for U the gain of one monopolist, and V the gain of the other :—

$$U = p_1F(m_1p_1 + m_2p_2);$$
$$V = p_2F(m_1p_1 + m_2p_2).$$

According to Cournot the prices are determined by the simultaneous equations

$$(1)\ \left(\frac{dU}{dp_1}\right) = 0 \quad (2)\ \left(\frac{dV}{dp_2}\right) = 0$$

(the price p_1 only being varied in U, and p_2 only in V). To which it may be objected that these equations cannot hold good simultaneously. Suppose, for instance, that the first holds good, then the second will not. For why should the second monopolist stop at the point at which the partial differential coefficient $\left(\frac{dV}{dp_2}\right) = 0$? He will go on varying the price p_2 up to the point at which the *complete* differential coefficient of V is zero. That is

$$\left(\frac{dV}{dp_2}\right) + \left(\frac{dV}{dp_1}\right)\frac{dp_1}{dp_2} = 0;$$

where $\frac{dp_1}{dp_2}$ is derived from equation (1). This equation combined with (1) will determine p_1 and p_2.

To adapt Cournot's illustration to our scheme of rectilinear demand-curves, we may, without loss of generality put

$$m_1 = m_2 = 1;$$

and write for the demand of the first commodity

$$x = 2N(1 - \xi - \eta);$$

and likewise for the second commodity

$$\eta = 2N(1 - \xi - \eta);$$

where ξ and η are the respective prices. Then the position of maximum profit to the seller of x for any assigned value of η is given by the equation

$$1 - 2\xi - \eta = 0,$$

* The reader may like to have a reference to a real case of complementary articles (links in a chain of canals) owned by different (monopolist) companies; of which one fixes a high rate which " obliges the other companies to reduce their rates." Report on Railways and Canals Amalgamation, 1846, p. 200 (Vol. XIII.), Part IV. The concrete case is, however, not so simple as the one above imagined.

represented by the dotted line Ba in the figure; and the corresponding locus for the seller of y is

$$1 - \xi - 2\eta = 0.$$

If we suppose that both these equations exist simultaneously we ought to have $\xi = \eta = Op = Op'$; with P as the position of equilibrium. If we suppose that one only of the equations holds good, the second, for example, but not the other, then, the first monopolist varying his price consistently with the satisfaction of the second equation, the position of equilibrium will be such that $\xi(1 - \xi - \eta)$ should be a *maximum, subject to the condition* that $1 - \xi - 2y = 0$; which gives that point on the line Ab for which $\xi = \frac{1}{2}$; that is, the point Q, if $OA = 1$. But it is the better opinion, I think, that neither of these suppositions is tenable. For clearly in the case of a single monopolist, when it is laid down as a fundamental principle that $pF(p)$ (less cost of production) should be a maximum, it is not supposed that the demand $F(p)$ should be subject to the condition that the prices of all the other articles should remain constant when there are other articles whose prices vary with p. We have already had an example in the international trade above described.* Here is a further somewhat fanciful illustration.

Suppose Nansen and Johansen are dragging their sledge over the Arctic plains (all their dogs having died). In the pursuit of different scientific aims one of them, Nansen, tries to get up on the ice as far as possible above the level of the sea, while the other strives to reach the position at which the depth of the sea measured from the sea-level is a maximum. With these different objects Nansen and Johansen do not act in concert; so much only of their old partnership remains that they do not act against each other, Nansen moves only in a line of latitude (in either direction), Johansen only in a line perpendicular thereto, a line of longitude, parallel to axis OB.

Under these conditions it is very possible that the two surfaces —of the ice and of the bottom of the sea—are crumpled in such wise that the sledge will never come to a point such that neither of the parties will want to get away from it. Such was the case above described with reference to rival commodities.

There is also possible another case. Suppose the principal ridge of ice on which Nansen wants to get as high as possible runs in the direction Ba (Fig. 3), and that the principal valley in the bottom of the sea above which Johansen wants to get as

* See above, p. 114.

high as possible runs in the direction bA. The intersection of these two lines at the point P might seem to be a position of equilibrium. From this point it is not the interest of Nansen to move either to the right or left; nor of Johansen to move either up or down. Nevertheless if Nansen were to move from this position—whether by accident in the polar darkness, or designedly foreseeing a future move of Johansen—say to the right to a neighbouring point P_1, not shown in the figure; then Johansen would tend to move downwards on the vertical line through P_1 to a point Q_2, where the depth of the valley measured from the sea-level is greatest. At this point it is probable that the height of the ice is greater than it was at the initial point P, since the " hog's-back " formed by the ice becomes higher as one moves towards OA along its crest, and accordingly as one moves near the crest, in that downward direction. Nansen will then be in a position to repeat his step to the right, whether induced by a knowledge of Johansen's motives, or simply by the fact that his first step to the right resulted in advantage to himself.* And so there may be reached a point on the line bA considerably below and to the right of the initial point P, the point at which it will no longer prove to the advantage of Nansen to take a step to the right. At this point, which proves to be that at which $\xi = \frac{1}{2}$, the point Q in Fig. 3, it may be thought that equilibrium will finally have been reached.

But it will not be a stable equilibrium, except on the extreme supposition that Nansen is perfectly intelligent and foreseeing, while Johansen, as the saying is, " cannot see beyond his nose." Otherwise let us suppose *first* that both proceed by tentative steps in the dark. At the point Q, or perhaps before getting so far from P, the immediate interest of Nansen may prompt him

---

* Let Q_1 be the point on the line Ba at which Johansen moving downwards from the point P_1 stops. The step PP_1 being short the position Q_1 must be more advantageous for Nansen than P from which he started. For Q_1 is *within* the curve of constant advantage, the indifference-curve, may we say, pertaining to Nansen defined by the equation $U = $ constant where $U = \xi 2N(1 - \xi - \eta)$. Whence

$$\frac{d\eta}{d\xi} = -\frac{du}{d\xi} \Big/ \frac{du}{d\eta} = -\frac{1 - 2\xi - \eta}{-\xi}.$$

Thus the tangent to Nansen's indifference-curve (which is concave towards the axis Oa) is horizontal at P (since at that point $\xi = \eta = \frac{1}{3}$); and at P_1 it slopes slightly downwards to the right, but not nearly so much as the line bA. Accordingly, if Nansen makes a second short step to the right from Q_1, say to P_2, and thence Johansen moves down to Q_2 on bA, the position Q_2 will be more advantageous for Nansen than Q_1. And it can be shown that this downward movement may continue on to the point Q where the tangent to the indifference-curve becomes coincident with the line bA.

to move to the left to a point on the line *Ba*. From this point Johansen will move upwards to a point on the line *bA*. And so on, until they regain perhaps the initial position *P*; ready to start on a second excursion, this time perhaps in an upward direction. *Secondly*, let us suppose that both are perfectly intelligent and aware of each other's motives. Then from the point *Q*, for instance, it is quite possible that Johansen may move *upwards ;* not that it is his immediate interest to move in this direction, but in the hope of inducing Nansen to move to the left to a position (on the line *bA*) more advantageous to Johansen than *Q*. Nansen, however, may not lend himself to this plan. And so the two may continue to make moves against each other; or if they stop, it will be only for a time, and not in a determinate position.*

To drop metaphor, it is certain in the case of rival articles offered by monopolists not in combination, and at least very probable in the case of complementary articles, that economic equilibrium is indeterminate.

It is unnecessary to point out how prevalent in the actual world are the relations of " rival " and " complementary." Let the reader consider the passages referred to in Professor Marshall's *Principles* under headings " Joint Demand," and " Substitutes." It will be sufficient here to mention two cases which, though they do not possess the essential characteristics of rival or complementary goods as above defined, yet have the property of rendering monopoly price unstable. The *summa genera* of necessary articles, food, clothes and so forth, may be regarded as complementary in a certain sense in so far as an increase in the price of one class tends to diminish that of the other class. For instance, it is said that during a dearth in one of our northern cities the price of old clothes diminished. Articles of consumption may also be rivals in a sense, though not capable of acting as substitutes for each other, if an increase in the price of one causes less money to be spent on it, and the money thus set free goes to increase the price of other articles.†

SECTION III.—Since then there is no theory of economic equilibrium in the case with which we have to do with different monopolists, we may confine ourselves to the case in which there is only one monopolist in the field. An important variety of this case occurs when there are two or three different markets

* For further illustrations of the indeterminateness which is characteristic duopoly see ECONOMIC JOURNAL, September 1922.

† *Cp.* below, p. 137.

furnished by one and the same monopolist with two or more articles of which the production is *joint* in this sense, that the increase of one renders the increase of the other (*a*) more, or (*b*) less, costly. In symbols let x and y be the respective quantities produced and $\varphi(x,y)$ the expenses, or, more generally, the pecuniary measure of the real cost of the productions of x and y together; we have then case (*a*) if $\dfrac{d^2\varphi}{dx,dy}$ is positive; if it is negative, case (*b*). These relations may be designated by the terms (*a*) rival production, (*b*) complementary production.

It should be observed that "complementary production" as here defined is not identical with joint production as used by some distinguished writers. If the expense incident to the production of two articles in the quantities x and y is $C + ax + by$, where C, a and b are constants, these articles would commonly be described as produced jointly, but they are not "complementary in our sense.*

(*a*) First, the production being rival, let the cost of producing x together with y be $\varphi(x,y)$ where $\dfrac{d^2\varphi}{dx^2}$, $\dfrac{d^2\varphi}{dy^2}$ (the law of increasing cost being assumed) and $\dfrac{d^2\varphi}{dx\,dy}$ are each positive. Let $f_1(x)$ be the price at which the quantity x is demanded in one market and $f_2(y)$ the price at which the quantity y is demanded in another market; then if V is the net advantage of the monopolist,

$$V = xf_1(x) + yf_2(y) - \varphi(x,y).$$

Now suppose a small tax of u per unit is imposed on the first commodity. If dx and dy are the consequent variations in the quantities furnished we have,

since $\qquad \left(\dfrac{dV}{dx}\right) = 0$, and $\left(\dfrac{dV}{dy}\right) = 0$,

$$dx\,\frac{d^2V}{dx^2} + dy\,\frac{d^2V}{dx\,dy} = u,$$

$$dx\,\frac{d^2V}{dx\,dy} + dy\,\frac{d^2V}{dy^2} = 0;$$

whence $dx = u\,\dfrac{d^2V}{dy^2} \div \varDelta$; $dy = -\,u\,\dfrac{d^2V}{dx\,dy} \div \varDelta$; where $\varDelta$ is the determinant $\dfrac{d^2V}{dx^2} \cdot \dfrac{d^2V}{dy^2} - \left(\dfrac{d^2V}{dx\,dy}\right)^2$, a quantity which must be positive in order that V should be a maximum. For the same

---

* Compare the definitions adopted by Pigou; as to which see passage referred to in Index, s.v. *Joint Production.*

reason $\dfrac{d^2V}{dx^2}$ must be negative. Also $\dfrac{d^2V}{dx,dy} = -\dfrac{d^2\varphi}{dx,dy}$ must be negative. Accordingly dx is negative, dy is positive; the purchasers of the taxed article are damnified, while the purchasers of the tax-free article are benefited. The proposition may be extended to any number of articles.

We might have reached the same conclusion if we had treated the *prices*, say ξ and η, as the independent variables; in which case it would be proper to substitute for x, $F_1(\xi)$ and for y, $F_2(\eta)$, likewise for $f_1(x)$ and $f_2(y)$ respectively ξ and η.

Analytical geometry may be usefully employed with either set of variables. Thus let V be represented by the height of a surface depending on the independent variables ξ and η. The position of maximum height is given by the simultaneous equations

$$(1)\ \left(\frac{dV}{d\xi}\right) = 0; \quad (2)\ \left(\frac{dV}{d\eta}\right) = 0$$

These equations are adequately represented, with respect to values of the variables, in the neighbourhood of the maximum by the curves AA' and BB' in Fig. 4. For both the curves in the neighbourhood of P will be inclined negatively to the axis of ξ; that is, the tangent $\dfrac{d\eta}{d\xi}$ will be for both negative. Further, that tangent *in absolute quantity* will be greater for AA' than for BB'. For with respect to AA'

$$\frac{d\eta}{d\xi} = -\left(\frac{d^2V}{d\xi^2}\right) \div \left(\frac{d^2V}{d\xi\,d\eta}\right)\left(\text{since } \left(\frac{dV}{d\xi}\right) = 0\right)$$

The numerator of this fraction is positive since V is a maximum (at the point P). Also the denominator is negative, as may be seen by substituting $F_1(\xi)$ and $F_2(\eta)$ for x and y in $\varphi(x,y)$. By parity of reasoning the tangent for BB'

$$= -\left(\frac{d^2V}{d\xi\,d\eta}\right) \div \left(\frac{d^2V}{d\eta^2}\right) < 0.$$

These values of $\left(\dfrac{d\eta}{d\xi}\right)_1$ and $\left(\dfrac{d\eta}{d\xi}\right)_2$ as they may respectively be called, are now to be combined with the *third* condition required in order that V may be a maximum, viz. $\dfrac{d^2V}{d\xi^2}\cdot\dfrac{d^2V}{d\eta^2} > \left(\dfrac{d^2V}{d\xi\,d\eta}\right)^2$. Whence $-\left(\dfrac{d\eta}{d\xi}\right)_1 \Big/ -\left(\dfrac{d\eta}{d\xi}\right)_2 > 1$; and $\left[\left(\dfrac{d\eta}{d\xi}\right)\right]_1$ in absolute quantity, $> \left[\left(\dfrac{d\eta}{d\xi}\right)\right]_2$. Thus $\left(\dfrac{d\eta}{d\xi}\right)_1$ and $\left(\dfrac{d\eta}{d\xi}\right)_2$

being both negative, the curves ought to be (in the neighbourhood of the *maximum*) inclined to the axes and to each other
as represented in Fig. 4.

Now let a (small) tax of u *ad valorem* * be imposed on the x
commodity. The curve AA' will be displaced to the right as
in the figure; while the curve BB' remains unchanged. Thus
while ξ is increased η is diminished; a conclusion identical with
that reached above, since the prices and quantities vary inversely.*

If we had treated x and y as the independent variables, the
loci $\left(\dfrac{dV}{dx}\right) = 0$, and $\left(\dfrac{dV}{dy}\right) = 0$ would still have been related like

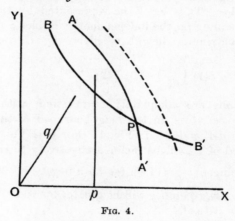

FIG. 4.

the curves AA' and BB' in Fig. 4; while the displaced curve
would lie on the *left* of AA'.

Conversely it may be shown that a bounty to one of the
commodities will prejudice the consumers of the other.

The effects of other kinds of governmental control may be
studied by a similar procedure. Thus let there be prescribed a
maximum price or a *fixed* price for one of the articles, a price less
than what would have been reached if monopoly were allowed free
play. If ξ in Fig. 4 is limited to Op, less than OP, the position of
equilibrium will be the highest point on the curve formed by the
intersection of the surface ($z = V$) with a plane through p perpendicular to the axis OX. The ordinate of the curve BB' formed by
its intersection with a perpendicular through p (in the plane of $\xi\eta$)

---

 * The conclusion is readily extended to a specific tax by substituting in the
above for $\Delta\xi$, considered as a small percentage of ξ, the increment $\Delta x \dfrac{d\xi}{dx}$. Like
reasoning applies to other small taxes.

to the axis OX (the price η) will evidently be greater than the ordinate intersecting at P. Of course if Op is considerably less than OP it might happen that the vertical plane through p does not meet the surface above the plane of $\xi\eta$. The value of V then becomes negative or impossible; the business cannot go on.

Very similar is the effect of the condition that one price should not exceed the other by more than a certain proportion. This condition is exemplified by the American short-haul clause; which enacts that if D_1 the distance of one station (from the terminus) is less than D_2, the distance of another station, and $\xi\eta$ are the respective fares per mile, then $D_1\xi$ shall not exceed $D_2\eta$.

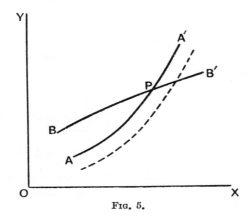

Fig. 5.

In other words, $\dfrac{\xi}{\eta}$ is not greater than $\dfrac{D_2}{D_1}$. This limit may be expressed by a line through the origin such as Oq in Fig. 4.

A line not passing through the origin may represent the condition that the *difference* between the two prices should not exceed a certain maximum.

(b) Corresponding propositions may be demonstrated for articles of which the production is complementary. We have simply to change the sign of $\dfrac{d^2\varphi}{dx\,dy}$; and accordingly the inclination of the price-curves, which will now be inclined and related as AA' and BB' in Fig. 5. The displacement caused by a tax on the x commodity is represented by a dotted curve on the right of AA' (on the understanding that the axes represent prices). Whence it appears that a tax on one of the complementary articles will cause the price of *both* to rise.

So far, supposing that the consumers of x and y constitute two distinct classes.[1]

Let us now suppose that the separation of classes no longer exists; and first let us suppose that x and y are quantities of rival commodities offered on a single market. For instance, x and y may denote respectively travelling on a railway by first or second class. (For simplicity we may suppose that there are only two classes, as commonly now in England; though they are commonly called first and *third*). This case is analogous to the preceding in so far as a tax on one commodity diminishes the quantity thereof which will be put on the market. But it does not now follow that the consumers of the substitute will be benefited. The consumers *in globo*, for instance, travellers on the railway as a body, may be prejudiced by a tax on one of the commodities, say travelling by first class; but it is also possible that they should be *benefited* thereby. The first proposition is self-evident; the second is a paradox which can only be demonstrated with the aid of mathematics.

Let $f_1(x,y)$ be the price of the first commodity when x and y are the quantities of the respective commodities that are taken by the market. Then $\frac{df_1}{dx}$ is, of course, negative. Also $\frac{df_1}{dy}$ is negative, since the increased consumption of x diminishes the demand for the substitute y. Let $f_2(xy)$ likewise represent the price of y. Then for the total net profit of the monopolist we have

$$V = xf_1(x,y) + yf_2(x,y) - \varphi(x,y).$$

For Δx and Δy, that is, the increments of the commodities due to a small tax τ on x, we have as before

$$\Delta x \frac{d^2V}{dx^2} + \Delta y \frac{d^2V}{dx\,dy} = \tau$$

$$\Delta x \frac{d^2V}{dx\,dy} + \Delta y \frac{d^2V}{dy^2} = 0.$$

From which it appears as before that $\Delta x \left(= \tau \frac{d^2V}{dy^2} \middle/ D \right.$ where D is positive) is negative. But Δy may be either positive or

<hr>

[1] An important variety of this case occurs when a monopolist fixes different prices for the same article as consumed by different classes; for instance, a ticket for a theatre may bear a different price according as it admits a soldier or a civilian, a man or a woman. Many interesting examples of this type are adduced by Neumann in Schönberg's *Handbuch* (see an example given by *Dupuit*, below II. 404).

negative. All that can be said with certainty about its sign is that it will be contrary to the sign of $\frac{d^2V}{dx\,dy}$. But nothing is known about this second differential, except that it must satisfy the condition for V being a maximum, viz.—

$$\left(\frac{d^2V}{dx^2}\right)\left(\frac{d^2V}{dy^2}\right) - \left(\frac{d^2V}{dx\,dy}\right)^2 > 0;$$

a condition which does not depend on the *sign* of the quantity which is squared.* This condition is compatible with the supposition that not only should Δy be positive, but also $x\Delta\xi + y\Delta\eta$,[1] the approximate expression for the decrement of Consumers' Surplus, should be negative; that is, the consumers as a whole should be advantaged by the tax.

As, even with respect to mathematics, " seeing is believing," I subjoin a numerical example of the special case.** Let x and y be the quantities of two commodities which are rivals in consumption (partial substitutes for each other). Let the law of demand of these commodities be as follows, p_1 and p_2 being the respective prices

$$p_1 = 1\cdot6053 - \cdot2x - \tfrac{2}{3}(x - \cdot96)^{\frac{3}{2}} - \tfrac{1}{2}y$$
$$p_2 = 3\cdot918 - 2(y - \cdot6975)^{\frac{1}{2}} - \tfrac{1}{2}x$$

for values of x and y in the neighbourhood of the vaules $x = 1$ and $y = 1$. This is a rational supposition, since there exists a function U such that $\left(\frac{dU}{dx}\right) = p_1$ $\left(\frac{dU}{dy}\right) = p_2$; and U is suited

---

* Nothing can be learnt about the sign in question from the laws of utility, since they tell us only that, if U is the Total Utility or Consumers' Surplus (*cp.* note to p. 117), $\frac{dU}{dx} > 0,\ \frac{dU}{dy} > 0,\ \frac{d^2U}{dx^2} < 0,\ \frac{d^2U}{dy^2} < 0,\ \frac{d^2U}{dx^2}\frac{d^2U}{dy^2} - \frac{d^2U}{dx\,dy} > 0;$ whereas $\frac{d^2V}{dx\,dy}$ involves *third* differentials of U, about which nothing is given.

[1] The total net utility accruing to the consumers or the Consumers' Surplus obtained from the purchase of the quantities x and y at the prices ξ and η respectively, may be written $U - x\xi - y\eta$; where U is identical with $F(x,y)$, as defined on p. 117 above. The total net utility when $x + \Delta x$ is substituted for x and for y $y + \Delta y$, becomes (approximately)

$$U + \Delta x\left(\frac{dU}{dx}\right) + \Delta y\left(\frac{dU}{dy}\right) - (x + \Delta x)(\xi + \Delta\xi) - (y + \Delta y)(\eta + \Delta\eta)$$

$$= U - x\xi - y\eta + \Delta x\left(\frac{dU}{dx} - \xi\right) + \Delta y\left(\frac{\Delta U}{dy} - \eta\right) - (x\Delta\xi + y\Delta\eta).$$

Whence the increment to the total net utility due to the increments of x and y is $-(x\Delta\xi + y\Delta\eta)$ (since $\left(\frac{dU}{dx}\right) = \xi$ and $\left(\frac{dU}{dy}\right) = \eta$).

** The numerical data here used are not exactly the same as those given in the example as originally set forth in the *Giornale*. The figures are now taken from a simplified version of that example (presented below, **F**, p. 148). Further fortification of the theory is offered at II. 93, **S**; and a fresh example at II. 400, ζ.

to represent the total utility (above a certain minimum) derived from the possession of the quantities of x and y distributed as described above (p. 117). For as $\left(\frac{dp_1}{dx}\right) = \left(\frac{d^2U}{dx^2}\right)$ is negative in the neighbourhood of the values $x = 1$, $y = 1$ (for which values $\left(\frac{dp_1}{dx}\right) = -\cdot 4$), there is, as there ought to be, a limit to the quantity of x which the consumers will take at that price, supposing the price of y to be fixed. There is a corresponding limit to the increase of y since $\left(\frac{dp_2}{dy}\right)$ is negative $(= -1\cdot 81)$. Further, supposing both quantities to vary simultaneously, there is, as there ought to be, a limit to the amount of *sandwiches* of the form $lx + my$ which the consumers at any assigned (pair of) prices will demand; since the remaining condition for U being a maximum holds good, for $x = 1$, $y = 1$ (and in the neighbourhood), viz.—

$$\left(\frac{d^2U}{dx^2}\right), \ \left(\frac{d^2U}{dy^2}\right) - \left(\frac{d^2U}{dx\,dy}\right)^2 > 0.$$

Such being the laws of demand, we have for the monopoly profit $V = xp_1 + yp_2$, *i. e.* supposing at first that there are no expenses of production; which is a maximum when $x = 1$, $y = 1$, since then

$$\left(\frac{dV}{dx}\right) = 1\cdot 605\dot{3} - \cdot 4x - \tfrac{2}{3}(x - \cdot 96)^{\frac{1}{2}} - x(x - \cdot 96)^{\frac{1}{2}} - y = 0,$$

$$\left(\frac{dV}{dy}\right) = 3\cdot 91\dot{8} - 2(y - \cdot 6975)^{\frac{1}{2}} - y(y - \cdot 6975)^{-\frac{1}{2}} - x = 0;$$

while the second differential coefficients of V fulfil the remaining condition for a maximum; for

$$\left(\frac{d^2V}{dx^2}\right) = -3\cdot 3$$

$$\left(\frac{d^2V}{dy^2}\right) = -\cdot 6311$$

$$\left(\frac{d^2V}{dx\,dy}\right) = -1$$

$$(-3\cdot 3) \times (-\cdot 6311) - 1^2 = 1\cdot 0826 > 0.$$

If now a small tax of τ per unit is imposed on the first commodity we have for the increments of quantity (above, p. 131)

$$-3\cdot 3\,\varDelta x - \varDelta y = \tau$$
$$-\varDelta x - \cdot 6311\,\varDelta y = 0.$$

Whence

$$\varDelta x = -\tau\cdot 6311 \div 1\cdot 0826 = -\cdot 5829\tau; \quad \varDelta y = 1 \div 1\cdot 0826 = +\cdot 9237\tau.$$

Accordingly the *decrement* of Consumers' Surplus

$$= x\Delta p_1 + y\Delta p_2 \text{ (approximately)}$$

$$= \Delta x\left(x\frac{dp_1}{dx} + y\frac{dp_2}{dx}\right) + \Delta y\left(x\frac{dp_1}{dy} + y\frac{dp_2}{dy}\right)$$

$$= - \cdot 583\,(- \cdot 4 - \cdot 5)\tau + \cdot 9237\,(- \cdot 5 - 1\cdot 81)\tau$$

$$= - 1\cdot 626\tau.$$

Since then the *decrement* of the *Consumers' Surplus* is negative, there is a positive increment of advantage to the consumers in consequence of the tax. Or is it easier to say that as *both* the prices are reduced, the purchasers must be gainers ? *

The conclusion becomes *a fortiori* when there are expenses of production; for then we have at our disposal more functions with which to manipulate a favourable example.**

Thus a tax on first-class tickets may have the effect of lowering the fares for both first and third class, and so benefiting passengers in general. The number of travellers by first class will, however, be diminished notwithstanding the attractions of a lower fare; the counter attractions of the lowered second-class fares predominating.

The paradox which has been exhibited is presented by many other kinds of taxation, or more generally governmental regulation relative to commodities that are correlated in consumption. The correlated commodities need not be *rivals*, as in the preceding example; they may be *complementary*, such as the carriage of a passenger's luggage and the carriage of the passenger himself. Likewise a bounty on one of the correlated commodities may prove *injurious* to the consumers.*** Again, the limitation of the monopoly profit to a fixed percentage of the cost (including interest on capital) is not necessarily advantageous to the consumer. For the problem is then to maximise V subject to the condition that **** $V \not> i\varphi(x,\ y)$, where i is a given fraction. Then beginning with the case in which the fraction i is such that the limitation is only just beginning to be operative, we shall find as before that the variations in the Consumers' Surplus consequent upon the limitation depend upon the sign of the magnitude $\left(\dfrac{d^2V}{dx,dy}\right)$

(or the corresponding second differential coefficient with respect

---

* $\Delta p_1 = - \cdot 229\tau,\ \Delta p_2 = - 1\cdot 4\tau.$

** The example is modified so as to illustrate this point in the article dated 1899, which is republished below, F, p. 149; where the ξ and η are used in the same sense as x and y in the present context.

*** Not stated explicitly in the original.

**** The symbol $\not>$ (not greater than) expresses the limitation better than the symbol $=$ used in the original.

to ξ and η); which in general is not given. The principle applies very generally to the taxation of correlated consumable articles in a regime of monopoly.*

These paradoxes may be somewhat diminished by the use of a principle which Economics is entitled to borrow from the kindred science of Probabilities, or the " Art of Conjecturing." This is the presumption that in certain cases a quantity of which we do not know the sign may be treated as zero. In the leading case before us, if, as before, $f_1(x_1y)$ is the price of the first commodity and $f_2(xy)$ that of the second (when the quantities x and y are taken by the market), $\varphi(x_1y)$ is the total cost of producing x and y, and V the net advantage of the monopolist, we have

$$V = xf_1(xy) + yf_2(xy) - \varphi(xy);$$

$$\frac{d^2V}{dx\,dy} = \left[\left(\frac{df_1}{dy}\right) + \frac{df_2}{dx}\right] + \left[x\frac{d^2f_1}{dx\,dy} + y\frac{d^2f_2}{dx\,dy}\right] - \left[\frac{d^2\varphi}{dx\,dy}\right].$$

Of the three parts or terms of this expression (distinguished by square brackets), we know that the first is positive or negative according as the demand is complementary or rival; and that the third (with its sign) is positive or negative according as the production is complementary or rival. But we do not know the sign of the second term; and are therefore perhaps justified in ignoring it; especially when the sum of the two other terms is considerable, as may well be if production and consumption are either both rival or both complementary.

So far in this section we have been supposing that the monopolist, true to his etymology, is only a *seller*. But the method which has been indicated may readily be extended to the case in which the monopolist is the *buyer* of two or more correlated commodities. Thus it is possible that he may have a rival or complementary demand for goods supplied by distinct groups of producers. Or he may purchase goods of which the production is rival or complementary. And at the same time he may have a rival or complementary demand for those goods.

We may form any number of combinations with the attributes of which the properties have been deduced; always excepting those cases in which two or more monopolists are in the field.

SECTION IV.—In conclusion I now propose to restate in plain

* The exposition in the original is interrupted by the statement of two well-known or obvious propositions : (*a*) A progressive (as well as a simply proportional) tax on the profits of the monopolist does not affect the consumers (even in the case of correlated consumption). (*b*) The effect of limiting the monopoly profit to a fixed amount is indeterminate; consumers may be either benefited or prejudiced by the limitation.

words the principal results of the preceding mathematical analysis. They consist, as might be expected, rather in general views than in particular rules.

1. One of the principal uses of mathematics to the economist is, in the words of Professor Marshall, " to make sure that he has enough and only enough premisses for his conclusions (*i. e.* that his equations are neither more nor less in number than his unknowns)." This criterion applied to monopoly shows that frequently—I think it may almost be said normally—there is not a sufficient number of conditions to render economic equilibrium determinate, in the general case of a system of bargains in which more than one monopolist takes part. This may be affirmed with peculiar confidence in the case where two or more monopolists who are in competition deal with a great number of customers who also are competing with each other; for example, two railways which ply between the same points. The instability is due not merely to the hope of one monopolist to ruin a rival by " cutting prices," a case that has often been described; but also to a more fundamental, though less obvious cause. The instability does not cease in cases where it is not possible for one monopolist to drive the other completely off the field. Such might be the case if workmen of two nationalities—say Anglo-Saxons and Chinese—united respectively in two combinations, had to deal with competitive entrepreneurs, or with foreign customers. The proposition clearly stated by Cournot,[1] and to all appearance generally admitted, that in such a system the action of economic forces would tend to a definite position of equilibrium, a determinate set of values,—this plausible proposition is proved to be unfounded. In the regime of competition, as Mill or someone has said, things are always seeking their level. It is not so in the regime of monopoly.

The character of perpetual instability may likewise be affirmed of conditions in which the two competing monopolists deal not in identical, but rival, articles; for example, in the cases just now instanced it may be supposed that the services of the two railways, or the work of the two nationalities, though not quite identical, are capable of acting as more or less perfect substitutes for each other.

This theory is less evident, the opinion of Cournot is more plausible, in cases where the competing monopolists are dealing

---

[1] " Il est bien évident que dans l'ordre des faits réels et lorsque l'on tient compte de toutes les conditions d'un système économique, il n'y a pas de denrée dont le prix ne soit complètement déterminé."

not in rival but "complementary" articles; for example, if the rolling-stock of a railway were possessed by one company and the railway-stations by another, or if the common labour necessary for the production of an article were monopolised by one combination, and the more highly skilled work without which the manual labour would be useless by another combination. Professor Marshall seems to contemplate this case when he supposes that a mill belongs to one monopolist and the water for driving it to another.[1]

Let us suppose that the two lettings are yearly; beginning at the middle of the year for the mill, and at the end of the year for the water-supply. If at midsummer the owner of the premises, when renewing his contract with the lessee, estimates what such a one can pay, on the basis of what he pays and will pay for the next six months for the use of the water—if the owner of the mill ignores the possible action of the owner of the water at the end of the year—then perhaps the reasoning of Cournot in a similar case will hold good. There will be a determinate equilibrium characterised by the curious property that the tenant will be worse off than if both had belonged to the same individual. That is, supposing that there are a number of mills at the disposal of the landlord, and a number of millers competing with each other.

But ought we to suppose that the proprietor, when renewing his contract, does not take into consideration possible future events? Will he not, theoretically, fix the rent at that figure which will be the most advantageous for him *in view of the rent which the owner of the water-supply may fix the next winter?* It is thus that a chess-player when making his move takes account of the move which his adversary will probably make. And, as in chess, when only the two kings and one of the inferior pieces remain on each side, may not the two monopolists go on making moves against each other to all eternity?

Those who adhere to Cournot's reasoning may be confronted with the supposition that one of the two monopolised articles, for instance, the water-power in the above example, passes into the hands of competitors. There will then be a regular market for water-power, offered by the competing owners to competing millers. Accordingly, given the rent of the mill, the payment for water-power will be determined by the usual equation between demand and supply (the total supply of water-power may be supposed a fixed quantity). According to the opinion

[1] *Principles of Economics*, third ed., Book V. ch. x.

here disputed, when once the charge for water-power has been settled by the market, the monopolist will treat this price as something sacred, and will only vary the rent of his premises *subject to the condition that the charge for water-power should not be disturbed*. But surely the general rule is that he will continue to vary the price of the monopolised article as long as that price multiplied by the quantity sold at that price—less the cost of production—continues to increase. It does not matter to him that the customers, in view of his changing that price, are obliged to modify their bargains with a third party. What difference can it make to the motives of the monopolist that the third party consists of a monopolist, not of individuals competing against each other? In both cases, indifferent to the interests of the third party, he will vary his price by successive steps in the direction which promises him an increase of profit. The only difference between the cases is that when the third party consists of competitors, a definite position of equilibrium will be reached (the tentatives of the single monopolist must come to a stop, or at least hover about a determinate point); whereas when the third party consists of a second monopolist, the conditions which bring about the equation of demand and supply in a competitive market are wanting. That is, excepting the arbitrary supposition that the second monopolist is such a fool as to act in the manner ascribed to him by Cournot's equation. But even if he were to do so, though there would exist a definite position of equilibrium, it would not be the one assigned by the theory here combated.*

This theoretical difference between the regime of monopoly and that of competition may have some bearing on practical issues, affecting as it does our views about trade unions and similar combinations. I have seen it proposed as an economic ideal that every branch of trade and industry should be formed into a separate union. The picture has some attractions. Nor is it at first sight morally repulsive; since, where all are monopolists, no one will be the victim of monopoly. But an attentive consideration will disclose an incident very prejudicial to industry —instability in the value of all those articles the demand for which is influenced by the prices of other articles; a class which is probably very extensive.

Among those who would suffer by the new regime there would be one class which particularly interests the readers of this Journal, namely the abstract economists, who would be

---

* It would correspond to the point *Q*, not to *P*, in Fig. 3.

deprived of their occupation, the investigation of the conditions which determine value. There would survive only the empirical school, flourishing in a chaos congenial to their mentality.

2. Professor Marshall exemplifies another use of mathematical reasoning when by means of his curves he demonstrates that it might be advisable to tax one kind of commodity and employ the proceeds in bountying another kind.[1] The abstract reasoning serves as a corrective to what has been called the " metaphysical incubus " of dogmatic *laisser faire*. In the case of monopoly indeed this incubus has not been serious : " it has never been supposed that the monopolist in seeking his own advantage is naturally guided in that course which is most conducive to the well-being of society regarded as a whole." Nevertheless, in so far as something similar to the old doctrine of economic harmony seems to be reappearing among the apologists for railway administration, a certain interest may attach to propositions unexpectedly favourable to the intervention of Government in businesses subject to monopoly. Such is the proposition above proved, that when the supply of two or more correlated com-modities—such as the carriage of passengers by rail first class or third class—is in the hands of a single monopolist, a tax on one of the articles—*e. g.* a percentage of first-class fares—may prove advantageous to the consumers as a whole. Thus in the instance given the advantage would accrue not only to those who before the tax travelled third class, and continue to do so afterwards, but the travelling public in general, including first-class passengers. The fares for *all* the classes might be reduced.

3. To obtain rules directly applicable to practice there would be required a knowledge of concrete details beyond what the present writer can command. Still, some suggestions bearing on the control of monopolies by governmental interposition may be derived from the preceding analysis.

A first step in this direction was made by Cournot when he proved that a tax of an ordinary kind on a monopolised product has the effect of increasing the price. This is contrary to the judgment of some distinguished writers who hold that, the monopolist having already done his worst against the customer, the burden of the latter cannot be increased by a tax. There is, however, a limiting case in which the popular opinion is correct ; namely, where a monopolist buyer deals with sellers of an article which is absolutely limited in quantity (land, for instance), or can only be increased with great difficulty. A building syndicate

---

[1] *Principles*, Book V. ch. xii. pp. 555–7. *Ibid.* ch. xiii. (third ed.)

buying up land from uncombined owners may afford an example.

Cases specially favourable for the application of mathematical analysis occur where we have to deal with *correlated* (connected) supply and demand. Suppose, first, the supply only connected, as when a railway company, the greater part of whose expenditure (interest on capital, cost of repairs, etc.) cannot be attributed exclusively to one branch of the business, serves two classes of customers whose interests are quite separate, say traders requiring their goods to be carried and passengers other than commercial travellers. Here we must distinguish two classes : (a) *complementary* products, in the case of which the production of one article becomes less difficult and expensive by the increased production of the other article (" joint " products as defined by Mill are included in this class); (b) *rival* products, in the case of which the production of one article becomes more costly according as the production of the other is increased. The first case usually occurs where the law of increasing returns rules; for instance, if the general expenses of a railway do not increase in proportion to the traffic, the increase of one kind of traffic tends to make the increase of the other kind more remunerative (see above a more exact definition). Contrariwise, when the land or the capital at the disposal of the company is fully occupied, it is possible that the increase of one service may render another less profitable than it would otherwise have been. The proprietors of a railway with only one or two tracks may find that the increase of the goods traffic causes the passenger traffic to be attended with greater expense; the fuel of the company and the labour of its employees being wasted while the passenger trains have to wait in side tracks to avoid collisions.

It is very possible that both tendencies may be present, not coincidently, but with reference to a different extent of variation in the products under consideration. Thus a certain increase in the goods traffic by crowding the present line as above described might act in *rivalry* to the passenger traffic; but with reference to a large increase in the goods traffic, such as to make it profitable to have an additional track and so obtain the economies of production on a large scale, the goods traffic may be considered as *complementary* to the passenger traffic.* I do not pretend to discern to which of the two categories each concrete case belongs; I only wish to distinguish their properties in the abstract.

Among methods of governmental control, one of the most

* See Index, *sub voce* Joint Production.

important is that which consists in fixing a maximum tariff; provided that the maximum is not suspended on high, but is such as really to restrain the action of the monopolist; in which case its operation is nearly similar to that of a fixed tax. Suppose now that the price of one product is fixed, but not so that of another; or, what is more probable, that there is an effective maximum for one article and an inoperative maximum for another. The effect on the price of the second article will differ according as the products are *complementary* or *rival*. If they are complementary, the lowering of the price of the first is followed by the lowering of the price of the second; the benefit in respect of one commodity is a benefit also in respect of the other commodity. If the products are rival, there is a benefit to one class of consumers and a loss to another; provided, of course, that the loss to the monopolist is not so great as to induce him to give up the business.

The same rule applies to the effects of a law which requires that the price of an article in one market should not exceed its price in another by more than a certain percentage.[1] What is a benefit in respect of one commodity will be also a benefit in respect of the other, if the products are complementary; but a loss in the case of rival production.

A corresponding rule applies to a tax of the kind called " specific," that is, of so much per unit of commodity. The loss to one class of consumers will be a loss to the other class in case of complementary products; but a gain in the case of rival products.

The case of connected *demand* does not admit of equally definite rules. It is probable, but not certain, that the rules enounced for rival and complementary production hold good respectively for complementary and rival demand. Thus a maximum which lowers the rate for the terminal services of a railway tends probably to raise the rates for carriage since the demands for the two services are complementary. But a maximum which lowers the fare for third-class passengers tends probably to lower the fares for the first class, since the demands for the two kinds of tickets are rival.

The probability increases when the tendency of demand is in the same direction as that of production, and diminishes in the contrary case.

These propositions respecting the influence of demand may

[1] Generalising the conceptions of the American " *Short-haul Clause*," as it is commonly understood.

be applied to a law against differential charges and to a specific tax.

A tax proportional to the profits of the monopolist falls entirely upon him, as Cournot and Professor Marshall have proved. It should be added that a " progressive " tax on monopoly profit acts similarly.[1]

The effect of limiting the profit of the monopolist to a fixed amount is generally indeterminate. It may be advantageous or detrimental to some or all or none of the various groups of his customers. The fixing a (*bonâ fide*) maximum rate of profit on the capital expended acts to the advantage of the consumer.

I am not blind to the practical difficulties which stand in the way of a tax on the net profits of a monopolist, and of other measures that are here discussed. It cannot be too often repeated that the rules derived from mathematical reasoning are essentially abstract and require in practice to be largely diluted with common sense.

[1] Since this article was printed I have found that Knut Wicksell had preceded me in pointing this out.

[6]

Econometrica, Vol. 56, No. 3 (May, 1988), 571–599

A THEORY OF DYNAMIC OLIGOPOLY, II: PRICE COMPETITION, KINKED DEMAND CURVES, AND EDGEWORTH CYCLES

By Eric Maskin and Jean Tirole[1]

We provide game theoretic foundations for the classic kinked demand curve equilibrium and Edgeworth cycle. We analyze a model in which firms take turns choosing prices; the model is intended to capture the idea of reactions based on short-run commitment. In a Markov perfect equilibrium (MPE), a firm's move in any period depends only on the other firm's current price. There are multiple MPE's, consisting of both kinked demand curve equilibria and Edgeworth cycles. In any MPE, profit is bounded away from the Bertrand equilibrium level. We show that a kinked demand curve at the monopoly price is the unique symmetric "renegotiation proof" equilibrium when there is little discounting.

We then endogenize the timing by allowing firms to move at any time subject to short-run commitments. We find that firms end up alternating, thus vindicating the *ad hoc* timing assumption of our simpler model. We also discuss how the model can be enriched to provide explanations for excess capacity and market sharing.

KEYWORDS: Tacit collusion, Markov perfect equilibrium, kinked demand curve, Edgeworth cycle, excess capacity, market sharing, endogenous timing.

1. INTRODUCTION

MODELING PRICE COMPETITION has posed a major challenge for economic research ever since Bertrand (1883). Bertrand showed that, in a market for a homogeneous good where two or more symmetric firms produce at constant cost and set prices simultaneously, the equilibrium price is competitive, i.e., equal to marginal cost. This classic result seems to contradict observation in two ways. First, in markets with few sellers, firms apparently do not typically sell at marginal cost. Second, even in periods of technological and demand stability, oligopolistic markets are not always stable. Prices may fluctuate, sometimes wildly.

Of course, one reason for these discrepancies between theory and evidence is that the Bertrand model is static, whereas dynamics may be an important ingredient of actual price competition.[2] Indeed, two classic concepts in the industrial organization literature, the Edgeworth cycle and the kinked demand curve equilibrium, offer dynamic alternatives to the Bertrand model.

In the Edgeworth cycle story, firms undercut each other successively to increase their market share (price war phase) until the war becomes too costly, at which point some firm increases its price. The other firms then follow suit (relenting phase), after which price cutting begins again. The market price thus

---

[1] We thank David Kreps, Robert Wilson, two referees, and especially John Moore, for very helpful comments. This work was supported by the Sloan Foundation and the National Science Foundation.

[2] Another possible explanation for lack of perfect competition—indeed, the most common theoretical one—is that products of different firms are not perfect substitutes. Alternatively, as Edgeworth (1925) suggested, firms may be capacity-constrained.

evolves in cycles. The concept is due to Edgeworth (1925), who, in his criticism of Bertrand, showed that static price equilibrium does not in general exist when firms face capacity constraints. His resolution of this nonexistence problem was the cycle.

By contrast with the Edgeworth cycle, the market price for a kinked demand curve (Hall and Hitch (1939), Sweezy (1939)) is stable in the long run. This "focal" price is sustained by each firm's fear that, if it undercuts, the other firms will do so too. A firm has no incentive to charge more than the focal price because it believes that, in that case, the other firms will *not* follow.

Despite their long history, the Edgeworth cycle and kinked demand curve have received for the most part only informal theoretical treatments. The primary purpose of this paper is to provide equilibrium foundations for these two types of dynamics.

The basis of our analysis is a model of duopoly where firms take turns choosing prices (see Section 2). The alternating move assumption is meant to capture the idea of short-run commitment; see our companion piece for motivating discussion. A firm maximizes the present discounted value of its profit. Its strategy is assumed to depend only on the physical state of the system (i.e., to be Markov). In our model, the state is simply the other firm's current price.

We first show through examples that an equilibrium of this model may be a kinked demand curve or a price cycle[3] (Section 3). Section 4 examines the general nature of equilibrium in our model. In particular, it establishes that any equilibrium must be either of the kinked demand type (where the market price converges in finite time to a unique focal price) or the Edgeworth cycle variety (in which the market price never settles down).

Section 5 proves that there exists a multiplicity of kinked demand curve equilibria. Specifically, we exhibit the exact range of possible equilibrium focal prices when the discount factor is near 1. This range—a closed interval containing the monopoly price—lies well above the competitive price. We argue in Section 6, however, that only one of these—the monopoly price equilibrium (which is unique)—is "renegotiation proof" in the sense that firms would never find it to their advantage to move to another equilibrium. We go on to investigate firms' adjustment to stochastic shifts in demand, showing, in particular, that an increase in demand may well trigger a price war.

Section 7, which treats Edgeworth cycles, is the counterpart of Section 5 on kinked demand curves. It demonstrates, by construction, the existence of Edgeworth cycle equilibria if the discount factor is sufficiently near 1 and proves that, in any such symmetric equilibrium, average aggregate profit must be no less than half the monopoly level.

In Section 8 we compare the qualitative nature of equilibrium in this paper with that of Part I of our study, which models competition in quantities/capacities. Whereas here there are many equilibria, symmetric equilibrium is unique in the companion paper. The respective comparative statics, moreover, are com-

---

[3] Unlike Edgeworth's treatment, price cycles in our model do not rely on capacity constraints.

pletely opposed. These contrasts can be traced to differences in the behavior of the cross partial derivative of the instantaneous profit function.

We acknowledge in Part I of this study that a model where firms' relative timing is imposed is unduly artificial. Accordingly, in Section 9, we show that the fixed timing analysis through Section 7 continues to hold when embedded in either of the endogenous timing frameworks discussed in our companion piece.

Our modeling methodology contrasts sharply with that of the well-established supergame model of tacit collusion. In Section 10 we draw a detailed comparison between the two approaches.

Finally, in Section 11, we discuss how our model can be extended to accommodate competition in quantities as well as prices. In particular, we provide explanations of two prominent market phenomena: excess capacity and market sharing.

2. THE MODEL

In this section we describe the main features of the exogeneous-timing duopoly model. Competition between the two firms ($i = 1, 2$) takes place in discrete time with an infinite horizon. Time periods are indexed by t ($t = 0, 1, 2, \ldots$). The time between consecutive periods is T. At time t, firm i's instantaneous profit π^i is a function of the two firms' current prices p_t^1 and p_t^2, but not of time: $\pi^i = \pi^i(p_t^1, p_t^2)$. We will assume that the goods produced by the two firms are perfect substitutes, and that firms share the market equally when they charge the same price. The price space is discrete, i.e., firms cannot set prices in units smaller than, say, a penny.[4] In most of the paper we assume that firms have the same unit cost c. Letting $D(\cdot)$ denote the market demand function, define

(1) $\Pi(p) \equiv (p - c)D(p)$.

The total profit function $\Pi(p)$ is assumed to be strictly concave. Let p^m denote the monopoly price, i.e., the value of p maximizing (1). From our assumptions,

$$\pi^i(p_t^1, p_t^2) = \begin{cases} \Pi(p_t^i), & \text{if } p_t^i < p_t^j, \\ \Pi(p_t^i)/2, & \text{if } p_t^i = p_t^j, \\ 0, & \text{if } p_t^i > p_t^j. \end{cases}$$

Firms discount the future with the same interest rate r; thus their discount factor is $\delta \equiv \exp(-rT)$. Because one expects that ordinarily firms can change prices fairly quickly, we will often think of T as being small and, therefore, of δ as being close to one. Firm i's intertemporal profit at time t is

$$\sum_{s=0}^{\infty} \delta^s \pi^i(p_{t+s}^1, p_{t+s}^2).$$

---

[4] The reason for this restriction is to ensure that optimal reactions exist. In a static Bertrand model, for example, best responses to prices above marginal cost are not defined when the price space is a continuum.

ERIC MASKIN AND JEAN TIROLE

As in our companion paper, we begin by assuming that firms move alternately. In odd-numbered periods t, firm 1 chooses its price, which remains unchanged until period $t + 2$. That is, $p_{t+1}^1 = p_t^1$ if t is odd. Similarly, firm 2 chooses prices only in even-numbered periods, so that $p_{t+1}^2 = p_t^2$ if t is even. As in Part I, we impose the Markov assumption: a firm's strategy depends only on the payoff-relevant state, those variables that directly enter its payoff function. In our model, the payoff-relevant state is just the price the other firm set last period. Hence, firm i's strategy is a dynamic reaction function, a (possibly random) function $R^i(\cdot)$, where $p_t = R^i(p_{t-1})$ is the firm's price in period t given that the other firm set p_{t-1} in period $t - 1$.

We are interested in *Markov perfect equilibria* (MPE): pairs of dynamic reaction functions forming perfect equilibria. From dynamic programming[5] (see Maskin–Tirole (1988) for details), a pair (R^1, R^2) is an MPE if, for all prices $\hat{p}$,

$$(2) \qquad V^1(\hat{p}) = \max_p \left[\pi^1(p, \hat{p}) + \delta W^1(p) \right],$$

and

$$(3) \qquad W^1(\hat{p}) = E_p \left[\pi^1(\hat{p}, p) + \delta V^1(p) \right],$$

where $R^1(\hat{p})$ is a maximizing choice of p in (2), the expectation in (3) is taken with respect to the distribution of $R^2(\hat{p})$, and where the symmetric conditions hold for firm 2. The expression, $V^i(p)$ is firm i's valuation (present discounted profit) if (a) it is about to move, (b) the other firm's current price is p, and (c) firms henceforth play according to (R^1, R^2). The expression $W^i(p)$ is firm i's valuation if *last* period it played p, the other firm is about to move, and firms use (R^1, R^2) forever after.

Most of our results will be demonstrated for discount factors close to one, which, as we already suggested, is often a reasonable assumption for price competition. Thus, a typical proposition will hold for all δ greater than a given $\delta < 1$. We sometimes also require the set of possible prices to be sufficiently "fine."

3. KINKED DEMAND CURVES AND EDGEWORTH CYCLES: EXAMPLES

This section exhibits two examples of Markov Perfect Equilibria, one a "kinked demand curve," the other an "Edgeworth cycle." In both examples the market demand curve is given by $D(p) = 1 - p$, and production is costless. Firms can charge any of seven prices: $p(i) = i/6$ for $i = 0, 1, \ldots, 6$. The corresponding profits, $\Pi(p(i)) = p(i)(1 - p(i))$ are proportional, respectively, to 0, 5, 8, 9, 8, 5, 0. The monopoly price is $p^m = p(3) = 1/2$.

Suppose that dynamic reaction functions are symmetric and described by Table I, where $\beta(\delta) \equiv (5 + \delta)/(5\delta + 9\delta^2)$.

---

[5] Because the set of available prices is finite, the instantaneous profit functions are bounded, which is sufficient for dynamic programming to be applicable.

TABLE I

A KINKED DEMAND CURVE

$\Pi(p)$	p	$R(p)$
0	$p(6)$	$p(3)$
5	$p(5)$	$p(3)$
8	$p(4)$	$p(3)$
9	$p(3)$	$p(3)$
8	$p(2)$	$p(1)$
5	$p(1)$	$\begin{cases} p(1) \text{ with probability } \beta(\delta) \\ p(3) \text{ with probability } 1 - \beta(\delta) \end{cases}$
0	$p(0)$	$p(3)$

CLAIM 1: The pair of strategies (R, R), where R is given by Table I, forms an MPE for discount factors close to one.

To prove Claim 1, it suffices to check that (2) and (3) are satisfied by the strategies in Table I. Let us verify two representative computations. To see that when the current price is $p(3)$ a firm does not want to undercut to $p(2)$, observe that staying at the monopoly price yields $V(3) = 4.5(1 + \delta + \delta^2 + \cdots) = 4.5/(1 - \delta)$. Undercutting to $p(2)$ gives $8 + \delta \cdot 0 + \delta^2 V(1) = 8 + \delta^2 \cdot (4.5) \cdot (\delta + \delta^2 + \cdots) < V(3)$ for δ close to one (note that to compute $V(1)$, we have used the fact that at $p(1)$, one of the firm's best actions is to raise the price to $p(3)$). We next check that at $p(2)$, a firm prefers to continue the price war rather than relenting and returning to $p(3)$. The former yields $5 + \delta W(1)$, whereas the latter gives $\delta(4.5)/(1 - \delta)$. Now, at $p(1)$, each firm is indifferent between staying at $p(1)$ and raising the price to $p(3)$. Thus, $V(1) = \delta(4.5)/(1 - \delta) = 2.5 + \delta W(1)$, and so undercutting from $p(2)$ to $p(1)$ yields $2.5 + \delta(4.5)/(1 - \delta) > \delta(4.5)/(1 - \delta)$.

Notice that ultimately the market price reaches $p(3)$, the monopoly price, and thereafter remains there. To see why this equilibrium resembles that of the traditional kinked demand curve, suppose that the market price were $p(3)$ and that firm 1 contemplated charging a higher price. Firm 1 would predict that firm 2 would not follow suit—i.e., would keep its price at $p(3)$. Firm 1 would thus anticipate losing all its customers by raising its price and so would find such a move undesirable. Alternatively, suppose that firm 1 contemplated undercutting to $p(2)$. In that first period, its market share would rise, and its profit would increase from 4.5 to 8. However, this action would trigger a price war: firm 2, in turn, would undercut to $p(1)$. At $p(1)$ a war of attrition would begin. Each firm i would like j to relent (to return to $p(3)$) first so that i could earn positive profit in the short run by charging $p(1)$. The probability $\beta(\delta)$ is chosen so that a firm is just indifferent between raising and not raising the price itself.

Because price falls significantly in a price war, intertemporal profits are lower than had the price remained at $p(3)$, even for firm 1, who triggered the war. Hence, it is not in the long run interest of a firm to undercut the monopoly price. Because of our perfection requirement, the length of a price war must strike a balance. On the one hand, it must be long enough to deter price cutting. On the

TABLE II

AN EDGEWORTH CYCLE

p	$R(p)$	
$p(6)$	$p(4)$	
$p(5)$	$p(4)$	
$p(4)$	$p(3)$	
$p(3)$	$p(2)$	
$p(2)$	$p(1)$	
$p(1)$	$p(0)$	
$p(0)$	$\begin{cases} p(0) & \text{with probability } \alpha(\delta) \\ p(5) & \text{with probability } 1 - \alpha(\delta) \end{cases}$	

other hand, it must not be so costly that, when one firm cuts its price, the other firm is unwilling to carry on with the war and instead prefers to relent immediately. Despite these conflicting requirements, we shall see below that kinked demand curve equilibria always exist, at least for discount factors that are not too low.

Our model permits a discussion of how firms react to cost and demand shifts. Scherer (1980, p. 168) observes that "prices tend to be at least as rigid downward as they are upward in well-disciplined oligopolies." From this empirical finding he concludes that if kinked demand curve theory is to explain pricing behavior, "the price must initially have been set below the profit-maximizing level if the subsequent emergence of a kink makes the price rigid against both upward and downward cost curve shifts." If other firms exactly match a cut in price, this conclusion is correct. Given that the initial price maximized joint profits, a firm can induce a shift to a new monopoly price if costs fall simply by cutting its price and waiting for the others to follow.

In the kinked demand curve of Table I (and in the more formal treatment of Section 5), however, such a shift may not be possible. This is because price cuts are *more* than matched by the other firm. Thus even if the monopoly price fell from $p(3)$ to $p(2)$, the market price might remain at $p(3)$ from firms' fear of starting a price war. (This argument relies on a particular choice of equilibrium when costs change, for which we have no theoretical justification. For a better grounded equilibrium selection model, predicting quite different behavior, see Section 6.)

Consider next the dynamic reaction function given by Table II, where $\alpha(\delta) \equiv (3\delta^2 - 1)(1 + \delta^2 + \delta^4)/(8 + 7\delta^2 + 2\delta^4 + 3\delta^6)$.

CLAIM 2: The pair of strategies (R, R), where R is given by Table II, forms a MPE for discount factors close to one.[6]

In the equilibrium of Table II, firms undercut each other successively until the price reaches the competitive level, $p(0)$, at which point some firm eventually reverts to the high price $p(5)$. Market dynamics thus consist of a price war

---

[6] Again, to prove Claim 2 it suffices to check that the strategies satisfy the dynamic programming equations (2) and (3) when the discount factor is high.

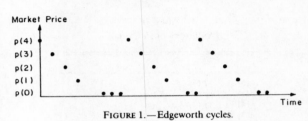

FIGURE 1.—Edgeworth cycles.

followed by a relenting phase. This second phase is a "war of attrition" at $p(0)$ in which each firm waits for the other to raise its price (relent). One may wonder why firms attach positive probability to maintaining the competitive price, where they make no profit. The explanation is that relenting is a public good from the firms' point of view. Both firms wish to raise their prices, but each would like the other to raise its price first so as to be able to undercut. Therefore, mixed strategies, where each firm relents with probability less than one, are quite natural as a resolution to this free-rider problem.

Notice that during the price war phase, a firm undercuts not simply to increase market share but because, with good reason, it does not trust its rival. That is, it anticipates that maintaining its price will not prevent the other firm from being aggressive. In that sense, mistrust is a self-justifying attitude.

Table II implies that a market onlooker would observe a cyclical path of market prices resembling that in Figure 1. We should emphasize that, unlike Edgeworth, we do not require capacity constraints to obtain this cycle. Nevertheless, we call this kind of price path an *Edgeworth cycle*.

Examples 1 and 2 together demonstrate that a kinked demand curve and an Edgeworth cycle can coexist for the same parameter values. As we shall see below, this is quite a general phenomenon.

4. EQUILIBRIUM PRICE COMPETITION

We now turn to an analysis of our general model. Recall that firms can charge any of n prices, which constitute the price grid. To simplify notation we will assume that the monopoly price p^m belongs to the price grid, and that the grid is subdivided into equal intervals of size k (this is not essential). Taking a finer grid consists of shrinking k. Some of our results will depend on the grid being "fine," i.e., on k being "small enough."

In this section we begin our characterization of equilibrium behavior. We first provide a few simple lemmas that are used repeatedly in the proofs of our propositions. We then consider long run equilibrium dynamics and show that whether or not the market price ultimately reaches a steady state is independent of initial conditions.

Some Useful Lemmas

Consider an MPE with valuation functions V^i and W^i for $i = 1, 2$.

LEMMA A: *The valuation function $V^i(\cdot)$ is nondecreasing.*

PROOF: For convenience, suppose that $i = 1$. Consider two prices $p < \hat{p}$. Let $\hat{\hat{p}}$ belong to the support of $R^1(p)$. We have

$$V^1(p) = \pi^1(\hat{\hat{p}}, p) + \delta W^1(\hat{\hat{p}}) \leqslant \pi^1(\hat{\hat{p}}, \hat{p}) + \delta W^1(\hat{\hat{p}}) \leqslant V^1(\hat{p}),$$

where the first inequality follows from the fact that a firm's profit is nondecreasing in its opponent's price, and the second inequality from the fact that $\hat{\hat{p}}$ is a feasible reaction to $\hat{p}$. Q.E.D.

A price is "focal" for a pair of strategies if, once it is set, firms continue to charge it forever. Thus a focal price p^f satisfies

$$p^f = R^1(p^f) = R^2(p^f).$$

LEMMA B: *If p^f is focal price, then $\Pi(p^f) > 0$.*[7]

PROOF: Suppose that, starting from p^f, firm 1, say, raises its price to $p > p^f$, where $\Pi(p) > 0$. If, contrary to the Lemma, $\Pi(p^f) \leqslant 0$ (in which case $V^1(p^f) = V^2(p^f) \leqslant 0$), the existence of p (we will handle the case where no such p exists below) implies that $p^f < p^m$ and so $\Pi(\tilde{p}) \leqslant 0$ for all $\tilde{p} \leqslant p^f$. Because firm 2 has the option of reacting to p with p itself, $V^2(p) > 0$. If, in fact, it reacts with a price below p^f (it cannot react with p^f since it would then earn nonpositive profit), it would therefore profit from cutting its price at p^f, a contradiction. Thus, there exists a price $\hat{p} > p^f$ with $\Pi(\hat{p}) > 0$ such that with positive probability firm 2 reacts to p with $\hat{p}$. (If for all p such that $\Pi(p) > 0$, $\Pi(\hat{p}) \leqslant 0$ for all $\hat{p}$ in $R^2(p)$, then $V^2(p) \leqslant 0$ for all such p, a contradiction.) But then firm 1 can earn positive profit by also playing $\hat{p}$, and so raising its price to p guarantees it positive expected profit. Thus $\Pi(p^f) > 0$.

If the firm cannot raise its price to p where $\Pi(p) > 0$, then $p^f > p^m$. In this case, however, the firm can always undercut and make a positive profit. Q.E.D.

For an equilibrium pair of dynamic reaction functions (R^1, R^2), a semi-focal price is a price p^f such that p^f is in the support of both $R^1(p^f)$ and $R^2(p^f)$.

LEMMA C: *If $\Pi(p^f) > 0$, a firm never reacts to a price p above a focal or semi-focal price, p^f, by undercutting to a price $\hat{p} < p^f$ or by raising its price. Thus the support of $R^i(p)$ lies in the interval $[p^f, p]$.*

PROOF: Let p^f be a focal (or semi-focal) price. Assume that firm i reacts to $p > p^f$ by charging $\hat{p} < p^f$. We have

$$\Pi(\hat{p}) + \delta W^i(\hat{p}) \geqslant \Pi(p^f) + \delta W^i(p^f),$$

since firm i could have undercut to p^f. But p^f is a semi-focal price. Thus, firm i does not gain by undercutting to $\hat{p}$ when the other firm charges p^f:

$$\Pi(\hat{p}) + \delta W^i(\hat{p}) \leqslant \frac{\Pi(p^f)}{2} + \delta W^i(p^f).$$

But these two inequalities are inconsistent if $\Pi(p^f) > 0$.

---

[7] I.e., p^f exceeds marginal cost but is not so high as to choke off demand.

Imagine next that, for some i, there exists $\hat{p} \in R^i(p)$ with $\hat{p} > p > p^f$. Since firm i could instead have set p^f, we have:

$$\delta W^i(\hat{p}) \geqslant \Pi(p^f) + \delta W^i(p^f),$$

which implies that

$$\delta W^i(\hat{p}) > \frac{\Pi(p^f)}{2} + \delta W^i(p^f).$$

But this implies that p^f is not a semi-focal price, since it tells us that at p^f it is in firm i's interest to raise the price to $\hat{p}$.   Q.E.D.

Ergodic Equilibrium Behavior

Consider (possibly mixed) strategies R^1 and R^2. In any period the market can be in any of $2n$ states. A state specifies (a) the firm that is currently committed to a price and (b) the price to which it is committed. The Markov strategies induce a Markov chain in this set of states. Let $x_{hg}(t)$ denote the t-step transition probability between states h and g for this Markov chain. The states h and g (with h possibly equal to g) *communicate* if there exist positive t_1 and t_2 such that $x_{gh}(t_1) > 0$ and $x_{hg}(t_2) > 0$. An *ergodic class* is a maximal set of states each pair of which communicate (see, e.g., Derman (1970)). A *recurrent state* is a member of some ergodic class.

Rather than considering states, we focus on the market price, the minimum of the two prices in a given period. The market price does not form a Markov chain, but, abusing terminology, we shall refer nonetheless to recurrent market prices and ergodic classes of market prices. A set of prices forms an *ergodic class of market prices* if it corresponds to an ergodic class of states.[8] A *recurrent market price* is a member of an ergodic class.

We are interested in long run properties of Markov perfect equilibria, i.e., in their ergodic classes. An MPE is a *kinked demand curve equilibrium* if it has an ergodic class consisting of a single price[9] (a "focal ergodic class"); it is an *Edgeworth cycle equilibrium* if it has an ergodic class of market prices that is not a singleton ("Edgeworth ergodic class").

A natural first question is whether an MPE can have several ergodic classes. This question is partially answered by Propositions 1 and 2.

---

[8] Formally, let $P(h)$ denote the set of potential market prices when the state is h (remember that mixed strategies are allowed). A set P of prices is an ergodic set of market prices if and only if there exists a set of states H such that (i) H is an ergodic set of states and (ii) $P = \bigcup_{h \in H} P(h)$.

[9] We have labelled an MPE with a singleton ergodic class a "kinked demand curve equilibrium" because, as in the classic concept, no firm will wish to deviate from the focal price and because any such equilibrium has at least some of the salient properties of the example of Table I (whether it has all such properties remains an open question). As we shall see below (Propositions 1 and 2) each such MPE (for δ near 1) *does* share the attractive feature of the example that, regardless of the starting point the market price eventually winds up at a unique steady-state p^f (the focal price). Moreover, Lemma C ensures that a firm will react to a price p above p^f with a price between p and p^f. We conjecture that there always exists a price $\underline{p} < p^f$ such that, at a price between $\underline{p}$ and p^f, a firm undercuts but that at prices below $\underline{p}$, the firm raises its price to a level not less than p^f.

580   ERIC MASKIN AND JEAN TIROLE

PROPOSITION 1: *For a given price grid, an MPE cannot have two focal ergodic classes if the discount factor is close enough to* 1.

PROOF: Consider a fixed price space. First note that, if $\Pi(p_1) \neq \Pi(p_2)$, p_1 and p_2 cannot both be focal prices for a given MPE if δ is sufficiently close to 1, as it would be in either firm's interest to jump to the high profit from the low profit focal price. Assume therefore that p_1 and p_2 are focal prices for which $\Pi(p_1) = \Pi(p_2)$. If $p_1 < p_2$ then, at p_2, a firm gains from reducing its price to p_1 since it thereby gets the whole market to itself for one period (from Lemma B, $\Pi(p_1) > 0$).   *Q.E.D.*

PROPOSITION 2: *An MPE cannot possess both a focal and an Edgeworth ergodic class.*

PROOF: Suppose that an MPE has both a focal price p^f and an Edgeworth ergodic class P. Let $\bar{p}$ be the highest price in P (recall that P is bounded). Because P is ergodic, there exist $p \in P$ ($p < \bar{p}$) and firm i such that

(8) $\bar{p}$ is in the support of $R^i(p)$.

If $\bar{p} > p^f$, then P lies entirely above p^f; otherwise, at some price in P above p^f, one of the firms will undercut to a price below p^f, a contradiction of Lemma C. But if P lies above p^f, then (8) also contradicts Lemma C. Thus $\bar{p} < p^f$.

For the firm i satisfying (8),

(9) $$\delta W^i(\bar{p}) \geq \frac{\delta \Pi(p^f)}{2(1-\delta)},$$

because it could have reacted to p by setting p^f. But because p^f is a focal price, firm i does not gain by lowering its price from p^f to $\bar{p}$:

(10) $$\frac{\Pi(p^f)}{2(1-\delta)} \geq \Pi(\bar{p}) + \delta W^i(\bar{p}).$$

Inequalities (9) and (10) imply that

(11) $\Pi(p^f) \geq 2\Pi(\bar{p})$,

which in turn implies that $\bar{p}$ is lower than p^m (otherwise, from the strict quasi-concavity of Π, $\bar{p}$ would exceed p^f). Now, in the class P, the market price is never above $\bar{p}$. Therefore,

$$\frac{\Pi(\bar{p})}{1-\delta} > W^i(\bar{p}),$$

which, with (9), implies that

$$2\Pi(\bar{p}) > \Pi(p^f),$$

a contradiction of (11).   *Q.E.D.*

We have not yet been able to prove that an MPE cannot possess two Edgeworth ergodic classes. But Propositions 1 and 2 show that, in any case, Markov perfect equilibria can be subdivided into two categories that are independent of initial conditions. In one category, the market price converges in finite time to a focal price. In the other, the market price never settles down.

Actually, we believe that the structure of Edgeworth cycle equilibria can be made more precise. As currently defined, an Edgeworth cycle is simply an equilibrium without a focal price. We conjecture that in any Edgeworth cycle with a sufficiently fine grid, there exist prices $\bar{p}$ and $\underline{p}$ $(\underline{p} < \bar{p})$ such that, for any $p > \bar{p}$, $R^i(p) = \bar{p}$; and for any $p \in (\underline{p}, \bar{p}]$, $\underline{p} \leq R^i(p) \leq p$.

5. KINKED DEMAND CURVES: GENERAL RESULTS

In this section we completely characterize equilibrium focal prices (i.e., the steady-states of kinked demand curve equilibria) for fine grids and high discount factors. We first define two prices x and y $(x < p^m < y)$ that will play a crucial role in this characterization. Let x and y be the elements of the price grid (recall that p^m belongs to the price grid) such that

$$\Pi(x) > \tfrac{4}{7}\Pi(p^m) \geq \Pi(x-k) \quad \text{and} \quad x < p^m$$

and

$$\Pi(y) > \tfrac{2}{3}\Pi(p^m) \geq \Pi(y+k) \quad \text{and} \quad y > p^m.$$

Thus profits at x and y are approximately four sevenths and two thirds of monopoly profit. We now study the set of prices that are focal prices of some MPE. This set is characterized in two steps.

PROPOSTION 3 (Necessary Conditions): *If p^f is a focal price of some MPE, then for a high discount factor, (i) $p^f \leq y$; (ii) and for a sufficiently fine grid, $p^f \geq x$.*

PROPOSITION 4 (Sufficient Conditions): *For a given (sufficiently fine) grid and a price p belonging to this grid and to the interval $[x, y]$, p is the focal price of some MPE for a discount factor near one.*

Propositions 3 and 4 determine the set of possible focal prices for fine grids when firms place sufficient weight on the future. We should emphasize two aspects of this characterization. First, focal prices are bounded away from the competitive price (zero profit level); firms must make at least four-sevenths of the monopoly profit in equilibrium. Second, there is a nondegenerate interval of prices that can correspond to a kinked demand curve equilibrium. This multiplicity accords well with the informal story behind the kinked demand curve. As this story is usually told, if other firms imitate price cuts but do not imitate price rises, a firm's marginal revenue curve will have a discontinuity at the current price. As long as the marginal cost curve passes through the interval of discontinuity, the current price can be an equilibrium (see Scherer (1980)).

582   ERIC MASKIN AND JEAN TIROLE

For complete proofs of these propositions, see Maskin–Tirole (1985). Here we attempt only to elucidate some of the ideas underlying Proposition 3 (see the Appendix for a sketch of a proof of Proposition 4).

PROOF OF PROPOSITION 3(i): That a focal price must not exceed y is readily seen. Remaining at p^f yields profit $\Pi(p^f)/2(1-\delta)$. If p^f exceeds y, undercutting to the monopoly price yields at least $\Pi(p^m) + \delta^3\Pi(p^f)/2(1-\delta)$, because the undercutting firm can always move the market price back to the steady state by returning to p^f two periods hence. Thus, for equilibrium, we have:

$$\tfrac{1}{2}\Pi(p^f)(1 + \delta + \delta^2) \geqslant \Pi(p^m),$$

which means that for δ near 1, a focal price above the monopoly price must yield at least two-thirds the monopoly profit.

PROOF OF PROPOSITION 3(ii): We shall content ourselves with showing that in a pure strategy MPE (where each R^i is deterministic), a focal price p^f below p^m must yield at least two-thirds the monopoly profit (allowing for mixed strategies reduces the lower bound to four-sevenths[10]). Let us fix the price grid, i.e., the interval k between prices. With pure strategies, Lemma C implies that

$$(12) \qquad \text{for } p > p^f \text{ and } \Pi(p) > \Pi(p^f), \quad R^i(p) < p \quad i = 1,2$$

(if $R^i(p) = p$ for some i, firm j can guarantee itself $\delta\Pi(p)/2(1-\delta) > \Pi(p^f)/2(1-\delta)$ for δ close to 1, by relenting from p^f to p and staying at p forever, and hence p^f is not a focal price). Suppose, to the contrary, that $\Pi(p^f) < (2/3)\Pi(p^m)$. Let $\bar{p} > p^f$ be the smallest price such that

$$(13) \qquad \Pi(\bar{p}) \geqslant \Pi(p^f)\left(1 + \frac{\delta}{2}\right),$$

i.e.,

$$(14) \qquad \Pi(\bar{p}) + \delta^2\frac{\Pi(p^f)}{2(1-\delta)} \geqslant \Pi(p^f) + \frac{\delta\Pi(p^f)}{2(1-\delta)}.$$

For a fine enough grid, (13) implies that $\bar{p} \in (p^f, p^m)$. We claim first that

$$(15) \qquad R^i(p) = p^f \quad \text{for all} \quad p \in (p^f, \bar{p}], \quad i = 1,2.$$

Suppose to the contrary that there existed a price violating (15). Let $\hat{p}$ be the smallest such price. Then $p^f < R^i(\hat{p}) < \hat{p}$ for some i, implying

$$(16) \qquad V^i(\hat{p}) = \Pi(R^i(\hat{p})) + \frac{\delta^2\Pi(p^f)}{2(1-\delta)}.$$

---

[10] This is because mixing allows the possibility of semi-focal prices. Consider an MPE where p^f is a focal price and $\bar{p}(> p^f)$ is a semi-focal price. If, at p^f, a firm should raise its price to $\bar{p}$ or above, the market price eventually returns to p^f. Suppose, however, we ruled out mixing. Then $\bar{p}$ would have to be a full-fledged focal price itself, and thus the market price, once raised above $\bar{p}$, would *not* return to p^f. The fact that the market price would remain at $\bar{p}$ would give a firm a greater incentive to raise its price. Thus p^f cannot be as low in a pure strategy as in a mixed strategy MPE.

By definition of $\bar{p}$, $V^i(\hat{p})$ is less than the right side of (13), a contradiction since the firm could always choose the price p^f. Hence, (15) holds.

Now, in view of (15) and the definition of $\bar{p}$, $R^i(\bar{p}+k)$ cannot lie in $(p^f, \bar{p})$ because firm i would do better to charge price p^f. But, from (13), it does still better to charge $\bar{p}$. Hence

(17) $R^i(\bar{p}+k) = \bar{p}$, $i = 1, 2$.

We next argue that

(18a) $R^i(\bar{p}+2k) = \bar{p}+k$, $i = 1, 2$.

From the above argument, $R^i(\bar{p}+2k) \in \{\bar{p}, \bar{p}+k\}$. Now, if, at $\bar{p}+2k$, firm i cuts its price to $\bar{p}$, its profit is

$$\Pi(\bar{p}) + \frac{\delta^2 \Pi(p^f)}{2(1-\delta)}.$$

However, if, instead, it reduces its price to $\bar{p}+k$, (17) implies that its profit is

$$\Pi(\bar{p}+k) + \delta^2 \left(\Pi(p^f) + \frac{\delta \Pi(p^f)}{2(1-\delta)} \right),$$

which is bigger. Hence, (18a) holds. Similarly

(18b) $R^i(\bar{p}+3k) = \bar{p}+2k$.

Because p^f is a focal price,

$$V^i(p^f) = \frac{\Pi(p^f)}{2(1-\delta)}, \quad i = 1, 2.$$

However, if, at p^f, firm i raises its price to $\bar{p}+3k$, (17), (18a), and (18b) imply that its payoff is no less than

$$\delta^2 \Pi(\bar{p}+k) + \delta^4 \Pi(p^f) + \frac{\delta^5 \Pi(p^f)}{2(1-\delta)},$$

which, from (14), is greater than $V^i(p^f)$ for δ near 1, a contradiction. Thus, as long as the grid is fine enough so that $\bar{p}+3k < p^m$, $p^f \geq x$ for δ near 1. *Q.E.D.*

Although this proof of the second part of Proposition 3 applies only to pure strategies, it should convey the intuition behind the result. If a putative price p^f is too low, a firm does better by raising its price well above p^f. If it does so, it can ensure that the price remains high long enough for it to recoup the loss it suffers from raising its price first.

When the focal price is p^m, there is a particularly simple kinked demand curve equilibrium in which each firm (i) cuts its price to p^m when the market price is above p^m, (ii) cuts its price immediately to a relenting price $\underline{p}$ when the market price is between $\underline{p}$ and p^m; and (iii) raises its price to p^m when the price is below $\underline{p}$. We shall call this the *simple monopoly kinked demand curve equilibrium*

(SMKE), and it will figure prominently below. Formally, the SMKE is given by

(19) $\qquad R^*(p) = \begin{cases} p^m, & \text{if } p \leqslant \underline{p} \text{ or } p \geqslant p^m, \\ \underline{p}, & \text{if } p \in (\underline{p}, p^m), \end{cases}$

where $\underline{p}$ satisfies

(20) $\qquad 4\Pi(\underline{p}) \geqslant \Pi(p^m) > 4\Pi(\underline{p} - k).$

(Notice that the existence of $\underline{p}$ is ensured by a sufficiently fine price grid.) The first inequality in (20) guarantees that, at a price between $\underline{p}$ and p^m, a firm would rather cut its price to $\underline{p}$ (where it earns $\Pi(\underline{p})(1 + \delta) + (\delta^2\Pi(p^m))/2(1 - \delta)$), the first term of which is approximately $2\Pi(\underline{p})$ when δ is near 1) than raise the price to p^m (where it earns $(\delta\Pi(p^m)/2) + (\delta^2\Pi(p^m)/2(1 - \delta))$, the first term of which is approximately $\Pi(p^m)/2$ when δ is near 1). Similarly, the second inequality in (20) ensures that, at $\underline{p}$ or below, a firm would prefer to raise its price to p^m than to undercut, if δ is near 1. The rest of the verification that the SMKE is an MPE proceeds in much the same way.

The SMKE not only sustains joint monopoly profit but is the only MPE, even among those outside the kinked demand curve class, to *approximate* this profit level, as our next result shows.

PROPOSITION 5: *For a sufficiently fine grid, there exists $\underline{\delta} < 1$ and $\epsilon > 0$ such that, for all $\delta \geqslant \underline{\delta}$, the unique MPE for which, at some price p, aggregate profit per period*

(21) $\qquad (1 - \delta)(V^i(p) + W^j(p))$

is within ϵ of $\Pi(p^m)$, is the SMKE (given by (19) and (20)).

The proof of Proposition 5 is fairly involved and so is relegated to the Appendix. It is not difficult, however, to see the main idea. If an MPE (R^1, R^2) generates nearly the monopoly profit and δ is near 1, the market price must equal p^m a high fraction of the time along the equilibrium path. This implies that when the market price is p^m, both firms will react by playing p^m with high probability. This already tells us that the MPE must be (very nearly) a kinked demand curve equilibrium with monopoly focal price and that a firm's payoff per period is very nearly $\Pi(p^m)/2$. The reason equilibrium takes the form given by (19) and (20) is that these strategies ensure that, should the market price ever deviate from the monopoly level, it will return to p^m quickly. Thus, for example, when the market price p exceeds p^m, firms react to p by cutting immediately to p^m. A quick return to the monopoly price is an essential property of equilibrium since a firm always has the option of charging p^m, providing a lower bound on its payoff of $\delta W^i(p^m)$ (which, when δ is near 1, translates into a payoff of very nearly $\Pi(p^m)/2$ per period). Of course, when $p \in (\underline{p}, p^m)$, the price cannot return *too* quickly (i.e., it must first fall to $\underline{p}$ before returning to p^m), otherwise a firm might find undercutting the monopoly price worthwhile.

6. RENEGOTIATION AND DEMAND SHIFTS

An equilibrium is sometimes interpreted as a "self-enforcing agreement." Given that firms have "agreed" to play equilibrium strategies, no individual firm has the incentive to renege. In models with many equilibria, this interpretation has particular appeal as a way of explaining how firms know *which* equilibrium is to be played: the matter is negotiated, either openly or tacitly.

Although the multiplicity of equilibria in our model accords neatly with the traditional kinked demand curve story, most of these equilibria do not hold up well as self-enforcing agreements. To see why, consider a kinked demand curve equilibrium in which a price cut precipitates a costly price war. Firms' strategies in the price war form an MPE, but it is difficult to see how such a war could come about if firms were able to negotiate. Specifically, after the initial price cut, firms might "talk things over." If there existed an alternative MPE in which *both* firms did better than in the price war, why would they settle for the war? Why should they not agree to move to the alternative (or some even better) MPE? But if firms renegotiated in this way, they could destroy the deterrent to cut prices in the first place. If a firm realized that lowering its price would not touch off a price war, it might find such a cut advantageous. Hence, our kinked demand curve equilibrium would collapse.

The same criticism can be levelled against much of the analysis of tacit collusion in the supergame literature. Consider a repeated Bertrand price-setting game. It has long been recognized that the monopoly outcome (cooperation) can be sustained as an equilibrium outcome (assuming sufficiently little discounting) through strategies that prescribe cooperation until some firm deviates and marginal cost pricing thereafter. But if someone actually *did* deviate, firms would face an eternity of zero profits,[11] a prospect that they might try to improve upon (by moving to a better equilibrium) were they really able to collude.

To study behavior that is *not* subject to this attack, we will define an MPE to be *renegotiation-proof* if, at any price, p, there exists no alternative MPE that Pareto-dominates it.[12] Essentially, the concept applies subgame perfection to the renegotiation process itself.

The requirement of renegotiation-proofness drastically reduces the set of equilibria in our model. Remarkably, under the hypotheses of Proposition 4, the *unique* symmetric renegotiation-proof MPE is the simple monopoly kinked demand curve equilibrium we constructed in the preceding section.

PROPOSITION 6: *For a sufficiently fine grid, there exists $\underline{\delta} < 1$ such that, for all $\delta > \underline{\delta}$, the unique symmetric renegotiation-proof MPE when firms have discount factor δ is the kinked demand curve equilibrium (R^*, R^*) given by (19)–(20).*

---

[11] The fact that in this example punishments last forever is inconsequential. Punishments of finite duration as in Abreu (1986) and Fudenberg–Maskin (1986) are subject to the same criticism.

[12] Basically the same criterion has been studied in the supergames literature by Rubinstein (1980) and Farrell–Maskin (1987). Actually, our concept here is a bit stronger than that of Farrell–Maskin because we do not require that the alternative MPE be renegotiation-proof itself.

PROOF: For δ near 1 and any price p,

$$(22) \qquad (1 - \delta)(V^*(p) + W^*(p)) \approx \Pi(p^m),$$

where V^* and W^* are the valuation functions corresponding to MPE (R^*, R^*) (given by (19)–(20)). If at some price p there exists an alternative MPE (R^1, R^2) that Pareto dominates (R^*, R^*), then $(1 - \delta)(V^i(p) + W^j(p))$ is also nearly $\Pi(p^m)$, and so, from Proposition 5, (R^1, R^2) equals (R^*, R^*). Hence (R^*, R^*) is renegotiation-proof.

Suppose that $(\hat{R}, \hat{R})$ is a symmetric MPE for δ near 1. Then $(1 - \delta)\hat{V}(p)$ nearly equals $(1 - \delta)\hat{W}(p)$ for any p. If $(1 - \delta)(\hat{V}(p) + \hat{W}(p))$ is appreciably less than $\Pi(p^m)$, therefore, we have $V^*(p) > \hat{V}(p)$ and $W^*(p) > \hat{W}(p)$, implying that $(\hat{R}, \hat{R})$ is not renegotiation-proof. If, on the other hand, $(1 - \delta)(\hat{V}(p) + \hat{W}(p))$ nearly equals $\Pi(p^m)$, Proposition 5 implies that $\hat{R} = R^*$. Hence (R^*, R^*) is the only renegotiation-proof equilibrium for δ near 1.   *Q.E.D.*

Proposition 6 has implications for the way we might expect firms to react to shifts in demand. Suppose that the current monopoly price is p^m, but that in the future, the monopoly price might shift (either permanently or for a long period of time) to $p_+^m > p^m$ or $p_-^m < p^m$. Let us suppose that the probability of either such change in any given period is ρ. If ρ is small enough, it will not affect current behavior at all. Thus, if (R, R) is the renegotiation-proof MPE of Proposition 6, such behavior remains in equilibrium even with the prospect of a shift in demand (but before the shift actually occurs) as long as ρ is sufficiently small (alternatively, we could simply suppose that future shifts in demand are completely unforeseen). We will assume that after a shift occurs, firms move to the renegotiation-proof equilibrium (R_-, R_-) if the shift is downward, and to (R_+, R_+) if the shift is upward.

Imagine that firms begin by behaving according to (R, R) and that eventually there is a downward shift in the monopoly price p_-^m. Hence, if firms were at the steady-state price, i.e., at p^m, beforehand, they can move directly to the new renegotiation-proof steady state afterwards. Thus price will fall from p^m to p_-^m once and for all.

If, instead, there is an upward shift, the new monopoly price p_+^m exceeds p^m. If the shift is large, so that p^m is less than the new "relenting" price p_+ (the price below which firms return to focal price p_+^m), then firms simply raise their prices directly to p_+^m, and that is the end of the story. If, however, the shift is smaller, so that p^m exceeds p_+, the first firm to respond will *cut* its price (to gain a larger market share). This will be followed by an ultimate price rise to p_+^m. Thus, comparatively small increases in demand temporarily *lower* prices (i.e., induce price wars) as firms scramble to take advantage of the larger demand. In the end, however, the higher demand induces a higher price.

The possibility of price wars during "booms" in our model is consistent with the results of Rotemberg–Saloner (1986). However, their price wars arise for quite a different reason. In their model, which takes the supergame route, a cartel's price must be (relatively) low in periods of booms because the temptation to deviate from collusive behavior is higher in a period of high demand.

Our assumption that the probability of future demand shocks is small enough not to affect current behavior (or, alternatively, that future shocks are unanticipated) is strong. It would be desirable to extend the model to permit anticipated shocks that *do* influence the present. We feel, however, that the general conclusions of this section would be robust to such extensions. Shocks that call for a price reduction will tend to be accommodated swiftly, because downward adjustments are not costly. By contrast, raising one's price involves a short-run loss in market share, so that such adjustments are likely to be delayed. This fear of losing market share by raising one's price during booms, we feel, is the essence of the traditional kinked demand curve story.

7. EDGEWORTH CYCLES: GENERAL RESULTS

We now turn to Edgeworth cycles. We begin by establishing the general existence of Edgeworth cycles.

PROPOSITION 7: *Assume that the profit function* $\Pi(p)$ *is strictly concave. For a fine grid and a discount factor near* 1, *there exists an Edgeworth cycle.*

For a proof of Proposition 7, see our discussion paper. It may be instructive to consider the equilibrium strategies used in the proof. In this equilibrium, there exist two prices $\underline{p}$ and $\bar{p}$ ($\underline{p} < \bar{p}$) on which the following symmetric strategies are based:

$$(23) \qquad R(p) = \begin{cases} \bar{p} & \text{for } p > \bar{p}, \\ p - k & \text{for } \bar{p} \geqslant p > \underline{p}, \\ c & \text{for } \underline{p} \geqslant p > c, \\ \left. \begin{array}{l} c \quad \text{with probability } \mu(\delta) \\ \bar{p} + k \quad \text{with probability } 1 - \mu(\delta) \end{array} \right\} & \text{for } p = c, \\ c & \text{for } p < c, \end{cases}$$

where c is the marginal cost.

Thus, beginning at $\bar{p}$, the equilibrium involves a gradual price war until an intermediate price, $\underline{p}$, is reached, at which point the firms undercut to the competitive price, where each firm tries to "induce" the other firm to relent first. The reader may wonder why, below marginal cost, firms raise the price only to c (which yields zero profit in the short-run). The explanation is the same as for the war of attrition at the competitive price in Table II of Section 3; a firm is willing to accept low profit today in the hope of making a killing should the other firm relent first.

We now examine the question of how low profits can be in an Edgeworth cycle. For symmetric equilibria we have the following result.

PROPOSITION 8: *For a discount factor near* 1 *and a sufficiently fine grid, at least one firm earns average profit no less than (just under) a quarter of monopoly profit,* $\Pi(p^m)$, *in an MPE. Hence, in a symmetric equilibrium, this must be true of both firms.*

PROOF: Consider an MPE (R^1, R^2) for a fine grid and δ near 1. Take $\bar{p} = p^m + k$. Firm i reacts to $\bar{p}$ either (i) by lowering its price, in which case its payoff is $\max_{p < \bar{p}} (\Pi(p) + \delta W^i(p))$; or (ii) by keeping the same price, leading to payoff $(\Pi(\bar{p})/2) + \delta W^i(\bar{p})$; or by (iii) raising its price, which yields payoff $\max_{p > \bar{p}} \delta W^i(p)$. Let p_*^i be the smallest price that maximizes firm i's payoff over these three alternatives. Then firm i reacts to $\bar{p}$ with a price no lower than p_*^i. Suppose, without loss of generality, that

$$(24) \qquad p_*^1 \leqslant p_*^2.$$

We will show that firm 1's payoff is bounded below by (slightly less than) $\Pi(p^m)/4$.

Case (a): $p_*^2 \geqslant p^m$. In this case, firm 1's equilibrium payoff is at least

$$(25) \qquad \delta^2[\Pi(p^m - k) + \delta W^1(p^m - k)],$$

since it could raise its price to $\bar{p}$ and, after firm 2's reaction, undercut to $p^m - k$. For the same reason, we have

$$(26) \qquad W^1(p^m - k) \geqslant \delta^3(\Pi(p^m - k) + \delta W^1(p^m - k)).$$

From (26), (25) is at least

$$(27) \qquad \frac{\delta^2 \Pi(p^m - k)}{1 - \delta^4}.$$

Thus firm 1's payoff per period is at least $\Pi(p^m - k)/4$ (minus ε) if δ is sufficiently close to 1.

Case (b): $p_*^2 < p^m$. In this case, for all $p < p_*^2$, $\Pi(p_*^2) + \delta W^2(p_*^2) > \Pi(p) + \delta W^2(p)$ (since p_*^2 is the smallest maximizer). Moreover,

$$(28) \qquad \Pi(p_*^1) + \delta W^1(p_*^1) \geqslant \Pi(p^m) + \delta W^1(p^m).$$

The first inequality and the fact that $p_*^1 \leqslant p_*^2$ imply that, at a price above p_*^2 (e.g., p^m), firm 2 will never set a price below p_*^1. Therefore,

$$(29) \qquad W^1(p^m) \geqslant \frac{\delta \Pi(p_*^1)}{2} + \delta^2 W^1(p_*^1).$$

Combining (28) and (29), we obtain

$$(30) \qquad (1 - \delta) W^1(p^m) \geqslant \frac{\delta}{1 + \delta}\left(\Pi(p^m) - \frac{\Pi(p_*^1)}{2}\right),$$

which implies that for δ near 1,

$$(31) \qquad (1 - \delta)W^1(p^m) \geqslant \frac{\Pi(p^m)}{4}.$$

But $(1 - \delta)W^1(p^m)$ provides a lower bound for firm 1's profit per period, since the firm has the option of setting p^m. Hence $\Pi(p^m)/4$ also is a lower bound.

Q.E.D.

Thus regardless of the equilibrium, the average market price must be bounded away from the competitive price. We showed above that in a kinked demand curve equilibrium, aggregate profit per period must exceed four-sevenths of the monopoly profit. This result and Proposition 8 show that one should not expect low prices in equilibrium if firms place enough weight on future profit. This conclusion contrasts with the properties of an MPE in the *simultaneous-move* price-setting game, where profits are very close or equal to zero (Bertrand equilibrium).[13]

8. COMPARISON WITH THE QUANTITY MODEL

We have seen that our price model can give rise to a considerable multiplicity of equilibria: a range of kinked demand curve equilibria as well as Edgeworth cycles. By contrast, the model of capacity/quantity competition in our companion piece, although ostensibly very similar in structure, has a unique symmetric MPE.

The technical reason for this striking discrepancy is that the cross partial derivative of the instantaneous profit function π^i behaves quite differently in the two models. In the quantity model, we assumed that $(\partial^2 \pi^i)/(\partial q^1 \partial q^2)$ is negative —so that a firm's marginal profit is declining in the other firm's quantity. This implies that dynamic reaction functions are negatively sloped. The explanation for this negative slope is much the same as that for the downward sloping reaction functions in the static Cournot model: if marginal profit decreases as the other firm increases its quantity, then the quantity satisfying the first-order conditions for profit-maximization also decreases. (Were the cross partial always positive, reaction functions would be positively sloped.) Such nicely behaved reaction functions make the possibility of a multiplicity of symmetric equilibria a nonrobust pathology.

By contrast, the cross partial in our price model changes sign: when the other firm's price is sufficiently low (i.e., lower than its own price), a firm's marginal profit is zero; when the two prices are equal, marginal profit is negative (since

---

[13] Assume that both firms are forced to play simultaneously (in odd periods, say). Then there is no payoff-relevant variable at the time firms make their decisions. Assume that the profit function is strictly concave in the firm's own price. If S^2 is the mixed strategy of firm 2, firm 1's profit can be written $\sum_p Pr\{S^2 = p\}\pi^1(p^1, p)$. This function has a unique maximum or possibly two consecutive optima p^* and $p^* + k$. The same holds for firm 2. A standard argument establishes that the maximum equilibrium price is $c + k$.

raising one's price drives away all customers); finally, when the other firm's price is higher, a firm's marginal profit is positive if its price is below the monopoly level. This nonmonotonicity of marginal profit gives rise to dynamic reaction functions that are decidedly nonmonotonic. In the kinked demand curve described by (19)–(20), a firm will respond to a price cut above the relenting price $\underline{p}$ by lowering its own price. But below $\underline{p}$ a price cut induces it to raise its price to p^f.

The price and quantity models also differ diametrically in their comparative statics. In the quantity model, an increase in the discount factor δ means that firm 1 places greater weight on the future reduction of firm 2's quantity induced by a current increase in 1's own quantity. Firm 1 therefore has the incentive to choose a correspondingly higher current quantity. Since the same reasoning also applies to firm 2, we conclude that an increase in δ induces an increase in equilibrium quantities, i.e., a more competitive outcome.

An increase in δ in the price model, by contrast, makes it more worthwhile for a firm to sacrifice current clientele by raising its price today in the expectation of future profit when the other firm follows suit. Thus an increase in δ may well *detract* from the competitiveness of the outcome. This is most clearly seen when we compare equilibrium for $\delta = 0$ (the only possible equilibrium price in the long run is very nearly marginal cost) with that for δ near 1 (perfect collusion becomes possible).

Finally, the price and quantity models differ according to the value that length of commitment confers on a firm. We mentioned in the introduction to Part I of this study that contractual agreements may account for the sort of short-run commitment we have been discussing. The length of a contract, however, is in part a matter of choice, and so it is of some interest to consider the relative desirability of alternative commitment periods. In the quantity model, it is clear that the incumbent firm is made better off as the length of its commitment grows. In the limit, it can attain monopoly profit by committing itself indefinitely. Thus, for contestability-like results to follow from a model where contracts form the basis of commitment, one must introduce some cost associated with lengthy contracts to prevent commitment of infinite duration.

In our price model, on the other hand, commitment serves as impediment to firms. To the extent that a firm is committed to a price, it will find it difficult to recapture lost market share should it be undercut. Thus, in this model, a firm will opt for contracts of the shortest possible length.

9. ENDOGENOUS TIMING

We now turn to the issue of alternating moves, and briefly examine how this timing might be derived rather than imposed. The first model is the discrete time framework with null actions described in Section 4 of Part I. Thus, a firm is free to set a price in any period where it is not already committed. Once it chooses a price, it remains committed for two periods. It also has the option of not setting a price at all, in which case it is out of the market for one period.[14] Thus a Markov strategy for firm i takes the form $\{R^i(\cdot), S^i\}$, where $R^i(p)$ is, as before, i's reaction to the price p, and S^i is its action when the other firm is not currently committed to a price.

We are interested in whether the alternating structure we imposed in Sections 2–8 emerges as equilibrium behavior in our expanded model. Accordingly, we will say that an MPE (R^1, R^2) of the fixed-timing (alternating move) game is *robust to endogenous timing* if there exist strategies S^1 and S^2 such that (i) $(\{R^1, S^1\}, \{R^2, S^2\})$ is an MPE of the endogenous timing game; (ii) starting from the simultaneous mode, firms switch to the alternating mode in finite time with probability one. Notice that because R^1 and R^2 are equilibrium strategies of the fixed timing game, they never entail choice of the null strategy. Hence, once firms reach the alternating mode, they stay there forever.

Analogously, if (S^1, S^2) is an MPE of the game in which firms are constrained to move simultaneously, we shall say that it is robust to endogenous timing if there exist reaction functions R^1 and R^2 such that (iii) $(\{R^1, S^1\}, \{R^2, S^2\})$ is an MPE of the endogenous-timing game; (iv) starting from the alternating mode, firms switch to the simultaneous mode in finite time with probability one. Our principal result of this section, proved in the Appendix, is the observation that symmetric alternating-move but not simultaneous-move MPE's are robust.

PROPOSITION 9: *For a sufficiently fine grid and a discount factor near enough* 1, *any symmetric alternating-move MPE* (R, R) *but no simultaneous-move MPE* (S^1, S^2) *is robust to endogenous timing.*

The idea behind Proposition 9 is that, as we observed in footnote 13, firms earn very nearly zero profit in a simultaneous mode equilibrium, whereas, from Proposition 8, they earn at least a quarter of monopoly profit each in the alternating mode if δ is near 1. Thus, in the simultaneous mode, a firm has the incentive to play the null action and move into the alternating mode. By the same token, neither firm has the incentive to upset alternating timing.

Of course, the endogenous-timing model of this section is only one of many possibilities. An even simpler, but perhaps less reasonable (for price competition), model that also leads to equilibrium alternation is a continuous time model with random (specifically, Poisson) commitment lengths.[15] If every time a firm set a price, it remained committed to that price during the interval Δt with probability $1 - \lambda \Delta t$, then the two periods of commitment in our discrete-time model

---

[14] We thus assume that retailers, say, who do not receive a new price list, do not carry the firm's product. One alternative would be to assume that retailers continue to charge the old price. Gertner (1985) shows that the conclusions are robust to this specification. Another interesting aspect of Gertner's paper is that it allows menu costs of price changes exceeding the one-period monopoly profit (undercutting never pays in the short run, but reactions to price cuts are also very costly). This reflects the possibility that decision periods are very short.

[15] For a fuller description of this example see our companion paper.

592 ERIC MASKIN AND JEAN TIROLE

correspond exactly to the *mean* commitment length in the stochastic model. Moreover, all our results for the former model go through for the latter.

10. COMPARISON WITH SUPERGAMES

Several of the results of this paper underscore the relatively high profits that firms can earn when the discount factor is near 1. Thus our model can be viewed as a theory of tacit collusion. There is, of course, a variety of other such theories. The literature on incomplete information in dynamic games, for example, has shown that high prices may be sustained by oligopolists' desire to mislead their rivals. Kreps–Milgrom–Roberts–Wilson (1982) demonstrate the advantages of cultivating a reputation for being intrinsically cooperative. The firms in (the price interpretation of) Riordan (1985) secretly charge high prices today to signal to their competitors that demand is high, so as to induce them to charge high prices tomorrow.

Another (more closely-related) alternative is the well-established supergame approach to oligopoly. Starting with Friedman (1977), the theory has produced many interesting applications, among them Brock–Scheinkman (1985), Green–Porter (1984), and Rotemberg–Saloner (1986), and undergone several developments, e.g., Anderson (1984) and Kalai–Stanford (1985). We feel, however, that our approach may offer certain advantages over the supergame line.

nature. A firm conditions its behavior on past prices *only* because other firms do so. If we eliminate the bootstrap equilibria, we are left with lack of collusion. Moreover, the strategies in the supergame literature typically have a firm reacting not only to other firms but to what it did *itself*.[16] By contrast, a Markov strategy has a firm condition its action only on those variables that are relevant in all cases of other firms' behavior. Thus, in a price war, a firm cuts its price not to punish its competitor (which would involve keeping track of its own past behavior as well as that of the competitor) but simply to regain market share. It strikes us that these straightforward Markov reactions often resemble the informal concept of reaction stressed in the traditional industrial organization discussion of business behavior (e.g., the kinked demand curve story) more closely than do their supergame counterparts.

Second, supergame equilibria rely on an infinity of repetitions. They break down even for long but finite horizons.[17] For example, any finite number of repetitions of the Bertrand price-setting game yields the competitive price at every iteration.[18] We have not yet been able to prove that equilibrium in the finite period version of our price model converges to the infinite period equi-

---

[16] Indeed, this "self-reactive" property is often essential to obtaining collusion (see Section 3B of Maskin–Tirole (1982)).

[17] Unless there are multiple equilibria in the constituent game (see Benoit–Krishna (1985)).

[18] One can preserve supergame equilibria by replacing the infinite horizon with a reasonably high probability in each round that the game will continue another period. But this extension does not cover the case where the horizon length is determined fairly well in advance.

librium as the horizon lengthens.[19] But we have at least shown that for a long enough finite horizon, equilibrium is not "close" to the competitive equilibrium, a result similar to Propositions 3 and 8.

Third, the supergame approach is plagued by an enormous number of equilibria. In the repeated Bertrand price game, any feasible pair of nonnegative profit levels can arise in equilibrium with sufficiently little discounting. Our model too has a multiplicity of equilibria but a smaller one. Propositions 3 and 7 demonstrate, for example, that profits must be bounded away from zero. Moreover, from Proposition 5, there is only a single equilibrium[20] that sustains monopoly profits (whereas there is a continuum of such equilibria in the supergame framework).

Finally, the supergame approach makes little distinction between price and quantity games: in either case any profit level between pure competition and pure monopoly is achievable for δ near 1. As we suggested in Section 9, however, our approach does distinguish between the two. Quantity/capacity games are marked by downward sloping reactions functions and an increase in competition as the number of interactions between firms increases (or the future becomes more important), whereas price games exhibit nonmonotonic reaction functions and a decrease in competition as δ rises. (In the terminology of Bulow et al. (1985), quantities are strategic substitutes, while prices are strategic complements for a range of prices and strategic substitutes for another.)

11. EXCESS CAPACITY AND MARKET SHARING

Although important, price is only one dimension in which oligopolists compete. In particular firms also make quantity decisions. In Maskin–Tirole (1985), we provide two simple examples that show how our model can be extended to provide explanations of excess capacity and market sharing.

Excess Capacity

In the kinked demand curve equilibrium of Example 1, undercutting the monopoly price is deterred by the threat of a price war. Recall, however, that in this example firms are not capacity constrained. Once we introduce such constraints, it is easy to see that the monopoly price may not be sustainable if firm 2 has only enough capacity to supply half the demand at the monopoly price. Indeed, firm 1 will wish to undercut if it has more than this capacity, and firm 2 will not be able to respond effectively because it cannot expand output at lower prices to reduce the first firm's market share. Thus the threat of a price war is a significant deterrent to price cutting only if firms have more capacity than they will use when price is at the monopoly level.

---

[19] We *have*, however, obtained just such a convergence result for the Cournot competition version of the model (Maskin–Tirole (1987)).

[20] This equilibrium is, in fact, renegotiation-proof.

In the extended model of Maskin–Tirole (1985), firms choose capacities simultaneously and once-and-for-all; they then compete through prices as in Section 3. We exhibit an MPE in which firms accumulate capacities above the level necessary to supply half the market at the monopoly price, and yet charge the monopoly price forever. That is, the firms accumulate capacities that they never use simply to make undercutting less attractive for their rivals.

Market Sharing

In a static model, a firm always supplies the demand it faces as long as price exceeds its marginal cost. In a dynamic framework, however, a firm may temper its rival's aggressiveness by voluntarily giving up some of its market share. In Maskin–Tirole (1985), we construct an example in which firm 1 has a marginal cost lower than that of firm 2. When a firm chooses a price, it also chooses a selling constraint, i.e., the maximum quantity that it can supply at its chosen price (corresponding, for example, to the extent of its inventory). In the MPE, the firms charge a price above the monopoly price of firm 1 but below that of firm 2. To avoid triggering price-cutting by the low-cost firm, firm 2 imposes a market share less than one-half on itself. It thus "bribes" firm 1 to accept a comparatively high market price.[21]

Department of Economics, Harvard University, Cambridge, MA 02138, U.S.A.
and
Department of Economics, MIT, Cambridge, MA 02139, U.S.A.

Manuscript received June, 1985; final revision received July, 1987.

APPENDIX

PROOF OF PROPOSITION 4: We must show that any price in $[x, y]$ is a focal price for sufficiently high discount factors. To do this, we will consider three cases depending on the relative magnitudes of $\Pi(p^f)$ and $(2/3)\Pi(p^m)$ and of p^f and p^m, where p^f is the focal price candidate in $[x, y]$. In each case, we will exhibit the equilibrium strategies giving rise to p^f.

Case (a): $\Pi(p^f) > (2/3)\Pi(p^m)$ and $p^f \leqslant p^m$. In this case, equilibrium consists of both players using the strategy

$$R(p) = \begin{cases} p^f, & \text{for } p \geqslant p^f, \\ \underline{p}, & \text{for } p^f > p > \underline{p}, \\ p^f, & \text{for } p \geqslant \underline{p}, \end{cases}$$

where $\underline{p}$ is chosen so that

$$4\Pi(\underline{p}) \geqslant \Pi(p^m) > 4\Pi(\underline{p} - k)$$

(notice that the existence of $\underline{p}$ is ensured by a sufficiently fine price grid).

---

[21] This is an example of a "puppy-dog" strategy: remain small so as not to trigger aggressive behavior by one's rival (see Fudenberg–Tirole (1984)).

Case (b): $\Pi(p^f) > (2/3)\Pi(p^m)$ and $p^f > p^m$. In this case the equilibrium strategy for each player is

$$R(p) = \begin{cases} p^f, & \text{for } p \geqslant p^f, \\ p_1, & \text{for } p^f > p > p_1, \\ \left. \begin{array}{l} p_1, \quad \text{with probability } \alpha \\ \underline{p}, \quad \text{with probability } 1 - \alpha \end{array} \right\} \text{for } p = p_1, \\ \underline{p}, & \text{for } p_1 > p > \underline{p}, \\ p^f, & \text{for } p \leqslant \underline{p}, \end{cases}$$

where $p^f > p^m > p_1 > \underline{p}$ and

$$\Pi(\underline{p})(1 + \delta) \geqslant \delta \frac{\Pi(p^f)}{2} > \Pi(\underline{p} - k)(1 + \delta),$$

$$\Pi(\underline{p})(1 + \delta) + \alpha \frac{(\delta^2 + \delta^3)}{2} \Pi(p^f) = \frac{\Pi(p_1)}{2} + \alpha \left(\delta \frac{\Pi(p_1)}{2} + \frac{\delta^2 + \delta^3}{2} \Pi(\underline{p}) \right),$$

$$\Pi(p_1) = \Pi(p^f) - \varepsilon,$$

for ε small.

Case (c): $\Pi(p^f) \leqslant (2/3)\Pi(p^m)$ and $p^m > p^f \geqslant x$. Now we take

$$R(p) = \begin{cases} \bar{p}, & \text{if } p > \bar{p}, \\ \left. \begin{array}{l} \bar{p}, \quad \text{with probability } \alpha \\ p^f, \quad \text{with probability } 1 - \alpha \end{array} \right\} \text{if } p = \bar{p}, \\ p^f, & \text{if } \bar{p} > p \geqslant p^f, \\ \underline{p}, & \text{if } p^f > p > \underline{p}, \\ \bar{p}, & \text{if } \underline{p} \geqslant p, \end{cases}$$

where $p^m > \bar{p} > p^f > \underline{p}$ and

$$\Pi(\bar{p}) \geqslant \Pi(p^f)\left(1 + \frac{\delta}{2}\right) > \Pi(\bar{p} - k),$$

$$V(\bar{p}) = \frac{\Pi(\bar{p})}{2} + \delta W(\bar{p}) = \Pi(p^f) + \delta \frac{\Pi(p^f)}{2(1 - \delta)},$$

$$\Pi(\underline{p})(1 + \delta) + \delta^2 V(\bar{p}) \geqslant \delta W(\bar{p}) > \Pi(\underline{p} - k)(1 + \delta) + \delta^2 V(\bar{p}),$$

$$\alpha = \frac{(2 + \delta)\Pi(p^f) - \Pi(\bar{p})}{\delta \Pi(\bar{p}) + \delta^2 \Pi(p^f)}.$$

Here $V(p)$ is the valuation of a firm when its rival has just played p, and $W(p)$ is the firm's valuation when it itself has just played p. Notice that $\bar{p}$ as defined above exists and is unique, since $\Pi(p^f) \leqslant (2/3)\Pi(p^m)$. For δ large and k small, α is approximately equal to one fifth.

For the straightforward verification that the strategies defined in Cases (a)–(c) form equilibria, see Maskin–Tirole (1985).   *Q.E.D.*

PROOF OF PROPOSITION 5: Fix the price grid. Assume for convenience that:

(A0)   there exists no feasible price p such that $\Pi(p) = \Pi(p^m)/2$.

For any $\alpha \in (0, 1)$, there exist $\varepsilon > 0$ and $\underline{\delta} < 1$ such that, if (R^1, R^2) is an MPE (with discount factor

596   ERIC MASKIN AND JEAN TIROLE

$\delta > \underline{\delta}$) such that

(A1) $(1 - \delta)(V^1(p) + W^2(p)) > \Pi(p^m) - \varepsilon$ for some p,

then

(A2) $\text{Prob}\left\{ R^i(p^m) \geqslant p^m \right\} > \alpha$ for $i = 1, 2$.

If ε is small and δ is near 1, then (A1) implies that the market price is p^m most of the time. But then the reaction to p^m must, with high probability, be a price p no less than p^m (if $p < p^m$, then p becomes the market price).

Formula (A2) ensures that, for α near 1, a firm can guarantee itself a payoff of nearly $\Pi(p^m)/2$ per period simply by always setting the price p^m. Indeed, if $\text{Prob}\{ R^i(p^m) > p^m \}$ is near 1, firm j can obtain nearly $\Pi(p^m)$ per period from this strategy. Hence, for ε small and δ near 1, an MPE (R^1, R^2) satisfying (A1) also satisfies

(A3) $\Pi(p^m)/2 \approx V^i(p^m)(1 - \delta) > \Pi(p)/2$,   for all $p \neq p^m$,

and

(A4) $\text{Prob}\left\{ R^i(p^m) = p^m \right\} > 0$, $i = 1, 2$.

Formula (A4) implies that p^m is a semi-focal price.
We first claim that if (R^1, R^2) satisfies (A1) for ε small and δ near 1, then

(A5) $\hat{p} > p^m$ implies $R^i(\hat{p}) = p^m$ for $i = 1, 2$.

Let p be in the support of $R^i(\hat{p})$ for some i and $\hat{p} > p^m$. Because p^m is a semi-focal price,

(A6) $p \in [p^m, \hat{p}]$.

Suppose that $\hat{p}$ is the smallest price such that $p \in (p^m, \hat{p}]$ for some realization p of $R^i(\hat{p})$. If $p < \hat{p}$, then

(A7) $V^i(\hat{p}) = \Pi(p) + \delta^2 V^i(p^m)$,

which contradicts the facts that $V^i(\hat{p}) \geqslant V^i(p^m)$ and $V^i(p^m)(1 - \delta) \approx \Pi(p^m)/2$ for δ close to 1. If $p = \hat{p}$, then

$$V^i(\hat{p}) \leqslant (1/2)\Pi(\hat{p})(1 + \delta) + \delta^2 V^i(\hat{p}),$$

since $R^j(\hat{p}) \leqslant \hat{p}$ and $V^i(\cdot)$ is nondecreasing. Hence $V^i(\hat{p})(1 - \delta) \leqslant \Pi(\hat{p})/2$, which again contradicts (A3). We conclude that (A5) holds after all.
We next argue that, for the MPE under consideration,

(A8)   if $\hat{p} < p^m$ and p is a realization of $R^i(\hat{p})$, then $p \leqslant p^m$.

If instead $p > p^m$, then from (A5)

(A9) $\delta^2 V^i(p^m) \geqslant \delta W^i(p^m)$.

But from (A4),

(A10) $V^i(p^m) = \Pi(p^m)/2 + \delta W^i(p^m)$.

Formulas (A9) and (A10) imply that

$$W^i(p^m)(1 - \delta) \leqslant \delta \frac{\Pi(p^m)}{2(1 + \delta)},$$

which contradicts (A3) and (A10). Hence, (A8) holds.
Next we demonstrate that

(A11)   if $\hat{p} < p^m$ and $p(> \hat{p})$ is a realization of $R^i(\hat{p})$, then $p = p^m$.

Clearly, if p is a realization of $R^i(\hat{p})$ and $p > \hat{p}$, we have

(A12) $W^i(p) \geqslant W^i(p^m)$.

From (A8) $p \leqslant p^m$, and so, if $p \neq p^m$,

(A13) $\Pi(p^m)/2 + \delta W^i(p^m) \geqslant \Pi(p) + \delta W^i(p)$.

Thus (A0), (A12), and (A13) imply that

(A14) $\dfrac{\Pi(p^m)}{2} > \Pi(p)$.

Now, $R^j(p) \leqslant p^m$. Hence, because $V^i(\cdot)$ is nondecreasing and p^m is a realization of $R^i(p^m)$,

(A15) $W^i(p) \leqslant \Pi(p) + \delta V^i(p^m) = \Pi(p) + \delta\dfrac{\Pi(p^m)}{2} + \delta^2 W^i(p^m)$.

From (A12) and (A15) we infer

$$W^i(p^m)(1 - \delta) \leqslant \left(\Pi(p) + \delta\dfrac{\Pi(p^m)}{2}\right)\Big/(1 + \delta),$$

which, in view of (A14), contradicts (A3) and (A10). Hence (A11) holds.

We next argue that

(A16)   for all $p \leqslant \underline{p}$, $R^i(p) = p^m$, $i = 1, 2$,

where $\underline{p}$ is defined by (20). For $i = 1, 2$, define $\underline{p}^i$ so that

(A17) $(1 + \delta)\Pi\left(\underline{p}^i\right) + \dfrac{\delta^2 \Pi(p^m)}{2} + \delta^3 W^i(p^m)$

$$\geqslant \delta W^i(p^m) > (1 + \delta)\Pi\left(\underline{p}^i - k\right) + \dfrac{\delta^2 \Pi(p^m)}{2} + \delta^3 W^i(p^m).$$

Rearranging, we obtain

(A18) $(1 + \delta)\Pi\left(\underline{p}^i - k\right) + \dfrac{\delta^2 \Pi(p^m)}{2} < \delta(1 + \delta)W^i(p^m)(1 - \delta)$

$$\leqslant (1 + \delta)\Pi\left(\underline{p}^i\right) + \delta^2\dfrac{\Pi(p^m)}{2}.$$

Now, for δ near 1, the middle expression of (A18) is nearly $\Pi(p^m)$. Hence, for such δ, $\underline{p}^i = \underline{p}$, $i = 1$, 2. Consider firm i when the current market price p is less than or equal to $\underline{p}$. If it chooses a price no higher than $\underline{p}$, then an upper bound on its payoff is the right side expression of (A17), since the best it can hope for is that the other firm reacts by raising its price to p^m. If, instead, firm i raises its price to p^m, it obtains the middle expression of (A17). The second inequality of (A17), therefore, establishes (A16).

We must now show that

(A19)   for $p \in \left(\underline{p}, p^m\right)$ $R^i(p) = \underline{p}$, $i = 1, 2$.

Consider $p \in (\underline{p}, p^m)$. From the first inequality in (A17), a firm is better off cutting its price to $\underline{p}$ than raising it to p^m when the current price is p. The only other possibility is that the firm could choose some price in $(\underline{p}, p]$. Let $\hat{p}$ be the smallest price in $(\underline{p}, p^m]$ for which for some firm i there exists $p^* \in (\underline{p}, \hat{p}]$ in the support of $R^i(\hat{p})$. Then, from (A16),

(A20) $V^i(\hat{p}) \leqslant \Pi(\hat{p}) + \delta^3 W^i(p^m)$.

If, however, firm i raises its price directly to p^m from $\hat{p}$, it obtains $\delta W^i(p^m)$, which (since $(1 - \delta)W^i(p^m)$ is nearly $\Pi(p^m)/2$) is greater than the right side of (A20), a contradiction. We conclude that (A19) holds after all.

We have demonstrated that for ε small and δ near 1, an MPE (R^1, R^2) satisfying (A1) also satisfies (19) for $p \neq p^m$. It remains to show that $R^i(p^m) = p^m$. Let p be a realization of $R^i(p^m)$. If $p > p^m$, then (A5) implies that $V^i(p^m) = \delta^2 V^i(p^m)$, which is clearly false. The argument of the previous paragraph ((A20) in particular) demonstrates that p cannot lie in $(\underline{p}, p^m)$. Suppose $p = \underline{p}$.

598   ERIC MASKIN AND JEAN TIROLE

Then $V(p^m) = \Pi(p)(1 + \delta) + \delta^2 V(p^m)$, which implies $(1 - \delta)V(p^m) = \Pi(p)$, a contradiction of the fact that $(1 - \delta)V(p^m)$ is near $\Pi(p^m)/2$. Thus, we conclude that $R^i(p^m) = p^m$.   Q.E.D.

PROOF OF PROPOSITION 9: Consider a symmetric MPE (R, R) of the alternating-move model, and let $V(p)$ and $W(p)$ be the associated valuation functions. Let $\hat{p}$ denote the smallest price that maximizes $\Pi(p) + \delta W(p)$. We will construct a strategy S^* for the simultaneous mode such that $(\{R, S^*\})$ forms an MPE for the endogeneous-timing game.

For the moment, suppose that firms, when in the simultaneous mode, can choose either (a) the null action or (b) a price no greater than $\hat{p}$ (we will admit the possibility of firms' choosing prices greater than $\hat{p}$ later on). Once we specify firms' behavior in this mode, then their payoffs are completely determined, assuming they play according to R in the alternating mode. Thus we can think of firms in the simultaneous mode as playing a one-shot game in which they choose mixed strategies S^1 and S^2 and their payoffs are determined by $(\{R, S^1\}, (R, S^2))$. Because this is a symmetric game there exists a symmetric equilibrium (S^*, S^*). Let U^* be a firm's corresponding present discounted profit. We claim that $(\{R, S^*\}, \{R, S^*\})$ is an MPE for the endogenous-timing game.

We first note that S^* must place positive probability on the null action. If this were not the case, then firms would remain in the simultaneous mode forever. But, as we argued in footnote 13, any simultaneous-mode equilibrium must entail (essentially) zero profit. By contrast, if a firm played the null action and thereby moved the firms into the alternating mode, Proposition 8 would guarantee it at least a quarter of monopoly profit, which is clearly preferable. Thus S^* must indeed assign the null action positive probability.

We next observe that, in the simultaneous mode, firm i cannot gain from choosing a price p greater than $\hat{p}$, given that firm j sticks to S^*. If firm j does not choose the null action—i.e., it selects a price—then firm i sells nothing with a price greater than $\hat{p}$. If firm j *does* select the null action, then the firms move into the alternating mode, and firm i's payoff is $\Pi(p) + \delta W(p)$, which, by definition of $\hat{p}$, is no greater than that from choosing $\hat{p}$. Hence a firm has no incentive to choose prices greater than $\hat{p}$ in the simultaneous mode.

It remains only to show that, in the alternating mode, a firm has no incentive to play the null action. If it did so, its payoff would be δU^*, since the firm would then be in the simultaneous mode. Now, because, as we have noted, it is optimal for a firm to play the null action in the simultaneous mode,

$$U^* \leqslant \delta V(\hat{p}).$$

Hence, by playing the null action in the alternating mode, a firm obtains a payoff less than $\delta^2 V(\hat{p})$. If instead it chooses a price $p > \hat{p}$, the other firm will react with a price no lower than $\hat{p}$, and so its payoff is at least $\delta^2 V(\hat{p})$. Hence the null action is not preferable.

To see that a simultaneous-move MPE (S^1, S^2) cannot be robust to endogenous timing, recall that in such an equilibrium, $S^i \leqslant c + k$ for $i = 1, 2$. Now if (S^1, S^2) were robust, there would exist reaction functions R^1 and R^2 such that, starting from the alternating mode, firms switch to the simultaneous mode in finite time and remain there forever. But, using much the same argument as in the proof of Proposition 8, we can show that at least one firm can obtain a per period equilibrium payoff that is bounded well away from zero, which contradicts the upper bound of $\Pi(c + k)/2$ it earns in the simultaneous mode.   Q.E.D.

REFERENCES

ABREU, D. (1986): "Extremal Equilibria of Oligopolistic Supergames," *Journal of Economic Theory*, 39, 191–225.
ANDERSON, R. (1984): "Quick Response Equilibrium," IP323, Center for Research in Management, University of California-Berkeley.
BENOIT, J. F., AND V. KRISHNA (1985): "Finitely Repeated Games," *Econometrica*, 53, 890–904.
BERTRAND, J. (1883): "Review of 'Theorie Mathematique de la Richesse Sociale et Recherches sur les Principes Mathematiques de la Richesse'," *Journal des Savants*, 499–508.
BROCK, W., AND J. SCHEINKMAN (1985): "Price Setting Supergames with Capacity Constraints," *Review of Economic Studies*, 52, 371–382.
BULOW, J., J. GEANAKOPLOS, AND P. KLEMPERER (1985): "Multimarket Oligopoly: Strategic Substitutes and Complements," *Journal of Political Economy*, 93, 488–511.
DERMAN, C. (1970): *Finite State Markovian Decision Processes*. New York: Academic Press.

EDGEWORTH, F. (1925): "The Pure Theory of Monopoly," in *Papers Relating to Political Economy*, Vol. 1. London: MacMillan, pp. 111–142.

FARRELL, J., AND E. MASKIN (1987): "Renegotiation in Repeated Games," mimeo, Harvard University.

FRIEDMAN, J. (1977): *Oligopoly and the Theory of Games*. Amsterdam: North-Holland.

FUDENBERG, D., AND J. TIROLE (1984): "The Fat-Cat Effect, the Puppy-Dog Ploy, and the Lean and Hungry Look," *American Economic Review*, 74, 361–366.

FUDENBERG, D., AND E. MASKIN (1986): "The Folk Theorem in Repeated Games with Discounting or with Incomplete Information," *Econometrica*, 54, 533–554.

GERTNER, R. (1985): "Dynamic Duopoly with Price Inertia," mimeo, MIT.

GREEN, E., AND R. PORTER (1984): "Noncooperative Collusion under Imperfect Price Information," *Econometrica*, 52, 87–100.

HALL, R., AND C. HITCH (1939): "Price Theory and Business Behavior," *Oxford Economic Papers*, 2, 12–45.

KALAI, E., AND W. STANFORD (1985): "Conjectural Variations Strategies in Accelerated Cournot Games," *International Journal of Industrial Organization*, 3, 133–152.

KREPS, D., P. MILGROM, J. ROBERTS, AND R. WILSON (1982): "Rational Cooperation in the Finitely-Repeated Prisoner's Dilemma," *Journal of Economic Theory*, 27, 245–252.

MASKIN, E., AND J. TIROLE (1982): "A Theory of Dynamic Oligopoly, I: Overview and Quantity Competition with Large Fixed Costs," MIT Working Paper #320.

——— (1985): A Theory of Dynamic Oligopoly, Part II: Price Competition," MIT Working Paper 373.

——— (1987): "A Theory of Dynamic Oligopoly, Part III: Cournot Competition," *European Economic Review*, 31, 947–968.

——— (1988): "A Theory of Dynamic Oligopoly, Part I: Overview and Quantity Competition with Large Fixed Costs," *Econometrica*, 56, 549–569.

RIORDAN, M. (1985): "Imperfect Information and Dynamic Conjectural Variations," *Rand Journal of Economics*, 16, 41–50.

ROTEMBERG, J., AND G. SALONER (1986): "A Supergame-Theoretic Model of Business Cycles and Price Wars During Booms," *American Economic Review*, 76, 390–407.

RUBINSTEIN, A. (1980): "Strong Perfect Equilibrium in Supergames," *International Journal of Game Theory*, 9, 1–12.

SCHERER, F. (1980): *Industrial Market Structure and Economic Performance*, Second Edition. Rand McNally.

SWEEZY, P. (1939): "Demand Under Conditions of Oligopoly," *Journal of Political Economy*, 47, 568–573.

[7]

Quantity precommitment and Bertrand competition yield Cournot outcomes

David M. Kreps*

and

José A. Scheinkman**

Bertrand's model of oligopoly, which gives perfectly competitive outcomes, assumes that: (1) there is competition over prices and (2) production follows the realization of demand. We show that both of these assumptions are required. More precisely, consider a two-stage oligopoly game where, first, there is simultaneous production, and, second, after production levels are made public, there is price competition. Under mild assumptions about demand, the unique equilibrium outcome is the Cournot outcome. This illustrates that solutions to oligopoly games depend on both the strategic variables employed and the context (game form) in which those variables are employed.

1. Introduction

■ Since Bertrand's (1883) criticism of Cournot's (1838) work, economists have come to realize that solutions to oligopoly games depend critically on the strategic variables that firms are assumed to use. Consider, for example, the simple case of a duopoly where each firm produces at a constant cost b per unit and where the demand curve is linear, $p = a - q$. Cournot (quantity) competition yields equilibrium price $p = (a + 2b)/3$, while Bertrand (price) competition yields $p = b$.

In this article, we show by example that there is more to Bertrand competition than simply "competition over prices." It is easiest to explain what we mean by reviewing the stories associated with Cournot and Bertrand. The Cournot story concerns producers who simultaneously and independently make production quantity decisions, and who *then* bring what they have produced to the market, with the market price being the price that equates the total supply with demand. The Bertrand story, on the other hand, concerns producers who simultaneously and independently name prices. Demand is allocated to the low-price producer(s), who *then* produce (up to) the demand they encounter. Any unsatisfied demand goes to the second lowest price producer(s), and so on.

There are two differences in these stories: how price is determined (by an auctioneer in Cournot and by price "competition" in Bertrand), and when production is supposed to take place. We demonstrate here that the Bertrand outcome requires both price competition and production after demand determination. Specifically, consider the following

---

* Harvard University.

** University of Chicago.

The authors are grateful to an anonymous referee and the Editorial Board for helpful comments. Professor Kreps' research is supported by NSF Grant SES-8006407 to Stanford University and Office of Naval Research Contract N00014-77-C-0518 to Yale University. Professor Scheinkman's research is supported by NSF Grant SES-7926726 to the University of Chicago.

game between expected profit maximizing producers: In a first stage, producers decide independently and simultaneously how much they will produce, and this production takes place. They then bring these quantities to market, each learns how much the other produced, and they engage in Bertrand-like price competition: They simultaneously and independently name prices and demand is allocated in Bertrand fashion, with the proviso that one cannot satisfy more demand than one produced for in the first stage.

In this two-stage game, it is easy to produce one equilibrium. Let each firm choose the Cournot quantity. If each firm does so, each subsequently names the Cournot price. If, on the other hand, either chooses some quantity other than the Cournot quantity, its rival names price zero in the second stage. Since any defection in the first stage will result in one facing the demand residual from the Cournot quantity, and since the Cournot quantity is the best response to this residual demand function, this is clearly an equilibrium. What is somewhat more surprising is that (for the very special parameterization above and for a large class of other symmetric parameterizations) the Cournot outcome is the unique equilibrium outcome. Moreover, there is a perfect equilibrium that yields this outcome. (The strategies above constitute an imperfect equilibrium.) This note is devoted to the establishment of these facts.

One way to interpret this result is to see our two-stage game as a mechanism to generate Cournot-like outcomes that dispenses with the mythical auctioneer. In fact, an equivalent way of thinking about our game is as follows: *Capacities* are set in the first stage by the two producers. Demand is then determined by Bertrand-like price competition, and production takes place at zero cost, subject to capacity constraints generated by the first-stage decisions. It is easy to see that given capacities for the two producers, equilibrium behavior in the second, Bertrand-like, stage will not always lead to a price that exhausts capacity. But when those given capacities correspond to the Cournot output levels, in the second stage each firm names the Cournot price. And for the entire game, fixing capacities at the Cournot output levels is the unique equilibrium outcome. This yields a more satisfactory description of a game that generates Cournot outcomes. It is this language that we shall use subsequently.

This reinterpretation in terms of capacities suggests a variant of the game, in which both capacity creation (before price competition and realization of demand) and production (to demand) are costly. Our analysis easily generalizes to this case, and we state results for it at the end of this article.

Our intention in putting forward this example is not to give a model that accurately portrays any important duopoly. (We are both on record as contending that "reality" has more than one, and quite probably more than two, stages, and that multiperiod effects greatly change the outcomes of duopoly games.) Our intention instead is to emphasize that solutions to oligopoly games depend on both the strategic variables that firms are assumed to employ and on the context (game form) in which those variables are employed. The timing of decisions and information reception are as important as the nature of the decisions. It is witless to argue in the abstract whether Cournot or Bertrand was correct; this is an empirical question or one that is resolved only by looking at the details of the context within which the competitive interaction takes place.

2. Model formulation

■ We consider two identical firms facing a two-stage competitive situation. These firms produce perfectly substitutable commodities for which the market demand function is given by $P(x)$ (price as a function of quantity x) and $D(p) = P^{-1}(p)$ (demand as a function of price p).

The two-stage competition runs as follows. At the first stage, the firms simultaneously and independently *build capacity* for subsequent production. Capacity level x means that up to x units can be produced subsequently at zero cost. The cost to firm i of (initially) installing capacity level x_i is $b(x_i)$.

After this first stage, each firm learns how much capacity its opponent installed. Then the firms simultaneously and independently name prices p_i chosen from the interval $[0, P(0)]$. If $p_1 < p_2$, then firm 1 sells

$$z_1 = \min (x_1, D(p_1)) \tag{1}$$

units of the good at price p_1 (and at zero additional cost), for a net profit of $p_1 z_1 - b(x_1)$. And if $p_1 < p_2$, firm 2 sells

$$z_2 = \min (x_2, \max (0, D(p_2) - x_1)) \tag{2}$$

units at price p_2 for a net profit of $p_2 z_2 - b(x_2)$. If $p_2 < p_1$, symmetric formulas apply. Finally, if $p_2 = p_1$, then firm i sells

$$z_i = \min \left(x_i, \frac{D(p_i)}{2} + \max \left(0, \frac{D(p_i)}{2} - x_j \right) \right) = \min \left(x_i, \max \left(\frac{D(p_i)}{2}, D(p_i) - x_j \right) \right) \tag{3}$$

at price p_i, for net profits equal to $p_i z_i - b(x_i)$. (In (3), and for the remainder of the article, subscript j means *not* i. Note the use of the *capacity* and *subsequent production* terminology.)

Each firm seeks to maximize the expectation of its profits, and the above structure is common knowledge between the firms. At this point the reader will notice the particular rationing rule we chose. Customers buy first from the cheapest supplier, and income effects are absent. (Alternatively, this is the rationing rule that maximizes consumer surplus. Its use is not innocuous—see Beckmann (1965) and Levitan and Shubik (1972).)

The following assumptions are made:

Assumption 1. The function $P(x)$ is strictly positive on some bounded interval $(0, X)$, on which it is twice-continuously differentiable, strictly decreasing, and concave. For $x \geq X$, $P(x) = 0$.

Assumption 2. The cost function b, with domain $[0, \infty)$ and range $[0, \infty)$, is twice-continuously differentiable, convex, and satisfies $b(0) = 0$ and $b'(0) > 0$. To avoid trivialities, $b'(0) < P(0)$—production at some level is profitable.

3. Preliminaries: Cournot competition

■ Before analyzing the two-stage competition formulated above, it will be helpful to have on hand some implications of the assumptions and some facts about Cournot competition between the two firms. Imagine that the firms engage in Cournot competition with (identical) cost function c. Assume that c is (as b), twice-continuously differentiable, convex, and nondecreasing on $[0, \infty)$. Note that from Assumption 1, for every $y < D(0)$ the function $x \rightarrow xP(x + y) - c(x)$ is strictly concave on $[0, y - x)$. Define

$$r_c(y) = \underset{0 \leq x \leq X-y}{\mathrm{argmax}}\ xP(x + y) - c(x).$$

That is, $r_c(y)$ is the *optimal response function* in Cournot competition if one's rival puts y on the market. It is the solution in x of

$$P(x + y) + xP'(x + y) - c'(x) = 0. \tag{4}$$

Lemma 1. (a) For every c as above, r_c is nonincreasing in y, and r_c is continuously differentiable and strictly decreasing over the range where it is strictly positive.
(b) $r'_c \geq -1$, with strict inequality for y such that $r_c(y) > 0$, so that $x + r_c(x)$ is nondecreasing in x.

(c) If c and d are two cost functions such that $c' > d'$, then $r_c < r_d$.

(d) If $y > r_c(y)$, then $r_c(r_c(y)) < y$.

Proof. (a) For any y, we have

$$P(r_c(y) + y) + r_c(y)P'(r_c(y) + y) - c'(r_c(y)) = 0.$$

Increase y in the above equation while leaving $r_c(y)$ fixed. This decreases the (positive) first term and decreases the second (it becomes more negative). Thus the concavity of $xP(x + y) - c(x)$ in x implies that, to restore equality, we must decrease $r_c(y)$. Where P is strictly positive, the decrease in $r_c(y)$ must also be strict. And the differentiability of r_c follows in the usual fashion from the smoothness of P and c.

For (b), increase y by h and decrease $r_c(y)$ by h in the equation displayed above. The first (positive) term stays the same, the second increases (becomes less negative), and the third increases. Thus the left-hand side, at $y + h$ and $r_c(y) - h$, is positive. The strict concavity of the profit function ensures, therefore, that $r_c(y + h) > r_c(y) - h$ (with the obvious qualifications about values y for which $r_c(y) = 0$).

For (c) and (d), arguments similar to (b) are easily constructed.

Because of (d), the picture of duopoly Cournot competition is as in Figure 1. For every cost function c, there is a unique Cournot equilibrium, with each firm bringing forward some quantity $x^*(c)$. Moreover, for c and d as in part (c) of the lemma, it is clear that $x^*(c) < x^*(d)$. In the next section, the case where c is identically zero plays an important role. To save on subscripts and arguments, we shall write $r(y)$ for $r_0(y)$ and x^* for $x^*(0)$. Also, we shall write $R(y)$ for $r(y)P(r(y) + y)$, the revenue associated with the best response to y when costs are identically zero.

FIGURE 1

THE PICTURE OF COURNOT COMPETITION UNDER THE ASSUMPTIONS OF THE MODEL

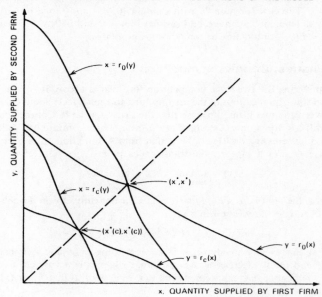

(The astute reader will notice that the analysis to follow does not require the full power of Assumptions 1 and 2. All that is really required is that, for each $y < D(0)$, the functions $x \to xP(x + y) - b(x)$ and $x \to xP(x + y)$ are strictly quasi-concave (on $(0, X - y)$), and that r_b and r appear as in Figure 1. The former does require that $p \to pD(p)$ is strictly concave where it is positive, but this is not quite sufficient. In any event, we shall continue to proceed on the basis of the assumptions given, as they do simplify the arguments that follow.)

4. The capacity-constrained subgames

■ Suppose that in the first stage the firms install capacities x_1 and x_2, respectively. Beginning from the point where (x_1, x_2) becomes common knowledge, we have a *proper subgame* (using the terminology of Selten (1965)). We call this the (x_1, x_2) capacity-constrained subgame—it is simply the Edgeworth (1897) "constrained-capacity" variation on Bertrand competition. It is not *a priori* obvious that each capacity-constrained subgame has an equilibrium, as payoffs are discontinuous in actions. But it can be shown that the discontinuities are of the "right" kind. For subgames where $x_1 = x_2$, the existence of a subgame equilibrium is established by Levitan and Shubik (1972) in cases where demand is linear and marginal costs are constant. Also for the case of linear demand and constant marginal costs, Dasgupta and Maskin (1982) establish the existence of subgame equilibria for all pairs of x_1 and x_2, and their methodology applies to all the cases that we consider. (We shall show how to "compute" the subgame equilibria below.)

The basic fact that we wish to establish is that for each (x_1, x_2), the associated subgame has unique expected revenues in equilibrium. (It is very probably true that each subgame has a unique equilibrium, but we do not need this and shall not attempt to show it.) Moreover, we shall give formulas for these expected revenues.

For the remainder of this section, fix a pair of capacities (x_1, x_2) and an equilibrium for the (x_1, x_2) subgame. Let $\bar{p}_i$ be the supremum of the support of the prices named by firm i; that is, $\bar{p}_i = \inf \{p\text{:firm } i \text{ names less than } p \text{ with probability one}\}$. And let p_i be the infimum of the support. Note that if $\min_i x_i \geq D(0)$, then, as in the usual Bertrand game with no capacity constraints, $\bar{p}_i = p_i = 0$. And if $\min_i x_i = 0$, we have the monopoly case. Thus we are left with the case where $0 < \min_i x_i < D(0)$.

Lemma 2. For each i, $p_i \geq P(x_1 + x_2)$.

Proof. By naming a price p less than $P(x_1 + x_2)$, firm i nets at most px_i. By naming $P(x_1 + x_2)$, firm i nets at worst $P(x_1 + x_2)(x_1 + x_2 - x_j) = P(x_1 + x_2)x_i$.

Lemma 3. If $\bar{p}_1 = \bar{p}_2$ and each is named with positive probability, then

$$p_i = \bar{p}_i = P(x_1 + x_2) \quad \text{and} \quad x_i \leq r(x_j), \quad \text{for} \quad \text{both} \quad i = 1 \quad \text{and} \quad i = 2.$$

Proof. Suppose that $\bar{p}_1 = \bar{p}_2$ and each is charged with positive probability. Without loss of generality, assume $x_1 \geq x_2$, and suppose that $\bar{p}_1 = \bar{p}_2 > P(x_1 + x_2)$. By naming a price slightly less than $\bar{p}_1$, firm 1 strictly improves its revenues over what it gets by naming $\bar{p}_1$. (With positive probability, it sells strictly more, while the loss due to the lower price is small.) Thus $\bar{p}_1 = \bar{p}_2 \leq P(x_1 + x_2)$. By Lemma 2, we know that $\bar{p}_i = p_i = P(x_1 + x_2)$ for $i = 1, 2$.

By naming a higher price p, firm i would obtain revenue $(D(p) - x_i)p$, or, letting $x = D(p) - x_j$, $xP(x + x_j)$. This is maximized at $x = r(x_j)$, so that were $r(x_j) < x_i$, we would not have an equilibrium.

Lemma 4. If $x_i \leq r(x_j)$ for $i = 1, 2$, then a (subgame) equilibrium is for each firm to name $P(x_1 + x_2)$ with probability one.

Proof. The proof of Lemma 3 shows that naming a price greater than $P(x_1 + x_2)$ will not profit either firm in this case. (Recall that $xP(x + x_j)$ is strictly concave.) And there is no incentive to name a lower price, as each firm is selling its full capacity at the equilibrium price.

Lemma 5. Suppose that either $\bar{p}_1 > \bar{p}_2$, or that $\bar{p}_1 = \bar{p}_2$ and $\bar{p}_2$ is not named with positive probability. Then:

(a) $\bar{p}_1 = P(r(x_2) + x_2)$ and the equilibrium revenue of firm 1 is $R(x_2)$;
(b) $x_1 > r(x_2)$;
(c) $p_1 = p_2$, and neither is named with positive probability;
(d) $x_1 \geq x_2$; and
(e) the equilibrium revenue of firm 2 is uniquely determined by (x_1, x_2) and is at least $(x_2/x_1)R(x_2)$ and at most $R(x_2)$.

Proof. For (a) and (b): Consider the function

$$\Xi(p) = p \cdot [\min (x_1, \max (0, D(p) - x_2))].$$

In words, $\Xi(p)$ is the revenue accrued by firm 1 if it names p and it is undersold by its rival. Under the hypothesis of this lemma, firm 1, by naming $\bar{p}_1$, nets precisely $\Xi(\bar{p}_1)$, as it is certain to be undersold. By naming any price $p > \bar{p}_1$, firm 1 will net precisely $\Xi(p)$. If firm 1 names a price $p < \bar{p}_1$, it will net at least $\Xi(p)$. Thus, if we have an equilibrium, $\Xi(p)$ must be maximized at $\bar{p}_1$.

We must dispose of the case $x_2 \geq D(0)$. Since (by assumption) $D(0) > \min_i x_i$, $x_2 \geq D(0)$ would imply $D(0) > x_1$. Thus, in equilibrium, firm 2 will certainly obtain strictly positive expected revenue. And, therefore, in equilibrium, $\bar{p}_2 > 0$. But then firm 1 must obtain strictly positive expected revenue. And if $x_2 \geq D(0)$, then $\Xi(\bar{p}_1) = 0$. That is, $x_2 \geq D(0)$ is incompatible with the hypothesis of this lemma.

In maximizing $\Xi(p)$, one would never choose p such that $D(p) - x_2 > x_1$ or such that $D(p) < x_2$. Thus, the relevant value of p lies in the interval $[P(x_1 + x_2), P(x_2)]$. For each p in this interval, there is a corresponding level of x, namely $x(p) = D(p) - x_2$, such that $\Xi(p) = x(p)P(x(p) + x_2)$. Note that $x(p)$ runs in the interval $[0, x_1]$. But we know that

$$\operatorname*{argmax}_{x(p)\in[0, x_1]} x(p)P(x(p) + x_2) = r(x_2) \wedge x_1,$$

by the strict concavity of $xP(x + x_2)$. If the capacity constraint x_1 is binding (even weakly), then $\bar{p}_1 = P(x_1 + x_2)$, and Lemma 2 implies that we are in the case of Lemma 3, thus contradicting the hypothesis of this lemma. Hence it must be the case that the constraint does not bind, or $r(x_2) < x_1$ (which is (b)), $\bar{p}_1 = P(r(x_2) + x_2)$, and the equilibrium revenue of firm 1 is $R(x_2)$ (which is (a)).

For (c): Suppose that $p_i < p_j$. By naming p_i, firm i nets $p_i(D(p_i) \wedge x_i)$. Increasing this to any level $p \in (p_i, p_j)$ nets $p(D(p) \wedge x_i)$. Thus, we have an equilibrium only if $D(p_i) < x_i$ and p_i is the monopoly price. (By the strict concavity of $xP(x)$, moving from p_i in the direction of the monopoly price will increase revenue on the margin.) That is, $p_i = P(r(0))$. But $p_i < \bar{p}_1 = P(r(x_2) + x_2) < P(r(0))$, which would be a contradiction. Thus $p_1 = p_2$. We denote this common value by p in the sequel. This is the first part of (c).

For the second part of (c), note first that $p > P(x_1 + x_2)$. For if $p = P(x_1 + x_2)$, then by naming (close to) p, firm 1 would make at most $P(x_1 + x_2)x_1$. Since $x_1 > r(x_2)$ and the equilibrium revenue of firm 1 is $R(x_2)$, this is impossible.

Suppose that the firm with (weakly) less capacity named p with positive probability. Then the firm with higher capacity could, by naming a price slightly less than p, strictly increase its expected revenue. (It sells strictly more with positive probability, at a slightly lower price.) Thus, the firm with weakly less capacity names p with zero probability. Since $\underline{p}$ is the infimum of the support of the prices named by the lower capacity firm, this firm must therefore name prices arbitrarily close to *and above* $\underline{p}$. But if its rival named $\underline{p}$ with positive probability, the smaller capacity firm would do better (since $\underline{p} > P(x_1 + x_2)$) to name a price just below $\underline{p}$ than it would to name a price just above $\underline{p}$. Hence, neither firm can name $\underline{p}$ with positive probability.

For (d) and (e): By (c), the equilibrium revenue of firm i must be $\underline{p}(D(\underline{p}) \wedge x_i)$. We know that $\underline{p} < \bar{p}_1 = P(x_2 + r(x_2))$, so that $D(\underline{p}) > D(P(x_2 + r(x_2))) = x_2 + r(x_2)$, and thus $D(\underline{p}) > x_2$. Hence, firm 2 certainly gets $\underline{p}x_2$ in equilibrium. Firm 1 gets no more than $\underline{p}x_1$, so that the bounds in part (e) are established as soon as (d) is shown.

Suppose that $x_2 > x_1$. Then $D(\underline{p}) > x_1$, and firm 1's equilibrium revenue is $\underline{p}x_1$. We already know that it is also $R(x_2)$, so that we would have $\underline{p} = R(x_2)/x_1$, and firm 2 nets $R(x_2)x_2/x_1$. By naming price $P(r(x_1) + x_1)$ $(>\underline{p}_1 = P(r(x_2) + x_2))$, firm 2 will net $R(x_1)$. We shall have a contradiction, therefore, if we show that $x_1 > r(x_2)$ implies $x_1 R(x_1) > x_2 R(x_2)$.

Let $\Theta(x) = xR(x) = xr(x)P(r(x) + x)$. We have

$$\Theta'(x) = r(x)P(r(x) + x) + xr'(x)P(r(x) + x) + xr(x)P'(r(x) + x)(r'(x) + 1)$$

$$= (r(x) - x)P(r(x) + x) + x(r'(x) + 1)(P(r(x) + x) + r(x)P'(r(x) + x)).$$

The last term is zero by the definition of $r(x)$, so that we have

$$\Theta'(x) = (r(x) - x)P(r(x) + x).$$

Thus $x_2 R(x_2) - x_1 R(x_1) = \Theta(x_2) - \Theta(x_1) = \int_{x_1}^{x_2} (r(x) - x)P(r(x) + x)dx$. The integrand is positive for $x < x^*$ and strictly negative for $x > x^*$. We would like to show that the integral is negative, so that the worst case (in terms of our objective) is that in which $x_1 < x^*$ and x_2 is as small as possible. Since $x_1 > r(x_2)$, for every $x_1 < x^*$ the worst case is where x_2 is just a bit larger than $r^{-1}(x_1)$. We shall thus have achieved our objective (of contradicting $x_2 > x_1$, by showing that the integral above is strictly negative) if we show that for all $x < x^*$, $\Theta(x) - \Theta(r^{-1}(x)) \geq 0$.

But $\Theta(x) - \Theta(r^{-1}(x)) = xr(x)P(x + r(x)) - r^{-1}(x)xP(r^{-1}(x) + x)$. This is nonnegative if and only if $r(x)P(x + r(x)) - r^{-1}(x)P(r^{-1}(x) + x) \geq 0$, which is certainly true, since $r(x)$ is the best response to x.

Lemma 6. If $x_1 \geq x_2$ and $x_1 > r(x_2)$, there is a (mixed strategy) equilibrium for the subgame in which all the conditions and conclusions of Lemma 5 hold. Moreover, this equilibrium has the following properties. Each firm names prices according to continuous and strictly increasing distribution functions over an (coincident) interval, except that firm 1 names the uppermost price with positive probability whenever $x_1 > x_2$. And if we let $\Psi_i(p)$ be the probability distribution function for the strategy of firm i, then $\Psi_1(p) \leq \Psi_2(p)$: firm 1's strategy stochastically dominates the strategy of firm 2, with strict inequality if $x_1 > x_2$.

Remarks. The astute reader will note that the first sentence is actually a corollary to the previous lemmas and to the (as yet unproven) assertion that every subgame has an equilibrium. The actual construction of an equilibrium is unnecessary for our later analysis, and the casual reader may wish to omit it on first reading. It is, however, of sufficient independent interest to warrant presentation. In the course of this construction, we obtain the second part of the lemma, which is also noteworthy. At first glance, it might be thought that firm 1, having the larger capacity, would profit more by underselling its rival, and therefore it would name the (stochastically) lower prices. But (as is usual with equilibrium logic) this is backwards: Each firm randomizes in a way that keeps the other firm indifferent among its strategies. Because firm 1 has the larger capacity, firm 2 is more "at risk" in terms of being undersold, and thus firm 1 must be "less aggressive."

Proof. Refer to Figure 2. There are five functions depicted there: $pD(p)$, $p(D(p) - x_2)$, $p(D(p) - x_1)$, px_1, and px_2. Note that:

(i) $px_1 = p(D(p) - x_2)$ and $px_2 = p(D(p) - x_1)$ at the same point, namely $P(x_1 + x_2)$.

(ii) $px_1 = pD(p)$ at the point where $p(D(p) - x_1)$ vanishes, and similarly for 2.

(iii) The first three functions are maximized at $P(r(0))$, $P(r(x_2) + x_2)$, and $P(r(x_1) + x_1)$, respectively.

(iv) Because P is concave, the first three functions are strictly concave on the range where they are positive. And every ray from the origin of the form px crosses each of these three functions at most once. (The latter is a simple consequence of the fact that $D(p)$ is decreasing.)

Now find the value $p = P(r(x_2) + x_2)$. This is $\bar{p}_1$. Follow the horizontal dashed line back to the function $p(D(p) \wedge x_1)$. We have drawn this intersection at a point p where $D(p) > x_1$, but we have no guarantee that this will happen. In any event, the level of p at this intersection is $\underline{p}$. Follow the vertical dashed line down to the ray px_2. The height $\underline{p}x_2$ will be the equilibrium revenue of firm 2. Note that even if the first intersection occurred at a point where $x_1 > D(p)$, this second intersection would be at a level $\underline{p}$ where $D(\underline{p}) > x_2$, since $x_2 = D(p)$ at $P(x_2)$, which is to the right of $P(r(x_2) + x_2)$. Also, note that these intersections occur to the right of $P(x_1 + x_2)$, since $R(x_2) > x_1P(x_1 + x_2)$.

Suppose that firm 1 charges a price $p \in [\underline{p}, \bar{p}_1]$. If we assume that firm 2 does not charge this price p with positive probability, then the expected revenue to firm 1 is

$$E_1(p) = \Phi_2(p)p(D(p) - x_2) + (1 - \Phi_2(p))p(D(p) \wedge x_1),$$

where Φ_2 is the distribution function of firm 2's strategy. A similar calculation for firm 2 yields

$$E_2(p) = \Phi_1(p)p[\max (D(p) - x_1, 0)] + (1 - \Phi_1(p))px_2.$$

(Note that for $p \in [\underline{p}, \bar{p}_1]$, we know that $D(p) - x_2 > 0$.)

Solve the equations $E_1(p) = R(x_2)$ ($= \underline{p}(D(\underline{p}) \wedge x_1)$) and $E_2(p) = \underline{p}x_2$ in $\Phi_2(p)$ and $\Phi_1(p)$, calling the solutions $\Psi_2(p)$ and $\Psi_1(p)$, respectively. Note that:

(v) Both functions are continuous and begin at level zero.

FIGURE 2

DETERMINING THE SUBGAME EQUILIBRIUM

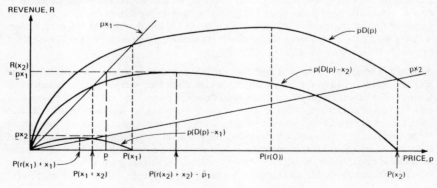

(vi) The function $\Psi_2(p)$ is strictly increasing and has value one at $\bar{p}_1$. To see this, note that $p(D(p) - x_2)$ is getting closer to, and $p(D(p) \wedge x_1)$ is getting further from, $R(x_2)$ as p increases. And $R(x_2) = \bar{p}_1(D(\bar{p}_1) - x_2)$.

(vii) The function $\Psi_1(p)$ is strictly increasing, everywhere less than or equal to one, and strictly less than one if $x_1 > x_2$. (If $x_1 = x_2$, then it is identical to $\Psi_2(p)$.) To see this, note first that for $p \geq P(x_1)$, $\Psi_1(p) = 1 - \underline{p}/p$. And for values of p in the range $\underline{p} \leq p < P(x_1)$, we have $R(x_2) = \underline{p}x_1$, and, thus,

$$\Psi_1(p) = \frac{(\underline{p} - p)x_2}{p(D(p) - x_1 - x_2)},$$

and

$$\Psi_2(p) = \frac{(\underline{p} - p)x_1}{p(D(p) - x_1 - x_2)}.$$

That is, for p between $\underline{p}$ and $P(x_1)$, $\Psi_1 = x_2\Psi_2/x_1$. Noting step (vi), the result is obvious.

(viii) $\Psi_1(p) \leq \Psi_2(p)$ for all p. This is immediate from the argument above for p in the range $\underline{p} \leq p < P(x_1)$. For $p \geq P(x_1)$, note that $pD(p)$ is receding from $R(x_2)$ more quickly than px_2 is receding from $\underline{p}x_2$ [since $p(D(p) - x_2)$ is still increasing], and $p(D(p) - x_2)$ is increasing, hence approaching $R(x_2)$ more quickly than the constant function zero is approaching $\underline{p}x_2$.

(ix) $\underline{p}x_2 \geq R(x_1)$. To see this, note first that $\underline{p}x_1 \geq R(x_2)$. Thus $\underline{p}x_2 \geq x_2R(x_2)/x_1$. To get the desired result, then, it suffices to show that $\bar{R}(x_1) \leq x_2R(x_2)/x_1$, or $x_1R(x_1) \leq x_2R(x_2)$ (with strict inequality if $x_1 > x_2$.) Recall that $x_1 > x_2$. If $x_2 \geq x^*$, then the result follows easily from the formula $x_1R(x_1) - x_2R(x_2) = \int_{x_2}^{x_1} (r(x) - x)P(r(x) + x)dx$. If $x_2 < x^*$, then $x_2 > r(x_1)$ (since $(x_1 > r(x_2))$), and the argument from the previous lemma applies.

Putting all these points together, we see that we have an equilibrium of the desired type if firm 1 names prices according to the distribution Ψ_1, and firm 2 names them according to Ψ_2. Each firm is (by construction) indifferent among those strategies that

FIGURE 3

THE DIFFERENT TYPES OF SUBGAME EQUILIBRIA

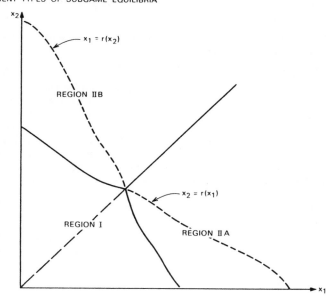

are in the support of their (respective) distribution functions. The levels of $\bar{p}_1$ and $\underline{p}$ are selected so that firm 1 has no incentive to name a price above the first or below the second. Since firm 2 gets no more than $R(x_1)$, it has no incentive to go above $\bar{p}_1$; neither (by construction) will it gain by naming a price below $\underline{p}$.

Since the construction of the equilibrium took us rather far afield of our main objective, we end this section by compiling the results established above that are important to subsequent analysis:

Proposition 1. (Refer to Figure 3.) In terms of the subgame equilibria, there are three regions of interest.

(a) If $x_i \leq r(x_j)$ for both $i = 1$ and $i = 2$ (which is labelled as region I in Figure 3), the unique equilibrium has both firms naming price $P(x_1 + x_2)$ with certainty. The equilibrium revenues are, therefore, $x_i P(x_1 + x_2)$ for firm i.

(b) If $x_1 \geq x_2$ and $x_1 > r(x_2)$ (labelled region IIA in Figure 3), then, in equilibrium, firm 1 has expected revenue $R(x_2)$, and firm 2 has expected revenue determined by (x_1, x_2) and somewhere between $R(x_2)$ and $x_2 R(x_2)/x_1$. If $x_2 < D(0)$, the equilibrium is the randomized one constructed in Lemma 6; if $x_2 \geq D(0)$, both firms net zero and name price zero with certainty.

(c) If $x_2 \geq x_1$ and $x_2 > r(x_1)$ (labelled region IIB in Figure 3), then, in equilibrium, firm 2 has expected revenue $R(x_1)$, and firm 1 has expected revenue determined by (x_1, x_2) and somewhere between $R(x_1)$ and $x_1 R(x_1)/x_2$. Similar remarks apply concerning $x_1 \lessgtr D(0)$ as appear in (b).

(d) The expected revenue functions are continuous functions of x_1 and x_2.

4. Equilibria in the full game

■ We can now show that in the full game there is a unique equilibrium outcome. We state this formally:

Proposition 2. In the two-stage game, there is a unique equilibrium outcome, namely the Cournot outcome: $x_1 = x_2 = x^*(b)$, and $p_1 = p_2 = P(2x^*(b))$.

Proof. The proposition is established in four steps.

Step 1: preliminaries. Consider any equilibrium. As part of this equilibrium firm i chooses capacity according to some probability measure μ_i with support $S_i \subseteq R$. Let us denote by $\Phi_i(x_1, x_2)$ the (possibly mixed) strategy used by firm i in the (x_1, x_2) subgame. Except for a $\mu_1 \times \mu_2$ null subset of $S_1 \times S_2$, $\Phi_i(x_1, x_2)$ must be an optimal response to $\Phi_j(x_1, x_2)$. That is, $\Omega_i = \{(x_1, x_2): \Phi_i(x_1, x_2)$ is an optimal response to $\Phi_j(x_1, x_2)\}$ is such that $(\mu_1 \times \mu_2)(\Omega_1 \cap \Omega_2) = 1$. (For subgame perfect equilibria $\Omega_1 \cap \Omega_2 = R^2$, but we do not wish to restrict attention to such equilibria.) In particular, if $E(x_i) = \{x_j:(x_1, x_2) \in \Omega_1 \cap \Omega_2\}$ and $\hat{X}_i = \{x_i \in S_i: \mu_j(E(x_i)) = 1\}$, then $\mu_i(\hat{X}_i) = 1$. Let π_i denote the expected profit of firm i in this equilibrium and $\pi_i(x_i)$ the expected profit when capacity x_i is built. If $X_i = \{x_i \in \hat{X}_i: \pi_i(x_i) = \pi_i\}$, then again $\mu_i(X_i) = 1$. Let $\bar{x}_i$ and $\underline{x}_i$ denote the supremum and infimum of X_i. Because the subgame equilibrium revenue functions are continuous in x_1 and x_2, and because revenues are bounded in any event, $\bar{x}_i$ and $\underline{x}_i$ must yield expected profit π_i if firm j uses its equilibrium quantity strategy μ_j and firms subsequently use subgame equilibrium price strategies.

Assume (without loss of generality) that $\bar{x}_1 \geq \bar{x}_2$.

Step 2: $\bar{x}_1 \geq r_b(\underline{x}_2)$. Suppose contrariwise that $\bar{x}_1 < r_b(\underline{x}_2)$. For every $x_1 < \bar{x}_1$, the subgame equilibrium revenue of firm 2, if it installs capacity $\underline{x}_2$, is $\underline{x}_2 P(x_1 + \underline{x}_2)$. That is,

$$\pi_2 = \int_{\underline{x}_1}^{\bar{x}_1} (\underline{x}_2 P(x_1 + \underline{x}_2) - b(\underline{x}_2)) \mu_1(dx_1).$$

If firm 2 increases its capacity slightly, to say, $x_2 + \epsilon$, where it remains true that $\bar{x}_1 < r_b(x_2 + \epsilon)$, then the worst that can happen to firm 2 (for each level of x_1) is that firm 2 will net $(\underline{x}_2 + \epsilon)P(x_1 + \underline{x}_2 + \epsilon) - b(\underline{x}_2 + \epsilon)$. Since for all $x_1 < \bar{x}_1$, $\underline{x}_2 + \epsilon < r_b(x_1)$, it follows that $(\underline{x}_2 + \epsilon)P(x_1 + \underline{x}_2 + \epsilon) - b(\underline{x}_2 + \epsilon) > \underline{x}_2 P(x_1 + \underline{x}_2) - b(\underline{x}_2)$, and this variation will raise firm 2's profits above π_2. This is a contradiction.

Step 3: $\bar{x}_1 \le r_b(\bar{x}_2)$. Suppose contrariwise that $\bar{x}_1 > r_b(\bar{x}_2)$. By building $\bar{x}_1$, firm 1 nets revenue (as a function of x_2) $R(x_2)$ if $\bar{x}_1 > r(x_2)$ and $\bar{x}_1 P(\bar{x}_1 + x_2)$ if $\bar{x}_1 \le r(x_2)$, assuming that a subgame equilibrium ensues. That is,

$$\pi_1 = \int_{(r^{-1}(\bar{x}_1),\bar{x}_2]} (R(x_2) - b(\bar{x}_1))\mu_2(dx_2) + \int_{[\underline{x}_2, r^{-1}(\bar{x}_1)]} (\bar{x}_1 P(\bar{x}_1 + x_2) - b(\bar{x}_1))\mu_2(dx_2). \quad (5)$$

Consider what happens to firm 1's expected profits if it lowers its capacity from $\bar{x}_1$ to just a bit less—say, to $\bar{x}_1 - \epsilon$, where $\bar{x}_1 - \epsilon > r_b(\bar{x}_2)$. Then the worst that can happen to firm 1 is that firm 2 (after installing capacity according to μ_2) names price zero. This would leave firm 1 with residual demand $D(p) - x_2$ (where $x_2 \le \bar{x}_2$). Firm 1 can still accrue revenue $R(x_2)$ if $\bar{x}_1 - \epsilon > r(x_2)$ and $(\bar{x}_1 - \epsilon)P(x_2 + \bar{x}_1 - \epsilon)$ otherwise. Thus, the expected profits of firm 1 in this variation are at least

$$\int_{[r^{-1}(\bar{x}_1 - \epsilon),\bar{x}_2]} (R(x_2) - b(\bar{x}_1 - \epsilon))\mu_2(dx_2)$$

$$+ \int_{[\underline{x}_2, r^{-1}(\bar{x}_1 - \epsilon))} ((\bar{x}_1 - \epsilon)P(x_2 + \bar{x}_1 - \epsilon) - b(\bar{x}_1 - \epsilon))\mu_2(dx_2). \quad (6)$$

We shall complete this step by showing that for small enough ϵ, (6) exceeds (5), thereby contradicting the assumption.

The difference (6) minus (5) can be analyzed by breaking the integrals into three intervals: $[r^{-1}(\bar{x}_1 - \epsilon), \bar{x}_2]$, $[\underline{x}_2, r^{-1}(\bar{x}_1)]$, and $(r^{-1}(\bar{x}_1), r^{-1}(\bar{x}_1 - \epsilon))$. Over the first interval, the difference in integrands is

$$(R(x_2) - b(\bar{x}_1)) - (R(x_2) - b(\bar{x}_1 - \epsilon)) = \epsilon b'(\bar{x}_1) + o(\epsilon).$$

Note well that $b'(\bar{x}_1)$ is strictly positive. Over the second interval, the difference in integrands is

$$((\bar{x}_1 - \epsilon)P(\bar{x}_1 - \epsilon + x_2) - b(\bar{x}_1 - \epsilon)) - (\bar{x}_1 P(\bar{x}_1 + x_2) - b(\bar{x}_1))$$

$$= \epsilon(b'(\bar{x}_1) - \bar{x}_1 P'(\bar{x}_1) - P(\bar{x}_1 + x_2)) + o(\epsilon).$$

Here the term premultiplied by ϵ is strictly positive except possibly at the lower boundary (where it is nonnegative), since by step 2, $\bar{x}_1 \ge r_b(\underline{x}_2) \ge r_b(x_2)$. Over the third interval, the difference in the integrands is no more than $O(\epsilon)$, because of the continuity of $xP(x + x_2) - b(x)$. Thus as ϵ goes to zero, the integral over the first interval will be strictly positive $O(\epsilon)$ if μ_2 puts any mass on $(r^{-1}(\bar{x}_1), \bar{x}_2]$. The integral over the second interval will be strictly positive $O(\epsilon)$ if μ_2 puts any mass on $(r_b^{-1}(\bar{x}_1), r^{-1}(\bar{x}_1)]$. The integral over the third interval must be $o(\epsilon)$, since it is the integral of a term $O(\epsilon)$ integrated over a vanishing interval. The hypothesis $\bar{x}_1 > r_b(\bar{x}_2)$ implies that μ_2 puts positive mass on either $(r_b^{-1}(\bar{x}_1), r^{-1}(\bar{x}_1)]$ or on $(r^{-1}(\bar{x}_1), \bar{x}_2]$ (or both). Hence for small enough ϵ, the difference between (6) and (5) will be strictly positive. This is the desired contradiction.

Step 4. The rest is easy. Steps 2 and 3 imply that $\bar{x}_1 = r_b(\bar{x}_2) = r_b(\underline{x}_2)$, and hence that firm 2 uses a pure strategy in the first round. But then firm 1's best response in the first round is the pure strategy $r_b(x_2)$. And firm 2's strategy, which must be a best response to this, must satisfy $x_2 = r_b(x_1) = r_b(r_b(x_2))$. This implies that $x_2 = x^*(b)$, and, therefore, $x_1 = r_b(x^*(b)) = x^*(b)$. Finally, the two firms will each name price $P(2x^*(b))$ in the second round (as long as both firms produce $x^*(b)$ in the first round, which they will do with probability one); this follows immediately from Step 1 and Proposition 1.

5. The case $b \equiv 0$

■ When $b \equiv 0$ it is easy to check that the Cournot outcome is an equilibrium. In this case, however, there are other equilibria as well. If imperfect equilibria are counted, then one equilibrium has $x_1 = x_2 = D(0)$ (or anything larger) and $p_1 \equiv p_2 \equiv 0$. Note well that each firm names price zero regardless of what capacities are installed. This is clearly an equilibrium, but it is imperfect, because if, say, firm 1 installed a small capacity and the subgame equilibrium ensued, each would make positive profits.

There are also other perfect equilibria, although it takes a bit more work to establish them. Let $x_1 \geq D(0)$. If firm 2 installs capacity greater than $D(0)$, it will net zero profits (assuming a subgame equilibrium follows). If it installs $x_2 < D(0)$, then its profits (in a perfect equilibrium) are $\underline{p}(x_2)x_2$, where $p(x_2) \leq p(0)$ solves the equation $\underline{p}(x_2)D(\underline{p}(x_2)) = R(x_2)$. Hence, in any perfect equilibrium where $x_1 \geq D(0)$, x_2 must be selected to maximize $\underline{p}(x_2)x_2 = R(x_2)x_2/D(\underline{p}(x_2))$. The numerator in the last expression is increasing for $x_2 \leq x^*$ and is decreasing thereafter. (See the proof of Lemma 5.) And as $\underline{p}(x_2)$ decreases in x_2, the denominator increases in x_2. Thus, the maximizing x_2 is less than x^*. But as long as firm 2 chooses capacity less than x^*, the best revenue (in any subgame equilibrium) that firm 1 can hope to achieve is $R(x_2)$, which it achieves with any $x_1 \geq D(0)$. Thus, we have a perfect subgame equilibrium in which firm 1 chooses $x_1 \geq D(0)$ and firm 2 chooses x_2 to maximize $\underline{p}(x_2)x_2$.

6. When both capacity and production are costly

■ In a slightly more complicated version of this game, both capacity (which is installed before prices are named and demand is realized) and production (which takes place after demand is realized) would be costly. Assuming that each of these activities has a convex cost structure and that our assumptions on demand are met, it is easy to modify our analysis to show that the unique equilibrium outcome is the Cournot outcome computed by using the sum of the two cost functions. (This requires that capacity is costly on the margin. Otherwise, imperfect equilibria of all sorts and perfect equilibria of the sort given above will also appear.) It is notable that the cost of capacity need not be very high relative to production cost: the only requirement is that it be nonzero on the margin. Thus, situations where "most" of the cost is incurred subsequent to the realization of demand (situations that will "look" very Bertrand-like) will still give the Cournot outcome. (A reasonable conjecture, suggested to us by many colleagues, is that "noise" in the demand function will change this dramatically. Confirmation or rejection of this conjecture must await another paper.)

References

BECKMANN, M. "Edgeworth-Bertrand Duopoly Revisited" in R. Henn, ed., *Operations Research-Verfahren, III,* Meisenheim: Verlag Anton Hein, 1965, pp. 55–68.

BERTRAND, J. "Theorie Mathématique de la Richesse Sociale." *Journal des Savants* (1883), pp. 499–508.

COURNOT, A. *Recherches sur les Principes Mathématiques de la Théorie des Richesses.* Paris: 1838 English translation: (N. Bacon, trans.), *Researches into the Mathematical Principles of the Theory of Wealth,* New York: Macmillan & Company, 1897.

DASGUPTA, P. AND MASKIN, E. "The Existence of Equilibrium in Discontinuous Economic Games, 2: Applications." Draft, London School of Economics, 1982.

EDGEWORTH, F. "La Teoria Pura del Monopolio." *Giornale degli Economisti,* Volume 40 (1897), pp. 13–31. Reprinted in English as "The Pure Theory of Monopoly," in F. Edgeworth, *Papers Relating to Political Economy,* Vol. 1, London: MacMillan & Co., Ltd., 1925, pp. 111–142.

LEVITAN, R. AND SHUBIK, M. "Price Duopoly and Capacity Constraints." *International Economic Review,* Vol. 13 (1972), pp. 111–122.

SELTEN, R. "Spieltheoretische Behandlung eines Oligopolmodells mit Nachfragetragheit." *Zeitschrift für die gesamte Staatswissenschaft,* Vol. 121 (1965), pp. 301–324.

[8]

ON THE EXISTENCE OF BERTRAND–EDGEWORTH EQUILIBRIA WITH DIFFERENTIATED COMMODITIES

JEAN-PASCAL BENASSY*

CNRS, CEPREMAP and Ecole Normale Supérieure, Paris, France

1. Introduction

The most rigorous description of the functioning of competitive market economies is certainly the recent formalization of the Walrasian model of General Equilibrium, developed notably by Arrow and Debreu (1954) and Debreu (1959). There it is shown rigorously how the agents make quantity decisions on the basis of price signals, and how the price mechanism can bring about an overall consistency between all these independent decisions. In this model, as in all competitive models, the price system itself is implicitly determined by the "Walrasian auctioneer", and in recent years economists have searched for foundations of competitive behavior where agents themselves would be responsible for price making.

A quite popular and lively area of research on such foundations of competition is that associated with the name of Bertrand (1883). The basic idea behind it is that prices are used as strategic variables in competition, obviously quite a realistic assumption (which of course does not preclude that other variables as well be used for competition). In his initial review of Cournot (1838), Bertrand showed that "competitive" price undercutting would lead to the perfect competition outcome as soon as there were at least two competitors. This was challenged however by Edgeworth (1897), who showed that the introduction of productive capacities could prevent the existence of an equilibrium in pure price strategies. All this generated quite an abundant and interesting literature: First the non-existence results for pure strategies were refined.[1] Then alterna-

---

*I wish to thank Andreu Mas-Colell for his perceptive comments on a first draft of this paper. Useful remarks were also made by participants in the research seminar of the Laboratoire d'Economie Politique at Ecole Normale Supérieure.
[1]Shubik (1959); see also Dixon (1984b).

tive solutions were sought in various directions: (i) mixed stochastic strategies,[2] (ii) strategic behavior on the side of buyers,[3] (iii) approximate equilibria.[4]

All of the above contributions have considered the traditional extreme case where all goods produced are perfect substitutes, the usual assumption if one wants to study perfect competition. We want in this article to revert to the initial Bertrand–Edgeworth problem of the existence of a pure strategies equilibrium, but examine it in the case of *differentiated products*.[5] As we shall see, quantity signals (of which the Edgeworthian capacities are a particular case) play a most important rôle for existence, as well as the timing of the various price–quantity decisions.[6] The corresponding effects do not seem, though, to have been investigated in the imperfect competition literature which is concerned with such differentiated commodities. Before going to the more formal presentation, we shall review briefly the original Bertrand–Edgeworth arguments.

The Bertrand–Edgeworth story

We shall develop here the arguments of the two authors, using the simple case depicted by Figure 1. Consider first the Bertrand story, and assume there are two price-setting firms with unlimited productive capacities at constant marginal cost c, and a market demand curve represented by the curve DD'. Bertrand shows that the only equilibrium configuration is that where both firms set their price equal to c, i.e., the competitive market clearing price.

To show this let us first remark that no firm would set a price below c, since this would yield negative profits. Now if the prices are both above c, but different, then the highest pricer does not sell anything, and he can make a positive profit by undercutting the other, still remaining above c; if the prices are equal, but above c, at least one of the two firms does not sell all the demand, and it can improve its profits just by infinitesimally undercutting and appropriating all demand; finally if one firm sets the price equal to c, the other being above c, the first sells all demand but does not make any profit, and it can improve its situation by setting a price higher than c, but lower than the other price. The only possible equilibrium is thus one where both firms set a price equal to c and share the demand. This is easily verified to be actually an equilibrium.

[2] Shubik (1959), Levitan and Shubik (1972), Dasgupta and Maskin (1982), Kreps and Scheinkman (1983), Allen and Hellwig (1983).
[3] Dubey (1982), Simon (1984a), Benassy (1984).
[4] Dixon (1984b).
[5] Bertrand competition with differentiated products is studied by Simon (1984b), but with a quite different approach.
[6] For a recent and interesting contribution on timing in the pure substitutes cases, see Kreps and Scheinkman (1983).

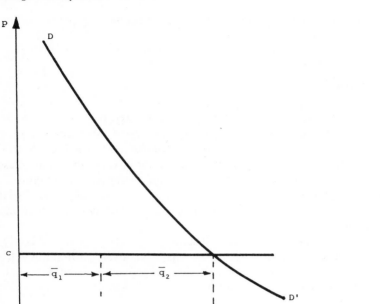

Figure 1

Now following Edgeworth assume that the two firms have productive capacities, $\bar{q}_1$ and $\bar{q}_2$ respectively (cf. Figure 1). Adapting a little the above "undercutting" argument, it is easy to show that the only possible equilibrium would be one where both firms set their price equal to c, firm 1 produces and sells $\bar{q}_1$, firm 2 produces and sells $\bar{q}_2$. But now imagine that starting from this position firm 1 deviates and sets a price $p_1 > c$. Because firm 2 cannot produce (and thus sell) more than the quantity $\bar{q}_2$ it already sells, there will be a strictly positive residual demand going to firm 1, which will thus make profits, and the initial situation cannot be Nash. There is thus no Nash equilibrium in pure strategies.

Of course the above example is very special, but it has been shown that the inexistence result carries to much more general circumstances,[7] with more than two agents, and more general cost–capacity configurations than the one considered in the example. The analysis generally retains, though, the assumptions that the produced commodities are perfect substitutes. We shall now

[7]Shubik (1959), Dixon (1984b).

extend the above considerations to a multi-firm setting with differentiated commodities.

2. The model

We shall consider here n competing firms, indexed by $i = 1, \ldots, n$. Each of these firms produces a quantity q_i of a single good, also indexed by i. The monetary price of good i is p_i, and is decided upon by firm i. Each firm has a particular cost function $C_i(q_i)$. We shall generally assume that these cost functions are continuous and display increasing marginal costs (Figure 2a). We may also introduce a capacity constraint $\bar{q}_i$ (Figure 2b). The Bertrand–Edgeworth example corresponds to this last case, with constant marginal cost up to capacity.

Most often in such models the demand side is represented directly by a demand function. However, since we shall be investigating the effects of quantity signals we need a more basic representation, and we shall thus represent the "demand side" as an aggregate representative consumer[8] with a utility function:

$$U(x, m),$$

where $x \in R_+^n$ is the n-dimensional vector of the consumer's goods purchases, and m represents the quantity of money saved. The household has an initial quantity of money $\bar{m}$ coming from previous savings or other sources of income, a datum in the period. The utility function is assumed to be continuously differentiable and *strictly* concave in x, in order to reflect the differentiation of the n products. We shall moreover assume that all the goods are normal.

Walrasian demand

The Walrasian demand of the consumer is naturally obtained as the solution in x of the usual program:

maximize $U(x, m)$,

subject to $px + m = \bar{m}$.

---

[8]The arguments below could actually be worked out with many consumers, but this would make the exposition quite tedious without much conceptual gain.

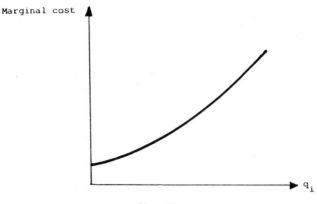

Figure 2a

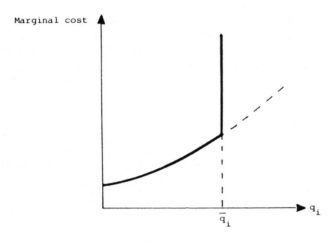

Figure 2b

This program has a unique solution because of the strict concavity of U in x, and we shall denote the Walrasian demand functionally as

$$x = \hat{D}(p) = \hat{D}(p_1, \ldots, p_n).$$

In what follows it will often be convenient to write the component i of this vector, i.e., the Walrasian demand for good i, as

$$\hat{D}_i(p_i, p_{-i}),$$

where

$$p_{-i} = \{ p_j | j \neq i \}.$$

The function $\hat{D}_i$ will be assumed to be continuously differentiable and decreasing in p_i in its positive range.

3. Existence of a Bertrand–Nash equilibrium with differentiated commodities

We shall study in this section the Nash equilibrium of the game where the firms use prices only as strategies (thus a "Bertrand–Nash" game) and where all firms assume that the demand facing them is the *Walrasian demand* (this last assumption will be criticized below).

Though p_i only is used as a strategic variable, firm i must choose both its price p_i and production q_i. These are chosen so as to maximize profits $p_i s_i - C_i(q_i)$, where s_i is the level of sales for firm i. These sales are equal to the minimum of the quantity put on the market by the firm, i.e., q_i since we do not consider any inventories, and of demand, which we take equal to the Walrasian one $\hat{D}_i(p_i, p_{-i})$, so that

$$s_i = \min \{ q, \hat{D}_i(p_i, p_{-i}) \}.$$

The optimal price–production decisions of the firm are thus given by the following program (A_i):

$$\begin{aligned}
&\text{maximize} \quad p_i s_i - C_i(q_i), \\
&\text{subject to} \quad s_i = \min \{ q_i, \hat{D}_i(p_i, p_{-i}) \}.
\end{aligned} \tag{A_i}$$

We shall call $\beta_i(p_{-i})$ the set of prices p_i solution of the above program. We may note here that the program (A_i) is a little different from alternative programs commonly found in the literature on imperfect competition, where it is assumed that the firm serves all demand, whatever its level, and adjusts production to it. According to this more traditional alternative approach the optimizing program of firm i should be the following program (B_i):

$$\begin{aligned}
&\text{maximize} \quad p_i s_i - C_i(q_i), \\
&\text{subject to} \quad q_i = s_i = \hat{D}_i(p_i, p_{-i}).
\end{aligned} \tag{B_i}$$

Note that this last way of formulating the problem is not a priori satisfactory, since the hypothesis that the firm satisfies demand under all circumstances might entail that the firm produces and sells beyond its profit-maximizing production level, which would not be individually rational.

But fortunately it turns out that the solutions of the two programs (A_i) and (B_i) are the same, since the firm will always choose a price sufficiently high to be willing to serve all demand and produce the corresponding quantity. More precisely we have the following simple proposition:[9]

Proposition 1. The solutions of programs (A_i) and (B_i) are the same. In particular the optimal p_i and q_i in program (A_i) are chosen such that

$$q_i = s_i = \hat{D}_i(p_i, p_{-i}).$$

Proof. Remember program (A_i) is

$$\text{maximize} \quad p_i s_i - C_i(q_i),$$
$$\text{subject to} \quad s_i = \min\{q_i, \hat{D}_i(p_i, p_{-i})\}.$$

If the optimal solution did not satisfy the equalities in the proposition, then we would have one of the two following situations:

– $s_i = \hat{D}_i(p_i, p_{-i}) < q_i$,

  but in this case the firm could reduce costs and increase profits by reducing production to s_i.

– $s_i = q_i < \hat{D}_i(p_i, p_{-i})$,

  but in this case the firm could increase slightly its price without having to change s_i or q_i, which would increase its profits (note that continuity of the demand function is quite crucial in this step).

Since none of the two above situations is profit-maximizing, the optimal plan in (A_i) must satisfy

$$q_i = s_i = \hat{D}_i(p_i, p_{-i}).$$

This implies immediately that the solutions of (A_i) and (B_i) are the same as the set of feasible (s_i, q_i, p_i) of program (A_i) strictly contains the corresponding set for (B_i), and the maximands of the two programs are the same. $\square$

[9]A similar proposition for a firm producing several products is found in Benassy (1976, 1982). See also Böhm, Maskin, Polemarchakis and Postlewaite (1983).

The common set of solutions in p_i of the programs (A_i) and (B_i) is thus $\beta_i(p_{-i})$ defined above.

Bertrand–Nash equilibrium

With the above definitions it is now easy to give the definition of a Bertrand–Nash equilibrium:

Definition. A Bertrand–Nash equilibrium is a set of prices p_i^*, $i = 1, \ldots, n$, such that

$$p_i^* \in \beta_i(p_{-i}^*), \qquad i = 1, \ldots, n.$$

We now turn to the problem of existence of such an equilibrium.

Existence of a Bertrand–Nash equilibrium

We shall give here a few conditions under which a Bertrand–Nash equilibrium exists. Since what we want to emphasize is the possibility of inexistence due to quantity signals, we shall make here assumptions sufficiently strong to ensure existence whenever these signals are ignored. As usual we need assumptions leading to boundedness and continuity of the price reaction function. The assumption for boundedness is:

Assumption 1. There exist some maximum prices $\bar{p}_i$, $i = 1, \ldots, n$, such that

$$\forall p_{-i}, \quad \hat{D}_i(p_i, p_{-i}) = 0 \quad \text{if} \quad p_i \geq \bar{p}_i.$$

Such a boundedness property can be obtained by assuming, for example, that for all values of x and m,

$$\frac{\partial U/\partial x_i}{\partial U/\partial m} \leq \bar{p}_i, \qquad i = 1, \ldots, n.$$

We shall secondly make a concavity assumption on the "profit function" which ensures upper semicontinuity of the optimal price response:

Assumption 2. The profit function

$$p_i \hat{D}_i(p_i, p_{-i}) - C_i[\hat{D}_i(p_i, p_{-i})]$$

is quasi-concave in p_i.

We should note that Assumption 2 is implied by the traditional assumptions of decreasing marginal revenue and increasing marginal cost. Indeed define the function $\rho_i(q_i, p_{-i})$ by

$$p_i = \rho_i(q_i, p_{-i}) \Leftrightarrow q_i = \hat{D}_i(p_i, p_{-i}).$$

The profit function in Assumption 2 can be written as a function of q_i as

$$q_i \rho_i(q_i, p_{-i}) - C_i(q_i),$$

which is total revenue minus total cost. Decreasing marginal revenue and increasing marginal cost imply that this function is strictly concave, and thus a fortiori quasi-concave. Since q_i and p_i are negatively and monotonously related in their positive range, the function in Assumption 2 is also quasi-concave.

We can now prove easily the following theorem:[10]

Theorem 1.   *Under Assumptions 1 and 2 a Bertrand–Nash equilibrium exists.*

Proof.   An equilibrium will be constructed as a fixed point of the mapping:

$$p_i \rightarrow \beta_i(p_{-i}), \qquad i = 1, \ldots, n.$$

Because of Assumption 1, we can restrict each price p_i to the interval $(0, \bar{p}_i)$, which thus yields a mapping from a compact convex set into itself. Now, as we indicated above, the optimal price response of firm i is solution in p_i of the program (A_i):

maximize $p_i s_i - C_i(q_i)$,

subject to $s_i = \min\{q_i, \hat{D}_i(p_i, p_{-i})\}$.

By Proposition 1 above, the optimal solutions of this program are such that

$$q_i = s_i = \hat{D}_i(p_i, p_{-i}),$$

so that the optimal p_i is solution of

maximize $p_i \hat{D}_i(p_i, p_{-i}) - C_i[\hat{D}_i(p_i, p_{-i})]$.

---

[10] This theorem is of course not very novel, and mainly serves as an introduction to the results in Sections 4 and 5 below. There are indeed already numerous theorems of similar inspiration in the literature, starting with the seminal contribution by Negishi (1961). See, for example, the survey by Friedman (1982).

Because of Assumption 2 the optimal price correspondence $\beta_i(p_{-i})$ is an upper hemicontinuous correspondence with convex values. The mapping considered at the beginning of this proof is thus an upper hemicontinuous, convex-valued correspondence from a compact convex set into itself. By Kakutani's theorem it has a fixed point, which yields a Bertrand–Nash equilibrium. □

A critique

Though the above existence theorem does not apply directly to the original Bertrand–Edgeworth example with capacities (cf. Section 1) because the demands there are discontinuous,[11] it is easy to see by direct computation that in that example a Bertrand–Nash equilibrium exists, and that it is the competitive one. This of course conflicts with the Edgeworth non-existence result seen above, and suggests that an important point has been forgotten in our description of the Bertrand–Nash game as a game of price competition (as well as in the literature on imperfect competition with differentiated products). As we shall see, the problem lies with the use of the Walrasian demand, or similar demand functions disregarding quantity signals.

Indeed the implicit presumption in the use of the Walrasian demand in the firms' programs is that all firms will be willing to serve all demands addressed to them under any circumstance. We actually showed in Proposition 1 that each firm would be willing to do so *in an equilibrium situation*, but the Edgeworth example above shows us that we cannot assume this to hold under any price configuration. Notably a firm cannot assume that *others* will always serve demand if we consider deviations from a potential Nash equilibrium. Indeed, going back to the example of Figure 1, if starting from the situation where both firms quote c firm 1 increases its price p_1, then firm 2 will not be able to satisfy all the demand addressed to it (which is $\bar{q}_1 + \bar{q}_2$). While the Walrasian demand addressed to firm 1 would be zero for price increases above c, the true residual demand is actually strictly positive, hence it is the interest of firm 1 to deviate from this "competitive" position, and this is the cause of inexistence in this example.

The assumption that demand is always served, notably by the other firms, is thus generally not admissible (except in the extreme Bertrand case where capacity would be infinite at a constant marginal cost), and we shall now construct more consistent games which take this problem into account by introducing quantity signals into the demand functions.

[11] Fixed capacities, however, can be integrated in Proposition 1 and Theorem 1.

4. Inexistence of an equilibrium in a one-stage Bertrand–Edgeworth game

We want now to introduce explicitly quantity signals into the above game and show that their consideration may entail problems of existence similar to that uncovered by Edgeworth. We may note that in the above Bertrand–Nash game each firm makes price *and* production decisions, but ignores the quantity decisions of the others and takes only into account their price decisions. The simplest manner to introduce quantity signals, which we shall now investigate, is to assume that the strategic variables for each firm are its price p_i and production q_i. Thus the quantity put on the market by each firm is known to others, and we shall assume that all firms draw the full implications of this information. On each market sales s_i are given as before by

$$s_i = \min(q_i, d_i),$$

where d_i is the demand for good i. How is this demand now determined? Firm i is aware that on the other markets $j \neq i$ the other firms will not serve more than q_j. The maximum sales that firm i can make is thus the level of purchases of good i which maximizes the utility of the consumer, subject to the budget constraint and the constraints that purchases be less than or equal to q_j on the other markets $j \neq i$, i.e., the demand of good i is the solution in x_i of the following program:

$$\text{maximize} \quad U(x, m),$$
$$\text{subject to} \quad px + m = \bar{m},$$
$$x_j \leq q_j, \quad j \neq i.$$

We recognize here a notion very similar to the effective demand function of non-Walrasian theory.[12] The demand for good i defined by the above program will be denoted functionally as

$$D_i(p_i, p_{-i}, q_{-i}),$$

where

$$q_{-i} = \{q_j | j \neq i\}.$$

---

[12] Cf. Benassy (1975, 1982) for definition, properties, and alternative uses. That this is the appropriate concept to use in such context has also been noted by Dixon (1984a, 1984b).

Now, as we said above, we assume that firm i knows perfectly both the function D_i, and the price and quantity decisions of the others, p_{-i} and q_{-i}. Its program for price and production determination is thus

$$\text{maximize} \quad p_i s_i - C_i(q_i),$$
$$\text{subject to} \quad s_i = \min\{q_i, D_i(p_i, p_{-i}, q_{-i})\},$$

which yields the set of optimal solutions in p_i and q_i, denoted as

$$\phi_i(p_{-i}, q_{-i}).$$

Now a Nash equilibrium in this one-stage Bertrand–Edgeworth game is a set of p_i^*, q_i^*, $i = 1, \ldots, n$, such that

$$(p_i^*, q_i^*) \in \phi_i(p_{-i}^*, q_{-i}^*) \quad \text{for all } i.$$

Inexistence of a Nash equilibrium

We shall now see that the introduction of these quantity signals seriously jeopardizes the existence of an equilibrium since, even making the fairly strong Assumptions 1 and 2, no Nash equilibrium exists if the goods are *gross substitutes* (remember the original Edgeworth case deals with *perfect* substitutes), and if the cost functions are continuously differentiable. More precisely we have the following theorem:

Theorem 2. Make Assumptions 1 and 2. If all goods are normal and strictly gross substitutes,[13] and the cost functions are continuously differentiable, then the above one-stage Bertrand–Edgeworth game has no Nash equilibrium in pure strategies.

Proof. In order to prove this theorem we shall characterize through a few lemmas the potential Nash equilibria, and then show they cannot actually be equilibria.

Lemma 1. At a potential Nash equilibrium one must have, for all i,

$$s_i = q_i = \hat{D}_i(p_i, p_{-i}).$$

---

[13] By strictly gross substitutes we mean that $\partial \hat{D}_i / \partial p_j > 0$, $\forall j \neq i$.

Proof. The proof goes in two easy steps. The first one is to show that, for all i,

$$q_i = s_i = D_i(p_i, p_{-i}, q_{-i}).$$

The method of proof is exactly the same as that of Proposition 1 above, and is thus not repeated here. Now if the above equalities hold for all i, this means that actually none of the constraints q_j is binding in the programs giving the effective demands. With no binding constraint we know that effective demand is equal to Walrasian demand and thus, for all i,

$$q_i = s_i = \hat{D}_i(p_i, p_{-i}). \quad \square$$

We may note however that, even though no constraint is actually binding, we are at the "limit point" where tightening of any constraint would make it binding, because the constraint is exactly equal to the unconstrained demand. We must thus expect the demand function $D_i(p_i, p_{-i}, q_{-i})$ to have discontinuous derivatives at the potential Nash equilibrium, which is made precise through the following lemma:

Lemma 2. *At the potential Nash equilibrium we have, for all i,*

$$(\partial D_i/\partial p_i)^- < (\partial D_i/\partial p_i)^+.$$

Proof. We shall successively compute the left and right derivatives of the function D_i with respect to p_i, remembering all goods are assumed to be strictly gross substitutes.

Consider first a decrease in the price p_i. Because all goods are gross substitutes, the household would demand less of every good $j \neq i$, and thus none of the constraints q_j, $j \neq i$, would be binding, which means that

$$(\partial D_i/\partial p_i)^- = \partial \hat{D}_i/\partial p_i.$$

But if on the contrary p_i increases, the household would like to purchase more of the goods $j \neq i$, and then all constraints q_j become binding. Tobin and Houthakker (1950) have provided a formula for computing the partial derivatives when the constraints are "just binding", which is the case here.[14] Their formula 6.2 (p. 145), which is the appropriate one to use here, becomes with our notation:

$$(\partial D_i/\partial p_i)^+ - \partial \hat{D}_i/\partial p_i = - \sum_{j \neq i} (\partial D_i/\partial q_j)(\partial \hat{D}_j/\partial p_i),$$

---

[14] See also, for example, Pollak (1969), Howard (1977), Neary and Roberts (1980) for other properties of the constrained demand function.

where the terms $\partial D_i/\partial q_j$ represent partial derivatives when the constraints q_j are just binding. It is shown by Tobin and Houthakker (1950, formula 3.8, p. 142) that $\partial D_i/\partial q_j$ is negative if goods i and j are substitutes, which is the case here. Moreover because the goods are strictly gross substitutes:

$$\partial \hat{D}_j/\partial p_i > 0, \quad \forall j \neq i,$$

and thus the second term of the equality is strictly positive, which yields

$$(\partial D_i/\partial p_i)^+ > \partial \hat{D}_i/\partial p_i = (\partial D_i/\partial p_i)^-. \quad \square$$

We can now establish that the potential Nash equilibria which we partly characterized are *not* equilibria. Indeed let us rewrite the program of profit maximization:

maximize $\quad p_i s_i - C_i(q_i),$

subject to $\quad s_i = \min\{q_i, D_i(p_i, p_{-i}, q_{-i})\}.$

We know already that the optimal solution of this program is such that

$$q_i = s_i = D_i(p_i, p_{-i}, q_{-i}).$$

So, calling π_i the profit of firm i, this is equal to

$$\pi_i = p_i D_i(p_i, p_{-i}, q_{-i}) - C_i[D_i(p_i, p_{-i}, q_{-i})].$$

We can compute the left and right derivatives of this profit at a potential Nash equilibrium:

$$(\partial \pi_i/\partial p_i)^+ = D_i + [p_i - C_i'](\partial D_i/\partial p_i)^+,$$
$$(\partial \pi_i/\partial p_i)^- = D_i + [p_i - C_i'](\partial D_i/\partial p_i)^-,$$

where C_i' is the (finite) derivative of the cost function. At a potential Nash equilibrium we have necessarily $p_i \geq C_i'$. Thus two situations might arise:

(a) If $p_i = C_i'$, then

$$(\partial \pi_i/\partial p_i)^+ = (\partial \pi_i/\partial p_i)^- = D_i > 0,$$

and profits are not maximized.

(b) If $p_i > C_i'$, then

$$(\partial \pi_i / \partial p_i)^+ > (\partial \pi_i / \partial p_i)^-,$$

and profits cannot be maximum at such a point either.

We thus see that profits are never maximized at any of the potential Nash equilibria. There is thus no Nash equilibrium. □

A possible counterexample: The case of fixed capacities

Let us now assume that there are fixed capacities for each firm, denoted by $\bar{q}_i$. The two lemmas of Theorem 2 still hold, but the end of the proof is modified in a way which leaves open the possibility that a pure strategies Nash equilibrium exists. Indeed the program of profit maximization is now written as

$$\text{maximize} \quad p_i s_i - C_i(q_i),$$
$$\text{subject to} \quad s_i = \min \{ q_i, D_i(p_i, p_{-i}, q_{-i})\},$$
$$q_i \leq \bar{q}_i.$$

If the potential Nash equilibrium corresponds to full capacity production $q_i = \bar{q}_i$, then we have, considering small variations of p_i,

$$q_i = s_i = D_i(p_i, p_{-i}, q_{-i}) \qquad \text{for price increases,}$$
$$q_i = s_i = \bar{q}_i < D_i(p_i, p_{-i}, q_{-i}) \quad \text{for price decreases.}$$

And thus:

$$(\partial \pi_i / \partial p_i)^+ = D_i + [p_i - C_i'](\partial D_i / \partial p_i)^+,$$
$$(\partial \pi_i / \partial p_i)^- = \bar{q}_i > 0.$$

With a strictly positive left derivative, it is possible that a Nash equilibrium exists. A necessary condition is that

$$(\partial \pi_i / \partial p_i)^+ \leq 0,$$

which may happen if capacity is "sufficiently" small, a traditional case in Edgeworth duopoly.

5. A two-stage Bertrand–Edgeworth game

We have studied successively two versions of Bertrand-type games where prices are used as strategic variables. In the first one, the Bertrand–Nash game, only prices signals were considered and existence was obtained, but at the price of incorrectly omitting any kind of quantity signal. The second game, the one-stage Bertrand–Edgeworth game, highlighted most clearly the role of quantity signals, but the implicit timing of commitments (prices and production together) made existence of a Nash equilibrium quite problematic.[15]

We shall now consider a game with a different timing, a two-stage game, which is closer to the intuitions of the original Bertrand and Edgeworth models. The idea is that agents choose prices in a first stage, and then productions in a second stage. The equilibrium concept we shall obtain is thus close to the notion of perfect equilibrium.[16] One should note that, in spite of production levels being decided upon at a later stage, quantity signals will appear in the first-stage price game since, for a given cost function and/or capacity, commitment to a price by a firm implies that it will never serve more than a given quantity, as we shall now see more precisely by studying the second-stage game.

The second-stage game

With prices being set in the first period, the second stage equilibrium will be a fix-price equilibrium,[17] which we shall now characterize briefly.

Consider first a firm i with a cost function $C_i(q_i)$ and a maximum capacity $\bar{q}_i$ (the Edgeworthian special case is thus included). Imagine this firm is faced with a demand d_i. The program determining the production of the firm is

$$\text{maximize} \quad p_i s_i - C_i(q_i),$$
$$\text{subject to} \quad s_i = \min\{q_i, d_i\},$$
$$q_i \leq \bar{q}_i,$$

where p_i is given from the first stage. The solution of this program is

$$s_i = q_i = \min\{d_i, k_i(p_i)\},$$

---

[15] Note however that it is in this particular Bertrand–Edgeworth setting that simultaneous price–quantity decision poses existence problems. Strategic market games with simultaneous price–quantity decisions have Nash equilibria under fairly weak conditions [see Benassy (1984)].
[16] Selten (1975).
[17] For a general definition and properties, see Benassy (1982).

with

$$k_i(p_i) = \min\{\bar{q}_i, C_i'^{-1}(p_i)\}.$$

This formula tells us that firm i is willing to serve demand up to the quantity $k_i(p_i)$, which is somehow the "profitable capacity" at the second stage, given the first-stage choice of a price p_i. The quantity constraints that the consumer faces in the second stage of this game are thus these $k_i(p_i)$, and the demand for good i is

$$d_i = D_i(p_i, p_{-i}, k_{-i}),$$

where

$$k_{-i} = \{k_j(p_j)|j \neq i\},$$

so that sales and productions in the second stage are given by the formula

$$s_i = q_i = \min\{k_i(p_i), D_i(p_i, p_{-i}, k_{-i})\}.$$

The second-stage equilibrium is now completely characterized, and we shall study the first-stage game.

The first-stage game

In the first stage the program of firm i is to choose p_i, knowing that sales and production will be given by the above formulas. Firm i solves thus the following program in p_i:

maximize $p_i s_i - C_i(q_i),$

subject to $q_i = s_i = \min\{k_i(p_i), D_i(p_i, p_{-i}, k_{-i})\}.$

The optimal solution is a function of p_{-i} and k_{-i}, but since k_{-i} is itself a function of p_{-i}, we shall write the optimal price correspondence as $\Psi_i(p_{-i})$. A Nash equilibrium of the first-stage game is a set of p_i^*, $i = 1, \ldots, n$, such that

$$p_i^* \in \Psi_i(p_{-i}^*), \qquad i = 1, \ldots, n.$$

A characterization of equilibria

We shall consider here the case where there are no capacity constraints and thus where the cost functions are strictly convex and differentiable. As we shall now see the only potential Nash equilibria of this game are the Bertrand–Nash equilibria which were described in Section 3 of this paper. Moreover we shall see that Bertrand–Nash equilibria are *locally Nash*, by which it is meant that the corresponding strategy yields a *local* profit maximum, given the others' strategies (though not necessarily a global maximum). We shall now make this precise through the following theorem:

Theorem 3. Make Assumptions 1 and 2, and assume strictly convex cost functions. Bertrand–Nash equilibria are the only possible pure strategies equilibria of the game. A Bertrand–Nash equilibrium is moreover locally Nash.

Proof. Recall first the program of firm i in the first stage:

$$\text{maximize} \quad p_i s_i - C_i(q_i),$$
$$\text{subject to} \quad q_i = s_i = \min\{k_i(p_i), D_i(p_i, p_{-i}, k_{-i})\}.$$

We want to show first that the constraints k_i are actually not binding at a potential Nash equilibrium. This is done through the following lemma:

Lemma 3. At a potential equilibrium,

$$k_i(p_i) > D_i(p_i, p_{-i}, k_{-i}), \qquad i = 1, \ldots, n.$$

Proof. We shall prove it by reductio ad absurdum. Assume first that

$$k_i(p_i) < D_i(p_i, p_{-i}, k_{-i}),$$

then for any small price increase or decrease in p_i we will have

$$q_i = s_i = k_i(p_i),$$

and thus:

$$\partial \pi_i / \partial p_i = k_i(p_i) + [p_i - C_i'](\partial k_i / \partial p_i).$$

Because there are no capacity constraints $p_i = C_i'$ and thus $\partial \pi_i / \partial p_i > 0$, which means that this case cannot yield the optimal solution.

Assume now that

$$k_i(p_i) = D_i(p_i, p_{-i}, k_{-i}),$$

and consider a small price increase, in which case we will have

$$q_i = s_i = D_i(p_i, p_{-i}, k_{-i}),$$

and thus:

$$(\partial \pi_i / \partial p_i)^+ = D_i + [p_i - C_i'](\partial D_i / \partial p_i)^+.$$

Again $p_i = C_i'$ and $(\partial \pi_i / \partial p_i)^+ > 0$, which shows that this situation cannot be optimal either. The only possibility left is thus that

$$k_i(p_i) > D_i(p_i, p_{-i}, k_{-i}). \quad \square$$

Since the constraints k_i are *strictly* non-binding at the potential Nash equilibrium, they must be also non-binding in a neighborhood. More precisely consider the set of prices

$$\Omega = \{ p_i, i = 1, \ldots, n | \hat{D}_i(p_i, p_{-i}) \le k_i(p_i), i = 1, \ldots, n \}.$$

For prices in this set none of the constraints k_i is binding, and thus:

$$D_i(p_i, p_{-i}, k_{-i}) = \hat{D}_i(p_i, p_{-i}), \qquad i = 1, \ldots, n.$$

From the above lemma this set Ω contains potential Nash equilibria in its interior. Now consider such a potential equilibrium p_i^*, $i = 1, \ldots, n$. The strategy p_i^* must be a local maximum of the program:

maximize $p_i s_i - C_i(q_i)$,

subject to $q_i = s_i = \hat{D}_i(p_i, p_{-i}^*).$

More precisely p_i^* must dominate every strategy p_i such that $(p_i, p_{-i}^*) \in \Omega$. Under Assumption 2 a local maximum of this program is also a global maximum, and thus, with the notations of Section 3, at a potential Nash equilibrium:

$$p_i^* \in \beta_i(p_{-i}^*), \qquad i = 1, \ldots, n,$$

which shows that the potential Nash equilibrium must be a Bertrand–Nash equilibrium. We also saw that p_i^* is preferred to any price p_i in the set

$$\{ p_i | (p_i, p_{-i}^*) \in \Omega \}.$$

Since this set contains p_i^* in its interior, the Bertrand–Nash equilibrium is locally Nash. □

Of course p_i^* may be a profit-maximizing strategy over a larger set than the one defined above, and may even be a global maximum. We may thus have the following possibilities: (i) All strategies p_i^* are actually global maxima, in which case the Bertrand–Nash equilibrium is a proper Nash equilibrium in pure strategies. (ii) One of the strategies p_i^* is not a global maximum, in which case the two-stage game has no Nash equilibrium in pure strategies. A characterization of the conditions under which each case occurs should be the subject of future research.

6. Conclusions

In this paper we have extended the Bertrand–Edgeworth framework from the traditional pure substitutes case to the more general case of differentiated commodities. This was clearly needed as up to now there was somehow a dichotomy between the treatments of the pure substitutes and the differentiated products cases of competition by prices. In the pure substitutes case each firm was assumed to take both the price and quantity decisions of other firms into account (the Bertrand–Edgeworth story), while for differentiated products (cf. most literature on imperfect competition) one was dealing with price signals only, demands being assumed to be served by all firms under any circumstance. This paper bridges the gap between these two lines of research by building models of price competition with differentiated products where each firm considers *both* the price and quantity decisions of its competitors.

The introduction of such quantity signals into the modelling of price competition has numerous consequences. First the existence of an equilibrium in a price–quantity game may be seriously jeopardized, just as in the pure substitutes case. Secondly the timing of commitments in prices and quantities is extremely important, and we have in particular constructed a model of two-stage decision very close to the spirit of Bertrand, where prices are chosen in a first stage and quantities in a second stage. In this model we could prove the existence of locally Nash strategies, thus leaving the problem of existence or non-existence fairly open.

Now of course all this invites the question of how the existence of a pure strategies Nash equilibrium can be obtained in such more sophisticated models of imperfect competition. A potentially quite fruitful way emerges from our second model, where it appears intuitively that chances are higher for a local maximum of profit to be a global maximum, the higher the competitors' unused capacities are. This suggests that a "large number" of competitors should be favourable to the existence of a proper Nash equilibrium in pure strategies. One thus meets again the traditional theme of the relation between large numbers and competition. This will be explored precisely in a forthcoming paper.

References

Allen, B. and M. Hellwig, 1983, Bertrand–Edgeworth oligopoly in large markets, Discussion paper (University of Bonn, Bonn).

Arrow, K.J. and G. Debreu, 1954, Existence of an equilibrium for a competitive economy, Econometrica 22, 265–290.

Benassy, J.P., 1975, Neo-Keynesian disequilibrium theory in a monetary economy, Review of Economic Studies 42, 503–523.

Benassy, J.P., 1976, The disequilibrium approach to monopolistic price setting and general monopolistic equilibrium, Review of Economic Studies 43, 69–81.

Benassy, J.P., 1982, The Economics of Market Disequilibrium (Academic Press, New York).

Benassy, J.P., 1984, On competitive market mechanisms, Econometrica, forthcoming.

Bertrand, J., 1983, Théorie des richesses, Journal des Savants, 499–508.

Böhm, V., E. Maskin, H. Polemarchakis and A. Postlewaite, 1983, Monopolistic quantity rationing, Quarterly Journal of Economics 98, Suppl., 189–197.

Cournot, A., 1838, Recherches sur les Principes Mathématiques de la Théorie des Richesses (Hachette, Paris).

Dasgupta, P. and E. Maskin, 1982, The existence of equilibrium in discontinuous economic games, 1: Theory, 2: Applications (ICERD, London School of Economics, London).

Debreu, G., 1959, Theory of Value (Wiley, New York).

Dixon, H., 1984a, The general theory of household and market contingent demand (Birkbeck College, London).

Dixon, H., 1984b, Approximate Bertrand equilibria in a replicated industry (Birkbeck College, London).

Dubey, P., 1982, Price–quantity strategic market games, Econometrica 50, 111–126.

Edgeworth, F., 1897, La teoria pura del monopolio, Giornale degli Economisti 40, 13–31. [English translation, 1925, The pure theory of monopoly, in: Papers Relating to Political Economy, Vol. 1 (Macmillan, London).]

Friedman, J.W., 1982, Oligopoly theory, in: K.J. Arrow and M.D. Intriligator, eds., Handbook of Mathematical Economics, Vol. 2 (North-Holland, Amsterdam).

Howard, D.H., 1977, Rationing, quantity constraints and consumption theory, Econometrica 45, 399–412.

Kreps, D. and J.A. Scheinkman, 1983, Quantity precommitment and Bertrand competition yield Cournot outcomes, Bell Journal of Economics 14, 326–337.

Levitan, R. and M. Shubik, 1972, Price duopoly and capacity constraints, International Economic Review 13, 111–123.

Neary, J.P. and K. Roberts, 1980, The theory of household behaviour under rationing, European Economic Review 13, 25–42.

Negishi, T., 1961, Monopolistic competition and general equilibrium, Review of Economic Studies 28, 196–201.

Pollak, R.A., 1969, Conditional demand functions and consumption theory, Quarterly Journal of Economics 83, 60–78.

Selten, R., 1975, Reexamination of the perfectness concept for equilibrium points in extensive games, International Journal of Game Theory 4, 448–460.

Shubik, M., 1959, Strategy and Market Structure (Wiley, New York).

Simon, L., 1984a, Bertrand, the Cournot paradigm and the theory of perfect competition, Review of Economic Studies 51, 209–230.

Simon, L., 1984b, Comparison shopping and local perfection in a Bertrand model with differentiated commodities (University of California, Berkeley, CA).

Tobin, J. and H.S. Houthakker, 1950, The effects of rationing on demand elasticities, Review of Economic Studies 18, 140–153.

[9]

Cartel Problems

By D. K. OSBORNE*

A cartel faces one external and four internal problems. The external problem, to which we here give only passing attention, is to predict (and if possible, discourage) production by nonmembers. The internal problems are, first, to locate the contract surface; second, to choose a point on that surface (the sharing problem); third, to detect, and fourth, to deter, cheating. Of these we are concerned with the problems of sharing the output and deterring cheating.

Locating the contract surface and detecting cheating are evidently serious problems. Indeed, they are the *only* serious internal problems. Solve them and the cartel will be internally stable. This might seem surprising. Standard theory teaches us that cartels are inherently *unstable*, mainly because of the sharing and deterring problems. Apart from the rare conditions of identical profit functions, the members will disagree about the appropriate point on the contract surface; some members will feel victimized and be tempted to cheat. Even those who don't feel victimized will have powerful incentives to cheat, because of the positive marginal profits (*ceteris paribus*) at the output quota. The reasoning can be explained in terms of the two-member case diagrammed in Figure 1: x_i^q is the output quota of member i ($i=1,2$); q is the point selected by the cartel as best on the contract curve; $I_i^1, \ldots, I_i^4$ are portions of four of member i's isoprofit contours, with profit along I_i^1 being greater than profit along $I_i^2, \ldots$, and

* Federal Reserve Bank of Dallas. The views expressed in this article are solely those of the author and do not necessarily represent those of the Federal Reserve System.

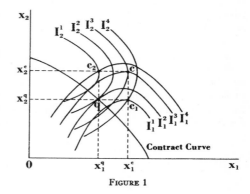

FIGURE 1

profit along I_i^3 being greater than the profit along I_i^4. Member i's profit at the cartel point q is $F_i(x_1^q, x_2^q)$. As is well known, and illustrated by the diagram,

$$\frac{\partial F_i(x_1^q, x_2^q)}{\partial x_i} > 0$$

If member i expects the other to observe the quota x_j^q he can maximize his profit by producing x_i^c; that is,

$$(1) \qquad F_1(x_1^c, x_2^q) > F_1(x_1^q, x_2^q)$$

$$F_2(x_1^q, x_2^c) > F_2(x_1^q, x_2^q)$$

If each expects the other to observe the quota, and produces x_i^c, they will end up at the cheating point c, where the profits are $F_i(x_1^c, x_2^c)$. Evidently,

$$(2) \qquad F_1(x_1^q, x_2^q) > F_1(x_1^c, x_2^c)$$

$$F_2(x_1^q, x_2^q) > F_2(x_1^c, x_2^c)$$

and so both members will be worse off at c than at q. However, it is also true that

$$(3) \qquad F_1(\overset{c}{x_1},\overset{c}{x_2}) > F_1(\overset{q}{x_1},\overset{c}{x_2})$$

$$F_2(\overset{c}{x_1},\overset{c}{x_2}) > F_2(\overset{c}{x_1},\overset{q}{x_2})$$

If one member cheats the other is better off cheating than observing the quota. Since the other is better off cheating even when the one observes the quota, it appears that cheating dominates observing the quota.

If we think of the cartel members as playing a game of strategy, where each member must choose one of two strategies (observe the quota or cheat), and regard the profits made at the points q, c_1, c_2, and c as payoffs, we can set up the following payoff matrix:

	member 2	
member 1	observe the quota	cheat
observe the quota	$F_1(\overset{q}{x_1},\overset{q}{x_2})$, $F_2(\overset{q}{x_1},\overset{q}{x_2})$	$F_1(\overset{q}{x_1},\overset{c}{x_2})$, $F_2(\overset{q}{x_1},\overset{c}{x_2})$
cheat	$F_1(\overset{c}{x_1},\overset{q}{x_2})$, $F_2(\overset{c}{x_1},\overset{q}{x_2})$	$F_1(\overset{c}{x_1},\overset{c}{x_2})$, $F_2(\overset{c}{x_1},\overset{c}{x_2})$

Choosing eight convenient numbers satisfying relations (1)–(3) we get

	observe	cheat
observe	4,3	2,4
cheat	5,1	3,2

Whether the outcome is in column 1 or 2, member 1 prefers to cheat; and whether the outcome is in row 1 or 2, member 2 prefers to cheat. Of the four strategy vectors, only (cheat, cheat) is Pareto dominated; the other three belong to the Pareto optimal set for this game. But since each of these Pareto optimal strategy vectors has at least one dominated component, it appears that the cartel faces a prisoners' dilemma.[1]

A prisoners' dilemma can be resolved satisfactorily by an enforceable contract. If such is available, the cartel can pool

revenues and share them out according to some negotiated rule. This is the device used by what Joe Bain calls *perfect cartels*, the theory of which was given by Don Patinkin. *Imperfect* cartels (those without revenue pooling) are not able to resolve their dilemma in this manner and, apparently, are thus doomed to collapse.

This reasoning certainly seems plausible; and it tends to comfort. If the cartel is inherently unstable because of the sharing and deterring problems, let us wait a while and it will go away. Indeed, when the Organization of Petroleum Exporting Countries (*OPEC*) formed their cartel in October 1973, many economists (myself included) predicted that it would collapse within a year. It is now thirty-six months later, and the cartel seems pretty healthy.[2] Of course not all of the returns are in yet, and everything must crumble eventually (entropy); but how much time must pass before the theory is proved wrong? While we are waiting perhaps we should reexamine the theory which led us to predict so poorly.

I shall argue that the problems of sharing and deterring are easily solved if the locating and detecting problems are solved—that for all its plausibility, the reasoning along the prisoners' dilemma line is incorrect. From this argument we will see that a cartel is not inherently unstable internally unless the locating and detecting problems are inherently insoluble; and we will see how mistaken are the proposals of civil servants and political leaders in the oil-importing countries to create a central international buying agency to deal with *OPEC*. If carried out these proposals would have the effect of solving the detecting problem for the car-

---

[1] A prisoners' dilemma is a game in which no Pareto optimal outcome can be reached unless at least one player plays a dominated strategy. See R. D. Luce and H. Raiffa for a discussion.

[2] Crude oil prices began to fall a bit early in 1975. Far from being a sign of imminent collapse of the cartel this is more likely an adjustment to the greater long-run demand elasticity, and might be a sign of successful adjustment to change.

tel, and thus remove its most important internal source of instability; they would almost certainly support the price of crude oil at a large multiple of long-run marginal cost.[3]

I. Definitions and Assumptions

Let us assume that the nonmember, locating, and detecting problems are solved, so that the cartel has located the contract surface and always knows the outputs of all members, who together produce the entire industry output. Let us also assume the following, where f_j is the inverse demand function and F_j is the profit function of member j $(j=1, \ldots, n)$, and $x=(x_1, \ldots, x_n)$ is the vector of outputs:[4]

ASSUMPTION 1: *For* $j=1, \ldots, n$, $F_j(x)$ *is differentiable, strictly concave in* x_j, *and concave and decreasing in* $x_i(i \neq j)$; *i.e.,* $F_j(x)$ *is concave in* x.

ASSUMPTION 2: $\partial f_j/\partial x_i = \partial f_i/\partial x_j$ *for* $i,j=1, \ldots, n$; *i.e., the effect of member* i's *output on member* j's *demand equals the effect of member* j's *output on member* i's *demand.*

These effects are made up of the cross-substitution and cross-income effects. Since the cross-substitution effects are always equal, Assumption 2 implies that the cross-income effects are either equal or negligible (see John Hicks, p. 310).

From Assumption 2 and the relation

$$\frac{\partial F_j}{\partial x_i} = x_j \frac{\partial f_j}{\partial x_i} \text{ for } i \neq j$$

we get

(4) $$x_i \frac{\partial F_j}{\partial x_i} = x_j \frac{\partial F_i}{\partial x_j}$$

[3] Morris Adelman estimates the long-run marginal cost, inclusive of a 20 percent rate of return on investment, at about 10 cents per barrel in 1968 prices.

[4] The analysis is not limited to profit maximization, but holds for any set of objective functions $F_1, \ldots, F_n$ of which Assumptions 1–3 are true.

Note that (4) does not imply

$$x_2 \frac{\partial F_1}{\partial x_2} = x_3 \frac{\partial F_1}{\partial x_3} = \ldots = x_n \frac{\partial F_1}{\partial x_n}$$

The cross effect between members i and j need not equal the cross effect between members j and k. Assumption 2 permits but does not imply perfect substitutes.

ASSUMPTION 3: $F(x) \equiv F_1(x) + \ldots + F_n(x)$ *has an interior maximum (not necessarily unique).*

Because of Assumption 1, F is the sum of concave functions and is thus itself concave. Therefore, the first-order conditions for an interior maximum are also sufficient conditions, and Assumption 3 implies:

x^0 maximizes $F(x)$ if and only if

(5) $$\sum_{j=1}^{n} \frac{\partial F_j(x^0)}{\partial x_i} = 0 \text{ for } i = 1, \ldots, n$$

Let M be the set of points maximizing $F(x)$. The concavity of F implies that M is connected, from which it follows that exactly one maximizer x^0 has the property

(6) $Var\ [F_1(x^0), \ldots, F_n(x^0)]$ is minimal in M

We shall use this fact to derive an optimal quota rule for the cartel.

The *contract surface* C is the set of points (output vectors x) that maximize $F_i(x)$ for constant $F_j(x)$, $i,j=1, \ldots, n$, $j \neq i$. At a point on C member i's isoprofit surface is tangent to a hyperplane H_i. The hyperplanes $H_1, \ldots, H_n$ intersect in a line L to which the n isoprofit surfaces are mutually tangent. Thus to each point $x \in C$ there corresponds one line $L(x)$ to which the isoprofit surfaces are tangent at x. See Figure 2 for an illustration in two dimensions.

A point $\bar{x} \in C$ has the *ray property* whenever $L(\bar{x})$ is a ray from the origin (as in Figure 2). All points on the boundary of C have the ray property (for example, the monopoly points $(x_1^m,0)$ and $(0,x_2^m)$ in Fig-

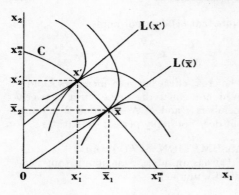

FIGURE 2

ure 2) but it is not obvious that any interior points have this property.

Define *grad $F_i(x)$* as

$$(\partial F_i(x)/\partial x_1, \ldots, \partial F_i(x)/\partial x_n)$$

the gradient vector of member i's profit function at the point x. This vector is normal to member i's isoprofit surface at x; hence it is orthogonal to the line $L(x)$. If x lacks the ray property $L(x)$ does not pass through the origin; in that case the output vector x does not lie on $L(x)$ and is thus not orthogonal to *grad $F_i(x)$* for any i. But each output vector $\bar{x}$ with the ray property is orthogonal to *grad $F_i(\bar{x})$*, i.e., $\bar{x} \cdot grad \, F_i(\bar{x}) = 0$ for $i = 1, \ldots, n$ if and only if $\bar{x}$ has the ray property. Hence the following system of equations holds if and only if $\bar{x}$ has the ray property:

$$(7) \qquad \sum_{j=1}^{n} \bar{x}_j \frac{\partial F_i(\bar{x})}{\partial x_j} = 0 \text{ for } i = 1, \ldots, n$$

Now let us return to system (5) and multiply equation i of that system by x_i^0.

$$(8) \qquad \sum_{j=1}^{n} x_i^0 \frac{\partial F_j(x^0)}{\partial x_i} = 0 \text{ for } i = 1, \ldots, n$$

Because of Assumption 3, system (8) holds if and only if system (5) does. Now use (4) to rewrite (8) in the equivalent form:

$$(9) \qquad \sum_{j=1}^{n} x_j^0 \frac{\partial F_i(x^0)}{\partial x_j} = 0 \text{ for } i = 1, \ldots, n$$

This system holds if and only if x^0 is an interior maximizer of $F(x)$; it evidently has the same solutions as (7), which holds if and only if $\bar{x}$ has the ray property. Hence an interior point maximizes joint profits if and only if it has the ray property. (Thus $\bar{x}$ in Figure 2 maximizes joint profits.)

The *cartel point* is the unique point $x^0 \in C$ which satisfies (6).

II. A Quota Rule

If the cartel were merely to assign the quota x_i^0 to member i, where x^0 is the cartel point, it would maximize joint profits provided no member cheated. But of course each member would gain by cheating, even if found out. The assignment would not resolve the prisoners' dilemma. To resolve that dilemma the cartel must assign each member a quota *rule*, an operating rule incorporating a deterrent to cheating; and the deterrent must take the form of a credible threat of retaliation. The cartel has such a rule, and that rule solves the sharing problem as well.

Let

$$s_i = \frac{x_i^0}{\sum_{j=1}^{n} x_j^0}$$

be member i's market share at the cartel point, and consider the following

(10)   *Quota Rule for Member i*: Produce

$$\max\{x_i^0, \; x_i^0 + \frac{s_i}{s_j} \Delta x_j\}$$

where Δx_j is the amount by which member j's output deviates from his quota x_j^0.[5]

[5] A more complete rule is, "Produce

$$\max\{x_i^0, \; x_i^0 + s_i \sum_{j \in J} \Delta x_j / \sum_{j \in J} s_j\}$$

where each member j in J deviates from his quota by Δx_j." The ensuing discussion applies, *mutatis mutandis*, to this rule as well.

Upon discovering that member j cheats, member i increases his output so that when all the other loyal members increase their outputs according to rule, all market shares are preserved. This rule operates to keep the output vector x on the ray $L(x^0)$; it gives the smallest increase in output that can be shared *pro rata* between the loyal members and that will punish the cheater; it is a "cheapest deterrent."

Member j will not cheat if he expects the other members to obey their quota rules; he (and the other members) would end up somewhere beyond x^0 on the line $L(x^0)$, thus losing profits. The n quota rules, regarded as strategies, form a Nash equilibrium point in the space of all strategies; i.e., no member can gain by a unilateral departure *of any kind* from his assigned quota rule.

Moreover, member j has every reason to expect the other members to follow their quota rules and retaliate to his cheating, for in so doing they will lose less than by standing pat at x_i^0. This important fact can be understood with the help of Figure 3.

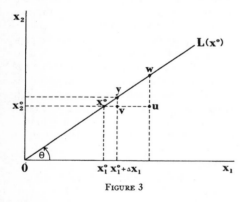

FIGURE 3

If member 1 increases his output by a small amount Δx_1 and member 2 retaliates according to rule, the output vector will move to y. Member 2's profit will change by the amount $\Delta x_1 D_v F_2(x^0)$, where

$$D_y F_2(x^0) = \cos\theta\, \partial F_2(x^0)/\partial x_1$$
$$+ \sin\theta\, \partial F_2(x^0)/\partial x_2$$

is the directional derivative, in the direction from x^0 to y, of F_2 at x^0. Let

$$d = \sqrt{(x_1^0)^2 + (x_2^0)^2}$$

so that $\cos\theta = \overset{0}{x_1}/d$, $\sin\theta = \overset{0}{x_2}/d$

then the directional derivative has the form

$$D_y F_2(x^0) = \frac{\overset{0}{x_1}}{d}\frac{\partial F_2(x^0)}{\partial x_1} + \frac{\overset{0}{x_2}}{d}\frac{\partial F_2(x^0)}{\partial x_2}$$

On the other hand, if member 2 stands pat the output vector will move to v and his profit will change by $\Delta x_1 D_v F_2(x^0)$, where

$$D_v F_2(x^0) = \partial F_2(x^0)/\partial x_1$$

is the directional derivative in the direction of v. Member 2 will lose less by retaliating than by standing pat if $D_y F_2(x^0) > D_v F_2(x^0)$, i.e., if

$$(11) \qquad \frac{\partial F_2(x^0)}{\partial x_2} > \frac{d - \overset{0}{x_1}}{x_2^0}\frac{\partial F_2(x^0)}{\partial x_1}$$

This inequality certainly holds because the left side is positive and the right side is negative. Hence $F_2(y) > F_2(v)$ and member 2 is better off retaliating than not. The quota rule thus incorporates a credible threat.

It is true that member 2 will not necessarily lose less by retaliating in full to a *large* increase in x_1 (i.e., $F_2(u)$ might be greater than $F_2(w)$, see Figure 3); but he is better off retaliating at least in part, because of (11). And the cheater will lose money by *any* retaliation: since $L(x^0)$ is tangent to his isoprofit surface at x^0 any outward movement along it will reduce his profit. Unlike the prisoners' dilemma, no member is tempted to cheat unless he can escape detection by all members. The quota rule therefore solves the problem of deterring.

840   THE AMERICAN ECONOMIC REVIEW   DECEMBER 1976

The rule also solves the problem of sharing. This is particularly obvious if $F(x)$ has a unique maximizer x^0. Let x' be any proposed solution of the sharing problem. In order to get his cooperation the cartel must allow member i to earn as much per period at x' as he could earn by buying up the other members and becoming a monopolist.[6] As a monopolist member i would obtain $F(x^0)$ per period; to buy out the other members would cost him the capitalized value of their per period profits

$$\sum_{\substack{j=1 \\ j \neq i}}^{n} F_j(x')$$

Hence x' must have the property

$$\frac{F_i(x')}{r} \geq \frac{F(x^0)}{r} - \left[\frac{F_1(x') + \ldots + F_{i-1}(x') + F_{i+1}(x') + \ldots F_n(x')}{r} \right]$$

for $i = 1, \ldots, n$, where r is the appropriate rate of interest (assuming an infinite time horizon for simplicity). This implies

$$\sum_{i=1}^{n} F_i(x') \geq F(x^0)$$

and since x^0 maximizes $F(x)$ the cooperation can be obtained only at the joint maximum.

A deeper reason why the quota rule solves the sharing problem is found in the ray property of x^0. If a proposed sharing solution x' lacked the ray property then the cartel would have more trouble with the deterring problem. Suppose $L(x')$ is not a ray and let s'_i be member i's market share at x'. If, *first*, the cartel told member i to produce

$$\max\left\{ x'_i, \, x'_i + \frac{s'_i}{s'_j} \Delta x_j \right\}$$

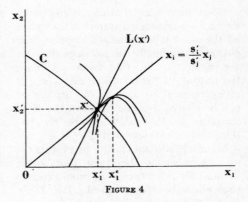

FIGURE 4

then at least one member j would be tempted to cheat even if he were certain to be caught; for in that case x'_j would not maximize $F_j(x)$ against the quota rules of the other members.[7] The ray through x' would intersect a better isoprofit surface of member j than the isoprofit surface through x' (see Figure 4, illustrating how, given member 2's observance of his quota rule, member 1 could get more profit by producing x_1^c than by producing x'_1). Only when a market-sharing quota rule is expressed in terms of a point with the ray property will this temptation disappear. If, *second*, the cartel told member i to produce x'_i if every other member j produces x'_j but to move out along the line $L(x')$ if the others produce more, then some members will lose market share by retaliating. (Only along a ray are the market shares constant.) Those members standing to lose market share would have a less credible threat, and so the deterrent would be weaker.

In case more than one point maximizes joint profits, the unique point that minimizes the variance of profits in M also minimizes jealousy and resentment; it is an obvious "focal point" (see Thomas Schelling).

VOL. 66 NO. 5   *OSBORNE: CARTEL PROBLEMS*   841

The quota rule (10) thus neatly solves the sharing and deterring problems in one fell swoop. We cannot expect it to be overlooked by cartels which are able to solve their other problems. Their managers may have been to Harvard Business School.

III. Nonmember and Locating Problems

Part of the problem of locating the contract surface is to predict the behavior of the firms that remain outside the cartel. Variations in the total output of these firms change the members' profit functions and thus shift the contract surface about. As these variations are likely to depend on the cartel's output the contract surface is not exogenously given, but varies with cartel production. In the best case—from the point of view of a cartel which cannot control it—the external production is wholly predictable, a known function of cartel production. To each cartel output there will then correspond one position of the contract surface, and the cartel will be able to choose the output which places the surface in the best position.

The external firms are likely to behave as Cournot followers. The cartel can then act as a Stackelberg leader, maximizing its profit subject to the Cournot reaction functions of the external firms. In this position, though its profit will be lower than it would be if no external firms existed, the cartel is doing the best it can subject to the existence of such firms. Total industry profit will not be maximized, but it will be positive.[8] We should not underestimate this problem, but neither should we exaggerate it; it does not appear to be a source of inherent instability in itself, but is most serious in connection with the detection problem.

The other, and more important, parts of the location problem are not so much

sources of instability to actual cartels as obstacles that many potential cartels never overcome. Bjarke Fog has reported some of the differences of opinion that prevent the formation of cartels. People have differing views about the availability of substitutes, differing expectations about the future course of the market, and differing time preferences. The latter is especially troublesome. If some member j takes a longer view than the majority, more lightly discounting the future, he might well think that the contract surface is higher, i.e., that F is maximized by a larger x than the majority thinks. He will reckon the present value of his earnings to be higher at an output larger than x_j^0; he will "cheat" and be better off (in his own view) even if the other members retaliate according to rule. Obviously, if the members can't agree on the joint profit-maximizing output they will not agree on their shares.[9] Still, these differences are sometimes resolved. Cartels do get formed. In any case public policy can do little to exacerbate the locating problem. Perhaps we could adopt a policy of deliberate misinformation, making demand appear to be more elastic than it is.[10]

IV. Detecting

It is to the problem of detecting cheating that we must turn for a source of instability more amenable to public policy. This problem is not inherently insoluble (suppose there are only two members), but it is difficult. George Stigler has studied

---

[8] If new entry can occur the cartel might practice limit pricing, along the lines considered by Morton Kamien and Nancy Schwartz, or the author.

[9] Cartels composed of national and private firms are especially prone to this source of disagreement. The nationalized firms, especially in underdeveloped countries, are likely to take the *shorter* view. Owing to frequent changes of government, the civil servants and politicians who make the decisions must discount the future very heavily.

[10] With respect to the demand for crude oil, the opposite effect is achieved by the civil servants and political figures in the consuming countries who soberly extrapolate the yearly growth of consumption of $3 oil to determine the "national needs" for $10 oil.

some aspects of the problem; to his excellent discussion I have only a little to add.

With respect to output a cartel could find itself in one of four positions. First, it could know the output of each member (perhaps after a brief lag). In this position the cartel has solved the detection problem completely, and can adopt the quota rule explained above. Second, the cartel can know the total output of all members taken together, but not the output of individual members. In this second-best position the cartel can modify the quota rule and still preserve some of its deterrent effect.

(12) *Modified Quota Rule for Member* i:

Produce $\max\{x_i^0, x_i^0 + ns_i z\}$

where $1/n$ is the average quota share and z is the amount by which cartel output deviates from

$$\sum_{i=1}^{n} x_i^0$$

Member i is thus told to assume that the unknown cheater has an average quota, and to increase output accordingly.

This modified rule operates to keep the *expected* output vector on $L(x^0)$; it incorporates a credible threat, just as rule (10) does, and thus deters cheating on the average, but it might not deter cheating by any member with an exceptionally small quota. Such a member might still gain profit by cheating because his actual market share increases enough to overmatch the price depressing effect of the greater total cartel output. This problem is more severe the greater the variance of quota shares. One possible solution is to modify rule (10) in a different manner—to tell member i to produce the larger of x_i^0 and $x_i^0 + (s_i/s^*)z$, where s^* is the smallest quota share. This will deter, but perhaps at a cost which is unnecessarily high (an unduly large increase in cartel output). Other modifica-

tions could be considered, but none can be wholly effective. This second position is therefore a true second best.

Third, the cartel could know the total industry output, but not the total output of the cartel. Evidently, this position can arise only when some producers remain outside the cartel; with respect to the detection problem it is equivalent to the fourth position, in which the cartel is ignorant of total industry output. These are the positions in which public policy must try to place cartels.

Given the fondness of the bureaucracy of all developed nations for publishing output statistics (some of them useful), public policy cannot place *domestic* cartels in the third or fourth positions. But if some important producers remain independent, the situation is different in the case of international cartels. We can illustrate with reference to the *OPEC* cartel.

With only the shortest of lags, world shipments of crude oil are known by all interested parties. The information is collected and reported by trade journals and various national and international agencies, and could in any case be inferred from a number of sources (for example, tanker charterings). All producers know their current market shares to a high degree of accuracy, and can thus learn if someone is cheating; they cannot so easily learn *who* is cheating. The members are sovereign states; they can attempt to keep their sales statistics secret if they wish. And some important producers (for example, Mexico) remain outside the cartel. *OPEC* thus finds itself in the third of the four positions. The likely consequences are a matter for speculation, but the following events are possible.

An increase in world shipments reduces the market shares of the loyal members who, however, cannot detect its source. If they assume the source to be external and remain at x_i^0 they will, in effect, demonstrate the profitability of cheating; those least loyal to the cartel will then secretly increase their output. On the other hand, if the loyal members assume the source to be internal and obey their quota rules (however modified), they will risk a needless increase in cartel output. With either choice the additional cartel output, added to the original increase from the unknown source, reduces prices. Distrust grows. Discipline weakens generally, and can be expected ultimately to disappear. Each member must look out for himself. Plenty of business can be done at a dollar under the cartel price; but it must be done quickly, for the buyers are daily demanding better terms. There is a general scurry for orders, and long-term commitments are made at $1, then $2, then $5 and $6 under the cartel price. The cartel has collapsed.

This outcome is by no means certain; it is possible, and we must nurture the possibility. It will be *impossible* if the consuming nations establish a central purchasing agency through which all orders are funneled. Sellers will be identified. Undetected cheating will be impossible and known by all to be impossible. The agency will have solved the severest problem that the cartel faced, thus placing it in the first of the four positions. In these circumstances who would be rash enough to predict anything but a *stable* oil cartel?

V. Summary

A cartel is inherently unstable only if it faces inherently insoluble problems. Of the five problems that we noticed, the three most serious are those of locating the contract surface, which requires information about demand and costs, predicting and if possible discouraging production by external firms (which affects the demands for members' output and is thus a species of the location problem), and detecting cheating by members. We considered these problems only in enough detail to see that,

while difficult, they are not inherently insoluble. The two remaining problems are to determine quotas and deter cheating. We treated them jointly because a good solution of the one also solves the other, and we saw that a quota rule expressed in terms of the ray through the cartel point deters cheating (unless it is undetected) and embodies a credible threat of retaliation. This rule has the further advantages of being the simplest rule with that property and requiring the smallest retaliatory increase in output that can be shared *pro rata* by the loyal members. Thus the sharing and deterring problems are not inherently insoluble either. A cartel is not inherently unstable.

From this it does not follow that a cartel is stable. Though it can solve its problems in principle, it might nevertheless fail to solve them in practice. But to recognize that a cartel might collapse because it cannot control external production or detect cheating is quite different from believing that all are necessarily doomed. So much depends on the particular features of their environments that no general prediction about the durability of cartels is justified.[11]

---

[11] Note added in proof: Further research into cartel history, undertaken after this article was written, convinces me that there is one justifiable prediction: a cartel will last—possibly succumbing to epidemics of cheating from time to time, but soon thereafter re-forming itself—until new substitutes appear at a price near its marginal cost. I can find no record of a cartel which died of internal problems alone, but plenty which fell to new substitutes. I therefore regret my suggestion that external production is a problem comparable to the internal ones. It is not; it is the one fatal problem. But this does not mean that collective purchasing would only be a trivial mistake. It would still delay and shorten the outbreaks of price competition that normally occur from time to time even in cartels protected from substitutes; but more significantly, it would also delay, and possibly prevent, the development of substitutes. The delegates to the collective purchasing agencies would sooner or later vest their interest in the orderly operation of established arrangements, and would perceive new substitutes as nothing more than a threat to settled practice. This they naturally would resist.

A cartel of raw material producers is well placed with respect to the nonmember problem. Its chief difficulty is the detection of cheating, a problem that public policy should exacerbate if possible and avoid solving in any case. The correct policy here as in so many areas is more easily expressed in negative than in positive terms: Take no action that will lead to the identification of individual transactors—it will only discourage cheating and preserve the cartel.

Though we considered the detection problem with reference to *OPEC* the analysis applies more generally. The success of this cartel has planted seeds in many minds in those countries which export primary materials. We can expect some of them to bear fruit, the more so if an international oil-buying agency keeps *OPEC* in business. We will hear proposals for the establishment of international agencies to present a "united front" to the banana, coffee, copper, tin, . . . , and bauxite cartels, to share the reduced output "on an equitable basis," or, depending on who does the proposing, to guarantee to the cartel an "orderly marketing arrangement" in ex-change for a dollar or two off its price. These proposals are gravely mistaken.

REFERENCES

M. A. Adelman, *The World Petroleum Market,* London, Baltimore 1972.

J. S. Bain, "Output Quotas in Imperfect Cartels," *Quart. J. Econ.,* Aug. 1948, *62,* 617–22.

B. Fog, "How Are Cartel Prices Determined?," *J. Ind. Econ.,* Nov. 1956, *5,* 16–23.

J. R. Hicks, *Value and Capital,* 2d ed., Oxford 1946.

M. I. Kamien and N. L. Schwartz, "Limit Pricing and Uncertain Entry," *Econometrica,* May 1971, *39,* 441–54.

R. D. Luce and H. Raiffa, *Games and Decisions,* New York 1957.

D. K. Osborne, "On the Rationality of Limit Pricing," *J. Ind. Econ.,* Sept. 1973, *22,* 71–80.

D. Patinkin, "Multi-Plant Firms, Cartels, and Imperfect Competition," *Quart. J. Econ.,* Feb. 1947, *61,* 173–205.

T. Schelling, *The Strategy of Conflict,* Cambridge 1960.

G. J. Stigler, "A Theory of Oligopoly," *J. Polit. Econ.,* Feb. 1964, *72,* 44–61.

Professor D. K. Osborne

Professor of Finance and Mangerial Economics
The University of Texas at Dallas
School of Management
Box 830688
Richardson
Texas 75083-0688
USA

[10]

A Non-cooperative Equilibrium for Supergames [1,2]

JAMES W. FRIEDMAN
University of Rochester

I. INTRODUCTION

John Nash has contributed to game theory and economics two solution concepts for nonconstant sum games. One, the non-cooperative solution [9] is a generalization of the minimax theorem for two person zero sum games and of the Cournot solution; and the other, the cooperative solution [10], is completely new. It is the purpose of this paper to present a non-cooperative equilibrium concept, applicable to supergames, which fits the Nash (non-cooperative) definition and also has some features resembling the Nash cooperative solution. "Supergame" describes the playing of an infinite sequence of "ordinary games" over time.[3] Oligopoly may profitably be viewed as a supergame. In each time period the players are in a game, and they know they will be in similar games with the same other players in future periods.

The most novel element of the present paper is in the introduction of a completely new concept of solution for non-cooperative supergames. In addition to proposing this solution, a proof of its existence is given. It is also argued that the usual notions of "threat" which are found in the literature of game theory make no sense in non-cooperative supergames. There is something analogous to threat, called "temptation", which does have an intuitive appeal and is related to the solution which is proposed.

In section II the ordinary game will be described, the non-cooperative equilibrium defined and its existence established. Section III contains a description of supergames and supergame strategies. In section IV a definition and discussion of a non-cooperative equilibrium for supergames is given. This equilibrium shares some of the attributes of the Nash-Harsanyi [10, 6] cooperative solution, and is very much in the spirit of the solution proposed several years ago by Professor Robert L. Bishop in the *American Economic Review* [2]. In section V existence will be proved, in section VI some assumptions will be relaxed, and in section VII economic applications will be discussed.

II. THE GAME AND THE NASH NON-COOPERATIVE EQUILIBRIUM

An "ordinary game" is a game in which each player has a set of strategies which is a compact, convex subset of a Euclidean space of finite dimension, there are a finite number of players and the payoff to each player is a function of the chosen strategies of all players. In this section, the ordinary game will be described in detail. A proposition, due originally to Nash [9], will be proved. It establishes the existence of a non-cooperative equilibrium for the ordinary game. Although this result was previously known, it is included for completeness. A game is said to be "non-cooperative" if it is not possible for the players to form coalitions or make agreements.

[1] *First version received, May* 1969; *final version received March* 1970 (*Eds*).
[2] The author gratefully acknowledges the support of the National Science Foundation in the research reported here.
[3] Some discussion of early work on supergames may be found in Luce and Raiffa [8], and some interesting developments in cooperative supergames, by Aumann, is begun in [1].

1

2   REVIEW OF ECONOMIC STUDIES

Denote the strategy of the ith player by s_i, a vector in r_i-dimensional Euclidean space, R^{r_i}. The strategy set of the ith player is taken to be a compact, convex subset of R^{r_i}, denoted S_i. There is a fixed, finite number of players, n, and the strategy set of the game S, is $S_1 \times ... \times S_n$, the Cartesian product of the individual strategy sets. A vector of strategies, one for each player, is denoted $s = (s_1, ..., s_n)$ and $\bar{s}_i$ denotes the strategy vector $(s_1, ..., s_{i-1}, s_{i+1}, ..., s_n)$. Thus $\bar{s}_i$ consists of the strategy choices of all players except the ith, and $s = (\bar{s}_i, s_i)$.

Payoff to the ith player is a real valued function of strategy, s, and is denoted $\pi_i(s)$. A vector of payoffs, associated with a given vector of strategies, may be denoted

$$\pi(s) = (\pi_1(s), ..., \pi_n(s)) \in R^n.$$

Assumptions made on the strategy space S and the payoff functions are:

A1 S_i is compact and convex $(i = 1, ..., n)$;

A2 The payoff functions, $\pi_i(s)$, are continuous and bounded on S, for all i;

A3 The payoff functions $\pi_i(s) = \pi_i(\bar{s}_i, s_i)$ are quasi-concave functions of s_i, for all i.

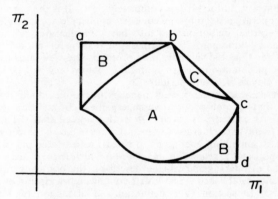

FIGURE 1

A point in the payoff space $(\pi_1(s^*), ..., \pi_n(s^*)) = \pi(s^*)$ is said to be " Pareto optimal " if

(i) $s^* \in S$ and
(ii) there is no $s \in S$ for which $\pi_i(s) > \pi_i(s^*)$ $(i = 1, ..., n)$.

Denote by H, the set of attainable payoffs: $H = \{\pi(s) \mid s \in S\}$. Denote by $H^* \subset H$, the set of Pareto optimal payoffs.

A4 If $\pi' \leq \pi''$ (i.e., $\pi_i' \leq \pi_i''$, $i = 1, ..., n$) and $\pi', \pi'' \in H$, then $\pi \in H$ where $\pi' \leq \pi \leq \pi''$;

A5 H^* is concave.

Most of the assumptions above are both reasonable and clear. The least so is A4, which will be discussed in section VI. Fig. 1 illustrates the meaning of certain of the assumptions. Region " A " is an arbitrary compact set. Compactness is required by A1 and A2. By A4, the regions denoted " B " are added, and by A5, region " C " is added. H^* is the heavy outer boundary *abcd*. Assumptions A4 and A5 mean that sets $H(\pi') = \{\pi \mid \pi > \pi', \pi \in H\}$ are convex, and for any $\pi \in H$ any non-negatively sloped ray through π will intersect H^* at exactly one point. This property will prove convenient in sections IV and V.

It remains in this section to define " non-cooperative equilibrium ", and prove its existence for ordinary games of the sort under study in this section. s^* is a non-cooperative equilibrium strategy vector if $s^* \in S$ and

$$\pi_i(s^*) = \max_{s_i \in S_i} \pi_i(\bar{s}_i^*, s_i), \quad i = 1, \ldots, n.$$

Proposition 1. *Any game satisfying A1, A2 and A3 has a non-cooperative equilibrium.*

Proof.[1] Define $\mu(s) = \mu_1(\bar{s}_1) \times \mu_2(\bar{s}_2) \times \ldots \times \mu_n(\bar{s}_n)$ as follows:

$$\mu_i(\bar{s}_i) = \{t_i \mid t_i \in S_i, \pi_i(\bar{s}_i, t_i) = \max_{s_i \in S_i} \pi_i(\bar{s}_i, s_i)\}, \quad (i = 1, \ldots, n), \quad s \in S;$$

$\mu_i(\bar{s}_i)$ is clearly compact and convex. As $\mu_i(\bar{s}_i) \subset S_i$, it is bounded. That $\mu_i(\bar{s}_i)$ is closed follows from the continuity of π_i, and convexity follows from the quasi-concavity of π_i in s_i. As this holds for all i, the sets $\mu(s) = \mu_1(\bar{s}_1) \times \mu_2(\bar{s}_2) \times \ldots \times \mu_n(\bar{s}_n)$ are compact, convex and subsets of S.

If it can be shown that the correspondence $\mu \colon S \to S$ is upper semi-continuous, the Kakutani [7] fixed point theorem may be applied. A fixed point of μ is a non-cooperative equilibrium. Let $\bar{s}_i^l \in \bar{S}_i, l = 1, 2, \ldots$, be a sequence of strategies converging to $\bar{s}_i^0$. $\mu_i(\bar{s}_i)$ is upper semi-continuous if, when

(a) $s_i^l \in \mu_i(\bar{s}_i^l), \quad l = 1, 2, \ldots,$ and

(b) $\lim_{l \to \infty} \bar{s}_i^l = \bar{s}_i^0$ and $\lim_{l \to \infty} s_i^l = s_i^0$ then

(c) $s_i^0 \in \mu_i(\bar{s}_i^0).$

Assume a sequence as described in (a) and (b), but assume (c) is false (i.e., $s_i^0 \notin \mu_i(\bar{s}_i^0)$). If $s_i^0 \notin \mu_i(\bar{s}_i^0)$, then $\pi_i(\bar{s}_i^0, s_i^0) < \pi_i(\bar{s}_i^0, s_i')$ for $s_i' \in \mu_i(\bar{s}_i^0)$. Say $\pi_i(\bar{s}_i^0, s_i') - \pi_i(\bar{s}_i^0, s_i^0) = \varepsilon > 0$. Now consider $\pi_i(\bar{s}_i^l, s_i^l)$. By the continuity of π_i, it is possible to choose an arbitrary $\delta > 0$ such that for $l \geq \mathcal{L}(\delta)$ ($\mathcal{L}(\delta)$, finite),

$$\pi_i(\bar{s}_i^0, s_i') - \delta < \pi_i(\bar{s}_i^l, s_i^l) < \pi_i(\bar{s}_i^0, s_i') + \delta.$$

Choosing $\delta < \varepsilon$ leads to a contradiction; hence, $s_i^0 \in \mu_i(\bar{s}_i^0)$ and μ_i is upper semi-continuous. As this holds for all i, μ is upper semi-continuous and has a fixed point. Let such a fixed point be $s^* \in \mu(s^*)$. By the definition of the μ_i,

$$\max_{s_i \in S_i} \pi_i(\bar{s}_i^*, s_i) = \pi_i(s^*), \quad i = 1, \ldots, n,$$

therefore s^* is a non-cooperative equilibrium strategy vector and $\pi(s^*)$ a non-cooperative equilibrium payoff vector.

It may be noted in passing that when the payoff functions are profit functions, the players are firms and the strategies are prices or quantities, the game is a (single period) oligopoly. The non-cooperative equilibrium becomes the same as the " Cournot solution " [3]. In this instance S_i is merely the interval of prices (or quantities) among which the firm is allowed to choose. Frank and Quandt [5] proved the existence of the Cournot equilibrium for a quantity model. Their result is, of course, a special case of Proposition 1, above, and, *a fortiori*, a special case of the theorem of Debreu [4].

Before proceeding to the next section, a final characteristic of the payoff space will be noted: let $\rho = (\rho_1, \ldots, \rho_n)$ be a vector such that $\rho_i \geq 0, i = 1, \ldots, n$ and $\sum_{i=1}^{n} \rho_i = 1$.

---

[1] This proposition is an easy generalization of the Nash [9] theorem, which deals with S_i which are finite sets of pure strategies, together with all mixed strategies attainable from them. The proposition is, on the other hand, a special case of a theorem of Debreu [4], which, so far as the author is aware, is the most general statement of existence of non-cooperative equilibria in finite strategy spaces.

4   REVIEW OF ECONOMIC STUDIES

If k is a scalar, then the points $\pi(s)+k\rho$ $(-\infty < k < \infty)$ form a ray through $\pi(s)$ having non-negative slope. By A4, for any ρ there is a unique $k(\rho) \geqq 0$ such that

$$\pi(s)+k(\rho)\cdot\rho \in H^*$$

for any $s \in S$. In particular, this property holds when s is a non-cooperative equilibrium.

III. SUPERGAMES AND SUPERGAME STRATEGIES

The games of the preceding section have been dealt with in the " normal " form—the form in which there is a payoff function for each player giving his payoff as a function of a strategy vector, $\pi_i(s)$. It is convenient now to define " supergame " in extensive form; i.e., in the form in which each " move " is described. An " ordinary " game may be termed a "finite " game because the strategy sets of the players are compact and reside in a finite space.

Now consider a sequence of ordinary games with strategy sets $S_{i1}, S_{i2}, ..., S_{it}, ...$ and payoff functions $\pi_{it}(s_t)(s_t \in S_t)$; $t = 1, ...$; $i = 1, ..., n$. The tth game has $S_{1t} \times ... \times S_{nt} = S_{nt} = S_t$ as its strategy set and $\pi_{it}(s_t)$ $(i = 1, ..., n)$ as its payoff functions. A " supergame " is a game in which the tth move $(t = 1, ...)$ is the playing of the tth ordinary game in the sequence. At each move a payoff is received and, if the strategy sequence $s_1, ..., s_t, ...$ is played, the payoff to the ith player in the supergame is

$$\sum_{t=1}^{\infty} \alpha_{it}\pi_{it}(s_t),$$

where α_{it} is the discount parameter of the ith player in the tth time period. It is obvious that a " supergame " in which the number of moves is finite is merely a finite game; hence, attention will be restricted to supergames as defined above, which have a countably infinite number of moves.

The general definition of a supergame strategy for the ith player is as follows:

$$s_{it} = f_{it}(s_1, ..., s_{t-1}), \quad t = 2, 3, ...,$$
$$= s_{i1}, \quad\quad\quad\quad t = 1.$$

$f_{it}(t = 2, 3, ...)$ is a sequence of functions which map all preceding ordinary game strategies of all players into the present (tth) ordinary game strategy of the ith player. As there is no past information available in the initial period, there must be a particular initial move. Then $(s_{i1}, f_{i2}, f_{i3}, ...)$ is a supergame strategy for the ith player. Existence of non-cooperative equilibria in the supergame is no problem. Indeed the problem is the reverse; it is easy to show existence of a large number. The principle task of this paper is to choose among these in a particular way and single out certain equilibria as being of special interest.

IV. EQUILIBRIUM STRATEGIES IN THE SUPERGAME

This section is devoted to describing a very large class of supergame strategies, to showing when members of this class are non-cooperative equilibria and to introducing a new solution concept.

The exposition will be simplified by using four additional assumptions: (A6) all constituent games of the supergame are identical, (A7) the discount parameters are the same in all periods, (A8) the ordinary game has only one non-cooperative equilibrium, and (A9) the non-cooperative equilibrium is not Pareto optimal. All of these assumptions may be removed with only minor effect on the results. This will be done in section VI.

Denote by σ_i a supergame strategy for the ith player, and denote the non-cooperative equilibrium of the ordinary game by s^c. The " Cournot strategy " is denoted σ^c and is defined by $\sigma_i^c = (s_i^c, s_i^c, ...), (i = 1, ..., n)$. The Cournot strategy is the repeated choice of the non-cooperative equilibrium of the ordinary game. It is immediate that

$$\sigma^c = (\sigma_1^c, ..., \sigma_n^c)$$

is a non-cooperative equilibrium in the supergame. Should any single player in any periods choose moves other than s_i^c he will (by definition of s^c) reduce his payoff in those periods and leave unaffected his payoff in the periods when he still chooses s_i^c.

Now a new class of non-cooperative equilibrium supergame strategies will be specified and discussed.

Let

$$B = \{s \mid s \in S, \pi_i(s) > \pi_i(s^c), \quad i = 1, ..., n\}.$$

B consists of all ordinary game strategies which dominate the ordinary game non-cooperative equilibrium. Let $s' \in B$. Now define a strategy for the ith player, σ_i', as follows:

$$s_{i1} = s_i',$$

$$s_{it} = s_i' \text{ if } s_{j\tau} = s_j' \quad j \neq i, \tau = 1, ..., t-1, t = 2, 3, ...,$$

$$s_{it} = s_i^c \text{ otherwise.}$$

Thus, the ith player chooses s_i' in period 1 and will continue to choose s_i' indefinitely, unless someone else chooses something other than $s_j'(j \neq i)$. If any player in any period chooses $s_j \neq s_j'(j \neq i)$, then in each succeeding period the ith player chooses s_i^c. The supergame strategy vector $\sigma' = (\sigma_1', ..., \sigma_n')$ is a non-cooperative equilibrium if:

$$\sum_{\tau=0}^{\infty} \alpha_i^\tau \pi_i(s') > \pi_i(\bar{s}_i', t_i) + \sum_{\tau=1}^{\infty} \alpha_i^\tau \pi_i(s^c), \quad i = 1, ..., n,$$

or

$$\frac{\alpha_i}{1-\alpha_i} [\pi_i(s') - \pi_i(s^c)] > \pi_i(\bar{s}_i', t_i) - \pi_i(s'), \quad i = 1, ..., n,$$

where $t_i \in S_i$ and $\pi_i(\bar{s}_i', t_i) = \max_{s_i \in S_i} \pi_i(\bar{s}_i', s_i)$.

To see whether σ_i' is the best strategy for the ith player, given $\bar{\sigma}_i'$, consider his alternatives. One is to choose σ_i', which results in using s_i' in every period, while all other players will choose $s_j'(j \neq i)$ and the discounted payoff stream will be

$$\sum_{\tau=0}^{\infty} \alpha_i^\tau \pi_i(s') = \frac{\pi_i(s')}{1-\alpha_i}.$$

Another is to choose $s_{i1} = t_i$, and $s_{it} = s_i^c(t > 1)$. t_i will yield the maximum possible payoff in period 1 (given the other players will choose $s_j'(j \neq i)$). After period 1 all other players will revert to the Cournot strategy, so the payoff maximizing choice after period 1 is $s_{it} = s_i^c$. Any other strategy is weakly dominated by one of the two just described, when the other players are using $\sigma_j'(j \neq i)$.

Which strategy to adopt simply depends upon which discounted profit stream is the larger. I.e., if the gain in the first period of maximizing against $\bar{s}_j' [\pi_i(\bar{s}_i', t_i) - \pi_i(s')]$ is less than the discounted loss from being at the Cournot point in all succeeding periods

$$\left(\frac{\alpha_i}{1-\alpha_i} [\pi_i(s') - \pi_i(s^c)] \right),$$

then σ_i' is the strategy which maximizes discounted payoff for the ith player, given that the strategy choices of the other players are $(\sigma_j', j \neq i)$.

As the discount parameter approaches one from below (discount rate falls to zero), the discounted loss from being at the Cournot point goes to infinity, while the single period gain from choosing t_i is finite and unchanging. So for any $s' \in B$ there is a lower bound for α_i, $\alpha_i(s')$, (such that $\alpha_i(s') < 1$) and if $s' \in B$ and $\alpha_i > \alpha_i(s')$, then σ'_i is optimal against $\bar{\sigma}'_i$. If these conditions hold for $i = 1, \ldots, n$, then $(\sigma'_1, \ldots, \sigma'_n)$ is a non-cooperative equilibrium.

Certain of the $s \in B$ are of special interest. There is a subset $B^* \subset B$ of move vectors which give rise to Pareto optimal payoff vectors:

$s^* \in B^*$ if

(a) $s^* \in B$ and

(b) $\pi(s^*) \in H^*$.

In considering a move vector (i.e. an ordinary game strategy vector), $s^* \in B^*$, why might a player cease choosing s_i^* if he has reason to believe the others will continue choosing $s_j^*(j \neq i)$? Clearly, he may feel a temptation to choose t_i (which maximizes the single period payoff against $\bar{s}_i^*$) because of the extra payoff which may be gained in the short run $[\pi_i(\bar{s}_i^*, t_i) - \pi_i(s^*)]$. Because the players should never, in the long run, receive less than $\pi(s^c)$ per period and because they may follow strategies which send them to π^c under some circumstances, it is intuitively appealing to measure the temptation associated with s^* in relation to $\pi_i(s^*) - \pi_i(s^c)$. Associated with the equilibrium proposed in this paper is the equilibrium move vector, s^*, which satisfies:

$$s^* \in B^*, \qquad\qquad\qquad\qquad \ldots(1)$$

$$\frac{\pi_i(\bar{s}_i^*, t_i) - \pi_i(s^c)}{\pi_i(s^*) - \pi_i(s^c)} = \frac{\pi_j(\bar{s}_j^*, t_j) - \pi_j(s^c)}{\pi_j(s^*) - \pi_j(s^c)}, \quad i, j = 1, \ldots, n. \qquad \ldots(2)$$

This point is Pareto optimal and leaves each player equally tempted (in the sense of the preceding paragraph) to maximize against $\bar{s}_i^*$. An alternative way of expressing (2) is

$$\frac{\pi_i(\bar{s}_i^*, t_i) - \pi_i(s^*)}{\pi_i(s^*) - \pi_i(s^c)} = \frac{\pi_j(\bar{s}_j^*, t_j) - \pi_j(s^*)}{\pi_j(s^*) - \pi_j(s^c)}, \quad i, j = 1, \ldots, n. \qquad \ldots(2')$$

Thus, if $\dfrac{\alpha_i}{1 - \alpha_i} > \dfrac{\pi_i(\bar{s}_i^*, t_i) - \pi_i(s^*)}{\pi_i(s^*) - \pi_i(s^c)}$, $(i = 1, \ldots, n)$, then the strategies $\sigma^* = (\sigma_1^*, \ldots, \sigma_n^*)$ form a non-cooperative equilibrium, where σ_i^* is defined by

$$s_{i1} = s_i^*,$$

$$s_{it} = s_i^* \text{ if } s_{j\tau} = s_j^*(j \neq i), \tau = 1, \ldots, t-1, t > 1,$$

$$s_{it} = s_i^c \text{ otherwise.}$$

It should be emphasized that σ^*, in addition to being a non-cooperative equilibrium, is Pareto optimal. s^c, the non-cooperative equilibrium of the basic game need not be Pareto optimal, and, as students of oligopoly theory are aware, its oligopoly counterpart, the Cournot solution, is generally *not*. It remains to show that ordinary game strategies satisfying (1) and (2) above do, in fact, exist. Before turning to that task, some comments will be made concerning properties of this concept of solution.

It is natural to ask if the proposed solution possesses any appealing properties and and also whether one might expect a cooperative solution to emerge (such as the Nash-Harsanyi [10, 6] even though the game is non-cooperative. While the Nash-Harsanyi solution applies to ordinary games, one could propose the sequence of Nash-Harsanyi solutions of the ordinary games as the solution of the supergame. The main reason for rejecting this, and other, cooperative solutions is that they rely on features of games which are peculiar to cooperative games and absent in non-cooperative. These revolve about the notion of " threat ".

It is often part of a cooperative game that the players name threat strategies and then, if they fail to come to agreement, they are forced to carry out these threat strategies. If he were not forced, a player would do better in the absence of agreement to maximize against the strategies he expects the others to use. Applying this reasoning to all players, one would expect them to choose the non-cooperative equilibrium—if they were not forced to carry out threats. This undermines the credibility of the threats.

Now consider the cooperative game from another vantage point. When a single player (or a subset forming a coalition) calculates the best payoff he can get by himself, he does so on the assumption that all other players will band together and adopt a strategy aimed at minimizing his payoff. Even in a cooperative game, this may appear an unduly costly way for the others to act; however, as a threat to coerce the player into an agreement with all other players, it has some appeal. By contrast, in the non-cooperative game coalitions are ruled out, players cannot talk and bargain with one another; hence, it is foolish to think other players wish to minimize one's own payoff. Each will want to maximize his own payoff and will not really care about payoffs to others. In other words, threats are out of place in non-cooperative games because they cannot be clearly and effectively voiced, and because they are not credible. They need not be carried out and there is no incentive to do so.

The notion of " temptation " in the supergame is slightly analogous to threat. If a player can increase his single period profit for a period or so, he may be tempted to do so, but the other players are, in response, likely to revert to a " safe " position. This is a position in which no one has any temptation to move for the sake of short term gain.

There are certain properties which one might like an equilibrium to possess:

$\alpha 1$, The solution should be unique, and always exist;

$\alpha 2$, The solution should be independent of irrelevant alternatives;

$\alpha 3$, The solution should be Pareto optimal;

$\alpha 4$, The solution should be symmetric;

$\alpha 5$, The solution should be invariant to a positive linear transformation of a payoff function;

$\alpha 6$, The solution should be a non-cooperative equilibrium.

The Nash cooperative solution satisfies $\alpha 2$-$\alpha 5$. The solution proposed here satisfies $\alpha 3$-$\alpha 6$. Properties $\alpha 3$ and $\alpha 6$ are obviously fulfilled, as is $\alpha 5$ (note that equation (2) is free of origin and scale). The meaning of $\alpha 4$ is that the solution should not depend on who is called player 1, who player 2, etc. That $\alpha 1$ is not met is obvious already, as existence depends on the discount parameter not being too small. It will be seen that if the α_i are sufficiently near one, an equilibrium must exist. Neither the present equilibrium nor the Nash-Harsanyi need be unique (except for the $N-H$ when $n = 2$).

The irrelevant alternatives assumption, $\alpha 2$, deserves special mention. Its meaning is that if you enlarge the set of available strategies, S, to a set $A \supset S$, then one of two conditions will hold: (i) the solution to the enlarged game will be the same as in the smaller game, or (ii) the solution will be a point, $y \in A$, which was not previously available ($y \notin S$). In other words the addition of new strategies cannot affect the solution unless one of the new strategies is the new solution. Thus the solution depends only on local properties of the payoff surface in the neighbourhood of the solution. This is very restrictive.

With the solution concept presented here one can well imagine $\alpha 2$ being violated. For example, enlarge the move space from S to $A = A_1 \times \ldots \times A_n$. Conceivably one or more players find that, while the old solution $s^* \in S$, is still Pareto optimal (and s^c is still the only single period non-cooperative equilibrium), the t_i do not satisfy

$$\max_{s_i \in A_i} \pi_i(\bar{s}_i^*, s_i) = \pi_i(\bar{s}_i^*, t_i).$$

Should this happen, the point, y^*, which is the new equilibrium, might be in S, although the associated t_i will not all be in S.[1] It is good that the solution offered in this paper is not restricted by $\alpha 2$.

V. EXISTENCE OF EQUILIBRIUM

The existence proof is based upon a fixed point argument which, while it guarantees existence, does not guarantee uniqueness. The fixed point argument will be used to show that points s^* exist such that

$$\frac{\pi_i(\bar{s}_i^*, t_i) - \pi_i(s^*)}{\pi_i(s^*) - \pi_i(s^c)} = \frac{\pi_j(\bar{s}_j^*, t_j) - \pi_j(s^*)}{\pi_j(s^*) - \pi_j(s^c)}, \quad (i, j = 1, ..., n).$$

A point s^* has n points $(\bar{s}_i^*, t_i)$ associated with it. The t_i are determined by

$$\pi_i(\bar{s}_i^*, t_i) = \max_{s_i \in S_i} \pi_i(\bar{s}_i^*, s_i).$$

In fact $\bar{s}_i^* \in \bar{S}_i$ is mapped into π_i. Denote this mapping ϕ_i. A preliminary result will now be proved.

Proposition 2. *The mappings ϕ_i are continuous, for all i.*

Without loss of generality, the proposition may be proved with specific reference to ϕ_1. Let $\bar{s}_1^0$ be any point in $\bar{S}_1$ and let $s_1^0 \in S_1$ be chosen so that $\pi_1(\bar{s}_1^0, s_1^0) = \phi_1(\bar{s}_1^0)$. Let $\bar{s}_1^l (l = 1, 2, ...)$ be a sequence of points in $\bar{S}_1$ such that $\bar{s}_1^l \to \bar{s}_1^0$ as $l \to \infty$. By definition of ϕ_1, there is a s_1^l associated with $\bar{s}^l$ such that $\pi_1(\bar{s}_1^l, s_1^l) = \phi_1(\bar{s}_1^l)$, $(l = 1, 2, 3, ...)$. It must now be shown that

$$\lim_{l \to \infty} \phi_1(\bar{s}_1^l) = \phi_1(\bar{s}_1^0).$$

Clearly $\lim_{l \to \infty} \phi_1(\bar{s}_1^l) \geqq \lim_{l \to \infty} \pi_1(\bar{s}_1^l, s_1^0)$. But $\lim_{l \to \infty} \pi_1(\bar{s}_1^l, s_1^0) = \pi_1(\bar{s}_1^0, s_1^0) = \phi_1(\bar{s}_1^0)$ by continuity of π_1. But if $\lim_{l \to \infty} \phi_1(\bar{s}_1^l) > \phi_1(\bar{s}_1^0)$, there would be a value of $\bar{s}_1 = \lim_{l \to \infty} s_1^l$ such that $\pi_1(\bar{s}_1^0, \bar{s}_1) > \pi_1(\bar{s}_1^0, s_1^0)$, due to continuity of π_1. This, of course, contradicts the definition of ϕ_1; hence the function of ϕ_1 is continuous. The same argument may be repeated for the remaining ϕ_i.

With the continuity of the ϕ_i established, it is now possible to prove the existence of a Pareto optimal move s^*, satisfying the condition

$$\frac{\pi_i(\bar{s}_i^*, t_i) - \pi_i(s^c)}{\pi_i(s^*) - \pi_i(s^c)} = \frac{\pi_j(\bar{s}_j^*, t_j) - \pi_j(s^c)}{\pi_j(s^*) - \pi_j(s^c)},$$

$\pi_i(\bar{s}_i^*, t_i) = \phi_i(\bar{s}_i^*)$.

Proposition 3. *There exists a move $s^* \in S$ such that $\pi(s^*)$ is Pareto optimal and*

$$\frac{\phi_i(\bar{s}_i^*) - \pi_i(s^c)}{\pi_i(s^*) - \pi_i(s^c)} = \frac{\phi_j(\bar{s}_j^*) - \pi_j(s^c)}{\pi_j(s^*) - \pi_j(s^c)}, \quad (i, j = 1, ..., n).$$

For any $\rho = (\rho_1, ..., \rho_n)$, $(\rho_i \geqq 0, \Sigma \rho_i = 1)$ there is one Pareto optimal point $\pi(s_\rho)$ such that

$$\frac{\pi_i(s_\rho) - \pi_i(s^c)}{\sum_{j=1}^{n} [\pi_j(s_\rho) - \pi_j(s^c)]} = \rho_i, \quad i = 1, ..., n.$$

[1] Strictly speaking, this is necessarily true if the original equilibrium s^* is unique. If s^* and y^* are both equilibria of the smaller game, it is possible that enlarging the move space eliminates s^*, leaves y^* unaffected and creates no new equilibrium points. This still violates $\alpha 2$.

The condition of Pareto optimality ensures that this mapping from points on the unit simplex, ρ, to certain Pareto optimal profit vectors (i.e. from the unit simplex to points in the closure of B^*) is one-one and onto. Now define a mapping Ω as follows:

Ω maps a point ρ on the unit simplex into δ where:

$$\delta_i = \frac{\phi_i(\bar{s}_{i\rho}) - \pi_i(s^c)}{\sum\limits_{j=1}^{n} [\phi_j(\bar{s}_{j\rho}) - \pi_j(s^c)]} = \Omega_i(\rho), \quad i = 1, ..., n.$$

Clearly δ is a point on the n-dimensional unit simplex, for $\delta_i \geq 0$ because

$$\phi_i(\bar{s}_{i\rho}) \geq \pi_i(s_\rho) \geq \pi_i(s^c).$$

Continuity of the ϕ_i implies continuity of Ω; therefore the Brouwer fixed point theorem may be applied. Any point, $s^* = s_\rho$, such that $\rho = \Omega(\rho)$, satisfies the conditions of the proposition.

While existence is assured, uniqueness is not. Furthermore, existence of a point s^* does not, by itself, assure existence of an equilibrium strategy vector $(\sigma_1^*, ..., \sigma_n^*)$, satisfying (1) and (2). This depends, additionally, on the discount rates of the players, $\dfrac{1-\alpha_i}{\alpha_i}$, not being too large. In particular, existence is assured if

$$\frac{1-\alpha_i}{\alpha_i} < \frac{\pi_i(s^*) - \pi_i(s^c)}{\phi_i(\bar{s}_i^*) - \pi_i(s^c)}.$$

Thus, the following proposition is established:

Proposition 4. *If A1-A9 are true, then a supergame strategy, σ^*, which satisfies* (1) *and* (2) *exists and is, in addition, a non-cooperative equilibrium when*

$$\frac{1-\alpha_i}{\alpha_i} < \frac{\pi_i(s^*) - \pi_i(s^c)}{\phi_i(\bar{s}_i^*) - \pi_i(s^c)}, \quad i = 1, ..., n.$$

When σ^* is a non-cooperative equilibrium it might be called the " balanced temptation solution ", for its characteristic (apart from being both Pareto optimal and a non-cooperative equilibrium) is that the ratio of short term gain from maximizing against $\bar{s}_i^*$ to the loss per period of having done so is identical for all players. I.e.:

$$\frac{\pi_i(\bar{s}_i^*, t_i) - \pi_i(s^*)}{\pi_i(s^*) - \pi_i(s^c)} = \frac{\pi_j(\bar{s}_j^*, t_j) - \pi_j(s^*)}{\pi_j(s^*) - \pi_j(s^c)} \text{ for all } i \text{ and } j.$$

An equivalent statement is that σ^* is defined so that $\alpha_i(s^*) = \alpha_j(s^*)$, for all i and j. That is, the discount parameter which makes the ith player indifferent between choosing σ_i^* and choosing $(t_i, s_i^c, s_i^c, ...)$ against the σ_j^* is the same for all players.

VI. THE RELAXATION OF ASSUMPTIONS

The first assumptions to be dropped are those made at the beginning of section IV: (A6), all constituent games of the supergame are identical; (A7), the discount parameters are the same in all periods; (A8), the basic game has only one non-cooperative equilibrium; and (A9) the non-cooperative equilibrium is not Pareto optimal.

Taking (A9) first, it is immediate that if $\pi(s^c) \in H^*$, then it is the only element of H^*. By default, the supergame equilibrium strategy would be for each player to always choose $s_i^c (i = 1, ..., n)$. Relaxing the remaining assumptions, let S_{it} be the strategy set of the ith player in the ordinary game of period t, let $C_t \subset S_t = S_{it} \times ... \times S_{nt}$ be the set of non-cooperative equilibria of the ordinary game of period t, and let α_{it} be the present value of the discount parameter of the ith firm in period t. That is, if the one period discount rates are $r_{i1}, ..., r_{it}, ...,$ then

$$\alpha_{it} = \prod_{\tau = 1}^{t-1} \frac{1}{1+r_{i\tau}} = \frac{\alpha_{i,t-1}}{1+r_{i,t}}, \quad t = 2, 3, ...,$$

$$\alpha_{i1} = 1.$$

If $C = C_1 \times C_2 \times ...,$ then $c = (c_1, c_2, ...) \in C$ is an infinite sequence of ordinary game non-cooperative equilibria, where c_t is a non-cooperative equilibrium in the game described by (S_t, π_t). Proposition 3 proves a result about ordinary games: if $c_t \in C_t$, then the set of points $p_t \in P_t(c_t)$ such that

$$\frac{\phi_{it}(\bar{p}_{it}) - \pi_{it}(c_t)}{\pi_{it}(p_t) - \pi_{it}(c_t)} = \frac{\phi_{jt}(\bar{p}_{jt}) - \pi_{jt}(c_t)}{\pi_{jt}(p_t) - \pi_{jt}(c_t)}, \quad i, j = 1, ..., n; \; t = 1, 2, ..., \qquad \qquad ...(3)$$

$$\pi_t(p_t) \in H_t^*, \; \pi_t(p_t) \geqq \pi_t(c_t), \qquad t = 1, 2, ..., \qquad \qquad ...(4)$$

is not empty. The symbols π_{it} and ϕ_{it} are defined as before, except that they are in relation to the game of the tth period.

Let t_{it} be defined as follows:

$$\pi_{it}(\bar{p}_{it}, t_{it}) = \max_{s_{it} \in S_{it}} \pi_i(\bar{p}_{it}, s_{it}).$$

Let $p \in P(c) = P_1(c_1) \times ... \times P_t(c_t) \times ...$ be a sequence of points satisfying conditions (3) and (4), above. In relation to a given $c \in C$ and $p \in P(c)$, the supergame strategy $\sigma_i(c, p)$ is defined for the ith player:

$$s_{i1} = p_{i1}, \qquad \qquad ...(5)$$

$$s_{it} = p_{it} \text{ if } s_{j\tau} = p_{j\tau}, \quad j = 1, ..., n; \; \tau = 1, ..., t-1, t \geqq 2, \qquad \qquad ...(6)$$

$$s_{it} = c_{it} \text{ otherwise.} \qquad \qquad ...(7)$$

$\sigma(c, p) = [\sigma_1(c, p), ..., \sigma_n(c, p)]$ is a non-cooperative equilibrium for the supergame if:

$$\sum_{\tau = t}^{\infty} \alpha_{i\tau} \pi_{i\tau}(p_\tau) > \alpha_{it} \pi_{it}(\bar{p}_{it}, t_{it}) + \sum_{\tau = t+1}^{\infty} \alpha_{i\tau} \pi_{i\tau}(c_\tau), \quad i = 1, ..., n, \quad t = 1, 2, ... \qquad ...(8)$$

If these conditions are met, the actual moves chosen will be $p (= p_1, p_2, ...)$. Here it must be true that no player in any period finds it more profitable to maximize against $\bar{p}_{it}$ and see the future moves be $c_{t+1}, ...$ Of course, this was true previously; however, when the same game is repeated in each period and discount rates are invariant over time, it is either never profitable to choose t_i, or most profitable to do so in the first period of the supergame.

If $p_t = c_t$ for all but a finite number of time periods, σ cannot be an equilibrium, and, if that were true for all $c \in C$, the only supergame non-cooperative equilibria would be strategies in which basic game non-cooperative equilibria were repeated.

Thus Proposition 4 is now extended to supergames, satisfying only A1-A5:

Proposition 5. *If A1-A5 are true, then a supergame strategy satisfying (3)-(7) exists and is a non-cooperative equilibrium for the supergame if (8) is satisfied.*

A4 might be weakened to say that for given $c_t \in C_t$ and $(\rho_1, ..., \rho_n)$ exactly one member of the family of vectors $[k(\rho_1, ..., \rho_n) + \pi_t(c_t)]$, $\rho_i \geqq 0, i = 1, ..., n, \Sigma \rho_i = 1, k \geqq 0$ coincides with a point on the payoff possibility frontier. Thus a surface such as is found in Fig. 2 would be possible. Proposition 3 is still valid. There will be at least one point on the profit frontier, in the segment from a to b. which will map into itself. Such a point provides the basis for a non-cooperative equilibrium which satisfies axioms $\alpha4-\alpha6$. Pareto optimality cannot be guaranteed. Now two possibilities emerge. (*a*) Do not require Pareto optimality of the solution, merely require that it lie on the frontier. (*b*) If the solution found by (*a*), preceding, is not Pareto optimal, substitute for it the nearest Pareto optimal point which has a larger payoff to each player.

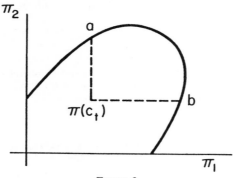

FIGURE 2

VII. COMMENTS ON ECONOMIC APPLICATIONS

A promising area of application for the equilibrium concept developed here is to the theory of oligopoly. With the game interpreted as an oligopoly, the Cournot, or ordinary game non-cooperative, equilibrium is not a Pareto optimal point. Considerable dissatisfaction has been voiced over the years with this equilibrium as a viable outcome in oligopoly. Even though out and out explicit collusion is difficult in a nation having antitrust legislation, because agreements are not legally binding and even meetings to attempt agreement may be illegal; still it seems unsatisfactory for firms to achieve only the profits of the Cournot point when each firm must realize more can be simultaneously obtained by each.

This line of argument often leads to something called " tacit collusion " under which firms are presumed to act as if they colluded. How they do this is not entirely clear, though one explanation is that their market moves are interpretable as messages. They converse in a code, as it were. Another explanation is that the " tacit collusion " is spontaneous. Everyone is so aware of the shortsightedness of Cournot behaviour that they simply behave better.

Yet, despite these misgivings, the Cournot solution has never been entirely in disrepute. It remains, neither wholeheartedly accepted, nor firmly rejected. No doubt this is because no acceptable alternative has been proposed, and because a non-cooperative equilibrium possesses attractive properties which are hard to entirely forego.

The equilibrium presented here is a sort of reconciliation. It provides an equilibrium which is both Pareto optimal and a non-cooperative equilibrium. Thus, it is possible to see the firm as selfish, willing to make any alteration in its behaviour which will increase its (discounted) profits, and, at the same time, all firms are jointly earning a Pareto optimal vector of profits. They are neither foregoing profit, nor behaving in a way which exposes firms to being " double-crossed ".

In the preceding section, it was found that there may be many basic game non-cooperative equilibria and, for each such point, many Pareto optimal points which could form part of a supergame non-cooperative equilibrium. Were this so, it would be impossible to choose one supergame equilibrium and regard it as a " natural " game solution, i.e., a particular set of strategies one should expect the players to adopt. It is possible,

12   REVIEW OF ECONOMIC STUDIES

however, that in application to oligopoly, the additional knowledge of the structure of
the game may be such as to guarantee existence of only one equilibrium. A unique
equilibrium would be a natural solution. Likewise, the difficulty that Proposition 3 could
lead to a point on the profit frontier which is not Pareto optimal may turn out impossible
in oligopoly models.

The implications of the supergame equilibrium for oligopoly will be explored in
more detail in a subsequent paper.

REFERENCES

[1] Aumann, R. J. "Acceptable Points in General Cooperative *n*-person Games",
     Contributions to the Theory of Games IV, Annals of Mathematics Study 40 (Princeton
     University Press, 1959) 287-324.

[2] Bishop, R. L. "Duopoly: Collusion or Warfare", *American Economic Review*
     (1960), 933-961.

[3] Cournot, A. *Researches into the Mathematical Principles of the Theory of Wealth*,
     trans. by N. T. Bacon (Kelley, New York, 1960).

[4] Debreu, G. "A Social Equilibrium Existence Theorem", *Proceedings of the
     National Academy of Science* (1952), 886-893.

[5] Frank, C. R. and Quandt, R. E. "On the Existence of Cournot Equilibrium",
     International Economic Review (1963) 92-96.

[6] Harsanyi, J. C. "A Simplified Bargaining Model for the *n*-Person Cooperative
     Game", *International Economic Review* (1963), 194-220.

[7] Kakutani, S. "A Generalization of Brouwer's Fixed Point Theorem", *Duke
     Mathematical Journal* (1941), 457-459.

[8] Luce, R. D. and Raiffa, H. *Games and Decisions* (Wiley, New York, 1957).

[9] Nash, J. "Noncooperative Games", *Annals of Mathematics*, **54** (1951), 286-295.

[10] Nash, J. "Two Person Cooperative Games", *Econometrica* (1953), 128-140.

[11]

A THEORY OF OLIGOPOLY

GEORGE J. STIGLER[1]

University of Chicago

N
O ONE has the right, and few the ability, to lure economists into reading another article on oligopoly theory without some advance indication of its alleged contribution. The present paper accepts the hypothesis that oligopolists wish to collude to maximize joint profits. It seeks to reconcile this wish with facts, such as that collusion is impossible for many firms and collusion is much more effective in some circumstances than in others. The reconciliation is found in the problem of policing a collusive agreement, which proves to be a problem in the theory of information. A considerable number of implications of the theory are discussed, and a modest amount of empirical evidence is presented.

I. THE TASK OF COLLUSION

A satisfactory theory of oligopoly cannot begin with assumptions concerning the way in which each firm views its interdependence with its rivals. If we adhere to the traditional theory of profit-maximizing enterprises, then behavior is no longer something to be assumed but rather something to be deduced. The firms in an industry will behave in such a way, given the demand-and-supply functions (including those of rivals), that their profits will be maximized.

The combined profits of the entire set of firms in an industry are maximized when they act together as a monopolist. At least in the traditional formulation of the oligopoly problem, in which there are no major uncertainties as to the profit-maximizing output and price at any time, this familiar conclusion seems inescapable. Moreover, the result holds for any number of firms.

Our modification of this theory consists simply in presenting a systematic account of the factors governing the feasibility of collusion, which like most things in this world is not free. Before we do so, it is desirable to look somewhat critically at the concept of homogeneity of products, and what it implies for profit-maximizing. We shall show that collusion normally involves much more than "the" price.

Homogeneity is commonly defined in terms of identity of products or of (what is presumed to be equivalent) pairs of products between which the elasticity of substitution is infinite. On either definition it is the behavior of buyers that is decisive. Yet it should be obvious that products may be identical to any or every buyer while buyers may be quite different from the viewpoint of sellers.

This fact that every transaction involves two parties is something that economists do not easily forget. One would therefore expect a definition of homogeneity also to be two-sided: if the products are what sellers offer, and the purchase commitments are what the buyers offer, full homogeneity clearly involves infinite elasticities of substitution between both products and purchase

[1] I am indebted to Claire Friedland for the statistical work and to Harry Johnson for helpful criticisms.

44

commitments. In other words, two products are homogeneous to a buyer if he is indifferent between all combinations of x of one and (say) $20 - x$ of the other, at a common price. Two purchase commitments are homogeneous to a seller if he is indifferent between all combinations of y of one and (say) $20 - y$ of the other, at a common price. Full homogeneity is then defined as homogeneity both in products (sellers) and purchase commitments (buyers).

The heterogeneity of purchase commitments (buyers), however, is surely often at least as large as that of products within an industry, and sometimes vastly larger. There is the same sort of personal differentia of buyers as of sellers—ease in making sales, promptness of payment, penchant for returning goods, likelihood of buying again (or buying other products). In addition there are two differences among buyers which are pervasive and well recognized in economics:

1. The size of purchase, with large differences in costs of providing lots of different size.
2. The urgency of purchase, with possibly sufficient differences in elasticity of demand to invite price discrimination.

It is one thing to assert that no important market has homogeneous transactions, and quite another to measure the extent of the heterogeneity. In a regime of perfect knowledge, it would be possible to measure heterogeneity by the variance of prices in transactions; in a regime of imperfect knowledge, there will be dispersion of prices even with transaction homogeneity.[2]

The relevance of heterogeneity to collusion is this: It is part of the task of maximizing industry profits to employ a

price structure that takes account of the larger differences in the costs of various classes of transactions. Even with a single, physically homogeneous product the profits will be reduced if differences among buyers are ignored. A simple illustration of this fact is given in the Appendix; disregard of differences among buyers proves to be equivalent to imposing an excise tax upon them, but one which is not collected by the monopolist. A price structure of some complexity will usually be the goal of collusive oligopolists.

II. THE METHODS OF COLLUSION

Collusion of firms can take many forms, of which the most comprehensive is outright merger. Often merger will be inappropriate, however, because of diseconomies of scale,[3] and at certain times and places it may be forbidden by law. Only less comprehensive is the cartel with a joint sales agency, which again has economic limitations—it is ill suited to custom work and creates serious administrative costs in achieving quality standards, cost reductions, product innovations, etc. In deference to American antitrust policy, we shall assume that the collusion takes the form of joint determination of outputs and prices by ostensibly independent firms, but we shall not take account of the effects of the legal prohibitions until later. Oligopoly existed before 1890, and has existed in countries that have never had an antitrust policy.

The colluding firms must agree upon the price structure appropriate to the transaction classes which they are prepared to recognize. A complete profit-maximizing price structure may have

---

[2] Unless one defines heterogeneity of transactions to include also differences in luck in finding low price sellers; see my "Economics of Information," *Journal of Political Economy*, June, 1961.

[3] If the firms are multiproduct, with different product structures, the diseconomies of merger are not strictly those of scale (in any output) but of firm size measured either absolutely or in terms of variety of products.

almost infinitely numerous price classes: the firms will have to decide upon the number of price classes in the light of the costs and returns from tailoring prices to the diversity of transactions. We have already indicated by hypothetical example (see Appendix) that there are net profits to be obtained by catering to differences in transactions. The level of collusive prices will also depend upon the conditions of entry into the industry as well as upon the elasticities of demand.

Let us assume that the collusion has been effected, and a price structure agreed upon. It is a well-established proposition that if any member of the agreement can secretly violate it, he will gain larger profits than by conforming to it.[4] It is, moreover, surely one of the axioms of human behavior that all agreements whose violation would be profitable to the violator must be enforced. The literature of collusive agreements, ranging from the pools of the 1880's to the electrical conspiracies of recent times, is replete with instances of the collapse of conspiracies because of "secret" price-cutting. This literature is biased: conspiracies that are successful in avoiding an amount of price-cutting which leads to collapse of the agreement are less likely to be reported or detected. But no conspiracy can neglect the problem of enforcement.

Enforcement consists basically of detecting significant deviations from the agreed-upon prices. Once detected, the deviations will tend to disappear because they are no longer secret and will be matched by fellow conspirators if they are not withdrawn. If the enforcement is weak, however—if price-cutting is detected only slowly and incompletely—

the conspiracy must recognize its weakness: it must set prices not much above the competitive level so the inducements to price-cutting are small, or it must restrict the conspiracy to areas in which enforcement can be made efficient.

Fixing market shares is probably the most efficient of all methods of combating secret price reductions. No one can profit from price-cutting if he is moving along the industry demand curve,[5] once a maximum profit price has been chosen. With inspection of output and an appropriate formula for redistribution of gains and losses from departures from quotas, the incentive to secret price-cutting is eliminated. Unless inspection of output is costly or ineffective (as with services), this is the ideal method of enforcement, and is widely used by legal cartels. Unfortunately for oligopolists, it is usually an easy form of collusion to detect, for it may require side payments among firms and it leaves indelible traces in the output records.

Almost as efficient a method of eliminating secret price-cutting is to assign each buyer to a single seller. If this can be done for all buyers, short-run price-cutting no longer has any purpose. Long-run price-cutting will still be a serious possibility if the buyers are in competition: lower prices to one's own customers can then lead to an expansion of their share of their market, so the price-cutter's long-run demand curve will be more elastic than that of the industry. Long-run price-cutting is likely to be important, however, only where sellers are providing a major cost component to the buyer.

There are real difficulties of other sorts

---

[4] If price is above marginal cost, marginal revenue will be only slightly less than price (and hence above marginal cost) for price cuts by this one seller.

[5] More precisely, he is moving along a demand curve which is a fixed share of the industry demand, and hence has the same elasticity as the industry curve at every price.

to the sellers in the assignment of buyers. In general the fortunes of the various sellers will differ greatly over time: one seller's customers may grow threefold, while another seller's customers shrink by half. If the customers have uncorrelated fluctuations in demand, the various sellers will experience large changes in relative outputs in the short run.[6] Where the turnover of buyers is large, the method is simply impracticable.

Nevertheless, the conditions appropriate to the assignment of customers will exist in certain industries, and in particular the geographical division of the market has often been employed. Since an allocation of buyers is an obvious and easily detectible violation of the Sherman Act, we may again infer that an efficient method of enforcing a price agreement is excluded by the antitrust laws. We therefore turn to other techniques of enforcement, but we shall find that the analysis returns to allocation of buyers.

In general the policing of a price agreement involves an audit of the transactions prices. In the absence or violation of antitrust laws, actual inspection of the accounting records of sellers has been employed by some colluding groups, but even this inspection gives only limited assurance that the price agreement is adhered to.[7] Ultimately there is no substitute for obtaining the transaction prices from the buyers.

An oligopolist will not consider making secret price cuts to buyers whose purchases fall below a certain size relative to his aggregate sales. The ease with which price-cutting is detected by rivals is decisive in this case. If p is the probability that some rival will hear of one such price reduction, $1 - (1 - p)^n$ is the probability that a rival will learn of at least one reduction if it is given to n customers. Even if p is as small as 0.01, when n equals 100 the probability of detection is .634, and when n equals 1000 it is .99996. No one has yet invented a way to advertise price reductions which brings them to the attention of numerous customers but not to that of any rival.[8]

It follows that oligopolistic collusion will often be effective against small buyers even when it is ineffective against large buyers. When the oligopolists sell to numerous small retailers, for example, they will adhere to the agreed-upon price, even though they are cutting prices to larger chain stores and industrial buyers. This is a first empirical implication of our theory. Let us henceforth exclude small buyers from consideration.

The detection of secret price-cutting will of course be as difficult as interested people can make it. The price-cutter will certainly protest his innocence, or, if this would tax credulity beyond its taxable capacity, blame a disobedient subordinate. The price cut will often take the indirect form of modifying some nonprice dimension of the transaction. The customer may, and often will, divulge price reductions, in order to have them matched by others, but he will learn from experience if each disclosure is followed by the withdrawal of the lower price offer. Indeed the buyer will frequently

[6] When the relative outputs of the firms change, the minimum cost condition of equal marginal costs for all sellers is likely to be violated. Hence industry profits are not maximized.

[7] The literature and cases on "open-price associations" contain numerous references to the collection of prices from sellers (see Federal Trade Commission, *Open-Price Trade Associations* [Washington, 1929], and cases cited).

[8] This argument applies to size of buyer relative to the individual seller. One can also explain the absence of higgling in small transactions because of the costs of bargaining, but this latter argument turns on the absolute size of the typical transaction, not its size relative to the seller.

48   GEORGE J. STIGLER

fabricate wholly fictitious price offers to test the rivals. Policing the collusion sounds very much like the subtle and complex problem presented in a good detective story.

There is a difference: In our case the man who murders the collusive price will receive the bequest of patronage. The basic method of detection of a price-cutter must be the fact that he is getting business he would otherwise not obtain. No promises of lower prices that fail to shift some business can be really effective—either the promised price is still too high or it is simply not believed.

Our definition of perfect collusion, indeed, must be that no buyer changes sellers voluntarily. There is no competitive price-cutting if there are no shifts of buyers among sellers.

To this rule that price-cutting must be inferred from shifts of buyers there is one partial exception, but that an important one. There is one type of buyer who usually reveals the price he pays, and does not accept secret benefices: the government. The system of sealed bids, publicly opened with full identification of each bidder's price and specifications, is the ideal instrument for the detection of price-cutting. There exists no alternative method of secretly cutting prices (bribery of purchasing agents aside). Our second empirical prediction, then, is that collusion will always be more effective against buyers who report correctly and fully the prices tendered to them.[9]

It follows from the test of the absence of price competition by buyer loyalty— and this is our third major empirical prediction—that collusion is severely limited (under present assumptions excluding

⁹ The problem implicitly raised by these remarks is why all sales to the government are not at collusive prices. Part of the answer is that the government is usually not a sufficiently large buyer of a commodity to remunerate the costs of collusion.

market-sharing) when the significant buyers constantly change identity. There exist important markets in which the (substantial) buyers do change identity continuously, namely, in the construction industries. The building of a plant or an office building, for example, is an essentially non-repetitive event, and rivals cannot determine whether the successful bidder has been a price-cutter unless there is open bidding to specification.

The normal market, however, contains both stability and change. There may be a small rate of entry of new buyers. There will be some shifting of customers even in a regime of effective collusion, for a variety of minor reasons we can lump together as "random factors." There will often be some sharing of buyers by several sellers—a device commending itself to buyers to increase the difficulty of policing price agreements. We move then to the world of circumstantial evidence, or, as it is sometimes called, of probability.

III. THE CONDITIONS FOR DETECTING SECRET PRICE REDUCTIONS

We shall investigate the problem of detecting secret price-cutting with a simplified model, in which all buyers and all sellers are initially of equal size. The number of buyers per seller—recalling that we exclude from consideration all buyers who take less than (say) 0.33 per cent of a seller's output—will range from 300 down to perhaps 10 or 20 (since we wish to avoid the horrors of full bilateral oligopoly). A few of these buyers are new, but over moderate periods of time most are "old," although some of these old customers will shift among suppliers. A potential secret price-cutter has then three groups of customers who would increase their patronage if given secret price cuts: the old customers of rivals;

the old customers who would normally leave him; and new customers.

Most old buyers will deal regularly with one or a few sellers, in the absence of secret price-cutting. There may be no secret price-cutting because a collusive price is adhered to, or because only an essentially competitive price can be obtained. We shall show that the loyalty of customers is a crucial variable in determining which price is approached. We need to know the probability that an old customer will buy again from his regular supplier at the collusive price, in the absence of secret price-cutting.

The buyer will set the economies of repetitive purchase (which include smaller transaction costs and less product-testing) against the increased probability of secret price-cutting that comes from shifting among suppliers. From the viewpoint of any one buyer, this gain will be larger the larger the number of sellers and the smaller the number of buyers, as we shall show below. The costs of shifting among suppliers will be smaller the more homogeneous the goods and the larger the purchases of the buyer (again an inverse function of his size). Let us label this probability of repeat purchases p. We shall indicate later how this probability could be determined in a more general approach.

The second component of sales of a firm will be its sales to new buyers and to the floating old customers of rivals. Here we assume that each seller is equally likely to make a sale, in the absence of price competition.

Let us proceed to the analysis. There are n_0 "old" buyers and n_n new customers, with $n_n = \lambda n_0$ and n_s sellers. A firm may look to three kinds of evidence on secret price-cutting, and therefore by symmetry to three potential areas to practice secret price-cutting.

1. *The behavior of its own old customers.*—It has, on average, n_0/n_s such customers, and expects to sell to $m_1 = pn_0/n_s$ of them in a given round of transactions, in the absence of price cutting. The variance of this number of customers is

$$\sigma_1{}^2 = \frac{(1-p)\,pn_0}{n_s}.$$

The probability of the firm losing more old customers than

$$\frac{(1-p)\,n_0}{n_s} + k\sigma_1$$

is given by the probability of values greater than k. The expected number of these old customers who will shift to any one rival is, say,

$$m_2 = \frac{1}{n_s - 1}\left[\frac{(1-p)\,n_0}{n_s} + k\sigma_1\right],$$

with a variance

$$\sigma_2{}^2 = \frac{n_s - 2}{(n_s - 1)^2}\left[\frac{(1-p)\,n_0}{n_s} + k\sigma_1\right].$$

The probability that any rival will obtain more than $m_2 + r\sigma_2$ of these customers is determined by r. We could now choose those combinations of k and r that fix a level of probability for the loss of a given number of old customers to any one rival beyond which secret price-cutting by this rival will be inferred. This is heavy arithmetic, however, so we proceed along a less elegant route.

Let us assume that the firm's critical value for the loss of old customers, beyond which it infers secret price-cutting, is

$$\frac{(1-p)\,n_0}{n_s} + \sigma_1$$

$$= \frac{(1-p)\,n_0}{n_s}\left[1 + \sqrt{\left(\frac{p}{1-p}\frac{n_s}{n_0}\right)}\right]$$

$$= \frac{(1-p)\,n_0}{n_s}(1+\theta),$$

GEORGE J. STIGLER

that is, one standard deviation above the mean. Any one rival will on average attract

$$m_2 = \frac{1}{n_s - 1}\left[\frac{(1-p)n_0}{n_s} + \sigma_1\right]$$

of these customers, with a variance of

$$\sigma_2{}^2 = \frac{n_s - 2}{(n_s - 1)^2}\left[\frac{(1-p)n_0}{n_s} + \sigma_1\right].$$

Let the rival be suspected of price-cutting if he obtains more than $(m_2 + \sigma_2)$ customers, that is, if the probability of any larger number is less than about 30 per cent. The joint probability of losing one standard deviation more than the average number of old customers and a rival obtaining one standard deviation more than his average share is about 10 per cent. The average sales of a rival are n_0/n_s, ignoring new customers. The maximum number of buyers any seller can obtain from one rival without exciting suspicion, minus the number he will on average get without price-cutting $([1 - p]n_0/n_s \ [n_s - 1])$, expressed as a ratio to his average sales, is

$$\frac{[\theta(1-p)n_0/(n_s-1)n_s + \sigma_2]}{n_0/n_s}.$$

This criterion is tabulated in Table 1.

TABLE 1

PERCENTAGE GAINS IN SALES FROM UNDETECTED PRICE-CUTTING BY A FIRM

$$Criterion\ I: \frac{1}{(n_s - 1)}\left[\theta(1-p) + \sqrt{\frac{n_s(n_s - 2)(1-p)(1+\theta)}{n_0}}\right] \qquad \theta = \sqrt{\frac{p}{1-p}}\frac{n_s}{n_0}$$

PROBABILITY OF REPEAT SALES (p)	No. OF BUYERS (n_0)	No. OF SELLERS					
		2	3	4	5	10	20
$p=0.95$	20	6.9	11.3	11.3	11.4	11.8	12.7
	30	5.6	8.9	8.8	8.8	9.0	9.6
	40	4.9	7.5	7.4	7.4	7.5	7.9
	50	4.4	6.6	6.5	6.4	6.5	6.8
	100	3.1	4.4	4.3	4.3	4.2	4.4
	200	2.2	3.0	2.9	2.8	2.8	2.8
	400	1.5	2.1	2.0	1.9	1.8	1.8
$p=0.90$	20	9.5	14.8	14.7	14.6	14.8	15.7
	30	7.8	11.7	11.5	11.4	11.4	12.0
	40	6.7	10.0	9.7	9.6	9.5	9.9
	50	6.0	8.8	8.6	8.4	8.3	8.6
	100	4.2	6.0	5.8	5.6	5.4	5.5
	200	3.0	4.1	3.9	3.8	3.6	3.6
	400	2.1	2.8	2.7	2.6	2.4	2.4
$p=0.80$	20	12.6	19.3	18.9	18.7	18.6	19.4
	30	10.3	15.4	15.0	14.7	14.5	15.0
	40	8.9	13.1	12.7	12.5	12.2	12.5
	50	8.0	11.6	11.2	11.0	10.6	10.8
	100	5.7	8.0	7.7	7.4	7.1	7.1
	200	4.0	5.5	5.3	5.1	4.8	4.7
	400	2.8	3.8	3.6	3.5	3.2	3.2
$p=0.70$	20	14.5	22.3	21.8	21.5	21.2	21.9
	30	11.8	17.8	17.3	17.0	16.6	16.9
	40	10.2	15.2	14.8	14.5	14.0	14.2
	50	9.2	13.5	13.1	12.8	12.3	12.4
	100	6.5	9.3	9.0	8.7	8.2	8.2
	200	4.6	6.5	6.2	6.0	5.6	5.5
	400	3.2	4.5	4.3	4.2	3.8	3.7

The entries in Table 1 are measures of the maximum additional sales obtainable by secret price-cutting (expressed as a percentage of average sales) from any one rival beyond which that rival will infer that the price-cutting is taking place. Since the profitability of secret price-cutting depends upon the amount of business one can obtain (as well as upon the excess of price over marginal cost), we may also view these numbers as the measures of the incentive to engage in secret price-cutting. Three features of the tabulation are noteworthy:

a) The gain in sales from any one rival by secret price-cutting is not very sensitive to the number of rivals, given the number of customers and the probability of repeat sales. The aggregate gain in sales of a firm from price-cutting—its total incentive to secret price-cutting— is the sum of the gains from each rival, and therefore increases roughly in proportion to the number of rivals.

b) The incentive to secret price-cutting falls as the number of customers per seller increases—and falls roughly in inverse proportion to the square root of the number of buyers.

c) The incentive to secret price-cutting rises as the probability of repeat purchases falls, but at a decreasing rate.

We have said that the gain to old buyers from shifting their patronage among sellers will be that it encourages secret price-cutting by making it more difficult to detect. Table 1 indicates that there are diminishing returns to increased shifting: The entries increase at a decreasing rate as p falls. In a fuller model we could introduce the costs of shifting among suppliers and determine p to maximize expected buyer gains. The larger the purchases of a buyer, when buyers are of unequal size, however, the greater is the prospect that his shifts will induce price-cutting.

In addition it is clear that, when the number of sellers exceeds two, it is possible for two or more firms to pool information and thus to detect less extreme cases of price-cutting. For example, at the given probability levels, the number of old customers that any one rival should be able to take from a firm was shown to be at most

$$(1-p)\frac{n_0(1+\theta)}{n_s-1},$$

with variance

$$\frac{(n_s-2)(1-p)(1+\theta)}{(n_s-1)^2}\,n_0.$$

At the same probability level, the average number of old customers that one rival should be able to take from T firms is at most

$$\frac{T(1-p)n_0}{n_s-T}\left(1+\frac{\theta}{\sqrt{T}}\right),$$

with the variance

$$\frac{(n_s-T-1)}{(n_s-T)^2}(1-p)\left(1+\frac{\theta}{\sqrt{T}}\right)n_0T.$$

Each of these is smaller than the corresponding expression for one seller when expressed as a fraction of the customers lost by each of the firms pooling information.

There are of course limits to such pooling of information: not only does it become expensive as the number of firms increases, but also it produces less reliable information, since one of the members of the pool may himself be secretly cutting prices. Some numbers illustrative of the effect of pooling will be given at a later point.

2. *The attraction of old customers of other firms is a second source of evidence of price-cutting.*—If a given rival has not cut prices, he will on average lose $(1-p)$ (n_0/n_s) customers, with a variance of σ_1^2. The number of customers he will retain with secret price-cutting cannot exceed

a level at which the rivals suspect the price-cutting. Any one rival will have little basis for judging whether he is getting a fair share of this firm's old customers, but they can pool their information and then in the aggregate they will expect the firm to lose at least $(1 - p)$ $(n_0/n_s) - 2\sigma_1$ customers, at the 5 per cent probability level. Hence the secret price-cutter can retain at most $2\sigma_1$ of his old customers (beyond his average number),

TABLE 2

OLD CUSTOMERS THAT A SECRET PRICE-CUTTER CAN RETAIN, AS A PERCENTAGE OF AVERAGE SALES

Criterion II: $2\sqrt{\dfrac{p(1-p)}{2}}\dfrac{n_s}{n_0}$

PROBABILITY THAT OLD CUSTOMER WILL REMAIN LOYAL (p)	No. of OLD CUSTOMERS PER SELLER (n_0/n_s)			
	10	20	50	100
0.95.......	13.8	9.7	6.2	4.4
.90.......	19.0	13.4	8.5	6.0
.85.......	22.6	16.0	10.1	7.1
.80.......	25.3	17.9	11.3	8.0
.75.......	27.4	19.4	12.2	8.7
.70.......	29.0	20.5	13.0	9.2
.65.......	30.2	21.3	13.5	9.5
.60.......	31.0	21.9	13.9	9.8
.55.......	31.5	22.2	14.1	10.0
0.50.......	31.6	22.4	14.1	10.0

ber), which as a fraction of his average sales (ignoring new customers) is

$$\frac{2\sigma_1}{n_0/n_s} = 2\sqrt{\frac{(1-p)pn_s}{n_0}}.$$

This is tabulated as Table 2.

If the entries in Table 2 are compared with those in Table 1,[10] it is found that a price-cutter is easier to detect by his gains at the expense of any one rival than by his unusual proportion of repeat sales. This second criterion will therefore seldom be useful.

3. *The behavior of new customers is a* *third source of information on price-cutting.*—There are n_n new customers per period,[11] equal to λn_0. A firm expects, in the absence of price-cutting, to sell to

$$m_3 = \frac{1}{n_s}\lambda n_0$$

of these customers, with a variance of

$$\sigma_3{}^2 = \left(1 - \frac{1}{n_s}\right)\frac{\lambda n_0}{n_s}.$$

If the rivals pool information (without pooling, this area could not be policed effectively), this firm cannot obtain more than $m_3 + 2\sigma_3$ customers without being deemed a price-cutter, using again a 5 per cent probability criterion. As a percentage of the firm's total sales, the maximum sales above the expected number in the absence of price cutting are then

$$\frac{2\sigma_3}{n_0(1+\lambda)/n_s} = \frac{2}{1+\lambda}\sqrt{\frac{(n_s-1)\lambda}{n_0}}.$$

We tabulate this criterion as Table 3.

Two aspects of the incentive to cut prices (or equivalently the difficulty of detecting price cuts) to new customers are apparent: the incentive increases rapidly with the number of sellers[12] and the

[10] For example, take $p = .95$. The entry for 10 customers per seller is 13.8 in Table 2—this is the maximum percentage of average sales that can be obtained by price reductions to old customers. The corresponding entries in Table 1 are 6.9 (2 sellers, 20 buyers), 8.9 (3 and 30), 7.4 (4 and 40), 6.4 (5 and 50), 4.2 (10 and 100), etc. Multiplying each entry in Table 1 by $(n_s - 1)$, we get the maximum gain in sales (without detection) by attracting customers of rivals, and beyond 2 sellers the gains are larger by this latter route. Since Table 1 is based upon a 10 per cent probability level, strict comparability requires that we use 1.6 σ, instead of 2 σ, in Table 2, which would reduce the entries by one-fifth.

[11] Unlike old customers, whose behavior is better studied in a round of transactions, the new customers are a flow whose magnitude depends much more crucially on the time period considered. The annual flow of new customers is here taken (relative to the number of old customers) as the unit.

[12] And slowly with the number of sellers if customers per seller are held constant.

incentive increases with the rate of entry of new customers. As usual the incentive falls as the absolute number of customers per seller rises. If the rate of entry of new buyers is 10 per cent or more, price-cutting to new customers allows larger sales increases without detection that can be obtained by attracting customers of rivals (compare Tables 1 and 3).

Of the considerable number of directions in which this model could be enlarged, two will be presented briefly.

The first is inequality in the size of firms. In effect this complication has al-

ready been introduced by the equivalent device of pooling information. If we tabulate the effects of pooling of information by K firms, the results are equivalent to having a firm K times as large as the other firms. The number of old customers this large firm can lose to any one small rival (all of whom are equal in size) is given, in Table 4, as a percentage of the average number of old customers of the small firm; the column labeled $K = 1$ is of course the case analyzed in Table 1.

The effects of pooling on the detection of price-cutting are best analyzed by

TABLE 3

Maximum Additional New Customers (as a Percentage of Average Sales) Obtainable by Secret Price-cutting

$$\text{Criterion III: } \frac{2}{1+\lambda} \sqrt{\frac{\lambda(n_s - 1)}{n_0}}$$

Rate of Appearance of New Buyers (λ)	No. of Old Buyers (n_0)	No. of Sellers					
		2	3	4	5	10	20
1/100	20	4.4	6.3	7.7	8.9	13.3	19.3
	30	3.6	5.1	6.3	7.2	10.8	15.8
	40	3.1	4.4	5.4	6.3	9.4	13.6
	50	2.8	4.0	4.8	5.6	8.4	12.2
	100	2.0	2.8	3.4	4.0	5.9	8.6
	200	1.4	2.0	2.4	2.8	4.2	6.1
	400	1.0	1.4	1.7	2.0	3.0	4.3
1/10	20	12.9	18.2	22.3	25.7	38.6	56.0
	30	10.5	14.8	18.2	21.0	31.5	45.8
	40	9.1	12.9	15.8	18.2	27.3	39.6
	50	8.1	11.5	14.1	16.3	24.4	35.4
	100	5.8	8.1	10.0	11.5	17.2	25.1
	200	4.1	5.8	7.0	8.1	12.2	17.7
	400	2.9	4.1	5.0	5.8	8.6	12.5
1/5	20	16.7	23.6	28.9	33.3	50.0	72.6
	30	13.6	19.2	23.6	27.2	40.8	59.3
	40	11.8	16.7	20.4	23.6	35.4	51.4
	50	10.5	14.9	18.3	21.1	31.6	46.0
	100	7.4	10.5	12.9	14.9	22.4	32.5
	200	5.3	7.4	9.1	10.5	15.8	23.0
	400	3.7	5.3	6.4	7.4	11.2	16.2
1/4	20	17.9	25.3	31.0	35.8	53.7	78.0
	30	14.6	20.7	25.3	29.2	43.8	63.7
	40	12.6	17.9	21.9	25.3	38.0	55.1
	50	11.3	16.0	19.6	22.6	33.9	49.3
	100	8.0	11.3	13.9	16.0	24.0	34.9
	200	5.7	8.0	9.8	11.3	17.0	24.7
	400	4.0	5.7	6.9	8.0	12.0	17.4

54   GEORGE J. STIGLER

comparing Table 4 with Table 1. If there are 100 customers and 10 firms (and $p = 0.9$), a single firm can increase sales by 5.4 per cent by poaching on one rival, or about 50 per cent against all rivals (Table 1). If 9 firms combine, the maximum amount the single firm can gain by secret price-cutting is 28.9 per cent (Table 4). With 20 firms and 200 customers, a single firm can gain 3.6 per cent from each rival, or about 30 per cent from 9 rivals; if these rivals merge, the corresponding figure falls to 14.0 per cent. The pooling of information therefore reduces substantially the scope for secret price-cutting.

This table exaggerates the effect of inequality of firm size because it fails to take account of the fact that the number of customers varies with firm size, on our argument that only customers above a certain size relative to the seller are a

TABLE 4

PERCENTAGE GAINS IN SALES FROM UNDETECTED PRICE-CUTTING BY A SMALL FIRM

Criterion IV:

$$\frac{1}{n_s - K}\left[\theta(1-p)\sqrt{K} + \sqrt{\frac{n_s K(1-p)(n_s - K - 1)(1 + \theta/\sqrt{K})}{n_0}}\right]$$

$$\theta = \sqrt{\frac{p}{1-p}\frac{n_s}{n_0}}$$

PROBABILITY OF REPEAT SALES (p)	NO. OF FIRMS ($n_s - K + 1$)	BUYERS PER SMALL SELLER (n_0/n_s)	SIZE OF LARGE FIRM (K)			
			1	2	5	9
$p=0.9$	2	10	9.5	13.4	21.2	28.5
		30	5.5	7.7	12.2	16.4
		50	4.2	6.0	9.5	12.7
	3	10	11.7	15.8	23.9	31.4
		30	6.3	8.7	13.3	17.6
		50	4.8	6.6	10.2	13.5
	4	10	9.7	13.1	19.7	25.7
		30	5.2	7.1	10.9	14.4
		50	4.0	5.4	8.3	11.0
	10	10	5.4	7.2	10.7	14.0
		30	2.9	3.9	5.9	7.7
		50	2.2	2.9	4.5	5.9
$p=0.8$	2	10	12.6	17.9	28.3	37.9
		30	7.3	10.3	16.3	21.9
		50	5.7	8.0	12.6	17.0
	3	10	15.4	21.0	32.1	42.3
		30	8.4	11.6	18.0	23.9
		50	6.4	8.9	13.8	18.4
	4	10	12.7	17.3	26.3	34.7
		30	6.9	9.5	14.7	19.5
		50	5.3	7.3	11.3	15.0
	10	10	7.1	9.5	14.4	18.9
		30	3.8	5.2	8.0	10.6
		50	2.9	4.0	6.1	8.1

feasible group for secret price-cutting. The small firm can find it attractive to cut prices to buyers which are not large enough to be potential customers by price-cutting for the large seller.

The temporal pattern of buyers' behavior provides another kind of information: What is possibly due to random fluctuation in the short run cannot with equal probability be due to chance if repeated. Thus the maximum expected loss of old customers to a rival in one round of transactions is (at the 1σ level)

$$\frac{n_0}{(n_s-1)n_s}(1-p)(1+\theta),$$

but for T consecutive periods the maximum expected loss is (over T periods)

$$\frac{T}{n_s-1}(1-p)\frac{n_0}{n_s}[1+\theta\sqrt{T}],$$

with a variance of

$$\sigma_5{}^2=\frac{(n_s-2)}{(n_s-1)^2}T(1-p)\frac{n_0}{n_s}[1+\theta\sqrt{T}].$$

This source of information is of minor efficacy in detecting price-cutting unless the rounds of successive transactions are numerous—that is, unless buyers purchase (enter contracts) frequently.

Our approach has certain implications for the measurement of concentration, if we wish concentration to measure likelihood of effective collusion. In the case of new customers, for example, let the probability of attracting a customer be proportional to the firm's share of industry output (s). Then the variance of the firm's share of sales to new customers will be $n_n s(1-s)$, and the aggregate for the industry will be

$$C=n_n\sum_1^r s(1-s)$$

for r firms. This expression equals $n_n (1-H)$, where

$$H = \Sigma s^2$$

is the Herfindahl index of concentration. The same index holds, as an approximation, for potential price-cutting to attract old customers.[13]

The foregoing analysis can be extended to non-price variables, subject to two modifications. The first modification is that there be a definite joint profit-maximizing policy upon which the rivals can agree. Here we may expect to encounter a spectrum of possibilities, ranging from a clearly defined optimum policy (say, on favorable legislation) to a nebulous set of alternatives (say, directions of research).[14] Collusion is less feasible, the less clear the basis on which it should proceed. The second modification is that

---

[13] A similar argument leads to a measure of concentration appropriate to potential price-cutting for old customers. Firm i will lose

$$(1-p)n_0 s_i$$

old customers, and firm j will gain

$$(1-p)n_0\frac{s_i s_j}{1-s_i}$$

of them, with a variance

$$(1-p)n_0\frac{s_i s_j}{1-s_i}\left(1-\frac{s_j}{1-s_i}\right).$$

If we sum over all $i\ (\neq j)$, we obtain the variance of firm j's sales to old customers of rivals

$$(1-p)n_0 s_j(1+H-2s_j),$$

to an approximation, and summing over all j, we have the concentration measure,

$$(1-p)n_0(1-H).$$

The agreement of this measure with that for new customers is superficial: that for new customers implicitly assumes pooling of information and that for old customers does not.

[14] Of course, price itself usually falls somewhere in this range rather than at the pole. The traditional assumption of stationary conditions conceals this fact.

GEORGE J. STIGLER

the competitive moves of any one firm will differ widely among non-price variables in their detectability by rivals. Some forms of non-price competition will be easier to detect than price-cutting because they leave visible traces (advertising, product quality, servicing, etc.) but some variants will be elusive (reciprocity in purchasing, patent licensing arrangements). The common belief that non-price competition is more common than

TABLE 5

RESIDUALS FROM REGRESSION OF ADVERTISING RATES ON CIRCULATION*

No. of Evening Papers	n	Mean Residual (Logarithm)	Standard Deviation of Mean
One..................	23	0.0211	0.0210
With morning paper.	10	− .0174	.0324
Without morning paper.............	13	.0507	.0233
Two.................	30	−0.0213	0.0135

* The regression equation is

log R

$$= 5.194 - 1.688 \log c + .139 (\log c)^2 ,$$
$$(.620) \qquad (.063)$$

where R is the 5 M milline rate and c is circulation.

Source: American Association of Advertising Agencies, *Market and Newspaper Statistics*, Vol. VIIIa (1939).

price competition is therefore not wholly in keeping with the present theory. Those forms that are suitable areas for collusion will have less competition; those which are not suitable will have more competition.

IV. SOME FRAGMENTS OF EVIDENCE

Before we seek empirical evidence on our theory, it is useful to report two investigations of the influence of numbers of sellers on price. These investigations have an intrinsic interest because, so far as I know, no systematic analysis of the effect of numbers has hitherto been made.

The first investigation was of newspaper advertising rates, as a function of the number of evening newspapers in a city. Advertising rates on a milline basis are closely (and negatively) related to circulation, so a regression of rates on circulation was made for fifty-three cities in 1939. The residuals (in logarithmic form) from this regression equation are tabulated in Table 5. It will be observed that rates are 5 per cent above the average in one-newspaper towns and 5 per cent below the average in two-newspaper towns, and the towns with one evening paper but also an independent morning paper fall nearly midway between these points. Unfortunately there were too few cities with more than two evening newspapers to yield results for larger numbers of firms.

The second investigation is of spot commercial rates on AM radio stations in the four states of Ohio, Indiana, Michigan, and Illinois. The basic equation introduces, along with number of rivals, a series of other factors (power of station, population of the county in which the station is located, etc.). Unfortunately the number of stations is rather closely correlated with population ($r^2 = .796$ in the logarithms). The general result, shown in Table 6, is similar to that for newspapers: the elasticity of price with respect to number of rivals is quite small ($-.07$). Here the range of stations in a county was from 1 to 13.

Both studies suggest that the level of prices is not very responsive to the actual number of rivals. This is in keeping with the expectations based upon our model, for that model argues that the number of buyers, the proportion of new buyers, and the relative sizes of firms are as important as the number of rivals.

To turn to the present theory, the only test covering numerous industries so far

A THEORY OF OLIGOPOLY 57

devised has been one based upon profitability. This necessarily rests upon company data, and it has led to the exclusion of a large number of industries for which the companies do not operate in a well-defined industry. For example, the larger steel and chemical firms operate in a series of markets in which their position ranges from monopolistic to competitive. We have required of each industry that the earnings of a substantial fraction of the companies in the industry (measured by output) be determined by the profit-

given in Table 8. The various concentration measures, on the one hand, and the various measures of profitability, on the other hand, are tolerably well correlated.[15] All show the expected positive relationship. In general the data suggest that there is no relationship between profitability and concentration if H is less than 0.250 or the share of the four largest firms is less than about 80 per cent. These data, like those on advertising rates, confirm our theory only in the sense that they support theories which

TABLE 6

REGRESSION OF AM SPOT COMMERCIAL RATES (26 TIMES)
AND STATION CHARACTERISTICS, 1961

($n = 345$)

Independent Variables*	Regression Coefficient	Standard Error
1. Logarithm of population of county, 1960..........	.238	0.026
2. Logarithm of kilowatt power of station...........	.206	.015
3. Dummy variables of period of broadcasting:		
a) Sunrise to sunset............................	−.114	.025
b) More than (*a*), less than 18 hours	−.086	.027
c) 18–21 hours.................................	−.053	.028
4. Logarithm of number of stations in county........	−.074	0.046
	$R^2 = .743$	

* Dependent variable: logarithm of average rate, May 1, 1961 (dollars).

Source: "Spot Radio Rates and Data," *Standard Rate and Data Service, Inc.*, Vol. XLIII, No. 5 (May 1961).

ability of that industry's products, that is, that we have a fair share of the industry and the industry's product is the dominant product of the firms.

Three measures of profitability are given in Table 7: (1) the rate of return on all capital (including debt), (2) the rate of return on net worth (stockholders' equity); (3) the ratio of market value to book value of the common stock.

In addition, two measures of concentration are presented: (1) the conventional measure, the share of output produced by the four leading firms; and (2) the Herfindahl index, H.

The various rank correlations are

assert that competition increases with number of firms.

Our last evidence is a study of the prices paid by buyers of steel products in 1939, measured relative to the quoted prices (Table 9). The figure of 8.3 for hot-

[15] The concentration measures have a rank correlation of .903. The profitability measures have the following rank correlations:

	Return on All Assets	Ratio of Market to Book Value
Return on net worth......	.866	.872
Ratio of market to book value.................	.733	....

TABLE 7

PROFITABILITY AND CONCENTRATION DATA

INDUSTRY*	CONCENTRATION (1954)		AVERAGE RATE OF RETURN (1953–57)		RATIO OF MARKET VALUE TO BOOK VALUE (1953–57)
	Share of Top 4	H†	All Assets	Net Worth	
Sulfur mining (4)	98	0.407	19.03	23.85	3.02
Automobiles (3)	98	.369	11.71	20.26	2.30
Flat glass (3)	90	.296	11.79	16.17	2.22
Gypsum products (2)	90	.280	12.16	20.26	1.83
Primary aluminum (4)	98	.277	6.87	13.46	2.48
Metal cans (4)	80	.260	7.27	13.90	1.60
Chewing gum (2)	86	.254	13.50	17.06	2.46
Hard-surface floor coverings (3)	87	.233	6.56	7.59	0.98
Cigarettes (5)	83	.213	7.23	11.18	1.29
Industrial gases (3)	84	.202	8.25	11.53	1.33
Corn wet milling (3)	75	.201	9.17	11.55	1.48
Typewriters (3)	83	.198	3.55	5.39	0.84
Domestic laundry equipment (2)	68	.174	9.97	17.76	1.66
Rubber tires (9)	79	.171	7.86	14.02	1.70
Rayon fiber (4)	76	.169	5.64	6.62	0.84
Carbon black (2)	73	.152	8.29	9.97	1.40
Distilled liquors (6)	64	0.118	6.94	7.55	0.77

* The number of firms is given in parentheses after the industry title. Only those industries are included for which a substantial share (35 per cent or more) of the industry's sales is accounted for by the firms in the sample, and these firms derive their chief revenues (50 per cent or more) from the industry in question.

† H is Herfindahl index.

TABLE 8

RANK CORRELATIONS OF MEASURES OF PROFITABILITY AND MEASURES OF CONCENTRATION

MEASURE OF CONCENTRATION	MEASURE OF PROFITABILITY		
	Rate of Return on All Assets	Rate of Return on Net Worth	Ratio of Market Value to Book Value
Share of output produced by four largest firms	.322	.507	.642
Herfindahl index (H)	.524	.692	.730

TABLE 9

PRICES OF STEEL PRODUCTS, 1939, AND INDUSTRY STRUCTURE, 1938

PRODUCT CLASS	PRICES, 2D QUARTER, 1939 (PER CENT)		HERFINDAHL INDEX	OUTPUT IN 1939 RELATIVE TO 1937
	Average Discount from List Price	Standard Deviation		
Hot-rolled sheets	8.3	7.3	0.0902	1.14
Merchant bars	1.2	4.5	.1517	0.84
Hot-rolled strip	8.5	8.3	.1069	0.56
Plates	2.6	4.8	.1740	0.85
Structural shapes	3.2	4.3	.3280	0.92
Cold-rolled strip	8.8	9.8	.0549	0.88
Cold-rolled sheets	5.8	5.0	.0963	1.14
Cold-finished bars	0.9	3.4	0.0964	0.83

Source: Prices: "Labor Department Examines Consumers' Prices of Steel Products," *Iron Age*, April 25, 1946; industry structure: 1938 capacity data from *Directory of Iron and Steel Works of the United States and Canada*; output: *Annual Statistical Report, American Iron and Steel Institute* (New York, 1938, 1942).

rolled sheets, for example, represents an average of 8.3 per cent reduction from quoted prices, *paid by buyers*, with a standard deviation of 7.3 per cent of quoted prices. The rate of price-cutting is almost perfectly correlated with the standard deviation of transaction prices, as we should expect: the less perfect the market knowledge, the more extensive the price-cutting.

In general, the more concentrated the industry structure (measured by the Herfindahl index), the larger were the price reductions. Although there were no extreme departures from this relationship, structural shapes and hot-rolled strip had prices somewhat lower than the average relationship, and cold finished bars prices somewhat higher than expected, and the deviations are not accounted for by the level of demand (measured by 1939 sales relative to 1937 sales). The number of buyers could not be taken into account, but the BLS study states:

The extent of price concessions shown by this study is probably understated because certain very large consumers in the automobile and container industries were excluded from the survey. This omission was at the request of the OPA which contemplated obtaining this information in connection with other studies. Since a small percentage of steel consumers, including these companies, accounts for a large percentage of steel purchased, prices paid by a relatively few large consumers have an important influence upon the entire steel price structure. Very large steel consumers get greater reductions from published prices than smaller consumers, often the result of competitive bidding by the mills for the large volume of steel involved. One very large steel consumer, a firm that purchased over 2 pct of the total consumption of hot and cold-rolled sheets in 1940, refused to give purchase prices. This firm wished to protect its suppliers, fearing that "certain transactions might be revealed which would break confidence" with the steel mills. However, this company did furnish percent changes of prices paid for several steel products which showed that for some products prices advanced markedly, and in one case, nearly 50 pct. The great price advances for this company indicate that it was receiving much larger concessions than smaller buyers.[16]

These various bits of evidence are fairly favorable to the theory, but they do not constitute strong support. More powerful tests will be feasible when the electrical equipment triple-damage suits are tried.[17] The great merit of our theory, in fact, is that it has numerous testable hypotheses, unlike the immortal theories that have been traditional in this area.

[16] See "Labor Department Examines Consumers' Prices of Steel Products," *op. cit.*, p. 133.

[17] For example, it will be possible to test the prediction that prices will be higher and less dispersed in sales on public bids than in privately negotiated sales, and the prediction that price-cutting increases as the number of buyers diminishes.

APPENDIX

The importance of product heterogeneity for profit-maximizing behavior cannot well be established by an a priori argument. Nevertheless, the following simple exposition of the implications for profitability of disregarding heterogeneity may have some heuristic value. The analysis, it will be observed, is formally equivalent to that of the effects of an excise tax on a monopolist.

Assume that a monopolist makes men's suits, and that he makes only one size of suit. This is absurd behavior, but the picture of the sadistic monopolist who disregards consumer desires has often made fugitive appearances in the literature so the problem has some interest of its own. The demand curve of a consumer for suits that fit, $f(p)$, would now be reduced because he would have to incur some alteration cost a in order to wear the suit. His effective demand would therefore decline to $f(p + a)$. Assume further that the marginal cost of suits is constant (m), and that it would be the same if the monopolist were to make suits of various sizes.

60   GEORGE J. STIGLER

The effect on profits of a uniform product—
uniform is an especially appropriate word here—
can be shown graphically (Fig. 1). The decrease
in quantity sold, with a linear demand curve, is

$$MB = \tfrac{1}{2} a f'(p) .$$

The decrease in the price received by the
monopolist is

$$DN = \frac{MB}{f'(p)} - a = -\frac{a}{2},$$

so if π is profit per unit, and q is output, the
relative decline in total profit is approximately

$$\frac{\Delta \pi}{\pi} + \frac{\Delta q}{q},$$

or

$$\frac{MB}{OB} + \frac{ND}{AD}.$$

Since

$$OB = \frac{f(m)}{2}$$

$$AD = -\frac{p}{\eta},$$

where η is the elasticity of demand, the relative
decline of profits with a uniform product is

$$\frac{a f'(p)}{f(m)} + \frac{a\eta}{2p} = \frac{a\eta}{2p} + \frac{a\eta}{2p}$$

$$= \frac{a\eta}{p}.$$

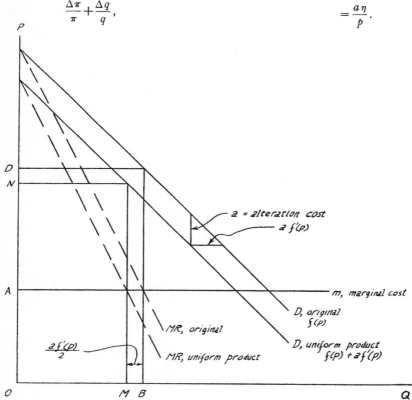

SIMPLE MONOPOLY
Price = OD
Quantity = OB
Profits = OB × AD

UNIFORM PRODUCT MONOPOLY
Price = ON
Quantity = OM
Profits = OM × AN

FIG. 1

A THEORY OF OLIGOPOLY

The loss from imposed uniformity is therefore proportional to the ratio of alteration costs to price.

Our example is sufficiently unrealistic to make any quantitative estimate uninteresting. In general one would expect an upper limit to the ratio a/p, because it becomes cheaper to resort to other goods (custom tailoring in our example), or to abandon the attempt to find appropriate goods. The loss of profits of the monopolist will be proportional to the average value of a/p, and this will be smaller, the smaller the variation in buyers' circumstances.

Still, monopolists are lucky if their long-run demand curves have an elasticity only as large as -5, and then even a ratio of a to p of 1/40 will reduce their profits by 12 per cent. The general conclusion I wish to draw is that a monopolist who does not cater to the diversities of his buyers' desires will suffer a substantial decline in his profits.

[12]

THE NATURE AND SIGNIFICANCE OF PRICE LEADERSHIP

By Jesse W. Markham*

That the Supreme Court's decision in the *Tobacco* Case[1] of 1946 attaches a new significance to price leadership in oligopolistic markets seems beyond reasonable doubt. The *Tobacco* decision constitutes a reversal of the stand taken by the Court in the *U. S. Steel* and *International Harvester* cases, where the Court ruled that the acceptance of a price leader by the rest of the industry did not constitute a violation of the Sherman Act by the price leader.[2] If we accept the full meaning of what the court has really said, that parallel pricing, whether implemented by an agreement or not, is now illegal, pricing policies prevailing in markets where sellers are few will henceforth be subjected to a much closer examination than they have been in the past.

Accomplished students of the monopoly problem, anticipating what such oligopolistic market studies might be expected to reveal, have predicted the possibility of some sweeping changes in the conduct of American business enterprise. Professor Rostow, for example, sees in the *Aluminum* and *Tobacco* decisions, when viewed collectively, the possible foundations for a new Sherman Act "which promises drastically to shorten and simplify antitrust trials" since they represent a triumph of the economic over the more cumbersome legal approach to the antitrust problem.[3] Professor Rostow points out specifically that such tacit parallelism, as evidenced by the practice of following a price leader, now lies within the scope of the antitrust laws.[4] Professor Nicholls cautiously points out that the assumptions which he made in his recent appraisal of the *Tobacco* decision,[5] namely, (1) that the

* The author is assistant professor of economics at Vanderbilt University. He expresses indebtedness to Professors George W. Stocking and George J. Stigler for their critical appraisal of this essay and for their many helpful suggestions.

[1] *American Tobacco Co., et al.,* v. *United States,* 148 F. 2d 416 (1944); 328 U. S. 781 (1946).

[2] *United States* v. *United States Steel Corporation,* 251 U. S. 417 (1920); and *United States* v. *International Harvester Company,* 274 U. S. 693 (1927).

[3] Eugene V. Rostow, "The New Sherman Act," *University of Chicago Law Review* (June, 1947) pp. 567-600. For a warier appraisal of the *Aluminum* and *Tobacco* decisions, see Edward H. Levi, "The Antitrust Laws and Monopoly," *ibid.,* pp. 172 ff.

[4] Rostow, *ibid.,* p. 577.

[5] William H. Nicholls, "The Tobacco Case of 1946," *Am. Econ. Rev.,* Vol. XXXIX, No. 3 (May, 1949), pp. 284-96.

Courts really said what he believed them to have said and (2) that they will carry to their logical conclusion the legal implications of that decision, may rest upon dubious grounds. Nevertheless, he concedes the possibility that such *modi operandi* as price leadership, the presence of which was perhaps the most important piece of incriminating evidence in the *Tobacco* case, are now illegal.

If the legal implications of the *Tobacco* decision as interpreted by Professors Rostow, Nicholls and others be accepted, the economic consequences of price leadership and the specific conditions likely to render it an effective weapon against price competition in oligopolistic markets need to be re-examined. Because the Court has not yet faced up to the problem of providing appropriate remedies, the question of wherein lies the most fruitful remedial action should at least be raised. It is primarily to this task that this article is addressed. Since, however, there is always the danger of assigning unwarranted homogeneity to such an economic phenomenon, its significance will be appraised on the basis of (1) the particular types of price leadership which prevail in industrial markets and (2) the extent to which each type might conceivably circumvent forces of competition.

Professor Stigler has distinguished between two kinds of price leadership: (1) that associated with a dominant firm and (2) that of the barometric type.[6] Since, however, one of the market conditions that the barometric firm's price is supposed to reflect is both secret and open price-cutting,[7] it is not always possible to determine whether the barometric firm should be viewed as the "price leader" or as one of the first "price followers." Hence, for purposes of this discussion, the above otherwise satisfactory dichotomy will be augmented by a third type of price leadership which may be viewed either as an extreme form of the barometric type or simply as price leadership in lieu of overt collusion.

"Models" of Price Leadership

Although most of the vast volume of economic literature on price practices and policies conveys the impression that price leadership is a logical and effective means for eliminating price competition among rival sellers, theoretical treatment of the topic has been cast in rather simple static terms and limited to three special cases.[8]

[6] George J. Stigler, "The Kinky Oligopoly Demand Curve and Rigid Prices," *Jour. Pol. Econ.*, Vol. LV, No. 5 (Oct., 1947) pp. 444-45.

[7] See Professor Stigler's illustrative case, *ibid.*, p. 445.

[8] The number of institutional and other conditions under which the prices set by one firm in an industry might be used by all others is probably very large, but only three sets of conditions seem to make price leadership of some sort inevitable and at the same time identify the price leader.

MARKHAM: NATURE AND SIGNIFICANCE OF PRICE LEADERSHIP 893

Perhaps the most familiar theoretical model of price leadership is centered upon the dominant firm or partial monopolist. Starting from the assumption that an industry comprises one large producer and a number of smaller ones, no one of which produces a high enough percentage of total output to influence the price, it logically follows that the rôle of price-making falls to the dominant firm. This is true because each small firm regards its own demand schedule as perfectly elastic at the price set by the dominant firm and thus behaves as though it operates under conditions of perfect competition. The dominant firm might set any price it chooses, but presumably would set one which maximizes its profits by equating its own marginal cost with its marginal revenue as derived from the market demand schedule and the summation of the individual marginal cost curves of the independent small producers.

Professor Boulding[9] has presented two other theoretical models of price leadership. One relates to an industry comprising one low-cost high-capacity firm and one or more high-cost low-capacity firms, the other to an industry comprising at least two firms having identical cost curves but different shares in the market. In the former case, because no price can equate marginal cost with marginal revenue for both (or all) firms, a conflict in price policy inevitably arises. However, since the price preferred by the low-cost high-capacity firm is lower than the price preferred by the high-cost low-capacity firm (or firms), the low-cost firm can impose its price policy on the industry. In the other case, under assumptions described by Professor Boulding as "rather peculiar," that marginal cost curves for all firms are identical and that each firm's relative share in the market is different from that of all other firms and remains unchanged over the entire range of possible prices, marginal cost and marginal revenue are equated at a lower price for the firm having the smallest share in the market than for any other firm. Hence, the firm having the smallest share in the market at all possible prices can impose the price most acceptable to it on the rest of the industry. Professor Boulding makes no claim that the latter model is built upon sufficiently realistic assumptions to throw much light upon price policies generally but suggests that it might explain price behavior in the retail gasoline industry.

It is worthwhile to point out that in none of the above three models is price leadership a result of collusion; in fact, in each of the models price leadership is an inevitable consequence of a particular cost or demand phenomenon which precludes price collusion among sellers as a possible solution. Moreover, in none of the three models is the absence of competition attributable to the presence of a price leader. In

[9] Kenneth E. Boulding, *Economic Analysis*, rev. ed. (New York, 1948). For a diagrammatical presentation of the two models, see pp. 582, 586.

each of the three cases, conditions in either the factor or product market are already assumed to be inconsistent with the assumptions associated with highly competitive industries. Since the empirical evidence presented in a later section also suggests that effective price leadership, for the most part, is a result of monopoly rather than a cause of it, it is important that these two observations be borne in mind when it comes to prescribing appropriate remedies for industries having price leaders.

Dominant Firm Price Leadership

Contrary to the general belief that price leadership, because it eliminates the kink in the oligopoly demand curve, makes for a higher degree of price flexibility, Professor Stigler has presented evidence to show that "Except for the number of price changes of two-firm industries . . . , the prices of industries with price leaders are less flexible than those of industries without price leaders . . . ."[10] Significant though this discovery may be as evidence of the nonexistence of kinked oligopoly demand curves, it should be pointed out that the basic conclusion reached by Professor Stigler applies to a particular type of oligopolistic market and, hence, is not conclusive evidence that price leadership, regardless of type, leads to less flexible prices. For example, Professor Stigler limits the industries characterized by price leadership to those in which a dominant firm (one that produces a minimum of 40 per cent of the total output of an industry and more if the second largest firm is large) is present. Hence, industries characterized by other types of price leadership were included among those having no price leader. Moreover, the average number of firms in industries classified as having a price leader was slightly less than one-half of the average number of firms in industries not so classified. It is not surprising, therefore, that the former group shows a higher degree of price inflexibility than the latter for two reasons.

First, the rationale of price-making by the dominant firm or partial monopolist differs but little from that employed by the pure monopolist. They both, presumably, have complete control over prices, but the partial monopolist, unlike the pure monopolist, must take account of the quantity that the competitive sector of the industry will offer at any price he may set. However inadequate classical theory might be in explaining the rigidity of monopoly prices, given the empirical evidence that monopoly prices are relatively inflexible, it probably follows that prices controlled by partial monopolists assume similar ridigities.

Secondly, the greatest number of firms in any industry classified

[10] Stigler, *op. cit.*, p. 446.

among those having a price leader was four; the average number of firms in such industries was three. On the other hand, one industry not classified among those having a price leader contained as many as twelve firms and another contained eleven; the average number of firms in industries classified as having no price leader was over six. However, since many of the excluded industries such as the rayon, newsprint, copper, gasoline, plate glass, window glass and plow industries possess barometric price leaders and a larger number of firms than those having a partial monopolist, Professor Stigler's findings could also be interpreted as evidence that (1) prices are more flexible under barometric than dominant firm price leadership and (2) price flexibility increases as the number of firms is increased. Professor Stigler isolated and very adequately treated the latter relationship himself;[11] the former will be discussed more fully below.

In the light of the formal theoretical construction employed to explain the rationale of dominant firm price leadership, a fairly strong argument can be made against even including markets where prices are set by a dominant firm among those containing a "price leader." Formal solutions which yield an equilibrium price in such markets preclude all possibilities of the failure of small firms to follow the dominant firms' price change, and, hence, from the viewpoint of the dominant firm, increase the probability of their following to absolute certainty. That is to say, whether the dominant firm attempts to maximize profits in the short-run by equating its own marginal cost and derived marginal revenue schedules or pursues some other price policy, so long as it produces at a rate of output which clears the market at its own price, the remaining firms in the industry have no choice but to equate their marginal costs with the price it sets. Essentially, therefore, the pure dominant firm market presents a problem of monopoly price control rather than one of price leadership.

For purposes of public policy, to draw such a distinction between monopoly pricing and price leadership involves more than a mere question of definition. Price "leadership" in a dominant firm market is not simply a *modus operandi* designed to circumvent price competition among rival sellers but is instead an inevitable consequence of the industry's structure. Hence, the only obviously effective remedy for such monopoly pricing is to destroy the monopoly power from which it springs, *i.e.*, dissolve, if economically and politically feasible, the dominant firm. Public policy should hardly be directed toward this end, however, before the foundations of the dominant firm's existence have been thoroughly examined. Nearly every major industry in the American economy has, in its initial stages of development, been dominated

[11] *Ibid.*, p. 444.

by a single firm—the Slater Mill in cotton textiles, the Firestone Company in rubber tires, Birdseye in frozen foods, the American Viscose Corporation in rayon yarn, etc., to mention only a few. The monopoly power of the initial dominant firm in most industries, however, was gradually reduced by industrial growth and the entrance of new firms. It is not at all certain that public policy measures could have either hastened or improved upon the process. Where forces of competition do not eliminate such power, however, (Professor Stigler has suggested the aluminum and scotch tape industries to me as possible examples), it is highly improbable that a mere declaration of the illegality of price leadership by the courts offers itself as a sufficient or even a possible remedial measure. The dominant firm would simply be confronted with the dilemma of (1) changing prices frequently and reminding the public with each price change that it sets the price for the industry or (2) simply varying its output and risk the attendant onus of price fixing. Hence, should all dominant firms accept the implications of the recent *Tobacco* decision at their face value, there would be no reason to conclude *a priori* whether prices in markets dominated by a particular firm would henceforth be more or less flexible, or would more closely approximate prices which one would expect under more competitive conditions.

Barometric Firm Price Leadership

Unlike price leadership of the dominant firm type, there is no explanatory hypothesis which identifies the barometric price leader. In contrast to the dominant firm, the barometric firm "commands adherence of rivals to his price only because, and to the extent that, his price reflects market conditions with tolerable promptness."[12] Hence, the reasons why a particular firm is the barometric firm must be found in the historical background of an industry and the institutional and other features which have shaped its development.

It is worthwhile to note in passing that in a large number of industries which do not contain a partial monopolist, the price leader is frequently but not always the largest firm. In the newsprint industry, for example, International Paper, the largest producer, has led most price changes in markets east of the Rocky Mountains and Crown Zellerbach, the largest western producer, has usually announced new prices on the west coast. The price leadership of International, however, has sometimes been challenged by Great Northern, another large producer. American Viscose, which at one time completely dominated the rayon industry, has continued to be the accepted list-price leader although it had lost its dominant firm position as early as

[12] *Ibid.*, p. 446.

MARKHAM: NATURE AND SIGNIFICANCE OF PRICE LEADERSHIP 897

1930. On the other hand, Phelps Dodge, only the third largest producer of copper in 1947, has been quite active in setting copper prices since OPA controls were removed in November, 1946.

Patently, it is not possible in every case to judge when barometric price leadership is monopolistic and when it is competitive in character without making a thorough investigation, but there are certain visible market features associated with competitive price leadership. For example, unless a particular firm has demonstrated unusual adeptness at adjusting prices to market forces, in the absence of conspiracy one would certainly expect occasional changes in the identity of the price leader. Moreover, unless the lines of price communication are extremely efficient, prices are not likely to be uniform among sellers in a specific market area for a short period immediately following the date the price leader announces a new price. A "wait and see" policy on the part of several sellers not only gives rise to occasional price differentials, but also suggests the absence of even tacit collusion. Furthermore, if new prices are communicated among buyers more rapidly than among sellers, there would be frequent changes in the ratios of sales (and, depending upon inventory policies, of production) of particular firms to the total volume of sales (or production) for the industry as a whole. In the rayon and textile industries, where each large fabricator buys yarn and cloth from several sellers simultaneously, this is usually the case. Buyers iron out price differentials among sellers by refusing to buy at old prices if the price leader has announced a price reduction and buy heavily at old prices if the price leader has announced a price increase.

The price histories of copper and rayon yarn illustrate fairly well most of the outward manifestations one would expect of competitive barometric price leadership. Immediately upon the removal of OPA controls Kennecott Copper took the lead in advancing domestic copper prices from the controlled 14.375 cents per pound to the world price of 17.5 cents per pound.[13] All other producers followed. Eight days later, on November 20, 1946, Phelps Dodge advanced its price to 19.5 cents per pound and was followed by the rest of the industry. On January 28, 1947, American Smelting and Refining Company advanced its domestic price to 20.5 cents; however, other producers continued to sell at the old price until Phelps Dodge increased its price to 21.5 cents on March 3. American Smelting and Refining Company matched the new price but Kennecott Copper announced a firm price policy on March 27 and stated that it would continue to make shipments at the old price. Large copper buyers announced three weeks later, however, that in their opinion "Kennecott had 'reluctantly' advanced their prices

[13] Company prices are from various issues of the *New York Times*.

to meet present levels and the present action to fix prices at present levels meant that Kennecott would be unlikely to follow any further upward price revisions from other sources."[14] In the latter part of June the price of copper settled at 21.5 cents after several weeks of varying prices among sellers. Around the end of July, 1948, several smaller companies increased their prices to 23.5 cents; the larger producers did not follow immediately but withdrew all offerings from the market. On August 3 Phelps Dodge and Anaconda jointly raised their prices to 23.5 cents and Kennecott followed on August 11.

Of the five major copper price changes which occurred between November, 1946, and December, 1948, therefore, Phelps Dodge, a medium-sized producer, initiated three. Competitive factors, however, such as the import tariff on sales made in the United States by foreign producers and price movements of scrap, tin, and aluminum, probably exerted much more influence on copper prices during the twenty-six month period than did the arbitrary judgment of the firm initiating the price changes.[15]

Until 1930 American Viscose was the dominant firm in the rayon yarn industry. Since then the company has produced from only 30 per cent to 35 per cent of the total domestic output of rayon yarn but has first announced over 75 per cent of all list-price revisions. The price leader can exercise only negligible control over rayon prices, however, since they are largely determined by the prices of such close substitutes as silk, cotton, wool, nylon, orlon, and vinyon, each of which competes strongly with rayon in a number of market areas. Moreover, small rayon producers do not hesitate to sell at less than their quoted price when inventories commence to accumulate, a practice which has prompted most of the downward revisions announced by American Viscose. On the other hand, rayon list prices are seldom increased unless the industry is operating close to full capacity and inventories are still declining. For list-price movements, however, American Viscose plays the rôle of the barometric firm.

Barometric price leadership which follows the above lines probably does not greatly circumvent the public interest nor is it likely that the *Tobacco* decision has brought this type of price leadership within the reach of the antitrust laws. The barometric firm possesses no power to coerce the rest of the industry into accepting its price and, in most such industries, it simply passes along information to the "Big Three"

[14] *New York Times*, March 29, 1947, p. 23.

[15] Copper producers seem to feel that their prices are largely dependent upon the prices of such competing metals as aluminum and tin. Between March, 1947, and August, 1948, Kennecott publicly denounced further price increases since it believed they would induce fabricators to substitute tin and aluminum for copper. *Cf. New York Times*, May 5, 1948, p. 41, and August 3, 1948, p. 29.

or the "Big Four" on what the rest of the industry is doing in a declining market, and proceeds with initiating price increases in a market revival only so rapidly as supply and demand conditions dictate.

For purposes of prescribing appropriate remedial action it is important also to differentiate between actual collusive price leadership and "apparent" collusive price leadership which stems more from overt selling arrangements than from simply following price changes announced by a rival firm. In the steel, cement, glass container, and fertilizer industries, what has appeared at times to be barometric price leadership was in fact a natural consequence of basing point and zone pricing systems. Under a single basing point system, if recognized and adhered to by all producers, giving the appearance of following a price leader is inevitable since the pricing policies of all sellers are unalterably geared to the base mill. The same is true of a multiple basing point system if all base mills are owned by a single seller. Identical prices among producers in an industry operating under a multiple basing point system where the base mills are owned by different producers is not clearly a necessary consequence of the basing point system but one should, on economic grounds, expect all prices at least to move in the same direction. A decrease in the base price in one area allows all producers abiding by this base price to further invade adjacent areas until mills in adjacent areas meet the price reduction; an increase in the base price in one area increases the demand for the commodity from mills in adjacent areas, thereby encouraging corresponding price increases. Hence, a sufficient explanation for similar price movements among producers abiding by a basing point system is the presence of the basing point system itself. The best evidence that this is so is the undisciplined pricing which occurs when the basing point system temporarily breaks down.[16]

For the most part, therefore, the barometric price leader, as defined by Professor Stigler and as visualized for purposes of this paper, appears to do little more than set prices that would eventually be set by forces of competition. In such industries as the copper and rayon industries, *i.e.*, oligopolies within monopolistically competitive markets, these prices are largely dependent upon the prices of closely competing products. In more clearly delineated oligopolistic industries, particularly where the number of firms is fairly large, price leadership of the barometric type has seldom if ever been a sufficiently strong instrument alone to insure price discipline among rivals. Price leadership in the steel and fertilizer industries has been a subordinate feature of a basing point system. The glass container industry implemented price leadership by inaugurating a zone pricing and market sharing system.

[16] *Cf.* Temporary National Economic Committee, Monograph No. 42, p. 3.

In spite of this, many firms were not faithful price followers.[17] In the tin can industry, where American Can Company has frequently been identified as the price leader, a recent study suggests that American's list price (computed principally from the price of tin plate) has only established the base line of competition for other can producers.[18] Moreover, American Can's influence over the price of tin cans is as much attributable to its quasi-monopsonistic position in the tin plate market as it is to the company's share of the tin can market.

From the standpoint of public policy the real problem in such markets as those discussed above, therefore, centers upon economic forces which support price leadership rather than upon price leadership *per se*. In industries dominated by a strong partial monopolist, parallel pricing among firms stems from the monopoly power possessed by the partial monopolist and not from the tacit adoption of a price leader to circumvent price competition. The competitive sector of the industry often has no choice but to accept the partial monopolist's price. In oligopolies which form segments of larger monopolistically competitive industries, such as those which conform to the pattern of the rayon and copper industries, the barometric firm "leads" price changes only in the limited sense that its price movements are presumed by its rivals to have resulted from a synthesis of all the available market information. Price decreases initiated by firms selling closely competing products and by smaller firms within its own segment of the industry usually prompt downward list-price revisions by the barometric firm. List-price increases occur only after the market forces have been reversed. In most markets of an intermediate character the evidence indicates that price leadership has been decidedly a subordinate feature of a pricing policy built upon the much stronger foundations of trade association activity, zone pricing, basing point agreements, etc.[19]

A comprehensive study embracing the tacit and overt pricing arrangements among sellers in a wide variety of industries more or less oligopolistic in character would undoubtedly point up to more meaningful conclusions than those suggested by the above evidence. Nevertheless, there is some basis for believing that the mere adoption of a price leader is not nearly such an effective means for eliminating price competition among the few as many economists are prone to believe.

[17] *Cf.* Robert L. Bishop, "The Glass Container Industry," in *The Structure of American Industry*, edited by Walter Adams (New York, 1950), pp. 407-8.

[18] Charles H. Hession, *The Tin Can Industry* (privately published), p. 362.

[19] An examination of recent industry studies [including those reproduced in part in *The Structure of American Industry, op. cit.*, and in Walter Adams and Leland E. Traywick, *Readings in Economics* (New York, 1948)] reveals little evidence that price leadership, when not buttressed by stronger means of preserving price discipline, prevented price competition among oligopolists in times of market crisis.

MARKHAM: NATURE AND SIGNIFICANCE OF PRICE LEADERSHIP 901

Except for the type of price leadership discussed below, the evidence suggests that the power of the price leader to preserve price discipline derives less from his ostensible status as the barometric firm than from the more overt arrangements which support it. Where such supporting arrangements are not found, the barometric firm seems to do little more than respond to forces of competition. If this is so, the *Tobacco* decision may have far less importance than has been attributed to it, but at the same time the search for remedial action in similar future cases may not be nearly so fruitless as is generally believed. The elimination of supports to effective price leadership, most of which are not particularly elusive targets, might very well eliminate the effectiveness of price leadership itself.

Price Leadership in Lieu of an Overt Agreement

In industries which possess certain specific features, however, one would expect *a priori* a type of price leadership of a much different nature and considerably more inimical to the public interest than that of the barometric type discussed above. In such industries price leadership may conceivably be so effective as to serve all the ends of a strong trade association or of a closely knit domestic cartel and, hence, in a political environment where overt collusion is illegal, may be the only feasible means of assuring parallel action among sellers. In view of the foregoing discussion, the most important market features prerequisite to effective price leadership of this type would seem to be as follows:

1. Firms must be few in number and each firm must be sufficiently large to be compelled to reckon with the indirect as well as the direct effects of its own price policy. If there are several very small firms in the industry but no dominant firm, they, through ignoring their indirect influence on price, are likely to engage in promiscuous price cutting whenever market crises occur and, hence, at least for downward price adjustments, usurp the rôle of price leader. Moreover, such firms are not likely to follow the lead in upward price revisions unless they are completely satisfied with their expected volume of sales at the new price.

2. Entry to the industry must be severely restricted in the price set by the price leader is to remain close to a rationalized oligopolistic price for any significant length of time. If the long-run cost curve for the new entrant is substantially the same as those which confront entrenched firms, price rationalization can be only temporary since the rationalized price will attract new entrants which, in turn, will bid the price down.[20] If, however, the time lag between investment decisions and actual investment in the industry is significant, price

[20] For an imperfect example, see discussion of cigarette industry, *infra*.

rationalization for the duration of the lag may suggest itself as a profitable possibility.

3. The "commodity" produced by the several firms need not be perfectly homogeneous but each producer must view the output of all other firms as extremely close substitutes for his own. If this condition is not fulfilled, each producer is likely to view his product as distinctive in character and the "market" will not be characterized by a single price policy but by several. Examples of such individual pricing policies may be found in the automobile and brand-name men's clothing markets. Where the output of each firm is differentiated to the extent that it is only a moderately good substitute for the output of other firms, price leadership, of course, is meaningless.

4. The elasticity of the market demand schedule for the output of the industry as described in (3) above must not greatly exceed unity. If demand for the output of the industry is elastic because the oligopoly is only a segment of a larger monopolistically competitive market, the prices of closely competing products severely limit or possibly even eliminate the gains to be derived from adopting a price leader. Moreover, if demand for the output of the oligopoly is highly elastic, firms are not likely to adhere to the price leader's price if to do so would result in substantially less than capacity operations, since each firm could still stimulate its own sales considerably by lowering its price, even though all other firms met the new price. The price history of the domestic rayon industry and the postwar price history of the copper industry furnish particularly good evidence of the validity of this point. Whenever declining silk and cotton prices have commenced to reduce the volume of rayon sales at existing list prices, rayon producers, if the price leader had not already reduced his price, have sold at less than list price in order to move accumulating inventories and to maintain operations at near-capacity output. Similarly, copper producers appear to follow the price leader only if they believe his new price is in line with prevailing scrap, aluminum, and tin prices.

5. Individual-firm cost curves must be sufficiently similar so that some particular price allows all firms to operate at a satisfactory rate of output. If, for example, the industry is composed of several high-cost low-capacity firms and several low-cost high-capacity firms, the resulting conflict in price and output policies cannot be resolved by adopting a price leader so long as all firms remain in the industry.[21] Low-cost firms will not accept the price leadership of high-cost firms since there is a better option in the form of a lower price and a higher rate of output open to them. They can therefore force the high-cost

---

[21] For the theoretical analysis relevant to an industry containing several firms but only one low-cost high-capacity firm, see Boulding, *supra*, fn. 9.

sector of the industry to adopt the lower price but, if the differences in costs between high-cost and low-cost firms are significant, high-cost firms will not recover full costs and will gradually be eliminated from the industry. Hence, the conflict will have been resolved and the condition that all producers be confronted with reasonably similar cost curves will then be fulfilled.

It might be argued that the foregoing conditions are fully as necessary for any form of effective parallel action, such as price maintenance agreements, strong trade associations, or even unimplemented oligopolistic rationalization, as they are for effective price leadership. Such an argument, of course, would be entirely valid for, it will be recalled, the type of price leadership being examined is but one of a number of possible forms of conscious parallelism, all of which presumably stem from a common source, namely, the identity between the long-run interests of each individual firm and those of the industry as a whole.

Moreover, conditions other than those discussed above bear significantly upon the likelihood of effective price leadership ever arising and maintaining price discipline in an industry. Among those that first come to mind are the extent of tariff protection, the rate of technological change, the stability of demand, and the aggressiveness of management. An examination of the available price histories of industries in which the number of sellers is not large indicates, however, that price leadership is most likely to serve the ends of a collusive agreement when the above five conditions are fulfilled. Or, stated another way, effective price discipline seems to have been rarely achieved by the tacit means of price leadership alone when one or several of these conditions did not exist.

The Tobacco Decision Reappraised

Had the Department of Justice diligently searched the American economy for an industry which most nearly contained all the conditions prerequisite to effective price leadership, it could hardly have found a better example than the cigarette industry. The entrenched position of the "Big Three" brand-names had made entry to the cigarette industry exceedingly difficult. Moreover, parallel action in the leaf tobacco market had insured fairly comparable if not equal cost conditions among the three large cigarette producers; and, although each of them viewed the output of the other two as such perfect substitutes for his own that none would risk a retail price differential, demand for their output collectively, at least in the short run, was inelastic. Furthermore, in 1929 the Big Three controlled over 90 per cent of the domestic cigarette market and, with Lorillard, they controlled 98 per cent. Hence, for all practical purposes, the number of cigarette producers was very small.

Also, the large cigarette producers had had ample opportunity as well as compelling reasons for working out a *modus operandi* which would identify their individual interests with those of the Big Three collectively. In substance, counsel for Liggett and Myers probably described the attitude of all the large producers of cigarettes when he stated, ". . . in making price decisions the management of Liggett and Myers has acted in response to a long experience of non-identical prices as well as identical prices."[22]

In spite of such ideal conditions for securing parallel action by adopting a price leader, however, the Big Three soon discovered that even their market was subject to economic forces that put an upper limit on exploitation. The *long-run* demand for their collective output was elastic, hence complete exploitation of the cigarette market was limited to a short-time period. With low tobacco prices and high cigarette prices in the latter half of 1931 and 1932, competitive forces began to assert their influence. Whereas the 10-cent brands had been virtually unknown (accounting for only 1.5 per cent of all cigarettes sold) in the first half of 1931, output of small independents began to increase rapidly after the price increase led by Reynolds in June, 1931. By December, 1932, they accounted for 22 per cent of total cigarette sales. In the meantime, the sales of Reynolds, American, Liggett and Myers and Lorillard had been drastically reduced. By February, 1933, their vulnerability to competition had become sufficiently evident to the Big Three to induce reductions in popular brand cigarette prices to the lowest level since 1918. Hence, simple price leadership, even under such ideal conditions as those afforded by the cigarette industry, had failed to preserve the rationalized oligopoly (or monopoly) market solution.

In the light of their alleged strategy after 1933, perhaps no one was more aware than the Big Three themselves of the long-run ineffectiveness of price leadership when not implemented by other safeguards from competition. Although price leadership continued to play an important rôle in cigarette pricing, its effectiveness after 1933 was largely dependent upon the successful effort of the Big Three to manipulate the leaf tobacco market.

If unimplemented price leadership proved to be an exploitative weapon of limited effectiveness in the cigarette industry, and its usefulness confined to a time period scarcely exceeding several years, it is highly improbable that tacit parallel pricing in oligopolistic markets offers itself *per se* as either a fruitful or fertile field for antitrust in-

---

[22] *American Tobacco Company* v. *United States*, 147 Fed. 2nd 93 (1945), Liggett and Myers' Brief, p. 264; *ibid.*, Reynolds' Brief, p. 390; and American Tobacco's Brief, pp. 94-95.

vestigation. Hence the *Tobacco* decision, particularly when viewed against a background in which appropriate remedial action is conspicuously absent, is not likely to have far-reaching consequences. The appropriate question before economists, the business community, and the courts alike, therefore, is not how far tacit parallel pricing in oligopolistic markets can proceed before it becomes illegal, but rather what implementing devices and market conditions make price leadership both possible and effective. In most oligopolistic industries where the record of pricing techniques is fairly complete, there are good reasons for suspecting that price leadership is essentially a shadow of more insidious pricing devices and trade restraints. When the devices which buttress price leadership have been destroyed, price leadership as an exploitative practice may well have ben emasculated.

In view of the extraordinary conditions prerequisite to the more effective type of price leadership, it is not likely that the *Tobacco* decision, as a legal precedent, can or will either measurably influence the behavior of prices in markets where sellers are few in number nor will it greatly broaden the scope of the antitrust laws. Along these lines, the recent basing point and similar future decisions would appear to be a much more profitable line of approach to monopoly problems posed by industries comprising relatively few sellers.

Part II
Entry Barriers

[13]

THE IMPORTANCE
OF THE CONDITION OF ENTRY

This book analyzes the character and significance of the "condition of entry" to manufacturing industries; it is based on an investigation of the force of latent competition from potential new sellers in twenty such industries in the United States.

The investigation was made because of two beliefs: (1) that most analyses of how business competition works and what makes it work have given little emphasis to the force of the potential or threatened competition of possible new competitors, placing a disproportionate emphasis on competition among firms already established in any industry; (2) that so far as economists have recognized the *possible* importance of this "condition of entry," they have no very good idea of how important it actually is.

If these are reasonable beliefs, it seems important to do two things — to develop systematic theory concerning the potential importance of the condition of entry as an influence on business conduct and performance, and to assess, in those ways that are open, the extent and nature of its actual importance. These are the main tasks of this book. In addition, we may read from our tentative findings some directions for the formulation of public policy toward business monopoly and competition. First, however, let us survey the facts and concepts which we are about to explore.

Actual competition versus the threat of entry

When competition is named as a regulator of enterprise outputs and prices, it is usually the competition among the firms already established in this or that industry which is emphasized. On the level of market conduct, detailed attention is given to whether the price-calculating policies of established firms are formulated independently or in the light of a "recognized interdependence" with each other, whether or not there is collusion among these firms, and the extent to which collusion, if found,

2   **BARRIERS TO NEW COMPETITION**

is imperfect. On the level of market structure, much emphasis is placed
on those characteristics of the industry that presumably influence competitive conduct as among established rivals, and particularly on the
number and size distribution of these rival sellers and on the manner in
which their products are differentiated from one another. The immediate
competition among established firms gets most of the attention.

This is true both of abstract economic theory and of the empirical
investigations which implement, test, or apply it. When conventional
price theory treats the working of business competition, it devotes nearly
all of its detailed analysis to the consequences of rivalry within various
alternative conformations of established sellers, so much so that the effects
of the actual or threatened entry of new sellers are generally mentioned,
if at all, cryptically and almost as an afterthought. Similarly, empirical
studies of market structure commonly center on seller concentration
within established groups, product differentiation within these groups,
and other determinants of the character of competition among established
sellers. Most studies of individual industries refer, when discussing competition, almost entirely to rivalry among established firms.

Correspondingly, the condition of entry has generally received only
nominal attention as a regulator of market conduct and performance.
Typical versions of abstract price theory do recognize the long-run impact
of an assumed "free" or "easy" entry of new firms to industries with many
small sellers. But when they turn to the very important category of
oligopolistic industries, they ordinarily fail to distinguish numerous
possible alternative situations with respect to the condition of entry,
and to identify and develop appropriate assumptions relative to the
structural determinants of the condition of entry. They thus fail to offer
any systematic predictions concerning the effect of variations in the
condition of entry on the market conduct of established sellers and on
industry performance in the long term. The theory of pricing in non-
atomistic markets is generally too oversimplified to identify or distinguish
potentially large and significant variations of behavior within the
oligopolistic sector of industries.

Much empirical investigation of business structure and competition
has followed the lead of abstract theory, and has been hindered by the
fact that abstract theory provided few leads in the area of the condition
of entry. Although investigations of the extent of existing seller concentration in various industries have become widespread in government
agencies and elsewhere, measurement of the height and nature of barriers
to entry has never been systematically undertaken. Studies of competitive
conduct and performance have paid much attention to such matters as
the role of the price leader in eliminating or canalizing competition among
established sellers and in influencing the ultimate relation of price to

IMPORTANCE OF THE CONDITION OF ENTRY   3

cost in his industry, but ordinarily they have given much less attention to the extent to which established firms shape price policies in the light of their anticipation of new entry, by deciding whether or not to try to forestall it. In brief, neither the theoretically possible nor the actual significance of variations in the condition of entry has received much attention from economists.

A strong emphasis on actual competition among existing sellers is of course appropriate. Such competition, with its determinants, is most probably of first importance as a regulator of business activity. But the substantial neglect of the condition of entry is definitely unfortunate, since there is considerable evidence of the importance of the condition of entry as a co-regulator of business conduct and performance.

Let us understand the term "condition of entry" to an industry to mean something equivalent to the "state of potential competition" from possible new sellers. Let us view it moreover as evaluated roughly *by the advantages of established sellers in an industry over potential entrant sellers, these advantages being reflected in the extent to which established sellers can persistently raise their prices above a competitive level without attracting new firms to enter the industry.* As such, the "condition of entry" is then primarily a structural condition, determining in any industry the intra-industry adjustments which will and will not induce entry. Its reference to market conduct is primarily to potential rather than actual conduct, since basically it describes only the circumstances in which the potentiality of competition from new firms will or will not become actual. If we understand the condition of entry in this way, its possible importance as a determinant of competitive behavior is clear.

Conventional price theory has been quite explicit concerning the effects of one type of condition of entry — *free* or *easy* entry. It has deduced from reasonable premises the valid conclusion that in markets with many small sellers, easy entry in the long run will force price to equality with minimal average costs and will bring output to a level sufficient for supplying all demands at this price. When price theory has turned to markets with few sellers and to conditions of entry other than easy, it has ordinarily been inexplicit, cryptic, or silent. But relatively elementary elaborations of received theory make it clear that variations in the condition of entry as it departs from the "easy" pole may have a substantial influence on the performance of established firms in any industry.

Even in atomistically organized industries, barriers to entry may, under certain conditions, result in a long-term elevation of prices and profits and a restriction of output; if established firms are restricted in number and encounter diseconomies of scale, entry will operate to limit prices only after they exceed a certain super-competitive level. In

4   BARRIERS TO NEW COMPETITION

oligopolistic industries, something additional is generally true. Each of the few large established sellers — whether they act collectively or singly — will appraise the condition of entry and, anticipating that entry may occur if price exceeds a given level, will regulate his price policies accordingly. There will thus be a sort of "recognized interdependence" of actions not only among established sellers but between established sellers and potential entrants. In this event, variations in the condition of entry may be expected to have substantial effects on the behavior of established sellers, *even though over long intervals actual entry seldom or never takes place.* Elementary extensions of the deductive logic of conventional price theory thus suggest an important role of the condition of entry, and emphasize the desirability of finding how much in fact it does vary from industry to industry.

Empirical observation reinforces the impression that the condition of entry may be an important determinant of market behavior, especially in the case of oligopolistic industries. Examination of any considerable number of concentrated industries reveals great differences in market conduct and performance among them, in spite of the fact that in each a recognized interdependence among established sellers definitely appears to be present. Variations in the degree of seller concentration or of product differentiation among oligopolies may explain a part of these differences in behavior, but not all of them. The other most evident structural variation among oligopolies is that of the condition of entry, and from casual observation this variation seems to be at least loosely associated with variations in behavior. A more systematic empirical study of the importance of the condition of entry is thus indicated.

The meaning of the condition of entry

As suggested above, the condition of entry is a structural concept. Like some other aspects of market structure, it may be viewed as potentially subject to quantitative evaluation in terms of a continuous variable. This variable is the percentage by which established firms can raise price above a specified competitive level without attracting new entry — a percentage which may vary continuously from zero to a very high figure, with entry becoming "more difficult" by small gradations as it does so. As the difficulty of entry (thus understood and evaluated) increases, some systematic variations in the behavior of established firms may be anticipated.

The preceding description is obviously unspecific in numerous details. On the ground that this is primarily an empirical study dealing with available data, and that we do not wish to fashion a precision instrument for use in ditch-digging, it does not seem profitable here to develop a very polished and detailed definition of the condition of entry. (The writer

IMPORTANCE OF THE CONDITION OF ENTRY 5

has taken some steps in that direction in an earlier article,[1] and even the moderate degree of detail and precision attempted there seems out of place in the present setting.) Nevertheless, it seems useful to be somewhat more explicit by simply stating, without a detailed theoretical discussion, what is to be understood by various terms and notions expressed or implied in the definition so far presented.

As stated, the condition of entry may be evaluated by the extent to which established sellers can persistently raise their prices above a competitive level without attracting new firms to enter the industry. The first term needing consideration is "attracting new firms to enter the industry." This implies some specific definition of the concept of *entry*, involving both the notion of the "new firm" and of the meaning of the verb "to enter." As a first approximation, entry of a new firm may be taken to mean here the combination of two events: (1) the establishment of an independent legal entity, new to the industry, as a producer therein; and (2) the concurrent building or introduction by the new firm of physical production capacity that was not used for production in the industry prior to the establishment of the new firm. An addition to industry capacity already in use, plus emergence of a firm new to the industry, are thus required.

This definition excludes two related events from the concept of "entry." The first is the acquisition of existing producing capacity by a new legal entity, whether by purchase from a preëxisting firm, by reorganization involving a change of corporate name and structure, or through other means. Simple change of ownership or control of existing operating capacity is not considered as entry. The second exclusion is the expansion of capacity by an established firm. If, for example, a small established firm doubles its capacity, this is to be considered as a phase of competition among established firms rather than an act of entry. Growth of an already established rival firm in an industry is thus not considered as entry to that industry. Both of these exclusions are in some degree arbitrary, since the introduction of a new owner of old capacity may constitute a distinct change in a competitive situation, and since expansion of an established competitor may, from the standpoint of another established firm, have about the same significance as entry of a new firm with new capacity. Nevertheless, present purposes call for distinguishing competition among established competitors from the entry of new competitors, and we thus draw the lines indicated. As we proceed, we will have occasion to refer to the significance of events closely related to entry as defined.

Given these exclusions, a firm new to the industry may enter that industry by building new capacity to produce, by converting for use in

[1] See J. S. Bain, "Conditions of Entry and the Emergence of Monopoly," *Monopoly and Competition and Their Regulation*, edited by E. H. Chamberlin (London, 1954), pp. 215–241.

6   **BARRIERS TO NEW COMPETITION**

this industry plants previously used in another industry, or by reactivating capacity that has been previously used in the instant industry but is currently idle. Any of these acts by a new firm, singly or in combination, will constitute entry, according to the definition, and will continue to do so, even though the new firm also acquires operating capacity from an already established firm. Acquisition of a going concern by a new firm, together with expansion of the facilities of the going concern, thus constitutes entry to the extent of the expansion. Detailed implementation of this definition would require further specifications, such as the duration of the idleness required to distinguish "idle" plant from "operating" plant, but from the preceding the general intent of our definition should be clear.

Thus we see that the condition of entry may be evaluated by the degree to which established firms can raise their prices above a competitive level without inducing new firms to bring added capacity into use in the industry. How many new firms or how big? For the moment we may say "one or more" new firms and "any size," although we will treat the subject directly when we consider the difference between the *immediate* and the *general* condition of entry.

The second crucial concept is the "competitive level of prices," which, by definition, established firms may exceed more and more *without attracting entry* as the condition of entry becomes progressively more difficult. The "competitive level of prices" is defined here as the minimum attainable average cost of production, distribution, and selling for the good in question, such cost being measured to include a normal interest return on investment in the enterprise.

In effect, this is equivalent to the level of price hypothetically attributed to long-run equilibrium in pure competition. If equilibrium were of the stationary sort frequently described in theory textbooks, in which each firm produced regularly and uninterruptedly at its most efficient output, then this competitive price would equal the minimum attainable average cost (interest returns included) for the most efficient scale of firm when its capacity is always utilized at the optimal rate. In actual situations, where demand is unstable and uncertain and equilibrium is necessarily an adjustment to an average of varying situations over time, the competitive level of price and cost is elevated sufficiently to cover, for the most efficient scale of firm, the added costs of resulting periodic deviations from an optimal rate of utilization, and those coming from unavoidable errors in estimates of future demands, costs, and the like.[2]

---

[2] Minimal costs as defined presuppose the use of optimal available production techniques. Where product differentiation and sales promotion are encountered, such costs also include sales-promotion costs as incurred according to profit-maximizing criteria. The distinction between the lowest attainable average cost for the firm (supposedly attained in purely competitive long-run equilibrium) and the close approximation to that lowest cost supposedly attained in equilibrium in monopolistic

IMPORTANCE OF THE CONDITION OF ENTRY 7

This competitive or minimum-cost level of price is a useful reference point for evaluating the condition of entry. Completely easy or unimpeded entry involves the inability of established firms to raise price above this level at all — persistently or on the average through time — without attracting new entry. If price may persistently exceed this level at all without inducing entry, then entry is somewhat impeded. The greater the persistent percentage excess attainable without inducing entry, the more difficult entry may be said to be.

It will be noted that this measure of the condition of entry refers to an independently defined standard of cost and not necessarily to the actual costs of firms established in the industry. It thus is a measure not simply of the profit margins they are able to establish without inducing entry, but rather of the margin between an entry-inducing price and minimal competitive costs as defined. There will tend to be a direct relationship between the two margins. But it is quite possible, for example, that in an industry where price could be substantially elevated above a competitive level without inducing entry, profits could nevertheless be absent because established firms were built to inefficient sizes.

A third term that must be considered is "persistently." We refer for our measure to the height of price which can be *persistently* attained by established sellers without inducing entry. This condition is inserted deliberately to give a long-run and structural aspect to our definition of the condition of entry, rather than to make it merely reflect transitory and varying short-term conditions from year to year. By a persistent elevation of price relative to a competitive level, therefore, we mean one maintained on the average over a substantial period of time, long enough to encompass a typical range of varying conditions of demand, factor prices, and the like. Such a period might normally be thought of as five or ten years. The definition thus refers, in brief, to the average relationship of the actual with a competitive price that can be maintained over a number of years without attracting entry. The relationship to entry of the short-run level of price — set only for a few months or year, for example — is deliberately neglected as erratic and without much significance in most industries.

We turn now to a very necessary elaboration of our definition of the condition of entry, designed to take into account (1) differences among established firms in an industry, and (2) differences among potential entrant firms. So far, we have referred to all established firms in an industry as an aggregate, and to entrant firms without reference to their number

---

competition will be neglected in defining minimal cost throughout the following discussion. Hypothetically, the basic minimal cost level from which the condition of entry is measured should refer alternatively to the two levels, depending upon whether or not product differentiation is present.

8   **BARRIERS TO NEW COMPETITION**

or identity. In so doing, we have spoken as if generally all established
firms in an industry would charge a single price and have a single common
competitive level of price or of minimum cost. Also, we have not recognized the existence or consequences of possible cost and other differences
among potential entrant firms. Although both suppositions could be
adopted for purposes of simplified theorizing, neither will be supported
by fact, and thus it is necessary to elaborate the definition.

With respect to established firms, the complications are two. There
may be a type of differentiation among their products which supports
some system of differentials among their prices, so that actually they
will at no time charge a single common price but rather maintain a certain
regimen of different prices. And they may have somewhat different
minimal costs to be used in defining the "competitive" level of price,
since there may be quality differences among their products or differential
advantages in cost. In view of these cost and price differences, then, how
do we define the maximum excess of price over competitive cost at which
entry may be forestalled?

There is no simple answer, since existence of the sort of cost and price
differences noted actually means that the condition of entry to an industry
has become intrinsically a more complicated concept and cannot be fully
measured by any single firm's difference between an actual and a competitive price. It could be measured fully only through an array of individual differences for all individual firms — i.e., margins of actual prices
above minimal costs — which would be encountered when all firms had
concurrently raised their prices just short of the point that would induce
new entry. Since this theoretically satisfactory procedure of complex
measurement is not practically useful, an arbitrary simplification is required.

We will tentatively suggest that, where interfirm differences exist
within the industry, the condition of entry may be conveniently evaluated
in the following terms. First, the relevant gap between price and minimal
cost (just short of that sufficient to induce entry) will be the one encountered when all established firms elevate their prices concurrently by
similar amounts or proportions, maintaining any customary competitive
price differentials. (It will not refer to gaps associated with isolated hypothetical price increases by one or a few firms, since these would be
relatively uninteresting.) Second, the condition of entry may then be
measured specifically as the maximum gap between price and minimal
cost at which entry may be forestalled, for the most favored established
firm or firms in the industry, supposing concurrent price elevations by
all established firms. (The "most favored firm" may be identified as that
with the largest price-minimal cost gap.) This single measure may be
elaborated by any information revealing a significantly different gap for

IMPORTANCE OF THE CONDITION OF ENTRY 9

other established firms. Closer or more elaborate approximations seem unlikely to be implemented with data that are or can be made available.

Our next problem concerns differences among potential entrant firms. The condition of entry is measured by the long-run gap between minimal cost and price which the most favored firms can reach without attracting entry — but whose entry and how much? Do we assume that all entrants are alike and that there will be an unlimited and perfectly elastic supply of entrant firms if the entry-inducing gap is exceeded? If not, what do we assume about the number and size of entrants attracted as an entry-inducing gap is reached?

It is not realistic to assume that all potential entrants are alike either in their capacity to enter or with respect to the gap which will just induce them to enter. Nor can we assume that established firms are confronted by an indefinitely large supply of entrant firms if they exceed some critical price-to-minimal-cost gap. The more plausible assumptions are (1) that potential entrant firms may differ as to the gap which will induce them to enter, conceivably to the point where every potential entrant differs from every other in this respect; and (2) that any specific entry-inducing gap may induce only the entry of a finite number of firms. Then for any industry the condition of entry is fully measured only by a succession, within any range conceivably relevant to market behavior, of successively higher entry-inducing price-minimal cost gaps that will attract successive firms or groups of firms to enter the industry.

We may therefore establish two complementary concepts: *the immediate condition of entry* and *the general condition of entry*. The *immediate condition of entry* refers to the impediments to entry by the firm or firms that can most easily or readily be induced to enter the industry in a given situation. This immediate condition is evaluated by the long-run price-minimal cost gap (for the most favored established firms) which is just short of sufficient (just sufficient at the margin) to induce the entry of what we may call the most favored potential entrant or entrants. At any stage in its development, each industry has some immediate condition of entry thus defined and evaluated, although the number of potential entrant firms referred to by the measure could vary greatly from industry to industry.

The *general condition of entry* then refers to the succession of values of the immediate condition of entry as entry to the industry occurs — to the distribution of price-minimal cost gaps just necessary to induce successively less favored firms or groups of firms to enter an industry consecutively, beginning with the most favored firm. At any stage in its development, each industry has a general condition of entry in prospect (as well as one past, or one faced by various established firms before entering the industry), reflecting the succession of entry-inducing long-run price-

10   **BARRIERS TO NEW COMPETITION**

minimal cost gaps at which successive increments to entry are expected to occur. At one extreme, this condition might be represented in the sustained repetition of a single value of the immediate condition of entry, reflecting in effect a perfectly elastic supply of entry. At the other, it might be represented in a series of different values each of which referred to the entry of only a single firm. In most cases, the general condition of entry to an industry should be expected *a priori* to lie between these two extremes.

If the condition of entry refers to the conditions for the inducement to entry of successive finite numbers of firms, it should also logically refer to the *size* of each entry, viewed either as realized *ex post* or anticipated *ex ante*. That is, a full measure of each *immediate* condition of entry (successions of which define the *general* condition) must include not only a measure of the long-run price-minimal cost gap for principal established firms necessary to induce some increment to entry, but also a measure of the long-run scale (attained *ex post* or expected to be attained *ex ante*) of the firms included in that increment. Such a measure of scale might be expressed as a percentage of total industry output. If the scale to be attained by entrants is a range of alternative values depending on the choice alternative policies open to established sellers, then the condition of entry is measured in part by such a range of values.

The last elaboration on the measure of the condition of entry represents a refinement of an order not very useful for application to actual data. Nevertheless, it may be possible in evaluating various conditions of entry to make some general appraisal of the comparative scales likely to be attained by potential entrants if they enter, and of the circumstances, if any, that would limit their sizes.

The preceding elaborations and definitions of terms should make the general meaning of the condition of entry to an industry sufficiently explicit for our purposes here. It refers to advantages which established firms in an industry have over potential entrant firms; it is evaluated in general by measures of the heights of entry-inducing prices relative to defined competitive levels. One major matter that has not received attention in this definition, however, concerns the "lags of entry," or time intervals consumed by entrants in making their entries effective.

Given any particular immediate condition of entry, as evaluated by some entry-inducing excess of price over a competitive level, there is still room for variation in the length of time an entrant firm requires to make its entry effective. For purposes of a first approximation we may say that entry is initiated when a new firm has taken more or less irrevocable steps to establish and use new capacity in an industry, and is completed when the firm has established and "broken in" all production and other facilities necessary to permit it to produce in routine fashion at its planned

IMPORTANCE OF THE CONDITION OF ENTRY 11

rate of output. The "lag period," then, is the time interval between these two dates, and may vary greatly from industry to industry. In the women's garment industry it might be only a few months; in the cement industry it might be a year or two; in the distilled liquor industry, more than four years would be required to develop aged stocks of whiskey.

The longer the lag period in question, the less influence any given threat of entry will be likely to have on established sellers. The fact that establishing a price at some given level may induce three new firms to enter the industry is more likely to deter established firms from setting so high a price if the entry will be made effective in six months than if it will be made effective in six years. The *effect* of any given condition of entry on market behavior will therefore be likely to vary with the length of the entry lags which accompany it.

Whether the "value" of the condition of entry should be modified to reflect the length of entry lags seems principally a semantic issue. Because there is logically no unique method of combining measures of an entry-inducing price gap and an entry lag, we will follow the convention here of defining or evaluating the condition of entry to any industry without reference to entry lags — i.e., in terms of the excess of an entry-inducing price over a competitive level, whatever the lag. We will, however, consider data on entry lags as supplementary information useful in predicting the consequences of the condition of entry as defined. This procedure seems to place entry lags in their proper role in analysis.

The determinants of the condition of entry

Once the condition of entry has been so defined and measured, the next question is what *determines* the condition of entry to any industry. What is the nature of the advantages that established firms may possess, and what technological or institutional circumstances give rise to these advantages?

The identity of the immediate determinants of the condition of entry is suggested by considering the characteristics ordinarily attributed to a situation of theoretical "easy entry." In modern price theory, "easy entry" is ordinarily conceived as a situation in which there is no impediment to the entry of new firms, in which established firms possess no advantages over potential entrant firms, or in which, more precisely, established firms cannot persistently elevate price by any amount above the competitive minimal-cost level without attracting sufficient new entry to bring price back to that level. The condition of entry, as we have seen, can be measured by the percentage by which the prices of established firms can exceed the competitive level without attracting entry. Then with easy entry, the immediate condition of entry has a value of *zero* at every point in any possible sequence of entry (each added entrant firm has no dis-

12   **BARRIERS TO NEW COMPETITION**

advantage relative to those already established), and the general condition of entry is correspondingly represented by a single zero value. Entry,
of course, ceases to be easy and becomes more difficult as values of the
condition of entry progressively in excess of zero are encountered, or as
at one point or another in the progression of entry established firms can
receive super-competitive prices without inducing entry.

The essential characteristics of the situation in which easy entry prevails should furnish a direct clue to the determinants of the condition of
entry in general. For easy entry, three conditions must in general be
simultaneously fulfilled. At any stage in the relevant progression of entry
(1) *established firms have no absolute cost advantages* over potential
entrant firms; (2) *established firms have no product differentiation advantages* over potential entrant firms; and (3) *economies of large-scale
firm are negligible*, in the sense that the output of a firm of optimal
(lowest-cost) scale is an insignificant fraction of total industry output.
Let us see briefly what each of these conditions means and why it is important.

The condition that with easy entry established firms should have no
absolute cost advantages means that, for a given product, potential
entrant firms should be able to secure just as low a minimal average cost
of production after their entry as established firms had prior to this entry.
This in turn implies (a) that established firms should have no price or
other advantages over entrants in purchasing or securing any productive
factor (including investible funds); (b) that the entry of an added firm
should have no perceptible effect on the going level of any factor price;
and (c) that established firms have no preferred access to productive
techniques. If these conditions are fulfilled, then established firms, if
they should wish to elevate price above the competitive level without
attracting entry, have no ability to do so by virtue of the fact that the
level of their costs is any lower than potential entrant firms will be able to
secure. Established firms (before entry) and the entrant (after entry)
have costs on the same level for any given product. If product differentiation exists, the equivalent of this condition must be fulfilled.

The condition that with easy entry there should be no product differentiation advantage to established firms means either that there must be
no product differentiation or that, if product differentiation is present,
potential entrant firms should be able to secure a relationship of price to
cost just as favorable as that enjoyed by established firms. Generally, if
the possibility of differences in products, production costs, and selling
costs is recognized, the potential entrant firm should always be able to
secure as favorable a relation of price to unit production plus selling cost
as established firms, so that established firms can never make a profit
when an entrant could not, or break even when entrant would lose

IMPORTANCE OF THE CONDITION OF ENTRY 13

money. For this to be true, there must be no net price or selling cost advantage accruing to established firms by reason of buyer preferences for their products, and also no price advantages in securing factors of production. The condition of lack of product differentiation advantages is obviously essential to easy entry, since otherwise established firms could raise their prices somewhat above the competitive level without creating a situation in which potential entrants could sell profitably.

The condition that there should be no significant economies to the large scale firm means of course that an entrant firm, even if it enters at an optimal or lowest-cost scale, will add so little to industry output that its entry will have no perceptible effect on going prices in the industry. In order to avail itself of the lowest costs available to established firms, the entrant need not augment industry output enough to make the industry price less attractive; thus, the pursuit of economies of scale to the ultimate is possible and provides no deterrent to entry. The importance of this condition is evident when we consider the opposite possibility.

If, in order to enter at optimal scale, a firm must add a significant fraction to industry output, several possibilities are open. If established firms maintain their going outputs, entry at such a scale will tend in general to bring about a reduction of industry price. If they maintain or increase their prices, the obtainable market share for the entrant may very well be insufficient to permit optimal scale operations. Furthermore, retaliatory pricing by established firms may be engendered, and entry at a scale small enough not to disturb the market will require suboptimal scale and higher costs.

In one way or another, entry tends to be deterred sufficiently so that established firms are probably enabled to elevate price at least somewhat above the lowest-cost level without inducing entry. The potential entrant, if he enters at significantly large scales himself, will probably expect or fear either an industry price after entry which is somewhat below that which prevails before entry, or a market share involving costs above those of optimal scale.[3] Thus he will probably not be induced to enter by a somewhat super-competitive industry price. If he considers entry at insignificant scales, he will have costs above the competitive level and thus again will not be induced to enter by a somewhat supercompetitive price. Significant economies of scale thus tend to impede entry, and their absence is generally essential to easy entry.

The three conditions just described are both necessary and sufficient

[3] Instances are logically conceivable in which a market share permitting lowest-cost scale could be secured by an entrant — e.g. where established firms were generally of super-optimal scale before entry, so that sellers in general would not be forced to suboptimal scales by sharing the market among more of them. But that this, plus the absence of some retaliation in price by established firms, should be found seems unlikely.

14   **BARRIERS TO NEW COMPETITION**

for easy entry to exist. If this is true, it is clear that we have by implication identified the sources of departure from easy entry and the immediate determinants of the condition of entry as defined.

Departures of the condition of entry from the "zero pole" of easy
entry must be attributable to one or more of the following: (1) absolute
cost advantages of established firms; (2) product differentiation advantages of established firms; and (3) significant economies of large-scale
firms. Correspondingly, the heights of barriers to entry, or the "values"
of the condition of entry (expressed as the percentages by which established firms can set prices above a competitive level while forestalling
entry), will clearly depend on the degree of these absolute cost and
product differentiation advantages and on the extent of scale economies
to large firms. The specific nature of these determinants of the condition
of entry are presumably more or less obvious, but a brief summary of
their character will serve to suggest the character of the institutional and
other conditions from which they arise.

Absolute cost advantages to established firms will in general arise
from one of three things: (1) the entry of a single firm may perceptibly
elevate one or more factor prices paid by both established firms and
the entrant firm, thus raising the level of costs; (2) established firms may
be able to secure the use of factors of production, including investible
funds, at lower prices than potential entrants can; (3) established firms
may have access to more economical techniques of production than
potential entrants, thus enabling them to secure lower costs. Such absolute cost advantages tend to give established firms a lower level of costs
than the potential entrant, and thus enable them to set prices above a
competitive level while still forestalling entry.

Product differentiation advantages of established firms result, of
course, from the preferences of buyers for established as compared to
new entrant products. What will constitute an effective product differentiation advantage will depend on the importance of economies of scale
in production and selling in the industry. If there are no economies of
scale, so that unit production plus selling costs are not increased by restricting output to very small amounts, a potential entrant firm may be
said to be without disadvantage if he can receive as high a price relative
to unit cost as established firms *at some output*, even though he is able
to do so only at a much smaller output than established firms. (Existence
of a large number of such potential entrants — even though each was
restricted in sales volume — would provide easy entry.) Conversely,
possession of an advantage by established firms in the case of no scale
economies requires their ability to secure at some output a higher price
or lower selling cost — or generally a higher ratio of price to production
plus selling cost — than the most favored potential entrants can secure at

IMPORTANCE OF THE CONDITION OF ENTRY　　15

any output.[4] Existence of such product differentiation advantages is possible and would confer on established firms the ability to elevate price above a competitive level while forestalling entry.

If there are some systematic economies of scale to the firm, so that unit costs of production plus selling decline relative to price over some range of outputs, absence of advantage to established sellers requires the ability of entrants in general to attain not only comparable prices but also to obtain them at comparable sales volumes and thus to secure comparable costs as well. Conversely, the possession of advantage by established firms would require only that they be able to sell at a higher price than potential entrants can at approximately optimal scales, even though potential entrants could gain a price parity at small and inefficient scales. In effect, entrants, in order to lack disadvantage, must not only get parity in price, but must get it at economically large sales volumes.

Not much more need be said of the nature of advantages to established firms that are inherent in substantial economies to the large-scale firm. The fact that an entrant must add significantly to industry output to attain lowest costs, and would have perceptibly higher costs at smaller outputs, bestows on established firms the ability to elevate price somewhat above the competitive level without attracting entry. The economies in question may be either those of large-scale production and distribution, or, as suggested in the preceding footnote, those of large-scale sales promotion. Clearly, the advantage of established firms is increased and the condition of entry becomes more difficult both as the optimal scale of the firm becomes larger relative to the market, and as the rise of costs at smaller scales becomes steeper.

A question related to these immediate determinants of the condition of entry as we have defined it concerns the identity of the basic institutional and technological circumstances that give rise to the various immediate deterrents to entry. No exhaustive treatment is required here, but the following tabulation suggests the sorts of circumstances which typically give rise to impeded entry and which may logically be the subject of an investigation bearing generally upon the condition of entry:

I. *Typical circumstances giving rise to an absolute cost advantage to established firms.*

    A. Control of production techniques by established firms, via either patents or secrecy. (Such control may permit exclusion of entrants

---

[4] A variant of this is that the potential entrants could, in the absence of scale economies *other than* price or selling-cost advantages of large-scale sales promotion, secure an equivalent price relative to unit costs, but only at an output constituting a significant fraction of the market. In this event the established firms would also enjoy some net advantage, although it would be attributable in some sense to the significance of scale economies *per se.*

16   BARRIERS TO NEW COMPETITION

from access to optimal techniques, or alternatively the levying of a discriminatory royalty charge for their use.)

B. Imperfections in the markets for hired factors of production (e.g. labor, materials, etc.) which allow lower buying prices to established firms; alternatively ownership or control of strategic factor supplies (e.g. resources) by established firms, which permits either exclusion of entrants from such supplies, driving entrants to use inferior supplies, or discriminatory pricing of supplies to them.

C. Significant limitations of the supplies of productive factors in specific markets or submarkets for them, relative to the demands of an efficient entrant firm. Then an increment to entry will perceptibly increase factor prices.

D. Money-market conditions imposing higher interest rates upon potential entrants than upon established firms. (These conditions are apparently more likely to be effective as a source of advantage to established firms as the absolute capital requirement for an efficient entrant increases.)

II. *Typical circumstances giving rise to a product differentiation advantage to established firms.*

A. The accumulative preference of buyers for established brand names and company reputations, either generally or except for small minorities of buyers.

B. Control of superior product designs by established firms through patents, permitting either exclusion of entrants from them or the levying of discriminatory royalty charges.

C. Ownership or contractual control by established firms of favored distributive outlets, in situations where the supply of further outlets is other than perfectly elastic.

III. *Typical circumstances discouraging entry by sustaining significant economies of the large-scale firm.*

A. Real economies (i.e. in terms of quantities of factors used per unit of output) of large-scale production and distribution such that an optimal firm will supply a significant share of the market.

B. Strictly pecuniary economies (i.e. monetary economies only, such as those due to the greater bargaining power of large buyers) of large-scale production, having a similar effect.

C. Real or strictly pecuniary economies of large-scale advertising or other sales promotion, having a similar effect.

These circumstances are in a sense the ultimate determinants of the

IMPORTANCE OF THE CONDITION OF ENTRY 17

condition of entry to an industry. We have emphasized throughout that the condition of entry is a structural concept, and that it is evaluated by the extent to which established firms can, on the average over a long period, elevate price above a long-run competitive level while still forestalling entry. Consistently, the ultimate determinants of the condition of entry either reflect or refer directly to long-run structural characteristics of markets, and it is these which determine the condition of entry as we have defined it here.

If these are the determinants of the condition of entry, we should be equally clear about the things that are *not* its determinants. The true determinants are the things that determine for established firms the possible price-cost relations which would and would not induce entry; they are not those things determining whether or not actual entry takes place at a particular time. Thus, although the persistent product-differentiation advantage of established firms is a true determinant of the condition of entry, the current and transitory relation of industry demand to capacity is not.

It is true, of course, that if an industry is currently plagued with heavy excess capacity (caused, for example, by a secular decline in demand against long-lived plants) prices may average below costs and no entry may take place for many years. But this does not necessarily mean that the condition of entry is therefore difficult, for it does not remove the fact that a persistent slight excess of price above minimal long-run average costs (perhaps unlikely to occur in this situation) could be sufficient to induce entry. We must thus in general reject current secular or cyclical movements of demand, capacity, and cost as determinants of the condition of entry to an industry, just as we reject the current record of accomplished entry as direct or conclusive evidence of what the condition of entry is. Such things as the relationship of demand to capacity in an industry would affect the condition of entry as defined only so far as they persisted in a given state for some time, and so far as, in addition, they affected the manner in which potential entrants would react to given persistent differences between the actual price and a competitive price.[5]

We have by now frequently noted that the condition of entry to an industry is a structural and long-term condition. But that does not mean it is necessarily permanent and immutable. The basic structural characteristics of a market can change, and the condition of entry may then change in response. Thus the discovery of new deposits of a given natural

[5] The principal possible exception would occur if monotonic long-term secular movements in demand or cost, followed by lagging adjustments of industry capacity, caused potential entrants to react differently to given persistent differences between the prices of established firms and their minimal costs. That the reaction of potential entrants might be affected in this way seems entirely possible.

18   BARRIERS TO NEW COMPETITION

resource might undercut the absolute cost advantage held by established processing firms which had controlled all previously known deposits; the development of a new product design by an outsider might reduce the product-differentiation advantages of established sellers of similar products; technological changes might either increase or decrease the economies of large-scale production in any line at any time. When such changes take place, the condition of entry to any industry will tend to be altered.

This raises the question whether the condition of entry and its determinants are sufficiently stable through time so that they may be viewed provisionally as quasi-independent long-run determinants of market behavior. If the condition of entry and its determinants change slowly through time and are not easily subject to deliberate alteration by the action of potential entrants, and if they thus represent primarily a structural framework for market behavior rather than a result of this behavior, this is a legitimate view. On the other hand, of course, is the possibility that the condition of entry is a sort of unstable will-o'-the-wisp rapidly changing through time, or that it is readily altered by the action of potential entrants. In this event, it should hardly be studied as a long-run structural determinant of market behavior.

It is definitely posited for purposes of the present study — on the basis of extensive empirical observation — that the condition of entry as defined and its ultimate determinants are usually stable and slowly changing through time, and are not generally susceptible to alteration by prospective entrants to various markets. Thus the condition of entry and the various specific advantages of established firms which fix its value may in general be viewed as long-run structural determinants of enterprise action.

This generalization, like many others about economic affairs, is, of course, true only subject to exceptions, or as a representation of a general tendency. Certainly the condition of entry has shifted fairly rapidly over time in a few industries, and certainly potential entrants periodically have succeeded in changing it to their advantage in some cases. Nevertheless, these exceptions seem infrequent and unusual enough to justify our proceeding on the basis of our assumption.

Only one specific exception may deserve special attention as we study various industries. In some industries (though definitely not in a majority of them), the ability of potential entrants to make effective product innovations has periodically broken down the product advantages of established firms and effectively eased entry to the markets in question. Here, the role of existing product preferences as structural determinants of action can be questioned. It will be interesting to see if we can identify some more fundamental determinants of the condition of entry in this area, in the shape of those things which determine whether or not poten-

IMPORTANCE OF THE CONDITION OF ENTRY 19

tial entrants are likely to be in a position to make effective product innovations.

Theory concerning effects of the condition of entry

Our reason for paying so much attention to the condition of entry is our belief in its substantial influence on market behavior or performance in various industries. The force of potential competition, that is, may be viewed as a regulator of prices and outputs of an importance comparable to that of actual competition. But in what ways? What impact may the condition of entry be expected to have on market performance in an industry, and how will variation in the condition of entry from one industry to another cause market performance to differ between them?

These questions may be approached in two ways — through theorizing or deductive logic, and through empirical testing. Later we will attempt a few empirical tests for the effect of the condition of entry, so far as available data permit. Unfortunately, these data as yet do not permit very much, so that no comprehensive or conclusive empirical testing is possible. We are thus forced at this time to rely on *a priori* theory as the primary source for our knowledge of the consequences of the condition of entry.

If we approach the prediction of the consequences of the condition of entry as a full-dress problem in formal theory, a very complicated and elaborate system of hypotheses may emerge through simple extensions of received doctrine. The condition of entry is intrinsically a very complex idea and can assume a wide range of significantly different "values" with significantly different probable effects; in addition the consequences of the condition of entry will vary with variations in the structure of any market as among established sellers. Thus a very considerable variety of formal theoretical models could be constructed in order to distinguish (1) a large number of variant patterns of the "general condition of entry"; (2) different sources of impediments to entry, so far as these differences are significant; and (3) different structural situations as among established sellers.

Some beginnings in this direction were made in an earlier article.[6] It does not seem desirable here to reproduce or to extend the full theoretical arguments or the relatively elaborate range of theoretical hypotheses developed there. Such hypotheses are too detailed for even tentative testing and verification with data now on hand or likely to be available in the near future. It does seem desirable, however, to set down as a tentative guide to our investigations some simplified and compressed hypotheses concerning the effects of the condition of entry.

Three things seem to be of primary importance in determining the

---

[6] Bain, "Conditions of Entry and the Emergence of Monopoly."

20   BARRIERS TO NEW COMPETITION

probable effect of the condition of entry. The first is the *value* of the condition of entry, as measured by the percentage by which established firms may set price above a competitive level while forestalling entry.[7] This "value" may be construed as a single value for the immediate condition of entry when calculated with reference to the most favored potential entrant or entrants, or as a series of successive values for the general condition of entry when calculated with reference to successive potential entrants or groups thereof of a progressively less favored status. The second thing is the degree of concentration among sellers already established in the market, the corresponding existence or nonexistence of a recognized interdependence or of express or tacit collusion among them, and the corresponding *degree* of interdependence among them or degree of imperfection of their express or tacit collusion. The third thing is the source of the departure from easy entry, and in particular whether or not the departure involves the existence of significant economies to the large-scale firm.

The interaction of the three determinants mentioned should, hypothetically, determine the effect of the condition of entry. A fourth potential determinant, neglected here, is whether or not established firms will ever encounter *diseconomies* of large scale; i.e. rising unit costs because the firm exceeds a certain size. We neglect this possibility as improbable, and will assume approximately constant unit costs as firm size exceeds the minimum necessary for lowest costs.

The "value" of the condition of entry — and we will refer here primarily to the succession of individual values encompassed in the general condition of entry — is obviously important because it potentially places a limit on the level that prices in an industry can maintain in the long run. In this connection, two distinctions among different general conditions of entry may be drawn.

The first distinction refers to differences among various potential entrants. First, there is potentially the general condition of entry in which, in a given situation or after a given stage in the development of an industry has been reached, all potential entrant firms are in the same status or have the same disadvantage relative to established firms, and will moreover continue in this status regardless of how many of them enter the industry. In effect, there is then a perfectly elastic supply of entry at a given entry-inducing price-to-minimal-cost gap; the immediate condition of entry will remain at the same value for each successive entrant in turn; and the general condition of entry will thus be represented by a single value of the immediate condition of entry (representing the excess of industry price over a given level of competitive price) regardless of how

[7] For purposes of theorizing, the percentage may be identified as that for the most favored established firm.

IMPORTANCE OF THE CONDITION OF ENTRY   21

much entry occurs. Such a situation might occur, for example, if established firms selling a given product had a ten per cent advantage in production cost over all potential entrants by virtue of patent rights (economies of scale being negligible), and if an indefinitely large number of new firms could enter only with this ten per cent cost disadvantage.

Second, there is the general condition of entry reflecting differential advantages among successive potential entrants, such that the disadvantage of potential entrants, as registered by the entry-inducing gap, is successively greater or becomes so as one after another actually enters the industry. Thus, by individuals or by groups, the potential entrants are classified, and as we proceed through the classes the percentage by which actual prices may exceed a given competitive level without inducing entry becomes greater. This may result either because the potential entrants have differential disadvantages *ab initio*, or because the actual further entry of one or more makes the condition of entry more difficult for remaining potential entrants.

The second distinction refers to the height of the barrier to entry. This distinction should be made separately in the cases of the "constant" general condition of entry, where all potential entrants are and remain in the same state of disadvantage relative to established firms, and the "progressive" general condition of entry, where successive potential entrants suffer progressively greater disadvantages.

Suppose there is a constant general condition of entry to an industry, represented by a single value of the immediate condition of entry. Then, after the industry reaches a given stage, there is a single percentage by which industry prices may persistently exceed a given competitive level while forestalling entry, regardless of how many new firms actually enter the industry; if the percentage excess becomes and remains greater, all potential entrants (to an indefinitely large number) will be ready to enter the industry. A given core of established firms thus has a more or less mutable advantage over any and all potential entrants. (As we will see below, a constant condition of entry can occur only where economies of large scale firm are absent or negligible, so that established and potential entrant firms' costs will not be perceptibly elevated by the reduction of their market shares as entry ensues.[8]) In this situation, the condition of entry may assume any of four sorts of values, each designated by a special term hereafter used only with the special meaning about to be set forth.

(1) *There may be "easy" entry*, so that price in the long-run cannot at all exceed the competitive cost level of all established firms without attracting entry.

(2) The value of the condition of entry may be positive (as measured

---

[8] The reader will remember the assumption of no diseconomies of large scale.

22   BARRIERS TO NEW COMPETITION

with reference to the most favored established firms) but so low that certain consequences ensue. That is, there may be what we will refer to as *"ineffectively impeded"* entry in the following sense: The most favored established firms could raise their prices (prices of other firms in the industry moving concurrently) somewhat above the competitive level without attracting entry, but they could make greater long-run profits by setting their prices above the entry-forestalling level and attracting further entrants to some point than they could make by setting prices low enough to forestall entry. This implies that the entry-forestalling price permits these firms only a rather small profit and similarly small percentage excess of price over minimal cost. It implies further that if entry is induced by higher prices, it will take place with sufficient lags to permit these established firms more attractive profits during an interval in which entrants are becoming established. This situation is appropriately characterized as having an *ineffectively impeded* entry.[9]

(3) The value of the condition of entry may be positive and there may be *"effectively impeded"* entry in the following sense: The most favored established firms could raise their prices (other prices in the industry moving concurrently) enough above their competitive level without attracting entry to make their long-run profits at the best entry-forestalling price greater than if they charged higher prices and induced entry (thus sharing the market with further sellers). At the same time, the best entry-forestalling price *is below that which would maximize their profits if there were no threat of entry.* This implies that the entry-forestalling price is moderately above costs, but not as high as a "monopolistic" price would be in the absence of any threat of entry.

(4) The value of the condition of entry may be positive and *entry may be effectively "blockaded"* — in the sense that the entry-forestalling level of industry prices is above that which would maximize the profits of the most-favored firms in the absence of any entry threat. They therefore have no virtual incentive to raise prices high enough to induce entry.

The preceding refers to four sorts of value of the condition of entry if the value is always at a single level for any number of successive entrants. So far as such a constant general entry condition is encountered, the sort of value may obviously influence market performance within an industry. Before exploring these influences, let us consider the possible values of the condition of entry when there is a "progressive" general condition of entry.

---

[9] It is clear that the longer the lags encountered in inducing entry the greater an excess of entry-forestalling price over cost will be considered as ineffectively impeding entry.

IMPORTANCE OF THE CONDITION OF ENTRY 23

In this instance, there is a differential advantage among successive potential entrants — either *ab initio* or developing as further entry occurs — so that the immediate condition of entry, as measured with reference to the initial minimal costs of the most favored established firms, becomes higher as successive firms or groups thereof enter the industry. Then if the percentage by which industry price may exceed that designated competitive level, while just forestalling the entry of the most favored potential entrant or entrants, is at a certain value, the percentage excess attainable while forestalling the entry of the next most favored potential entrant is larger, and so forth. The general condition of entry is represented by some succession of values of the immediate condition of entry referring to successively less favored entrants.

There are generally two possible sources of a "progressive" condition of entry. First, different potential entrant firms may have differential advantages in absolute cost or from product differentiation. These may be either advantages which exist initially before any firms enter, or advantages which develop as entry occurs — for example, the entrants who are "first in" the industry thereby secure advantages over the remainder. In either event, some potential entrants will tend to be able to secure higher prices or lower costs than others, thus leading to a progression in the value of the immediate condition of entry as entry occurs.

Second, there may be significant economies of scale, in the sense that an optimal-sized firm will supply a significant fraction of the total market and that unit costs for a firm will become progressively larger at progressively smaller scales. In this event, a progression in the absolute value of the condition of entry is more or less inevitable as further entry occurs, even though all established and potential entrant firms might have precisely the same cost conditions. This is because successive entry will successively tend to force all established firms to significantly smaller market shares and significantly higher costs, and to confront all remaining potential entrants with the prospect of smaller market shares and higher costs. Therefore, higher and higher prices (relative to minimal attainable costs) will be required to attract further entry as additional entry raises the going level of costs by forcing more and more uneconomical sizes on firms entered in the industry. Thus, where there are significant scale economies, a progressive condition of entry is more or less automatically encountered.

What of the possible values of the progressive general condition of entry? It is at this point that theorizing becomes especially difficult, since an indefinitely large number of different patterns of the condition of entry is logically possible. For purposes of initial rough generalization, however, it may be sufficient to distinguish a few general patterns. These are briefly listed, in each case with the supposition that the immediate con-

24   **BARRIERS TO NEW COMPETITION**

dition of entry is measured with reference to the minimal costs of the most favored established firms:

(5) *The immediate condition of entry is initially at a small absolute value; with successive entry assumes only slightly larger absolute values; and at every step in a relevant sequence of entry is ineffectively impeded from the standpoint of the most favored established firms.* In other words, the condition of entry is always low enough so that a higher entry-inducing price would be more profitable to established firms in the long run than the best entry-forestalling price.

(6) *The immediate condition of entry is initially at a small absolute value and progresses to successively larger absolute values with successive entry; but in the course of increasing it progresses from ineffectively impeded to effectively impeded from the standpoint of the most favored established firms* (and possibly later to a *blockaded* value). That is, entry becomes effectively impeded in the sense that the highest entry-forestalling price would in the long run be more profitable to them than a higher price which would induce entry.

(7) *The immediate condition of entry is initially at a value regarded as effectively impeded by established firms;* in increasing with progressive entry it either remains *effectively impeded* or becomes *blockaded.*

(8) *The immediate condition of entry is initially at a blockaded value* — that is, the highest entry-forestalling price exceeds that which would maximize the profits of established firms.

(9) *The immediate condition of entry is at a relatively small absolute value initially, but with successive entry steadily progresses to substantially larger absolute values. Nevertheless, the condition of entry continues through a sequence of entry to be regarded as ineffectively impeded by established firms and never reaches an effectively impeded value.* This is because with successive entry the rise of the entry-forestalling price relative to minimal costs is matched by a rise in their actual costs, so that higher and higher entry-forestalling prices do not offer adequate profits. (This pattern should be found only where there are substantial economies of scale. In this instance, established firms in a long sequence of entry never find it most profitable to set price low enough to exclude entry.) [10] The sequence of ineffectively impeded values would tend to be followed ultimately in the progression of entry by a blockaded value at the point where the most profitable price only permits established firms to break even and will not attract entry.

[10] When they do, the scale-economies case would fall under 6, 7, or 8 above.

IMPORTANCE OF THE CONDITION OF ENTRY   25

We have thus listed five main sorts of the "progressive" general condition of entry, in addition to four sorts of "constant" condition. The total list may be shortened, however, by combining cases of which the predicted effects will not differ significantly. In effect, case 5 above, in which the value of the condition of entry will remain small and be regarded as ineffectively impeded indefinitely does not differ significantly from case 2. Similarly, case 7 involving progressions from an initial effectively impeded condition of entry, merges with case 3, representing a constant effectively impeded condition of entry, without important loss of detail in analysis; case 8 similarly merges with case 4. Thus only cases 6 and 9 need to be added to our initial list of four. The combined list may now be renumbered to read as follows:

I. Constantly *easy* entry.

II. Continual *ineffectively impeded* entry, either at a single constant small absolute value of the condition of entry or at a succession of small but increasing absolute values.

III. Initial *effectively impeded* entry, followed in a progression of entry by either *effectively impeded* or *blockaded* entry. (The absolute value of the immediate condition of entry may remain constant or increase with progressive entry.)

IV. Initial *ineffectively impeded* entry, at small absolute values of the condition of entry, progressing to somewhat higher absolute values and to *effectively impeded* entry.

V. Initial *ineffectively impeded* entry at small absolute values of the condition of entry, followed by substantially higher absolute values as entry ensues, but with the condition of entry nevertheless regarded as *ineffectively impeded* throughout a substantial progression of entry — and never reaching an *effectively impeded* value.

VI. Continually *blockaded* entry, either at a single absolute constant value of the condition of entry or at a succession of increasing absolute values.

So much for the classification of entry conditions *per se*. As indicated above, the effects of the condition of entry should depend upon two more things: the degree of concentration among established sellers in any market, and the presence or absence of significant economies to the large-scale firm.

The degree of seller concentration is essentially important because it may be expected to determine whether or not, or to what extent, the established sellers in a market will in effect act collectively in determining

26   BARRIERS TO NEW COMPETITION

their prices. "Collective" market-policy determination or pricing action may, in the sense we use the term here, result from express collusion or consensus of established sellers, from a tacit understanding based on the past experience of rival firms with each other's policies, or from a recognized interdependence such that each seller alters his price significantly or makes other significant alterations of policy only in the expectancy of some more or less predictable concurrent action or reaction of his rivals.

However it may result, collective action means in general that the principal sellers in an industry will change price concurrently, and in addition that every principal seller will change his price significantly only to match rival changes or with the anticipation that there will be, in response to his change, concurrent and. similar changes of other prices in the industry. Therefore, the consequences to him of his own major price changes will become the consequences of a similar general change in the level of industry prices, including his own. The emergence of "collective action" patterns generally requires that the principal sellers in the market control substantial individual shares of the market, so that the price adjustments of any one will clearly affect the others and produce the requisite interdependence and the recognition of it. From this it follows that as seller concentration increases, and thus the shares of the market controlled by individual sellers, collective action among sellers becomes more probable.

The pattern of market conduct opposite to collective action is strictly independent action. In this case the individual seller will act, in pricing and other market activities, non-collusively and with substantial neglect of the possible reactions of his competitors. He will not necessarily follow his rivals, nor anticipate that his rivals will follow him or match his policies. This is typically because his own actions will have no perceptible effect on his rivals (or theirs on his), and in turn that is because the individual seller supplies a negligible fraction of the market. We thus see the converse of our last proposition, namely that collective action becomes less probable as seller concentration decreases.

The presence or absence of what we have called "collective action" has long been recognized in economic theory as strategic to the character of competition among established sellers. Markets in which there is a significant concentration of sellers have been designated as *oligopolistic*, as distinguished from the atomistic markets in which sellers are many and individually small. It has been argued in general that in oligopolistic industries there is a definite tendency (via express or tacit collusion or recognized interdependence) for sellers to act "collectively" or in unison in establishing prices and outputs, whereas in atomistic industries any attempted collusion will fail and every seller will act independently in

IMPORTANCE OF THE CONDITION OF ENTRY 27

adjusting himself to a market price and output which he feels to be outside of his influence of control. Correspondingly, it has been argued that the "collective action" pattern of conduct in oligopoly tends to lead in the direction of monopolistic or quasi-monopolistic price and output results, although these may be tempered or poorly approximated so far as collusion is imperfect, as express or tacit agreements cannot be reached, or as forays of independent action are undertaken. The "independent" pattern of conduct in atomistic markets, on the other hand, tends to lead to results that feature lower industry prices and larger industry outputs, and that are designated as "competitive."

The additional question posed here concerns what influence, if any, the presence or absence of "collective action" has upon the way in which the condition of entry to an industry affects market performance in that industry. In effect, will the established sellers in an industry behave any differently in the face of a given condition of entry if they are few and have developed a conduct-pattern of collective action than if they are many and pursue a conduct-pattern of independent action?

The presence or absence of a collective-action pattern of conduct should have one major influence in this regard. Suppose that all sellers, or at any rate the principal sellers, in an industry act collectively, in the sense that each views his own price changes as equivalent to similar changes by the whole industry. Then each will regard the effect of his own price changes on entry (whether he is leading others or following others and thus validating their leadership) as similar to the effect of a concurrent industry-wide price change on entry. And if this is so, two things follow. First, the individual seller will always calculate, in considering his own price adjustments, as if his own price adjustment had a definite (and in a sense maximum) effect on entry, since his own adjustment is effectively equivalent to an industry-wide price adjustment of similar magnitude. He will be led to consider that his own price adjustments can alternatively forestall or induce entry to the industry. Second, the seller will be led, in making his own price adjustments, to consider the effect upon industry profits, via entry, of an industry-wide price adjustment equivalent to his own, and upon his share of these profits.

In consequence, he will be led to consider the alternatives of forestalling or attracting entry through his own price adjustments, and this primarily in terms of the anticipated effect of industry-wide price adjustments on entry and of such entry upon industry profits and his share of them. This should be true, as a general tendency, whether the seller is operating as a member of a cartel trying to agree on price, or as an independent seller in an oligopoly, operating subject to tacit collusion or a strong recognized interdependence with rivals. Finally, industry price adjustments will tend to be made only in the full recognition of their effects in inducing entry, and of such entry on industry profits and on the individual seller's share of them.

Suppose alternatively that every seller in the industry acts independently, on the supposition that his own price and output adjustments will not and cannot perceptibly influence his established rivals. That is, any first seller supposes that each of his competitors will do whatever he would have done otherwise (whether to hold to his going price or to make some adjustment) regardless of what he, the first seller, does. (He thus effectively accepts market-price movements as data beyond his control.) This sort of attitude will generally result from the fact that each seller controls a negligible fraction of the total market in which he sells. *If this is so, it will also be true in general that no seller will take account of the possible influence of his price adjustments on entry, since he will correctly believe such an influence to be negligible.* Thus the entry-forestalling or entry-inducing effects of individual price adjustments will not be taken into account by those making them. It will therefore also be true that the effect upon industry profits of the inducement of or discouragement to entry attributable to individual price adjustments will not be considered by any seller or by sellers in general. Industry-wide price movements — the result of many individual and independent movements — will therefore emerge without regard to their effects on entry and thus on industry profits, since no price-determining unit will take account of these effects. This will be true even though all the many individual prices in an industry will in fact generally move concurrently (though independently) in response to broad economic determinants.

We thus have two general types of situations. In the first, the effects of industry-wide price adjustments on entry and of entry on industry profits are taken into account by sellers individually or collectively. In the second, these effects are not taken into account and do not influence pricing decisions, because of independence of action and the fact that each seller is a negligible factor in the market.

These are of course typical or polar situations, and between them many variant or modified situations may exist. Thus we have collective action tempered by sporadic independent action in pricing, so that sellers usually but not always act as if their own price changes were more or less equivalent to industry-wide changes. Or we may have independent action tempered by some slight recognition of interdependence. For purposes of predicting very roughly the general effects of the condition of entry, however, it should be enough to distinguish the two general patterns of conduct so far mentioned — collective action and independent action. Correspondingly, we may distinguish (a) seller concentration sufficiently high to implement or lead to collective-action patterns of conduct; and (b) seller concentration low enough to lead to substantial independence

IMPORTANCE OF THE CONDITION OF ENTRY   29

of action by individual sellers. A more detailed classification, recognizing modified and in-between cases, may be neglected for present purposes.

The third general determinant of the effect of the condition of entry is whether or not significant economies of the large-scale firm are found in an industry. As already noted above, the primary significance of the existence of significant scale economies (such that a firm of optimal scale will supply an appreciable fraction of industry output and that smaller firms will have distinctly higher costs) is that it tends to lead more or less automatically to a progressively higher barrier to entry as progressive entry occurs. It leads, that is, to a specific and especially troubling type of pattern of the general condition of entry — troubling both because the impediment to further entry tends to be increased by entry itself and because the source of the impediment (advantages of size inherent in techniques of production or commerce) is not easily attacked or modified by policy measures when the impediment to entry is undesirable. Barriers to entry resting on product differentiation or absolute cost considerations, on the other hand, do not *per se* or necessarily result in the progressive heightening of barriers to entry as further entry occurs, or in steeply "progressive" patterns of the general condition of entry.

A second significance of the existence of significant scale economies is that this will ordinarily tend to be associated with moderate to high concentration among established sellers — a phenomenon the possible significance of which has been suggested in preceding paragraphs. In predicting the effects of the condition of entry, therefore, it is useful to make a definite distinction between cases where significant economies of scale are and are not present.

Given the three major determinants of the effect of the condition of entry on market performance — i.e., the value of the condition of entry, the degree of seller concentration, and the source of the departure from easy entry — we may now turn directly to these effects, at least so far as they are predictable by *a priori* economic theory. Through elaborations of this theory, certain deductions may be drawn concerning the probable effect of the condition of entry on the price policies and on other aspects of the market conduct of established sellers, and thereby on their ultimate market performance so far as that is reflected in such things as the degree of monopolistic output restriction attained within the industry, the excess of prices over actual costs (as measured by the size of profits), the efficiency of production, and the size of selling costs. Although we will not attempt any full or formal development of the relevant theoretical arguments here, it is useful to state and explain briefly the general content of available theoretical predictions concerning such effects of the condition of entry.

In doing so, a primary distinction must be drawn between industries

30   **BARRIERS TO NEW COMPETITION**

of high and low seller concentration. If there is an atomistic structure in an industry, no seller will presume that he can influence the course of entry to the industry by his own market adjustments; he can himself neither attract nor forestall entry thereby. The condition of entry (reflecting the relation of an entry-forestalling industry-wide level of price to minimal costs) will tend to be neglected by sellers in an atomistic industry; their market policies will be uninfluenced by it. Industry-wide price movements will occur without regard to whether or not they will induce entry. The condition of entry then will serve in atomistic industries only as a sort of automatic regulator of market performance, setting limits to long-run movements of the industry-wide relation of price to cost by imposing the corrective effect of entry if the movements exceed these limits.

Given this general rule, it is not difficult to perceive the effects of the six sorts of general condition of entry (listed on page 25) on the market performance of atomistic industries. If there were constantly easy entry to an industry, so that any number of firms could enter at no price or cost disadvantage as compared to previously established firms, price could never in the long run exceed the common minimal costs of production for all established firms. (As we have seen, differential advantages among established firms are not consistent with completely easy entry.) Any tendency for price to rise higher would induce sufficient new entry to bring it back to the competitive level. Correspondingly, there could never persist in the long run any monopolistic output restriction, any profits in excess of a normal interest return on investment, and none other than "competitive" selling costs (arrived at through a multitude of independent selling policies).

A more interesting question is whether, with atomistic market structures, conditions of entry that involve some advantages of established over potential entrant firms can lead in the long run to prices higher than are encountered with easy entry. Elementary price analysis suggests that in an atomistic market structure, and *in the absence of diseconomies of large scale to the firm*, the competition of established firms will tend to bring about a competitive level of prices regardless of barriers to entry, as they increase their outputs relative to market demand and reduce their prices until their marginal and average costs are equal to their selling prices.[11] Entry is not requisite to a full competitive adjustment, since the ability of all firms to expand indefinitely without exceeding minimal costs (or incurring equivalent disadvantages), plus the independent pricing attributable to atomism, lead to the result even without entry. In this

---

[11] With product differentiation, it should do so to a close approximation. The difference between this case and that without product differentiation will be neglected here as relatively insignificant.

IMPORTANCE OF THE CONDITION OF ENTRY   31

case, therefore, it may be argued that the existence of various degrees and types of impediment to entry (numbers II through VI, page 25) will not make the long-run industry performance significantly different than it would be under completely easy entry.

We have just said that in the atomistic situations outlined, and with no diseconomies to large-scale firms, competition should in the long run bring price to a minimal cost level with or without entry. But whose minimal cost level, if there are significant differential advantages among established firms? Formally, this is an inappropriate question, since the significant differential advantages among established firms which it supposes to exist could not survive with atomistic competition in the long run if there were no diseconomies or equivalent disadvantages of large-scale firms. Instead, competition would force prices to the level of minimal average costs for a group of most-advantaged firms and drive all other firms from the industry through losses. Then all surviving firms would enjoy substantially equivalent minimal cost levels, and prices would equal these cost levels for all firms simultaneously. It follows from this that the coexistence of (a) atomism, (b) no disadvantages of large scale of firm, and (c) significant differential advantages as among established firms connotes an unstable market structure. With or without entry this structure will evolve toward elimination of differential advantages among surviving firms, and possibly toward the elimination of the atomistic structure. In the latter event, the predictions developed here for atomistic structures with impeded entry would of course no longer apply.

Atomistic market structures, within which differential advantages among established firms exist, should, if they are not unstable and in transition to something else, be attributable to the existence of diseconomies to or other disadvantages of large-scale firms. We have argued that such diseconomies are unlikely to be important and may be in general assumed away for a simplified theoretical argument. But if significant diseconomies to the expansion of established firms are encountered in atomistic markets, then a competitive course of market conduct involving independent adjustments by each seller may lead to results somewhat different from those just predicted. Each individual firm is then unable to extend its output indefinitely at minimal costs, and encounters progressively rising average and marginal costs as output extends beyond an "optimal" scale. As soon as the demand for industry output at prices equal to the minimal costs of the most favored established firms exceeds the sum of the optimal outputs for these firms, this excess will lead to a competitive extension of their outputs with rising average and marginal costs and prices. Such a price rise will be accompanied, according to the condition of entry, by the entry of further sellers as the prices rise high enough to induce them to enter in spite of their disadvantages. The increase of output by entry

32   **BARRIERS TO NEW COMPETITION**

and enlargement of the output of established firms will proceed until a competitively determined supply is equal to demand at a price in excess of the minimal average costs of the most favored sellers, and perhaps also of other sellers. In this situation, the more favored sellers will tend to make excess profits and to operate at scales in excess of the optimum. The amount of these excesses will tend to become greater as their advantages over other established firms and potential entrants is greater, or as the general condition of entry proceeds more quickly in a progression of entry to a high value. On the other hand, the long-run price finally arrived at will not in general exceed the minimal average cost of the most favored excluded entrant. Whether the condition of entry would be regarded as blockaded, effectively impeded, or ineffectively impeded is not relevant, since individual sellers in any event disregard the condition of entry. But the progression of absolute values of the immediate condition of entry represented in the general condition of entry will be strategic to the final price-cost adjustment.

Too much emphasis, however, could be given to the logical possibilities just described. Observation suggests that the existence of atomistic market structures is closely related to the existence of relatively easy entry, and that atomistic structures do not commonly emerge mainly because of diseconomies of scale and in spite of substantial entry barriers. If this is so, variations in the condition of entry are likely to be relatively unimportant as influences on market performance in industries of atomistic structure.[12]

[12] Two further questions concerning the condition of entry to atomistic markets may be mentioned briefly. First, need distinctions be drawn as to source of barriers to entry? Generally no, because significant economies of scale will not persistently be found in conjunction with atomistic market structures. Except for unstable market structures in transition, only product differentiation advantages or absolute cost advantages of established firms will constitute barriers to entry in atomistic markets. And there are no important theoretical distinctions to draw between the effects of product differentiation and of absolute cost advantages as entry barriers.

Second, will the condition of entry have any influence on the *short-run* behavior of atomistic markets — that is, upon the way in which they adapt to fluctuations or secular movements in demand, technology, and so forth? The predictions discussed above refer entirely to long-run "equilibrium" tendencies in atomistic markets, or to the destination or ultimate resting point which industry market adjustments seek relative to any given set of governing economic conditions. We have argued that variations in the condition of entry from one atomistic market to another should not *a priori* be expected to be important determinants of variations in such long-run tendencies among atomistic industries. It has frequently been held, however, that very easy entry to atomistic industries is a primary source of recurring and even chronic difficulties in adapting to changes in demand, cost, and the like over time. The general tenor of the argument is that such easy entry permits a large and excessive number of small enterprises to crowd into such industries in times of peak demand and general prosperity, failing to anticipate subsequent declines in demand, increases in productivity, and so forth, and that thereafter changes of this sort make for redundant capacity and destructive competition, which is not eliminated easily because of the long lives of fixed plants and the reluctance of firms to exit from the industry.

That periodic or chronic maladjustments have been encountered in atomistic

IMPORTANCE OF THE CONDITION OF ENTRY 33

Conversely, the condition of entry will tend to have its major effect in concentrated or oligopolistic industries. In these, (1) collusion or interdependent pricing tends to permit deliberate elevation of prices to the extent allowed by the condition of entry, the height of which thus becomes strategic; (2) firms individually and collectively will calculate the effects of their policies in inducing or forestalling entry; and (3) concentration may, unlike atomism, be expected to be accompanied by numerous alternative patterns of the condition of entry.

Given these tendencies, the condition of entry may have a major influence on market conduct and performance in oligopolistic industries, although detailed and precise predictions of its effects are hazardous for a number of reasons. One of these is that oligopolistic collusion of either the express or tacit variety may be imperfect in various degrees, especially because of secret defections from agreed-upon or common prices or because of disagreement on the most desirable price. A second is that there may be differential advantages among established sellers or differences in their views of strategic market variables which lead them to different opinions concerning the desirability of attracting or forestalling entry via pricing, or concerning what prices will and will not forestall entry. There must thus be some allowance for uncertainty in theories that concern the policy established settlers will follow and whether or not it will succeed. Nevertheless, predictions of general tendencies inherent in oligopolistic situations may be developed by adopting certain simplifying assumptions.

To this end, we will generally assume that there is effective concurrence of market action by established sellers in establishing some approximation to a joint-profit-maximizing price, referring to the effects of possible imperfections of express or tacit collusion parenthetically. We will also assume that, so far as there are differential advantages among established firms and as these lead to differences in opinion regarding the desirability of attracting or forestalling entry, the largest or principal firms will effectively determine the industry policy. We will presume, moreover, that they will in general be the most favored established firms. We will assume finally that the dominant established firms are in general correct in their appraisals of what will attract and forestall entry, and thus do not inadvertently do one thing when the other is intended. Exceptions to this rule may be recognized parenthetically. At this point we

---

industries with easy entry and historically declining demands is well known. And it is conceivable that more substantial barriers to entry — almost never found in such atomistic industries — would have some retarding influence on the periodic development of overcapacity. Unless we wish to fashion a special theory to rationalize certain observed events, however, it is not readily deduced that variations in the condition of entry are primarily accountable for variations in the performance of atomistic industries in this regard. We will therefore leave the issue open for the time being.

34   **BARRIERS TO NEW COMPETITION**

may also reiterate the earlier assumption that diseconomies of large-scale firms are generally negligible or absent.

Given these assumptions, let us consider the effect in oligopolistic industries of the six sorts of entry conditions listed on page 25, in each case recognizing any significant distinctions which depend on the source of the barrier to entry.

With constantly *easy* entry (I), with which no established firms can ever enjoy any long-run advantage over potential entrants, price will in the long run not tend persistently to exceed the minimal-cost level of established firms. The pressure of entry will always drive price back toward this level. But several complications require note.

First, the attainment of oligopolistic seller concentration is nevertheless possible — for example, by merger. Second, the development of concentration may seem advantageous to established sellers if there are entry lags which will permit them to elevate prices and earn supernormal profits during a period before the entry, attracted by such prices, takes place. Third, if such industries become concentrated they may then tend to experience periods of pricing at super-competitive levels, followed by the attraction of entry, by a resulting approach to atomistic structure, and thus by pricing at the competitive level. The instability of market structure which is thus implicit in the conjoining of oligopolistic concentration and very easy entry may recur in cycles (though not necessarily); it will, for example, if the atomism produced by attracting entry is later remedied by new mergers.

Fourth, if structural instability of the market is induced by monopolistic pricing over short intervals, there will be not only higher prices at times, but also excess capacity from redundant plant, the latter persisting even with a return to competitive pricing until some plants wear out. If plants are long-lived, the concentrated industry with easy entry may be chronically plagued with the "short-run" excess capacity which is attracted and reattracted by recurring episodes of monopolistic pricing. Severe social wastes may then result. This may be true even though, as is necessarily true with easy entry, there are no significant long-run economies of large-scale firms.

Fifth, approximately the same tendencies may be inherent in governmentally imposed or sponsored cartels, like those frequently found in agriculture. The major difference is that a government agency may have the power (where a private agreement does not) to elevate price and attract redundant capacity indefinitely, or to blockade entry arbitrarily in order to preserve the working of the cartel. Finally, large sellers in concentrated markets faced with easy entry will of course try to erect barriers to entry in various ways, for instance by attempting to establish product differentiation. It is difficult to predict how frequently seller con-

IMPORTANCE OF THE CONDITION OF ENTRY 35

centration will actually be conjoined with completely easy entry, but the logical possibility is clearly open, and especially so if entry lags are long.

A closely related condition of entry (II) appears where, in any relevant progression of potential entry, there is always a small absolute value of the immediate condition of entry and where entry is always "ineffectively impeded." Price can exceed the minimal costs of the most favored established firms a little but never very much without attracting some further entry,[13] and these firms continually, through any sequence of entry, will anticipate greater long-run profits from setting a high entry-inducing price, reaping extra profits during a lag period, and attracting further entry, than from setting a lower entry-forestalling price. This is presumably because lags encountered in inducing entry are appreciable and because the long-run profit margin at the best entry-forestalling price is not large.

This condition of entry is effectively confined to cases where economies of the large-scale firm are absent or negligible, since otherwise the progressive attraction of entry would force a progressive and ultimately substantial rise in the absolute barrier to entry as firms had to operate at distinctly uneconomical small scales. The only important barriers to entry are therefore those of the absolute cost advantages or product differentiation advantages of established over potential entrant firms. But product differentiation is not reflected, for example, in significant economies of large-scale advertising.[14]

[13] The absolute value may or may not increase a little with further entry.

[14] It may be noted that large-scale economies must be insignificant in category II in the usual sense but not in another sense. That is, the output of a firm of optimal or lowest-cost scale must be a small or negligible fraction of total industry output (even though the firm may experience higher unit costs at still smaller scales), so that the attraction of a unit of entry will not significantly affect the market shares or unit costs of established and further potential entrant firms. (If it did, the barrier to entry would become progressively and significantly larger as each successive unit of entry was attracted.)

But scale economies may be significant in the following sense and still permit of a condition of entry which remains at a small absolute value (potentially even a constant value) through a progression of entry. In effect, we may have the situation where (1) although the output of a firm of optimal scale is a negligible fraction of total industry output, there are substantial economies of scale (declining costs) as the firm's output increases up to this optimum; and (2) *over the same output range the potential entrant's absolute cost or product differentiation disadvantage increases.* Then in order to avoid or minimize his absolute cost or product differentiation disadvantage, the entrant would have to enter at a suboptimal scale where costs were elevated because of small size, whereas in order to avoid diseconomies of unduly small scale he would have to suffer a magnified absolute cost or product differentiation disadvantage. In this case economies of scale on the one hand and product differentiation or absolute cost disadvantages *which are related to scale* on the other combine to fix a minimum inescapable disadvantage, even though optimal scale itself might be a negligible or relatively unimportant consideration. This case can properly fall under entry cases II, III, IV, or VI, in none of which scale economies need be significant in the usual sense.

36   BARRIERS TO NEW COMPETITION

The prospect for market conduct and performance is much the same as if entry were easy. Price cannot in the long run persistently exceed the minimal costs of the most favored firms by very much, although it can do so by a relatively small absolute percentage, and possibly by one that increases somewhat as the inducement of entry progresses. But since the possibility of forestalling entry by relatively low prices will in general be less attractive to the most favored and other established firms than that of reaping larger temporary profits at higher prices (which will induce entry), concentrated markets in this category will tend to be afflicted, like those in the first category, with the periodic emergence of prices substantially above the competitive level, with consequent structural instability tending toward atomism, and with periodic or chronic excess plant capacity.

As in the first case, the attraction of entry may ultimately lead to stability with an atomistic structure and competitive pricing. But any induced atomism is just as likely to be followed by a regrouping of structure through mergers or otherwise, and by the beginning of another cycle of high pricing and excessive entry. The latter possibility is perhaps stronger in this second case, since here relatively few established firms may have small differential advantages of absolute cost or product differentiation over all others. Then the emergence of competitive pricing following the attraction of entry will tend to result in their regaining a dominance of the market, reinstating high concentration, and thereafter setting off another cycle of high, entry-inducing pricing.

The major possible escape from these tendencies is that at some point the market will reach, through induced entry, a low enough concentration so that independence of pricing or imperfection of collusion will keep price below the entry-inducing level, while at the same time (1) the differential advantages of the firms now established are small enough that a stable structure will persist, and (2) the propensity of these established firms to reconcentrate through merger is checked by failure to agree or by law.

The third sort of condition of entry to be considered is that in which, with a concentrated market, the condition of entry is initially "effectively impeded" (and thereafter the same or "blockaded") at moderate absolute values. In this case, the most favored established firms can set a price that is moderately above the competitive level but below the industry joint-profit-maximizing level and that will forestall further entry to the industry. Moreover, by not exceeding the best entry-forestalling price and thus restricting the number of competitors, these firms expect greater long-run profits than they could get by establishing a higher price and ultimately attracting further entrants to share their market. This is evidently because long-run profits, while forestalling entry, are appreciable

IMPORTANCE OF THE CONDITION OF ENTRY 37

as compared to the temporary higher profits which entry lags would permit at higher prices.

The predicted course of action here is distinctly different from that for the cases of easy entry and of ineffectively impeded entry. Further entry, that is, will not tend to be attracted, since prices will be kept low enough to discourage it. There will thus be a relatively stable market structure except for possible shifts in market shares among established sellers. Price will tend appreciably to exceed the minimal level of costs unless imperfections of collusion or neglect of interdependence in pricing keep it lower, but it will nevertheless be only moderately above the competitive level and clearly lower than that of a monopolist protected from entry. It is quite conceivable, for example, that few dominant established firms might be willing to forestall entry at a price only a very few percentage points above cost if entry lags were short and if a substantial quantity of entry might be attracted by higher prices.

So much for tendencies relative to structural stability and the relationship of prices to minimal costs. What of accompanying tendencies in efficiency, in profits, and in selling costs? In predicting such performance in this category, distinctions must be drawn between barriers to entry that do and do not involve significant economies of the large-scale firm.

If significant scale economies are absent or negligible, so that the effectively impeded entry results solely from the product differentiation or absolute cost advantages of established firms, established firms can in general attain minimal costs at any of a wide range of scales. Two things then tend to follow. When such firms have settled into the position of pricing to forestall entry, all in general will operate at scales consistent with minimal costs. And the excess of price over minimal costs attained in the entry-forestalling equilibrium will be the same as the excess of price over actual costs, or the profit margin. Therefore excess profits equivalent per unit to the price-to-minimal-cost gap will be earned in the long run. Since there will in this instance be no periodic inducement of excessive entry, as there might be in cases I and II, there will be no corresponding tendency toward periodic or chronic losses from excess plant capacity.

If the preferences of buyers for the products of established as compared to new entrant firms are the primary bases of the "effectively impeded" entry — as may well be the case in numerous concentrated consumer-goods industries — then substantial advertising and other selling costs will ordinarily be incurred in sustaining the preferred product positions of established sellers. This tendency may also be present in similar industries under case II when the impediment to entry inheres in product differentiation, but the incentive to maintenance of barriers through continued advertising and sales promotion seems likely to be greater when

38   BARRIERS TO NEW COMPETITION

the barriers offer a more valuable protection, as in the present case.

If the barrier to entry rests on the absolute cost advantages of established firms, such as result from resource control, and patent control of techniques, no similar tendency toward excessive selling costs is noted, although there might be a parallel stimulus toward enlarged expenditures on industrial research and technological development.

If significant economies of scale are present as a source of impediment to entry, structural stability with pricing to forestall entry is still to be expected, and a moderate excess of price over minimal costs will tend to persist if collusion is effective or interdependence strong. But conclusions with respect to efficiency and to profits are potentially different. The number of firms which can operate with maximal efficiency is distinctly limited. Thus if an efficient firm will supply at least one-fourth of the total market at prices likely to be charged, no more than four firms can operate with optimal efficiency of scale. If entry is attracted to increase the number of firms beyond this limit, some or all firms will operate at suboptimal scales and with higher actual costs. Generally this will in turn elevate the barrier to further entry a bit (further potential entrants anticipating higher actual costs), but in any event efficiency among established firms will be impaired.

Given this, the question in point is what the degree of seller concentration or number of sellers will be, relative to the efficiency ideal, when established sellers come to regard the immediate condition of entry as "effectively impeded." Will the number of firms be optimal, thus permitting lowest-cost operations, or will it be excessive, thus elevating the general level of costs through the inefficiencies of insufficient scale? Either may be the case. The structure of the industry may accidentally be such that established firms are generally of optimal scale, and the barrier to entry may then be large enough to encourage them to forestall further entry at a price moderately above minimal cost. In this event efficiency of scale will be optimal, and also the profit margin will be the same as the excess of price above minimal cost. Or the structure of the industry may initially be such that firms are smaller than is most economical, either "by accident" or because entry was deliberately attracted by high prices when firms were fewer. In this event, given a presently effectively impeded entry, actual costs will persistently remain above the minimal level and the profit margin will be smaller than the excess of price over minimal costs. However, some excess profits will presumably still be earned if the entry-forestalling price is to be regarded as attractive. In this latter case, larger absolute gaps between price and minimal cost may be required to provide effectively impeded entry, and fairly serious departures from optimal scale are theoretically possible. Elimination of these inefficiencies will not come through entry (which would worsen

IMPORTANCE OF THE CONDITION OF ENTRY   **39**

matters if it were attracted), and will not necessarily come about through a "rationalization" by mergers or other devices aimed at reducing the number of firms. A secularly growing industry demand would, of course, be a welcome corrective.

The exploration of case III has enabled us to discover two tendencies in price and market behavior which could be found extensively in concentrated markets. First, with the barriers to entry at some moderate level such that established firms can forestall entry at a price which allows some excess profit but is well below a theoretical monopoly level, long-run price policies designed to forestall entry may emerge, with a resultant structural stability of the market, only moderately super-competitive prices, and moderate excess profits. The second tendency, associated with the existence of significant economies of the large-scale firm, is that it is *possible* for oligopolistic responses to the conditon of entry, when it includes barriers resulting from scale economies, to lead toward a stable market structure in which further entry is forestalled and in which some inefficiencies of insufficient scale are chronic. On the other hand, it is at least equally possible that entry will be forestalled at a point where established firms are in general at efficient scales. The tendencies just described carry over into the remaining cases (IV, V, and VI), which may be analyzed much more quickly, by simple extensions of the arguments so far developed.

Suppose (case IV) that in concentrated markets there is initially "ineffectively impeded" entry as calculated with reference to the prices that will induce one or a few firms to enter the industry. But suppose also that after one or a few units of entry have been brought in, the barrier to entry becomes absolutely higher for further entrants and is effectively impeded from the standpoint of the most favored established firms. Then the market structures will be initially unstable, as entry will be attracted through prices above the entry-forestalling level. But the attraction of a finite and limited number of entrants will result, together with an increase in the price which will just forestall further entry, so that it will stand enough above minimal and actual costs to make it profitable to forestall further entry. At this point the structure of the market will become stable and the results will be similar to those predicted for case III above, with the same distinctions according to the sources of impediment to entry applying unchanged. Development of "case IV" into "case III" industries through structural change will fail only if imperfection of collusion or similar phenomena preclude the attraction of entry which will initially be desired by established firms.

Case V is that in which the entry-forestalling price rises higher and higher above minimal costs as entry occurs but never exceeds an "ineffectively impeded" value — that is, it never exceeds actual costs by

40   **BARRIERS TO NEW COMPETITION**

enough to make the forestalling of entry attractive — until finally a point is reached in the progression of entry where the most profitable price only allows established firms to break even, and thus precludes further inducement of entry. This can occur only where there are significant scale economies (which elevate actual costs as entry progresses), and where in addition the relation of cost to scale is such as to give rise to a peculiar succession of values of the immediate condition of entry. Predicted behavior in this case leads obviously to the progressive attraction of a great excess of entry, terminating at or near a point where price is far above minimal cost but equal to actual cost for established firms, and where great diseconomies of small scale (or of an excessive number of firms) are encountered. In general this seems, from both observation and logic, to be an extreme, limiting, and unlikely case, although it illustrates the pole toward which the tendency observed in case IV may lead when economies of scale are important. It deserves special mention perhaps in order to emphasize that it illustrates a somewhat bizarre case, rather than a tendency for much of oligopoly, as Professor Chamberlin might have had it.[15]

In the sixth case established firms are at the outset and thereafter protected by blockaded entry conditions, in the sense that the level of industry prices which would maximize their profits if they were completely protected from entry is lower than that which will attract further entry. Established firms may pursue a joint-profit-maximizing policy while entirely neglecting the possibility of induced entry. In this case, we tend to get (1) a stable market structure, and (2) a large excess of price over minimal cost. If significant economies of scale are absent we also tend to get maximal efficiency in scale of firms and high excess profits. If significant scale economies are present, the same efficiency and profit results may ensue, or it is equally possible that inefficiencies of insufficient scale and reduced profits may be encountered. If product differentiation advantages of established firms are strategic in impeding entry, large selling costs to maintain these advantages may in general be anticipated.

In markets where there is an oligopolistic concentration of sellers, the condition of entry should thus be expected to have a distinct impact upon the market conduct of established sellers and upon the ultimate market performance which emerge. A primary distinction may be drawn among three sorts of cases: (A) those where barriers to entry are absent or where entry is ineffectively impeded through any relevant progression of entry (I and II); (B) those where entry is effectively impeded or becomes so after the attraction of a limited amount of entry (III and IV); and (C) those where entry is either blockaded initially or approaches a

---

[15] E. H. Chamberlin, *Theory of Monopolistic Competition*, 1st edition (Cambridge, Mass., 1933), pp. 92 ff.

IMPORTANCE OF THE CONDITION OF ENTRY   41

blockaded limit through an unbroken succession of ineffectively impeded values (V and VI).

In situation A, oligopolistic pricing is likely to lead to a chronic instability of market structure, wastes of periodic or chronic excess capacity, and periodic monopolistic pricing episodes interspersed with returns of price toward a competitive level. Stability at reasonably competitive prices will occur only if oligopolistic collusion or the recognition of interdependence by sellers is quite imperfect, or if the attraction of entry brings about an atomistic structure which remains. The emergence of oligopoly in these cases (which do not admit of important scale economies) is potentially unfortunate from a social standpoint, but by no means unlikely to occur.

In situation B, the prospect is for a stable market structure with entry forestalled, initially or after a certain progression of entry; and also for a long-run price moderately in excess of a competitive level, but lower than monopolistic prices would be in the absence of a threat of entry, and for moderate excess profits. If significant economies of large-scale firm are not involved, long-run efficiency at optimal scales and an absence of wasteful excess capacity are in prospect. If such scale economies are involved, slight to moderate departures from optimal efficiency, due to suboptimal scales, either may or may not emerge, depending on the character of the general condition of entry.

In situation C, extreme monopolistic excesses of price over minimal cost, with a stable market structure, are generally in prospect. If scale economies are not significant, similarly high excess profits and optimal efficiency in scale will result. If they are, it is possible though not necessarily probable that moderate to severe wastes of insufficient scale may be encountered, together with the reduction or elimination of excess profits.

To this is may be added that the existence of barriers to entry resting on the preference of buyers for the products of established sellers may be expected frequently to be accompanied by excesses of selling expenditures by established firms, aimed at maintaining these barriers to entry. On the other hand, variations in the condition of entry seem unlikely *a priori* to be major determinants of variations in behavior in unconcentrated or atomistic markets, although this is in part because relatively easy entry is generally common to such markets.

This prediction, and the more complex prediction concerning the effects of the condition of entry in oligopoly, deserve some testing or verification from available empirical data. Even if they cannot be fully tested at present, the framework of hypotheses provides a rationale for investigating what the actual conditions of entry are in our industries.

Let us now turn to the empirical findings of our study.

[14]

Contestable Markets: An Uprising in the Theory of Industry Structure

By William J. Baumol*

The address of the departing president is no place for modesty. Nevertheless, I must resist the temptation to describe the analysis I will report here as anything like a revolution. Perhaps terms such as "rebellion" or "uprising" are rather more apt. But, nevertheless, I shall seek to convince you that the work my colleagues, John Panzar and Robert Willig, and I have carried out and encapsulated in our new book enables us to look at industry structure and behavior in a way that is novel in a number of respects, that it provides a unifying analytical structure to the subject area, and that it offers useful insights for empirical work and for the formulation of policy.

Before getting into the substance of the analysis I admit that this presidential address is most unorthodox in at least one significant respect—that it is not the work of a single author. Here it is not even sufficient to refer to Panzar and Willig, the coauthors of both the substance and the exposition of the book in which the analysis is described in full. For others have made crucial contributions to the formulation of the theory—most notably Elizabeth Bailey, Dietrich Fischer, Herman Quirmbach, and Thijs ten Raa.

But there are many more than these. No uprising by a tiny band of rebels can hope to change an established order, and when the time for rebellion is ripe it seems to break out simultaneously and independently in a

variety of disconnected centers each offering its own program for the future. Events here have been no different. I have recently received a proposal for a conference on new developments in the theory of industry structure formulated by my colleague, Joseph Stiglitz, which lists some forty participants, most of them widely known. Among those working on the subject are persons as well known as Caves, Dasgupta, Dixit, Friedlaender, Grossman, Hart, Levin, Ordover, Rosse, Salop, Schmalensee, Sonnenschein, Spence, Varian, von Weiszäcker, and Zeckhauser, among *many* others.[1] It is, of course, tempting to me to take the view that our book is the true gospel of the rebellion and that the doctrines promulgated by others must be combatted as heresy. But that could at best be excused as a manifestation of the excessive zeal one comes to expect on such occasions. In truth, the immediate authors of the work I will report tonight may perhaps be able to justify a claim to have offered some systematization and order to the new doctrines—to have built upon them a more comprehensive statement of the issues and the analysis, and to have made a number of particular contributions. But, in the last analysis, we must look enthusiastically upon our fellow rebels as comrades in arms, each of whom has made a crucial contribution to the common cause.

Turning now to the substance of the theory, let me begin by contrasting our results with those of the standard theory. In offering this contrast, let me emphasize that much of the analysis rests on work that appeared considerably earlier in a variety of forms.

*Presidential address delivered at the ninety-fourth meeting of the American Economic Association, December 29, 1981. I should like to express my deep appreciation to the many colleagues who have contributed to the formulation of the ideas reported here, and to the Economics Program of the Division of Social Sciences of the National Science Foundation, the Division of Information Science and Technology of the National Science Foundation, and the Sloan Foundation for their very generous support of the research that underlies it.

[1]Such a list must inevitably have embarassing omissions—perhaps some of its author's closest friends. I can only say that it is intended just to be suggestive. The fact that it is so far from being complete also indicates how widespread an uprising I am discussing.

We, no less than other writers, owe a heavy debt to predecessors from Bertrand to Bain, from Cournot to Demsetz. Nevertheless, it must surely be acknowledged that the following characterization of the general tenor of the literature as it appeared until fairly recently is essentially accurate.

First, in the received analysis perfect competition serves as the one standard of welfare-maximizing structure and behavior. There is no similar form corresponding to industries in which efficiency calls for a very limited number of firms (though the earlier writings on workable competition did move in that direction in a manner less formal than ours).

Our analysis, in contrast, provides a generalization of the concept of the perfectly competitive market, one which we call a "perfectly contestable market." It is, generally, characterized by optimal behavior and yet applies to the full range of industry structures including even monopoly and oligopoly. In saying this, it must be made clear that perfectly contestable markets do not populate the world of reality any more than perfectly competitive markets do, though there are a number of industries which undoubtedly approximate contestability even if they are far from perfectly competitive. In our analysis, perfect contestability, then, serves not primarily as a description of reality, but as a benchmark for desirable industrial organization which is far more flexible and is applicable far more widely than the one that was available to us before.

Second, in the standard analysis (including that of many of our fellow rebels), the properties of oligopoly models are heavily dependent on the assumed expectations and reaction patterns characterizing the firms that are involved. When there is a change in the assumed nature of these expectations or reactions, the implied behavior of the oligopolistic industry may change drastically.

In our analysis, in the limiting case of perfect contestability, oligopolistic structure and behavior are freed entirely from their previous dependence on the conjectural variations of *incumbents* and, instead, these are generally determined uniquely and, in a manner that is tractable analytically, by the pressures of *potential* competition to which Bain directed our attention so tellingly.

Third, the standard analysis leaves us with the impression that there is a rough continuum, in terms of desirability of industry performance, ranging from unregulated pure monopoly as the pessimal arrangement to perfect competition as the ideal, with relative efficiency in resource allocation increasing monotonically as the number of firms expands.

I will show that, in contrast, in perfectly contestable markets behavior is sharply discontinuous in its welfare attributes. A contestable monopoly offers us some presumption, but no guarantee, of behavior consistent with a second best optimum, subject to the constraint that the firm be viable financially despite the presence of scale economies which render marginal cost pricing financially infeasible. That is, a contestable monopoly has some reason to adopt the Ramsey optimal price-output vector, but it may have other choices open to it. (For the analysis of contestable monopoly, see my article with Elizabeth Bailey and Willig, Panzar and Willig's article, and my book with Panzar and Willig, chs. 7 and 8.)

But once each product obtains a second producer, that is, once we enter the domain of duopoly or oligopoly for each and every good, such choice disappears. The contestable oligopoly which achieves an equilibrium that immunizes it from the incursions of entrants has only one pricing option—it must set its price exactly *equal* to marginal cost and do *all* of the things required for a first best optimum! In short, once we leave the world of pure or partial monopoly, any contestable market must behave ideally in every respect. Optimality is *not* approached gradually as the number of firms supplying a commodity grows. As has long been suggested in Chicago, two firms can be enough to guarantee optimality (see, for example, Eugene Fama and Arthur Laffer).

Thus, the analysis extends enormously the domain in which the invisible hand holds sway. In a perfectly contestable world, it seems to rule almost everywhere. Lest this seem to be too Panglossian a view of reality, let me offer two observations which make it clear that we emphatically do not believe that all need be for the best in this best of all possible worlds.

First, let me recall the observation that real markets are rarely, if ever, perfectly contestable. Contestability is merely a broader ideal, a benchmark of wider applicability than is perfect competition. To say that contestable oligopolies behave ideally and that contestable monopolies have some incentives for doing so is not to imply that this is even nearly true of all oligopolies or of unregulated monopolies in reality.

Second, while the theory extends the domain of the invisible hand in some directions, it unexpectedly restricts it in others. This brings me to the penultimate contrast I wish to offer here between the earlier views and those that emerge from our analysis.

The older theoretical analysis seems to have considered the invisible hand to be a rather weak intratemporal allocator of resources, as we have seen. The mere presence of unregulated monopoly or oligopoly was taken to be sufficient per se to imply that resources are likely to be misallocated *within* a given time period. But *where the market structure is such as to yield a satisfactory allocation of resources within the period*, it may have seemed that it can, at least in theory, do a good job of intertemporal resource allocation. In the absence of any externalities, persistent and asymmetric information gaps, and of interference with the workings of capital markets, the amounts that will be invested for the future may appear to be consistent with Pareto optimality and efficiency in the supply of outputs to current and future generations.

However, our analysis shows that where there are economies of scale in the production of durable capital, intertemporal contestable monopoly, which may perform relatively well in the single period, cannot be depended upon to perform ideally as time passes. In particular, we will see that the least costly producer is in the long run vulnerable to entry or replacement by rivals whose appearance is inefficient because it wastes valuable social resources.

There is one last contrast between the newer analyses and the older theory which I am most anxious to emphasize. In the older theory, the nature of the industry structure was *not* normally explained by the analysis. It was, in effect, taken to be given exogenously, with the fates determining, apparently capriciously, that one industry will be organized as an oligopoly, another as a monopoly and a third as a set of monopolistic competitors. Assuming that this destiny had somehow been revealed, the older analyses proceeded to investigate the consequences of the exogenously given industry structure for pricing, outputs, and other decisions.[2]

The new analyses are radically different in this respect. In our analysis, among others, an industry's structure is determined explicitly, endogenously, and simultaneously with the pricing, output, advertising, and other decisions of the firms of which it is constituted. This, perhaps, is one of the prime contributions of the new theoretical analyses.

I. Characteristics of Contestable Markets

Perhaps a misplaced instinct for melodrama has led me to say so much about contestable markets without even hinting what makes a market contestable. But I can postpone the definition no longer. A contestable market is one into which entry is absolutely free, *and exit is absolutely costless.* We use "freedom of entry" in Stigler's sense, not to mean that it is costless or easy, but that the entrant suffers no disadvantage in terms of production technique or perceived product quality relative to the incumbent,

---

[2] Of course, any analysis which considered the role of entry, whether it dealt with perfect competition or monopolistic competition, must implicitly have considered the determination of industry structure by the market. But in writings before the 1970's, such analyses usually did not consider how this process determined whether the industry would or would not turn out to be, for example, an oligopoly. The entry conditions were studied only to show how the *assumed* market structure could constitute an equilibrium state. Many recent writings have gone more explicitly into the determination of industry structure, though their approaches generally differ from ours.

and that potential entrants find it appropriate to evaluate the profitability of entry in terms of the incumbent firms' pre-entry prices. In short, it is a requirement of contestability that there be no cost discrimination against entrants. Absolute freedom of exit, to us, is one way to guarantee freedom of entry. By this we mean that any firm can leave without impediment, and in the process of departure can recoup any costs incurred in the entry process. If all capital is salable or reusable without loss other than that corresponding to normal user cost and depreciation, then any risk of entry is eliminated.

Thus, contestable markets may share at most one attribute with perfect competition. Their firms need not be small or numerous or independent in their decision making or produce homogeneous products. In short, a perfectly competitive market is necessarily perfectly contestable, but not *vice versa*.

The crucial feature of a contestable market is its vulnerability to hit-and-run entry. Even a very transient profit opportunity need not be neglected by a potential entrant, for he can go in, and, before prices change, collect his gains and then depart without cost, should the climate grow hostile.

Shortage of time forces me to deal rather briefly with two of the most important properties of contestable markets—their welfare attributes and the way in which they determine industry structure. I deal with these briefly because an intuitive view of the logic of these parts of the analysis is not difficult to provide. Then I can devote a bit more time to some details of the oligopoly and the intertemporal models.

A. *Perfect Contestability and Welfare*

The welfare properties of contestable markets follow almost directly from their definition and their vulnerability to hit-and-run incursions. Let me list some of these properties and discuss them succinctly.

First, a contestable market never offers more than a normal rate of profit—its economic profits must be zero or negative, even if it is oligopolistic or monopolistic. The reason is simple. Any positive profit means that a transient entrant can set up business,

replicate a profit-making incumbent's output at the same cost as his, undercut the incumbent's prices slightly and still earn a profit. That is, continuity and the opportunity for costless entry and exit guarantee that an entrant who is content to accept a slightly lower economic profit can do so by selecting prices a bit lower than the incumbent's.

In sum, in a perfectly contestable market any economic profit earned by an incumbent automatically constitutes an earnings opportunity for an entrant who will hit and, if necessary, run (counting his temporary but supernormal profits on the way to the bank). Consequently, in contestable markets, zero profits must characterize any equilibrium, even under monopoly and oligopoly.

The second welfare characteristic of a contestable market follows from the same argument as the first. This second attribute of any contestable market is the absence of any sort of inefficiency in production in industry equilibrium. This is true alike of inefficiency of allocation of inputs, X-inefficiency, inefficient operation of the firm, or inefficient organization of the industry. For any unnecessary cost, like any abnormal profit, constitutes an invitation to entry. Of course, in the short run, as is true under perfect competition, both profits and waste may be present. But in the long run, these simply cannot withstand the threat brandished by potential entrants who have nothing to lose by grabbing at any opportunity for profit, however transient it may be.

A third welfare attribute of any long-run equilibrium in a contestable market is that no product can be sold at a price, p, that is less than its marginal cost. For if some firm sells y units of output at such a price and makes a profit in the process, then it is possible for an entrant to offer to sell a slightly smaller quantity, $y - \varepsilon$, at a price a shade lower than the incumbent's, and still make a profit. That is, if the price p is less than MC, then the sale of $y - \varepsilon$ units at price p must yield a total profit $\pi + \Delta\pi$ which is greater than the profit, π, that can be earned by selling only y units of output at that price. Therefore, there must exist a price just slightly lower than p which enables the entrant to undercut the incumbent and yet to earn at least as much as the incumbent, by eliminating the unprofitable marginal unit.

This last attribute of contestable equilibria —the fact that price must always at least equal marginal cost—is important for the economics of antitrust and regulation. For it means that in a perfectly contestable market, no cross subsidy is possible, that is, no predatory pricing can be used as a weapon of unfair competition. But we will see it also has implications which are more profound theoretically and which are more germane to our purposes. For it constitutes half of the argument which shows that when there are two or more suppliers of any product, its price must, in equilibrium, be exactly equal to marginal cost, and so resource allocation must satisfy all the requirements of first best optimality.

Indeed, the argument here is similar to the one which has just been described. But there is a complication which is what introduces the two-firm requirement into this proposition. $p < MC$ constitutes an opportunity for profit to an entrant who drops the unprofitable marginal unit of output, as we have just seen. It would seem, symmetrically, that $p > MC$ also automatically constitutes an opportunity for profitable entry. Instead of selling the y-unit output of a profitable incumbent, the entrant can now offer to sell the slightly larger output, $y + \varepsilon$, using the profits generated by the marginal unit at a price greater than marginal cost to permit a reduction in price below the incumbent's. But on this side of the incumbent's output, there is a catch in the argument. Suppose the incumbent is a monopolist. Then output and price are constrained by the elasticity of demand. An attempt by an entrant to sell $y + \varepsilon$ rather than y may conceivably cause a sharp reduction in price which eliminates the apparent profits of entry. In the extreme case where demand is perfectly inelastic, there will be no positive price at which the market will absorb the quantity $y + \varepsilon$. This means that the profit opportunity represented by $p > MC$ can crumble into dust as soon as anyone seeks to take advantage of it.

But all this changes when the market contains two or more sellers. Now $p > MC$ does always constitute a real opportunity for prof-

itable entry. The entrant who wishes to sell a bit more than some one of the profitable incumbents, call him incumbent A, need not press against the industry's total demand curve for the product. Rather, he can undercut A, steal away all of his customers, at least temporarily, and, in addition, steal away ε units of demand from any other incumbent, B. Thus, if A and B together sell $y_a + y_b > y_a$, then an entrant can lure away $y_a + \varepsilon > y_a$ customers, for ε sufficiently small, and earn on this the incremental profit $\varepsilon(p - MC) > 0$. This means that the entrant who sells $y_a + \varepsilon$ can afford to undercut the prevailing prices somewhat and still make more profit than an incumbent who sells y_a at price p.

In sum, where a product is sold by two or more firms, any $p > MC$ constitutes an irresistible entry opportunity for hit-and-run entry in a perfectly contestable market, for it promises the entrant supernormal profits even if they accrue for a very short period of time.

Consequently, when a perfectly contestable market contains two or more sellers, neither $p < MC$ nor $p > MC$ is compatible with equilibrium. Thus we have our third and perhaps most crucial welfare attribute of such perfectly contestable markets—their prices, in equilibrium, must be equal to marginal costs, as is required for Pareto optimality of the "first best" variety. This, along with the conclusion that such markets permit no economic profits and no inefficiency in long-run equilibrium, constitutes their critical properties from the viewpoint of economic welfare. Certainly, since they do enjoy those three properties, the optimality of perfectly contestable equilibria (with the reservations already expressed about the case of pure monopoly) fully justifies our conclusion that perfect contestability constitutes a proper generalization of the concept of perfect competition so far as welfare implications are concerned.

B. *On the Determination of Industry Structure*

I shall be briefer and even less rigorous in describing how industry structure is determined endogenously by contestability analysis. Though this area encompasses one of its most crucial accomplishments, there is no way I can do justice to the details of the analysis in an oral presentation and within my allotted span of time. However, an intuitive view of the matter is not difficult.

The key to the analysis lies in the second welfare property of contestable equilibria—their incompatibility with inefficiency of any sort. In particular, they are incompatible with inefficiency in the *organization* of an industry. That is, suppose we consider whether a particular output quantity of an industry will be produced by two firms or by a thousand. Suppose it turns out that the two-firm arrangement can produce the given output at a cost 20 percent lower than it can be done by the 1,000 firms. Then one implication of our analysis is that the industry cannot be in long-run equilibrium if it encompasses 1,000 producers. Thus we already have some hint about the equilibrium industry structure of a contestable market.

We can go further with this example. Suppose that, with the given output vector for the industry, it turns out that *no* number of firms other than two can produce at as low a total cost as is possible under a two-firm arrangement. That is, suppose two firms can produce the output vector at a total cost lower than it can be done by one firm or three firms or sixty or six thousand. Then we say that for the given output vector the industry is a *natural duopoly*.

This now tells us how the industry's structure can be determined. We proceed, conceptually, in two steps. First we determine what structure happens to be most efficient for the production of a given output vector by a given industry. Next, we investigate when market pressures will lead the industry toward such an efficient structure in equilibrium.

Now, the first step, though it has many intriguing analytic attributes, is essentially a pure matter of computation. Given the cost function for a typical firm, it is ultimately a matter of calculation to determine how many firms will produce a given output most efficiently. For example, if economies of scale hold throughout the relevant range and there are sufficient complementarities in the production of the different commodities sup-

plied by the firm, then it is an old and well-known conclusion that single firm production will be most economical—that we are dealing with a natural monopoly.

Similarly, in the single product case suppose the average cost curve is U shaped and attains its minimum point at an output of 10,000 units per year. Then it is obvious that if the industry happens to sell 50,000 units per year, this output can be produced most cheaply if it is composed of exactly five firms, each producing 10,000 units at its point of minimum average cost.

Things become far more complex and more interesting when the firm and the industry produce a multiplicity of commodities, as they always do in reality. But the logic is always the same. When the industry output vector is small compared to the output vectors the firm can produce at relatively low cost, then the efficient industry structure will be characterized by very few firms. The opposite will be true when the industry's output vector is relatively far from the origin. In the multiproduct case, since average cost cannot be defined, two complications beset the characterization of the output vectors which the firm can produce relatively efficiently. First, since here average cost cannot be defined, we cannot simply look for the point of minimum average costs. But we overcome this problem by dealing with output bundles having fixed proportions among commodity quantities—by moving along a ray in output space. Along any such ray the behavior of average cost *is* definable, and the point of minimum ray average cost (RAC) is our criterion of relatively efficient scale for the firm. Thus, in Figure 1 we have a ray average cost curve for the production of boots and shoes when they are produced in the proportion given by ray OR. We see that for such bundles y^m is the point of minimum RAC. A second problem affecting the determination of the output vectors the firm can produce efficiently is the choice of output proportions —the location of the ray along which the firm will operate. This depends on the degree of complementarity in production of the goods, and it also lends itself to formal analysis.

We note also that the most efficient number of firms will vary with the location of the

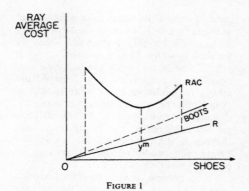

FIGURE 1

industry's output vector. The industry may be a natural monopoly with one output vector, a natural duopoly with another, and efficiency may require seventy-three firms when some third output vector is provided by the industry.

This, then, completes the first of the two basic steps in the endogenous determination of industry structure. Here we have examined what industry structure is least costly for each given output vector of a given industry, and have found how the result depends on the magnitudes of the elements of that output vector and the shape of the cost function of the typical firm. So far the discussion may perhaps be considered normative rather than behavioral. It tells us what structure is most efficient under the circumstances, not which industry structure will emerge under the pressures of the market mechanism.

The transition toward the second, behavioral, stage of the analysis is provided by the observation that the optimal structure of an industry depends on its output vector, while that output vector in turn depends on the prices charged by its firms. But, since pricing depends on industry structure, we are brought full circle to the conclusion that pricing behavior and industry structure must, ultimately, be determined simultaneously and endogenously.

We are in no position to go much further than this for a market whose properties are unspecified. But, for a perfectly contestable market, we can go much further. Indeed, the properties of perfect contestability cut

through every difficulty and tell us the equilibrium prices, outputs, and industry structure, all at once.

Where more than one firm supplies a product, we have already characterized these prices precisely. For we have concluded that each equilibrium price will equal the associated marginal cost. Then, given the industry's cost and demand relationships, this yields the industry's output quantities simultaneously with its prices, in the usual manner. Here there is absolutely nothing new in the analysis.

But what is new is the format of the analysis of the determination of industry structure. As I have already pointed out, structure is determined by the efficiency requirement of equilibrium in any contestable market. Since no such equilibrium is compatible with failure to minimize industry costs, it follows that the market forces under perfect contestability will bring us results consistent with those of our normative analysis. Whatever industry structures minimize total costs for the equilibrium output vector must turn out to be the only structures consistent with industry equilibrium in the long run.

Thus, for contestable markets, but for contestable markets *only*, the second stage of the analysis of industry structure turns out to be a sham. Whatever industry structure was shown by the first, normative, portion of the analysis to be least costly must also emerge as the industry structure selected by market behavior. No additional calculations are required by the behavioral analysis. It will all have been done in the normative cost-minimization analysis and the behavioral analysis is pure bonus.

Thus, as I promised, I have indicated how contestability theory departs from the older theory which implicitly took industry structure to be determined exogenously in a manner totally unspecified and, instead, along with other recent writings, embraces the determination of industry structure as an integral part of the theory to be dealt with simultaneously with the determination of prices and outputs.

At this point I can only conjecture about the determination of industry structure once we leave the limiting case of perfect contestability. But my guess is that there are no sharp discontinuities here, and that while the industry structures which emerge in reality are not always those which minimize costs, they will constitute reasonable approximations to the efficient structures. If this is not so it is difficult to account for the similarities in the patterns of industry structure that one observes in different countries. Why else do we not see agriculture organized as an oligopoly in any free market economy, or automobiles produced by 10,000 firms? Market pressures must surely make any very inefficient market structure vulnerable to entry, to displacement of incumbents by foreign competition, or to undermining in other ways. If that is so, the market structure that is called for by contestability theory may not prove to be too bad an approximation to what we encounter in reality.

II. On Oligopoly Equilibrium

I should like now to examine oligopoly equilibrium somewhat more extensively. We have seen that, except where a multiproduct oligopoly firm happens to sell some of its products in markets in which it has no competitors, an important partial monopoly case which I will ignore in what follows, all prices must equal the corresponding marginal costs in long-run equilibrium. But in an oligopoly market, this is a troublesome concept. Unless the industry output vector happens to fall at a point where the cost function is characterized by locally constant returns to scale, we know that zero profits are incompatible with marginal cost pricing. Particularly if there are scale economies at that point, so that marginal cost pricing precludes financial viability, we can hardly expect such a solution to constitute an equilibrium. Besides, we have seen that long-run equilibrium requires profit to be precisely zero. We would thus appear to have run into a major snag by concluding that perfect contestability always leads to marginal cost pricing under oligopoly.

This is particularly so if the (ray) average curve is U shaped, with its minimum occurring at a single point, y^m. For in this case that minimum point is the only output of the firm consistent with constant returns to scale

and with zero profits under marginal cost pricing. Thus, dealing with the single product case to make the point, it would appear, say, that if the AC-minimizing output is 1,000, in a contestable market, equilibrium is possible if quantity demanded from the industry happens to be exactly 2,000 units (so two firms can produce 1,000 units each) or exactly 3,000 units or exactly 4,000 units, etc. But suppose the demand curve happens to intersect the industry AC curve, say, at 4,030 units. That is, then, the only industry output satisfying the equilibrium requirement that price equals zero profit. But then, at least one of the four or five firms in the industry must produce either more or less than 1,000 units of output, and so the slope of its AC curve will not be zero at that point, precluding either MC pricing or zero profits and, consequently, violating one or the other of the requirements of equilibrium in a perfectly contestable market.

It would appear that equilibrium will be impossible in this perfectly contestable market unless by a great piece of luck the industry demand curve happens to intersect its AC curve at 2,000 or 3,000 units or some other integer multiple of 1,000 units of output.

There are a variety of ways in which one can grapple with this difficulty. In his dissertation at New York University, Thijs ten Raa has explored the issue with some care and has shown that the presence of entry costs of sufficient magnitude, that is, irreversible costs which must be borne by an entrant but not by an incumbent, can eliminate the existence problem. The minimum size of the entry cost required to permit an equilibrium will depend on the size of the deviation from zero profits under marginal cost pricing and ten Raa has given us rules for its determination. He has shown also that the existence problem, as measured by the required minimum size of entry cost, decreases rapidly as the equilibrium number of firms of the industry increases, typically attaining negligible proportions as that number reaches, say, ten enterprises. For, as is well known, when the firm's average cost curve is U shaped the industry's average cost curve will approach a horizontal line as the

VOL. 72 NO. 1   BAUMOL: CONTESTABLE MARKETS   9

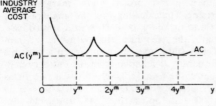

FIGURE 2

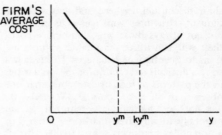

FIGURE 3

size of industry output increases. This is shown in Figure 2 which is a standard diagram giving the firm's and the industry's AC curves when the former is U shaped. As a result, the deviations between average cost and marginal cost will decline as industry output increases and so the minimum size of the entry cost required to preserve equilibrium declines correspondingly.

However, here I want to describe another approach offered in our book to the problem of existence which I have just described—the difficulty of satisfying simultaneously the zero-profit requirement and the requirement of marginal cost pricing. This second avenue relies on the apparently unanimous conclusion of empirical investigators of the cost function of the firm, that AC curves are not, in fact, characterized by a unique minimum point as they would be if they had a smooth U shape. Rather, these investigators tell us, the AC curve of reality has a flat bottom—an interval along which it is horizontal. That is, average costs do tend to fall at first with size of output, then they reach a minimum and continue at that level for some range of outputs, after which they may begin to rise once more. An AC curve of this variety is shown in Figure 3. Obviously, such a flat segment of the AC curves *does* help matters because there is now a *range* of outputs over which MC pricing yields zero profits. Moreover, the longer the flat-bottomed segment the better matters are for existence of equilibrium. Indeed, it is easy to show that if the left-hand end of the flat segment occurs at output y^m and the right-hand end occurs at ky_m, then if k is greater than or equal to 2 the existence problem disappears altogether, because the industry's AC curves will be horizontal for any output greater than y_m. That

is, in any contestable market in which two or more firms operate the industry AC curve will be horizontal and MC pricing will always yield zero profits. To confirm that this is so, note that if, for example, the flat segment for the firm extends from $y = 1,000$ to $y = 2,000$, then any industry output of, say, $9,000 + \Delta y$ where $0 \leqslant \Delta y \leqslant 9,000$ can be produced by nine firms, each of them turning out more than 1,000 but less than 2,000 units. Hence, each of them will operate along the horizontal portion of its AC curve, as equilibrium requires.

Thus, if the horizontal interval (y^m, ky_m) happens to satisfy $k \geqslant 2$, there is no longer any problem for existence of equilibrium in a contestable market with two or more firms. But fate may not always be so kind. What if that horizontal interval is quite short, that is, k is quite close to unity? Such a case is shown in our diagram where for illustration I have taken $k = 4/3$.

I should like to take advantage of your patience by dealing here not with the simplest case—that of the single product industry—but with the multiproduct problem. I do this partly to offer you some feeling of the way in which the multiproduct analysis, which is one of the hallmarks of our study, works out in practice.

Because, as we have seen, there is no way one can measure average cost for all output combinations in the multiproduct case, I will deal exclusively with the total cost function. Figure 4 shows such a total cost function for the single firm, which is taken to manufacture two products, boots and shoes.

Let us pause briefly to examine its shape. Along any ray such as OR, which keeps

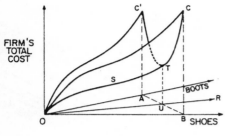

FIGURE 4

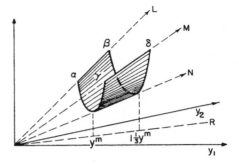

FIGURE 5

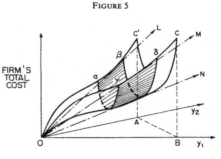

FIGURE 6

output proportions constant, we have an ordinary total cost curve, OST. With one exception, which I will note soon, I have drawn it to have the usual sort of shape, with marginal costs falling near the origin and rising at points much further from the origin. On the other hand, the trans ray cut above AB yields a cross section $C'TC$ which is more or less U shaped. This means that it is relatively cheaper to produce boots and shoes together (point U) than to produce them in isolation (point A or point B). That is, this convex trans ray shape is enough to offer us the complementarity which leads firms and industries to turn out a multiplicity of products rather than specializing in the production of a single good.

Now what, in such a case, corresponds to the flat bottom of an AC curve in a single product case? The answer is that the cost function in the neighborhood of the corresponding output must be linearly homogeneous. In Figure 5 such a region, $\alpha\beta\gamma\delta$, is depicted. It is linearly homogeneous because it is generated by a set of rays such as L, M, and N. For simplicity in the discussion that follows, I have given this region a very regular shape—it is, approximately, a rectangle which has been moved into three-dimensional space and given a U-shaped cross section.

Now Figure 6 combines the two preceding diagrams and we see that they have been drawn to mesh together, so that the linearly homogeneous region constitutes a portion of the firm's total cost surface. We see then that the firm's total cost does have a region in which constant returns to scale occur, and which corresponds to the flat-bottomed segment of the AC curve.

Moreover, as before, I have deliberately kept this segment quite narrow. Indeed, I have repeated the previous proportions, letting the segment extend from a distance y^m from the origin to the distance $1\frac{1}{3}y^m$ along any ray on the floor of the diagram.

Let us now see what happens in these circumstances when we turn to the total cost surface for the *industry*. This is depicted in Figure 7 which shows a relationship that may at first seem surprising. In Figure 7 I depict only the linearly homogeneous portions of the industry's cost surface. There we see that while for the firm linear homogeneity prevailed only in the interval from y^m to $1\frac{1}{3}y^m$, in the case of industry output linear homogeneity also holds in that same interval but, in addition, it holds for the interval $2y^m$ to $2\frac{2}{3}y^m$ and in the region extending from $3y^m$ to infinity. That is, everywhere beyond $3y^m$ the industry's total cost function is linearly homogeneous. In this case, then, we have three regions of local linear homogene-

VOL. 72 NO. 1   BAUMOL: CONTESTABLE MARKETS   11

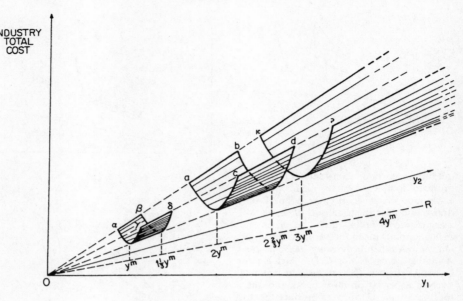

FIGURE 7

ity in the industry's cost function, $\alpha\beta\gamma\delta$, which is identical with that of the individual firm, the larger region $abcd$, and the infinite region $aleph\ beth$....

Before showing why this is so we must pause to note the implications of the exercise. For it means that even a relatively small region of flatness in the AC curve of the individual firm, that is, of linear homogeneity in its total cost function, eliminates the bulk of the existence problem for oligopoly equilibrium in a contestable market. The problem does not arise for outputs nearer to the origin than y_m because such outputs are supplied most efficiently by a monopoly which is not required to price at marginal cost in a contestable market equilibrium. The problem also does not arise for any industry output greater than $3y^m$ in this case, because everywhere beyond that marginal cost pricing yields zero profits. There are two relatively narrow regions in which no equilibrium is, indeed, possible, but here we may conjecture that the vicissitudes of disequilibrium will cause shifts in the demand relationships as changing prices and changing

consumption patterns affect tastes, and so the industry will ultimately happen upon an equilibrium position and remain there until exogenous disturbances move it away. Thus we end up with an oligopoly equilibrium whose prices, profits, and other attributes are determined without benefit of the conjectural variation, reaction functions, and the other paraphernalia of standard oligopoly analysis.

To complete this discussion of oligopoly equilibrium in a contestable market, it only remains for me to explain why the regions of linear homogeneity in the industry's cost function are as depicted in Figure 7. The answer is straightforward. Let $C(y)$ be the firm's total cost function for which we have assumed for expository simplicity that in the interval from y^m to $1\frac{1}{3}y^m$ along each and every ray, total cost grows exactly proportionately with output. Then two firms can produce $2y^m$ at the same unit cost, and three firms can produce $3y^m$ at that same unit cost for the given output bundle, etc. But by exactly the same argument, the two firms together, each producing no more than $1\frac{1}{3}y^m$, can turn out anything up to $2\frac{2}{3}y^m$ without affecting unit costs, and three firms can produce as much as $3\frac{3}{3}y^m$, that is, as much as $4y^m$. In sum, the intervals of linear homogeneity for the industry are the following:

Interval 1: from y^m to $1\frac{1}{3}y^m$
Interval 2: from $2y^m$ to $2\frac{2}{3}y^m$
Interval 3: from $3y^m$ to $4y^m$
Interval 4: from $4y^m$ to $5\frac{1}{3}y^m$
Interval 5: from $5y^m$ to $6\frac{2}{3}y^m$

. . . .

That is, each interval begins at an integer multiple of y^m and extends $1/3$ y^m further than its predecessor. Thus, beyond $3y^m$ successive intervals begin to touch or overlap and that is why linear homogeneity extends everywhere beyond $3y^m$ as I claimed.[3]

There is one complication in the multiproduct case which I have deliberately slid over, feeling the discussion was already complicated enough. The preceding argument assumes implicitly that the firms producing the industry output all employ the same output proportions as those in the industry output vector. For otherwise, it is not legitimate to move outward along a single ray as the number of firms is increased. But suppose increased industry output were to permit savings through increased specialization. Might there not be constant returns with fixed output proportions and yet economies of scale for the industry overall? This problem is avoided by our complementarity assumption used to account for the industry's multiproduct operation—our U-shaped trans-ray cross section. This, in effect, rules out such savings from specialization in the regions where linear homogeneity also rules out savings from increased scale.

This, then, completes my discussion of oligopoly equilibrium in perfectly contestable markets, which we have seen, yields a determinate set of prices and outputs that is not dependent upon assumptions about the

[3] The reader can readily generalize this result. If the flat-bottomed segment for the firm extends from y^m to $y^m(1+1/w)$, where w is an integer, then there will be w regions of linear homogeneity in the industry cost function and it will be linearly homogeneous for any output $y \geqslant wy^m$.

nature of incumbent firm's expectations relating to entrants' behavior and offers us a concrete and favorable conclusion on the welfare implications of contestable oligopoly.

III. Intertemporal Vulnerability to Inefficient Entry

Having so far directed attention to areas in which the invisible hand manifests unexpected strength, I should like to end my story by dealing with an issue in relation to which it is weaker than some of us might have expected. As I indicated before, this is the issue of intertemporal production involving durable capital goods.

The analysis is far more general than the following story suggests, but even the case I describe is sufficiently general to make the point. We deal with an industry in which a product is offered by a single firm that provides it period after period. The equilibrium quantity of the commodity that is demanded grows steadily with the passage of time in a manner that is foreseen without uncertainty. Because of economies of scale in the production of capacity the firm deliberately builds some excess capacity to take care of anticipated growth in sales volume. But there is some point, let us say, $z = 45$ years in the future, such that it would be uneconomic to take further growth in sales volume into account in the initial choice of capacity. This is so because the opportunity (interest) cost of the capacity that remains idle for 45 or more years exceeds the savings made possible by the economies of scale of construction. Thus, after 45 years it will pay the firm to undertake a second construction project to build the added capacity needed to produce the goods demanded of it.

Suppose that in every particular period our producer is a natural monopolist, that is, he produces the industry's supply of its one commodity at a cost lower than it can be done by any two or more enterprises. Then considering that same product in different periods to be formally equivalent to different goods we may take our supplier to be an intertemporal natural monopolist in a multiproduct industry. That is, no combination of two or more firms can produce the industry's intertemporal output vector as cheaply as he. I will prove now under a set of remarkably unrestrictive assumptions that despite its cost advantages, there exists no intertemporal price vector consistent with equilibrium for this firm. That is, whatever his price vector, his market will at some time be vulnerable to partial or complete takeover by an entrant who has neither superior skills nor technological superiority and whose entrance increases the quantities of resources used up in production. In other words, here the invisible hand proves incapable of protecting the most efficient producing arrangement and leaves the incumbent producer vulnerable to displacement by an aggressive entrant. I leave to your imaginations what, if anything, this says about the successive displacements on the world market of the Dutch by the English, the English by the Germans and the Americans, and the Americans, perhaps, by the Japanese.

The proof of our proposition on the intertemporal vulnerability of incumbents to entry that is premature from the viewpoint of cost minimization does require just a little bit of algebra. To keep our analysis simple, I will divide time into two periods, each lasting $z = 45$ years so that capacity in the first period is, optimally, just sufficient to satisfy all demand, but in the second, it requires the construction of added capacity to meet demand growth because, by assumption, anticipatory construction to meet growth more than z years in the future simply is too costly. Also for simplicity, I will assume that there are no costs other than cost of construction. Of course, neither this nor the use of only two periods really affects the argument in any way. My only three substantive assumptions are that demand is growing with time, that there are economies of scale, that is, declining average costs in construction, and that there exists some length of time, z, so great that it does not pay in the initial construction to build capacity sufficient for the growth in quantity demanded that will occur beyond that date.

The argument, like the notation, is now straightforward. Let y_t be output in period t,

p_t be price in period t, and $K(y)$ be the cost of construction of capacity sufficient to produce (a maximum of) y units per period. Here, both p_t and $K(y)$ are expressed in discounted present value.[4]

Then, by assumption, our firm will construct at the beginning of the first period capacity just sufficient to produce output y_1 at cost $K(y_1)$ and at the beginning of the second period it will produce the rest of the capacity it needs, $y_2 - y_1 > 0$, at the cost $K(y_2 - y_1)$.

The first requirement for the prices in question to be consistent with equilibrium is that they permit the incumbent to cover his costs, that is, that

$$(1) \qquad p_1 y_1 + p_2 y_2 \geqslant K(y_1) + K(y_2 - y_1).$$

Second, for these prices to constitute an equilibrium they must protect the incumbent against any and all possible incursions by entrants. That is, suppose an entrant were to consider the possibility of constructing capacity y_1 and not expanding in the future, and, by undercutting the incumbent, selling the same output, y_1, in each period. Entry on these terms will in fact be profitable unless the prices are such that the sale of y_1 in each period does not bring in revenues sufficient to cover the cost, $K(y_1)$, of the entrant's once-and-for-all construction. That is, entry will be profitable unless

$$(2) \qquad p_1 y_1 + p_2 y_1 \leqslant K(y_1).$$

Thus, the prices in question cannot constitute an equilibrium unless (2) as well as (1) are satisfied.

Now, subtracting (2) from (1) we obtain immediately

$$p_2(y_2 - y_1) \geqslant K(y_2 - y_t)$$

or

$$(3) \qquad p_2 \geqslant K(y_2 - y_1)/(y_2 - y_1),$$

---

[4] That is, if p_1^*, p_2^*, represent the undiscounted prices, $p_1 = p_1^*, p_2 = p_2^*/(1+r)$, where r is the rate of interest, etc.

but, by the assumption that average construction cost is declining, since $y_1 > 0$,

(4) $\quad K(y_2 - y_1)/(y_2 - y_1) > K(y_2)/y_2.$

Substituting this into (3) we have at once

$$p_2 > K(y_2)/y_2$$

or

(5) $\qquad\qquad p_2 y_2 > K(y_2).$

Inequality (5) is our result. For it proves that any prices which satisfy equilibrium requirements (1) and (2) must permit a second-period entrant using the same techniques to build capacity y_2 from the ground up, at cost $K(y_2)$, to price slightly below anything the incumbent can charge and yet recover his costs; and that in doing so, the entrant can earn a profit.

Thus, our intertemporal natural monopolist cannot quote, *at time zero*, any prices capable of preventing the takeover of some or all of his market. Moreover, this is so despite the waste, in the form of replication of the incumbent's plant, that this entails. That, then, is the end of the formal argument, the proof that here the invisible hand manifests weakness that is, perhaps, unexpected.

You will all undoubtedly recognize that the story as told here in its barest outlines omits all sorts of nuances, such as entrants' fear of responsive pricing, the role of bankruptcy, depreciation of capital, and the like. This is not the place to go into these matters for it is neither possible nor appropriate here for me to go beyond illustration of the logic of the new analysis.

IV. Concluding Comments

Before closing let me add a word on policy implications, whose details must also be left to another place. In spirit, the policy conclusions are consistent with many of those economists have long been espousing. At least in the intratemporal analysis, the heroes are the (unidentified) potential entrants who exercise discipline over the incumbent, and who do so most effectively when entry is free. In the limit, when entry and exit are completely free, efficient incumbent monopolists and oligopolists may in fact be able to prevent entry. But they can do so only by behaving virtuously, that is, by offering to consumers the benefits which competition would otherwise bring. For every deviation from good behavior instantly makes them vulnerable to hit-and-run entry.

This immediately offers what may be a new insight on antitrust policy. It tells us that a history of absence of entry in an industry and a high concentration index may be signs of virtue, not of vice. This will be true when entry costs in our sense are negligible. And, then, efforts to change market structure must be regarded as mischievous and antisocial in their effects.

A second and more obvious conclusion is the questionable desirability of artificial impediments to entry, such as regulators were long inclined to impose. The new analysis merely reinforces the view that any proposed regulatory barrier to entry must start off with a heavy presumption against its adoption. Perhaps a bit newer is the emphasis on the importance of freedom of exit which is as crucial a requirement of contestability as is freedom of entry. Thus we must reject as perverse the propensity of regulators to resist the closing down of unprofitable lines of activity. This has even gone so far as a Congressional proposal (apparently supported by Ralph Nader) to require any plant with yearly sales exceeding $250,000 to provide fifty-two weeks of severance pay and to pay three years of taxes, before it will be permitted to close, and that only after giving two years notice!

There is much more to the policy implications of the new theory, but I will stop here, also leaving its results relating to empirical research for discussion elsewhere.

Let me only say in closing that I hope I have adequately justified my characterization of the new theory as a rebellion or an uprising. I believe it offers a host of new analytical methods, new tasks for empirical research, and new results. It permits reexamination of the domain of the invisible hand, yields contributions to the theory of oligopoly, provides a standard for policy that is far broader and more widely applicable than that of perfect competition, and leads to a theory that analyzes the determination of industry structure endogenously and simultaneously with the analysis of the other variables more traditionally treated in the theory of the firm and the industry. It aspires to provide no less than a unifying theory as a foundation for the analysis of industrial organization. I will perhaps be excused for feeling that this was an ambitious undertaking.

REFERENCES

Bain, Joe S., *Barriers to New Competition*, Cambridge: Harvard University Press, 1956.

Baumol, William J., Bailey, Elizabeth E., and Willig, Robert D., "Weak Invisible Hand Theorems on the Sustainability of Multiproduct Natural Monopoly," *American Economic Review*, June 1977, *67*, 350–65.

_____, Panzar, John C., and Willig, Robert D., *Contestable Markets and the Theory of Industry Structure*, San Diego: Harcourt Brace Jovanovich, 1982.

Bertrand, Jules, Review of *Théorie Mathematique de la Richesse* and *Récherches sur les Principes Mathématiques de la théorie des Richesses*, *Journal des Savants*, 1883, 499–508.

Cournot, A. A., *Researches into the Mathematical Principles of the Theory of Wealth*, New York: A. M. Kelley, 1938; 1960.

Demsetz, Harold, "Why Regulate Utilities?," *Journal of Law and Economics*, April 1968, *11*, 55–65.

Fama, Eugene F. and Laffer, Arthur B., "The Number of Firms and Competition," *American Economic Review*, September 1972, *62*, 670–74.

Panzar, John C. and Willig, Robert D., "Free Entry and the Sustainability of Natural Monopoly," *Bell Journal of Economics*, Spring 1977, *8*, 1–22.

ten Raa, Thijs, "A Theory of Value and Industry Structure," unpublished doctoral dissertation, New York University, 1980.

Reprinted from

THE AMERICAN ECONOMIC REVIEW

[15]

Reprinted for private circulation from

THE JOURNAL OF POLITICAL ECONOMY

Vol. LXVI, No. 3, June 1958

PRINTED IN U.S.A.

NEW DEVELOPMENTS ON THE OLIGOPOLY FRONT[1]

FRANCO MODIGLIANI

Carnegie Institute of Technology

I

IN MY opinion the two books reviewed in this article represent a welcome major breakthrough on the oligopoly front. These two contributions, which appeared almost simultaneously, though clearly quite independently, have much in common in their basic models and method of approach to the problem. But, fortunately, they do not significantly repeat each other; for, having started from the same point of departure, the authors have followed divergent paths, exploring different implications of the same basic model.

Sylos deals almost exclusively with *homogeneous* oligopoly defined as a situation in which all producers, actual and potential, are able to supply the identical commodity (more generally, commodities that are perfect substitutes for each other) and have access to the very same long-run cost function. He thus focuses on barriers to entry resulting from economies of scale. Bain, on the other hand, also analyzes the effect of competitors being altogether unable to produce perfect substitutes—that is, product-differentiation barriers—or being able to do so only at higher costs—absolute cost-advantage barriers. Furthermore, Bain's book is greatly enriched by fascinating empirical data, painstakingly collected

through a variety of means, and by a courageous attempt at an empirical verification of the implications of his model. However, Bain is concerned primarily with the analysis of long-run market equilibrium, while Sylos devotes more than half of his book to examining the implications of his model for many other issues, such as (1) the effect of short-run or cyclical variations in demand and costs, (2) the validity of the so-called full-cost pricing model, (3) the effect of technological progress, and (4) the impact of oligopolistic structures on the formation and reabsorption of unemployment. His analysis is primarily theoretical and does not purport to provide new empirical evidence, with one rather significant exception. In an appendix to the introductory chapter Sylos presents indexes of concentration for various sectors of the American economy, based on the Gini coefficient.[2] Sylos finds that, according to this measure, concentration has tended to increase appreciably over the period considered—generally from the first decade of the century to the end of the 1940's—for all but one of the distributions analyzed. These include the distribution of plants by value added and by value of sales for manufacturing as a whole and by size of labor force for all manufacturing and for selected industries[3] and the distribution of cor-

[1] A review article of Paolo Sylos Labini, *Oligopolio e progresso tecnico* ("Oligopoly and Technical Progress"). Milan: Giuffrè, 1957. Pp. 207. L. 1,000. Joe S. Bain, *Barriers to New Competition*. Cambridge, Mass.: Harvard University Press, 1956. Pp. xi+329. $5.50. A preliminary edition of Sylos' book was published in 1956 for limited circulation. References in this article are to the final edition.

[2] The Gini coefficient is a measure of the area lying between the actual Lorenz curve and the equidistribution Lorenz curve.

[3] The individual industries, chosen on the ground that their definition has remained reasonably stable over time, are: (1) steel works and rolling mills;

porations by size of assets. These findings are rather striking, since they run counter to widely accepted views based on well-known studies of the share of the market of the four or eight largest firms. They will undoubtedly deserve close scrutiny by the experts on the subject.

It would be impossible within the scope of a review article to summarize adequately the content of both books and take a good look at the promising new horizons they open. Under these conditions it appears wise to devote primary attention to Sylos' work. The reader can do full justice to Bain's contribution by reading the original, while in the case of Sylos this possibility is open only to the "happy few." With respect to Bain's book, therefore, my only goal will be to whet the reader's appetite.

II

Until quite recently little systematic attention has been paid in the analysis of monopoly and oligopoly to the role of entry, that is, to the behavior of potential competitors. This neglect is justified for monopoly, which is generally defined as the case of a single actual as well as potential producer whose demand curve is not significantly influenced, either in the short or in the long run, by his price policy. Oligopoly could also be defined to exclude entry, fewness being then the result of the impossibility, for firms not now in the group, of producing the commodity—whether for physical or legal reasons. And, undoubtedly, the impossibility of entry is frequently

at least implicitly assumed in the analysis of oligopoly, following the venerable example of Cournot, with his owners of mineral wells. But such a narrow definition leaves out the far more interesting case where fewness is the result of purely economic forces, entry being prevented by—and within the limits of—certain price-output policies of existing producers. This is precisely the essence of homogeneous oligopoly analyzed by both Sylos and Bain.

One might suppose that, as long as potential entrants have access to a long-run cost function identical in all respects to that of existing firms, entry must tend to occur whenever the market price is higher than the minimum long-run average cost. (Cost is used hereafter in the sense of opportunity cost, including therefore an appropriate allowance for "normal" profits.) But then long-run market equilibrium would have to involve a price equal to minimum average cost and a corresponding output[4] and would be undistinguishable from perfectly competitive equilibrium. This supposition is, however, invalid whenever the output of an optimum size firm represents a "non-insignificant" fraction of pre-entry output. The price that is relevant to the potential entrant is the price *after* entry. Even if the pre-entry price is above the lowest achievable cost, the additional output he proposes to sell may drive the price below cost, making the entry unprofitable.

Unfortunately for the theorist, the exact anticipated effect of the entry on

(2) electrical machinery; (3) petroleum refining; (4) lumber and timber products; and (5) shipbuilding and iron and steel. For these industries indexes are given for 1914 and 1947. The distribution for lumber is the single instance in which concentration has decreased.

[4] This is, in fact, the conclusion reached by H. R. Edwards, "Price Formation in Manufacturing Industry and Excess Capacity," *Oxford Economic Papers*, VII, No. 1 (February, 1955), 194–218, sec. 4.2, which is, in turn, an elaboration of the model developed by P. W. S. Andrews in *Manufacturing Business* (London: Macmillan & Co., 1949). In other respects Edwards' stimulating analysis anticipates many of the conclusions of Sylos and Bain.

NEW DEVELOPMENTS ON THE OLIGOPOLY FRONT 217

price is not independent of the (anticipated) reaction of existing producers. The more they are willing to contract their output in response to the entry, the smaller will be the fall in price; in the limiting case the price may even be completely unaffected. Both authors have wisely refused to be stopped by this difficulty. They have instead proceeded to explore systematically the implications of the following well-defined assumption: that potential entrants behave as though they expected existing firms to adopt the policy most unfavorable to them, namely, the policy of maintaining output while reducing the price (or accepting reductions) to the extent required to enforce such an output policy. I shall refer to this assumption as "Sylos' postulate" because it underlies, more or less explicitly, most of his analysis, whereas Bain has also paid some attention to the possibility of potential entrants, assuming a less belligerent behavior on the part of existing firms.

The significance of Sylos' postulate lies in the fact that it enables us to find a definite solution to the problem of long-run equilibrium price and output under homogeneous oligopoly, or at least a definite upper limit to the price, to be denoted by P_0 and a corresponding lower limit to aggregate output, say, X_0. Both authors have essentially reached this conclusion, though through somewhat different routes.

I shall not attempt to reproduce faithfully their respective arguments, but shall instead concentrate on developing the logical essence of their approach. To this end, let $X = D(P)$ denote the market demand curve for the product and let P' denote the pre-entry price, $X' = D(P')$ being then the corresponding aggregate output. Under Sylos' postulate the prospective entrant is confronted not by an infinitely elastic demand at the price P' but by a sloping demand curve which is simply *the segment of the demand curve to the right of* P'. I shall refer to this segment as the marginal demand curve. Note that it is uniquely determined by the original demand curve and the pre-entry price P'. Suppose P' to be such that the corresponding marginal demand curve is *everywhere* below *the* long-run average cost function. Clearly, under these conditions, entry will not be profitable; that is, such a P' is an *entry-preventing price*. The critical price P_0 is then simply the *highest* entry-preventing price, and the critical output X_0 is the corresponding aggregate demand, $D(P_0)$. Under perfect competition, where the output of an optimum size firm is negligible relative to market demand, the marginal demand curve is itself infinitely elastic *in the relevant range;* hence the familiar conclusion that the long-run equilibrium price cannot exceed minimum average cost. But, where the output of an optimum plant is not negligible, P_0 will exceed minimum cost to an extent which depends on the nature of the demand and the long-run cost function.

In order to explore the factors controlling P_0, let us denote by $\bar{x}$ the optimum scale of output, that is, the scale corresponding to the lowest point of the long-run average cost curve. (If this scale is not unique, $\bar{x}$ will mean the smallest scale consistent with minimum cost.) If k denotes the corresponding minimum average cost, then the perfectly competitive equilibrium price is $P_c = k$, and the corresponding equilibrium output is $X_c = D(P_c) = D(k)$. Finally, let us define the size of the market, S, as the ratio of the competitive output to the optimum scale; $S = X_c/\bar{x}$. (This definition is not the same as that of either

Sylos or Bain; it appears, however, to be the most convenient for theoretical purposes, even though it may have drawbacks for empirical investigations.)

Now, following Bain, consider first the simplest case in which the technology of the industry is such that, at a scale less than $\bar{x}$, costs are prohibitively high, so that an entrant can come in only at a scale $\bar{x}$ or larger. In this case the entry-preventing output X_0 is readily found to be

$$X_0 = X_c - \bar{x} = X_c\left(1 - \frac{\bar{x}}{X_c}\right)$$
$$= X_c\left(1 - \frac{1}{S}\right), \tag{1}$$

or $(100/S)$ per cent below the competitive output. Suppose in fact that aggregate output were smaller; it would then be profitable for a firm of scale $\bar{x}$ to enter. Indeed, the post-entry output would then still be smaller than X_c, and hence the post-entry price would be larger than P_c, which is in turn equal to the entrant's average cost. By the same reasoning an output X_0 (or larger) would make entry unattractive. The critical price P_0 corresponding to X_0 can be read from the demand curve or found by solving for P the equation $X_0 = D(P)$. The relation between P_0 and the competitive equilibrium price P_c can be stated (approximately) in terms of the elasticity of demand in the neighborhood of P_c; if we denote this elasticity by η, we have

$$P_0 \simeq P_c\left(1 + \frac{1}{\eta S}\right),$$

or $100/\eta S$ per cent above P_c.[5]

We can now replace the very special

cost function assumed so far with the more conventional one, falling, more or less gradually, at least up to $\bar{x}$. In this general case the critical output may be somewhat larger, and the critical price may be lower, than indicated in the previous paragraph. Indeed, while at the output X_0 given by (1) it is not profitable to enter at the scale $\bar{x}$, it *may* still be profitable to come in at a *smaller* scale.

This possibility and its implications can be conveniently analyzed by means of the graphical apparatus presented in Figure 1. (This graphical device is not to be found in either of the books under review, but I believe that it is quite helpful in bringing out the essence of the authors' arguments.)[6] In panels *IA* and *IIA*, the light lines falling from left to right are the (relevant portions of the) market demand curve. For the sake of generality it is convenient to take $\bar{x}$ (the optimum scale) as the unit of measurement for output X and to take k (the corresponding minimum cost) as the unit of measurement for price, P. It follows that the competitive equilibrium price is, by definition, unity, while the corresponding output is precisely the size of the market S. Thus panel *IA* of Figure 1 relates to an industry of size 2 and panel *IIA* to an industry of size 10. The two demand curves have constant unit elasticity in the range shown, but, as will become apparent, the effect of different assumptions about the elasticity of demand can readily be handled.

The two heavy lines in each of the two panels represent alternative cost curves, graphed on the same scale as the demand curve, for outputs up to $\bar{x}$ (that is, for values of X up to 1). Because of the choice of units, each curve shows the

---

[5] This approximation will not be very satisfactory for small values of S. In particular, if the demand curve has constant elasticity, then, for small values of S, the extent of price rise will be significantly underestimated.

[6] In the case of Sylos, I am less sure of my ground, since his argument rests almost entirely on a detailed analysis of two numerical examples.

NEW DEVELOPMENTS ON THE OLIGOPOLY FRONT   219

behavior of costs, in percentage of minimum cost, as a function of plant scale, expressed in percentage of optimum scale. The steeper of the two curves is the kind of traditional, well-behaved cost function that underlies Bain's analysis and involves marked economies of scale. It is, in fact, based on the information reported by him for the cement industry, which appears to have more marked economies of scale than any other of the twenty industries analyzed in his book. It is obtained by joining with a smooth curve the data provided there for discrete scale sizes. The other cost curve, involving less pronounced economies of scale, depicts the kind of cost function that underlies Sylos' numerical examples. Sylos explicitly assumes, on grounds of presumed realism, the existence of very pronounced discontinuities in the available technologies. Plants can thus have only sizes that are very specific and far apart—only three sizes in his examples and in my graph. The rounded

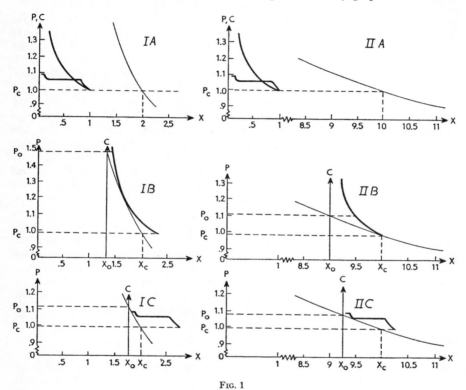

Fig. 1

portions of the curve result from the fact that, beyond certain critical outputs, it pays to shift to a plant of a larger size, even though such a plant could not be utilized to capacity.[7]

[7] If Sylos' assumption is taken literally, the portions of the curves shown as straight lines parallel to the X-axis should really have a scalloped shape. This refinement can, however, be ignored, since it does not affect the results.

220   FRANCO MODIGLIANI

The critical price and output, P_0 and X_0, for a given cost curve can now be readily located by means of the following simple device. Slide the cost curve to the right parallel to itself, together with its co-ordinate axis, until no point of this curve lies inside the demand curve. This step is illustrated in panels IB and IIB for the steeper cost curve and in panels IC and IIC for the flatter one. The point at which the Y-axis so displaced cuts the demand curve represents P_0; the point at which it cuts the X-axis is X_0. For, clearly, the portion of the demand curve to the right of the displaced axis is precisely the marginal demand curve when the aggregate output of the existing firms is X_0. If the cost curve is nowhere below this marginal demand curve, there is no possibility of profits for a new entrant.

As can be seen from Figure 1, the cost curve in its terminal position may be either tangent to the demand curve, as in IB, or may touch it at a "corner," as in IC and IIC, or, finally, may touch it at its lower extreme, as in IIB.[8] The X co-ordinate of the point where the two curves touch, referred to the axis of the cost curve, indicates the size of firm which represents the most immediate threat of entry. Where this immediate threat comes from an optimum size plant, as in IIB, X_0 is precisely that given by formula (1) above; it is now seen that this possibility represents a limiting case—and that, in general, the formula provides only a lower bound to X_0.

With the help of Figure 1 we can also establish several interesting propositions in comparative statics. First, by comparing panel IB with IC and IIB

with IIC, we see that, for given market size, P_0 will tend to be higher the steeper the cost curve, that is, the greater the economies of scale. The common sense of this result is apparent: when economies of scale are important, the effective threat will tend to come from large-scale plants, which must widen the gap between X_0 and X_c. Similarly, by comparing IB with IIB and IC with IIC, it appears that, for a given cost curve and elasticity of demand, P_0 will tend to fall with the size of the market; it will, in fact, approach unity (the competitive price) as the size of the market approaches infinity. Furthermore, since, for given size S, a higher elasticity of demand implies a rotation of the cost curve in a counterclockwise direction around the competitive point, it is apparent that a higher elasticity will act in the same direction as a larger size with given elasticity; that is, it will tend to lower P_0.

In summary, under Sylos' postulate there is a well-defined, maximum premium that the oligopolists can command over the competitive price, and this premium tends to increase with the importance of economies of scale and to decrease with the size of market and the elasticity of demand.[9]

III

I have now laid down the basic long-run equilibrium model common to both Bain and Sylos. Hereafter, their roads part, and I shall first follow Sylos in his explorations of some of the fascinating implications of the model.

The first of these implications refers to the size distribution of firms (or, more

---

[8] It may, of course, also have several discrete points of contact with the demand curve or overlap a portion of it.

[9] As Bain points out, it is conceivable, though not likely, that P_0 will be higher than the price that "maximizes the profit" of the existing firms, in which case it will have no bearing on long-run equilibrium. See below, Sec. VIII.

precisely, of plants) within the group—its *internal structure*, as I shall call it. If we look, for example, at panel *IC*, we see that the price P_0 is considerably above the average cost of the medium-size firms and even slightly above that of the smallest. If then any such firm *happened* to be a member of the group—Sylos here, in good Walrasian tradition, speaks of the initial structure as "criée par hasard"—it could survive and even prosper.

But would it not be profitable for the larger firms to expand, eliminating the smaller ones and securing for themselves the small firms' share of the market? In Sylos' model this possibility can be largely dismissed, thanks to his assumption of sharp technological discontinuities. Suppose, for instance, that there are only two possible scales: (*a*) large plants, producing 10,000 units, and (*b*) small plants, producing 500 units. Suppose further that X_0 is 15,000 and that this output is initially produced by one large firm and ten small ones. There is, then, no real incentive for the large firm to drive the small ones out of the market, for, in order to produce the extra 5,000 units, it would, in fact, have to operate ten small plants (at least as long as the average cost of a small plant is less than the average incremental cost of producing an extra 5,000 units by operating two large plants at 75 per cent of capacity). But the cost of a small firm must be such as to yield very little, if any, abnormal profit at the price P_0. In fact, this price must be such as not to give an inducement to enter the market with a small plant. Hence there will generally be no incentive for the large firm to undertake the price war necessary to eliminate the smaller firms.

If there existed a technology of inter-

mediate size, say, size 5,000, the situation might look somewhat different, since at price P_0 such a plant would make some profits. However, even in this case the elimination of small firms would involve a costly price war. The price would have to be kept below prime cost of the small firms for a time long enough to induce them to fold up or below their average cost until their fixed plant wears out. Sylos suggests that usually the war will not be worth the prize and that it will be preferable for the larger firms not to disturb the delicate balance that always prevails in a homogeneous oligopoly structure.

Are we then to conclude that any structure, "criée par hasard," will tend to perpetuate itself as long as it is consistent with a price not higher than P_0? Sylos does not investigate this issue systematically, confining himself to illustrating various possibilities on the basis of his specific numerical examples. I suggest, however, that with the help of Sylos' model it is possible to throw some interesting light on this question. To this end I shall first introduce a definition. Consider any two structures *A* and *B* consistent with no inducement to entry: let us say that *A* is more rational than *B* if the total profits accruing to the members of the group are larger under structure *A* than under *B*.[10] It follows from this definition and our previous analysis that there exists a *most rational* structure, namely, that structure (not necessarily unique) which produces at the smallest total cost the output X_0 that can be sold at price P_0.[11] This

[10] It is apparent that this notion bears a close affinity to that of *dominance* in the theory of games.

[11] This statement is valid only to a first approximation. It is possible that the output X_0 cannot be produced with an integral number of plants of various sizes working at capacity, in which case profit maximization may involve an output somewhat

most rational structure has two features worth mentioning. (1) From a welfare point of view, it has certain optimal properties in that X_0 is being produced at the smallest (social) cost; but it still involves a departure from the usual conditions of Pareto optimality in that the output X_0 is, generally, too small and P_0 too high. (2) From a technological point of view, it has the property that the total capacity of the plants of a given size must necessarily be no larger than the capacity of one plant of the next larger size.

It seems reasonable to suppose that, if a structure B is less rational than a structure A, it will be less likely to be observed. For there is some incentive to a shift from B to A, since such a shift is accompanied by a net gain; that is, losses, if any, are more than compensated by gains. But there will be no corresponding incentive to move back from A to B. It does not follow, however, that structures other than the most rational have no chance at all of ever existing or surviving. As Sylos rightly points out, moving from one structure to another generally involves costs—at best, the cost of reaching an agreement; at worst, that of war—and the potential gain may not be worth the cost, especially when the gain, and even more the cost, may be problematic and uncertain.

The conclusions to which we are led are therefore, as it were, of a probabilistic nature. Less rational structures are less likely to be observed than more rational ones, and very irrational structures are unlikely to maintain themselves for any length of time. But certainly structures

other than the most rational can exist and survive, especially in a world that is moving and in which the most rational structure is itself continuously changing. Similar considerations apply to the price; while we should not expect prices higher that P_0 to be long maintainable, lower prices may have a certain degree of permanence. But, again, a gap between P and P_0 will provide a stimulus to reorganization of the structure, and this stimulus will be more powerful, and hence more likely to produce a response, the greater the gap.

By drawing together the analysis of market equilibrium and that of internal structure, we may venture some tentative conclusions about the factors which, according to Sylos' model, tend to control the degree of scatter in the size distributions of firms. We already know that only those sizes can survive whose average cost is no larger than P_0. From an analysis of the figure it can therefore be inferred that the possible range of the scatter of sizes will tend to be greater the smaller (a) the economies of scale, (b) the size of the markets, and (c) the elasticity of demand.

These implications, as well as those relating to P_0, are in principle testable. Indeed, it is to both Bain's and Sylos' credit that, by moving us away from conjectural variations and similar subjective notions and focusing instead on objective market and technological data, they have provided us with theories rich in empirical content and capable of being disproved by the evidence. To be sure, such tests may not be easy to carry out, especially with the information presently available, as is amply attested by Bain's gallant efforts in this direction. But, with a clear theoretical framework available as a guide in the collection of data, one may hope that more reliable

---

above X_0. However, the departure from X_0 will tend to be negligible, at least as long as the output of the smallest size consistent with P_0 represents a minor fraction of X_0.

and abundant evidence will sooner or later accumulate.

Even at this stage, ingenuity can do much to remedy inadequacies of the data. For instance, in order to compute the actual value of P for a given industry, one would need to know not only the market price but also the minimum average cost of an optimal plant. Bain ingeniously suggests that, even in the absence of precise information on this point, some notion of the relative height of P for various industries may be gotten by ranking them in terms of the rate of profits of the largest firms in each industry, since the average cost of such firms will presumably tend to be reasonably close to the minimum.[12] It should be noted, however, that, contrary to what Bain seems to imply in some of his empirical tests, there is no reason to expect any simple association between P_0 (or its proxy, the rate of profit) and the degree of scatter in plant sizes, at least within Sylos' model. While it is true that a large scatter is not to be

expected when P_0 is very close to unity— for then only firms of near-optimum size can survive—it does not follow that there is a positive association between P_0 and scatter. The only safe statement we can make is that, for given P_0, the scatter should tend to be smaller the steeper the cost curve and that, for given cost curve, the association between P_0 and scatter should be positive, both variables tending to decline as the size of the market and the elasticity of demand increase. A cursory examination of Bain's data for those industries in which product-differentiation and absolute-cost advantages are not supposed to be dominant does not seem to contradict this inference conspicuously. Unfortunately, the data in question provide no information on the elasticity of demand and, what is more serious, leave too much room for personal judgment in ranking industries in terms of any variable.

IV

It is tempting to explore the extent to which the implications we have derived from Sylos' model would be affected if we relaxed some of his very rigid assumptions. This question is especially pressing with respect to his assumption of technological discontinuities. Indeed, Bain has emerged from his empirical investigation with a strong conviction that, although there exists a fairly definite scale $\bar{x}$ at which average cost reaches its minimum, costs do not generally tend to rise for scales larger than $\bar{x}$. This possibility in no way affects our analysis of long-run equilibrium price and output but has considerable bearing on the conclusions concerning the size structure. Clearly, under a Bain-type cost function, the "most rational structure" must be such that all the output X_0 is produced by plants of size $\bar{x}$ or

[12] In his book and in earlier contributions Bain measures the rate of profit as the rate of return, net of taxes, on the book value of equity. It would seem preferable to use the rate of return before taxes and interest on the book value of assets, since such a measure is not affected by financial structure. Perhaps a still more relevant measure, for the purpose of testing the model, could be derived from the rate of profit on sales. In fact, letting p denote the market price, we have

$$P = \frac{p}{k} = \frac{px}{kx} = \frac{\text{Sales}}{\text{Sales} - \text{Profit}} = \frac{1}{1 - \dfrac{\text{Profit}}{\text{Sales}}}.$$

By profit I mean here earnings over and above a "normal" rate of return on the book value of assets, which may not be easy to estimate in practice. One may also have some reservations about the assumption that minimum long-run average cost can be approximated from the actual average cost of the dominant firms in the industry. Franklyn Fisher has suggested that a better approximation may be obtained by utilizing, at least as supplementary evidence, the rate of profit on sales of the most profitable firms.

larger. It would follow that structures involving smaller plant sizes would tend to be unstable, especially where the cost function is steep in the range of (relative) costs from 1 to P_0.

The reader can decide for himself just how serious this conclusion is for Sylos' construction.[13] I shall limit myself to suggesting that Sylos' case may be considerably strengthened when we recognize the existence of product differentiation of a type not altogether inconsistent with the notion of homogeneous oligopoly, such as spatial differentiation or modifications in product design to meet customers' specifications. Under these conditions the area of the market supplied by smaller firms may be such that the dominant firms would have little to gain by capturing it, either because they have no cost advantage or because this would require an unprofitable price policy on other lines of product.

Consider, for example, the case of spatial differentiation. Suppose the large firm has a cost of 10 and the cost of transportation to a given distant market is 1. Suppose further that the highest f.o.b. price preventing entry that the large firm can charge is 12. The delivered price in the given market is then 13, and it may well be that, at this price, the market can be profitably supplied by a small local firm at, say, a cost of 12.5. In order to capture that relatively small market, the large firm would have to keep the price well below 11.5 for some considerable length of time and then keep it no higher than 11.5 in-

definitely—a policy which may well be unprofitable.[14] There is thus room for smaller firms in the industry, but this room is generated by market "exploitation" on the part of the large firm, and all customers are paying a higher price (by 2 per unit) than under competitive equilibrium.

Consider next the case of product modifications. It may well be that a class of customers is willing to pay an extra premium of 1 for a specific variation of the standard product. If the large firm charges 12 for the standard line, even though it has a cost of 10, these customers are therefore willing to pay 13. Now, suppose that, given the size of the market for the specialty, the average cost of the product is again, say, 12.5, whether it is produced by the larger firm or by a smaller one specializing in that line. If such a smaller firm exists, it is not worthwhile for the large firm to try to capture the market. But note once more that the existence of the smaller firm is made possible by the larger firm's oligopoly power. Under competitive conditions the small firm could not exist, since, if customers could get the standard product for 10, they would not be willing to pay enough for the specialty to cover its production cost of 12.5.

In short, in many situations the presence of a variety of sizes may be rendered reasonably stable by the fact that the larger firms find it advantageous to skim the fattest segment of the market, leav-

---

[13] Rosenstein-Rodan has pointed out to me that Bain's long-run cost function may not be too relevant where plant is very long lived. For, even though it may be possible to design a plant having cost k at sizes larger than $\bar{x}$, nonetheless an existing firm wishing to undertake a moderate expansion may have to utilize a smaller-scale technique with higher costs.

[14] It is assumed that the alternative, and more profitable, course of quoting a delivered price of 12.5 is not available. It is interesting to note in this connection that the prohibition of freight absorption as an antitrust measure will have a desirable effect if it induces the producer to choose a lower price in order not to lose distant markets to smaller local firms but that it will have an undesirable outcome if the producer finds it more advantageous to abandon those markets, in which case the demand will be supplied at a higher social cost.

NEW DEVELOPMENTS ON THE OLIGOPOLY FRONT 225

ing it for smaller firms to supply less profitable pockets. Nor should one forget altogether, even within the realm of pure theory, the public relations advantages that tend to accrue to the large firms from the coexistence of smaller and weaker partners. The argument that prices cannot be lowered without playing havoc with large numbers of honest and industrious small enterprises is always one of great public appeal. And, where antitrust laws are a potential threat, the advantages of having smaller competitors is even more evident.[15]

V

Before closing the subject of long-run static analysis, I must report one more observation on which Sylos lays a great deal of stress and which has to do with the effects of technological progress. While improvements in technology that are applicable to all scales must necessarily tend to depress price and expand output, he argues that improvements applicable only at, or near, the largest scale will not affect the critical price and hence will tend to result in higher profits for the larger firms. Furthermore, Sylos seems to feel that technological changes are very commonly of

this type, and he is inclined to account in this fashion for a presumed tendency of the profit margin of large firms to grow over time. Here, however, I cannot avoid feeling that Sylos is going too far. For, in the first place, even a change that affects only the largest scale may well lower P_0 when the immediate threat is, in fact, from firms of size $\bar{x}$; and, in the second place, any innovation that affects only plants of suboptimal size (and such innovations are by no means inconceivable) will also result in a fall in the critical price and thus will reduce the profit of the largest firms whose costs have remained unchanged. There is therefore serious doubt whether Sylos' argument can account for a long-run relative rise in large firms' profits, not to mention the equally serious doubt whether such a relative rise has in fact occurred. The model does suggest, however, that changes in technology may cause radical changes in the most rational structure and thus eventually may lead to pervasive changes in the actual structure, including the possible elimination of whole layers of small-scale plants.

VI

I now proceed to consider with Sylos some implications of the model for the effect of short-run changes in demand and cost conditions. Note, first, that in the analysis of market equilibrium I have made no mention of the standard categories of monopolistic competition theories, namely, marginal cost and marginal revenue. To be sure, with sufficient ingenuity, the analysis could be forced into that cast,[16] but such an undertaking would be merely an exercise in semantics

---

[15] The considerations of this section clearly point to the importance of factors other than those discussed in Sec. III above in controlling the scatter of the size distribution of firms and plants. In particular, under a Bain-type cost function, the model has nothing to say about the size distribution of firms above the optimum size $\bar{x}$. Here one may have to fall back on stochastic models of the type advanced, for example, by H. Simon in *Models of Man* (New York: John Wiley & Sons, 1957), chap. ix. In any event the analysis presented casts most serious doubts on the argument advanced by some authors and well exemplified by the following quotation: "Actually, we find that in most industries firms of very different sizes survive, and we may infer that commonly there is no large advantage or disadvantage to size over a very considerable range of outputs" (George Stigler, *The Theory of Price* [New York: Macmillan Co., 1952], p. 144).

[16] For such an attempt see, for example, J. R. Hicks, "The Process of Imperfect Competition." *Oxford Economic Papers*, VI (February, 1954), 41–54.

and formal logic and would in no way increase our understanding of what is involved. On the other hand, our result can readily be recast in the framework of the so-called full-cost pricing principle. According to this principle, prices are determined by adding to prime cost a markup to cover overhead per unit and by adding further an "appropriate" profit margin. So far, however, it has never been convincingly explained just at what level of output the overhead charge is computed or what determines the "appropriate" profit margin. Sylos' and Bain's models do provide answers to both questions. The large firms, which typically set the pace in the market, must base their price on long-run average cost (so that the overhead must normally be computed at capacity operation, with due allowance for normal seasonal and cyclical variations in the rate of utilization) and apply to this cost the largest profit markup that "the traffic will bear," namely, the markup P_0—for P_0, it will be recalled, is precisely the ratio of the highest possible price to average cost.

The usefulness of translating the result of the static analysis into the language of full-cost pricing becomes fully apparent when we proceed to examine the effects of a variation, say, an increase, in some element of prime cost. Such a change will generally affect all firms and hence will raise the long-run cost curve more or less uniformly. This development in turn will raise the level of the critical price and make it profitable to raise the actual price to this new level. Now it can be verified that, at least for moderate variations in costs and well-behaved demand functions, a good approximation of the new critical price can be obtained precisely by adding to the new average cost the very same profit margin that prevailed before the

change; and nearly as good an approximation can be obtained by applying to the new prime cost the original total percentage markup. Thus full-cost pricing may well represent a very useful rule of thumb in reacting to cost changes affecting the entire industry, at least as long as such changes are not too drastic.

Now that we have a solid rationale for the full-cost principle, we need not have qualms about acknowledging two other sets of factors that tend to give it further sanction. (1) In an oligopolistic situation, with its precarious internal equilibrium, there is much to be gained from simple and widely understood rules of thumb, which minimize the danger of behavior intended to be peaceful and cooperative being misunderstood as predatory or retaliatory.[17] (2) The experience of those who, like myself, have conducted extensive personal interviews with executives suggests that these respondents have a strong propensity to explain their behavior in terms of simple mechanical principles, especially when they feel that these principles are blessed by general respectability.

So much about the effect of variations in costs. Let us now turn to the effect of cyclical variations in demand. For the sake of concreteness, let us start out from the prosperity phase, in which plants are being operated at, or near, capacity rates. If the demand curve now shifts to the left as a result of a fall in aggregate income, our model suggests that the optimum markup may have a slight tendency to increase. There are two main reasons for this contention:

[17] See, for example, A. Henderson, "The Theory of Duopoly," *Quarterly Journal of Economics*, LXVIII (November, 1954), 576–79, Sec. VII, and T. C. Schelling "Bargaining, Communication, and Limited War," *Conflict Resolution*, I (March, 1957), 19–36.

NEW DEVELOPMENTS ON THE OLIGOPOLY FRONT 227

(1) the critical price P_0 tends to rise when the size of the market falls and (2), with substantial idle capacity and sharply reduced profits, or even losses, prevailing in the industry, even a price somewhat higher than P_0 is not likely to encourage entry, especially where the effective threat is from plants large enough to require a substantial investment. This tendency for the critical markup to rise may partly be offset or even more than offset if, as the demand shifts, its elasticity increases; it will be reinforced if the elasticity falls—a case which Sylos regards as more typical, though, in our view, not very convincingly.

On the whole, then, the critical price P_0 may have some mild tendency to rise; but this does not mean that the actual markup will necessarily rise, for, with much idle capacity, the temptation for individual members of the oligopolistic group to secure a larger share of the shrunken business is very strong. Thus the self-discipline of the group may well tend to break down, with a resultant fall in the effective price if not in the officially quoted one.

In the course of the recovery the markup will of course tend to retrace the path followed in the contraction. But here some new interesting possibilities arise which Sylos himself has not considered. In an expanding economy the recovery will tend to push demand to levels higher than previous peaks. As a result of a rise in demand that is rapid and larger than expected, or as a result of circumstances beyond its control, such as war, the industry may be caught with capacity inadequate to satisfy the demand at the critical price P_0. In terms of traditional patterns of thinking, one would expect firms in the industry to be eager to exploit the situation by charging higher prices. But such

a price policy may not be so appealing to the larger firms whose long-run interest is to secure for themselves as much as possible of the additional demand at the profitable price P_0. A higher price may tend to encourage entry, which would not only reduce their share but possibly also threaten the maintenance of self-discipline in periods of depressed demand. Thus the dominant firms may have an incentive to "hold the price line" by such devices as lengthening delivery schedules and informal rationing (even at the risk of gray markets), while at the same time expanding capacity—but only to an extent that seems warranted by the anticipated long-run demand at the price P_0. These considerations may help to explain the otherwise rather puzzling behavior of certain important sectors of the economy in the early postwar period.[18]

On the whole it would appear that no very definite general conclusion can be reached about the cyclical behavior of the markup, although the model may have a good deal to say for well-defined classes of situations. One might, however, go along with Sylos on the following two tentative generalizations: (1) on the average, the markup is not likely to change much in the course of the cycle, but one should expect some scatter around this central tendency, and (2)

---

[18] A similar explanation is advanced in Edwards, *op. cit.*, and in Kuh and Meyer, *The Investment Decision* (Cambridge, Mass.: Harvard University Press, 1957), esp. chap. xii. It has also been suggested that the price policies in question may be explained by the concern that higher prices and consequent higher profits would have led to irresistible pressure for wage concessions, difficult to reverse. By contrast, the abnormally high profits of dealers or gray-market operators could be counted on to disappear automatically as the supply gradually caught up with demand. I am indebted to Albert G. Hart and Richard Cyert for stimulating discussions on the relevance of Sylos' model to the explanation of the postwar experience.

prices should tend on the average to fluctuate more in relation to prime cost where there is more chance for the discipline of the group to break down, and this chance presumably should tend to increase with the size of the group and decrease with degree of concentration (in Sylos' sense). These generalizations appear to be consistent with the evidence assembled by Stigler in his well-known criticism of the kinky demand curve,[19] though they may be less easy to reconcile with certain empirical studies of price flexibility.[20]

Sylos attempts to dispose of the latter evidence by an ingenious argument which is not entirely convincing in this context but which is of interest on its own merit. Specifically, he suggests that, where the full-cost principle is widely adhered to, it may be in the interest of the larger firms to sustain the prices of factors entering into prime cost; in fact, provided that the shifted demand curve has a sufficiently low elasticity, such a policy will increase the over-all profit of the industry. Where the large firms are themselves important producers of some critical raw materials, they may best achieve this purpose by sustaining these particular prices; where this is not possible, they may acquiesce to an increase in real wages.[21] However, the advantage of an increase in prime costs is realized only where full-cost pricing is adhered to in spite of widespread excess capacity. Hence this policy can be sensi-

ble only where discipline is maintained, which, as suggested earlier, may be related to small number and heavy concentration. Sylos suggests that these considerations may help to explain certain empirical results indicating a positive association between cyclical wage rigidity and degree of concentration.[22]

VII

The last two parts of Sylos' book expound the thesis that monopolistic and oligopolistic market structures are an important factor contributing to the development of unemployment, especially technological unemployment. In spite of the importance of the subject, this part will be reviewed in very sketchy form, both for lack of space and because Sylos' argument is not so convincing as his partial equilibrium analysis.

The main thread of his argument in Part II seems to run as follows. Starting from a stationary situation with full employment, a labor-saving innovation initially displaces labor. The reabsorption of this unemployment requires some net saving to be invested in the equipment necessary to outfit the displaced workers. (The alternative possibility of a fall in real wages leading to an appropriate change in capital coefficients is excluded by assumption.) Under perfectly competitive market structures, the fall in cost would lead to higher real income for all those who have not lost their

[19] George Stigler, "The Kinky Oligopoly Demand Curve and Rigid Prices," *Journal of Political Economy*, LV (October, 1947), 432–49.

[20] Richard Ruggles, "The Nature of Price Flexibility and Determinants of Relative Price Changes in the Economy," in *Business Concentration and Price Policy* (A Conference of the Universities–National Bureau Committee for Economic Research [Princeton, N.J.: Princeton University Press, 1955]), pp. 441–505.

[21] Note that this argument is applicable even to long-run equilibrium analysis. That is, when the market demand is sufficiently inelastic, an increase in wage rates may increase the total excess of receipts over (opportunity) costs accruing to the group. It may then be profitable for existing firms to tolerate high wages, as long as these are enforced by a trade union strong enough to impose the same wage scale on any potential entrant.

[22] The major piece of evidence quoted in this connection is J. W. Garbarino, "A Theory of Interindustry Wage Structure Variation," *Quarterly Journal of Economics*, LXIV (May, 1950), 282–305.

employment, and this rise in real income, especially profits, supposedly produces the saving and investment necessary for the reabsorption. On the other hand, under oligopolistic structures, the fall in cost will frequently not be accompanied by a proportionate fall in prices and will thus result in an increase in the value added of the sector where costs have fallen. (I have already expressed some doubt about the validity of this conclusion in Sec. V above.) To the extent that the increase in value added is absorbed by higher wages, the necessary saving will not be forthcoming, since, by an assumption which is particularly unpalatable to me, workers have a marginal propensity to consume equal to 1. To the extent that the increase in value added results in higher profits— and even if these profits give rise to savings—there may still be difficulties. Sylos suggests in fact that the entrepreneurs to whom the profits accrue will be disinclined to invest outside their own industry, whereas the investment required should be spread throughout the economy.

The conclusion Sylos draws is that, with widespread oligopolistic market structures, the forces making for reabsorption, though not entirely absent, will be lagging and weak. In a world of continous technological change this weakness is sufficient, in his view, to account for a substantial permanent pool of unemployment, whose continuing existence is therefore an essentially dynamic phenomenon. He further argues that the kind of innovations the larger firms in the oligopolistic group will be inclined to adopt are likely to aggravate the technological displacement of labor. He maintains in fact that, though these firms will tend to be quite progressive in searching for, and adopting, innovations that cut

costs at current level of output, they will nonetheless shun improvements that would cut costs only at a large scale of operation. But this argument is not quite consistent with his own model, since the new, larger-scale, and cheaper technique may itself become the immediate threat to entry. Nor is it clearly relevant—for it does not per se establish a bias in favor of labor-saving innovations.

Part III purports to explore the implications of the previous analysis for the standard Keynesian theory of effective demand. This part again contains many interesting observations but also has its shortcomings. In particular, the author does not seem to be sufficiently aware that the implications of the analysis of Part III are profoundly different for an economy poor in capital and savings like the Italian economy and for one in which the main threat to unemployment springs from a lack of effective demand. In the former case, labor-saving innovations may indeed tend to aggravate the problem of unemployment, especially when coupled with powerful unions and downward wage rigidity. But, in the latter case, such innovations are, as it were, a blessing, since they increase the required stock of capital and thus make possible the absorption of full-employment saving.

This sketch of Parts III and IV may well fail to do justice to Sylos' argument. But such a failure would serve to confirm the earlier statement that these final chapters do not quite match the high level of performance that characterizes the rest of this remarkable book.

VIII

Let us now look briefly at that part of Bain's analysis that does not overlap Sylos'.

Still with respect to barriers from economies of scale, Bain makes a halfhearted attempt to explore the consequences of dropping Sylos' postulate (see Sec. II). Unfortunately, as long as we are dealing with homogeneous oligopoly, it is hard to find a well-defined sensible alternative. Certainly, the diametrically opposite assumption that existing firms will adopt a policy of maintaining price, by contracting their output, would generally be a rather foolish one for the entrant to make. It implies that established firms will graciously allow the entrant to carve out for himself whatever slice of the market he pleases, while suffering losses on two accounts: (1) by losing sales and (2) by incurring a higher average cost, at least in the short run and possibly even in the long run, if their original plant was of no more than optimal size. Furthermore, such a policy, if consistently followed, would unavoidably result in the original members' being gradually squeezed out of the market.

The only alternative systematically explored by Bain is for the entrant to assume that price will be maintained but only provided he is contented with a share of the market no larger than that of the existing firms—which are conveniently assumed, for this purpose, to be all of equal size. There is, then, in general, a well-defined critical price (and corresponding output) such that entry is unprofitable even if a prospective entrant proceeds on the stated "optimistic" assumption.[23]

As Bain is well aware, this alternative assumption is but one of a large class of assumptions that could be constructed and explored. But he has wisely refrained from following this line, which is rather unpromising at this stage. For the moment, at least, we must be satisfied with the conclusion that there exists a well-

defined upper limit to the price that can be maintained under oligopoly in the long run, and this upper limit is P_0, obtained under Sylos' postulate. It is the upper limit because, at a price higher than this, entry will be profitable even if the existing firms are bent on doing the entrant as much damage as they possibly can.[24] But a price lower than P_0 cannot be excluded a priori, even in the long run, especially where P_0 would cover the cost at a scale of output which represents a small fraction of X_0 and where a plant of such scale would require a relatively small investment. But, broadly speaking, these are precisely the conditions under which P_0 is close to 1, and the classical competitive model may provide a reasonable approximation. Conversely, Sylos' postulate may well provide a reasonable approximation precisely where it makes a real difference —where it implies a value of P_0 appreciably above unity.

Dropping the assumption that all producers, actual and potential, have access

[23] It is easy to verify that the stated critical price, say, p_0, and corresponding output are given by the simultaneous solution of the following two equations:

$$X = D(p) \qquad (1)$$

$$p = c\,\frac{X}{(n+1)}, \qquad (2)$$

where $c(q)$ denotes the minimum long-run average cost of producing the quantity q, and n is the number of plants. In general, p_0 is an increasing function of n and is larger than the competitive price, at least as long as n is larger than S. Furthermore, for sufficiently large n, each firm is of less than optimal size, and the equilibrium bears a close resemblance to that described by Chamberlin in *Monopolistic Competition*, chap. v, sec. 5.

[24] A somewhat higher price could conceivably be maintained if the industry produced an output smaller than X_0, but had enough capacity to produce X_0 or more and a record of readiness to exploit the extra capacity to *expand* output in the face of entry. Such behavior would presumably require more or less open collusion, of a nature likely only with a very small and well-disciplined group.

NEW DEVELOPMENTS ON THE OLIGOPOLY FRONT 231

to identical cost functions enables us to analyze another set of forces which can account for a long-run excess of price over cost, and which Bain labels "absolute cost advantages." Such differential costs, arising from factors like control of scarce resources, patents and trade secrets, and generally superior technical and managerial know-how, have already been extensively analyzed and understood in the received body of theory. They underlie the traditional theory of monopoly, oligopoly without entry, and rents. Of course, with cost differential in the picture, there is no longer a specific entry-forestalling price, even under Sylos' postulate. Rather the critical price depends on the cost of the most efficient potential entrant and, hence, on just which firms are already in the group. It may then not be in the interest of existing firms to try to prevent the entry of very efficient producers, since this might require an unprofitably low price. When the price-output policy of existing firms is not intended to discourage potential entrants, Bain speaks of "ineffectively impeded" entry, in contrast to "effectively impeded" entry, in which price and output policy is designed to make entry unprofitable, and to "blockaded entry," in which the price and output policy that is most advantageous to the group, without regard to entry, happens to make entry unattractive.

But Bain's most significant finding about absolute cost barriers is probably at the empirical level. He finds in fact that, at least for his sample of twenty industries, such barriers are generally not important. Natural scarcity appears to be a significant factor in at most two industries—copper and possibly steel. In only three other cases do patents and/or technical know-how possibly play some role and apparently not a major one.

Bain also provides a valuable tabulation of available information on the size of the investment required by a new entrant (with an optimum scale plant). These capital requirements represent a somewhat special type of barrier to entry whose possible significance has been repeatedly mentioned earlier.

The remaining barrier to entry—resulting from the inability of potential competitors to produce a commodity that is a perfect substitute for the product of existing firms—is again one that has received considerable attention in the past. Bain's new contribution in this area consists of a penetrating empirical investigation of the specific barriers that impede the production of perfect or near-perfect substitutes for each industry and their consequences. The main factors may be classified roughly as follows: (1) Allegiance to brands, supported by large advertising outlays, and possibly also, by a long record of reliability; this factor is found to provide the main barrier, and a significant one, almost only in the case of inexpensive durable or non-durable consumers' goods such as cigarettes, liquor, and soap. (2) Control by the manufacturer of an extensive and exclusive dealers' organization attending to the sale and the servicing of the product; as one might expect, this phenomenon is of major importance for expensive durable goods, such as automobiles, typewriters, and tractors and other farm machinery, but it is apparently also of some significance for other commodities, such as petroleum and rubber tires. (3) Patents protecting some feature of the product or related auxiliary services. (4) Special services provided to customers. These last two factors are rarely mentioned and generally do not seem to offer very effective protection.

It is worth noting that factors (2) and (3), and in part also factor (1), could be largely treated as economies of scale in marketing. Both Bain and Sylos are aware of this possibility; in fact, the latter—though he pays only passing attention to product differentiation fostered by advertising—hints that the effect of this type of barrier could be analyzed along lines similar to those utilized in the homogeneous oligopoly model. That is, a new entrant could hope to match the profit performance of the successful large firms only by securing a market of the same absolute size. But, given the over-all size of the market, even if the entrant succeeded in capturing a share comparable to that of existing firms, each member would be left with too small a market, so that the final result of the entry would be to make the business unattractive for all.

After evaluating for his twenty industries the over-all barriers to entry resulting from the joint effect of economies of scale, absolute cost advantages, and product differentiation and after summarizing the effects that these over-all barriers should have on various aspects of market performance on the basis of his theoretical analysis, Bain proceeds to check his deductions against available evidence on actual performance. To be sure, the present evidence on barriers to entry as well as on market performance is frequently far from adequate, and one may have reservations about the details of some of the test procedures. Nonetheless, Bain's courageous attempt at systematic testing and his candid admission of occasional failures of his predictions is a highly welcome novelty and one whose importance can hardly be overestimated.

Finally, the implications of the analysis for public policy designed to foster workable competition are set forth in a very cautious and restrained spirit in the concluding chapter viii. On the whole, the outlook for effective public policy is not too optimistic, although it is by no means as gloomy as that of Sylos. But, then, Sylos' gloom is understandable. His inspiration comes from the Italian economy, where markets are naturally small and are made still smaller by tariffs and other artificial restrictions. According to his own model, the tendency to oligopolistic structures, and their power of market exploitation, will tend to be greater the smaller the size of the market.

I hope I have succeeded in justifying the glowing statement with which this review begins and in showing how well the two books complement each other. To be sure, much work still remains to be done in the area of oligopolistic market structures. In particular, the analysis of both authors is still largely limited to a static framework, and there is reason to believe that certain aspects of oligopolistic behavior can be adequately accounted for only by explicitly introducing dynamic elements into the analysis.[25] In my view, the real significance of Bain's and Sylos' contributions lies not merely in the results that they have already reached but at least as much in their having provided us with a framework capable of promising further developments and leading to operationally testable propositions. In addition, Bain deserves high credit for having led the way on the path of empirical testing.

[25] Some promising beginnings in this direction are already to be found in Sylos and, even more, in Bain. The latter's notion of ineffectively impeded entry, for example, is an essentially dynamic one. Similarly, Sylos hints that, where demand is growing, existing firms, to discourage entry, may have to keep their capacity somewhat larger than X_0 and their markup somewhat below P_0. Needless to say, the mere emphasis on the problem of entry is, per se, a significant movement in the direction of a dynamic analysis.

[16]

JOURNAL OF ECONOMIC THEORY 3, 306–322 (1971)

Dynamic Limit Pricing: Optimal Pricing under Threat of Entry

DARIUS W. GASKINS, JR.

Received July 31, 1970

INTRODUCTION

This paper attempts to determine the optimal pricing strategy for a dominant firm or a group of joint profit maximizing oligopolists faced by potential entry into the product market. The models explored here have broader applications, but we limit our discussion to a dominant firm able to deduce a residual demand schedule through knowledge of the output of a well-behaved competitive fringe. Contemporary writings on this subject for the most part contend that the dominant firm will maximize its present value by either charging the short-run profit maximizing price and allowing its market share to decline or by setting price at the limit price and precluding all entry.[1] A firm practicing short-run profit maximization would have to ignore continually the reality of induced entry. Conversely, a firm charging the limit price has to be convinced that its prevailing market share is optimal. There has been no analytic justification for this strategic dichotomy, and intuition suggests that the optimal strategy would entail a balancing between current profits and future market share.

The basic premise of this study is that the rate of entry of rival producers into a particular market is a function of current product price. Mansfield has shown that the variation in rate of firms entering or exiting an industry is positively correlated with the level of industry profits.[2] It follows that a dominant firm with high current price and profit levels is sacrificing some future profits through erosion of its market share. The dependence of future market share on the current price level means that the dominant firm's pricing strategy can only be determined in a dynamic framework.

The Basic Model

In general terms, the optimal pricing strategy will maximize the present value of firm profits, as given by Eq. (1) below:

$$V = \int_0^\infty [p(t) - c] \, q(p(t), t) \, e^{-rt} \, dt, \tag{1}$$

where V = present value of firm's profit stream, $p(t)$ = product price, c = average total cost of production (assumed to be constant over time), $q(p(t), t)$ = dominant firm's output, r = dominant firm's discount rate.

The specific functional dependence of sales on time is determined by the nature of the entry phenomenon. We assume that the level of the dominant firm's current sales can be decomposed into additive univariate functions of price and time, respectively,

$$q(p(t), t) = f(p(t)) - x(t), \tag{2}$$

where $f(p)$ = initial demand curve and $x(t)$ = the level of rival sales.

The residual demand curve $q(p(t), t)$ at any specific instant is found by subtracting the output of the competitive fringe from the total market demand. Equation (2) indicates that the net effect of rival entry into the product market is to shift the dominant firm's residual demand curve laterally. This would be the case if rival producers' short-run supply curve is completely inelastic.[3] The rate of entry of rival producers $[\dot{x}(t)]$ is surely determined by their expected rate of return. If potential entrants view current product price as a proxy for future price, the rate of entry will be a monotonically nondecreasing function of current price. We assume that this relationship between rate of entry and current price is linear, as shown by Eq. (3),[4]

$$\dot{x}(t) = k[p(t) - \bar{p}], \qquad x(0) = x_0, \qquad \bar{p} \geq c, \tag{3}$$

$\bar{p}$ = limit price (a constant),[5] k = response coefficient ≥ 0, x_0 = initial output of the competitive fringe.

The limit price $\bar{p}$ is defined in this model as that price level at which net entry is equal to zero. The model implies therefore that pricing below $\bar{p}$ will cause negative entry or exit from the product market by rival producers. The difference between the limit price and the dominant firm's average total cost is a measure of the cost advantage enjoyed by the dominant firm. It seems reasonable to restrict the limit price to be greater than or equal to the dominant firm's average total cost. While there may be examples of dominant firms with cost disadvantages, their fate is obvious with or without optimal pricing.

To expedite the analysis further, we assume that the dominant firm's initial demand schedule $f(p(t))$ is downward sloping and twice differentiable with respect to output. With these simplifying assumptions, it is possible to determine the optimal pricing strategy analytically using the mathematics of optimal control. In the language of modern control theory, we wish to maximize the functional

$$V = \int_0^\infty [p(t) - c][f(p) - x(t)] e^{-rt} dt \qquad (4)$$

subject to

$$\dot{x}(t) = k(p(t) - \bar{p}), \qquad x(0) = x_0. \qquad (3)$$

In the control theory framework, $x(t)$ is the state variable and $p(t)$ is the control variable.

We may derive necessary conditions for the optimal path by using Pontryagin's maximum principle. The Hamiltonian for this problem is given by

$$H = (p(t) - c)(f(p) - x(t)) e^{-rt} + z(t) k(p(t) - \bar{p}). \qquad (5)$$

The adjoint variable $z(t)$ appearing in the Hamiltonian is equal to $\partial V/\partial x \,(t)$ and can be interpreted as the shadow price of an additional unit of rival entry at any point in time.[6] The first term of Eq. (5) (the integrand of Eq. (4)) is the change in present value accruing from current sales. The second term which is the product of $\dot{x}(t)$ and $z(t)$ reflects the effect of current entry on future profits. Intuitively, maximizing the Hamiltonian with respect to $p(t)$ involves balancing the flows of present value from present and future sales. The maximum principle states that for a maximum V to exist, it is necessary that there exists a $z(t)$ such that:

(i) $\dot{x}^*(t) = k(p^*(t) - \bar{p}), \qquad x^*(0) = x_0$;

(ii) $\dot{z}^*(t) = -\dfrac{\partial H}{\partial x} (x^*(t), z^*(t), p^*(t), t);$

$\qquad = (p^*(t) - c) e^{-rt}, \lim_{t \to \infty} z^*(t) = 0;$

(iii) $H(x^*(t), z^*(t), p^*(t), t) = \max_{\text{w.r.t. } p(t)} H (x^*(t), z^*(t), p(t), t).$

The superscript * denotes variables along the optimal trajectory. It is easily shown that condition (iii) implies

$$\frac{\partial H}{\partial p(t)} = 0,$$

as long as

$$2 f'(p) + (p - c) f''(p) < 0, \qquad \text{where the prime denotes } \partial/\partial p.$$

This basic inequality will always hold if profit is a smooth concave function of price along the initial demand curve. We assume that such is the case. This assumption which assures the concavity of $H(x(t), z(t), p(t), t)$ with respect to p and x is sufficient to guarantee the existence of an optimal path.[7]

The necessary conditions produce the two simultaneous ordinary differential equations:

$$\dot{x}^*(t) = k(p^*(t) - \bar{p}), \qquad x^*(0) = x_0, \tag{5}$$

$$\dot{z}^*(t) = (p^*(t) - c) e^{-rt}, \qquad \lim_{t \to \infty} z^*(t) = 0, \tag{6}$$

where

$$z^*(t) = \frac{(x^*(t) - f(p^*) - (p^*(t) - c) f'(p^*)) e^{-rt}}{k}. \tag{7}$$

We can eliminate the adjoint variable $z(t)$ from these equations and write the necessary condition as the simultaneous differential equations in $p(t)$ and $x(t)$:

$$\dot{x}(t) = k(p(t) - \bar{p}), \qquad x(0) = x_0, \tag{8}$$

$$\dot{p}(t) = \frac{k(\bar{p} - c) + r[x - f(p) - (p - c) f'(p)]}{-2f'(p) - (p - c) f''(p)}. \tag{9}$$

These two equations generate a family of trajectories in the $x - p$ plane. Unfortunately the terminal condition $\lim z^*(t) = 0$, as $t \to \infty$, cannot be translated into an explicit condition of $x(t)$ or $p(t)$ and therefore it is not immediately obvious which of these trajectories satisfies (satisfy) the necessary conditions.

We argue from a phase-plane portrait of Eqs. (8) and (9) that there is a unique trajectory meeting all the necessary conditions. Figure 1 presents

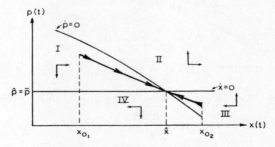

FIG. 1.   Phase plane for the basic model.

the locii of $\dot{p} = \dot{x} = 0$ in the $x - p$ plane. These two locii divide the $x - p$ plane into four distinct regions. It is apparent that the intersection of these locii denoted $(\hat{x}, \hat{p})$ is a saddlepoint. Any trajectory entering or originating in regions II or IV will remain in that region. Further, x and p will increase without bound along any trajectory in region II and decrease without bound along a path in region IV. Inspection of the dominant firms objective function $V(p(t), x(t), t)$ indicates that no trajectory in region II or IV could be an optimal path. In region II ever increasing $x(t)$ and $p(t)$ would generate an increasing stream of losses after some point in time. Similarly, in region IV a steadily decreasing $p(t)$ and $x(t)$ will eventually generate an ever increasing stream of negative profits (i.e., when $p(t) < c$).

We now verify that any path reaching the equilibrium point $(\hat{x}, \hat{p})$ will satisfy the terminal boundary condition $\lim z^*(t) = 0$, as $t \to \infty$. At $(\hat{x}, \hat{p})$ both $\dot{x}$ and $\dot{p}$ are zero. Equation (7) indicates that at this point $z^*(t) = (\hat{x} - f(\hat{p}) - f'(\hat{p})(\hat{p} - c) e^{-rt})/k$ is an exponential function of time that declines to zero, therefore a trajectory reaching this equilibrium point will trivially satisfy the terminal boundary condition. Since the functions $\dot{x}(x, p)$ and $\dot{p}(x, p)$ are both continuous and continuously differentiably in the $x - p$ plane $(2f'(p) + f''(p)(p - c) < 0)$, there will be only two trajectories (labeled (1) and (2) in the figure) which terminate at $(\hat{x}, \hat{p})$. All other trajectories originating in region I or III will eventually enter either region II or IV.

The optimal pricing strategy will therefore be to move along either trajectory (1) or (2) depending on the original size of the competitive fringes output x_0. For $x_0 < \hat{x}$ we conclude that the dominant firm will maximize its present value by gradually lowering product price towards the limit price $\bar{p}$. Such a pricing policy will induce rival entry and continually reduce the dominant firm's market share. Conversely, when x_0 is greater than $\hat{x}$ the optimal strategy is to price below the limit price, continuously driving out rivals.

We are able to prove that the optimal price level will always be below the short run profit maximizing price at every point along the optimal path. If the dominant firm has been moving along the optimal path, instantaneous profit is given by the function

$$\pi(p) = (p(t) - c)(f(p) - x^*(t)). \tag{10}$$

The myopic profit maximizing price $p_m(t)$ is the solution to the equation

$$\frac{\partial \pi(p)}{\partial p_m} = f'(p_m)(p_m(t) - c) + f(p_m) - x^*(t) = 0. \tag{11}$$

We have previously seen that maximization of the Hamiltonian at every point along the optimal path implies that

$$-z(t) = (f'(p^*)(p^*(t) - c) + f(p^*) - x^*(t)) e^{-rt}/k, \qquad (12)$$

where $z(t)$ the shadow price of additional rival entry is necessarily negative. By prior assumption $\partial^2 \pi(p)/\partial^2 p_m < 0$ and therefore, Eqs. (11) and (12) are both satisfied only if $p_m(t) > p^*(t)$.

Comparative Statics and Dynamics of the Optimal Trajectory

We now attempt to establish the effects of variation in the model parameters, k, c, $\bar{p}$, r and x_0 on the optimal path. The equilibrium level of rival output $\hat{x}$ is seen to be an important characteristic of the optimal pricing strategy. Setting Eqs. (8) and (9) equal to zero and solving simultaneously for $\hat{x}$ we find that

$$\hat{x} = (\bar{p} - c)f'(\bar{p}) + f(\bar{p}) - \frac{k(\bar{p} - c)}{r}. \qquad (13)$$

The market share of the dominant firm at any point in time is $s(t) = (f(p) - x(t))/f(p)$. It is clear that as $p(t)$ and $x(t)$ approach $\hat{p}$ and $\hat{x}$, respectively, $s(t)$ will approach an equilibrium $\hat{s}$.

The optimal strategy in fact may be viewed as pricing to achieve a long-run optimal market share equal to:

$$\hat{s} = \frac{f(\bar{p}) - \hat{x}}{f(\bar{p})} = \frac{k(\bar{p} - c)/r - f'(\bar{p})(\bar{p} - c)}{f(\bar{p})}. \qquad (14)$$

Differentiating Eqs. (13) and (14) we establish the following results:

(a) $\dfrac{d\hat{x}}{d\bar{p}} < 0,$

(b) $\dfrac{d\hat{x}}{dc} > 0 \Rightarrow \dfrac{d\hat{s}}{dc} < 0,$

(c) $\dfrac{d\hat{x}}{dr} \geqslant 0 \Rightarrow \dfrac{d\hat{s}}{dr} \leqslant 0,$

(d) $\dfrac{d\hat{x}}{dk} \leqslant 0 \Rightarrow \dfrac{d\hat{s}}{dk} \geqslant 0$ (see Ref. 8),

(e) $\text{sgn} \dfrac{d\hat{s}}{d\bar{p}} = \text{sgn}[f(\bar{p})(k/r - f''(\bar{p})(\bar{p} - c) - f'(\bar{p}))$
$$\qquad\qquad\qquad\qquad - f'(\bar{p})(k(\bar{p} - c)/r - f'(\bar{p})(\bar{p} - c))],$$

(f) $\dfrac{d\hat{x}}{dx_0} = \dfrac{d\hat{s}}{dx_0} = \dfrac{d\hat{p}}{dx_0} = 0.$

The first two of these conditions jointly indicate that the dominant firm will price to allow less entry as its cost advantage ($\bar{p} - c$) increases. We argue that $\bar{p}$ will vary directly with the average level of rival costs. A very large ($\bar{p} - c$) will justify pricing to rationalize the relevant industry by driving out "inefficient" producers ($\hat{x} < x_0$).

An important practical case is the dominant firm which enjoys no cost advantage over rival producers. We model such a case by setting $\bar{p} = c$. In this case Eq. (13) indicates that in response to optimal pricing by the dominant firm the output of the competitive fringe will asymptotically approach $f(c)$, the total industry output. The dominant firm in this case prices itself out of the market in the long-run. While it is acknowledged that our model will lose its validity at some point as the dominant firm's market share declines the conclusion remains that dominant firms with little or no cost advantage decline if they strive to maximize their present value.

Condition (c) indicates that as the dominant firm's discount rate increases it will sacrifice a portion of its long-run market share. A higher discount rate indicates that future profits become relatively less important.

Condition (d) indicates that the more rapidly rivals respond to price signals the larger will be the dominant firms long-run market share. This result is at first glance counter-intuitive and would seem to question the efficacy of any public policy designed to increase the responsiveness of potential entrants. We demonstrate below that a concomitant result is that an increase in k will necessarily lower the optimal price trajectory at least in the short run.

Because r, k, and c don't affect $\bar{p}$ the change in the dominant firms equilibrium market share in response to variation in these parameters will be of the opposite sign of the change in $\hat{x}$. A change in $\bar{p}$ however will affect $f(\bar{p})$ as well as $\hat{x}$ and therefore complicate the determination of the sgn $d\hat{s}/d\bar{p}$. Condition (e) indicates that the sign of $d\hat{s}/d\bar{p}$ depends on the sign of an expression which contains only one term which can be negative, i.e., $-f''(\bar{p})(\bar{p} - c)$. We conclude that if either the curvature of the demand curve near $\bar{p}$ is relatively small or that the dominant firm has a small cost advantage the dominant firms long run market share will increase as $\bar{p}$ increases.

Condition (f) merely restates the obvious point that the long-run optimal price level and market share are independent of the initial output of the competitive fringe.

We now attempt to establish the effect of variation of the model parameters on the optimal trajectory away from the equilibrium point. Because our model still includes the general function $f(p)$ it is not possible to find the explicit form of the whole optimal path. The phase-plane can be used however to obtain certain comparative dynamic results without further model specification.

Figure 2 indicates the effect of a positive increase in the response coefficient k on the phase portrait. We see that the new equilibrium

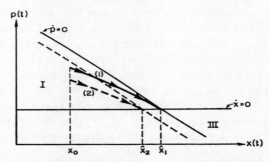

FIG. 2. Comparative dynamic effect of a change in the response coefficient.

point $(\hat{x}_2, \bar{p})$ has been moved to the left in accordance with condition (d) above. It is easily shown that the slope of trajectories in region I will be increased at every point by an increase in k. The slope of any trajectory in the $x - p$ plane designated $G(x, p)$ is equal to

$$G = \frac{dp}{dx} = \frac{\dot{p}}{\dot{x}} = \frac{k(\bar{p} - c) + r(x - f(p) - f'(p)(p - c))}{k(p - \bar{p})(-2f'(p) - f''(p)(p - c))}. \quad (15)$$

By differentiation we find that

$$\frac{dG}{dk} = \frac{-r(x - f(p) - f'(p)(p - c))}{(p - \bar{p})(-2f'(p) - f''(p)(p - c))}. \quad (16)$$

Recalling from Eq. (7) that the shadow price of entry $z^*(t)$ is proportional to the quantity $(x - f(p) - f'(p)(p - c)) e^{-rt}$, we argue that the numerator of Eq. (16) is positive since an additional unit of rival entry at any time will surely lower the present value of the dominant firm. By previous assumption $(-2f'(p) - f''(p)(p - c)) > 0$, and we conclude that sgn $dG/dk = \text{sgn}(p - \bar{p})$.

If we examine the situation in region I of the phase plane it is apparent that the new optimal path (2) must lie below the original optimal trajectory (1). At points along the old path the slope has been increased by the increase in k and therefore any trajectory passing through a point on (1) must move above (1) as x increases. No such path could possibly reach the new equilibrium point $(\hat{x}_2, \bar{p})$. In a similar fashion, we can demonstrate that if the original optimal path was in region III (i.e., $x_0 > \hat{x}_1$) the optimal trajectory will move downward as k increases.

We have shown that the optimal trajectory in the $x - p$ plane will always be lowered by an increase in the responsiveness of rival producers to price signals. While it follows that the initial portion of the dominant firm's optimal price trajectory will be lowered by increasing k we are not assured that the whole time path $p^*(t)$ has been lowered.[9] By similar arguments we are able to establish the following comparative dynamic results:

(g) $\quad \dfrac{dp^*}{dr}(t) > 0;$

(h) $\quad \dfrac{dp^*}{dc}(t) > 0, \quad$ if $\ f''(p) \approx 0;$

(i) $\quad \dfrac{dp^*}{dx_0}(t) < 0.$

Each of these conditions indicates the *short term* effect of variation of a particular model parameter. In addition, since variation in x_0 the initial output of the competitive fringe only affects the starting point of the optimal path, the last condition holds for the whole time path of $p^*(t)$.

Unfortunately, it is not possible to assess the impact of small changes in $\bar{p}$ on the initial portion of the optimal path in this general model. We have demonstrated elsewhere that for a linear demand curve the response of the optimal price at any point in time is such that:

(j) $\quad \dfrac{dp^*(t)}{d\bar{p}} < 0 \quad$ (see Ref. 10).

Conditions (h) and (j) jointly indicate that the dominant firm will lower its price in response to an increase in its relative cost advantage. We have the somewhat ironic result that a policy which lowers existing barriers to entry (e.g., mandatory licensing of a vital patent) will raise prices in the short run if dominant firms price according to this model.

The economic justification for this seemingly perverse result is that the optimal long-run market share of the dominant firm is increased as its cost advantage increases (we previously saw that $d\hat{x}/d(\bar{p} - c) < 0$). As the dominant firm becomes increasingly efficient it will strive to drive out more of the inefficient producers and it does this by lowering the product price in the short run. We observe however that if the change in the cost advantage is due to an increase in $\bar{p}$ the long run price will be increased.

The most sanguine conclusion from this model remains that dominant firms with little or no market power ultimately decline. We find much to our chagrin however that growth of the product market destroys this consoling result.

MARKET GROWTH MODEL

The American economy with its growing population and increasing per capita income is not consistent with the static product market assumed by the basic model. More realistically dominant firms are faced by markets which are growing as the economy expands. We now explore a model in which the output of the dominant firm is assumed to be of the form

$$q(p(t), t) = f(p(t)) e^{\gamma t} - x(t), \tag{17}$$

where $\gamma =$ the market growth rate.

It is postulated that product demand is increasing exponentially. This particular growth model which has the property that the price elasticity at a given price remains constant over time seems to be consistent with steady growth of disposable income rather than the secular growth of any single product market.[11] Consonant with growing disposable income, we also assume that the entry response coefficient k is now the growing exponential function of time

$$k(t) = k_0 e^{\gamma t}. \tag{18}$$

An increase of disposable income should cause a proportional increase in the quantity of resources available to potential entrants for investment in any product market. Under this growth model, the dominant firm attempts to maximize the present value of its stream of profits

$$V = \int_0^\infty (p(t) - c)(f(p(t)) e^{\gamma t} - x(t)) e^{-rt} \, dt; \qquad \gamma < r,^{[12]} \tag{19}$$

subject to

$$\dot{x}(t) = k_0 e^{\gamma t}(p(t) - \bar{p}), \qquad x(0) = x_0. \tag{20}$$

The necessary conditions for a maximum V generate the simultaneous differential equations[13]:

$$\dot{x}^*(t) = k_0 e^{\gamma t}(p^*(t) - \bar{p}), \qquad x^*(0) = x_0, \tag{21}$$

$$\dot{z}^*(t) = (p^*(t) - c) e^{-rt}, \qquad \lim_{t \to \infty} z^*(t) = 0, \tag{22}$$

316   GASKINS

where

$$z^*(t) = (x^*(t) e^{-\gamma t} - f(p^*) - (p^*(t) - c) f'(p^*)) e^{-rt}/k.^{14}$$

This system of differential equations can be converted into an autonomous system by making the substitution $w(t) = x(t) e^{-\gamma t}$ and eliminating $z(t)$. The resulting equations are

$$\dot{w}(t) = k_0(p(t) - \bar{p}) - \gamma w(t), \qquad w(0) = x_0, \tag{23}$$

$$\dot{p}(t) = \frac{k_0(\bar{p} - c) - r(f(p) - w(t) + f'(p)(p(t) - c)) + \gamma w(t)}{(-2f'(p) - f''(p)(p(t) - c))}. \tag{24}$$

The phase plane portrait of these equations is shown in Fig. 3. It is clear from the figure and our previous arguments about the phase-plane portrait of the basic model that there is a unique optimal path which will take one of four possible shapes determined by the values of $\hat{w}$ and $w(0) = x_0$.

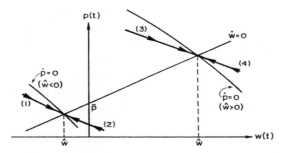

FIG. 3. Phase plane for the growth model.

The trajectory labeled (1) in the figure will be the optimal path when $x_0 < \hat{w} < 0$. Such a case is of no interest for our particular problem since the initial rival output x_0 is surely nonnegative. Trajectory (2), which occurs when $x_0 > \hat{w} < 0$, is similarly not a valid result under this model since it implies that $x(t) = w(t) e^{rt}$ will eventually become negative along the optimal path. A negative output by rival producers is not a feasible solution.[15]

We conclude that the trajectories (3) and (4) are the only optimal paths of interest and that the equilibrium optimal price $\hat{p}$ is necessarily greater than $\bar{p}$. We see that just as under the basic model the optimal pricing strategy results in a constant long-run market share for the dominant firm. For this model the dominant firms market share $s(t)$ at any time is given by

$$s(t) = \frac{f(p) e^{\gamma t} - w(t) e^{\gamma t}}{f(p) e^{\gamma t}} = \frac{f(p) - w(t)}{f(p)}. \tag{25}$$

It is clear that as $p(t)$ and $w(t)$ approach their equilibrium levels $\hat{p}$ and $\hat{w}$ the dominant firm's market share approaches the constant $\hat{s} = 1 - [\hat{w}/f(\hat{p})]$. To find the equilibrium values $\hat{w}$ and $\hat{p}$ we set Eqs. (23) and (24) equal to zero which yields the simultaneous equations

$$\gamma \hat{w} = k_0(\hat{p} - \bar{p}), \tag{26}$$

$$(\gamma + r) \hat{w} = r(f(\hat{p}) + f'(\hat{p})(\hat{p} - c)) - k_0(\bar{p} - c). \tag{27}$$

Equation (27) clearly indicates that for $\gamma > 0$, $\hat{w}$ is strictly less than $f(\hat{p})$. In contrast to the basic model we now find that a dominant firm with no cost advantage (i.e., $\bar{p} = c$) will not price itself out of the market asymptotically. It can be shown that if the curvature of the demand curve at the equilibrium price is not too great ($f''(\hat{p}) \lesssim 0$) an increase in the growth rate γ will always increase $\hat{s}$.[16]

This is a disturbing result because growth of the product market not only raises the long run price level ($\hat{p} > \bar{p}$) but it also allows dominant firms with insignificant cost advantages to maintain a constant market share over the long haul. It is of some interest therefore to establish the quantitative effects of growth on a specific model. Table I below presents the long-run optimal price and market share of a dominant firm selling in a growing product market. The model analyzed here postulates that the residual demand curve is linear specifically: $q(t) = (100 - p(t)) e^{\gamma t} - x(t)$, and that $c = 10$, $r = 0.1$, $k_0 = 1$, $x_0 = 0.$[17] The table presents the equilibrium values of $\hat{s}$ and $\hat{p}$ for a dominant firm with a substantial cost advantage ($\bar{p} = 15$) and for a firm with no cost advantage ($\bar{p} = 10 = c$).

TABLE I

Long Run Optimal Price and Market Share with Market Growth
(Linear Demand Curve)

	$\gamma = 0$	$\gamma = 0.02$	$\gamma = 0.04$	$\gamma = 0.08$
$\bar{p} = 15$	$\hat{p} = 15$	$\hat{p} = 15.48$	$\hat{p} = 15.76$	$\hat{p} = 16.22$
	$\hat{s} = 0.647$	$\hat{s} = 0.716$	$\hat{s} = 0.778$	$\hat{s} = 0.817$
$\bar{p} = 10$	$\hat{p} = 10$	$\hat{p} = 11.45$	$\hat{p} = 12.43$	$\hat{p} = 13.67$
(no cost advantage)	$\hat{s} = 0$	$\hat{s} = 0.181$	$\hat{s} = 0.306$	$\hat{s} = 0.468$

The first column represents the case of a static product market. The quantitative difference between the results shown in that column and the other columns are solely attributable to growth of the product market. The striking conclusion from this table is a moderate rate of growth ($\gamma = 0.04$) enables a dominant firm with no cost advantage to set the long run price 24% above the limit price and still maintain 30% of the total market. Further, we see that increasing the rate of growth increases the equilibrium price level and raises the long-run market share of the dominant firm.

COMPARATIVE STATICS AND DYNAMICS OF THE GROWTH MODEL

Differentiation of Eqs. (25), (26), and (27) with respect to various structural parameters of the growth model yields the following results:

(k) $\dfrac{d\hat{s}}{d\bar{p}} > 0,$

(l) $\dfrac{d\hat{s}}{dc} < 0,$

(m) $\dfrac{d\hat{s}}{dr} < 0,$

(n) $\operatorname{sgn} \dfrac{d\hat{s}}{dk_0} = \operatorname{sgn} \left[2f'(\hat{p}) + f''(\hat{p})(\hat{p} - c) + \dfrac{k_0}{r} \left(\dfrac{\bar{p} - c}{\hat{p} - \bar{p}} \right) \right.$
$$\left. - \dfrac{f'(\hat{p}) k_0}{f(\hat{p})} \left(\dfrac{\hat{p} - c}{r} + \dfrac{\hat{p} - \bar{p}}{\gamma} \right) \right]$$

(o) $\dfrac{d\hat{p}}{d\gamma} > 0,$

(p) $\dfrac{d\hat{p}}{dk_0} < 0,$

(q) $\dfrac{d\hat{p}}{dc} > 0,$

(r) $\dfrac{d\hat{p}}{dr} > 0,$

(s) $1 > \dfrac{d\hat{p}}{d\bar{p}} > 0.$

The first three of these conditions are identical to the results under a static product market. An increase in the dominant firm's cost advantage or a decrease in the discount rate will both increase the long-run optimal market share.

Condition (n) indicates that the sign of $d\hat{s}/dk_0$ depends upon a host of model parameters. For the specific model considered in Table 1 above it can be shown that $d\hat{s}/dk_0$ will be positive if the dominant firm enjoys a relatively larger cost advantage ($\bar{p} > c$) and becomes negative as $\bar{p}$ approaches c. It is also clear that the term $k_0/r((\bar{p} - c)/(\hat{p} - \bar{p}))$ dominates the sign of $d\hat{s}/dk_0$ for small values of γ because ($\hat{p} - \bar{c}$) approaches zero and ($\hat{p} - \bar{p})/\gamma = \hat{w}/k$ remains bounded as γ approaches zero. This result is consistent with the comparative static result of the basic model which indicated that $d\hat{s}/dk$ was proportional to ($\bar{p} - c$). We conclude that if the dominant firm enjoys a large cost advantage that an increase in the response of rivals to price signals will likely increase its long-run market share.

Under the growth model we find that the equilibrium price $\hat{p}$ varies with each of the model parameters. We are disturbed to observe that an increase in the rate of market growth will always increase $\hat{p}$. Conversely, the existence of any positive growth rate is sufficient to prevent an increase in $\bar{p}$ from being fully reflected in the equilibrium price level. Further, under this growth model an increase in the responsiveness of rival producers to price signals (k_0) will result in a lower long-run product price. The sign of $d\hat{p}/dc$ is consistent with the result under a naive static profit maximizing model.

It is possible to demonstrate by phase plane analysis of the optimal paths the following general comparative dynamic results:

(t) $\quad \dfrac{dp^*}{dk_0}(t) < 0,$

(u) $\quad \dfrac{dp^*}{dr}(t) > \quad ,$

(v) $\quad \dfrac{dp^*}{dc}(t) > 0,$ if $f''(p) \lessgtr 0,$

(w) $\quad \dfrac{dp^*}{dx_0}(t) < 0.$

Just as under the basic model it is not possible to determine the sign of $dp^*/d\bar{p}(t)$ for a general demand curve. It is true, however, that for a linear demand curve an increase in the limit price at any point in time will result in a lower optimal price in the short run.[17] We conclude that the comparative dynamics for the growth model are qualitatively identical to the results found under the basic model.

320   GASKINS

The major substantive changes in the optimal pricing strategy resulting from growth of the product market are that the equilibrium price is raised above the limit price, and that dominant firms with no cost advantage no longer price themselves out of the market in the long-run.

MODEL IMPLICATIONS

These models have mixed implications for economic policy. Initially we were reassured to find that optimizing dominant firms will ultimately decline if they have no substantial long-run cost advantage. Steady growth of the product market unfortunately mitigates the decline of dominant firms and causes the long-run product price to be above the average cost of production. By-products of faster economic growth are increased concentration levels and higher prices in dominated industries.

The comparative statics and dynamics of these models have conflicting implications for patent policy. If, for example, the effectiveness of existing patents was weakened by mandatory licensing the immediate effect would be to lower $\bar{p}$ the limit price in dominated industries. This would decrease the long-run market shares and product prices but probably would raise prices in the short-run.

A policy to increase the responsiveness of potential entrants to price signals by improving the information flow or eliminating capital market imperfections would lower prices both in the short-run and long-run. But such a policy would ultimately lead to larger market shares for dominant firms, if the dominant firms enjoyed substantial long-run cost advantages.

ACKNOWLEDGMENT

I am especialling indebted to Frederick M. Scherer for seminal discussions of this topic. In addition, I would like to thank Steven Goldman, Harl Ryder, Lester Taylor, and Sidney Winter for useful comments and suggestions on previous drafts.

REFERENCES

1. See, for example, DALE OSBORNE, The role of entry in oligopoly theory, *J. Political Econ. LXXII* (1964), 396.
2. E. MANSFIELD, Entry, Gibrat's Law, innovation and the growth of firms, *Amer. Econ. Rev. LII* (1962), 1026
3. The residual demand curve will also shift laterally if a more general rival supply curve shifts laterally as rival producers enter or exit.

4. This can be viewed as a first-order approximation of a more complicated functional relationship between $\dot{x}$ and $(p(t) - \bar{p})$. It can be shown that if rival producers, attempting to maximize the present value of their profit stream, expect the product price to remain constant and are faced by an increasing marginal cost of expansion, then the rivals will expand at a rate proportional to $(p - \bar{p})^\gamma$ (where $\gamma \geqslant 0$). A quadratic entry model which allows asymmetric entry and exit and holds that the rate of entry increases more than proportionally as price increases has been explored in my dissertation "Optimal Pricing by Dominant Firms" unpublished Ph.D. dissertation, University of Michigan, 1970. This more realistic entry model did not alter qualitatively any of the following results.

5. Cases involving continuous variation and discrete jumps in $\bar{p}$ have been considered in my dissertation, Ref. 4, Chap. 3.

6. Strictly speaking this interpretation requires finding a twice differentiable solution to the Hamilton–Jacobi partial differential equation for this problem. This has been done for a linear version of this problem and may be found in Ref. 4, Chap. 4.

7. Formally, there are problems involved in optimizing a functional when it is an indefinite integral. The major difficulty for our purposes is that most existence theorems have been proved only for optimization over finite time intervals. This difficulty is avoided in this particular case by making the substitutions;

   (1) $\tau = 1 - e^{-dt}$,

   (2) $\delta(t) = (p(t) - \bar{p}) e^{dt}$, d is an arbitrary positive constant less than r.

The first substitution maps the time interval $(0, \infty)$ into the τ interval $(0, 1)$ and therefore transforms the original indefinite integral into a definite integral with respect to τ. The second substitution is required to maintain a well-behaved differential constraint over the interval $(0 \leqslant \tau \leqslant 1)$. We may now use the existence theorem due to LAMBERTO CESARI *in* Existence theorems for optimal solutions in Pontryagin and Lagrange problems, *SIAM J. Control* 3 (1966), 478–79. This existence theorem also requires that the state variable $x(t)$ and control variable $\delta(t)$ of the transformed problem are contained in compact sets. We can satisfy this by imposing constraints on $x(t)$ and $\delta(t)$, respectively. As long as trajectories satisfying necessary conditions for optimality do not exceed these constraints we may apply this existence theorem. We note that $\delta(t)$ is bounded only if $\lim_{t\to\infty} (p^*(t) - \bar{p}) e^{dt}$ is finite, and that $p^*(t)$ must approach $\bar{p}$ at least as fast as a declining exponential.

8. The strict inequalities will hold only when the dominant firm has no cost advantage, i.e., $\bar{p} = c$.

9. The velocity $\dot{p}^*(t)$ along the new path has also changed and it cannot be shown that it will always be less than the velocity along the original optimal path.

10. This result is demonstrated in Ref. 4, p. 13. It also may be shown that this result holds for a demand curve of constant unitary elasticity. No counterexamples have been found.

11. A growth model under which price elasticity steadily declines is explored in Ref. 4, Chap. 4.

12. The assumption that the growth rate of disposable income, γ is less than the discount rate r is required to guarantee convergence of the present value integral.

13. We are unable to prove existence of an optimal path in this case. The method of transformation used to prove existence for the basic model is inappropriate for this model because the new control variable $\delta(t)$ is unbounded since $\lim p^*(t) \neq \bar{p}$.

14. We again assume that $f''(p)(p(t) - c) + 2f'(p) < 0$, which guarantees an interior solution.

322   GASKINS

15. This result which is also possible under the basic model leads us to consider a model under which the state variable $x(t)$ is constrained to be positive. Such a model is analyzed in Ref. 4, Chap. 5.

16. Differentiating $\hat{s}$ with respect to γ we find that

$$\frac{d\hat{s}}{d\gamma} = \frac{k_0(\hat{p} - \bar{p})}{\gamma^2} \left[\frac{f(\hat{p})[2f'(\hat{p}) + f''(\hat{p})(\hat{p} - c) - k_0/r] - \hat{w}f'(\hat{p})}{2f'(\hat{p}) + f''(\hat{p})(\hat{p} - c) - k_0 \left(\dfrac{1}{r} + \dfrac{1}{\gamma} \right)} \right].$$

Since $\hat{w} < f(\hat{p})$, the numerator of the second term is strictly less than $f(\hat{p})(f'(\hat{p}) + f''(\hat{p})(\hat{p} - c) - k_0/r)$. This expression will certainly be negative if $f''(\hat{p}) \lesssim 0$. The denominator of $d\hat{s}/d\gamma$ is negative by prior assumption and we conclude that $f''\hat{p} \lesssim 0 \Rightarrow d\hat{s}/d\gamma > 0$.

17. The optimal price trajectory for this model is found in Ref. 4, Chap. 4.

[17]

On Entry Preventing Behavior and Limit Price Models of Entry[1])

By *J.W. Friedman*, Rochester[2])

Abstract: Formally, the market is regarded as a supergame in which one established firm and one potential entrant are players. Both players know all relevant demand and cost functions, and throughout the paper, noncooperative behavior is assumed. The model has two distinct stages: pre- and post entry. In the pre-entry stage, the monopolist chooses his price and capital stock so as to maximize his discounted profits, noting that his investment decision may affect the entry plans of the entrant. Existence of equilibrium is proved, entry preventing behavior is characterized and conditions are shown under which it will be employed.

1. Introduction

Probably the first "limit price" discussions of entry occur in *Bain* [1949] and *Harrod* [1952]. To see what is meant by a limit price, suppose a monopolistic industry into which there is free entry. A price, p^*, is a limit price if no new firm would enter the industry when the monopolist charges p^* or less, and if entry would occur when a price above p^* were used. In deciding what price to adopt, the monopolist compares three per period profit rates, π^m, π^* and π^a. They are, respectively, the highest profit the firm could get as a monopolist (before entry of a new firm), the largest profit attainable when the monopolist keeps his price at or below p^* and the profit which the monopolist believes it would have if entry occurred. If these profit levels are ordered $\pi^m > \pi^* > \pi^a$ then the firm may maximize discounted profits by selecting an entry preventing price and obtaining a profit of π^* per period. Letting $\alpha = 1 / (1 + r)$, where r ($\geqslant 0$) is the firm's discount rate, and assuming entry would take place in period t if entry preventing prices were not chosen earlier, then entry prevention is optimal if

$$\frac{1}{1 - \alpha} \pi^* > \frac{1 - \alpha^t}{1 - \alpha} \pi^m + \frac{\alpha^t}{1 - \alpha} \pi^a. \tag{1}$$

⊦ This model prompts a number of questions. For example, how is p^* determined? It ought to arise as the result of an optimization process undertaken by the potential

[1]) I am grateful to Professor Vernon Smith for the opportunity to present an earlier version of this work at the Arizona Conference on Experimental Economics in March, 1977, and to Mordecai Kurz for a suggestion leading to an improvement in exposition and in the proof of theorem 1. I retain responsibility for any remaining errors.

[2]) Prof. *James W. Friedman*, The University of Rochester, College of Arts and Science. Dept of Economics, Rochester, N.Y. 14627, USA.

entrant[3]). How do results change if the market is characterized by oligopoly or by monopolistic competition? How is entry affected if knowledge of future demand and/ or cost conditions is incomplete? Or subject to stochastic elements? I hope to deal with all of these questions in the present paper and in subsequent papers. In the present paper, the assumption is maintained throughout that, prior to the entry of new firms, the market is characterized by monopoly. Also, there are no stochastic elements in the model, and both the established firm and the entrant know the demand and cost functions which prevail before and after entry.

The notion of an entry preventing price has wide appeal; yet in the models examined below an entrant has no direct interest in an established firm's pre-entry price policy. What matters to him is the price pattern which would emerge after he were to come in. That is, he wants to know what equilibrium behavior in the market would be if he were in, and he wants to know what profits he would have under such an equilibrium.

Now, after entry occurs, the established firm and the entrant are in a two person game whose structure and form are entirely independent of the pre-entry price policy of the established firm; hence, whose equilibria are independent of the pre-entry price policy of the established firm. If both participants are fully informed at the outset concerning the profit functions which would prevail after entry, then it is difficult to see the relevance of pre-entry prices to the plans of the entrant.

Though pre-entry price policy has no role in the models examined here, the pre-entry capital policy may be relevant. Imagine that active firms make both price and investment decisions and consider, again, that both firms know in advance what profit functions would prevail after entry. Any equilibria for the model as of the entry time would depend upon the amount of capital held by the established firm just prior to entry. Presumably, before making a commitment to enter, the entrant would check on the size of the established firm's capital, and refrain from entering if the equilibria associated with that capital afforded him negative profits. Thus the established firm may be able to carry out an entry preventing investment policy. The crucial difference between price and investment is, of course, that today's investment decision makes an inevitable change in the future circumstances one will face; but today's price decisions only affect today. In particular, under the assumptions made below, the optimal price for a firm is inversely related to the size of its own capital stock; hence, by choosing a large capital stock, it may force its optimal price to be low. This, in turn, tends to lower the demand of a rival firm.

The model described in section 2, is one in which there is a monopolist and one potential entrant. As long as the potential entrant is not in the market, he uses a criterion, known to the monopolist, upon which to decide whether or not to enter. Once he has come into the market, the model becomes one of duopoly with no possibility of entry by additional firms. Either or both of the firms may leave the market; however, once a firm leaves, he may not enter again. In section 3, the model of section 2 is restricted somewhat, which allows some additional results, and section 4 has a few concluding comments.

---

[3]) To avoid clumsy locutions, I refer to the potential entrant as the entrant, even if he has not decided to come into the industry.

2. Entry and Exit Under Certainty

Imagine a monopolist who chooses his price and the size of his capital stock for each period in a discrete time model. He knows the cost and demand functions which he faces as a monopolist; and he knows what his demand function would be if an entrant came into his market. He also knows the demand and cost functions which the entrant would have. There is one potential entrant whose information is like that of the monopolist. He knows the cost and demand functions he would have if he entered the industry, and he knows the cost and demand functions prevailing for the monopolist both before and after entry. The senses in which the model is characterized by certainty are: a) the information conditions above and b) no stochastic terms enter the cost or demand functions. Throughout the paper, it is assumed that the firms never collude or cooperate in any way.

The model has two distinct stages. These correspond to pre- and post entry. In the pre-entry stage, the monopolist chooses his price and capital stock so as to maximize his discounted profits, taking into account that his investment decision may have a bearing on the plans of the entrant. In the post entry stage, the two firms are in a two person game, with the extra provision that one or both of the firms may leave the market at any time. The entrant will come into the industry if there is any time at which entry would bring positive profits. The time of entry is the one for which discounted profits are maximized. The model which is outlined above is presented in detail in Section 2.1. Following that, in section 2.2, existence and characteristics of equilibrium are discussed.

2.1 A Model of Monopoly with Entry and Exit

The monopolist faces a demand function, $q_{1t} = f(p_{1t})$. p_{1t} is the monopolist's price in period t and q_{1t}, his output and sales level. The entrant's price and output are denoted p_{2t} and q_{2t}. After entry his demand function would be $f_2(p_{1t}, p_{2t}) = f_2(p_t)$ and the (former) monopolist would face $f_1(p_{1t}, p_{2t})$. Both of them know f_1 and f_2. The monopolist is sometimes called "firm 1" and the entrant, "firm 2."

Let $\overset{\circ}{A}_i$ denote the subset of the price space within which f_i is positive[4]):

$$\overset{\circ}{A}_i = \{p \mid p \geqslant 0, \; f_i(p) > 0\}, \qquad i = 1, 2. \tag{2}$$

Let $\overset{\circ}{A} = \overset{\circ}{A}_1 \cap \overset{\circ}{A}_2$ and let A be the closure of $\overset{\circ}{A}$ and A_i the closure of $\overset{\circ}{A}_i$. R_+^2 denotes the non-negative orthant of the two dimensional Euclidean space, R^2. The conditions imposed upon the demand functions are given in A1 and A2.

A1. $f_i(p)$ *is continuous, bounded and non-negative for all* $p \in R_+^2$. *For* $p \in \overset{\circ}{A}_i$, f_i *has continuous second partial derivatives with respet to* p_i. *For* $p \in \overset{\circ}{A}$, f_i *is twice continuously differentiable. Where the indicated derivatives exist, the following hold:*

---

[4]) The notational conventions for vector inequalities are: $p^0 > p^1$ means $p_i^0 > p_i^1$, $i = 1, \ldots, n$, $p^0 > p^1$ means $p^0 \geqslant p^1$ and $p^0 \neq p^1$, and, finally, $p^0 \gg p^1$ means $p_i^0 > p_i^1$, $i = 1, \ldots, n$.

On Entry Preventing Behavior 239

$$f_i^i < 0, f_i^j > 0 \text{ (for } i \neq j), \text{ and } f_i^1 + f_i^2 < 0. \quad i, j = 1, 2. \tag{3}$$

Furthermore, A is bounded.

Under A1, it is known that A contains a unique maximal element, $p^+ = (p_1^+, p_2^+)$. [See *Friedman*, 1977, theorem 3.1]. A1 insures that a firm's sales decline as its own price rises and rise as its rival's price rises. As both prices rise together, both firms suffer a decline in sales. There is a price (p_i^+) for each firm above which nothing is sold, no matter what price is chosen by the rival. It remains to impose a consistency requirement on f_1 which recognizes that if $p_2 \geqslant p_2^+$, then firm 1 must necessarily face the same demand function which it faced as a monopolist.

A2. *If $p_2 \geqslant p_2^+$, then $f_1 (p_1, p_2) = f(p_1)$ for all $p_1 \geqslant 0$.*

A2 implies that $f(p_1^+) = 0$ and, for any $p_1 < p_1^+, f(p_1) > 0$.

The cost of production in period t is given by $C_i (q_{it}, K_{i,t-1})$ where $K_{i,t-1}$ is the capital of the firm as of the start of the period. Gross investment is denoted I_{it}; hence, total costs of all types for period t are $C_i (q_{it}, K_{i,t-1}) + I_{it}$. The capital stock available at the start of period $t + 1$ is $K_{it} = (1 - \delta) K_{i,t-1} + I_{it}$. The capital stock available at the start of period $t + 1$ is $K_{it} = (1 - \delta) K_{i,t-1} + I_{it}$, where δ is a depreciation rate between zero and one. The initial capital, K_{i0}, equals initial investment, I_{i0}. The full statement of cost assumptions is in A3 and A4.

A3. *The cost of production, $C_i (q_{it}, K_{i,t-1})$, is defined, non-negative and convex on R_+^2, and is twice continuously differentiable on the interior of R_+^2. In addition,*
a) $C_i (0, 0) = 0$, b) $\lim_{q \to 0} C_i^2 (q, K) > 0$, *when* $K > 0$, c) $C_i^1 (q, K) > 0$,

d) $C_i^1 (q, K) \to \infty$ *as* $K \to 0$, e) $C_i^{12} (q, K) < 0$, *and* f) *for* $0 < K_2 < K_1 < \infty$ *there is* $q = \phi_i (K_1, K_2)$ *such that* $C_i (\phi_i (K_1, K_2), K_1) = C_i (\phi_i (K_1, K_2), K_2)$. $i = 1.2$.

A4. $K_{i0} = I_{i0}$. *For* $t \geqslant 1, K_{it} = (1 - \delta) K_{i,t-1} + I_{it}$. $\delta \in [0, 1]$. $I_{it} \geqslant 0$ *for* $t = 1, 2, \ldots,$ *and* $i = 1, 2$. $I_{20} \geqslant I_2' > 0$ [5]).

The cost function specified in A4 shows positive marginal cost of production (from c)) and increasing marginal cost as output increases, for given capital (from convexity of C_i). At zero output and zero capital, production cost is nil; however, any positive amount of capital has associated with it a level of fixed cost, $C_i (0, K)$, which rises as K increases (from b)). Marginal cost of production goes to infinity as the capital stock of the firm goes to zero (from d)). Condition e) insures that, for a fixed level of output, the marginal cost of production declines as capital increases. Condition f) guarantees that, for any pair of positive capital stock levels, there is an output level above which the total production costs associated with the larger capital stock are less than those associated with the smaller.

For period $t \geqslant 1$, the firm's profit is

$$\pi_i (p_t, K_{i,t-1}, K_{it}) = p_{it} f_i (p_t) - C_i (f_i (p_i), K_{i,t-1}) - (K_{it} - (1 - \delta) K_{i,t-1}). \tag{4}$$

Let $\alpha_i \in (0, 1)$ be the discount parameter of firm i. The discounted profit stream for a firm, if both are in the market from the outset, is

---

[5]) Of course, if firm 2 does not enter the market until t_0, his investment is zero in every period up to that time.

$$-I_{i0} + \sum_{t=1}^{\infty} \alpha_i^t \, \pi_i \, (p_t, K_{i,t-1}, K_{it}). \tag{5}$$

There is a final assumption made on the π_i.

A5. *For any p and K_i such that $p_i \geqslant C_i^1 \, (f_i \, (p), K_i)$, then*
$2f_i^i + (p_i - C_i^1 \, (f_i \, (p), K_i)) f_i^{ii} < 0, \quad i = 1, 2.$

Together with convexity of C_i, A5 insures that the functions π_i are concave with respect to (p_i, K_i) in the region of A where the firm's price is no less than its marginal cost.

2.2 Existence of an Entry-Exit Equilibrium

Entry and exit are each treated separately before considering a model in which both are possible. Section 2.2.1 deals with a model in which only entry can occur, in section 2.2.2, an exit model is considered and section 2.2.3 takes up a model in which both entry and exit are possible.

2.2.1 A Model With Entry and Without Exit

First, it is necessary to be precise about the timing of decisions. In time zero, the established firm chooses only K_{10}, his initial capital stock, which is also his initial investment, I_{10}, and is the capital *in place* for period 1. It is in period 1 that he can first produce and sell. Thus, from period 1 onward, he chooses both a price and a capital stock. For the entrant, his decision to enter cannot be made earlier than period 1. If he decides to enter in period $t_0 \geqslant 1$, this means a) that he chooses only an investment level in period t_0, I_{2,t_0}, which is also his initial capital K_{2,t_0} and which is his capital in place in period $t_0 + 1$; b) his *announcement* that he will enter in period t_0 is assumed to be made *before* firm 1 makes his period t_0 choices; and c) firm 2 cannot sell or make price choices until period $t_0 + 1$.

The strategy of the established firm may be thought of as having two major parts. The first consists of a sequence of capital and price decisions which it follows as long as it is alone in the market. The second consists of the capital and price decisions which it follows from the moment of entry of the second firm. The latter necessarily depends upon the capital the estiablished firm possesses when the entrant announces his intention to come in. For the entrant, there is the choice of whether to enter the market. If a date of entry is chosen, then there must be a sequence of capital and price decisions.

The first step of analysis is to look at the subgame which begins at the moment when firm 2 commits himself to enter the market. Most of the present section is devoted to showing that this subgame has a non-cooperative equilibrium. Due to the stationary character of the model, the announcement of entry may be assumed at $t = 1$. Initial capital for the established firm is $K_{10} = I_{10}$. The entrant invests first in period 1 and has sales first in period 2. Thus the two discounted payoff streams for the time period 1 onward are

On Entry Preventing Behavior 241

$$-I_{11} + A^* + \sum_{t=2}^{\infty} \alpha_1^{t-1} \pi_1 (p_t, K_{1,t-1}, K_{1t}) \qquad (6)$$

$$-I_{21} + \sum_{t=2}^{\infty} \alpha_2^{t-1} \pi_2 (p_t, K_{2,t-1}, K_{2t}) \qquad (7)$$

where A^* accounts for the effects of period 0 investment and period 1 sales.

For firm 1 a *strategy* may be written $\sigma_1 = (p_{11}, K_{11}, p_{12}, K_{12}, \dots)$ and for firm 2, $\sigma_2 = (K_{21}, p_{22}, K_{22}, p_{23}, K_{23}, \dots)$. A strategy pair is written $\sigma_1 = (\sigma_1, \sigma_2)$. These strategies are *simple* in the sense that the actions taken in any given time period by a firm are not contingent in any way upon the decisions prior to that time. An equilibrium in simple strategies is also an equilibrium in a game in which the strategy sets are enlarged. The payoff stream given by equation (6) may be denoted $G_1 (\sigma)$ and that for equation (7) by $G_2 (\sigma)$.

Let the strategy set for player i, from which σ_i is drawn, be denoted by S_i. S_i is the set of all simple strategies for firm i and is defined precisely below. A non-cooperative equilibrium is defined by: $(\sigma_1^*, \sigma_2^*) = \sigma^*$ is a non-cooperative equilibrium if

$$\sigma_i^* \in S_i, \quad i = 1, 2 \qquad (8)$$

$$G_i (\sigma^*) = \max_{\sigma_i \in S_i} G_i (\sigma_i, \sigma_j^*), \quad i \neq j, \quad i = 1, 2. \qquad (9)$$

That the post-entry subgame has a non-cooperative equilibrium is proved below in theorem 1. Prior to theorem 1, the notion of *best reply* is defined: σ_2' is the best reply to σ_1' for firm 2 if

$$G_2 (\sigma_1', \sigma_2') = \max_{\sigma_2} G_2 (\sigma_1', \sigma_2). \qquad (10)$$

A non-cooperative equilibrium is also defined by $\sigma^* = (\sigma_1^*, \sigma_2^*)$ such that σ_1^* is a best reply to σ_2^* for firm 1 and σ_2^* is a best reply to σ_1^* for firm 2.

Theorem 1: The no entry, no exit two person subgame satisfying A1 − A5, with discounted profits given by equations (6) and (7), and with firm 1 having an initial capital of K_{10} has a non-cooperative equilibrium.

Proof: The steps of the proof are: a) show that the strategy sets of the firms are convex and compact, b) show that the best reply mapping of each firm is defined, single valued and continuous for each strategy of the other, and c) show that a) and b) imply the existence of a non-cooperative equilibrium.

a) Note first that $p_{1t} \in [0, p_1^+]$ and $K_{1t} \in [0, K_1^+]$ where it must now be assured that K_1^+ is finite. Because revenue is bounded, profit per period is bounded by π_2^+, a finite upper bound on revenue per period. Non-negative profit is impossible if I_{1t} exceeds $\pi_1^+/(1 - \alpha_1)$; hence, K_1^+ may be taken as $\pi^+/((1 - \alpha_1)(1 - \delta))$. Let $K_1 = (\{K_{10}, K_{11}, K_{12}, \dots \}), 0 \leqslant K_{10} \leqslant K_1^+$ and $(1 - \delta) K_{1,t-1} \leqslant K_{1t} \leqslant K_1^+$,

$t = \{1, 2, \ldots\}$, $P_1 = \overset{\infty}{\underset{t=1}{X}} [0, p_1^+]$ and let $S_1 = K_1 \times P_1$. S_1 is the strategy space for firm 1. Both K_1 and P_1 are convex; hence S_1 is convex. Compactness of S_1 may be seen from the following norm for $\sigma_1 \in S_1$.

$$\| \sigma_1 \| = \sum_{t=1}^{\infty} \alpha_1^{t-1} (p_{1t} + K_{1t}) \tag{11}$$

The same argument may be used for S_2, defined in a parallel fashion to S_1.

b) That the best reply mapping of a firm is defined for any strategy of the other firm is immediate because G_i is a continuous function of σ_i and σ_i has a compact set as its domain; hence, G_i takes a maximum. Single valuedness and continuity of one firm's best reply with respect to the strategy of the other remains to be proved. These follow from the concavity conditions imposed in A1 − A5. Whenever the optimal price is so high that demand is zero, the best reply is taken to be the lowest price at which demand is zero. Letting a_1 denote the points in R_+^2 which are in A_1, but are not in $\overset{\circ}{A}_1$, the best reply price of firm 1 in period t is given by $\pi_{1t}^1 = 0$, if any price satisfies this condition, and by p_{1t} such that $p_t \in a_1$, if no price satisfies $\pi_{1t}^1 = 0$ [6]). This best reply price depends only on p_{2t} and $K_{1,t-1}$ and may be denoted

$$p_{1t} = \psi_1 (K_{1, t-1}, p_{2t}). \tag{12}$$

$$p_{2t} = \psi_2 (K_{2, t-1}, p_{1t}) \tag{13}$$

may be analogously defined. Note that

$$\frac{\partial \psi_1}{\partial K_{1,t-1}} = \psi_1^1 = \frac{-\pi_1^{13}}{\pi_1^{11}} \quad \text{if } f_1 > 0 \\ \left. \begin{array}{cc} \end{array} \right\} \tag{14}$$
$$= 0 \qquad \text{otherwise}$$

If $f_1 > 0$, then $\psi_1^1 < 0$, which means that the larger is the firm's capital, the lower is its optimal price, due to the effect which the larger capital has on lowering marginal cost.

With ψ_1 substituted for p_{1t}, $\pi_1 (p_t, K_{1,t-1}, K_{1t}) = \pi_1 (\psi_1, p_{2t}, K_{1,t-1}, K_{1t})$,

$$\frac{\partial \pi_1}{\partial K_{1,t-1}} = \pi_1^1 \psi_1^1 + \pi_1^3 \tag{15}$$

and

$$\frac{\partial^2 \pi_1}{\partial K_{1,t-1}^2} = \psi_1^1 (\pi_1^{11} \psi_1^1 + \pi_1^{13}) + \pi_1^1 \psi_1^{11} + \pi_1^{31} \psi_1^1 + \pi_1^{33}. \tag{16}$$

_____

[6]) Superscripts are used to denote partial derivatives. The "t" subscript denotes the time period to which the demand and cost functions pertain.

The term $\pi_1^1 \, \psi_1^{11} = 0$; for, if $f_1 > 0$, then $\pi_1^1 = 0$ and if $f_1 = 0$, then $\psi_1^{11} = 0$. Equation (16) is clearly strictly negative. Again, if $f_1 = 0$, then $\pi_1^1 = 0$, leaving only π_1^{33}, which is negative. Otherwise, recalling that $\psi_1^1 = -\pi_1^{13}/\pi_1^{11}$, equation (16) reduces to

$$\pi_1^{11} \, (\psi_1^1)^2 + 2 \, \pi_1^{13} \, \psi_1^1 + \pi_1^{33} = \frac{\pi_1^{11} \, \pi_1^{33} - (\pi_1^{13})^2}{\pi_1^{11}} < 0. \tag{17}$$

Because the only term of G_1 into which $K_{1,t-1}$ enters non-linearly is $\pi_1 \, (p_t, K_{1,t-1}, K_{1t})$, the strict concavity of π_1 in $K_{1,t-1}$ implies strict concavity of G_1 in $(K_{10}, K_{11}, K_{12}, \ldots)$.

c) Let the best reply functions of the two firms be denoted $\sigma_1 = r_1 \, (\sigma_1)$ and $\sigma_2 = r_2 \, (\sigma_1)$. The two functions, taken together, are a function from $S = S_1 \times S_2$ into S and may be written

$$\sigma' = r \, (\sigma) = (r_1 \, (\sigma_2), r_2 \, (\sigma_1)). \tag{18}$$

Any fixed point of r is a non-cooperative equilibrium and any non-cooperative equilibrium is a fixed pint of r. Thus, if r has a fixed point, the subgame has an equilibrium. By Brouwer's fixed point theorem, the fixed point exists and the theorem is proved. □

The equilibrium of theorem 1 is not, in general, unique; however, in section 3 additional conditions are given under which it is. The lack of uniqueness is an inconvenience which is circumvented by making an arbitrary selection. For each possible value of $K_1 \in [0, K_1^+]$, the capital held by the established firm at the time of entry, choose an arbitrary non-cooperative equilibrium and denote the i-th firm's discounted payoff under the chosen equilibrium, discounted to the announcement period, by $F_i \, (K_1)$.

It is now possible to characterize the entry game in which, if the entrant decides in period t to come in, his payoff for the whole game, discounted to period t is $F_2 \, (K_{1,t-1})$. The payoff to the established firm, given entry in period t, and discounted to period 0 is

$$-I_{10} + \sum_{\tau=1}^{t-1} \alpha_1^\tau \, \pi_1 \, (p_{1\tau}, p_2^+, K_{1,\tau-1}, K_{1\tau}) + \alpha_1^t F_1 \, (K_{1,t-1}). \tag{19}$$

The strategy of firm 1 has been partly specified already — for that part of the game which commences from the entry announcement of the entrant. Firm 1 must also specify a sequence $\{p_{1t}, K_{1,t-1}\}_{t=1}^\infty$ which it follows as long as it is alone in the market. To see how the entrant behaves in equilibrium, imagine an arbitrary price-capital sequence for firm 1 which it follows prior to entry. Clearly, if there is at least one t such that $F_2 \, (K_{1t}) > 0$, then the entrant will come in at some time; however, it need not be in the entrant's best interest to come in at the very first period for which F_2 is positive. Consider the situation as of period 0, and look at the sequence $\{\alpha_2^t \, F_2 \, (K_{1t})\}$. Firm 2 enters at time t' if the discounted payoff at that time is positive and if further waiting will not increase his discounted payoff. For any given strategy of the established firm, there is a best reply for the entrant, characterized below:

Lemma 1: The entrant comes into the market at time t' if a) $F_2 (K_{1t'}) > 0$, b) $\alpha_2^{t'} F_1 (K_{1t'}) \geqslant \alpha_2^t F_2 (K_{1t})$ *for all* $t > t'$ *and* c) $\alpha_2^{t'} F_2 (K_{1t'}) > \alpha_2^t F_2 (K_{1t})$ *for all* $t < t'$. *If there is at least one t such that* $F_2 (K_{1t}) > 0$, *then there is a unique* t' *which satisfies* a) − c). *If there is no t such that* $F_2 (K_{1t}) > 0$, *then the entrant never comes into the market.*

Proof: The only thing in the lemma which requires proof is the assertion that if there is at least one t such that $F_2 (K_{1t}) > 0$, then there is a unique t' satisfying a) − c). The conditions a) − c) specify that the entrant comes in at the time at which his discounted profits are maximized, and that, if there are two or more such times, he comes in at the earliest of them; hence, proof reduces to showing that if discounted profits are ever positive, then at some time they are maximized.

By hypothesis there is some t'' such that $F_2 (K_{1t''}) > 0$. Because F_2 is bounded, there is t_0 such that

$$\alpha_2^{t''} F_2 (K_{1t''}) \geqslant \alpha_2^t F_2 (K_{1t}) \tag{20}$$

for all $t > t^0$. Therefore t' must be a member of the set $\{0, \ldots, t''\}$ which is finite; hence, $\alpha_2^t F_2 (K_{1t})$ takes a maximum on the set. If the maximum is attained for more than one t, then t' is the smallest. Otherwise, it is the time of the unique maximum.

$\square$

For the established firm, only an ϵ-optimal strategy can be assured. That is a strategy such that no other strategy yields a discounted payoff higher by more than an arbitrary positive ϵ. To see this, consider any $\sigma_1 = \{p_{1t}, K_{1,t-1}\}_{t=1}^{\infty}$ specifying the firm's behavior in the absence of entry, and note that the discounted profits of the established firm need not be continuous in σ_1. The set of attainable payoffs is bounded, but not closed; hence, it has a least upper bound which need not be attainable. Thus:

Theorem 2: In the two firm market with one established firm and one entrant, satisfying A1 − A5, with entry allowed, but not exit, there exists an ϵ-equilibrium. This equilibrium is characterized by a pair of strategies such that the entrant's strategy is a best reply to the strategy of the established firm, and no other strategy of the established firm, given that the entrant is always assumed to use a best reply to the choice of the established firm, yields more by at least ϵ.

To see whether the established firm engages in entry preventing behavior, it is necessary to determine the behavior the firm would follow if the entrant did not exist. Let σ_1^* denote a strategy which maximizes the discounted profits of the firm on the assumption that entry is impossible. Let $\{K_{1t}^*\}$ be the associated sequence of capital stocks. If $F_2 (K_{1t}^*) \leqslant 0$ for all t, then the firm's optimal choice is to follow σ_1^* and entry will not occur. It is also possible that $F_2 (K_{1t}^*) > 0$ for some t; however, no alternative policy for the established firm yields higher profits. In this case too entry preventing behavior would not be followed.

Now consider circumstances in which the established firm will wish to affect or prevent entry. First, assume that there are some values of K_1 for which F_2 is non-positive and others for which it is positive. Assume also that at least one of the K_{1t}^* yields positive F_2. Then if the firm follows a policy such that F_2 is never positive, it is engaging in entry preventing behavior. Such behavior need not be in the firm's best interests; however, under the circumstances sketched above, it is at least possible. It also provides a workable definition of entry preventing behavior.

Now consider an equilibrium in which the entrant does come in at t_0 and the strategy followed by the established firm is not σ_1^*. If entry under σ_1^* would occur at t^* and $t^* \neq t_0$, then the behavior of the established firm is influenced by (the threat of) entry. Even if $t_0 > t^*$, it does not seem reasonable to say that the firm is engaging in entry preventing behavior. It is engaging in entry delaying behavior, but it is not preventing entry.

2.2.2 A Model With Exit and Without Entry

The situation considered here is one in which two firms are in the market at the outset and one or both may leave the market at any time and not return. Assume that both firms make their initial investment in period 0, but that firm 1 may start with an initial capital which is positive. Assume, further, that if either firm left the market, the remaining one would certainly find it profitable to continue. If, for example, firm j leaves the market at the end of period $t - 1$ and, at that time, firm i has a capital stock of $K_{i,t-1}$, then the maximum discounted profit which firm i can earn from t onward, discounted back to t, is denoted $H_i (K_{i,t-1})$. It is immediate that this maximum exists and depends only on the capital which firm i possesses when it becomes a monopolist having no threat of entry.

Exit from the market is handled by assuming that each firm in each period decides on a probability, v_{it}, of remaining in the market in the next period. That is, if firm i is in the market in period t, it chooses p_{it}, K_{it} and v_{it}, where $v_{it} \in [0, 1]$ is the probability that firm i will continue in the market in period $t + 1$, given that it was in the market in period t. Thus, from the time of entry of firm 2, the market is a two player exit game as in *Friedman* [1979]. It remains to define an equilibrium for such a game and to show existence. The equilibrium concept which is employed is the weak non-cooperative equilibrium of *Friedman* [1979]. Letting $V_{it} = \overset{t}{\underset{\tau=1}{\pi}} v_{i\tau}$, the profit function of the i-th firm is

$$G_i (\sigma) = -I_{i0} + A_i^* + \alpha_i V_{10} V_{20} \pi_i (p_1, K_{i0}, K_{i1})$$

$$+ \overset{\infty}{\underset{t=2}{\Sigma}} \alpha_i^t V_{i,t-1} V_{j,t-2} [v_{j,t-1} \pi_i (p_t, K_{i,t-1}, K_{it})$$

$$+ (1 - v_{j,t-1}) H_i (K_{i,t-1})], \ i \neq j. \tag{21}$$

$A_1^* = A^*, A_2^* = 0$, and $V_{10} = V_{20} = 1$.

To picture the strategy of firm i, recall that firm i knows in any period whether its rival is still active and knows that if the rival leaves the market he (firm i) is thenceforth alone. The firm must, then, name a sequence of prices and capital levels. $K_{i0}, p_{i1}, K_{i1}, p_{i2}, K_{i2}, \ldots$ which specify what it chooses as long as the rival is in the market. It must also specify the choices to be followed from period $t + 1$ onward, given that the rival's last period in the market is period t; however, these need not be formally spelled out because the firm would merely face a simple maximization problem. The strategy, σ_i, consists of the sequence $(K_{i0}, p_{i1}, K_{i1}, v_{i1}, p_{i2}, K_{i2}, v_{i2}, \ldots) = = (\underline{K}_i, \underline{p}_i, \underline{v}_i)$ together with the implicitly understood behavior to be followed in the event the firm becomes a monopolist.

A particular strategy pair, (σ_1^*, σ_2^*) is a *weak non-cooperative equilibrium* if σ_i^* is in the strategy set of player i ($i = 1, 2$), and

$$G_i(\sigma^*) = \max_{\underline{p}_i, \underline{K}_i} G_i(\underline{K}_i, \underline{p}_i, \underline{v}_i^*, \sigma_j^*) = \max_{\underline{v}_i} G_i(\underline{K}_i^*, \underline{p}_i^*, \underline{v}_i, \sigma_j^*),$$
$$i = 1, 2, \quad i \neq j. \tag{22}$$

That is, neither player can increase his discounted payoff by changing his "survival" probabilitites, $\underline{v}_i$, nor can he increase his payoff by changing his price-capital policy. Joint changes of $\underline{v}_i$ and $(\underline{p}_i, \underline{K}_i)$ are not considerd, which is what distinguishes the *weak* non-cooperative equilibrium from a non-cooperative equilibrium. Existence of a non-cooperative equilibrium cannot be assured in this model because the payoff of a firm (G_i) is not, in general, a quasi-concave function of its own strategy (σ_i).

Theorem 3: In any exit model satisfying A1 − A5, *the game which commences when the entrant comes into the market has a weak non-cooperative equilibrium.*

Proof: For a weak non-cooperative equilibrium in a two player game, there are four *best reply* functions. Each is defined in this way: Let $(\sigma_1, \underline{K}_2, \underline{p}_2)$ be given. Then, for firm 2 there is a $\underline{v}_2$ which maximizes its payoff, given the other actions. This $\underline{v}_2$ is said to be a *best reply* to $(\sigma_1, \underline{K}_2, \underline{p}_2)$. If the best reply is always unique, then there is a best reply function, and when the best reply need not be unique, the relation is a best reply correspondence. A second best reply relation is that which gives the (set of) optimal $(\underline{K}_2, \underline{p}_2)$ for any σ_1 and $\underline{v}_2$. Another two best reply relations may be analogously defined for $\underline{v}_1$ and $(\underline{K}_1, \underline{p}_1)$. These four best reply relations are all defined for all possible strategies and form a mapping, Φ, from the product of the two players' strategy sets to itself. That is

$$\sigma' \quad = (\underline{K}_1', \underline{p}_1', \underline{v}_1', \underline{K}_2', \underline{p}_2', \underline{v}_2') \in \Phi(\sigma) \text{ is defined by}$$

$$\Phi(\sigma) \quad = \Phi(\underline{K}_1, \underline{p}_1, \underline{v}_1, \underline{K}_2, \underline{p}_2, \underline{v}_2) \tag{23}$$

$$= \Phi_1(\underline{p}_1, \underline{K}_1, \sigma_2) \times \Phi_2(\underline{v}_1, \sigma_2) \times \Phi_3(\sigma_1, \underline{p}_2, \underline{K}_2) \times \Phi_4(\sigma_1, \underline{v}_2)$$

where Φ_1, Φ_2, Φ_3 and Φ_4 are the four best reply mappings. Φ_2 and Φ_4 are, in fact functions.

$$\underline{y}_1' \in \Phi_1 \ (\underline{p}_1, \underline{K}_1, \sigma_2), (\underline{p}_1', \underline{K}_1') = \Phi_2 \ (\underline{V}_1, \sigma_2),$$

$$\underline{y}_2' \in \Phi_3 \ (\sigma_1, \underline{p}_2, \underline{K}_2), \text{ and } (\underline{p}_2', \underline{K}_2') = \Phi_4 \ (\sigma_1, \underline{y}_2). \tag{24}$$

Because the payoffs are linear in the probabilities, the two best reply mappings (σ_1 and Φ_3) which determine $\underline{y}_1$ and $\underline{y}_2$ are upper semi-continuous and they have convex image sets. On this, see *Friedman* [1979]. That the other two best reply mappings are continuous functions is known from the proof of theorem 1; hence, by the Kakutani fixed point theorem, Φ has a fixed point and such a fixed point is a weak non-cooperative equilibrium. ☐

2.2.3 Entry and Exit Under Certainty

It remains now to put the two pieces together. Note first that the equilibrium whose existence is proved in theorem 4 is not, in general, unique; hence, one equilibrium is selected for each K_1 whenever more than one exists. Denote the selected equilibrium payoffs by $F_1^* (K_1)$ and $F_2^* (K_1)$.

The situation is parallel to that discussed at the end of section 2.2.1 for the model with entry and no exit. The differences are that the F_i of section 2.2.1 are replaced with the F_i^* and the ϵ-non-cooperative equilibrium with an ϵ-weak non-cooperative equilibrium. Earlier proofs go through, subject to the modifications just given. Thus the following Lemma and theorem are proved.

Lemma 2: The entrant comes into the market at time t' if a) $F_2^* (K_{1t'}) > 0$, b) $\alpha_2^{t'} F_2^* (K_{1t'}) \geqslant \alpha_2^t F_2^* (K_{1t})$ for all $t > t'$ and c) $\alpha_2^{t'} F_2^* (K_{1t'}) > \alpha_2^t F_2^* (K_{1t})$ for all $t < t'$. If there is at least one t such that $F_2^* (K_{1t}) > 0$, then there is a unique t' which satisfies a) – c). If there is no t such that $F_2^* (K_{1t}) > 0$, then the entrant never comes into the market.

Theorem 4: In the two firm market with one established firm and one entrant, satisfying A1 – A5, with both entry and exit allowed, there exists an ϵ-equilibrium. This equilibrium is characterized by: a) The equilibrium strategies yield a weak non-cooperative equilibrium for any subgame commencing with the time the entrant comes into the market. b) Subject to a), the entrant's strategy is a best reply to the strategy of the established firm. c) Given that the entrant always may choose a best reply to the established firm's strategy, the established firm chooses a strategy such that no other strategy could achieve at least ϵ greater discounted profit.

3. Equilibrium in a Special Case of the Model

If some additional assumptions are made, equilibrium is unique in the two firm model with neither entry nor exit. This model is developed in section 3.1 and in section 3.2 some results on entry prevention are obtained, where it is shown that the entrant's equilibrium profit in the market falls as the capital stock of the monopolist, held at the moment of entry, rises. This is what is intuitively expected; however, relaxation of some of the assumptions would results in the contrary.

3.1 Equilibrium in the Two Firm Market with Neither Entry nor Exit

Consider the subgame centered about the choices made in period t. Then

$$\pi_i\,(p_t,\,K_{i,t-1},\,K_{it}) + \alpha_i\,\pi_i\,(p_{t+1},\,K_{it},\,K_{i,t+1}) = \pi_{it} + \alpha_i\,\pi_{i,t+1} \tag{25}$$

is that part of the i-th firm's objective function into which decisions of time t enter. It is possible to think of a single period game in which $(K_{i,t-1},\,p_{i,t+1},\,K_{i,t+1})$, $i = 1, 2$, are given, the two firms choose $(p_{it},\,K_{it})$, respectively, and equation (25) gives their objective functions. The non-cooperative equilibria of such a game may be denoted by $\phi\,(p_{t-1},\,p_{t+1},\,K_{t-1},\,K_{t+1})$. Such games have been studied in *Friedman* [1977, chapter 9]. If, for each $(p_{t-1},\,p_{t+1},\,K_{t-1},\,K_{t+1})$ there is exactly one equilibrium and the function ϕ is a contraction, then the equilibrium has some special features. Irrespective of the nature of ϕ, a non-cooperative equilibrium for the game (i.e., the original infinite period game) satisfies the function ϕ in each period. Even without further assumptions, ϕ is known to be more specialized than the form given above. In particular,

$$\left.\begin{array}{l} p_{1t} = \phi_1\,(K_{t-1}), p_{2t} = \phi_2\,(K_{t-1}) \\[2mm] K_{1t} = \phi_3\,(p_{t+1},\,K_{1,t-1}), K_{2t} = \phi_4\,(p_{t+1},\,K_{2,t-1}) \end{array}\right\} \tag{26}$$

ϕ_1 and ϕ_2 are derived from equations (12) and (13). $\phi_3\,(p_{t+1},\,K_{1,t-1})$ is the solution to $(\partial\,/\,\partial K_{1t})\,(\pi_{1t} + \alpha_1\,\pi_{1,t+1}) = 0$ if that solution is no smaller than $(1-\delta)K_{1,t-1}$. When $\phi_3\,(p_{t+1},\,K_{1,t-1}) > (1-\delta)\,K_{1,t-1}$, then K_{1t} depends only on p_{t+1}. Otherwise, $\phi_3\,(p_{t+1},\,K_{1,t-1}) = (1-\delta)\,K_{1,t-1}$. Similarly for ϕ_4. Furthermore, if the optimal values of the variables are in the interior of their domains, then the derivatives of ϕ are

$$\left.\begin{array}{llll} \dfrac{\partial p_{1t}}{\partial K_{1,t-1}} = \dfrac{-\pi_{1t}^{13}\,\pi_{2t}^{22}}{\pi_{1t}^{11}\,\pi_{2t}^{22} - \pi_{1t}^{12}\,\pi_{2t}^{21}} & & \dfrac{\partial p_{it}}{\partial K_{2,t-1}} = \dfrac{\pi_{1t}^{12}\,\pi_{2t}^{23}}{\pi_{1t}^{11}\,\pi_{2t}^{22} - \pi_{1t}^{12}\,\pi_{2t}^{21}} \\[5mm] \dfrac{\partial p_{2t}}{\partial K_{1,t-1}} = \dfrac{\pi_{1t}^{13}\,\pi_{2t}^{21}}{\pi_{1t}^{11}\,\pi_{2t}^{22} - \pi_{1t}^{12}\,\pi_{2t}^{21}} & & \dfrac{\partial p_{2t}}{\partial K_{2,t-1}} = \dfrac{-\pi_{2t}^{23}\,\pi_{1t}^{11}}{\pi_{1t}^{11}\,\pi_{2t}^{22} - \pi_{1t}^{12}\,\pi_{2t}^{21}} \\[5mm] \dfrac{\partial K_{1t}}{\partial p_{1,t+1}} = \dfrac{-\pi_{1,t+1}^{31}}{\pi_{1,t+1}^{33}} & & \dfrac{\partial K_{1t}}{\partial p_{2,t+1}} = \dfrac{-\pi_{1,t+1}^{32}}{\pi_{1,t+1}^{33}} \\[5mm] \dfrac{\partial K_{2t}}{\partial p_{1,t+1}} = \dfrac{-\pi_{2,t+1}^{31}}{\pi_{2,t+1}^{33}} & & \dfrac{\partial K_{2t}}{\partial p_{2,t+1}} = \dfrac{-\pi_{2,t+1}^{32}}{\pi_{2,t+1}^{33}} \end{array}\right\} \tag{27}$$

On Entry Preventing Behavior   249

where

$$\pi_{1t}^{11} = (P_{1t} - C_{1t}^1) f_{1t}^{11} + (2 - C_{1t}^{11} f_{1t}^1) f_{1t}^1 < 0$$

$$\pi_{1t}^{12} = (P_{1t} - C_{1t}^1) f_{1t}^{12} + (1 - C_{1t}^{11} f_{1t}^1) f_{1t}^2 > 0 \qquad (28)$$

$$\pi_{1t}^{13} = -C_{1t}^{12} f_{1t}^1 < 0, \; \pi_{1t}^{23} = -C_{1t}^{12} f_{1t}^2 > 0, \; \pi_{1t}^{33} = -C_{1t}^{22} < 0$$

and analogously for firm 2. If the optimal K_{1t} is a boundary value, then $\partial K_{1t} / \partial p_{1,t+1} = \partial K_{1t} / \partial p_{2,t+1} = 0$. If the optimal value of p_{2t} is high enough that $f_{2t} = 0, f_{1t}^{12} = f_{1t}^2 = f_{2t}^1 = f_{2t}^2 = f_{2t}^{11} = f_{2t}^{12} = f_{2t}^{22} = 0$ and some of the derivatives in equation (28) are adjusted accordingly, and the various derivatives must be recalculated. The derivatives with altered values are

$$\frac{\partial p_{1t}}{\partial K_{2,t-1}} = \frac{\partial p_{2t}}{\partial K_{1,t-1}} = \frac{\partial p_{2t}}{\partial K_{2,t-1}} = 0, \; \frac{\partial p_{1t}}{\partial K_{1,t-1}} = \frac{-\pi_{1t}^{13}}{\pi_{1t}^{11}},$$

$$\frac{\partial K_{1t}}{\partial p_{2,t+1}} = \frac{\partial K_{2t}}{\partial p_{1,t+1}} = \frac{\partial K_{2t}}{\partial p_{2,t+1}} = 0. \qquad (29)$$

Should ϕ be a contraction, then from *Friedman* [1977, chap. 9], there is a unique non-cooperative equilibrium for the game, given the initial capital the firms hold. ϕ is a contraction if the following conditions hold:

A6. *For p such that* f^{ii} *and* f^{12} *exist,* $f_i^{ii} \leq 0$ *and* $f_i^{ii} + |f_i^{12}| \leq 0$. *In addition* $C_i^{12} \geq -1$ *and* $-C_i^{12} / C_i^{22} (|f_i^1| + |f_i^2|) < 1, \; i = 1, 2.$

Lemma 3: If A1 $-$ A6 *hold, then* ϕ *is a contraction.*

Proof: ϕ is a contraction if $|\phi_j^1| + |\phi_j^2| < 1$ for $j = 1, \ldots, 4$. Consider first $j = 1$. From equation (29) it is seen that $|\phi_1^1| + |\phi_1^2| = 0$ if $f_1 = 0$; and $|\phi_1^1| + |\phi_1^2| = = \pi_{1t}^{13} / \pi_{1t}^{11}$ if $f_1 > 0$ and $f_2 = 0$. $\pi_{1t}^{13} / \pi_{1t}^{11} < 1$ is equivalent to

$$(P_{1t} - C_{1t}^1) f_{1t}^{11} + (1 - C_{1t}^{11} f_{1t}^1) f_{1t}^1 + (1 - C_{1t}^{12}) f_{1t}^1 < 0 \qquad (30)$$

which clearly holds. If f_1 and f_2 are positive, then $|\phi_1^1| + |\phi_1^2| < 1$ is equivalent to

$$\pi_{1t}^{13} \pi_{2t}^{22} - \pi_{1t}^{12} \pi_{2t}^{23} < \pi_{1t}^{11} \pi_{2t}^{22} - \pi_{1t}^{12} \pi_{2t}^{21} \qquad (31)$$

which, in turn, is equivalent to

$$0 < (\pi_{1t}^{11} - f_{1t}^1)(\pi_{2t}^{22} - f_{2t}^2) - \pi_{1t}^{12} \pi_{2t}^{21} + f_{2t}^2 (\pi_{1t}^{11} - f_{1t}^1 - C_{2t}^{12} \pi_{1t}^{12}) +$$

$$+ f_{1t}^1 \pi_{2t}^{22} (1 + C_{1t}^{12}) \qquad (32)$$

That equation (32) holds may be seen by recalling that $-1 \leqslant C_{it}^{12} \leqslant 0$, $\pi_{it}^{12} > 0$ and $\pi_{it}^{ii} - f_{it}^{i} + \pi_{it}^{12} < 0$. An analogous argument can be made to show that $|\phi_2^1| + |\phi_2^2| < 1$.

Turning now to $|\phi_3^1| + |\phi_3^2| < 1$, when no boundary conditions are in effect, the condition is satisfied when

$$\frac{C_{1t}^{12} f_{1t}^1 - C_{1t}^{12} f_{1t}^2}{C_{1t}^{22}} = \frac{-C_{1t}^{12}}{C_{1t}^{22}} (f_{1t}^2 - f_{1t}^1) < 1 \tag{33}$$

holds. Equation (33) is one of the conditions stated in A6. As to boundary conditions, if $f_{2t} = 0$, then ϕ_3^1 is unchanged and $\phi_3^2 = 0$, so the requirement is still met. If $K_{1,t-1}$ is at a value so high that the choice is zero investment, then $\phi_3^1 = \phi_3^2 = 0$. Again, an analogous argument may be made to show that $|\phi_4^1| + |\phi_4^2| < 1$.   □

And now the existence theorem may be given:

Theorem 5: In a two firm market, without entry and exit, which satisfies A1 − A6, *there is a unique non-cooperative equilibrium.*

Proof: Virtually all the elements of proof have been given. It remains to note that the unique $\{p_t, K_t\}$ sequence which satisfies ϕ is clearly a non-cooperative equilibrium. This holds because any equilibrium sequence satsfies ϕ and, due to the concavity of G_i, the given sequence is the only sequence to do so.   □

The special structure of the model may be exploited further. The four equations of equation (26) may be condensed into two.

$$\left. \begin{array}{l} K_{1t} = \phi_3 \, (\phi_1 \, (K_t), \phi_2 \, (K_t), K_{1,t-1}) \\[2mm] K_{2t} = \phi_4 \, (\phi_1 \, (K_t), \phi_2 \, (K_t), K_{2,t-1}) \end{array} \right\} . \tag{34}$$

The optimal K_t is a fixed point of the system above. Note, however, that if the system of equations is a contraction, the fixed point is unique for a given K_{t-1} and may be written

$$K_{1t} = \psi_3 \, (K_{t-1}), \quad K_{2t} = \psi_4 \, (K_{t-1}) \tag{35}$$

Recall that $K_{1,t-1}$ enters ϕ_3 only as a boundary condition which stipulates that the capital stock of the firm cannot fall by a fraction larger than δ in each period. Thus, when the boundary constraints on K_{1t} and K_{2t} are not binding, $\psi_3 \, (K_{t-1}) = K_1^*$ and $\psi_4 \, (K_{t-1}) = K_2^*$, a pair of constants. It is surprising that the optimal capital stocks, away from the lower boundary, do not depend on the past history of the market or the length of the firms' horizons, as long as the horizons both extend at least through $t + 1$. Associated with the optimal capital stocks $K^* = (K_1^*, K_2^*)$ are prices $p^* = (\phi_1 \, (K^*), \phi_2 \, (K^*))$.

Note what would happen if one firm began in the market with an arbitrary initial capital which exceeded the optimal level by a large amount. Say it were firm 1. Its starting capital is K'_{10} and its subsequent capital levels are $K'_{1t} = (1 - \delta) K'_{1,t-1}$ as long as $(1 - \delta) K'_{1,t-1} \geqslant K^*_1$. For all periods afterward, the optimal level is constant at K^*_1. The capital stock choice of firm 2 and the two firms' prices are found by solving

$$K_{2t} = \phi_4 \left(\phi_1 \left(K'_{1t}, K_{2t} \right), \phi_2 \left(K'_{1t}, K_{2t} \right), K_{2,t-1} \right) \tag{36}$$

for the fixed point value of K_{2t}, with K'_{1t} and $K_{2,t-1}$ given, and then using ϕ_1 and ϕ_2 to find the prices for period $t + 1$. This process is followed by starting in the last period for which $K'_{1t} > K^*_1$ and working backward to the earliest period in which firm 2 is active.

3.2 Some Observations on Entry Prevention

In section 2.2.1, there is some discussion of entry preventing behavior in which it is noted that if the monopolist can choose an investment policy under which the entrant will never come in, and that policy is not what it would pursue in the absence of an entry threat, then it can engage in entry preventing behavior. It remains to understand whether the equilibrium profits of the entrant, given entry at time t, would rise or fall as K_{1t} increases. Intuition is confirmed, as is seen below:

Theorem 6: In a two firm market with no exit, which satisfies A1 — A6, let firm 2 use a best reply strategy to firm 1's strategy and let firm 1 use prices which are optimal given its capital and the strategy of firm 2. Then, given strategies such that no boundary conditions are in effect, the discounted payoff of firm 2 falls as K_{1t} rises.

Proof: Proof comes down to evaluating the sign of

$$\frac{dF_2}{dK_{1t}} = \frac{\partial F_{2t}}{\partial K_{2t}} \frac{\partial K_{2t}}{\partial K_{1t}} + \sum_{j=1}^{2} \frac{\partial F_2}{\partial p_{j,t+1}} \left[\frac{\partial p_{j,t+1}}{\partial K_{1t}} + \frac{\partial p_{j,t+1}}{\partial K_{2t}} \frac{\partial K_{2t}}{\partial K_{1t}} \right]. \tag{37}$$

As the evaluation is made at a point where firm 2 is in equilibrium and firm 1 is choosing optimal prices, both $\partial F_2 / \partial p_{2,t+1}$ and $\partial F_2 / \partial K_{2t}$ are zero and equation (37) becomes

$$\frac{dF_2}{dK_{1t}} = \frac{\partial F_2}{\partial p_{1,t+1}} \left[\phi^1_1 + \phi^2_1 \frac{dK_2}{dK_1} \right]. \tag{38}$$

As $\partial F_2 / \partial p_{1,t+1} > 0$, equation (38) has the same sign as the term in brackets. dK_2 / dK_1 is obtained by differentiating ϕ_4 and equals

$$\frac{\phi^1_4 \phi^1_1 + \phi^2_4 \phi^1_2}{1 - \phi^1_4 \phi^2_1 - \phi^2_4 \phi^2_2} \tag{39}$$

which makes equation (37) equivalent to

$$\frac{\phi_1^1 - \phi_4^2 \, (\phi_1^1 \, \phi_2^2 - \phi_1^2 \, \phi_2^1)}{1 - \phi_4^1 \, \phi_1^2 - \phi_4^2 \, \phi_2^2}. \tag{40}$$

The numerator of equation (40) is

$$-\frac{\pi_1^{13} \, (\pi_2^{22} \, \pi_2^{33} - \pi_2^{23} \, \pi_2^{23})}{\pi_2^{33} \, (\pi_1^{11} \, \pi_2^{22} - \pi_1^{12} \, \pi_2^{21})} < 0. \tag{41}$$

The denominator is

$$\frac{\pi_1^{11} \, (\pi_2^{22} \, \pi_2^{33} - \pi_2^{23} \, \pi_2^{23}) + \pi_1^{12} \, (\pi_2^{13} \, \pi_2^{23} - \pi_1^{12} \, \pi_2^{33})}{\pi_2^{33} \, (\pi_1^{11} \, \pi_2^{22} - \pi_1^{12} \, \pi_1^{21})} > 0. \tag{42}$$

It is perhaps not transparent that the denominator, equation (42) is positive. That fact may be seen in the following way: Equation (42) is in the form

$$\frac{A_1 \, B_1 + A_2 \, B_2}{E} \tag{43}$$

where A_1 and E are negative and the remaining terms are positive. $|A_1| > A_2$ and $B_1 > B_2$, making $A_1 \, B_2 + A_1 \, B_2 < 0$ and equation (43) positive. Thus, the sign of equation (40) is negative, making dF_2/dK_{1t} negative. $\qquad\square$

In the model it is clear from equations (27) and (28) that the optimal capital for a monopolist who has no fear of entry is larger than the optimal capital K_1^* which would obtain if there were two firms. Letting the former capital be denoted K_1^{**}, it is possible that if the firm had capital of K_1^{**} prior to the entry of firm 2 that, depending on the relative sizes of K_1^{**}, K_1^* and δ, it might take several periods for the firm's capital to fall from K_1^{**} to K_1^*. So it is possible that it would not be profitable for firm 2 to enter the market even though it could make positive profits when the two capital stocks are $K^* = (K_1^*, K_2^*)$.

Another aspect of the model is that if entry preventing behavior is possible, it involves firm 1 choosing its capital stock at or above some critical value, $\bar{K}_1$. Precisely because the high capital stock cannot be reduced at a faster rate than δ per period, the firm is forced to have too much capital during an adjustment interval of several periods. During this interval, it has lower marginal cost at any output level than at K_1^*; hence, it follows a lower price policy and, as a result, lowers the demand of firm 2.

Taking into account both the foregoing remarks and theorem 6, it is clear that entry preventing behavior, or entry forestalling behavior, consists of choosing levels of capital which are above the level which is optimal for the monopolist when he does not take entry into account. The latter level is above the level which would prevail after entry, so the entry preventing intention is unambiguous.

4. Concluding Comments

The most intuitively plausible entry preventing behavior in the present paper is that associated with the entry model of section 3. In it there is the possibility of the established firm preventing entry by choosing its capital so high that an entrant could not make a positive profit. In general it need not be that such a capital level for firm 1 exists, nor, if it does exist, that it is profitable for firm 1 to adopt it. Nonetheless, the means of entry prevention, where it can be practiced, is clear in the model. Note that adopting a very large, entry preventing, capital is like making a credible threat to the entrant. The threat is to use a price so low that he will not make a positive profit, should he come in. What makes the threat credible is that the firm's capital is so high that the "threat price" is simply the ordinary equilibrium price which is natural for the firm to choose after entry and in the light of the capital it would have. This may be contrasted with a model in which there is no capital and the established firm makes a general public announcement that it will switch to some particular (non-equilibrium) low price if any new firm should enter its industry. In this case, after entry, it has no incentive to charge its previously announced price.

The present paper is, I believe, a start on analyzing entry and exit with explicit account taken of the entrants — that is, with the entrant being an active, rational, decision making economic agent. The only earlier work along these lines of which I am aware is *Shubik's* [1959] *firm-in-being*. The present paper is an elaboration of that idea. Whether any of the results here still obtain, and if so, in what form, after the model is further generalized remains to be seen.

References

Bain, J.S.: A Note on Pricing in Monopoly and Oligopoly. Amer. Econ. Rev. 39, 1949, 448–464.
Friedman, J.W.: Oligopoly and the Theory of Games. 1977.
−: Non-cooperative Equilibrium for Exit Supergames. Int. Econ. Rev. 20, forthcoming, 1979.
Harrod, R.F.: Theory of Imperfect Competion Revised. Economic Essays, chapt. 8, London 1952.
Hoggatt, A.C.: Response of Paid Student Subjects to Differential Behaviour of Robots in Bifurcated Duopoly Games. Rev. of Econ. Stud. 36, 1969, 417–432.
Shubik, M.: Strategy and Market Structure. New York 1959.

[18]

The Economic Journal, **90** (March 1980), 95–106
Printed in Great Britain

THE ROLE OF INVESTMENT IN
ENTRY-DETERRENCE*

The theory of large-scale entry into an industry is made complicated by its game-theoretic aspects. Even in the simplest case of one established firm facing one prospective entrant, there are some subtle strategic interactions. The established firm's pre-entry decisions can influence the prospective entrant's view of what will happen if he enters, and the established firm will try to exploit this possibility to its own advantage.

The earliest treatments met these problems by adopting the Bain–Sylos postulate, where the prospective entrant was assumed to believe that the established firm would maintain the same output after entry as its actual pre-entry output. Then the established firm naturally acquired a Stackelberg leadership role. However, the assumption is dubious on two opposing counts. First, faced with an irrevocable fact of entry, the established firm will usually find it best to make an accommodating output reduction. On the other hand, it would like to threaten to respond to entry with a predatory increase in output. Its problem is to make the latter threat credible given the prospective entrant's knowledge of the former fact. (A detailed exposition of the Bain–Sylos model and its critique can be found in Scherer (1970, ch. 8).)

In a seminal treatment of games involving such conflicts, Schelling (1960, ch. 2) suggested that a threat which is costly to carry out can be made credible by entering into an advance commitment which makes its fulfilment optimal or even necessary. This was applied to the question of entry by Spence (1977), who recognised that the established firm's prior and irrevocable investment decisions could be a commitment of this kind. He assumed that the prospective entrant would believe that the established firm's post-entry output would equal its pre-entry capacity. In the interests of entry-deterrence, the established firm may set capacity at such a high level that in the pre-entry phase it would not want to utilise it all, i.e. excess capacity would be observed.

The Bain–Sylos and Spence analyses were extended in Dixit (1979) by considering whether the established firm will find it best to prevent entry or to allow it to occur. However, the basic assumptions concerning the post-entry developments were maintained.

Since it is at best unclear whether such assumptions will be valid, it seems useful to study the consequences of some alternatives. In reality, there may be no agreement about the rules of the post-entry game, and there may be periods of disequilibrium before any order is established. Financial positions of the firms may then acquire an important role. However, even when the two have a common understanding of the rules of the post-entry duopoly, there are several possibilities. An obvious case is where a Nash equilibrium will be established

* I am grateful to Gunnar Bramness and Michael Waterson for useful comments on an earlier version.

after entry, either in quantities as in Cournot (see also Wenders (1971)) or in prices as in Bertrand. Yet another case is where the entrant is destined to take over Stackelberg leadership in setting quantities (see Salop (1978)).

In this paper I examine some of these possibilities. The basic point is that although the *rules* of the post-entry game are taken to be exogenous, the established firm can alter the *outcome* to its advantage by changing the initial conditions. In particular, an irrevocable choice of investment allows it to alter its post-entry marginal cost curve, and thereby the post-entry equilibrium under any specified rule. It will be seen that it can use this privilege to exercise limited leadership.

I. THE MODEL

The basic point is most easily seen in a simplified model. I shall reduce the dynamic aspects to the barest essentials by ignoring all lags. Either entry does not occur at all, in which case the established firm continues in a stationary state, or else it occurs at once, and the post-entry equilibrium is also established at once, so that the resulting duopoly continues in its stationary state. It is as if the two players see through the whole problem and implement the solution immediately.[1] The result is that we can confine attention to the constant streams of profits, avoiding the complication of reducing a varying pair of profit flows to discounted present values. However, once the underlying principle is understood, an added complication in this respect is not difficult to admit in principle.

The second simplification made in the main body of the analysis is with regard to the costs of production. Let the subscript 1 denote the established firm and 2 the prospective entrant. Each firm will be supposed to have a constant average variable cost of output, and a constant unit cost of capacity expansion, and a set-up cost. If firm i has capacity k_i and is producing output x_i (with $x_i \leqslant k_i$), its cost per period will be

$$C_i = f_i + w_i x_i + r_i k_i, \qquad (1)$$

where f_i is the fixed set-up cost, r_i the constant cost per unit of capacity (both expressed in per period or flow terms), and w_i the constant average variable cost for output. The possibility that the two firms have the same cost functions ($f_1 = f_2$, etc.) is not excluded. The special form (1) has some analytical and empirical merit; I examine a more general cost function in Section III.

The revenues per period for the two firms will be functions $R^i(x_1, x_2)$. Each will be increasing and concave in that firm's output. Also, each firm's total and marginal revenue will be decreasing in the other's output.

The rules of the game are as follows. The established firm chooses a pre-entry capacity level k_1. This may subsequently be increased, but cannot be reduced. If the other firm decides to enter, the two will achieve a duopoly Cournot-Nash equilibrium with quantity-setting. Otherwise the established firm will prevail as a monopoly.

---

[1] Compare the exchange between Moriarty and Holmes in *The Final Problem*: 'All that I have to say has already crossed your mind', said he. 'Then possibly my answer has crossed yours', I replied.

First suppose that firm 1 has installed capacity k_1. If it is producing output within this limit, i.e. if $x_1 \leqslant k_1$, its total costs are

$$C_1 = f_1 + r_1 k_1 + w_1 x_1.$$

However, if it wishes to produce greater output, it must acquire additional capacity. If $x_1 > k_1$, therefore,

$$C_1 = f_1 + (w_1 + r_1) x_1.$$

Correspondingly, firm 1's marginal cost is w_1 so long as its output does not exceed k_1, and $(w_1 + r_1)$ thereafter. Firm 2 has no prior commitment in capacity. For all positive levels of output x_2, it acquires capacity k_2 to match, yielding

$$C_2 = f_2 + (w_2 + r_2) x_2$$

and a marginal cost of $(w_2 + r_2)$. The choice of k_1 thus affects the shape of the marginal cost curve of firm 1, which in turn affects its reaction curve. When the two firms interact, the resulting duopoly equilibrium depends on k_1, and therefore so do the profits of the two firms in it. If the profits for the second firm are positive, it will enter; otherwise it will not. Bearing this in mind, firm 1 will choose that k_1 which maximises its profit. Whether this is done by preventing entry or by allowing it to occur remains to be seen. However, I shall assume for simplicity of exposition that the established firm's maximum profit is positive, i.e. exit is not its best policy.

The analysis follows the scheme just outlined. For a given k_1, Fig. 1 shows the marginal cost curve for the established firm, MC_1, as the heavy kinked line.

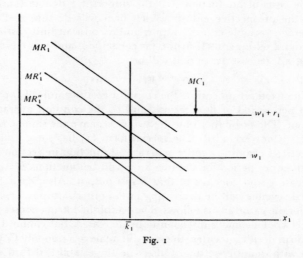

Fig. 1

It equals w_1, the marginal cost when there is spare capacity, up to the output level k_1 and $(w_1 + r_1)$, the marginal cost including capacity expansion cost, thereafter. On this we superimpose the marginal revenue curve, the position of which depends on the assumed output level x_2 of the other firm. For a sufficiently low value of x_2, the curve is in a position like the one labelled MR_1, and the first firm's profit-maximising choice of x_1 lies to the right of its previously fixed capacity level. For successively higher levels of x_2, the marginal revenue curve shifts downwards to occupy positions like MR_1' and MR_1'', yielding choices of x_1 at, or below, the capacity level. This response of x_1 to x_2 is just the established firm's reaction function to the entrant's output.

This function can be shown in a more familiar direct manner in the space of two quantities, and this is done in Fig. 2. I have shown two 'reference' curves MM' and NN'. The first becomes the reaction function if capacity expansion costs matter, and the second if there is spare capacity. Therefore the first is relevant for outputs above k_1 and the second for outputs below this level. For fixed k_1, then, the reaction function is the kinked curve shown in heavy lines.

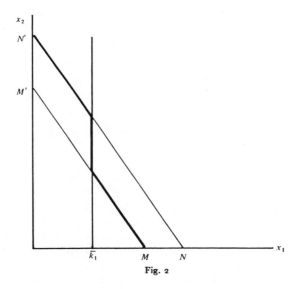

Fig. 2

Let the points M and N have respective coordinates $(M_1, 0)$ and $(N_1, 0)$. The quantities M_1 and N_1 can be interpreted as follows. Both are profit-maximising quantity choices of firm 1 when the output level of firm 2 is held fixed at zero, i.e. when the possibility of entry is ignored. However, M_1 is the choice when capacity expansion costs matter, and N_1 is relevant when there is sufficient capacity already installed and only variable costs matter.

Since firm 2 has no prior commitment in capacity, its reaction function RR' is straightforward. I assume that it intersects both MM' and NN' in a way that corresponds to the usual 'stable' Cournot solution, in order to minimise complications other than those of immediate interest (see Fig. 3).

For given k_1, we have a duopoly Nash equilibrium at the intersection of the two reaction functions. However, the established firm has the privilege of choosing k_1 in advance, and thus determining which reaction function it will present in the post-entry duopoly. Suppose firm 2's reaction function meets MM' at $T = (T_1, T_2)$ and NN' at $V = (V_1, V_2)$ as shown in Fig. 3. Clearly T and V can be interpreted as Nash equilibria under alternative extreme circumstances, T when capacity expansion costs matter for firm 1, and V when

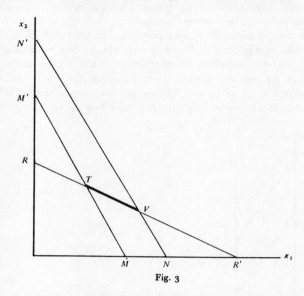

Fig. 3

they do not. It is then evident on comparing Figs. 2 and 3 that for a choice of $k_1 \leqslant T_1$, the post-entry equilibrium will be at T, while for $k_1 \geqslant V_1$, it will occur at V. Most importantly, for $T_1 \leqslant k_1 \leqslant V_1$, it will occur at the appropriate point on the heavy line segment of the entrant's reaction function lying between T and V. Here the established firm will produce output $x_1 = k_1$, and the entrant will produce the same output as would a Stackelberg follower faced with this x_1. It is in this sense that, even when the post-entry game is accepted as leading to a Nash equilibrium, the established firm can exercise leadership over a limited range by using its capacity choice to manipulate the initial conditions of that game.

However, the qualification of the limited range is important. In particular, it means that capacity levels above V_1 are not credible threats of entry-deterrence. When a prospective entrant is confident of its ability to sustain a Nash equilibrium in the post-entry game, it does not fear such levels. And when the established firm knows this, it does not try out the costly and empty threats.

Since $N_1 > V_1$, we see a fortiori the futility of maintaining capacity levels above N_1 as threats to deter entry. Nor are such capacity levels justified by considerations of pre-entry production; in fact a monopolist saddled with capacity above N_1 will choose to leave the excess idle. Under the rules of the game assumed here, therefore, we will not observe the established firm installing capacity above N_1. The Spence excess capacity strategy will not be employed.

Nor will we ever see the established firm installing pre-entry capacity of less than T_1: if entry is to occur it will want more capacity, and if entry is not to occur it will want capacity of at least $M_1 > T_1$.

In the model used by Spence, it is simply assumed that a prospective entrant expects the established firm will respond to entry by producing an output level equal to its pre-entry capacity, no matter how high that may be. It is then possible that constrained monopoly profits made by keeping capacity at the entry-deterring level and producing at N exceed what is possible with a lower capacity leading to a Stackelberg duopoly equilibrium. This is the excess-capacity strategy of entry prevention. When the credibility of the threat is questioned, matters can be different, and the above argument shows that they are indeed different under the particular modification of the rules of the game.

II. CLASSIFICATION OF OUTCOMES

The discussion so far was confined to the post-entry duopoly, i.e. both firms were assumed to have incurred the set-up costs. When we come to the ex ante decision about whether to enter, set-up costs matter, and the choice is governed by the sign of the profits net of them. (Dixit (1979) uses an alternative geo-metric approach involving discontinuous reaction functions.)

We have seen above that at all points that are ever going to be observed without or with entry, the established firm will be producing an output equal to its chosen pre-entry capacity. Therefore we may write the profits of the two firms as functions of their outputs alone, i.e.

$$\pi_i(x_1, x_2) = R^i(x_1, x_2) - f_i - (w_i + r_i) x_i.$$

It will often be convenient to indicate the point of evaluation (x_1, x_2) by a letter label such as that used in the corresponding figure. I have assumed that the maximum value of π_1 is always positive. Depending on the sign of π_2, various cases arise. Note that along firm 2's reaction function, its profit decreases monotonically from T to V. Therefore we can classify the possibilities as follows:

Case 1. $\pi_2(T) < 0$. Now the prospective entrant cannot make a profit in any post-entry equilibrium. So it will not try to enter the industry at all. Entry being irrelevant, the established firm will enjoy a pure monopoly by setting its capacity and output at M_1.

Case 2. $\pi_2(V) > 0$. Here the prospective entrant will make a positive profit in any post-entry equilibrium, so the established firm cannot hope to prevent entry. It can only seek the best available duopoly position. To this end, it will compute its profit along the segment TV. Since all these choices involve output equal to capacity, we can simply use the conventional iso-π_1 contours in (x_1, x_2) space and find the highest contour along the segment TV. If there is a Stackelberg tangency to the left of V, that is firm 1's best choice. However, if the conventional tangency occurs to the right of V, we now have a corner solution at V, which can then be thought of as a sort of generalised Stackelberg leadership point.

Case 3. $\pi_2(T) > 0 > \pi_2(V)$. This presents the richest set of possibilities. Now there is a point $B = (B_1, B_2)$ along such TV that $\pi_2(B) = 0$. If the established firm sets its capacity above B_1, the prospective entrant will reckon on making a negative profit in the post-entry Nash equilibrium, and therefore will not enter. Thus the capacity level B_1 is the entry-barring level. Knowing this, firm 1 wants to know whether it is worth its while to prevent entry.

Sub-case i. If $B_1 < M_1$, then the established firm's monopoly choice is automatically sufficient to deter entry. In Bain's terminology, entry can be said to be blockaded.

If $B_1 > M_1$, the established firm can only bar entry by maintaining capacity (and output) at a level greater than it would want to as a monopolist; thus it is faced with a calculation of the costs and benefits of entry-prevention. To prevent entry, it needs a capacity of just greater than B_1. Since $B_1 < V_1 < N_{1,,}$ we know that it will want to use all this capacity in its monopoly choice of output, so its profit will be $\pi_1(B_1, 0)$. The alternative is to allow entry and settle for the best duopoly point, which may be a tangency in the segment TV, or a corner solution at V. Whichever it is, call it the generalised Stackelberg point S, with coordinates (S_1, S_2). Then we have:

Sub-case ii. $\pi_1(S) < \pi_1(B_1, 0)$, when it is better to prevent entry by choosing a limit-capacity or limit-output at B_1. There is a corresponding limit-price. In Bain's usage, entry is effectively impeded. Incidentally, for this sub-case to arise, it is sufficient to have $S_1 \geqslant B_1$. For, with $B_1 > M_1$, we have $\pi_1(S_1, S_2) < \pi_1(S_1, 0) \leqslant \pi_1(B_1, 0)$.

Sub-case iii. $\pi_1(S) > \pi_1(B_1, 0)$, when it is better to allow entry, i.e. entry is ineffectively impeded, and a duopoly solution is observed at S. Remember that S is the post-entry Nash equilibrium.

An alternative way of distinguishing between the sub-cases *ii* and *iii* is to draw the iso-π_1 contour through S and see if it intersects the x_1-axis to the right or the left of B_1. This would follow Dixit (1979), except for one new feature: the Stackelberg point S can be at the corner solution V.

For particular demand functions, we can evaluate all these profit expressions explicitly, and thereby express the classification of outcomes in terms of the underlying parameters.

III. EXTENSIONS AND MODIFICATIONS

Of the numerous extensions conceivable, I consider three. The first involves an alternative and rather extreme post-entry equilibrium, where the rules of the game are that the entrant acquires the role of quantity leadership (see Salop (1978)). Thus firm 2 chooses a point on firm 1's post-entry reaction function to maximise its own profit. However, firm 1, by its initial commitment to capacity, can decide which reaction function to present to the entrant, and can manipulate this choice to its own advantage.

Fig. 4 shows the possibilities. The notation is the same as in Fig. 3, with some additions. Let $F = (F_1, F_2)$ be the ordinary Stackelberg point where firm 2 is the leader and firm 1 the follower, taking into account capacity expansion costs, i.e. using the reference curve MM'. If firm 1 sets its capacity k_1 at a level less than F_1, then its reaction function as drawn in Fig. 2 will drop from NN' to MM' at k_1 to the left of F. Firm 2's profit will then be maximised on this reaction function at the tangency point F. For k_1 between F_1 and T_1, there will be a maximum at the kink in firm 1's reaction function where it meets MM', yielding an equilibrium at the appropriate point along the segment FT.

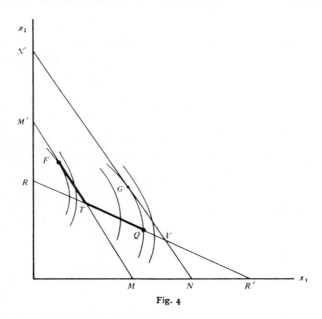

Fig. 4

For a while to the right of T, we will have a tangency solution along TV, an iso-π_2 contour being tangential to the vertical portion of firm 1's reaction function. Let G be the point where an iso-π_2 contour is tangential to NN', and let this contour meet RR' at $Q = (Q_1, Q_2)$. Then the vertical tangency will be the best choice for firm 2 so long as $k_1 \leqslant Q_1$. For $k_1 > Q_1$, however, it will prefer the tangency at G.

By its choice of k_1, the established firm can therefore secure as the post-entry equilibrium any point along the kinked line segment FTQ, shown in heavy ink in the figure, and the isolated point G. In other words, even though the rules of the game require it to surrender post-entry quantity leadership, the established firm can use its commitment to capacity to seize a limited initiative back from the entrant. It remains to choose the best available point. Now G is clearly inferior from the point of view of firm 1 to the point directly below it on the segment TQ. Similarly, all points along FT are worse than T. However, there is a genuine choice to be made, i.e. leadership exercised, along the segment TQ. This is smaller than the segment TV which was available when the post-entry rules led to a Nash equilibrium. But the qualitative features are unchanged, and all of my earlier analysis applies on replacing V by Q throughout.

The second extension I consider allows a more general cost function. The form (1), up to the given capacity level, has marginal cost constant at the level w_1, and since capacity cannot be exceeded, the marginal cost of output can be said to jump to infinity where output hits capacity. An increase in capacity then lowers marginal cost from infinity to w_1 over the added range. Now I replace this by a form which has a more flexible notion of capacity. Let

$$C_1 = C^1(x_1, k_1). \tag{2}$$

This will be increasing in x_1, and convex at least beyond a certain point. For each x_1 there will be a cost-minimising choice of k_1, so C^1 will be decreasing in k_1 up to this level and increasing thereafter. Finally, a higher level of k_1 will lower marginal cost of output, i.e.

$$C^1_{x_1 k_1} < 0, \tag{3}$$

with subscripts denoting partial derivatives in the usual way. All this follows the theory of the familiar textbook short-run cost functions. This is similar to the more general model in Spence (1977) except that price discipline does not break down completely after entry.

Begin with the post-entry Nash equilibrium given that firm 1 has set its capacity variable at the level k_1. Firm 2's reaction function is again straight-forward. That for firm 1 is found by choosing x_1 to maximise

$$R^1(x_1, x_2) - C^1(x_1, k_1)$$

for given x_2 and k_1. This has the first-order condition

$$R^1_{x_1}(x_1, x_2) - C^1_{x_1}(x_1, k_1) = 0 \tag{4}$$

and the second-order condition

$$R^1_{x_1 x_1}(x_1, x_2) - C^1_{x_1 x_1}(x_1, k_1) < 0. \tag{5}$$

Equation (4) defines firm 1's post-entry reaction function, and also tells us how it shifts as k_1 changes. Total differentiation gives

$$dx_1 = [-R^1_{x_1 x_2}/(R^1_{x_1 x_1} - C^1_{x_1 x_1})] dx_2 + [C^1_{x_1 k_1}/(R^1_{x_1 x_1} - C^1_{x_1 x_1})] dk_1.$$

Given our assumption that the commodities are substitutes in the sense that an increased quantity of the second lowers the marginal revenue for the first, and using (5), we see that the reaction function slopes downward. Also, using (3) and (5), we see that it shifts to the right as k_1 increases.

Fig. 5 shows a collection of firm 1's reaction functions for different choices of k_1, as a set of dashed lines. Where each meets firm 2's reaction function RR', there is a post-entry Nash equilibrium for the appropriate choice of k_1. Thus, once again, firm 1 by its choice of capacity can achieve any one of a range of points along firm 2's reaction function. This is almost as if it acquired the privilege of quantity leadership. There are two limitations. First, the possible reaction functions found by varying k_1 may trace out only a limited part of firm 2's reaction function, as happened in the case of Section I. Secondly, in any post-entry Nash equilibrium, the k_1 which achieves it is not the ideal choice for producing the x_1 that prevails there; so the policy involves a cost that does not appear in straightforward quantity leadership. To see this, we must examine the equilibrium in more detail. Firm 2 maximises $R^2(x_1, x_2) - C^2(x_2)$ in obvious notation, so its reaction function is given by

$$R^2_{x_2}(x_1, x_2) - C^2_{x_2}(x_2) = 0. \tag{6}$$

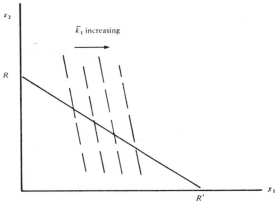

Fig. 5

Then (4) and (6) define the duopoly equilibrium as a function of k_1. Differentiating the equations totally, we have

$$\begin{bmatrix} R^1_{x_1 x_1} - C^1_{x_1 x_1} & R^1_{x_1 x_2} \\ R^2_{x_1 x_2} & R^2_{x_2 x_2} - C^2_{x_2 x_2} \end{bmatrix} \begin{bmatrix} dx_1 \\ dx_2 \end{bmatrix} = \begin{bmatrix} C^1_{x_1 k_1} dk_1 \\ 0 \end{bmatrix}. \tag{7}$$

Write Δ for the determinant of the coefficient matrix; it is positive by the stability condition for the equilibrium. Then we have the solution

$$\begin{bmatrix} dx_1 \\ dx_2 \end{bmatrix} = \frac{1}{\Delta} \begin{bmatrix} R^2_{x_2 x_2} - C^2_{x_2 x_2} \\ -R^1_{x_1 x_2} \end{bmatrix} C^1_{x_1 k_1} dk_1. \tag{8}$$

Firm 1 uses this in its choice to k_1 to maximise its profit, therefore

$$d\pi_1 = (R^1_{x_1} - C^1_{x_1}) dx_1 + R^1_{x_2} dx_2 - C^1_{k_1} dk_1$$
$$= -(R^1_{x_2} R^2_{x_1 x_2} C^1_{x_1 k_1}/\Delta + C^1_{k_1}) dk_1. \tag{9}$$

At the best duopoly point, the coefficient of dk_1 in (9) is zero. Since all three factors in the numerator of the first term are negative while Δ is positive, we see that at this point,

$$C^1_{k_1} > 0,$$

i.e. firm 1 carries its capacity to a point beyond what is optimum for producing its output.

Once again the analysis can be completed by examining the sign of firm 2's profits, and the desirability of entry-prevention for firm 1. This more flexible notion of capacity can be interpreted in terms of other types of investment such as dealer networks and advertising, and this provides a basis for arguments that such expenditures can be used by an established firm in its efforts to deter entry. This counters recent expressions of pessimism (e.g. Needham (1978) pp. 177–9) concerning the effectiveness of such tactics.

For the last modification, I revert to a rigid concept of capacity, but consider price-setting in the post-entry duopoly, the solution rule being the Bertrand–Nash equilibrium. Some added complications can arise due to possible non-convexities even with reasonable demand and cost functions, but I ignore these and show the simplest possible case. This is done in Fig. 6, with notation analogous to the corresponding quantity-setting case of Fig. 3.

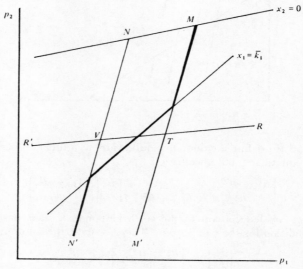

Fig. 6

The prospective entrant's reaction function is RR'. For the established firm, we have two reference curves MM' and NN', the former when capacity expansion costs matter and the latter when they do not. Their relative positions are naturally reversed as compared to the quantity-setting case. The former is relevant for $x_1 \geq k_1$ and the latter for $x_1 \leq k_1$, where x_1 is found from the demand function $D^1(p_1, p_2)$. The boundary curve $x_1 = k_1$ is shown for a particular k_1, and the corresponding reaction function for the established firm is shown by the heavy lines. It is then clear that by varying k_1, the established firm can secure any point along the segment TV of the prospective entrant's reaction function as the post-entry Nash equilibrium. Once again, we observe a limited leadership possibility arise by virtue of the established firm's advantage in being the first to make a commitment to capacity.

IV. CONCLUDING COMMENTS

The theme of the paper is that the role of an irrevocable commitment of investment in entry-deterrence is to alter the initial conditions of the post-entry game to the advantage of the established firm, for any fixed rule under which that game is to be played. This was illustrated in several simple models. Prominent among the conclusions was the observation that if the post-entry game is agreed to be played according to Nash rules, the established firm will not wish to install capacity that would be left idle in the pre-entry phase. This contrasts with the results of Spence (1977), where the post-entry game involves leadership by the established firm, and its threat of producing at a level equal to its pre-entry capacity is assumed to be believed by the prospective entrant. It is not possible to claim universal validity for either of these models. However, in the absence of any asymmetrical advantage possessed by the established firm in the post-entry phase, the Nash solution has considerable appeal.

Salop (1979) provides some examples of similar prior commitments that create an advantage for the established firm. Spence (1979) can be thought of as developing the same theme. In this model, capacity can only be acquired slowly, and the two firms differ in their abilities in this regard. This difference governs how the industry evolves, including issues of whether the second firm will enter, and what kind of equilibrium will result if it does. Much of the interesting dynamics is lost in my formulation, but the compensating advantage is that the basic idea becomes much more transparent. It is hoped that the distinction between the *rules* of the post-entry game and its *initial conditions* will prove useful in future work. I have assumed the rules to be understood and accepted by both firms. Investment then helps deter entry by changing the initial conditions. Within this framework, there is scope for several extensions: several periods and firms could be introduced, and constraints arising from capital markets could be imposed. The question of whether one firm can change the rules in its own favour is more interesting, but much more difficult.

University of Warwick   **AVINASH DIXIT**

Date of receipt of final typescript: July, 1979

REFERENCES

Dixit, A. (1979). 'A model of duopoly suggesting a theory of entry barriers.' *Bell Journal of Economics*, vol. 10, no. 1 (Spring) pp. 20–32.
Needham, D. (1978). *The Economics of Industrial Structure, Conduct and Performance*. London: Holt, Rinehart and Winston.
Salop, S. (1978). 'A note on self-enforcing threats and entry deterrence'. University of Pennsylvania, Discussion Paper No. 14.
——(1979). 'Strategic entry deterrence.' *American Economic Review*, Papers and Proceedings.
Schelling, T. C. (1960). *The Strategy of Conflict*. Cambridge, Mass.: Harvard University Press.
Scherer, F. M. (1970). *Industrial Market Structure and Economic Performance*. Chicago: Rand-McNally.
Spence, M. (1977). 'Entry, investment and oligopolistic pricing.' *Bell Journal of Economics*, vol. 8, no. 2 (Autumn), pp. 534–44.
—— (1979). 'Investment, strategy and growth in a new market.' *Bell Journal of Economics*, vol. 10, no. 1 (Spring), pp. 1–19.
Wenders, T. (1971). 'Collusion and entry.' *Journal of Political Economy*, vol. 79, no. 6 (November–December), pp. 1258–77.

[19]

Exit barriers are entry barriers: the durability of capital as a barrier to entry

B. Curtis Eaton*

and

Richard G. Lipsey**

We argue that the effectiveness of capital as an entry barrier depends critically on its durability and that this aspect of capital has been largely ignored. We examine strategic decisions with respect to capital durability in two models. In a broad range of cases an active policy with respect to durability and replacement of capital is necessary to maintain a position of market power. Such policies will result in capital that is "too durable" or "too soon replaced" or "too well maintained" relative to the cost minimizing solution (for a given time path of output).

1. Introduction

■ In his seminal essay on bargaining, Thomas Schelling (1956) distinguishes threats and commitments. Both are designed to influence a competitor by impressing him with the consequences of his actions. Both take the same form: "If you take action X, I shall take action Y, which will make you regret X." The distinguishing characteristic of a threat is that the actor has no incentive to carry out action Y either before or after action X. The distinguishing characteristic of a commitment is that, X having occurred, it is in the actor's self-interest to take action Y. A fanatic may carry out a threat, and may thus make "credible threats." A maximizer would not carry out his threats and thus cannot make his threats credible. There would seem, therefore, to be little place for threats in maximizing models.

In this paper we examine the use of product-specific capital goods as vehicles for entry-deterring *commitments*. It may seem surprising that there is anything left to say on this subject in view of such works as Caves and Porter (1977), Dixit (1979, 1980), Eaton and Lipsey (1978, 1979), Schmalensee (1978), and Spence (1977, 1979). These papers deal, however, with what may be called the atemporal aspect of capital as a barrier to entry: a monopolist strategically commits a quantity of capital which is sufficient to produce a negative *flow* of profits to a new entrant. This may be called a *type-A artificial monopoly* (*A*

---

* University of British Columbia and Yale University.

** Queen's University and Yale University.

This is a shortened version of Eaton and Lipsey (1980), in which proofs may be found of results asserted in the present article. We are indebted to G. C. Archibald, Y. Kanemoto, and J. Roemer for comments and suggestions.

for "atemporal"). *Type-A natural monopoly* occurs when nonstrategic profit-maximizing behavior commits enough capital to produce a negative flow of profits to an entrant. Capital indivisibilities and decreasing costs are at the heart of this analysis. One firm can profitably serve such a market but two cannot.

The point of this paper is that it is not indivisibilities and decreasing costs *per se* which create barriers to entry. Rather, it is the intertemporal commitment of specific capital to a market, in combination with decreasing costs which creates an entry barrier. We thus focus on the durability of capital in the creation of entry barriers. We define a *type-T natural monopoly* (*T* for "temporal") to be one in which *cost minimizing* decisions with respect to durability, replacement, and maintenance of capital imply that there is no point in time at which entry is profitable, and a *type-T artificial monopoly* to be one in which *strategic decisions* with respect to capital prevent there being any point in time at which entry is profitable.

To see the potential importance of durability as an entry barrier, first consider two extreme cases under static demand and cost conditions. At one extreme is a type-*A* natural monopolist who has no sunk costs. (This would arise, for example, if capital were not product-specific and could be bought, sold, and rented on perfect markets.) Although only one firm can serve this market profitably, there exists no vehicle for commitment to the market. With no sunk costs the market is "up for grabs" at each instant. The absence of capital fixity and associated fixed costs thus seems to imply chaos. At the other extreme, the durability of capital (plant) is exogenous and infinite. Now a type-*A* natural monopolist has a permanent commitment to the market: as long as he can cover his avoidable costs he will remain in the market. As a result, he need never consider the possibility of the entry of new firms.

Second, consider the intermediate case in which a type-*A* natural monopolist's plant has an exogenous and finite durability, $0 < H < \infty$. When unconcerned about entry, the monopolist replaces his plant every *H* years. But a potential new entrant could establish plant just as the monopolist was about to renew his plant. The market would then belong to the new entrant. But foreseeing that strategy, the existing monopolist would renew his plant a little sooner. But foreseeing this, a potential new entrant would establish his plant sooner yet, and so on. In this case it is clear that the type-*A* natural monopolist must concern himself with the threat of entry; he is not a type-*T* natural monopolist.

In this article we study the strategic use of capital to create a type-*T* artificial monopoly. It is useful in analytical studies to separate strategic decisions with respect to the creation of the two types of monopoly. To isolate the creation of type-*A* artificial monopoly, it is convenient to assume type-*T natural* monopoly by letting the durability of capital be infinite (Spence, 1979; Dixit, 1980). Similarly, to isolate the creation of type-*T* artificial monopoly, it is convenient in this article to assume a type-*A natural* monopoly. (Our results extend in a fairly obvious way to a firm that has erected entry barriers to create a type-*A* artificial monopoly as well as to oligopolists who wish to maintain their place in the market.)

Our analysis shows that the textbook, type-*A* natural monopoly is not necessarily a type-*T* natural monopoly and that it is impossible for the monopolist to separate cost-minimizing decisions from profit-maximizing ones.

This results because capital produces a revenue to the firm by acting both as a factor of production and as a barrier to entry.

2. Model 1: one-hoss shay capital

■ The basic assumptions of model 1 are as follows. There is an indivisible, product-specific capital good, called plant, which is large enough that a monopolist would require only one unit of it. There are constant returns to the variable factor up to plant capacity.

If there were two firms in the market, each with one unit of plant, their common capacity and common short-run marginal costs would imply a symmetric resolution of the duopoly problem. The symmetric resolution might be Cournot-Nash, or it might be based on some conjectural-variation formulation. Indeed any symmetric resolution will allow us to define what we require: R_1 *is the rate of flow of revenues over variable costs when one firm serves the market; R_2 is the rate of flow of revenues over variable costs for either firm when two firms serve the market.* We assume that R_1 and R_2 are time invariant, that firms know them with certainty, and that $R_1 > 2R_2 > 0$. These inequalities imply that the resolution of the duopoly pricing problem is not joint profit maximizing and that duopolists cover variable costs.

In model 1 plant of durability H costs $C(H)$ and requires no maintenance. We assume that

$$\lim_{H \to 0} C(H) > 0, \qquad C'(H) > 0, \qquad \text{and} \qquad C''(H) \geq 0 \text{ for } H > \hat{H}. \tag{1}$$

These restrictions guarantee that H will always be chosen to be positive and finite. The deterioration of this "one-hoss shay" capital depends on its age and is independent of intensity of use. Since R_2 is positive, a firm which has plant is committed (in Schelling's sense of the word) to stay in the market until its plant expires.

If a monopolist replaced plant of durability H every $H - \Delta$ periods, its minimum commitment to the market would be Δ. The discounted present value of this policy to a monopolist would be

$$V(\Delta, H) = \frac{R_1}{r} - \frac{C(H)}{1 - \exp[-r(H - \Delta)]}. \tag{2}$$

It is, of course, Δ that is the deterrent to entry and, given Δ, H will be chosen to maximize profits. Define

$$\bar{V}(\Delta) = \frac{R_1}{r} - \frac{C(h(\Delta))}{1 - \exp[-r(h(\Delta) - \Delta)]}, \tag{3}$$

where $h(\Delta)$ is the profit-maximizing (or cost-minimizing) value of H, given Δ. It can be shown that $h'(\Delta) > 0$. Let $\hat{H} = h(0)$. Type-A natural monopoly requires that

$$\bar{V}(0) = \frac{R_1}{r} - \frac{C(\hat{H})}{1 - \exp[-r\hat{H}]} > 0 > \frac{R_1}{2r} - \frac{C(\hat{H})}{1 - \exp[-r\hat{H}]}. \tag{4}$$

The first inequality implies that one firm could more than cover costs and the second implies that two could not.

We assume that entry will occur if and only if the discounted present value of an entrant's profits is greater than zero, and thus we adopt the following definitions. An entry-preventing policy (EPP) is a policy such that the discounted present value of an entrant's profits is always less than or equal to zero. An optimal, entry-preventing policy (OEPP) is an EPP that maximizes the monopolist's present value evaluated at any point in time when he is replacing his plant.

To provide an intuitive explanation of the problem we *assume* that an OEPP exists, denoted by Δ^*, and that potential entrants consider only this policy. Subsequently we show directly the existence of an OEPP with $0 < \Delta^* < h(\Delta^*)/2$. The present value of an entrant's pursuing policy Δ^* is

$$E(\delta,\Delta^*) = -C(h(\Delta^*)) + R_2 \int_0^\delta \exp[-rt]dt$$

$$+ R_1 \int_\delta^{h(\Delta^*)-\Delta^*} \exp[-rt]dt + V(\Delta^*) \exp[-r(h(\Delta^*) - \Delta^*)],$$

where δ is the length of time until the sitting monopolist's plant expires. To interpret this expression let the origin in time be the time of entry. The entrant's initial plant would cost $C(h(\Delta^*))$ and he would earn R_2 from time 0 to δ. Since Δ^* is, by assumption, an EPP, the sitting monopolist would not renew plant and entry would be deterred at all future times. Thus the entrant would earn R_1 from δ to $h(\Delta^*) - \Delta^*$ at which time he would renew his plant and his present value would be $V(\Delta^*)$. $E(\delta,\Delta^*)$ can be rewritten as

$$E(\delta,\Delta^*) = \hat{V}(\Delta^*) - (R_1 - R_2) \int_0^\delta \exp[-rt]dt. \tag{5}$$

The second term is the new entrant's "price of admission": the difference between profits when the market is served by two firms rather than one firm for the length of time until the sitting monopolist exits. This is also, of course, the measure of the barrier to entry at any point in time. Let Δ be the sitting monopolist's policy. Then

$$E(\Delta,\Delta^*) = \max_\delta E(\delta,\Delta^*) = \hat{V}(\Delta^*) - (R_1 - R_2) \int_0^\Delta \exp[-rt]dt, \tag{6}$$

which is the maximum present value of an entrant.

Thus the monopolist's problem is

$$\max_\Delta \hat{V}(\Delta)$$

subject to

$$E(\Delta,\Delta^*) \le 0. \tag{7}$$

Both $\hat{V}(\Delta)$ and $E(\Delta,\Delta^*)$ are decreasing in Δ, and thus the maximization problem posed in (7) is solved by finding $\tilde{\Delta}$ such that $E(\tilde{\Delta},\Delta^*) = 0$. But Δ^* is an OEPP by assumption and thus $\tilde{\Delta} = \Delta^*$. So, if it exists, Δ^* must satisfy $E(\Delta^*,\Delta^*) = 0$. $E(0,0) = \hat{V}(0)$, which is positive by the first inequality in (4). $E(\Delta,\Delta)$ is decreasing in Δ and goes to $-\infty$ as Δ goes to ∞. Thus, there exists a unique $\Delta^* > 0$ such that $E(\Delta^*,\Delta^*) = 0$. It can be shown that the second inequality in (4) implies that $\Delta^* < h(\Delta^*)/2$. Intuitively, if Δ^* were greater than $h(\Delta^*)/2$, costs of plant would exceed the costs of having two units of plant in the market at all times, which could not be profitable, given our definition of natural monopoly.

At the outset we assumed existence of Δ^*, and thus the argument above is only an intuitive argument. We can however use the result that Δ^* is the unique value of Δ such that $E(\Delta,\Delta)$ is equal to zero to show directly that Δ^* is the unique OEPP. Note first that $E(\Delta_m,\Delta_e)$ is the maximum present value of an entrant with policy Δ_e, if Δ_e is an EPP, when the sitting monopolist's policy is Δ_m. Note that the first derivatives of E with respect to Δ_m and Δ_e are negative. We use a proof by contradiction to demonstrate that Δ^* is the unique OEPP.

Proof: (i) Assume $\Delta_1 < \Delta^*$ is an EPP and that the sitting monopolist's policy is Δ_1. Then, since Δ_1 is an EPP, $E(\Delta_1,\Delta_1) \le 0$, otherwise an entrant adopting policy Δ_1 would not be deterred. But we have shown that for $\Delta_1 < \Delta^*, E(\Delta_1,\Delta_1) > 0$, which contradicts our assumption that Δ_1 is an EPP. Thus $\Delta_1 < \Delta^*$ is not an EPP. (ii) Now assume that Δ^* is not an EPP and that the sitting monopolist's policy is Δ^*. Since Δ^* is not an EPP, there exists an EPP, Δ_2, such that $E(\Delta^*,\Delta_2) > 0$. But since $E(\Delta^*,\Delta^*) = 0$ and E is decreasing in its second argument, $\Delta_2 < \Delta^*$. But, by the argument in (i), $\Delta_2 < \Delta^*$ cannot be an EPP, a contradiction. Thus Δ^* is an EPP.[1] (iii) The argument in (ii) implies that any policy, $\Delta > \Delta^*$, is an EPP. But since $\bar{V}(\Delta)$ is decreasing in Δ, Δ^* is the unique OEPP. *Q.E.D.*

For completeness we must show that the monopolist prefers the OEPP to the policy of "graceful exit": allowing entry to occur and then exiting when his plant expires. In the absence of entry prevention, entry would occur $\Delta^* - \epsilon$ periods before the sitting monopolist's plant expired, where ϵ is arbitrarily small. As ϵ goes to zero, the present value of graceful exit approaches

$$G(\Delta^*) = R_2 \int_0^{\Delta^*} \exp[-rt]dt > 0. \tag{8}$$

Note that

$$\bar{V}(\Delta^*) - E(\Delta^*,\Delta^*) = (R_1 - R_2) \int_0^{\Delta^*} \exp[-rt]dt.$$

But since $E(\Delta^*,\Delta^*) = 0$, we have

$$\bar{V}(\Delta^*) = (R_1 - R_2) \int_0^{\Delta^*} \exp[-rt]dt, \tag{9}$$

and since $R_1 > 2R_2$, we have $V(\Delta^*) > G(\Delta^*) > 0$.

We have shown in model 1 that an active policy of entry prevention is necessary—that type-A natural monopoly does not imply type-T natural monopoly—and that this strategy is profitable. Protecting this monopoly position involves the dissipation of monopoly rents and is wasteful of scarce resources, since the monopolist replaces plant before it is economically obsolete. The dissipation of monopoly rents through early replacement of capital and the resulting resource waste will be smaller the stronger is duopoly price competition, and the smaller are the monopoly profits (*ceteris paribus* the smaller is

---

[1] This argument assumes that the entrant considers only entry-preventing policies. We show in Eaton and Lipsey (1980), footnote 2, that nonentry-preventing strategies are never profitable.

R_2 or R_1). Regulation that reduces monopoly profits may thus reduce the social waste analyzed in this paper.

Since $\Delta^* > 0$ and $h'(\Delta) > 0$, it follows that $h(\Delta^*) > \bar{H}$. In other words, the strategy of entry deterrence leads the monopolist to choose plant which is more durable than the cost-minimizing durability. This result does not reflect an additional burden since, given Δ^*, durability is chosen to minimize costs.

3. Model 2: maintaining plant

■ In model 2 we assume that plant costs K, $K > 0$, and that maintenance costs, m, are a convex function of age of plant, a:

$$m = g(a), \qquad g'(a) > 0, \qquad g''(a) \geq 0. \tag{10}$$

Notice that we have three categories of costs in this model: sunk costs of plant; costs of maintaining plant which are avoidable only by not producing and which are invariant with respect to output; and the constant marginal costs of production. Define $C(S)$ to be the discounted present cost of a new plant over a service life of S periods. Then

$$C(S) = K + \int_0^S g(a) \exp[-ra]da. \tag{11}$$

The restrictions on $g(a)$ imply that $C'(S) > 0$ and $C''(S) > 0$.

$C(S)$ satisfies the restrictions on the cost function in model 1, and it follows immediately that the monopolist could create a minimum commitment to the market, Δ, by replacing plant, *with a prepaid maintenance contract of S periods*, every $S - \Delta$ periods. By analogy with model 1 there exists a Δ^* which maximizes profits, subject to entry's being unprofitable. Further, it is easily demonstrated that the optimal service life associated with Δ^* is less than the cost-minimizing service life, so that plant is replaced before its economic life is over.

Our purpose in model 2 is to explore another entry-preventing strategy when plant is maintainable. Accordingly, define S to be the policy of replacing plant every S periods. The present value to a monopolist of this policy is

$$V(S) = \frac{R_1}{r} - \frac{C(S)}{1 - \exp[-rS]}. \tag{12}$$

$V(S)$ is pseudoconcave in S, decreases without bound as S goes to zero and as S goes to infinity, and therefore has a unique maximum.[2] Let $\bar{S}$ be the value of S which maximizes $V(S)$.

We wish to argue that, in the event of entry, the sitting monopolist would stay in the market until his maintenance costs rose to R_2. We argue as follows: if $g(a)$ were less than R_2, and if the monopolist paid $g(a)$, then he and the entrant would face identical avoidable costs, the resolution of the duopoly problem would be symmetric, and the monopolist would enjoy the flow R_2; therefore, the monopolist will incur the maintenance costs if and only if $g(a) \leq R_2$. Alternatively, in the event of entry the monopolist could sign a binding maintenance contract with a third party, and his avoidable costs would then be just

---

[2] Pseudoconcavity of $V(S)$ requires that when $V'(S) = 0$, $V''(S) < 0$, which is easily verified. See Diewert, Avriel, and Zang (1977) for a useful taxonomy of concavity.

the marginal costs of production. An optimal maintenance contract would run until $g(a) = R_2$.

Let A be the age of plant such that $g(A) = R_2$. Then if the monopolist chooses a policy $S \leq A$, his minimum commitment to the market is $A - S$. If he chooses $S > A$, his minimum commitment to the market is zero.

Then we seek the existence of a policy S^* which solves

$$\max_{S} V(S)$$

subject to

$$E(S, S^*) \leq 0,$$

$$(13)$$

where

$$E(S, S^*) = \begin{cases} V(S^*) - (R_1 - R_2) \int_0^{A-S} \exp[-rt]dt, & \text{if} \quad S \leq A, \\ V(S^*), & \text{if} \quad S > A. \end{cases} \quad (14)$$

$E(S, S^*)$ is interpreted as the present value of an entrant's pursuing policy S^* when the monopolist's policy is S.

Several cases require attention. First, suppose the monopolist adopts policy $\tilde{S}$. It is clear from (14) that if A is large enough relative to $\tilde{S}$, the monopolist need not pursue an active policy of entry prevention. Let $\tilde{A}$ be the value of A in (14) such that $E(\tilde{S}, \tilde{S}) = 0$. Then, if $A \geq \tilde{A}$, $S^* = \tilde{S}$, and entry prevention is costless. This is a case of type-T natural monopoly.

Denote by S_1 and S_2 the minimum and maximum values of S such that $V(S) = 0$. Pseudoconcavity of $V(S)$ then implies that $V(S) > 0$ in the open interval (S_1, S_2) and $V(S) < 0$ for $S < S_1$ and for $S > S_2$. When $A \leq S_1$, the constraint in (13) cannot be satisfied in the profitable range of production. Thus $S^* = S_1$ and $S^* = S_2$ are the only solutions to the problem posed in (13) and $V(S^*) = 0$. In this case it is clear that the use of a prepaid maintenance contract to deter entry is the preferred strategy.

Finally, consider the case when $S_1 < A < \tilde{A}$. $E(S_1, S_1) < 0$, since $S_1 < A$, and $E(\tilde{S}, \tilde{S}) > 0$, since $A < \tilde{A}$. Both $V(S)$ and $E(S, S^*)$ are increasing in S when $S_1 < S < \tilde{S}$, and thus S^* must satisfy $E(S^*, S^*) = 0$. Since $E(S, S)$ is increasing in S in this interval, there exists a unique S^*, $S_1 < S^* < \tilde{S}$ such that $E(S^*, S^*) = 0$. An argument parallel to that in model 1 shows that S^* is the unique OEPP. Since $S^* < \tilde{S}$, plant is replaced before its economically useful life is over.

We have shown that when plant is maintainable, there exist circumstances where entry deterrence is costless, the case of type-T natural monopoly. When an active policy of entry deterrence is necessary, the monopolist has two options, both of which require the replacement of plant before its economically useful life is over. Since a potential entrant has the same options, the monopolist must choose the more profitable option.

4. Conclusions

■ Our analysis suggests a need for revision of the concept of natural monopoly. A fully insulated natural monopoly must have both type-A and type-T natural monopoly. If it has only the former, it may be able to use specific capital to create a type-T artificial monopoly.

Profit maximization does not imply cost minimization in our models. Thus, when one is considering the creation of artificial barriers to entry, taking minimized costs as a primitive can be misleading. Product-specific capital is a natural vehicle for commitment, and firms who so use it will violate cost minimization.

It may be useful to consider the argument that a successful entry-preventing strategy must be based on commitment, not threat, in the context of the creation of a type-T monopoly. To make an entry-deterring threat in model 1, the sitting monopolist must threaten that in the event of entry, he will stay in the market *long enough* that the entrant's present value at time of entry will be nonpositive. "Long enough" is Δ^* periods. If the sitting monopolist's plant has at least Δ^* periods of remaining economic life, then the threat is a commitment, because the sitting monopolist's plant can more than cover its variable costs. If his plant has less than Δ^* periods of remaining economic life, the threat is not a commitment: fulfilling it would require building new plant at a time when it promises a negative present value. Δ^* can be interpreted as the monopolist's minimum commitment to the market or as the minimum *barrier to his exit*. It is in this sense that barriers to exit are barriers to entry.

The intuitive appeal of our results suggests to us that they will survive generalization of our assumptions with respect to capital. Two obvious possibilities are capital that decays exponentially or capital that decays only with use. Specific capital is a natural vehicle for commitment to the market, and commitment is valuable to the firm, since it inhibits entry. Accordingly a profit-maximizing firm will choose the specifications of specific capital (its durability and/or time of replacement and/or level of maintenance, etc.), so that marginal cost is equal to a positive marginal value in inhibiting entry. This choice will often result in specific capital that is "too durable" or "too soon replaced" or "too well maintained" relative to the unconstrained cost-minimizing solution.

The entry-deterring strategies that we have analyzed would be relatively easy to detect in a world of static demand and technology. They would, however, be much harder to detect in the real world of changing demand and technology. The entry-preventing firm may then appear as the "alert" firm, establishing capacity to meet growing demand, and as the "progressive" firm, investing early in new technologies.

Application to policy is clearly premature. The purpose of this article is to reveal a gap in our present theories of natural and artificial monopoly. To do this we use stark concepts of capital. At a minimum, analysis of more "realistic" assumptions with respect to capital and corroborating empirical work are necessary before the social waste that occurs in our models can be held to be likely and/or significant. In this context it is important to note that although waste of capital always occurs in model 1, it may be unnecessary in model 2.[3]

References

CAVES, R.E. AND PORTER, M.E. "Barriers to Exit" in R.T. Masson and P.D. Qualls, eds., *Essays on Industrial Organization in Honor of Joe S. Bain*, Cambridge: Ballinger, 1976.
—— AND ——. "From Entry Barriers to Mobility Barriers: Conjectural Decisions and Contrived Deterrence to New Competition." *Quarterly Journal of Economics* (May 1977), pp. 241–261.

---

[3] Since writing this paper, our attention has been drawn to Caves and Porter (1976), in which the issues discussed in this paper are foreshadowed. See especially their pages 44–45.

DIEWERT, W.E., AVRIEL, M., AND ZANG, I. "Nine Kinds of Quasi Concavity and Concavity." Discussion Paper 77-31, University of British Columbia, 1977.

DIXIT, A. "A Model of Duopoly Suggesting a Theory of Entry Barriers." *Bell Journal of Economics* (Spring 1979), pp. 20–32.

———. "The Role of Investment in Entry Deterrence." *Economic Journal* (March 1980), pp. 95–106.

EATON, B.C. AND LIPSEY, R.G. "The Theory of Market Preemption: The Persistence of Excess Capacity and Monopoly in Growing Spatial Markets." *Economica* (May 1977).

——— AND ———. "Freedom of Entry and the Existence of Pure Profit." *Economic Journal* (September 1978), pp. 455–469.

——— AND ———. "Exit Barriers Are Entry Barriers." University of British Columbia Discussion Paper No. 80-3, February 1980.

SCHELLING, T.C. "An Essay on Bargaining." *American Economic Review* (June 1956), pp. 281–306.

SCHMALENSEE, R. "Entry Deterrence in the Ready-to-Eat Breakfast Cereal Industry." *Bell Journal of Economics* (Autumn 1978), pp. 305–327.

SPENCE, A.M. "Entry, Capacity, Investment, and Oligopolistic Pricing." *Bell Journal of Economics* (Autumn 1977), pp. 534–544.

———. "Investment Strategy and Growth in a New Market." *Bell Journal of Economics* (Spring 1979), pp. 1–19.

[20]

The Fat-Cat Effect, The Puppy-Dog Ploy, and the Lean and Hungry Look

By Drew Fudenberg and Jean Tirole*

Let me have about me men that are
fat....   *Julius Caesar*, Act 1, Sc. 2

The idea that strategic considerations may provide firms an incentive to "overinvest" in "capital" to deter the entry or expansion of rivals is by now well understood. However, in some circumstances, increased investment may be a strategic handicap, because it may reduce the incentive to respond aggressively to competitors. In such cases, firms may instead choose to maintain a "lean and hungry look," thus avoiding the "fat-cat effect." We illustrate these effects with models of investment in advertising and in *R&D*. We also provide a taxonomy of the factors which tend to favor over- and underinvestment, both to deter entry and to accommodate it. Such a classification, of course, requires a notion of what it means to overinvest; that is, we must provide a benchmark for comparison. If entry is deterred, we use a monopolist's investment as the basis for comparison. For the case of entry accommodation, we compare the incumbent's investment to that in a "precommitment" or "open-loop" equilibrium, in which the incumbent takes the entrant's actions as given and does not try to influence them through its choice of preentry investment. We flesh out the taxonomy with several additional examples.

Our advertising model was inspired by Richard Schmalensee's (1982) paper, whose results foreshadow ours. We provide an example in which an established firm will

*University of California, Berkeley, CA 94707, and CERAS, Ecole Nationale des Ponts et Chaussées, 75007 Paris, France. Much of this paper is drawn from our survey (1983b). We would like to thank John Geanakoplos, Jennifer Reinganum, and Richard Schmalensee for helpful conversations. Research support from the National Science Foundation is gratefully acknowledged.

underinvest in advertising if it chooses to deter entry, because by lowering its stock of "goodwill" it establishes a credible threat to cut prices in the event of entry. Conversely, if the established firm chooses to allow entry, it will advertise heavily and become a fat cat in order to soften the entrant's pricing behavior. Thus the strategic incentives for investment depend on whether or not the incumbent chooses to deter entry. This contrasts with the previous work on strategic investment in cost-reducing machinery (Michael Spence, 1977, 1979; Avinash Dixit, 1979; our 1983a article) and in "learning by doing" (Spence, 1981; our 1983c article) in which the strategic incentives always encourage the incumbent to overaccumulate. Our *R&D* model builds on Jennifer Reinganum's (1983) observation that the "Arrow effect" (Kenneth Arrow, 1962) of an incumbent monopolist's reduced incentive to do *R&D* is robust to the threat of entry so long as the *R&D* technology is stochastic.

Our examples show that the key factors in strategic investment are whether investment makes the incumbent more or less "tough" in the post-entry game, and how the entrant reacts to tougher play by the incumbent. These two factors are the basis of our taxonomy. Jeremy Bulow et al. (1983) have independently noted the importance of the entrant's reaction. Their paper overlaps a good deal with ours.

I. Advertising and Goodwill

In our goodwill model, a customer can buy from a firm only if he is aware of its existence. To inform consumers, firms place ads in newspapers. An ad that is read informs the customer of the existence of the firm and also gives the firm's price. In the first period, only the incumbent is in the market; in the second period the entrant may enter. The crucial assumption is that some of the customers who received an ad in the first period do not bother to read the ads in the second period, and therefore buy only from the incumbent. This captive market for the incumbent represents the incumbent's accumulation of goodwill. One could derive such captivity from a model in which rational consumers possess imperfect information about product quality, as in Schmalensee (1982), or from a model in which customers must sink firm-specific costs in learning how to consume the product.

There are two firms, an incumbent and an entrant, and a unit population of *ex ante* identical consumers. If a consumer is aware of both firms, and the incumbent charges x_1, and the entrant charges x_2, the consumer's demands for the two goods are $D^1(x_1, x_2)$ and $D^2(x_1, x_2)$, respectively. If a consumer is only aware of the incumbent (entrant), his demand is $D^1(x_1, \infty)$ and ($D^2(\infty, x_2)$). The (net of variable costs) revenue an informed consumer brings the incumbent is $R^1(x_1, x_2)$ or $R^1(x_1, \infty)$ depending on whether the consumer also knows about the entrant or not, and similarly for the entrant. We'll assume that the revenues are differentiable, quasi concave in own-prices, and they, as well as the marginal revenue, increase with the competitor's price (these are standard assumptions for price competition with differentiated goods).

To inform consumers, the firms put ads in the newspapers. An ad that is read makes the customer aware of the product and gives the price. The cost of reaching a fraction K of the population in the first period is $A(K)$, where $A(K)$ is convex for strictly positive levels of advertising, and $A(1) = \infty$.[1] There are two periods, $t = 1, 2$. In the first period, only the incumbent is in the market. It advertises K_1, charges the monopoly price, and makes profits $K^1 \cdot R^m$. In the second period the entrant may enter.

To further simplify, we assume that all active firms will choose to cover the remaining market in the second period at cost A_2.

[1] See Gerard Butters (1977), and Gene Grossman and Carl Shapiro (1984) for examples of advertising technologies.

Then assuming entry, the profits of the two firms, Π^1 and Π^2, can be written

$$(1) \quad \Pi^1 = \left[-A(K_1) + K_1 R^m \right]$$
$$+ \delta \left[K_1 R^1(x_1, \infty) \right.$$
$$\left. + (1 - K_1) R^1(x_1, x_2) - A_2 \right]$$
$$\Pi^2 = \delta \left[(1 - K_1) R^2(x_1, x_2) - A_2 \right],$$

where δ is the common discount factor.

In the second period, the firms simultaneously choose prices. Assuming that a Nash equilibrium for this second-stage game exists and is characterized by the first-order conditions, we have

$$(2) \quad K_1 R_1^1(x_1^*, \infty)$$
$$+ (1 - K_1) R_1^1(x_1^*, x_2^*) = 0;$$
$$(3) \qquad\qquad R_2^2(x_1^*, x_2^*) = 0,$$

where $R_j^i \equiv \partial R^i(x_1, x_2)/\partial x_j$, and x_i^* is the equilibrium value of x_i as a function of K_1.

From equation (2), and the assumption that $R_{ij}^i > 0$, we see that

$$R_1^1(x_1^*, \infty) > 0 > R_1^1(x_1^*, x_2^*).$$

The incumbent would like to increase its price for its captive customers, and reduce it where there is competition; but price discrimination has been assumed impossible.

Differentiating the first-order conditions, and using $R_{ij}^i > 0$, we have

$$(4) \quad \partial x_1^*/\partial K_1 > 0, \qquad \partial x_1^*/\partial x_2^* > 0,$$
$$\partial x_2^*/\partial K_1 = 0, \qquad \partial x_2^*/\partial x_1^* > 0.$$

The heart of the fat-cat effect is that $\partial x_1^*/\partial K_1 > 0$. As the incumbent's goodwill increases, it becomes more reluctant to match the entrant's price. The large captive market makes the incumbent a pacifistic "fat cat." This suggests that if entry is going to occur, the incumbent has an incentive to increase K_1 to "soften" the second-period equilibrium.

To formalize this intuition we first must sign the *total* derivative dx_1^*/dK_1. While one would expect increasing K_1 to increase the incumbent's equilibrium price, this is only true if firm 1's second-period reaction curve is steeper than firm 2's. This will be true if $R_{11}^1 \cdot R_{22}^2 > R_{12}^1 \cdot R_{21}^2$. If dx_1^*/dK_1 were negative the model would not exhibit the fat-cat effect.

Now we compare the incumbent's choice of K_1 in the open-loop and perfect equilibria. In the former, the incumbent takes x_2^* as given, and thus ignores the possibility of strategic investment. Setting $\partial \pi^1 / \partial K_1 = 0$ in (1), we have

$$(5) \quad R^m + \delta \big(R^1 (x_1^*, \infty)$$
$$- R^1 (x_1^*, x_2^*) \big) = A'(K_1).$$

In a perfect equilibrium, the incumbent realizes that x_2^* depends on K_1, giving first-order conditions

$$(6) \quad R^m + \delta \big(R^1 (x_1^*, \infty) - R^1 (x_1^*, x_2^*)$$
$$+ (1 - K_1) R_2^1 (dx_2^*/dK_1) \big) = A'(K_1).$$

As R_2^1 and dx_2^*/dK_1 are positive, for a fixed K_1 the left-hand side of (6) exceeds that of (5), so if the second-order condition corresponding to (6) is satisfied, its solution exceeds that of (5).

The fat-cat effect suggests a corollary, that the incumbent should underinvest and maintain a "lean and hungry look" to deter entry. However, while the "price effect" of increasing K_1 encourages entry, the "direct effect" of reducing the entrant's market goes the other way. To see this, note that

$$(7) \quad \Pi_K^2 = \delta \big[(1 - K_1) R_1^2 (dx_1^*/dK_1) - R^2 \big].$$

The first term in the right-hand side of (7) is the strategic effect of K_1 on the second-period price, the second is the direct effect. One can find plausible examples of demand and advertising functions such that the indirect effect dominates. This is the case, for example, for goods which are differentiated by their location on the unit interval with linear

"transportation" costs, if first-period advertising is sufficiently expensive that the incumbent's equilibrium share of the informed consumers is positive. In this case, entry deterrence requires underinvestment.

II. Technological Competition

We now develop a simple model of investment in $R\&D$ to illustrate the lean and hungry look, building on the work of Arrow and Reinganum. In the first period, the incumbent, firm 1, spends K_1 on capital, and then has constant average cost $\bar{c}(K_1)$. The incumbent receives the monopoly profit $V^m(\bar{c}(K_1))$ in period 1. In the second period, both the incumbent and firm 2 may do $R\&D$ on a new technology which allows constant average cost c. If one firm develops the innovation, it receives the monopoly value $V^m(c)$. Thus the innovation is "large" or "drastic" in Arrow's sense. If both firms develop the innovation, their profit is zero. If neither firm succeeds, then the incumbent again receives $V^m(\bar{c})$. The second-period $R\&D$ technology is stochastic. If firm i spends x_i on $R\&D$, it obtains the new technology with probability $\mu_i(x_i)$. We assume $\mu_i'(0) = \infty$, $\mu_i' > 0$, $\mu_i'' < 0$. The total payoffs from period 2 on are

$$(9) \quad \Pi^1 = \mu_1 (1 - \mu_2) V^m(c)$$
$$+ (1 - \mu_1)(1 - \mu_2) V^m(\bar{c}) - x_1,$$
$$\Pi^2 = \mu_2 (1 - \mu_1) V^m(c) - x_2.$$

The first-order conditions for a Nash equilibrium are

$$(10) \quad \mu_1' [V^m(c) - V^m(\bar{c})] (1 - \mu_2) = 1,$$
$$\mu_2' V^m(c)(1 - \mu_1) = 1.$$

We see that since the incumbent's gain is only the difference in the monopoly profits, it has less incentive to innovate than the entrant. This is the Arrow effect.[2] We have

[2] For large innovations, the monopoly price with the new technology is less than the average cost of the old one. Richard Gilbert and David Newbery (1982) showed

derived it here in a model with each firm's chance of succeeding independent of the other's, so that we have had to allow a nonzero probability of a tie. Reinganum's model avoids ties, because the possibilities of "success" (obtaining the patent) are not independent.

Because $\mu_i' > 0$ and $\mu_i'' < 0$, the reaction curves in (10) slope downward—the more one firm spends, the less the other wishes to. Since increasing K_1 decreases the incumbent's gain from the innovator's we expect that the strategic incentive is to reduce K_1 to play more aggressively in period 2. As in our last example, this is only true if the reaction curves are "stable," which in this case requires $\mu_1'' \mu_2'' (1 - \mu_1)(1 - \mu_2) > (\mu_1' \mu_2')^2$. This is true for example for $\mu_i(x) = \max(1, bx^{1/2})$, with b small. We conclude that to accommodate entry the incumbent has a strategic incentive to underinvest. Because K_1 has no direct effect on Π^2, we can also say that to deter entry the incumbent has an incentive to underinvest.[3]

III. Taxonomy and Conclusion

In the goodwill model the incumbent could underinvest to deter entry, while in the $R\&D$ model the strategic incentives always favored underinvestment. To relate these results to previous work, we next present an informal taxonomy of pre-entry strategic investment by an incumbent. In many cases, one might expect both "investment" and "production" decisions to be made post-entry. We have restricted attention to a single post-entry variable for simplicity. We should point out

that this involves some loss of generality. Strategic underinvestment requires that the incumbent not be able to invest after entry, or more generally that pre- and post-entry investments are imperfectly substitutable. This was the case in both of our examples. However, if investment is in productive machinery and capital costs are linear and constant over time, then underinvestment would be ineffective, as the incumbent's post-entry investment would make up any previous restraint.

Before presenting the taxonomy, it should be acknowledged that since Schmalensee's (1983) article, several authors have independently noticed the possibility of underinvestment. J. Baldani (1983) studies the conditions leading to underinvestment in advertising. Bulow et al. present a careful treatment of two-stage games in which either production or investment takes place in the first period, with production in the second, and costs need not be separable across periods. They focus on cost minimization as the benchmark for over- and underinvestment. The starting point for the Bulow et al. paper was the observation that a firm might not to enter an apparently profitable market due to strategic spillovers on other product lines. This point is developed in more detail in K. Judd (1983).

Our taxonomy classifies market according to the signs of the incentives for strategic investments. Because only the incumbent has a strategic incentive, given concavity, we can unambiguously say whether the incumbent will over- or underinvest to accommodate entry (compared to the open-loop equilibrium).[4] We continue to denote the incumbent's first-period choice K_1, the post-entry decisions x_1 and x_2, and the payoffs Π^1 and Π^2. For entry deterrence there are

---

that for "small" innovations, because the sum of the duopoly profits is (typically) less than $\Pi'''(c)$, the incumbent loses more than the entrant gains if the entrant obtains the patent. With a deterministic $R\&D$ technology, the incumbent's incentive to innovate thus exceeds the entrant's, because the incumbent's current patent is certain to be superceded and thus the current profits are not "sacrificed" by the incumbent's $R\&D$. Reinganum showed that with stochastic $R\&D$ and a small innovation, either effect can dominate. In her $R\&D$ model the reaction curves slope up.

[3] For small innovations the direct effect goes the other way.

[4] This does not generalize to the case in which both firms make strategic decisions. In our paper on learning by doing (1983c), we give an example in which one firm's first-period output declined in moving from the precommitment to the perfect equilibrium. The problem is that if, as expected, firm 1's output increases when it plays strategically, firm 2's strategic incentive to increase output can be outweighed by its response to firm 1's change.

two effects, as we noted before: the "direct effect" $\partial \Pi^2/\partial K_1$, and the "strategic effect" $\partial \Pi^2/\partial x_1^* \cdot \partial x_1^*/\partial K_1$. We saw in the goodwill case that these two effects had opposite signs, and so the overall incentives were ambiguous. In all the rest of our examples, these two effects have the same sign.

In Table 1, first the entry-accommodating strategy and then the entry-deterring one is given. The fat-cat strategy is overinvestment that accommodates entry by committing the incumbent to play less aggressively post-entry. The lean and hungry strategy is underinvestment to be tougher. The top dog strategy is overinvestment to be tough; this is the familiar result of Spence and Dixit.

Last, the puppy-dog strategy is *underinvestment* that accommodates entry by turning the incumbent into a small, friendly, nonaggressive puppy dog. This strategy is desirable if investment makes the incumbent tougher, and the second-period reaction curves slope up.

One final caveat: the classification in Table 1 depends as previously on the second-period Nash equilibria being "stable," so that changing K_1 has the intuitive effect on x_2^*.

Our goodwill model is an example of Case I: goodwill makes the incumbent soft, and the second-period reaction curves slope up. The *R&D* model illustrates Case II. Case III is the "classic" case for investing in productive machinery and "learning by doing" (Spence, 1981; our paper, 1983c) with quantity competition. Case IV results from either of these models with price competition (Bulow et al.; our paper, 1983b; Judith Gelman and Steven Salop, 1983). A more novel example of the puppy-dog ploy arises in the P. Milgrom and J. Roberts (1982) model of limit pricing under incomplete information, if we remove their assumption that the established firm's cost is revealed once the entrant decides to enter, and replace quantity with price as the strategic variable. To accommodate entry, the incumbent then prefers the entrant to believe that the incumbent's costs are relatively high.

We conclude with two warnings. First, one key ingredient of our taxonomy is the slope of the second-period reaction curves. In many

TABLE 1

Slope of Reaction Curves	Investment Makes Incumbent:	
	Tough	Soft
Upward	Case IV	Case I
	A: Puppy Dog D: Top Dog	A: Fat Cat D: Lean and Hungry
Downward	Case III	Case II
	A: Top Dog	A: Lean and Hungry
	A: Top Dog	A: Lean and Hungry

Note: A = Accommodate entry; D = Deter entry.

of our examples, downward slopes correspond to quantity competition and upward slopes to competition in prices.[5] These examples are potentially misleading. We do not intend to revive the Cournot vs. Bertrand argument. As David Kreps and José Scheinkman (1983) have shown, "Quantity Precommitment and Bertrand Competition Yield Cournot Outcomes." Thus, "price competition" and "quantity competition" should not be interpreted as referring to the variable chosen by firms in the second stage, but rather as two different reduced forms for the determination of both prices and outputs. Second, our restriction to a single post-entry stage eliminates many important strategic interactions. As our 1983a paper shows, such interactions may reverse the over- or underinvestment results of two-stage models.

---

[5]Bulow et al. point out that while these are the "normal" cases, it is possible, for example, for reaction curves to slope up in quantity competition.

REFERENCES

Arrow, Kenneth, "Economic Welfare and the Allocation of Resources to Innovation," in R. Nelson, ed., *The Rate and Direction of Economic Activity,* New York: National Bureau of Economic Research, 1962.

Baldani, J., "Strategic Advertising and Credible Entry Deterrence Policies," mimeo.,

Colgate University, 1983.

Bulow, J., Geanakoplos, J. and Klemperer, P., "Multimarket Oligopoly," Stanford Business School R. P. 696, 1983.

Butters, Gerard, "Equilibrium Distributions of Sales and Advertising Prices," *Review of Economic Studies*, October 1977, *44*, 465–96.

Dixit, A., "A Model of Duopoly Suggesting a Theory of Entry Barriers," *Bell Journal of Economics*, Spring 1979, *10*, 20–32.

Fudenberg, D. and Tirole, J., (1983a) "Capital as a Commitment: Strategic Investment to Deter Mobility," *Journal of Economic Theory*, December 1983, *31*, 227–50.

_____ and _____, (1983b) "Dynamic Models of Oligopoly," IMSSS T. R. 428, Stanford University, 1983.

_____ and _____, (1983c) "Learning by Doing and Market Performance," *Bell Journal of Economics*, Autumn 1983, *14*, 522–30.

Gelman, J. and Salop, S., "Judo Economics," mimeo., George Washington University, 1982.

Gilbert, R. and Newbery, D., "Preemptive Patenting and the Persistence of Monopoly," *American Economic Review*, June 1982, *72*, 514–26.

Grossman, G. and Shapiro, C., "Informative Advertising with Differentiated Goods," *Review of Economic Studies*, January 1984, *51*, 63–82.

Judd, K., "Credible Spatial Preemption," MEDS D. P. 577, Northwestern University, 1983.

Kreps, D. and Scheinkman, J., "Quantity Precommitment and Bertrand Competition Yield Cournot Outcomes," mimeo., University of Chicago, 1983.

Milgrom, P. and Roberts, J., "Limit Pricing and Entry under Incomplete Information," *Econometrica*, 1982, *50*, 443–60.

Reinganum, Jennifer, "Uncertain Innovation and the Persistence of Monopoly," *American Economic Review*, September 1983, *73*, 741–48.

Schmalensee, Richard, "Product Differentiation Advantages of Pioneering Brands," *American Economic Review*, June 1982, *72*, 349–65.

_____, "Advertising and Entry Deterrence: An Exploratory Model," *Journal of Political Economy*, August 1983, *90*, 636–53.

Spence, A. Michael, "Entry, Capacity, Investment, and Oligopolistic Pricing," *Bell Journal of Economics*, Autumn 1977, *8*, 534–44.

_____, "Investment Strategy and Growth in a New Market," *Bell Journal of Economics*, Spring 1979, *10*, 1–19.

_____, "The Learning Curve and Competition," *Bell Journal of Economics*, Spring 1981, *12*, 49–70.

[21]

Sequential location among firms with foresight

Edward C. Prescott

Professor of Economics
Graduate School of Industrial Administration
Carnegie-Mellon University

and

Michael Visscher

Assistant Professor of Economics
Ohio State University

Existing theory poorly describes the product diversity in a modern market economy largely because such theory is founded on an inadequate concept of equilibrium. Standard analysis regards decision makers as naive in their anticipations of the response of rivals to their decisions and neglects the substantial costs of relocating in the product characteristic space. In this paper, we construct an equilibrium model of firms in which each firm locates in sequence with correct expectations of the way its decisions influence the decisions of firms yet to locate. The nature of the equilibrium is explored in a series of familiar examples taken from the literature.

1. Introduction

■ The modern theory of the firm seems ill-equipped to cope with some aspect of firms' market decisions. The bulk of this theory is designed to describe the nature of market equilibrium in a well-defined industry that produces a well-defined product. Existing theory has difficulty with the diversity of product characteristics offered in a market where products are differentiated. When nonconvexities are unimportant, of course, a result much like perfect competition—with the product space filled by a complete spectrum of product varieties and the particular tastes of each consumer satisfied—can be expected (Rosen, 1974; Visscher, 1975). However, there exist cases in which imperfect competition is of interest. Most product differentiation occurs in industries with some economies of scale that limit the extent of product variety. The perfectly competitive model modified to permit product variety is thus only a benchmark. The significance of deviations from the perfect competition benchmark cannot be judged until an adequate model is found to describe the firm's product characteristic choice in *imperfectly* competitive markets.

Chamberlin's model (1933) posited imperfectly competitive mar-

We would like to acknowledge helpful comments of participants of the NBER-NSF Industrial Organization Seminar, Carnegie-Mellon University, March 1976. The comments of Gerard Butters, Timothy W. McGuire, and Steve Salop were particularly valuable. We also acknowledge helpful comments of an anonymous referee and the Editorial Board.

kets in which products are differentiated, but he made no predictions about the variety of products one should expect to see in market equilibrium. Discussion of product differentiation in oligopoly, the other market structure marked by nonhomogeneous products, is limited essentially to work stemming from the plant location model of Lösch (1954) and the famous duopoly location model of Hotelling (1929).

The Hotelling model has been an obvious foundation on which to build a theory of location in product characteristic space. Hotelling analyzed the behavior of duopolists locating a single store on a finite one-dimensional geographical market. The concept of location extends easily to any choice of a product characteristic. For example, firms often "locate" along a single dimension in choosing product durability and quality (sudsiness, softness, cleaning power, absorbency, etc.). Hotelling asserted that in his problem the duopolists, able to make costless relocations, attain a noncooperative equilibrium back-to-back in the center of the market.

The Hotelling model has been adopted with some success by Downs (1964) to explain centralist tendencies in political platforms and by Steiner (1961) to explain similarities in television programming on different channels. But a fundamental assumption of the Hotelling solution—that location, like price, can be altered costlessly—makes it inappropriate for the study of much actual market product differentiation. There may well be firms like the proverbial ice cream vendors on the beach that face small costs of relocating as Hotelling assumed. But it commonly seems that the costs of relocation are quite substantial. Relocation in product characteristic space may mean retooling dies, changing consumer images via advertising, or moving a plant site.

Given these not inconsequential relocation costs, it may be more reasonable to model firms as making location decisions once-and-for-all, one firm at a time, with firms being aware of the relative permanence of their decisions and thus taking some care to anticipate the decision rules firms entering later in the sequence will follow.[1] We offer such a model here and argue that theory must go in this direction to advance further the usefulness of models of the firm.

Firms in our model locate one at a time. It can be argued that firms enter in sequence because some entrants become aware of a profitable market before others or require longer periods of time in which to "tool up." Further, each firm's location decision is once-and-for-all; relocation is assumed prohibitively expensive. Moving a store after witnessing the location choices of others or retooling product dies as new products enter is a very costly procedure. Each firm is assumed to choose the profit maximizing market position based on the observed choices of firms already located and the location *rules* that subsequent, equally rational entrants and potential entrants will use. Thus, each firm takes into consideration the effect of its location decision upon the ultimate configuration of the industry.

Each firm in our solution recognizes that other potential entrants into the market are not unlike itself; no firm mistakenly considers itself a profit-maximizer in a world of fools. The expectations of the firm

---

[1] Hay (1976) has independently derived the infinite line equilibrium for our example I below by using the foresighted sequential solution concept.

about the response of other firms to its own decisions are rational in the sense that the expectations are consistent with the predictions of the model. In this way we are able to avoid incompatible incentives among firms that mark most other oligopoly models. Other oligopoly models offer a wide variety of *ad hoc* reaction functions, each with the property that in equilibrium each firm has incorrect expectations about the reaction of rival firms to changes in its own decision.

Further advantages of such a model are several. First, entry into the market can be endogenous in this model. Unlike many oligopoly theories, we need not assume that a specific number of firms enter, assign reaction functions to each firm, and solve for equilibrium locations. Instead, we can allow firms to enter sequentially and then determine simultaneously the equilibrium locations *and* the equilibrium number of firms. The resulting equilibrium may have all successful entrants making positive profits and yet further entry is deterred because the ensuing price competition would leave the further entrants with negative profits. Thus, the foresighted sequential entry solution makes formal the notion introduced in the limit-pricing literature (cf. Sherman, 1974, Ch. 14) of barriers to entry due to the threat of potential competition. Second, this model should provide a better description of behavior for some problems than other models provide. The test of any model is the accuracy of its predictions. We do not test our model rigorously, but we believe that it is likely to predict behavior better than other models in many cases. In part, this hunch is due to the assumed sophistication of the economic agents in our theory, together with the observation that when much is at stake and bad decisions are not easily corrected, it pays agents to be sophisticated in their decision making. Armchair perceptions of the world are, at least, not inconsistent with our model. Firms do not try to imitate an existing product when introducing a new product line, but rather aim for the "gaps" in the existing product spectrum.[2] Similarly, we find in our model that firms space themselves and do not cluster in the Hotelling fashion.

To introduce our proposed solution concept, in Section 2 we examine a series of examples that display important aspects of market equilibrium. The first example is the so-called "Hotelling problem" of a fixed number of firms competing on a finite linear market by location alone, but we employ our solution concept rather than the conventional one. That is, the firms enter sequentially and once-and-for-all with each entering firm correctly anticipating the decision of the remaining firms in the sequence of entrants.

The second example embellishes the first by making entry endogenous and unrestricted. Firms are spaced evenly in equilibrium at a distance determined by the fixed setup cost required for entry, with no tendency for firms to pair up back-to-back as in the Hotelling solution. The solution is unique in further contrast to the Hotelling solution where either no equilibrium exists (with three firms) or multiple equilibria can exist.[3]

The third example is the true Hotelling problem in which firms

---

[2] A plethora of marketing models are now available to determine the "locations" of such gaps and the size of the market the gap represents. See Kotler (1971, Chapter 17).

[3] As Gerard Butters observed at the March 1976 NBER-NSF Conference on Theoretical Industrial Organization, there exist multiple equilibria in the "Hotelling" solution when the number of firms exceeds five.

compete noncooperatively on the basis of both location and price. There is no noncooperative solution to the original Hotelling problem because of a discontinuity in the reaction function of each firm. After modifying the Hotelling structure to ensure continuity and using numerical methods, we find that duopolists seek maximum separation rather than the minimum separation claimed by Hotelling. With three firms, no noncooperative equilibrium in pure (nonrandomized) strategies was obtained even for this modified Hotelling structure.

In the fourth example, however, we assume sequential entry and employ our recursive solution concept for the modified Hotelling structure to obtain a unique equilibrium without reliance on randomized strategies. Endogenous entry by firms is easily admitted to this model.

The final example studies an industry in which entrants choose in sequence only production capacities. In this example with restricted entry, complete monopoly results.

Section 3 notes the tendency to monopoly in the sequential entry equilibrium when the number of locations a firm can occupy is not arbitrarily constrained. Section 3 also presents potential reasons for the apparent limit to the number of positions a firm can occupy.

■ The following examples help illustrate the solution concept we offer. The examples represent familiar structures in the literature. The object is to point out the nature of the equilibrium when firms locate sequentially and to contrast the result with that from other well-known solutions.

2. Some examples

□ **Example 1.** The first example will be what is commonly called the Hotelling (1929) spatial location problem but with sequential location. The space of potential locations is the unit interval, and the uniform density of customers is N. Customers patronize the nearest store and purchase one unit (price is set exogenously and is equal at each store). Initially we follow Hotelling (or, for more than two firms, Eaton and Lipsey, 1975) and limit entry to a fixed number of firms, n. In sequence firms each locate one store on the unit interval to maximize profits, given the location of firms already located, knowledge that firms yet to enter will attempt to maximize profit, and knowledge of the fixed number of firms that will be permitted to enter.

The nature of the solution, assuming that the fixed cost of entry is sufficiently small that n firms can locate profitably, is obtained by backward inductive reasoning from the location decision of firm n to that of firm 1. The problem of firm n is simply to maximize its profits (proportional to the length of the interval that it serves) by choice of its location given the locations of the $n - 1$ firms that have already located. Since firm n is a profit maximizer, there is a decision rule it should follow in deciding where to locate. Because firm $n - 1$ *knows* firm n is a profit maximizer, firm $n - 1$ can use the rule firm n will apply to predict how firm n will locate as it varies its own position. Given that it can predict the response by firm n to its choice of position, firm $n - 1$ can determine a profit maximizing decision rule for itself as a function of the $n - 2$ occupied locations it observes when it locates. Firm $n - 2$ can use the decision rules it knows firms n and $n - 1$ will use to predict how their locational choices will respond as it varies its own position. Given that it can predict the response to its choice by n and $n - 1$, firm $n - 2$ obtains a decision rule for itself as a function of the $n - 3$ occupied positions it sees. Working backward this way, the decision of the first firm can be found, and from that, the ultimate structure of the industry is determined.

For example, suppose the number of firms is two. After the first firm has located, the second firm will have a choice of locating in one of two disjoint intervals on either side of the first firm. The profit maximizing decision rule of the second firm is clearly to choose the larger interval and to locate as closely as possible to the position of firm 1. As Hotelling first noted, the second firm captures the trade of all consumers in the "hinterland" from it to the end of the market and must split the consumers between it and the other firm, so the best position is that which maximizes the size of the hinterland. Recognizing that this is the decision rule firm 2 will apply, the first firm can do no better than to locate in the market center and face an equal probability of firm 2's locating on either side an epsilon distance away (like Hotelling we assume no firm can locate on top of another).

Consider now the three-firm case. No Hotelling equilibrium exists (firms continue to leapfrog to obtain an outside position), but a well-defined equilibrium exists assuming foresighted sequential entry. Given the symmetry of the problem, we assume without loss of generality that x_1, the location of the first firm, is less than ½. The optimal decision rule for the third firm conditional upon the decisions of firms 1 and 2 is as follows:

(i) If $x_2 \leq$ ½, locate just to the right of $\max(x_1, x_2)$.
(ii) If $x_2 >$ ½ and $x_1 > \max[1 - x_2, (x_2 - x_1)/2]$, locate just to the left of x_1.
(iii) If $x_2 >$ ½ and $1 - x_2 > \max[x_1, (x_2 - x_1)/2]$, locate just to the right of x_2.
(iv) If $x_2 >$ ½ and $(x_2 - x_1)/2 \geq \max[x_1, 1 - x_2]$, locate at $(x_1 + x_2)/2$. [Actually the third firm is indifferent among all points between x_1 and x_2 so our selection of the midpoint is somewhat arbitrary.]

Given this rule for firm 3 and the location of firm 1, the best location rule for the second firm is

$$x_2 = \tfrac{2}{3} + \tfrac{1}{2} x_1 \qquad \text{if } x_1 \leq \tfrac{1}{4}$$

or

$$x_2 = 1 - x_1 \qquad \text{if } \tfrac{1}{4} < x_1 \leq \tfrac{1}{2}.$$

Given these rules for firms 2 and 3, the optimal location for firm 1 is ¼. Therefore, the equilibrium locations for firms 1 and 2 are at ¼ and ¾ and the third firm locates between them. Clustering is thus avoided for all intents and purposes.[4]

□ **Example 2.** The method used to analyze the previous example becomes impractical when there are more than a few firms. However, we are able to characterize the solution when there are an infinite

---

[4] It is perhaps worth noting that this solution invites mutually beneficial side payments, if they can be arranged. Observe that each of the first two entrants gains in market share ½ of any further distance it can persuade the third firm to move away from it, and the third firm's market share is the same at all locations between the two initial entrants.

number of potential entrants and a fixed cost of locating. The infinite number of potential entrants assumption is admittedly unrealistic, but we need not apologize because the assumption imposes the same restrictions upon observed market structure as would be obtained for any finite n-firm problem for which n exceeds the number of firms which the market can profitably support. Letting α be market share needed to cover fixed costs, $[1/\alpha]$ is a bound on the number of firms which this market can profitably support.

To evaluate the profitability of a location decision, a firm must have expectations as to the way the industry structure will develop conditional upon its decision and the existing structure. We conjecture (and later verify that the conjecture is consistent with maximizing behavior on the part of subsequent potential entrants) that the firm locating on the unit interval expects the following to occur:

(i) If two firms are located at x_A and x_B, where $x_A < x_B$, and there are no firms located between them, then $x_B - x_A \leq 2\alpha$ implies that no firms will ever locate in the $[x_A, x_B]$ interval, $2\alpha < x_B - x_a \leq 4\alpha$ implies that a subsequent firm will locate at $(x_A + x_B)/2$, and $x_B - x_A > 4\alpha$ implies that the next firm to locate in the interval will locate with equal probability at $x_A + 2\alpha$ or $x_B - 2\alpha$.

(ii) If a firm is located at x and no other firm is located to its left, then $x < \alpha$ implies that no firm will ever locate in the $[0,x]$ interval, and $x > \alpha$ implies that the next firm to locate in the $[0,x]$ interval will choose the point α.

(iii) If a firm is located at x and no other firm is located to its right, then $1 - x \leq \alpha$ implies that no firm will ever locate in the $[x,1]$ interval, and $1 - x > \alpha$ implies that the next firm to locate in the $[x,1]$ interval will choose point $1 - \alpha$.

Given this expectations conjecture, we now characterize the optimal location rule for a firm conditional upon industry structure at the time of its decision.

Given the conjecture above, the firm can predict its ultimate market share conditional upon its location decision and the set of locations already occupied. Its (expected) market share will be divided into sales to customers located to its left and sales to customers located to its right. The left- (right-) hand share depends only upon the distance z to its nearest existing left- (right-) hand competitor or to the end point if there is no such competitor. The left- (right-) hand market share is denoted by $w(z,e)$, where $e = 0$ if there is a competitor to the left (right) and $e = 1$ if there is not.

The left-hand value function $w(z,0)$ must satisfy the functional equation

$$w(z,0) = \begin{cases} \frac{1}{2} w(z - 2\alpha, 0) + \frac{1}{2}\alpha & \text{if } z > 4\alpha \\ \frac{1}{4} z & \text{if } 2\alpha < z \leq 4\alpha \\ \frac{1}{2} z & \text{if } 0 < z \leq 2\alpha, \end{cases} \tag{1}$$

where z is the distance to the nearest existing left-hand competitor. If this distance exceeds 4α, the conjecture implies that the next firm to locate between them will choose with equal probability a point 2α from either the nearest left-hand rival or the firm in question. In the former case the distance to the nearest left-hand competitor is reduced to $z - 2\alpha$. In the latter case the distance becomes 2α, and no further reduction to the nearest left-hand competitor occurs. Consequently, its realized left-hand market share would be α under the latter contingency. This explains the first relationship. When $2\alpha < z \le 4\alpha$, the conjecture implies that one additional firm will locate at the midpoint between the firm and its nearest existing left-hand rival. If $z \le 2\alpha$, no subsequent firm will locate in that interval. This explains the remaining relations in (1). By an identical argument, the right-hand market share must also satisfy the functional equation (1) when z is defined to be the distance to the nearest right-hand competitor.

We can now write the explicit function satisfying the functional equation (1). Let l be the integer part of $z/2\alpha$ and r the remainder. Then

$$w(z,0) = (1 - 2^{-l})\alpha + 2^{-l-1}r. \tag{2}$$

Another function $w(z,1)$ is needed to specify the expected market share conditional upon selecting a point for which there is no existing nearest competitor to the left (right). By the conjecture, if $x > l$, the first firm to locate between 0 and x will choose location α. If on the other hand $x \le \alpha$, no subsequent firm will locate to its left. Thus

$$w(z,1) = \begin{cases} w(z - \alpha,0) & \text{if } z > \alpha \\ z & \text{if } z \le \alpha. \end{cases} \tag{3}$$

The same function specifies right-hand market share when there is no existing right-hand competitor, with z denoting the distance from x to the right-hand end point 1.

Let $x_1, x_2, \ldots, x_k$ be the locations on [0,1] that k previous firms have already occupied, where $x_i > x_j$ if $i > j$ (the size of the subscript here does *not* refer to the order of entry over time). The end points of the interval are $x_0 \equiv 0$ and $x_{k+1} \equiv 1$. Let $e(j) = 0$ for $j = 1, \ldots, k$ and $e(j) = 1$ for $j = 0, k + 1$. This function indicates whether the point x_j is or is not an end point.

The expected value of the firm if it locates at point x between x_j and x_{j+1} is then the sum of left- and right-hand market share less the fixed cost of locating α; that is,

$$v_j(x) = w[|x - x_j|,e(j)] + w[|x_{j+1} - x|,e(j + 1)] - \alpha.$$

The optimal location x conditional upon entry between x_j and x_{j+1} is (see Figure 1)

$$\begin{array}{ll} x = \alpha & \text{if } e(j) = 1 \text{ and } x_{j+1} > \alpha; \\ x = 1 - \alpha & \text{if } e(j + 1) = 1 \text{ and } x_j < 1 - \alpha; \\ x = x_j + 2\alpha \text{ or } x = x_{j+1} - 2\alpha & \\ & \text{if } x_{j+1} - x_j > 4\alpha \text{ and } e(j) = 0; \\ x = (x_j + x_{j+1})/2 & \text{if } 2\alpha < x_{j+1} < x_j \le 4\alpha. \end{array} \tag{4}$$

The optimum decision under any other circumstance is not to locate.

Subsequent firms to enter face essentially the same decision problem as that outlined above (there may be additional points occupied and, therefore, a different k, of course). Given that all firms share the conjecture, maximizing behavior on their part implies that their location decisions will satisfy (4). As (4) implies the expectations conjecture, the conjecture and maximizing behavior on the part of subsequent firms are consistent. Therefore, our conjecture is an equilibrium conjecture.

The equilibrium rule is not completely determined until we specify

FIGURE 1

THE w VALUE FUNCTION

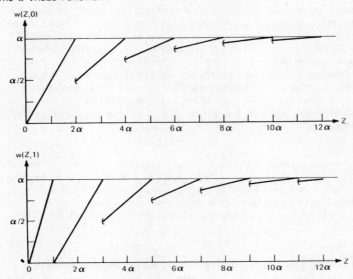

how to choose among the $k + 1$ intervals. Let

$$v_j = \text{maximum } v_j(x)$$
$$x_j < x < x_{j+1}.$$

If the maximum v_j is 0, the firm does not locate. If the maximum v_j is positive, the firm chooses in any way among the j for which v_j is greatest. Letting the chosen j be j^*, the firm locates optimally in the $[x_{j^*}, x_{j^*+1}]$ interval. This decision rule maximizes expected profits.

With this equilibrium rule the first firm will locate α from one end (assuming $\alpha \leq \frac{1}{2}$) and the second firm will locate α from the other end (assuming $\alpha < \frac{1}{2}$). Subsequent firms locate 2α from the nearest competitor until this is no longer possible. If $1/\alpha$ happens to be an even integer or $1/\alpha < 4$, no subsequent firms enter. Otherwise, a final firm locates at the midpoint of that remaining unoccupied interval with length exceeding 2α. Except for the last firm, the spacing is uniform. Firms locate as far away from their nearest competitor as is possible without inviting entry in between.[5]

□ **Example 3.** Although a duopoly model with competition by location only (and not by price) on a finite, one-dimensional market is sometimes referred to as "the Hotelling problem," the true Hotelling structure admits noncooperative price determination as well. Indeed, there is a bit of a sequential element in the manner in which the duopolists' locations and prices are determined in the original Hotelling problem. *Given* any duopolists' locations, Nash equilibrium prices are determined. *Given* that prices will be determined in this noncooperative manner after locations are chosen, profits can be

---

[5] This location principle is appropriate, but spacing is not uniform, if the density of customers is not uniform.

written as a function of locations alone, and Nash equilibrium locations are then sought. The difficulty with this solution concept, as others have noted (Smithies, 1941; Eaton, 1976; and Salop, 1976), is that when locations in Nash are sufficiently close, Nash equilibrium prices will not exist. The nonexistence of equilibrium is a problem that frequently arises when reaction functions are, as in this case, discontinuous. The source of the discontinuity in the price reaction function here is that a lower price by one of the firms does not always gain the firm market share in a smooth continuous fashion. A price sufficiently low can capture the entire market, whereas a price slightly higher loses the rival firm's entire "hinterland."

In this example, we drop the foresighted sequential solution concept temporarily to look more carefully at the Hotelling problem and its original solution concept. We modify the Hotelling structure to avoid discontinuities in firms' price reaction functions, yet maintain the spirit of the Hotelling problem. Rather than locating stores in geographical space, consider firms that choose, in addition to price, a level of product quality (or rather defectiveness) to be thought of as customer waiting time at a retail outlet. Given the manner in which this product quality characteristic is admitted to our model, the price setting game is concave so price reaction functions are continuous; this is sufficient to insure the existence of equilibrium prices, given locations.

Each firm is constrained arbitrarily to offering a single waiting time. The profits of firm i are

$$\pi_i = [p_i - C(x_i)]q_i - F,$$

where p_i is price at outlet i, $C(x_i)$ is cost per unit sold when waiting time is x_i, F is the fixed cost of entry, and q_i is the quantity sold at outlet i. Consumers are indexed by their valuation of the (dis)amenity, to be thought of in this example as value of waiting time, $0 \leq v \leq V_m$, and are distributed uniformly over this interval with density N.

Consumer of type v purchases one unit from the outlet offering the smallest total price

$$p_i + vx_i.$$

If firm h offers the next shorter waiting time, x_h, and higher price, p_h, and firm j offers the next longer waiting time, x_j, and lower price, p_j, then sales q_i to firm i offering x_i and p_i are

$$q_i = N\left[\frac{p_h - p_i}{x_i - x_h} - \frac{p_i - p_j}{x_j - x_i}\right],$$

or the length of the value of time interval served by firm i multiplied by N. If no firm offers a longer wait, then

$$q_i = N\left[\frac{p_h - p_i}{x_i - x_h}\right].$$

If no firm offers a shorter wait, then

$$q_i = N\left[V_m - \frac{p_i - p_j}{x_j - x_i}\right].$$

In this revised Hotelling problem, each firm always gains or loses market share with small changes in price in a continuous fashion, thus eliminating the troublesome aspect of the original Hotelling structure.

Equilibrium prices, given location, are now assured. Therefore, equilibrium overall is more likely than in Hotelling's formulation. Using numerical methods, we obtain equilibrium prices and waiting time "locations" of duopolists employing Hotelling's adjustment mechanism in a sample problem. The cost function employed was of the form

$$C(x_i) = A/(A + Bx_i),$$

where A and B are constants.[6] The equilibrium found in the sample problem examined is unique. However, more startling than the existence of a unique equilibrium where Hotelling's problem offers none is the nature of the equilibrium obtained. In contrast to the minimum differentiation Hotelling claimed, duopolists in the revised Hotelling problem have equilibrium locations far apart! The results of the exercise are displayed in Table 1. An intuitive explanation for the sig-

TABLE 1

HOTELLING EQUILIBRIUM

NUMBER OF FIRMS	x_i	$C(x_i)$	P_i	q_i	π_i
2	1.000	0.500	3.854	3.500	11.717
	0.040	0.962	7.208	6.500	40.640

nificant equilibrium spread between the duopolists' locations can be given. Locations too close together (i.e., products that are too close a substitute for one another) make price cutting appear too lucrative, given the naive expectations of Hotelling-like competitors. When the duopolists are close together, small decreases in one firm's price yield large increases in the market share captured from its competitors. Intense price competition, then, when the firms are in close proximity makes such locations undesirable from the point of view of either firm, even though if price competition could be avoided, those locations would be chosen as Hotelling asserted.[7]

Despite the modification in the structure of the Hotelling problem that makes equilibrium more likely, existence of an equilibrium still cannot be guaranteed. An example with three firms and the same parameters as the previous example produced no equilibrium. In the sample problem, when two firms begin far apart as in the two-firm equilibrium and a third firm is between the two widely separated firms, then the two firms with the longest waiting times proceed to jump over each other, attempting to offer a slightly shorter wait until one competitor gets too close to the firm offering the shortest wait. At that point the remaining firm lengthens his wait time dramatically to capture the portion of the market that has now been vacated. This permits the middle firm to increase its wait time somewhat (and avoid stiff price

---

[6] In the sample problem, $N = 1$, $V_m = 10$, $A = 2$, $B = 2$, and $0.040 \leq x_i \leq 1.000$.

[7] McGuire and Staelin (1976) show that wholesale dealers may use distributorships to buffer themselves from extreme price competition in much the same way as the duopolists in our example seek a buffer zone of waiting time locations between them to avoid aggressive price cutting.

competition with the shortest wait firm), whereupon the leapfrog process back to the shortest waiting time begins again.

This nonexistence problem with the Hotelling solution concept in pure (nonrandomized) strategies[8] does not enhance the appeal of the theory. An added benefit of considering firms to locate in sequence once-and-for-all is the virtual guarantee of a well-defined equilibrium.

☐ **Example 4.** The modified Hotelling structure (waiting time example) introduced in the previous section is used here as a vehicle for examining the nature of the equilibrium when firms with foresight enter sequentially and once-and-for-all.

If both waiting time "location" *and* price were chosen once-and-for-all, there would be difficulties with the sequential choice solution concept as severe as the nonexistence of an equilibrium using the Hotelling solution concept. For, if the first entrant must make an irreversible choice of both "location" and price, then the second entrant can always do at least as well as the first entrant, thus making entry later in the sequence preferred to entry earlier. The second entrant can always do at least as well as the first in this case, because the second firm always has the option available of choosing the same "location" as the first at an arbitrarily smaller price, leaving the first firm no market share at all. Therefore, if firm 2 considers a location at which its profits would be more than a very small amount less than firm 1, then firm 2 can do better by choosing the firm 1 location and a price slightly less than that of firm 1, in which case firm 2 will then have profits greater than firm 1 with certainty. The sequential "equilibrium" in this case would involve the second entrant's being more profitable than the first. As it now stands, the model has no means of predicting when or whether the first of the potential entrants will enter rather than wait when, as in this case, each potential entrant would prefer entering second to entering first. Thus, the sequential solution concept appears inappropriate when later entry is preferred to earlier entry.

Fortunately, the choice of price is generally not so inflexible as the choice of product quality characteristics. Consequently, while it may be reasonable to assume that product quality is chosen sequentially and once-and-for-all, it may be better to assume that price can be costlessly varied by each firm after witnessing the price choice of all other firms. Therefore, in the example of this section, we compute the equilibrium in which each firm is assumed to locate by offering one waiting time, given the observed waiting times chosen by firms already in, the correct expectations of the *way* the waiting times of firms yet to enter will be chosen, and the knowledge that prices will be determined non-cooperatively in Nash fashion once waiting time offerings are chosen. The assumption that prices are costlessly changed by each firm in response to the decisions of other firms eliminates much (not all) of the indeterminacy in achieving equilibrium that was noted above when each firm's price was assumed permanent.

The equilibrium waiting times in our example can be obtained by recursive methods. The procedure is as follows. Solve for the decision rule of firm $n + 1$, the first firm failing to enter successfully. This rule

---

[8] Eaton (1976) documents similar difficulties with the original Hotelling structure when nonexistence due to discontinuities in the reaction functions of each firm is assumed away. Salop (1976) analyzes the Hotelling structure when the linear market is a circle and finds nonexistence is still pervasive.

defines the choice (including the choice not to enter) of waiting time by firm $n + 1$, given the previous choices of other firms. Substitute that decision rule for the expected choice of firm $n + 1$ in the maximization problem of firm n, the last firm to enter successfully. Solve for the profit maximizing decision rule of firm n as a function only of the choices of the $n - 1$ firms already entered. Proceed until the decision of the first firm is obtained. Use the decision rules derived to deduce the industry structure and confirm that firm $n + 1$ indeed fails to enter.

Table 2 describes the equilibria computed for $n \leq 3$ for specific assumptions about the size of the fixed costs of entry and demand.[9]

TABLE 2

SEQUENTIAL EQUILIBRIUM

FIXED COST OF ENTRY F	EQUILIBRIUM NUMBER OF FIRMS	ORDER OF ENTRY	x_i	$C(x_i)$	P_i	q_i	π_i
0.300	2	1	0.500	1.000	1.548	6.101	3.041
		2	0.590	0.848	1.198	3.899	1.064
0.200	2	1	0.500	1.000	1.311	6.062	1.685
		2	0.551	0.907	1.109	3.938	0.595
0.160	3	1	0.500	1.000	1.356	5.555	1.818
		2	0.564	0.886	1.071	3.569	0.500
		3	0.833	0.600	0.836	0.875	0.040

Several aspects of the sequential equilibrium are evident in the results of this example. As one might expect, the size of the fixed setup cost acts as a barrier to entry; the greater is the fixed cost, the smaller is the number of firms that enter. However, a change in the size of the fixed cost alters the "location" choices of the entrants, even when the change is not sufficient to influence the number of successful entrants. For example, the affect of an increase in the fixed cost from 0.20 to 0.30 does not merely decrease the profits of the two successful entrants without affecting location. Indeed profits of both firms actually increase! Closer scrutiny of the results produces the reason. When the fixed cost is at the lower level, the second entrant must locate closer to the first to forestall further entry by a third firm that would lower profits even more. The second entrant would prefer to locate farther from the first if entry could be artificially restricted to two firms, because price competition between rivals near one another is intense, and prices then get cut to less profitable levels. A higher fixed cost of entry, therefore, permits the second entrant to move farther from the first, where it can enjoy more of a monopoly position and higher equilibrium prices without attracting further entry. Thus, paradoxically, a higher fixed cost within certain limits actually increases a firm's profitability because of its value as a barrier to entry.

Table 2 also shows that when fixed costs are reduced to a certain level (0.16 in the example computed), a third firm successfully enters. At that level of fixed cost, firm 1 and firm 2 "location" choices which are close enough together to limit further entry are no longer consistent with profit maximizing behavior. The equilibrium sequence is

[9] A listing of the FORTRAN computer program used to compute these equilibria is available upon request from the authors. For the results in the tables, $N = 1$, $V_m = 10$, $A = 40$, $B = 1$, $0.5 \leq x_i \leq 1.0$, all i.

characterized by successive entrants' choosing successively longer waiting times and no firm's choosing a waiting time arbitrarily close to the choice of any other firm. Profits and market share are larger the earlier in the sequence that a firm enters; i.e., it pays to be first in the market. It is worth noting that the three-firm equilibrium in Table 2 is the unique equilibrium in the example computed for any number of potential entrants greater than or equal to three. Since the fourth firm in the sequence does not enter profitably, neither does any other firm later in the sequence. Therefore, for the equilibrium described in Table 2, no specific number of potential entrants need be assumed initially as long as the number exceeds three. Without loss of generality, the number of potential entrants can be assumed infinite.

It is conceivable that there are cases in which it pays a firm to enter later rather than earlier. In such an instance, a firm may delay entry in the hope that some other firm will go first. A similar kind of indeterminacy is sometimes mentioned in discussions of the incentives to innovate in the absence of a patent law. Rather than devote resources in new product innovation, firms may wait for some other firm to innovate first in the hope of appropriating costlessly the value of the innovation by using the information thus revealed about the innovation by the first firm (cf. Sherman, 1974, pp. 180–185). The sequential solution concept is inappropriate in this case unless the gaming aspects of firms strategically delaying entry are treated explicitly.

In practice, the indeterminacy in such a situation might be resolved by a single firm's obtaining sufficient venture capital to locate at multiple positions such that no remaining potential position offers profits. The result in this case is complete monopoly. Indeed, sequential foresighted entry results in monopoly anytime the number of locations any one firm can choose is not restricted because all equilibrium locations are profitable, and we expect the first firm in the sequence to choose all profitable locations if possible.

☐ **Example 5.** This example emphasizes our contention that making entry into the industry endogenous is crucial and further demonstrates the proposition asserted in the previous example that without a constraint on the number of "locations" any one firm may occupy, the resulting industry structure is monopoly. "Location" by a firm in this example will correspond to a choice of physical plant capacity. Firms produce a homogeneous product, and market price is determined by the total amount of plant capacity in the industry. Assume that industry marginal revenue is a decreasing function of industry capacity, $F > 0$ is the fixed cost of entering the industry, and C is the constant marginal cost of additional capacity.

With a large number of potential entrants, the equilibrium capacity selection rule is to build just sufficient capacity to insure that no subsequent firm can enter profitably. That is, the first firm should be a "limit capacity" monopolist. Suppose the first firm stops short and thus invites further successful entry. The market price is the demand price corresponding to the total industry capacity. The first firm captures sales equal to the size of its capacity choice. Had the first firm chosen the entire industry capacity, however, market price would be no different, further entry would still be forestalled, yet the first firm would sell more than had it chosen smaller capacity; firm 1 clearly profits more by extending capacity to the ultimate industry size. This is the equivalent of the first firm in example 4 opting for as many locations as necessary to preclude subsequent entry unless otherwise constrained.

A very different solution may result if, rather than unfettered endogenous entry, a predetermined, fixed, finite number of entrants is assumed and the fixed cost of entry is then assumed small enough to permit that number to enter successfully. This is the conventional (and we think unsatisfactory) procedure for modeling a market equilibrium. The resulting capacity choices, given foresighted sequential entry, may differ significantly from the case above. If the capacity choices of earlier firms permit firm n to enter with positive profit, then firm n will not drive market price down to the limit entry level as in the previous case. The demand curve faced by firm n is that portion of the market demand remaining after the first $n - 1$ firms make their capacity choices. Firm n *can* induce by its capacity choice any demand price less than that corresponding to industry capacity after $n - 1$ firms have "located"; the market price it *elects* to induce is that which maximizes its profits. Thus, earlier firms in the sequence choose capacity small enough so that profit maximizing firms "locating" later in the sequence elicit the market price most favorable to the earlier firms.[10]

■ The "foresighted sequential entry" equilibrium we obtain in each of the previous examples guarantees nonnegative wealth to all successful entrants and positive wealth to some. This raises the following interesting question: since firms move sequentially, why does the first firm to enter not locate at all positions in the equilibrium industry structure and obtain all potential profits in the market rather than be content with only the first location and less profits? In other words, why should the first firm not be a monopoly?

3. An observation and concluding remarks

Foresighted sequential entry would appear to imply more monopoly market structure than is common in the economy. It is worth considering amendments that would bring the predictions of the model closer to reality. One possibility is that there are costs to occupying multiple locations not yet in the model. Alternatively, perhaps firms *do* occupy all profitable locations initially, but as time passes, additional locations become desirable, yet the first entrant into the market has no special incentive to expand into these locations. We shall discuss briefly how each of these possibilities might be incorporated into our model.

There are several potential constraints on the number of different locations a firm might want to occupy. A constraint may be financial. It is well known that firms exhibit preference for financing new ventures from internal retained earnings rather than external equity or debt capital. The reason for this preference may not be an internal cost of capital that is significantly lower than the market rate of interest. It could be merely that confidentiality is worth a premium. Borrowing by the firm or interesting investors in new equity shares involves revealing investment plans. Therefore, obtaining the financ-

---

[10] If the demand is linear, the number of potential entrants is limited to n, and the fixed cost of entry is sufficiently small, then the sequential entry solutions can be determined analytically. Letting a be the intercept of the inverse industry demand curve and c be the constant marginal cost of production, capacity of the ith firm is $(a - c)/2^i$. Thus the first firm to enter is twice the size of the second, which is twice the size of the third, etc.

ing necessary to locate in enough positions to exhaust all profitable market opportunities through external means may in itself eliminate those market opportunities by forcing the firm to divulge too much information. This could be an argument for a model in which the number of potential locations a firm can occupy is limited by cash flow. In this spirit, Spence (1977) imposes financial constraints in a dynamic setting and shows that monopoly does not result.

Alternatively, a constraint on the potential locations available to any individual firm may ultimately result in diseconomies of scale. The question is, why can a big firm not do everything that a small firm can do? Williamson (1975) explores the hypothesis that there are limits to the effective reach of the managerial hierarchy. The burgeoning literature on the internal organizations of the firm may soon indicate the pervasiveness of such scale diseconomies. Yet to be resolved if we are to rely on span of control explanations of multiple firm markets is why we observe such widely disparate firm sizes and why, as suggested by Williamson's research, the use of relatively autonomous divisions cannot reduce such diseconomies.

There are other potential costs to monopolizing when the market is "discovered." The first firm may be uncertain about the extent of the market. If the firm is risk averse, it may sample the market initially to obtain information even though to do so provides information to other potential entrants and relinquishes its monopoly position. Another possibility is that rapid adjustment of firm size is more costly than slow adjustment.[11] The first firm might then find it more profitable to add capacity slowly, even though such a policy invites loss of market share. Similar results were found by Flaherty (1976) and Kydland (1976) in dynamic equilibrium analyses with costly adjustment. Even though the assumption of increasing cost of adjustment is standard in investment demand theory (see Lucas, 1967), the origins of these costs have not been explored. One appealing justification is that adding productive capacity requires new personnel that must be screened. Conceivably, the likelihood of mistakenly accepting the wrong job candidate increases the larger is the ratio of screening rate to the current size of the organization. The argument here is not that there is a limit to the span of control within the firm, but rather that the effectiveness of screening job applicants to find a good "match" to existing tasks and personnel depends on the time horizon over which the screening proceeds. This hypothesis warrants further study.

Thus, elaborations of the sequential location model developed can add explanatory power to the theory. As the above discussion indicates, much useful work remains in the development of the theory of sequential location. Yet, as an alternative to other *solution concepts,* the nature of the market equilibrium described here has something substantial to offer. Market agents in this model make choices based on the *way* they think choices of all other agents will be made conditional on their own decision, rather than based simply on the observed current choices of their present rivals. It is only when firms consider the potential influence of their decisions on choices of competitors that in equilibrium no firm can improve its situation by adopting a different decision rule. Equilibrium defined in this fashion is

[11] We thank Oliver Williamson for this suggestion.

appealing if firms realize that competitors have motivations similar to their own. And if one argues that firms are unaware of rivals' motives and can be modeled most successfully with that assumption, then we must explain why more economists are not managing firms.

References

BROCK, W. "On Models of Expectations That Arise from Maximizing Behavior of Economic Agents over Time." *Journal of Economic Theory*, Vol. 5 (1972), pp. 348–376.

CHAMBERLIN, E. *The Theory of Monopolistic Competition*. Cambridge: Harvard Univ. Press, 1933 (1948, 6th ed.).

DOWNS, A. *An Economic Theory of Democracy*. New York: Harper and Row, 1957.

EATON, B. C. "Free Entry in One Dimensional Models: Indeterminacy and the Nonexistence of Equilibrium." Queens University Discussion Paper, Kingston, Ontario, 1976.

EATON, B. C. AND LIPSEY, R. "The Principle of Minimum Differentiation Reconsidered: Some New Developments in the Theory of Spatial Competition." *Review of Economic Studies*, Vol. 42, No. 129 (1975), pp. 27–50.

FLAHERTY, M. T. "Industry Structure and Cost-Reducing Investment: A Dynamic Equilibrium Analysis." Unpublished Ph.D. dissertation, Carnegie-Mellon University, February 1976.

HAY, D. A. "Sequential Entry and Entry-Deterring Strategies." *Oxford Economic Papers* (July 1976), pp. 240–257.

HOTELLING, H. "Stability in Competition." *Economic Journal*, Vol. 39 (March 1929), pp. 41–57.

KOTLER, P. *Marketing Decision Making: A Model Building Approach*. New York: Holt, Rinehart, and Winston, 1971.

KYDLAND, F. E. "A Dynamic Dominant Firm Model of Industry Structure." Department of Economics, University of Minnesota, August 1976.

LERNER, A. AND SINGER, H. "Some Notes on Duopoly and Spatial Competition." *Journal of Political Economy*, Vol. 45 (February 1941), pp. 423–439.

LOSCH, A. *The Economics of Location*. New Haven: Yale Univ. Press, 1954.

LOVELL, M. C. "Product Differentiation and Market Structure." *Western Economic Journal*, Vol. 8 (June 1970), pp. 120–143.

LUCAS, R. E., JR. "Adjustment Cost and the Theory of Supply." *Journal of Political Economy*, Vol. 75 (August 1967), pp. 322–334.

——— AND PRESCOTT, E. C. "Investment under Uncertainty." *Econometrica*, Vol. 39 (September 1971), pp. 659–681.

McGUIRE, T. W. AND STAELIN, R. "An Industry Equilibrium Analysis of Downstream Vertical Integration." Carnegie-Mellon University Working Paper, 73-75-76, 1976.

ROSEN, S. "Hedonic Prices and Implicit Markets." *Journal of Political Economy*, Vol. 82 (January/February 1974), pp. 34–55.

SALOP, S. "Monopolistic Competition Reconsidered." Federal Reserve Board of Governors, Washington, D.C., 1976.

SHERMAN, R. *The Economics of Industry*. Boston: Little, Brown and Co., 1974.

SMITHIES, A. "Optimum Location in Spatial Competition." *Journal of Political Economy*, Vol. 49 (February 1941), pp. 423–439.

SPENCE, M. "Firm Investment Strategies and Market Equilibrium." Paper presented at the Industrial Organization Seminar, Bell Laboratories, Holmdel, N.J., March 1977.

STEINER, P. O. "Monopoly and Competition in Television: Some Policy Issues." *The Manchester School of Economic and Social Studies*, Vol. 29, No. 2 (May 1961), pp. 107–131.

VISSCHER, M. "The Value of Consumers' Waiting Time in Supply of Goods." Unpublished Ph.D. dissertation, University of Virginia, Charlottesville, 1975.

WILLIAMSON, O. E. *Markets and Hierarchies*. New York: Free Press, 1975.

Part III
Product Differentiation

[22]

THE

QUARTERLY JOURNAL
OF ECONOMICS

| Vol. LXVII | February, 1953 | No. 1 |

THE PRODUCT AS AN ECONOMIC VARIABLE*

By Edward H. Chamberlin

I. Introduction: the inadequacy of mere price-quantity analysis; possible relationships between the four variables of price, product, advertising and quantity, 1. — II. Products *are* variable; the meaning of product determination, 8. — III. Three main determinants of products: custom, 12; standards, 14; profit maximization, 17.

I

The recognition that the fundamental structure of the economic world which the economist must explain is one of competition between monopolists, each with a product different in some degree from those of his rivals, may be regarded as having a twofold impact upon traditional economic theory. In the first place, it forces an integration into a single system of the two separate theories of monopoly and of competition, no longer to be looked upon as mutually exclusive alternatives, but as partial aspects of a much more complex structure. In the second place, it opens up broad new areas for investigation.

It is the first of those mentioned which has attracted almost exclusive attention, and the reason is not far to seek, for here at least we remain in the familiar territory of price-quantity relationships. The theory of pure competition, which has traditionally explained the economy, is a system of such relationships, as is the traditional theory of monopoly. It is clear by now that the integration of these two theories through the recognition of product heterogeneity and of oligopolistic forces creates a new way of looking at the economic system, raising a host of new problems and yielding new solutions for old ones. Yet it remains true that *mere* integration may still take place within a framework limited to the familiar variables of price and quantity.

* The substance of this article has been presented to successive generations of graduate students at Harvard since 1935, and a number of them have since carried the analysis much further than is done here. The present manuscript is a revision of one prepared and almost completed in 1936.

A note on bibliography appears at the end of the article.

1

But the recognition of heterogeneity in the output of the economic system further transforms and enlarges economic theory by opening it to new variables of major importance. The managements of individual firms will seek in their control of their market relationships not only to choose price most advantageously, but with it to combine (1) the best choice of the "product" itself in its various qualitative aspects, and (2) the optimum expenditure for advertising and selling.

"Non-price competition" is a term which has come to be rather widely accepted to describe the area covered by these new variables, the "product" and selling costs. They are "new" in the sense that they are inconsistent with pure competition and therefore emerge only when the assumption of pure competition is dropped. They might, of course, be ruled out in a system of heterogeneous products by further assumptions carefully designed to exclude them, but such a procedure would be arbitrary indeed, and would require strong justification in view of their vital importance in the real economic world which the economist is charged with explaining. They have both from the beginning been part and parcel of the theory of monopolistic competition,[1] and any formulation of this theory which does not include them is no more than a piece of partial analysis — a facet of the whole theory.

The main concern of this paper is with the "product" as a

1. They are not a part of the theory of imperfect competition as developed by Mrs. Robinson. Alfred Sherrard, in his article "Advertising, Product Variation, and the Limits of Economies" (*Journal of Political Economy*, April 1951) seems to recognize that they are not (p. 126, note 1), yet gratuitously includes Mrs. Robinson (also Stackelberg) in his adverse criticisms of this type of theory. Surely this is a new level of absurdity in the history of this slip-shod tradition which glosses over all differences between the two theories. Sherrard says that "if Chamberlin's interpretation of Mrs. Robinson were accepted, her theory would have to be excluded from consideration in this article altogether, on the ground that 'imperfect competition' does not encompass product variation." But this is not my "interpretation" — it is simply a fact. Mrs. Robinson herself would be the last to make any claim to have dealt with the subject, and in fact *necessarily* excludes it by defining the commodity coextensive with her imperfectly competitive market as "homogeneous" (*Imperfect Competition*, p. 17) and consistently interpreting it in this way. Indeed there is no reason to suppose that she would be any more sympathetic towards the "product as a variable" than is Sherrard. She should therefore be spared his criticisms.

Sherrard cites Triffin in support of his rejection of my "interpretation." But Triffin's authority on this seemingly controversial matter is to the contrary. With reference to product variation and selling outlays Triffin states that in "the expositions of Mrs. Robinson, von Stackelberg and Pareto . . . no attention is given to these problems." Perhaps it is for this reason that he neglects them himself, and warns his readers that this neglect "must be borne in mind when comparing *The Theory of Monopolistic Competition* with the expositions [in question]." (*Monopolistic Competition and General Equilibrium Theory*, p. 21, note 6.) Unfortunately Mr. Sherrard failed to bear it in mind, and thereby contributed his bit to the prevailing obfuscation.

THE PRODUCT AS AN ECONOMIC VARIABLE 3

variable.[2] But since it is necessary to view the problem in its whole setting, let us first look briefly at the many-sided nature of "competition" in which four variables, instead of the familiar two of quantity and price, play a part.

If all four are truly variable, the functional relationships of any two of them, important as they may be, cannot be accepted as more than a partial explanation of the whole. It is not enough, for instance, to concern oneself with the proposition that the demand for a *given* product (under given selling outlays) varies with its price; one must also take into account that the demand at a *given* price (and under given selling outlays) varies with its "quality." One must take it into account because products[3] are not in fact "given"; they are continuously changed — improved, deteriorated, or just made different — as an essential part of the market process.

It may be said that the reactions of buyers to quality are so obvious that there is nothing to be said about them. Yet they may be as complicated in their ramifications as are the equally "obvious" reactions of buyers (and sellers) to prices, upon which the whole structure of economic theory has been built. Certainly they cannot be ignored in any realistic description of how the economic system works. In the same way the question of the behavior of *each* variable relative to the others inevitably poses itself. The quantity of a product which can be sold depends in part upon the price which is asked for it, in part upon its "product" attributes, and in part upon the amount spent to persuade people to buy it. And any one of the four may be regarded as dependent upon the other three in a similar manner.

Where the variables are two (price and quantity), there arises only the question of their relationships to each other. But when they are four, the number of possible paired relationships expands to six, as follows:

1. Price-quantity.
2. Product-quantity.
3. Advertising[4]-quantity.

2. Product variation must not be confused with the familiar analysis of "product differentiation" in which the products of different sellers, although different, are all *given*, so that the only variables studied are price and quantity.

3. "Product" is used in the broad sense to include all aspects of the good or service exchanged, whether arising from materials or ingredients, mechanical construction, design, durability, taste, peculiarities of package or container, service, location of seller, or any other factor having significance for the buyer. Cf. *Monopolistic Competition*, pp. 56, 71, 78.

4. Advertising is used here for convenience as a more concise term to cover all forms of selling costs. The definition of these latter is discussed in *Monopolistic Competition*, chap. VI.

4. Price-product.
5. Price-advertising.
6. Advertising-product.

Such a table must be regarded merely as a symbol, especially with reference to the "product," which is seen at once to be a composite made up of a more or less indefinite number of aspects, such as location, size, design, workmanship, nutritive value, etc., depending on the nature of the product in question. But it is a very useful symbol. For instance, it indicates at once what an absurdly small part of a very broad problem is the first pair of variables — price-quantity relationships — to which economic theory has traditionally limited itself. And it provides sub-headings under which the general nature of the expansion in subject matter may be conveniently indicated. Passing over the first of these sub-headings as familiar, let us look briefly at each of the other five.

Product-quantity relationships. It may be helpful at this point merely to suggest two of the many ways in which familiar concepts of price-quantity analysis may be taken as a starting point in analyzing the phenomena of this new area. First, elasticity of demand, in its general sense of the degree of responsiveness of demand to a change in price, is evidently applicable to the product as a variable, where the question becomes that of the responsiveness of demand to a change in the product. How much, for instance, will an improvement — better materials or some technical addition — (price remaining the same) increase the amount demanded; and how much will a little poorer materials or a few corners cut here and there diminish it? In addition to an analysis based on perfect knowledge, it is especially important here to admit also the highly realistic assumption of imperfect knowledge. If the product can be deteriorated in ways not easily detected, the demand may be quite inelastic with reference to such a change and the temptation will be strong to go ahead; but if the change is easily discovered, buyers will shift in greater numbers to something else. The special problem of "product elasticity of demand" in the face of consumer ignorance is one of those brought into the open by the recognition of the product as a variable. It is relatively easy for the buyer to know the *price* of a product; but as to its *qualities* and their significance to him, perfect ignorance would often be a better assumption than perfect knowledge — and one leading to very different theoretical conclusions as to how products are "determined," as will be seen later on.

As a second example, "cut-throat" price competition has its counterpart in product-quantity relations. In price analysis this

THE PRODUCT AS AN ECONOMIC VARIABLE 5

term has referred to a severe struggle for business in which prices are cut to disastrous levels far below costs; in product analysis it would refer to a struggle in which products are improved with resulting higher costs until costs are above prices. Such a result may easily follow in any type of product competition where an improvement or an added service by one seller succeeds sufficiently well to oblige his rivals to "follow suit," and thus opens the way to a series of adjustments. A simple example may be found in the element of speed in transportation. Speed is a qualitative aspect of the product in this case, excluded from economic analysis unless the product is admitted as a variable; yet increased speed of transport has probably been as revolutionary in its effects upon the economic system as has lower costs. Our concern for the moment is with speed as a basis of competition, and in particular, of "cut-throat" competition. There have been some famous "speed wars" in the history of rail transport, with reference in particular to passenger transport. A reduction in the number of hours between, say, New York and Chicago, is a way of attracting customers, just as is a reduction in the price of a ticket. Increased speed increases costs (after an optimum has been reached) in terms of road ballast, fuel consumption, design of power units and trains, safety measures, lawsuits where safety measures fail, etc. Speed wars can be (and have been) as "ruinous" as rate wars. But apart from this particularly dramatic aspect of speed as an element of competition, it is evident that we have here a very simple, run-of-the-mill example of the product as a variable, one which is of major importance, perfectly measurable, and as capable of analysis in terms of cost and demand functions, profit maximization, etc., as is the conventional variable of price.[5]

Advertising-quantity relationships. With given prices and products, demand will vary with selling expenditures. The manner of its variation is highly complex and is only beginning to be studied and to be integrated into the main body of economic analysis. Selling costs must likewise be related to the general (production) cost analysis of economic theory. An attempt to develop a systematic analysis of these problems and to relate them to the other variables involved is contained in Chapter VII of *Monopolistic Competition*. It may be added here that the two problems just discussed with reference to product-quantity relationships as illustrative of the application of familiar concepts to these areas obviously have their counterparts in

---

5. Many of the problems of this area have been examined by Herbert Ashton in an unpublished Ph.D. thesis, *Economic Analysis of the Element of Speed in Transportation*, Harvard University, 1936.

advertising-quantity relationships. The recognition of advertising as a means of creating and altering demands evidently introduces the distinction between demands as they are found by producers and economically created demands. Economic theory has concerned itself only with the former.

Price-product relationships. Advertising outlay and quantity sold remaining the same, how will price vary with changes in the product? This type of relationship may be difficult to visualize in its isolated form because it would rarely happen in actuality that variations in price and in product would be unaccompanied by a change in advertising outlay and would take place in such a way as not to alter the amount sold. But the functional relationship exists as a part of the whole problem, and it is one of the most important. In general, it is elementary common sense that there will be a rough correlation between the quality of the product and its price, although the conventional analysis of price competition completely passes over such a correlation by confining its attention to price changes for *given* products. We have here a prime example of one of the pitfalls of partial analysis if it is not used with care. *Reasoning from a given product*, economists are much given to scolding business men because they are not sufficiently active in their (price) competition. The admission of the product as a variable not only adds to the picture an alternative area in which competition may in fact be quite active; it does much more than this: it supplies a powerful new force working *against* price competition. If products were actually "given," people would rush to buy from the seller whose price was cheapest because they would know they were getting the same thing for less money. Since products in the real world are not "given," people will naturally recognize that the lower price may be accompanied by poorer quality and their response to it will be diminished; it may even be negative. Furthermore intense price competition puts strong pressure on business men actually to lower the quality of their products, and the desire to maintain certain standards emerges as a natural and commonplace (partial) explanation of why business men do not like price competition. Neglect of price-product relationships gives a warped picture indeed of the actual competitive process.

Price-advertising and advertising-product relationships. Analytically, each of these may be separated from the complex whole in the same way that price-quantity relationships are ordinarily isolated — by holding constant the other two variables in the problem. In real life they do not stand out as clearly as the others for the reason that they do not so often vary in perfect isolation. Let us consider, for

THE PRODUCT AS AN ECONOMIC VARIABLE 7

example, advertising and quality. There is no difficulty about conceiving of the price as held constant, for many products have fixed prices over long periods of time. But the quantity sold is so sensitive to changes both in selling expenditure and in quality that it is difficult to conceive in actuality of advertising and quality varying in such a way as exactly to offset each other, thereby leaving the quantity sold a constant amount. Nevertheless, we know that advertising is often used to maintain sales volume in the face of quality deterioration. And many firms choose to devote resources to improving their products as an alternative to advertising. It is also true that advertising and quality are often positively correlated, and it is a familiar maxim that "it doesn't pay to advertise a poor product." What is indicated by these apparently contradictory observations is not, as will at once be said, "general indeterminateness," but rather a state of general ignorance for lack of study. We know very little about the functional relationships involved for the simple reason that economic theory has been so conceived as to exclude them from its province. As soon as they are accepted as legitimate objects of analysis it seems not too much to hope that our knowledge of the forces involved and hence of the whole competitive process will improve. Clearly, equilibrium in any particular case must involve an optimum relationship between advertising and the product as well as between the other variables in question. Similarly, for a product of given quality, any particular output may be achieved by many possible different combinations of advertising outlay and price. The higher the price the greater must be the advertising outlay (and vice versa) in order to produce the demand necessary to take the given output from the market. Total profit will vary with different combinations and equilibrium must involve an optimum relationship between advertising and price as well as between the other variables. The isolation of price-advertising and advertising-product relationships suggests among other things studies as to the comparative qualities and prices of advertised as against non-advertised goods on the market.

The above discussion has been framed in terms of *pairs* of variables as a familiar type of simplified partial analysis, but evidently three or more variables may be studied together by more complicated methods, and any *final* picture of the forces at work either for a firm, a group of firms, or the whole economy must embrace *all* the forces at work. The principles involved here are no different from those of economic analysis generally.

In looking into new problems opened up by the recognition of the "product" and of advertising (in addition to price and quantity) as economic variables, a word may be said about variations over time. Time series of prices and of quantities produced or consumed (either for individual commodities or in the form of indexes) are, of course, among the most familiar of economic data. Familiar, too, are the difficulties encountered both in the construction and interpretation of such series because of the qualitative changes over time in the products which compose them. It is not necessary, then, to argue for the existence of such changes. What is necessary is to recognize them as variations of vital importance in themselves, rather than as disturbing elements in the problem of price and quantity indexes. We know next to nothing about the history, even the recent history, of the qualitative improvement or deterioration of products, either individually, by classes, or in general. There is a limitless field for investigation here. Of course, to a considerable extent, descriptions of product changes would have to be in non-quantitative terms, but the extent to which quality may be reduced to quantitative terms is apt to be underestimated.[6] The nutritive qualities of food stuffs, tensile strength and thread count of materials, durability and performance of mechanical devices, are simple examples of tests highly relevant to the capacities of goods to satisfy wants. Even such elusive aspects of quality as taste, appearance, etc., have been successfully reduced to quantitative terms in some of the products (as butter) for which standards and grades have already been promulgated by the Federal government. Quality series could be related to the business cycle (To what extent are products deteriorated in time of depression?); and data bearing on quality could be related to the growth of competition or monopoly, to the scale of production, to the growth of production for the market as opposed to production for direct use, and to many other familiar economic categories in a way which would tremendously increase our knowledge of the working of the economic system.

II

Let us turn now to one part of the whole process considered up to this point — that part having to do specifically with the product as a variable. In view of the generally sanctioned procedure of studying price-quantity relationships for *given* products it is of the utmost importance at the outset to realize that there is literally no such thing as a *given* product. Products are actually the most volatile things in the economic system — much more so than prices. To begin with, almost every "product" has at least a variable element in the circum-

6. It was definitely underestimated in *Monopolistic Competition*, p. 79.

THE PRODUCT AS AN ECONOMIC VARIABLE   9

stances surrounding its sale: convenience of location, peculiarities of shop and environment, personalities, service, methods of doing business, etc. These factors are, of course, of varying importance in the individual case.

As for products in the narrower sense, evidently consumers' goods may be of different materials, design or standards of workmanship, whether we are speaking of furniture, clothing or household equipment. The preparation of food for sale, whether by canning, baking, or other type of manufacture for consumption at home, or by cooking and serving in a restaurant, affords infinite possibilities of variation with respect to the selection of ingredients, their quality and the manner in which they are combined and prepared. The perfect and infinite variability of such "products" as services — public utility, professional and personal — is evident. In the case of barber shops, beauty parlors, laundries, cleaning establishments, etc., the quality of what is sold is a major element in the consumer's decision to buy from one seller rather than another — his choice is made as much on the basis of "product" as of price, and probably much more so.

Moving back in the productive process from consumers' goods to capital goods, it is evident without further elaboration that similar considerations apply, and that *all* products beyond the raw material stage are highly variable, for the most part on a continuous scale.

Where, then, do we find fixed products? It would seem that when we get back to raw materials, we might find something given by nature — perhaps some metals in their pure form. But agricultural products can be varied a great deal — the quality of meat is obviously varied by feeding, by breeding, and so on; grains, fruits and vegetables are changed a great deal by human control of seed, methods of culture, etc.; and all these things are done constantly in order to improve profits by the people who are producing them. A student once suggested that the "given" product we were looking for was an egg. This might have been a good illustration before the scientific age. But eggs are actually among the most variable of products and nowadays are *made* to vary in size, color, chemistry of contents, hardness of shell, freshness, etc., to say nothing of such newfangled inventions as that described in the following item: "Government experts claim to have developed an egg with a non-porous shell that will remain edible about twice as long as the average egg."[7]

If products are in fact so elusive, how can we as economists justify freezing them at some arbitrary point, and consider that we

7. From *Looking Ahead Toward the Better World of Tomorrow*, a monthly bulletin published by the State Street Trust Co., Boston.

have done our job when we have explained prices and outputs *for the particular resulting entities?* There can be no true equilibrium until products themselves as well as prices and outputs have been determined; and they are in fact determined along with these latter by the interaction of entrepreneurs' decisions in the face of market forces, often with the familiar objective of maximizing profits. The study of these "non-price" aspects of the economic system should add substantially to our knowledge of how it operates, as compared with the limited partial picture we get when we assume that everything is "given" except price and quantity.

It may be said by some that traditional economic theory already contains a theory of products, holding as it does, at least implicitly, that entrepreneurs will engage in the production of those goods for which, in the light of demand and cost conditions, there are the greatest possibilities of profit. But the proposition that products are determined by the maximum profit decisions of entrepreneurs reveals itself as no more than a plausible initial assumption. It is inadequate to explain products for the same reason that the bare proposition that prices will be such as to maximize profits does not constitute a theory of value. The system of products may actually be much more intricate and complicated in its functional relationships than is the system of prices.

To appreciate fully what is meant by the problem of "product determination" it will be helpful to elaborate the idea of a wide range of product "possibilities" only a few of which are realized in actuality. We are accustomed to thinking of wants as expressing themselves in the market in terms of demand curves or schedules for the particular goods there offered. Yet it must be evident at once that these are only a fragment of the whole system of wants. Just as the demands for any particular good at prices other than the one actually ruling make up a part of the system, so with the demands for products other than those actually produced. After all, the only wants which *actually* express themselves, even for the given products, are those at the prices which *actually* come into existence. If the demands for these same products at other prices constitute a part of the system, so equally do the demands for other products at the same prices (and therefore at other prices as well). The wants in which we are interested, then, are those for all possible products at all possible prices. Only with this conception clearly before us do the same potentialities for product variation appear as are always recognized for prices in the familiar demand curve.[8]

8. There is no reason to dismiss such a notion on the ground that it involves an infinity of possibilities which are absurdly remote and which the entrepreneur

THE PRODUCT AS AN ECONOMIC VARIABLE 11

The diversity of these wants is disguised by the degree of uniformity present in the goods brought forth in the market.[9] The explanation of such uniformity lies, of course, in economies of scale, economies which vary widely in importance as between products. If all products were "made to order," production would clearly be very much less efficient and fewer wants would be satisfied. But they would be satisfied with greater precision.

This failure of actual "products" to satisfy wants exactly may be visualized by imagining all buyers to be distributed uniformly along a line in space and considering the product of all to be homogeneous except for the single element of convenience. The variety of "product" desired by each would be produced only if there were a shop at every point on the line, and this would be the case (barring obstacles to "entry") if there were no economies of scale. Where such economies exist, a maximum of *efficiency* for each firm would be realized only if there were such a limited number of them that each was producing at the minimum point on its cost curve. But since willingness to pay something for convenience means that the demand curve for the product of each firm is tipped from the horizontal, the number of firms would in our example adjust itself by familiar principles so that their demand and cost curves would be tangent; their size would be smaller and there would be more of them than under conditions of maximum efficiency.[1] The exact number of shops in any particular case would evidently be larger the greater the importance which buyers attached to convenience, and smaller the greater the importance of the economies of scale. Even if we suppose the equilibrium number of shops in this final adjustment to be located at equal intervals along the line so as to give a maximum of convenience, the only buyers who are getting *exactly* what they want are those few located at the identical points with the shops. The others purchase at the nearest shop because it affords the next best substitute.

In this example the diversity of wants was infinitely graded on a scale of distance. When we pass to other phases of the "product," and recognize that no two individuals are either identical in tastes or identically situated relative to their environment, we might by anal-

would never consider. The same is true of prices. Realistically the entrepreneur will naturally not waste his time in considering remote product possibilities any more than he will waste it in considering whether or not to set a price of $1,000 on a lead pencil.

9. By uniformity is meant, not merely that sometimes existing as between producers, but, what is much more important, uniformity in the product of any one producer as compared with the diversity of wants on the part of those who purchase from him.

1. Cf. *Monopolistic Competition*, p. 84.

ogy regard buyers as distributed along symbolical lines in multi-dimensional space with respect to other aspects of the product. Certain it is that they are not concentrated at precise points corresponding to the particular "products" actually produced. The demands for products "in between" those actually upon the market are analogous to those for locations in between those actually established on the line of distance.[2] The economic problem of "products," like that of prices, is simply to discover and elaborate the principles that determine which of the many potential products (prices) become, or tend to become, actual.

III

It is possible in the remainder of this article, to present only a few suggestions for a theory of products, and to develop some of them in a limited way.[3] Let us distinguish three main determinants of products under the general headings of (1) custom, (2) standards, and (3) profit maximization.

The first will be passed over quickly. Many products and some aspects of almost all products are determined by custom — and let us add, inertia; sometimes for long periods, more often for short periods.[4] Here a comparison with prices is highly suggestive. Economists, believing on the whole in the "law of supply and demand," and recognizing, as they must, that supply and demand conditions change more or less constantly, have been much concerned with explaining the phenomenon of rigid, or "sticky," prices — prices which remain unchanged over any substantial period of time. At the same time, since the possible variation in products has been covered up by the device of *assuming* them constant, the "stickiness"

2. Because we usually become habituated to what we can get and accept it without too much grumbling, the extent to which products fail to satisfy our wants is underestimated. Yet it is a familiar experience not to find exactly what one wants upon the market. Many "in-between" products might be as profitable to produce as others actually on the market if the "surrounding products" were different.

3. Product decisions are evidently made with reference to the whole range of time periods; and there is no reason to think that the element of time is of any less importance here than in price theory. But it will not be developed in what follows, except incidentally. It may be remarked in passing that a product, say an automobile, by reason of its many aspects, may, at any one time (unlike a price) be a *composite* of decisions made with reference to different time periods.

4. It is of interest to recall that John Stuart Mill clearly (and correctly) distinguished custom from "competition" in value theory. It is a force separate and distinct from the laws of supply and demand and of cost, and he gave it great importance, both in the long and in the short run. (*Principles of Political Economy*, Ashley Edition, Book II, chap. 4 and *passim*.)

THE PRODUCT AS AN ECONOMIC VARIABLE   13

of these latter over time has been taken as a matter of course. Once the product has been recognized as a variable, a parallel treatment of prices and products is suggested. "Sticky" products, equally with prices, require explaining. If rigid prices over a period of time raise suspicions of an antisocial price agreement, then rigid products suggest the possibility of an equally antisocial product agreement. Similarly, if it is a matter of no concern that certain aspects of products become "frozen" over periods of time by reason of custom or inertia, the same forces may explain why prices too do not move for substantial periods. It is suggested that active price competition with "given" products may in general be not more or less "competitive" than active product competition with "given" prices. When competition takes place over an area which includes both prices and products, rigidity in *any* portion of this area, whether caused by a monopolistic agreement, by custom or by inertia, is at least not inconsistent with flexibility in other portions of it and even with intense competition. Finally, it would seem that new light on all the problems of this area is to be had by recognizing the fundamental variability of both products and prices and hence the possible parallels in the explanations of their failures to vary.

We may discuss at this point two other explanations of short-run product rigidity logically independent of custom, yet involving it finally in the form of generally accepted, industry-wide procedures. The first is the influence of technical change on the frequency with which types or models of certain products are altered; the second is the style factor.

It happens that both of these may be illustrated by the automobile industry. In the United States automobile models are changed yearly. Why once a year instead of once a month, or once every five years? What determines the period during which this particular product becomes fixed? There would perhaps be disagreement as to whether the period of one year in the automobile industry is in fact predominantly the result of technological or of style considerations. But let us for the moment turn attention merely to the former. Research is constantly going on, of course, and possible improvements over the model which is in production accumulate. If, for the sake of incorporating such improvements, producers were to set up new models, say every week, they would never produce very many of any particular one; and so, in order to realize the economies which come with large aggregate production of a particular type on a production line basis, they have to freeze the product for a substantial period. If the period is too long, the gains from cheap production are more than offset by the deficiencies of the product relative to the developing state of technical knowledge.[5] From this point of view the annual change of models is simply the compromise which has been worked out between the conflicting objectives of low cost and improved quality.

There are similar problems in connection with style. Here the issue is not technical but aesthetic "improvement," in the sense that human beings tire of a particular design, whether of automobiles or of clothing, and are refreshed by a change, the new product being in this sense an "improvement" (again for a time). This fundamental desire for variety is of course greatly accentuated in its influence by the social interdependence of want satisfactions, illustrated by the satisfaction derived (or the dissatisfaction avoided) from being "in style" once the cycle has been established. Be this as it may, the style cycle for many products, of which women's clothing is perhaps the best example, represents again a compromise between the conflicting objectives of frequent change ("improvement") and of low cost, the latter resulting not only from the popularization and quantity output of a particular design or general type of product, but also from a period of use on the part of the purchaser sufficiently long to reduce to a reasonable level the cost to him per unit of time. The style cycle is full of special problems and is certainly one of the most interesting and important aspects of the product as an economic variable.[6]

The second determinant of products may be called "standards," and they are of various kinds. Speaking generally, a certain conception of what a product ought to be often exists, and although it may be freely variable in a "technical" sense, there is disapproval of variations which involve a departure from, and in particular a deterioration of, the standard set. Perhaps the simplest example of such a standard is one established and maintained by organized society through the machinery of the state. Thus legal enactments in the form of building codes determine in great detail the types of houses that may be constructed, laws and commission regulations set stand-

5. The related problem of just when to freeze the production of a particular model of airplane or tank for military purposes is one which similarly involves the foregoing of subsequent improvements in order to gain quantity output. Its "solution" is, of course, quite different because of the totally different objective of optimum defense, which introduces important new variables such as the relative strength of the enemy, the time when he is most likely to attack, and the inevitable oligopolistic element of his probable reaction to any decision taken.

6. The problem of "variety over time" bears an obvious analogy to that discussed above of variety in general, and illustrated by a spatial example.

ards of service for transport and public utilities, public authority regulates sizes and shapes of food containers and in diverse respects the qualitative aspects of food and drug products themselves, etc., etc. For the most part (but not entirely) the imposition of such legal standards seems to be explained by the alternative dramatic deterioration of "products" in a system where they are determined by profit maximization. The circumstances under which such deterioration is "normal" are discussed further on.

Standards are also established and maintained by various classes and subgroups within society, as well as by firms and individuals. Thus there are professional standards, and the conception of the "professions" as an area of activity in which objectives other than profit maximization prevail is familiar. With reference to the "product" this means, to take medicine as an example, that a doctor is restrained by the weight of generally accepted professional practice from depreciating the quality of his medical services, even where such depreciation, combined with the proper price policy, might increase his income. Indeed the taboo on commercialism in the form both of advertising and of "price competition" is a part of a system designed to protect a standard-determined service from being put on the scale of profit maximization.

Closely related to standards in the professions are artistic, ethical and moral standards, and standards of purity, of quality or of workmanship. An artist or writer may be faithful to his best creative ideals — a standard — or he may deliberately alter his product in favor of what will sell more readily. In like manner the character of sports will be vitally affected by whether the persons taking part in them are competing for the sake of the sport itself or to make money, and so we have the distinction (increasingly difficult to maintain) between amateur and professional sports. Even where all participants are amateur, profit maximization by other control units may enter in, as illustrated by the recent crisis in college football in which leading American universities suddenly became aware that their eagerness to exploit the market possibilities of great football spectacles had altered the "product" in numerous undesirable respects.[7]

The services of the politician may be dedicated uncompromisingly to the public interest, or they may depart from this standard in all degrees by reason of inducements pressed upon him by those who

---

7. Typically, however, the "maximum profits" from football since they were used to offset the losses in other sports, were consistent with no profits (or a deficit) for the athletic program as a whole.

seek to influence his views or to obtain political favors: in our terminology the "product" (his services) is in the latter case no longer
determined by a standard of integrity but has been altered in favor
of income maximization.[8] Similarly, maple syrup, the product of the
maple tree, may be produced and marketed as such or it may be
allowed to depart from this standard by diluting it in various degrees
with cheaper cane syrup. This latter may seem a less serious "loss
of integrity," than in the case of the politician, and one which would
be fairly well taken care of by informing the purchasers of what had
been done, but analytically the contrast between a product determined by a standard on the one hand or by profit maximization on
the other is the same in the two cases.

Individual business men, of course, constantly set standards for
their products or services, and, as has been noted, their aversion to
price competition is in some part explained by the downward pressure
it puts upon quality. Typically a trade-marked product is carefully
defined and its quality scrupulously maintained so that buyers will
get exactly what they have come to expect. However, although the
product definition *may* involve a standard independent of profit
maximization (consistent, incidentally, with the determination of
price by this latter principle), more often it will merely represent the
"freezing" of a product determined by the maximization principle.

As an example of "standards of workmanship" I may mention
a recent article by a French chef explaining how he made several of
his most famous dishes, in which he began with the comment that
if you permitted yourself to think about money you were "ruined
from the start." Here the standard appears to be the "maximum
excellence of the product," a "maximum" about which we read
nothing in economic literature although it would seem to be a category
which should figure prominently in welfare economics. A "standard
of workmanship" implies a feeling strongly held that a product
"ought" by its very nature to be made in a certain way. The artisan
who feels thus and who revolts at the idea of cutting corners in

8. There has been much discussion of this particular problem in the United
States recently. In the revelations of gifts to public servants by interested
parties, an accused income tax official startled the community by his defense of
accepting a ham on the ground that it weighed only twelve pounds. A politician
is in fact up against a perplexing problem in protecting his "product." Since
"gifts" are constantly pressed upon him which range from a casual cigarette or
a luncheon to expensive entertainment and articles of great value, the important
practical question is raised of where to draw the line in order not to be a prig
and yet to maintain a satisfactory standard of ethics. Senator Paul H. Douglas
has discussed the practical and ethical aspects of the question and mentioned
his own rule-of-thumb limit, designed to avoid "major involvements," as $2.50.
(*Ethics in Government*, Harvard University Press, 1952, pp. 45–49.)

THE PRODUCT AS AN ECONOMIC VARIABLE 17

order to make his product more cheaply still exists but he is increasingly difficult to find.

This all-too-brief discussion of standards with its few scattered illustrations may at least serve the purpose of emphasizing that products, which are by their nature highly variable, are often determined by important forces other than the maximizing of profits.[9] It seems clear that, at least in this area, profit maximization is not nearly as universal as it is commonly assumed to be in price-quantity analysis. And, by analogy, one may be led to wonder whether it is actually as important as has been thought in this latter area as well, or if other determinants should not receive more attention.

The third of our main determinants of products is profit maximization. Here we are on familiar ground so far as the objective goes, but not with respect either to the variables manipulated or to the variety of functional relationships which describe the paths along which they may move. Only a few of many types of problems may be mentioned here. First of all, the whole subject of product agreements must be passed over, although, as with price theory, collusive action opens up a broad area for study.

Let us begin by returning to the subject of spatial location. Space is in fact one of the leading aspects of product differentiation and of product variation. It is obviously mensurable, and many of the leading problems of monopolistic competition may helpfully be conceived, by analogy, as spatial problems.[1] Although location in the economic system is normally a matter of two dimensions, we may, without loss of generality for our present purpose, limit our brief comments to the simplified one-dimensional version already mentioned — that of the distribution of sellers along a line. It is a familiar problem with a substantial and growing literature, to which the reader is referred for a more extended discussion.[2]

We assume at first that buyers are uniformly distributed along

9. The economist may of course restrict himself to describing; but if he permits himself to pass judgments he will probably recognize that, in some fields at least, preserving standards seems preferable to maximizing profits. Education (in which he himself is usually engaged) is perhaps a clear example. The disturbing question is raised of the criteria by which such areas are to be distinguished from those in which standards are thought to be of no importance.

1. Although space is given substantial importance in *Monopolistic Competition*, it appears (with small exceptions) simply as one of the many types of product differentiation. In "Monopolistic Competition Revisited," *Economica*, Nov. 1951, it is used as a device to develop by analogy the whole conception of a monopolistically competitive economic system.

2. In addition to the several sources mentioned here, many more will be found among the items indicated in the bibliographical note at the end of this article.

the line, which may be thought of as a street. Prices are given and uniform for all sellers, and products are homogeneous except for location, so that there is no basis of competition other than convenience, each buyer trading with the seller who locates nearest to him. The actual number of sellers on any such line would of course be worked out as always by the interplay of the desire for "diversity" (in this case, more convenience) on the one hand, and economies of scale on the other, as expressed by the demand and cost curves involved.[3] But this problem may be abstracted from in discussing the location of any particular number of sellers.

The major problem is whether the sellers will concentrate at a point on the line or whether they will be dispersed over its length, as are the buyers. If we assume, with Hotelling,[4] that the distribution of sales as between sellers is a function of location, but that *aggregate* sales on the line are a constant, a single seller would locate anywhere at all. But two sellers would be concentrated at the center[5] instead of dispersed at the quartile points, where convenience would be maximized. This is because either one would, by the general principle that the market of each extends half way to his nearest rival in any direction, increase his sales by moving towards the other; and if, when they met, they were not already at the center, the one nearer to an end of the line, and hence with the smaller market of the two, would gain by moving around to the other side of his rival. Such movements would continue until they were side by side in the middle of the line where, their markets being equal, neither one could improve his position by a further adjustment. A substantial development of the problem has taken place for this special case of duopoly, including the obvious possibility of oligopolistic reactions, both as to location and as to price.[6] But let us pass on to larger numbers where the issue of concentration vs. dispersion appears in more general form. Assuming two sellers already grouped together, Hotelling argued that a third would also maximize his market by closing in on them as explained above, and that a fourth and a fifth and so on would likewise pile up at the same spot, the general conclusion being excessive concentration. The reasoning was extended

3. Cf. above, p. 11.
4. "Stability in Competition," *Economic Journal*, March 1929.
5. Hotelling argues merely that two or a larger number of sellers will "cluster unduly." Since he never *isolates* the spatial factor as we have done, he reaches no conclusion as to *where* the cluster will take place.
6. I mention specifically only two of the numerous articles: A. P. Lerner and H. W. Singer, "Some Notes on Duopoly and Spatial Competition," *Journal of Political Economy*, April 1937, and Arthur Smithies, "Optimum Location in Spatial Competition," *Ibid.*, June 1941.

THE PRODUCT AS AN ECONOMIC VARIABLE   19

by analogy to cider, political parties and even to religions: products in general are "too homogeneous."

The falsity of this result for more than two sellers was argued in my own Appendix C,[7] where the general principle of dispersion along the line was established for three or more sellers, it being held that groups of two were possible, but not groups of three (or more). Groups of three are impossible because the "one who is caught between the other two will move to the outer edge of the group, and a series of such moves, always by the one left in the center, will disperse the group." Groups of two, however, are possible because any seller located *between two others* will make the same total sales wherever he locates within the limits of their positions, and hence *may* locate next to one of them. In general, n sellers must be dispersed so that "the space between the last sellers at either end and the ends of the line can never exceed $1/n$ . . . and that the space between any two sellers can never exceed $2/n$ (taking the length of the line as unity), this limit being reached only in the extreme case where the sellers are grouped by twos." The dispersion would, of course, go even further if groups of two did not come into being.

Lerner and Singer, in addition to presenting an elaborate analysis of the duopoly case, also discuss the general problem for larger numbers, and, although expressing strong dissent from my own conclusions, seem with two exceptions to agree with them.[8] The first exception is the case of three (and only three) sellers where an intriguing alternative possibility is suggested of the three milling about indefinitely at the center of the line or possibly waltzing up and down it in an "unstable cycle." The second exception is the discovery that, although "groups" of sellers may in general consist of either one or two, the *end* groups must necessarily consist of two sellers.[9] The necessity arises from the fact that a lone seller at either end would always gain by closing in on his neighbor until he was as near him as possible, just as in the case of two sellers described above. This is a correction of greater importance than seemed to be realized, for it now appears that when there are only two sellers on the line, they will crowd together at a point not because they are duopolists, but because they are a special case of the "end problem." That this is so can be seen at once by getting rid of the ends.

The ends may be got rid of by the expedient of bending them around and joining them, in other words by assuming a "circular

7. *Monopolistic Competition*, Appendix C, "Pure Spatial Competition."
8. *Op. cit.*, pp. 176–82. See especially diagram on p. 177.
9. *Ibid.*, p. 181.

street." This is of course only a symbol, but as a symbol it is probably more meaningful than a line with ends, since the idea of a "chain of substitutes" without sharp breaks and which therefore "defies subdivision"[1] has become a commonplace. On a circular street the first seller would locate at any place on the circle, as would the second, since in any event total sales would be split between them by the familiar principle that each sells half way to the other. Thus with two sellers equilibrium no longer *requires* their concentration, since if they were dispersed there would be no gain for either one by moving towards the other. But there would also be no loss, and in general, with two or more sellers, we still have the *possibility*, as on the straight line, of sellers grouping "accidentally" by twos (but not by threes) for the reason explained earlier that any seller may wander about between his two neighbors, even coming up very close to one of them, without effect upon the size of his market.

However, this latter type of indeterminacy disappears at one stroke when the unrealistic assumption is dropped that *aggregate* demand on the line is the same regardless of the number and location of the sellers. In general people do take space into account in some degree in deciding whether to buy at all, so that if the product is too far away and it is too much trouble to obtain it they will do without it. For this reason one seller will sell more if he locates at the center of the line than if he locates anywhere else. "Convenience" is maximized at that point (more generally, the discrepancy between products and wants is minimized), and just as demand is greater at a lower price, so it is greater if "convenience" is increased. Similarly two sellers located one each at the quartile points on the line will sell more than two located side by side at the mid-point.[2] And similarly a seller will always increase his sales by choosing the mid-point between his neighbors in either direction. The way is opened to further instructive analysis in the case of duopoly (also oligopoly) on a line with ends, as Lerner and Singer and particularly Smithies have shown; but if we rid ourselves of the "end problem" by some device such as the "circular street," it is clear that two or any larger number of sellers will always adjust themselves to a pattern involving

1. *Monopolistic Competition*, p. 103.
2. Thus, although two sellers on a line with ends will, if "competing" in the sense of ignoring their mutual dependence, move towards the center, the solution of "mutual dependence recognized" will lead them to move to the quartile points, where their joint sales are a maximum. A product (location) agreement would also put them at the quartile points. Agreement in this case is socially preferable to "competition" — a result most distressing to any competitive theorist.

THE PRODUCT AS AN ECONOMIC VARIABLE 21

equal spacing. There remains one small element of indeterminacy — there is no answer to the question of *where* sellers will locate; all we know is that they will be equally far apart. If there are four, for instance, they may be at 12, 3, 6 and 9 o'clock on the circle, or they may be at 1, 4, 7 and 10. This conclusion in its general application appears to present a major difficulty for welfare economics. In the special case of one seller, he may again locate anywhere.

All the discussion so far has assumed buyers to be distributed *evenly* along the line, and has established the *general* principle (contrary to Hotelling) of an adjustment of sellers roughly conforming to buyers' locations. The problem takes on new and important developments when it is recognized that buyers are in fact unevenly distributed and often highly concentrated at certain points. The locations of sellers and the sizes of firms will of course adapt themselves to such concentrations, and there will be some rather complicated interactions and cumulative effects which are passed over here.[3] But it is clear that the piling up of sellers and the growth in their scale of output at any point or in any area will usually be explained by the fact that buyers are concentrated there instead of being dispersed as we have been assuming up to now. Such "concentrations of population" are obvious for the spatial problem in the literal sense, and a moment's reflection will show that they exist very generally too in "economic space" and yield important general conclusions for the way in which products are determined. "Concentrations of buyers" around a successful type of economics textbook, of beach costume or of toothpaste (chlorophyl!) bring sellers rushing to the area and result in an outpouring of products which are "close together" in certain leading characteristics, although divergent in others.

Consider for example the scale of taste in general terms. By the reasoning already developed, one would expect products to be distributed over a wide range of human tastes; but we must also expect them to be concentrated wherever tastes are concentrated, and especially heavily where there is the greatest concentration of all — the mass market. So it is for example with the entertainment field generally, where it is significant that even in the case of classic literary productions where one might hope that the product would be determined once for all by a standard of fidelity, reproduction for the moving pictures under principles of profit maximization will usually lead to substantial alterations being made in the interest of "widening the market." For similar reasons the most sensational and/or catastrophic news of the day is heavily exploited by most

3. Some of these are discussed in *Monopolistic Competition*, Appendix C.

newspapers in the belief, apparently borne out by the facts, that mass tastes are concentrated at this level. In a highly penetrating discussion of these and related matters, H. A. Overstreet has commented that "where money-making is the paramount interest, a constant search will be made to discover what most people *as they are* can be relied upon to like most of the time," with little or no interest in "what a few discriminating people like," "what many people might eventually like" or "what most people like once in awhile."[4] Evidently maximum profits do not lie in these areas where the "population" is thinly distributed. Fundamentally the reason for this must go back to economies of scale. In fields of activity where small scale production is not too heavily penalized so that there can be a large number of sellers over the field as a whole, it is likely that the thinly populated areas will not be left out entirely. But it is, after all, familiar and rather obvious that the economies of mass production require the existence (or the development) of mass tastes, and put heavy pressure on all others for survival.[5]

Another example is furnished by the scale of incomes, with its heavy concentration at the lower end. Since there is a "concentration of population" at levels of moderate or low incomes, profit maximization requires, by principles already developed, that the great mass of products be determined *qualitatively* with reference to what people of such incomes can afford to pay. Indeed, to take the extreme, one of the simple and obvious results of a complete leveling down of incomes would seem to be the complete disappearance from the market of goods of the highest quality and most skilled workmanship — goods which are expensive to make and which only those of high incomes can afford to buy. But even long before this extreme has been reached, the economies of scale play heavily in favor of the mass market and against those products higher up the scale of quality which could be bought only by those in the thinly populated income areas.

A corollary to these effects of income distribution on the determination of products is the pressure on quality exerted by the outpouring of new products. The appearance on the market of every new product creates pressure in some degree on the markets for others,

4. *The Mature Mind* (New York: W. W. Norton & Co., 1949), p. 206. Italics in original.

5. An interesting study of the adaptation of "products" to preferences in the field of radio broadcasting has been made by Peter O. Steiner in his article, "Program Patterns and Preferences and the Workability of Competition in Radio Broadcasting," this *Journal*, May 1952. A field which seems to the author to cry out for analysis from this point of view is that of book publishing; also that of magazine publishing.

THE PRODUCT AS AN ECONOMIC VARIABLE 23

and when products are variable and determined by profit maximization some of this pressure is bound to be exerted on quality in order to maintain prices which people can afford to pay. Thus in a world whose technology is constantly creating new products, it should not be surprising to find that a part of the whole process is the deterioration of other products in order to make room for the new ones at the mass market level where the population is concentrated.

Who is there who has not heard many times the observation that "they don't make them that way any more"? Any reader could supply his own illustrations; but let me mention several from recent personal experience. A plumber (who ought to know about such matters) inspected a water boiler in my cellar and informed me that if it had been made more recently it would already be worn out, but being an "old-timer" it still had many years of life in it. Again, an honest but apparently unenterprising radio dealer has repeatedly advised me against discarding a small radio purchased twenty years ago, for the reason that it "has better stuff in it" than those currently on the market at double the price. And a jeweler recently informed me on his own initiative that the really beautifully made watch is virtually extinct because, as he put it, nowadays all watches are "made to sell at a price." One feels foolish substantiating by illustration what is a commonplace to most people, but my impression is that in this matter, whereas most people are quite aware of what goes on, economists on the whole are deluded. Perhaps they have been blinded as the joint result of (1) a system of thought which takes products as data and hence does not even raise the question of how they are determined, and (2) an unconsciously held conviction that, since we live in an age of "progress," whenever products do change they must change for the better. One might add (3) a technique of welfare analysis which (at least for the unwary, and how few are not!) seems to grind out the answer that so long as free choice is preserved we are bound to get the best of all possible worlds. Let it be noted that I am not denying that technology often gives us new and better products, but only insisting that its equally notable achievement in giving us poorer ones whenever these will maximize profits must not be overlooked.

Let us leave the family of problems flowing from the spatial analogy and look briefly at profit maximization in two other settings. The first of these has to do with durability. Durability is an aspect of products which is exceedingly variable, and incidentally quite measurable, like space, speed of transportation, and others we have discussed. Since it is variable, the producer has to face the question of how durable to make his product. Evidently if he makes it too durable, as soon as people have bought one unit they will not need another for a substantial period during which there will be no "repeat demand" for his product.[6] He has an interest then in making it less durable so that people will come back that much sooner to buy another unit. On the other hand, just as he must not set his price too high, so he must not offer a product which wears out too fast in comparison with others on the market. The problem is to find that length of life for his product which will maximize his profit.

I have been told by people who ought to know, that it is possible to make at reasonable cost a razor blade which would last a lifetime. I will not vouch for the fact — let us take it merely as a hypothetical illustration. What is clear is that if razor blades of this kind were made, as soon as everybody had one there would be no more sold. Probably most products not consumed in a single use could be made more durable than they are at somewhat higher cost. On the other hand, in some cases — as when there is a style factor — buyers do not want durability beyond a certain point. The question is raised: what governs the durability of different types of products, and under different conditions of competition and monopoly; and how does the optimum defined by profit maximization compare with standards defined by a public interest or welfare criterion?

Finally, let us raise explicitly the question of imperfect knowledge, and begin with an example. In 1934 a letter was received by the Consumers' Advisory Board of the NRA from a manufacturer of mayonnaise in Texas which read substantially as follows: "I started making mayonnaise several years ago. I was making it out of the best ingredients and selling it at a fair profit. Everything went all right for a while until a competitor came in and started making mayonnaise with about 10 per cent gum arabic in it and lowering the price. I had to lower the price along with him in order to stay in business, and so I had to put in 10 per cent gum arabic too because I couldn't produce 100 per cent good mayonnaise at this lower price. What did my competitor do but increase the gum arabic to 20 per cent and lower the price again. Of course I had to do the same thing in order not to lose my customers. This has been going on until I am now putting in 55 per cent gum arabic with 45 per cent mayonnaise. Can't you do something so that I can go back again to making a good product?" As it happened, the Consumers' Advisory Board

6. Thus an executive of the men's apparel industry recently observed that "the business suffers from a lack of obsolescence." The subject of durability is evidently (or should be) closely linked to Keynesian economics, since aggregate demand may fall off and unemployment result if products last too long.

THE PRODUCT AS AN ECONOMIC VARIABLE 25

could do nothing (about this or anything else); but what interests us here is the principle of product determination involved.

The phenomenon of product deterioration has already received substantial discussion and explanation, but without any particular reference to the consumer's imperfect knowledge of products. An added element of major importance now appears in the recognition of the fact that this knowledge is extremely limited. With respect to food products, consumers are not chemists as a rule, and therefore cannot test them to find out about their ingredients. What is perhaps more to the point is that even if they had the necessary technical knowledge and equipment, and the necessary passion for testing things, they would be unable individually to find out about even a small fraction of the myriad varieties of products and services made available by modern industry for them to purchase. They have of course some limited defenses, as in the case of food the faculty of taste, but these are feeble indeed when pitted against the achievements of modern science.[7] In particular it often happens that alterations in products may be effected so gradually that small changes cannot be detected at all. In any such situation the logic of profit maximization leads to definite and clear-cut results. Any producer, by deteriorating his product slightly, can reduce his cost and increase his profits, either by selling at the same price as before, which would give him a greater profit per unit, or by combining the deterioration with a lower price, which is what happens more usually, and thereby increasing profits by taking business away from his rivals. In a succession of such moves there appears to be no limit until the technological possibilities of deterioration have been exhausted — in the case at hand, if the producer had put any more gum arabic in the mayonnaise, it would probably have disintegrated.

The general principle may be formulated as follows: assuming profit maximization and complete lack of knowledge with respect to certain aspects of products, these aspects will undergo such qualitative change as will reduce cost, until a limit set by *technological* considerations is reached. In actuality, since knowledge is hardly ever either perfect or completely lacking, deterioration will be carried further in some cases than in others, and intermediate equilibria may be defined in any particular case by demand considerations reflecting buyers' expected responses to further deterioration, as governed by their knowledge or suspicions as to what is happening and in particular by the question of whether the situation is general or whether sub-

7. It is this situation of course which provides a market for the services of the consumers' counsel and testing agencies.

stitute products *of assured quality* are available. The general tendency described might be termed Gresham's Law of products: bad products drive good products off the market.

Let us look at one more example. Alsberg, in his pioneering and authoritative study in this field,[8] has described the process by which sole leather came over the years to be "weighted" more and more by leaving in excessive amounts of tanning extract, or by impregnating the leather with glucose or epsom salts; those who introduced these practices being able in the early stage "to sell tanning extract, glucose or epsom salts, as the case might be, at the price of sole leather . . . The limit for water-soluble substances," he says, "has climbed continuously upward" until "in the federal specifications for sole leather . . . [it] is now [1931] being raised to 33 per cent to conform with 'good commercial practice.' The figure cannot well go much higher, because the tanner cannot get much more into the leather without risk of resulting trouble from spewing of the load." Again, the limit is technological.

To what extent in real life are products determined in this way? Certainly the average citizen (whose lack of knowledge is what accounts for the phenomenon!) is in no position to answer, and in the absence of an unmitigated faith in the virtues of "free enterprise" no reason presents itself for supposing that the two examples mentioned are in any way exceptional. On the contrary, since the results in both cases followed from the two main conditions of (a) profit maximization and (b) imperfect knowledge, and since these conditions are widespread, a presumption would seem to be established that they are typical. It should not be forgotten that what is involved is not merely major and spectacular changes, but also countless lesser ones, sometimes of subsidiary importance for particular products, sometimes compounded into a significant aggregate, and often overshadowed by an "improvement" of some sort to which the buyer's attention is directed by skillful advertising.

The principle must of course be understood as one operating in the absence of measures designed to offset it; and substantial evidence as to its validity and importance is to be had by observing the extent to which it has in fact led to countervailing action on the part of government to protect consumers from its consequences. The regulation of service and safety in the public utility and transport industries is a familiar example. Standards of safety, for instance, are set and enforced by governments because it is recognized that if they

8. C. R. Alsberg, "Economic Aspects of Adulteration and Imitation," this *Journal*, Nov. 1931. The discussion of sole leather is on pp. 8–11.

THE PRODUCT AS AN ECONOMIC VARIABLE   27

were not, private companies would, in order to maximize their profits, avoid the outlays necessary for this purpose. Similarly, standards of container fill for food products are established because when they were not, some producers had a tendency to maximize profits by converting a given amount of food into more cans of food through putting less food into each can. Similarly, informative labeling as to ingredients is required for some food and drug products as a means of preventing or discouraging certain types of adulteration, and as an aid to the consumer in detecting and judging the acceptability of others in the light of lower price and other considerations. All that was said earlier[9] about the determination of products by government standards should be recalled at this point. The principle of product deterioration explains such measures of social control in just the same way that the principle of monopoly profits explains the regulation of monopoly.

There are of course factors other than those of government control which operate against product deterioration, and which similarly attest to its importance in the sense that they have arisen or continue as countervailing forces. They include in general all the alternatives to profit maximization, especially "standards" in all the senses of this word discussed above,[1] of which those established by governments are only one. They include the attempts of producers to avoid price competition in so far as these represent attempts to avoid pressure on "products." They include such monopoly elements as trade-marks, names, etc., in their role of guarantors of quality. And they include all informational activity designed to improve the state of knowledge of consumers. The net result is difficult to evaluate, but in any event the importance of the principle in question is not to be judged by the amount of product deterioration that remains after a few of the worst instances of it have been counteracted by regulation, any more than the importance of the principle of monopoly price is to be judged by the residuum after some degree of monopoly control. There seems on the whole to be no reason to doubt that the tendencies described are an important part of the larger subject of product determination.

By way of general summary, it seems difficult to understand how the economist can pretend to explain (or to prescribe for) the economic system and leave products out of the picture. Why not leave prices out? And why is one more important than the other? It is perhaps

9. Above, pp. 14–15.
1. Pp. 14–17.

28   *QUARTERLY JOURNAL OF ECONOMICS*

unnecessary to argue the point, since "non-price competition" seems
already to have achieved some substantial recognition in the literature.[2] But many are still afraid of it, in particular the traditionalists
who do not like to "rock the boat."[3] From their point of view I
think they are right. One thing seems certain — non-price competition will not stay quietly in a separate compartment, leaving the
rest of economic theory to go its way unaffected and undisturbed
by its recognition. For it pervades, and pervades vitally, the whole
competitive process.[4]

2. Non-price competition has its counterpart in other areas, as for instance
in the field of incomes, where, in particular, "nonwage" elements in the labor
bargain are always important and often more important than the wage itself,
both from a private and a public point of view. Yet they have been completely
passed over in wage theory until quite recently, when they have begun to receive
some small attention.

3. I cannot refrain in this connection from again referring to the position
taken by Professor Hicks who, reasoning that "a general abandonment of the
assumption of perfect competition . . . must have very destructive consequences
for economic theory," concludes, "Let us, then, return to the case of perfect
competition." (*Value and Capital*, pp. 83–85.) Perhaps the new areas of analysis
suggested in this article will provide a partial answer to his apprehensions. There
appears to be no threat of intellectual unemployment for economic theorists in
the foreseeable future.

4. *Bibliographical Note.* A convenient way to indicate bibliography for
the subject of the product as a variable, including spatial competition, is to give
the numbers of the items in the general bibliography at the end of *The Theory of
Monopolistic Competition* which deal with this subject. They are as follows:

Fourth and later editions: 4, 5, 7, 9, 17, 18, 22, 23, 30, 50, 51, 52, 57, 66,
69, 78, 84, 85, 92, 95, 98, 100, 118, 131, 139, 148, 157, 187, 190, 191, 199, 207,
229, 233, 273, 290, 296, 308, 309, 310, 314, 325, 353, 354, 355, 364, 372, 382, 383,
393, 394, 404, 413, 425, 449, 450, 454.

Sixth edition ("Supplement: May 1948"; also appeared in this *Journal*,
August 1948): 464, 485, 498, 509, 510, 526, 527, 537, 540, 541, 543, 554, 555, 580,
583, 590, 591, 592, 601, 602, 616, 630, 651, 656, 658, 680.

No effort has been made to extend the *general* bibliography beyond 1948,
but a few items dealing with product and spatial competition which have come
to my attention since that date are listed below. Unfortunately the list must
be far from complete. The outpouring after 1948 of articles on basing points is
not included here.

Becker, Arthur P., "Psychological Production and Conservation," this
Journal, 63:577 (1949).

Brems, Hans, *Product Equilibrium under Monopolistic Competition*, Cambridge, Mass., 1951.

Brems, Hans, "Employment, Prices, and Monopolistic Competition,"
Review of Economics and Statistics, 34:314 (1952).

Brown, T. H., "Quality Control," *Harvard Business Review*, 29, No. 6: 69
(November 1951).

Chamberlin, Edward H., "Product Heterogeneity and Public Policy,"
American Economic Review, 40 (sup.): 85 (1950).

Chamberlin, Edward H., "Monopolistic Competition Revisited," *Economica*,
18 (new series): 343 (1951).

THE PRODUCT AS AN ECONOMIC VARIABLE   29

Dreyfuss, Henry, "The Industrial Designer and the Business Man," *Harvard Business Review*, 28, No. 6: 77 (November 1950).

Enke, Stephen, "Resource Malallocation within Firms," this *Journal*, 63:572 (1949).

Fellner, William, *Competition Among the Few*, New York, 1949.

Gill, F. W. and Bates, G. L., *Airline Competition*, Boston, 1949.

Greenhut, Melvin L., "The Size and Shape of the Market Areas of a Firm," *Southern Economic Journal*, 19:37 (1952).

Houthakker, H. S., "The Econometrics of Family Budgets," *Journal of the Royal Statistical Society, Series A*, 1952, p. 1 (especially Section 4).

Houthakker, H. S., "Compensated Changes in Quantities and Qualities Consumed," *Review of Economic Studies*, 19:155 (1952–53).

Houthakker, H. S. and Prais, S. J., "Les Variations de Qualité dans les Budgets de Famille," *Economie Appliquée*, 5: 65 (1952).

Innis, H. A., *The Press, a Neglected Factor in the Economic History of the Twentieth Century*. London, 1949.

Isard, Walter, "The General Theory of Location and Space-Economy," this *Journal*, 63:476 (1949).

Isard, Walter, "Distance Inputs and the Space Economy, Part I: The Conceptual Framework; Part II: The Locational Equilibrium of the Firm," this *Journal*, 65:181 and 373 (1951).

Kaldor, Nicholas, "The Economic Aspects of Advertising," *Review of Economic Studies*, 18:1 (1949–50).

Leyland, N. H., "A Note on Price and Quality," *Oxford Economic Papers*, 1 (new series): 269 (1949).

Oxenfeldt, Alfred R., "Consumer Knowledge: Its Measurement and Extent," *Review of Economics and Statistics*, 32:300 (1950).

Picton, G., *Commercial Agreements. The Form and Content of Some Agreements between Firms*. Cambridge, England, 1952.

Sherrard, Alfred, "Advertising, Product Variation and the Limits of Economics," *Journal of Political Economy*, 59:126 (1951).

Solo, Carolyn S., "Innovation in the Capitalist Process: A Critique of the Schumpeterian Theory," this *Journal*, 65:417 (1951).

Steiner, Peter O., "Program Patterns and Preferences, and the Workability of Competition in Radio Broadcasting," this *Journal*, 66:194 (1952).

Theil, H., "Qualities, Prices and Budget Enquiries," *Review of Economic Studies*, 19:129 (1952–53).

Wadsworth, H. E., "Utility Cloth and Clothing Scheme," *Review of Economic Studies*, 16:82 (1949–50).

Yolande, Sister Mary, "Some Economic and Ethical Considerations for Legislation Protecting the Consumer," *Review of Social Economy*, March 1949.

EDWARD H. CHAMBERLIN.

HARVARD UNIVERSITY

[23]

GROUP EQUILIBRIUM

Let us turn now to what we may call the group problem, or the adjustment of prices and "products" of a number of producers whose goods are close substitutes for each other. The group contemplated is one which would ordinarily be regarded as composing one imperfectly competitive market: a number of automobile manufacturers, of producers of pots and pans, of magazine publishers, or of retail shoe dealers. From our point of view, each producer within the group is a monopolist, yet his market is interwoven with those of his competitors, and he is no longer to be isolated from them. The question now to be asked is: what characterizes the system of relationships into which the group tends to fall as a result of their influence one upon another? The conclusions reached will be especially illuminating when considered alongside of those yielded by the theory of pure competition, ordinarily applied to the same phenomena.

One difficulty encountered in describing the group equilibrium is that the widest variations may exist in all respects between the different component firms. Each "product" has distinctive features and is adapted to the tastes and needs of those who buy it. Qualitative differences lead to wide divergences in the curves of cost of production, and buyers' preferences account for a corresponding variety of demand curves, both as to shape (elasticity) and as to position (distance from the x and y axes). The result is heterogeneity of prices, and variation over a wide range in outputs (scales of production) and in profits. Many such variations are, of course, temporary, and are constantly in process of being eliminated. We are concerned, however, only with those which persist over a long period of time. To a very considerable extent

82   *THEORY OF MONOPOLISTIC COMPETITION*

the scheme of prices is the result of conditions unique to each product and to its market — it defies comprehensive description as a "group" problem, even when monopolistic forces are given their full value in the explanation.

The matter may be put in another way by saying that the "imperfection" of competition is not uniform throughout what is regarded as an imperfectly competitive market. It is not as though a few elements of friction, such as imperfect knowledge, or partial indifference to economic gain, spread an even haze over the whole; nor as though immobility of resources gave a general tendency for "normal" results to be retarded in working themselves out. These factors would apply with equal force in all portions of the field, at least over periods long enough for chance short time irregularities to be ironed out. But the differentiation of the product is not, so to speak, "uniformly spaced"; it is not distributed homogeneously among all of the products which are grouped together. Each has its own individuality, and the size of its market depends on the strength of the preference for it over other varieties. Again, if high average profits lead new competitors to invade the general field, the markets of different established producers cannot be wrested from them with equal facility. Some will be forced to yield ground, but not enough to reduce their profits below the minimum necessary to keep them in business. Others may be cut to the minimum, and still others may be forced to drop out because only a small demand exists or can be created for their particular variety of product. Others, protected by a strong prejudice in favor of theirs, may be virtually unaffected by an invasion of the general field — their monopoly profits are beyond the reach of competition.

These variations will give no real difficulty in the end. Exposition of the group theory is facilitated, however, by ignoring them for the present. We therefore proceed under the heroic assumption that both demand and cost curves for all the "products" are uniform throughout the group. We shall return later [1] to a recognition of their diversity, and to the manner in which allowance for it is to be made. Meanwhile, it may be remarked that diversity

[1] P. 110.

DIFFERENTIATION AND THEORY OF VALUE   83

of "product" is not entirely eliminated under our assumption. It is required only that consumers' preferences be evenly distributed among the different varieties, and that differences between them be not such as to give rise to differences in cost. This might be approximately true where very similar products were differentiated by trade-marks. It is also approximately realized in the fairly even geographical distribution of small retail establishments in the outlying districts of a city.[1]

Another complication in the group problem arises in connection with the number of competitors included within the group and the manner in which their markets "overlap." If numbers are few, complexities similar to those described in Chapter III become important. This complication may be adequately recognized by considering first the case where numbers are very large, then the case where they are small. Specifically, we assume for the present that any adjustment of price or of "product" by a single producer spreads its influence over so many of his competitors that the impact felt by any one is negligible and does not lead him to any readjustment of his own situation. A price cut, for instance, which increases the sales of him who made it, draws inappreciable amounts from the markets of each of his many competitors, achieving a considerable result for the one who cut, but without making incursions upon the market of any single competitor sufficient to cause him to do anything he would not have done anyway.

As in the case of individual equilibrium, we shall first focus attention upon the price adjustment by assuming "products" stable; then reverse the process; and finally combine the two results.

Let the demand and cost curves for the "product" of *each* of the competing monopolists in the group be DD' and PP' respectively (Fig. 12). Each seller will at once set his price at AR, since his profits, $GHRE$, at that point are a maximum. In spite of the extra profit which all are enjoying, there is no reason for any one to reduce his price below this figure, since the business gained would not make up for the price sacrifice. The extra profit will,

---

[1] The concentration of population (at the time of making purchases) in the center would make it untrue there. Cf. Appendix C.

84   *THEORY OF MONOPOLISTIC COMPETITION*

however, attract new competitors into the field, with a resulting shift in the demand curves and possibly in the cost curves. The demand curve for the "product" of each seller will be moved to the left, since the total purchases must now be distributed among a larger number of sellers. The cost curve we shall assume for the moment to be unaffected. With each shift in the demand curve will come a price readjustment so as to leave the area correspond-

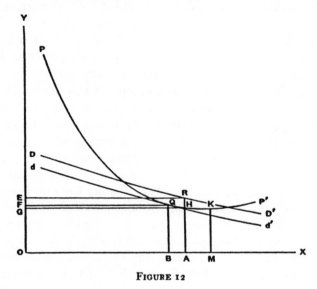

FIGURE 12

ing to *GHRE* a maximum, the process continuing until the demand curve for each "product" is tangent to its cost curve, and the area of surplus profit is wiped out. The price is now *BQ*, and the ultimate demand curve, *dd'*. The same final adjustment would have been reached if the original demand curve had lain to the left of and below *dd'*, through an exodus of firms caused by the general realization of losses, and the movement of the demand curve to the right and upwards as the total sales were shared by a smaller number of competitors, until it settled in the position of *dd'*. Here is a position of equilibrium. Price equals cost of production and any seller will lose by either raising or lowering it; it is therefore stable. There will be no further flow of resources into

DIFFERENTIATION AND THEORY OF VALUE 85

or out of the field, since profits are just adequate to maintain the amount then invested.

Let us now return to the question of the cost curves in the adjustment. As new resources flow into the field, these curves may be raised (by an increase in the price of the productive factors employed); they may be lowered (by improvements in the organization of the group as a whole — "external economies"); or they may remain the same (owing to the absence of both of these tendencies or to their cancellation one against the other). These three possibilities correspond respectively to the familiar increasing, decreasing, and constant cost of competitive theory. In the simple illustration just given no allowance was made for a shift in the curves; in other words, the assumption was implicitly made that conditions of constant cost obtained for the group as a whole. This assumption will be continued throughout, and for two reasons: (1) the theory in this form is widely applicable to the facts, and (2) where it is not applicable, its extension to cover cases of increasing and decreasing cost for the group is easily made.

First, as to its applicability. It has already been explained (see above, p. 22) why variations in output by a single producer will, if he is one of many producers, have a negligible effect upon the total output for all and hence upon cost tendencies for the product as a whole. Similarly, whenever the quantity of resources employed in one field of production is small relative to their quantity employed generally, an increase or decrease in output within this one field will have a negligible effect upon the prices of the productive factors employed and hence upon costs. An increase in the manufacture of scissors will not appreciably affect the price of steel. Nor will an increased output of rubber boots raise the price of rubber. What conditions obtain in any particular case is, of course, a question of fact. It is only meant to point out that tendencies towards increasing (or decreasing) cost with respect to particular kinds of resources or factors of production are transmitted to finished products almost always with diminished force and often with a force which is negligible.[1] To this must be added

[1] The extent to which they are transmitted depends partly on the breadth of the class of finished product considered (the cost tendency for lumber would be trans-

the fact that the resources themselves may be obtainable at fairly constant cost. If increased supplies of cement, sand, and gravel are readily available, expansion of the building industry will be possible at constant costs so far as these materials are a factor. In sum, it is likely that many fields of production are subject to conditions of approximately constant cost so far as the prices of the resources involved are concerned.

Do improvements in the organization of resources with larger output — "external economies" — result generally in a tendency to diminishing cost? The answer is yes, where they are appreciable. But it must be realized that such economies include only those made possible by the expansion of this particular field, exclusive of (*a*) those arising from the expansion of smaller fields (the individual establishments) within it — "internal economies" — and (*b*) those arising from the expansion of larger fields of which it is a part — the largest of which would be industry generally. The former are excluded because they may be realized to the full, independently of the output of the group (see above, p. 22); the latter, for a similar reason, because, since the group in question is small relative to larger fields of which it is a part, its expansion or contraction has a negligible effect upon economies in this larger field.[1] To illustrate, an expansion of the retail grocery trade does not enable the individual grocer to approximate any more closely the most effective conditions of production within his own shop; neither does it contribute appreciably to such economies as are made possible by a large volume of retailing generally. In the

mitted to furniture more than it would be to chairs), and partly on the number of uses to which the particular resource is put (the cost tendency for wheat would be transmitted to flour to a greater extent than that for lumber would be to furniture, since most wheat becomes flour, whereas lumber is put to many important uses other than furniture).

[1] Cf. Sraffa, "The Laws of Returns Under Competitive Conditions," *Economic Journal*, Vol. XXXVI, especially pp. 538–541. The literature on cost and supply curves has expanded rapidly in recent years. A bibliography is to be found in an article by Dr. Morgenstern, "Offene Probleme der Kosten- und Ertragstheorie," *Zeitschrift für Nationalökonomie*, Band II, Heft 4 (March, 1931), to which may be added: Harrod, "Notes on Supply," *Economic Journal*, Vol. XL (1930), and "The Law of Decreasing Costs," *Economic Journal*, Vol. XLI (1931); Viner, "Cost Curves and Supply Curves," *Zeitschrift für Nationalökonomie*, Band III, Heft 1 (1931); and Schneider, "Zur Interpretation von Kostenkurven," *Archiv für Sozialwissenschaft*, Band LXV, Heft 2, (1931) and "Kostentheoretisches zum Monopolproblem," *Zeitschrift für Nationalökonomie*, Band III, Heft 2 (1932).

group problem, then, the only economies which may be admitted as lowering the cost curves with increase of output are those which are due to the expansion of the group itself. Whether such economies exist in any particular case is, again, a matter of fact. Wherever they do not or where they are of only negligible importance, the result is a tendency to constant cost for the group.

The theory as developed for the case of constant cost may also be applicable if there are opposing tendencies of increasing and decreasing cost which approximately offset each other. Thus, expansion of the automobile industry may lead to (1) higher costs because of increased demand for materials, and (2) lower costs because of improved organization within the industry, the two roughly balancing each other and giving a net result of constant cost.

Secondly, the theory is not developed to include the cases of increasing and decreasing cost for the group because to do so in detail is not necessary. Where increasing costs obtain, the curves of all producers will rise as the resources employed in the field are increased, and fall as they are diminished, equilibrium being reached at a higher or at a lower point as the case may be. (Rents will be affected as in purely competitive theory, and are here to be included within the cost curves of the individual producers.) Similarly, in the case of decreasing cost the curves of all producers will fall as resources are increased and rise as they are diminished, the equilibrium being correspondingly lower or higher. These observations need not be repeated at every stage of the argument. Regardless of the cost tendency for the group, the equilibrium is always defined in the same manner with respect to the individual curves, and the divergences from the norms of purely competitive theory are always of the same sort. Our interest lies primarily in these matters, and they are most clearly revealed in the simple case of constant cost, to which attention will be confined from this point on.

Before introducing further complications, we may note some general conclusions as to monopolistic competition which follow from the first very simple putting of the case. In the first place, we see the necessity for distinguishing carefully between competi-

88   *THEORY OF MONOPOLISTIC COMPETITION*

tive prices and competitive profits. If there were no monopoly
elements, prices would correspond to the cost of production under
the most efficient conditions, *MK* in the figure. The demand
curve for the product of any single producer would be a horizontal
line, and would be lowered by competition until it was tangent
to *PP'* at *K*. The monopoly elements inevitably carry it higher,
although the profits made by the individual producer are no
greater, costs being exactly covered in both cases. Competition,
in so far as it consists of a movement of resources into the industry, reduces profits to the competitive level, but leaves prices
higher to a degree dependent upon the strength of the monopoly
elements. Competitive profits, then, never mean competitive
prices under monopolistic competition, for the demand curve is
never tangent to the cost curve at its lowest point.

In the second place, the price is inevitably higher and the scale
of production inevitably smaller under monopolistic competition
than under pure competition. It might be argued that a price
reduction on the part of one seller, although it would increase his
sales only within limits, would conceivably increase them to *OM*,
and that successive moves on the part of all would establish the
price *MK*. But this is impossible. It is true that for the position
of *DD'* shown in Fig. 13 a reduction, if made, would in fact give
the price of *MK* and the most efficient scale of production, *OM*.
But such a reduction would not be made, for any seller could increase his profits by raising his price to *AR*, where *FHRE* is a
maximum; and equilibrium will be reached, as described earlier,
when *DD'* has moved to the left until it is tangent to *PP'*, the
price at this point being higher than *MK* and the scale of production smaller than *OM*.

A third conclusion is that general uniformity of price proves
nothing as to the freedom of competition from monopoly elements. The general explanation of such tendency towards a uniform price as exists in actuality is that the demand curve for the
product of each seller is of about the same elasticity, so that each
finds his maximum profit at the same point. In the field of retailing, for instance, if the market of each seller is a random sample
of the whole population, prices in an entire area will be fairly uni-

DIFFERENTIATION AND THEORY OF VALUE   89

form, and grouped about a modal, or most prevalent, price according to the law of probability. Of course, such freedom of movement as exists among buyers contributes to this result, for the more elastic the demand schedules, the more closely will price deviations be grouped about the mode.[1] But apart from such freedom of movement (the elasticity of demand), they will also be grouped more closely about the mode as each sample is more

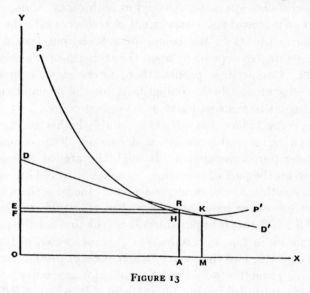

FIGURE 13

nearly the same in composition as the whole. If each dealer's market were made up of exactly the same proportion of rich and poor, and of those of different tastes and preferences, prices would everywhere be the same, even though a wall separated the province of each seller, isolating his market completely from those of his competitors. General uniformity of prices, therefore, proves nothing as to the purity of competition, or, we might say, as to the relative proportions of monopoly and competition in the admixture.

Let us return to the main thread of the argument. The nature of the equilibrium adjustment pictured in Fig. 12 will be better

---

[1] I. e., the standard deviation will approach more closely to zero.

understood if another route by which it may be reached is described. The maladjustment which was corrected in the movement towards this equilibrium was one of an unduly small number
of firms, which gave to each one a larger market and the possibility of profits above the minimum level. It was corrected by an
influx of new firms until markets were diminished and the extra
profits eliminated. Let us now suppose the number of firms to be
that corresponding to the equilibrium adjustment and to remain
unchanged while a ruling price higher than the equilibrium one is
corrected. Graphic representation of this situation requires the
introduction of a new type of demand curve.

The curve *DD'*, as heretofore drawn, describes the market for
the "product" of any one seller, *all* "products" and *all other*
prices being given.[1] It shows the increase in sales which he could
realize by cutting his price, *provided* others did not also cut theirs;
and conversely, it shows the falling off in sales which would attend
an increase in price, *provided* other prices did not also increase.
Another curve may now be drawn which shows the demand for
the product of any one seller at various prices on the assumption
that his competitors' prices are always identical with his. Evidently
this latter curve will be much less elastic than the former, since
the concurrent movement of all prices eliminates incursions by one
seller, through a price cut, upon the markets of others. Such a
curve will, in fact, be a fractional part of the demand curve for the
general class of product, and will be of the same elasticity. If
there were 100 sellers, it will show a demand at each price which
will be exactly 1/100 of the total demand at that price (since we
have assumed all markets to be of equal size). Let *DD'* in Fig. 14
be such a curve, and let the price asked by all producers be, for
the moment, *BQ*. The sales of each are *OB*, and the profits of each
(in excess of the minimum contained within the cost curve) are
FHQE. Now let *dd'* be drawn through *Q*, showing the increased
sales which any one producer may enjoy by lowering his price,

[1] Its *position* naturally depends upon the values given to these constant factors
which define it. Its *elasticity* may, however, without sensible error, be taken as the
same regardless of position, since it expresses the preference of buyers for the
"product" of one seller over that of the others. There seems to be no especial reason
why this should be stronger at higher than at lower prices, or vice versa.

DIFFERENTIATION AND THEORY OF VALUE   91

provided the others hold theirs fast at *BQ*.[1] Evidently, profits
may be increased for any individual seller by moving to the right
along *dd'*; and he may do this without fear of ultimately reducing
his gains through forcing others to follow him[2] because his competitors are so numerous that the market of each of them is in-
appreciably affected by his move. (Each loses only 1/99 of the
total gained by the one who cuts his price.) The same incentive of

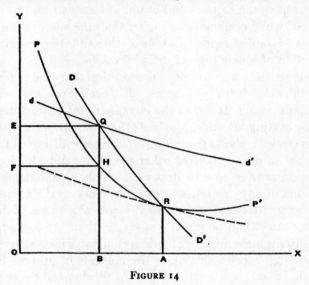

FIGURE 14

larger profits which prompts one seller to reduce his price leads
the others to do likewise. The curve *dd'*, then, explains why each
seller is led to reduce his price; the curve *DD'* shows his actual

---

[1] It may seem that anyone reducing his price from *BQ* would enjoy all the additional demand at the lower price for the entire market, i. e., 100 times that shown by
DD' in Fig. 14; and that this fact alone would, by the reasoning developed in connection with pure competition, make the curve *dd'* virtually horizontal. This is not the
case, however. The increased demand when all lower their prices, indicated by the
so-called demand curve for the general market, contains its due proportion of those
who prefer each variety of the product, and the lower price offer by one producer
will attract only a portion of them. In fact, the very concept of a demand curve for
the general market of a differentiated product is open to the objection that people do
not demand the product "in general," but particular varieties of it, so that the
amount which any buyer will take depends not only upon the price but upon the
variety which is offered him.

[2] Cf. above, pp. 46 ff.

92   *THEORY OF MONOPOLISTIC COMPETITION*

sales as the *general* downward movement takes place. The former curve "slides" downwards along the latter as prices are lowered, and the movement comes to a stop at the price of *AR*. Evidently it will pay no one to cut beyond that point, for his costs of producing the larger output would exceed the price at which it could be sold.

The position of *DD'* depends upon the number of sellers in the field. It lies further to the left as there are more of them, since the

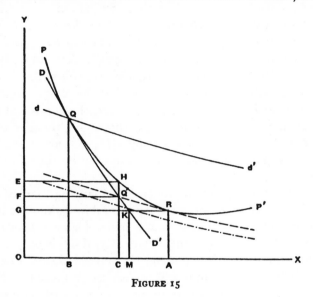

FIGURE 15

share of each in the total is then smaller; and further to the right as there are fewer of them, since the share of each in the total is then larger. It was drawn through *R*, the point of tangency of *dd'* with *PP'*, in the example just given, since the number of sellers was assumed to be that consistent with the final equilibrium adjustment. Let us now suppose that, at prices in the neighborhood of *BQ*, temporarily prevailing, additional sellers are attracted by the high profits, and intrench themselves in the field before the price-cutting corrective takes place. Such an inflow of resources may conceivably continue until *DD'* is pushed leftwards to a position of tangency with *PP'*, as in Fig. 15, the price being *BQ* and the output per firm *OB*. Here cost exactly equals price, be-

DIFFERENTIATION AND THEORY OF VALUE   93

cause the uneconomical scale at which each is producing has raised
costs to meet it. The situation is unstable, however, because of
the possibility of increased profits, represented for any producer
by the demand curve dd', drawn through Q. That each, and
hence all, will cut prices is evident from dd'; and that each, and
hence all, are involved in ever increasing losses as the process continues is evident from DD', which shows the sales of each as the
prices of all are lowered. When the price has fallen to CQ', for
instance, the sales of each are OC, and his losses $FQ'HE$. An
escape is offered to anyone by further cuts, however, as is indicated by the dotted line passing through Q'. Any seller, by cutting to AR, will avoid losses and exactly cover his costs. It might
seem that equilibrium has been reached at this point, since dd' is
now tangent to PP', as required. However, the number of sellers
is so great that when all cut to AR, as they must, the sales of each
are not OA, but OM, as indicated by DD', and losses are larger
than ever. Equilibrium can be achieved only by the elimination
of firms.

Before this takes place, however, price cutting may continue
still further. Although, for positions of dd' lower than the dotted
line, it is no longer possible to escape losses of some magnitude, it
is still possible to reduce them. Evidently, if dd' is only slightly
lower than the dotted line passing through R, this will be true.
Soon, however, a lower limit will be reached, represented by the
dot-dash line, where departure by any one from the adjustment
for all on DD' will no longer diminish his losses, and here the
movement will stop.

The curve dd' having reached any position below that of tangency, there is no escape from general losses until the number of
firms is reduced. As this takes place, DD' will move to the right,
and the movement must continue until it passes through R—in
other words, until the output of each producer when all are
charging the same price is OA. Equilibrium, then, is defined by
two conditions: (*a*) dd' must be tangent to PP', and (*b*) DD' must
intersect both dd' and PP' at the point of tangency.

We may regard the elasticity of dd' as a rough index of buyers'
preferences for the "product" of one seller over that of another.

The equilibrium adjustment becomes, then, a sort of ideal. With fewer establishments, larger scales of production, and lower prices it would always be true that buyers would be willing to pay more than it would cost to give them a greater diversity of product; [1] and conversely, with more producers and smaller scales of production, the higher prices they would pay would be more than such gains were worth. In Fig. 14 this is evident from drawing a curve of the elasticity of dd' through a point on PP' to the right of R for the first case, and to the left of R for the second case. In either case there would be a gain in the surplus, over cost, of what buyers are willing to pay, by an adjustment towards R, for dd' would lie above PP' in that direction.

We pass to consideration of the second variable, the "product." The meaning of product variation has already been described, and the difficulties in its quantitative representation must be recalled. In order to retain the precision of statement which is possible only if the markets of all the competing sellers are alike, we must imagine, consistent with continued differences between the "products" of all sellers, possibilities of product variation which are uniform for all, so that the adjustments of *each* may be represented by a single graph, as in the price analysis. This is not so difficult as it sounds. A concrete instance is that of spatial differentiation in retailing, where each seller offers a "product," adapted by convenience of location to those buyers who are nearest to him geographically; yet the possibilities of a change in location are open to each, and an inflow or outflow of resources in the general field will decrease or increase the average distance between stores, and hence the size of the market enjoyed by each. Again, differentiation with regard to location often remains unchanged while "products" are altered by competition based upon service, or upon other qualitative factors. Still another instance, in the manufacturing field, is that of a number of products continually distinguished by trade-marks while qualitative changes are made in them.

[1] In retailing, this greater "diversity" would, in part, take the form of the location of stores at smaller intervals, thus giving to buyers greater convenience. The necessity of interpreting the terminology to fit the different aspects of product differentiation must be constantly borne in mind.

Product variation is isolated by the device, already explained, of holding the price for all the "products" constant. Let it be *OE* in Fig. 16, which will display the adjustments of any one seller; and let a horizontal line, *EZ*, be drawn at this height. As already pointed out, it does not indicate indefinite demand at this price, but will serve as a line along which the demands for each

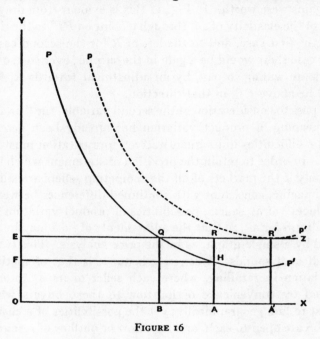

FIGURE 16

variation of the "product" may be measured. Curves of cost of production for different variations in the "product" of any seller may now be drawn, as in the earlier case of "product" variation where it was sought to define the individual equilibrium, and that variation offering the largest total profits will be chosen by each seller, as before. Let *PP'* represent the cost of production for such an optimum variation of the "product." The demand for it we will suppose to be *OA*. The total cost of producing this volume is *OAHF*, and the total profit (above the minimum included under *PP'*) is *FHRE*. The elimination of this profit, which is essential to an equilibrium adjustment, may take place in either or all of several ways. Since, by definition, this is the optimum variation for each seller, there will be no further "product adjustment." The extra profit will, however, attract new competitors to the field, and reduce the sales of each until they reach *OB*, where, cost being equal to price, there will be no further movement. Similarly, if the number of competitors were so great that the market of each was reduced below *OB*, losses would drive them from the field until those remaining had markets equal to *OB*, and were again meeting their costs.

In addition to the flow of resources into and out of the field, something analogous to price cutting may take place among those who occupy it at any one time. If any seller can increase his profits by improving his "product" (analogous to lowering his price), while the products of his competitors remain unaltered, he will do so. Such an improvement would increase demand along *EZ* and also increase costs, shifting *PP'* upwards and to the right. A new and larger profit area would result for the new "product." But when, with the same objective, his competitors made the same move, the increase in sales enjoyed by each would be only his proportionate share of the total increase for the general class of product on account of its general improvement (analogous to the increase in demand for a given class of product when all producers lower their prices). Higher costs remain, however (just as lower prices remain after everyone has cut his price), and the profit of each has been reduced by the general movement. The process may now be repeated, and will, in fact (as under price cutting), continue so long as it is possible for any seller to increase his gains in this way. What is the position of *PP'* when the limit has been reached? Evidently, it cannot be higher than the dotted curve, *pp'*, in Fig. 16, for if it were, the product could not be produced at all. It may, in fact, be lower; for it must not be forgotten that *EZ* is not a demand line (indicating indefinite demand at the price of *OE*), and that the mere fact that the cost curve descends below it does not indicate that greater profits are possible by an adjustment of output to achieve minimum costs. The demand for any one variation of the "product" is definitely

DIFFERENTIATION AND THEORY OF VALUE   97

limited; it cannot (under the present hypothesis) be increased by a price reduction, and its increase by improvement of the "product" involves altered cost conditions. There is no reason to suppose (especially when the cost curve for each has risen to a position only slightly below that of pp') that further improvement of the "product" of any one seller, which would shift his cost curve to the position of pp', would result in a demand for it of OA'.[1] The difficulties of representing graphically the variation of "product" render hazardous any attempt to define with precision the exact point of equilibrium. It would seem that the most that can be said is that it will be characterized by (1) the equation of cost and price, and (2) the impossibility of a "product" adjustment by anyone which would increase his profits. It will involve either the intersection of the price line with the curve of cost of production, or its tangency to it.

If "product" and price are both variable, however, it is easily shown that the cost curve must cut below the horizontal line drawn at the height of the equilibrium price. This may be seen at once in Fig. 16, by imagining a sloping demand curve drawn through the point R'. Such a curve would evidently lie above pp' immediately to the left of R', since it would have a negative slope as it passed through R', whereas pp' has a slope of zero. Profits could be increased by raising the price slightly and reducing the sales. (Cf. Fig. 13, page 89, where profits of zero at the price of MK are increased to $FHRE$ by raising the price to AR, thereby reducing sales from OM to OA.) An influx of new competitors would then push the demand curve for the product of each to the left until equilibrium was reached when it was tangent to pp'. The conclusion is that, although when price is *actually* fixed (as by custom, or, for the retailer, by the manufacturer) the improvement of "product" *may* be carried to the point where the most efficient conditions of production are realized, when it is not actually fixed (but only assumed so for logical purposes of isolation) it will not be carried that far. When the seller is free to vary

---

[1] However, if this proposed variation of the "product" were *arbitrarily assumed*, together with a fixed price of OE, the ingress or egress of firms would establish an output per firm of OA'.

either "product" or price or both, his adjustments will not stop until all possibilities of increasing his profit are exhausted. The impossibility of production under the most efficient conditions is settled once and for all by the shape of the demand curve.

When both "product" and price are variable, an equilibrium adjustment will be reached for both which is a combination of that for each in isolation. Under given conditions with regard to the "products" and prices of his competitors, each seller will choose that combination of price and "product" for himself which will maximize his profit. For each variety of "product" possible to him there will be a price which will render his profit a maximum *relative* to that "product." From these relative maxima he will choose the largest of all. Readjustments will be necessary as his competitors do the same thing, until finally a point is reached, as for each variable in isolation, where no one can better his position by a further move. At the same time, resources will flow into the field in order to reduce profits which are higher than the competitive minimum, or out of it in order to raise them to this minimum, so that the number of producers finally occupying the field will be such as to leave the costs of each exactly covered and no more.

A graphic summary of this comprehensive equilibrium is attempted in Fig. 17, although, in fact, because of the difficulties of reducing "product" variation to graphic terms, it shows little more than the price equilibrium of Fig. 12. *PP'* must be regarded as the cost curve for the optimum "product" and *dd'* as the demand curve for it. (Let the dotted line *pp'* be ignored for the moment.) The equilibrium price is *AR*, for, *R* being the point at which *dd'* and *PP'* are tangent to each other, it is evident that either a higher or a lower price would give unit costs in excess of price. Since, by definition, the "product" is the optimum one, either a better or a poorer "product" would likewise leave unit costs, for the amount which could be sold, in excess of the price *OE*. A better "product" would, by raising the cost curve, move its intersection with *EZ* further to the right than it would move the demand (measured along *EZ*). A poorer "product" would similarly, by lowering the cost curve, move its intersection with

DIFFERENTIATION AND THEORY OF VALUE   99

EZ to the left by a shorter distance than it would decrease the demand (measured along *EZ*). The total output in the field under these conditions of equilibrium will be *OA* multiplied by the number of producers.

The conclusion seems to be warranted that just as, for a given "product," price is inevitably higher under monopolistic than under pure competition, so, for a given price, "product" is inevi-

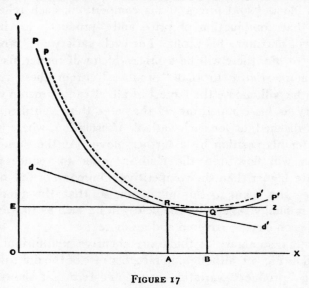

FIGURE 17

tably somewhat inferior. After all, these two propositions are but two aspects of a single one. If a seller could, by the larger scale of production which is characteristic of pure as compared with monopolistic competition, give the same "product" for less money, he could, similarly, give a better "product" for the same money. This is illustrated in Fig. 17. If competition were pure, *dd'* would be horizontal, and competitive pressure would lower it to the point of tangency with *PP'* at *Q*, where the price would be *BQ*, lower than *AR*. But if the price were now held constant at *AR*, and any seller could dispose of any amount he pleased at that price (as under pure competition), each would expand his output to approximately *OB*, and the extra profits there being realized

100   *THEORY OF MONOPOLISTIC COMPETITION*

would be reduced, not by a fall in price, which is impossible by hypothesis, but by general improvement of the "product" with consequent rise in cost curves to the position of the dotted line pp', whose minimum point equals AR. It follows that the impossibility of selling all he pleases at the going price creates a tendency not only towards higher prices, but also towards inferior product. Against these forces must, of course, be offset the gain through increased variety and freedom of choice.

E H CHAMBERLIN

[24]

Monopolistic Competition and Optimum Product Diversity

By Avinash K. Dixit and Joseph E. Stiglitz*

The basic issue concerning production in welfare economics is whether a market solution will yield the socially optimum kinds and quantities of commodities. It is well known that problems can arise for three broad reasons: distributive justice; external effects; and scale economies. This paper is concerned with the last of these.

The basic principle is easily stated.[1] A commodity should be produced if the costs can be covered by the sum of revenues and a properly defined measure of consumer's surplus. The optimum amount is then found by equating the demand price and the marginal cost. Such an optimum can be realized in a market if perfectly discriminatory pricing is possible. Otherwise we face conflicting problems. A competitive market fulfilling the marginal condition would be unsustainable because total profits would be negative. An element of monopoly would allow positive profits, but would violate the marginal condition.[2] Thus we expect a market solution to be suboptimal. However, a much more precise structure must be put on the problem if we are to understand the nature of the bias involved.

It is useful to think of the question as one of quantity versus diversity. With scale economies, resources can be saved by producing fewer goods and larger quantities of each. However, this leaves less variety, which entails some welfare loss. It is easy and probably not too unrealistic to model scale economies by supposing that each

potential commodity involves some fixed set-up cost and has a constant marginal cost. Modeling the desirability of variety has been thought to be difficult, and several indirect approaches have been adopted. The Hotelling spatial model, Lancaster's product characteristics approach, and the mean-variance portfolio selection model have all been put to use.[3] These lead to results involving transport costs or correlations among commodities or securities, and are hard to interpret in general terms. We therefore take a direct route, noting that the convexity of indifference surfaces of a conventional utility function defined over the quantities of all potential commodities already embodies the desirability of variety. Thus, a consumer who is indifferent between the quantities (1,0) and (0,1) of two commodities prefers the mix (1/2,1/2) to either extreme. The advantage of this view is that the results involve the familiar own- and cross-elasticities of demand functions, and are therefore easier to comprehend.

There is one case of particular interest on which we concentrate. This is where potential commodities in a group or sector or industry are good substitutes among themselves, but poor substitutes for the other commodities in the economy. Then we are led to examining the market solution in relation to an optimum, both as regards biases within the group, and between the group and the rest of the economy. We expect the answer to depend on the intra- and intersector elasticities of substitution. To demonstrate the point as simply as possible, we shall aggregate the rest of the economy into one good labeled 0, chosen as the numeraire. The economy's endowment of it is normalized at unity; it can be thought of as the time at the disposal of the consumers.

*Professors of economics, University of Warwick and Stanford University, respectively. Stiglitz's research was supported in part by NSF Grant SOC74-22182 at the Institute for Mathematical Studies in the Social Sciences, Stanford. We are indebted to Michael Spence, to a referee, and the managing editor for comments and suggestions on earlier drafts.
[1] See also the exposition by Michael Spence.
[2] A simple exposition is given by Peter Diamond and Daniel McFadden.

[3] See the articles by Harold Hotelling, Nicholas Stern, Kelvin Lancaster, and Stiglitz.

The potential range of related products is labeled 1,2,3, ... Writing the amounts of the various commodities as x_0 and $x = (x_1, x_2, x_3 ...,$ we assume a separable utility function with convex indifference surfaces:

$$(1) \qquad u = U(x_0, V(x_1, x_2, x_3...))$$

In Sections I and II we simplify further by assuming that V is a symmetric function, and that all commodities in the group have equal fixed and marginal costs. Then the actual labels given to commodities are immaterial, even though the total number n being produced is relevant. We can thus label these commodities 1,2, ... , n, where the potential products $(n + 1)$, $(n + 2)$, ... are not being produced. This is a restrictive assumption, for in such problems we often have a natural asymmetry owing to graduated physical differences in commodities, with a pair close together being better mutual substitutes than a pair farther apart. However, even the symmetric case yields some interesting results. In Section III, we consider some aspects of asymmetry.

We also assume that all commodities have unit income elasticities. This differs from a similar recent formulation by Michael Spence, who assumes U linear in x_0, so that the industry is amenable to partial equilibrium analysis. Our approach allows a better treatment of the intersectoral substitution, but the other results are very similar to those of Spence.

We consider two special cases of (1). In Section I, V is given a *CES* form, but U is allowed to be arbitrary. In Section II, U is taken to be Cobb-Douglas, but V has a more general additive form. Thus the former allows more general intersector relations, and the latter more general intrasector substitution, highlighting different results.

Income distribution problems are neglected. Thus U can be regarded as representing Samuelsonian social indifference curves, or (assuming the appropriate aggregation conditions to be fulfilled) as a multiple of a representative consumer's utility. Product diversity can then be interpreted either as different consumers using different

varieties, or as diversification on the part of each consumer.

I. Constant-Elasticity Case

A. *Demand Functions*

The utility function in this section is

$$(2) \qquad u = U\left(x_0, \left\{\sum_i x_i^\rho\right\}^{1/\rho}\right)$$

For concavity, we need $\rho < 1$. Further, since we want to allow a situation where several of the x_i are zero, we need $\rho > 0$. We also assume U homothetic in its arguments.

The budget constraint is

$$(3) \qquad x_0 + \sum_{i-1}^n p_i x_i = I$$

where p_i are prices of the goods being produced, and I is income in terms of the numeraire, i.e., the endowment which has been set at 1 plus the profits of the firms distributed to the consumers, or minus the lump sum deductions to cover the losses, as the case may be.

In this case, a two-stage budgeting procedure is valid.[4] Thus we define dual quantity and price indices

$$(4) \qquad y = \left\{\sum_{i-1}^n x_i^\rho\right\}^{1/\rho} \qquad q = \left\{\sum_{i-1}^n p_i^{-1/\beta}\right\}^{-\beta}$$

where $\beta = (1 - \rho)/\rho$, which is positive since $0 < \rho < 1$. Then it can be shown[5] that in the first stage,

$$(5) \qquad y = I\frac{s(q)}{q} \qquad x_0 = I(1 - s(q))$$

for a function s which depends on the form of U. Writing $\sigma(q)$ for the elasticity of substitution between x_0 and y, we define $\theta(q)$ as the elasticity of the function s, i.e., $qs'(q)/s(q)$. Then we find

$$(6) \qquad \theta(q) = \{1 - \sigma(q)\}\,\{1 - s(q)\} < 1$$

but $\theta(q)$ can be negative as $\sigma(q)$ can exceed 1.

---

[4] See p. 21 of John Green.
[5] These details and several others are omitted to save space, but can be found in the working paper by the authors, cited in the references.

Turning to the second stage of the problem, it is easy to show that for each i,

$$(7) \qquad x_i = y\left[\frac{q}{p_i}\right]^{1/(1-\rho)}$$

where y is defined by (4). Consider the effect of a change in p_i alone. This affects x_i directly, and also through q; thence through y as well. Now from (4) we have the elasticity

$$(8) \qquad \frac{\partial \log q}{\partial \log p_i} = \left(\frac{q}{p_i}\right)^{1/\beta}$$

So long as the prices of the products in the group are not of different orders of magnitude, this is of the order $(1/n)$. We shall assume that n is reasonably large, and accordingly neglect the effect of each p_i on q; thus the indirect effects on x_i. This leaves us with the elasticity

$$(9) \qquad \frac{\partial \log x_i}{\partial \log p_i} = \frac{-1}{(1-\rho)} = \frac{-(1+\beta)}{\beta}$$

In the Chamberlinian terminology, this is the elasticity of the dd curve, i.e., the curve relating the demand for each product type to its own price with all other prices held constant.

In our large group case, we also see that for $i \neq j$, the cross elasticity $\partial \log x_i / \partial \log p_j$ is negligible. However, if all prices in the group move together, the individually small effects add to a significant amount. This corresponds to the Chamberlinian DD curve. Consider a symmetric situation where $x_i = x$ and $p_i = p$ for all i from 1 to n. We have

$$(10) \qquad y = xn^{1/\rho} = xn^{1+\beta}$$
$$q = pn^{-\beta} = pn^{-(1-\rho)/\rho}$$

and then from (5) and (7),

$$(11) \qquad x = \frac{ls(q)}{pn}$$

The elasticity of this is easy to calculate; we find

$$(12) \qquad \frac{\partial \log x}{\partial \log p} = -[1 - \theta(q)]$$

Then (6) shows that the DD curve slopes downward. The conventional condition that the dd curve be more elastic is seen from (9) and (12) to be

$$(13) \qquad \frac{1}{\beta} + \theta(q) > 0$$

Finally, we observe that for $i \neq j$,

$$(14) \qquad \frac{x_i}{x_j} = \left[\frac{p_j}{p_i}\right]^{1/(1-\rho)}$$

Thus $1/(1-\rho)$ is the elasticity of substitution between any two products within the group.

B. Market Equilibrium

It can be shown that each commodity is produced by one firm. Each firm attempts to maximize its profit, and entry occurs until the marginal firm can only just break even. Thus our market equilibrium is the familiar case of Chamberlinian monopolistic competition, where the question of quantity versus diversity has often been raised.[6] Previous analyses have failed to consider the desirability of variety in an explicit form, and have neglected various intra- and intersector interactions in demand. As a result, much vague presumption that such an equilibrium involves excessive diversity has built up at the back of the minds of many economists. Our analysis will challenge several of these ideas.

The profit-maximization condition for each firm acting on its own is the familiar equality of marginal revenue and marginal cost. Writing c for the common marginal cost, and noting that the elasticity of demand for each firm is $(1+\beta)/\beta$, we have for each active firm:

$$p_i\left(1 - \frac{\beta}{1+\beta}\right) = c$$

Writing p_e for the common equilibrium price for each variety being produced, we have

$$(15) \qquad p_e = c(1+\beta) = \frac{c}{\rho}$$

[6]See Edwin Chamberlin, Nicholas Kaldor, and Robert Bishop.

The second condition for equilibrium is that firms enter until the next potential entrant would make a loss. If n is large enough so that 1 is a small increment, we can assume that the marginal firm is exactly breaking even, i.e., $(p_n - c)x_n = a$, where x_n is obtained from the demand function and a is the fixed cost. With symmetry, this implies zero profit for all intramarginal firms as well. Then $I = 1$, and using (11) and (15) we can write the condition so as to yield the number n_e of active firms:

$$(16) \qquad \frac{s(p_e n_e^{-\beta})}{p_e n_e} = \frac{a}{\beta c}$$

Equilibrium is unique provided $s(p_e n^{-\beta})/p_e n$ is a monotonic function of n. This relates to our earlier discussion about the two demand curves. From (11) we see that the behavior of $s(pn^{-\beta})/pn$ as n increases tells us how the demand curve DD for each firm shifts as the number of firms increases. It is natural to assume that it shifts to the left, i.e., the function above decreases as n increases for each fixed p. The condition for this in elasticity form is easily seen to be

$$(17) \qquad 1 + \beta\theta(q) > 0$$

This is exactly the same as (13), the condition for the dd curve to be more elastic than the DD curve, and we shall assume that it holds.

The condition can be violated if $\sigma(q)$ is sufficiently higher than one. In this case, an increase in n lowers q, and shifts demand towards the monopolistic sector to such an extent that the demand curve for each firm shifts to the right. However, this is rather implausible.

Conventional Chamberlinian analysis assumes a fixed demand curve for the group as a whole. This amounts to assuming that $n \cdot x$ is independent of n, i.e., that $s(pn^{-\beta})$ is independent of n. This will be so if $\beta = 0$, or if $\sigma(q) = 1$ for all q. The former is equivalent to assuming that $\rho = 1$, when all products in the group are perfect substitutes, i.e., diversity is not valued at all. That would be contrary to the intent of the whole analysis. Thus, implicitly, conventional analysis assumes $\sigma(q) = 1$. This gives a con-

stant budget share for the monopolistically competitive sector. Note that in our parametric formulation, this implies a unit-elastic DD curve, (17) holds, and so equilibrium is unique.

Finally, using (7), (11), and (16), we can calculate the equilibrium output for each active firm:

$$(18) \qquad x_e = \frac{a}{\beta c}$$

We can also write an expression for the budget share of the group as a whole:

$$(19) \qquad s_e = s(q_e)$$

where
$$q_e = p_e n_e^{-\beta}$$

These will be useful for subsequent comparisons.

C. *Constrained Optimum*

The next task is to compare the equilibrium with a social optimum. With economies of scale, the first best or unconstrained (really constrained only by technology and resource availability) optimum requires pricing below average cost, and therefore lump sum transfers to firms to cover losses. The conceptual and practical difficulties of doing so are clearly formidable. It would therefore appear that a more appropriate notion of optimality is a constrained one, where each firm must have nonnegative profits. This may be achieved by regulation, or by excise or franchise taxes or subsidies. The important restriction is that lump sum subsidies are not available.

We begin with such a constrained optimum. The aim is to choose n, p_i, and x_i so as to maximize utility, satisfying the demand functions and keeping the profit for each firm nonnegative. The problem is somewhat simplified by the result that all active firms should have the same output levels and prices, and should make exactly zero profit. We omit the proof. Then we can set $I = 1$, and use (5) to express utility as a function of q alone. This is of course a decreasing function. Thus the problem of maximizing u becomes that of minimizing q, i.e.,

$$\min_{n,p} pn^{-\beta}$$

subject to

$$(20) \qquad (p - c)\frac{s(pn^{-\beta})}{pn} = a$$

To solve this, we calculate the logarithmic marginal rate of substitution along a level curve of the objective, the similar rate of transformation along the constraint, and equate the two. This yields the condition

$$(21) \qquad \frac{\dfrac{c}{p-c} + \theta(q)}{1 + \beta\theta(q)} = \frac{1}{\beta}$$

The second-order condition can be shown to hold, and (21) simplifies to yield the price for each commodity produced in the constrained optimum, p_c, as

$$(22) \qquad p_c = c(1 + \beta)$$

Comparing (15) and (22), we see that the two solutions have the same price. Since they face the same break-even constraint, they have the same number of firms as well, and the values for all other variables can be calculated from these two. Thus we have a rather surprising case where the monopolistic competition equilibrium is identical with the optimum constrained by the lack of lump sum subsidies. Chamberlin once suggested that such an equilibrium was "a sort of ideal"; our analysis shows when and in what sense this can be true.

D. *Unconstrained Optimum*

These solutions can in turn be compared to the unconstrained or first best optimum. Considerations of convexity again establish that all active firms should produce the same output. Thus we are to choose n firms each producing output x in order to maximize

$$(23) \qquad u = U(1 - n(a + cx), xn^{1+\beta})$$

where we have used the economy's resource balance condition and (10). The first-order conditions are

$$(24) \qquad -ncU_0 + n^{1+\beta}U_y = 0$$

$$(25) \qquad -(a + cx)U_0 + (1 + \beta)xn^\beta U_y = 0$$

From the first stage of the budgeting problem, we know that $q = U_y/U_0$. Using (24) and (10), we find the price charged by each active firm in the unconstrained optimum, p_u, equal to marginal cost

$$(26) \qquad p_u = c$$

This, of course, is no surprise. Also from the first-order conditions, we have

$$(27) \qquad x_u = \frac{a}{c\beta}$$

Finally, with (26), each active firm covers its variable cost exactly. The lump sum transfers to firms then equal an, and therefore $I = 1 - an$, and

$$x = (1 - an)\frac{s(pn^{-\beta})}{pn}$$

The number of firms n_u is then defined by

$$(28) \qquad \frac{s(cn_u^{-\beta})}{n_u} = \frac{a/\beta}{1 - an_u}$$

We can now compare these magnitudes with the corresponding ones in the equilibrium or the constrained optimum. The most remarkable result is that the output of each active firm is the same in the two situations. The fact that in a Chamberlinian equilibrium each firm operates to the left of the point of minimum average cost has been conventionally described by saying that there is excess capacity. However, when variety is desirable, i.e., when the different products are not perfect substitutes, it is not in general optimum to push the output of each firm to the point where all economies of scale are exhausted.[7] We have shown in one case that is not an extreme one, that the first best optimum does not exploit economies of scale beyond the extent achieved in the equilibrium. We can then easily conceive of cases where the equilibrium exploits economies of scale too far from the point of view of social optimality. Thus our results undermine the validity of the folklore of excess capacity, from the point of view of the

[7]See David Starrett.

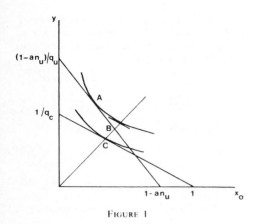

unconstrained optimum as well as the constrained one.

A direct comparison of the numbers of firms from (16) and (28) would be difficult, but an indirect argument turns out to be simple. It is clear that the unconstrained optimum has higher utility than the constrained optimum. Also, the level of lump sum income in it is less than that in the latter. It must therefore be the case that

$$(29) \qquad q_u < q_c = q_e$$

Further, the difference must be large enough that the budget constraint for x_0 and the quantity index y in the unconstrained case must lie outside that in the constrained case in the relevant region, as shown in Figure 1. Let C be the constrained optimum, A the unconstrained optimum, and let B be the point where the line joining the origin to C meets the indifference curve in the unconstrained case. By homotheticity the indifference curve at B is parallel to that at C, so each of the moves from C to B and from B to A increases the value of y. Since the value of x is the same in the two optima, we must have

$$(30) \qquad n_u > n_c = n_e$$

Thus the unconstrained optimum actually allows more variety than the constrained optimum and the equilibrium; this is another point contradicting the folklore on excessive diversity.

Using (29) we can easily compare the budget shares. In the notation we have been using, we find $s_u \gtrless s_c$ as $\theta(q) \gtrless 0$, i.e., as $\sigma(q) \gtrless 1$ providing these hold over the entire relevant range of q.

It is not possible to have a general result concerning the relative magnitudes of x_0 in the two situations; an inspection of Figure 1 shows this. However, we have a sufficient condition:

$$x_{0u} = (1 - an_u)(1 - s_u) < 1 - s_u \leq 1 - s_c$$
$$= x_{0c} \text{ if } \sigma(q) \geq 1$$

In this case the equilibrium or the constrained optimum use more of the numeraire resource than the unconstrained optimum. On the other hand, if $\sigma(q) = 0$ we have L-shaped isoquants, and in Figure 1, points A and B coincide giving the opposite conclusion.

In this section we have seen that with a constant intrasector elasticity of substitution, the market equilibrium coincides with the constrained optimum. We have also shown that the unconstrained optimum has a greater number of firms, each of the same size. Finally, the resource allocation between the sectors is shown to depend on the intersector elasticity of substitution. This elasticity also governs conditions for uniqueness of equilibrium and the second-order conditions for an optimum.

Henceforth we will achieve some analytic simplicity by making a particular assumption about intersector substitution. In return, we will allow a more general form of intrasector substitution.

II. Variable Elasticity Case

The utility function is now

$$(31) \qquad u = x_0^{1-\gamma}\left\{\sum_i v(x_i)\right\}^\gamma$$

with v increasing and concave, $0 < \gamma < 1$. This is somewhat like assuming a unit intersector elasticity of substitution. However, this is not rigorous since the group utility $V(\underline{x}) = \sum_i v(x_i)$ is not homothetic and therefore two-stage budgeting is not applicable.

It can be shown that the elasticity of the dd curve in the large group case is

$$(32) \quad -\frac{\partial \log x_i}{\partial \log p_i} = -\frac{v'(x_i)}{x_i v''(x_i)} \quad \text{for any } i$$

This differs from the case of Section I in being a function of x_i. To highlight the similarities and the differences, we define $\beta(x)$ by

$$(33) \quad \frac{1 + \beta(x)}{\beta(x)} = -\frac{v'(x)}{x v''(x)}$$

Next, setting $x_i = x$ and $p_i = p$ for $i = 1, 2, \ldots, n$, we can write the DD curve and the demand for the numeraire as

$$(34) \quad x = \frac{I}{np}\,\omega(x), \qquad x_0 = I[1 - \omega(x)]$$

where

$$(35) \quad \omega(x) = \frac{\gamma\rho(x)}{[\gamma\rho(x) + (1 - \gamma)]}$$

$$\rho(x) = \frac{x v'(x)}{v(x)}$$

We assume that $0 < \rho(x) < 1$, and therefore have $0 < \omega(x) < 1$.

Now consider the Chamberlinian equilibrium. The profit-maximization condition for each active firm yields the common equilibrium price p_e in terms of the common equilibrium output x_e as

$$(36) \quad p_e = c[1 + \beta(x_e)]$$

Note the analogy with (15). Substituting (36) in the zero pure profit condition, we have x_e defined by

$$(37) \quad \frac{c x_e}{a + c x_e} = \frac{1}{1 + \beta(x_e)}$$

Finally, the number of firms can be calculated using the DD curve and the break-even condition, as

$$(38) \quad n_e = \frac{\omega(x_e)}{a + c x_e}$$

For uniqueness of equilibrium we once again use the conditions that the dd curve is more elastic than the DD curve, and that entry shifts the DD curve to the left. However, these conditions are rather involved and opaque, so we omit them.

Let us turn to the constrained optimum.

We wish to choose n and x to maximize u, subject to (34) and the break-even condition $px = a + cx$. Substituting, we can express u as a function of x alone:

$$(39) \quad u = \gamma^\gamma (1 - \gamma)^{(1-\gamma)} \frac{\left[\dfrac{\rho(x)v(x)}{a + cx}\right]^\gamma}{\gamma\rho(x) + (1 - \gamma)}$$

The first-order condition defines x_c:

$$(40) \quad \frac{c x_c}{a + c x_c} = \frac{1}{1 + \beta(x_c)} - \frac{\omega(x_c) x_c \rho'(x_c)}{\gamma\rho(x_c)}$$

Comparing this with (37) and using the second-order condition, it can be shown that provided $\rho'(x)$ is one-signed for all x,

$$(41) \quad x_c \gtrless x_e \text{ according as } \rho'(x) \lessgtr 0$$

With zero pure profit in each case, the points (x_e, p_e) and (x_c, p_c) lie on the same declining average cost curve, and therefore

$$(42) \quad p_c \lessgtr p_e \text{ according as } x_c \gtrless x_e$$

Next we note that the dd curve is tangent to the average cost curve at (x_e, p_e) and the DD curve is steeper. Consider the case $x_c > x_e$. Now the point (x_c, p_c) must lie on a DD curve further to the right than (x_e, p_e), and therefore must correspond to a smaller number of firms. The opposite happens if $x_c < x_e$. Thus,

$$(43) \quad n_c \lessgtr n_e \text{ according as } x_c \gtrless x_e$$

Finally, (41) shows that in both cases that arise there, $\rho(x_c) < \rho(x_e)$. Then $\omega(x_c) < \omega(x_e)$, and from (34),

$$(44) \qquad\qquad x_{0c} > x_{0e}$$

A smaller degree of intersectoral substitution could have reversed the result, as in Section I.

An intuitive reason for these results can be given as follows. With our large group assumptions, the revenue of each firm is proportional to $x v'(x)$. However, the contribution of its output to group utility is $v(x)$. The ratio of the two is $\rho(x)$. Therefore, if $\rho'(x) > 0$, then at the margin each firm finds it more profitable to expand than what would be socially desirable, so $x_e > x_c$.

Given the break-even constraint, this leads to there being fewer firms.

Note that the relevant magnitude is the elasticity of utility, and not the elasticity of demand. The two are related, since

$$(45) \qquad x \, \frac{\rho'(x)}{\rho(x)} = \frac{1}{1 + \beta(x)} - \rho(x)$$

Thus, if $\rho(x)$ is constant over an interval, so is $\beta(x)$ and we have $1/(1 + \beta) = \rho$, which is the case of Section I. However, if $\rho(x)$ varies, we cannot infer a relation between the signs of $\rho'(x)$ and $\beta'(x)$. Thus the variation in the elasticity of demand is not in general the relevant consideration. However, for important families of utility functions there is a relationship. For example, for $v(x) = (k + mx)^j$, with $m > 0$ and $0 < j < 1$, we find that $-xv''/v'$ and xv'/v are positively related. Now we would normally expect that as the number of commodities produced increases, the elasticity of substitution between any pair of them should increase. In the symmetric equilibrium, this is just the inverse of the elasticity of marginal utility. Then a higher x would correspond to a lower n, and therefore a lower elasticity of substitution, higher $-xv''/v'$ and higher xv'/v. Thus we are led to expect that $\rho'(x) > 0$, i.e., that the equilibrium involves fewer and bigger firms than the constrained optimum. Once again the common view concerning excess capacity and excessive diversity in monopolistic competition is called into question.

The unconstrained optimum problem is to choose n and x to maximize

$$(46) \qquad u = [nv(x)]^\gamma [1 - n(a + cx)]^{1-\gamma}$$

It is easy to show that the solution has

$$(47) \qquad\qquad p_u = c$$

$$(48) \qquad\qquad \frac{cx_u}{a + cx_u} = \rho(x_u)$$

$$(49) \qquad\qquad n_u = \frac{\gamma}{a + cx_u}$$

Then we can use the second-order condition to show that

$$(50) \quad x_u \lessgtr x_c \text{ according as } \rho'(x) \gtrless 0$$

This is in each case transitive with (41), and therefore yields similar output comparisons between the equilibrium and the unconstrained optimum.

The price in the unconstrained optimum is of course the lowest of the three. As to the number of firms, we note

$$n_c = \frac{\omega(x_c)}{a + cx_c} < \frac{\gamma}{a + cx_c}$$

and therefore we have a one-way comparison:

$$(51) \qquad \text{If } x_u < x_c, \text{ then } n_u > n_c$$

Similarly for the equilibrium. These leave open the possibility that the unconstrained optimum has both bigger and more firms. That is not unreasonable; after all the unconstrained optimum uses resources more efficiently.

III. Asymmetric Cases

The discussion so far imposed symmetry within the group. Thus the number of varieties being produced was relevant, but any group of n was just as good as any other group of n. The next important modification is to remove this restriction. It is easy to see how interrelations within the group of commodities can lead to biases. Thus, if no sugar is being produced, the demand for coffee may be so low as to make its production unprofitable when there are set-up costs. However, this is open to the objection that with complementary commodities, there is an incentive for one entrant to produce both. However, problems exist even when all the commodities are substitutes. We illustrate this by considering an industry which will produce commodities from one of two groups, and examine whether the choice of the wrong group is possible.[8]

Suppose there are two sets of commodities beside the numeraire, the two being perfect substitutes for each other and each having a constant elasticity subutility function. Further, we assume a constant budget share

---

[8] For an alternative approach using partial equilibrium methods, see Spence.

for the numeraire. Thus the utility function is

(52)

$$u = x_0^{1-s}\left\{\left[\sum_{i_1=1}^{n}x_{i_1}^{\rho_1}\right]^{1/\rho_1} + \left[\sum_{i_2=1}^{n_2}x_i^{\rho_2}\right]^{1/\rho_2}\right\}^s$$

We assume that each firm in group i has a fixed cost a_i and a constant marginal cost c_i.

Consider two types of equilibria, only one commodity group being produced in each. These are given by

(53a) $\bar{x}_1 = \dfrac{a_1}{c_1\beta_1}, \bar{x}_2 = 0$

$\bar{p}_1 = c_1(1 + \beta_1)$

$\bar{n}_1 = \dfrac{s\beta_1}{a_1(1 + \beta_1)}$

$\bar{q}_1 = \bar{p}_1\bar{n}_1^{-\beta_1} = c_1(1 + \beta_1)^{1+\beta_1}\left(\dfrac{a_1}{s}\right)^{\beta_1}$

$\bar{u}_1 = s^s(1 - s)^{1-s}\bar{q}_1^{-s}$

(53b) $\bar{x}_2 = \dfrac{a_2}{c_2\beta_2}, \bar{x}_1 = 0$

$\bar{p}_2 = c_2(1 + \beta_2)$

$\bar{n}_2 = \dfrac{s\beta_2}{a_2(1 + \beta_2)}$

$\bar{q}_2 = \bar{p}_2\bar{n}_2^{-\beta_2} = c_2(1 + \beta_2)^{1+\beta_2}\left(\dfrac{a_2}{s}\right)^{\beta_2}$

$\bar{u}_2 = s^s(1 - s)^{1-s}\bar{q}_2^{-s}$

Equation (53a) is a Nash equilibrium if and only if it does not pay a firm to produce a commodity of the second group. The demand for such a commodity is

$$x_2 = \begin{cases} 0 & \text{for } p_2 \geq \bar{q}_1 \\ s/p_2 & \text{for } p_2 < \bar{q}_1 \end{cases}$$

Hence we require

$$\max_{p_2}(p_2 - c_2)x_2 = s\left(1 - \dfrac{c_2}{\bar{q}_1}\right) < a_2$$

or

(54) $\bar{q}_1 < \dfrac{sc_2}{s - a_2}$

Similarly, (53b) is a Nash equilibrium if and

only if

(55) $\bar{q}_2 < \dfrac{sc_1}{s - a_1}$

Now consider the optimum. Both the objective and the constraint are such as to lead the optimum to the production of commodities from only one group. Thus, suppose n_i commodities from group i are being produced at levels x_i each, and offered at prices p_i. The utility level is given by

(56) $u = x_0^{1-s}\{x_1n_1^{1+\beta_1} + x_2n_2^{1+\beta_2}\}^s$

and the resource availability constraint is

(57)

$$x_0 + n_1(a_1 + c_1x_1) + n_2(a_2 + c_2x_2) = 1$$

Given the values of the other variables, the level curves of u in (n_1, n_2) space are concave to the origin, while the constraint is linear. We must therefore have a corner optimum. (As for the break-even constraint, unless the two $q_i = p_in_i^{-\beta_i}$ are equal, the demand for commodities in one group is zero, and there is no possibility of avoiding a loss there.)

Note that we have structured our example so that if the correct group is chosen, the equilibrium will not introduce any further biases in relation to the constrained optimum. Therefore, to find the constrained optimum, we only have to look at the values of $\bar{u}_i$ in (53a) and (53b) and see which is the greater. In other words, we have to see which $\bar{q}_i$ is the smaller, and choose the situation (which may or may not be a Nash equilibrium) defined in (53a) and (53b) corresponding to it.

Figure 2 is drawn to depict the possible equilibria and optima. Given all the relevant parameters, we calculate $(\bar{q}_1, \bar{q}_2)$ from (53a) and (53b). Then (54) and (55) tell us whether either or both of the situations are possible equilibria, while a simple comparison of the magnitudes of $\bar{q}_1$ and $\bar{q}_2$ tells us which is the constrained optimum. In the figure, the nonnegative quadrant is split into regions in each of which we have one combination of equilibria and optima. We only have to locate the point $(\bar{q}_1, \bar{q}_2)$ in this space to know the result for the given

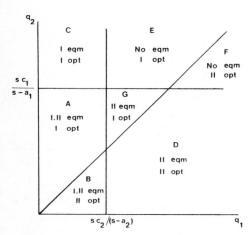

FIGURE 2. SOLUTIONS LABELED I REFER TO
EQUATION (53a); SOLUTIONS LABELED II
REFER TO EQUATION (53b)

parameter values. Moreover, we can compare the location of the points corresponding to different parameter values and thus do some comparative statics.

To understand the results, we must examine how $\bar{q}_i$ depends on the relevant parameters. It is easy to see that each is an increasing function of a_i and c_i. We also find

$$(58) \qquad \frac{\partial \log \bar{q}_i}{\partial \beta_i} = -\log \bar{n}_i$$

and we expect this to be large and negative. Further, we see from (9) that a higher β_i corresponds to a lower own-price elasticity of demand for each commodity in that group. Thus $\bar{q}_i$ is an increasing function of this elasticity.

Consider initially a symmetric situation, with $sc_1/(s - a_1) = sc_2/(s - a_2)$, $\beta_1 = \beta_2$ (the region G vanishes then), and suppose the point $(\bar{q}_1, \bar{q}_2)$ is on the boundary between regions A and B. Now consider a change in one parameter, say, a higher own-elasticity for commodities in group 2. This raises $\bar{q}_2$, moving the point into region A, and it becomes optimal to produce commodities from group 1 alone. However, both (53a) and (53b) are possible Nash

equilibria, and it is therefore possible that *the high elasticity group is produced in equilibrium when the low elasticity one should have been.* If the difference in elasticities is large enough, the point moves into region C, where (53b) is no longer a Nash equilibrium. But, owing to the existence of a fixed cost, a significant difference in elasticities is necessary before entry from group 1 commodities threatens to destroy the "wrong" equilibrium. Similar remarks apply to regions B and D.

Next, begin with symmetry once again, and consider a higher c_1 or a_1. This increases $\bar{q}_1$ and moves the point into region B, making it optimal to produce the low-cost group alone while leaving both (53a) and (53b) as possible equilibria, until the difference in costs is large enough to take the point to region D. The change also moves the boundary between A and C upward, opening up a larger region G, but that is not of significance here.

If both $\bar{q}_1$ and $\bar{q}_2$ are large, each group is threatened by profitable entry from the other, and no Nash equilibrium exists, as in regions E and F. However, the criterion of constrained optimality remains as before. Thus we have a case where it may be necessary to prohibit entry in order to sustain the constrained optimum.

If we combine a case where $c_1 > c_2$ (or $a_1 > a_2$) and $\beta_1 > \beta_2$, i.e., where commodities in group 2 are more elastic and have lower costs, we face a still worse possibility. For the point $(\bar{q}_1, \bar{q}_2)$ may then lie in region G, where only (53b) is a possible equilibrium and only (53a) is constrained optimum, i.e., the market can produce only a low cost, high demand elasticity group of commodities when a high cost, low demand elasticity group should have been produced.

Very roughly, the point is that although commodities in inelastic demand have the potential for earning revenues in excess of variable costs, they also have significant consumers' surpluses associated with them. Thus it is not immediately obvious whether the market will be biased in favor of them or against them as compared with an optimum. Here we find the latter, and independent findings of Michael Spence in other contexts confirm this. Similar remarks apply to differences in marginal costs.

In the interpretation of the model with heterogenous consumers and social indifference curves, inelastically demanded commodities will be the ones which are intensively desired by a few consumers. Thus we have an "economic" reason why the market will lead to a bias against opera relative to football matches, and a justification for subsidization of the former and a tax on the latter, provided the distribution of income is optimum.

Even when cross elasticities are zero, there may be an incorrect choice of commodities to be produced (relative either to an unconstrained or constrained optimum) as Figure 3 illustrates. Figure 3 illustrates a case where commodity A has a more elastic demand curve than commodity B; A is produced in monopolistically competitive equilibrium, while B is not. But clearly, it is socially desirable to produce B, since ignoring consumer's surplus it is just marginal. Thus, the commodities that are not produced but ought to be are those with inelastic demands. Indeed, if, as in the usual analysis of monopolistic competition, eliminating one firm shifts the demand curve for the other firms to the right (i.e., increases the demand for other firms), if the con-

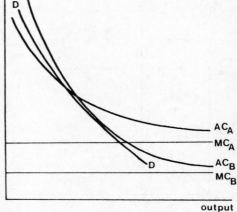

FIGURE 4

sumer surplus from A (at its equilibrium level of output) is less than that from B (i.e., the cross hatched area exceeds the striped area), then constrained Pareto optimality entails restricting the production of the commodity with the more elastic demand.

A similar analysis applies to commodities with the same demand curves but different cost structures. Commodity A is assumed to have the lower fixed cost but the higher marginal cost. Thus, the average cost curves cross but once, as in Figure 4. Commodity A is produced in monopolistically competitive equilibrium, commodity B is not (although it is just at the margin of being produced). But again, observe that B should be produced, since there is a large consumer's surplus; indeed, since were it to be produced, B would produce at a much higher level than A, there is a much larger consumer's surplus. Thus if the government were to forbid the production of A, B would be viable, and social welfare would increase.

In the comparison between constrained Pareto optimality and the monopolistically competitive equilibrium, we have observed that in the former, we replace some low fixed cost-high marginal cost commodities with high fixed cost-low marginal cost commodities, and we replace some commodities

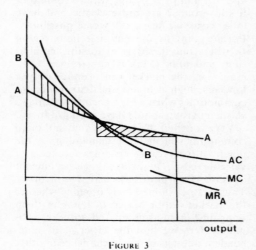

FIGURE 3

with elastic demands with commodities with inelastic demands.

IV. Concluding Remarks

We have constructed in this paper some models to study various aspects of the relationship between market and optimal resource allocation in the presence of some nonconvexities. The following general conclusions seem worth pointing out.

The monopoly power, which is a necessary ingredient of markets with nonconvexities, is usually considered to distort resources away from the sector concerned. However, in our analysis monopoly power enables firms to pay fixed costs, and entry cannot be prevented, so the relationship between monopoly power and the direction of market distortion is no longer obvious.

In the central case of a constant elasticity utility function, the market solution was constrained Pareto optimal, regardless of the value of that elasticity (and thus the implied elasticity of the demand functions). With variable elasticities, the bias could go either way, and the direction of the bias depended not on how the elasticity of demand changed, but on how the elasticity of utility changed. We suggested that there was some presumption that the market solution would be characterized by too few firms in the monopolistically competitive sector.

With asymmetric demand and cost conditions we also observed a bias against commodities with inelastic demands and high costs.

The general principle behind these results is that a market solution considers profit at the appropriate margin, while a social optimum takes into account the consumer's surplus. However, applications of this principle come to depend on details of cost and demand functions. We hope that the cases presented here, in conjunction with other studies cited, offer some useful and new insights.

REFERENCES

R. L. Bishop, "Monopolistic Competition and Welfare Economics," in Robert Kuenne, ed., *Monopolistic Competition Theory*, New York 1967.

E. Chamberlin, "Product Heterogeneity and Public Policy," *Amer. Econ. Rev. Proc.*, May 1950, *40*, 85–92.

P. A. Diamond and D. L. McFadden, "Some Uses of the Expenditure Function In Public Finance," *J. Publ. Econ.*, Feb. 1974, *82*, 1–23.

A. K. Dixit and J. E. Stiglitz, "Monopolistic Competition and Optimum Product Diversity," econ. res. pap. no. 64, Univ. Warwick, England 1975.

H. A. John Green, *Aggregation in Economic Analysis*, Princeton 1964.

H. Hotelling, "Stability in Competition," *Econ. J.*, Mar. 1929, *39*, 41–57.

N. Kaldor, "Market Imperfection and Excess Capacity," *Economica*, Feb. 1934, *2*, 33–50.

K. Lancaster, "Socially Optimal Product Differentiation," *Amer. Econ. Rev.*, Sept. 1975, *65*, 567–85.

A. M. Spence, "Product Selection, Fixed Costs, and Monopolistic Competition," *Rev. Econ. Stud.*, June 1976, *43*, 217–35.

D. A. Starrett, "Principles of Optimal Location in a Large Homogeneous Area," *J. Econ. Theory*, Dec. 1974, *9*, 418–48.

N. H. Stern, "The Optimal Size of Market Areas," *J. Econ. Theory*, Apr. 1972, *4*, 159–73.

J. E. Stiglitz, "Monopolistic Competition in the Capital Market," tech. rep. no. 161, IMSS, Stanford Univ., Feb. 1975.

[25]

Market Imperfection and Excess Capacity

By Nicholas Kaldor

OF all the doctrines emerging from recent work on the economics of imperfect competition, none appears more intellectually striking or more significant from a practical point of view than the doctrine of " excess capacity." It is intellectually striking, because it admits possibilities which the traditional " laws of economics " seem to have excluded: e.g. that an increase in " supply " may be followed by a rise in price.[1] And it is practically significant, because if the main contentions of the theory are found to be correct, it affords some reasons for interfering with the " free play of competitive forces " on grounds upon which traditional economic theory would have dismissed the case for interference. The theory envisages a situation, where, on the one hand the market facing a group of competing firms is, for one reason or another, not absolutely " perfect," while on the other hand the entry of resources into the " industry " is free, and it shows that under such conditions " competition " (i.e. the free flow of resources into uses where they expect to obtain the largest net remuneration) will drive each producer to a situation in which it is not using its resources to the best advantage; and it will thus lead to a reduction of the physical productivity of resources all round. In a sense, it thus reverses the old argument about " increasing returns " and monopoly; it not only says that falling costs will lead to monopoly but that a monopolistic or rather a pseudo-monopolistic situation[2] will automatically lead each firm to a position where it is faced with

---

[1] Since Marshall, we are aware of the fact that given certain cost conditions an increase in demand may be followed by a fall in price. But neither the Marshallian, nor, so far as the present writer is aware, any other theoretical system left room for the possibility that under certain market conditions, an increase in the number of sources of supply (an inflow of resources into the " industry ") could lead to a rise in prices.

[2] We shall see later what precisely the term " monopolistic " implies in this connection.

33

falling average costs.[1] It is a highly ingenious and one might almost say revolutionary doctrine: it shows up " free competition " (i.e. the freedom of entry into any trade or industry) not in the traditional and respectable role as the eliminator of the unfit but in the much more dubious role as the creator of excess capacity. It affords an excellent theoretical background for the age-old cry of business men about the " wastes of competition "—so far completely neglected by the economists. It is worth while therefore to examine this theory in some detail.

The theory is put forward both in Professor Chamberlin's recent work and also in Mrs. Robinson's book.[2] Closer inspection reveals, however, that Mrs. Robinson's version possesses a merely formal similarity with Professor Chamberlin's theory. For Mrs. Robinson includes in her " cost curves " such profits which are not competed away by the entry of new producers; and under the circumstances, her statement that " demand curves will be tangential to cost curves " and that firms will be of " less than their optimum size " is merely a statement of a tautology.[3] It does not imply " excess capacity " or anything of that sort. In the subsequent analysis we shall follow therefore mainly Professor Chamberlin's statement of the theory.

II

The main argument can be stated briefly. Although not stated so explicitly, it is really based on four assumptions.

[1] " Falling average costs," if they are to be regarded as the criterion of " excess capacity " should be interpreted that in the relevant output, costs are falling *in a state of long-period equilibrium* (after *all* adjustments have been made to that output), which also implies that *variable costs* are falling (since in the long run the supply of all factors— even the resources supplied by the entrepreneur himself—can be assumed variable and consequently there are no " fixed " costs). Since in a state of full equilibrium "short-run " cost curves must be tangential to the long-run cost curve : falling long-period costs also imply that short-run total costs are falling. But the converse is not necessarily true; falling short-run total costs (the " fixed costs " being calculated on a " historic " basis) need not involve falling long-run costs, for the same output, and consequently these are no safe criteria for the prevalence of excess capacity.

[2] Chamberlin, *The Theory of Monopolistic Competition*, Ch. V. Mrs. Robinson, *The Economics of Imperfect Competition*, Ch. 7. The theory of course, is by no means completely new. Wicksell already stated it (*Lectures*, p. 86) and it is also to be found, in essentials, in Cairnes' *Political Economy*, p. 115. It was outlined in P. Sraffa's well-known article (" The Laws of Returns under Competitive Conditions," *Economic Journal*, 1926). The first systematic exposition is, however, Chamberlin's.

[3] Cf. on this point G. F. Shove, " The Imperfection of the Market " (*Economic Journal*, March, 1933), an article, which in the present writer's view, contains one of the most penetrating analyses so far published on this whole subject.

Firstly, it is assumed that there are a large number of independent producers, each selling one product only, which is " slightly different " from the products of the rest of the producers. The words " slightly different " imply, that while the demand for the product of any of the producers is highly sensitive to the prices charged by the others, yet this sensitiveness is never so great as to compel all producers to sell at the same price. It implies that a producer, by lowering his price relatively to his competitors' prices, will attract away some, but not *all* their customers; or alternatively, that he will lose some, but not all of his own customers, if he raises his price relatively to the rest.[1] It is assumed, secondly, that " *consumers' preferences are fairly evenly distributed among the different varieties*,"[2] and since there are a large number of them " any adjustment of price or of ' product ' by a single producer spreads its influence over so many of his competitors that the impact felt by any one is negligible and does not lead him to any readjustment of his own situation." [3] Thus, given the prices of all the others, a " demand curve " can be drawn up with respect to the product of each.[4] Thirdly, it is assumed that no producer possesses an " institutional monopoly " over any of the varieties produced and thus the entry of new producers " into the field in general and every portion of it in particular is free and unimpeded." Fourthly, the long-run cost curves of all producers are assumed to be falling up to a certain rate of output; in other words, it is assumed that up to a certain output, there are " economics of scale " (Professor Chamberlin's cost curves are U-shaped, i.e. they begin to

[1] In technical terms this implies that the consumer's "elasticity of substitution " between the different producers' products is large, but not infinite; which is the same thing as saying that the " cross-elasticities of demand " (the elasticity of demand for one producer's product with respect to another producer's price) are considerable but not infinite. Looking at it in this way, "monopoly " and " perfect competition " appear as the two limiting cases, where the " cross-elasticities " are zero or infinite, respectively; and there can be little doubt that the large majority of industrial producers in the real world are faced with imperfect markets in this sense.

[2] Which implies, in the above terminology, that the cross-elasticity of the demand for the product of any producer is of the same order of magnitude with respect to the price of *any* of his competitors. Cf. my article, " Mrs. Robinson's Economics of Imperfect Competition," ECONOMICA, August, 1934, p. 339.

[3] Chamberlin, p. 83. Mrs. Robinson does not state this so definitely, but her analysis is implicitly based on the same assumptions. Professor Chamberlin states (pp. 82-3) that he only makes these assumptions temporarily in order to facilitate the exposition, and removes them later on (pp. 100-11). But, as I shall try to show, the theory, in its rigid form at any rate, really stands or falls with these assumptions.

[4] In the absence of these assumptions one can speak of a demand curve only in the sense of an " imagined demand curve," cf. below.

rise after a certain point. But while the legitimacy of the latter assumption in the case of long-run curves appears doubtful,[1] it does not affect his argument, which merely requires that costs should be falling over a certain range.) The elasticities of the demand curve and the cost curves of each producer are also assumed to be the same, but this, as I shall try to show, is not essential to the main argument so long as " institutional monopolies " are assumed to be absent. Now, given these two curves each producer will try to produce that output which will maximise his own profits, i.e. equate marginal revenue with marginal cost. But since marginal revenue is less than price, price will be higher than average cost (including under the latter the displacement cost of the resources supplied by the entrepreneur himself) unless average cost is also, and to a corresponding degree, higher than marginal cost (which it can only be if average costs are falling). Let us assume that this is not the case initially. Entrepreneurs in the industry will then make " monopoly profits," i.e. remuneration for their own resources will be higher than that which similar resources could earn elsewhere. This will attract such resources into the " industry "; new firms will come in, producing new substitutes, which will reduce the demand for all existing producers; and this process will continue, until profits are reduced to normal, i.e. the difference between the actual earnings and the displacement costs of the entrepreneur's own resources is eliminated. In the position of final equilibrium not only will marginal cost be equal to marginal revenue, but average cost will also be equal to price. The demand curve will thus be " tangential " to the cost curve. The effect of the entry of new competitors will not necessarily reduce the price of existing products; it may even raise them. The profits which the entrepreneur no longer earns will thus not be passed on to the consumer in the form of lower prices but are mainly absorbed in lower productive efficiency. The producers, *as a body*, could of course prevent this from occurring by reducing their prices *in anticipation* of the entry of new competitors. But since the appearance of any *single* new producer will only affect the demand of a *single* existing producer very slightly, while similarly the reduction of price of a *single* existing producer will only slightly affect the profits which a potential producer can expect, no producer could

[1] Cf. my article, " The Equilibrium of the Firm," *Economic Journal*, March, 1934, p. 70.

take these indirect effects on his own price policy into consideration.

There can be little doubt that given these assumptions the theory is unassailable. Any criticism therefore must be directed against the usefulness and the consistency of the assumptions selected.

III

1. The first of these concerns the assumptions made about the interrelations of the demand for the products of various producers (which are substantially the same as those underlying Mrs. Robinson's conception of an " imperfectly competitive industry " [1]). No doubt, in most cases, the products of various producers selling the same sort of goods are not " perfect substitutes " to each other in the sense that the slightest price difference would eliminate all demand for the products of higher-price producers. The reasons for such " market imperfection " may be classed under one of three headings. There may either be slight differences in the products themselves (as in the case of motor cars, wireless sets, etc., the absence of " standardisation "); or differences in the geographical location of producers in cases where the consumers themselves are distributed over an area; or finally, there may exist a certain " inertia " on behalf of the buyers themselves who will require either some time, or a certain magnitude in the price-difference, before they make up their minds to buy from another seller—even if they are quite indifferent as between the products of different sellers.[2] Whatever the cause, the effect, from the analytical point of view, will be the same: the " cross elasticities " of demand

---

[1] Cf. *The Economics of Imperfect Competition*, Ch. 1. Cf. on this point my review, *op. cit.*, p. 339.

[2] It might be objected that anything which causes a lack of indifference between buyers will make the products " imperfect substitutes " in relation to each other (since the consumers' attitude is the final criterion for classifying " products ") and consequently no distinction can be made out between " buyers' inertia " and " product-differentiation " as causes of market imperfection. There is, however, a very good reason for keeping them separate. Whereas in the ordinary case of imperfectly substitutable commodities the consumers' " elasticity of substitution " between two products is symmetrical (i.e. a given change in the price ratio will cause a given change in the relative quantities demanded, whichever of the two prices has moved relatively to the other) this is by no means the case when the lack of indifference is merely due to the inertia of buyers. In the latter case, one cannot even speak of a given " marginal rate of substitution," since this rate will be different according to the direction of the change.

will have a positive finite value. But is there any justification
for the further assumption that they will also be of the same
order of magnitude with respect to the prices of *any* group of
rival products ? Can we say that any adjustment of price or of
" product " by a single producer will spread its influence
evenly over all his competitors ? No doubt, cases are conceivable when it would. When the " imperfection of the market "
is due to sheer buyers' inertia *and nothing else*, we could invoke
the law of large numbers and say that the buyers who no
longer buy from A, will pair themselves more or less evenly
with B, C, D. . . . But buyers' inertia, though an important
factor in practice, is rarely found in isolation as a cause of
market-imperfection. It is generally coupled with either or
both of the other causes.[1] And in these cases, it is clear that
the different producers' products will never possess the same
degree of substitutability in relation to any particular product.
Any particular producer will always be faced with rivals who
are nearer to him, and others who are "farther off." In fact,
he should be able to class his rivals, *from his own point of view*,
in a certain order, according to the influence of their prices
upon his own demand (which will not be necessarily the same
order as that applying to any particular rival of his). This is
clear in the case where " market imperfection " is merely due
to differences in the geographical location of producers. It is
equally true in cases of " product-differentiation." Savile
Row tailors will be most influenced by Savile Row prices;
they will be less concerned with fluctuations in the price of
East-end clothes.[2]

    " Pseudo-monopolists "—distinguished from the old-
fashioned " real monopolists " merely by the fact that the
" cross-elasticities of demand " for their product is large—
thus cannot be grouped together in a lump but can at best
be placed into a series. Each " product " can be conceived
as occupying a certain position on a " scale "; the scale being
so constructed that those products are neighbouring each

---

[1] Moreover, the case where market-imperfection is *merely* due to buyers' inertia
is not a very good one from the point of view of this theory: since it always implies
the presence of " institutional monopoly " as well. Cf. p. 45.

[2] It is conceivable that the " scale of preferences " of different consumers should differ
in just that degree as to eliminate the differences in the degree of substitutability of
different products for the body of consumers as a whole. (If individual X regards
product B as a nearer substitute to A than either C or D, but Y regards C as a nearer
substitute than either B or D, while Z regards D as the nearest substitute to A, then
the prices B, C, D may have the same influence on the demand for A.) But this is a
rather improbable supposition.

other between which the consumers' elasticity of substitution is the greatest (a " product " itself can be defined as a collection of objects between which the elasticity of substitution of all relevant consumers is infinite). Each producer then is faced on each side with his nearest rivals; the demand for his own product will be most sensitive with respect to the prices of these; less and less sensitive as one moves further away from him. "Product variation " by an individual producer can then itself be represented as a movement *along* the scale; and, given the position of all other producers, each producer will tend to settle at that point on the scale where his anticipated profits are the greatest. New entrants must also occupy a position on that scale, and will thus necessarily make the chain of substitutes " tighter."

The idea of such a " scale " can best be envisaged in the case of the simplest type of market-imperfection: the distribution of consumers over an area. Let us assume that all consumers are situated along a road (a kind of " ribbon development "), they are of an even degree of density, and all of them have an equal desire to buy. They are completely indifferent as between the products of different sellers; or rather the only difference consists in respect to transport costs (which can be equally regarded to be borne either by the buyers or the sellers). Under such conditions, sellers will tend to settle at equidistant points from each other along the road,[1] and thus they are all " pseudo-monopolists," since no two producers sell from the same spot.[2] Looked at from the point of view of any seller, a change of price by any other particular seller (the prices of the rest being assumed as given) is less and less important for him, the further away that particular seller is situated.

It follows from this, first, that even when the number of producers is large (the chain of substitutes tight) it cannot be assumed that the effect of a single producer's action will spread itself *evenly* over a large number of his rivals and will be negligible for each of them individually. The other producers'

---

[1] If only there are more than two of them, cf. Chamberlin p. 196, where Professor Hotelling's relevant theorem is corrected.

[2] The assumption that " institutional monopolies " are absent, implies in this case, that any seller *could*, if he wanted to, move to the same spot as that occupied by any other seller (or so near to it as to eliminate differences in transport costs) and thus make his own product " indistinguishable " from that of the other. Neglect to distinguish between these two cases of " monopolies " has been the source of much confusion in the past.

prices and " products " thus cannot be assumed as " given " in drawing up the demand schedule for the first; and the real demand curve for a single producer's product is thus indeterminate (depending on any of the large numbers of possible reactions in which his rivals might indulge).[1] The problems of " duopoly " are thus not merely concomitants of a situation where there are a " small number of producers " but arise in all cases where producers are selling substitute products, since the fact of " imperfect substitutability " necessarily involves the presence of the " scale " and thus of the " small number." " Duopoly " is thus seen not as a special class by itself but rather as " the leading species of a large genus."

Secondly, it can just as little be assumed that " new products " (the products of new or prospective entrants) will stand in the same or similar relation with *all* existing products. A new product must necessarily be placed in between two existing products; and will thus make considerable inroads into the markets of his nearest neighbours. Thus a producer, if far-sighted, will take the effect of his own actions not merely on his existing competitors into consideration but also on his *potential competitors*.[2] He will act on the basis of an " imagined demand curve " which shows the amount he can sell at different prices in *the long run*, under the assumption that his competitors' products, prices, and the number of his competitors are all adjusted to his price. If a producer knows that if he charges a high price to-day a competitor will appear to-morrow whose mere existence will put him in a *permanently worse position*, he will charge a price which will afford him only a low profit, if only he hopes to secure this profit

[1] Which does not imply that each producer will not base his policy upon certain ideas concerning the relation between the demand of his product and its price. But this " imagined demand curve " is based on certain expectations concerning his rivals' behaviour as a result of changes in his own policy; irrespectively whether these expectations are correct or not. Such an " imagined demand curve " is always determinate (since something must always exist in the producer's own mind). But it is a different sort of thing from the " demand curves " of traditional analysis which always implied an *objective* relationship between price and the quantity demanded. For a fuller treatment of the distinction between a real and an imagined demand curve, cf. my previous article quoted above (ECONOMICA, August, 1934, p. 340.).

[2] If a producer takes into account the consequences of his own policy on his *existing* competitors, this will probably induce him to charge a higher price than otherwise (will make his " imagined demand curve " less elastic). But if he takes *potential competition* into account, this will probably induce him to charge a price lower than otherwise (make his imagined demand curve more elastic). " Potential competition " implies both (*a*) the appearance of a new rival, (*b*) the possibility of " product-adjustment " rather than price-adjustment by an existing rival.

permanently; i.e. he will act in a manner *as if* his own demand curve were very much more elastic than it is. And this " foresight " will, or at any rate may, prevent him from being driven to a state of " excess capacity." [1]

2. Moreover, it can be shown that even if none of the producers takes the indirect effects of his own policy into consideration[2] " potential competition " will never succeed in making the individual demand and cost curves tangential, if " economies of scale " exist; while the possibility of " product-differentiation " will by itself never prevent the establishment of " perfect competition " if " economies of scale " are completely absent. Demand curves and cost curves therefore will only become necessarily " tangential " to each other when " demand curves " have also become horizontal.

In order to prove this, let us again take the simplest case of market imperfection which is at the same time the one most favourable to the " excess capacity " theory: when it exists solely on account of the spreading of consumers over a large area. Let us again assume that consumers are evenly distributed over the whole area; that they have no preferences whatever as between the different sellers; and that the cost functions of all producers are identical. The demand curves of individual sellers will be " downward sloping " solely on account of the increase in transport costs as more is sold. Let us assume that producers are situated at equal distances from each other and that they all make " profits " (sell at prices which more than cover average displacement costs). Let us assume that new producers enter the field. Each producer's market will be smaller; the elasticity of demand, at any price, higher than before. But if we assume that economies of scale are completely absent (i.e. long-run cost curves are horizontal) profits will never be eliminated altogether so long

[1] Whether it will do so or not, will depend on the relative willingness and ability of bearing losses—on behalf of the " existing producer " and the " new entrant." For let us assume that a producer reduces his price in anticipation of the entrance of new competitors. If the " new producer " comes in nevertheless, *at the ruling price*, both will be involved in losses. But there will be some higher price at which both will make some profits; and if the new entrant can induce the old producer to raise his price to that level he can thereby secure his place on the " scale " permanently. If on the other hand, the old producer persists in charging the low price, one of them will have to drop out. (In so far as " buyers' inertia " is present at all, there is always a presumption that such a price-war will cost less to the old producer than the new one.)

[2] I.e. they all act on the basis of an " imagined demand curve " which corresponds to a " real demand curve " drawn on the assumption that the prices and " products " of all other producers remain the same, irrespectively of what the first producer is doing (which is the assumption underlying Professor Chamberlin's demand curves).

as the elasticity of demand is less than infinite. For each producer can always recover some of his lost profits by reducing output up to the point where marginal revenue equals marginal cost (which in this case, also equals average cost). The inflow of new producers will continue, leading to a continuous reduction in the output of existing producers and a continuous increase in the elasticities of their demand until the latter becomes infinite and prices will equal " average costs." There the movement will stop. But each " firm " will have reduced his output to such an extent that he has completely lost his hold over the market.

We see therefore that the mathematical economists in making " perfect competition " as their starting point, weren't such fools after all. For they assumed perfect divisibility of everything; and where everything is perfectly divisible, and consequently economies of scale completely absent, " perfect competition " must necessarily establish itself solely as a result of the " free play of economic forces." No degree of " product-differentiation " and no possibility of further and further " product-variation " will be sufficient to prevent this result, so long as all kinds of " institutional monopolies " and all kinds of indivisibilities are completely absent.

Let us now introduce indivisibilities and economies of scale. The movement of new " firms " into the field will then not continue until the elasticities of demand for individual producers become infinite; it will be stopped long before that by the increase in costs as the output of producers is reduced. *But there is no reason to assume that it will stop precisely at the point where the demand and cost curves are tangential.* For, on account of the very reason of " economies of scale " the potential producer cannot hope to enter the field profitably with less than a certain magnitude of output; and that additional output may reduce demand, both to his nearest neighbours and to him, to such an extent that the demand curves will lie *below* the cost curves and all will be involved in losses. The interpolation of a third producer in between any two producers may thus transform " profits " into " losses." *The same reason therefore which prevents competition from becoming " perfect "—i.e. indivisibles—will also prevent the complete elimination of " profits."* It will secure a " monopolistic advantage " to anybody who is first in the field and merely by virtue of priority. The ultimate reason for this being that it is not the original resources themselves, but the various uses

to which they are put that are indivisible—you can divide
" free capital " but you cannot invest *less* than a certain amount
of it in a machine—and consequently the investment of
resources cannot be so finely distributed as to equalise the
level of marginal productivities.[1]

The above argument does not hold, if we assume as
Professor Chamberlin assumed at the start, that consumers'
preferences are *evenly distributed* over the whole field; and
consequently the entry of a new firm affects *all* existing firms
to an equal degree. Then the demand for each is only reduced
by an insignificant amount by a single new entrant; and
consequently the number of firms could increase with im-
punity until profits are completely wiped out and the demand
curves become " tangential."

That Professor Chamberlin is aware of our first objection is
clear from his analysis of chain-relationships on pp. 102-4
of his book. That he is also aware of the second is clear from
certain remarks in connection with spatial competition on
p. 199. It would be most unfair therefore to criticise him on a
point of logic—since the logic of Professor Chamberlin's
analysis is indeed excellent. What he does not seem to be
aware of is the degree of unreality involved in his initial
assumptions; and the extent to which his main conclusions
are dependent on those assumptions.

3. So far we have not mentioned the most frequent and
conspicuous objection against the " excess capacity " theory:
that it assumes " identical cost and demand curves " for the
different producers. In our view, this is no valid criticism
on Professor Chamberlin's assumptions. The identity of
the demand curves merely ensures that the *prices* of different
producers will be identical. But since producers are free to
vary the quality of their product as well as their price, differences in elasticity will not save producers from being driven
to a position of " tangency "—although they may reach this
position by selling at different prices. The identity of the cost
curves—*in the required sense*—follows on the other hand from
the assumption of the absence of ány " institutional monopoly."
It is assumed, that is to say, that every producer, *could*, if he

[1] This brings out clearly also the objection against Mrs. Robinson's " normal
profits." We see how the level of profits in each firm—the difference between its actual
remuneration and the displacement cost of its earnings—is determined by the degree
of indivisibility which acts as a " protective shield " against intruders. There is no
more reason to assume these profits to tend to a " normal " level than there is to assume
that the extent of indivisibilities is the same in all cases.

wanted to, produce commodities completely identical to those
of any other producer—if he does not, this is merely because
he would not find it profitable to do so.[1] [2] Such "institutional
monopolies" may consist of patents, copyrights, trade-marks
or even a trade-name. They may be conferred by law, by
ownership, or merely by the will of the public. If the public
prefers to buy from Messrs. Smith and Robinson and thus the
name of the seller becomes part of the " quality of the product,"
then Messrs. Smith and Robinson have an "institutional
monopoly" of their products. They possess something which
others cannot possess. Similarly, if the enterpreneur *owns*
resources which are *relatively* better fitted for the production
of some varieties than the resources over which other entrepreneurs have command, he has exclusive control over
resources which to that extent are unique: and this also implies
the presence of some "institutional monopoly."[3] Consequently, in the absence of these, since the relative costs of producing
different varieties must be the same for the different producers,
their cost curves, *for each single variety*, must also be identical.

It might be objected, that "institutional monopoly" thus
defined, covers a much larger number of cases than what is
generally understood by this term. Indeed, one could make
out a nice distinction between the possession of an "absolute"
monopoly (when no other producer is able to produce a
completely identical product at *any* cost) or a comparative or
"partial" monopoly (when no other producer is able to
produce the same product at the same relative cost). But as
all "products" are more or less close substitutes for one
another, this distinction becomes analytically unimportant
since it comes to the same thing whether producer B can
produce merely a "more or less close substitute" to A—
or whether he can produce the *same* product but only at a
higher cost than A.[4] Anything therefore which imposes
higher costs on one producer than another (whether it is due

---

[1] Professor Chamberlin does not state this explicitly; but this is the only logically
consistent interpretation one can give to his assumption that "the entry of new
producers into the field in general and every portion of it in particular is free and
unimpeded."

[2] This implies in our terminology that every producer is free to move along and
settle at any point of the "scale," he can get therefore "as near to" the products of
any other producer as he wants without incurring higher *relative* costs.

[3] In order to avoid misunderstanding it must be pointed out that the absence of
"institutional monopoly" does not imply that the abilities of each entrepreneur, and
consequently the *absolute level* of their costs, are identical.

[4] In both cases producer B will obtain smaller total receipts for the same total outlay.

to the possession of " unique " resources by one entrepreneur or whether it is merely due to " buyers' inertia " [1] imposing a special " cost of entry " on new producers) implies, to that extent, the presence of " institutional monopoly."

Such " institutional monopolies " of course are never completely absent. Their presence—though as we have seen in the last section, is by no means essential—may even be directly responsible for a large part of market imperfection— as Professor Chamberlin himself so convincingly shows in his appendix in favour of " unfair trading." They cannot therefore usefully be assumed absent when a situation is analysed which is often largely bound up with them. And what does the situation look like when they are not absent ?

If the " scale of differentiation " of the consumers can be regarded as given (as e.g. in the previous example, when the degree of substitutability of different " products " was rigidly determined by the level of transport costs) institutional monopoly, to the extent to which it is present, will prevent the generation of " excess capacity "—since to that extent, " profits " earned by one producer cannot be competed away by another producer. Many types of " institutional monopolies " however, by themselves increase the degree of market imperfection, and to that extent are favourable to the generation of " excess capacity." [2] The sudden appearance of buyers' inertia, for example, has the double effect of reducing the elasticity of demand for the individual products and of imposing a cost of entry on potential competitors; these two opposing tendencies may cancel out, or the net effect may go in either direction.

---

[1] What we designated above as " sheer buyers' inertia " (i.e. that consumers require either a certain lapse of time, or a certain minimum of price-difference before they change over from one seller to another, even if they are otherwise completely indifferent between the different sellers' products) is merely a special case of " institutional monopoly "; since it always imposes a differential advantage on the existing producer relatively to the new entrant. The mere existence of specialised durable plant, however, does not imply such a differential advantage in the long run, although it may prevent adjustments being undertaken in the short run.

[2] The difference between these two types of " institutional monopolies " (the one which affects merely the relative costs of different producers, and the other which affects the elasticities of the demand curves for products as well) can best be elucidated by examples. A legal patent for a certain cheap process of producing ordinary window glass will not lead the consumers to differentiate between glass produced by one process or another. It will merely have the effect of imposing higher costs upon anybody who does not possess the patent. A trade-mark protecting a certain soap or medicine may lead, however, the consumers to differentiate between different soaps or medicines ; and thus reduce the elasticity of demand for the products of each producer.

To sum up the results of the above argument. The extent to which " excess capacity " may be generated as a result of " free competition " (under the assumption that the existence of " economies of scale " will prevent this competition from becoming " perfect ") will depend : (i) On the degree of " short-sightedness " or " far-sightedness " of producers (how far they take potential competition into account in deciding upon their price- and product-policy). This is a question of business psychology rather than economics. (ii) The extent to which " institutional monopolies " are present. This, as we have seen, will tend to prevent the generation of " excess capacity " if it leaves the scale of differentiation unaffected; while it will have an uncertain effect if it increases the scale of differentiation as well. (iii) The extent to which the market-situation resembles a " chain relationship " (in Professor Chamberlin's terminology), i.e. the extent to which the various " cross-elasticities " of demand differ in order of magnitude. Only in the special case when they are all of the same order of magnitude will Professor Chamberlin's conclusion (that demand curves will be tangential to cost curves) necessarily follow. At the same time, there is a presumption that some degree of " excess capacity " will be generated even if profits will not be completely competed away: since " indivisibilities," by themselves, will not offer a strong enough shield to prevent *some* rise in costs as a consequence of the intrusion of new competitors. Many of the objections therefore which can be brought against the theory if put forward in its *rigid* form (that demand curves will tend to become " tangential " with the cost curves), do not affect the fundamental proposition that the effect of the competition of " new entrants " and consequent reduction of the level of profits earned may take the form of a rise in costs rather than a reduction of prices.[1]

---

[1] Professor Chamberlin's analysis is most valuable also in throwing light upon the probable consequences of all monopolistic agreements which refer to selling prices rather than quantities produced. It explains why, if a uniform taxi-fare is imposed, one will find too many empty taxis about. Or if the code of " professional etiquette " prevents doctors and lawyers from undercutting each other, sooner or later they will all complain that they are " under-employed." Or if manufacturers' cartels or trade associations impose a uniform price or a uniform " profit-margin " on retailers, one will find too many tobacco-shops round the streets. It should also make us very sceptical about any remedying of the evils of " imperfect competition " by compulsory rationalisation, cartellisation, or any type of interference with price-competition. For measures which intend to prevent the alleged evils of " price-cutting " not infrequently tend to aggravate the real evils which they are supposed to remedy.

4. So far we have not touched upon another abstract assumption which Professor Chamberlin has made, i.e. that each producer produces only a single " product." In reality the majority of producers produce a series of different products, if products are to be defined by the same rigid market-criteria as were applied in the earlier parts of this article. And at first sight at any rate, it does appear as if the spreading of production over a series of different products is the way in which producers can overcome the effect of those " indivisibilities " which form the *conditio sine qua non* of imperfect competition. If there is not a sufficiently great demand to produce one product on an " optimal scale," the producer may still utilise his plant fully by producing two or more products, rather than building a smaller, sub-optimal plant or leaving his existing plant under-employed. In this way, " indivisibilities " will be overcome; and consequently " excess capacity " will not make its appearance either. The effect of " competition from outside " will be to induce producers to produce a larger series of products, rather than to reduce the scale of output as a whole.

In our view this line of reasoning is not strictly accurate; for even if it is admitted that varying the number of different kinds of products produced provides one line of adjustment for the entrepreneur, this does not imply that the essential consequences of this type of situation (that increased competition will lead to an increase in costs) can thereby be avoided. Whether they will or not, will depend on the nature of the cost-function of the jointly produced products.

Commodities, of course, will only be produced jointly if it is cheaper to produce them jointly than separately. For certain commodities (such as wheat and straw) this is always the case: whatever is the amount produced of each (or rather whatever is the amount of resources engaged in producing them); irrespectively therefore whether the economies due to scale are attained or not. These are the cases of " by-products "; where more than one commodity emerges as a result of single productive process. Certain other commodities, however, may be jointly produced simply because the demand for any of them is not large enough to be produced on a scale which should enable the realisation of the economies of scale; while some of these economies can be retained by utilising a larger " plant " for the production of several commodities. For such commodities " joint production " will only be profitable as certain outputs, and will become unprofitable as soon as the demand for each or any of them is sufficiently large to enable the " economies of scale " to be secured in case of separate production. This is the case simply because the " indivisible factors " (buildings, machinery, etc.) which are responsible for these economies, are never completely specialised; and can be used, more or less effectively, for the production of several things simultaneously.

Since, however, in most cases, " indivisible factors " are not completely unspecialised either, such a "spreading of production " is always attended with some cost; i.e. the physical productivity of a *given* quantity of resources calculated in terms of *any* of the products will always be less, the greater the number of separate commodities they are required simultaneously to produce. That this is the case for a large proportion of jointly produced commodities is shown by the fact that the development of an " industry " is always attended by " specialisation " or " disintegration," i.e. the reduction of the number of commodities produced by single firms.[1]

Assuming that the cost-functions of jointly produced commodities are of this nature, how does the equilibrating process work itself out under our previous assumptions ? For simplicity, we can postulate that there are a given number of firms, and initially each of them produce only one product and all are making profits (not necessarily to the same degree). Let us suppose that one of them finds it profitable to produce another commodity, highly competitive with the products of some other producers. These latter producers will now find the demand for their products reduced; and *this* may make it profitable for them to engage in the production of a second, or even a third, commodity—even if this was not profitable before. This in turn will induce other producers (possibly our " first " producer) to do the same, which in turn will lead to a further " spreading of production " by competing producers. Assuming always that producers merely take the *direct* effects of their actions into consideration (i.e. act upon an " imagined demand curve " which regards the prices and the " products " of all other producers as given[2]) this process will continue, so long as producers continue to make some profits;

[1] Cf. Allyn Young, " Increasing Returns and Economic Progress," *Economic Journal,* 1929.

[2] This implies in this case that producers ignore not only any adjustment of price or of product by other producers as a result of their own policy, but also any effect upon the demand for some of the other commodities produced by themselves.

and so long as the loss caused by a reduction in the amount of resources engaged (if the reduction in the output of one commodity were not compensated by an increase in the output of another) is greater than the loss caused by a further " spreading of output." A precise formulation of this process would require either some very cumbrous language or some rather involved mathematics; but without resorting to either, it is easy to see what conditions the final equilibrium will involve. The demand curve for each single " product," will have become very much more elastic[1] (since each producer now produces a very much smaller share of each product, or " type of product ") ; profits will have been wiped out and the general level of costs for each product, or type of product, will have become higher. There will not be much " excess capacity " in the sense, that given the *number* of different products produced simultaneously by each firm, an increase in the output of all of them would reduce costs per unit. Yet there will be a " technical wastage," since the physical productivity of resources will be less than what it would be if each producer produced a smaller number of products and a large proportion of the total output of each; a policy they undoubtedly would prefer, if all of them would foresee the ultimate, as distinct from the immediate, consequences of their actions.[2]

IV

We have seen therefore that in all cases where economies of scale are present over certain ranges of output and where market imperfection exists (in the sense that highly and yet imperfectly substitutable commodities are on sale), "increased competition " (i.e. an increase in the number of firms in a particular industrial field) might lead to a reduction of technical efficiency rather than to a reduction in price or an increase in aggregate output; while in cases where firms can vary the number of different products produced, this might come about even without an inflow of " new firms." In both

[1] It can become infinitely elastic only when the " spreading of output " involves *no* additional cost at all. In this case the "economies of scale " refer to the amount of resources used by single firms rather than those engaged in the production of certain products ; and for each single product, conditions of perfect competition might be brought about even if the total number of firms is small.

[2] There may be another reason, apart from this type of " short-sightedness," why producers would prefer a policy of many-product production: and this is the reduction of risk, especially important in cases of " fashionable " articles, where they cannot calculate with any precision how the public will take any particular " variety."

cases this result was seen to depend on a certain " short-sightedness " of producers who act on the basis of the immediate industrial situation confronting them rather than follow out the further consequences of their own policy. The prevalence of such short-sightedness can be sufficiently accounted for, however, partly by the producers' ignorance of those further consequences and partly by the uncertainty as to the extent of far-sightedness with which their actual and potential competitions are endowed.

It is extremely difficult to deduce any general conclusions from the above analysis as to the effect of the generation of " excess capacity " upon economic welfare in general—in whatever arbitrary way this concept may be defined. If the money-value of the National Dividend is to be made its criterion (calculated on the basis of some *given* price-level), then no doubt, it could be increased, in some fields quite considerably, by compulsory " standardisation," cartel-agreements, the restriction of entry or any similar measure enabling producers to realise more fully the " economies of scale." The recognition of this fact, however, as yet far from warrants the advocacy of such measures. Apart from the ill-effects on distribution (and in a world of wage-rigidities, upon employment) which such processes of monopolisation inevitably involve, the public would be offered finally larger amounts of a smaller number of commodities; and it is impossible to tell how far people prefer quantity to diversity or vice versa.

Neither is it permissible to argue, on the other hand, that the generation of " excess capacity " is itself the result of consumers' choice; since it only comes about by creating a greater diversity of commodities: and consequently its emergence is evidence that the public, to that extent, prefer " variety " to " cheapness." This line of reasoning would only be permissible if consumers were actually confronted with the choice of having *either* a smaller range of commodities at lower prices *or* a larger range at higher prices. In fact, they never are in a position to choose between these alternatives: they are offered either the one or the other, but never both. To expect the consumers to be so " far-sighted " as to concentrate on the purchase of a few varieties merely in the hope of thereby reducing prices in the future, is an assumption which even the highest level of abstraction should avoid.

[26]

SPATIAL COURNOT OLIGOPOLY

MARTIN J. BECKMANN

Brown University and the University of Munich

As everyone knows, in location theory one is forced to work with simple assumptions in order to get any results at all. Yet in the study of spatial oligopoly, the usual assumptions are not simple enough—results are so complicated that there is controversy over the meaning and implications of the hexagon hypothesis, the consequences of free entry, and so forth. In this paper I shall reexamine the theory of spatial markets under mill pricing using a rectangular demand function, the simplest one that has ever been used (Fig. 1):

$$\text{quantity} = \begin{cases} 1 & \text{price} \leq 1 \\ 0 & \text{price} > 1 \,. \end{cases}$$

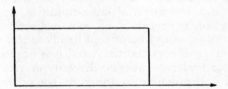

FIGURE 1. A SIMPLE DEMAND CURVE

The operational implication of this demand curve is that quantity consumed depends in an all-or-nothing fashion on distance: below a critical distance the quantity is positive and constant, beyond the critical distance it is zero. Such a curve might represent the demand for a necessity, of which a fixed amount is absorbed by a household or nothing at all—certain durables, medical services, and types of clothing. Another possibility is that a perfect local substitute exists at a given price.

I propose to study Cournot oligopoly in a spatially homogeneous market in terms of this demand function. The noncooperative case appears to be the one most appropriate for a study of markets with free entry—the closest approximation we have to perfect competition in a spatially dispersed industry and Cournot mill pricing the simplest strategy.

To avoid unnecessary mathematical work I shall standardize the units of distance, quantity, and price, and the intercept of the demand function such that:

Research for this paper was supported by National Science Foundation Grant No. 3280. I am indebted to Tridib Biswas for assistance with the calculations.

$k = 1$ transportation cost per unit quantity and unit distance is one;
$a = 1$ maximum amount of quantity demanded per unit area is one;
$c = 0$ the proportional cost of production is zero.

Since we are not concerned directly with problems of free entry, the fixed costs of production will in general be disregarded.

COURNOT OLIGOPOLY

Consider first, two firms in a one-dimensional market. If the distance between the two firms is sufficiently small (the exact bound to be determined) and the markets on the other side are unbounded, the first firm considering price p_2 of its rival as given and unchanging will calculate its profits to be

$$G = G(p, q) = p_1(1 - p_1) + p_1\frac{D_1 + p_2 - p_1}{2}$$

where D_1 denotes that distance and p_1 its own price. Maximization of profit with respect to p yields

$$p_1 = \frac{1}{3} + \frac{D + p_2}{6}. \tag{1}$$

Consider now an ith firm with two neighbors, at distances D_{i-1} and D_i charging mill prices p_{i-1} and p_{i+1}, respectively. Profit is now

$$G(p_{i-1}, p_i, p_{i+1}) = \left(\frac{D_{i-1} + D_i}{2} + \frac{p_{i-1} + p_{i+1}}{2} - p_i\right)p_i$$

and this is maximized by

$$p_i = \tfrac{1}{4}(D_{i-1} + D_i) + \tfrac{1}{4}(p_{i-1} + p_{i+1}) = \tfrac{1}{2}\bar{D}_i + \tfrac{1}{2}\bar{p}_i$$

where

$$\bar{D}_i = \tfrac{1}{2}(D_{i-1} + D_i)$$
$$\bar{p}_i = \tfrac{1}{2}(p_{i-1} + p_{i+1}). \tag{2}$$

In fact, consider a firm in a transportation network. Distances to the various neighbor firms in this industry are D_{ij} and we assume that all firms are sufficiently close for markets to overlap. Then the same analysis shows that profits are

$$G = p\left(\sum_j \frac{D_{ij} + p_j}{2} - \frac{n}{2}p\right)$$

where n is the number of neighbors and the sum is extended over all of these. The profit maximizing mill price is

$$\bar{p}_i = \frac{1}{2}\frac{1}{n}\sum_j D_{ij} + \frac{1}{2}\frac{1}{n}\sum_j p_j \tag{3}$$

yielding

$$p_i = \tfrac{1}{2}\bar{D}_i + \tfrac{1}{2}\bar{p}_i \tag{4}$$

as before, where the bar denotes the average. The system of linear equation (4) augmented by boundary conditions (1) determines the Cournot equilibrium solution. Our assumption about market overlap assures the existence of such a solution.

That this solution is stable may be shown as follows. Consider the adjustment equations (t denotes time)

$$p_{i,t+1} = \tfrac{1}{2}\bar{D}_i + \tfrac{1}{4}(p_{i-1,t} + p_{i+1,t})$$

and introduce the deviations from equilibrium

$$u_{i,t} = p_{i,t} - p_i \,.$$

The $u_{i,t}$ satisfy

$$u_{i,t+1} = \tfrac{1}{4}(u_{i-1,t} + u_{i+1,t}) \,.$$

This is a diffusion equation whose solution will dissipate to zero.

When average distances between firms equal D and there are no endpoints (i.e., the economy is a closed circle or extends along an unbounded line), then in equilibrium all prices are equal:

$$p = \tfrac{1}{2}D + \tfrac{1}{2}p \quad \text{or}$$

$$p = D \tag{5}$$

provided market areas overlap, i.e.,

$$p + \frac{D}{2} \le 1 \,,$$

or, using (5),

$$D \le \tfrac{2}{3} \,. \tag{6}$$

When $\tfrac{2}{3} < D \le 1$, then, since markets do not overlap,

$$G = 2p\,(1 - p) \quad \text{provided} \quad 1 - p \le \frac{D}{2} \,.$$

Since $dG/dp = 2 - 4p > 0$ p is pushed to its maximal admissible value $p = 1 - D/2$ and this solution is valid as long as

$$p \ge \tfrac{1}{2} \,,$$

i.e., $$D \le 1 \,.$$

When $D \ge 1$ the monopoly price $p = \tfrac{1}{2}$ is charged. Figure 2 shows the Cournot oligopoly price as a function of distance.

These results are readily extended to a two-dimensional market, where transportation takes place on a rectangular grid so that transportation cost is equal to the sum of the absolute values of the coordinate differences.   Assume that neighbors

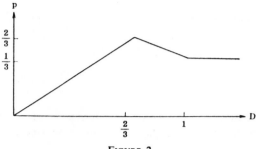

FIGURE 2

are located along transport lines.   When $D_i \leq \frac{2}{3}$, then the market areas may be shown to be rectangles with edges running in the principal directions of the transportation system.   The market area is easily calculated in Figure 3.

$$A = \left(\frac{D_1 + q_1 + D_3 + q_3}{2} - p\right)\left(\frac{D_2 + q_2 + D_4 + q_4}{2} - p\right)$$
$$= (\bar{D}_1 + \bar{q}_1 - p)(\bar{D}_2 + \bar{q}_2 - p), \text{ say.}$$

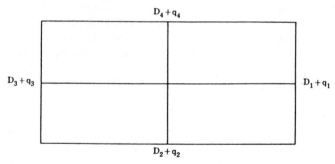

FIGURE 3

Maximizing profit pA with respect to p, assuming the q_i to be given and unchanging, yields:

$$0 = (\bar{D}_1 + \bar{q}_1 - p)(\bar{D}_2 + \bar{q}_2 - p) - p(\bar{D}_1 + \bar{q}_1 - p) - p(\bar{D}_2 + \bar{q}_2 - p),$$

a quadratic equation in p.

In the special case of equal average distances, $\bar{D}_i = D$, the solution p is given by

$$D^2 - 2pD = 0$$

$$p = \frac{D}{2} \tag{7}$$

and markets overlap as long as

$$p + \frac{D}{2} \leqq 1 - p,$$

or, using (7)

$$D \leqq \tfrac{2}{3}.$$

When $\tfrac{2}{3} < D$ and market areas overlap, the derivative of profit with respect to price is positive so that prices are pushed to the point where overlap ceases,

$$p = 1 - \frac{D}{2}. \tag{8}$$

Then the market areas are squares whose edges run at a 45-degree angle to the transportation system and at prices (8) there is room for four additional firms with a 45-degree edge separating their market areas.

The two-dimensional case with Euclidian distance is of particular interest. It is this case presumably that is at the basis of the Löschian theory of market areas. It is this assumption which the theory of monopolistic competition rests on, namely, that other firms' prices are given, rather than, say, their market areas are retained. This latter case, customer retention, will not be examined in this paper.

We shall study the case when all firms are spaced equally and have identical costs, hence will have equal prices in equilibrium. To determine the equilibrium position, it will be necessary, however, to examine behavior in the face of price differences.

Let A denote the size of our market area. Profits are

$$G = pA.$$

Consider the condition for profit maximization, given that price q of our rival is assumed to be unchanging,

$$0 = \frac{dG}{dp} = A + p\frac{dA}{dp}$$

$$= A + p\frac{\partial A}{\partial \theta} \cdot \frac{d\theta}{dp}$$

where θ is given by Figure 4.

$$(1 - q)^2 = D^2 + (1 - p)^2 - 2D(1 - p)\cos\theta. \quad \text{Now}$$

$$A = (\pi - \theta)(1 - p)^2 + 2\int_0^\theta \int_0^{R(\phi, p)} r \, dr \, d\phi$$

$$\frac{dA}{dp} = -2(\pi - \theta)(1 - p) + 2\int_0^\theta R(\phi, p) \cdot \frac{\partial R}{\partial p} d\phi$$
$$+ \left[-(1-p)^2 + 2\int_0^{R(\theta,p)} r\, dr \right] \frac{d\theta}{dp}. \tag{9}$$

Here $R(\phi, p)$ is given by the condition that Figure 4

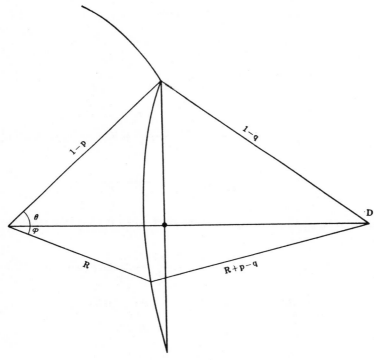

FIGURE 4

$$F \equiv (R + p - q)^2 - R^2 - D^2 + 2\cos\phi \cdot RD = 0. \tag{10}$$

In Figure 4 it is seen that

$$R(\theta) = 1 - p.$$

Therefore, the bracket in (9) vanishes.   Implicit differentiation of (10) yields

$$\frac{\partial R}{\partial p} = -\frac{F_p}{F_R} = -\frac{2(R + p - q)}{2(R + p - q) - 2R + 2D\cos\phi}. \quad \text{Substituting}$$

$$\frac{dA}{dp} = -2(\pi - \theta)(1 - p) - 2\int_0^\theta \frac{R(\phi)[R(\phi) + p - q]}{p - q + D\cos\phi} d\phi.$$

Suppose that equilibrium has been reached.   Since cost and demand functions are the same for both firms, $q = p$.   Then

$$\frac{dR}{dp} = \frac{-R}{D \cos \phi}$$

$$\frac{dA}{dp} = -2(\pi - \theta)(1 - p) - 2\int_0^\theta \frac{R^2}{D \cos \phi} d\phi \ .$$

Now $R(\phi) = D/(2 \cos \phi)$ when $p = q$, and so

$$-2\int_0^\theta \frac{R^2}{D \cos \phi} d\phi = -\frac{D}{2} \int_0^\theta \frac{1}{\cos^3 \theta} d\phi$$

$$= -\frac{D}{4}\left[\frac{\sin \theta}{\cos^2 \theta} + \log\left(\frac{1}{\cos \theta} + \tan \theta\right)\right].$$

Substituting

$$\frac{dA}{dp}\bigg|_{q=p} = -2(\pi - \theta)(1 - p) - \frac{D}{4}\left[\frac{\sin \theta}{\cos^2 \theta} + \log\left(\frac{1}{\cos \theta} + \tan \theta\right)\right].$$

Also

$$A\big|_{q=p} = (\pi - \theta)(1 - p)^2 + \frac{D}{2}\sqrt{(1 - p)^2 - \frac{D^2}{4}}.$$

The equilibrium condition for Cournot prices when distance between firms is D is, therefore,

$$(\pi - \theta)(1 - p)^2 + \frac{D}{2}\sqrt{(1 - p)^2 - \frac{D^2}{4}} - 2(\pi - \theta)p(1 - p)$$

$$- p\frac{D}{4}\left[\frac{\sin \theta}{\cos^2 \theta} + \log\left(\frac{1}{\cos \theta} + \tan \theta\right)\right] = 0$$

where

$$\theta = \text{arc cos} \frac{D}{2(1 - p)} \ .$$

Suppose now that six plants are equidistant from the given firm and from nearest neighbors at distance D.   Then the equilibrium condition is

$$0 = (\pi - 6\theta)(1 - p)^2 + 3D\sqrt{(1 - p)^2 - \frac{D^2}{4}}$$

$$- 2(\pi - 6\theta)p(1 - p) - \frac{3}{2}pD\left[\frac{\sin \theta}{\cos^2 \theta} + \log\left(\frac{1}{\cos \theta} + \tan \theta\right)\right] \qquad (11)$$

where

$$\theta = \text{arc cos} \frac{D}{2(1 - p)} \ . \qquad (12)$$

Eliminating p between (11) and (12) yields D as a function of θ

$$D = \frac{6b(\theta) + 4\dfrac{\pi - 6\theta}{\cos \theta}}{3\dfrac{\pi - 6\theta}{\cos^2 \theta} + 6 \tan \theta + 3\dfrac{b(\theta)}{\cos \theta}} \tag{13}$$

where

$$b(\theta) = \frac{\sin \theta}{\cos^2 \theta} + \log\left(\frac{1}{\cos \theta} + \tan \theta\right).$$

This equilibrium condition applies when

$$0 \le \theta \le \frac{\pi}{6}. \quad \text{Substituting } \frac{\pi}{6} \text{ in (13)}$$

$$D\left(\frac{\pi}{6}\right) = \frac{\sqrt{3b\left(\dfrac{\pi}{6}\right)}}{1 + b\left(\dfrac{\pi}{6}\right)} = 0.959$$

and $p = 0.45$.

At distances $D \le .95$
the size of the market is independent of p and depends only on D, the area of the hexagon being

$$A = \frac{\sqrt{3}}{2}D^2. \tag{14}$$

Equation (11), the derivative of profit with respect to price, assumes the form

$$0 = \frac{\sqrt{3}}{2}D^2 - \frac{3}{2}pD\left[\frac{\sin \dfrac{\pi}{6}}{\cos^2 \dfrac{\pi}{6}} + \log\left(\frac{1}{\cos \dfrac{\pi}{6}} + \tan \dfrac{\pi}{6}\right)\right]$$

from which

$$p = 0.476D. \tag{15}$$

As in the one-dimensional case, for sufficiently small distances the Cournot duopoly price is proportional to distance between firms. It reaches a maximum $p = 0.451$ at $D = 0.95$. Beyond that range, price is a decreasing function of distance. Monopoly becomes possible when distances equal or exceed $\frac{4}{3}$, and the monopoly price is $\frac{2}{3}$.

Figure 5 shows the angle θ of the polynomial part of the market area as a function of the (equal) distance between firms D. Figure 6 shows the Cournot price (and profit) as a function of distance.

It can be verified that the equilibrium is stable, at any rate for distances $D \approx 1$.

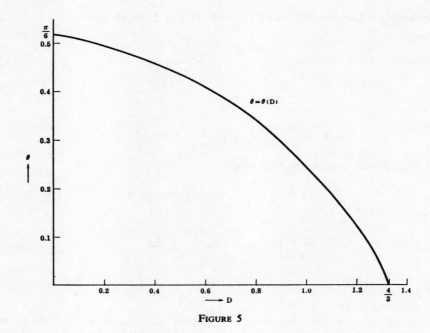

FIGURE 5

To calculate profits (before fixed cost) as a price of distance substitute p in the appropriate function for G.

$$G = pA = (\pi - 6\theta)(1 - p)^2 p + 12p \int_0^\theta \int_0^{R(\phi,p)} r\, dr\, d\phi\ .$$

When $\quad 0 \le \theta \le \dfrac{\pi}{2}\quad \dfrac{D}{2(1-p)} = \cos\theta$

$$G = p\frac{\sqrt{3}}{2}D^2 \quad \text{when}\quad \theta = \frac{\pi}{2}$$

$$= 0.476 \cdot \frac{\sqrt{3}}{2}D^3 \quad \text{using (15)}$$

$$= 0.4175\, D^3\ .$$

Figure 6 shows profit before fixed cost as a function of distance. It is a monotonically increasing function of distance reaching a maximum at $D = \frac{4}{3}$, the minimum distance for monopolists. Under free entry that distance is attained in long-run equilibrium for which profit just equals fixed cost. The higher the level of fixed cost the greater the equilibrium distance of firms to long-run market areas.

In order to study the dependence of price, profit, and equilibrium spacing on cost and demand characteristics, rewrite the profit function $G = pA$ in terms of

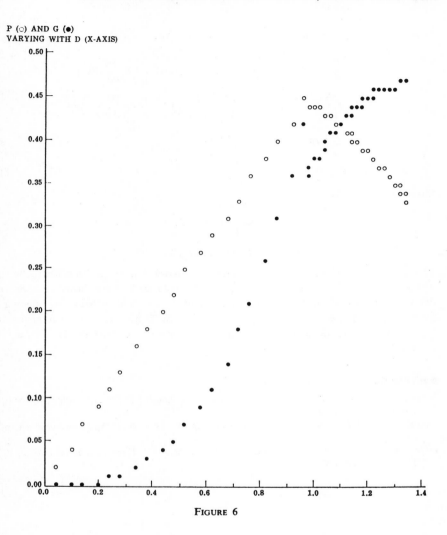

FIGURE 6

nonstandardized variables. *b* is the maximum demand price.

$$G = (p - c)a\left[(\pi - 6\theta)\left(\frac{b-p}{k}\right)^2 + 2\int_0^\theta \int_0^{R(\phi)} r\, dr\, d\phi \right]$$

where $\left(R + \dfrac{p-q}{k}\right)^2 - R^2 - D^2 + 2\cos\phi\, RD = 0$.

In the case of hexagonal market areas

$$G = (p - c)a \cdot 6 \int_0^{\pi/6} R^2(\phi)d\phi$$

$$0 = \frac{dG}{dp} = 6a \int_0^{\pi/6} R^2(\phi)d\phi + (p - c)a \cdot 2 \int_0^{\pi/6} R\frac{\partial R}{\partial p}d\phi$$

$$0 = \frac{\sqrt{3}}{2}D^2 + (p - c)2 \int_0^{\pi/6} \frac{D}{2\cos\phi}\left(-\frac{1}{k}\frac{R^2}{D\cos\phi}\right)d\phi$$

$$0 = \frac{\sqrt{3}}{2}D^2 + \frac{1}{2}(p - c)D\frac{1}{k}\int_0^{\pi/6} \frac{d\phi}{\cos^3\phi}$$

$$p - c = 0.476 \cdot kD . \tag{16}$$

Substituting in (16)

$$G = ak\, D^3\, 0.476 \cdot \frac{\sqrt{3}}{2}$$

$$= 0.4175\, ak\, D^3 .$$

This shows that profits are proportional to demand density per unit area, the rate of transportation cost, and the third power of distance between firms. Under free entry, a fall in transportation cost or demand density will increase the spacing of firms, *ceteris paribus*. To double the number of firms, distance in a hexagonal lattice must be reduced to $\sqrt{3}/2$ and hence density increased to $(2/\sqrt{3})^3 \approx 1.54$ their values.

REFERENCES

Beckmann, M. J. "Equilibrium Versus Optimum: Spacing of Firms and Patterns of Market Areas," mimeo., 1971.

Greenhut, M. *A Theory of the Firm in Economic Space.* New York: Appleton Century-Crofts, 1971.

Lovell, M. C. "Product Differentiation and Market Structure," *Western Economic Journal*, VIII, No. 2, 1970, pp. 120–143.

[27]

STABILITY IN COMPETITION [1]

AFTER the work of the late Professor F. Y. Edgeworth one may doubt that anything further can be said on the theory of competition among a small number of entrepreneurs. However, one important feature of actual business seems until recently to have escaped scrutiny. This is the fact that of all the purchasers of a commodity, some buy from one seller, some from another, in spite of moderate differences of price. If the purveyor of an article gradually increases his price while his rivals keep theirs fixed, the diminution in volume of his sales will in general take place continuously rather than in the abrupt way which has tacitly been assumed.

A profound difference in the nature of the stability of a competitive situation results from this fact. We shall examine it with the help of some simple mathematics. The form of the solution will serve also to bring out a number of aspects of a competitive situation whose importance warrants more attention than they have received. Among these features, all illustrated by the same simple case, we find (1) the existence of incomes not properly belonging to any of the categories usually discussed, but resulting from the discontinuity in the increase in the number of sellers with the demand; (2) a socially uneconomical system of prices, leading to needless shipment of goods and kindred deviations from optimum activities; (3) an undue tendency for competitors to imitate each other in quality of goods, in location, and in other essential ways.

Piero Sraffa has discussed [2] the neglected fact that a market is commonly subdivided into regions within each of which one seller is in a quasi-monopolistic position. The consequences of this phenomenon are here considered further. In passing we remark that the asymmetry between supply and demand, between buyer and seller, which Professor Sraffa emphasises is due to the condition that the seller sets the price and the buyers the quanti-

[1] Presented before the American Mathematical Society at New York, April 6, 1928, and subsequently revised.

[2] " The Laws of Returns Under Competitive Conditions," ECONOMIC JOURNAL, Vol. XXXVI. pp. 535–550, especially pp. 544 ff. (December 1926).

ties they will buy. This condition in turn results from the large number of the buyers of a particular commodity as compared with the sellers. Where, as in new oil-fields and in agricultural villages, a few buyers set prices at which they will take all that is offered and exert themselves to induce producers to sell, the situation is reversed. If in the following pages the words " buy " and " sell " be everywhere interchanged, the argument remains equally valid, though applicable to a different class of businesses.

Extensive and difficult applications of the Calculus of Variations in economics have recently been made, sometimes to problems of competition among a small number of entrepreneurs.[1] For this and other reasons a re-examination of stability and related questions, using only elementary mathematics, seems timely.

Duopoly, the condition in which there are two competing merchants, was treated by A. Cournot in 1838.[2] His book went apparently without comment or review for forty-five years until Walras produced his *Théorie Mathématique de la Richesse Sociale*, and Bertrand published a caustic review of both works.[3] Bertrand's criticisms were modified and extended by Edgeworth in his treatment of duopoly in the *Giornale degli Economisti* for 1897,[4] in his criticism of Amoroso,[5] and elsewhere. Indeed all writers since Cournot, except Sraffa and Amoroso,[6] seem to hold that even apart from the likelihood of combination there is an essential instability in duopoly. Now it is true that such competition lacks complete stability; but we shall see that in a very general class of cases the independent actions of two competitors not in collusion lead to a type of equilibrium much less fragile than in the examples of Cournot, Edgeworth and Amoroso. The solution which we shall obtain can break down only in case of an express or tacit understanding which converts the supposed

---

[1] For references to the work of C. F. Roos and G. C. Evans on this subject see the paper by Dr. Roos, " A Dynamical Theory of Economics," in the *Journal of Political Economy*, Vol. XXXV. (1927), or that in the *Transactions of the American Mathematical Society*, Vol. XXX. (1928), p. 360. There is also an application of the Calculus of Variations to depreciation by Dr. Roos in the *Bulletin of the American Mathematical Society*, Vol. XXXIV. (1928), p. 218.

[2] *Recherches sur les Principes Mathématiques de la Théorie des Richesses.* Paris (Hachette). Chapter VII. English translation by N. T. Bacon, with introduction and bibliography by Irving Fisher (New York, Macmillan, 1897 and 1927).

[3] *Journal des Savants* (1883), pp. 499–508.

[4] Republished in English in Edgeworth's *Papers Relating to Political Economy* (London, Macmillan, 1925), Vol. I. pp. 116–26.

[5] ECONOMIC JOURNAL, Vol. XXXII. (1922), pp. 400–7.

[6] *Lezioni di Economia Mathematica* (Bologna, Zanichelli, 1921).

competitors into something like a monopoly, or in case of a price war aimed at eliminating one of them altogether.

Cournot's example was of two proprietors of mineral springs equally available to the market and producing, without cost, mineral water of identical quality. The demand is elastic, and the price is determined by the total amount put on the market. If the respective quantities produced are q_1 and q_2 the price p will be given by a function

$$p = f(q_1 + q_2).$$

The profits of the proprietors are respectively

$$\pi_1 = q_1 f(q_1 + q_2)$$

and

$$\pi_2 = q_2 f(q_1 + q_2).$$

The first proprietor adjusts q_1 so that, when q_2 has its current value, his own profit will be as great as possible. This value of q_1 may be obtained by differentiating π_1, putting

$$f(q_1 + q_2) + q_1 f'(q_1 + q_2) = 0.$$

In like manner the second proprietor adjusts q_2 so that

$$f(q_1 + q_2) + q_2 f'(q_1 + q_2) = 0.$$

There can be no equilibrium unless these equations are satisfied simultaneously. Together they determine a definite (and equal) pair of values of q_1 and q_2. Cournot showed graphically how, if a different pair of q's should obtain, each competitor in turn would readjust his production so as to approach as a limit the value given by the solution of the simultaneous equations. He concluded that the actual state of affairs will be given by the common solution, and proceeded to generalise to the case of n competitors.

Against this conclusion Bertrand brought an "objection péremptoire." The solution does not represent equilibrium, for either proprietor can by a slight reduction in price take away all his opponent's business and nearly double his own profits. The other will respond with a still lower price. Only by the use of the quantities as independent variables instead of the prices is the fallacy concealed.

Bertrand's objection was amplified by Edgeworth, who maintained that in the more general case of two monopolists controlling commodities having correlated demand, even though not identical, there is no determinate solution. Edgeworth gave a variety of examples, but nowhere took account of the stabilising effect of masses of consumers placed so as to have a natural

preference for one seller or the other. In all his illustrations of
competition one merchant can take away his rival's entire
business by undercutting his price ever so slightly. Thus discontinuities appear, though a discontinuity, like a vacuum, is
abhorred by nature. More typical of real situations is the case
in which the quantity sold by each merchant is a continuous
function of two variables, his own price and his competitor's.
Quite commonly a tiny increase in price by one seller will send
only a few customers to the other.

I

The feature of actual business to which, like Professor Sraffa,
we draw attention, and which does not seem to have been generally
taken account of in economic theory, is the existence with reference to each seller of groups of buyers who will deal with him
instead of with his competitors in spite of a difference in price.
If a seller increases his price too far he will gradually lose business
to his rivals, but he does not lose all his trade instantly when he
raises his price only a trifle. Many customers will still prefer to
trade with him because they live nearer to his store than to the
others, or because they have less freight to pay from his warehouse
to their own, or because his mode of doing business is more to
their liking, or because he sells other articles which they desire,
or because he is a relative or a fellow Elk or Baptist, or on account
of some difference in service or quality, or for a combination of
reasons. Such circles of customers may be said to make every
entrepreneur a monopolist within a limited class and region—
and there is no monopoly which is not confined to a limited class
and region. The difference between the Standard Oil Company
in its prime and the little corner grocery is quantitative rather
than qualitative. Between the perfect competition and monopoly of theory lie the actual cases.

It is the gradualness in the shifting of customers from one
merchant to another as their prices vary independently which is
ignored in the examples worked out by Cournot, Amoroso and
Edgeworth. The assumption, implicit in their work, that all
buyers deal with the cheapest seller leads to a type of instability
which disappears when the quantity sold by each is considered
as a continuous function of the differences in price. The use of
such a continuous function does, to be sure, seem to violate the
doctrine that in one market there can at one time be only one
price. But this doctrine is only valid when the commodity in
question is absolutely standardised in all respects and when the

" market " is a point, without length, breadth or thickness. It is, in fact, analogous to the physical principle that at one point in a body there can at one time be only one temperature. This principle does not prevent different temperatures from existing in different parts of a body at the same time. If it were supposed that any temperature difference, however slight, necessitates a sudden transfer of all the heat in the warmer portion of the body to the colder portion—a transfer which by the same principle would immediately be reversed—then we should have a thermal instability somewhat resembling the instability of the cases of duopoly which have been discussed. To take another physical analogy, the earth is often in astronomical calculations considered as a point, and with substantially accurate results. But the precession of the equinoxes becomes explicable only when account is taken of the ellipsoidal bulge of the earth. So in the theory of value a market is usually considered as a point in which only one price can obtain; but for some purposes it is better to consider a market as an extended region.

Consider the following illustration. The buyers of a commodity will be supposed uniformly distributed along a line of

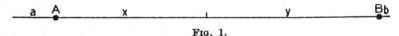

FIG. 1.

Market of length $l = 35$. In this example $a = 4, b = 1, x = 14, y = 16$.

length l, which may be Main Street in a town or a transcontinental railroad. At distances a and b respectively from the two ends of this line are the places of business of A and B (Fig. 1). Each buyer transports his purchases home at a cost c per unit distance. Without effect upon the generality of our conclusions we shall suppose that the cost of production to A and B is zero, and that unit quantity of the commodity is consumed in each unit of time in each unit of length of line. The demand is thus at the extreme of inelasticity. No customer has any preference for either seller except on the ground of price plus transportation cost. In general there will be many causes leading particular classes of buyers to prefer one seller to another, but the ensemble of such consideration is here symbolised by transportation cost. Denote A's price by p_1, B's by p_2, and let q_1 and q_2 be the respective quantities sold.

Now B's price may be higher than A's, but if B is to sell anything at all he must not let his price exceed A's by more than the cost of transportation from A's place of business to his own. In fact he will keep his price p_2 somewhat below the figure p_1 —

$c(l - a - b)$ at which A's goods can be brought to him. Thus he will obtain all the business in the segment of length b at the right of Fig. 1, and in addition will sell to all the customers in a segment of length y depending on the difference of prices and lying between himself and A. Likewise A will, if he sells anything, sell to all the buyers in the strips of length a at the left and of length x to the right of A, where x diminishes as $p_1 - p_2$ increases.

The point of division between the regions served by the two entrepreneurs is determined by the condition that at this place it is a matter of indifference whether one buys from A or from B. Equating the delivered prices we have

$$p_1 + cx = p_2 + cy.$$

Another equation between x and y is

$$a + x + y + b = l.$$

Solving we find

$$x = \tfrac{1}{2}\left(l - a - b + \frac{p_2 - p_1}{c}\right),$$

$$y = \tfrac{1}{2}\left(l - a - b + \frac{p_1 - p_2}{c}\right),$$

so that the profits are

$$\pi_1 = p_1 q_1 = p_1(a + x) = \tfrac{1}{2}(l + a - b)p_1 - \frac{p_1^2}{2c} + \frac{p_1 p_2}{2c},$$

and $$\pi_2 = p_2 q_2 = p_2(b + y) = \tfrac{1}{2}(l - a + b)p_2 - \frac{p_2^2}{2c} + \frac{p_1 p_2}{2c}.$$

If p_1 and p_2 be taken as rectangular co-ordinates, each of the last equations represents a family of hyperbolas having identical asymptotes, one hyperbola for each value of π_1 or π_2. Some of these curves are shown in Fig. 2, where (as also in Fig. 1) we have taken $l = 35, a = 4, b = 1, c = 1$.

Each competitor adjusts his price so that, with the existing value of the other price, his own profit will be a maximum. This gives the equations

$$\frac{\partial \pi_1}{\partial p_1} = \tfrac{1}{2}(l + a - b) - \frac{p_1}{c} + \frac{p_2}{2c} = 0,$$

$$\frac{\partial \pi_2}{\partial p_2} = \tfrac{1}{2}(l - a + b) + \frac{p_1}{2c} - \frac{p_2}{c} = 0,$$

from which we obtain

$$p_1 = c\left(l + \frac{a - b}{3}\right),$$

$$p_2 = c\left(l - \frac{a - b}{3}\right);$$

and
$$q_1 = a + x = \tfrac{1}{2}\left(l + \frac{a-b}{3}\right),$$

$$q_2 = b + y = \tfrac{1}{2}\left(l - \frac{a-b}{3}\right).$$

The conditions $\partial^2\pi_1/\partial p_1{}^2 < 0$ and $\partial^2\pi_2/\partial p_2{}^2 < 0$, sufficient for a maximum of each of the functions π_1 and π_2, are obviously satisfied.

If the two prices are originally the co-ordinates of the point Q in Fig. 2, and if A is the more alert business man of the two, he

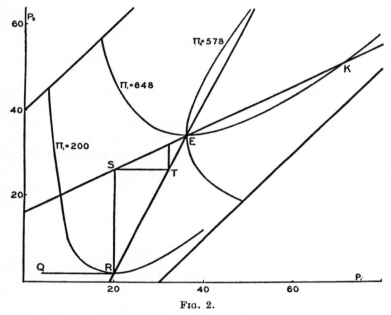

FIG. 2.

Conditions of competition for the market of Fig. 1. The co-ordinates represent the prices at A's and B's shops for the same article. The straight lines through E are the two lines of maximum profit. On one of the curves through E, A's profit is everywhere 648; on the other, B's is 578. The lower curve is the locus on which A's profit is 200.

will change his price so as to make his profit a maximum. This is represented graphically by a horizontal motion to the point R on the line $\partial\pi_1/\partial p_1 = 0$. This line has the property that every point on it represents a greater profit for A than any other point having the same ordinate. But presently B discovers that his profits can be increased by a vertical motion to the point S on his own line of maximum profit. A now moves horizontally to T. Thus there is a gradual approach to the point E at the intersection of the two lines; its co-ordinates are given by the values of p_1 and

p_2 found above. At E there is equilibrium, since neither merchant can now increase his profit by changing his price. The same result is reached if instead of Q the starting point is any on the figure.[1]

Now it is true that prices other than the co-ordinates of the equilibrium point may obtain for a considerable time. Even at this point one merchant may sacrifice his immediate income to raise his price, driving away customers, in the hope that his rival will do likewise and thus increase both profits. Indeed if A moves to the right from E in Fig. 2 he may reasonably expect that B will go up to his line of maximum profit. This will make A's profit larger than at E, provided the representing point has not gone so far to the right as K. Without this proviso, A's position will be improved (and so will B's as compared with E) if only B will sufficiently increase p_2. In fact, since the demand is inelastic, we may imagine the two alleged competitors to be amicably exploiting the consumers without limit by raising their prices. The increases need not be agreed upon in advance but may proceed by alternate steps, each seller in turn making his price higher than the other's, but not high enough to drive away all business. Thus without a formal agreement the rivals may succeed in making themselves virtually a monopoly. Something of a tacit understanding will exist that prices are to be maintained above the level immediately profitable in order to keep profits high in the long run.

But understandings between competitors are notoriously fragile. Let one of these business men, say B, find himself suddenly in need of cash. Immediately at hand he will have a resource : Let him lower his price a little, increasing his sales. His profits will be larger until A decides to stop sacrificing business

---

[1] The solution given above is subject to the limitation that the difference between the prices must not exceed the cost of transportation from A to B. This means that E must lie between the lines $p_1 - p_2 = \pm c(l - a - b)$ on which the hyperbolic arcs shown in Fig. 2 terminate. It is easy to find values of the constants for which this condition is not satisfied (for example, $l = 20$, $a = 11$, $b = 8$, $c = 1$). In such a case the equilibrium point will not be E and the expressions for the p's, q's and π's will be different; but there is no essential difference either in the stability of the system or in the essential validity of the subsequent remarks. A's locus of maximum profit no longer coincides with the line $\partial\pi_1/\partial p_1 = 0$, but consists of the portion of this line above its intersection with $p_1 - p_2 = c(l - a - b)$, and of the latter line below this point. Likewise B's locus of maximum profit consists of the part of the line $\partial\pi_2/\partial p_2 = 0$ to the right of its intersection with $p_2 - p_1 = c(l - a - b)$, together with the part of the last line to the left of this point. These two loci intersect at the point whose co-ordinates are, for $a > b$,

$$p_1 = c(3l - 3a - b), \quad p_2 = 2c(l - a),$$

and the type of stability is the same as before.

and lowers his price to the point of maximum profit. B will now be likely to go further in an attempt to recoup, and so the system will descend to the equilibrium position E. Here neither competitor will have any incentive to lower his price further, since the increased business obtainable would fail to compensate him.

Indeed the difficulties of maintaining a price-fixing agreement have often been remarked. Not only may the short-sighted cupidity of one party send the whole system crashing through price-cutting; the very fear of a price cut will bring on a cut. Moreover, a price agreement cannot be made once for all; where conditions of cost or of demand are changing the price needs constant revision. The result is a constant jarring, an always obvious conflict of interests. As a child's pile of blocks falls to its equilibrium position when the table on which it stands is moved, so a movement of economic conditions tends to upset quasi-monopolistic schemes for staying above the point E. For two independent merchants to come to an agreement of any sort is notoriously difficult, but when the agreement must be made all over again at frequent intervals, when each has an incentive for breaking it, and when it is frowned upon by public opinion and must be secret and perhaps illegal, then the pact is not likely to be very durable. The difficulties are, of course, more marked if the competitors are more numerous, but they decidedly are present when there are only two.

The details of the interaction of the prices and sales will, of course, vary widely in different cases. Much will depend upon such market conditions as the degree of secrecy which can be maintained, the degree of possible discrimination among customers, the force of habit and character as affecting the reliance which each competitor feels he can put in the promises of the other, the frequency with which it is feasible to change a price or a rate of production, the relative value to the entrepreneur of immediate and remote profits, and so on. But always there is an insecurity at any point other than the point E which represents equilibrium. Without some agreement, express or tacit, the value of p_1 will be less than or equal to the abscissa of K in Fig. 2; and in the absence of a willingness on the part of one of the competitors to forgo immediate profits in order to maintain prices, the prices will become the co-ordinates of E.

One important item should be noticed. The prices may be maintained in a somewhat insecure way *above* their equilibrium values but will never remain *below* them. For if either A or B has a price which is less than that satisfying the simultaneous equations it will pay him *at once* to raise it. This is evident from the figure. Strikingly in contrast with the situation pictured by Bertrand, where prices were for ever being cut below their calculated values, the stabilising effect of the intermediate customers who shift their purchases gradually with changing prices makes itself felt in the existence of a pair of minimum prices. For a prudent investor the difference is all-important.

It is, of course, possible that A, feeling stronger than his opponent and desiring to get rid of him once for all, may reduce his price so far that B will give up the struggle and retire from the business. But during the continuance of this sort of price war A's income will be curtailed more than B's. In any case its possibility does not affect the argument that there is stability, since stability is by definition merely the tendency to return after *small* displacements. A box standing on end is in stable equilibrium, even though it can be tipped over.

II

Having found a solution and acquired some confidence in it, we push the analysis further and draw a number of inferences regarding a competitive situation.

When the values of the p's and q's obtained on p. 46 are substituted in the previously found expressions for the profits we have

$$\pi_1 = \frac{c}{2}\Big(l + \frac{a - b}{3}\Big)^2, \quad \pi_2 = \frac{c}{2}\Big(l - \frac{a - b}{3}\Big)^2.$$

The profits as well as the prices depend directly upon c, the unit cost of transportation. These particular merchants would do well, instead of organising improvement clubs and booster associations to better the roads, to make transportation as difficult as possible. Still better would be their situation if they could obtain a protective tariff to hinder the transportation of their commodity between them. Of course they will not want to impede the transportation of the supplies which come to them; the object of each is merely to attain something approaching a monopoly.

Another observation on the situation is that incomes exist which do not fall strictly within any of the commonly recognised categories. The quantities π_1 and π_2 just determined may be classified as monopoly profits, but only if we are ready to extend the term " monopoly " to include such cases as have been considered, involving the most outright competition for the marginal customer but without discrimination in his favour, and with no sort of open or tacit agreement between the sellers. These profits certainly do not consist of wages, interest or rent, since we have assumed no cost of production. This condition of no cost is not essential to the existence of such profits. If a constant cost of production per unit had been introduced into the calculations above, it would simply have been added to the prices without affecting the profits. Fixed overhead charges are to be subtracted from π_1 and π_2, but may leave a substantial residuum. These gains are not compensation for risk, since they represent a minimum return. They do not belong to the generalised type of " rent," which consists of the advantage of a producer over the marginal producer, since each makes a profit, and since, moreover, we may suppose a and b equal so as to make the situation symmetrical. Indeed π_1 and π_2 represent a special though common sort of profit which results from the fact that the number of sellers is finite. If there are three or more sellers, income of this kind will still exist, but as the number increases it will decline, to be replaced by generalised " rent " for the better-placed producers and poverty for the less fortunate. The number of sellers may be thought of as increasing as a result of a gradual increase in the number of buyers. Profits of the type we have described will exist at all stages of growth excepting those at which a new seller is just entering the field.

As a further problem, suppose that A's location has been fixed but that B is free to choose his place of business. Where will he set up shop? Evidently he will choose b so as to make

$$\pi_2 = \frac{c}{2}\left(l + \frac{b-a}{3}\right)^2$$

as large as possible. This value of b cannot be found by differentiation, as the value thus determined exceeds l and, besides, yields a minimum for π_2 instead of a maximum. But for all smaller values of b, and so for all values of b within the conditions of the problem, π_2 increases with b. Consequently B will seek to make b as large as possible. This means that he will come just as close to A as other conditions permit. Naturally, if A is not exactly in the centre of the line, B will choose the side of A towards the more extensive section of the market, making b greater than a.[1]

[1] The conclusion that B will tend to gravitate *infinitesimally* close to A requires a slight modification in the particular case before us, but not in general. In the footnote on p. 48 it was seen that when A and B are sufficiently close together, the analytic expressions for the prices, and consequently the profits,

This gravitation of B towards A increases B's profit at the expense of A. Indeed, as appears from the expressions on p. 46, if b increases so that B approaches A, both q_2 and p_2 increase while q_1 and p_1 diminish. From B's standpoint the sharper competition with A due to proximity is offset by the greater body of buyers with whom he has an advantage. But the danger that the system will be overturned by the elimination of one competitor is increased. The intermediate segment of the market acts as a cushion as well as a bone of contention ; when it disappears we have Cournot's case, and Bertrand's objection applies. Or, returning to the analogy of the box in stable equilibrium though standing on end, the approach of B to A corresponds to a diminution in size of the end of the box.

It has become common for real-estate subdividers in the United States to impose restrictions which tend more or less to fix the character of future businesses in particular locations. Now we find from the calculations above that the total profits of A and B amount to

$$\pi_1 + \pi_2 = c\left[l^2 + \left(\frac{a-b}{3}\right)^2 \right].$$

Thus a landlord or realtor who can determine the location of future stores, expecting to absorb their profits in the sales value of the land, has a motive for making the situation as unsymmetrical as possible; for, the more the lack of symmetry, the greater is $(a - b)^2$, which appears in the expression above for $\pi_1 + \pi_2$.

Our example has also an application to the question of capitalism *v.* socialism, and contributes an argument to the socialist side. Let us consider the efficiency of our pair of merchants in serving the public by calculating the total of transportation charges paid by consumers. These charges for the strip of length a amount to $c\int_0^a t\,dt$, or $\frac{1}{2}ca^2$. Altogether the sum is

$$\tfrac{1}{2}c(a^2 + b^2 + x^2 + y^2).$$

are different. By a simple algebraic calculation which will not here be reproduced it is found that B's profits π_2 will increase as B moves from the centre towards A, only if the distance between them is more than four-fifths of the distance from A to the centre. If B approaches more closely his profit is given by $\pi_2 = bc(3l - a - 3b)$, and diminishes with increasing b. This optimum distance from A is, however, an adventitious feature of our problem resulting from a discontinuity which is necessary for simplicity. In general we should consider q_1 and q_2 as continuous functions of p_1 and p_2, instead of supposing, as here, that as $p_2 - p_1$ falls below a certain limit, a great mass of buyers shift suddenly from B to A.

Now if the places of business are both fixed, the quantities a, b and $x + y$ are all determined. The minimum total cost for transportation will be achieved if, for the given value of $x + y$, the expression $x^2 + y^2$ is a minimum. This will be the case if x and y are equal.

But x and y will not be equal unless the prices p_1 and p_2 are equal, and under competition this is not likely to be the case. If we bar the improbable case of A and B having taken up symmetrical positions on the line, the prices which will result from each seeking his own gain have been seen to be different. If the segment a in which A has a clear advantage is greater than b, then A's price will be greater than B's. Consequently some buyers will ship their purchases from B's store, though they are closer to A's, and socially it would be more economical for them to buy from A. If the stores were conducted for public service rather than for profit their prices would be identical in spite of the asymmetry of demand.

If the stores be thought of as movable, the wastefulness of private profit-seeking management becomes even more striking. There are now four variables, a, b, x and y, instead of two. Their sum is the fixed length l, and to minimise the social cost of transportation found above we must make the sum of their squares as small as possible. As before, the variables must be equal. This requires A and B to occupy symmetrical positions at the quartiles of the market. But instead of doing so they crowd together as closely as possible. Even if A, the first in the field, should settle at one of these points, we have seen that B upon his arrival will not go to the other, but will fix upon a location between A and the centre and as near A as possible.[1] Thus some customers will have to transport their goods a distance of more than $\frac{1}{2}l$, whereas with two stores run in the public interest no shipment should be for a greater distance than $\frac{1}{4}l$.

If a third seller C appears, his desire for as large a market as possible will prompt him likewise to take up a position close to A or B, but not between them. By an argument similar to that just used, it may be shown that regard only for the public interest would require A, B and C each to occupy one of the points at distances one-sixth, one-half and five-sixths of the way from one end of the line to the other. As more and more sellers of the same commodity arise, the tendency is not to become distributed in the socially optimum manner but to cluster unduly.

The importance and variety of such agglomerative tendencies

[1] With the unimportant qualification mentioned in the footnote on p. 48.

become apparent when it is remembered that distance, as we have used it for illustration, is only a figurative term for a great congeries of qualities. Instead of sellers of an identical commodity separated geographically we might have considered two competing cider merchants side by side, one selling a sweeter liquid than the other. If the consumers of cider be thought of as varying by infinitesimal degrees in the sourness they desire, we have much the same situation as before. The measure of sourness now replaces distance, while instead of transportation costs there are the degrees of disutility resulting from a consumer getting cider more or less different from what he wants. The foregoing considerations apply, particularly the conclusion that competing sellers tend to become too much alike.

The mathematical analysis thus leads to an observation of wide generality. Buyers are confronted everywhere with an excessive sameness. When a new merchant or manufacturer sets up shop he must not produce something exactly like what is already on the market or he will risk a price war of the type discussed by Bertrand in connection with Cournot's mineral springs. But there is an incentive to make the new product very much like the old, applying some slight change which will seem an improvement to as many buyers as possible without ever going far in this direction. The tremendous standardisation of our furniture, our houses, our clothing, our automobiles and our education are due in part to the economies of large-scale production, in part to fashion and imitation. But over and above these forces is the effect we have been discussing, the tendency to make only slight deviations in order to have for the new commodity as many buyers of the old as possible, to get, so to speak, *between* one's competitors and a mass of customers.

So general is this tendency that it appears in the most diverse fields of competitive activity, even quite apart from what is called economic life. In politics it is strikingly exemplified. The competition for votes between the Republican and Democratic parties does not lead to a clear drawing of issues, an adoption of two strongly contrasted positions between which the voter may choose. Instead, each party strives to make its platform as much like the other's as possible. Any radical departure would lose many votes, even though it might lead to stronger commendation of the party by some who would vote for it anyhow. Each candidate " pussyfoots," replies ambiguously to questions, refuses to take a definite stand in any controversy for fear of losing votes. Real differences, if they ever exist, fade gradually with time though the issues may be as important as ever.   The Democratic party, once opposed to protective tariffs, moves gradually to a position almost, but not quite, identical with that of the Republicans.   It need have no fear of fanatical free-traders, since they will still prefer it to the Republican party, and its advocacy of a continued high tariff will bring it the money and votes of some intermediate groups.

The reasoning, of course, requires modification when applied to the varied conditions of actual life.   Our example might have been more complicated.   Instead of a uniform distribution of customers along a line we might have assumed a varying density, but with no essential change in conclusions.   Instead of a linear market we might suppose the buyers spread out on a plane.   Then the customers from one region will patronise A, those from another B.   The boundary between the two regions is the locus of points for which the difference of transportation costs from the two shops equals the difference of prices, *i.e.* for which the delivered price is the same whether the goods are bought from A or from B.   If transportation is in straight lines (perhaps by aeroplane) at a cost proportional to the distance, the boundary will be a hyperbola, since a hyperbola is the locus of points such that the difference of distances from the foci is constant.   If there are three or more sellers, their regions will be separated from each other by arcs of hyperbolas.   If the transportation is not in straight lines, or if its cost is given by such a complicated function as a railroad freight schedule, the boundaries will be of another kind; but we might generalise the term hyperbola (as is done in the differential geometry of curved surfaces) to include these curves also.

The number of dimensions of our picture is increased to three or more when we represent geometrically such characters as sweetness of cider, and instead of transportation costs consider more generally the decrement of utility resulting from the actual commodity being in a different place and condition than the buyer would prefer.   Each homogeneous commodity or service or entrepreneur in a competing system can be thought of as a point serving a region separated from other such regions by portions of generalised hyperboloids.   The density of demand in this space is in general not uniform, and is restricted to a finite region.   It is not necessary that each point representing a service or commodity shall be under the control of a different entrepreneur from every other.   On the other hand, everyone who sells an article in different places or who sells different articles in the same place may be said to control the prices at several points of the symbolic space. The mutual gravitation will now take the form of a tendency of the outermost entrepreneurs to approach the cluster.

Two further modifications are important. One arises when it is possible to discriminate among customers, or to sell goods at a delivered price instead of a fixed price at store or factory plus transportation. In such cases, even without an agreement between sellers, a monopoly profit can be collected from some consumers while fierce competition is favouring others. This seems to have been the condition in the cement industry about which a controversy raged a few years ago, and was certainly involved in the railroad rebate scandals.

The other important modification has to do with the elasticity of demand. The problem of the two merchants on a linear market might be varied by supposing that each consumer buys an amount of the commodity in question which depends on the delivered price. If one tries a particular demand function the mathematical complications will now be considerable, but for the most general problems elasticity must be assumed. The difficulty as to whether prices or quantities should be used as independent variables can now be cleared up. This question has troubled many readers of Cournot. The answer is that either set of variables may be used; that the q's may be expressed in terms of the p's, and the p's in terms of the q's. This was not possible in Cournot's example of duopoly, nor heretofore in ours. The sum of our q's was constrained to have the fixed value l, so that they could not be independent, but when the demand is made elastic the constraint vanishes.

With elastic demand the observations we have made on the solution will still for the most part be qualitatively true; but the tendency for B to establish his business excessively close to A will be less marked. The increment in B's sales to his more remote customers when he moves nearer them may be more than compensation to him for abandoning some of his nearer business to A. In this case B will definitely and apart from extraneous circumstances choose a location at some distance from A. But he will not go as far from A as the public welfare would require. The tempting intermediate market will still have an influence.

In the more general problem in which the commodities purveyed differ in many dimensions the situation is the same. The elasticity of demand of particular groups does mitigate the tendency to excessive similarity of competing commodities, but not enough. It leads some factories to make cheap shoes for the poor and others to make expensive shoes for the rich, but all the shoes are too much alike. Our cities become uneconomically large and the business districts within them are too concentrated. Methodist and Presbyterian churches are too much alike; cider is too homogeneous.

HAROLD HOTELLING

Stanford University,
California.

[28]

Econometrica, Vol. 53, No. 4 (July, 1985)

THE PRINCIPLE OF MINIMUM DIFFERENTIATION HOLDS UNDER SUFFICIENT HETEROGENEITY

By A. de Palma, V. Ginsburgh, Y. Y. Papageorgiou,
and J.-F. Thisse[1]

The so-called Principle of Minimum Differentiation, stated by Hotelling, has been challenged by many authors. This paper restores the Principle by showing that *n* firms locate at the center of the market and charge prices higher than the marginal cost of production when heterogeneity in consumers' tastes is "large enough."

1. INTRODUCTION

It was Hotelling's [12] belief, subsequently shared by many others, that competition between two sellers of an homogeneous product leads to their agglomeration at the center of a linear, bounded market. The underlying idea is that any firm would gain, through an increase of its market share, by establishing close to its competitor on the larger side of the market. This apparently reasonable process was shown to be invalid by Lerner and Singer [15] in the case of three firms. Indeed, given two firms at the center of the market, the third will locate immediately outside either. The firm squeezed between the other two, in turn, will experience a vanishing market. Consequently, it will itself move immediately outside either, thus generating instability. Furthermore, whenever price is a decision variable, Hotelling's prediction does not hold even in the case of two firms (d'Aspremont, Gabszewicz, and Thisse [5]). When both firms locate together, price competition à la Bertrand drives down to zero equilibrium prices, hence profits. Thus firms have an advantage to spatially differentiate so as to enjoy the benefits of a local monopoly. All this destroys the so-called Principle of Minimum Differentiation.[2]

We reformulate here the Hotelling problem and show that the Principle is restored when *products and consumers are sufficiently heterogeneous*. More precisely, we recognize that (1) inherent characteristics of firms cause differentiation in their products, (2) consumers have specific preferences for these products, and (3) firms cannot determine a priori differences in consumers' tastes. At the individual level, since now firms cannot predict with certainty the decision of a particular consumer, they endow him with a probabilistic choice rule. At the aggregate level, it is assumed that the probability functions predict the actual frequencies perfectly well. This approach agrees with recent advances in discrete choice theory, which are especially relevant to choices involving location and quality.[3] Introducing therefore random behavior in the theory of spatial competi-

---

[1] The author would like to thank J. Jaskold Gabszewicz, W. B. MacLeod, C. Manski, J. Sutton, the participants of the Microeconomic Workshop at Queen's University, and two referees for their comments.

[2] For a detailed discussion of Hotelling and his successors, see Graitson [11].

[3] General references to discrete choice theory include Luce [17], Manski and McFadden [18], McFadden [19], and Tversky [25]. Examples of locational choice include Carlton [1] and Leonardi [14]. Examples of quality choice include Shocker and Srinivasan [23] and Urban and Hauser [26].

tion seems natural. Although a large number of models are available as alternative representations of such behavior, only a few have been found useful in applications. Of these, we retain the logit model since it admits simple expressions. In consequence, individual demands are smoothly distributed between firms which, in turn, give rise to overlapping market areas supported by casual experience. Building the demand system from these individual demands, it is shown that the Principle holds when the degree of heterogeneity is sufficiently large.

Spatial competition theory with homogeneous products and consumers displays several examples of nonexistence of equilibrium (see e.g. d'Aspremont, Gabszewicz and Thisse [4], Eaton and Lipsey [7], Economides [8]). This has led some to introduce mixed strategies to re-establish existence (Dasgupta and Maskin [2], Shaked [22]). However, Gal-Or [9] has shown that mixed strategies in the Hotelling model are not sufficient to ascertain the Principle of Minimum Differentiation. By contrast, our approach permits restoration of both the existence property and the Principle within a more natural framework to the extent that, intuitively, mixed strategies do not have sufficient predictive power to account for most locational decisions.[4]

Our paper is organized as follows. In Section 2, the model is described and illustrated for two firms competing in location. Instead of patronizing a single firm, as under homogeneity, consumers now distribute their purchases between firms according to a probability rule which appears to fit observed shopping behavior. Section 3 is devoted to the model of spatial competition between n firms when prices are parametric and uniform. It is shown that firms do agglomerate at the center of the market when the variation in tastes is sufficiently large. In this result, we observe that the likelihood of a central agglomeration decreases for higher average transportation costs and more firms. Section 4 deals with price competition between identically located firms. By contrast with the Bertrand case, equilibrium prices are shown to be strictly positive and proportional to the degree of heterogeneity. Competition in both location and price is handled in Section 5, where the results of Sections 3 and 4 are extended. Finally, Section 6 displays conclusions and possible extensions.

2. THE LOCATION MODEL FOR TWO FIRMS

2.1. The space X is the interval $[0, l]$. Locations and distances from the origin are identically denoted by $x \in X$.

ASSUMPTION 1: *Every unit interval in X generates a unit demand for a given product.*

There are two firms. Firm 1 locates at x_1 and firm 2 at x_2, where $x_1 \leq x_2$. The sub-intervals $[0, x_1]$, $[x_1, x_2]$, $[x_2, l]$ are named regions 1, 2, and 3 respectively.

---

[4] Probabilistic models have similarly proved useful in restoring transitivity of the majority rule (Denzau and Kats [6]), and in establishing the existence of equilibrium under variable returns to scale (Miyao and Shapiro [20]).

ASSUMPTION 2: *The product is produced at no cost and is sold at a given price p by firms.*

Following Hotelling, it is common practice in the theory of spatial competition to represent the (indirect) utility of a consumer located at x and purchasing from firm i as $v_i[x] = a - p - c|x - x_i|$, where a is the valuation of the product and c the transportation rate (recall that each consumer buys one unit of the product). That the valuation is invariant over products and consumers reflects the hypothesis of *homogeneity* made by Hotelling and his successors.

In this paper, the point is made that both products and consumers are *heterogeneous*. Products are differentiated by inherent attributes of firms, and consumers are endowed with specific tastes about these attributes. This implies that each consumer now possesses a system of different valuations which are not observable a priori. Hence firms cannot predict with certainty the behavior of a *particular* consumer. In other words, the utility of a consumer located at x and purchasing from firm i can be determined up to a probability distribution as

(1) $u_i[x] = v_i[x] + \mu \varepsilon_i,$

where ε_i is a random variable with zero mean and unit variance, and μ is a positive constant. It is perhaps worth noticing, at this stage, that the utility of a particular consumer is treated as a random variable in order to account for a lack of information on the part of firms regarding the tastes of that consumer, and not (necessarily) in order to reflect a lack of rationality in his behavior.

We now assume that the variations in valuations can be captured by choosing an appropriate distribution for ε_i. In consequence, firms can predict *aggregate* consumer behavior perfectly. Since firms do not price-discriminate, such knowledge is sufficient to determine their policy.

Given that consumers maximize utility, the probability $P_i[x]$ that a consumer located at x will purchase the product from firm i is defined by $\Pr(u_i[x] \geq u_j[x]; i \neq j)$. To obtain some simple expression for $P_i[x]$, we suppose, following McFadden and others (see Manski and McFadden [18]), that the ε_i terms in (1) are identically, independently Weibull-distributed. Accordingly, $P_i[x]$ is given by the logit model:

ASSUMPTION 3:

$$P_i[x] = \frac{e^{(a-p-c|x-x_i|)/\mu}}{\sum\limits_{j=1}^{2} e^{(a-p-c|x-x_j|)/\mu}}.$$

In our model, the value of μ reflects the degree of heterogeneity in consumer tastes: the larger the latter, the larger the former. From now on we concentrate on firm 1.

2.2. Using Assumption 3, the probability of purchasing from firm 1 is

(2) $P_1^1 = \dfrac{1}{1+H},$ $P_1^2 = \dfrac{1}{1 + e^{-(c/\mu)(\delta + 2(x_1 - x))}},$ $P_1^3 = \dfrac{1}{1+K}$

770   A. DE PALMA, V. GINSBURGH, Y. Y. PAPAGEORGIOU, AND J.-F. THISSE

for a consumer in region 1, 2, and 3 respectively, where $\delta \equiv |x_1 - x_2|$ is the distance separating the two firms, $H \equiv \exp(-c\delta/\mu)$, and $K \equiv \exp(c\delta/\mu)$.

Using (2), the probability of purchasing from firm 1 is constant over the regions 1 and 3 and monotonic over region 2. Furthermore $P_1^3 = 1 - P_1^1 = P_2^1$. Finally

(3) $\dfrac{\partial}{\partial x} P_1^2 < 0$ and $\text{sign} \dfrac{\partial^2}{\partial x^2} P_1^2 = \text{sign} \left(e^{-(c/\mu)(\delta + 2(x_1 - x))} - 1 \right).$

The inflexion point of P_1^2 is at

(4) $\bar{x} = x_1 + \dfrac{\delta}{2}.$

Thus if $x_1 < x < x_1 + \delta/2$, then P_1^2 is strictly concave and if $x_1 + \delta/2 < x < x_2$ it is strictly convex.

Consider Figure 1. The origin of the graph associated with P_1 is on the SW corner and the origin of the graph associated with P_2 is on the NE corner. It can be seen that each probability function is derived from the other as a composition of two reflections, one around the vertical axis passing through $\bar{x}$ (which corresponds to exchanging names) and another around the horizontal axis passing through $1/2$ (which corresponds to $P_1 + P_2 = 1$). Hence the two shaded areas are the same. This type of symmetry is justified because any two consumers symmetrically located relative to $\bar{x}$ face the same distribution of distances from firms, the only difference being the exchange of names between firms. The invariance of probabilities in regions 1 and 3 is a direct consequence of the assumptions that transportation cost is linear in distance and that utility is linear in transportation cost. More generally, the spatial structure of P_1 is consistent with the "law of intervening opportunities" (Stouffer [24]): the probability of purchasing from a firm is high where one necessarily encounters that firm *before* any other, and low where one necessarily encounters that firm *after* another. This, for firm 1, refers

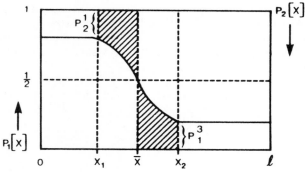

FIGURE 1.

MINIMUM DIFFERENTIATION   771

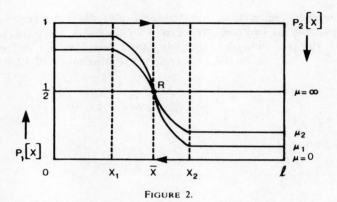

FIGURE 2.

to regions 1 and 3 respectively. Probabilities in region 2 on the other hand, where no intervening opportunities exist, are determined by the distance from the two competing firms in a way which agrees with experience (Golledge [10]).

Using (2)

(5) $\dfrac{\partial}{\partial \mu} P_1[x] \lessgtr 0$ for $x \lesseqqgtr \bar{x}.$

Symmetry and (5) imply that $P_1 = \tfrac{1}{2}$ at the midpoint between x_1 and x_2 which, here, is also the inflexion point $\bar{x}$. This, in turn, defines the areas of dominance for the two firms, i.e. the areas over which the probability of patronizing a firm is higher than that of the other. Furthermore

(6) $\displaystyle \lim_{\mu \to 0} P_1[x] = \begin{cases} 1 & \text{for } x < \bar{x}, \\ 0 & \text{for } x > \bar{x}, \end{cases}$

(7) $\displaystyle \lim_{\mu \to \infty} P_1[x] = \tfrac{1}{2}$ for $x \in X.$

An intuitive explanation of (6) and (7) is that, as μ approaches zero, costs (including transportation costs) become an increasingly important determinant of utility relative to the differentiated product characteristics. The opposite happens when μ approaches infinity. These results are summarized in Figure 2 where $0 < \mu_1 < \mu_2 < \infty$.

2.3. Without loss of generality, let $p = 1$. Using Assumptions 1 and 2, and (2), the *profit* of firm 1 is

(8) $\pi_1 = \pi_1^1 + \pi_1^2 + \pi_1^3 = \displaystyle\int_0^{x_1} P_1^1[x]\, dx + \int_{x_1}^{x_2} P_1^2[x]\, dx + \int_{x_2}^{l} P_1^3[x]\, dx$

$$= \frac{x_1}{1 + H} + \frac{\delta}{2} + \frac{l - x_2}{1 + K}.$$

It is worth noticing that π_1 is now a continuous function of x_1 over X as long as $\mu > 0$. In other words, *heterogeneity eliminates discontinuities in the profit function.* This is to be contrasted with the homogeneity case in which discontinuities arise when firms cross each other. Moreover, in Figure 2, increasing μ favors firm 1. This remains true as long as firm 2 is more centrally located because the profit loss of firm 1 in region 1 due to increasing μ is more than compensated by the corresponding gain in region 3. As the degree of heterogeneity becomes arbitrarily large, the profit of firm 1 approaches $l/2$ from below. On the other hand, since differences in profits are generated only within the regions of intervening opportunities 1 and 3, $\pi_2 - \pi_1$ decreases for smaller δ. At the limit, when there are no intervening opportunities left, $\pi_1 = \pi_2 = l/2$.

2.4. Consider the best location reply (BLR) of firm 1 relative to firm 2, in other words the profit-maximizing location for firm 1 given the location x_2 of firm 2. Toward this purpose, we use (8) to obtain

(9) $$\frac{\partial}{\partial x_1} \pi_1 = \frac{\mu(K - H) + 2c(l - x_1 - x_2)}{2\mu(1 + K)(1 + H)}.$$

Assume that $x_2 \geq l/2$. (The case $x_2 \leq l/2$ obtains by symmetry.) When $\mu = 0$ there is no BLR. That is, firm 1 aspires to follow as close as possible firm 2 in order to capture as much as possible of the market. But for any $x_1 < x_2$ there is a location in-between which yields a higher profit for firm 1. On the other hand, for every positive μ there is BLR, typically corresponding to a location quite distinct from x_2. The way such BLR varies can be determined as follows. Totally differentiating (9) at x_1^*, we obtain

(10) $$\frac{\partial x_1^*}{\partial x_2} > 0 \quad \text{and} \quad \frac{\partial x_1^*}{\partial \mu} < 0,$$

where x_1^* is the BLR. Furthermore, as μ varies on $]0, \infty[$, x_1^* varies on $]l/2, x_2[$; and x_1^* is a continuous, decreasing function of μ. Thus, for every $x_1 \in]l/2, x_2[$, there is a $\bar{\mu} \in]0, \infty[$ such that $x_1^*|_{\bar{\mu}} = x_1$. These results are summarized in Figure 3 which describes the BLR of firm 1 for $0 \leq x_2 \leq l$ and for $0 < \mu_1 < \mu_2 < \infty$.

3. THE LOCATION MODEL

3.1. In this section we discuss conditions under which an agglomeration of n non-cooperating firms occurs, when firms decide only upon their location. This is a special case in which prices are supposed to be given and equal (to one by normalization). Let $x_1, \ldots, x_n$ be the location of firms $1, \ldots, n$. A *Nash location equilibrium* (NLE) is an n-tuple $(x_1^*, \ldots, x_n^*)$ such that $\pi_i[x_1^*, \ldots, x_i^*, \ldots, x_n^*] \geq \pi_i[x_1^*, \ldots, x_i, \ldots, x_n^*]$ for any $x_i \in [0, l]$ and $i = 1, \ldots, n$. An *agglomerated Nash location equilibrium* (ANLE) is an NLE with $x_1^* = \cdots = x_n^*$. Thus, in the case of an ANLE, the above condition for equilibrium amounts to $\pi_i[x^*|x_j^* = x^*$ for $j = 1, \ldots, n$ and $i \neq j] \geq \pi_i[x_i|x_j^* = x^*$ for $j = 1, \ldots, n$ and $i \neq j]$ for any $x_i \in [0, l]$ and $i = 1, \ldots, n$. For our purpose it is therefore sufficient to consider the case in which one firm, say firm 1, locates at x_1 and the rest locate at x_2. Given that (1) holds for all firms, Assumption 3 is now replaced by Assumption 3':

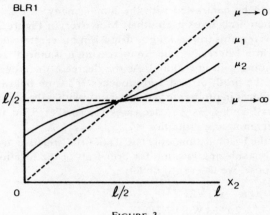

FIGURE 3.

ASSUMPTION 3′: $P_1[x] = e^{v_1[x]/\mu}/(e^{v_1[x]/\mu} + (n-1) e^{v_2[x]/\mu})$.

Using this assumption, we obtain

(11)

$$P_1^1 = \frac{1}{1+(n-1)H}, \qquad P_1^2 = \frac{1}{1+(n-1) e^{-(c/\mu)(\delta+2(x_1-x))}},$$

$$P_1^3 = \frac{1}{1+(n-1)K},$$

and, consequently, (8) becomes

(12) $$\pi_1 = \frac{x_1}{1+(n-1)H} + \delta - \frac{\mu}{2c} \ln \frac{1+(n-1)K}{1+(n-1)H} + \frac{l-x_2}{1+(n-1)K}.$$

The type of symmetry identified in Figure 2 is now lost because, for $n > 2$, x_1 and x_2 are no longer equally attractive. The general form of (4) is

(13) $$\bar{x} = x_1 + \frac{\delta}{2} - \frac{\mu}{2c} \ln (n-1).$$

The inflexion point $\bar{x}$ of P_1^2 moves along the line $P_1 = \frac{1}{2}$ toward x_1 with increasing n. As long as there is an inflexion point, it continues to partition X in two areas of dominance. For $n \geq 1 + \exp(c\delta/\mu)$, however, P_1^2 becomes strictly convex over region 2 and there is no area of dominance corresponding to firm 1, i.e., the probability of patronizing x_1 is everywhere lower than that of x_2. These results are summarized in Figure 4. Figure 5, on the other hand, illustrates variations in heterogeneity where $0 < \mu_1 < \mu_2 < \mu_3 < \infty$. The impact of increasing heterogeneity on both the inflexion point and the shape of curves in region 2 is similar to that of an increasing number of firms.

774   A. DE PALMA, V. GINSBURGH, Y. Y. PAPAGEORGIOU, AND J.-F. THISSE

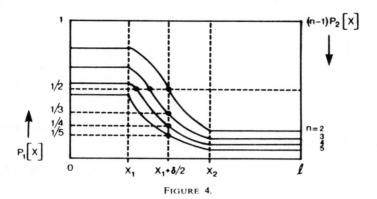

FIGURE 4.

3.2. Using (12)

(14) $$\operatorname{sign} \frac{\partial}{\partial x_1} \pi_1 = \operatorname{sign} \left(K - H - \frac{2x_1 c((n-1)+H)}{\mu(1+(n-1)H)} \right.$$
$$\left. + \frac{2(l-x_2)c((n-1)+K)}{\mu(1+(n-1)K)} \right).$$

This will serve as a basis for most arguments of the section.

PROPOSITION 1: *If μ is finite, then an ANLE can exist only at the center.*

PROOF: It suffices to establish that, for any peripheral agglomeration of n firms, a firm will benefit by moving slightly toward the center if the location of the rest is fixed. This is obvious for $\mu = 0$ where the profit of the displaced firm will change from l/n to larger than $l/2$. For $\mu > 0$, consider $n - 1$ firms at $x_2 < l/2$ and the remaining firm 1 at $x_2 + \xi$ with $\xi > 0$ and arbitrarily small. Since δ is now arbitrarily small, $H = 1 - c\xi/\mu$ and $K = 1 + c\xi/\mu$ are approximately true. Replace

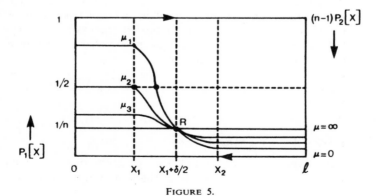

FIGURE 5.

those in (14) and take the limit as $\xi \to 0$ to obtain

(15) $\left. \text{sign} \dfrac{\partial}{\partial x_1} \pi_1 \right|_{x_2} = \text{sign} \dfrac{1}{\mu}(n-1)(l-2x_2).$

Thus, if $\mu < \infty$, the profit of a firm increases by moving slightly toward the center if the location of the rest is fixed.   *Q.E.D.*

Clearly, the agglomeration of two firms at the center is an NLE for any $\mu \geq 0$. However, we have the following proposition.

PROPOSITION 2: *For $n > 2$, if $\mu < cl(1-2/n)/2$, then there is no ANLE.*

PROOF: We shall first demonstrate that, under these circumstances, a firm will benefit by moving slightly away from the central agglomeration of n firms. For $\mu > 0$ and $n > 2$, consider $n-1$ firms at $l/2$ and the remaining firm 1 at $l/2 - \xi$. Using the approximation of H and K in Proposition 1 on (14) yields, for ξ arbitrarily small,

(16) $\left. \text{sign} \dfrac{\partial}{\partial x_1} \pi_1 \right|_{l/2-\xi} = \text{sign} \left(2 + \dfrac{cl(2-n)}{\mu n} \right).$

Hence the profit of a firm increases by moving slightly away from the central agglomeration if and only if

(17) $2 + \dfrac{cl(2-n)}{\mu n} < 0.$

The result then follows immediately from Proposition 1.   *Q.E.D.*

PROPOSITION 3: *If $\mu \geq cl(1-2/n)$, then the central agglomeration of n firms is an NLE.*

PROOF: It suffices to establish that a firm at $x_1 < l/2$ will benefit by moving slightly toward the central agglomeration of $n-1$ firms. Upon replacement of $2x_1$ with l in (14) we obtain a lower bound for the right-hand side of this expression on $[0, l/2[$. In consequence $\partial \pi_1/\partial x_1$ will be positive if that lower bound is nonnegative. This, in turn, holds if and only if

(18) $1 + (n-1)(H+K) + (n-1)^2 \geq \dfrac{cl}{\mu}(n^2 - 2n).$

Since $H + K \geq 2$,

(19) $1 + (n-1)(H+K) + (n-1)^2 \geq n^2$

for $0 \leq x_1 < l/2$. Combining (18) and (19) we conclude that if $\mu \geq cl(1-2/n)$, then the profit of a firm increases if it joins the central agglomeration.

                                                                        Q.E.D.

In order to clarify our results, assume that a firm decides to move away from the central agglomeration to establish at $x < l/2$. The firm is now closer to those located in the interval $[0, x + \delta/2]$. When tastes are similar, the firm captures almost everyone over $[0, x + \delta/2[$, but almost none over $]x + \delta/2, l]$. Consequently the firm gains from leaving its competitors. Once tastes become more heterogeneous, the firm expects to capture a smaller fraction of the customers in the first interval, but to realize more business in the second. Actually, for $\mu < cl(1 - 2/n)/2$, the gain on $[0, x + \delta/2[$ is larger than the loss on $]x + \delta/2, l]$ so that it is in the firm's interest to abandon the agglomeration. When $\mu \geq cl(1 - 2/n)$, the opposite becomes true and the central agglomeration emerges as an equilibrium. This happens because consumer's choice is now influenced more by tastes and less by the objective characteristics of firms (here delivered price). Then the best choice for firms is central agglomeration. The above necessary and sufficient conditions do not coincide. However, numerical experiments undertaken for three firms suggest that the profit function of, say, firm 1 is single-peaked at $l/2$ for $cl/6 \leq \mu < cl/3$ when firms 2 and 3 are at $l/2$. How suggestive this result is for the n-firm case remains to be seen.

In general, we do not know whether other equilibrium configurations exist. Yet, when μ is large enough, but finite, the central agglomeration can be shown to be the only possible equilibrium. This can be understood as follows. Note first that the demand addressed to a firm is elastic with respect to the location of that firm and to the location of all its competitors. As μ increases, the relative impact of competitors on demand declines, until it becomes significantly affected by that firm's location only. Under these circumstances, as suggested by Figure 3, the center becomes increasingly attractive for any locational pattern of competitors. In consequence, every peripheral firm is inevitably drawn toward the center.

4. THE PRICE MODEL

In this section we keep the location of n firms fixed at a common point and we investigate the case in which the prices are no longer given but chosen by firms. Let p_i denote the price of firm i. Since from now on p_i is a decision variable, we replace Assumption 2 with the following assumption.

ASSUMPTION 2': *The product is produced at no cost and is sold at a price p_i to be determined by firm i. Therefore, $v_i[x] = a - p_i - c|x_i - x|$.*

Changes in profits as given by (12) are easily made. Indeed using an obvious extension of Assumption 3, it follows that

$$(20) \qquad P_i = e^{-p_i/\mu} \Big/ \sum_{j=1}^{n} e^{-p_j/\mu},$$

hence that

$$(21) \qquad \pi_i = p_i l \Big/ \left(1 + e^{p_i/\mu} \sum_{j \neq i} e^{-p_j/\mu}\right).$$

Thus the profit is continuous with respect to p_i which, once more, must be contrasted with the Bertrand case where a discontinuity appears at the undercutting price.

A *Nash price equilibrium* (NPE) is an *n*-tuple $(p_1^*, \ldots, p_n^*)$ such that $\pi_i[p_1^*, \ldots, p_i^*, \ldots, p_n^*] \geqslant \pi_i[p_1^*, \ldots, p_i, \ldots, p_n^*]$ for any $p_i \geqslant 0$ and $i = 1, \ldots, n$.

PROPOSITION 4: $p_1^* = \cdots = p_n^* = p^* = \mu n/(n-1)$ *is the only NPE for an agglomeration of n firms.*

PROOF: Let $p_1 \leqslant p_2 \leqslant \cdots \leqslant p_n$. From (21)

(22) $\text{sign} \dfrac{\partial}{\partial p_1} \pi_1 = \text{sign} \left(1 - \dfrac{p_1}{\mu} \Big/ \left(1 + e^{-p_1/\mu} \Big/ \sum_{j=2}^{n} e^{-p_j/\mu} \right) \right).$

Since

(23) $e^{-p_1/\mu} \Big/ \sum_{j=2}^{n} 1^{-p_j/\mu} \geqslant \dfrac{1}{n-1},$

it follows that $\partial \pi_1/\partial p_1 > 0$ if $p_1 < \mu n/(n-1)$. Thus there can be no price lower than $\mu n/(n-1)$ at NPE. Using a similar argument on p_n we also conclude that there can be no price higher than $\mu n/(n-1)$ at NPE.   Q.E.D.

Heterogeneity in consumer's reactions slows down the undercutting of prices stressed by Bertrand in a way that market prices are stabilized at a positive, common value. The reason is that every firm faces a positive and finite elasticity over its entire demand schedule. Not surprisingly, the resulting equilibrium price depends on μ and tends to zero as we approach Bertrand.

5. THE LOCATION-PRICE MODEL

In this section we combine and extend our previous results when both location and price are decision variables. Under these circumstances a *Nash equilibrium* (NE) is an *n*-tuple $((x_1^*, p_1^*), \ldots, (x_n^*, p_n^*))$ such that

$$\pi_i[(x_1^*, p_1^*), \ldots, (x_i^*, p_i^*), \ldots, (x_n^*, p_n^*)]$$

$$\geqslant \pi_i[(x_1^*, p_1^*), \ldots, (x_i, p_i), \ldots, (x_n^*, p_n^*)]$$

for any $x_i \in [0, l]$, $p_i \geqslant 0$, and $i = 1, \ldots, n$. An *agglomerated Nash equilibrium* (ANE) is an NE with $x_1^* = \cdots = x_n^*$.

PROPOSITION 5: *If μ is finite, then an ANE can exist only at the center.*

PROOF: Using Proposition 4, $p_1^* = \cdots = p_n^* = p^*$ holds for any ANE. The claim then follows from Proposition 1 which implies that, for any peripheral agglomeration of *n* firms with prices fixed at p^*, a firm will benefit by moving slightly toward the center if the location of the rest is fixed.   Q.E.D.

When firm 1 locates at x_1 with price p_1 and the rest locate at x_2 with price p^*, the probability of purchasing from firm 1 becomes

(24)
$$P_1^1 = \frac{1}{1+(n-1)\,e^\lambda H}, \qquad P_1^2 = \frac{1}{1+(n-1)\,e^\lambda\,e^{-c/\mu(\delta+2(x_1-x))}},$$

$$P_3^1 = \frac{1}{1+(n-1)\,e^\lambda K},$$

where $\lambda = (p_1 - p^*)/\mu$. Consequently the profit function becomes

(25)
$$\pi_1 = \frac{x_1}{1+(n-1)\,e^\lambda H} + \delta - \frac{\mu}{2c}\ln\frac{1+(n-1)\,e^\lambda K}{1+(n-1)\,e^\lambda H} + \frac{l-x_2}{1+(n-1)\,e^\lambda K}$$

and

(26)
$$\operatorname{sign}\frac{\partial}{\partial x_1}\pi_1 = \operatorname{sign}\left(K - H - \frac{2x_1 c((n-1)\,e^\lambda + H)}{\mu(1+(n-1)\,e^\lambda H)}\right.$$

$$\left.+\frac{2(l-x_2)c((n-1)\,e^\lambda + K)}{\mu(1+(n-1)\,e^\lambda K)}\right).$$

PROPOSITION 6: *For $n > 2$, if $\mu < cl(1-2/n)/2$, then there is no ANE.*

PROOF: For $\mu > 0$ and $n > 2$, consider $n-1$ firms at $l/2$ with prices p^* given in Proposition 4 and the remaining firm 1 at $l/2 - \xi$ with price $p_1 > 0$. Using the approximation of H and K in Proposition 1 on (26) we obtain

(27)
$$\operatorname{sign}\frac{\partial}{\partial x_1}\pi_1 = \operatorname{sign}\left(2+\frac{cl(1-(n-1)\,e^\lambda)}{\mu(1+(n-1)\,e^\lambda)}\right).$$

Thus there is no central ANE if

(28)
$$\mu < \frac{cl}{2}\left(1-\frac{2}{1+(n-1)\,e^\lambda}\right).$$

The result then follows immediately from Proposition 5 and the observation that (28) holds for $p_1 = p^*$.   Q.E.D.

PROPOSITION 7: *If $\mu \geq cl$, then the central agglomeration of n firms with $p_1^* = \cdots = p_n^* = \mu n/(n-1)$ is an NE.*

PROOF: For $\mu > 0$, we consider once more $n-1$ firms at $l/2$ with prices p^* and the remaining firm 1 at $x_1 < l/2$ with price $p_1 \geq 0$. Upon replacement of $2x_1$ with l in (26) we obtain a lower bound analogous to that of Proposition 3, which implies that $\partial\pi_1/\partial x_1 > 0$ if and only if

(29)
$$1+(n-1)\,e^\lambda(H+K)+(n-1)^2\,e^{2\lambda} \geq \frac{cl}{\mu}((n-1)^2\,e^{2\lambda}-1).$$

Since

(30) $1+(n-1) e^{\lambda}(H+K)+(n-1)^2 e^{2\lambda} \geq (1+(n-1) e^{\lambda})^2$,

it follows that if

(31) $\mu \geq cl\left(1-\dfrac{2}{1+(n-1) e^{\lambda}}\right)$,

then the profit of firm 1 increases if it moves toward the central agglomeration. This must hold for any $p_1 \geq 0$. Once at the center, by Proposition 4, firm 1 will charge p^*.   *Q.E.D.*

Now that profits are no longer driven down to zero when firms are clustered, we may expect that the counter-argument given by d'Aspremont et al. [5] becomes irrelevant in some cases. Indeed, even though strong competition lessens the equilibrium market price under agglomeration, it may not render it low enough to overcome the advantage of higher market share at the center. This happens whenever μ is larger than cl, thus restoring Hotelling's Principle of Minimum Differentiation.

6. CONCLUSIONS

By introducing the spatial dimension, Hotelling expected to smooth market reactions to changes in the strategy of firms, hence to avoid price competition à la Bertrand. We know how discontinuities in demands destroy his reasonable hope. A lot has been subsequently written on non-existence of equilibria, existence of spatial arrangements strongly sensitive to the number of competitors, and the like. At the foundation of all this lies the sharpness of spatial behavior generated by the standard assumptions of perfect homogeneity. We believe however that the world is pervasively heterogeneous, and we have made it clear how, in a particular model, this restores smoothness. Furthermore the Hotelling conjecture has been obtained by further introducing enough heterogeneity in both firms and consumers. Here, this amounts to adding a second, non-spatial dimension which arises from differences in products and tastes. Since firms are not informed about the details of such differences, heterogeneity operates as a hidden dimension in our model. This has a deep effect on market structure because it creates some kind of sluggishness which, in turn, may stabilize competition.[5] Not surprisingly, the degree of heterogeneity required to sustain a central agglomeration increases for larger markets and higher transportation rates. This generates a trade-off leading to the clustering of firms for μ/cl relatively large and to the dispersion of firms for μ/cl relatively small.

Our study is limited in several respects. Firstly, keeping as close as possible to Hotelling, we have assumed a linear market, a uniform distribution of consumers and a perfectly inelastic individual demand. Nevertheless we hope that

---

[5] This idea is not entirely new: Dasgupta and Stiglitz [3] obtained a similar conclusion in patent race games.

the idea of heterogeneity is sufficient to render our existence results valid for some such extensions. Secondly, for a wide range of μ, we have no analytical results about the existence and nature of equilibria other than the central agglomeration. In particular, the question of dispersed equilibria remains open. Nevertheless a numerical analysis of the 3-firm case, suggests that such equilibria may exist either alone or together with an agglomerated equilibrium.

Our approach to spatial competition can be connected with some other issues in economic theory.

(1) The "Folk Theorem" for competitive markets states that if firms are small relative to the market, then the market solution is approximately competitive.[6] Here, we know that the market price prevailing in the agglomeration is greater than a strictly positive constant whatever the number of firms. To the extent that μ as a function of n does not go to zero, our analysis provides a counter-example to the Folk Theorem when firms are price-makers. Indeed, in this case, the equilibrium prices decrease but do not reach the competitive level—although at the same time the equilibrium profits converge to zero. The reason is that, under these circumstances, the products provided by the new firms are different enough from the existing ones, to preserve some monopoly power for each firm.

(2) The outcome of the Lancester [13] entry process results in a regular spacing of products over a linear space of characteristics. This is to be contrasted with the following. Assume that a clustering of products already exists at $l/2$ and consider the problem faced by new entrants. If μ remains large enough, i.e. $\mu \geq cl$, new firms will select products close to the existing ones and no firm wants to re-design its product. The entry process stops when the marginal profit net of the entry cost becomes negative. Over the spatial realm, an analogous contrast can be drawn with the Löschian [16] firm entry process.

(3) Hotelling's contribution was seminal to many other theories, including party competition and voting theory. Clearly, our approach could be extended to such topics. In particular, this could avoid the standard nonexistence outcome encountered in dealing with the n-dimensional version of the spatial competition model. Results already obtained by Wittman [27] are very promising.

Queens University,
Université Libre de Bruxelles,
McMaster University,
          and
Université Catholique de Louvain

Manuscript received July, 1983; final revision received August, 1984.

REFERENCES

[1] CARLTON, D. W.: "The Location and Employment Choices of New Firms: An Econometric Model with Discrete and Continuous Endogenous Variables," *The Review of Economics and Statistics*, 65(1983), 440–449.

[6] A rigorous proof of this result has been given by Novshek [21] when firms are quantity-setters.

[2] DASGUPTA, P., AND E. MASKIN: "The Existence of Equilibrium in Discontinuous Economic Games, 2: Applications," ICERD Discussion Paper 55, London School of Economics, 1982.
[3] DASGUPTA, P., AND J. E. STIGLITZ: "Uncertainty, Industrial Structure and the Speed of R & D," *Bell Journal of Economics*, 11(1980), 1-28.
[4] D'ASPREMONT, C., J. JASKOLD GABSZEWICZ, AND J.-F. THISSE: "On Hotelling's 'Stability in Competition'," *Econometrica*, 47(1979), 1145-1150.
[5] ——: "Product Differences and Prices," *Economics Letters*, 11(1983), 19-23.
[6] DENZAU, A. T., AND A. KATS: "Expected Plurality Voting Equilibrium and Social Choice Functions," *Review of Economic Studies*, 44(1977), 227-233.
[7] EATON, B. C., AND R. G. LIPSEY: "The Principle of Minimum Differentiation Reconsidered: Some New Developments in the Theory of Spatial Competition," *Review of Economic Studies*, 42(1975), 27-49.
[8] ECONOMIDES, N. S.: "Nash Equilibrium in Oligopolistic Competition in Prices and Varieties," Discussion Paper 150, Department of Economics, Columbia University, 1982.
[9] GAL-OR, E.: "Hotelling's Spatial Competition as a Model of Sales," *Economics Letters*, 9(1982), 1-6.
[10] GOLLEDGE, R. G.: "Conceptualizing the Market Decision Process," *Journal of Regional Science*, 7(1967), 239-258.
[11] GRAITSON, D.: "Spatial Competition à la Hotelling: A Selective Survey," *Journal of Industrial Economics*, 31(1982), 13-26.
[12] HOTELLING, H.: "Stability in Competition," *Economic Journal*, 39(1929), 41-57.
[13] LANCASTER, K.: *Variety, Equity and Efficiency.* Oxford: Basil Blackwell, 1979.
[14] LEONARDI, G.: "The Use of Random-Utility Theory in Building Location-Allocation Models," in *Locational Analysis of Public Facilities*, ed. by J.-F. Thisse and H. G. Zoller. Amsterdam: North-Holland, 1983.
[15] LERNER, A., AND H. SINGER: "Some Notes on Duopoly and Spatial Competition," *Journal of Political Economy*, 45(1937), 145-186.
[16] LÖSCH, A.: *The Economics of Location.* New Haven: Yale University Press, 1954.
[17] LUCE, R. D.: *Individual Choice Behavior.* New York: John Wiley and Sons, 1959.
[18] MANSKI, C. F., AND D. MCFADDEN: *Structural Analysis of Discrete Data with Econometric Applications.* Cambridge, Massachusetts: MIT Press, 1981.
[19] MCFADDEN, D.: "Conditional Logit Analysis of Qualitative Choice Behavior," in *Frontiers in Econometrics*, ed. by P. Zarembka. New York: Academic Press, 1973.
[20] MIYAO, T., AND P. SHAPIRO: "Discrete Choice and Variable Returns to Scale," *International Economic Review*, 22(1981), 257-273.
[21] NOVSHEK, W.: "Cournot Equilibrium with Free Entry," *Review of Economic Studies*, 47(1980), 473-486.
[22] SHAKED, A.: "Existence and Computation of Mixed Strategy Nash Equilibrium for 3-Firms Location Problem," *Journal of Industrial Economics*, 31(1982), 93-96.
[23] SHOCKER, A. D., AND V. SRINIVASAN: "A Consumer-Based Methodology for the Identification of New Product Ideas," *Management Science*, 20(1974), 921-937.
[24] STOUFFER, S. A.: "Intervening Opportunities: A Theory of Relating Mobility and Distance," *American Sociological Review*, 5(1940), 845-867.
[25] TVERSKY, A.: "Elimination by Aspects: A Theory of Choice," *Psychological Review*, 79(1972), 281-299.
[26] URBAN, G. L., AND J. R. HAUSER: *Design Marketing of New Products.* Englewood Cliffs, N.J.: Prentice-Hall, 1980.
[27] WITTMAN, D.: "Candidate Motivation: A Synthesis of Alternative Theories," *American Political Science Review*, 77(1983), 142-157.

[29]

JOURNAL OF ECONOMIC THEORY 22, 327–338 (1980)

Entry (and Exit) in a Differentiated Industry*

J. Jaskold Gabszewicz and J.-F. Thisse

Center for Operations Research & Econometrics,
Université Catholique de Louvain, Louvain-la-Neuve 1348, Belgium

Received August 6, 1979

The entry process in an industry embodying more or less close substitutes is considered. One examines whether the increase in the number of substitutes induces pure competition when prices are chosen noncooperatively. It is shown that there exists an upper bound on the number of firms which can compete in the market: when this upperbound is reached, any further entry entails the exit of an existing firm. In spite of this fact, new entries imply the decrease of prices to the competitive ones.

Since Cournot [3], there has been a long-standing tradition according to which entry into a homogeneous market, where oligopolists use quantity strategies, restores pure competition (see, for instance, [5] or [7]). Intuitively, when the number of firms increases, the ability of each oligopolist to alter the value of the inverse demand function through his own strategic choice must necessarily diminish, and vanishes at the limit. By contrast, if the firms use price strategies on the same market, it has been known since Bertrand [1] that pure competition obtains already with two firms. Clearly the loss induced by undercutting the competitor's price is broadly compensated by capturing the whole demand. With Hotelling [4] and Chamberlin [2], the idea was developed that firms operate through product differentiation in order to avoid price competition "à la Bertrand." Nevertheless, within such a context, the problem remains open whether, by analogy with the homogeneous case, the increase in the number of substitutes in the industry induces pure competition when prices are chosen noncooperatively.

In order to deal with this problem, the approach employed for the homogeneous case suggests starting out with an entry process where the entrants arrive in the industry with products which are more or less close substitutes for the existing ones, and then studying the asymptotic behavior of noncooperative prices when the number of entrants tends to infinity. It is the purpose of this article to show through an example that this procedure

* The major part of this work was done while the first author was visiting Bonn University. Financial support from the Sonderforschungsbereich 21 is gratefully acknowledged.

327

0022-0531/80/020327–12$02.00/0

cannot be transposed as such to the case of a differentiated industry with price strategies.

Our example suggests that *the number of firms which can coexist in a differentiated industry cannot exceed a finite value n** (in our example, the number n^* is determined by a set of parameters which describe our simple economy, inspired by a previous work of the authors [6]). Surprisingly, if more than n^* firms try to remain on the market, they will necessarily jostle each other, and this struggle will provoke the exit of one of them. Still more surprising is that *this upper bound on the number of firms does not preclude that entry reinforces the tendency toward pure competition.*

In fact, the entry process decomposes into three successive phases. The first one corresponds to the situation where the number of firms is such that the whole market is not supplied at the equilibrium prices. The second obtains when the whole market is served, but where room is left for the entry of some additional firms. In the third, and last, phase, the number of potential firms is larger than n^*. It will be shown that in both the first and second phases, new entries entail decreases in prices of the products already sold on the market. As for the third phase, a new entry is now necessarily accompanied by the exit of another firm. But, in spite of the fixed number of firms still allowed on the market, equilibrium prices must necessarily decrease to the competitive ones when the number of entrants increases.

Finally, it must be noted that competition can also be restored with means other than the number of firms, because product differentiation adds a new dimension to the rivalry among firms. Our example suggests that, more than from the number of firms, perfect competition could emerge from the close substitutability among the products, thus confirming the "objection péremptoire" of Bertrand against Cournot.

The authors have recently proposed a model for dealing with a situation of differentiated duopoly [6]. Its extension to an arbitrary number of firms can provide a natural framework for settling an example in which the above questions can be discussed.

Imagine an industry constituted by *n firms*, indexed by k, $k = 1,..., n$; firm k sells, at no cost, product k; all these products are more or less close substitutes for each other. Let $T = [0, 1]$ be the set of *consumers*, which are assumed to be ranked in T by order of increasing income, and let the income $R(t)$ of consumer $t \in T$ be given by

$$R(t) = R_1 + R_2 t, \qquad R_1 > 0, R_2 \geqslant 0.$$

Consumers are also assumed to make indivisible and mutually exclusive purchases. Thus if consumer t decides to buy one of the products, k, he buys that product only, and a single unit of it.

Let us denote by $u(k, R)$ the utility of having one unit of product k and an income R, and by $u(0, R)$ the utility of having no unit of any product and an income R. In our example we take the further specification[1]

$$u(k, R) = u_k \cdot R = u_1 \cdot [1 + \alpha(k - 1)] \cdot R, \qquad \alpha \geqslant 0, \qquad (1)$$

and

$$u(0, R) = u_0 \cdot R \qquad (2)$$

with $u_1 > u_0 > 0$.

In this specification, u_k is a "utility index" which ranks the quality of the products: if $k > h$, product k is more desired than product h. The parameter α is a measure of the substitutability between products k; thus, for $\alpha = 0$ all products are perfect substitutes, and substitutability decreases when α increases.

Let p_k be the price quoted by oligopolist k; product k would be bought by customer t rather than product j, $j \neq k$, if and only if

$$\begin{aligned} u(k, R(t) - p_k) = u_1 \cdot [1 + \alpha(k - 1)](R_1 + R_2 t - p_k) \\ \geqslant u_1 \cdot [1 + \alpha(j - 1)](R_1 + R_2 t - p_j) = u(j, R(t) - p_j). \end{aligned} \qquad (3)$$

To be sure that t buys product k, we must further have

$$\begin{aligned} u(k, R(t) - p_k) = u_1 \cdot [1 + \alpha(k - 1)](R_1 + R_2 t - p_k) \\ \geqslant u_0 \cdot (R_1 + R_2 t) = u(0, R(t)). \end{aligned} \qquad (4)$$

(The consumer must prefer to buy product k rather than nothing.)

In what follows we want to characterize a noncooperative price equilibrium for the above framework. By this we mean an n-tuple of prices such that no firm can increase its profit by any unilateral deviation and such that each of the n products obtains a positive market share. To this end, let us derive the contingent demand function for each oligopolist, under the assumption that each of the n firms has a positive market share. Let $M_k(\bar{p}_1, ..., p_k, ..., \bar{p}_n)$ be the *market share* of firm k defined by

$$M_k(\bar{p}_1, ..., p_k, ..., \bar{p}_n) = \{t \mid t \text{ buys product } k \text{ at prices } (\bar{p}_1, ..., p_k, ..., \bar{p}_n)\},$$

and let (t, τ) be a pair of consumers such that $t < \tau$ (which implies that t is poorer than τ). Using (1), it is easily seen that if t chooses to buy product k, then τ will not choose to buy a product $k - j$ of lower quality, with $j \in$

---

[1] Note that this formulation does not imply any restriction with respect to our analysis in [6], when $n = 2$.

$\{1,..., k - 1\}$. Similarly, again using (1), if τ chooses to buy product k, then t will not choose to buy a product $k + j$ of higher quality, with $j \in \{1,..., n-k\}$. It follows that $M_k(\bar{p}_1 ,..., p_k ,..., \bar{p}_n)$ is defined by an interval I_k of $[0, 1]$ and that the intervals I_k are ranked from the left to the right of $[0, 1]$ in an increasing order. Given our hypothesis that each consumer of brand k buys only a single unit of that product, the contingent demand function of oligopolist k is equal to the length of the interval I_k. To determine that length, it is sufficient to identify both extremities of I_k. First, let k be a product such that $1 < k < n$. The lower extremity of I_k is given by the consumer who is just indifferent between buying product k or product $k - 1$, since by assumption all the firms are on the market. Similarly the upper extremity is defined by the consumer who is just indifferent between purchasing product k or product $k + 1$. According to (3), the lower and upper extremities of I_k are consequently given by

$$t_k(\bar{p}_1 ,..., p_k ,..., \bar{p}_n) \underset{\text{def}}{=} \frac{u_k p_k - u_{k-1} p_{k-1}}{(u_k - u_{k-1}) R_2} - \frac{R_1}{R_2} \tag{5}$$

and

$$t_{k+1}(\bar{p}_1 ,..., p_k ,..., \bar{p}_n) \underset{\text{def}}{=} \frac{u_{k+1} p_{k+1} - u_k p_k}{(u_{k+1} - u_k) R_2} - \frac{R_1}{R_2}, \tag{6}$$

so that the demand function $\mu[M_k(\bar{p}_1 ,..., p_k ,..., \bar{p}_n)]$ is equal to

$$\mu[M_k(\bar{p}_1 ,..., p_k ,..., \bar{p}_n)] = t_{k+1}(\bar{p}_1 ,..., p_k ,..., \bar{p}_n) - t_k(\bar{p}_1 ,..., \bar{p}_n). \tag{7}$$

Let us now consider the case of product n. Since no brand of higher quality exists, the upper extremity of I_n is provided by the richest customer $t = 1$, so that the demand function of oligopolist n is given by

$$\mu[M_n(\bar{p}_1 ,..., \bar{p}_k ,..., p_n)] = 1 - t_n(\bar{p}_1 ,..., \bar{p}_k ,..., p_n)$$

$$= 1 - \frac{u_n p_n - u_{n-1} p_{n-1}}{(u_n - u_{n-1}) R_2} + \frac{R_1}{R_2}. \tag{8}$$

Finally let us envision the case of product 1. Since no brand of lower quality is offered and if the whole market is not served, the lower extremity of I_1 is provided by the consumer who is just indifferent between buying product 1 or buying nothing, i.e., using (4) with $k = 1$,

$$t_1(p_1 ,..., \bar{p}_k ,..., \bar{p}_n) \underset{\text{def}}{=} \frac{u_1 p_1}{(u_1 - u_0) R_2} - \frac{R_1}{R_2} ; \tag{9}$$

the demand function of oligoplist 1 is then given by

$$\mu[M_1(p_1 ,..., \bar{p}_k ,..., \bar{p}_n)] = t_2(p_1 ,..., \bar{p}_k ,..., \bar{p}_n) - t_1(p_1 ,..., \bar{p}_k ,..., \bar{p}_n). \tag{10}$$

On the other hand, if the whole market is served, the lower extremity of I_1 is defined by the poorest customer $t = 0$, so that the demand function of oligopolist 1 is then equal to

$$\mu[M_1(p_1, ..., \bar{p}_k, ..., \bar{p}_n)] = t_2(p_1, ..., \bar{p}_k, ..., \bar{p}_n). \tag{11}$$

Denote by $P_k(\bar{p}_1, ..., p_k, ..., \bar{p}_n) = p_k \cdot \mu[M_k(\bar{p}_1, ..., p_k, ..., \bar{p}_n)]$ the profit function of firm k. A *noncooperative price equilibrium* is defined as an n-tuple of prices $(p_1^*, ..., p_k^*, ..., p_n^*)$ such that no firm k can increase its profit by any unilateral deviation from p_k^* when other firms j stick to prices $p_j^*, j \neq k$, and $\mu[M_k(p_1^*, ..., p_k^*, ..., p_n^*)] > 0, \forall k = 1, ..., n.$[2]

Let us now determine the equilibrium prices, successively, when the whole market is not served ($\sum_{k=1}^{n} \mu[M_k(p_1^*, ..., p_n^*)] < 1$) and when it is entirely served ($\sum_{k=1}^{n} \mu[M_k(p_1^*, ..., p_n^*)] = 1$). In the first case, the demand functions are described by (7), (8), and (10). Assuming that there exists a noncooperative price equilibrium, the following first-order conditions must be satisfied:

$$\frac{\partial P_1}{\partial p_1}\bigg|_{(p_1^*, ..., p_n^*)} = \frac{(1 + \alpha) u_1 p_2^* - 2u_1 p_1^*}{\alpha u_1 R_2} - \frac{2u_1 p_1^*}{(u_1 - u_0) R_2} = 0,$$

$$\frac{\partial P_k}{\partial p_k}\bigg|_{(p_1^*, ..., p_n^*)} = \frac{(1 + \alpha k) u_1 p_{k+1}^* - 2[1 + \alpha(k - 1)] u_1 p_k^*}{\alpha u_1 R_2}$$
$$- \frac{2[1 + \alpha(k - 1)] u_1 p_k^* - [1 + \alpha(k - 2)] u_1 p_{k-1}^*}{\alpha u_1 R_2} = 0,$$
$$k = 2, ..., n - 1,$$

$$\frac{\partial P_n}{\partial p_n}\bigg|_{(p_1^*, ..., p_n^*)} = 1 - \frac{2[1 + \alpha(n - 1)] u_1 p_n^* - [1 + \alpha(n - 2)] u_1 p_{n-1}^*}{\alpha u_1 R_2}$$
$$+ \frac{R_1}{R_2} = 0,$$

[2] The contingent demand functions we have derived above are only valid in the restricted domains of price strategies for which all the n oligopolists obtain a positive market share. Without this assumption the possibility should indeed be recognized that, for any group of products, n-tuples of prices can be found which would cancel the demand for any product in that group. Nevertheless, it can be shown that the equilibrium prices calculated in the restricted domains are in fact equilibrium prices over the whole domains. The reason is that the profit function of each oligopolist is quasi-concave over the whole domain of its strategies, so that a local best reply is also a global one. This subject will be dealt in a forthcoming paper.

which reduce to the system of difference equations:

$$(1 + \alpha)(u_1 - u_0)\, p_2^* - 2[(u_1 - u_0) + \alpha u_1]\, p_1^* = 0,$$

$$(1 + \alpha k)\, p_{k+1}^* - 4[1 + \alpha(k - 1)]\, p_k^* + [1 + \alpha(k - 2)]\, p_{k-1}^* = 0,$$

$$k = 2,..., n - 1,$$

$$-2[1 + \alpha(n - 1)]\, p_n^* + [1 + \alpha(n - 2)]\, p_{n-1}^* = -\alpha(R_1 + R_2).$$

Using the change of variables defined by

$$x_k = [1 + \alpha(k - 1)]\, p_k^* \tag{12}$$

the above system can be rewritten as

$$(u_1 - u_0)\, x_2 - 2[(u_1 - u_0) + \alpha u_1]\, x_1 = 0,$$

$$x_{k+1} - 4x_k + x_{k-1} = 0, \qquad k = 2,..., n - 1, \tag{1}$$

$$-2x_n + x_{n-1} = -\alpha(R_1 + R_2),$$

the solution of which is

$$x_k = A_n(2 + 3^{1/2})^k + B_n(2 - 3^{1/2})^k$$

with

$$A_n = \cfrac{\alpha(2 - 3^{1/2})[3^{1/2}(u_1 - u_0) + 2\alpha u_1](R_1 + R_2)}{\left(\begin{aligned}(3u_1 - 3u_0 + 2\cdot 3^{1/2}\alpha u_1)(2 + 3^{1/2})^{n-1}\\ - (3u_1 - 3u_0 - 2\cdot 3^{1/2}\alpha u_1)(2 - 3^{1/2})^{n-1}\end{aligned}\right)}$$

and

$$B_n = \cfrac{\alpha(2 + 3^{1/2})[3^{1/2}(u_1 - u_0) - 2\alpha u_1](R_1 + R_2)}{\left(\begin{aligned}(3u_1 - 3u_0 + 2\cdot 3^{1/2}\alpha u_1)(2 + 3^{1/2})^{n-1}\\ - (3u_1 - 3u_0 - 2\cdot 3^{1/2}\alpha u_1)(2 - 3^{1/2})^{n-1}\end{aligned}\right)}.$$

Given (12), we finally obtain

$$p_k^* = \frac{1}{[1 + \alpha(k - 1)]}\, [A_n(2 + 3^{1/2})^k + B_n(2 - 3^{1/2})^k]. \tag{13}$$

These prices are only valid when the whole market is not served. In order to guarantee that this condition is satisfied, we must have, in particular, that the equilibrium price p_1^* for oligopolist 1 obtained from (13) is larger than $[(u_1 - u_0)/u_1]\, R_1$ (by (4) with $k = 1$), i.e.,

$$\frac{R_1}{R_2} < \cfrac{2u_1\alpha\, 3^{1/2}}{\left(\begin{aligned}3(u_1 - u_0)[(2 + 3^{1/2})^{n-1} - (2 - 3^{1/2})^{n-1}]\\ + 2u_1\alpha\, 3^{1/2}[(2 + 3^{1/2})^{n-1} + (2 - 3^{1/2})^{n-1} - 1]\end{aligned}\right)}. \tag{14}$$

DIFFERENTIATED INDUSTRY 333

In the case where the whole market is served, the demand functions are defined by (7), (8), and (11). Hence an interior noncooperative price equilibrium must verify the first-order conditions

$$\frac{\partial P_1}{\partial p_1}\bigg|_{(p_1^*,\ldots,p_n^*)} = \frac{(1+\alpha)\,u_1 p_2^* - 2u_1 p_1^*}{\alpha u_1 R_2} - \frac{R_1}{R_2} = 0,$$

$$\frac{\partial P_k}{\partial p_k}\bigg|_{(p_1^*,\ldots,p_n^*)} = \frac{(1+\alpha k)\,u_1 p_{k+1}^* - 2[1+\alpha(k-1)]\,u_1 p_k^*}{\alpha u_1 R_1}$$

$$- \frac{2[1+\alpha(k-1)]\,u_1 p_k^* - [1+\alpha(k-2)]\,u_1 p_{k-1}^*}{\alpha u_1 R_2} = 0,$$

$$k = 2,\ldots, n,$$

$$\frac{\partial P_n}{\partial p_n}\bigg|_{(p_1^*,\ldots,p_n^*)} = 1 - \frac{2[1+\alpha(n-1)]\,u_1 p_n^* - [1+\alpha(n-2)]\,u_1 p_{n-1}^*}{\alpha u_1 R_2}$$

$$+ \frac{R_1}{R_2} = 0,$$

which, for the change of variables (12), are equivalent to the system of difference equations

$$x_2 - 2x_1 = \alpha R_1,$$
$$x_{k+1} - 4x_k + x_{k-1} = 0, \qquad k = 2,\ldots, n-1, \qquad \{2\}$$
$$-2x_n + x_{n-1} = -\alpha(R_1 + R_2),$$

whose solution is given by

$$x_k = A_n'(2 + 3^{1/2})^k + B_n'(2 - 3^{1/2})^k$$

with

$$A_n' = \frac{(3 - 2\cdot 3^{1/2})[\alpha(2-3^{1/2})^{n-1}\,R_1 - \alpha(R_1 + R_2)]}{3[(2+3^{1/2})^{n-1} - (2-3^{1/2})^{n-1}]}$$

and

$$B_n' = \frac{(3 + 2\cdot 3^{1/2})[\alpha(2+3^{1/2})^{n-1}\,R_1 - \alpha(R_1 + R_2)]}{3[(2+3^{1/2})^{n-1} - (2-3^{1/2})^{n-1}]}$$

so that p_k^* is defined by

$$p_k^* = \frac{1}{[1+\alpha(k-1)]}\,[A_n'(2+3^{1/2})^k + B_n'(2-3^{1/2})^k]. \qquad (15)$$

These prices are only valid when the market is entirely served and when each oligopolist gets a positive market share. To this effect, the equilibrium

334   GABSZEWICZ AND THISSE

price p_1^* of oligopolist 1 given by (15) must be smaller than or equal to $[(u_1 - u_0)/u_1] R_1$, i.e.,

$$\frac{2u_1\alpha \, 3^{1/2}}{\left(\begin{array}{c}3(u_1 - u_0)[(2 + 3^{1/2})^{n-1} - (2 - 3^{1/2})^{n-1}] \\ + u_1\alpha \, 3^{1/2}[(2 + 3^{1/2})^{n-1} + (2 - 3^{1/2})^{n-1} - 2]\end{array}\right)} \leqslant \frac{R_1}{R_2} \qquad (16)$$

and $\mu[M_1(p_1^*,..., p_k^*,..., p_n^*)]$ must be positive, i.e.,

$$\frac{R_1}{R_2} < \frac{2}{(2 + 3^{1/2})^{n-1} + (2 - 3^{1/2})^{n-1} - 2} \, . \qquad (17)$$

So far, we have characterized equilibrium prices in an industry embodying n firms selling products whose respective utility indices satisfy relationship (1). Equipped with this framework, we may now study the change in prices and market shares when the number of firms increases. To proceed in that direction, we shall assume that new firms always enter the market with higher-quality products, namely, that the $(n + 1)$st firm enters the market with a utility index u_{n+1} equal to $(1 + \alpha n) u_1$.[3]

To begin with, let us assume that the starting number n of firms is such that the whole market is not served. In this case, we know that condition (14) must hold and that equilibrium prices are given by (13). Defining $\bar{n}$ as the largest integer for which condition (14) is verified, it means that $n \leqslant \bar{n}$. If a new firm enters, then either $n + 1$ is still smaller than or equal to $\bar{n}$, or $n + 1$ is greater than $\bar{n}$. In the first alternative, it is easily verified that *the "after-entry" equilibrium prices for existing firms*, still given by (13), *are smaller than the "pre-entry" equilibrium prices*. Consequently, as long as the whole market is not served, equilibrium prices form a decreasing sequence of the number of the new entrants. In the second alternative, the whole market is served. Assuming that an interior noncooperative price equilibrium is observed with $(\bar{n} + 1)$ firms (which is fulfilled if condition (16) holds for $\bar{n} + 1$), the equilibrium prices are then given by (15). Computing $\partial p_k^*/\partial n$ from (15), we obtain the result that, as soon as the whole market is served, equilibrium prices again form a decreasing sequence when the number of entrants increases.

Our major finding is that this entry process cannot allow a continuously increasing number of firms with a positive market share. Indeed, for all the firms already on the market to maintain a positive share, we know that condition (17), among others, must be satisfied. As the right-hand side of (17) is a decreasing function of n, there exists a maximal number, say n^*, of firms for

---

[3] Although the use of this particular entry process entails some loss of generality, that loss is comparable with the loss of generality which follows from assuming that all firms are identical, a hypothesis usually made in the theory of entry with homogeneous products. Moreover, analogous processes are considered in the recent literature in location theory (see, for instance, [8]).

which (17) can still hold. For $n > n^*$, the converse of (17) must be verified: income disparities, as expressed in our model by the value of R_2, are no longer sufficient to sustain an industry embodying a larger number of firms. In other words, *the income distribution determines endogenously the maximal number of products which defines the industry*. It is our belief that the number n^* can be viewed as a kind of long-run equilibrium number of firms in the sense that, when this number is reached, no room is left for a larger number of products.

Does it mean that no other firm with a higher-quality product can enter when the long-run equilibrium number n^* is reached? The answer is no. Indeed the entry of a new firm can take place, provided, however, that it is accompanied by the exit of another. Assume that a firm selling a product with utility index $u_{n^*+1} = (1 + \alpha n^*) u_1$ decides to enter. It then follows from the definition of n^* that at least one other firm must necessarily obtain a null market share at the after-entry equilibrium. In fact, it can be shown that only one firm must exit at the after-entry equilibrium and that it can be only firm 1 (see the proposition given in the Appendix). Consequently, after entry of firm $n^* + 1$, the industry again embodies n^* firms, but now with indices $\{2,..., n^* + 1\}$. More generally, the entry of firm $n^* + m$, with utility index $u_{n^*+m} = [1 + \alpha(n^* + m - 1)] u_1$, would similarly lead to an industry profile defined by the firms $\{m + 1,..., n^* + m\}$. Interestingly, *the after-entry equilibrium prices form a sequence decreasing to the competitive prices as the number m of new entrants increases*. Indeed, the equilibrium price of firm k is given by

$$ p_k^* = \frac{1}{1 + \alpha(k - 1)} \, [A_{n^*}'.(2 + 3^{1/2})^{k-m} + B_{n^*}'.(2 - 3^{1/2})^{k-m}], $$

with $k = m + 1,..., m + n^*$ (again see the proposition of the Appendix). Among other things, this result implies that we may observe low prices in an industry embodying a fixed, and possibly small, number of firms provided m is large enough.

Let us illustrate the whole process we have just described when the long-run equilibrium number n^* is equal to 2. Let firm 1 initially be a monopolist in the industry and sell a product with utility index u_1. By the choice rule (4) with $k = 1$, one easily checks that the market share $M_1(p_1)$ is defined by the interval I_1 whose lower and upper extremities are respectively given by

$$ t_1(p_1) = \text{Max} \left\{ 0, \frac{u_1 p_1}{(u_1 - u_0) R_2} - \frac{R_1}{R_2} \right\} $$

and 1. The demand function $\mu[M_1(p_1)]$ faced by firm 1 is then

$$ \text{Min} \left\{ 1, 1 - \frac{u_1 p_1}{(u_1 - u_0) R_2} + \frac{R_1}{R_2} \right\}. $$

Assuming $R_1/R_2 < 1$, a simple calculation shows that the monopoly price is equal to $\frac{1}{2}[(u_1 - u_0)/u_1](R_1 + R_2)$. Since, at this price, all the consumers are not served, room is left for entry of firm 2 with utility index $u_2 = (1 + \alpha) u_1$. Assuming also that condition (16) holds for $n = 2$, namely,

$$\frac{\alpha}{3(u_1 - u_0) + \alpha u_1} \leqslant \frac{R_1}{R_2} ,$$

we deduce from the above that the whole market is supplied at the equilibrium prices

$$p_1^* = \frac{\alpha(R_2 - R_1)}{3} \quad \text{and} \quad p_2^* = \frac{\alpha(2R_2 + R_1)}{3(1 + \alpha)} ;$$

consequently, $\bar{n} = 1.$[4] Suppose further that condition (17) is not fulfilled for $n = 3$, namely, that $\frac{1}{6} \leqslant R_1/R_2$; accordingly, $n^* = 2$. Hence under the hypothesis

$$\max \left\{ \frac{\alpha}{3(u_1 - u_0) + \alpha u_1} , \frac{1}{6} \right\} \leqslant \frac{R_1}{R_2} < 1,$$

two firms, and only two firms, may remain in the industry forever. If firm 3 with utility index $u_3 = (1 + 2\alpha) u_1$ would in turn enter the market, then a new equilibrium would emerge at which firm 1 has been enforced to exit, with prices

$$p_2^* = \frac{\alpha(R_2 - R_1)}{3(1 + \alpha)} \quad \text{and} \quad p_3^* = \frac{\alpha(2R_2 + R_1)}{3(1 + 2\alpha)} .$$[5]

It remains to study the role of substitutability among the products at the equilibrium. First note that, whatever the fixed number of products, a value of α sufficiently small exists for condition (16) to be satisfied. In this case, equilibrium prices are then given by (15). Second, these equilibrium prices form a decreasing sequence which converges to zero as the substitutability between products increases, that is, as α tends to zero. As stated above, pure competition is the limit of a process where products become more and more homogeneous. At the limit this is nothing else but the "objection péremptoire" of Bertrand against Cournot.

APPENDIX

PROPOSITION.   *Let q and m be two arbitrary integers such that $q \leqslant m + 1$ and let the firms defined by the set of indices $\{q,..., n^*,..., n^* + m\}$. A non-*

---

[4] A more extensive discussion of the market solution for $n = 2$ is contained in [6].

[5] This illustration shows that the long-run equilibrium number is not necessarily very large. A priori, to any value of n, there corresponds an income distribution which authorizes a number of firms at most equal to this value. Possibly, with a high degree of income dispersion, a large number of products will be observed.

cooperative price equilibrium involves exactly n* firms given by the set of indices $\{m + 1,..., n^* + m\}$. *Furthermore, the equilibrium price of firm* k, *with* $k = m + 1,..., n^* + m$ *is given by*

$$p_k^* = \frac{1}{1 + \alpha(k - 1)} \cdot [A'_{n^*}(2 + 3^{1/2})^{k-m} + B'_{n^*}(2 - 3^{1/2})^{k-m}]. \quad (18)$$

Proof. Assume that the firms defined by $\{q,..., n^* + m\}$ have a positive market share at the equilibrium and that the firms defined by $\{1,..., q - 1\}$ have been put out of business. In this case, the equilibrium prices must verify the following first-order conditions:

$$(1 + \alpha q) p_{q+1}^* - 2[1 + \alpha(q - 1)] p_q^* - \alpha R_1 = 0,$$

$$(1 + \alpha k) p_{k+1}^* - 4[1 + \alpha(k - 1)] p_k^* + [1 + \alpha(k - 2)] p_{k-1}^* = 0,$$

$$k = q + 1 \cdots n^* + m - 1,$$

$$\alpha(R_1 + R_2) - 2[1 + \alpha(n^* + m - 1)] p_{n^*+m}^*$$
$$+ [1 + \alpha(n^* + m - 2)] p_{n^*+m-1}^* = 0.$$

Using the change of variables defined by (12), we obtain

$$x_{q+1} - 2x_q - \alpha R_1 = 0,$$
$$x_{k+1} - 4x_k + x_{k-1} = 0, \qquad k = q + 1,..., n^* + m - 1, \qquad \{3\}$$
$$\alpha(R_1 + R_2) - 2x_{n^*+m} + x_{n^*+m-1} = 0.$$

Furthermore, setting $j = k - q + 1$ yields the system

$$x_2 - 2x_1 - \alpha R_1 = 0,$$
$$x_{j+1} - 4x_j + x_{j-1} = 0, \qquad j = 2,..., n^* + m - q, \qquad \{4\}$$
$$\alpha(R_1 + R_2) - 2x_{n^*+m-q+1} + x_{n^*+m-q} = 0.$$

This system is identical to system $\{2\}$, with $n = n^* + m - q + 1$, so that its solution is given by

$$x_j = A'_{n^*+m-q+1}(2 + 3^{1/2})^j + B'_{n^*+m-q+1}(2 - 3^{1/2})^j,$$

$$j = 1,..., n^* + m - q + 1,$$

i.e.,

$$x_k = A'_{n^*+m-q+1}(2 + 3^{1/2})^{k-q+1} + B'_{n^*+m-q+1}(2 - 3^{1/2})^{k-q+1},$$

$$k = q,..., n^* + m,$$

338   GABSZEWICZ AND THISSE

which leads to

$$p_k^* = \frac{1}{1 + \alpha(k-1)}$$
$$\cdot [A'_{n^*+m-q+1}(2 + 3^{1/2})^{k-q+1} + B'_{n^*+m-q+1}(2 - 3^{1/2})^{k-q+1}]. \quad (19)$$

By definition of a noncooperative price equilibrium, each firm must have a positive market share. In particular, this must be true for firm q, so that

$$u_{q+1} p_{q+1}^* - u_q p_q^* > \alpha R_1 .$$

The latter condition is verified if and only if condition (17) holds for $n^* + m - q + 1$, which is impossible as long as $q < m + 1$. Consequently, firm q cannot afford a positive market share. As a similar argument applies to firms $k = q + 1,..., k = m$, *exactly* n^* firms, namely, the firms defined by $\{m + 1,..., n^* + m\}$, remain on the market and the corresponding equilibrium prices are provided by (19), where $q = m + 1$, i.e., by (18).   Q.E.D.

ACKNOWLEDGMENTS

We thank J. Drèze and an anonymous referee for their helpful comments.

REFERENCES

1. J. BERTRAND, Théorie mathématique de la richesse sociale, *J. Savants* (1883), 499–508.
2. E. H. CHAMBERLIN, "The Theory of Monopolistic Competition," 7th ed., Harvard Univ. Press, Cambridge, Mass. 1956.
3. A. A. COURNOT, "Recherches sur les principes mathématiques de la théorie des richesses," Librairie des Sciences politiques et sociales, M. Rivière et Cie, Paris, 1838.
4. H. HOTELLING, Stability in competition, *Econ. J.* 39 (1929), 41–57.
5. J. JASKOLD GABSZEWICZ AND J. P. VIAL, Oligopoly "à la Cournot" in a general equilibrium analysis, *J. Econ. Theory* 4 (1972), 381–400.
6. J. JASKOLD GABSZEWICZ AND J.-F. THISSE, Price competition, quality and income disparities, *J. Econ. Theory* 20 (1979), 340–359.
7. W. NOVSHEK AND H. SONNENSCHEIN, Cournot and Walras equilibrium, *J. Econ. Theory* 19 (1978), 223–266.
8. E. C. PRESCOTT AND M. VISSCHER, Sequential location among firms with foresights, *Bell J. Econ.* 8 (1977), 378–393.

[30]

Econometrica, Vol. 51, No. 5 (September, 1983)

NATURAL OLIGOPOLIES[1]

BY AVNER SHAKED AND JOHN SUTTON[2]

In a market where firms offer products which differ in quality, an upper bound may exist to the number of firms which can coexist at a noncooperative price equilibrium. We fully characterize the conditions under which this possibility arises.

1. BACKGROUND

THE PRESENT PAPER is concerned with the analysis of price competition in markets where consumers purchase a single unit of some good, the alternative brands of which differ in quality. The defining characteristic of this kind of product differentiation is that, were any two of the goods in question offered at the same price, then all consumers would agree in choosing the same one, i.e. that of "higher quality."

Little attention has been paid to the analysis of competition in this "vertical differentiation" case, in contrast to the widely studied case of "horizontal differentiation" where the defining characteristic is that consumers would differ as to their most preferred choice if all the goods in question were offered at the same price. The standard paradigm is that of the "locational" and associated models. In such models, the number of firms in the industry increases indefinitely as the fixed costs associated with entry decline, or, equivalently, as the size of the economy expands. That this can happen, depends in turn on the fact that the market can support an arbitrarily large number of firms, each with a positive market share and a price in excess of unit variable cost. This property is of fundamental importance: for, as firms become more closely spaced, price competition between them implies that prices approach the level of unit variable costs. It is this "Chamberlinian" configuration which forms the basis of the notion of "perfect monopolistic competition." (See [5].)

The central question posed in the present paper is whether this property will be available in the "vertical differentiation" case. In a large class of cases, it turns out not to hold; in such cases, no passage to an atomistic, competitive, structure will be possible. However low the level of fixed costs, and independently of any considerations as to firms' choices of product, the nature of price competition in itself ensures that only a limited number of firms can survive at equilibrium.

[1] This paper was presented at the "Agglomeration in Space" meeting (Habay-la-Neuve, Belgium, May 1982) organized with the financial support of the Fonds National de la Recherche Scientifique of Belgium.

Our thanks are due to the International Centre for Economics and Related Disciplines at LSE for financial support.

[2] We would like to acknowledge the help of two referees, whose comments prompted a considerable improvement in the exposition of these results.

2. INTRODUCTION

We will be concerned, in what follows, with elaborating a condition which is necessary and sufficient to allow an arbitrarily large number of firms to co-exist with positive market shares, and prices exceeding unit variable costs, at a Nash equilibrium in prices. It may be helpful to begin, in the present section, by setting out this condition in a quite informal manner.

Suppose a consumer with income Y purchases *one unit* of a product of quality u, at price $p(u)$, thereby achieving a level of utility given by, say, the function

$$u \cdot (Y - p(u)).$$

Let each of a number of firms produce one product of some quality u subject to constant unit variable cost, $c(u)$. We consider a hypothetical situation in which a number of products are offered at a price equal to their respective levels of unit variable cost. (The relevance of this case lies in the fact that some firms may not be able to achieve positive sales at a price which covers variable cost, and it is this which limits the number of firms surviving at equilibrium.)

Figure 1 shows the function $uc(u)$. Take a line of slope Y_1 through the point $(u, uc(u))$. Then the vertical intercept $AB = u \cdot (Y_1 - c(u))$ represents the utility attained by a consumer of income Y_1 in purchasing a product of quality u at price $c(u)$. Again referring to the Figure, the consumer of income Y_1 is indifferent between u at price $c(u)$ and v at price $c(v)$. Finally, we illustrate the optimal quality choice for a consumer of income Y_2, who can purchase any quality at unit variable cost, as the point of tangency q (chosen to maximize the associated intercept).

We are now in a position to identify a fundamental dichotomy which forms the basis of our subsequent analysis. Let consumer incomes lie in some range $[a, b]$ and suppose unit variable cost rises only slowly with quality. Then, if two products are made available at unit variable cost, all consumers will agree in

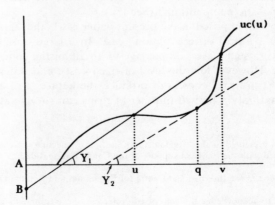

FIGURE 1.

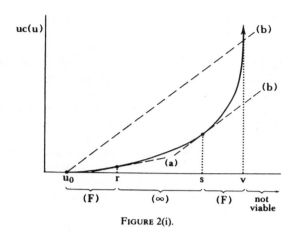

FIGURE 2(i).

preferring the higher quality product, i.e. all consumers rank the products in the same order. On the other hand, consider the cost function shown in Figure 2(i); here, we illustrate an example in which $uc(u)$ is convex, and we identify two points of tangency r and s where the slope of the curve coincides with our extreme income values a and b. Here, if any set of products lying in the interval below r is made available at unit variable cost, all consumers will agree in ranking them in increasing order of quality; and for a set of qualities drawn from the interval above s, and sold at unit variable cost, consumers will agree in ranking them in decreasing order of quality. In the intermediate quality range, however, consumers will differ in their ranking of products, at unit variable cost. Now this is reminiscent of the "location" paradigm noted above, and we shall show in the sequel that the basic property alluded to earlier continues to hold good here—an unbounded number of firms may coexist with positive market shares and prices exceeding unit variable cost, at equilibrium.

Now, in this "location-like" situation, the manner in which an arbitrarily large number of firms may be entered, is straightforward: for, within a certain interval, we can always insert an additional firm (product) *between* two existing firms, without precipitating the exit of any other firm.

A second, and quite distinct, kind of situation may arise, however, which is also consistent with the coexistence of an unbounded number of competing firms. While many subcases of this possibility arise, all are quite analogous, and a clear illustration of the mechanism involved is provided by the following example. Suppose costs were zero; and suppose further that the range of incomes extends downwards to zero. In this case, an unbounded number of products may be entered: for no product can have zero profits at equilibrium unless some higher quality product sells for price zero (remember the consumer of income zero is indifferent between all products at price zero, so any product can otherwise find some positive price at which it can earn positive profits). But it now suffices to notice that the highest quality product in the sequence will *not* be sold at price zero; for clearly there exists some price at which it can earn positive profits.

Hence in this situation, an infinite number of products may again be entered—but now, the method by which they are entered is by introducing new products of successively lower quality at the end of the existing range.

What characterizes this situation, and all analogous subcases, is the presence of a consumer—here the consumer of income zero—who is (locally) indifferent between alternative products, at unit variable cost (i.e. the derivative of his utility score with respect to product quality is zero).

The condition which we develop below is designed to exclude these two types of situation. Where that condition is satisfied, all consumers will be agreed in ranking the products in the same strict order, at unit variable cost. When this is so, it follows that one firm could set a price which would drive the remaining firms out of the market. This will not in general occur at equilibrium, however. (For an elementary example, see [4].) What we show is that, in this case, *there will exist an upper bound independent of product qualities, to the number of firms which can coexist with positive market shares and prices exceeding unit variable costs, at a Nash Equilibrium in prices.*

It is worth stressing immediately that this property is extremely strong: the bound we define depends only on the pattern of tastes and income distribution and is independent of the qualities of the various products offered.

The mechanism through which the result comes about, is that whatever the set of products entered, competition between certain "surviving" products drives their prices down to a level where every consumer prefers either to make no purchase, or to buy one of these surviving goods *at its equilibrium price*, rather than switch to any of the excluded products, *at any price sufficient to cover unit variable cost*.

The implications of this "finiteness property" are far-reaching; for, if the technology is such that unit variable cost rises only slowly with quality, so that the "finiteness property" holds everywhere, then *irrespective of the manner in which product quality is chosen by firms*, the familiar "limiting process" by which we might arrive at a competitive outcome cannot occur. The number of firms which can coexist at equilibrium is no longer limited by the level of fixed costs, as in the familiar case, but is instead determined by the upper bound which we identify below. This means, in turn, that the effect of a further reduction in fixed costs, or an increase in the extent of the market, will, once that bound is attained, have no effect on the equilibrium number of firms in the industry.

It is this configuration, in which the finiteness property holds over the relevant quality range, which we label a *natural oligopoly*.

The "finiteness" property has already been demonstrated for a special case in which all costs are zero, by Jaskold Gabszewicz and Thisse [2]. The aim of the present paper is to provide a necessary and sufficient condition for such an outcome, where costs are present.

Finally, we emphasize that we shall not be concerned here with the question of optimal quality choice by firms; the "finiteness" property is independent of such considerations. The range of qualities available on the market will, in general, of course depend *inter alia* on the relation between *fixed costs* (including R & D), and product quality. (We have elsewhere examined this problem of quality choice [7, 8, 9].) Here, however, we will take qualities as given and all such costs as sunk costs; and so we will be concerned only with variable cost.[3]

The structure of the paper is as follows. Section 3 presents the model, and in Section 4 we examine price equilibrium. In Section 5 we present a necessary and sufficient condition for "finiteness;" Section 6 is devoted to a discussion of the results.

3. THE MODEL

A number of firms produce distinct, substitute, goods. We label their respective products by an index $k = 1, \ldots, n$, where firm k sells product k at price p_k. (We take the goods to be distinct, here, since if two or more goods are identical, then all have price equal to unit variable cost, at a Nash Equilibrium in prices, by the usual Bertrand argument. The case where some firms produce an identical quality level is considered in the proof of Proposition 3 below.)

Assume a continuum of consumers identical in tastes but differing in income; incomes are uniformly distributed over some range, $0 < a \leq t \leq b$.

Consumers make indivisible and mutually exclusive purchases from among our n substitute goods, in the sense that any consumer either makes no purchase, or else buys exactly one unit from one of the n firms. We denote by $U(t, k)$ the utility achieved by consuming one unit of product k and t units of "other things" (the latter may be thought of as a Hicksian "composite commodity," measured as a continuous variable), and by $U(t, 0)$ the utility derived from consuming t units of income only.

Assume that the utility function takes the form

$$(1) \qquad U(t, k) = u_k \cdot t \qquad\qquad\qquad (k = 1, \ldots, n)$$

and

$$U(t, 0) = u_0 \cdot t$$

with $0 < u_0 < u_1 < \cdots < u_n$ (i.e. the products are labelled in increasing order of quality).

(The particular forms of the utility function, and income distribution, used here, play no crucial part in what follows. See Section 6 below.) Let

$$r_{k-1,k} = \frac{u_k}{u_k - u_{k-1}}$$

(whence $r_{k-1,k} > 1$). Then we may define the income level t_k such that a consumer with this income will be indifferent between good k at price p_k and

---

[3] Labor, materials, and divisible capital equipment. It is of course *long run* unit variable costs which are relevant.

good $k - 1$ at price p_{k-1}, by setting

$$u_{k-1} \cdot (t_k - p_{k-1}) = u_k \cdot (t_k - p_k)$$

to obtain

$$(2) \qquad t_k = p_{k-1}(1 - r_{k-1,k}) + p_k r_{k-1,k}$$

$$= p_{k-1} + (p_k - p_{k-1}) \cdot r_{k-1,k}$$

and

$$t_1 = p_1 r_{0,1} \, .$$

It is immediate from inspection of our utility function that a consumer with income above t_k will strictly prefer the higher quality good k, and conversely: the function (1) is designed to capture the property that richer consumers are willing to pay more for a higher quality product.

Given any set of prices, then, certain firms have positive market shares bounded by marginal consumers (income levels), firm k selling to consumers of income t_k to t_{k+1} (t_k to b for firm n); the market shares of the higher quality firms corresponding to higher income bands. We shall find it convenient below to identify, sometimes, the set of firms with positive market shares; it is important to remember that a firm may be "just" excluded in the sense that $t_k = t_{k-1}$ so that it has market share zero: here an infinitesimal fall in its price, or an infinitesimal rise in the price set by either of this firm's neighbors, will cause its market share to become positive.

Let $c(u)$ represent the level of unit variable cost as a function of the quality of the product; it is assumed independent of the level of output. We will assume that $c(u)$ is continuously differentiable (but see Section 6 below). We will write $c(u_k)$ as c_k in what follows.

The profit of any firm k now becomes, for $k = 1, \ldots, n - 1$,

$$\pi_k = (p_k - c_k)(t_{k+1} - t_k), \qquad p_k \geq c_k,$$

$$\pi_k = 0 \qquad\qquad\qquad\qquad \text{otherwise.}$$

From this we may deduce a necessary condition for profit maximization. For firm k we require

$$(t_{k+1} - t_k) - (p_k - c_k)(r_{k,k+1} + r_{k-1,k} - 1) \leqq 0,$$

which is the requirement that an *increase* in k's price reduces profit. The corresponding inequality required to ensure that a *reduction* in k's price reduces profits splits into a number of cases according as k's nearest neighbor from above, and/or from below, has market share zero.

NATURAL OLIGOPOLIES   1475

4. PRICE EQUILIBRIUM

We seek a noncooperative price equilibrium (Nash Equilibrium), viz.: a vector of prices $p_n^*, p_{n-1}^*, \ldots, p_1^*$, such that, for all k, given the prices set by the remaining firms, p_k^* is the profit maximizing price for firm k.

We begin by establishing the existence of such an equilibrium:

LEMMA 1: *For any given products $u_1, u_2, \ldots, u_n$ and corresponding prices p_1, $p_2, \ldots, p_{k-1}, p_{k+1}, \ldots, p_n$, for all k, the profit of the kth firm is a single peaked function of its price.*

PROOF: Note that for p_k sufficiently high the sales of firm k are zero; similarly, for $p_k = c_k$ revenue equals zero. We establish that for intermediate values of p_k, profit π_k is a single peaked function of p_k.

We note that the market share of firm k is sandwiched between that of two neighboring firms, $k - 1$ and $k + 1$. As its price falls, it will at some point squeeze out one or both of these neighboring firms, thus acquiring a new "neighbor."

Consider the function

$$\pi_k = (p_k - c_k)(t_{k+1} - t_k)$$

which is formally defined for all p_k, and which coincides with the profit of firm k over that range of p_k such that firm k has a positive market share bounded by $(k - 1)$ and $(k + 1)$. We first show that any turning point of π_k is a maximum, i.e. π_k is single peaked. For, differentiating with respect to p_k we have

(3)
$$\pi_k' = (p_k - c_k)(1 - r_{k,k+1} - r_{k-1,k}) + t_{k+1} - t_k,$$
$$\pi_k'' = 2(1 - r_{k,k+1} - r_{k-1,k}) < 0.$$

Suppose now that p_k falls so far as to drive one of its neighbors, $k - 1$ say, out of the market. Then its new neighbors are $k - 2, k + 1$. Again, the profit function $\hat{\pi}_k$ for k sandwiched between $k - 2, k + 1$, is a single peaked function of p_k. Moreover, at the price at which the market share of $k - 1$ becomes zero, i.e. $t_k = t_{k-1}$, we shall show that

$$\hat{\pi}_k' > \pi_k'$$

so that if π_k is increasing at this point then a fortiori $\hat{\pi}_k$ is increasing. From this it follows that the profit function is globally single peaked.

To show that $\hat{\pi}_k' > \pi_k'$ we compare π_k' as defined by (3) with

$$\hat{\pi}_k' = (p_k - c_k)(1 - r_{k,k+1} - r_{k-2,k}) + t_{k+1} - t_{k-2}$$

and using $t_k = t_{k-1}$, and since (by inspection of the definitions of $r_{k-1,k}$) we have $r_{k-2,k} < r_{k-1,k}$, our result follows.   *Q.E.D.*

From this we obtain the following proposition.

PROPOSITION 1: *For any set of products* $1, \ldots, n$ *a noncooperative price equilibrium* $p_1, \ldots, p_n$ *exists.*

PROOF: This follows immediately by appealing to the fact that each firm's profit function is quasi-concave by virtue of Lemma 1 [1, p. 152].   *Q.E.D.*

5. THE FINITENESS PROPERTY

We proceed by defining the following property:

DEFINITION 1: An interval $[\underline{u}, \bar{u}]$ of qualities possesses the *finiteness property* if there exists a number K such that, at any Nash equilibrium involving a number of products drawn from this interval, at most K enjoy positive market shares and prices exceeding unit variable cost.

REMARK: K will depend on the range $[a, b]$ of consumer incomes.

We note that if this property does not hold, then it follows that for all N, there exists a sequence of at least N products coexisting with positive market shares, and prices exceeding unit variable cost, at a Nash Equilibrium in prices.

We now turn to the condition required to ensure this "finiteness" property.

We begin by defining a function $t(u, v)$, which is the income level at which a consumer is indifferent between goods u and v, where both are available at unit variable cost. Setting

$$u(t - c(u)) = v(t - c(v))$$

we have

$$t(u, v) = \frac{vc(v) - uc(u)}{v - u} = c(v)r_{uv} + c(u)(1 - r_{uv})$$

where $r_{uv} = v/(v - u)$.

Consumers of income above $t(u, v)$ strictly prefer the higher quality good; and conversely.

We begin by deleting from our interval $[\underline{u}, \bar{u}]$ any products for which $t(u_0, u) > b$; such products will not be viable in that even the richest consumer will prefer to make no purchase, rather than buy such a good, even at cost. In general this deletion will leave a number of closed subintervals of quality.

We now state a condition which will be shown, in Propositions 2, 3 below, to be necessary and sufficient for the finiteness property to hold on any such subinterval, whence it follows immediately that it is necessary and sufficient for finiteness on $[\underline{u}, \bar{u}]$.

We define the function $t(u, u)$,

$$t(u, u) = \lim_{v \to u} t(u, v).$$

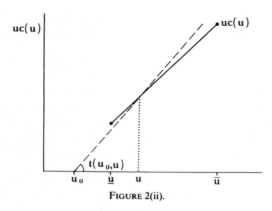

FIGURE 2(ii).

Since $c(u)$ is differentiable, and

$$t(u, u) = c(u) + uc'(u),$$

it follows that $t(u, u)$ is well defined.

Now $t(u, u)$ may be interpreted directly, as follows. If all goods are made available at unit variable cost, then a consumer of income $t(u, u)$ attains *either* a maximum, *or* a minimum, of utility, by choosing u. To see this, consider the problem

$$\max_u u(Y - c(u))$$

which leads to the first order condition (Figure 1)

$$Y = (uc(u))' = uc'(u) + c(u) = t(u, u).$$

Our condition for finiteness is that no such consumer is present; to exclude such cases we require that *either* (a) $t(u, u) \notin [a, b]$, *so that all such consumers lie outside our range of incomes*, or (b) $t(u, u) < t(u_0, u)$, *so that any such consumer strictly prefers to make no purchase, rather than buy u.* (The latter case is illustrated in Figure 2(ii).) Combining these two cases we obtain the following condition.

CONDITION (F): $t(u, u) \notin [\max(a, t(u_0, u)); b]$.

REMARK 1: Condition (F) implies that for all (u, v), $t(u, v) \notin [\max(a, t(u_0, u)); b]$.

This latter condition excludes the appearance of any consumer indifferent between two goods u and v, at unit variable cost. That it follows from (F) is immediate from inspection of Figure 1. (We might of course replace $t(u_0, u)$ here by $t(u_0, v)$, for if a consumer prefers u_0 to u, and is indifferent between u and v, he prefers u_0 to v also.)

REMARK 2: Since $t(u,v)$ is continuous, it follows that $t(u,v)$ is uniformly (in u,v) bounded away from its corresponding interval $[\max(a, t(u_0u)); b]$.

REMARK 3: We here note two cases which will be of interest below.

For any two goods u and v, with $v > u$: (i) If $t(u,v) < \max(a, t(u_0,u))$, then any consumer willing to buy u at cost (in the sense of preferring this to making no purchase) will certainly prefer to buy v rather than u, if both are made available at cost. (ii) If $t(u,v) > b$, then any consumer willing to buy v at cost, will prefer to buy u rather than v if both goods are made available at cost.

In the Introduction, we noted that there are two ways in which the "finiteness" property may fail to hold; we can now interpret the restriction imposed by Condition (F) in terms of these two possibilities.

The first way in which Condition (F) may be violated is by the appearance of some $u \in (\underline{u}, \overline{u})$, such that a consumer of some income $t \in (a,b)$ attains a *maximum* of utility by consuming u, all products being available at unit variable cost. This case violates the requirement that all consumers rank products in the same order at cost; it is analogous to the familiar "location" models, in that consumers with income above (below) t will prefer a quality above (below) u.

The remaining cases in which Condition (F) is violated are all analogous to the case noted in the Introduction, in which costs are zero, while the range of incomes extends to zero. These include the possibility that, for some $u \in (\underline{u}, \overline{u})$, a consumer of some income $t \in (a,b)$ attains a *minimum* of utility. (The analogy between this case to that in which the range of incomes extends to zero is developed in the proof of Proposition 3 below.) They also include a number of boundary cases; for example, where a consumer of income $t = a$ attains maximum utility at $u = \underline{u}$.

We now turn to our central results, showing that Condition (F) is necessary and sufficient for finiteness.

PROPOSITION 2 (Sufficiency): *Condition (F) implies the finiteness property.*

PROOF: First note, by virtue of the continuity of $t(u,v)$, and the differentiability of $c(u)$, that (F) implies that *either* $t(u,v) > b$ for all (u,v) *or* $t(u,v) < \max(a, t(u_0, u))$. (Note Remark 1 above.) In the former case, unit variable cost rises so steeply with quality that all consumers rank products (at cost) in decreasing order of quality; while in the latter case $c(u)$ is "sufficiently flat," and all consumers rank products (at cost) in increasing order of quality.

We here establish the result for the latter case; the proof for the former case being similar.

We establish the result by showing that there exists some $\epsilon > 0$ such that the market share of any good, whose price exceeds unit variable cost, is greater than ϵ.

We first note what happens if two or more goods have the same quality level. Then, by the familiar Bertrand argument, they have price equal to unit variable cost at equilibrium. Moreover, it then follows immediately from Condition (F) that all products of lower quality have a zero market share. Now if the highest quality level is offered by two or more firms, our result therefore follows. Otherwise, denote the highest quality level produced by more than one firm as u_s, where we set $u_s = u_0$ in the case where all products are distinct.

Consider any good $k, k > 1$, which has a price exceeding unit variable cost, and for which $t_k > a$. Then the first order condition for profit maximization by firm k implies

$$t_{k+1} - t_k \geq (p_k - c_k)(r_{k-1,k} + r_{k,k+1} - 1).$$

Clearly

$$t_k > \max(a, t(u_0, u_{k-1}), t(u_s, u_{k-1})) = m, \qquad \text{say.}$$

(Note $t_k > a$, and since the consumer of income t_k prefers good $k - 1$ at price $p_{k-1} \geq c_{k-1}$ to the zero good, we have $t_k > t(u_0, u_{k-1})$. Similarly, $t_k > t(u_0, u_s)$.) Hence

$$t_k = p_k r_{k-1,k} + p_{k-1}(1 - r_{k-1,k}) > m$$

or (remembering $r_{k-1,k} > 1$),

$$(p_k - c_k)r_{k-1,k} \geq m + p_{k-1}(r_{k-1,k} - 1) - c_k r_{k-1,k}$$

$$\geq m + c_{k-1}(r_{k-1,k} - 1) - c_k r_{k-1,k} = m - t(u_{k-1}, u_k).$$

But bearing in mind the first order conditions above, we have that the market share

$$(t_{k+1} - t_k) > (p_k - c_k)r_{k-1,k} \geq m - t(u_{k-1}, u_k)$$

$$> \max(a, t(u_0, u_{k-1})) - t(u_{k-1}, u_k).$$

By virtue of Remarks 1 and 2 above, this last expression is bounded away from zero, uniformly in u, from which our result follows.   *Q.E.D.*

PROPOSITION 3 (Necessity): *If Condition (F) is violated, then the finiteness property does not hold.*

PROOF: As we noted above, we may divide instances in which (F) is violated into two cases according as: (i) $t(u, u)$ maximizes his utility by choosing u (at cost) or (ii) $t(u, u)$ minimizes his utility by choosing u (at cost).

Now in both of these cases the same construction can be used to show how any number of products can be entered in the neighborhood of u; the essential property used is that there exists a consumer who is locally indifferent between a certain range of goods.

Each of these cases includes a number of subcases; we deal with one subcase, viz. $t(u, u) \in (a, b)$ and $u \in (\underline{u}, \bar{u})$ and $t(u_0, u) < t(u, u)$. The remaining "boundary" cases can be dealt with in an obvious manner.

CASE (i): Here the proof is immediate. We have some interval of qualities for which $t(q, q) \in (\max(a, t(u_0, q)), b)$ at each point q (from the differentiability of $uc(u)$ at q (Fig. 1)).

Thus each quality in this interval is preferred, at cost, to any alternative, by consumers of some income level (as in "location" models).

Hence, given any sequence of products $u_1, \ldots, u_n$ in this neighborhood, each good k certainly enjoys a positive market share at equilibrium. Thus any number of distinct products can coexist with positive market shares and prices exceeding variable cost, and the finiteness property does not hold.

CASE (ii): This case is more complicated; to show that there are n qualities which can coexist we need to choose these qualities close to u. The construction of such a set of qualities is carried out in the Appendix.

We here illustrate the intuition underlying this construction by describing a limiting case, as follows. Suppose there exists a consumer who is indifferent between an interval of qualities (i.e. $uc(u)$ is linear over this interval). Then consider any finite sequence $u_1, \ldots, u_n$ of qualities in this interval.

A product within this sequence will not be driven out of the market unless the seller of some higher quality product in the sequence sets price equal to cost. It suffices then to show that the top quality u_n is not sold at cost. But this is immediate, for this product can certainly earn positive profits by selling at a price exceeding cost.

This argument is of course analogous to that of the zero cost case, with $a = 0$, alluded to above. (As $t(u, u)$ is in the interior of the relevant interval, u_n can be sold to a richer consumer at a price above cost.)

The proof in the Appendix shows how this kind of argument extends to the case of a turning point of $uc(u)$ and thus establishes that the finiteness property does not hold.   *Q.E.D.*

6. DISCUSSION

The condition we have developed above is necessary and sufficient for the finiteness property. That condition refers to the relationship between consumers' willingness to pay for quality improvements, and the change in unit *variable* cost associated with those improvements; thus it involves the interplay of technology and tastes.

The "finiteness" condition is likely to hold in those industries where the main burden of quality improvement takes the form of R & D, or other fixed costs. Unit variable costs, on the other hand, being the sole costs relevant to our present concerns, may rise only slowly with increases in quality. Indeed, insofar as product innovation is often accompanied by concomitant process innovation, unit variable costs may even fall.

It is this situation, where the "finiteness" property holds along the relevant interval of qualities, which we have labelled a "natural oligopoly."

The finiteness condition does not *in itself* exclude an infinite number of firms; it is consistent with the presence of an arbitrarily large number of firms each selling an identical product at a price equal to unit variable cost, and a bounded number of firms offering a range of distinct, higher, qualities, at prices exceeding unit variable cost.

The implications of our present results are most clearly seen in the context of a model in which firms first incur some *arbitrarily small* fixed cost in entering the industry; then choose the qualities of their respective products, and then compete in price. Here, the presence of any fixed cost, however small, excludes the viability of firms whose prices are not strictly greater than unit variable cost at equilibrium. We have, in [7], characterized a perfect equilibrium[4] in this three stage game (entry; choice of quality; choice of price). The outcome is that, given a large number of entrants, only a bounded number (there, two) will choose to enter; they will produce distinct products, and both will earn strictly positive profits at equilibrium. Further reductions in fixed costs, or an expansion in the size of the economy (once our bound is attained), have no effect on the equilibrium number of firms in the industry.

We remark, finally, on a number of directions in which certain assumptions of the present model may be relaxed:

(i) *Linearity of utility functions; uniform income distribution*: The special forms of the utility function and income distribution used here do not play a critical role, and our results may be extended to a wider class of function. (For a full treatment of existence, and finiteness, in the zero cost case, see [3].)

(ii) *Identical consumers*: The assumption that consumers be identical can be relaxed, once some ranking of consumers in order of their willingness to pay is available.

(iii) *Smoothness of the cost function*: The analysis extends readily to the case in which $c(u)$ is kinked. In fact a new possible case of "finiteness" arises here, in that $c(u)$ may be "flat" up to some point, and "steep" thereafter, so that the finiteness property holds (consider the first and third zones in Figure 2(i) joined at a kink). Consumers will now rank products (at cost) in increasing order of quality to the left of the kink, but in decreasing order to the right.

(iv) *Multiproduct firms*: The restriction that each firm produces a single product can be relaxed. If we allow firms to produce a number of products, the finiteness property still holds, in that a bound will exist to the number of *firms* which can enjoy positive market shares at a Nash Equilibrium in prices.

London School of Economics

Manuscript received August, 1981; final revision received September, 1982.

APPENDIX

We here provide the construction referred to in the proof of Proposition 3 of the text. We show that where (F) is violated, then for any n, we can choose n distinct qualities sufficiently close to the point u at which (F) fails, such that all coexist with positive market share at a Nash Equilibrium in prices. This proof covers both the cases, (i) and (ii), referred to in Proposition 3; while a direct proof for case (i) is possible, the present construction is needed for case (ii). The fact that the present construction covers both cases demonstrates clearly that what enables an infinite number of products to coexist is the presence of a consumer who is locally (in quality) indifferent between products of differing qualities, where each is made available at cost.

The strategy of our construction is as follows: Choosing n qualities in a particular manner we write down the system of first order conditions which define equilibrium, and we show that a choice of qualities which are "sufficiently close" ensures that all have a positive market share at equilibrium.

[4]See [6].

Let u denote the quality at which (F) is violated. Choose $u_n = u$ and $u_k - u_{k-1} = \epsilon$. Note from the definition of $t_1, \ldots, t_k$, that we can express $p_k r_{k-1,k}$ as a function of $t_1, \ldots, t_k$, viz.

$$p_k r_{k-1,k} = t_k + \cdots + t_2 + t_1 \alpha$$

where $\alpha = (u_1 - u_0)/\epsilon$. Similarly, we can express $c_k r_{k-1,k}$ as:

$$c_k r_{k-1,k} = t(u_{k-1}, u_k) + \cdots + t(u_1, u_2) + t(u_0, u_1)\alpha.$$

To simplify the equation, we define a new variable

$$s_k = t_k - t(u_{k-1}, u_k).$$

Then the first order conditions (3) take the form:

$$\begin{cases} s_2 + t(u_1, u_2) - a = s_1\alpha, & s_1 \leq a - t(u_0, u_1), \\ s_2 + [t(u_1, u_2) - t(u_0, u_1)] = s_1(2 + \alpha), & s_1 \geq a - t(u_0, u_1), \end{cases}$$

$$s_{k+1} - s_k + [t(u_k, u_{k+1}) - t(u_{k-1}, u_k)] = 2(s_k + s_{k-1} + \cdots + s_2 + s_1\alpha)$$

$$(k = 2, \ldots, n-1),$$

$$b - s_n - t(u_{n-1}, u_n) = s_n + s_{n-1} + \cdots + s_2 + s_1\alpha.$$

(Note that the first order condition for firm 1 depends on whether 1's lower boundary is below a or not, i.e., whether all consumers buy one of the available products, or otherwise. Hence we have two equations for firm 1.)

From the first order condition for firm k, we may deduce that k's market share is

$$M^k = 2(s_k + \cdots + s_2 + s_1\alpha).$$

As $\epsilon \to 0$, the qualities chosen approach u and $\alpha \to \infty$, $t(u_k, u_{k+1}) \to t(u, u)$ for $k = 1, \ldots, n-1$ and $t(u_0, u_1) \to t(u_0, u)$.

We wish to show that in the limit as $\epsilon \to 0$, the market shares of all products are positive.

Since in any solution the s_k are bounded, it must be the case that s_1 approaches zero. Denote $s_1\alpha$ as $\bar{s}_1$, and write the equations for $\epsilon = 0$ (limit equations). Linearity and continuity guarantee that the solution of the limit system is the limit of the solutions. In the limit the relevant equation for firm 1 corresponds to the first of the pair cited above ($s_1 = 0$).

$$s_2 + [t(u, u) - a] = \bar{s}_1,$$

$$s_{k+1} - s_k = 2(s_k + \cdots + s_2 + \bar{s}_1) \qquad (k = 2, \ldots, n-1),$$

$$[b - t(u, u)] - s_n = s_n + \cdots + s_2 + \bar{s}_1.$$

Note that $b - t(u, u) > 0$ and $t(u, u) - a > 0$. To show that k's market share $M^k = 2(s_k + \cdots + s_2 + \bar{s}_1)$ is positive, we split the system of equations into two subsystems, and introduce the new variable M^k:

System (A)
$$\begin{cases} s_2 + [t(u, u) - a] = \bar{s}_1, \\ s_3 - s_2 = 2(s_2 + \bar{s}_1), \\ s_4 - s_3 = 2(s_3 + s_2 + \bar{s}_1), \\ \overline{} \\ s_k - s_{k-1} = 2(s_{k-1} + \cdots + s_2 + \bar{s}_1), \\ M^k = 2(s_k + \cdots + s_2 + \bar{s}_1), \end{cases}$$

System (B)
$$\begin{cases} s_{k+1} - s_k = M^k, \\ s_{k+2} - s_{k+1} = 2s_{k+1} + M^k, \\ \overline{} \\ s_n - s_{n-1} = 2(s_{n-1} + \cdots + s_{k+1}) + M^k, \\ b - t(u, u) - s_n = s_n + \cdots + s_{k+1} + M^k/2. \end{cases}$$

We show that the first system (A) defines s_k as an increasing linear function of M^k with a negative value at $M^k = 0$ and that the second system (B) defines s_k as a decreasing linear function with a positive value at $M^k = 0$. The two functions must therefore intersect at a positive M^k.

To verify these assertions, note that in (A) $s_2, s_3, \ldots, s_k, M^k$ are all strictly increasing linear functions of $\mathfrak{s}_1$; hence s^k can be written as an increasing linear function of M^k. To see that $s^k < 0$ when $M^k = 0$, set $M^k = 0$ in the last equation, and substitute this in the preceding equation, to obtain $s_{k-1} = 3s_k$. Continuing backwards, we represent each s_j in turn, for $j \geq 2$, as $q^j s_j$, where q^j is some positive constant, and $\mathfrak{s}_1$ as $q^2 s_2 + [t(u, u) - t(u_0, u)]$. Substituting this in the last equation, we have

$$(1 + q^2 + q^3 + \cdots q^{k-1})s_k + [t(u, u) - t(u_0, u)] = 0.$$

Hence $s_k(0) < 0$.

From system (B), beginning from the first equation, we can write $s_{k+1}, \ldots, s_n$ as linear functions of s_k, M^k, increasing in both arguments. Substituting this in the last equation, we find s^k as a decreasing function of M^k. This function is positive for $M^k = 0$ for (from the first equation) $s_{k+1} = s_k$, while from the second $s_{k+2} = 3s_k$, etc. All the s_k can be written as the product of a positive constant and s_k, whence from the last equation we have $s_k > 0$.

Hence the solution M^k is positive. This completes our construction.

REFERENCES

[1] FRIEDMAN, JAMES W.: *Oligopoly and the Theory of Games.* Amsterdam: North-Holland, 1977.
[2] JASKOLD GABSZEWICZ, J., AND J.-F. THISSE: "Entry (and Exit) in a Differentiated Industry," *Journal of Economic Theory*, 22(1980), 327–338.
[3] JASKOLD GABSZEWICZ, J., AVNER SHAKED, JOHN SUTTON, AND J.-F. THISSE: "Price Competition Among Differentiated Products: A Detailed Study of a Nash Equilibrium," ICERD Discussion Paper No. 37, London School of Economics, 1981.
[4] ———: "International Trade in Differentiated Products," *International Economic Review*, 22(1981), 527–534.
[5] LANCASTER, K.: *Variety, Equity and Efficiency.* New York: Columbia University Press, 1979.
[6] SELTEN, R.: "Re-examination of the Perfectness Concept for Equilibrium Points in Extensive Games," *International Journal of Game Theory*, 4(1975), 25–55.
[7] SHAKED, AVNER, AND JOHN SUTTON: "Relaxing Price Competition through Product Differentiation," *Review of Economic Studies*, 49(1982), 3–14.
[8] ———: "Natural Oligopolies and the Gains from Trade," ICERD Discussion Paper No. 48, London School of Economics, 1982.
[9] ———: "Natural Oligopolies and International Trade," in H. Kierzkowski (ed.), *Monopolistic Competition and International Trade.* Oxford: Oxford University Press, 1983.

Part IV
Incomplete Information

[31]

JOURNAL OF ECONOMIC THEORY 3, 156–168 (1971)

A Model of Price Adjustment

PETER A. DIAMOND

*Department of Economics, Massachusetts Institute of Technology,
Cambridge, Massachusetts 02139*

Received July 14, 1970

The limitations of equilibrium theory and of the stability analyses which justify it have led to considerable work on the development of a disequilibrium economics.[1] Of the criticisms of stability theory, there are three which have motivated the approach taken in this paper. First, the fundamental question seemingly underlying most stability analyses seems inappropriate. Most papers seem to explore the question of developing an adjustment process which will converge to competitive equilibrium. A more appealing approach is the development of adjustment processes which are designed to reflect some realistic process and then consideration of the long-run position of the market if the process is stable. Second, the economic agents in a disequilibrium process should be aware, at least in part, of the disequilibrium in the economy, and adjust their behavior in response to the altered opportunities which are present. Third, in most markets, all the agents are in the market for their own gain and prices get set by a demander or supplier rather than a nonparticipating auctioneer.

There are many models one might want to construct to reflect price adjustments in differently organized markets. In selecting the particular model presented here great weight has been given to mathematical tractability rather than trying to reflect some specific market (although many aspects are patterned after a retail consumer durable market). The purpose has been to develop a very simple model to permit straightforward analysis while hopefully having a framework which will lend itself to generalization. It is assumed that there are many identical firms and many consumers. Each period each firm sets a price and each consumer visits one firm. The consumer either purchases, according to an underlying demand curve, or concludes that the price is too high and leaves

---

[1] See, e.g., E. S. Phelps *et al.*, "Microeconomic Foundations of Employment and Inflation Theory," Norton, New York, 1970, and the references given there.

the store, to enter another the following period. Firms are assumed to know the demands they face (including the prices that cause people to walk out of the store) and to maximize profits separately each period. Consumers are uncertain about future prices and must compare the cost of searching further with the expected gain from finding a better price. The key dynamic element in the model is the consumer adjustment of cutoff prices for consumers entering the market for the first time. This adjustment is not analyzed in detail. Rather, plausible assumptions are made about it which are sufficient for the stability analysis.

The model does not converge to competitive equilibrium. In finite time, the price becomes that which maximizes joint profits. This particular price equilibrium rests heavily on several assumptions in the model. However it seems generally true that models of this sort will not converge to competitive equilibrium.

Consumer Behavior

This model will be constructed in discrete time, with the time period being the length of time it takes for a consumer to visit one store. We shall assume that prices change at a comparable rate, so that each period each store sets its price for that period. The consumer learns the price in a store only by entering it. He is aware that other stores may have different prices currently and, more important, may have different prices in the next period when he could reach another store. (The store he is currently shopping in may also have a different price the following period.) The nature of the commodity is such that the consumer purchases a quantity of it only once.[2] This rules out diversification, i.e., buying a little today and a little tomorrow as protection against making the entire purchase at a high price. It also rules out intertemporal interconnections of demand which would arise with a single budget constraint holding for present and future purchases.

Let us now consider a single consumer in a store at time t. Let us denote by

x the quantity of the good

p the price of the good

z the number of periods the consumer has spent
     checking prices of the good.

We assume that once the decision is made to purchase in a given period, the quantity purchased depends only on the price that period and is

---

[2] Thinking of the good as a durable, the different quantities might represent quality or size differences, as e.g., the dimensions of a television picture.

independent of the number of searches that have been made. Let us call the relationship between quantity and price, given the decision to purchase, the underlying demand curve and denote it by $x(p)$. Let us denote by Q the set of prices which will result in the consumer's purchasing in this period. Then, the actual demand, which we denote by $x^*(p)$ satisfies

$$x^*(p) = \begin{cases} x(p), & p \in Q \\ 0 & p \notin Q. \end{cases} \tag{1}$$

In general, we would expect Q to be fairly complicated. For example, we would expect very low prices to be in Q because the gain from finding a lower price (or even a zero price) would not be worth looking for another period. Somewhat higher prices might not be in Q because of the expectation of doing better in the future. However, even higher prices might be in Q because they signal a rising price trend (and so the desirability of purchasing now). Despite such possibilities, we shall assume that there is a single cutoff price q such that the consumer purchases at any price less than or equal to q:

$$x^*(p) = \begin{cases} x(p) & p \leq q \\ 0 & p > q. \end{cases} \tag{2}$$

Below we will discuss changes in q over time.

We can write the consumer's utility as a function of the price at which he purchases and the number of periods he looks before purchasing, $u(p, z)$. We assume that u is strictly decreasing in each argument. We assume further that the marginal disutility of search increases without limit so that if prices are bounded above there is a finite upper limit to the number of searches any consumer would make. We shall assume that different consumers have different cutoff prices and different utility functions but that all consumers have the same underlying demand. Further, we shall assume that the common underlying demand results in a revenue function which is continuous, strictly quasiconcave, and has its maximum at a finite price p^*. Thus, we are assuming

$px(p)$ increases for $p < p^*$ and

decreases for $p > p^*$.

Since we shall assume zero costs for the firm, this will give the same property to the underlying profit function. Thus, as we shall see, no firm will quote a price above p^*, giving rise to a finite maximum of the number of searches any consumer will make. We shall employ a double superscript $h\tau$ to identify individual consumers, the first index referring to the type of consumer and the second to the time period when he first entered the market to purchase the commodity. We shall employ a single subscript t to denote the time period in which the variable being considered is relevant. Thus, $q_t^{h\tau}$ is the cutoff price in time t for a consumer of type h who first entered the market at time τ.

Aggregate Demand

We assume that each period a new set of consumers enters the market, each set of consumers identically constituted in terms of consumer types; that is, h runs over the same index for each t. This implies that the utility functions of the same type are the same even though generations differ:

$$u^{h\tau}(p, z) = u^{h\tau+1}(p, z).$$

This does not imply that cutoff prices are necessarily the same, for the different generations have observed prices differently. Below we shall use the concept of similar approaches to cutoff prices of identical types to develop restrictions on the changes in aggregate demand over time.

Let us denote by $N_t^\tau(p)$ the number of consumers of generation τ who are willing to purchase in time t at price p. This is defined by counting the consumers with a cutoff price at least as large as p. From our assumptions above we see that N is nonincreasing and continuous from the left in p. Let us denote aggregate demand at time t by X_t, then

$$X_t(p) = x(p) \sum_\tau N_t^\tau(p). \tag{3}$$

Choice of Supplier

Before we can use the model of consumer behavior within a store we must determine which consumers enter each store. Let us assume that there are m stores in this market. Then, we shall assume that each firm faces the demand curve $(1/m) X_t(p)$ in each period. Below, we will also briefly consider the case where the fraction of aggregate demand confronting each firm depends on the firm's price reputation. Let us note some of the restrictions arising from this assumption. We are assuming that individual stores do not appeal to particular types of consumers either because of location, overhead expenditures, or other nonprice elements. Furthermore, we are ignoring the reasonable aspect of search that consumers, having decided not to purchase, will seek out a different store in the following period. If the number of stores is large relative to the number of stores a consumer visits, then the fraction of aggregate demand representing consumers who have been in a given store in the past is small and this aspect of the assumption is not very inaccurate.

Firm Behavior

Given the assumptions that the share of consumers going to each store is independent of history and that there are a large number of firms (and so no one firm considers the future demand by consumers who have walked out of its store), the firm can consider the problem of its best position separately in each period. One would like to parallel the uncertainty on the consumer side by giving firms the problems of estimating the demand curves they face and then of selecting an optimal action in this uncertain setting. A proper formulation of these problems seems very complicated in itself and one that would add to the difficulty of describing the time path of price adjustment. Rather than falling back on rules of thumb to describe firm behavior, it seems preferable to make the extreme assumption that firms know with certainty the demand curves they face each period. This also simplifies the choice of an objective function which can be taken to be profits. Ignoring the consumer share fraction (which being constant, does not affect the choice of price level) we can state the firm's problem as

$$\max_p pX_t(p) = px(p) \sum_\tau N_t^\tau(p). \tag{4}$$

We have assumed that the firm has no costs. (Constant costs would not affect the stability results given quasiconcavity of the profit function.) By assuming the same costs for all firms, we imply that they all face the same maximization problem and all select the same price. Since N_t^τ is continuous from the left, nonincreasing; $px(p)$, quasiconcave, and continuous with maximum at p^*, a finite price, this problem has a solution, which, however, need not be unique. This nonuniqueness would be troublesome for difference equation analysis of this model, but offers no problem for the stability analysis done here. Thus we shall assume that p_t is one of the profit maximizing prices; the statements to be made hold for any choice of p_t. The unique maximum of $px(p)$ at p^* will lead to a unique long-run equilibrium even though the time path may not be unique. Let us note a few preliminary results on profit maximizing price setting.

LEMMA 1. $p_t \leqslant p^*$.

Proof. For $p > p^*$, $p^*x(p^*) > px(p)$ and

$$N_t^\tau(p^*) \geqslant N_t^\tau(p) \qquad \text{for all} \quad \tau.$$

Let us define $\bar{p}_t$ as the greatest price which still results in all consumers buying:

$$\bar{p}_t = \min_{h,\tau} q_t^{h\tau}. \tag{5}$$

From this definition we see that for

$$p < \bar{p}_t, N_t^\tau(p) = N_t^\tau(\bar{p}_t).$$

We can use $\bar{p}_t$ for further restrictions on price setting.

LEMMA 2.   *For $\bar{p}_t \geqslant p^*, p_t = p^*$*

Proof.   By Lemma 1, $p_t \leqslant p^*$. For $p < p^*$ $p^*x(p^*) > px(p)$ and

$$N_t^\tau(p) = N_t^\tau(p^*) \qquad \text{for all} \quad \tau.$$

LEMMA 3.   *For $\bar{p}_t \leqslant p^*, p_t \geqslant \bar{p}_t$*

Proof.   By quasiconcavity, for $p < \bar{p}_t$, $px(p) < \bar{p}_t x(\bar{p}_t)$. By the definition of $\bar{p}_t$, $N_t^\tau(p) = N_t^\tau(\bar{p}_t)$ for all τ.

Changes in Cutoff Price

We have considered consumer and firm behavior within a single period. To develop a complete model, we must describe the change in parameters between successive periods. The supply side of the market and the underlying demand by each consumer are unchanged over time. The number of consumers and their cutoff prices change over time, however, as new consumers enter the market for the first time, as consumers make purchases and leave the market, and as consumers who have not purchased revise their cutoff prices in the light of the observed price and the increase in the marginal disutility of further search. A natural approach to this question would be to develop a theory of price awareness for individuals not in the market and a theory of expectation adjustment in response to observed prices. I did not want to face the formidable task of developing such a theory for these purposes and have chosen instead to look for reasonable restrictions on cutoff price changes for demanders remaining in the market and on the differences in cutoff prices between successive generations entering the market for the first time. These restrictions alone would not be sufficient to determine the full path of price adjustment, but will be sufficient to show convergence to equilibrium.

There are two separate questions which must be faced in determining cutoff prices. One is the change in cutoff prices for consumers remaining in the market. A second is the determination of cutoff prices for consumers in the market for the first time. It seems reasonable to assume that a consumer who does not purchase in one period raises his cutoff price for the next period. One reason for this is the price observed when the consumer does not buy, which was sufficiently high to make him feel it was worth waiting. A price which a consumer rejects will lead to a revision of price expectations. This revision seems likely to increase the price at which the consumer is willing to make a purchase without further searching.[3] A second reason for a rise in cutoff price from an unsuccessful attempt to purchase is the assumed increasing marginal disutility of search. Even if the consumer's price expectations are unchanged by the observed price, the increased cost of searching should make him willing to settle at a somewhat higher price than he was willing to settle for previously. Furthermore, we assume that there is a minimal response. Thus, we assume that a consumer continuing in the market in period $t + 1$ has a cutoff price which satisfies

$$q_{t+1}^{h\tau} > q_t^{h\tau} + \eta \qquad \text{for } \eta > 0 \text{ and independent of } h, \tau, \text{ and } t. \qquad (6)$$

Generational Differences

The pattern of cutoff prices for a consumer in the market is a relatively well-defined problem i.e., incorporating additional information into a well-defined maximization problem. The question of the initial cutoff price for a new entrant into the market is far less well-defined. More specifically, we are interested in the differences between successive generations of new entrants. One approach might be to assume that successive generations enter with the same set of cutoff prices for different types. Consumers of this type presumably receive no information on the price in this market. (It is natural to think of them as tourists, having no local information.) A second type of consumer (resident) receives some information on the price level in this market, even though he is not directly observing the price by trying to purchase. It would be interesting to develop models with both types of consumers and, I suspect, would result in a different structure of equilibrium from the one which will develop here with just resident types. (Surprisingly, it seems that the presence of tourists may lower the price for residents.)

To develop a dynamic model, we need to ask how consumers of each type entering the market for the first time in period $t + 1$ differ from those who entered for the first time in period t. In terms of our notation,

---

[3] This argument is not completely compelling. A consumer with a low dislike for searching may be heartened by finding a price close to his cutoff price in the early stages of searching and feel that this enhances his chances of finding even lower prices and so may lower his cutoff price. This case seems possible but unusual.

how does q_{t+1}^{ht+1} differ from q_t^{ht}? The prime difference in experience between these individuals is the occurrence of p_t. It is natural, then, to relate the difference between q_{t+1}^{ht+1} and q_t^{ht} to p_t and q_t^{ht}. A natural reaction would be to relate sign differences in the former to sign differences in the latter. This approach, however, is not completely appealing because of the presence of the cost of searching. If the price were expected to be at a given level next period (ignoring the remaining future), this would justify a cutoff price in excess of that price today, in response to the searching-cost saving from purchasing today rather than tomorrow. In the face of a price tomorrow of p, expected with certainty, the ideal cutoff price for today q^* would satisfy

$$u^h(q^{*h}, 1) = u^h(p, 2). \tag{7}$$

Considering the continuous functional relationship between q^* and p defined by this equation, the presence of search costs implies

$$q^{*h}(p) > p. \tag{8}$$

We shall now assume that the cutoff price for generation $t + 1$ lies in the interval defined by the cutoff price for generation t and the ideal cutoff price which p_t would have justified. Thus we have one of the following two cases

$$q^{*h}(p_t) \leqslant q_{t+1}^{ht+1} \leqslant q_t^{ht}$$

or

$$q_t^{ht} \leqslant q_{t+1}^{ht+1} \leqslant q^{*h}(p_t). \tag{9}$$

This restriction seems more appealing than one based on q_t^{ht} and p_t, although it is far from satisfactory. We shall further assume that the difference in cutoffs between successive generations does not become vanishingly small relative to the difference between cutoff and ideal cutoff. For some ϵ, $0 < \epsilon < 1$

$$| q_{t+1}^{ht+1} - q_t^{ht} | \geqslant \epsilon \min\{1, | q^{*h}(p_t) - q_t^{ht} |\} \tag{10}$$

for all h and t.

With these restrictions on cutoff price adjustment, we have restrictions on the movement of the minimum cutoff price for all the consumers in the market.

LEMMA 4. $p_t \geqslant \bar{p}_t$ *implies* $\bar{p}_{t+1} > \bar{p}_t$.

Proof. For all consumers in the market in $t + 1$ who were in the market previously, we have, by (6),

$$q_{t+1}^{h\tau} > q_t^{h\tau} \geqslant \bar{p}_t \qquad \text{since} \quad \bar{p}_t \text{ is the minimum of cutoff prices.}$$

For consumers in the market for the first time, we have, by (9),

$$q_{t+1}^{ht+1} \geqslant \min(q^{*h}(p_t), q_t^{ht}).$$

Since $q^{*h}(p_t) > p_t \geqslant \bar{p}_t$, we need only be concerned with a consumer type for which $q_t^{ht} = \bar{p}_t$. Then, by (10), $q_{t+1}^{ht+1} > q_t^{ht}$. Therefore all cutoff prices, and thus their minimum, are greater than $\bar{p}_t$.

LEMMA 5. $\bar{p}_t \geqslant p_t$ implies $\bar{p}_{t+1} \geqslant p_t$.

Proof. $p_t \leqslant \bar{p}_t$ implies that all consumers in the market at time t make their purchases. For consumers in the market for the first time in $t + 1$, $q_{t+1}^{ht+1} \geqslant \min(q^{*h}(p_t), q_t^{ht})$. By hypothesis, $q_t^{ht} \geqslant p_t$. From (8), $q^{*h}(p_t) > p_t$.

Stability

The assumptions made above are sufficiently strong to lead to convergence of p_t to p^* in finite time.

THEOREM.   *There exists a time t' such that $p_t = p^*$ for all $t \geqslant t'$.*

Proof. If at any time t, $\bar{p}_t \geqslant p^*$, then, by Lemma 2, $p_t = p^*$. By Lemma 5, $\bar{p}_{t+1} \geqslant p^*$, implying that the price would be p^* for all future time. Thus, if the theorem is false, $\bar{p}_t < p^*$ for all t. By Lemmas 1 and 4 it would then follow that $p_t \geqslant \bar{p}_t$ and $\bar{p}_{t+1} > \bar{p}_t$. Thus the sequence $\{\bar{p}_t\}$ would be increasing and bounded above. It would, therefore, converge to $\hat{p}$, say, with $\hat{p} \leqslant p^*$. Let us define $r = \min_{h,p}(q^{*h}(p) - p)$ for $\hat{p} - \epsilon \leqslant p \leqslant \hat{p}$, where ϵ is the value for the minimal response in q^h in (10). By assumption, $r > 0$. Then there would exist a time $\hat{t}$ such that

$$\hat{p} - \bar{p}_{\hat{t}} \leqslant \min\{\eta/2, \epsilon/2 \min(1, r)\},$$

where η is the value in (6).

For all consumers in the market at $\hat{t}$ and $\hat{t} + 1$, we would have

$$q_{\hat{t}+1}^{h\tau} > q_{\hat{t}}^{h\tau} + \eta \geqslant \bar{p}_{\hat{t}} + \eta > \hat{p}.$$

Now let us consider consumers in the market for the first time. By Lemma 3, we would have $p_{\hat{t}} \geqslant \bar{p}_{\hat{t}}$ and thus $q^{*h}(p_{\hat{t}}) \geqslant p_{\hat{t}} + r \geqslant \bar{p}_{\hat{t}} + r$.

For those consumer types with $q'^{hi}_i \geqslant q^{*h}(p_i)$, we have $q^{hi+1}_{i+1} \geqslant q^{*h}(p_i) \geqslant \bar{p}_i + r > \hat{p}$. For those consumer types with $q'^{hi}_i < q^{*h}(p_i)$, we have

$$q^{hi+1}_{i+1} \geqslant q^{hi}_i + \epsilon \min\{1, q^{*h}(p_i) - q^{hi}_i\}$$

$$= \min\{q^{hi}_i + \epsilon, q^{hi}_i + \epsilon(q^{*h}(p_i) - q^{hi}_i)\}$$

$$\geqslant \min\{\bar{p}_i + \epsilon, (1 - \epsilon)\bar{p}_i + \epsilon(p_i + r)\}$$

$$\geqslant \min\{\bar{p}_i + \epsilon, \bar{p}_i + \epsilon r\}$$

$$> \hat{p}.$$

Thus all consumers in the market in $\hat{t} + 1$ have a higher cutoff price than $\hat{p}$, which is a contradiction. Therefore, the price p^* is reached in finite time.

Equilibrium Analysis

Given convergence to a constant price position, it is easy to see that the joint profit maximizing price p^* will be the equilibrium price. In a steady state, consumers expect the price next period to equal the long-run value. They, therefore, have a cutoff price this period slightly above the long-run price, since it is worth a small sum to make the purchase this period rather than next period. Thus, in the neighborhood of the long-run price, the actual demand facing a firm is the same as the underlying demand. With constant shares of consumers each period, the firm is interested only in short-run profits. Thus the equilibrium position will be one of profit maximization of the underlying demand curve. With changing shares of consumers, this strong conclusion will not follow; however, it does not seem that consideration of future market shares would be sufficient to result in the competitive price. Let us briefly consider a model with changing shares and examine possible long-run equilibrium positions.

Varying Shares of Consumers

The assumption that the fraction of consumers entering any store is constant is both unrealistic and important for the above results. Without developing a dynamic model with varying shares to examine stability, let us consider equilibrium positions, assuming a steady state is reached. We must alter the above analysis to introduce determination of firm shares and to develop rules for firm decision making in this new setting. (We shall ignore the change needed in consumer analysis to incorporate the presence of different prices at different stores in any period.)

Let us denote by $\alpha_t = (\alpha_t^1, ..., \alpha_t^m)$ the vector of shares of consumers entering each of the m stores and by $\beta_t = (\beta_t^1,..., \beta_t^m)$ the prices set by each of the stores. It seems appropriate to have firm shares determined by price histories

$$\alpha_t^j = \psi^j(\beta_{t-1}, \beta_{t-2},...), \qquad j = 1, 2,..., m. \tag{11}$$

We might simplify this if we assume that the shares at time $t - 1$ summarize the impact of past prices on share development. Then we would have

$$\alpha_t^j = \phi^j(\alpha_{t-1}, \beta_{t-1}), \qquad j = 1, 2,..., m. \tag{12}$$

In keeping with the spirit of the above model we would want each firm to set its price in ignorance of the prices being set concurrently by other firms and with interest only in its own current profit and future share. If the firm is maximizing an additive function of current profits and expected future position we would have an objective function

$$\alpha_t^j \beta_t^j X_t(\beta_t^j) + V_t^j(\alpha_{t+1}^j), \tag{13}$$

where V is some expectation operator reflecting the evaluation in the future of starting $t + 1$ with share α_{t+1}^j and the probability of the different values of α_{t+1}^j given the choice of β_t^j and the subjective probabilities of other prices in the market. The dependence of V_t on β_t implies that prices are not chosen simply to maximize short-run profits. Since V should be decreasing in β, prices will tend to be less than they would be with single-period profit maximization in that period and the long-run price will be less than p^*. The greater the dependence of V on β in the long-run equilibrium position, the lower will the long-run price tend to be. Given a long-run equilibrium it does not seem possible that the competitive (zero) price will rule. In this extreme model of no costs a one period gain in profits above the zero level is worth a considerable drop in future shares, since there are no profits to be made in the future at the competitive price. More generally, if market shares depend smoothly on prices (rather than the sharp loss of all business in the standard competitive model), we would expect equilibrium to occur between the competitive and profit maximizing prices.

Demand Functions

The assumption of quasiconcavity of revenue functions played a key role in the uniqueness of long-run equilibrium. If there is a price p^1 such that $p^1 x(p^1) > px(p)$ for $p \leqslant p^1 + \max_h q^{*h}(p^1), p \neq p^1$, then the price p^1 is a possible long-run equilibrium. Thus without quasiconcavity there can be multiple equilibria, the initial set of cutoff prices determining the relevant one. Also the choice of a particular price p_t at a time when there are several profit maximizing prices can determine the long-run equilibrium. With some rules for choosing p_t among prices giving equal profits one can get cycling among local maxima of $px(p)$ which are near to each other (relative to $q^*(p)$). It is not clear whether there can be cycles involving prices that are not local maxima. Cycling can also occur in the case of differing demand curves among individuals even when it is assumed that each of the individual revenue functions are strictly quasi-concave. Thus it seems that a more general model will require additional assumptions to obtain stability.

Entry

The model presented above assumed a fixed set of firms. Since there was a tendency for the appearance of pure profits, it is natural to inquire about the entry of additional firms. It seems more realistic to include a fixed cost of setting up a firm in addition to the variable costs, which happened to be zero above. If the annual profits exceed the interest on fixed setup costs, it is natural for additional entrepreneurs to consider setting up a firm. The new element needed for a theory is the behavior of market shares when an additional firm appears. Let us first consider the model with fixed shares. It is natural to divide the consumers among $n + 1$ stores rather than the previous n; and to divide them evenly if there are no advantages of location. The presence of an additional firm does nothing, then, to change the pricing analysis done above. The possibility of an additional firm when industry profits are high should have no effect on the behavior of individual firms. Thus the price analysis is unchanged and profits per firm are decreased. Presumably this process continues until firms are just making normal return on the cost of setting up a firm. This outcome is very similar to that of monopolistic competition. Additional firms enter the market until there are no pure profits, but prices remain above marginal costs because of the downward slope of the demand curve caused in this case by the advantage of the product once a consumer is in a store.

The case of variable shares is naturally more complicated. In a model where new stores start with small shares and can only build them up over time and with lower prices, there will be less incentive for entry than in the model with fixed shares. Thus historical position gives a firm an element of goodwill to which one can impute part of the profits. The more difficult for additional rivals to reach a break-even position, the more valued the historical position. The process of equilibrium is nevertheless well-defined provided one describes the subjective probabilities of potential entrepreneurs toward future market conditions.

168   DIAMOND

Concluding Remarks

The mark of having been chosen more for mathematical tractability than for realism appears clearly on many of the assumptions in this paper. The directions in which the model needs to be generalized are fairly obvious. The basic question of stability which was asked in the paper is intrinsically less interesting than comparative static and welfare questions. Hopefully, it will be possible to consider these questions both for the long-run equilibrium position and for the single period positions during the adjustment process.

ACKNOWLEDGMENT

During most of the work on this paper I was a visitor successively at Hebrew University, Jerusalem, and Nuffield College, Oxford. I wish to thank both institutions for their hospitality.

I am indebted to J. A. Mirrlees and M. E. Yaari for many helpful discussions on this topic and to the National Science Foundation for financial support.

[32]

Bargains and Ripoffs: A Model of Monopolistically Competitive Price Dispersion

STEVEN SALOP

Federal Reserve Board

and

JOSEPH STIGLITZ

Stanford University and Oxford University

INTRODUCTION

This paper analyses an economy in which agents differ in their ability and willingness to make economical decisions in the market-place. On the one hand there are economists, bargain-hunters and other price-conscious consumers who carefully and analytically gather the information required to make wise purchases. Other agents are less rational and calculating in their decisions. Most people do not understand even the simplest laws of probability; for example, an overwhelming majority will bet " heads " after a run of " tails " in a coin-flipping game. Many people do not calculate unit-prices in the super-market. Disparity in incomes provides some further indirect evidence; because of differences in preference or ability, some agents perform much better than others in market decisions.

We explore this problem of heterogeneity of consumer rationality within a simple model of costly information-gathering. We assume that consumers differ in the " costs " of becoming perfectly informed. To make the model as simple and transparent as possible, the relevant information to gather and the flow of that information is highly unrealistic and oversimplified: only price information is gathered; consumers have " rational " though limited prior information; " perfect " information may be generated for some fixed cost. However, the model may be reinterpreted to include the more realistic cases of quality differentials and heterogenous commodity preferences and more complex information transmission such as sequential search, advertising and word-of-mouth.

The central implication of costly information-gathering is that the equilibrium will not occur at the perfectly competitive price. This is a fairly straightforward observation: Suppose every firm did charge the perfectly competitive price. Then some firm(s) could raise price slightly without losing any customers. Consumers would be unwilling to gather the extra information needed to switch stores or brands. Clearly there is a limit on the price increases at one store that consumers will tolerate without leaving. However, since the *relative* store prices determine the gains from a search, then as every store raises price slightly, the cycle of price rises by a few stores may occur again. Hence prices throughout the market continue to rise.

Akerlof's famous " Lemons Principle " [1] asserted that prices will continue to rise (or quality fall) until the market is destroyed. Diamond [4] realized that the prices may settle down at the pure monopoly price with each small firm acting as a complete monopolist

493

over its usual customers. In our model, we show that the market will not be destroyed, for, when prices get high enough, some firm can lower its price substantially and induce search. At this point there are two possibilities: either prices may cycle forever, or they may settle down to some equilibrium configuration.

We show that if prices do settle down, they will settle at the monopoly price (or, as Braverman [2] has pointed out, at a Chamberlinean monopolistically competitive price) or there may be permanent price dispersion in the range between the perfectly competitive and monopolistically competitive prices. The final spread of prices depends on the magnitude of information costs and degree of scale economies. For U-shaped average costs, higher-priced firms produce in the region of decreasing average costs; thus, there are too many small firms at equilibrium.

Moreover, the economy does not produce information efficiently. A " rational economic planner " could economize on information costs by eliminating the price dispersion; for with no price dispersion, there is no need for costly search. There is an informational externality at work between efficient and inefficient information-gatherers. Those agents who become informed give an external economy to the uninformed; the weight of their search keeps prices lower. In fact, if there are enough informed agents, the market price will settle down to the perfectly competitive price. On the other hand, by shopping at high-priced stores, the uninformed inflict an external diseconomy on the informed; these informed must gather costly information to obtain the lower price.

In this paper, a simplistic market with costly information-gathering for complete price-information will be studied. We will analyse an example in which there are only two groups of consumers by search costs. Four Nash equilibrium configurations can occur in this market:

   (i) A Single-Price Equilibrium (SPE) at the Competitive Price, p^*.

   (ii) A Single-Price Equilibrium at the Monopoly Price, u.

   (iii) A Two-Price Equilibrium (TPE) in which the lower price, p_l, is the competitive price, and the higher price, p_h, is no greater than the monopoly price.

   (iv) Non-existence of any Nash equilibrium.

Regions in which the four cases obtain are shown in Figure 1.

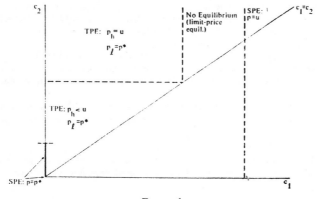

FIGURE 1

1. FORMAL MODEL

There are a large number, L, of consumers who form the potential market for a durable commodity. Each consumer has an identical inelastic demand curve for one and only one unit of the commodity. The maximum price a consumer will pay (the reservation price) is denoted by u^1; hence, u is the monopoly price. This assumption is made for simplicity; it has been generalized to downward sloping demand curves by Braverman [2].

The most crucial assumptions of the model are those describing the consumers' degree of information and the corresponding information flows among consumers and firms. In the formal model here, the commodities sold at the different stores are known by consumers to be identical. However, consumers do not have perfect information regarding the price charged at each store in the market; this information must be generated at a cost. Suppose there are n stores selling the commodity at prices $p = \{p_1, p_2, ..., p_n\}$ at locations $l = \{l_1, l_2, ..., l_n\}$. The usual competitive model assumes that consumers are freely endowed with perfect information regarding the $\{p, l\}$ set. This model will move only one step from perfect information. We will assume that the consumer is freely endowed with the price vector p; he knows the prices charged in the market. However, he does not know *a priori* the location vector l of these prices. That is, he knows what prices exist but he does not know which store charges which price. Clearly much of the information-gathering in markets attempts to discover locations, quality and other product characteristics as well as price. However, each of these variables affects the " effective " price a consumer pays per unit of a standard commodity bundle. The model could be generalized into a Lancasterian hedonic-price framework in which information increases a consumer's " net surplus ".

We will assume that only *complete information* may be gathered: Consumer i may gather complete information regarding the l-vector for a *fixed* cost c^i. Once l is known, he can then go costlessly to the minimum-price store and purchase the commodity there. This assumption could be thought of as follows: A newspaper exists that publishes full information; consumer i can purchase and process all the information in the newspaper for a cost c^i. Consumers differ in their information-gathering costs due to differences in analytic ability, the cost of time and preference for reading and processing information.

This complete information assumption is the central one in the model. It will be seen that it does generalize to include fixed-cost advertising. However, partial processing of information which generalizes to variable search costs (sequential search) and variable advertising costs lead to quite different results.[2] It is assumed that sequential sampling is quite costly and not economical for consumers to pursue.

Finally, we make the simplest assumption that there are only two groups of consumers distinguished by information-generating costs, a proportion, α, with cost c_1 and the rest, $(1-\alpha)$, with higher cost c_2; this assumption is made for analytic convenience only, it is not crucial to any of the results obtained. For models with a continuous cost distribution, see Salop and Stiglitz [12] and Braverman [2].

The consumer has two decisions to make. He must decide whether to enter the market at all. He must also decide whether to buy the newspaper to obtain perfect information or purchase at a randomly selected store. We will first analyse the information-gathering decision.

If consumer i buys the newspaper at cost c^i, he will be able to purchase at the lowest available price, which we denote by $p^{\min}$. His total expenditure will be E_S^i where

$$E_S^i = p^{\min} + c^i. \qquad \qquad ...(1)$$

Alternatively, he can purchase at a randomly selected store and on average pay a price equal to the mean price charged, $\bar{p}$. Thus, the total expected expenditure from the no-search strategy, E_N^i, is

$$E_N^i = \bar{p} = (1/n) \sum_{j=1}^{n} p_j.^3 \qquad \qquad ...(2)$$

Assuming the consumer is risk-neutral,[4] he will buy the newspaper if and only if

$$E_S^i < E_N^i,^5 \quad \Leftrightarrow p^{\min} + c^i < \bar{p}. \qquad \qquad ...(3)$$

Having decided on the optimal search strategy, a consumer will enter the market if and only if his total cost does not exceed his demand price, u, i.e. if and only if

$$u \geq \min \, [p^{\min} + c^i, \, \bar{p}]. \qquad \qquad ...(4)$$

It is also true that no consumer will pay a price greater than u. Thus, a store charging a price greater than u will obtain no sales at all.

There are n firms selling the durable commodity. Every firm has identical technology characterized by a fixed cost T and variable costs $v(q)$ which depend on the quantity q produced. Marginal cost is assumed to be increasing ($v'(q) > 0$). Thus, the average cost (AC) curve is U-shaped.

Firms do not have the information problem facing consumers. Like consumers, they are assumed to know the prices charged by other firms; they need not know the actual locations of other firms. Furthermore, we assume they know costlessly the distribution of consumers' search costs and thus can perfectly predict how many consumers will search. This is the information that is necessary for each firm to know its expected demand curves. L is assumed large enough for the law of large numbers to assure that actual demand always equals expected demand. Thus, firms face no uncertainty or any critical shortage of information.

It is assumed that firms follow " Nash " price-setting behaviour *vis-à-vis* other firms. That is, a firm takes all other firms' prices as given in maximizing its profits. Formally, for firm j, we have

$$\max_p \, \pi^j(p \mid p^{-j}), \, p^{-j} = \{p_1, \, p_2, \, ..., \, p_{j-1}, \, p_{j+1}, \, ..., \, p_n\}. \qquad ...(5)$$

On the other hand, each firm follows a " Stackleberg " strategy *vis-à-vis* consumers. Rather than taking the consumer search *decisions* as given, it takes the consumer search *rule* as given and takes into consideration exactly how consumer search decisions will depend on the price it chooses. More precisely, the firm knows that an individual with cost c^i will search if

$$c^i < \bar{p} - p^{\min}. \qquad \qquad ...(6)$$

Firm j calculates its effect on $\bar{p}$ and $p^{\min}$ in the following way.

$$\bar{p} = \frac{1}{n} \, p_j + \frac{1}{n} \sum_{i \neq j} p_i \qquad \qquad ...(7)$$

$$p^{\min} = \min \, \{p_j, \, p^{-j}\} \qquad \qquad ...(8)$$

From these three equations and the distributions of consumers by information-gathering costs, we may calculate the demand curve for firm j given the prices of the other $(n-1)$ firms. We denote this demand curve by $D(p_j \mid p^{-j})$. Note how the Nash and Stackleberg assumptions are contained in the demand curve. Firm j takes the other firms' prices p^{-j} as *given*. However, it considers how its price choice *induces* information-gathering by consumers.

Finally, we assume that entry occurs as long as profits are positive. This assumption assures that at equilibrium (if one exists), every firm makes identical zero profits. That is, denoting by $\hat{p}_j$ the price of firm j that comes from its profit-maximizing behaviour and by $\hat{p}^{-j}$ the other firms' optimal prices, we have

$$\pi(\hat{p}_j \mid \hat{p}^{-j}) = 0, \quad \text{for all} \quad j = 1, 2, ..., n. \qquad ...(9)$$

This condition is used to compute the number of firms in equilibrium. It simply states that in equilibrium price equals average cost for each firm.[6, 7] This is, of course, the monopolistic competition assumption.

Equilibrium. Given the assumptions just made, we may characterize the monopolistically competitive equilibrium in this market. An equilibrium is defined by a price vector $p^* = \{p_1^*, p_2^*, ..., p_n^*\}$, a number n^* of firms in the market, and a percentage of consumers that gather information α^* that obey the following conditions:

(i) *Profit Maximization.* Each firm chooses a price to maximize its profits given the prices of the other firms and the search strategy of consumers summarized in its demand curve. For every firm j, we have

$$\max_{p} \pi(p_j \mid p^{*-j}) = p_j D(p_j \mid p^{*-j}) - v[D(p_j \mid p^{*-j})] - T, \quad \text{for all } j = 1, 2, ..., n^*. \quad ...(10)$$

(ii) *Zero Profits.* Furthermore, the maximized value of profits for every firm j equals zero at equilibrium.

$$\pi(p_j^* \mid p^{*-j}) = 0, \quad \text{for all } \quad j = 1, 2, ..., n^*. \qquad ...(11)$$

Thus, an equilibrium is characterized by n^* firms charging identical or different prices and each producing and selling just enough output to place them on the downward sloping portion of their common average cost curve, with enough firms so that every customer obtains one unit of the commodity. Note that the zero profit and profit-maximization conditions jointly imply that each firm's demand curve lies below the AC-curve at every point except the equilibrium price chosen.

(iii) *Search Equilibrium.* At equilibrium, consumers gather information optimally.

$$\alpha^* = \begin{cases} 1 \text{ for } c_1 \leqq c_2 < \bar{p} - p^{\min} & ...(12) \\ \alpha \text{ for } c_1 < \bar{p} - p^{\min} \leqq c_2 & ...(13) \\ 0 \text{ for } \bar{p} - p^{\min} \leqq c_1 \leqq c_2 & ...(14) \end{cases}$$

2. OVERVIEW OF THE MODEL

Before turning to the technical details, it may be useful to summarize the argument in a more intuitive way. The basic TPE is pictured below: high-price, p_h, stores sell a smaller quantity, q_h, than do lower-priced, p_l, stores. Every store earns zero profits, $p = AC$. The TPE has the properties that: (a) the higher information-cost consumers $[(1-\alpha)L$ consumers with cost $c_2]$ *choose* to remain uninformed given the price dispersion in the market; they purchase randomly from the first store sampled, while (b) the lower information-cost consumers $[\alpha L$ consumers with cost $c_1 < c_2]$ choose to become informed, and hence purchase from a p_l store. This property constrains the possible price dispersion in the market.

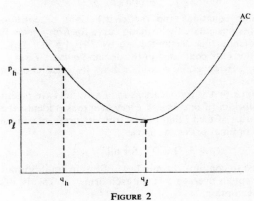

FIGURE 2

If a proportion, β, of the total stores, n, is low priced, and if consumers search optimally, it must be true that $c_1 < (1-\beta)(p_h - p_l) \leq c_2$, (where the expected gains from search are $(1-\beta)(p_h - p_l)$, and costs are c_i for a type-i consumer).

Given that only the c_1's become informed, p_h stores sell only to unlucky uninformed consumers while p_l stores sell to informed consumers and lucky uninformed consumers. As there are $(1-\beta)(1-\alpha)L$ unlucky c_2's and $(1-\beta)n$ high-priced stores we have

$$q_h = (1-\alpha)\frac{L}{n}. \qquad \qquad ...(15)$$

As each low-priced store gets a normal $(1/n)$th share of the $(1-\alpha)L$ uninformed c_2's and additionally the βn low-priced stores split the αL informed c_1's equally, we have

$$q_l = (1-\alpha)\frac{L}{n} + \frac{\alpha L}{\beta n}. \qquad \qquad ...(16)$$

Denoting the downward-sloping portion of the average cost curve by $AC = A(q)$, zero profits implies

$$p_h = A(q_h) \qquad \qquad ...(17)$$

$$p_l = A(q_l). \qquad \qquad ...(18)$$

The low price must equal the competitive price p^*. Otherwise, one low-priced store could shade its price slightly, obtain all the informed customers and even positive profits. Thus, we have

$$p_l = p^*. \qquad \qquad ...(19)$$

Substituting, we have the equilibrium conditions

$$p^* = A\left[\left(\frac{\alpha}{\beta} + (1-\alpha)\right)\frac{L}{n}\right]; \qquad \qquad ...(20)$$

$$p^* + \frac{c_2}{1-\beta} = A\left[(1-\alpha)\frac{L}{n}\right]. \qquad \qquad ...(21)$$

This is the essence of the model. Complications arise from the possibility of corner solutions and non-existence of a TPE or any equilibrium.

3. DERIVATION OF EQUILIBRIA

We will now derive the equilibrium prices for this market. The methodology is as follows. A " potential " equilibrium satisfying the zero profit condition is proposed. We first check to see that the consumer search equilibrium condition is satisfied. Then, we examine the behaviour of a " deviant " firm to see whether its profit-maximization condition is satisfied at the " potential " equilibrium. If a " deviant " firm increases its profits by charging a different price, then the " potential " equilibrium is not an equilibrium. Only if the deviant prefers the equilibrium price is the potential equilibrium an actual equilibrium. This is equivalent to assuming that firms experiment in their pricing decisions.

Lemma 1. *There are no Three-, Four-, . . .-Price Equilibria. Only Single-Priced Equilibria* (SPE) *and Two-Price Equilibria* (TPE) *are possible.*

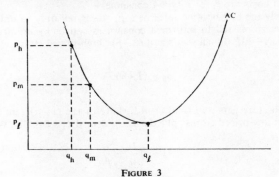

FIGURE 3
Three-price equilibrium.

Proof. At these prices, suppose some consumers find it worth while to purchase complete information; these consumers pay the low price p_l. Of those consumers that do not search, every firm obtains an equal $(1/n)$th share. Since the p_m and p_h firms sell only to uninformed consumers, their sales are identical. Thus, the p_h firms must obtain higher revenue, breaking the zero profit condition.[8]

This lemma holds for all distributions of consumer search costs, for the consumers can always be split into an informed and an uninformed group. Incomplete information-gathering is necessary for equilibria with more than two prices.

Two-price and single-price equilibria are possible. We will first examine single-price equilibria and show that there may only be single-priced equilibria at the monopoly price u and at the competitive price p^*.

Single-Price Equilibria

Lemma 2. *There is no single-price equilibrium at any price $\hat{p}$ in the open interval* $\hat{p} \in (p^*, u)$.

Proof. Consider a SPE at $\hat{p}$ in the open interval (p^*, u) obeying the zero profit condition as pictured below.

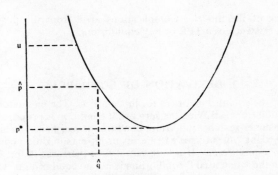

FIGURE 4
Interior single-price equilibrium.

Since there is no price dispersion, each of the n firms in production obtains equal sales, or $\hat{q} = L/n$. This defines the potential equilibrium number of firms. We will now show that it always pays a deviant to charge a price different from $\hat{p}$.

(a) *Local Price Rises.* Suppose a deviant raises his price slightly to $\hat{p} + \varepsilon$. From (9), this raises the mean price to $\bar{p}' = \hat{p} + (\varepsilon/n)$. The benefit of search becomes $b = \bar{p}' - p^{\min}$. Since $p^{\min} = \hat{p}$, we have a positive benefit or $b = (\varepsilon/n)$. Consumer i will gather information if and only if $c_i \leq b$.

If $c_2 \geq c_1 > 0$, there exists some small $\varepsilon > 0$ such that the deviant firm loses no customers; its demand curve is perfectly inelastic for some interval above $\hat{p}$. Thus, if it raises its price, its revenue rises. This breaks the profit-maximization equilibrium condition and thus the potential equilibrium. On the other hand, if $c_1 = 0$, even an ε-price change induces search and may make the deviant strategy unprofitable. However, in that case, price decreases will be profitable.

(b) *Local Price Decreases.* Suppose a deviant were to lower his price slightly to $\hat{p} - \varepsilon$. From (9) and (10), both $\bar{p}$ and $p^{\min}$ fall. $p^{\min}$ falls by more. Thus, we have

$$b = \bar{p}' - p^{\min} = \frac{n-1}{n} \varepsilon.$$

If $c_1 = 0$, those αL type 1 consumers will become informed and buy from the deviant. He will obtain a normal $(1/n)$th share of the $(1-\alpha)L$ uninformed type 2's and all the αL informed type 1's. His sales jump from L/n to

$$q_d = (1-\alpha)\frac{L}{n} + \alpha L = \frac{L}{n} + \alpha L \left(\frac{n-1}{n} \right).$$

Since his sales jump from this small price decrease, his profits become positive.[9] Once again, the profit-maximization condition is broken and the potential SPE is impossible.

At the monopoly price u,[10] the deviant strategy of raising price is not profitable; no consumer is willing to pay a price above u. Similarly, at the competitive price p^*, since $p^* = \min AC$, any price decreases must be unprofitable, regardless of the deviant's sales. As a result, there may be SPE's at u and p^*. We analyse the competitive price first.

Consider the potential SPE at the competitive price p^*. Zero profits implies that each firm must sell q^*, as pictured below. Since there is no dispersion, no search takes place at this equilibrium and the number of firms n^* is easily calculated from $q^* = L/n^*$. (Of course, we are assuming $u > p^*$. If $u < p^*$, no market can exist for this commodity.)

There are two cases in which p^* is a full equilibrium. If both groups can gather information costlessly ($c_1 = c_2 = 0$), then if a deviant raises price by $\varepsilon > 0$, he loses all his customers. This is the conventional result that the purely competitive price obtains if consumers are perfectly informed. On the other hand, if both groups face costly search ($c_1, c_2 > 0$), the SPE at p^* cannot obtain.

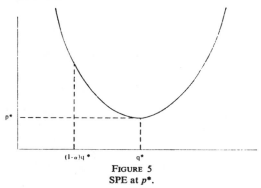

FIGURE 5
SPE at p^*.

Suppose the type 1's have perfect information ($c_1 = 0$), and the type 2's do not ($c_2 > 0$). If a deviant raises his price, he will lose all his type 1's and none of his type 2's. Since he will be earning a higher return on fewer sales, his profits may rise or fall. There is a limit on his price increase: if he chooses $p_d > u$, the type 2's will drop out of the market; if he chooses p_d such that type 2's find it worth while to gather information, he loses all his customers. If he charges p_d, the benefit of search is given by

$$b = \bar{p}' - p^{min} = \frac{1}{n^*}(p_d - p^*).$$

He loses no type 2 customers if he chooses a p_d such that $c_2 \geqq b$ and $p_d \leqq u$; that is, if $p_d \leqq \min [u, \; p^* + n^* c_2]$. Since the proportion of type 2's is $(1 - \alpha)$ his sales will be $q_d = (1 - \alpha)(L/n^*)$. Since $q^* = L/n^*$, we have $q_d = (1 - \alpha)q^*$. This deviant strategy will be profitable if $A(q_d)$, the average cost of producing q_d, is less than the price p_d. Thus, the SPE is *not broken* if and only if

$$A[(1 - \alpha)q^*] > \min (u, \; p^* + n^* c_2). \qquad \qquad ...(22)$$

(22) will hold for small u and c_2, for steep AC curves, and most crucially, for large α. This formalizes a notion that has always been implicit in competitive theory: *Every consumer need not have perfect information. If there are enough perfectly informed consumers (α high enough), the weight of their potential search keeps the market competitive. The informed exert a positive pecuniary externality on the uninformed.* As we shall see subsequently, this externality remains even when there is a price dispersion at equilibrium.

We now analyse the conditions under which a SPE obtains at the monopoly price u. If there is a SPE at u, every firm produces a quantity q_u as shown in Figure 6.

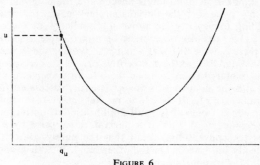

FIGURE 6

SPE at u.

As we argued previously, no firm will raise its price, for no consumer will pay more than u. If a deviant were to lower price to $p_d < u$, he lowers the minimum price more than he owers the mean price. Since $\bar{p}' = ((n - 1)/n)u + (1/n)p_d$, and $p^{min'} = p_d$, the benefit of search rises to

$$b = \bar{p}' - p^{min'} = \frac{n - 1}{n}(u - p_d).$$

If $b \geqq c_1$, the type 1's will search and the deviant's sales will jump to

$$q_d = (1 - \alpha)\frac{L}{n} + \alpha L = (1 - \alpha)q_u + \alpha L.$$

For large values of L,[11] this will be a profitable strategy if and only if

$$p_d \geqq p^*.$$

That is, a deviant firm can induce search by lowering price, but this will only lead to positive profits if the " search-inducing price ", p_d, is above the competitive price. Setting $c_1 = b$, we have the condition that this SPE is a full equilibrium if and only if

$$p_d = u - (n/(n-1))c_1 < p^*$$

or

$$u - p^* < \frac{n}{n-1} c_1. \qquad ...(23)$$

For $L \to \infty$, then $n \to \infty$ and we have

$$u - p^* \gtrsim c_1 \leqq c_2. \qquad ...(24)$$

This condition makes intuitive sense. If the deviant lowers price to p^*, the gains from search are (approximately) $u - p^*$. If the cost, c_1, of informing the type 1's of its location outweighs the benefit, the deviant will not induce search.

Two-Price Equilibria (TPE)

For the (c_1, c_2) discussed above, a SPE will obtain. For all other values of (c_1, c_2) either a TPE or no Nash-equilibrium obtains. The interaction between the three equilibrium conditions is seen most clearly in the analysis of a TPE. We will adopt the following notation. An equilibrium will be defined by a number of firms, n, of which a proportion, β, charge a low price, p_l, and the rest, a proportion $(1-\beta)$, charge a high price, p_h. A TPE with the property that $p_l = p^*$ was pictured previously in Figure 2.

(i) *Search Equilibrium.* For a TPE to obtain, it must be true that only those lower cost consumers become informed. (If all or none of the consumers become informed, every firm will obtain identical sales.) From the search rule in (6), we have the necessary condition

$$c_1 < \bar{p} - p^{\min} \leqq c_2.$$

Substituting the definition of $\bar{p}$, $\bar{p} = \beta p_l + (1-\beta)p_h$, we have

$$c_1 \leqq (1-\beta)(p_h - p_l) \leqq c_2. \qquad ...(25)$$

(ii) *Zero Profits.* Each of the n firms must earn zero profits. Given (25) the p_h firms sell only to uninformed consumers; the sales per firm-q_h is given by

$$q_h = (1-\alpha)\frac{L}{n}. \qquad ...(26)$$

The p_l firms obtain an identical share of the uninformed and share the informed consumers among themselves. Thus βn firms split up αL informed consumers, and each gets $\alpha L/\beta n$ of them. Each has sales given by

$$q_l = \left(1 - \alpha + \frac{\alpha}{\beta}\right)\frac{L}{n}. \qquad ...(27)$$

These sales must yield zero profits:

$$p_h = A\left((1-\alpha)\frac{L}{n}\right) \qquad ...(28)$$

$$p_l = A\left(\left(1 - \alpha + \frac{\alpha}{\beta}\right)\frac{L}{n}\right), \qquad ...(29)$$

where $A(q)$ is average costs.

(iii) *Maximum Profits.* As before, no deviant must be willing to break the TPE by charging a different price, either locally or globally. This consideration permits the following two Lemmas to be proved.

Lemma 3. $p_l = p^*$. *The low price is the competitive price.*

SALOP & STIGLITZ   COMPETITIVE EQUILIBRIUM   503

Proof. The proof of this proposition is straightforward. Consider a TPE in which $p_l > p^*$. If a deviant p_l firm were to shade its price slightly, it would obtain all the informed customers instead of only a proportion $(1/\beta n)$ of them. Its sales would jump and its profits would become positive. On the other hand, if $p_l = p^*$, then the deviant makes negative profits from price shading, regardless of the number of customers it obtains.

Lemma 4. $p_h = \min [u, p_l + (c_2/(1-\beta))]$. *Referring to (25), the high price is either the monopoly price or just high enough that the type 2's are indifferent between becoming informed and purchasing randomly.*

Proof. Suppose $p_h < p_l + (c_2/(1-\beta))$, that is, suppose $(1-\beta)(p_h - p_l) < c_2$. Then from (25), it is clear that the type 2 consumers prefer not to search. Thus, a deviant p_h firm could raise its price, lose no customers and increase its profits; this would break the TPE. Only if a deviant p_h firm loses its uninformed customers from price rises can the TPE obtain. This occurs only if small price rises induce them to exit from the market ($p_h = u$) or induce them to search, ($p_h = p^* + (c_2/1-\beta)$). Note that we follow the convention that if a consumer is indifferent between searching and purchasing randomly, he follows the latter strategy.

Substituting into (28) and (29) the results of Lemmas 3 and 4 for p_l and p_h, we summarize the TPE as follows:

$$A\left((1-\alpha)\frac{L}{n}\right) = \min\left(u, \ p^* + \frac{c_2}{1-\beta}\right) \qquad \qquad ...(30)$$

$$A\left(\left(1-\alpha+\frac{\alpha}{\beta}\right)\frac{L}{n}\right) = p^*. \qquad \qquad ...(31)$$

Further, since $p^* = A(q^*)$, we have

$$q^* = (1-\alpha-(\alpha/\beta))(L/n). \qquad \qquad ...(32)$$

Equations (30) and (31) may be solved for the equilibrium values of β and n. Note we also have the implicit constraint $0 < \beta < 1$.

A solution to these equations is a full equilibrium only if no firm can earn positive profits from globally deviating by charging a different price, for Lemmas 3 and 4 were local conditions only, and global deviance must also be checked. We will now solve (30)-(31) for β, n, and then check on globally deviant behaviour. We will find that profitable global deviance sometimes breaks the equilibrium.

The clearest method of the solution is to diagramme equations (30)-(32). Equation (31) is illustrated in Figure 7. It is easy to show the curve is downward sloping, since $d\beta/dn = -(\beta^2/n\alpha)(1-\alpha-(\alpha/\beta)) < 0$, where $(\alpha/\beta) > \alpha$ since $\beta < 1$.

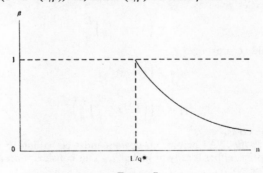

FIGURE 7

$\pi_l = 0.$

From (31), when $\beta = 1$, $A(L/n) = p^*$. From (32), we have $p^* = A(q^*)$, and, when $\beta = 1$, $n = L/q^*$ where q^* is the minimum average cost quantity.

The diagram of equation (30) is more difficult. There are two regions, depending on whether u or $p^* + (c_2/(1-\beta))$ is smaller. The boundary $(\hat{\beta})$ of these two regions may be positive or negative. Setting the two terms equal, we have

$$\hat{\beta} = 1 - \frac{c_2}{u - p^*}.$$

Setting $\hat{\beta} \gtreqless 0$, we have

$$\hat{\beta} \lesseqgtr 0 \Leftrightarrow c_2 \gtreqless u - p^*. \qquad \text{...(33)}$$

There are two β-regions to consider:

Region I $(\beta < 1 - c_2/(u-p^*))$. In this region, $p^* + (c_2/(1-\beta))$ is smaller, and the $\beta - n$ curve is upward sloping, since $d\beta/dn = -(1-\beta)^2 L(1-\alpha)A'/(c_2 n^2) > 0$. It is described by

$$p^* + \frac{c_2}{1-\beta} = A\left((1-\alpha)\frac{L}{n}\right).$$

The curve is asymptotic (as $\beta \to -\infty$) to $n = (1-\alpha)(L/q^*)$, from (32).

Region II $(\beta \geq 1 - c_2/(u-p^*))$. In this region, u is the minimum, and the equation is described by

$$u = A\left((1-\alpha)\frac{L}{n}\right). \qquad \text{...(34)}$$

Defining the quantity on the average cost curve at u by q_u, we have

$$q_u = (1-\alpha)\frac{L}{n}, \qquad \text{...(35)}$$

which defines an n_u such that

$$n_u = (1-\alpha)\frac{L}{q_u}. \qquad \text{...(36)}$$

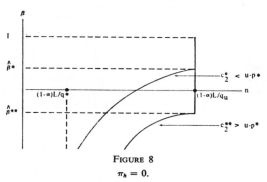

FIGURE 8

$\pi_h = 0$.

Equation (30) is shown in Figure 8 for two values of c_2. Possible TPE's occur where the curves cross. Noting that the minimum n in Figure 7 is L/q^* and maximum n in Figure 8 is $(1-\alpha)L/q_u$, then a necessary condition for a TPE arising from the interaction of the technology and the consumer distribution is given by

$$n_u = (1-\alpha)\frac{L}{q_u} > \frac{L}{q^*} \qquad \text{...(37)}$$

SALOP & STIGLITZ   COMPETITIVE EQUILIBRIUM   505

or rewriting

$$1-\alpha > \frac{q_u}{q^*}. \qquad \qquad ...(38)$$

Thus, a TPE will not exist for large α *or a steep average cost curve,* ((q_u/q^*) *large*). The intuition behind this result is as follows. Suppose the market consists primarily of low cost consumers (large α). The high-price firms, which sell only to unlucky high-cost consumers, will have a small market. If the average cost curve is steep enough, there will not be enough high-cost consumers to support even one high-price firm. As we will discuss subsequently, if this necessary condition is not met, there will be either no equilibrium or a SPE at the monopoly price, depending on (c_1, c_2).

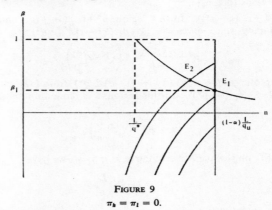

FIGURE 9
$\pi_h = \pi_l = 0.$

Assuming that this necessary condition is satisfied, a TPE exists as shown in Figure 9. If the equilibrium occurs at $n_u = (1-\alpha)L/q_u$ (at a point like E_1), then the high price equals the monopoly price, u. If the equilibrium occurs at a point like E_2, the high price is below the monopoly price. Given the technology, which equilibrium occurs will depend on c_2. When $\hat{\beta} < 0$, we certainly have E_1, or

$$p_h = u \quad \text{for} \quad c_2 > u - p^*. \qquad ...(39)$$

Intuitively, if c_2 is high enough, each high-price firm can raise its prices without inducing any c_2 customers to search. Thus, p_h will rise until the monopoly price is reached. (For $p > u$, c_2 customers will exit from the market. Thus, the rises in p_h stop at u.)

Referring to (30) and Figure 9, the TPE will occur at E_1, ($\beta = \beta_1$), if

$$p^* + \frac{c_2}{1-\beta_1} \gtreqless u, \qquad ...(40)$$

where β_1 is defined by (31) at $n_u = (1-\alpha)\dfrac{L}{q_u}$ by

$$\left(1-\alpha + \frac{\alpha}{\beta_1}\right)\frac{L}{n_u} = q^*. \qquad ...(41)$$

Substituting from n_u, we have

$$\beta_1 = \frac{\alpha}{1-\alpha}\left(\frac{1}{\dfrac{q^*}{q_u}-1}\right). \qquad ...(42)$$

If the necessary condition given by (38) holds, then $(q^*/q_u) - 1 > \alpha/(1 - \alpha)$. This defines a $\beta \in (0, 1)$, since $\beta_1 < 1$ follows from (42), and $\beta_1 > 0$ follows from $(q^*/q_u) > 0$. Substituting (42) into (40), we have

$$\beta = \beta_1, \quad p_h = u \quad \text{for} \quad c_2 \geq (1 - \beta_1)(u - p^*). \qquad \text{...(43)}$$

Similarly, from Figure 9,

$$\beta > \beta_1, \quad p_h < u, \quad \text{for} \quad c_2 < (1 - \beta_1)(u - p^*), \qquad \text{...(44)}$$

i.e. for smaller c_2, we have an equilibrium like E_2.

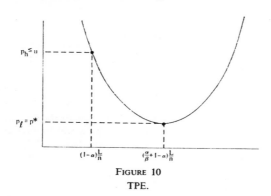

FIGURE 10

TPE.

Substituting into (26) and (27), we may calculate the number of firms. We have

$$n = (1 - \alpha) \frac{L}{q_h}. \qquad \text{...(45)}$$

We now confirm that these equations do define a full TPE. That is, we must show that in fact consumers are searching optimally, every firm is making zero profits, and every firm is maximizing profits.

(i) *Search Equilibrium.* From Lemmas 3 and 4, $c_2 \geq \bar{p} - p^{\min}$. Thus, c_2 consumers find it optimal to purchase randomly. At the $p_h < u$ TPE, since the c_2's are indifferent to search, then c_1 consumers do *prefer* to gather information, since $c_1 < c_2$. At the $p_h = u$ TPE, the necessary condition that the c_1 consumers do gather information is, of course, just opposite of the condition that the c_2 consumers do not search.

$$c_1 < (1 - \beta_1)(u - p^*) \qquad \text{...(46a)}$$

$$c_2 \geq (1 - \beta_1)(u - p^*). \qquad \text{...(46b)}$$

(ii) *Zero Profits.* By setting price equal to average cost, the TPE was constructed to obey the zero profit conditions.

(iii) *Maximum Profits.* We now show that no potentially deviant p_l or p_h firm can increase its profits by charging a different price. We examine a p_l deviant first.

Suppose a p_l deviant raises his price. The mean price $\bar{p}$ will rise without affecting $p^{\min}$, raising the benefits of search. Since the c_1 consumers were already searching, their behaviour will not change. The c_2 consumers could be induced to search. If they do, they will purchase from the non-deviant p_l firms. The p_l deviant's sales will fall to zero. Thus, p_l deviance is unprofitable.

Suppose a p_h deviant lowers his price to $p_d < p_h$. The mean price falls without affecting $p^{\min}$. This lowers the benefits from search. Since the c_2 consumers previously found it non-optimal to search, their behaviour is not affected. However, it is possible that the

SALOP & STIGLITZ   COMPETITIVE EQUILIBRIUM   507

benefits fall enough to make search by the c_1 consumers non-optimal. If they begin purchasing randomly, the p_h deviant's sales rise from $(1-\alpha)L/n$ to $q_d = (L/n)$.

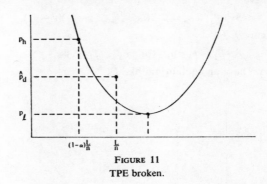

FIGURE 11
TPE broken.

Thus, if the $\hat{p}_d$ which eliminates search is high enough for the deviant to cover his average costs, large p_h deviance will be profitable and the TPE will be broken. This situation is shown in Figure 11. The necessary condition for such " global " p_h deviance to be unprofitable is given by

$$\hat{p}_d < A\left(\frac{L}{n}\right),\qquad\qquad\text{...(47)}$$

where $\hat{p}$ is the price such that

$$\bar{p}' - p^{\min} = c_1,\qquad\qquad\text{...(48)}$$

where

$$\bar{p}' = \beta p^* + \left(1-\beta-\frac{1}{n}\right)p_h + \frac{1}{n}\hat{p}_d.\qquad\qquad\text{...(49)}$$

Substituting (49) into (48) and using Lemmas 3 and 4, we have

$$\hat{p}_d = \begin{cases} p_h - n(c_2 - c_1) & \text{for } p_h < u \\ p_h - n[(1-\beta_1)(u-p^*) - c_1] & \text{for } p_h = u. \end{cases}\qquad\text{...(50)}$$

For large values of L, n will be large and (47) will be satisfied. Intuitively, if there are many firms, a p_h deviant will have a very small effect on the average price; thus, it will be unable to stop the c_1 consumers from gathering information. Note that this condition assumed that only one firm deviated. If a significant number of p_h firms colluded in jointly lowering price, they could break the TPE more easily. This raises the possibility that duopoly may lead to lower prices than competition.

We have derived regions of (c_1, c_2) under which there are SPE, TPE and no equilibria. We summarized these regions in Figure 1. Under the assumption that $L\to\infty$, the regions do not overlap and the equilibrium (if it exists) is unique for all $c_2 \geq c_1 \geq 0$.[12]

If the technology is such that $\beta_1 \geq 1$ (i.e. $1-\alpha \leq (q_u/q^*)$), there is a SPE at $p = u$ for $c_1, c_2 \geq u-p^*$ and no equilibrium for lower c_1, c_2.[13]

Non-existence of Equilibrium

For certain values of $(\alpha, q_u, q^*, c_1, c_2)$ we have shown that no equilibrium exists, because if some deviant changes his price substantially, he will earn positive profits. If firms engaged only in " local " price experiments, but not in " global " price experiments, the non-existence region would not occur. Alternatively, if the deviant realizes that others will react to his deviance, then he may not break the equilibrium. With this in mind, a " limit price " equilibrium concept can be defined as follows. There exists some price p^L and associated quantity q^L for every firm such that (i) profits are zero, (ii) no deviant can break the equilibrium with price decreases and (iii) if any firm attempts to increase short-run profits by raising price, another deviant can lower its price discretely and capture all the c_1 consumers (and possibly the c_2 consumers as well). Thus, this limit price equilibrium is a reaction function equilibrium.

p^L is derived as follows for the case in which $c_1 = c_2 = c$.[14]

$$p^L = A(q^L). \quad \text{(zero profits)} \qquad \qquad \text{...(51)}$$

$$q^L = \frac{L}{n}. \quad \text{(equal market shares)} \qquad \qquad \text{...(52)}$$

$$\frac{n-1}{n}(p^L - p^*) = c. \qquad \text{(search equilibrium)} \qquad \qquad \text{...(53)}$$

Equation (53) expresses the notion that if some deviant lowers price to p^*, he will just induce search. Rewriting, we have

$$p^L = p^* + \frac{n}{n-1}c, \qquad \qquad \text{...(54)}$$

where (51) and (52) define n. For large n, $n/(n-1) \cong 1$, and we have

$$p^L \cong p^* + c. \qquad \qquad \text{...(55)}$$

Note that p^L is not a " Nash " equilibrium with respect to deviant price increases. A single firm could raise price slightly without losing any customers. However, this would then induce another deviant to lower price. That is, if a firm acts in its *short-run* interest, it will destroy the equilibrium by allowing other firms drastically to cut prices to induce search. Prices may then begin to oscillate between the competitive price p^* and the limit price. The exact dynamics will depend on the dynamic learning process of consumers and firms. In general, prices may creep up slowly to slightly above the limit price, inducing a price war down to p^*, only to again begin the upward creep. The frequency and regularity of the cycle will depend on the adjustment speeds of price changes, entry, and the learning by consumers. In that smaller more competitive firms will be more likely to act in their short-run interests at the expense of the long-run, this leads to the notion that competitive markets will be more unstable than oligopolistic markets.

CONCLUSIONS

In this paper, we have analysed the industry equilibrium for an economy in which imperfectly informed consumers can only become perfectly informed at a cost. This assumption leads to a monopolistically competitive equilibrium and generally to price dispersion as well, even though the commodity produced by each firm is identical.

The price dispersion here is different from that analysed by Grossman and Stiglitz [5] and Mortensen [6], where costly information leads to incomplete market adjustments to exogenous shocks. Such markets are incompletely arbitraged. Furthermore, the price dispersion generated here is specifically associated with a market economy; a socialist economy with exactly the same information and production technology would require all stores to charge the same price.

This paper is one of a series dealing with the effects of costly information on market equilibrium. These studies differ with respect to the technology of information acquisition and the characteristics of consumers and producers. In the model examined here, con-sumers differ only in their costs of information acquisition. In Salop [10] and Salop and Stiglitz [13] individuals differ also in their demand functions. A further reason for price dispersion arises there. Firms attempt to act as discriminating monopolists. The costs of information allows them to exercise this kind of discrimination, which they would be unable to do in a competitive market with perfect information. Finally, in Salop and Stiglitz [13], Butters [3] and Stiglitz [17], even when individuals are identical *ex ante* in both search costs and demand functions, price dispersion may occur.

Finally, one shortcoming with this model is that possible " indirect information " contained in the prices and market shares are ignored by consumers. Low-priced stores have larger market shares, since they sell to informed as well as uninformed buyers. If uninformed buyers observed the market shares of firms, then purchasing according to market shares would assure them the lower price. This is an example of the more general notion that in the presence of some informed consumers, uninformed consumers ought to " buy with the market "; price will reflect quality and market shares will reflect the overall " best buys ".[15]

If there is no heterogeneity in preferences, advertising, or differential costs of production, this result is true in our model. However, in general there will be other " noise " in the market so that there is still a net benefit to becoming informed; Grossman and Stiglitz have shown that generally an equilibrium with price dispersion will still obtain.

First version received April 1975; *final version accepted October* 1976 (*Eds.*).

The views expressed herein are those of the authors and do not necessarily represent the views of the Board of Governors of the Federal Reserve System. We are grateful to Avi Braverman, Andy Weiss, Larry Weiss and other participants at the IMSSS Conference at Stanford University and Steve Salant, Peter von zur Muehlen and Roger Waud at the Federal Reserve Board for helpful conversations. Stiglitz's work was supported by National Science Foundation Grant No. SOC74-22182 at the Institute for Mathematical Studies in the Social Sciences, Stanford University.

NOTES

1. u may be thought of as the marginal utility in dollar terms of the unit of the durable.
2. Cf. G. Butters [3], P. von zur Muehlen [18], Stiglitz [17] and Salop and Stiglitz [13]. The basic result on the existence of equilibrium with price distributions remains valid in these models.
3. Note that $\bar{p}$ is not weighted by sales of each store. It is not the mean price measured in the price dispersion literature. For a model in which consumers know market shares, see Smallwood and Conlisk [15].
4. Risk aversion is effectively captured in c^i.
5. If $E_S^i = E_N^i$, the consumer is just indifferent. We follow the convention that indifferent consumers do not buy the newspaper. This assumption is not crucial. If the opposite convention were followed or it were assumed indifferent consumers flipped a coin, the equilibrium prices would change only by an arbitrarily small epsilon.
6. Its output is the lower of the two outputs which share a common AC. Thus, each firm's output is demand-constrained at equilibrium (it would like to sell more if it could) unless the firm charges the competitive price.
7. More precisely, we have, for a finite n^*,

$$\pi(\hat{p}_j \mid \hat{p}^{-j}) \geqq 0, \quad \text{for all} \quad j = 1, 2, ..., n^*$$
$$\pi(\hat{p}_j \mid \hat{p}^{-j}) \leqq 0, \quad \text{for all} \quad j = 1, 2, ..., n^*+1.$$

8. If no consumers search, every firm has identical sales and the p_h firm has highest profits. If consumers all search, the p_m and p_h firms have no sales at all.
9. It is possible that q_d is so large that $p_d < AC(q_d)$. That is, the deviant is swamped with customers. This is a potential problem for any competitive model. Cf. Salop [11].
10. With downward-sloping demand curves, this would be at the Chamberlinean monopolistically competitive price. See Braverman [2].
11. We assume L is very large so as to not bias the case against perfect competition. Once again, we ignore the fact that the deviant will be swamped with customers.
12. For finite L, there are regions in which both a SPE at u and a TPE exist. See equations (16) and (46).
13. We effectively move the axes of Figure 1 over to $(1-\beta_1)(u-p^*)$.
14. Note that if $c_1 = c_2$, a TPE must have the property that all consumers are just indifferent to search. If we follow the convention that indifference implies no search, then a TPE is impossible. On the other hand, if we assume that an indifferent consumer chooses to search with probability α, then a different TPE obtains for each α. For an example of such a model, see Stiglitz [17]. Shilony [14] derives a similar mixed strategy equilibrium.
15. This has been explored by Nelson [7] and Smallwood and Conlisk [15].

510   REVIEW OF ECONOMIC STUDIES

REFERENCES

[1]   Akerlof, G.   " The Market for ' Lemons ':   Qualitative Uncertainty and the Market Mechanism ",
      Quarterly Journal of Economics (1970).
[2]   Braverman, A.   " Price Dispersion in Monopolistic Competition " (Ph.D. Dissertation, Stanford
      University, 1976).
[3]   Butters, G.   " Equilibrium Distributions of Sales and Advertising Prices ", (this volume).
[4]   Diamond, P.   " A Model of Price Adjustment ", *Journal of Economic Theory* (1971).
[5]   Grossman, S. and Stiglitz, J.   " Information and Competitive Price Systems ", *American Economic
      Review, Papers and Proceedings* (May 1976).
[6]   Mortensen, D. T.   " Search Equilibrium in a Simple Multi-Market Economy " (Center for Mathe-
      matical Studies, Discussion Paper No. 54, Northwestern University, October 1973).
[7]   Nelson, P.   " Information and Consumer Behavior ", *Journal of Economic Theory* (1970).
[8]   Phelps, E. and Winter, S.   " Optimal Price Policy Under Atomistic Competition ", in Phelps, E.,
      et al., *Microeconomic Foundations of Inflation and Employment Theory* (New York, 1970).
[9]   Rothschild, M.   " A Two-Armed Bandit Theory of Market Pricing ", *Journal of Economic Theory*
      (1974).
[10] Salop, S.   " The Noisy Monopolist ", (this volume).
[11] Salop, S.   " On the Non-Existence of Competitive Equilibrium " (Federal Reserve Board, 1976).
[12] Salop, S. and Stiglitz, J.   " A Framework for Analyzing Monopolistically Competitive Price Dis-
      persion " (Federal Reserve Board, 1975).
[13] Salop, S. and Stiglitz, J.   " A Theory of Sales " (Stanford University, 1976).
[14] Shilony, Y.   " Mixed Pricing in Locational Oligopoly ", (Berkeley, 1975).
[15] Smallwood, D. and Conlisk, J.   " Produce Quality in Markets Where Consumers are Imperfectly
      Informed and Naive "(UCSD, 1975).
[16] Stigler, G.   " The Economics of Information ", *Journal of Political Economy* (1961).
[17] Stiglitz, J.   " Equilibrium Wage Distributions " (Technical Report No. 154, Economics Series,
      Institute for Mathematical Studies in the Social Science, Stanford University, 1974).
[18] von zur Muehlen, P.   " Sequential Search and Price Dispersion in Monopolistic Competition ",
      (Federal Reserve Board, 1976).

[33]

Econometrica, Vol. 52, No. 1 (January, 1984)

NONCOOPERATIVE COLLUSION UNDER IMPERFECT PRICE INFORMATION

By Edward J. Green and Robert H. Porter[1]

Recent work in game theory has shown that, in principle, it may be possible for firms in an industry to form a self-policing cartel to maximize their joint profits. This paper examines the nature of cartel self-enforcement in the presence of demand uncertainty. A model of a noncooperatively supported cartel is presented, and the aspects of industry structure which would make such a cartel viable are discussed.

1. INTRODUCTION

LONG-STANDING QUESTIONS about how widespread is the occurrence of collusion in industries having several firms, and about the extent to which the performance of industries experiencing such collusion departs from the competitive norm, continue to provoke spirited debate. In this paper we offer a theory of collusive industry equilibrium which will provide a means of clarifying these questions.

In his classic paper "A Theory of Oligopoly" [15], George Stigler appealed to dynamic considerations to explain how apparently cooperative industry performance might result from noncooperative motives. According to this theory, the firms of an industry form a cartel, which is designed to enforce monopolistic conduct in a self-policing way. "Self-policing" means precisely that the agreed-upon conduct is noncooperatively viable and that it remains so over time.

Stigler's theory differs markedly from traditional oligopoly theories based on static equilibrium concepts (e.g., Cournot and Stackelberg). This difference is particularly striking in the case of an industry structure which is essentially immune from entry. The traditional theories would suggest that the performance of such an industry should be largely determined by its degree of concentration —the number of firms in the industry and their relative sizes—and by the extent to which substitute goods are available. In contrast, Stigler suggested that the greatest obstacle to collusion in the absence of entry would be what he character-ized as "secret price cutting." By informally relating concentration and various other features of industry structure to the immunity of a cartel from entry and to its ability to deter inimical firm behavior, and by assuming that industry profitability reflects successful operation of a cartel, he justified the use of cross-industry regressions to test his theory.

The obvious interpretation of Stigler is that he made explicit a theory of oligopoly which implicitly conceived of a cartel as a "policeman" which with some frequency is required to punish destabilizing "offenses" of individual cartel

[1] We have accepted the generous help of many colleagues in the course of this research. We would particularly like to thank C. Berry, T. Bresnahan, J. Friedman, J. Mirrlees, S. Salop, H. Sonnenschein, and R. Willig. Robert Porter's research received support from a Sloan Foundation grant to the University of Minnesota Economics Department.

members. The somewhat different interpretation of this paper is that Stigler had a view of cartel organization as an instance of an optimization problem: to design an institution which achieves an efficient equilibrium outcome subject to the constraint that agents in the institution behave noncooperatively. On this interpretation, the optimal cartel structure may be one which provides member firms with strong positive incentives which make collusive behavior attractive, rather than one which provides insufficient incentives and which severely punishes defecting firms after the fact.

In fact, two formulations of the cartel problem exist already which treat noncooperative collusion in a rigorous way. Osborne [8] proposes a reaction function equilibrium in which firms respond to changes in output by other firms in order to maintain their proportionate share of industry output. (See also the extensions of Spence [13, 14].) Knowing that other firms will respond in this manner, each firm will realize that it does not pay to deviate from the collusive output level.

Friedman [3], on the other hand, outlines a strategy in which firms respond to suspected cheating, which they infer from a drop in the market price below the price that obtains when all firms produce at agreed-upon levels, by producing at Cournot levels thereafter. If future profit streams are discounted sufficiently slowly, then a firm would reduce the discounted value of its returns by failing to collude. Therefore, for all firms to adopt the collusive strategy would be a noncooperative equilibrium.

The trouble with these formulations, from an applied industrial organization viewpoint, is that incentives in these equilibria are so perfect that the deterrent mechanisms are never observed. Then it may be difficult to infer from econometric time-series evidence whether the observed market data is the outcome of a quasicompetitive or collusive equilibrium (cf. T. Bresnahan [2]). The substance of the present contribution is that this perfection is an artifact of the certainty world in which these models are formulated. When the considerations of imperfect information, which played a decisive role in Stigler's theory, are reintroduced, optimal incentive structures may involve episodic recourse to the kind of short-run unprofitable conduct which would have been characterized as "price wars" or "punishment" previously.

Our argument has three parts. First, we frame a precise definition of collusion in terms of industry conduct. Second, we show that collusive conduct may, in a particular industry structure, result in a pattern of industry performance marked by recurrent episodes in which price and profit levels sharply decrease. Thus we reject the received view that performance of this type necessarily indicates an industry where firms are engaging in a sequence of abortive attempts to form a cartel. Since this opinion is often used as a basis to deny the need for intervention to promote competition in such industries (because the market purportedly is already withstanding the collusive assaults), our argument suggests the need to re-examine a widely-held assumption about policy.

Third, we point out that the distinctive character of the phenomenon just discussed and the necessary appearance of this phenomenon if collusion is to take place (given the particular industry structure in question) make it possible to draw clear-cut conclusions about the presence or absence of collusion in some specific industries on the basis of market data. This is a singular opportunity to learn about whether collusion does indeed exist in situations where it might plausibly occur, without having to face the many problems of interpretation surrounding the usual cross-industry tests of its extent.[2]

2. COLLUSION UNDER UNCERTAINTY

Collusive equilibria exhibiting stable performance may possibly characterize some industries. For instance, a market might be segmented geographically because firms have divided it. As long as this agreement was adhered to, each firm would be a monopolist within its area. Moreover, poaching by one firm in another's territory would be quickly and surely detected, and would invite retaliation. In that situation, no one would poach. All that would ever be "observed" is monopolistic conduct.[3]

Similarly, in an industry in which contracts are awarded by competitive bidding, a scheme to rotate winning bids might be perfectly enforceable. Each firm would act as a monopolist when its turn came, and would clearly see that bidding low out of turn would jeopardize a profitable arrangement. Again, only monopolistic conduct would ever be "observed."[4]

We will study a model in which demand fluctuations not directly observed by firms lead to unstable industry performance. Intuitively firms will act monopolistically while prices remain high, but they will revert for a while to Cournot behavior when prices fall. Specifically, it will be assumed that firms agree on a "trigger price" to which they compare the market price when they set their production.[5] Whenever the market price dips below the trigger price while they have been acting monopolistically, they will revert to Cournot behavior for some fixed amount of time before resuming monopolistic conduct.

Suppose that, at a given time, firms are supposed to be colluding (i.e., they expect one another to collude). If a firm produces more than its share of the monopoly output, its net return at that time will increase. However, by increasing the probability that the market price will fall below the trigger price, the firm incurs a greater risk that the industry will enter a reversionary episode during which profits will be low for everyone. For producing its monopolistic share to be

---

[2] These problems, involving both the nature of the cross-industry data and also the logical difficulties of using it as a basis for inference are described in the essays by J. McGee, H. Demsetz, and L. Weiss in [4].

[3] A referee has suggested that the U.S. steel industry employed such an enforcement device in the first half of this century.

[4] For example, a "phases of the moon" system has been used to allocate low-bidding privileges in the high voltage switchgear industry. (See Scherer [12, Chapter 6].)

[5] It is logically possible for this agreement to be a tacit one which arises spontaneously. Nevertheless, in view of the relative complexity of the conduct to be specified by this particular equilibrium and of the need for close coordination among its participants, it seems natural to assume here that the equilibrium arises from an explicit agreement.

the firms' noncooperatively optimal action, the marginal expected loss in future profits from possibly triggering a Cournot reversion must exactly balance (in terms of present discounted value) the marginal gain from over-producing. For appropriate distributions of the demand disturbance, reversionary episodes will sometimes occur without any firm defecting, simply because of low demand. Thus, over a long period, both Cournot behavior and collusive behavior will be observed at various times. In this respect, collusion under uncertainty differs markedly from the collusive equilibria under certainty discussed earlier. The fact that both monopolistic and Cournot performance are observed will make it possible to identify statistically the collusive equilibrium under uncertainty.

We now address the question of exactly what sort of industry our model might appropriately describe. Such an industry would have a structure possessing four features.

First, the industry is presumed to be stable over time. Temporal stability is required if the assumption that firms have rational expectations—an assumption which underlies the use of Nash equilibrium—is to be credible. On a more technical level, it justifies the use of stationary dynamic programming to characterize equilibrium.[6]

Second, output quantity is assumed to be the only decision variable which firms can manipulate. In particular, firms should not be able to engage in product differentiation or have ability to divide their market regionally. With firm decisions so restricted, asymmetric cartel incentive schemes are ruled out. In particular, even if one firm were suspected of violating a cartel agreement, other firms would have no way of isolating it and punishing it differentially.

Third, except for each firm's private knowledge about its present and past production, information about the industry and its environment is public. The Nash equilibrium assumption presupposes that firms have an accurate idea of their competitor's cost functions, for example. Also, for firms to coordinate effectively in keeping track of whether the industry is in a collusive or a reversionary state, they must all observe the realization of a common variable.

Fourth, the information which firms use to monitor whether the cartel is in a collusive or reversionary state must be imperfectly correlated with firms' conduct. Otherwise, if compliance were optimal for firms in collusive periods, reversion would never occur. Price is not the only information variable which could be used for monitoring—price data with correction for a systematic demand component, or market share information, would also be subject to error. However, this assumption of imperfect information is incompatible with transactions in the industry being few and publicly announced (e.g., with individual contracts being awarded on the basis of sealed-bid auctions) or with completely accurate and current market-share information being available to firms.

---

[6] Radner [11] considers the case of time-average utilities. His work relies essentially on the measurability of utility in the tail sigma-field of payoffs, which asymptotic-average utility satisfies. In contrast, discounted utility is not measurable with respect to the tail sigma-field, so that our work is not directly comparable to [11].

In our model firms monitor market price, which imperfectly reflects the output levels of other firms. We assume that the products of the firms are of homogeneous quality, and so they face a common market price. This structure is adopted for expositional ease. An environment in which firms monitored their own market share, which imperfectly reflected the price choices of other firms, would be more in the spirit of Stigler's paradigm.

We now give a formal description of collusion under uncertainty as a Nash equilibrium in contingent strategies. Consider an oligopoly of n firms which produce an undifferentiated product in a stationary and time separable environment. This environment is like that described in Friedman [3], except that demand is subject to multiplicative uncertainty. Specifically, i, j range over *firms* $1, \ldots, n$. $\pi_i : R_+^2 \to R$ is the *return function* of i. $\pi_i(x_i, p)$ is i's net return from producing x_i units and selling at price p. β is the discount rate. Firms are risk neutral and maximize $E[\sum_{t=0}^{\infty} \beta^t \pi_i(x_{it}, p_t)]$. Observed price $p_t = \theta_t p(\sum_{i=1}^{n} x_{it})$, where $p : R_+ \to R_+$. The random variables θ_t are i.i.d. with c.d.f. F having continuous density f. $E(\theta) = 1$. Each θ_t is a demand shock which firms cannot observe directly.[7]

A *contingent strategy* for firm i is an infinite sequence $s_i = (s_{i0}, s_{i1}, \ldots)$, where s_{i0} is a determinate initial output level x_{i0}, and $s_{it+1} : R_+^{t+1} \to R_+$ determines i's output level at time $t + 1$ as a function of past prices by $s_{it+1}(p_0, \ldots, p_t) = x_{it+1}$. The choice of domain reflects the assumption that firms do not observe rivals' production levels directly.

A strategy profile $(s_1, \ldots, s_n)$ determines recursively a stochastic process of prices, which in turn induces a probability distribution on the space of infinite sequences of prices. Expectation with respect to this distribution will be denoted by $E_{s_1 \ldots s_n}$.

A Nash equilibrium is a strategy profile $(s_1^*, \ldots, s_n^*)$ which satisfies

(1) $$E_{s_1^* \ldots s_i \ldots s_n^*} \left[\sum_{t=0}^{\infty} \beta^t \pi_i(s_{it}(p_0, \ldots, p_{t-1}), p_t) \right]$$

$$\leq E_{s_1^* \ldots s_i^* \ldots s_n^*} \left[\sum_{t=0}^{\infty} \beta^t \pi_i(s_{it}^*(p_0, \ldots, p_{t-1}), p_t) \right]$$

for all firms i and feasible strategies s_i.

Now consider how the industry might produce at a monopolistic level most of the time (i.e., except during reversionary episodes) in a Nash equilibrium in trigger price strategies. Firms will initially produce their respective shares of this restricted industry output, and will continue to do so until the market price falls below a trigger price $\bar{p}$. Then they will produce Cournot outputs for the duration (we will specify this to be $T - 1$ periods) of a reversionary episode, regardless of

---

[7]James Friedman has suggested to us that the variables θ_t might alternatively be specified to be a martingale, so that the prices p_t would also be a martingale. This property ought to be satisfied if the good is a durable, or if consumption is perfectly substitutable across times. We retain the i.i.d. specification which makes the analysis simpler, but acknowledge that it is restrictive.

what happens to prices during this time. At the conclusion of the episode, T periods after the price drop, they will resume monopolistic production. This will continue until the next time that $p_t < \bar{p}$, and so forth.[8]

Formally, let $y = (y_1, \ldots, y_n)$ be a profile of restricted outputs, and let $z = (z_1, \ldots, z_n)$ be a Cournot output profile. Choose a price level $\bar{p}$ and a length of time T. Define time t to be *normal* if (a) $t = 0$, or (b) $t - 1$ was normal and $\bar{p} \leq p_{t-1}$, or (c) $t - T$ was normal and $p_{t-T} < \bar{p}$. Define t to be *reversionary* otherwise. Define strategies for firms by

$$x_{it} = \begin{cases} y_i & \text{if } t \text{ is normal,} \\ z_i & \text{if } t \text{ is reversionary.} \end{cases}$$

These are well-defined policy strategies.

Each firm faces a stationary two-state (normal and reversionary) T-stage Markov dynamic programming problem. Its optimal policy is to produce z_i in reversionary periods, and to produce some fixed quantity r in normal periods. Let $V_i(r)$ be the expected discounted present value of firm i if it sets $x_{it} = r$ in normal periods. Define

$$w_i = \sum_{j \neq i} y_j, \quad \gamma_i(r) = E_\theta \pi_i(r, \theta p(r + w_i)), \quad \delta_i = E_\theta \pi_i \left[z_i, \theta p \left(\sum_{j \leq n} z_j \right) \right].$$

In normal periods, i anticipates that the aggregate output of the other firms will be w_i, and so $\gamma_i(r)$ is the expected profit of then producing r. The expected profit in reversionary periods is δ_i. Let $Pr(\cdot)$ denote probability with respect to the distribution of θ. We assume that $\gamma_i(y_i) > \delta_i$ for each firm i. Then V_i satisfies the functional equation

$$(2) \qquad V_i(r) = \gamma_i(r) + \beta Pr(\bar{p} \leq \theta p(r + w_i)) V_i(r)$$

$$+ Pr(\theta p(r + w_i) < \bar{p}) \left[\sum_{t=1}^{T-1} \beta^t \delta_i + \beta^T V_i(r) \right].$$

$Pr(\theta p(r + w_i) < \bar{p}) = F(\bar{p}/p(r + w_i))$, so (2) is equivalent to

$$(3) \qquad V_i(r) = \frac{\gamma_i(r) + F(\bar{p}/p(r + w_i))((\beta - \beta^T)/(1 - \beta))\delta_i}{1 - \beta + (\beta - \beta^T)F(\bar{p}/p(r + w_i))}$$

$$= \frac{\gamma_i(r) - \delta_i}{1 - \beta + (\beta - \beta^T)F(\bar{p}/p(r + w_i))} + \frac{\delta_i}{1 - \beta}.$$

Thus the expected discounted present value of firm i equals what it would be in a Cournot environment, plus the single-period gain in returns to colluding, appropriately discounted. Inequality (1), the defining condition for Nash equilib-

---

[8] For simplicity, we are considering only the simplest variant of a trigger price strategy. For example, firms might condition T on the amount by which $\bar{p}$ exceeds the observed market price.

rium, can now be rewritten

(4) $V_i(r) \leq V_i(y_i)$ for all r and i.

The first-order condition for (4) is

(5) $V_i'(y_i) = 0$ for all i.

Using the fact that $(f/g)' = 0$ if and only if $f'g - fg' = 0$, (5) is equivalent to

(6) $$0 = \left[1 - \beta + (\beta - \beta^T) F\left(\bar{p} / p\left(\sum_{j \leq n} y_j \right) \right) \right] \gamma_i'(y_i)$$

$$+ (\beta - \beta^T) f\left(\bar{p} / p\left(\sum_{j \leq n} y_j \right) \right) \left[\bar{p} p'\left(\sum_{j \leq n} y_j \right) \middle/ \left(p\left(\sum_{j \leq n} y_j \right) \right)^2 \right]$$

$$\times (\gamma_i(y_i) - \delta_i)$$

for all i.

Equation (6) states that the marginal return to a firm from increasing its production in normal periods $(\gamma_i'(y_i))$ must be offset exactly by the marginal increase in risk of suffering a loss in returns $(\gamma_i(y_i) - \delta_i)$ by triggering a reversionary episode. When this condition holds for all firms, n differential constraints are placed on the n-dimensional vector y of restricted outputs in equilibrium. Thus, the assertion that an equilibrium which satisfies an additional constraint exists will require careful justification. In particular, the output profile which maximizes total returns to the industry may not be supportable in equilibrium.[9]

There are two related final observations about the formal model of collusion under uncertainty. First, no firm ever defects from the cartel. More precisely, no firm i has any private information that would lead it to assess its return function π_i more accurately than its competitors do. Thus, every competitor is able to figure out what i will do to maximize profits. The market price reveals information about demand only, and never leads i's competitors to revise their beliefs about how much i has produced. In equilibrium, the frequency of reversion from normal states will be given by $F(\bar{p}/p(\sum y_j))$.

Second, despite the fact that firms know that low prices reflect demand conditions rather than overproduction by competitors, it is rational for them to participate in reversionary episodes.[10] Basically, a reversionary episode is just a temporary switch to a Nash equilibrium in noncontingent strategies. It does not pay any firm to deviate unilaterally from its Nash strategy in this temporary

---

[9]In [9] it is shown that, for symmetric firms under imperfect price information, the output profile for normal periods which will maximize discounted industry profits in a noncooperative equilibrium in trigger price strategies is different from the profile which would be chosen if the industry were a monopoly. I.e., firms forego some profits in normal periods in order to reduce the frequency and duration of reversion needed to provide appropriate incentives, if $\bar{p}$ and T are chosen to maximize expected discounted profits subject to the incentive compatibility constraint (5).

[10]To be precise, we argue here that the equilibrium is perfect or sequentially rational. A formal statement and proof of this assertion are given in [5].

situation, any more than it would if the industry were permanently a Cournot industry. It might be asked why Cournot equilibrium is appropriate at all. If firms know at a particular time that a low price has been observed in the past, and that the cartel has had a perfect record of monopolistic conduct, why do firms not disregard the price and continue to act monopolistically? The answer is that everyone understands the incentive properties of equilibrium. If firms did not revert to Cournot behavior in response to low prices, equation (5) would not hold the rest of the time, so monopolistic behavior would cease to be individually optimal for firms.

We realize that the assumptions about industry structure are quite restrictive. We emphasize that the particular Nash equilibrium we are studying is not the only sort of Nash equilibrium which would be collusive according to the definition offered in this section, and that evidence that this particular Nash equilibrium occurs in a specific industry is not the only evidence relevant to forming an opinion about the extent of collusion in various sectors of the economy. However, even though the direct applicability of our model is severely limited, it would be valuable to examine an industry for which it would be appropriate. We believe that the American rail freight industry in the 1880's was one example of an industry which satisfies our structural conditions quite well. Studies of that industry by Paul MacAvoy [7] and Thomas Ulen [16, 17] have produced qualitative conclusions which are consistent with our model. Recent econometric work by Porter [10] (based on the extensive time series data collected by Ulen) strengthens these conclusions.

3. PRICE PROCESSES GENERATED BY COLLUSION

The equilibrium discussed in the preceding section is noteworthy because it reverses the traditional interpretations of a certain kind of industry price pattern. According to these traditional interpretations, an episode in which price drops sharply, remains low for some time, and then sharply rises again without there being an apparent cost or demand shock would indicate one of two possible events. The episode might be a symptom of the predatory reaction of incumbent firms to a threatened entry. Alternatively, it might signal (as in Stigler's theory) a breakdown of a cartel agreement followed by the reestablishment of the agreement. In either case, such evidence would indicate the fragility of collusion among the incumbents. Thus, in the formulation of policy, it has sometimes been argued that intervention to promote competition would likely be redundant in markets where these episodes are already occurring.

In marked contrast, such episodes play an essential role in the maintenance of an ongoing scheme of collusive incentives in the model presented here. While the traditional views would predict the transience of collusion in a market marked by these episodes of price depression, and with the demise of collusion also the cessation of the price instability which it engendered, our model suggests that industries having certain structural characteristics (i.e., the four characteristics enumerated in the previous section) will exhibit price instability as a feature of a stable, time-stationary pattern of prices if its member firms are colluding. This observation raises the question of whether it is possible to estimate consistently, from the stochastic process of prices generated by a collusive equilibrium of the form described in Section 2, the trigger price $\bar{p}$ and the reversionary length T which determine that equilibrium. The answer to this question is affirmative. Moreover, there also exists an estimator which is computationally attractive and which has only a small asymptotic bias if the interval between price observations is short relative to both the length of reversionary episodes and the expected length of normal episodes—the situation which one would expect to encounter in an industry where collusion actually did confer significant market power on firms.

While a discussion of estimation *per se* lies beyond the scope of this paper, we characterize in the Appendix the stochastic process of prices which arises in the equilibrium of the model presented in Section 2. It can be shown that any data series of prices may be treated as a sample path of a stationary ergodic process. This result provides a foundation for the study of asymptotic properties of estimation of the model, because it justifies the use of the ergodic theorem [1, Theorem 6.28] to generalize the role which the law of large numbers plays in the estimation theory of independent processes.[11] (In particular, the existence of consistent estimators of $\bar{p}$ and T is a consequence of the ergodic theorem.) In the Appendix, the price process will be compared to an alternative process which is a Markov version of the well-known Bernoulli switching process (cf. [6]). It can be shown that a data series of prices may be regarded as a "contaminated sample path" of the alternative process, and the degree of contamination will be computed as a function of the true parameters of the equilibrium.

Federal Reserve Board
        and
University of Minnesota

Manuscript received September, 1982; final revision received March, 1983.

APPENDIX

To begin, consider a very general definition of the class of stochastic processes which will be under consideration. The observed price process $\{X_t\}_{t\in\mathbb{N}}$ will be determined by two processes $\{Y_t\}_{t\in\mathbb{N}}$, the price process which would ensue if all periods were normal (i.e., if the industry were to produce the restricted output vector y at all times), and $\{Z_t\}_{t\in\mathbb{N}}$, the price process which would ensue if all periods were reversionary (i.e., if the industry were to operate in Cournot equilibrium at all times, producing the output vector z). Whether the observed price is drawn from the normal or the reversionary distribution is determined by a process $\{W_t\}_{t\in\mathbb{N}}$, which specifies whether the industry is in a normal or a reversionary state. Note that $\{X_t\}_{t\in\mathbb{N}}$ is the only component of the joint process $\{(W_t, X_t, Y_t, Z_t)\}_{t\in\mathbb{N}}$ which is observed.

---

[11] A stochastic process is ergodic if every event definable in terms of the tails of sample paths (e.g., the set of sample points having convergent paths) has probability zero or one. The ergodic theorem extends the strong law of large numbers to such processes.

96   E. J. GREEN AND R. H. PORTER

Formally, define a *switching process* to be determined by a probability space (Ω, β, m), a state space S, a subset $N \subseteq S$, and four sequences of random variables $\{W\} = \{W_t : \Omega \to S\}_{t \in \mathbb{N}}$, $\{X\} = \{X_t : \Omega \to \mathbb{R}\}_{t \in \mathbb{N}}$, $\{Y\} = \{Y_t : \Omega \to \mathbb{R}\}_{t \in \mathbb{N}}$, and $\{Z\} = \{Z_t : \Omega \to \mathbb{R}\}_{t \in \mathbb{N}}$ which satisfy

(A1) $\{Y\} \cup \{Z\}$ is a set of independent r.v.'s,

(A2) $\{Y\}$ is identically distributed with c.d.f. G,

(A3) $\{Z\}$ is identically distributed with c.d.f. H,

(A4) $\{W\}$ is a Markov process with stationary transition probabilities,

(A5) $\forall t \; S_t \in N \Rightarrow X_t = Y_t$, w.p.1,

(A6) $\forall t \; S_t \notin N \Rightarrow X_t = Z_t$, w.p.1.

Note that the special case of a switching process usually studied occurs when $S = \{0, 1\}$, $N = \{0\}$, and $\{W\}$ is a Bernoulli process which is independent of $\{Y\} \cup \{Z\}$.
    In the case of a collusive price process, G and H are the c.d.f.'s of the normal and reversionary price distributions, respectively. $S = \{0, \ldots, T - 1\}$ and $N = \{0\}$. (I.e., $W_t = 0$ signifies that the industry is in a normal period at time t.) The Markov process $\{W\}$ is defined recursively by starting with an arbitrary $W_0 : \Omega \to S$, and then imposing

(A7)   if $W_t(\omega) = 0$ and $Y_t(\omega) \geq \bar{p}$, then $W_{t+1}(\omega) = 0$,

(A8)   if $W_t(\omega) = 0$ and $Y_t(\omega) < \bar{p}$, then $W_{t+1}(\omega) = 1$,

(A9)   if $W_t(\omega) = k$, $1 \leq k < T - 1$, then $W_{t+1}(\omega) = k + 1$,

(A10)   if $W_t(\omega) = T - 1$, then $W_{t+1}(\omega) = 0$.

The process $\{W\}$ defined by (A7)–(A10) is Markov with stationary transition probabilities because, by (A1) and (A2), $\{Y\}$ is i.i.d. The transition graph of $\{W\}$ is shown in Figure 1, in which each arrow is labeled with its transition probability.
    The aim is to show that W_0 can be chosen in such a way that $\{X\}$ will be a stationary ergodic process. Conditions (A5) and (A6) show that $X_t(\omega)$ is a function of $(W_t(\omega), Y_t(\omega), Z_t(\omega))$, so by [1, Proposition 6.32] it is sufficient to show that the joint process $\{W, Y, Z\}$ is ergodic. By [1, Theorem 7.16], this process is ergodic if it is a stationary Markov process having a unique invariant distribution (i.e., a unique distribution such that, if W_1 is defined by (A7)–(A10), then $\{W_0, Y_0, Z_0\}$ and $\{W_1, Y_1, Z_1\}$ have identical joint distributions). This follows from [1, Theorem 7.18], completing the proof that $\{X\}$ is ergodic.

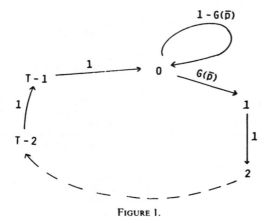

FIGURE 1.

NONCOOPERATIVE COLLUSION   97

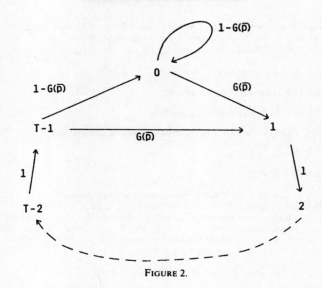

FIGURE 2.

In **[10]**, a maximum likelihood estimator for a switching process somewhat different from (A1)–(A10) is used to study the pre-ICC rail freight cartel in the U.S. That process is obtained by replacing (A1), (A2), and (A7)–(A10) with

(A11)
$\{Y\}$ is identically distributed with c.d.f.,

$$J(p) = \max\Big[(1 - G(\bar{p}))^{-1}(G(p) - G(\bar{p})), 0\Big].$$

(I.e., J is the distribution of p according to G, conditional on $p \geq \bar{p}$.)

(A12) $\{W\} \cup \{Y\} \cup \{Z\}$ is a set of independent random variables,

and

(A13) $\{W\}$ is a stationary Markov process having the transition probabilities

specified by Figure 2.[12]

That is, this process is defined by relaxing the usual assumption that the switching process is Bernoulli, while retaining the assumption that it is independent of the underlying variables which determine the observed prices. Call the process defined by (A1)–(A10) the *price process*, and that defined by (A3)–(A5), (A11)–(A13) the *approximating process*.

The advantage of the approximating process over the price process is that it permits adaptation of much of the work which has been done on maximum-likelihood estimation of the Bernoulli switching process. In particular, it is possible both to compute the ML estimator economically and to appeal to theoretical results asserting its consistency and asymptotic normality. The crucial question raised by use of the approximating process is of how seriously misspecified it is as a model for data actually generated by the price process. We now address this question.

The basis for comparing the two processes is that, given a stationary price process $\{W, X, Y, Z\}$ with parameters $(\bar{p}, T, G, H)$, a stationary approximating process $\{W', X', Y', Z'\}$ with the same

---

[12]Using extensive information including industry prices, macroeconomic variables, and firm-specific quantity data, Porter estimates the structural equations of a detailed industry model. His method may be viewed as an imposition of prior constraints on the reduced-form estimation described here.

parameters can be obtained by a kind of censoring. Looking at the matter from the opposite perspective, the sample paths of Z can be viewed as a contaminated (by reinsertion of the censored observations) version of the approximating process. The extent of the contamination is easily computable from the parameters of the process. If it is slight, and if the ML estimator is regarded as robust, then the ML estimator of the approximating process should also be considered to have small asymptotic bias as an estimator of the price process.

The approximating process $\{W', X', Y', Z'\}$ is defined from $\{W, X, Y, Z\}$ simply by censoring the triggering events (i.e., the events in which $W_t = 0$ and $Y_t < \bar{p}$). Formally, this is done by means of a sequence of stopping times $\{\tau_t : \Omega \to \mathbf{N}\}_{t \in \mathbf{N}}$. Define

$$(A14) \qquad \tau_0(\omega) = \begin{cases} 1 & \text{if } W_0(\omega) = 0 \text{ and } Y_0(\omega) < \bar{p}, \\ 0 & \text{otherwise,} \end{cases}$$

and

$$(A15) \qquad \tau_{t+1}(\omega) = \begin{cases} \tau_t(\omega) + 2 & \text{if } W_{\tau_t(\omega)+1}(\omega) = 0 \text{ and } Y_{\tau_t(\omega)+1}(\omega) < \bar{p}, \\ \tau_t(\omega) + 1 & \text{otherwise.} \end{cases}$$

Then define

$$(A16) \qquad W_t'(\omega) = W_{\tau_t(\omega)}(\omega), \quad X_t'(\omega) = X_{\tau_t(\omega)}(\omega), \quad \text{and} \quad Z_t'(\omega) = Z_{\tau_t(\omega)}(\omega).$$

Finally, take a set $\{Y_t''\}_{t \in \mathbf{N}}$ which are identically distributed with c.d.f. J and such that $\{Y\} \cup \{Z\} \cup \{Y''\}$ is independent, and define

$$(A17) \qquad Y_t'(\omega) = \begin{cases} Y_{\tau_t(\omega)}(\omega) & \text{if } W_t'(\omega) = 0, \\ Y_t''(\omega) & \text{if } W_t'(\omega) > 0. \end{cases}$$

(N.B. The definition of the observed component $\{X'\}$ of the approximating process is the same whether $\{Y'\}$ is defined by (A17) or by $Y_t'(\omega) = Y_{\tau_t(\omega)}(\omega)$ for all ω. The reason for using (A17) is both to satisfy (A11) and to keep $\{W'\}$ and $\{Y'\}$ independent so that (A12) is satisfied. Under the simpler definition, (A15) would have introduced dependency between them.)

The effect of (A15) and (A16) is to continue to let a low realization of Y_t be the event which causes the state to change from zero to one, but to censor this event if it occurs. Thus the dependence of W_{t+1} on $\{W_t, Y_t\}$ in the price process is removed, and (A12) holds. By the strong Markov property [1, Proposition 7.8], the censored process is a stationary Markov process, so (A13) holds. I.e., $\{W', X', Y', Z'\}$ is an approximating process with parameters $(\bar{p}, T, J, H)$.

It remains to calculate how much censoring of the price series $X(\omega)$ is required to construct the approximating series $X'(\omega)$. (Alternatively, how much contamination of $X'(\omega)$ is required to reconstruct $X(\omega)$?) Formally, what is $\lim_{t \to \infty} (\tau_t(\omega) - t)/\tau_t(\omega)$? If this quotient is close to zero for almost every ω, then the asymptotic bias of the approximating-process ML estimator applied to data generated by the price process should be small.

To calculate the quotient, first define $\sigma(W, Y) = 1$ if $W = 0$ and $Y < \bar{p}$, and $\sigma(W, Y) = 0$ otherwise. By (A14) and (A15), $\tau_t(\omega) = t + \sum_{u=0}^{\tau_t(\omega)} \sigma(W_u(\omega), Y_u(\omega))$, or

$$(A18) \qquad \frac{\tau_t(\omega) - t}{\tau_t(\omega)} = \frac{1}{\tau_t(\omega)} \sum_{u=0}^{\tau_t(\omega)} \sigma(W_u(\omega), Y_u(\omega)).$$

By the ergodic theorem,

$$(A19) \qquad \lim_{t \to \infty} \frac{1}{\tau_t(\omega)} \sum_{u=0}^{\tau_t(\omega)} \sigma(W_u(\omega), Y_u(\omega)) = m(\{W_0 = 0, Y_0 < \bar{p}\}) G(\bar{p}) \qquad \text{a.s.}$$

(Recall that m is the stationary measure on Ω.) Combining (A18) and (A19), and appealing to the fact that the stationarity of the price process forces W_0 and Y_0 to be independent, yields

$$(A20) \qquad \lim_{t \to \infty} \frac{\tau_t(\omega) - t}{\tau_t(\omega)} = m(\{W_0 = 0\}) G(\bar{p}) \qquad \text{a.s.}$$

The calculation of $m(\{ W_0 = 0\})$ is an easy matter. For $1 \leq k < T - 1$, by (A9) and stationarity, we have

(A21) $m(\{ W_0 = k \}) = m(\{ W_1 = k + 1 \}) = m(\{ W_0 = k + 1 \})$.

Also, by (A7) and stationarity, we have

(A22) $m(\{ W_0 = 1 \}) = m(\{ W_1 = 1 \}) = m(\{ W_0 = 0 \})G(\bar{p})$.

Since the probabilities of the states sum to unity, (A21) and (A22) yield

(A23) $m(\{ W_0 = 0 \}) = [1 + (T - 1)G(\bar{p})]^{-1}$.

Thus, by (A22) and (A23),

(A24) $\displaystyle \lim_{t \to \infty} \frac{\tau_t(\omega) - t}{\tau_t(\omega)} = G(\bar{p})[1 + (T - 1)G(\bar{p})]^{-1}$.

For example, consider a hypothetical industry in which a trade association disseminates weekly price data to its members. I.e., the appropriate interpretation of a period in the discrete-time model is one week. Suppose that the parameters of this industry were estimated using the ML estimator for the approximating process, with the results that $\hat{G}(\hat{p}) = .025$ and $\hat{T} = 11$. Since the expected duration of an episode of normal conduct is $(G(\bar{p}))^{-1}$, these estimates indicate that a reversionary episode occurs once a year on average, and lasts ten weeks. Thus there is (on average) one price observation a year (that being the observation of the price which triggers the reversionary episode), which would not be included if the approximating process were really generating the data. This is a contamination ratio of one in fifty, or $(.025)[1 + .25]^{-1}$ which is the expression which is obtained from (A24).

The ML estimator is computed by dividing the data into two sub-samples, one of which is presumed to have been drawn from distribution G and the other from H, and then estimating these distributions from the respective subsamples. If the "contaminating" observations were to comprise equal proportions of the two subsamples, then each subsample is being estimated with 2 per cent contamination, and one might reasonably suppose the discrepancy between the price process and the approximating process to be rather small. If all of the "contaminating" observations were assigned to the subsample presumed to be generated by normal conduct, then this subsample would have $2\frac{1}{2}$ per cent contamination, which still might reasonably be ignored. However, if the "contaminating" observations were all included in the subsample presumed to reflect reversionary conduct, then that subsample would have a 10 per cent contamination level. In this worst case, it is easy to imagine that the observations actually drawn from the lower tail of G would seriously bias the estimation of H.

The parameter estimates for the example just given are approximately the same as those reported by Porter [10] for the rail freight industry. Thus, while the foregoing analysis is insufficiently precise to rule out the worst-case assumption concerning bias of his estimator relative to the price process, it has shown that under more optimistic assumptions the bias would plausibly be slight. While we acknowledge that there is an inevitable element of subjective judgment in a situation such as this, we suggest that Porter's study provides presumptive evidence that the rail freight industry may have exemplified the kind of equilibrium which has been studied here.

REFERENCES

[1] BREIMAN, L.: *Probability*. Reading: Addison-Wesley, 1968.
[2] BRESNAHAN, T.: "The Oligopoly Solution Concept is Identified," *Economics Letters*, 10(1982), 87–92.
[3] FRIEDMAN, J. W.: "A Non-cooperative Equilibrium for Supergames," *Review of Economic Studies*, 28(1971), 1–12.
[4] GOLDSCHMID, H. J., H. M. MANN, AND J. F. WESTON (EDS.): *Industrial Concentration: The New Learning*. Boston: Little, Brown and Co., 1974.
[5] GREEN, E. J.: "Non-cooperative Price Taking in Large Dynamic Markets," *Journal of Economic Theory*, 22(1980), 155–182.
[6] KIEFER, N. M.: "A Note on Switching Regressions and Logistic Discrimination," *Econometrica*, 48(1980), 1065–1069.
[7] MACAVOY, P. W.: *The Economic Effects of Regulation*. Cambridge: MIT Press, 1965.
[8] OSBORNE, D. K.: "Cartel Problems," *American Economic Review*, 66(1976), 835–844.

[9] PORTER, R. H.: "Optimal Cartel Trigger-Price Strategies," *Journal of Economic Theory*, 29(1983), 313–338.

[10] ———: "A Study of Cartel Stability: The Joint Executive Committee 1880–1886," *Bell Journal of Economics*, to appear.

[11] RADNER, R.: "Collusive Behavior in Noncooperative Epsilon-Equilibria With Long But Finite Lives," *Journal of Economic Theory*, 22(1980), 136–154.

[12] SCHERER, F. M.: *Industrial Market Structure and Economic Performance*, Second Ed. Chicago: Rand McNally, 1980.

[13] SPENCE, M.: "Tacit Coordination and Imperfect Information," *Canadian Journal of Economics*, 11(1978), 490–505.

[14] ———: "Efficient Collusion and Reaction Functions," *Canadian Journal of Economics*, 11(1978), 527–533.

[15] STIGLER, G. J.: "A Theory of Oligopoly," *Journal of Political Economy*, 72(1964), 44–61.

[16] ULEN, T. S.: "Cartels and Regulation," unpublished Ph.D. dissertation, Stanford University, 1978.

[17] ———: "The Market for Regulation: The ICC from 1887 to 1920," *American Economic Review, Papers and Proceedings*, 70(1980), 306–310.

[34]

REINHARD SELTEN

THE CHAIN STORE PARADOX

ABSTRACT. The chain store game is a simple game in extensive form which produces an inconsistency between game theoretical reasoning and plausible human behavior. Well-informed players must be expected to disobey game theoretical recommendations.

The chain store paradox throws new light on the well-known difficulties arising in connection with finite repetitions of the prisoners' dilemma game. Whereas these difficulties can be resolved by the assumption of secondary utilities arising in the course of playing the game, a similar approach to the chain store paradox is less satisfactory.

It is argued that the explanation of the paradox requires a limited rationality view of human decision behavior. For this purpose a three-level theory of decision making is developed, where decisions can be made on different levels of rationality. This theory explains why insight into the rational solution of a decision problem does not necessarily mean that the corresponding course of action will be taken.

It is the purpose of this paper to present the example of a simple game in extensive form where the actual behavior of well-informed players cannot be expected to agree with the clear results of game theoretical reasoning. A story about a fictitious chain store and its potential competitors is a convenient way to describe the game. This expositional device should not be misunderstood as a model of a real situation.[1] In view of the story the game will be called 'the chain store game'. The disturbing disagreement between plausible game behavior and game theoretical reasoning constitutes the 'chain store paradox'.

The chain store paradox throws new light on the well-known difficulties which arise in connection with the finite super-game of the prisoners' dilemma game. A limited rationality approach seems to be needed in order to explain human strategic behavior. An attempt shall be made to discuss the possibility of a 'three-level theory of decision making' as an explanation of discrepancies between game theoretic analysis and human behavior.

1. THE CHAIN STORE GAME

Consider the following fictitious market situation: A chain store, also called player A, has branches in 20 towns, numbered from 1 to 20. In each of these towns there is a potential competitor, a small businessman who might raise

Theory and Decision 9 (1978) 127–159. *All Rights Reserved.*

money at the local bank in order to establish a second shop of the same kind. The potential competitor at town k is called player k. Thus the game has 21 players: the chain store, player A and its 20 potential competitors the players k with $k = 1, \dots, 20$. Apart from these 20 players the chain store does not face any other competition, neither now nor in the future.

Just now none of the 20 small business men has enough owned capital to be able to get a sufficient credit from the local bank but as time goes on, one after the other will have saved enough to increase his owned capital to the required amount. This will happen first to player 1, then to player 2, etc. As soon as this time comes for player k, he must decide whether he wants to establish a second shop in his town or whether he wants to use his owned capital in a different way. If he chooses the latter possibility, he stops being a potential competitor of player A.

If a second shop is established in town k, then player A has to choose between two price policies for town k. His response may be 'cooperative' or 'aggressive'. The cooperative response yields higher profits in town k, both for player A and for player k, but the profits of player A in town k are even higher if player k does not establish a second shop. Player k's profits in case of an aggressive response are such that it is better for him not to establish a second shop if player A responds in this way.

After this description of the fictitious market situation which yields a convenient economic interpretation of the chain store game, a more abstract and more precise description of the rules must be supplied in order to remove possible sources of misunderstanding. In this section we consider a first version of the chain store game. For some purposes, it is convenient to introduce a somewhat different second version of the game. This will be done in a later section. In both cases it will be useful to assume that there are m potential competitors, where m may be any positive integer. Nevertheless it is convenient to focus attention on $m = 20$, since the game changes its character if m becomes too small. The extensive form of the first version with m potential competitors will be denoted by Γ^1_m.

Rules for Γ^1_m, the first version of the chain store game

The game has $m + 1$ players, player A and players $1, \dots, m$. The game is played over a sequence of m consecutive periods $1, \dots, m$. At the beginning of period k, player k must decide between IN and OUT. (The decision IN means that a second shop is established by player k.) Player k's decision is immediately made known to all players. No further decisions are made in period k if player k's decision was OUT. If his decision was IN, the player A has to choose between COOPERATIVE and AGGRESSIVE (both words stand for possible price policies of player A in town k). This decision is immediately made known to all players, too. Then for $k = 1, \ldots, m - 1$ the period $k + 1$ begins and is played according to the same rules. The game ends after period m.

Player A's payoff is the sum of m partial payoffs for the periods $1, \ldots, m$. Player A's partial payoffs and the payoffs of the players $1, \ldots, m$ are given in Table I.

The game is played in a non-cooperative way. The players cannot commit themselves to threats or promises. No binding contracts are possible. Side payments are not permissible. The players are not allowed to talk during the game.

TABLE I

Player A's partial payoffs and player k's payoff.

player k's decision	player A's decision in period k	player k's payoff	player A's partial payoff for period k
IN	COOPERATIVE	2	2
IN	AGGRESSIVE	0	0
OUT	–	1	5

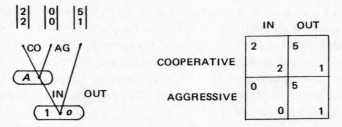

Fig. 1. The extensive form Γ_1^1 and the normal form of Γ_1^1. Player A's payoffs are above and player 1's payoffs are below. 'CO' and 'AG' stand for 'COOPERATIVE' and 'AGGRESSIVE'. The game begins at the origin o. Information sets are indicated by lines which encircle vertices belonging to the same information set. The player who has to make a choice at a given information set is indicated by the appropriate symbol. – In the representation of the normal form, player A's payoff is given in the upper left corner and player 1's payoff is given in the lower right corner.

REINHARD SELTEN

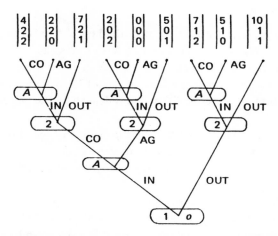

Fig. 2. The extensive form Γ_2^1. The components of the payoff vectors above the end-points refer to the payoffs of player A, 1 and 2 in that order from above to below. (For further explanations of the graphical representation see Figure 1.)

2. A FIRST VIEW OF THE PARADOX

In this section, the chain store paradox will be introduced in an intuitive way without making use of the formal tools of game theory.

Let us focus our attention on the case $m = 20$. Consider the situation of one of the players 1, ... , 20. Should he choose IN or OUT? The choice of OUT guarantees a payoff of 1. The choice of IN may yield a payoff of 2 if player A's response is COOPERATIVE but if the response is AGGRESSIVE, then the payoff is 0.

Consider the situation of player A. How should he respond to a choice of IN? The COOPERATIVE response yields a partial payoff of 2 and the AGGRESSIVE response yield a partial payoff of 0. In the short run the COOPERATIVE response is more advantageous but in the long run it may pay to choose the AGGRESSIVE response in order to discourage the choice of IN.

There are two different theories about the adequate behavior in the game. One will be called the 'induction theory' and the other will be called the 'deterrence theory'.

THE CHAIN STORE PARADOX   131

The induction theory

If in period 20 player 20 selects IN, then the best choice for player *A* is the COOPERATIVE response. The COOPERATIVE response yields a higher payoff. Long run considerations do not come in, since after period 20 the game is over. This shows that it is best for player 20 to choose IN. Obviously the strategic situation of period 20 does not depend on the players' decisions in period 1, ... , 19.

Now consider period 19. The decisions in period 19 have no influence on the strategic situation in period 20. If player 19 selects IN, then the CO-OPERATIVE response is best for player *A*. The AGGRESSIVE response would not deter player 20.

It is clear that in this way we can go on to conclude by induction that each player *k* should choose IN and each time player *A* should use the CO-OPERATIVE response. The strategic situation in the remainder of the game does not depend on the decisions up to period *k*. If it is already known that in periods *k* + 1, ... , 20 players *k* + 1, ... , 20 will choose IN and player *A* will always select the COOPERATIVE choice, then it follows that also in period *k* a choice of IN should lead to a COOPERATIVE response.

The induction theory comes to the conclusion that each of the players 1, ... , 20 should choose IN and player *A* should always react with his CO-OPERATIVE response to the choice of IN. If the game is played in this way, then each of the players 1, ... , 20 receives a payoff of 2 and player *A* receives a total payoff of 40.

The deterrence theory

Player A should not follow the reasoning of the induction theory. He can get more than 40. It is true that the reasoning of the induction theory is very compelling for the last periods of the game. Therefore player *A* cannot neglect these arguments completely. He should decide on the basis of his intuition for how many of the last periods he wants to accept the induction argument. Suppose he decides to accept the argument for the last 3 periods 18, 19 and 20, but not for the periods 1, ... , 17. Then, on the basis of this decision he should act according to the following strategy: In the periods 1, ... , 17 the response to a choice of IN is AGGRESSIVE, in periods 18, 19 and 20 the response to a choice of IN is COOPERATIVE.

Suppose that the players 1, ... , 20 expect that player *A* behaves according to this strategy. Then it is best for players 1, ... , 17 to choose OUT and it is best for players 18, 19, 20 to choose IN. If the game is played in this way, players 1, ... , 17 will receive a payoff of 1, players 18, 19 and 20 will receive a payoff of 2 and player A will receive a payoff of 91.

Even if some of the players 1, ... 20 have a different view of the force of the induction argument, player A will still be better off than the induction theory suggests. Suppose that not only the 3 players 18, 19 and 20, but also 10 of the players 1, ... , 17 choose IN, whereas the others choose OUT. In this case player A's payoff will be 41 which is still more than 40.

Suppose that early in the game 2 or 3 of the players 1, ... , 17 choose IN. If they are punished by Player A's AGGRESSIVE response, then most of the others will have learnt their lesson. It may still be true that player 17 feels that the induction argument applies to him, too, and the same may be true for player 16, but on the whole, it seems to be very improbable that more than 5 of the players 1, ... , 17 will choose IN. This means that it is very probable that player A will have a payoff of at least 66.

It may also happen that in spite of the fact that player A does not plan to react by his AGGRESSIVE response to choices of IN by players 18, 19 and 20, player 18 and maybe even player 19 will still be deterred by this threat.

Since the players 1, ... , 20 can expect that player A will follow the deterrence theory, they should behave accordingly. If up to period $k - 1$ not very many of the players 1, ... , $k - 1$ selected IN and player A's response was always AGGRESSIVE, then player k should select OUT unless he feels that period k is sufficiently near to the end of the game to make it probable that player A will acept the induction argument for period k.

The deterrence theory does not yield precise rules of behavior, since some details are left to the intuition of the players, but this does not impair the practical applicability of the theory.

Comparison of the two theories

As we shall see in section 8, only the induction theory is game theoretically correct. Logically, the induction argument cannot be restricted to the last periods of the game. There is no way to avoid the conclusion that it applies to all periods of the game.

Nevertheless the deterrence theory is much more convincing. If I had to play the game in the role of player A, I would follow the deterrence theory.

I would be very surprised if it failed to work. From my discussions with friends and colleagues, I get the impression that most people share this inclination. In fact, up to now I met nobody who said that he would behave according to the induction theory. My experience suggests that mathematically trained persons recognize the logical validity of the induction argument, but they refuse to accept it as a guide to practical behavior.

It seems to be safe to conjecture that even in a situation where all players know that all players understand the induction argument very well, player A will adopt a deterrence policy and the other players will expect him to do so.

The fact that the logical inescapability of the induction theory fails to destroy the plausibility of the deterrence theory is a serious phenomenon which merits the name of a paradox. We call it the 'chain store paradox'.

3. THE SECOND VERSION OF THE CHAIN STORE GAME

Consider a fictitious market situation similar to that described in section 1. Again the chain store, player A, has 20 branches in 20 towns and there is one potential competitor, player k in each town k. But now we assume that already at the beginning of the game every potential competitor has a sufficient amount of owned capital but there is only one bank where they all have to apply for credit if they want to establish a second shop. As long as there are any applicants, in every period the bank gives a credit to one of them who is selected randomly. Thus in every period exactly one of the players $1, \dots, 20$ establishes a second shop until a period arrives where there are no applicants. If this happens the game ends. Before the end of the game a player k who did not yet establish a shop may or may not apply for credit in every period; he may change his decision in the next period. In order to avoid misunderstandings, a more precisely formulated set of rules is given below. The extensive form of the second version of the game with m competitors will be denoted by Γ_m^2.

Rules for Γ_m^2, the second version of the chain store game

The game has $m + 1$ players, player A and players $1, \dots, m$. The game is played over a sequence of periods $t = 1, \dots, T$, where T is determined by the decisions of the players. In every period t some of the players $1, \dots, m$ are called 'outside' and others are called 'inside'. At the beginning, in period 1, all of them are outside. Let M_t be the set of outside players in period t.

In every period t, each player in M_t has to decide between IN and OUT. These decisions are made secretly. Let I_t be the set of all players in M_t who choose IN in period t. A random mechanism selects a player $j_t \in I_t$. Each of the players in I_t has the same probability to become the selected player j_t. In period $t + 1$ the player j_t becomes an inside player. M_{t+1} is the set $M_t - \{j_t\}$.

The players in M_t must make their decisions for period t without knowing the decisions of the other members of M_t for period t. Immediately after these decisions have been made, they are made known to all players.

If in period t the set I_t is empty, then period t is the last period T and player A does not have to make a decision for this period. This is not the only way in which the end of the game can be reached. It may happen that M_{t+1} is empty; then t is the last period T. (In this case we must have $T = m$.)

If I_t is not empty, then player A has to choose between a 'COOPERATIVE' and an 'AGGRESSIVE' response in period t. This decision is immediately made known to all players. Player A has full knowledge of all past decisions when he makes his choice.

Player j_t receives the payoff 2 if player A's choice in period t is CO-OPERATIVE; he receives 0 if player A's choice in period t is AGGRESSIVE. Let m_c be the number of periods where player A's decision was COOPERA-TIVE. Player A receives the payoff $2m_c + 5(m + 1 - T)$.

The Paradox in the second version of the game

Game theoretically, the induction theory holds for the second version of the game, too. If all players $1, \ldots, m$ with the exception of one already have chosen IN, then the last one can do so, too, since player A's best response is the COOPERATIVE one. Therefore, if two are left over in M_t, both of them should choose IN, etc.

For the discussion of the deterrence theory let us focus our attention on the case $m = 20$. Here the deterrence theory is even more convincing than for the first version of the game. It may easily happen that already in the first period none of the players $1, \ldots, 20$ dares to choose IN. In this case player A receives the payoff 100.

If in period 1, some of the players choose IN and player A takes his AGGRESSIVE response, then in period 2 the players in M_2 will have a very good reason to fear that the same will happen again. If in spite of this some

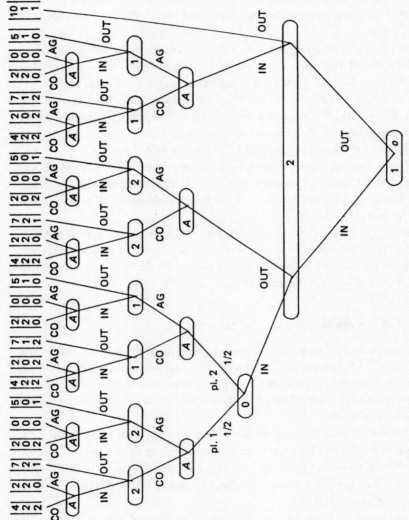

Fig. 3. The extensive Form Γ_2^2. (See explanations below Figures 1 and 2.) The symbol 0 refers to the random player who selects either player 1 or player 2 with probabilities 1/2.

players still choose IN in period 2 and player *A* again takes his AGGRESSIVE response, then in period 3 it will be very probable that nobody dares to choose IN.

It seems to be highly improbable that player *A* will have to take his AGGRESSIVE response more than 2 or 3 times. Thus it is very likely that he will get a payoff of at least 85 which is much more than the payoff of 40 which he should get according to the induction theory.

Player *A* does not have to worry about the question what will happen if the game should reach periods 18, 19 or 20, since this is highly improbable. In this respect player *A* has an easier decision problem in the second version of the game. If *m* is big enough, then he does not have to pay any attention to the induction argument. Only if one looks at the set of all games Γ_m^2 does this problem arise again. For which of the games Γ_m^2 is the number *m* sufficiently small to make the induction theory acceptable?

4. A LOOK AT THE FINITE SUPERGAME OF THE PRISONER'S DILEMMA GAME

If the same game in normal form is played again and again for a finite or infinite number of times by the same set of players, then a supergame of the original game in normal form results. The *k*-th repetition of the original game is also called period *k* of the supergame. In the following we shall only consider such supergames where after each repetition of the game, the strategy choices of all players are announced to all players; thus at the beginning of each period each player has a complete knowledge of the past history of the supergame. Moreover, we shall only consider finite supergames with a finite number of repetitions. The number of repetitions is assumed to be known to all players at the beginning of the supergame. The supergame payoff of a player is the sum of his payoffs for all repetitions. The original game which is repeated in a given supergame is also called the 'source game' of this supergame.

It is important to distinguish between the supergame and its source game. A supergame may have game theoretical properties which are not apparent from the analysis of the source game.

Prisoners' dilemma games are a much discussed class of symmetrical two-person games in normal form with 2 strategies for each of both players. For our purposes it is convenient to focus attention on the normal form represented in Figure 4 which is in this class.

THE CHAIN STORE PARADOX 137

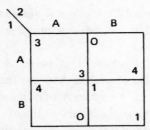

Fig. 4. A specific prisoner's dilemma game. Player 1's payoff is given in the upper left corner and player 2's payoff is given in the lower right corner of the fields representing the strategy combinations.

Let Γ_m^3 be the extensive form of the supergame which results from the m-fold repetition of the normal form of Figure 4. The graphical representation of Γ_2^3 is given in Fig. 5.

It is well known that for sufficiently large m, say $m = 100$, the analysis of Γ_m^3 leads to a result which is very similar to the chain store paradox.[2] In the same way as in the case of the chain store game, we are faced with a

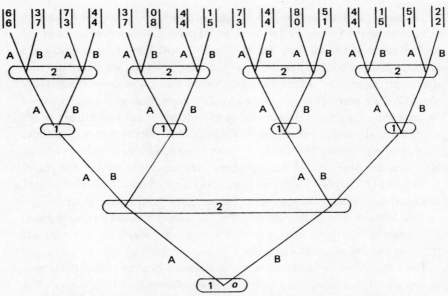

Fig. 5. The supergame Γ_2^3 which results from a 2-fold repetition of the specific prisoner's dilemma game of Figure 4.

conflict between two theories, an 'induction theory' and a 'cooperation theory'. (The cooperation theory corresponds to the deterrence theory.) The induction theory is the game theoretically correct one but the cooperation theory seems to be the better guide to practical behavior.

The conflict between the two theories is less serious than for the case of the chain store game. Practical recommendations for a laboratory situation, where the payoffs are money payoffs, can be given on the basis of a third kind of theoretical reasoning. It is plausible to assume that the utility payoffs of the players are different from the money payoffs. The 'benevolence theory', which will be presented below, is a theory of this type.[3] The practical conclusions of this theory are similar to those of the cooperation theory but contrary to the cooperation theory the benevolence theory does not face any logical difficulties. It is not necessary to reject the induction argument, since it does not apply.[4]

In the following we shall outline the three theories for Γ_m^3. We shall focus our attention on the case $m = 100$.

The induction theory

Clearly, in the last repetition of the game it is better to choose B, whatever the other player does. This determines the last period of Γ_{100}^3. Both players will choose B. Therefore the situation in the second last period is not different from that of the last one. Again it is clear that both should choose B. If it is already clear that for the last k periods both players will always choose B, then it follows that they should choose B in the $(k + 1)$-th last period, too. If both behave rationally, they will always choose B.

The cooperation theory

The reasoning of the induction theory is very compelling for the last periods of the supergame. A player must decide on the basis of his intuition for how many periods at the end of the supergame he should follow this reasoning. Suppose this number of periods is r. Then in the last r periods he should always choose B, no matter what the previous history of the supergame has been but for the first $100 - r$ he should behave differently. In the following we assume $r = 3$.

The exact nature of the supergame strategy up to period 97 is not very important. The strategy should be such that the other player has an incentive to choose A for as many periods as possible. In the following we shall describe one strategy of this kind but there are many other strategies which would serve the same purpose. The description will take the form of a recommendation to player 1 but it is meant to apply to player 2, too.

The recommendation for the periods $k = 1, \ldots , 97$ is as follows: player 1 should choose A in period 1. For $k = 2, \ldots , 97$ he should choose A in period k, unless in period $k - 1$ player 1 selected A and player 2 selected B; in this case player 1's choice in period k should be B.

This kind of behavior has the following interpretation: With the exception of the last 3 periods, player 1 is willing to use A as long as he observes that player 2 has chosen A. If player 2 deviates to B, then player 1 punishes this deviation by a selection of B in the next period but immediately afterwards he returns to A, in the expectation that player 2 will return to A, too. If this expectation is disappointed, a new punishment will follow. Each punishment lasts for one period only.

Suppose that player 2 knows that player 1 behaves in this way. What is his best reply? As we shall see it is best for player 2 to choose A in the first 96 periods and B in the 4 last ones.

We first consider a special kind of deviation from the proposed best reply. After a period k, where both players have chosen A, player 2 selected B for s consecutive periods and then returns to A. Here we assume $k + s < 97$. Figure 6 and 7 describe the results of two such deviations. In both cases the deviation does not pay. Obviously this is true for all deviations of the same kind. The deviation yields a payoff of at most 5/2 per deviation period whereas a choice of A yields 3 per period.

It can easily be seen that other kinds of deviations do not pay either. One can restrict one's attention to deviations for s consecutive periods $k + 1, \ldots , k + s$, which are such that both players never choose A at the same time and where both players select A in periods k and $k + s + 1$. The situation is essentially the same for $k = 0$ or $k + s + 1 = 97$. After the end of a deviation of this kind, player 1 will behave as if no deviation occurred. Whenever player 1 chooses A in the periods $k + 1, \ldots , k + s$, player 2 chooses B. Therefore in these periods player 1 alternates between A and B. The best payoff per deviation period which player 2 can get under these conditions is 5/2. In a period where player 1 chooses A, player 2 can get at most 4 and in a period where player 1 chooses B, player 2 can get at most 1. Moreover s must be an

140   R E I N H A R D   S E L T E N

period:	k	$k + 1$	$k + 2$	$k + 3$	$k + 4$	$k + 5$
player 1's choice:	A	A	B	A	B	A
player 2's choice:	A	B	B	B	B	A
player 2's partial payoffs:	3	4	1	4	1	3

Fig. 6. The result of a 4-period deviation.

period:	k	$k + 1$	$k + 2$	$k + 3$	$k + 4$	$k + 5$
player 1's choice:	A	A	B	A	B	A
player 2's choice:	A	B	B	B	A	A
player 2's partial payoffs:	3	4	1	4	0	3

Fig. 7. The result of a 3-period deviation.

even number, since player 1's choice in period $k + 1$ is A and A is always followed by B as long as the play does not return to a situation where both select A.

Suppose that both players follow the recommendations of the cooperation theory. Each player i selects a number r_i of periods at the end of the supergame where he plans to use B under all circumstances but in earlier periods he follows the pattern of one period punishments described above. Suppose that we have $r_1 = 3$ and $r_2 = 4$. As we have seen, in this case player 2 uses a best reply to player 1's strategy. More generally, we can say that player i uses a best reply to player j's strategy if $r_i = r_j + 1$. It is impossible that both players choose their numbers r_i in such a way that a game theoretical equilibrium results where each player uses a best reply against the other player's strategy, but it is possible that one of them uses a best reply to the other player's behavior. Therefore the cooperation theory does not recommend a specific number r_i. Each player i must decide on the basis of his intuition which r_i he wants to select. In order to do this he may try to optimize with respect to his subjective expectations about the other player. It is true that at least one of them must have wrong subjective expectations. Nevertheless both can try to do their best.

Suppose that player 1 selects $r_1 = 3$ and player 2 succeeds to 'outguess' him by the selection of $r_2 = 4$. Then player 1 receives a supergame payoff of 291. Player 2 receives 295. If both players would always choose B as the induction theory suggests, each of them gets 100. Clearly, for reasonably small r_t it is much more advantageous to be outguessed in the cooperation theory than to use a best reply in the induction theory.

The benevolence theory

Strictly speaking this theory is not a theory for Γ_{100}^3. It is a theory for a laboratory situation, where the payoffs are money payoffs. The utility payoffs are assumed to be the sum of two components, a 'primary' utility which depends linearly on the money payoffs and a 'secondary' utility which depends on the player's perception of his social relations with the other player. The perceived character of the social relationship is determined by the past history of the supergame and by the way in which the decisions influence the primary utilities. In the light of the primary utilities, past and future choices are interpreted as friendly or unfriendly acts. A friendly atmosphere is preferred to an unfriendly one.

The benevolence theory is only one specific theory which can be constructed on the basis of these general ideas. One should not overemphasize the details of the psychological mechanism which yields the secondary utilities. The exact nature of this mechanism cannot be clarified without empirical research. The assumptions which will be made below are purely speculative. They exemplify a certain type of explanation for a plausible pattern of behavior in the finite prisoners' dilemma supergame.

The secondary utilities are assumed to reflect the following tendencies: (1) A friendly social relationship is preferred to an unfriendly one. (2) A player does not want to be 'mean' in the sense that he disappoints the other player's trust.

The simplest way to model tendency (1) is the assumption that each of both players receives a secondary utility a for every period, where both players choose A. The constant a reflects the strength of the tendency. Since the selection of A by both players is the obvious cooperative solution of the game of Figure 4, it is reasonable to suppose that no other combination of choices creates the impression of a friendly relationship.

In order to make an assumption about the secondary utilities resulting from tendency (2), the notion of trust must be made more precise. Imagine that in period $t - s - 1$, at least one player selected B, but then for the s following periods up to period $t - 1$ both players selected A. In this situation

142   REINHARD SELTEN

a player shows 'trust' if he selects A in period t. If he selects B and the other selects A, then he 'disappoints the trust' of the other player. There is no disappointment of trust if both of them choose B, since in this case there was no trust in the first place.

Obviously there is more reason to expect trust and to extend trust after a long sequence of choice combinations (A,A) than after a short one. (The first symbol refers to the choice of player 1 and the second to that of player 2.) Therefore it is more objectionable to disappoint the trust of the other player after a long sequence of this kind than after a short one.

In view of these considerations, we assume that a player who selects B in a period t where the other player selects A experiences a negative secondary utility $-b_s$, where s is the number of periods with choice combinations (A,A) after the latest period $k < t$ such that in period k the choice combination was different from (A,A). (Obviously we have $s = t - 1 - k$). It is assumed that b_s is an increasing function of s.

If the secondary utilities are added to the primary utilities, then the original supergame Γ_m^3 is transformed into a new game which we denote by Γ_m^4. Player i's payoff in Γ_m^4 is the sum of all his primary and secondary payoffs for all m periods. Obviously Γ_m^4 does not have the structure of a supergame, since b_s depends on the past history of the play.

Suppose that in Γ_{100}^4 both players have chosen A for 99 periods. Then, up to the irrelevant additive constant $99 (3 + a)$, the last-period payoffs are given by the bimatrix in Figure 9. For $a + b_{99} \geqslant 1$, the bimatrix game of Figure 9 has two equilibrium points in pure strategies (A,A) and (B,B). The benevolence theory does not give a different result from the induction theory unless this is the case. Therefore in the following discussion we shall always assume $a + b_{99} \geqslant 1$.

As we shall see, under this assumption the game Γ_{100}^4 has equilibrium points which are such that both players always choose A if both of them stick

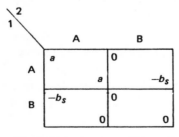

Fig. 8. Bimatrix of secondary utilities.

THE CHAIN STORE PARADOX 143

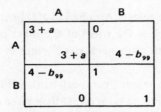

Fig. 9. Last-period payoffs after 99 periods with (A,A).

to their equilibrium strategies. An example is supplied by the following simple rule of behavior: In period t choose A if A was always selected by both players in periods $1, \ldots, t-1$; otherwise choose B.

If this rule is followed by the other player, then it does not pay to deviate to B in a period where B was not chosen before by at least one of the players. For $t < 100$ the sum of the primary utilities is already reduced by a deviation of this kind, and the secondary utilities make it even more disadvantageous. For $t = 100$ a deviation of this kind does not pay because $a + b_{99} \geq 1$. The situation is that of Figure 9.

Let $\bar{s}$ be the smallest integer with $a + b_{\bar{s}} \geq 1$. If $\bar{s}$ is sufficiently small, then it is possible to change the rule in the direction of a pattern of one-period punishments and returns to A, as described in our discussion of the cooperation theory, without destroying the equilibrium character of the strategy pair. Such possibilities will not be explored here. It is sufficient to demonstrate that the induction argument does not apply to Γ_m^4 if the influence of the secondary utilities is big enough.

Another way in which the strategy pair may be changed without destroying its equilibrium character is as follows: Suppose that we have $\bar{s} < 99$. Consider the following rule of behavior: For $t < 100$, choose A if A was chosen by both players in periods $1, \ldots, t-1$; otherwise choose B. In period 100 choose B.

Obviously for $\bar{s} < 99$, the players use an equilibrium pair of strategies for Γ_{100}^4 if both apply this rule. In the equilibrium play both choose A up to period 99 but in period 100 an 'end effect' takes place and both choose B. We may say that in period 100 the mutual trust breaks down.

Note that the strategy pair where both choose B under all circumstances is an equilibrium pair for Γ_{100}^4, too. The benevolence theory permits that trust is established between the players but it does not exclude the possibility that no trust is established.

144   R E I N H A R D   S E L T E N

Comparison of the three theories

The logical conclusions of the induction theory are inescapable if no secondary utilities are introduced and the game Γ_m^3 is taken literally. Nevertheless the recommendations of the cooperation theory are much more plausible. This does not necessarily mean that the induction argument fails to be behaviorally convincing. Probably one cannot form a sound intuitive judgement about the practical usefulness of different strategical recommendations without thinking about a concrete situation like a laboratory experiment where the payoffs are money payoffs. Therefore it may be impossible to avoid one's intuitions being influenced by the presence of secondary utilities. As soon as secondary utilities enter the picture, theories of the type of the benevolence theory provide rational reasons not to accept the induction argument. Intuitive judgement and game theoretical analysis are brought into agreement. Unfortunately, in the light of the chain store paradox this easy escape from the problems posed by the induction argument is less convincing than one may think if one looks at the finite prisoners' dilemma supergame in isolation.

A remark on the evidence from prisoners' dilemma experiments

Many experimental studies have been based on prisoners' dilemma supergames. Unfortunately in most cases the number of repetitions was not made known to the players at the beginning of the game. If the number of periods is not revealed, then the experimental situation is more like an infinite supergame. The infinite supergame has equilibrium points in pure strategies where the equilibrium play is such that the players always take the cooperative choice (in our case A). Suppose that the game of Figure 4 is repeated an infinite number of times and that the long run average payoff or more precisely the limit inferior of the average payoff is taken as the supergame payoff. (The ordinary limit may not exist.) It can easily be seen that an equilibrium point for this game Γ_∞^3 is obtained if the players always behave as recommended by the cooperation theory for the first $100 - r$ periods.

There are some experiments where the laboratory situation did correspond to the finite supergame with money payoffs. (See for example Lave 1962; Lave 1965; Morehous 1973; Rapoport and Dale 1973.)

The results do not show any obvious disagreement with the cooperation theory or the benevolence theory, at least if one is willing to make adjustments for the possibility that a sizable proportion of the subjects did not understand the strategic situation very well. In many cases the players manage to achieve cooperation in the sense that both of them take the cooperative choice for a long sequence of periods. It happens quite often that the cooperation breaks down in the last periods. Such end effects are predicted by the cooperation theory and not excluded by the benevolence theory.

The way in which the game is described to the players strongly influences the behavior of the subjects (Evans and Crumbaugh 1966; Pruitt 1967, 1970; Guyer, Fox and Hamburger 1973). According to these experiments one must expect that it makes a difference whether Γ_m^3 is described by Figure 4 or by a table of the kind in Figure 10. Here both players have the same table and each of the players receives as his payoff for one period the sum of what he 'takes for himself' and what the other player 'gives to him'. The representation of the game seems to influence the interpretation of the other player's choices in terms of his intentions. In Figure 10 choice A looks more 'cooperative' than in Figure 4. Looking at Figure 4, a subject may think: "he has selected A because he wanted to receive the payoff of 3", whereas Figure 10 suggests another kind of interpretation: "he has given 3 to me and has taken nothing for himself in order to show his good will". Presentation effects of this kind point in the direction of secondary utilities. Probably the benevolence theory does not provide the best explanation in terms of secondary utilities, but some psychological effects do come in.

Comparison with the chain store paradox

Since secondary utilities seem to be important for the prisoners' dilemma supergame, one may be tempted to try to apply the same kind of reasoning to the chain store game. What kind of assumptions about secondary utilities can be made in order to avoid the chain store paradox?

	I take for myself	and I give to him
A	0	3
B	1	0

Fig. 10. Alternative description of the game of Figure 4.

One could assume that human beings have some kind of 'internal commit-ment power'. Once somebody has made a plan, a negative utility will be attached to any change of the plan. This idea is in agreement with the theory of cognitive dissonance (Festinger 1957).

Suppose that player A in the first version of the chain store game makes an internal plan to react by his AGGRESSIVE response to a choice of IN up to period 17. Assume that the negative utility for a change of his plan is -3. Then he has a good reason to stick to his plan, since in period 17 it will be better to react by the AGGRESSIVE response. (As before, primary and secondary utilities are assumed to combine additively.)

If player A has this internal commitment power, it would be even better and just as feasible to make an internal commitment to take the AGGRESSIVE response up to the last period of the game. This is not very plausible. There-fore the 'internal commitment theory' which, by the way, would be applicable to the finite prisoners' dilemma game too, does not seem to be a reasonable theory for the chain store game.

Another possibility of introducing a secondary utility is as follows: if player A follows the behavior prescribed by the deterrence theory and never-theless many of the players 1, ... , 20 select IN, then player A will become very angry. As an angry person he will have a positive secondary utility for aggressive behavior. This is in agreement with the frustration-aggression hypo-thesis (Dollard, Doob, Miller, Mowres and Sears 1939). The 'anger theory' has implications similar to the internal commitment theory. Player A should be able to deter all players 1, ... , 20. The deterrence should not break down for some of the last players. Therefore the 'anger theory' is as implausible as the 'internal commitment theory'.

The game Γ_{100}^3 is a 2-person game where both players interact for a con-siderable number of periods. Some interpersonal relationship can be expected to develop. Contrary to this, the chain store game Γ_{20}^1 is a 21-person game where player A interacts with each of the players 1, ... , 20 at most once; there is no occasion for the development of interpersonal relationships. This is an important difference between both games which is partly responsible for the fact that plausible theories based on secondary utilities are much more difficult to construct for the chain store game.

On the basis of these considerations it seems to be justified to draw the following conclusion. Theories based on secondary utilities do not provide a satisfactory explanation for the fact that rational players refuse to accept the conclusions of the induction theory as a guide to practical behavior. It is necessary to look for a different explanation.

5. SKETCH OF A THREE-LEVEL THEORY OF DECISION MAKING

In this section, an attempt shall be made to develop an informal model of some aspects of the human decision process. The general approach is based on the idea that a decision may be reached on three different levels, the levels of routine, imagination and reasoning. The theory is speculative rather than based on empirical facts other than circumstantial evidence.

It is of course an oversimplification to assume that there are exactly three levels of decision making, neatly separable from each other. There cannot be any doubt about the fact that the decision process is much more complicated than the simplistic picture which we are going to paint. The three-level theory cannot claim to be more than a heuristic tool for the investigation of problems of limited rationality.

The level of routine

The level of routine may be thought of as a simple mathematical learning model where the possibilities with which one of k alternatives $1, \dots, k$ in a given decision problem is selected, depends on the experience with similar decision problems in the past.[5] On the routine level, decisions are made without any conscious effort. The underlying criteria of similarity between decision situations are crude and sometimes inadequate.

The level of imagination

On the level of imagination, the decision maker tries to visualize how the selection of different alternatives may influence the probable course of future events. The result of this process of imagination is the selection of one alternative which appears to be preferable to other alternatives. The decision maker does not know why he imagines one scenario rather than another. The imagination process is governed by a multitude of procedural decisions which are made on the routine level. We may say that the imagination level employs the routine level. The imagination process is similar to a computer simulation. The program of this simulation is determined on the routine level.

The level of reasoning

The level of reasoning is characterized by a conscious effort to analyse the situation in a rational way on the basis of explicit assumptions whose validity is examined in the light of past experience and logical thinking. The result of the reasoning process is the selection of an optimal alternative. The level of reasoning needs the help of the lower levels of imagination and routine. Ordinarily logical analysis is based on some kind of simplified model whose assumptions are products of imagination. Moreover, the results of the imagination process are used as heuristic hints which guide the process of reasoning.

The predecision

Suppose that a decision maker is confronted with a decision problem where he has to select among k alternatives $1, \ldots, k$. Which of the three levels are activated by this situation? Since the higher levels need the help of the lower levels there are only three possibilities. (1) Only the routine level is activated. We may say that the decision maker does not stop to think. (2) The routine level and the imagination level are activated. The decision maker visualizes the consequences of different alternatives but he does not transcend the level of imagination. (3) All three levels are activated. A conscious effort is made to analyse the situation in a rational way.

Obviously, a decision has to be made which of the three possibilities (1), (2) and (3) is selected. This decision will be called the 'predecision'. The predecision is made on the routine level.

The final decision

After the predecision has been made, those levels which have been activated will begin to operate. Normally each of these levels will produce one alternative which will be called a 'level decision'. We assume that the routine level always reaches a level decision but we do not exclude the possibility that the imagination process or the reasoning process are employed without reaching any conclusion. Time may be too short or the decision problem may be too difficult.

Suppose that several level decisions have been reached. Generally these level decisions will be different from each other. Obviously a decision has to be made which selects one of the level decisions. This decision is called the

THE CHAIN STORE PARADOX   149

'final decision'. The final decision determines the actual behavior. It is made on the routine level.

Note that we do not assume that a decision on a higher level automatically supersedes a decision on a lower level. No final decision would be needed if this were the case. It is an important feature of the three-level theory that a decision maker who has found the rational way of behavior may make the final decision to do something else.

The influence of past experience on predecision and final decision

Predecision and final decision are the results of learning processes which operate on the routine level. In both cases the decision is a decision between levels. The tendency to select one level rather than another will be influenced by the consequences of similar decisions in the past.

Let us first look at the final decision. If the final decision was made in favor of one level, e.g. the level of reasoning and it turns out that the behavior in the decision situation is rewarded by a success, then this will strengthen the tendency to make a final decision in favor of this level in case of a similar decision situation in the future. The tendency is weakened by the experience of a failure.

The tendency to make one predecision rather than another will also be influenced by the successes and failures experienced in similar decision situations in the past. If a final decision in favor of a certain level was successful, then the probability of a predecision which activates this level and the lower ones is increased. The probability is decreased by the experience of a failure.

It may happen that after the decision has been made, it turns out that it would have been better to take another level decision as the final decision. This will also influence the tendencies to select one level rather than another.

The short run character of success and failure

The way in which a learning process operates depends on the criteria which define what constitutes a success or a failure. The process cannot function well if there is a lack of feedback; successes and failures must be experienced sufficiently often. Therefore, the definition of success and failure must be based on short run criteria: within a reasonably short time after a decision has been made it must be possible to determine whether the consequences of the decision are favorable of unfavorable.

The short run character of success and failure does not exclude the pursuit of long run goals. Long run goals may be approached by short run measures of achievement. Each step in the right direction is experienced as a success.

There is no reason to suppose that the substitution of short run measures of achievement for the pursuit of long run goals will work in a similar way as a long run optimization in the sense of modern decision theory. Therefore one cannot expect that learning processes have the tendency to produce a way of behavior which approximates long run utility maximization.

Economy of decision effort

Decision time and decision effort are scarce commodities. In terms of these commodities, the imagination process is more costly than the routine process and the reasoning process is more costly than the imagination process. The predecision serves the purpose of allocating decision time and effort in a reasonable way.

In view of these considerations, one may ask the question why the final decision sometimes does not select the level decision produced by the highest activated level. After all, the decision effort has been spent already.

The answer is quite simple. It is not true that the higher level always yields the better decision. The reasoning process is not infallible. It is subject to logical and computational mistakes. The imagination process has its short-comings, too. Which level has the best chance to produce a successful decision will depend on the nature of the decision problem. Therefore it is necessary to gather experiences about the comparative merits of the decisions made on different levels. For such purposes it may be useful to produce a higher level decision in a situation where the final decision will select a lower level decision with a very high probability. The selection of the lower level decision does not mean that the decision effort spent on the higher level is wasted.

Why rational behavior cannot be learnt completely

Suppose that a decision maker is repeatedly confronted with the same kind of decision problem under uncertainty; assume that on the level of reasoning he is able to find the rational solution for a problem of this kind. In order to have something specific in mind, we may think of a sequence of investment decision situation where some amount of money can be invested in several different ways; the goal is the maximization of profit.

Since the decision is made under uncertainty, the rational solution in the sense of modern decision theory will involve the maximization of expected utility; in our specific example we may assume that this expected utility can be represented by expected profit.

If the decision has long run consequences, then the utility maximization will be long run; in our specific example the expected profit to be maximized will be a discounted sum of a stream of expected future profits or something similar. From our remarks on the short run character of success and failure it is clear that in this case it is not very probable that a long process of learning will lead to a decision behavior which approaches the rational solution. In the following discussion we shall assume that there are no such problems. The decision situation is supposed to be such that it is rational to maximize short run expected profit. As we shall see, even in this case a long process of learning may fail to approach the rational solution.

The learning process which determines the probabilities with which the final decision selects one level decision or another operates on the routine level. Since expected profit is not observed, the experience of actual profits will supply the criteria of success and failure which guide this learning process. Because of the uncertainty of the decision situation, it is unavoidable that sometimes the rational decision produced on the level of reasoning appears to be a failure, whereas the routine process or the imagination process may seem to be more successful. This will weaken the tendency to take the rational choice. Even if the rational choice has a much higher rate of success than the decisions produced on the other levels, failures will occur with some probability and the decision maker will never trust his reasoning process completely. From time to time he will not take his rational choice.

Consider a situation where in our specific example the decision maker had some very bad experiences with a certain kind of investment, say the investment in common stock. On the reasoning level he comes to the conclusion that this was due to some unforeseen events which had a very low probability when the decision was made, and that under the present circumstances the investment in common stock is the most profitable one. Nevertheless, he cannot help being impressed by his bad experience. He feels less inclined to trust his reasoning process. On the lower levels an investment in common stock does not seem to be advisable. On the routine level he has learnt to fear the repetition of his bad experiences. On the level of imagination he vividly visualizes the repetition of the unforeseen events which reduced the price of stock, in spite of the fact that on the level of reasoning he knows that now such events are even less probable than before. In the end he makes the final decision to choose another investment possibility.

6. THE INDUCTION PROBLEM IN THE LIGHT OF THE THREE-LEVEL THEORY OF DECISION MAKING

For the sake of shortness we use the term 'induction problem' in order to refer to the difficulties which arise in connection with the induction theories for the two versions of the chain store game and for the finite prisoners' dilemma supergame. In the following discussion, the ideas of the preceding section will be applied to this problem.

Why strategic decisions are likely to come from the level of imagination

Most of the strategic decision problems which occur in human life are quite complicated. Usually rational solutions are not easily available. Even in the case of relatively simple parlor games it is rarely possible to compute optimal strategies. Strategic decision problems of business and war are subject to the additional difficulty that the unstructured nature of such situations makes it very hard to analyse them in a rigorous way.

It is plausible to assume that under such circumstances the level of imagination has the best chance to produce a successful decision. Usually the visualization of the possible consequences of different choices will reveal some important structural details of the strategic situation which are not obvious enough to be recognized on the routine level. Therefore the imagination level is likely to produce better decisions than the routine level. In a game situation it is often important to put oneself into the situation of the other player in order to form an expectation about his behavior. This can be done on the level of imagination. A player who does not stop to think and makes his decision on the routine level is likely to make some mistakes which can be easily avoided by imagining oneself to be in the other player's position.

If a player tries to analyse the game situation in a rigorous way, then he will often find that the process of reasoning does not lead to any clear conclusion. This will weaken his tendency to activate the level of reasoning in later occasions of the same kind. It may also happen that the process of reasoning yields an inadequate decision which is the result of rigorous thinking about an oversimplified model of the situation. The decision situation itself is often not sufficiently well structured to permit the direct application of rigorous analysis. The analysis must be applied to a model of the situation. The level of reasoning needs the help of the level of imagination in order to construct the model. The imagination process is not unlikely to be more reliable as a generator of scenarios than as a generator of assumptions for a model of the situation.

On the basis of these considerations, one must expect that the final decision shows a strong tendency in favor of the level of imagination even in such cases where the situation is well structured and the application of rigorous thinking is not too difficult.

Application to the induction problem

Obviously the induction argument is a result of abstract thinking which is done on the level of reasoning. On the level of imagination a clear and detailed visualization of a sequence of two, three or four periods is possible – the exact number is not important. A similarly clear and detailed visualization of a sequence of 20 periods is not possible. For a small number of periods the conclusions of the induction argument can be obtained by the visualization of scenarios. For a large number of periods the scenarios will either be restricted to several periods, e.g. at the end of the game or the visualization will be vague in the sense that the individual periods are not seen in detail. A player may imagine that 'in the beginning' something else will happen than 'towards the end' without having any clear view of the extension of these vaguely defined parts of the game.

On the level of imagination, one cannot find anything wrong with the deterrence theory for the two versions of the chain store game and with the cooperation theory for the finite prisoners' dilemma supergame. On the contrary, the scenarios which support these theories appear to be very convincing.

The fact that the last periods appear to be different from the earlier ones is easy to understand with the help of the three-level theory. Theories based on secondary utilities do not exclude end effects but they do not really explain them. (See our discussion of the benevolence theory in section 4.) The three-level theory seems to be a very natural way to look at the induction problem.

154   R E I N H A R D   S E L T E N

7. PERFECT EQUILIBRIUM POINTS

In the following some game-theoretical concepts are introduced which are needed in order to make the induction argument precise. For the purposes of this section a game will always be a finite n-person game in extensive form with perfect recall.[6] Games with perfect recall can be analyzed with the help of behavior strategies. There is no need to consider other kinds of strategies.[7]

Definititions[8]

Let $\mathcal{U}_i$ be the set of all information sets of player i in a game Γ. *A behavior strategy*

(1) $q_i = \{q_U\}_{U \in \mathcal{U}_i}$

of player i in Γ assigns a probability distribution q_U over the choices of U to every information set of player i. If γ is a choice at U, then $q_U(\gamma)$ is the probability with which γ is chosen by q_i.

Let Q_i be the set of all behavior strategies q_i of player i in Γ. An n-tuple $q = (q_1, \dots, q_n)$ with $q_i \epsilon Q_i$ is called a *strategy combination for* Γ. The set of all strategy combinations for Γ is denoted by Q.

Since no other strategies are considered, in the following discussion behavior strategies often will be simply called strategies. For every strategy combination $q \epsilon Q$ an *expected payoff vector* $H(q) = (H_1(q), \dots, H_n(q))$ is defined in the usual way. $H_i(q)$ is player i's expected payoff under the condition that the strategies in q are used by the players.

If q is a strategy combination and q_i' is a strategy for player i, then the notation q/q_i' is used for the strategy combination $(q_1, \dots, q_i', \dots, q_n)$ which results from q if in q player i's strategy q_i is replaced by q_i', whereas all other strategies in q remain unchanged.

A strategy $\tilde{q}_i$ is called a *best reply to the strategy combination* $q = (q_1, \dots, q_n)$ if we have

(2) $H_i(q/\tilde{q}_i) = \max_{q_i' \epsilon Q_i} H_i(q/q_i').$

An equilibrium point is a strategy combination $q^* = (q_1^*, \dots, q_n^*)$ where for $i = 1, \dots, n$ the strategy q_i^* is a best reply to q^*.

THE CHAIN STORE PARADOX   155

Subgames

Let x be a vertex of the tree K of a game Γ. Let K_x be the subtree which contains x and all those parts of K which come after x in the sense that they can be reached by a play after x has been reached. K_x is the tree of a *subgame* Γ_x if and only if K_x has the following property: if an information set U contains at least one vertex of K_x, then every vertex in U belongs to K_x. — The subgame Γ_x results from Γ by restricting the rules of Γ to K_x: On K_x the information sets and the choices of the players, the probabilities of random choices and the payoffs are the same as in Γ.

A strategy q_{xi} of player i for a subgame Γ_x *of* Γ is called induced by a strategy q_i for Γ if on Γ_x the strategies q_{xi} and q_i prescribe the same behavior. A strategy combination $q_x = (q_{x1}, \ldots, q_{xn})$ for Γ_x is *induced* by a strategy combination $q = (q_1, \ldots, q_n)$ if for $1 = 1, \ldots, n$ the strategy q_{xi} is induced by q_i.

Perfect equilibrium points

A perfect equilibrium point $q^* = (q_1^*, \ldots, q_n^*)$ for a game Γ is an equilibrium point for Γ which induces an equilibrium point q_x^* ♭ $(q_{x1}^*, \ldots, q_{xn}^*)$ on every subgame Γ_x of Γ.

It has been argued elsewhere that a strictly non-cooperative solution of a game in extensive form must be a perfect equilibrium point.[9] A rational theory which specifies complete strategic recommendations for all players in a game Γ must prescribe a perfect equilibrium point for Γ. The theory must prescribe an equilibrium point, since otherwise at least one of the players can improve his payoff by a deviation from the theoretical recommendations, if the other players behave in the prescribed way. A situation of this kind should not only be excluded in the game as a whole but also in the subgames of the game. This is not automatically true for every equilibrium point since an equilibrium point for the whole game may induce a disequilibrium strategy combination on a subgame which is not reached if the equilibrium point for the whole game is played. It is clear that a rational theory should prescribe rational behavior in all parts of the game, even in those parts which cannot be reached if the game is played rationally.

The difference between a perfect equilibrium point and an imperfect one can be exemplified with the help of the game Γ_1^1 in Figure 1. As we can see from the bimatrix, this game has two equilibrium points in pure strategies;

156   REINHARD SELTEN

the equilibrium point COOPERATIVE/IN is perfect and the equilibrium point AGGRESSIVE/OUT is imperfect. After player 1 has selected IN, a subgame begins; this subgame has only one equilibrium point, namely the CO-OPERATIVE response of player A. It follows immediately that Γ_1^1 has one and only one perfect equilibrium point, the strategy combination COOPERA-TIVE/IN.

The imperfect equilibrium point AGGRESSIVE/OUT has an interesting interpretation: player A threatens to take the AGGRESSIVE response to the choice of IN. If this threat is believed by player 1, then it is better for him to choose OUT. Player A does not have to execute his threat if player 1 chooses OUT. The subgame after the choice of IN is not reached by AGGRESSIVE/OUT.

Player A's threat is not credible. Player 1 knows that it is not in the interest of player A to take the AGGRESSIVE response after a choice of IN. Therefore it is better for player 1 to choose IN. The imperfect equilibrium point is no rational alternative to the perfect one. Player 1 cannot be deterred.

8. PRECISE STATEMENT OF THE INDUCTION THEORY

A precise statement of the induction theory for the two versions of the chain store game and for the finite prisoners' dilemma supergame requires the concept of a perfect equilibrium point. The deterrence theory for the two versions of the chain store game is not incompatible with the idea of an equilibrium point. As we have seen in the preceding section, even in Γ_1^1 an imperfect equilibrium point is available where player 1 is deterred from choosing IN. The deterrence theory fails to be game-theoretically correct since it is incompatible with the concept of a perfect equilibrium point.

It is well known that in the case of the finite prisoners' dilemma supergame the cooperation theory is already incompatible with the equilibrium point concept.[10] Nevertheless, it is more adequate to apply the notion of a perfect equilibrium point.

The finite prisoners' dilemma supergame is a game in extensive form. Moreover, the natural way of reasoning from behind, first looking at the last period, then on the second last, etc. is closely connected to the requirement of perfectness. Among the imperfect equilibrium points of the finite prisoners' dilemma supergame there are many which in some unreached subgames prescribe the cooperative choice A in the last period.

THE CHAIN STORE PARADOX   157

The following theorem contains a precise statement of the induction theory.

THEOREM: *For* $m = 1, 2, \ldots$ *each of the games* Γ_m^1, Γ_m^2 *and* Γ_m^3 *has one and only one perfect equilibrium point. In the case of the two versions of the chain store game* Γ_m^1 *and* Γ_m^2, *the uniquely determined perfect equilibrium point requires that whenever one of the players* 1, $\ldots$, m *has to make a choice, he chooses IN and whenever player A has to make a choice, he chooses COOPERATIVE. In the case of the finite prisoners' dilemma supergame* Γ_m^3, *the uniquely determined perfect equilibrium point requires that each of both players selects B under all circumstances in every period.*

Proof: Let us first look at the two versions of the chain store game. There is no difference between Γ_1^1 and Γ_1^2. Our discussion in the preceding section has shown that as far as Γ_1^1 is concerned, the assertion of the theorem is correct. Assume that the theorem holds for $\Gamma_1^1, \ldots, \Gamma_{m-1}^1$ and for $\Gamma_1^2, \ldots,$ Γ_{m-1}^2. Up to the numbering of the players and up to some strategically irrelevant constants in the payoff function, the subgames of Γ_m^1 at the beginning of period 2 have the same structure as Γ_{m-1}^1. Analogously, the subgames at the beginning of period 2 of Γ_m^2 have essentially the same structure as Γ_{m-1}^2. In view of the definition of the perfectness requirement, it is clear that a perfect equilibrium point is induced on every subgame by a perfect equilibrium point. It follows from the induction assumption that the subgames at the beginning of period 2 have exactly one perfect equilibrium point each. The perfect equilibrium point of the whole game must induce these equilibrium points which prescribe the behavior required by the theorem. Since the behavior in the subgames does not depend on the outcome of period 1, there is only one way in which this behavior can be completed in order to construct a perfect equilibrium point for the whole game by adding prescriptions for period 1. In Γ_m^1, player 1 has to choose IN and player A has to take his COOPERATIVE response. In Γ_m^2 the players 1, $\ldots$, m must choose IN and player A has to take his COOPERATIVE response. It is clear that player A must behave in this way. He cannot influence the other players' behavior in later periods. If he would behave differently, the perfect equilibrium point would fail to induce an equilibrium point in the subgame which begins with player A's response in period 1. It follows that in period 1 it is better for player 1 in Γ_m^1 and for the players 1, $\ldots$, m in Γ_m^2 to choose IN. This shows that the theorem holds for Γ_m^1 and Γ_m^2.

158   REINHARD SELTEN

Let us now look at Γ_m^3. The assertion of the theorem holds for Γ_1^3. This game has only one equilibrium point, namely (B,B). Assume that the theorem is correct for $\Gamma_1^3, \dots, \Gamma_{m-1}^3$. Up to a strategically irrelevant additive constant in the payoff functions, the subgames of Γ_m^3 at the beginning of period 2 have the same structure as Γ_{m-1}^3. Therefore each of these subgames has exactly one perfect equilibrium point which prescribes the choice of B under all circumstances. A perfect equilibrium point Γ_m^3 must prescribe the same behavior for periods 2, ... , m. There is only one way in which this behavior can be completed by a prescription of choices for period 1 if one wants to construct an equilibrium point for the whole game: both players must choose B in period 1. Given the behavior in the subgames, in period 1 the choice of B yields a better payoff than the choice of A, independently of the other player's choice in period 1. This completes the proof of the theorem.

Institut für Mathematische Wirtschaftsforschung
Universität Bielefeld

NOTES

[1]   Nevertheless the industrial organization flavor of the story is not purely fortuitious. I became aware of the problem in the course of a conversation about the theory of entry preventing prices. I am grateful to Professor A. Gutowsky of the University of Frankfurt am Main with whom I had this very interesting interchange of ideas.

[2]   The book *Games and Decisions* by Luce and Raiffa contains a thorough discussion of the finite supergame of the prisoners' dilemma game (Luce–Raiffa 1957, pp. 97–102).

[3]   Luce and Raiffa are aware of the possibility of such theories, but their view is that of the cooperation theory. I think that they underemphasize the paradoxical nature of their recommendations (Luce–Raiffa 1957, pp. 97–102).

[4]   Luce and Raiffa suggest that this is not a solution of the problem, since it is possible to imagine a laboratory situation where the psychological effects are compensated by appropriate changes of the money payoffs (Luce–Raiffa 1957, p. 98n). This argument is not conclusive. It is very hard to imagine a laboratory situation of this kind. Therefore one might argue that one would be inclined to behave according to the induction theory if one were confronted with such a situation.

[5]   Since the appearance of the classic work by Bush and Mosteller (Bush and Mosteller 1955) many mathematical learning models of this kind have been explored in the literature (see e.g. Restle and Greeno 1970).

[6]   See Kuhn 1953 and Aumann 1964.

[7]   Kuhn has proved that in a game with perfect recall a payoff equivalent behavior strategy can be found for every ordinary mixed strategy. (Kuhn 1953, p. 213).

[8]   It will be assumed that the reader is familiar with the notion of a game in extensive form (see Kuhn 1953 or Selten 1960 and Selten 1964).

[9]   See Selten 1965, 1968 or 1973. The refined concept of 1975 is not used here.

[10]   See Luce–Raiffa 1957, pp. 99–100.

THE CHAIN STORE PARADOX   159

REFERENCES

Aumann, R. J., 'Mixed and Behavior Strategies in Infinite Extensive Games', in: M. Dresher, L. S. Shapley and A. W. Tucker (eds.), *Advances in Game Theory, Annals of Mathematics Studies* 52 (Princeton, 1964), pp. 627–650.

Bush, R. R. and F. Mosteller, *Stochastic Models for Learning* (New York, 1955).

Dollard, J. L. Doob, N. Miller, O. Mowres and R. Sears, *Frustration and Agression* (New Haven, 1939).

Evans, Gary W. and Charles M. Crumbaugh, 'Effects of Prisoner's Dilemma Format on Cooperative Behavior', *Journal of Personality and Social Psychology* 6 (1966), pp. 486–488.

Festinger, L., *A Theory of Cognitive Dissonance* (Evanston Ill., 1957).

Guyer, Melvin, John Fox and Henry Hamburger, 'Format Effects in the Prisoner's Dilemma Game', *Journal of Conflict Resolution* 17 (1973), pp. 719–743.

Kuhn, H. W., 'Extensive Games and the Problem of Information', in: H. W. Kuhn and A. W. Tucker (eds.), *Contributions to the Theory of Games*, Vol. II, *Annals of Mathematics Studies* 28 (Princeton, 1953), pp. 193–216.

Lave, Lester B., 'An Empirical Approach to the Prisoner's Dilemma', *Quarterly Journal of Economics* 76 (1962), pp. 424–436.

Lave, Lester B., 'Factors Affecting Cooperation in the Prisoner's Dilemma', *Behavioral Science* 10 (1965), pp. 26–38.

Luce, Duncan R. and Howard Raiffa, *Games and Decisions* (New York–London–Sidney, 1957).

Morehous, L. G., 'One-play, Two-play, Five-play and Ten-play Runs of Prisoner's Dilemma', *Journal of Conflict Resolution* 11 (1967), pp. 354–362.

Neumann, J.v. and O. Morgenstern, *Theory of Games and Economic Behavior*, Princeton, 1944.

Pruitt, D. G., 'Reward Structure and Cooperation: the Decomposed Prisoner's Dilemma Game', *Journal of Personality and Social Psychology* 7 (1967), pp. 21–27.

Pruitt, D. G., 'Motivational Processes in the Decomposed Prisoner's Dilemma Game', *Journal of Personality and Social Psychology* 14 (1970), pp. 227–238.

Rapoport, Anatol and Philip S. Dale, 'The "End" and "Start" Effects in the Iterated Prisoner's Dilemma', *Journal of Conflict Resolution* 11 (1967), pp. 354–462.

Restle, Frank and James G. Greeno, *Introduction to Mathematical Psychology* (Addison Wesley Publishing Company, 1970).

Selten, R., 'Bewertung strategischer Spiele', *Zeitschrift für die gesamte Staatwissenschaft* (1960), pp. 221–282.

Selten, R., 'Valuation of *n*-Person Games', in: *Advances in Game Theory, Annals of Mathematics Studies* 52 (Princeton N.J., 1964), pp. 565–578.

Selten, R., 'Spieltheoretische Behandlung eines Oligopolmodells mit Nachfrageträgheit', *Zeitschrift für die gesamte Staatswissenschaft* 121 (1965), Teil I, pp. 301–324, Teil II, pp. 667–689.

Selten, R., 'An Oligopoly Model with Demand Inertia', Working Paper No. 250 (Center for Research in Management Science, University of California, Berkeley, 1968).

Selten, R., 'A Simple Model of Imperfect Competition, Where 4 are Few and 6 are Many', *International Journal of Game Theory* 2 (1973), pp. 141–201.

Selten, R., 'Reexamination of the Perfectness Concept for Equilibrium Points in Extensive Games', *International Journal of Game Theory* 4 (1975), pp. 25–55.

[35]

JOURNAL OF ECONOMIC THEORY 27, 253–279 (1982)

Reputation and Imperfect Information

DAVID M. KREPS AND ROBERT WILSON

*Graduate School of Business, Stanford University,
Stanford, California 94305*

Received June 18, 1980; revised June 22, 1981

A common observation in the informal literature of economics (and elsewhere) is that in multistage "games," players may seek early in the game to acquire a reputation for being "tough" or "benevolent" or something else. But this phenomenon is not observed in some formal game-theoretic analyses of finite games, such as Selten's finitely repeated chain-store game or in the finitely repeated prisoners' dilemma. We reexamine Selten's model, adding to it a "small" amount of imperfect (or incomplete) information about players' payoffs, and we find that this addition is sufficient to give rise to the "reputation effect" that one intuitively expects. *Journal of Economic Literature*, Classification Numbers: 026, 213, 611.

1. INTRODUCTION

The purpose of this paper is to present some game-theoretic models that illustrate the role of a firm's reputation. Allusions to reputational effects recur in the industrial organization literature on imperfect competition, but formal models and analyses have been lacking. Scherer [21], for example, points to

> the demonstration effect that sharp price cutting in one market can have on the behavior of actual or would-be rivals in other markets. If rivals come to fear from a multimarket seller's actions in Market A that entry or expansion in Markets B and C will be met by sharp price cuts or other rapacious responses, they may be deterred from taking agressive actions there. Then the conglomerate's expected benefit from predation in Market A will be supplemented by the discounted present value of the competition-inhibiting effects its example has in Markets B and C. (page 338)

The intuitive appeal of this line of reasoning has, however, been called the "chain-store paradox" by Selten [24], who demonstrates that it is not supported in a straightforward game-theoretic model. We shall elaborate Selten's argument later, but the crux is that, in a very simple environment, there is no means by which thoroughly rational strategies in one market could be influenced by behavior in a second, essentially independent market.

253

0022-0531/82/040253-27$02.00/0

What is lacking, apparently, is a plausible mechanism that connects behavior in otherwise independent markets.

We show that imperfect information is one such mechanism. Moreover, the effects of imperfect information can be quite dramatic. If rivals perceive the *slightest* chance that an incumbent firm might enjoy "rapacious responses," then the incumbent's optimal strategy is to employ such behavior against its rivals in all, except possibly the last few, in a long string of encounters. For the incumbent, the immediate cost of predation is a worthwhile investment to sustain or enhance its reputation, thereby deterring subsequent challenges.

The two models we present here are variants of the game studied by Selten [24]; several other variations are discussed in Kreps and Wilson [8]. The first model can be interpreted in the context envisioned by Scherer: A multimarket monopolist faces a succession of potential entrants (though in our model the analysis is unchanged if there is a single rival with repeated opportunities to enter). We treat this as a finitely repeated game with the added feature that the entrants are unsure about the monopolist's payoffs, and we show that there is a unique "sensible" equilibrium where, no matter how small the chance that the monopolist actually benefits from predation, the entrants nearly always avoid challenging the monopolist for fear of the predatory response. The second model enriches this formulation by allowing, in the case of a single entrant with multiple entry opportunities, that also the incumbent is uncertain about the entrant's payoffs. The equilibrium in this model is analogous to a price war: Since the entrant also has a reputation to protect, both firms may engage in battle. Each employs its aggressive tactic in a classic game of "chicken," persisting in its attempt to force the other to acquiesce before it would itself give up the fight, even if it is virtually certain (at the outset) that each side will thereby incur short-run losses.

After reviewing Selten's model in Section 2, we analyze these two models in Sections 3 and 4, respectively. In Section 5 we discuss our results and relate them to some of the relevant literature. In particular, this issue of the *Journal* includes a companion article by Milgrom and Roberts [13] that explores many of the issues studied here in models that are richer in institutional detail. Their paper is highly recommended to the reader.

2. THE CHAIN-STORE PARADOX

The models we analyze are variations on the chain-store game studied by Selten [24]. Consider a sequential game with two players called the *entrant* (or potential entrant) and the *monopolist*. The entrant moves first, electing either to *enter* or to *stay out*. Following entry, the monopolist chooses either to *acquiesce* or to *fight*. If the entrant stays out, the incumbent is not called

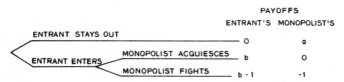

FIG. 1.   Selten's chain-store game.

upon to move. Payoffs to the players, depending on the moves selected, are given in Fig. 1. We consider the case that $a > 1$ and $0 < b < 1$.

How will this game be played? If the entrant enters, the monopolist chooses between the payoffs 0 if it acquiesces and -1 if it fights, so surely it will acquiesce. Anticipating this response, the entrant chooses between 0 if it stays out and b if it enters, and so it will enter. This is one Nash equilibrium of the game, but there is another: If the entrant were to anticipate that the monopolist would fight entry, then the entrant would want to stay out. Note that it costs the monopolist nothing to adopt the strategy "fight if entry" if no entry occurs. So this is a second Nash equilibrium. But this second equilibrium is not so plausible as the first. It depends on an expectation by the entrant of the monopolist's behavior that, faced with the *fait accompli* of entry, would be irrational behavior for the monopolist. In the parlance of game theory, the second equilibrium is *imperfect*. We suppose that the entrant adopts the "rational expectation" that the monopolist will acquiesce to entry, and we expect the first equilibrium to ensue.

Consider next the case that the game in Fig. 1 is played a finite number of times. A single monopolist plays a succession of N different entrants, where the monopolist's total payoff is the sum of its payoffs in the N stage games. Allow the later entrants to observe the moves in all earlier stages of the game. Scherer's reasoning predicts that in this case the "reputation" effect might come to life: The monopolist, by fighting any early entry, might convince later opponents that it will fight, thus deterring later entries. Indeed, if this were the case, then also the early round opponents would not enter, not wishing to be abused for demonstration purposes. However, as Selten argues, this does not withstand scrutiny. In the last stage the monopolist will not fight because there are no later entrants to demonstrate for. So in the last stage, entry will surely occur. But then in the penultimate stage, the monopolist again has no reason to fight—it is costly in the short run and has no effect on the last stage. The next-to-last entrant, realizing this, will surely enter. This logic can be repeated, unraveling from the back: In each stage entry and acquiescence will occur. To be precise, this is the unique perfect Nash equilibrium of the game; cf. Selten [22, 23, 24]. Apparently, this model is inadequate to justify Scherer's prediction that reputational effects will play a role.

3. ONE-SIDED UNCERTAINTY

Our contention is that this inadequacy arises because the model does not capture a salient feature of realistic situations. (This contention was made first by Rosenthal [17], whose work we shall discuss in Section 5.) In practical situations, the entrants cannot be *certain* about the payoffs to the monopolist. They may be unsure about the monopolist's costs, or they may be uncertain about nonpecuniary benefits that the monopolist reaps—this may be a monopolist who enjoys being tough. The latter might be more colorfully stated by saying that the monopolist plays tough "irrationally"; according to Scherer [21, p. 247], "... fear of irrational or avowedly rapacious action, then, rather than the expectation of rational pricing responses, may be what deters the potential new entrant from entering on a large scale." For whatever reason, the entrants may initially assess some positive probability p that the monopolist's payoffs are not as in Fig. 1 but rather (in the simplest case) as in Fig. 2, reflecting a short-term benefit from a fighting response. In this case, later entrants, observing earlier moves, will revise their assessment p on the basis of what they see. Perhaps in this case the reputation effect will come alive.

We model this formally as follows. There are $N + 1$ players, for N a positive integer. One of the players is the *monopolist*; the others are called *entrant* N, *entrant* $N - 1$,..., *entrant* 1. The monopolist plays the game in Fig. 1 against each entrant in turn: First it plays against entrant N, then $N - 1$, etc. (We always index time backwards, and we refer to stage n as that part of the game that involves entrant n.) The payoffs for each entrant are given in Fig. 1.

The monopolist's payoffs are more complex: Its total payoff is the sum (undiscounted for now) of its payoffs in each stage, where the stage payoffs are either *all* as in Fig. 1 or *all* as in Fig. 2. The monopolist knows which payoff structure obtains. The entrants, on the other hand, initially assess probability δ that the monopolist's payoff structure is the second one. As the game progresses, each entrant (and the monopolist) observes all prior moves. Consequently, the history of moves prior to stage n may enable entrant n to revise this assessment if the history reveals some information about the relative likelihoods of the monopolist's two possible payoff structures.

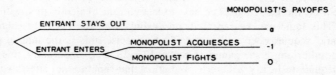

FIG. 2. Payoffs for a tough monopolist.

This model conforms to Harsanyi's [7] formulation of a game with incomplete information. Alternatively, it is a game with imperfect information (among the entrants) and perfect recall, in which "nature" initially determines the monopolist's payoff structure, and nature's move is observed by the monopolist but not the entrants. In line with the first interpretation, we refer to the *weak monopolist* or the *strong monopolist*, meaning the monopolist if its payoffs are as in Fig. 1 or Fig. 2, respectively.

Since the players have perfect recall, there is no loss of generality in restricting attention to behavior strategies (Kuhn [10]). We wish to identify a Nash equilibrium of this game and, moreover, we wish the equilibrium identified to be *perfect*. That is, we wish to exclude equilibria that are based on expectations by one player of another's behavior that would not be rational for the latter to carry out if called upon to do so. Because our games have incomplete information, Selten's [22] concept of subgame perfection is inadequate. His concept of "trembling-hand" perfection (Selten [23]), on the other hand, is difficult to employ in games with strategy spaces as complex as those present here. So we use an analogous equilibrium concept called a *sequential equilibrium*. This is a refinement for extensive games of the usual Nash equilibrium that captures the spirit of Selten's perfectness criterion but that is much easier to apply. General definitions and properties of sequential equilibria are given in Kreps and Wilson [9], which we summarize here.

There are three basic parts to the definition of a sequential equilibrium: (a) Whenever a player must choose an action, that player has some probability assessment over the nodes in its information set, reflecting what that player believes has happened so far. (b) These assessments are consistent with the hypothesized equilibrium strategy. For example, they satisfy Bayes' rule whenever it applies. (c) Starting from *every* information set, the player whose turn it is to move is using a strategy that is optimal for the remainder of the game against the hypothesized future moves of its opponent (given by the strategies) and the assessment of past moves by other players and by "nature" (given by the assessment over nodes in the information set). The difference between this and the standard concept of a Nash equilibrium is that (c) is required for *every* information set, including those that will not be reached if the equilibrium strategies are followed. So each player will be willing to carry out its strategy at *every* point in the game, if ever it is called upon to do so. The properties are: Sequential equilibria exist for all finite extensive games. They are subgame perfect Nash equilibria. For a fixed extensive form and probabilities of nature's moves, as we vary the payoffs it is generic that all strict sequential equilibria are trembling-hand perfect, and the equilibrium path of each sequential equilibrium is an equilibrium path for some trembling-hand perfect equilibrium. Every trembling-hand perfect equilibrium is sequential.

In the context of the game analyzed here, the definition of sequential equilibrium specializes as follows. An equilibrium comprises a (behavior) strategy for each player *and*, for each stage $n = N,..., 1$, a function p_n taking histories of moves up to stage n into numbers in $[0, 1]$ such that: (a) Starting from any point in the game where it is the monopolist's move, the monopolist's strategy is a best response to the entrants' strategies. (b) For each n, entrant n's strategy (contingent on a history h_n of prior play) is a best response to the monopolist's strategy *given that* the monopolist is strong with probability $p_n(h_n)$. (c) The game begins with $p_N = \delta$. (d) Each p_n is computed from p_{n+1} and the monopolist's strategy using Bayes' rule whenever possible. (We will not write (d) precisely—it will be transparent when we give the equilibrium below. That (d) implies "consistency of beliefs" in the sense of Kreps and Wilson |9| may not be apparent, but it does follow from the simple structure of the game being considered here.) The interpretation is that p_n gives the probability assessed by entrant n that the monopolist is strong as a function of how the game has been played up to stage n. Note that in (a) the monopolist's assessment over nodes in its information set is omitted, because all of its information sets are singletons.

We now give a sequential equilibrium for this game. This particular sequential equilibrium has the fortuitous property that, in terms of play from stage n on, p_n is a sufficient statistic for the history of play up to date n. That is, the choices of the players at stage n depend only on p_n and (for the monopolist) the move of entrant n; and p_n is a function of p_{n+1} and the moves at stage $n + 1$. We are lucky to be able to find a sequential equilibrium with this simple structure; it is not generally the case that one can find sequential equilibria for which the players' assessments are sufficient statistics for past play. (See remark (A) below.)

We begin by giving the functions p_n. Set $p_N = \delta$. For $n < N$, if the history of play up to stage n includes *any* instance that entry was met by acquiescence, set $p_n = 0$. If every entry so far has been met by fighting, and if k is the smallest index $(>n)$ such that there was entry at stage k, then set $p_n = \max(b^{k-1}, \delta)$. If there has been no entry, set $p_n = \delta$.

This corresponds to the following recursive definition:

(a) If there is no entry at stage $n + 1$, then $p_n = p_{n+1}$.

(b) If there is entry at stage $n + 1$, this entry is fought, and $p_{n+1} > 0$, then $p_n = \max(b^n, p_{n+1})$.

(c) If there is entry at stage $n + 1$ and either this entry is met by acquiescence or $p_{n+1} = 0$, then $p_n = 0$.

Now that we have described how p_n is computed at every node in the game tree, we can give the strategies of the players in terms of p_n.

Strategy of the Monopolist

(a) If the monopolist is strong, it always fights entry.

(b) If the monopolist is weak and entry occurs at stage n, the monopolist's response depends on n and p_n: If $n = 1$, the monopolist acquiesces. If $n > 1$ and $p_n \geqslant b^{n-1}$, the monopolist fights. If $n > 1$ and $p_n < b^{n-1}$, the monopolist fights with probability $((1 - b^{n-1})p_n)/((1 - p_n)b^{n-1})$ and acquiesces with the complementary probability. (Note that when $p_n = 0$, the probability of fighting is zero, and when $p_n = b^{n-1}$, the probability of fighting is one.)

Strategies of the Entrants

If $p_n > b^n$, entrant n stays out. If $p_n < b^n$, entrant n enters. If $p_n = b^n$, entrant n randomizes, staying out with probability $1/a$.

PROPOSITION 1. *The strategies and beliefs given above constitute a sequential equilibrium.*

Proof. We only sketch the proof, leaving details to the reader. In the context of this game, there are two things to verify: First, the beliefs of the entrants must be consistent with the strategy of the monopolist, in the sense that Bayes' rule holds whenever it applies. Second, starting from any information set in the game, no player has the incentive (in terms of the payoff for the remainder of the game) to change its selection of move at that information set. For entrants, this verification is made using the beliefs given above. (Once this is verified, the Bellman optimality principle together with the fact that beliefs are Bayesian consistent ensures that no player can unilaterally change its strategy and benefit starting from any point in the game tree.)

The verification of Bayesian consistency is easy. If no entry takes place at stage n, nothing is learned about the monopolist, and we have $p_{n-1} = p_n$ in such instances. If $p_n \geqslant b^{n-1}$, then the monopolist is supposed to fight entry. If $p_n = 0$, then the monopolist is supposed to acquiesce. So in these cases, Bayes' rule implies that $p_{n-1} = p_n$ (as long as the monopolist follows its strategy). In each case, this is what we have. Finally, for $p_n \in (0, b^{n-1})$, there are positive probabilities that the monopolist will acquiesce and that it will fight entry. It only acquiesces if it is weak, and, indeed, in this case we have $p_{n-1} = 0$. If it fights, Bayes' rule requires that

$$p_{n-1} = \text{Prob(monopolist strong} \mid \text{monopolist fights)}$$

$$= \text{Prob(monopolist strong and fights)}/\text{Prob(fights)}$$

$$= \frac{\text{Prob(fights} \mid \text{strong)} \cdot \text{Prob(strong)}}{\text{Prob(fights} \mid \text{strong)} \cdot \text{Prob(strong)} + \text{Prob(fights} \mid \text{weak)} \cdot P(\text{weak})}$$

$$= \frac{1 \cdot p_n}{1 \cdot p_n + [((1 - b^{n-1})p_n)/((1 - p_n)b^{n-1})][1 - p_n]} = b^{n-1},$$

which is what we have posited. Thus beliefs and strategies are Bayesian consistent.

Note that there are two instances in which Bayes' rule does not apply: $p_n \geqslant b^{n-1}$ and the monopolist acquiesces to entry; $p_n = 0$ and the monopolist fights. In each case we set $p_{n-1} = 0$. In words, we assume that any acquiescence is viewed by the entrants as "proof" that the monopolist is weak, and the entrants are unshakeable in this conviction once it is formed. This assignment of beliefs off the equilibrium path is *somewhat* arbitrary—there are other assessments that work as well. But this assignment is not wholly capricious—there are assessments that would not give an equilibrium. (This will be discussed more fully below.)

(Repeating an earlier contention, this set of assessments is consistent in the sense of Kreps and Wilson [9]. A direct proof is not difficult.)

Verification that the entrants are playing optimally is straightforward. If $p_n \geqslant b^{n-1}$, entrant n expects entry to be fought, and so it stays out. If $p_n \in (b^n, b^{n-1})$, acquiescence will occur with positive probability, but with probability less than $1 - b$. Again it is better to stay out. If $p_n = b^n$, acquiescence follows entry with probability $1 - b$, and the entrant is indifferent. If $p_n < b^n$, the probability of acquiescence exceeds $1 - b$, and the entrant enters.

To see that the strong monopolist is playing optimally, note that if the entrants follow the strategy above, acquiescence at any point results in more future entries than does fighting. In the short run fighting is better for the strong monopolist, and in the long run fewer entries are better, so the strong monopolist will always fight.

Finally, for the weak monopolist, one can verify inductively that given that these strategies are followed from stage n to stage 1, the expected payoff to the weak monopolist from stages n to 1 is given by the following function of p_n:

$$
\begin{aligned}
v_n(p_n) &= a(t - k(p_n) + 1) + 1 && \text{if } b^n < p_n = b^{k(p_n)-1}, \\
&= a(t - k(p_n) + 1) && \text{if } b^n < p_n < b^{k(p_n)-1}, \\
&= 1 && \text{if } p_n = b^n, \text{ and} \\
&= 0 && \text{if } p_n < b^n,
\end{aligned}
$$

where $k(p) = \inf\{n: b^n < p\}$ for $p > 0$, and $k(0) = \infty$. Now suppose that entry occurs at stage n. By acquiescing, the monopolist receives zero both in this stage and in the rest of the game (since p_{n-1} will be set equal to zero). By fighting, the monopolist receives -1 in this stage and future expected payoffs of 0 if $p_n = 0$, 1 if $p_n \in (0, b^{n-1}]$, and more than 1 if $p_n > b^{n-1}$. Thus the weak monopolist is happy to follow the strategy given above. ∎

It is easiest to understand the nature of this equilibrium by tracing through the play of the game for "typical" values of δ and b, say $\delta = 1/10$ and $b = 1/2$. Note that in this case, $k(\delta) = 4$. Refer to Fig. 3. At stage N (presumed to be greater than 4) the game begins with $p_N = \delta$. At this stage, the monopolist would fight entry regardless of its payoffs, so entry is forestalled. The game evolves along arrow (a) to the point $p_{N-1} = p_N = \delta$. Note that *if* there is entry, the monopolist is willing *ex post* to fight—to acquiesce moves the game along arrow (b) to $p_{N-1} = 0$, from which point the monopolist nets zero. Fighting costs 1 immediately, but acquiescing costs much more in the future. (Note that all that is necessary is that acquiescence cost at least one—as long as acquiescence resulted in $p_{N-1} \leqslant 1/16$ this would

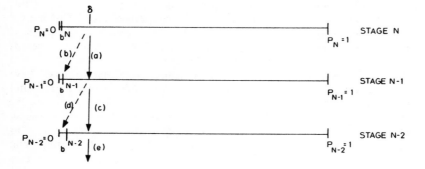

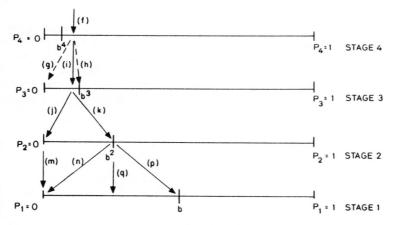

FIG. 3.   Temporal evolution of the game.

be so in this case. So here is one place where the non-Bayesian reassessments need not be *precisely* as specified above to have an equilibrium. But note that $p_{N-1} \leqslant 1/16$ is necessary—otherwise the weak monopolist would rather acquiesce than fight at this stage.) The game continues in this fashion (arrows (c), (e), and (f)) until date 4 $(=k(\delta))$. At this date the monopolist might acquiesce if it is weak and if it is challenged—the strategy of the weak monopolist is chosen so that following entry, acquiescence leads to $p_3 = 0$ (arrow (g)) and fighting leads to $p_3 = b^3$ (arrow (h)). But this does *not* give entrant 4 enough incentive to enter—the game actually evolves along arrow (i) to $p_3 = \delta$. At date 3 the weak monopolist again will randomize if challenged (so that arrows (j) and (k) give the posteriors), and now there is high enough probability of acquiescence for entrant 3 to enter. If the monopolist acquiesces, the game moves along arrow (j) to $p_2 = 0$. At this point the monopolist is known to be weak, and entrants 2 and 1 both enter with the monopolist acquiescing each time. The monopolist thereafter is supposed to acquiesce; if it fights instead at, say, date 2, entrant 1 disregards this and continues to believe that the monopolist is weak. That is, $p_1 = 0$ if either the monopolist acquiesces *or* if it fights. (Note that we could have $p_1 \leqslant 1/2$ if the monopolist fights, and still we would have an equilibrium. But if $p_1 > 1/2$, then the weak monopolist would prefer to fight, upsetting the equilibrium. Again there is some freedom in defining beliefs off the equilibrium path, but not complete freedom.) Back at stage 3, if the monopolist fights entry, the game moves along arrow (k) to $p_2 = 1/4$. At this point entrant 2 is indifferent between entering and staying out, and chooses between the two randomly. If entrant 2 enters, the weak monopolist randomizes between acquiescence (arrow (n)) and fighting (arrow (p)). If entrant 2 stays out, the game moves along arrow (q) to $p_1 = 1/4$ (and entrant 1 surely enters).

The remarkable fact about this equilibrium is that even for very small δ, the "reputation" effect soon predominates. Even if the entrants assess a one-in-one-thousand chance that the monopolist would prefer (in the short run) to fight, if there are more than ten stages to go the entrant stays out because the monopolist will *surely* fight to preserve its reputation. Note the "discontinuity" that this causes as the number of stages in the game goes to infinity:

$$\lim_{N \to \infty} v_N(\delta)/N = a \qquad \text{if} \quad \delta > 0, \text{ and}$$

$$= 0 \qquad \text{if} \quad \delta = 0.$$

The obvious question at this point is: To what extent is this equilibrium unique? It is not the case that it is the unique Nash equilibrium for this game, for the following four reasons.

(a) There are other Nash equilibria that are not sequential equilibria.

(That is, that are not, roughly speaking, perfect.) For example, it is a Nash equilibrium for the monopolist to fight any entry (regardless of its payoffs), and for the entrants never to enter. But this behavior is not "ex post rational" for the weak monopolist in stage one. In general, we wish to allow only sequential equilibria, and we confine attention to those for the remainder of this discussion.

(b) There are sequential equilibria where the strong monopolist acquiesces to entry. For example, if $N = 2$, $b = 1/2$, and $\delta = 2/3$ (very high probability that the monopolist is strong), it is a sequential equilibrium for entrant 2 to enter, the monopolist to acquiesce to this entry regardless of its payoffs, and for entrant 1 to adopt the strategy: Stay out if the monopolist acquiesces in stage 2; enter if the monopolist fights in stage 2. (In stage one, the monopolist responds with its ex post dominant action.) This is sequential because it is supported by the following beliefs of entrant 1:

$$\text{Prob(monopolist strong | acquiescence in stage 2)} = p_2 = 2/3,$$

$$\text{Prob(monopolist strong | fight in stage 2)} = 1/4.$$

For the given strategies, the first of these reassessments follows from Bayes' rule, and the second is "legitimate" because Bayes' rule does not apply: There is zero prior probability that the monopolist will fight in stage 2.

Although this is a sequential equilibrium, we contend that it is not very sensible. The flaw is in the beliefs of entrant one—if there is fighting in stage 2, entrant 1 revises *downward* the probability that the monopolist is strong. Intuitively it seems at least as likely that the strong monopolist would defect and fight as that the weak monopolist would do so. Thus it seems intuitive that entrant one will assess

$$\text{Prob(strong | fight)} \geqslant \text{Prob(strong | acquiesce)}.$$

But if we insist on this condition holding, then the equilibrium given immediately above is excluded.

Putting this formally, we will call the beliefs $\{p_n\}$ of the entrants *plausible* if given two histories h_n and h'_n of play up to stage n, if h_n and h'_n are the same except that some plays of "fight" in h_n are "acquiesce" in h'_n, then $p_n(h_n) \geqslant p_n(h'_n)$. We wish to allow only sequential equilibria that are supported by plausible beliefs. Note that this is not true of the equilibrium immediately above, but it is true of the equilibrium Proposition 1.

(c) In the sequential equilibrium given in this section, there is some freedom in describing what happens off the equilibrium path. For example, we have said that if $p_n = 0$ and the monopolist fights entry, then the entrants set $p_{n-1} = 0$. Thus once $p_n = 0$ in our equilibrium, every subsequent entrant enters. But we would also have an equilibrium if we set $p_{n-1} = b^{n-1}$ after such a defection from the equilibrium, and then entrant $n-1$ would randomize between entering and staying out. Note well, this concerns the behavior of entrant $n-1$ only off the equilibrium path, but in terms of strategies it is a different equilibrium. We cannot hope to have uniqueness off the equilibrium path.

(d) Finally, there is a bit of freedom in defining equilibria along the equilibrium path when $\delta = b^n$ for some $n \leqslant N$: The behavior of entrant n in this case need not conform to the strategy above—any randomization will work.

Except for these four problems, we do get uniqueness:

PROPOSITION 2. *If $\delta \neq b^n$ for $n \leqslant N$, then every sequential equilibrium with plausible beliefs has on-the-equilibrium-path strategies as described previously. Thus every sequential equilibrium with plausible beliefs has the value functions given above.*

The proof is by induction and is left to the reader. We simply note that in carrying out the induction one establishes the following:

(a) The value function of the strong monopolist (in equilibrium) will be a nondecreasing function of p_n, and the strong monopolist will therefore fight any entry.

(b) The value function of the weak monopolist will be a nondecreasing function of p_n and will be given by the formula in the proof of Proposition 1 for $\delta \neq b^n$, $m \leqslant n$.

(c) If there is entry at stage n and if the monopolist fights this entry, then entrant $n-1$ must stay out with probability exactly $1/a$.

By going through this proof, the reader will see the intuition behind this equilibrium, which we will try to summarize here. As long as beliefs are plausible, the strong monopolist will always fight entry. Thus any acquiescence is conclusive proof that the monopolist is weak. Moreover, such evidence once given must result in zero payoff for the monopolist—the argument of Selten that we have given in Section 1 applies (with minor modifications). If entrant n is to enter, then it must be that there is probability $1 - b$ (at least) that the monopolist will acquiesce, which requires that the weak monopolist is randomizing or simply acquiescing. This also requires that $p_n \leqslant b$, and, from Bayes' rule, that *if* this entry is met by fighting, then $p_{n-1} \geqslant p_n/b$. Thus if we begin with $\delta > b^m$, there can be *at most* m entrants who have a positive probability of entering. As N gets large, then, the value to either monopolist must asymptote to aN, and, for $N > 2m$, the weak monopolist would always wish to fight entry. (In fact, in the equilibrium in turns out that this is true for $N \geqslant m$.)

We close this section by listing several extensions and embellishments of the basic model.

(A)   We have dealt above with the case $a > 1$. If $0 < a \leqslant 1$, then the same basic structure for the equilibrium emerges, in that for sufficiently large n, entrants do not enter because the monopolist will fight with probability one. The play near the end of the game is more complicated however. In particular, one cannot obtain an equilibrium where entrant n's strategy depends only on p_n—it depends instead on p_n and the history of play in the last j rounds, where j is the smallest integer such that $ja > 1$.

(B)   If the monopolist discounts its payoffs by a factor ρ per period, the following results. If $\rho > 1/a$, then the equilibrium is *precisely* as above except that the randomizing probabilities of the entrants must change. If $\rho \leqslant 1/(a + 1)$, then the equilibrium is quite different—the weak monopolist acquiesces at the first entry, so entrants enter if $p_n < b$ and stay out if $p_n > b$. For ρ such that $1/(a + 1) < \rho \leqslant 1/a$, the basic character of the equilibrium is just as in the case of $\rho > 1/a$—for large enough n entrants stay out because the monopolist will fight any entry. But the equilibrium is complicated for small n, resembling the equilibrium in the undiscounted case where $a < 1$.

(C)   Suppose that instead of the sequential game depicted in Fig. 1, each stage consists of a two-by-two simultaneous move game, Table I, where the payoffs with probability $1 - \delta$ are shown in (a) and the payoffs with probability δ are shown in (b). (We assume $0 < b < 1$ and $a > 1$.) Otherwise the structure of the game is the same: One of these two bimatrices is chosen at the outset, according to the probabilities given. One monopolist plays against N entrants in sequence. The monopolist knows which bimatrix was chosen; the entrants do not.

For $\delta = 0$, the argument of Selten is easy adapted to show that the *unique* equilibrium (perfect or not) has row 2, column 1 played in each stage. This is because row 2 is strongly dominant in the stage game. But for $\delta > 0$ we get an equilibrium almost identical to the one discussed above: For stages n such that $b^n < \delta$, the monopolist plays row 1 regardless of which bimatrix was selected, and the entrant responds with column 2. (The play of the game is a bit different near the end of the game.) So we see that a little incomplete

TABLE I

	entrant column 1	entrant column 2		entrant column 1	entrant column 2
monopolist row 1	$-1, b-1$	$a-1, 0$	**monopolist** row 1	$0, b-1$	$a, 0$
row 2	$0, b$	$a, 0$	row 2	$-1, b$	$a-1, 0$

(a)   (b) information can not only make an imperfect equilibrium perfect (more accurately, sequential)—it can also make as part of a sequential equilibrium the play of an action that with very high probability is *strongly dominated* in the stage game.

(D) Paul Milgrom has pointed out to us that similar equilibria can be found even when every player in the game knows the payoffs of the monopolist, as long as this knowledge is not *common knowledge*. That is suppose all the entrants know the monopolist's payoffs, but they are not certain whether their fellow entrants have this information. Then (with the proper precise specification) they fear that the weak monopolist will fight (for large n), in order to maintain its reputation among the other entrants. This being so, the entrant will not enter. And the monopolist, even if it knows that all the entrants know that it is weak, may be willing to fight entry early on, in order to help "convince" subsequent entrants that it (the monopolist) is not sure that the entrants know this. (Precise arguments of this form are found in Milgrom and Roberts [13].) Selten's argument requires that it is common knowledge that the monopolist is weak. In real-life contexts this is a very strong assumption, and weakening it ever so slightly (more slightly than we have done above) can give life to the "reputation" effect.

(E) We have dealt exclusively with the case of a single monopolist playing against N different entrants. Another interesting case is where a single monopolist plays N times against a single entrant. For the game we have analyzed in this section, this turns out to have no effect on the equilibrium. (We leave this to the reader to verify.) But as we shall see in the next section, this is due (at least in part) to the fact that there is no uncertainty about the payoffs of the entrants.

4. Two-Sided Uncertainty

In this section we consider what happens when the monopolist is unsure about the payoffs of the entrants. The most interesting formulation of this problem is where a single monopolist plays the stage game of Fig. 1 a total of N times against a single opponent. The payoff to each player is the sum of the player's payoffs in each stage. The monopolist's payoffs are as in Fig. 1 or Fig. 2, with probabilities $1 - \delta$ and δ, respectively. The entrant's payoffs are as in Fig. 1, for some b such that $0 < b < 1$ with probability $1 - \gamma$ and for some other $b > 1$ with probability γ. Each player knows its own payoffs at the start of the game, and each is unsure of the payoffs of its opponent. The payoffs are statistically independent.

Continuing the terminology of Section 3, we shall refer to the weak entrant as the entrant if its payoffs satisfy $0 < b < 1$, and the strong entrant if its payoffs satisfy $b > 1$.

Note that the strong entrant does better to enter than to stay out in any stage, even if the monopolist is sure to fight. Because it seems plausible that entry will not decrease the probability that the monopolist will acquiesce subsequently, we look for equilibria where the strong entrant always enters. Thus any failure to enter brands the entrant as weak, at which point we are back to the situation of Section 3. (Recall that it did not matter there whether there was a single entrant or N entrants.) Similarly, we look for an equilibrium where the strong monopolist always fights. Thus any failure to fight brands the monopolist as weak, following which the entrant always enters and the monopolist always acquiesces. We search, then, for an equilibrium of the following sort: The strong entrant always enters. The strong monopolist always fights. The weak entrant chooses a strategy that is a mixture of "stopping rules": A stopping rule gives the date at which the entrant will "give in" and not enter if the monopolist has not acquiesced yet. (The entrant may later re-enter, as we will then follow the equilibrium of Section 3.) The weak monopolist will also mix among stopping rules: A stopping rule for the monopolist gives the date at which the monopolist will first acquiesce if the entrant has not retreated first. If one side or the other gives in, we move to either the situation of Section 3 or to where entry-acquiescence follows until the game ends.

Giving a complete specification of the equilibrium that is obtained is extraordinarily tedious, because it is based on some very involved recursions. Still, we can give a rough description of what happens. At any stage n the previous play of the game is summarized into two statistics: p_n, the probability assessed by the entrant that the monopolist is strong; q_n, the probability assessed by the monopolist that the entrant is strong. (The game begins with $p_N = \delta$ and $q_N = \gamma$.) Thus the "state space" of the game at stage n is the unit square, as depicted in Fig. 4. The edge $q_n = 0$ is the subject of

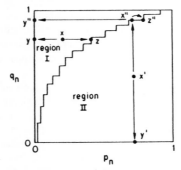

FIG. 4.   State space of the game at stage n.

Section 3. The edge $p_n = 0$ can be analyzed using the argument of Selten with the conclusion: The entrant always enters, and the weak monopolist always acquiesces.

The square is divided into two regions by a curve, as shown. If (p_n, q_n) lies in region I, say at the point x, then the entrant enters regardless of its payoffs, and the weak monopolist randomizes. If the weak monopolist acquiesces, the game evolves to the point y (actually, to this point in the *next* square—the square for stage $n - 1$). If it fights, or if it is strong and hence fights, the entrant uses Bayes' rule to compute p_{n-1}, landing at the point z on the curve, and just *beyond* the curve in region II of the next square. If (p_n, q_n) lies in region II, say at x', then the weak entrant randomizes. If it stays out, the equilibrium of Section 3 ensues—and the next stage begins a the point y'. If it enters (or if it is strong and therefore enters), the monopolist recomputes the probability that it is strong, landing at the point x'' along the curve. Then the monopolist randomizes (if weak), and the game evolves to y'' or to z''. Both z and z'' are in region II of the next square, so the next round begins with randomization by the weak entrant, and so on.

Except for the very start of the game, when $p_N = \delta$ and $q_n = \gamma$, most of the play takes place along the curve. (Actually, the curve shifts slightly as n changes.) So we see an initial jump to the curve (or to one of the two edges), followed by a slow climb up the curve with ever present the chance that a jump to one of the edges will occur. With probability one, a weak player will eventually give in, so we either jump to an edge eventually or, if both players are strong, we reach the point $p_0 = q_0 = 1$. This is a game of "chicken," where once begun, each side (if weak) randomizes between a small probability of giving in and a large probability of daring the other side for one more round. The relative size of these probabilities is required by the conditions of an equilibrium: Daring once more costs something this round, but giving in is costly for the rest of the game. So it must be that daring once more does not give either player a substantial chance of *immediate* gain; the opponent must be about to "dare" once again with large probability.

While it is tedious to give the exact equilibrium in the discrete time formulation, it is relatively simple to do so in a continuous time version of the game. So we shall now develop that continuous-time version. (We should forewarn the reader: We will be somewhat sloppy in what follows. But everything we say can be made exact.)

To begin, consider the game of Section 3 played against a single entrant over the time period N to 0. Instead of playing at times $N, N - 1,..., 1$, for the stakes (per stage) given in Section 3, we imagine that an integer K is given, and that the game is played "more frequently, for reduced stakes," with play at times $N, (KN - 1)/K, (KN - 2)/K,..., 1/K$, for stakes $1/K$ times the stakes given. It is the *number* of times that the monopolist has left to demonstrate its "toughness" that is decisive in Section 3, so we find that if $k(\delta) = n$, the entrant stays out (and the monopolist would surely fight) at all times $t > n/K$. As K goes to infinity, we see that the entrant stays out until "the very last instant" of time.

With this limiting result as motivation, we now consider the "continuous-time" version of the above game, played over a time interval T to 0. At each time $t \in [T, 0]$, the entrant chooses whether to enter or to stay out, and the monopolist chooses whether to fight entry or to acquiesce. A realization of the entrant's strategy is formalized as a (measurable) function $e: [T, 0] \to \{0, 1\}$, where $e(t) = 1$ means that the entrant is entering at date t. A realization of the monopolist's strategy is formalized as a function $f: [T, 0] \to \{0, 1\}$, where $f(t) = 1$ means that the monopolist is fighting at date t. (We have a "closed-loop" game, so pure strategies would be a pair of functions e and f where $e(t)$ is $F((e(s), f(s)), s < t)$-measurable, and $f(t)$ is $F(f(s), s < t; e(s), s \leqslant t)$-measurable. We shall not try to be more precise about this here; instead we trust the reader's ability to see how to formalize what follows.) Given realizations e and f, payoffs to each side are determined by measuring the lengths of times during which there is not entry ($e(t) = 0$), during which entry is fought ($e(t) = 1$, $f(t) = 1$), and during which there is acquiescence to entry ($e(t) = 1$, $f(t) = 0$), and assigning payoffs accordingly. For example, if λ denotes Lebesgue measure, then the weak monopolist's payoff is

$$\lambda\{e(t) = 0\} \cdot a - \lambda\{e(t) = 1, f(t) = 1\}.$$

In this game, an equilibrium calls for the entrant to stay out as long as the monopolist does not acquiesce and to always enter after any acquiescence is observed; for the strong monopolist to fight any entry; and for the weak monopolist to fight as long as it has not acquiesced yet and to acquiesce forever after an acquiescence. The reader can easily verify that this is an equilibrium. Moreover, if by some "mistake" the entrant entered before time 0, the weak monopolist would want to fight: By acquiescing it saves an "instantaneous" one unit, but then it invites entry for the remainder of the game—a substantial loss that outweighs the instantaneous savings.

(The reader is entitled to be somewhat skeptical about this. By moving to a continuous-time formulation, we have obtained some of the features of the supergame (infinitely repeated) formulation. For example, the equilibrium above is "perfect" even if $\delta = 0$, just as in the supergame with $\delta = 0$. But in the case $\delta = 0$, this equilibrium is not the limit of discrete-but-more-rapid equilibrium play. What justifies this particular equilibrium in the case $\delta > 0$ is that it is the limit of discrete equilibria. We shall return to this point after we discuss the case of two-sided uncertainty.)

Now consider the continuous-time game where there is uncertainty on both sides. The formulation is as above, but now there is uncertainty (at the outset) about the entrant's payoffs as a function of the realizations of e and f.

We are looking for an equilibrium with the following characteristics: (1) The strong monopolist always fights. (2) The strong entrant always enters. (3) By virtue of (1), if the monopolist ever declines to fight an entry, it is revealed as weak. Thereafter, the entrant always enters and the weak monopolist always acquiesces. (4) By virtue of (2), if the entrant ever fails to enter it is revealed as weak. Assuming that the monopolist has not previously been revealed as weak, the game proceeds as above, with the weak entrant staying out until the end and the monopolist always ready to fight.

Just as in the discrete time formulation, an equilibrium with these features can be recast as an equilibrium in "stopping rules" for the weak entrant and monopolist—each choosing the date at which it will "give in" if its opponent has not given in yet. If the entrant gives in first (at date t), then regime (4) above takes effect, with the weak monopolist obtaining at for the rest of the game, and the weak entrant receiving 0. If the monopolist gives in first at t, regime (3) ensues, with the weak entrant receiving bt and the weak monopolist receiving 0. Until one side or the other gives in, the weak monopolist receives -1 per unit of time, and the weak entrant receives $b - 1$ per unit of time. The equilibrium condition is that each player's stopping time should be optimal given the probability distribution of the other's, and given the assumption that the other player, if strong, will never give in. This game is very similar to the "war of attrition" game; cf. Riley [16] and Milgrom and Weber [14]. It is formally equivalent to a two-person competitive auction, where the stopping times are reinterpreted as bids. This observation will be especially useful later when we discuss the connection between this continuous-time formulation and the discrete-time formulation of the game. (We are indebted to Paul Milgrom for acquainting us with the "war of attrition" and for pointing out the relevance of his work with Weber.)

It is easiest and most illustrative to present the equilibrium using a diagram similar to Fig. 4. In Fig. 5 we have the "state space" of this game—the unit square, interpreted exactly as in Fig. 4. The bottom boundary is where the entrant is known to be weak. Along this boundary (excluding the left hand endpoint) the weak monopolist's payoff function (at date t) is $v_t(p, 0) = at$ and the weak entrant's is $u_t(p, 0) = 0$. The left hand boundary is where the monopolist is known to be weak—here (including the bottom endpoint) $v_t(0, q) = 0$ and $u_t(0, q) = bt$.

The nature of the equilibrium is just as in the discrete case: The state space is divided into two regions by a curve $f(p, q) = 0$ that passes through the points $(0, 0)$ and $(1, 1)$. If the initial data of the game place us in region I, then the game begins with the entrant entering for sure and the monopolist (if weak) randomizing between fighting and immediate capitulation. This randomization is such that if the monopolist does fight at time T, the entrant revises its assessment that the monopolist is strong so as

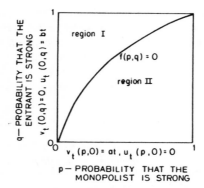

FIG. 5.   State space of the continuous-time game.

to go to the curve $f(p, q) = 0$. From region II it is the (weak) entrant that randomizes between immediate capitulation and entry—if it does enter, the monopolist revises its assessment that the entrant is strong up to a point where the curve $f(p, q)$ is reached. Thereafter, the weak monopolist and weak entrant randomize "continuously" between keeping up the fight and capitulating—this is done in a fashion so that as long as they continue to fight, the Bayesian reassessments of each side that the other is strong causes (p_t, q_t) to slide up along the curve toward $(1, 1)$. (Of course, if one side or the other capitulates, transition is made to the appropriate boundary.) There is a time $T^0 > 0$ such that by this time, one side or the other (if weak) has given in with probability one—if both sides are strong, at this time the point $(1, 1)$ has been reached, and we remain there until time $t = 0$.

The difference between this equilibrium and the one for the discrete time game (and the reason that this one is so much easier to compute) is that the curve $f(p, q) = 0$ does not change with t in the continuous-time case. This is so because in the continuous-time version of the game, a game of duration $T/2$ is strategically equivalent to a game of duration T, so long as the priors (δ, γ) are the same. All that changes is that everything takes place twice as rapidly—we could as well think of the game taking place at the same speed but for half the stakes. The values are half as large, but nothing else changes.

We now present a heuristic derivation of the equilibrium, assuming that it has the form outlined above. Note first that along the curve the value functions for each side must be identically zero. This is so because (by hypothesis) both sides are randomizing continuously, and one outcome of these randomizations transfers them to points (the lower boundary for the entrant and the left-hand boundary for the monopolist) where the value function is zero. Let $\pi_t(p_t, q_t)$ and $\rho_t(p_t, q_t)$ be the hazard rate functions associated with the weak monopolist's and entrant's randomizations at time t

with posteriors p_t and q_t lying along the curve. That is, in the time interval $(t, t - h)$ there is (up to terms of order $o(h)$) probability $(1 - p_t) \cdot \pi_t(p_t, q_t) \cdot h$ that the monopolist will give in, and $(1 - q_t) \cdot p_t(p_t, q_t) \cdot h$ that the entrant will give in. Assuming sufficient continuity, if the value functions are to be constant (and zero) along the curve, it is necessary that the expected change in value to the weak monopolist be zero. Up to terms of order $o(h)$, this is

$$-h + [(1 - q_t) \cdot p_t(p_t, q_t) \cdot h][at] = o(h).$$

That is, the weak monopolist's immediate cost $-h$ of keeping up the bluff should be offset by the small chance $(1 - q_t) \cdot p_t(p_t, q_t) \cdot h$ that the entrant will give in times the large gain at that will accrue in this event. The analogous argument for the entrant gives

$$(b - 1)h + (1 - p_t) \cdot \pi_t(p_t, q_t) \cdot hbt = o(h).$$

Dividing by h and passing to the limit, we get

$$p_t(p_t, q_t) = 1/(at(1 - q_t)) \qquad \text{and} \qquad \pi_t(p_t, q_t) = (1 - b)/(bt(1 - p_t)).$$

Consider next the evolution of the posteriors p_t and q_t. The probability table that the monopolist would construct at date t for the joint probability distribution that the entrant is weak or not and will give in or not in the interval $(t, t - h)$ is given in Table II (up to terms of order $o(h)$). Thus the conditional probability that the entrant is strong, conditional on not giving in over the interval $(t, t - h)$, is

$$q_{t-h} = q_t/[1 - (1 - q_t)p_t(p_t, q_t)h].$$

Thus, ignoring terms of order $O(h)$,

$$(q_t - q_{t-h})/h = q_t(1 - q_t)p_t(p_t, q_t).$$

Passing to the limit, this gives $\dot{q}_t = (q_t - q_t^2)p_t(p_t, q_t) = q_t/(at)$. Similarly $\dot{p}_t = p_t(1 - b)/(bt)$. Thus along the curve we must have

$$dq_t/dp_t = (q_t b)/((1 - b) a p_t).$$

TABLE II

	weak	strong	
give in	$(1 - q_t)p_t(p_t, q_t)h$	0	$(1 - q_t)p_t(p_t, q_t)h$
not	$(1 - q_t)(1 - p_t(p_t, q_t)h)$	q_t	$1 - (1 - q_t)p_t(p_t, q_t)h$
	$(1 - q_t)$	q_t	

This is independent of t, and it is easily integrated to give $q_t = k(p_t)^c$ where k is a constant of integration and $c = b/((1-b)a)$. To ensure that $(1, 1)$ is on the curve, we must have $k = 1$. Therefore the curve is given by

$$f(p, q) \equiv q^{(1-b)/b} - p^{1/a} = 0.$$

(Note well the normalization of k so that $(1, 1)$ is on the curve. This will be important later on.)

We can solve similarly for q_t and p_t. Integrating $\dot{q}_t = q_t/(at)$ yields $q_t = k't^{-1/a}$. Analogously, $p_t = k''t^{-(1-b)/b}$. The constants k' and k'' are determined by the initial conditions. Suppose, for example, that we initially have a prior (δ, γ) that lies in region II. Then the initial randomization is by the weak entrant and yields posterior $q_T = \delta^c$ if the entrant does enter. Solving for k' yields $k' = \delta^c T^{1/a}$. Solving for k'' yields $k'' = \delta T^{(1-b)/b}$. Thus

$$p_t = \delta(T/t)^{(1-b)/b} \qquad \text{and} \qquad q_t = \delta^c(T/t)^{1/a}.$$

Note that these yield $p_t = 1$ and $q_t = 1$ for $t = T\delta^{ac} = T\delta^{b/(1-b)}$. (Of course, both p_t and q_t hit one simultaneously as the curve has been normalized to pass through $(1, 1)$.) The point to note here is that in this equilibrium, the posterior $(1, 1)$ will be reached at a time T° strictly between T and 0 (unless $\delta = 0$ or 1) so long as neither player gives in previously. But of course, the posterior $(1, 1)$ can only be reached if with probability one both of the weak players would have given in. So, according to this equilibrium, if the two players are both strong, they will learn this before the game terminates. Put another way, the date T° previously referred to is $\delta^{b/(1-b)}T$ (for (δ, γ) in region II). The formulae change somewhat for (δ, γ) in region I, but the qualitative conclusions are the same.

Does this heuristic derivation hold up? That is, do we really have an equilibrium? There are two things to worry about. First, in several places the heuristic arguments that we give depend somewhat on sufficient regularity of the functions π_t and ρ_t. The reader can make these arguments rigorous for the functions that we derived. Second (and more substantially), the necessary conditions that were developed for π_t and ρ_t were necessary for the value functions to be *constant* along the curve. To have an equilibrium we require somewhat more: The value functions must be identically *zero* along this curve. This is where the normalization of the curve comes in: At the point $(1, 1)$, the value functions are clearly zero for each weak player, as each is certain that the other is strong. Put another way, suppose (once the curve is reached) that one side or the other is weak and decides *not* to randomize but simply to wait out its opponent. The conditions that gave us π_t and ρ_t ensure that the change in expected value is zero as this goes on. (For the technically minded, apply Dynkin's formula to the appropriate generalized Poisson process.) And at date T°, if nothing has happened the player that is waiting *knows* that its opponent is strong—it should immediately give in for a value of zero. Thus the value all along the curve is zero. This, with a little careful argument, suffices to show that we really do have an equilibrium.

Two final comments about this equilibrium seem in order. First, the value functions to each (weak) player are easily computed. In region II, they are $u_T(\delta, \gamma) = 0$ and $v_T(\delta, \gamma) = [(\delta^c - \gamma)/\delta^c] aT$; in region I, they are $u_T(\delta, \gamma) = [(\gamma^{1/c} - \delta)/\gamma^{1/c}] bT$ and $v_T(\delta, \gamma) = 0$. That is, they are simple linear interpolates of the value of zero along the curve and the values along the bottom boundary in region II and the left-hand boundary in region I.

Second, we noted earlier that the continuous-time formulation can introduce equilibria that are not limits of the equilibria for discrete-time models. We should like to know that the continuous-time equilibrium just presented is indeed the limit of the discrete-time equilibrium with which we began this section. We have not checked all the details, but we are quite sure that this is so. To see this, recall that the discrete time game can be posed as an optimal stopping problem where the entrant is limited to stopping at, say, discrete times $T, (TK - 1)/K, ..., 1/K$ and the monopolist is limited to stopping at times (say) $T - 1/(2K), (TK - 3/2)/K, ..., 1/(2K)$. The continuous-time problem is one where stopping at any time $t \in [T, 0]$ is possible. It is easy to move from the discrete-to-continuous-time versions of the problem when there is one-sided uncertainty, so we know that we have convergence of the value of "stopping" at particular times. As K goes to infinity, the sets of available strategies also converge, and the methods of Milgrom and Weber [14] apply to show convergence of the equilibria of the discrete games to the continuous-time version. (Indeed, Paul Milgrom has shown us how, by viewing the continuous-time game as a game in distributional strategies, it is simple to derive the equilibrium given above.)

Before concluding this section, we also note that this gives just one sort of formulation of the problem with two-sided uncertainty. We might consider what happens when a single monopolist plays against a succession of different entrants (each of whom plays the game once), where the monopolist is uncertain of the entrants' payoffs. In such a game we would have to specify the way in which the entrants' payoffs are related—they might all be identical (perfectly correlated, from the point of view of the monopolist), or they might be independently and identically distributed, or something between these two extremes. Both of these extreme cases are analyzed in detail in Kreps and Wilson [8]. The case of identical entrants gives the most interesting comparison with the model analyzed above: With identical entrants who only play the game once, the first entrant nearly always "tells the truth" by refusing to enter if weak, and the weak monopolist will with substantial probability fight the first few entries, just to keep the weak entrants "honest." What this illustrates is that the game of "chicken" that we see above requires *both* two-sided uncertainty *and* that each side has a stake in maintaining its reputation. When it is only one side that will participate in many stages, the other has little motivation to dissemble and will not fight too hard to attain/maintain its reputation. (Another interesting formulation of the problem is where there is a population of entrants and a population of monopolists, and in each round there is a random assignment of one monopolist to one entrant, in the manner of Rosenthal [18] and Rosenthal and Landau [19]. We have done no analysis of this formulation.)

5. Discussion

We have presented these simple examples to illustrate formally the power of "reputation" in finitely repeated games. That reputation is powerful in reality is very well appreciated: In the context of Industrial Organization, recall the quotation from Scherer in Section 1. Consider the importance of reputation in contract and labor negotiations; in a firm's employment practices; in a firm's "good name" for its product; in the maintenance of a cartel (or in the prisoners' dilemma game); in international diplomacy. To each of these contexts, our analytical structure can be applied to yield the conclusions: If the situation is repeated, so that it is worthwhile to maintain or acquire a reputation, and if there is some uncertainty about the motivations of one or more of the players, then that uncertainty can substantially affect the play of the game. There need not be much uncertainty for this to happen. The power of the reputation effect depends on the nature of one's opponents; notably on whether they also seek to acquire a reputation.

Phenomena that bear the interpretation of "reputation" are not entirely new to the literature of formal game theory. They are implicit in much of the literature on super-games, where the stage game is repeated infinitely often, or where there is always high enough probability of at least one more repetition (Rubinstein [20] is a representative citation). Indeed, Dybvig and Spatt [6] make explicit use of the reputation interpretation in a super-game context. What is new in this paper (and in Milgrom and Roberts [13]) is the observation that with a very little imperfect information, these effects come alive in finitely repeated games. Comparing the two approaches is difficult, but it is worth noting that in the models reported here, the problem of multiplicity of equilibria that plagues the super-game literature is substantially alleviated. Also, we believe that we have interesting models of the sorts of "wars" that might go on between players to see which equilibrium will ensue. But we are far from ready to make a very informed comparison of the two approaches—at this point, we can only claim that this seems to be an interesting alternative way to produce reputation effects.

A point made briefly in Section 3 is worth repeating here. To keep matters simple, we posited the simplest type of uncertainty: Players are uncertain about the payoffs of their fellows. But it does nearly as well if there is no uncertainty about players' payoffs, but there is uncertainty about whether this is so. In the parlance of game theory, for these effects to disappear, payoffs must be common knowledge. (Milgrom and Roberts [13] present formal models to back up this contention.) This is a very strong assumption for any real-life application.

The reader may object that in order to obtain the reputation effect, we have loaded the deck. That is, we have a model where reputation is easily shattered, making it all the more valuable; there are at most two types of each player; and each player has only two possible actions. To the first of these criticisms we plead guilty: The power of reputation seems to be positively related to its fragility. As for the second, the models of Milgrom and Roberts [13] have continua of types of monopolists, so this does not seem crucial to our conclusions. And to the third, we do admit that this has made it easy for us to get a "pooling equilibrium" (to borrow a term from the insurance literature), where one type successfully mimics another. The analysis of Milgrom and Roberts [12] shows that with a continuum of actions, one can also get screening equilibria in these sorts of models. But this is not necessary: Crawford and Sobel [3] investigate a class of models with a continua of actions where some pooling is necessary in any equilibrium. The assumption of only two actions makes things easier for us, but we doubt that it is crucial.

What is evident from our simple examples is that a very little uncertainty "destabilizes" game-theoretic analysis in games with a fairly large number of stages. The reader may suspect that something more is true: By cleverly choosing the nature of that small uncertainty (precisely—its support), one can get out of a game-theoretic analysis whatever one wishes. We have no formal proposition of this sort to present at this time, but we certainly share these suspicions. If this is so, then the game-theoretic analysis of this type of game comes down eventually to how one picks the initial incomplete information. And nothing in the *theory* of games will help one to do this.

This reinforces a point made by Rosenthal [17]. Rosenthal investigates the original chain-store game and makes the point with which we began: The paradoxical result in Selten's analysis is due to the complete and perfect information formulation that Selten uses. In a more realistic formulation of the game, the intuitive outcome will be predicted by the game-theoretic analysis. Rosenthal does not provide this analysis, despairing of the analyst's ability to solve an adequate formulation. Instead, he suggests an analysis using the paradigm of Decision Analysis, where one tries to assess *directly* how the entrants will respond to early round fighting by the monopolist. Such an analysis can certainly lead to the intuitive outcome, as shown by Macgregor [11]. But, as Rosenthal notes, the weakness in this approach is the *ad hoc* assessment of entrants' behavior. We have carried out a game-theoretic analysis of *one* very simple incomplete information formulation. We therefore have avoided *ad hoc* assumptions about the entrants' behavior. But we have made *ad hoc* assumptions about their information, and we have found that small changes in those assumptions greatly influence the play of the game. So at some level, analysis of this sort of situation may require *ad hoc* assumptions.

We have presented models in this paper that demonstrate the reputation effect as simply and as powerfully as possible. In order to do this, we have not tried to model realistic settings from Industrial Organization or some other economic context. (Milgrom and Roberts [13] rectify this deficiency: They concentrate somewhat more on the application of these ideas.) To illustrate how these ideas might be applied, we close with two examples.

The first concerns the problem of entry deterrence, especially the papers of Spence [26] and Dixit [4, 5]. These papers take the basic framework of Bain [1] and Sylos [27] and ask: What can the monopolist do prior to the entrant's decision point to make predation optimal in the short run? (The answers they give include such things as expanded capacity, sales networks, etc.) The relevance of this question is that the *threat* of predation is only credible if predation is *ex post* the optimal response, so the monopolist must make it so in order to forestall entry. What our model suggests (and what can be demonstrated formally) is that in repeated play situations, the actions taken by the monopolist need not make predation actually ex post optimal—what they must do is to make predation *possible* and, perhaps, increase the probability assessed by the entrants that it is *ex post* optimal. If deterrence is the objective, the appearance and not the reality of *ex post* optimal predation may be what is important.

The second context is that of a monopolist producer of a durable capital good where, for whatever reason, the monopolist is unable to maintain a rental market but must sell outright his product. In a multiperiod setting, where the monopolist is assumed to be sequentially optimizing, this can severely diminish the monopolist's market power. (See Bulow [2] and Stokey [25].) Supposing the monopolist produces subject to a capacity constraint, the monopolist is often *better off* with a tighter constraint. This is because the constraint prevents the monopolist from "over-producing." Then, if that constraint is the matter of private information for the monopolist, a monopolist with a loose constraint can successfully (in an equilibrium) masquerade as having a more stringent constraint, thereby recouping some of his lost market power. In essence, as the number of periods goes to infinity (as one comes closer to a continuous-time formulation), the monopolist can successfully attain the reputation of a "low capacity" producer even if his capacity is (with probability approaching one) high. Moorthy [15] presents an example along these lines.

278   KREPS AND WILSON

ACKNOWLEDGMENTS

The authors express their gratitude to John Harsanyi, Mary Macgregor, Paul Milgrom, John Roberts, Robert Rosenthal, Reinhart Selten, Sylvain Sorin and many other colleagues for their helpful comments and criticisms. This research has been supported in part by National Science Foundation Grants SOC77-07741-A01, SOC75-21820-A01, SOC77-0600-A01 and SES80-06407 to the Institute for Mathematical Studies in the Social Sciences and the Graduate School of Business, Stanford University.

REFERENCES

1. J. S. BAIN, "Barriers to New Competition," Harvard Univ. Press, Cambridge, Mass., 1956.
2. J. BULOW, Durable goods monopolists, Stanford Graduate School of Business, mimeo, 1979; *J. Pol. Econ.*, in press.
3. V. CRAWFORD AND J. SOBEL, Stategic information transmission, University of California at San Diego, mimeo, 1981.
4. A. DIXIT, A model of duopoly suggesting a theory of entry barriers, *Bell J. Econ.* **10** (1979), 20–32.
5. A. DIXIT, The role of investment in entry-deterence, *Econ. J.* **90** (1980), 95–106.
6. P. DYBVIG AND C. SPATT, Does it pay to maintain a reputation, Financial Center Memorandum No. 32, Princeton University, 1980.
7. J. HARSANYI, Games with incomplete information played by Bayesian players, Parts I, II, and III, *Manag. Sci.* **14** (1967–1968), 159–182, 320–334, 486–502.
8. D. KREPS AND R. WILSON, "On the Chain-Store Paradox and Predation: Reputation for Toughness," Stanford University Graduate School of Business Research Paper No. 551, 1981.
9. D. KREPS AND R. WILSON, Sequential equilibria, *Econometrica* **50** (1982).
10. H. KUHN, Extensive games and the problem of information, *in* "Contributions to the Theory of Games, Vol. 2" (H. Kuhn and A. Tucker, Eds.), pp. 193–216, Princeton Univ. Press, Princeton, N.J., 1953.
11. M. MACGREGOR, A resolution of the chain-store paradox, University of California at Berkeley, mimeo, 1979.
12. P. MILGROM AND J. ROBERTS, "Limit Pricing and Entry under Incomplete Information: An Equilibrium Analysis," *Econometrica* **50** (1982), 443–460.
13. P. MILGROM AND J. ROBERTS, Predation, reputation, and entry deterrence, *J. Econ. Theory* **27** (1982), 280–312.
14. P. MILGROM AND R. WEBER, Distributional strategies for games with incomplete information, Northwestern University Graduate School of Management, mimeo, 1980.
15. S. MOORTHY, The Pablo Picasso problem, Stanford University Graduate School of Business, mimeo, 1980.
16. J. RILEY, Strong evolutionary equilibria and the war of attrition, *J. Theoret. Biol.* **82** (1980).
17. R. W. ROSENTHAL, Games of perfect information, predatory pricing and the chain-store paradox, *J. Econ. Theory* **25** (1981), 92–100.
18. R. W. ROSENTHAL, Sequences of games with varying opponents, *Econometrica* **47** (1979), 1353–1366.
19. R. W. ROSENTHAL AND H. J. LANDAU, A game-theoretic analysis of bargaining with reputations, Bell Telephone Laboratories, mimeo, 1979.

20. A. RUBINSTEIN, Strong perfect equilibrium in supergames, *Internat. J. Game Theory* **9** (1979), 1–12.
21. F. SCHERER, "Industrial Market Structure and Economic Performance," 2nd ed., Rand McNally College Publishing Company, Chicago, 1980.
22. R. SELTEN, Spieltheoretische behandlung eines oligopolmodells mit nachfragetragheit, *Z. Staatswissenschaft* **121** (1965).
23. R. SELTEN, Reexamination of the perfectness concept for equilibrium points in extensive games, *Internat. J. Game Theory* **4** (1975), 25–55.
24. R. SELTEN, The chain-store paradox, *Theory and Decision* **9** (1978), 127–159.
25. N. STOKEY, Self-fulfilling expectations, rational expectations, and durable goods pricing, Northwestern University, mimeo, 1979.
26. A. M. SPENCE, Entry, capacity, investment and oligopolistic pricing, *Bell J. Econ.* **8** (1977), 534–544.
27. P. SYLOS-LABINI, "Oligopoly and Technical Progress," trans. E. Henderson, Harvard Univ. Press, Cambridge, Mass., 1962.

[36]

Econometrica, Vol. 50, No. 2 (March, 1982)

LIMIT PRICING AND ENTRY UNDER INCOMPLETE
INFORMATION: AN EQUILIBRIUM ANALYSIS[1]

By Paul Milgrom and John Roberts

Limit pricing involves charging prices below the monopoly price to make new entry appear unattractive. If the entrant is a rational decision maker with complete information, pre-entry prices will not influence its entry decision, so the established firm has no incentive to practice limit pricing. However, if the established firm has private, payoff relevant information (e.g., about costs), then prices can signal that information, so limit pricing can arise in equilibrium. The probability that entry actually occurs in such an equilibrium, however, can be lower, the same, or even higher than in a regime of complete information (where no limit pricing would occur).

1. INTRODUCTION

THE BASIC IDEA OF LIMIT PRICING is that an established firm may be able to influence, through its current pricing policy alone,[2] other firms' perceptions of the profitability of entering the firm's markets, and that the firm may thus set its prices below their short run maximizing levels in order to deter entry. As such, limit pricing has constituted a major theme in the industrial organization literature for at least the last thirty years, and during the past decade in particular it has been the subject of a number of papers employing formal models of maximizing behavior.[3] For the most part, these latter analyses have concentrated on the decision problem of the established firm, taking as given the limit-pricing assumption that a lower pre-entry price will deter or restrict entry. In this context, the typical conclusion is that an optimal price-output policy in the face of threatened entry will involve prices which are below the short-run monopoly level, but still above the level that would prevail after entry. This conclusion had led to some debate as to the appropriate public policy regarding such limit pricing, since there appears to be a trade-off between the benefits to society of lower pre-entry prices and the costs arising from entry being limited or deterred.

[1] Much of the work reported here first appeared in [11]. This work has been presented at a large number of conferences, meetings, and seminars, and we would like to thank our audiences at each of these events for their comments. We are particularly indebted to Eric Maskin, Roger Myerson, Steve Salop, Robert Wilson, and two referees for their helpful suggestions, to David Besanko for his excellent research assistance, and to Armando Ortega-Reichert, whose work on repeated competitive bidding [15] has influenced our thinking on the present subject. Finally, we gratefully acknowledge the financial support of the Graduate School of Business at Stanford, the J. L. Kellogg Graduate School of Management at Northwestern, and the National Science Foundation (Grants SOC 77-06000 to the IMSSS at Stanford and SOC 79-07542 and SES 80-01932 to Northwestern).
   [2] Although some recent treatments of entry deterrence incorporate other strategic variables, the standard, traditional approach is to treat the choice of the pre-entry price as the firm's only decision and to assume no dependence of post-entry profits on this choice.
   [3] The idea behind limit pricing can be traced back through the work of J. Bain [1] and J. M. Clark [2] at least to a paper by N. Kaldor [7]. The recent formal investigations begin with D. Gaskins [5], M. I. Kamien and N. L. Schwartz [8], and G. Pyatt [16]. See F. M. Scherer [18] and S. Salop [17] for further references.

P. MILGROM AND J. ROBERTS

In this paper we present a re-examination of the limit pricing problem. Our model differs from most of the existing literature in that we treat both the established firm and potential entrant as rational, maximizing economic agents. This naturally leads to a game-theoretic, equilibrium formulation. However, once one adopts this approach, it is not immediately obvious why limit pricing should emerge at all.

This point has been made explicitly by J. Friedman [3] in one of the few existing game-theoretic treatments of pricing in the face of potential entry of which we are aware. Friedman notes that, under the usual sort of assumptions on demand, the profits which would accrue should entry occur are completely independent of the pre-entry price. Since in Friedman's model both the established firm and the entrant are completely informed as to demand and cost conditions, these post-entry profits are fully known when the entry decision is made. Then the inescapable logic of (perfect) equilibrium (Selten [19]) requires that the entry decision be independent of the pre-entry price. This means that any attempt at limit pricing would serve only to squander pre-entry profits and so there would be no limit pricing.

Friedman's argument will be generally valid in any complete-information, game-theoretic model in which the established firm's pre-entry actions do not influence post-entry costs and demand. In such a model, then, the intuitive idea underlying the traditional concept of limit pricing—that potential entrants would read the pre-entry price as a signal concerning the price and market shares they can expect to prevail after entry—finds no formal justification. In contrast, a formalization of this intuition is the very heart of our model.

Specifically, we consider situations in which neither the established firm nor the potential entrant is perfectly informed as to some characteristic of the other which is relevant to the post-entry profits of both. The central example of such a characteristic, and the one on which we initially concentrate, is the other firm's unit costs. In such a situation, the pre-entry price may become a signal regarding the established firm's costs, which in turn are a determinant of the post-entry price and profits for the entrant. Thus the relationship assumed in the earlier literature emerges endogenously in equilibrium in our model: a lower price (by signalling lower costs) tends to discourage entry. Thus, too, limit-pricing behavior arises in equilibrium, with the established firm attempting to influence the entry decision by charging a pre-entry price which is below the simple monopoly level.

The entrant, meanwhile, will seek to infer the established firm's costs (and thus the profitability of entry) from observation of the pre-entry price. In making this inference, of course, it will have to employ some conjecture regarding the established firm's pricing policy, i.e., the relationship between the established firm's cost and the price it charges. In Nash equilibrium, this conjecture must be correct. Indeed the very definition of equilibrium in this context involves rational expectations by each firm about the other's behavior. Thus, the entrant will allow for limit pricing in making its inferences and its entry decision.

Thus, in equilibrium, the established firm practices limit pricing, but the entrant is not fooled by this strategy. Consequently, the probability that entry actually occurs in equilibrium need not be any lower than it would be in a world of full information, where limit pricing would not arise. Indeed, the probability of entry in the limit pricing equilibrium may even be higher than with complete information, even though the pre-entry price is lower. In particular, this means that the alleged trade-off for society between lower prices and delayed or deterred entry may never arise.

In the next section, we illustrate these claims in the context of a simple model with linear demand and constant unit costs. In this model we compute equilibria for two specific examples. One of these involves only two possible levels of costs for the entrants and for the established firm; the other involves a continuum of possibilities on each side. In Section 3 we consider a more general model. The final section contains our conclusions.

2. TWO EXAMPLES

Consider the market for a homogeneous good in which there is an established firm, denoted firm 1, and a potential entrant, firm 2. Initially, each firm knows its own unit cost, c_i, $i = 1, 2$, but it does not know the other firm's cost level. Firm 1 is a monopolist, and it must pick a quantity Q to produce (or a price to charge) as a monopolist, given its knowledge of c_1 and its beliefs about c_2. Firm 2 will observe this choice and then (knowing c_2 but not c_1) must either enter the market or decide to stay out. If it enters, it incurs an entry cost of K, each firm learns the other's cost, and then the two firms operate as Cournot duopolists. If it does not enter, firm 1 will henceforth enjoy its monopoly profits without further fear of entry.

We summarize the notation and profit formulae with linear demand and constant unit costs in Table I. To simplify the payoff formulae, we normalize the

TABLE I

Present value to i of \$1 accruing after entry	δ_i
Unit production cost of firm i	c_i
Fixed cost of entry for firm 2	K
Inverse demand	$P = a - bQ$
Simple monopoly output	$m(c_1) = (a - c_1)/2b$
First period profit for firm 1	$\Pi_1^0(Q, c_1) = (a - bQ - c_1)Q$
Monopoly profit for firm 1	$\Pi_1^M(c_1) = (a - c_1)^2/4b$
Cournot profit for firm i	$\Pi_i^C(c_1, c_2) = (a - 2c_i + c_j)^2/9b$
Reward to firm 1 from deterring entry	$R(c_1, c_2) = \Pi_1^M(c_1) - \Pi_1^C(c_1, c_2)$
Payoff to 1 if entry occurs	$\Pi_1^0(Q, c_1)$
Payoff to 1 if no entry	$\Pi_1^0(Q, c_1) + \delta_1 R(c_1, c_2)$
Payoff to 2 if entry	$\delta_2 \Pi_2^C(c_1, c_2) - K$
Payoff to 2 if no entry	0
Range of possible c_i values	$[\underline{c}_i, \bar{c}_i]$
Probability distribution function for c_i (j's beliefs about c_i)	H_i

P. MILGROM AND J. ROBERTS

post-entry profits of the established firm to be zero if entry occurs, so it receives only its first period profit as its payoff in this event. If entry does not occur, its payoff is its first period profit plus the discounted value of a reward to deterring entry. This reward is equal to the excess of its monopoly profit over its profit as a Cournot duopolist.

The extensive form game corresponding to this set-up is one of incomplete information, since the players do not know the numerical values of the payoffs corresponding to any pair of decisions they make. Attempting to analyze such a game directly would easily lead one into a morass of infinite regress. The approach we adopt instead is that proposed by Harsanyi [6], which involves replacing this *incomplete* information game by a game of *complete* but *imperfect* information.[4] One then treats the Nash equilibria of this second game as the equilibria of the original game.

The imperfect information game involves another player, "Nature," which is indifferent over all possible outcomes. Nature moves first and selects c_1 and c_2 according to the probability distributions, H_i, giving the players' beliefs. Then player i is informed about c_i but not about c_j, and for each realization of c_1 and c_2 the game tree unfolds as above.

In any extensive form game, a player's strategy is a specification of the action it will take in any information set, i.e., the player's actions at any point can depend only on what it knows at that point. Here, the information sets for firm 1 are defined by the realized values of c_1 (given by "Nature's move") and those for firm 2 by a realization of c_2 and a choice of Q by firm 1. Thus, a (pure) strategy for 1 is a map s from its possible cost levels into the possible choices of Q and a (pure) strategy for 2 is a map t from $\mathbb{R}^2$ into $\{0, 1\}$ giving its decision for each possible pair (c_2, Q), where we interpret 1 as "enter" and 0 as "stay out."

A pair of strategies constitutes an equilibrium if each maximizes the expected payoff of the player using it, given that the other is using its specified strategy. This is the standard Nash equilibrium notion. However, to accentuate the rational expectations character of Nash equilibrium, it is helpful to use the following, equivalent definition. An equilibrium consists of a pair of strategies (s^*, t^*) and a pair of conjectures $(\bar{s}, \bar{t})$ such that (i) firm 1's pricing policy s^* is a best response to its conjecture $\bar{t}$ about firm 2's entry rule, (ii) the strategy t^* is a best response for firm 2 to its conjecture $\bar{s}$, and (iii) the actual and conjectured strategies coincide. We formalize these conditions as follows: (i) for any $c_1 \in [\underline{c}_1, \bar{c}_1]$ and any $s : [\underline{c}_1, \bar{c}_1] \to \mathbb{R}_+$,

$$\Pi^0(s^*(c_1), c_1) + \delta_1 \int_{\underline{c}_2}^{\bar{c}_2} R(c_1, c_2)\big[1 - \bar{t}(c_2, s^*(c_1))\big] dH_2(c_2)$$

$$\geqq \Pi^0(s(c_1), c_1) + \delta_1 \int_{\underline{c}_2}^{\bar{c}_2} R(c_1, c_2)\big[1 - \bar{t}(c_2, s(c_1))\big] dH_2(c_2),$$

[4] An extensive form game has imperfect information if some player at some point must make a move without having been fully informed about all the previous moves made by the other players.

LIMIT PRICING AND ENTRY   447

(ii) for any $c_2 \in [\underline{c}_2, \bar{c}_2]$ and any $t : [\underline{c}_2, \bar{c}_2] \times \mathbb{R}_+ \to \{0, 1\}$,

$$\int_{\underline{c}_1}^{\bar{c}_1} \left[\delta_2 \Pi_2^C(c_1, c_2) - K \right] t^*(c_2, \bar{s}(c_1)) \, dH_1(c_1)$$

$$\geq \int_{\underline{c}_1}^{\bar{c}_1} \left[\delta_2 \Pi_2^C(c_1, c_2) - K \right] t(c_2, \bar{s}(c_1)) \, dH_1(c_1), \quad \text{and}$$

(iii) $(s^*, t^*) = (\bar{s}, \bar{t})$.

Given this framework, we first study a parameterized family of examples where the H_i are two-point distributions and, for specific values of the parameters, compute equilibria. Later in this section we will allow for a continuum of possible cost levels ("types") for the two firms.

Thus, suppose that the demand curve is $P = 10 - Q$, that $K = 7$, that $\underline{c}_1 = 0.5$, $\underline{c}_2 = 1.5$, $\bar{c}_1 = \bar{c}_2 = 2.0$, that $\delta_1 = \delta_2 = 1$, and that the costs are independently distributed with $H_2(c_2 = \bar{c}_2) = p = 1 - H_2(c_2 = \underline{c}_2)$ and $H_1(c_1 = \bar{c}_1) = q = 1 - H_1(c_1 = \underline{c}_1)$.

With these specifications, the payoffs are as follows:

$$
\begin{aligned}
R(\underline{c}_1, \underline{c}_2) &= 10.31, & \Pi_2^C(\underline{c}_1, \underline{c}_2) - K &= -0.75, \\
R(\underline{c}_1, \bar{c}_2) &= 9.12, & \Pi_2^C(\underline{c}_1, \bar{c}^2) - K &= -2.31, \\
R(\bar{c}_1, \underline{c}_2) &= 9.75, & \Pi_2^C(\bar{c}_1, \underline{c}_2) - K &= 2.00, \\
R(\bar{c}_1, \bar{c}_2) &= 8.89, & \Pi_2^C(\bar{c}_1, \bar{c}_2) - K &= 0.11, \\
m(\underline{c}_1) &= 4.75, & \Pi_1^M(\underline{c}_1) &= 22.56, \\
m(\bar{c}_1) &= 4.00, & \Pi_1^M(\bar{c}_1) &= 16.00.
\end{aligned}
$$

Note that if 1's costs were known to be $\underline{c}_1$, neither type of potential entrant would want to enter, while if c_1 were known to be $\bar{c}_1$, both would want to enter. Thus, the probability of entry, if the entrant were to be directly informed of the realized value of c_1, is simply q, the probability that $c_1 = \bar{c}_1$. Of course, if firm 2 were so informed, there would be no point to limit pricing and Q would simply be set at the short-run profit-maximizing level of $m(c_1)$.

Note, too, that if firm 2 were unable to observe Q and were uninformed about c_1, then it would want to enter if its expected profits were positive, i.e., if $q\Pi_2^C(\bar{c}_1, c_2) + (1 - q)\Pi_2^C(\underline{c}_1, c_2) - K \geq 0$. If $0.954 > q > 0.273$, then this inequality holds for $\underline{c}_2$ and not for $\bar{c}_2$, so the low cost entrant would come in and the high cost entrant would not. (For $q < 0.273$, neither would want to enter, and for $q > 0.954$, both would want to enter.)

In fact, if 2 is not directly informed about c_1 but can observe Q, it will attempt to make inferences about the actual value of c_1 from its observation of Q, using its conjectures about 1's behavior. Note that in equilibrium, the only values of Q which could be observed are $s^*(\underline{c}_1)$ and $s^*(\bar{c}_1)$. Now in this set-up there are only two possibilities: either $s^*(\underline{c}_1) = s^*(\bar{c}_1)$, or else the two values differ. An equilibrium with the first of these properties is called *pooling*, while in the other situation the equilibrium is *separating*. Thus, in pooling equilibrium, observing Q gives no information, while the observation of Q in a separating equilibrium allows the value of c_1 to be inferred exactly.

Thus, in a separating equilibrium (s^*, t^*), entry will occur if $s^*(\bar{c}_1)$ is observed and will not if $s^*(\underline{c}_1)$ is observed: *entry takes place in exactly the same circumstances as if the entrant had been informed about the value of* c_1, i.e., with prior probability q. Moreover, this will be true in any separating equilibrium of any model of this type: in any separating equilibrium, observing the equilibrium choice of the established firm allows a precise and accurate inference to be made about the firm's characteristic. Thus, in such an equilibrium, *limit pricing will not limit entry* relative to the complete information case (in which there would be no limit pricing because the possibility of influencing the entrant's decision does not arise).

In a pooling equilibrium, the entrant can infer nothing from observing Q and so enters if its expected profit is positive. Thus, as noted above, if $q \in (0.273, 0.954)$, only the low cost entrant will come in. Thus, in a pooling equilibrium, the probability of entry is $(1 - p)$, while in a separating equilibrium the probability of entry is q.

We now will show that, in this example, so long as p is not too small, there are both pooling and separating equilibria, that all equilibria involve limit pricing, and that the probability of entry in a pooling equilibrium may equal, exceed or fall short of that in a separating equilibrium (or, equivalently, under complete information).

First, we show that the following strategies constitute a separating equilibrium:

$$s^*(\underline{c}_1) = 7.2, \qquad s^*(\bar{c}_1) = m(\bar{c}_1) = 4.0,$$

$$t^*(c_2, Q) = \begin{cases} 1 & \text{if } Q < 7.2, \\ 0 & \text{otherwise.} \end{cases}$$

Note that since $s^*(\underline{c}_1) > m(\underline{c}_1)$, s^* is a limit pricing strategy. Notice too that from our earlier discussion, t^* is clearly a best response to s^*. Thus, we need to check that s^* is optimal, given t^*. First, note that unless the high cost established firm produces at least 7.2, it cannot deter any entry. But, this level is high enough that it is not worthwhile for $\bar{c}_1$ to produce it, even though in so doing it would eliminate all entry. To see this, note that producing $Q = s^*(\underline{c}_1)$ yields the payoff

$$\Pi_1^0(\bar{c}_1, s^*(\underline{c}_1)) + pR(\bar{c}_1, \bar{c}_2) + (1 - p)R(\bar{c}_1, \underline{c}_2) = 15.51 - 0.86p$$

while producing $m(\bar{c}_1)$ yields $\Pi_1^0(\bar{c}_1, m(\bar{c}_1)) = 16$, which exceeds $15.51 - 0.86p$ for all $p \geq 0$. Finally, note that the low cost firm has no reason to produce more than $s^*(\underline{c}_1)$. If it produces less, it is sure to face entry, and thus its best choice in this range would be $m(\underline{c}_1)$. But $s^*(\underline{c}_1)$ yields an expected payoff of $26.87 - 1.19p$, which for all $p \leq 1$ strictly exceeds the payoff $\Pi_1^M(\underline{c}_1) = 22.56$ from producing $m(\underline{c}_1)$. Thus, $s^*(\underline{c}_1)$ is also optimal.

LIMIT PRICING AND ENTRY

We now demonstrate the existence of a pooling equilibrium given by

$$s^*(\underline{c}_1) = s^*(\bar{c}_1) = m(\underline{c}_1) = 4.75,$$

$$t^*(\underline{c}_2, Q) = 1,$$

$$t^*(\bar{c}_2, Q) = \begin{cases} 0 & \text{if } Q \geqq 4.75, \\ 1 & \text{otherwise.} \end{cases}$$

Note again that our earlier discussion indicates that t^* is a best response to s^*, given $q \in (0.273, 0.954)$. Further, it is evident that s^* is optimal if $c_1 = \underline{c}_1$, since any increase in Q would not deter entry, and any decrease in output would both increase entry and reduce first period profits. Finally, if the established firm has $c_1 = \bar{c}_1$, it similarly has no incentive to increase output, while cutting output could at best yield the monopoly first period return, but would induce certain entry. This gives a payoff of 16.00, which is, for $p > 0.063$, less than its current return of $\Pi_1^0(\bar{c}_1, 4.75) + pR(\bar{c}_1, \bar{c}_2) = 15.44 + 8.89p$. Thus, if $p > 0.063$, this is also an equilibrium, and since $s^*(\bar{c}_1) > m(\bar{c}_1)$, it, too, involves limit pricing.

To summarize, our pooling equilibrium required that the probability p of the entrant having high costs exceed 0.063 and that q lie in $(0.273, 0.954)$, while our separating equilibrium existed for all p and q. In a separating equilibrium, the probability of entry is q, which is just the probability that the established firm is of the high cost type, while in our pooling equilibrium, the probability of entry is $1 - p$, the probability of the entrant having low costs.[5] Clearly, we may have $1 - p$ greater than, less than, or equal to q and still meet the requirements for existence of both equilibria. *Limit pricing equilibria may involve less, the same, or more entry than occurs in the full information (no limit pricing) case.*

It is, of course, true in either type of equilibrium that if the limit-pricing firm were to charge a higher price than is called for by the equilibrium strategy, then it would face a greater threat of entry. This is because the entrant would interpret this high price as meaning that the firm's costs were higher than they in fact are, and thus entry would appear more attractive. (Note that the entrant's inferences will be correct only if firm 1 adheres to its equilibrium strategy.) Indeed, it is this balancing of foregone first period profits against the reward to deterring entry which characterizes the equilibrium and it is this threat of increased entry which leads the established firm to maintain its expanded output. Thus, in this sense, limit pricing does limit entry.

A useful way to think about these results is to consider limit pricing as the outcome of competition between the types of the established firm, with high cost types attempting to mimic low cost ones and low cost firms attempting to distinguish themselves from the high cost ones. Then whether a pooling or a

---

[5] If $q < 0.273$, then there is a pooling equilibrium against which the probability of entry is zero. If $q > 0.954$, then entry would be certain if a pooling equilibrium were established. But then each type of established firm would find that its monopoly output represents a profitable deviation. Thus, there could be no such equilibrium.

separating equilibrium is established is a matter of whether it is the high or low cost type which is successful. This competition could, of course, be purely a conjectural one in the mind of the entrant, but it might also be more concrete. Specifically, one can imagine that there are a number of currently monopolized markets, all of which are identical except that a percentage p have high cost incumbents and the rest have low cost incumbents. There is also a limited supply of venture capital, which is available to an entrant whose costs are unknown a priori. Then the competition between types of established firms becomes real, with each established firm attempting to make entry into its market appear unattractive.[6]

The active role assigned to the entrant in this model and the corresponding significance of the beliefs and conjectures embodied in the entrant's strategy lead to the existence of a multiplicity of equilibria, both in this example and more generally. Our example actually has a continuum of both separating and pooling equilibria, where each class of equilibria is parameterized by the critical level of Q such that observation of a lower output than this level induces increased entry. In general, there is a large class of entrant's strategies t such that t and the best response to it constitute an equilibrium: many possible conjectures by the entrant as to the outcome of the competition among established firms are consistent with rational expectations. Thus, there is no unique limit price in these models.[7]

One way to attempt to narrow the set of equilibria is to place restrictions on the possible strategies for the entrant. For example, one could require that, conditional on observing *any* Q, the entrant assign probabilities to Q having been the choice of each type of established firm. Then one would require that, for each Q, $t^*(c_2, Q)$ be a best response, given these conjectures. This is the essence of the concept of sequential equilibrium due to David Kreps and Robert Wilson [10], and it is clearly in the spirit of the perfectness criterion for equilibria (Selten [19]).[8] However, as is easily verified, our equilibria already satisfy this condition, and still we have the unwanted multiplicity. Thus one might consider further restrictions on the entrant's conjectures. In particular, one might hypothesize that the entrant will not conjecture that the competition between types of established firm will be unnecessarily wasteful. This results in considering only those equilibria (s^*, t^*) for which there is no other equilibrium where the payoffs to the various types of established firms weakly dominate those under (s^*, t^*). The two particular equilibria we have identified here meet this condition. Other separating

---

[6]See E. Gal-or [4] for a more explicit model along these lines. Also see D. Kreps and R. Wilson [9] and P. Milgrom and J. Roberts [12] for multi-market models of entry deterrence through predation.

[7]There is a second source of non-uniqueness which involves the specification of $t^*(c_2, Q)$ for values of Q outside the range of s^*. Since such values of Q are observed with probability zero, the maximization of expected return places no constraint on t^* at these points. Then, even within the constraint that s^* be a best response to the entrant's strategy, there are typically many strategies t^* which constitute equilibria with s^*. However, all such t^* for a given s^* give the same evolution of the play of the game (the same Q values being chosen and the same entry decisions being made). Thus, this non-uniqueness is less crucial.

[8]This correspondence is not coincidence, as Kreps and Wilson [10] have shown: every perfect equilibrium is sequential.

equilibria all involve $s^*(\bar{c}_1) = m(\bar{c}_1)$ and $s^*(\underline{c}_1) > 7.2$,[9] other pooling equilibria must involve lower payoffs for the low cost established firm,[10] and neither equilibrium dominates the other.

Although there are no equilibria in this example where $s^* \equiv m$, the monopoly output, this strategy could arise in equilibrium with other specifications of the parameters. This would happen if the profit to a high cost firm in producing its monopoly output and then facing certain entry exceeded its profits from producing the monopoly output of the low cost firm and then avoiding all entry. However, if there are a continuum of types (cost levels) possible for the established firm and the H_i are atomless, this cannot happen: at most only a set of firms of measure zero could produce their monopoly outputs in equilibrium.

Both to establish this claim and to explore more completely the nature of the limit pricing problem in a framework with less discontinuity, we now examine a specification of the model with a continuum of possible cost levels. Thus, suppose that the distribution of c_j is given by a continuous density function $h_j(c_j)$ which is positive on $[\underline{c}_j, \bar{c}_j]$. We will initially concentrate on separating equilibria.

Assume that 2 conjectures that 1 will play some strategy $\bar{s}$. Then, for any Q in the range of $\bar{s}$, the entrant's best response is to act as if $c_1 \in \bar{s}^{-1}(Q)$, and to enter if and only if the expected value of $\delta_2 \Pi_2^C(c_1, c_2) - K$, conditional on $c_1 \in \bar{s}^{-1}(Q)$, is positive. If $\bar{s}$ is monotone decreasing, then $\bar{s}^{-1}(Q)$ is a singleton and so 2 should enter if and only if $c_2 \leqq \gamma(\bar{s}^{-1}(Q))$, where $\gamma(c_1) \equiv (a + c_1 - 3\sqrt{bK})/2$ is the highest level of c_2 permitting successful entry against a firm with costs c_1. Thus, for $Q \in$ range $\bar{s}$, 2's best response satisfies

$$t(c_2, Q) = \begin{cases} 1 & \text{if } c_2 \leqq \bar{g}(Q), \\ 0 & \text{otherwise,} \end{cases}$$

where $\bar{g} = \gamma \circ \bar{s}^{-1}$.

Now, suppose that 1's conjecture is that t is of this general form, so that 2 will be deterred from entering if c_2 exceeds some value $g(Q)$. Then 1's expected payoff is

$$G(c_1, Q) = \Pi_1^0(c_1, Q) + \delta_1 \int_{g(Q)}^{\bar{c}_2} R(c_1, c_2) h_2(c_2) \, dc_2.$$

Maximizing with respect to Q yields

$$0 = \frac{\partial \Pi_1^0}{\partial Q} - \delta_1 R(c_1, g(Q)) h_2(g(Q)) g'(Q).$$

---

[9]Note, in particular, that $s^* = m$ is not an equilibrium strategy, since the $\bar{c}_1$ firm would be willing to produce $m(\underline{c}_1)$ to eliminate all entry.

[10]While it might seem that any other pooling equilibrium would have $s^*(c_1) > m(\underline{c}_1)$, this need not be the case. However, if the entrant's conjectures regarding the value of c_1, given Q, are continuous in Q, pooling equilibria with higher than monopoly prices disappear. If, in addition, the probability assigned to $c_1 = \underline{c}_1$ rises sufficiently rapidly in Q, then only separating equilibria can exist. These continuity and monotonicity conditions are similar in spirit to Myerson's properness criterion [14].

452   P. MILGROM AND J. ROBERTS

But, in equilibrium, the conjectures must be correct (i.e., $\bar{s} = s^*$, $g = \gamma \circ s^{*-1}$), so we have that $s^*(c_1)$ must satisfy

(1) $$0 = \frac{\partial \Pi_1^0(c_1, s^*(c_1))}{\partial Q} - \frac{\delta_1 R(c_1, \gamma(c_1)) h_2(\gamma(c_1)) \gamma'(c_1)}{ds^*(c_1)/dc_1}$$

Note that, so long as $R(c_1, \gamma(c_1))$, $h_2(\gamma(c_1))$, and $\gamma'(c_1)$ are positive and $ds^*/dc_1 < \infty$ (i.e., s^* is differentiable at c_1), then this first order condition implies that $\partial \Pi_1^0/\partial Q < 0$. Thus, the simple monopoly solution $m(c_1)$, which is defined by $\partial \Pi_1^0/\partial Q = 0$, cannot arise in equilibrium. If the entrant were to conjecture $\bar{s} = m$ and respond optimally, then by increasing output slightly from $m(c_1)$ to, say, $m(c_1) + \epsilon = \bar{s}(c_1')$, the established firm can eliminate the threat of entry from firms in the interval $(\gamma(c_1'), \gamma(c_1)]$. This increase in output has a first-order effect on Π_1^0 of zero, since $\partial \Pi_1^0/\partial Q = 0$ at $m(c_1)$, but a non-negligible first-order effect on the expected value of the reward to deterring entry. Thus, in any model of this type, so long as: (i) it is more profitable to be a monopolist than to share the market, (ii) beliefs are given by a positive density, and (iii) higher costs for the established firm encourage entry, essentially all established firms must be limit pricing in a separating equilibrium.

Of course, in such an equilibrium, s^* is invertible and so there is the same entry as if c_1 were known directly.

Now, to obtain an explicit solution for a particular specification, suppose that $\underline{c}_i = 0$ and that h_2 has, for $c_2 \geq \gamma(0)$, the particular form

$$h_2(c_2) = 8bp / \left[4(a - c_2)\sqrt{bK} - 7bK \right],$$

where the parameter ρ reflects the probability of there being a viable potential competitor. Also, assume that $\bar{c}_i < a/2$, which insures that the usual first-order conditions define a Cournot equilibrium after entry. As well, assume that $a \geq 7\sqrt{bK}/2$, which both insures that h_2 is a density for any choice of $\bar{c}_2 < a/2$ and also implies that $\gamma(0) > 0$, so that even low cost established firms are threatened by entry. Finally, assume that $\gamma(\bar{c}_1) < \bar{c}_2$, so that $h_2(\gamma(\bar{c}_1)) \neq 0$.

Then, substituting for $R(c_1, \gamma(c_1)) = [2(a - c_1)\sqrt{bK} - bK]/4b$ and h_1 and rearranging terms yields

$$\frac{ds^*}{dc} = \frac{\delta_1 \rho}{\left[a - c_1 - 2bs^*(c_1) \right]}.$$

This differential equation was derived on the assumption that s^* was monotone decreasing on $[\underline{c}_1, \bar{c}_1]$. The solutions meeting this condition and satisfying the non-negativity condition for expected profits form a non-intersecting family parameterized by a boundary condition, which we may take to be the value of $s^*(\bar{c}_1)$. Since each member of this family with the appropriate specification of t^*

LIMIT PRICING AND ENTRY   453

can constitute an equilibrium,[11] the multiplicity of equilibria in the earlier
example carries over.

As suggested earlier, it seems reasonable to concentrate on solutions which are
Pareto efficient. There is a unique such solution among the separating equilibria.
In it, the highest cost firm, which will stand revealed as a weakling in any case,
does not limit price. Alternatively, we can also eliminate the multiplicity by
imposing the condition that an entrant whose costs exceed $\gamma(\bar{c}_1)$ will never enter,
no matter what value of Q is observed, since such an entrant could never expect
to recoup the entry cost K. Under either of these specifications, the boundary
condition becomes $s^*(\bar{c}_1) = m(\bar{c}_1) = (a - \bar{c}_1)/2b$. The corresponding solution of
the differential equation is then given implicitly by

$$0 = m(c_1) - s^*(c_1) + \delta_1\rho - \delta_1\rho \exp\left[\frac{m(\bar{c}_1) - s^*(c_1)}{\delta_1\rho}\right].$$

Now, let t^* be specified by $t(c_2, Q) = 1$ iff $c_2 \leqq \gamma(s^{*-1}(Q))$ for Q in the range
of s^* and, say, by $t(c_2, Q) = t(c_2, s^*(\underline{c}_1))$ for $Q > s^*(\underline{c}_1)$ and $t(c_2, Q) = t(c_2,$
$s^*(\bar{c}_1))$ for $Q < m(\bar{c}_1)$. For s^* and t^* to be an equilibrium it is clearly sufficient
that $G(c_1, Q)$ be pseudo-concave in Q for each c_1, so that the first order
condition (1) guarantees an optimum. For this, it is in turn sufficient (see [11])
that

$$\frac{ds^*(z)}{dz} \leqq \inf_{c \in [0, \bar{c}_1]} \frac{\delta_1\gamma'(z)[R(c_1, \gamma(z)) - R(z, \gamma(z))]h_1(\gamma(z))}{(z - c)}$$

$$= \inf_{c_1} \frac{\delta_1(1/2)[(z - c_1)(24\sqrt{bK} - 6a - z + 7c_1)/36b]}{(z - c_1)}$$

$$\times \left(\frac{8b\rho}{2(a - z)\sqrt{bK} - bK}\right) = \frac{\delta_1\rho[24\sqrt{bK} - 6a - z]}{9[2(a - z)\sqrt{bK} - bK]}.$$

Since $ds^*/dz = -1/[2b(1 - \exp[(m(\bar{c}_1) - s(z))/\delta_1\rho])]$ is strictly decreasing and
bounded above by $-1/(2b)$, if the right hand side of the inequality were always
positive, i.e., $6a + \sup z < 24\sqrt{bK}$, we would then be assured that (s^*, t^*) is an
equilibrium. Thus, since $\bar{c}_1 = \sup z < a/2$, $a < 48\sqrt{bK}/13$ provides a sufficient
condition.

It is straightforward to obtain comparative statics results for this example. Let
$A \equiv [m(\bar{c}_1) - s(c_1)]/(\delta_1\rho) \leqq 0$. Then

$$\partial s^*/\partial\rho = \delta_1 \frac{[1 + (A - 1)\exp A]}{1 - \exp A} > 0,$$

$$\partial s^*/\partial\delta_1 = \rho \frac{[1 + (A - 1)\exp A]}{1 - \exp A} > 0,$$

[11] So long as the first-order condition (1) actually gives a maximum.

454   P. MILGROM AND J. ROBERTS

and

$$\partial s^*/\partial \bar{c}_1 = \frac{\exp A}{2b(1 - \exp A)} > 0.$$

The intuition behind the first two results is clear. Regarding the third, the idea is that the possibility of there being higher cost firms leads the current $\bar{c}_1$ firm to limit price in order to distinguish itself, and then all lower cost firms must further increase their outputs.

Since the particular h function that we chose to permit computation resulted in $R(c_1, \gamma(c_1))h(\gamma(c_1))$ being constant, comparative statics with respect to a and b reveal the effects of changes in first period demand only. Note too that changes in these parameters affect both m and s^*, so interest centers on the effects on $s^* - m$. These are obtained by $\partial s^*/\partial a = 1/2b = \partial m/\partial a$, and $\partial s^*/\partial b < - (a - c_1)/2b^2 = \partial m/\partial b$: increases in a do not affect the amount of limit pricing, while increases in b reduce the amount of limit pricing by increasing the marginal cost of this activity (as measured by c_1 less the marginal revenue at $s^*(c_1)$) while leaving the marginal return (in the second period) unaffected.

Since the density function we used depends on K, comparative statics with respect to K cannot legitimately be interpreted in the natural way as indicating the effect of changing entry barriers.[12] To allow such an analysis, suppose instead that the established firm's beliefs are given by a density function which is independent of K. In this case, if $K = 0$, then $R(c_1, \gamma(c_1))h(\gamma(c_1)) \equiv 0$, and no limit pricing will occur. It is only the fact of positive K that causes the marginal entrant to enter with a strictly positive level of output. With no cost of entry, a marginal entrant comes in with an output which is essentially zero, and there is no return to deterring such entry. Similarly, if K is very large (Bain's blockaded entry case), no possible level of $\underline{c}_2$ will permit positive profits, the threat of entry disappears, and again no limit pricing will occur. In the particular example we calculated, K was such that $\gamma(\underline{c}_1) > \underline{c}_2$, so even low cost established firms were threatened and practiced limit pricing. A fourth possibility comes when K is high enough that $\gamma(\underline{c}_1) < \underline{c}_2$, so that there is a set $[\underline{c}_1, c_1^*)$ of firms against which no potential entrant would want to enter. An interesting aspect of our model is that even firms in this range may practice limit pricing. The essential cause of this is that, if $m(c_1') \leq s(c_1'')$ for some $c_1' < c_1^* < c_1''$, then by producing $m(c_1')$, the low cost firm becomes identified with higher cost firms which are subject to entry. These latter firms may be expected to be limit pricing, so $s^*(c_1'') > m(c_1'')$, and thus $m(c_1') = s^*(c_1'')$ is possible. By increasing output to (slightly more than) $s^*(c_1^*)$, which, to a first approximation, does not reduce the value of Π^0, the low cost firm can eliminate the threat of entry and thus increase second period expected returns.

Finally, we should mention that although we have concentrated on separating equilibria, other equilibria are possible in the continuum of types framework. A

----

[12] The possibility of normalizing 2's payoff means that lowering δ_2 corresponds to raising K.

result of Milgrom and Weber [13] indicates that we need not concern ourselves with mixed strategy equilibria in games of this type. However, pure pooling equilibria are conceptually possible, as are equilibria where s^* is a decreasing step function.[13] In any pooling equilibrium, all types of the established firm are better off producing the equilibrium output Q^* than they are changing their output and facing the different probability of entry this different value of Q implies. For example, if entry is relatively unlikely when $Q = Q^*$ (perhaps because low values of c_1 are very likely a priori), and any deviation from Q^* brings certain entry, then if the $\bar{c}_1$ type is willing to produce Q^*, a pooling equilibrium will be maintained. In general, the form of the entrant's conjectures (as embodied in its strategy) which is necessary to support a pooling equilibria is typically discontinuous in Q, and the same sort of discontinuities underlie step-function equilibria.

It is clear that the extended example we have been discussing involves a number of special features, such as the linearity of demand and cost, and the assumption that post-entry competition yields the full information Cournot outcome. However, these assumptions serve mainly to simplify arguments and facilitate computation; they do not drive the results. Indeed, so long as the entrant's post-entry profits decrease in c_2 and increase in c_1 while the established firm strictly prefers to be a monopolist than to share the market ($R(c_1, c_2) > 0$), our principal conclusions remain: if pre-entry price can be a signal for post-entry profits, even if it does not directly influence profitability, then limit pricing will emerge in equilibrium, but entry need not be deterred relative to the complete information case. Moreover, as we shall argue in the next section, even if we allow for much more general uncertainty and for post-entry profits being dependent on pre-entry actions, a similar conclusion is valid.

3. ENTRY DETERRENCE AND RATIONAL EXPECTATIONS

In this section we consider a fairly general two-period model of entry deterrence and entry under incomplete information. While we do not provide a complete analysis of this model, we do indicate some of the implications of equilibrium for the firms' behavior.

Rather than setting up a general formal model from scratch, let us re-interpret the model in Section 2 with some modifications. In particular, we now view c_1 and c_2 as belonging to some arbitrary measurable spaces, and we will view Q as an action belonging to some other arbitrary space. Suppose further that 2 observes only some variable q which is correlated with Q, and suppose, too, that the payoffs depend not only on c_1, c_2 and the action y taken by the entrant (which may also now belong to some arbitrary space), but also on Q and possibly on a random variable θ, the realization of which is not revealed until the firms make their choices. Finally, let all the random variables have some arbitrary joint distribution.

---

[13] The possible equilibria are characterized in [11].

This framework is obviously very general. In particular, it allows for capital investment which affects marginal costs, advertising and other means of achieving brand loyalty, general forms of demand and cost functions, varying scales and forms of entry, imperfect observability of actions, uncertainty as to how the post-entry game will be played, and arbitrary dependencies among all the random elements of the model.

As before, it is useful to analyze equilibrium via strategies, s^* and t^*, and conjectures, $\bar{s}$ and $\bar{t}$. (These may be taken to be either pure or mixed strategies.) Thus, firm 1 conjectures that 2's strategy is $\bar{t}$, for each value of c_1 it will select an action $Q = s(c_1)$ to maximize the expected value of its perceived payoff, conditional on c_1. Unless expected second-period payoffs are insensitive to Q, both through any direct effect on second period profits and also through the effect on 2's conjectured action, the solution for the established firm's maximization problem will not be the same as the solution to the problem of maximizing the expected value of first period profits. Thus, we would generally expect that the threat of entry will alter behavior: some generalized form of limit pricing will be a characteristic of equilibrium.

In making its decision, the entrant will seek to maximize its expected payoff conditional on its private information c_2 and its (imperfect) observation of Q, given its conjecture $\bar{s}$. Should it happen that the observation of the signal q in equilibrium permits a precise inference via $\bar{s}$ about c_1, then entry will of course occur in precisely the same circumstances as if c_1 had been directly announced. In this case, the only effect of the generalized limit pricing on entry will be through the direct effect of Q on 2's post-entry profits (as, for example, when the choice of Q affects demand or cost). If this effect is zero, then, as in the example in Section 2, limit pricing will still occur, but it need not deter entry relative to the complete information case.

However, the unrestricted dimensionalities allowed for c_1 and Q suggest that an invertible strategy s^* is unlikely. Moreover, so long as the random noise term relating q and Q is neither perfectly correlated with c_1 nor degenerate, then even if s^* is an invertible function of Q one would not expect a noisy observation of Q via q to permit a precise inference of the value of c_1. Thus one must expect that such exact inferences will be impossible in equilibrium, and that residual uncertainty will remain concerning c_1 when the entry decision is made. In this case, the entrant must base its entry decision y on the expected value of its profits, as a function of Q, y and the exogenous uncertainty θ, conditional on the values of c_2 and q, and given its conjecture $\bar{s}$ about 1's behavior. With some abuse of notation, let us write this as

(2) $E\big(\Pi_2(c_1,c_2,\bar{s}(c_1),y,\theta)\,|\,q(\bar{s}(c_1),\theta),c_2\big).$

Then the question is that of whether the established firm can, through its choice of Q, cause the entrant in equilibrium to lower its estimate of the profitability of entry.

Consider what 2's estimate of its prospects are a priori, knowing c_2 but before observing q. This is just the expectation of expression (2), conditional on c_2. Then, in equilibrium, where $\bar{s} = s^*$, so that 2's conjecture is correct, this a priori estimate is

(3) $E\big(E\big[\Pi_2(c_1, c_2, s^*(c_1), y, \theta) \,|\, q(s^*(c_1), \theta), c_2 \big] \,|\, c_2 \big).$

But, by a standard result in probability theory, expression (3) is equal to $E(\Pi_2(c_1, c_2, s^*(c_1), y, \theta) \,|\, c_2)$. But this, in turn, is simply what firm 2 would estimate its profits to be if it were to receive no information.

In this sense, then, the observation of the established firm's actions cannot, in equilibrium, systematically bias the entrant's expectations. If without any information it would have estimated its expected profits at $\overline{\overline{\Pi}}$ then the fact that it will receive the signal cannot lead it to expect to receive less than $\overline{\overline{\Pi}}$. Put a different way, if there are some values of c_1 and c_2 such that observing $s^*(c_1)$ (directly or indirectly) causes an entrant with characteristics c_2 to underestimate the profitability of entry, then there is an offsetting set of values for c_1 and c_2 where observing $s^*(c_1)$ causes the entrant to overestimate its prospects.

4. SUMMARY AND CONCLUSIONS

In his original analysis of limit pricing, Bain [1, p. 453] argued that although "current price ... need play no direct role [in the entry decision], since the anticipated industry price *after entry* and the entrant's anticipated market share are the strategic considerations," the potential entrant may "regard this price as an indicator" of post-entry profitability. Given this, Bain developed his theory of limit pricing, from which a large literature has emerged. A weakness of this literature has been the failure to model both the established firm and the entrant as strategic agents. However, if one models the situation described by Bain as a game of complete information, no limit pricing can emerge in equilibrium [3].

In this paper we model the problem considered by Bain of entry deterrence and entry as a game of incomplete information. In this game, Bain's arguments are valid: although pre-entry actions by the established firm may not influence post-entry profitability, they may become signals for some unobservable determinants of profits. Limit pricing, or, more generally, deviations from short run maximizing behavior, then emerge in equilibrium, just as earlier analyses had found. However, an unsuspected feature also emerges. Since the entrant will, in equilibrium, recognize the incentives for limit-pricing, its expectations of the profitability of entry will not be consistently biased by the established firm's behavior. Then, depending on the particular equilibrium that is established and the parameters of the model, the probability of entry may fall short of, equal, or even exceed what it would be if there were complete information and thus no limit pricing.

One conclusion of this analysis is for the appropriate public policy towards

458   P. MILGROM AND J. ROBERTS

limit-pricing. If pre-entry price does not influence post-entry demand and if the two-period modelling used here is appropriate, then limit pricing should not be discouraged, since it means lower prices and cannot, overall, limit entry. More generally, the admittedly incomplete analysis in Section 3 might suggest a stronger statement regarding strategic moves taken by established firms to deter entry. To the extent that these actions are not objectionable per se, but rather are of potential concern only because of signalling effects which it is feared may deter entry, then they are in fact benign. The question is whether either of these suggestions would stand up under a full examination of a richer model. In particular, it would seem that embedding the opportunity for limit pricing in a multi-period model where predation is possible and where reputations are a factor would be an important extension of the present analysis. This is a problem we hope to address in future work.

Northwestern University
and
Stanford University

Manuscript received March, 1980; revision received December, 1980.

REFERENCES

[1] BAIN, J.: "A Note on Pricing in Monopoly and Oligopoly," *American Economic Review*, 39(1949), 448–464.
[2] CLARK, J. M.: "Toward a Concept of Workable Competition," *American Economic Review*, 30(1940), 241–256.
[3] FRIEDMAN, J.: "On Entry Preventing Behavior," in *Applied Game Theory*, ed. by S. J. Brams, A. Schotter, and G. Schwodiauer. Wurzburg, Vienna: Physica-Verlag, 1979, pp. 236–253.
[4] GAL-OR, E.: "Limit Price Entry Prevention and its Impact on Potential Investors—A Game-Theoretic Approach," Ph.D. Dissertation, Northwestern University, 1980.
[5] GASKINS, D.: "Dynamic Limit Pricing: Optimal Pricing Under Threat of Entry," *Journal of Economic Theory*, 2(1971), 306–322.
[6] HARSANYI, J. C.: "Games with Incomplete Information Played by 'Bayesian' Players," Parts I, II and III, *Management Science*, 14 (November, 1967; January, 1968; and March, 1968), 159–182, 320–324, and 486–502.
[7] KALDOR, N.: "Market Imperfection and Excess Capacity," *Economica*, 2(1935), 33–50.
[8] KAMIEN, M. I., AND N. SCHWARTZ: "Limit Pricing and Uncertain Entry," *Econometrica*, 39(1971), 441–454.
[9] KREPS, D., AND R. WILSON: "On the Chain-Store Paradox and Predation: Reputation for Toughness," Discussion Paper 551, Graduate School of Business, Stanford University, 1980.
[10] ———: "Sequential Equilibria," Discussion Paper 584, Graduate School of Business, Stanford University, 1980.
[11] MILGROM, P., AND J. ROBERTS: "Equilibrium Limit Pricing Doesn't Limit Entry," Discussion Paper 399R, Center for Mathematical Studies in Economics and Management Science, Northwestern University, 1980.
[12] ———: "Predation, Reputation, and Entry Deterrence," Discussion Paper 427, Center for Mathematical Studies in Economics and Management Science, Northwestern University, 1980.
[13] MILGROM, P., AND R. WEBER: "Distributional Strategies for Games with Incomplete Information," Discussion Paper 428, Center for Mathematical Studies in Economics and Management Science, Northwestern University, 1980.
[14] MYERSON, R.: "Refinements of the Nash Equilibrium Concept," *International Journal of Game Theory*, 7(1978), 73–80.

[15] ORTEGA-REICHERT, A.: "Models for Competitive Bidding Under Uncertainty," Ph.D. dissertation, Stanford University, 1968.

[16] PYATT, G.: "Profit Maximization and the Threat of New Entry," *Economic Journal*, 81(1971), 242–255.

[17] SALOP, S. C.: "Strategic Entry Deterrence," *American Economic Review*, 69(1979), 335–338.

[18] SCHERER, F. M.: *Industrial Market Structure and Economic Performance*, Second Edition. Chicago: Rand McNally and Company, 1979.

[19] SELTEN, R.: "Reexamination of the Perfectness Concept for Equilibrium Points in Extensive Games," *International Journal of Game Theory*, 4(1975), 25–55.

[37]

MANAGEMENT SCIENCE
Vol. 25, No. 3, March 1979
Printed in U.S.A.

THE STRATEGIC ROLE OF INFORMATION ON THE DEMAND FUNCTION IN AN OLIGOPOLISTIC MARKET*

JEAN-PIERRE PONSSARD†

This paper investigates the incentives for cooperation in market surveys among competitive firms. The analysis relies on a game theoretic model. The main conclusion is that the value of information in a competitive market exhibits a sharp decrease as the number of firms that share the information increases. Thus, the advantage obtained through sharing the cost of a market survey may be upset by the loss due to the spreading of information among the competitors. The consumer's point of view is also studied showing that market surveys are advantageous in terms of consumer surplus, a usual indicator of the consumer's satisfaction.
(MARKETING; GAMES/GROUP DECISIONS; INFORMATION SYSTEMS)

1. Introduction

In recent years, there has been a growing interest in studying explicitly the role of information in economic situations. For example, Hirschleifer [6] and Marshall [10] investigated the social and private value of information in general equilibrium models in which there are uncertainties on the initial endowments. There has also been interest in some specific models including production (Arrow [1], Green [4]). In many such investigations, the strategic analysis of the role of information remains incomplete, in particular, it may not be specified whether uninformed agents are aware of the information acquisition obtained by others and may adapt to the new situation, or, the possible spreading of information (which may involuntarily take place through the informed agents' activity) may be ignored thus over-evaluating the value of private information. In a strategic analysis of information performed in a game theoretic framework, such factors may appear essential and could give rise to many counter-intuitive results such as bluff, signalling, negative value of information, controlled transmission of information and so on (Aumann and Maschler [3], Ponssard [12], Levine and Ponssard [8]). The corresponding game models belong to the class of games with incomplete information introduced by Harsanyi [5].

The subject of this paper is to study the strategic role of information in a partial equilibrium economic situation using as a model a game with incomplete information. Though the emphasis was not on the role of information, this class of games has already been used in the economic literature (d'Aspremont and Gerard-Varet [2], Wilson [13]). This paper may be seen as an attempt to use such models for bringing out specific insights about the role of information, e.g., market research.

The situation to be studied concerns an oligopolistic market for an homogenous product, the demand for which is uncertain. The questions of interest concern the incentives for firms to acquire private information. This will be shown to strongly depend on the number of firms who do so. The consumer's point of view will also be taken into account so that one may discuss the social value of information. This situation is modeled as a simple oligopolistic market game with linear demand and cost functions. The advantage of this model is that it is mathematically tractable (and it may not be an overstatement to say that games with incomplete information are complex due to the fact that a strategy is not a number but a function of the state of information). The drawback is of course that the results are constrained by the narrow assumptions.

* Accepted by Melvin F. Shakun, former Departmental Editor; received January 19, 1976. This paper has been with the author 5 months for 3 revisions.
† Centre de Recherche en Gestion, Ecole Polytechnique, France.

2. The Model and Its Solution

2.1. *Assumptions*

Consider the following simple oligopolistic market model for an homogenous product:

The *demand function* is linear, if p denotes the price, q the quantity, D and a two parameters, we have:

$$p = D - aq. \tag{1}$$

The parameter D *is a random variable* and $F(\cdot)$ is its distribution function. This may be interpreted as if a random perturbation with mean zero were added to a known demand function. Uncertainties of other types such as multiplicative shall not be considered here. The function $F(\cdot)$ is assumed to be known to the firms. The questions of interest are about the expected values of perfect information on the random parameter D. (Throughout this note, taking an expected value will be represented by the letter E, and a variance by Var so that ED stands for mean of D and Var D for the variance of D.)

There are N *competing firms*, $i = 1, \ldots, N$. The quantity produced by firm i, denoted x_i, is taken as its decision variable. The production functions, though different, will all be assumed to be linear, c_i denoting firm i's marginal cost.

The firms are maximizing their expected profit, no risk aversion will be taken into account. The resulting game is a *non cooperative game* with simultaneous moves. The solution concept to be used is the *Nash equilibrium* (Nash [11]), also called the Cournot solution in this context.

2.2. *Solutions*

2.2.1. *Solution of the no information game.* The calculation to derive the equilibrium point in this case is quite standard. Letting $\Pi_i(x_i)$ denote firm i's profit, we have:

$$\Pi_i(x_i) = (p - c_i)x_i. \tag{2}$$

Substituting for p its value according to (1), and letting $q = \sum_{j=1}^{N} x_j$, it follows that

$$\Pi_i(x_i) = \left(D - c_i - a \sum_{j=1}^{N} x_j \right) x_i. \tag{3}$$

Taking expected values,

$$E\Pi_i(x_i) = \left(ED - c_i - a \sum_{j=1}^{N} x_j \right) x_i. \tag{4}$$

An equilibrium point consists of a vector $(x_i^*)_{i=1,\ldots,N}$ such that the expected profit of firm i is maximal at x_i^* whenever the other firms produce $x_j^*, j \neq i$. Assume that x_i^* is not a corner solution,[1] it may be obtained by writing that the derivatives of the expected profits are zero. Then, the $(x_i^*)_{i=1,\ldots,N}$ satisfy the following set of linear equations:

$$a \sum_{j=1}^{N} x_j + ax_i = ED - c_i, \qquad i = 1, \ldots, N. \tag{5}$$

This set of equations is easily solved by adding up all equations to obtain $a \sum_{j=1}^{N} x_j$ and then substituting to find each value of x_i.

Then, there exists a unique equilibrium point in pure strategies (which dominates any randomized equilibrium since the payoff functions are convex). It is easily

---

[1] This will be so long as the solution $(x_i)_{i=1,\ldots,N}$ of (5) is nonnegative. The corresponding assumptions on the parameters' values will be assumed to hold.

THE DEMAND FUNCTION IN AN OLIGOPOLISTIC MARKET   245

calculated,

$$x_i^* = \left(\left(ED + \sum_{j=1}^{N} c_j\right) \Big/ (N+1) - c_i\right) \Big/ a. \tag{6}$$

The resulting price and its expected value are respectively

$$p^* = D - \left(NED - \sum_{j=1}^{N} c_j\right) \Big/ (N+1) \tag{7}$$

and

$$Ep^* = \left(ED + \sum_{j=1}^{N} c_j\right) \Big/ (N+1). \tag{8}$$

Finally, one obtains the expected profit of each firm at the equilibrium:

$$E\Pi_i^* = \left(\left(ED + \sum_{j=1}^{N} c_j\right) \Big/ (N+1) - c_i\right)^2 \Big/ a. \tag{9}$$

2.2.2. *The I_1 informed game and the firms' optimal profits.* In this section, it is assumed that firms $1, 2, \ldots, k$ $(k < N)$ acquire perfect information on the value taken by the random parameter D whereas firms $k+1, \ldots, N$ remain uncertain about d. This fact is known to all firms. How does this situation compare with the case in which no firm is informed?

This new situation may be modelled as a game in extensive form which starts by a chance move selecting the true value d of D according to the probability distribution $F(\cdot)$. Then this value d is exclusively revealed to informed firms whereas for the others it remains uncertain. All firms know the probability distribution according to which the true value d of D is selected. Such models are called games with incomplete information (Harsanyi [5]).

Let I_1 denote the subset of informed firms whereas I_2 denotes the subset of uninformed ones. For simplicity, we shall refer to this game as the I_1 informed game. An equilibrium point of the I_1 informed game is a vector of functions $(\bar{x}_1(\cdot), \ldots, \bar{x}_k(\cdot), \bar{x}_{k+1}, \ldots, \bar{x}_N)$, in which the informed firms select the quantity to be produced as a function of the true value d. The uninformed firms select only a point; note that for them the decisions taken by the informed firms will appear as random variables since they do not know d.

One may obtain the equilibrium point in this game, writing that informed firms maximize their profit conditional on d, whereas uninformed firms maximize expected profit (Harsanyi [5]).[2]

$$i \in I_1, \quad \Pi_i(x_i) = \left(d - c_i - a \sum_{j \in I_1} x_j(d) - a \sum_{j \in I_2} x_j\right) x_i(d), \tag{10}$$

$$i \in I_2, \quad E\Pi_i(x_i) = \left(ED - c_i - a \sum_{j \in I_1} Ex_j - a \sum_{j \in I_2} x_j\right) x_i. \tag{11}$$

---

[2] It should be noted at this point that the present Nash equilibrium, which is to be found by solving a set of simultaneous equations, cannot be interpreted as the stable point of usual tatônnement processes. For example, in a duopoly model a usual tatônnement process considers that each firm reacts myopically to the quantity produced by its competitor by maximizing its own profit given this quantity. Under some hypotheses, this process converges to the Nash equilibrium.

In the present case, the observation of the quantity produced by informed firms would clearly reveal some information about the true value of D to the uninformed firms and this transmission of information should be taken into account. If the situation to be modelled contains a true dynamic feature, it should be explicitly introduced into the model otherwise the role of information cannot be studied in a coherent game theoretic sense.

This note should be kept in mind for any interpretations of the results of this paper in a dynamic context.

Then, we may proceed as in §2.2.1, writing that the derivatives are zero (again assuming no corner solutions). The set of equations is as follows:
For all possible d and all $i \in I_1$,

$$a \sum_{j \in I_1} x_j(d) + a \sum_{j \in I_2} x_j + ax_i(d) = d - c_i, \tag{12}$$

for all $i \in I_1$.

$$a \sum_{j \in I_1} Ex_j + a \sum_{j \in I_2} x_j + ax_i = ED - c_i, \tag{13}$$

for all $i \in I_2$.

We are now in a position to state the following results:

THEOREM 1.[3]   *There exists a unique equilibrium point in the I_1 informed game,* $(\bar{x}_1(\cdot), \ldots, \bar{x}_k(\cdot), \bar{x}_{k+1}, \ldots, \bar{x}_N)$. *It satisfies:*

$$i \in I_1, \qquad E\bar{x}_i = x_i^*, \tag{14}$$

$$i \in I_2, \qquad \bar{x}_i = x_i^*, \tag{15}$$

in which $(x_i^*)_{i=1, \ldots, N}$ *is the solution of the no information game (cf. 2.2.1). Moreover, for each realized value d of the random parameter D, $[\bar{x}_i(d)]_{i \in I_1}$ is the Nash equilibrium of the oligopoly game with complete information, the demand function of which is given by*

$$p = d - a \left[q + \sum_{i \in I_2} x_i^* \right].$$

PROOF.   The set of equations $(12) + (13)$ may be solved along the following lines. One may take an expected value over all possible d for each $i \in I_1$ to obtain:

$$a \sum_{j \in I_1} Ex_j + a \sum_{j \in I_2} x_j + aEx_i = ED - c_i. \tag{12 bis}$$

Comparing (12 bis) + (13) and the set of equations (5) it follows that, if a solution exists, (14) and (15) hold. Now, the values of $\bar{x}_i(d)$ for each d may be obtained by solving the corresponding (12) in which the $x_i, i = k + 1, \ldots, N$, are replaced by their values, x_i^*. This procedure clearly defines a unique potential solution which is found to satisfy all equations.

THEOREM 2.   *Comparing with the case of no information, the expected profits at the equilibrium point of the I_1 informed game are increased by* $\operatorname{Var} D/a(k + 1)^2$ *for informed firms and unmodified for uninformed firms.*

PROOF.   This result will be proved as follows: first it will be shown to hold if $k = N$, i.e. all firms are informed; second, this will be extended for all values of k $(1 < k < N)$.

---

[3] The assumption of no corner solution is crucial for this theorem and if d is allowed to vary widely, it may easily be violated. It may also be interesting to note that the mathematical structure allowing this very simple result, which is the key to evaluating the expected values of information, is as follows: take an N person noncooperative game and let u_i be the utility function of player i, if u_i has the form

$$u_i(x_1, \ldots, x_N) = f(x_1, \ldots, x_N) + Dx_i$$

in which f is quadratic and D a random parameter, then Theorem 1 holds.

Finally, this theorem makes immaterial whether the acquisition of information is made privately or secretly (Levine and Ponssard [8]).

Let $k = N$, then the expected value of perfect information on the random parameter D is the difference between the expected profits knowing d, $E\Pi_i^*(D \mid D = d)$, and the expected profits not knowing d, $E\Pi_i^*(D)$. Using result (9), and the fact that if Y is a random variable and α and β two real numbers,

$$E[\alpha Y + \beta]^2 - [E[\alpha Y + \beta]]^2 = \alpha^2 \text{Var } Y,$$

we have:

$$E\Pi_i^*(D \mid D = d) - E\Pi_i^*(D)$$

$$= E\left(\left(D + \sum_{j=1}^{N} c_j\right)\Big/(N+1) - c_i\right)^2 \Big/ a - \left(\left(ED + \sum_{j=1}^{N} c_j\right)\Big/(N+1) - c_i\right)^2 \Big/ a$$

$$= \text{Var } D/a(N+1)^2. \tag{16}$$

For $1 < k < N$, using Theorem 1, one sees that the expected quantity on the market remains the same so that the expected price will also be the same. Since uninformed firms produce the same quantity in the two games (no information and I_1 informed respectively) their expected profits are unmodified.[4] To evaluate the change of profits for informed firms, one may simply consider that in the corresponding games, uninformed firms are passive players with their production levels fixed at $\bar{x}_i = x_i^*$. Then the comparison is exactly the one which resulted in (16) except that N is changed in k and that, in the demand function D is replaced by $D - aq_2$ where q_2 is the aggregate constant production of I_2 firms. This latter modification has no effect on the variance operation performed to obtain (16). This completes the proof.

2.2.3. *The consumer surplus in the I_1 informed game.* In partial equilibrium models such as the one considered in this paper, consumers are passive players with no strategic choice and no explicit utility functions. Nevertheless, it may be of interest to have an idea of how they may be affected by the acquisition of information by the firms. A possible approach to acquiring such an idea is to attribute to them an aggregate utility index such as the consumer surplus and see how it varies between the two games.

THEOREM 3. *Compared to the no information game, the expected consumer surplus in the I_1 informed game is increased by*

$$k^2 \text{Var } D/2a(k+1)^2. \tag{17}$$

PROOF. It may be useful to follow the reasoning using Figures 1, 2 and 3. Figure 1 gives the graphical definition of the consumer surplus, it is the area of the shaded triangle. Note that it may be calculated as $(d - p^*)q^*/2$, and since $p^* = d - aq^*$, it is simply $aq^{*2}/2$. In the no information game, the aggregate production is independent of the true value d; then, though the price and the demand function are modified depending on d, the consumer surplus remains exactly the same as if D were replaced by its expected value (Figure 2).

In the I_1 informed game, the aggregate production depends on the true value d through the production levels of the informed firms. Recall equation (12),

$$a \sum_{j \in I_1} x_j(d) + a \sum_{j \in I_2} x_j + ax_i(d) = d - c_i, \tag{12}$$

---

[4] It will be shown later that the variance of their profits decreases. This gives an indication that if risk aversion were introduced, they would enjoy a higher utility level by having the other firms being informed.

and denote by $\bar{q}(d)$ and q^* the optimal aggregate production levels in the I_1 informed game and in the no information game respectively. Using (12) one obtains (adding (12) over the subset I_1)

$$\bar{q}(d) - q^* = kd/a(k + 1). \tag{18}$$

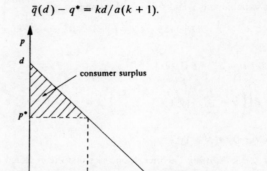

FIGURE 1.   Graphical Definition of the Consumer Surplus.

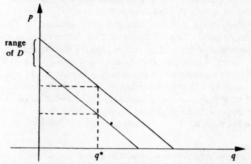

FIGURE 2.   The Consumer Surplus in the No Information Game.

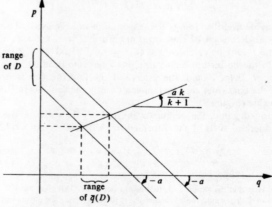

FIGURE 3.   The Consumer Surplus in the I_1 Informed Game.

[Note that the variance of the equilibrium price decreases as k increases (see Figure 3); it follows that the variance of expected profits of uninformed firms decreases as well.] Since the consumer surplus is $a\bar{q}(d)^2/2$ as a function of the true value d, its expected value is $E[a\bar{q}(D)^2/2]$. Using (18) concludes the proof.

3. Discussion of the Results

The results obtained in the context of the simple model detailed in §2 allow us to initiate a discussion of the strategic role of information on the demand function. First, the firms' point of view will be discussed then, we shall turn to the consumer's point of view.

Theorem 2 indicates that there is a positive incentive for each firm to acquire private information but that this incentive strongly depends on the number of firms that will do so. Namely, this incentive decreases as $1/(k + 1)^2$ where k is the number of informed firms. To develop an interpretation of this result it is interesting to make the following analogy:

—take a no information game with $N = 1$, it is a monopoly and its expected optimal profit is $(ED - c)^2/4a$; now let newcomers arrive in the market (for simplicity assume all marginal costs are equal). Then, if there are N firms altogether, each firm's optimal profit now is $(ED - c)^2/a(N + 1)^2$; note that profits decrease as $1/(N + 1)^2$;

—consider now the I_1 informed game, that is the oligopolistic market in which k firms know exactly the demand function; it may be seen as a two level game: at the first level, all firms compete in a market in which the demand function is the average demand function; at the second level, the informed firms, and only they, compete on the variance of the demand function; then, if there is only one informed firm it obtains a monopoly rent on the variance, that is var $D/4a$, if there are k informed firms, each obtain an oligopolistic rent of var $D/a(k + 1)^2$.

In other words, there is a complete similarity between entry of new firms in a market with a known demand function and the acquisition of information by firms in a market with uncertain demand function. This gives an idea of the competitive advantage associated with the precise knowledge of the demand function. It is clear that uninformed firms have an incentive to acquire information whereas informed firms have an incentive not to share the information. In the information market, a barrier to entry is the cost of acquiring information, which may typically be a fixed cost. Then, one may expect that if this fixed cost is not too high (relative to the competitive advantage associated with information), all firms could acquire information (they may even make a syndicate to share the cost of experimentation and this collusion, provided it stops there, would be socially valuable). However, if the fixed cost is high, only a limited number of firms would acquire information until its cost equals its marginal competitive advantage for the newcomer. In this type of game, there is an advantage in moving first and the situation recalls a battle of sexes game (Luce and Raiffa [9]). An interesting question would then be to explore a dynamic market model and see if the informed firms can keep their competitive advantage over time or if there is an inevitable diffusion of information through their past moves so that their competitive advantage would decrease as time goes on (for such a dynamic analysis in a zero sum context, see Ponssard [12]).

Turning now to the consumer's point of view, Theorem 3 indicates that the consumer surplus increases when the firms are acquiring information. Moreover, it increases as the number of informed firms increases. Given the interpretation in terms of entry in the information market, this result is not surprising. It is to the consumer's interest that the firms are informed and that their number be as high as possible. But, this does not necessarily mean that if the consumer is given a strategic variable such as the possibility of revealing or not revealing the demand function, he may use a sincere strategy that always reveals his true preferences. This may be an interesting question for further study.

Taking a global point of view, one may conclude by saying that the social value of information is positive since it is positive for every economic agent. However, the preceding discussion gives certainly a more precise idea of this statement showing the partially antagonistic point of views among firms for the information market as well as between firms and consumer for the number of informed firms.[5]

---

[5] Detailed comments by E. Kohlberg on an earlier version of this paper were very helpful.

References

1. ARROW, K. J., "Vertical Information and Communication," IMSSS, Technical report No. 145, Stanford University, Stanford, Calif., 1974.
2. D'ASPREMONT, CL. AND GERARD-VARET, L. A., "Individual Incentives and Collective Efficiency for an Externality Game with Incomplete Information," CORE, discussion paper No. 7519, 1975.
3. AUMANN, R. J. AND MASCHLER, M., "Repeated Games with Incomplete Information: A Survey of Recent Results," Report of the U.S. Arms Control and Disarmement Agency, Washington, D.C. ACDA/ST-116, prepared by Mathematica, Princeton, N. J., 1967.
4. GREEN, J. R., "On the Economics of Information with Incomplete Markets," mimeographed, 1976.
5. HARSANYI, J., "Games with Incomplete Information Played by 'Bayesian' Players," Part 1, 2, 3, *Management Sci.*, Vol. 14, No. 3, 5, 7 (1967).
6. HIRSCHLEIFER, J., "The Private and Social Value of Information and the Reward to Inventive Activity," *Amer. Econom. Rev.*, Vol. 61 (1971), pp. 561–573.
7. ———, "Where Are We in the Theory of Information?," *Amer. Econom. Rev.*, Vol. 63 (1973), pp. 31–39.
8. LEVINE, P. AND PONSSARD, J. P., "The Value of Information in Some Nonzero Sum Games," *Internat. J. Game Theory*, Vol. 6, No. 4, pp. 221–229.
9. LUCE, R. D. AND RAIFFA, H., *Games and Decisions*, Wiley, New York, 1957.
10. MARSHALL, J. M., "Private Incentives and Public Information," *Amer. Econom. Rev.*, Vol. 64 (1974), pp. 373–389.
11. NASH, J. F., "Non-Cooperative Games," *Ann. of Math.*, Vol. 54, No. 2 (1951).
12. PONSSARD, J. P., "On the Concept of the Value of Information in Competitive Situations," *Management Sci.*, Vol. 22, No. 7 (1976).
13. WILSON, R., "A Bidding Model of Perfect Competition," IMSSS, technical report No. 184, Stanford University, Stanford, Calif., 1975.

[38]

JOURNAL OF ECONOMIC THEORY **34**, 71–94 (1984)

Duopoly Information Equilibrium: Cournot and Bertrand

XAVIER VIVES*

*Department of Economics, University of Pennsylvania,
Philadelphia, Pennsylvania 19104*

Received August 3, 1983

In a duopoly model where firms have private information about an uncertain linear demand, it is shown that if the goods are substitutes (not) to share information is a dominant strategy for each firm in Bertrand (Cournot) competition. If the goods are complements the result is reversed. Furthermore the following welfare results are obtained:

   (i)   With substitutes in Cournot competition the market outcome is never optimal with respect to information sharing but it may be optimal in Bertrand competition if the products are good substitutes. With complements the market outcome is always optimal.

   (ii)   Bertrand competition is more efficient than Cournot competition.

   (iii)   The private value of information to the firms is always positive but the social value of information is positive in Cournot and negative in Bertrand competition. *Journal of Economic Literature* Classification Numbers: 022, 026, 611.   c 1984 Academic Press, Inc.

1. Introduction

Consider a symmetric differentiated duopoly model in which firms have private market data about the uncertain demand. We analyze two types of duopoly information equilibrium, Cournot and Bertrand, which emerge, respectively, from quantity and price competition, and show that the incentives for information sharing and its welfare consequences depend crucially on the type of competition, the nature of the goods (substitutes or complements), and the degree of product differentation.

The demand structure is linear and symmetric, and allows the goods to be substitutes, independent or complements. There is uncertainty only about the

* I am grateful to Marcus Berliant, Drew Fudenberg, Andreu Mas–Colell, Tom Palfrey, Leo Simon, Nirvikar Singh, and participants in seminar presentations at Harvard (Business School and Economics Department), Johns Hopkins, Pennsylvania and Wisconsin–Madison for helpful comments on the May 1982, September 1982, and present versions of the paper. Anonymous referees of the Journal provided useful suggestions. Dominique van der Mensbrugghe took good care of the graphs. Once the manuscript of the paper was completed some related work of Esther Gal–Or came to my attention.

71

common price intercept of the demand functions. Firm i receives a signal s_i which provides an unbiased estimate of the intercept and formulates a conjecture about the behavior of its competitor which together with its beliefs about the joint distribution of the intercept and the other firm's signal given it has received s_i determines the expected profit of any action firm i may take. We assume there is a joint Normal distribution of the intercept and the signals which is common knowledge to te firms. Firms have constant and equal marginal costs and are risk neutral. In this context a Bayesian Nash equilibrium requires that firms maximize expected profit given their conjectures, and that the conjectures be right.

We suppose that there is an agency, a trade association for example, which collects market data on behalf of each firm. Firm i may allow part of its private information to be put in a common pool available to both firms. The signal a firm receives is the best estimate of the price intercept given its private information and the information in the common pool. If there is no sharing of information the error terms of the signals are independent. Pooling of information correlates them positively. A firm, when sharing market data is, at the same time, giving more information to its rival and increasing the correlation of the signals.

Since we are interested in self-enforcing pooling agreements we consider a two-stage game where first the firms, prior to the market data collection, instruct the agency how much of their private information to put in the common pool. At the second stage market research is conducted and the agency sends the signals to the firms which choose an action (quantity or price). Therefore at the second stage a Bayesian (Cournot or Bertrand) game is played. We show that the two-stage game has a unique subgame perfect equilibrium in dominant strategies at the first stage. With substitutes it involves no pooling of information in Cournot competition and complete pooling in Bertrand competition. With complements the result is reversed.

When the goods are substitutes, in Cournot competition it turns out that increases in the precision of the rival's information and increases in the correlation of the signals have adverse effects on the expected profit of the firm and we find that not to share any information is a dominant strategy. Consequently the unique subgame perfect equilibrium of the two-stage game involves no information sharing. On the other hand, in Bertrand competition the two factors mentioned above have positive effects on the expected profit of the firm and to put everything in the common pool is a dominant strategy. This is true even when a firm's information is much better than the one of its rival. When the goods are complements the situation is reversed. Since, in any case, expected profit of firm i increases with the precision of its own information, with substitutes and in Bertrand competition the firms always obtain an efficient outcome (in profit terms). This is not the case in Cournot competition, where complete pooling of information may dominate in terms of profits the no sharing arrangement if the goods are not very good substitutes and therefore the firms are in a Prisoner's Dilemma type situation since not to share any information is a dominant strategy for each firm.

Consider now a symmetric situation where firms start with the same amount of information, neglect the resource cost of information and restrict attention to the two extreme arrangements: complete pooling of information and no pooling at all. If the goods are substitutes, then in welfare terms the market outcome (the outcome of the two-stage game) is never optimal with respect to information sharing in Cournot competition since pooling always dominates no pooling in terms of expected total surplus. In Bertrand competition it may be optimal if the goods are close enough substitutes. Then pooling dominates no pooling. Otherwise no pooling is better. This contrasts with the complements case, where the market outcome is always optimal: in either Cournot or Bertrand competition it maximizes expected total surplus with respect to information sharing.

We confirm in our incomplete information setting that Bertrand competition is more efficient (in expected total surplus terms, for example) than Cournot competition although with substitute products profits may be larger in the Bertrand case if we look at the outcome of the two-stage game.

We find that the private value of information to firm i is always positive and larger or smaller in Cournot than in Bertrand competition according to whether the goods are substitutes or complements. On the other hand the social value of information is positive in Cournot and negative in Bertrand competition.

In Section 2 we survey very briefly some related literature. Section 3 describes the model without uncertainty and states some results for this case. Section 4 extends the duopoly model to an incomplete information context. Section 5 deals with the two-stage game. Section 6 examines the welfare consequences of the two extreme information sharing arrangements. Efficiency and the value of information, private and social, are considered in Section 7. Concluding remarks including extensions and policy implications of the analysis follow in the last section.

2. Relationships with the Literature

Leland, in his paper about a monopoly facing an uncertain demand, states that "Although under certainty the choice of behavioral mode by a monopolistic firm is unimportant we show that it critically conditions performance under uncertainty" (Leland, 8, p. 278|). This paper can be seen, in part, as an extension to a duopoly context with incomplete information of this statement.

Strategic transmission of information is dealt with in an abstract setting

74   XAVIER VIVES

by Crawford and Sobel [3]. The oligopoly literature on uncertain demand and incomplete information focuses on Cournot competition with homogenous product. This is the case of the work briefly surveyed below. They also assume that demand is linear with a random intercept. Normality is assumed in all of the papers considered except the first one.

Novshek and Sonnenschein [11] consider a duopoly model with constant costs and examine the incentives for the firms to acquire and release private information. Our modelling of the signals of the firms is based on theirs.

Basar and Ho [1] consider a duopoly model with quadratic cost functions. They show existence and uniqueness of affine equilibrium strategies and that, in equilibrium, expected profits of firm i increase with the precision of its information and decrease with the precision of the rival's information.

Clarke [2] considers an n-firm oligopoly model and shows that there is never a mutual incentive for all firms in the industry to share information unless they may cooperate on strategy once information has been shared.

Harris and Lewis [6] consider a duopoly model where firms in period one decide on plant capacity before market conditions are known. In period two they choose a level of production contingent on the state of demand and their plant size. They argue that observed differences in firm size and market share may be explained by producers having access to different information at the time of their investment decisions.

Gal–Or [5] considers an oligopoly model with two stages. At the first firms observe a private signal and decide whether to reveal it to other firms and how partial this revelation will be. At the second, they choose the level of output. She shows that no information sharing is the unique Nash equilibrium of the game both when private signals are completely uncorrelated and when they are perfectly correlated.

In our model Cournot competition with a homogenous product is a particular case. Our findings for this case are consistent with those of the authors who use the Normal model.

The demand structure (with no uncertainty) we consider is a symmetric version of a duopoly model proposed by Dixit [4] the duality and welfare properties of which are analyzed in Singh and Vives [13].

3. THE CERTAINTY MODEL

In our economy we have, on the production side, a monopolistic sector with two firms, each one producing a differentiated good, and a competitive numéraire sector, and, on the consumption side, a continuum of consumers of the same type with utility function linear and separable in the numéraire good. The representative consumer maximizes $U(q_1, q_2) - \sum_{i=1}^{2} p_i q_i$, where

$q_i \geqslant 0$, $i = 1, 2$, are the amounts of the goods and p_i, $i = 1, 2$, their prices. U is assumed to be quadratic, (strictly) concave and symmetric in q_1 and q_2. $U(q_1, q_2) = \alpha(q_1 + q_2) - \frac{1}{2}(\beta q_1^2 + 2\gamma q_1 q_2 + \beta q_2^2)$ with $\alpha > 0$, $\beta > |\gamma| \geqslant 0$. The goods are substitutes, independent, or complements according to whether $\gamma \gtrless 0$. When $\beta = \gamma$ the goods are perfect substitutes. When $\beta = -\gamma$, "perfect complements." γ/β goes from 1 to -1. Note that the maximization problem of the consumer may not have a solution in the perfect complements case. Inverse demands are given by

$$p_1 = \alpha - \beta q_1 - \gamma q_2 \qquad \text{in the region of quantity space}$$
$$p_2 = \alpha - \gamma q_1 - \beta q_2 \qquad \text{where prices are positive.}$$

Letting $a = \alpha/(\beta + \gamma)$, $b = \beta/(\beta^2 - \gamma^2)$, and $c = \gamma/(\beta^2 - \gamma^2)$,

$$q_1 = a - b p_1 + c p_2 \qquad \text{in the region of price space where}$$
$$q_2 = a + c p_1 - b p_2 \qquad \text{quantities are positive.}$$

Firms have constant and equal marginal costs. From now on suppose prices are net of marginal cost. The Cournot equilibrium is the Nash equilibrium in quantities and the Bertrand equilibrium the one in prices. Profits of firm i are given by $\pi_i = p_i q_i$. Notice that since π_i is symmetric in p_i and q_i and the demand structure is linear, Cournot (Bertrand) competition with substitute products is the perfect dual of Bertrand (Cournot) competition with complements and they share similar strategic properties. For example, in both cases reaction functions slope downwards (upwards). A useful corollary is that we only need to compute equilibria for one type of competition and the other follows by duality. In the Cournot case there is a unique equilibrium given by $q_i = \alpha/(2\beta + \gamma)$, $i = 1, 2$, and correspondingly a unique Bertrand equilibrium given by $p_i = a/(2b - c)$, $i = 1, 2$, which equals $\alpha(\beta - \gamma)/(2\beta - \gamma)$.

In this context total surplus (TS) is just equal to $U(q_1, q_2)$. For future reference we give the equilibrium values of profits π, consumer surplus (CS), and total surplus for both types of competition.

Note that if q is the Cournot output and p the Bertrand price then $\pi_i^C = \beta q^2$ and $\pi_i^B = b p^2$, $i = 1, 2$, so that the profit formulae are perfectly dual. This is not the case for the other formulae. For example, (see Table I) the dual of $(\beta + \gamma) \alpha^2/(2\beta + \gamma)^2$ would be $(b - c) a^2/(2b - c)^2$ which equals $(\beta - \gamma)^2 \alpha^2/(2\beta - \gamma)^2 (\beta + \gamma)$ and not $\beta^2 \alpha^2/(2\beta - \gamma)^2 (\beta + \gamma)$. This is because the CS and TS functions do not treat prices and quantities symmetrically.

Note that when the goods are perfect substitutes ($\beta = \gamma$) the Bertrand price and profits are zero and we have the efficient outcome (price equal marginal cost). When the goods are perfect complements the Cournot consumer surplus is zero and the Bertrand magnitudes are not defined since at the Bertrand prices the consumer demands infinite quantities.

TABLE I

	π_i	CS	TS
Cournot	$\dfrac{\beta}{(2\beta-\gamma)^2}\,\alpha^2$	$\dfrac{\beta+\gamma}{(2\beta+\gamma)^2}\,\alpha^2$	$\dfrac{3\beta+\gamma}{(2\beta+\gamma)^2}\,\alpha^2$
Bertrand	$\dfrac{b}{(2b-c)^2}\,\alpha^2$	$\dfrac{\beta^2}{(2\beta-\gamma)^2\,(\beta+\gamma)}\,\alpha^2$	$\dfrac{\beta(3\beta-2\gamma)}{(2\beta-\gamma)^2\,(\beta+\gamma)}\,\alpha^2$

The following proposition, the proof of which is in Singh and Vives [13], states that Bertrand competition is more efficient than Cournot competition. In all the propositions that follow we assume, unless otherwise stated, that $\beta > |\gamma|$, that is, we forget about the two extreme cases.

PROPOSITION 1. *Consumer surplus and total surplus are larger in Bertrand than in Cournot competition except when the goods are independent, in which case they are equal. Profits are larger, equal or smaller in Cournot than in Bertrand competition according to whether the goods are substitutes, independent or complements.*

The intuition behind the proposition is simple. Firms have less capacity to raise prices above marginal cost in Bertrand competition because the perceived elasticity of demand of a firm when taking as given the price of the rival is larger than that which the same firm perceives when taking the quantity of the rival as given. The result is that in Bertrand competition and in equilibrium firms quote lower prices than the Cournot ones. This is always good for consumers. For firms it is bad if the goods are substitutes since low prices mean low profits, if the goods are complements the situation is reversed, to increase profits firms have to lower prices to gain market.

4. THE UNCERTAINTY MODEL

Consider the model advanced in the last section but now with α, the demand intercept, being a random variable normally distributed with mean $\bar{\alpha}$ and variance $V(\alpha)$. Firm i receives a signal s_i which consists of α plus some noise ε_i, $s_i = \alpha + \varepsilon_i$, $i = 1, 2$. We assume that the error terms $(\varepsilon_1, \varepsilon_2)$ follow a bivariate normal distribution, independent of α, with zero means and covariance matrix $\begin{bmatrix} v_1 & \sigma_{12} \\ \sigma_{12} & v_2 \end{bmatrix}$, with $v_i \geqslant \sigma_{12} \geqslant 0$, $i = 1, 2$. All this is common knowledge to the firms. Given these assumptions, $E(\alpha|s_i) = (1 - t_i)\,\bar{\alpha} + t_i s_i$ and $E(s_j|s_i) = (1 - d_i)\,\bar{\alpha} + d_i s_i$, where $t_i = V(\alpha)/(V(\alpha) + v_i)$ and $d_i = (V(\alpha) + \sigma_{12})/(V(\alpha) + v_i)$, $i = 1, 2$, $i \neq j$. Note that $1 \geqslant d_i \geqslant t_i \geqslant 0$, so that both conditional expectations are convex combinations of $\bar{a}$ and the received signal s_i. We say that signal s gives more precise information about α than signal s' if its mean squared prediction error is smaller, i.e., if $E\{\alpha - E(\alpha|s)\}^2 < E\{\alpha - E(\alpha|s')\}^2$. This is equivalent to saying that the variance of the error term of signal s is smaller than the one for s'. Therefore as v_i ranges from 0 to ∞ the signal goes from being perfectly informative to being not informative at all and at the same time t_i ranges from 1 to 0. When the information is perfect, $E(\alpha|s_i) = s_i$, when there is no information, $E(\alpha|s_i) = \bar{a}$.

A strategy for a firm is a Borel measurable function that specifies an action, price or quantity, for each possible signal the firm may receive. Firms are assumed to be risk neutral. Each firm makes a conjecture about the opponent's strategy. A Bayesian Nash equilibrium[1] is then a pair of strategies and a pair of conjectures such that (a) each firm strategy is a best response to its conjecture about the behavior of the rival and (b) the conjectures are right.

Cournot Equilibrium

In the Cournot game, firms set quantities and a strategy for firm i specifies a quantity for each signal the firm may receive. We show that there is a unique equilibrium with linear (affine, to be precise) strategies.[2]

PROPOSITION 2.   *The unique Bayesian equilibrium of the Cournot game is* $(\sigma_1^*(\cdot), \sigma_2^*(\cdot))$, *where* $\sigma_i^*(s_i) = A + B_i t_i(s_i - \bar{a})$ *with* $A = \bar{a}/(2\beta + \gamma)$ *and* $B_i = (2\beta - \gamma d_j)/(4\beta^2 - \gamma^2 d_1 d_2)$, $i = 1, 2, j \neq i$.

Proof.   We first show that if firm 1 uses $\sigma_1^*(s_1) = A + B_1 t_1(s_1 - \bar{a})$ the unique best response for firm 2 is to use $A + B_2 t_2(s_2 - \bar{a})$. To see this notice that the expected profit of firm 2 choosing the quantity q_2 given the signal s_2 if firm 1 uses $\sigma_1^*(s_1)$ is

$$E(\alpha - \gamma\sigma_1^*(s_1) - \beta q_2 | s_2) q_2.$$

So the optimal choice for firm 2 is

$$q_2^* = \frac{1}{2\beta} E(\alpha - \gamma\sigma_1^*(s_1) | s_2) = \frac{1}{2\beta}(E(\alpha | s_2) - \gamma E(\sigma_1^*(s_1) | s_2))$$

which, after some computations, equals $A + B_2 t_2(s_2 - \bar{a})$.

---

[1] See Harsanyi [7].

[2] Note that given our normality, assumption α and the signals may take negative values. Firms are constrained to choose positive princes and quantites. For convenience we ignore this and, given the firm's strategies that we derive, we can get negative prices and outputs for certain combinations of α and the signals. The probability of such an event can be made arbitrarily small by appropriately choosing the variances of the model.

Uniqueness follows similarly as in Basar and Ho |1| or Clarke |2|, using
the fact that $\beta \geqslant |\gamma|$.   Q.E.D.

Remark 4.1.   Suppose $v_i = v$, $i = 1, 2$, when the firms have no information at all. For $v = \infty$, the equilibrium strategy is constant and equal to
$\bar{a}/(2\beta + \gamma)$, the Cournot outcome when there is no uncertainty. As the information the firms receive improves, i.e., as v declines and t goes towards one,
the slope of the linear strategy increases till it reaches $1/(2\beta + \gamma)$ when $t = 1$.
Then $\sigma_1^*(s_1) = s_1/(2\beta + \gamma)$, which is the full information outcome.

Remark 4.2.   The expected Cournot output always equals the Cournot
certainty output (with $\bar{a}$). Since $\sigma_i^*(s_i) = A + B_i t_i(s_i - \bar{a})$ and $Es_i = \bar{a}$,
$E(\sigma_i^*(s_i)) = A$, which equals $\bar{a}/(2\beta + \gamma)$. Note that when $s_i = \bar{a}$, $\sigma_i^*(s_i) = A$ so
that equilibrium strategies always go through the point $(s_i, q_i) = (\bar{a}, \bar{a}/(2\beta + \gamma))$.

We would like to know how expected profits in equilibrium are affected by
variations in the precision and correlation of the signals the firms receive.
Expected   profits   in   equilibria   are   easy   to   compute. $E(\pi_1 \mid s_1) =$
$E((\alpha - \gamma\sigma_2^*(s_2) - \beta\sigma_1^*(s_1)) \mid s_1)\sigma_1^*(s_1) = |E(\alpha - \gamma\sigma_2^*(s_2) \mid s_1) - \beta\sigma_1^*(s_1)|\sigma_1^*(s_1)$,
but $E(\alpha - \gamma\sigma_2^*(s_2) \mid s_1) = 2\beta\sigma_1^*(s_1)$ according to the first order conditions,
therefore $E(\pi_1 \mid s_1) = \beta(\sigma_1^*(s_1))^2$ and $E\pi_1 = \beta E(\sigma_1^*(s_1))^2$. Substituting in
$\sigma_1^*(s_1) = A + B_1 t_1(s_1 - \bar{a})$ we get $E\pi_1 = \beta(A^2 + B_1^2 t_1 V(\alpha))$. The slope of the
linear strategy $\sigma_1^*(s_1)$, $B_1 t_1$, is the channel through which changes in the
precision and correlation of the signals get transmitted to expected profits.

LEMMA 1.   *The slope of $\sigma_i^*(\cdot)$*

(a)   *increases with the precision of the information of firm i.*

(b)   *decreases, is unaffected, or increases with the precision of its
competitor's information and with the correlation of the signals according to
whether the goods are substitutes, independent or complements.*

Proof.   The slope in question is $B_1 t_1 = ((2\beta - \gamma d_2)/(4\beta^2 - \gamma^2 d_1 d_2)) t_1$.
Noting that $d_i = t_i(1 + (\sigma_{12}/V(\alpha)))$ and $t_i = V(\alpha)/(V(\alpha) + v_i)$, $i = 1, 2$, and
using the fact that $d_i \leqslant 1$, $i = 1, 2$, we get by inspection that $B_1 t_1$ decreases
with v_1 and,   upon   differentiating,   that   sign $\partial B_1 t_1/\partial v_2 =$ sign $-\gamma =$
sign $\partial B_1 t_1/\partial\sigma_{12}$.   Q.E.D.

The intuition behind (a) is clear. As firm 1 gets better information it trusts
more the signal received and responds more to divergences of s_i and $\bar{a}$ (see
Remark 1). This is independent of the nature of the products. To understand
(b) note that the covariance between the signals is $V(\alpha) + \sigma_{12}$, which is
always positive and increasing in σ_{12} since $\sigma_{12} \geqslant 0$. Suppose the goods are
substitutes. If firm 1 observes a high signal, $s_1 > \bar{a}$ (recall that the signals are

positively correlated), this means that probably firm 2 has observed a high signal too. Now, firm 2, according to (a), will produce less if v_2 is high than if it is low. The optimal thing to do for firm 1 is to produce a high output since in Cournot competition with substitutes if you expect the competitor to produce low you want to produce high. Therefore $\partial B_1 t_1/\partial v_2 > 0$ in this case. To evaluate the impact of an increased correlation in the signals we can reason similarly. If firm 1 observes a high signal, $s_1 > \bar{a}$, it will produce less if σ_{12} is high than if it is low since in the former case the probability that the competitor has received a high signal too is larger and if firm 1 expects a high output of the competitor it has an incentive to reduce its own output. Therefore $\partial B_1 t_1/\partial \sigma_{12} < 0$.

We are now ready to state

PROPOSITION 3. *In equilibrium, the expected profit of firm i*

(a) *increases with the precision of its own information,*

(b) *decreases, is unaffected, or increases with the precision of the competitor's information and with the correlation of the signals according to whether the goods are substitutes, independent or complements.*

Proof. Recall that $E\pi_1 = \beta(A^2 + B_1^2 t_1 V(\alpha))$, then

(a) B_1 and t_1 decrease with v_1.

(b) Sign $\partial E\pi_1/\partial v_2 = $ sign $\partial B_1/\partial v_2 = $ sign γ according to Lemma 1.

(c) Sign $\partial E\pi_1/\partial \sigma_{12} = $ sign $\partial B_1/\partial \sigma_{12} = $ sign $-\gamma$ according to Lemma 1.

($\gamma > 0$ for substitutes and $\gamma < 0$ for complements.) Q.E.D.

Bertrand Equilibrium

In the Bertrand game firms set prices and a strategy for firm i specifies a price for each signal the firm may receive. The duality argument gives us the Bertrand equilibrium strategies. Identifying α with a, β with b, γ with $-c$, and s_i with $\hat{s}_i$, where $\hat{s}_i = s_i/(\beta + \gamma)$, we get

PROPOSITION 2a. *The unique Bayesian equilibrium of the Bertrand game is* $(\tau_1^*(\cdot), \tau_2^*(\cdot))$, *where* $\tau_i^*(\hat{s}_i) = \hat{A} + \hat{B}_i t_i(\hat{s}_i - \bar{a})$ *with* $\hat{A} = \bar{a}/(2b - c)$ *and* $\hat{B}_i = (2b + cd_j)/(4b^2 - c^2 d_1 d_2)$, $i = 1, 2, j \neq i$.

Remarks similar to Remark 1 and 2 apply to the Bertrand case and Lemma 1 and Proposition 2 hold replacing $\sigma_i^*(\cdot)$ by $\tau_i^*(\cdot)$ and exchanging substitutes for complements.

5. The Two-Stage Game

In Section 4 we assumed firms received signals satisfying certain properties. We provide now, along the lines of Novshek and Sonnenschein, a rationale for these signals.

Suppose firm i starts with an n_i independent observation sample $(r_{i1},...,r_{in_i})$ satisfying $r_{ik} = \alpha + u_{ik}$, where the u_{ik}'s are i.i.d. normal with mean zero and variance σ_u^2 and independent of α. Firm i decides to put $\lambda_i n_i$, $0 \leqslant \lambda_i \leqslant 1$, observations in a common pool. The signal firm 1 receives, s_1, is then the best (minimum variance unbiased) estimate of α based on $n_1 + \lambda_2 n_2$ observations, its own sample plus the observations put in the common pool by firm 2. This is just the average, $s_1 = \alpha + (1/(n_1 + \lambda_2 n_2))(\sum_{k=1}^{n_1} u_{1k} + \sum_k^{\lambda_2 n_2} u_{2k})$. With this information structure the error terms of the signals $(\varepsilon_1, \varepsilon_2)$ follow a bivariate normal distribution with zero means and covariance matrix $\left| \begin{smallmatrix} v_1 & \sigma_{12} \\ \sigma_{12} & v_2 \end{smallmatrix} \right|$, where $v_i = \sigma_u^2/(n_i + \lambda_j n_j)$, $i = 1, 2, j \neq i$ and $\sigma_{12} = ((\lambda_1 n_1 + \lambda_2 n_2)/(n_1 + \lambda_2 n_2)(n_2 + \lambda_1 n_1)) \sigma_u^2$. Note that $v_i \geqslant \sigma_{12} \geqslant 0$, $i = 1, 2$. λ_i is, thus, the proportion of observations firm i puts in the common pool. $\lambda_i \in \Lambda_i$, where $\Lambda_i = \{0, 1/n_i,..., (n_i - 1)/n_i, 1\}$, $i = 1, 2$. When $\lambda_1 = \lambda_2 = 0$ there is no pooling of information, $v_i = \sigma_u^2/n_i$, $i = 1, 2$, and $\sigma_{12} = 0$. When $\lambda_1 = \lambda_2 = 1$ there is complete pooling and $v_i = \sigma_{12} = \sigma_u^2/(n_1 + n_2)$, $i = 1, 2$. Information sharing has two effects: it decreases the variance of the error terms and it increases their correlation (and therefore the correlation of the signals).

LEMMA 2.   (a) v_i *decreases with* λ_j, $j \neq i$, *and is independent of* λ_i.

(b) σ_{12} *increases with* λ_i *if* $\lambda_j < 1$, $i = 1, 2, j \neq i$.

Otherwise is independent of λ_i.

Proof.   (a)   By inspection.

(b) $\sigma_{12} = ((\lambda_1 n_1 + \lambda_2 n_2)/(n_1 + \lambda_2 n_2)(n_2 + \lambda_1 n_1)) \sigma_u^2$. Differentiating with respect to λ, one gets $\partial \sigma_{12}/\partial \lambda_1 = ((1 - \lambda_2 n_1 n_2/(n_1 + \lambda_2 n_2)(n_2 + \lambda_1 n_1)^2) \sigma_u^2$. (In fact, λ_i is discrete but this does not matter here.)   Q.E.D.

Consider now a two-stage game where first firms decide how much information are they going to put in the common pool. We suppose there is an agency, a trade association, for example, that collects an $n_1 + n_2$ observation sample and that forms the signals according to the instructions of the firms, the λ_i's. At the first stage, then, firm i picks independently $\lambda_i \in \Lambda_i$ and communicates it to the agency. At the second stage, firms, knowing the selected pair (λ_1, λ_2), play the Bayesian (Cournot or Bertrand) game. For each pair (λ_1, λ_2) we have a well-defined (proper) subgame. We are interested in subgame perfect Nash equilibria of the two-stage game, where equilibrium strategies form a (Bayesian) Nash equilibrium in every subgame (see Selten [12]).

LEMMA 3. *In Cournot competition with substitutes (or Bertrand with complements) expected profits of firm i decrease with λ_i. In Bertrand competition with substitutes (or Cournot with complements) expected profits of firm i increase with λ_i and with λ_j, $j \neq i$. If the goods are independent $E\pi_i$ are increasing with λ_j and unaffected by λ_i, $j \neq i$, $i = 1, 2$.*

Proof. Consider the Cournot case. Increases in λ_i give better information to firm j, $j \neq i$, and increase (maybe weakly) the correlation of the firm's signals. If the goods are substitutes, according to Proposition 3, both effects decrease $E\pi_i$. If the goods are complements both effects increase $E\pi_i$. Increases in λ_j, $j \neq i$, give better information to firm i and increase (maybe weakly) the correlation of the firm's signals. If the goods are complements both effects increase $E\pi_i$. Note that if they are substitutes the second decreases $E\pi_i$ so that nothing can be said a priori except if $\lambda_i = 1$. Then the covariance of the signals cannot be increased and the first effect dominates. The Bertrand case, as usual, follows by the duality argument.   Q.E.D.

According to Lemma 3 in Cournot competition with substitutes to set $\lambda_i = 0$ is a dominant strategy for firm i since $E\pi_i$ decreases with λ_i whatever the value of λ_j, $j \neq i$. Symmetrically, in Bertrand competition to put all the information in the common pool is a dominant strategy for firm i. If the goods are independent $E\pi_i$ is unaffected by λ_i, $i = 1, 2$. Therefore we have established the following proposition.

PROPOSITION 4. *Suppose the goods are not independent. Then the two-stage game has a unique subgame perfect equilibrium in dominant strategies at the first stage. With substitutes it involves no pooling of information in Cournot competition and complete pooling in Bertrand competition. With complements the result is reversed.*

Remark 5.1. If the goods are independent any pair (λ_1, λ_2), $\lambda_i \in \Lambda_i$, $i = 1, 2$, is an equilibrium.

Remark 5.2. If the goods are perfect substitutes Proposition 4 holds for Cournot competition since in this case Lemma 3 holds as well. In Bertrand competition prices and expected profits are zero independently of the pooling decisions of the firms. Any pair (λ_1, λ_2) is an equilibrium in this case.

Remarks 5.3. Note that in Bertrand competition with substitute products to pool information is a dominant strategy for firm i even if the firm has much better information than its competitor, i.e., even if n_i is much larger than n_j, $j \neq i$.

TABLE II

Equilibrium Strategies for Firm i

	NP	P
C	$\dfrac{\bar{a}}{2\beta + \gamma} + \dfrac{t}{2\beta + \gamma t}(s_i - \bar{a})$	$\dfrac{1}{2\beta + \gamma}(\bar{a} + \tilde{t}(s_i - \bar{a}))$
B	$\dfrac{\bar{a}}{2b - c} + \dfrac{t}{2b - ct}(\hat{s}_i - \bar{a})$	$\dfrac{1}{2b - c}(\bar{a} + \tilde{t}(\hat{s}_i - \bar{a}))$

Remark 5.4. Suppose the goods are substitutes. Note that given that at the second stage a Bayesian Bertrand equilibrium is reached the firms obtain an efficient outcome by completely pooling their information since $E\pi_i$ is increasing in λ_i and λ_j, $j \neq i$, $i = 1, 2$, in this situation. When the second stage is Cournot the firms, by choosing noncooperatively not to share any information, may not reach an efficient outcome. If the products are not very good substitutes complete pooling may dominate, in profits terms, the no pooling arrangement.

The following proposition compares the profits for the firms under the two extreme information sharing situations when each firm has a sample of size n. (For the rest of the paper we are going to restrict attention to these cases.) Let $v = \sigma_u^2/n$, $t = V(\alpha)/(V(\alpha) + v)$ and $\tilde{t} = V(\alpha)/(V(\alpha) + v/2)$. When no information is pooled $v_j = v$, $i = 1, 2$, and $\sigma_{12} = 0$ so that $t_i = d_i = t$, $i = 1, 2$. With complete pooling, $v_i = \sigma_{12} = v/2$, $i = 1, 2$, so that $d_i = 1$ and $t_i = \tilde{t}$, $i = 1, 2$.

First, we give expressions for equilibrium strategies and expected profits of the four possible combinations of Cournot C, or Bertrand B; pooling P, or not pooling NP. Using Proposition 2 and the expressions for expected profits we get Tables II and III.

TABLE III

Equilibrium Expected Profits for Firm i

	NP	P
C	$\beta\left(\dfrac{\bar{a}^2}{(2\beta + \gamma)^2} + \dfrac{t}{(2\beta + \gamma t)^2}V(\alpha)\right)$	$\dfrac{\beta}{(2\beta + \gamma)^2}(\bar{a}^2 + \tilde{t}V(\alpha))$
B	$b\left(\dfrac{\bar{a}^2}{(2b - c)^2} + \dfrac{t}{(2b - ct)^2}V(\alpha)\right)$	$\dfrac{b}{(2b - c)^2}(\bar{a}^2 + \tilde{t}V(\alpha))$

DUOPOLY INFORMATION EQUILIBRIUM　　　83

Let $E\pi_i^P$ and $E\pi_i^{NP}$ denote, respectively, expected profits of firm i with complete pooling and with no pooling of information.

PROPOSITION 5.　*Let $v > 0$, then, in equilibrium,*

(a)　*in Bertrand competition with substitute products (or in Cournot with complements), $E\pi_i^P > E\pi_i^{NP}$, $i = 1, 2$;*

(b)　*in Cournot competition with substitutes (or in Bertrand with complements), letting $\mu = \gamma/\beta$,*

(i)　*If $|\mu| \geqslant 2(\sqrt{2} - 1)$ then $E\pi_i^{NP} > E\pi_i^P$, $i = 1, 2$.*

(ii)　*If $2(\sqrt{2} - 1) > |\mu| > \frac{2}{3}$ then $E\pi_i^P \gtreqless E\pi_i^{NP}$ iff*

$$\frac{v}{V(\alpha)} \gtreqless \frac{4 - 4\mu - 3\mu^2}{\mu^2 + 4\mu - 4}, \qquad i = 1, 2.$$

(iii)　*If $|\mu| \leqslant \frac{2}{3}$ then $E\pi_i^P > E\pi_i^{NP}$, $i = 1, 2$.*

(See Fig. 1.)

Remark 5.5.　When the goods are perfect substittes the proposition applies for the Cournot case. In the Bertrand case $E\pi_i$ are zero with pooling or no pooling.

Proof.　(a)　Follows from Lemma 3.

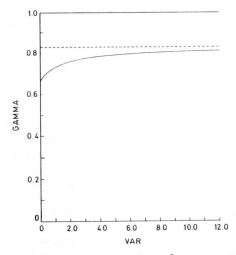

FIG. 1.　Cournot with substitutes. Expected profits. $E\pi_i^P$ greater (smaller) than $E\pi_i^{NP}$ below (above) the continuous line, (GAMMA $\equiv \gamma/\beta$, VAR $\equiv v/V(\alpha)$).

(b) We only have to compare $t/(2\beta + \gamma t)^2$ with $\tilde{t}/(2\beta + \gamma)^2$ in the Cournot case and $t/(2b - ct)^2$ with $\tilde{t}/(2b - c)^2$ in the Bertrand case. The second follows from the first, noting that c is negative for complements and $\gamma/\beta = c/b$. After some computations, in the Cournot case, we have that $E\pi_i^{NP} \gtreqless E\pi_i^P$ iff $3\mu^2 + 4\mu - 4 \gtreqless (v/V(\alpha))(4 - 4\mu - \mu^2)$. The values $\frac{2}{3}$ and $2(\sqrt{2} - 1)$ are, respectively, the unique roots in the $|0, 1|$ interval of the LHS and RHS. For $\mu < \frac{2}{3}$ the LHS is negative and the RHS positive. For $2(\sqrt{2} - 1) > \mu > \frac{2}{3}$ both are positive. For $\mu > 2(\sqrt{2} - 1)$ the LHS is positive and the RHS negative.   Q.E.D.

The proposition has an easy intuitive explanation. Complete pooling of information cuts the variance of the error terms of the signals the firms receive by half and correlates perfectly the strategies of the firms. In Cournot competition with substitutes the second effect is bad for expected profits, the first, the joint decrease in variance, it is easily seen to be good by differentiating $E\pi_i$ with respect to v.

Which effect dominates depends on the degree of product differentiation. If the goods are close substitutes, i.e., γ/β is close to one, the correlation effect is going to prevail since it is weighted precisely by γ/β and conversely if the goods are not good substitutes. There is also an intermediate region where it pays to pool information if the precision of the firm's information is poor enough. Note that if the goods are perfect substitutes, $\beta = \gamma = 1$, it never pays to share information. (See Fig. 1.) In view of Proposition 5 we see that when the goods are not very good substitutes, in Cournot competition, the firms face a Prisoner's Dilemma type situation since not to pool any information is a dominant strategy for each firm but by sharing information the firms would increase their profits.

6. WELFARE

We analyze the welfare consequences, in terms of expected consumer surplus ECS and expected total surplus ETS of two extreme situations, no sharing and complete sharing of information, when the firms have the same information to start with. Tables IV and V give the equilibrum values of ECS and ETS in the four possible cases we are considering. Note that the Cournot and Bertrand expressions are not "dual." To compute them note that the expected value of any equilibrium strategy is equal to the equilibrium strategy when $\bar{a}$ is known to obtain with certainty (see Remark 4.1). All the expressions decompose into two parts: one analogous to the certainty expression with $\bar{a}$ (see Section 3) and another obtained by taking deviations from the mean $\bar{a}$.

TABLE IV

Expected Consumer Surplus

	NP	P
C	$\dfrac{\beta + \gamma}{(2\beta + \gamma)^2} \bar{a}^2 + \dfrac{\beta + \gamma t}{(2\beta + \gamma t)^2} t V(a)$	$\dfrac{\beta + \gamma}{(2\beta + \gamma)^2} (\bar{a}^2 + \bar{t} V(a))$
B	$\dfrac{\beta^2}{(2\beta - \gamma)^2 (\beta + \gamma)} \bar{a}^2 + \dfrac{\beta[\beta(4 - 3t) - \gamma t(1 - t)]}{(2\beta - \gamma t)^2 (\beta + \gamma)} V(a)$	$\dfrac{\beta^2 \bar{a}^2 + [(2\beta - \gamma)^2 - (\beta - \gamma)(3\beta - \gamma) \bar{t}] V(a)}{(2\beta - \gamma)^2 (\beta + \gamma)}$

TABLE V

Expected Total Surplus

	NP	P
C	$\dfrac{3\beta + \gamma}{(2\beta + \gamma)^2} \bar{a}^2 + \dfrac{3\beta + \gamma t}{(2\beta + \gamma t)^2} t V(a)$	$\dfrac{3\beta + \gamma}{(2\beta + \gamma)^2} (\bar{a}^2 + \bar{t} V(a))$
B	$\dfrac{\beta(3\beta - 2\gamma)}{(2\beta - \gamma)^2 (\beta + \gamma)} \bar{a}^2 + \dfrac{\beta[\beta(4 - t) - t(3 - t)]}{(2\beta + \gamma t)^2 (\beta + \gamma)} V(a)$	$\dfrac{\beta(3\beta - 2\gamma) \bar{a}^2 + [(2\beta - \gamma)^2 - (\beta - \gamma)^2 \bar{t}] V(a)}{(2\beta - \gamma)^2 (\beta + \gamma)}$

Before making any welfare comparisons we will see how variations in the precision of the firm's information have very different welfare effects in Cournot or Bertrand competition. Note that we consider here exogenous variations in v, i.e., variations induced not by information sharing decisions but by changes in the size of the sample firms receive (equal by assumption for both firms) or by changes in σ_u^2.

PROPOSITION 6.   *If firms pool their information, ECS and ETS increase (decrease) with the precision of the information in Cournot (Bertrand) competition. If firms do not pool their information the same holds except when $(|\gamma|/\beta) t$ is greater (or equal) than $\frac{2}{3}$, then with complements ECS^C decreases (weakly), and with substitutes ETS^B increases (weakly), with the precision of the information.*

Proof.   In obvious notation, ECS$_P^C$ and ETS$_P^C$ increase and ECS$_P^B$ and ETS$_P^B$ decrease with $\bar{t}$ by inspection of the formulae in Tables IV and V. On the other hand, differentiating we get

$$\text{Sign}\left\{\frac{\partial ECS_{NP}^C}{\partial t}\right\} = \text{Sign}\{2\beta + 3\gamma t\}$$

which is positive if $\dfrac{\gamma}{\beta} t > -\dfrac{2}{3}$ and nonnegative otherwise.

$$\text{Sign}\left\{\frac{\partial ECS_{NP}^B}{\partial t}\right\} = \text{Sign}\{-(\beta - \gamma)(6\beta - \gamma t)\}$$

which is negative always.

$$\text{Sing}\left\{\frac{\partial ETS_{NP}^C}{\partial t}\right\} = \text{Sign}\{6\beta + \gamma t\}$$

which is positive always.

$$\text{Sign}\left\{\frac{\partial ETS_{NP}^B}{\partial t}\right\} = \text{Sign}\{(\beta - \gamma)(3\gamma t - 2\beta)\}$$

which is negative if $\dfrac{\gamma}{\beta} t < \dfrac{2}{3}$ and nonnegative otherwise.

Q.E.D.

Remark 6.1.   If the goods are perfect substitutes the proposition applies for the Cournot case. In the Bertrand case ECS and ETS, which are equal since $E\pi_i$ are zero, are not affected by the precision of the firm's information. This is clear since firms set prices equal to marginal cost anyway.

PROPOSITION 7. *Let* $\mu = \gamma/\beta$ *and* $\bar{\mu}$ *be the unique root of* $\mu^3 + \mu^2 - 8\mu + 4$ *in the interval* $|0, 1|$ $(\bar{\mu} \approx 0.56)$.

In Cournot competition, pooling dominates no pooling in terms of ECS *and* ETS *except maybe when the goods are complements. In that case:*

(a) *If* $|\mu| \geqslant 2(\sqrt{2} - 1)$, *then* $\text{ECS}_{\text{NP}} > \text{ECS}_{\text{P}}$.

(b) *If* $2(\sqrt{2} - 1) > |\mu| \geqslant \bar{\mu}$ *then* $\text{ECS}_{\text{NP}} \gtrless \text{ECS}_{\text{P}}$ *iff*

$$\frac{v}{V(\alpha)} \lesseqgtr \frac{4 + 8\mu + \mu^2 - \mu^3}{\mu^2 - 4\mu - 4}.$$

(See Fig. 2.)

In Bertrand competition, no pooling dominates pooling in terms of ECS *and* ETS *except maybe when the goods are substitutes. In that case:*

(a) *If* $\mu \geqslant 2(\sqrt{2} - 1)$ *then* $\text{ETS}_{\text{P}} > \text{ETS}_{\text{NP}}$.

(b) *If* $2(\sqrt{2} - 1) > \mu \geqslant \bar{\mu}$, *then* $\text{ETS}_{\text{P}} \gtrless \text{ETS}_{\text{NP}}$ *iff*

$$\frac{v}{V(\alpha)} \lesseqgtr \frac{4 - 12\mu + 9\mu^2 - \mu^4}{8\mu - 3\mu^2 - \mu^3 - 4}.$$

(See Fig. 3.)

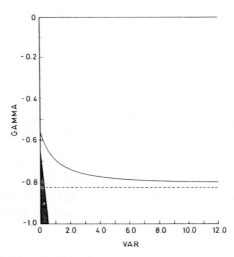

FIG. 2. Cournot with complements. Expected consumer surplus. In the interior of the shaded region $\partial \text{ECS}^{\text{NP}}/\partial t > 0$. ECS^{P} greater (smaller) than ECS^{NP} above (below) the continuous line. (GAMMA $\equiv \gamma/\beta$, VAR $\equiv v/V(\alpha)$.)

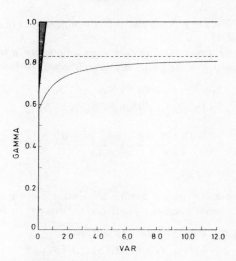

FIG. 3. Bertrand with substitutes. Expected total surplus. In the interior of the shaded region $\partial ETS^{NP}/\partial t > 0$. ETS^P greater (smaller) than ETS^{NP} above (below) the continuous line. (GAMMA $\equiv \gamma/\beta$, VAR $\equiv v/V(\alpha)$).

Proof. Let $f_2(\mu) = 4 - 12\mu + 9\mu^2 - \mu^4$ and $f_1(\mu) = 4 - 8\mu + \mu^2 + \mu^3$. Note that $f_2(\mu) = (1 - \mu)f_1(\mu)$. It is easily seen that $\bar{\mu}$ is the unique root of f_1 in $|0, 1|$ ($\bar{\mu} \approx 0.56$), so that $f_2(\bar{\mu}) = 0$. Also the unique root of $4 + 8\mu + \mu^2 - \mu^3$ in $|-1, 0|$ is $-\bar{\mu}$ since this function is equal to $f_1(-\mu)$. Let $g_2(\mu) = 8\mu - 3\mu^2 - \mu^3 - 4$ and $g_1(\mu) = \mu^2 + 4\mu - 4$. Note that $g_2(\mu) = (1 - \mu) g_1(\mu)$. The unique root of g_1 in $|0, 1|$ is $2(\sqrt{2} - 1)$ (which is 0.83 approximately), therefore $2(\sqrt{2} - 1)$ is also a root of g_2. Now, using the formulae in Tables IV and V and after some computations we obtain,

(i) $ECS_P^C \gtreqless ECS_{NP}^C$ iff $f_1(-\mu) \gtreqless (v/V(\alpha)) g_1(-\mu)$. For $\mu \geqslant -\bar{\mu}$ the LHS is nonnegative and the RHS negative. For $-\bar{\mu} > \mu > 2(1 - \sqrt{2})$ both are negative. For $\mu \leqslant 2(1 - \sqrt{2})$ the LHS is negative and the RHS is nonnegative.

(ii) $ETS_P^C \gtreqless ETS_{NP}^C$ iff $12 - 5\mu^2 - \mu^3 \gtreqless (v/V(\alpha))(3\mu^2 + 4\mu - 12)$. The LHS is always positive and the RHS is always negative. (Recall $|\mu| < 1$.)

(iii) $ECS_{NP}^B \gtreqless ECS_P^B$ iff $(12 + 3\mu^3 - 8\mu - 7\mu^2)(v/V(\alpha)) \gtreqless \mu^4 + 5\mu^2 + 12\mu - 6\mu^3 - 12$. The LHS is always positive and the RHS always negative. (Recall $|\mu| < 1$.)

(iv) $ETS_P^B \gtreqless ETS_{NP}^B$ iff $g_2(\mu)(v/V(\alpha)) \gtreqless f_2(\mu)$. For $\mu \leqslant \bar{\mu}$, the LHS is negative and the RHS nonnegative. For $\bar{\mu} < \mu < 2(\sqrt{2} - 1)$ both are negative. Otherwise the LHS is nonnegative and the RHS negative. (Note that $ECS_{NP}^B = ECS_P^B$ and $ETS_{NP}^B = ETS_P^B$ when $\mu = 1$.)   Q.E.D.

Remark 6.2. The proposition applies when the goods are perfect substitutes ($\mu = 1$) if Cournot competition prevails. In Bertrand competition pooling makes no difference in ECS or ETS. Prices equal marginal cost and consumers get the maximum surplus they can get in either case.

Remark 6.3. The exceptions in Proposition 6 and 7 are when we consider ECS^C or ETS^B. In Cournot competition, welfare, in terms of ECS or ETS, increases with the precision of information and is greater with pooling of information with the possible exception of ECS when the goods are strong complements. In Bertrand competition, welfare decreases with the precision of information and is greater with no information sharing except possibly in terms of ETS when the products are good substitutes. (See Figs. 2 and 3.)

To keep things simple and in the spirit of the welfare comparisons we are making suppose that firms can only choose to share completely or not share at all the information they own, i.e. they instruct the testing agency $\lambda_i \in \{0, 1\}$, $i = 1, 2$. We would like to compare in welfare terms the outcome of the two-stage game, the market outcome, with the outcome an authority or planner could induce either by not allowing the agency to form or by requiring that all information be disclosed, thus enforcing no pooling or complete pooling of information respectively. The objective of the planner would be to maximize ETS. We say an outcome is optimal (with respect to information sharing) if it gives at least as much ETS as the planner can obtain.

PROPOSITION 8. *If the goods are complements the market outcome is always optimal. If the goods are substitutes, in Cournot competition the market outcome is never optimal, in Bertrand competition it is optimal if the goods are close to perfect substitutes or if they are moderately substitutes and the precision of the information is low.*

Proof. For complements. In Cournot competition the market outcome involves pooling, $\lambda_i = 1$, $i = 1, 2$, and $ETS_{NP}^C < ETS_P^C$ from Proposition 7. In Bertrand, we have $ETS_{NP}^B > ETS_P^B$ and the market outcome involves no pooling, $\lambda_i = 0$, $i = 1, 2$.

For substitutes. In Cournot competition the market outcome is NP, but $ETS_{NP}^C < ETS_P^C$. In Bertrand competition the market outcome is P and $ETS_P^B > ETS_{NP}^B$ under (a) and (b) of Proposition 7.   Q.E.D.

Remark 6.4. If the goods are independent there are four equilibria in the two-stage game and therefore four possible market outcomes. Discarding the nonsymmetric ones, we will have that one of the remaining is going to be optimal in each type of competition. (The pooling one in Cournot and the no pooling one in Bertrand.)

Remark 6.5. If the goods are perfect substitutes Proposition 8 holds. In Bertrand competition any pooling arrangement is self-enforcing (i.e., it can be a market outcome) and optimal since in that case ETS is constant over arrangements.

7. Efficiency and the Value of Information

In this section we extend Proposition 1 to the incomplete information case, confirming thus that "Bertrand competition is more efficient than Cournot competition," and we compare the private and social value of information under the two types of competition.

PROPOSITION 9. *In welfare terms, either ECS or ETS, Bertrand is strictly better than Cournot. Furthermore, $E\pi_i^C \gtreqless E\pi_i^B$ according to whether the goods are substitutes, independent or complements. This holds comparing either the no pooling subgames or the complete pooling ones.*

Proof. First note that it is sufficient to show it when $\bar{a} = 0$. If $\bar{a} > 0$, then all the expressions have "certainty" terms (with $\bar{a}$) which we can rank according to the certainty proposition. Let then $\bar{a} = 0$. Using Tables III–V with $\bar{a} = 0$, the relevant inequalities follow noting that $|\gamma|/\beta$, t, and $\tilde{t}$ are between zero and one.   Q.E.D.

Remark 7.1. Notice that when the goods are independent and we have two monopolies expected profits are equal with price and quantity setting but, contrary to the certainty case, ECS qnd ETS are larger with price setting. Thus under uncertainty and incomplete information consumers and society have another reason to prefer price over quantity setting apart from the traditional one that firms have less monopoly power under Bertrand competition.

Remark 7.2. Bertrand competition is more efficient than Cournot competition (in terms of ETS even if we look at the outcomes of the two-stage game. Take the substitutes case. With Cournot the market outcome involves no pooling and with Bertrand, pooling. From Propositions 7 and 9 we know that $ETS_P^B > ETS_P^C > ETS_{NP}^C$, so that $ETS_P^B > ETS_{NP}^C$. It may happen though that Bertrand profits be larger than the Cournot ones. From Table III we get $E\pi_{NP}^C = \beta((\bar{a}^2/(2\beta + \gamma)^2) + (t/(2\beta + \gamma t)^2) V(\alpha))$ and $E\pi_P^B = (b/(2b - c)^2)(\bar{a}^2 + \tilde{t}V(a))$. We know that the "certainty" term (involving $\bar{a}$ or $\bar{a}$) will be larger in the Cournot case, but not very much if the products are very differentiated (γ small). The other term may be larger in the Bertrand case, and make up the difference, if the information of the firms is not very precise ($v/V(\alpha)$ not close to zero), and if there is enough basic uncertainty

DUOPOLY INFORMATION EQUILIBRIUM   91

TABLE VI

Private Value of Information to Firm i

	P	NP
C	$\dfrac{\beta}{(2\beta + \gamma t)^2} \, t V(\alpha)$	$\dfrac{\beta}{(2\beta + \gamma)^2} \, (\bar{t} - t) \, V(\alpha)$
B	$\dfrac{b}{(2b - ct)^2} \, t V(\alpha)$	$\dfrac{b}{(2b - c)^2} \, (\bar{t} - t) \, V(a)$

$(V(\alpha)$ not too small relative to $\bar{a}$). For example, if $\gamma = 0.1$, $\bar{a} = 10$, $V(\alpha) = v = 1$, then $E\pi_P^B > E\pi_{NP}^C$. Similarly, if the goods are complements one sees immediately that $\text{ETS}_{NP}^B > \text{ETS}_P^C$ but it may be the case that $E\pi_P^C > E\pi_{NP}^B$ for the same type of parameter configurations as above.

The Value of Information

Recall we are considering symmetric situations where both firms receive an n-sample. We define the private value of information to firm i, PVI as the difference in expected profits between receiving the n-sample and getting no information at all (the other firm gets an n-sample in either case). As before let $v = \sigma_u^2/n$ and $t = V(\alpha)/(V(\alpha) + v)$. When $n_1 = 0$ and $n_2 = n$, with no pooling $v_1 = \infty$, $v_2 = v$, and $\sigma_{12} = 0$ so that $d_1 = t_1 = 0$ and $d_2 = t_2 = t$; with pooling $v_i = \sigma_{12} = v$, $i = 1, 2$, so that $d_i = 1$, $t_i = t$, $i = 1, 2$. Now, recalling that the formulae for the Cournot expected profits is $\beta(A^2 + B_i^2 t_i V(\alpha))$ where $A = \bar{a}/(2\beta + \gamma)$ and $B_i = (2\beta - \gamma d_j)/(4\beta^2 - \gamma^2 d_1 d_2)$, $j \neq i$, and using the formulae in Table III we can get the PVI in the Cournot case. The Bertrand case follows by duality. Table VI gives the results.

We define the social value of information (SVI) as the difference in ETS between the firms receiving signals of the same finite variance v and the firms receiving no information at all. Using the formulae in Table V and noting that when t or $\bar{t}$ equal zero, ETS^C is just the Cournot certainty expression (with $\bar{a}$) while ETS^B is the Bertrand certainty expression plus $V(\alpha)/(\beta + \gamma)$, one gets Table VII.

TABLE VII

Social Value of Information

	NP	P
C	$\dfrac{3\beta + \gamma t}{(2\beta + \gamma t)^2} \, t V(\alpha)$	$\dfrac{3\beta + \gamma}{(2\beta + \gamma)^2} \, \bar{t} V(\alpha)$
B	$-\dfrac{(\beta - \gamma t)(\beta - \gamma)}{(2\beta - \gamma t)^2 \, (\beta + \gamma)} \, t V(\alpha)$	$-\dfrac{(\beta - \gamma)^2}{(2\beta - \gamma)^2 \, (\beta + \gamma)} \, \bar{t} V(\alpha)$

PROPOSITION 10. *The social value of informtion is positive in Cournot and negative in Bertrand competition. The private value of information to the firms is always positive and larger or smaller in Cournot than in Bertrand competition according to whether the goods are substitutes or complements. This holds comparing either the no pooling subgames or the pooling ones and also in the two-stage game where the information sharing decision is endogenous.*

Proof. From the proof of Proposition 9 it follows that $(\beta/(2\beta + \gamma t)^2) V(\alpha) \gtreqless (b/(2b - ct)^2) V(a)$ if and only if $\gamma \gtreqless 0$ and $(\beta/(2\beta + \gamma)^2) V(\alpha) \gtreqless (b/(2b - c)^2) V(a)$ if and only if $\gamma \gtreqless 0$, so that from Table VI we get that $PVC^C \gtreqless PVI^B$ if and only if $\gamma \gtreqless 0$ with either pooling or not pooling of information. Now, with substitutes $PVI_{NP}^C > PVI_P^C$ since $1/(2\beta + \gamma t)^2 > 1/(2\beta + \gamma)^2$ and $t > \bar{t} - t$ and therefore $PVI_{NP}^C > PVI_P^B$. With complements we get similarly that $PVI_{NP}^B > PVI_P^C$. The inequalities for the SVI follow by inspection of Table VII. Q.E.D.

Remark 7.3. When the goods are perfect substitutes the private and social value of information is zero in Bertrand competition since prices equal marginal cost independently of the information received.

6. CONCLUDING REMARKS: EXTENSIONS AND POLICY IMPLICATIONS

Extensions

We have considered a symmetric duopoly model. In principle there should be no difficulty in relaxing the symmetry assumption (and deal with a nonsymmetric model as in Singh and Vives |13|) or the duopoly assumption and deal with more than two firms. Computations would be very cumbersome, particularly when trying to relax both at the same time.

Note that the Cournot model can be reconsidered to accommodate the case where firms are uncertain about their common marginal costs and receive signals giving information about them. We could imagine a situation where firms have a common technology with only one variable input, oil, for example, the price of which is uncertain. The variable cost of producing one unit of output m is a constant times the price of oil. Letting $\hat{a} = a - m$ we can use our model with $\hat{a}$. The signals in this example could come from an energy forecasting agency. For the Bertrand case new computations need to be made.[3]

[3] A situation where two firms are bidding for a government contract can be thought as a Bertrand model. If the firms have the same (unknown) costs we are in the *common value* case of the auction literature. The incentives to gather and share information in this context (see |9, 10|) contrast sharply with the results we have obtained in the paper for Bertrand competition with substitutes. I am grateful to an anonymous referee for pointing this out.

Finally, a word about the Normality assumption. We use it for analytical convenience although in our context it would be more natural to use a distribution with compact support. In fact the property we need to get linear (affine) equilibrium strategies is that conditional expectations be linear (affine). The Normal is the most common distribution with this property. Note that if $E(\alpha \mid s_i) = T + ts_i$, for some constants T and t, and $Es_i = \bar{\alpha}$ then necessarily $T = (1 - t)\bar{\alpha}$ since $E\{E(\alpha \mid s_i)\} = \bar{\alpha}$ so that $\bar{\alpha} = T + t\bar{\alpha}$.

Policy Implications

We have seen that the market outcomes and optimal outcomes (with respect to information sharing) depend crucially on the type of competition, the nature of the goods and the degree of product differentation. This has immediate policy implications regarding information sharing. If the goods are complements the best policy is no intervention since the market outcome is already optimal. If the goods are substitutes and Cournot competition prevails, public policy should encourage information sharing. (It could do that by requiring, e.g., trade associations or testing agencies to disclose all information to the firms.) If Bertrand competition prevails and the goods are close substitutes no intervention is needed. If they are poor substitutes pooling of information should be avoided (no trade association allowed to form). In the intermediate region where the goods are moderately good substitutes if the precision of the firms' information is good enough no intervention is required, otherwise the authority should discourage the sharing of market data. Note that in this case the authority has no incentive to improve the precision of the firms' information (by subsidizing information acquisition, e.g.) since expected total surplus is decreasing with the precision of information.

We see therefore that policy prescriptions, or inferences of firm behavior, based on the Cournot model with homogenous product could be misleading when out of context. For example, if the goods are substitutes observing the firms pool information in Cournot competition is not evidence that they are setting quantities collusively if the goods are not very good substitutes. In this case pooling of information increases expected profits and although a pooling agreement is not self-enforcing in our two-stage game it could be in a repeated situation. Firms would be colluding then in their market research but not in setting outputs.

REFERENCES

1. T. BASAR AND V. C. HO, Informational properties of the Nash solutions of two stochastic nonzero-sum games, *J. Econom. Theory* **7** (1976), 370–387.
2. R. CLARKE, "Collusion and the Incentives for Information Sharing," working paper No. 8233, University of Wisconsin–Madison, 1983.

94   XAVIER VIVES

3. V. Crawford and J. Sobel, Strategic information transmission, *Econometrica* **50** (1982), 1431–1451.

4. A. K. Dixit, A model of duopoly suggesting a theory of entry barriers, *Bell J. Econom.* **10** (1979), 20–32.

5. E. Gal.–Or, "Information Sharing in Oligopoly," University of Pittsburgh, working paper, 1982.

6. R. Harris and T. Lewis, "Strategic Commitment under Uncertainty with Private Information," California Institute of Technology, working paper, 1982.

7. J. Harsanyi, Games with incomplete information played by Bayesian players, I, *Management Sci.* **14** (1967–78), 159–182; II, 320–334; III, 486–502.

8. H. Leland, Theory of the firm facing uncertain demand, *Amer. Econom. Rev.* **62** (1972), 278–291.

9. P. Milgrom and R. Weber, A theory of auctions and competitive bidding, *Econometrica* **50** (1982), 1089–1122.

10. P. Milgrom and R. Weber, The value of information in a sealed bid auction, *J. Math. Econom.* **10** (1982), 105–114.

11. W. Novshek and H. Sonnenschein, Fulfilled expectations Cournot duopoly with information acquisition and release, *Bell J. Econom.* **13** (1982), 214–218.

12. R. Selten, Re-examination of the perfectness concept for equilibrium points of extensive games, *Internat. J. Game Theory* **5** (1975), 25–55.

13. N. Singh and X. Vives, "Price and Quantity Competition in a Differentiated Duopoly," Discussion paper, No. 154, C.S.O.I., University of Pennsylvania, 1983.

Part V
General Equilibrium with Imperfect Competition

Econometrica, Vol. 41, No. 3 (May, 1973)

OLIGOPOLY IN MARKETS WITH A CONTINUUM OF TRADERS[1]

BY BENYAMIN SHITOVITZ[2]

It was suggested in [2] that an appropriate model for an oligopolistic economy is one in which the set of traders consists of some large traders and a continuum of small traders. The cores of such market models are analyzed here.

Some of the results are as follows: A duopolistic market in which the duopolists are of the same type is "perfectly competitive," i.e., its core coincides with the set of competitive allocations. At any allocation in the core of any oligopolistic markets, the value of the bundle received by a small trader does not exceed the value of his initial bundle; that is, small traders can never "gain money." Conditions are given under which small traders will not "lose money" either. In addition to the case of duopoly, other conditions are given under which an oligopolistic market will be perfectly competitive.

1. INTRODUCTION

RECENTLY, A NUMBER of authors [2, 4, 16, 18, 21, 22, 36] have considered market models with a continuum of traders. Such a model embodies the idea that the economy under consideration has a "very large" number of participants, and that the influence of each individual participant is "negligible;" this is precisely the notion of "perfect competition" which is prevalent in the treatment of economic equilibrium. However, in many real markets, such as monopolistic or more generally oligopolistic markets, the competition is far from being perfect; such markets are probably better represented by a mixed model, in which some of the traders are "small", i.e., individually insignificant, whereas others are "large," i.e., individually significant (compare [2, 12, 16, 25, 28, 34]).[3] The main purpose of this paper is to analyze such markets. In particular, we are interested in the following questions: To what extent can the large traders "exploit" the small ones, and how much can the small traders gain from possible competition between the large traders?

Two basic concepts that describe possible "outcomes" of the exchange process in a market are the core and the competitive allocations (allocations corresponding to competitive equilibria).

For markets with a continuum of small traders, Aumann proved in [2] the equivalence of the core and the set of competitive allocations. This theorem, which we shall call the "Equivalence Theorem," is the mathematical embodiment of the idea that such markets are competitive. Our efforts will be directed at seeing to what extent the equivalence theorem can be extended to markets in which at least some of the traders are "large." We shall restrict ourselves to pure exchange

---

[1] This paper is a part of the author's Ph.D. thesis prepared at the Hebrew University under the direction of Professor R. J. Aumann.

[2] I am very grateful to Professor R. J. Aumann for his helpful advise and his kind encouragement; I am also indebted to Professor D. Schmeidler whose suggestion led to a very considerable shortening of the proof of the theorems. I would also like to acknowledge G. Debreu, W. Hildenbrand, J. J. Gabszewicz, M. Maschler, B. Peleg, R. Selten, M. Yaari, and S. Zamir for valuable conversations.

[3] These lines are "borrowed" almost verbatim from [2, pp. 39 and 41].

468   BENYAMIN SHITOVITZ

economics (i.e., markets), though our results are true for general productive economics. We plan to publish this extension in a subsequent paper.

Mathematically, we shall represent the set of traders by a measure space in which the small traders form a non-atomic part and in which the large traders are atoms. Our main mathematical tools are separation theorems and Lyapunov's theorem [17, 23] on the range of a vector measure. We also use the concept of the integral of a set-valued function [3, 8], but very little of the theory of such integrals is needed.

The mathematical model is presented in Section 2, and the results are stated in Section 3. In Section 4 we give a verbal description of our results, and discuss them and their economic interpretation. Section 5 is devoted to the proof of Theorem A, and in Section 6 we give the proofs of Theorems B, C, and D. In Section 7 we present some examples and open problems. In Section 8, we review the literature on the subject and compare the present work with that of other authors. Section 9 is devoted to some concluding remarks.

If the reader prefers, he may skip at once to Section 4, as little or no use will be made of the more mathematical parts of our paper in the verbal treatment given in that section.

2. THE MATHEMATICAL MODEL

We shall be working in a Euclidean space R^n; the dimension n of the space represents the number of different commodities being traded in the market. Superscripts will be used exclusively to denote coordinates. Following standard practice, for x and y in R^n we write $x > y$ to mean $x^i > y^i$ for all i; we use $x \geqq y$ to mean $x^i \geqq y^i$ for all i; and we use $x \geq y$ to mean $x \geqq y$ but not $x = y$. The integral of a vector function is to be taken as the vector of integrals of the components. The scalar product $\Sigma_{i=1}^n x^i y^i$ of two members x and y in R^n is denoted $x \cdot y$. The symbol 0 denotes the origin in R^n as well as the real number zero; no confusion will result. The symbol $\setminus$ will be used for set-theoretic subtraction, whereas $-$ will be reserved for ordinary algebraic subtraction. The ith unit vector e_i is the vector in R^n whose ith coordinate is 1 and whose other coordinates vanish. We use $e = \Sigma_{i=1}^n e_i$ to denote the vector in R^n all of whose coordinates are 1.

Let $(T, \mathscr{B}, \mu)$ be a measure space of economic agents, i.e., T denotes a set (the traders), $\mathscr{B}$ denotes a σ-field of subsets of T (the family of coalitions), and μ denotes a totally finite complete positive σ-additive measure on $\mathscr{B}$. (Intuitively, the number $\mu(C)/\mu(T)$ represents the fraction of the totality of traders belonging to the coalition C.)

An atom of the measure space $(T, \mathscr{B}, \mu)$ is a coalition S with $\mu(S) > 0$ such that for each coalition $R \subseteq S$ we have either $\mu(R) = 0$ or $\mu(S \setminus R) = 0$. Let $S_1, S_2, \ldots$ be an enumeration[4] of all atoms. We say that $T_1 = \cup S_k$ is the set of the atoms whereas $T_0 = T \setminus T_1$ is the atomless part of T.

A *commodity bundle* x is a point in the nonnegative orthant Ω of R^n. An *assignment* (of commodity bundles to traders) is an integrable function x from T to Ω.

---

[4] The enumerability of the atoms follows from the fact that $\mu(T) < \infty$.

All integrals are with respect to the variable t (which stands for trader), and in most cases the range of integration is all of T. In an integral we will therefore omit the symbol $d\mu(t)$ and the indication of the dependence of the integrand on t, and will specifically indicate the range of integration only when it differs from all of T. Thus $\int x$ means $\int_T x(t)\,d\mu(t)$. A *null* set of traders is a set of measure 0. A statement asserted for "almost all" traders, or "almost each" trader, or "almost each" trader in a certain set, is to be understood to hold for all such traders except possibly for a null set of traders.

There is a fixed initial assignment[5] i. We assume

(2.1) $$\int i = 0.$$

This asserts that no commodity is totally absent from the market.

For each trader t a relation $\succ_t$ is defined on Ω, which is called the *preference relation* of trader t and satisfies the following conditions:

(2.2)   *Desirability (of the commodities)*: $x \geqslant y$ implies $x \succ_t y$.

(2.3)   *Continuity (in the commodities)*: For each $y \in \Omega$, the sets $\{x : x \succ_t y\}$ and $\{x : y \succ_t x\}$ are open (relative to Ω).

(2.4)   *Measurability*: If x and y are assignments, then the set $\{t : x(t) \succ_t y(t)\}$ is measurable in T.

(2.5)   *Convexity assumption on the large traders*: For each trader t belonging to an atom, the preference relation $\succ_t$ is convex, i.e., for each $y \in \Omega$, the set $\{x : x \succ_t y\}$ is convex.

Note specifically that $\succ_t$ is not assumed to be complete, nor even transitive. In some parts of the paper, we shall use the following assumption:

(2.6)   *Quasi-order assumption on the large traders*: For each trader t belonging to an atom, the preference relation $\succ_t$ is derived from a preference-or-indifference relation $\succsim_t$ on Ω, which is assumed to be a quasi-order, i.e., a reflexive, transitive and complete binary relation.

From $\succsim_t$ we derive relations $\succ_t$ and $\sim_t$ called preference and indifference, respectively, as follows:

$$x \succ_t y \quad \text{if} \quad x \succsim_t y \quad \text{but not} \quad y \succsim_t x,$$
$$x \sim_t y \quad \text{if} \quad x \succsim_t y \quad \text{and} \quad y \succsim_t x.$$

Note that together with the assumption that $\succsim_t$ is a quasi-order, the continuity assumption yields the existence of a continuous utility function $u_t(x)$ on Ω for each fixed large trader t (see [9]).

---

[5] The precise intuitive meaning of $i(t)$ will be discussed in Section 4.

An *allocation* (or "final assignment" or "trade") is an assignment x for which $\int x = \int i$. An assignment y *dominates* an allocation x *via* a coalition S (S is then said to *block* x) if $y(t) \succ_t x(t)$ for almost each $t \in S$, and S is effective for y, i.e., $\int_S y = \int_S i$. The *core* is the set of all allocations that are not blocked by any[6] non-null coalition.

A *price vector* p is an n-tuple of nonnegative real numbers, not all of which vanish. A *competitive equilibrium* (c.e.) is a pair (p, x) consisting of a price vector p and an allocation x, such that for almost all traders t, $x(t)$ is maximal with respect to $\succ_t$ in t's *budget set* $B_p(t) = \{x : p \cdot x \leqslant p \cdot i(t)\}$. A *competitive allocation* x is an allocation for which there exists a price vector p such that (p, x) is a competitive equilibrium.

An *efficiency equilibrium*[7] (e.e.) is a pair (p, x) consisting of a price vector p and an allocation x, such that for almost all traders t, $x(t)$ is maximal with respect to $\succ_t$ in t's *efficiency budget set* $B_p^*(t) = \{x : p \cdot x \leqslant p \cdot x(t)\}$. Note that every c.e. is an e.e., but not every e.e. is necessarily a c.e.

A price vector p is called an *efficiency price* with respect to an allocation x if (p, x) is an efficiency equilibrium.

3. STATEMENT OF THE THEOREMS

THEOREM A: *Assume* (2.1)–(2.5). *Let x be an allocation in the core. Then there exists a price vector p such that*: (i) (p, x) *is an efficiency equilibrium; and* (ii) $p \cdot i(t) \geqslant p \cdot x(t)$ *for almost all traders t in the atomless part T_0 of T.*

For the following, we shall assume all assumptions (2.1)–(2.6).

Two traders s and t are said to be of the same *type* if $i(t) = i(s)$ and for all $x, y \in \Omega$, $x \succ_t y$ if and only if $x \succ_s y$.

THEOREM B: *Assume that there are at least two large traders, and that all large traders are of the same type. Then the core coincides with the set of competitive allocations.*

Two large traders are said to be of the same *kind* if they are of the same type and have the same measure. Thus every market may be represented as $(T_0; A_1, A_2, \ldots)$, where T_0 is the atomless part of T, and $A_1, A_2, \ldots$ is a partition of the set of all atoms such that two atoms belong to the same A_k if and only if they are of the same kind. For $k = 1, 2, \ldots$, denote the number of atoms in A_k by $|A_k|$ (note that $|A_k| < \infty$).

THEOREM C: *Given a market $(T_0; A_1, A_2, \ldots)$, let m be the greatest common divisor (g.c.d.) of $|A_k|$, $k = 1, 2, \ldots$. If $m \geqslant 2$ and if x is an allocation in the core of the market, then there exists a price vector p such that*: (i) (p, x) *is an efficiency equilibrium*; (ii) $p \cdot i(t) = p \cdot x(t)$ *for almost all traders t in the atomless part T_0 of T; and* (iii) $p \cdot x(t) = p \cdot x(s)$ *for all large traders s and t of the same kind.*

---

[6] Note that allocations which are blocked by the set of all traders T are called Pareto optimal allocations (see Section 3).

[7] A "valuation equilibrium" in the terminology of Debreu [7].

Let W be an atom in a market M. The *split atom* W^* is a continuum of small traders such that $\mu(W) = \mu(W^*)$, and every trader $t \in W^*$ is of the same type as W. The market obtained from M after splitting a set ω of atoms will be denoted by M_ω.

THEOREM D: *Let M and M^* be two markets, and let m and m^* be the corresponding g.c.d.'s defined in Theorem C. If $m \geqq 2$ and $m^* \geqq 2$, and if $M^* = M_\omega$ where ω contains atoms of all kinds in M except possibly one kind, then in M^* the core coincides with the set of the competitive allocations.*

4. DISCUSSION OF THE THEOREMS

We begin our discussion with the concept of efficiency equilibrium. An *allocation* is a redistribution of the initial resources among the traders. A pair (p, x) consisting of a price system p and an allocation x is an *efficiency equilibrium* if, given the prices p, no trader t can improve his situation (i.e., get a bundle that he prefers to $x(t)$) by selling $x(t)$ and, with the proceeds, buying something else; in other words, $x(t)$ is the best that t can buy with the value of $x(t)$. It is this notion which gives meaning to the word "price;" surely, if a price system p can at all be associated with an allocation x, then (p, x) must be an efficiency equilibrium.

A *competitive equilibrium* is a special kind of efficiency equilibrium. Here we demand that $x(t)$ be not only the best that t can buy with the value of $x(t)$, but also the best that he can buy with the value of his initial bundle $i(t)$. If (p, x) is an efficiency equilibrium that is not competitive, a trader t may either regret having acquired $x(t)$ (Figure 1a), or he may have somehow acquired a bundle that he prefers to anything that he could have purchased with the value of $i(t)$ (Figure 1b). Nevertheless, the current situation, characterized by the allocation x and the prices p, may be said to be in equilibrium.

The concept of efficiency equilibrium appears in the literature under a number of different names.[8] We have used this particular name because the efficient allocations are the same as the Pareto optimal allocations. This is a classical theorem of welfare economics in the finite case under convexity of preferences [1, 9]; in the case of markets with a continuum of traders, it has been established by Hildenbrand [19].

Between the core and the competitive equilibrium there is a relationship that is more or less analogous to that between the Pareto optimum and the efficiency equilibrium: In markets consisting of a continuum of "small" traders and no "large" traders, the core coincides with the set of all competitive allocations. This is the "Equivalence Theorem" to which we referred in the introduction; unlike the theorem connecting efficiency equilibria and Pareto optima, this theorem does not hold for markets with finitely many traders. Our aim in this paper is to investigate under what conditions and to what extent this theorem continues to hold when some of the traders may be large. Our use of the term "large trader"[9]

---

[8] See footnote 7 in Section 2.

[9] A notion that is very similar to the notion of "giant" in [12].

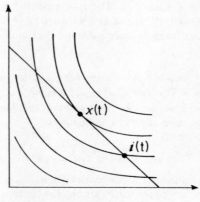

Competitive equilibrium

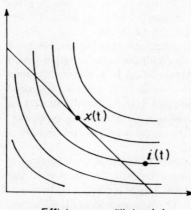

Efficiency equilibrium (a)

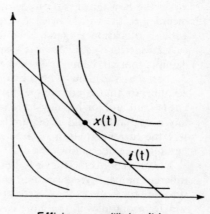

Efficiency equilibrium (b)

FIGURE 1

is very general; by it we simply mean a trader whose initial resources are large compared with the entire market. There is no implication that the large traders have any oligopolistic power in advance or have a "corner" on some good or goods, although, of course, this possibility is not excluded. Thus we are exclusively interested here in the effect of size and structure on the competitive properties of a market. Specifically, our results can be applied to investigate the effect of mergers on a market, i.e., what will happen when a set of traders combines to form a single "trader" (a single bargaining unit), or when a number of sets of traders combine (compare [12, 16]).

Among our theorems, perhaps the one with the most immediate intuitive appeal is Theorem B. This says that in a market in which there are at least two large traders, and all the large traders are of the same "type,"[10] all core allocations are competitive. Thus such a market is essentially indistinguishable from a perfectly competitive market; if all the large traders were to split into a continuum of small traders (of the same "type" as the original large traders), there would be essentially no change in the core. In this case, therefore, the presence of several large traders engenders such intense competition among them that the effect of the large traders' size is nullified.

To avoid misunderstandings, let us now say a word about the notion of "type." Two traders are of the same "kind" if they have the same initial bundle and the same preferences. If they are of the same kind they are also of the same type, but the notion of type is more general. For example, if we have three traders of the same kind, and two of them combine and form a single trader (i.e., a single bargaining unit), then the resulting two traders are of the same type, but not of the same kind. More generally, if we take any set of traders who are all of the same kind, divide them into two sets, and then let each of these two sets combine and form a single trader, we obtain two traders of the same type. This could serve as a definition of "type," if we admit the case in which the original set of traders was a continuum of small traders.[11]

Note that the preferences of two traders of the same type are in general *different*, unless the traders are also of the same kind.[12] It is probably best to think of traders of the same type as corporations of different size whose shareholders are of the same kind. Clearly the managers of these corporations, when acting for the corporations, will in general have different preferences; for example, the managers of a large and a small automobile company are not in the market for the same amount of steel. Also, the initial bundles of two traders of the same type are different, although they have the same direction (i.e., each is a scalar multiple of the other).

We now turn to Theorem A. Suppose x is an allocation in the core. Then it is in particular Pareto optimal, and so we may associate with it prices p so that (p, x) is an efficiency equilibrium. Let us now consider the value, under the prices p, of the bundle that is assigned by x to a trader t. If for all t this value is equal to the value of t's initial bundle, then (p, x) is a competitive equilibrium. This is, of course, not in general the case. What Theorem A says is that the efficiency price p can be chosen so that when t is a small trader, the value of this bundle is less than or

---

[10] This term will be explained in the sequel.

[11] This is necessary to cover the case in which the measures of the two traders have an irrational ratio.

[12] If x is an allocation, then $x(t)$ is *not* the bundle that is assigned to t, but the "bundle density." The actual bundle that is assigned to t is, in the case of a large trader, $x(t)\mu(\{t\})$. In Section 2 (and throughout the paper), preferences are formally defined on bundle densities, not on actual bundles. Since traders of the same type may have different measures, it follows that though the preferences of traders of the same type are the same on bundle densities, they will be different on bundles.

equal to the value of the initial bundle. In terms of value, therefore, the small traders lose, or at best they come out even. The large traders, of course, take up the slack; as a group, their profit is exactly equal to the sum of the losses of the small traders. About an individual large trader we can, however, say nothing; he may either lose or gain.

In brief, Theorem A says that "in general," it is advantageous in terms of value to be a large trader. Theorem B then says that the intense competition generated under the particular conditions of that theorem nullifies the advantage of the large traders.

Theorem A may be illustrated by a used car market: If an individual sells his car to a used car dealer, then in general the money he receives will not be sufficient to buy his car back.

Note that the equivalence theorem is a special case of Theorem A. If all traders are small, then there are no large traders, so in particular the total profit of the large traders is 0. This means that the total loss of the small traders is 0, and since none of the small traders can gain, each one loses nothing. Thus the value of the bundle assigned by x to each trader is equal to the value of his initial bundle, and so we have a competitive equilibrium (compare [2, 10, 11, 13, 18, 21, 22, 27, 36, and 37]).

Next, we discuss Theorem C. Let us call two groups of large traders *congruent* if there is a one-to-one correspondence between the two sets such that corresponding large traders are of the same kind. Theorem C says that if the large traders can be divided into two or more congruent groups, then the small traders do not lose, i.e., for each x in the core there are prices p such that (p, x) is an efficiency equilibrium and the value of each small trader's final bundle is equal to that of his initial bundle.

Incidentally, if we consider any *one* of the congruent groups, then the value of its *total* final bundle equals the value of its initial bundle. In particular, if each such group contains only one trader, then the value of each trader's final bundle equals that of his initial bundle, and so we have a competitive equilibrium; i.e., the equivalence theorem holds, as indeed we know from Theorem B. In general, though, each of the congruent groups contains more than one kind of traders; though the value of the total final bundle of such a group equals that of the initial bundle, this need not be true for the individual traders in the group, and so we will not in general get a competitive equilibrium. Specifically, in Theorem C, some of the large traders may lose, while others may gain.

For an example, suppose there are two types of large traders. Of the first type, there are two large traders of measure 1 each, and of the second type, there are three large traders, two of measure 1 and one of measure 2. Such a market does not obey the conditions of Theorem C, so that for all we know, the small traders may actually lose vis-a-vis the value of their initial bundle. But now, if in the second type, *either* the two traders of measure 1 consolidate, *or* the trader of measure 2 splits into two traders of measure 1, then Theorem C applies, so that the small traders can no longer lose.

Finally, we turn to Theorem D. Suppose we have a market satisfying the conditions of Theorem C, and that we take some of the large traders and "split" each of them into a continuum of small traders. Then we may conclude that the resulting market is competitive *if* the following two conditions are satisfied: First, large traders of all kinds, except possibly one kind, have been split; and second, the resulting market still satisfies the conditions of Theorem C.

To illustrate Theorem D, suppose that in the original market, the number of large traders of each kind is a multiple of 4. Then, if of each kind, except the first, we split exactly half the large traders into continua, the resulting market will be competitive.

Economically, Theorem D might be interpreted as pointing the way for a central agency, such as a government, that wishes to engage in "trust-busting," i.e., that wishes to modify a given economic structure in order to make it competitive. Theorem D shows that this can sometimes be done by splitting some of the large firms into "continua." It would not, however, always be necessary to do this; in some industries (such as retail businesses of various kinds), there are already large as well as small firms in the market, and a relatively minor adjustment in the market, possibly even including some mergers, might serve to turn a market that is not competitive into one that is competitive.

On a more mathematical level, Theorem D is useful in that it gives additional conditions under which the equivalence theorem holds; though the hypotheses of Theorem D sound a little special, it is, however, difficult to relax them, as we shall see by various examples in Section 7.

5. PROOF OF THEOREM A

Throughout this section we will assume, without loss of generality, that $\mu(T) = 1$.

In the following let $F, G, H, \ldots$ denote functions defined on T whose values are subsets of R^n, while $f, g, h, \ldots$ denote functions defined on T whose values are points in R^n.

For any set-valued function F define:

$$\mathcal{L}_F = \{f : f \text{ is integrable and } f(t) \in F(t) \quad \text{for almost all } t\}$$

and

$$\int F = \left\{ \int f : f \in \mathcal{L}_F \right\}.$$

According to Lyapunov's theorem [17, 23] the range of a non-atomic vector measure is convex. A result of Lyapunov's theorem is a theorem due to Richter (see [3, 8, 26]) which states that the integral of a set-valued function over a non-atomic measure space is convex. In this paper we shall use the following generalization of Richter's result to a general measure space (with atoms).

THEOREM 1: *Let F be a set-valued function such that $F(t)$ is convex for all traders t belonging to an atom. Then $\int F$ is convex.*

476   BENYAMIN SHITOVITZ

PROOF: Let T_1 be the set of all atoms and $T_0 = T \setminus T_1$ be the atomless part of T. Then $\int F = \int_{T_0} F_0 + \int_{T_1} F_1$, where F_0 and F_1 are the restrictions of the function F to T_0 and T_1 respectively. The integral $\int_{T_0} F_0$ is a convex set by Richter's theorem, whereas $\int_{T_1} F_1$ is convex by a direct application of our assumption. Hence $\int F$, as the sum of two convex sets, is convex.

The following set-valued function plays an important role in the analysis of markets. For a given assignment x, define

(5.1) $G(t) = \{x - x(t) : x \succ_t x(t)\}$.

This set-valued function G has some useful properties which we state in the following lemmas. Let us call an allocation x *individually rational* (i.r.) if $i(t) \nsucc_t x(t)$ for almost all traders t.

LEMMA 1: *Let x be an i.r. allocation, and let $0 \neq p \in R^n$. Then (p, x) is an efficiency equilibrium if and only if $p \cdot G(t) \geqq 0$ for almost all traders t.*[13]

PROOF: See Appendix A.

LEMMA 2: *For a given i.r. allocation x, let F be a set-valued function such that $G(t) \subseteq F(t)$ for almost all traders t. If p $(0 \neq p \in R^n)$ is such that $p \cdot \int F \geqq 0$, then (i) (p, x) is an efficiency equilibrium, and (ii) $p \cdot f(t) \geqq 0$ for all $f \in \mathscr{L}_F$ and almost all $t \in T$.*[14]

PROOF: See Appendix B.

COROLLARY 1 (Hildenbrand): *An i.r. allocation x is Pareto optimal if and only if there exists a price vector p such that (p, x) is an efficiency equilibrium.*

PROOF: Let x be i.r. Assume first that x is Pareto optimal. Then $\int G$ is convex (Theorem 1), and $0 \notin \int G$ by definition of Pareto optimality. Therefore, by the supporting hyperplane theorem, there exists a p $(0 \neq p \in R^n)$ such that $p \cdot \int G \geqq 0$. Hence, (p, x) is an efficiency equilibrium (Lemma 2). The converse direction is standard and is omitted. This completes the proof of the corollary.

The idea behind the proof of Theorem A is quite simple. Let x be an allocation in the core (the "final" allocation), let p be efficiency prices for x, and suppose that some small traders get positive profits at the prices p, i.e., for these traders, $p \cdot (x(t) - i(t)) > 0$. This means that their excess $x(t) - i(t)$ has positive value at the "market prices." Denote by S the set of all such small traders, and by $\int_S (x - i)$ their *aggregate* excess. Then for each small positive number ε we can find a subset εS of S such that the aggregate excess $\int_{\varepsilon S} (x - i)$ of εS is exactly equal to $\varepsilon \int_S (x - i)$. For this it is necessary to use Lyapunov's theorem, according to which the range

---

[13] For $p \in R^n$ and $G \subseteq R^n$, we write $p \cdot G \geqq 0$ $(p \cdot G > 0)$ to mean $p \cdot g \geqq 0$ $(p \cdot g > 0)$ for each $g \in G$.
[14] The exceptional set may, however, depend on f.

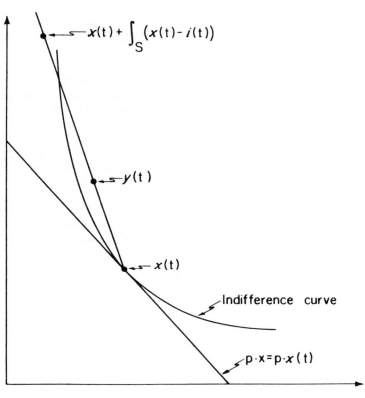

$$-s-x(t) + \int_S (x(t) - i(t))$$

$$-s-y(t)$$

$$-s-x(t)$$

Indifference curve

$$-s-p \cdot x = p \cdot x(t)$$

FIGURE 2

of a non-atomic vector measure is convex; intuitively, if we think of the traders in S as divided into types, what we must do is to take a proportion ε of each of the types. Now take εS and distribute its aggregate excess among the remaining traders $T \setminus \varepsilon S$. Then if ε is sufficiently small, the new allocation y obtained in this way will give the traders t in $T \setminus \varepsilon S$ a bundle $y(t)$ which is preferred to $x(t)$. On the other hand, the traders in $T \setminus \varepsilon S$ can guarantee y, since indeed their total bundle under y exactly equals their total bundle under i (this follows from the fact that x is an allocation). But then we have a contradiction to the fact that x is in the core (see Figure 2).

Note that it is essential in the above argument for ε to be small; therefore, the argument will not work for large traders, and they may get a positive as well as a negative profit.

We remark that though in this description of the proof of Theorem A, we started out with efficiency prices p, the proof itself does not proceed exactly in this way; rather, it constructs the prices p and at the same time shows that they have the asserted properties. The key to this procedure, one might say, is the definition of the set-valued function F (see (5.2)).

Now, in order to prove Theorem A, it will be more convenient to formulate the following modified version of Theorem A, and prove this version before the original one.

THEOREM A*: *Assume* (2.1)–(2.5). *Let x be an individually rational allocation. Then x is not blocked by any non-null coalition that contains all large traders if and only if there exists a price vector p such that* (i) (p, x) *is an efficiency equilibrium, and* (ii) $p \cdot i(t) \geqslant p \cdot x(t)$ *for almost all traders t in the atomless part T_0 of T.*

Since every allocation in the core is in particular an individually rational allocation and is not blocked by any non-null coalition at all, Theorem A follows from Theorem A*.

PROOF OF THEOREM A*: First, we demonstrate the "if" part. Let (p, x) be an e.e. such that $p \cdot i(t) \geqslant p \cdot x(t)$ for almost all $t \in T_0$. Suppose, contrary to the theorem, that x is dominated by an assignment y via a non-null coalition S which contains all large traders. Define

$$z = y\chi_S + i\chi_{S^*}$$

where $S^* = T \setminus S$.

By definition of e.e. we have

$$p \cdot z(t) = p \cdot y(t) > p \cdot x(t) \quad \text{for almost all} \qquad t \in S.$$

By our assumption (since $S^* \subseteq T_0$), we have

$$p \cdot z(t) = p \cdot i(t) \geqslant p \cdot x(t) \quad \text{for almost all} \qquad t \in S^*.$$

Therefore, since $\mu(S) > 0$ we have

$$p \cdot \int z = \int p \cdot z > \int p \cdot x = p \cdot \int x$$

and this contradicts

$$\int z = \int_S y + \int_{S^*} i = \int_S i + \int_{S^*} i = \int i = \int x.$$

Conversely, let x be an i.r. allocation that is not blocked by any non-null coalition which contains all large traders. Define

$$(5.2) \qquad F(t) = \begin{cases} G(t) & \text{for} \quad t \in T_1, \\ G(t) \cup \{i(t) - x(t)\} & \text{for} \quad t \in T_0. \end{cases}$$

LEMMA 3: 0 is not an interior point of $\int F$.

PROOF: We consider two cases.

(i) $\mu(T_1) > 0$. In this case $0 \notin \int F$. For suppose $0 \in \int F$, then $0 = \int f$ where $f \in \mathscr{L}_F$. Define $S = \{t : f(t) \in G(t)\}$, and let $y = f + x$. By definition of F we have $y(t) \succ_t x(t)$

for almost all $t \in S$ and $y(t) = i(t)$ for almost all $t \notin S$. Therefore $\int y = \int f + \int x = \int i$, and hence $\int_S y = \int_S i$. Since S contains all large traders, it follows that y dominates x via the coalition S, which is non-null (since $\mu(T_1) > 0$) and contains all large traders, contrary to assumption.

(ii) $\mu(T_1) = 0$. In this case $0 \notin \operatorname{int} \int F$. For suppose $0 \in \operatorname{int} \int F$; then there is a point $a > 0$ such that $-a \in \int F$, i.e., $-a = \int f$, where $f \in \mathscr{L}_F$. Define $A = \{t : f(t) \in G(t)\}$ and $A^* = T \setminus A$. Obviously, $\mu(A) > 0$ (since $a \neq 0$). Let

$$(5.3) \qquad F^*(t) = \begin{cases} G(t) & \text{for } t \in A, \\ F(t) & \text{for } t \in A^*. \end{cases}$$

By definition of A, we have $-a \in \int F^*$, and by desirability, $x(t) + a \succ_t x(t)$ for all traders t. Hence $\int [(x + a) - x] = a \in \int F^*$. Hence, since $\int F^*$ is convex, $0 \in \int F^*$, and this fact yields a contradiction in a similar way as in case (i) (by replacing T_1 by A and F by F^*). This proves the lemma.

We now proceed with the proof of Theorem A*. It follows from the convexity assumption (2.5) and from the definition of F that $\int F$ is convex (Theorem 1). We also have $0 \notin \operatorname{int} \int F$ (Lemma 3). Therefore, by the supporting hyperplane theorem, there exists p $(0 \neq p \in R^n)$ such that $p \cdot \int F \geqslant 0$. Hence, (p, x) is an e.e. (Lemma 2).

By desirability, $f = (i - x)\chi_{T_0} + e\chi_{T_1} \in \mathscr{L}_F$. Therefore, $0 \leqslant p \cdot f(t) = p \cdot i(t) - p \cdot x(t)$ for almost all $t \in T_0$ (Lemma 2), i.e., (p, x) is an efficiency equilibrium with prices that discriminate against the small traders. This completes the proof of Theorem A*.

6. PROOF OF THEOREMS B, C, AND D

Throughout this section we will assume, without loss of generality, that $\mu(T) = 1$.

In the following, it will be convenient to make use of a notion of domination which is slightly different from the usual one (see Section 2).

DEFINITION 1: An assignment y *dominates an allocation x via a coalition S (S is then said to *block x) if: (i) $\mu(R) > 0$ where $R = \{t \in S : y(t) \succ_t x(t)\}$; (ii) for almost each $t \in S \setminus R$, we have: either $y(t) \succsim_t x(t)$ (if the preference $\succ_t$ is derived from a quasi-order $\succsim_t$), or $y(t) = x(t)$; and (iii) $\int_S y = \int_S i$.

Note that if $\mu(S \setminus R) = 0$ then *domination coincides with domination. The *core is the set of all allocations that are not *blocked by any coalition.

LEMMA 4: *The core coincides with the* *core.

PROOF: See Appendix C.

PROOF OF THEOREMS B AND C: First, we give a heuristic argument. For simplicity in this description, let us assume that there are just two large traders W_1 and W_2, and that they are of the same kind. Since x is in the core, both large traders are indifferent between $x(W_1)$ and $x(W_2)$; this phenomenon is well-known (compare

480   BENYAMIN SHITOVITZ

[11, 16]).[15] In fact, we may go further; assume that both large traders actually get the same bundle,[16] i.e., that $x(W_1) = x(W_2)$. Therefore, by Lyapunov's theorem there exist two disjoint coalitions S_1 and S_2 of small traders trading with W_1 and W_2 respectively, i.e., $\int_R x = \int_R i$ for $R = S_1 \cup W_1$ and $R = S_2 \cup W_2$.[17] Intuitively, also, it is not unreasonable to assume that two identical large traders will split the market evenly between them. This means that the market is actually composed of two monopolistic submarkets whose traders are $S_1 \cup W_1$ and $S_2 \cup W_2$ respectively. Let $p(t) = p \cdot x(t) - p \cdot i(t)$ be the monetary profit of trader t at the "market prices" p. By Theorem A we have that each small trader t has a non-positive profit. Suppose now that one of the large traders, say W_1, has a positive profit. Then, since the total profit of each submarket is zero, there are small traders in S_1 who have been monetarily exploited. Therefore, by adding a sufficiently small part of these traders to the other submarket, and by distributing the excess $i(t) - x(t)$ of the part (whose value at the "market prices" is positive) among themselves and the traders of the other submarket, we obtain a new submarket whose traders t receive a new bundle in the neighborhood of $x(t)$ whose value at the "market prices" is more than the value of $x(t)$ (compare the description of the proof of Theorem A above). Therefore, the traders of this new submarket can block x, in contradiction to the assumption that x is in the core.

These ideas are formally embodied in Lemma 6, by way of the definition of the set-valued function H (see (6.2)). The rather strange definition of H actually expresses the fact that a small trader may contribute to the "kitty" either his initial bundle $i(t)$ (if he is in S_1) or his final bundle $x(t)$ (if he is in S_2), whereas the atom W_2 always contributes $x(t)$.

In very simple terms, what is happening is that if some of the "customers" of W_1 are "losing money," then it will be worthwhile for W_2 to "steal" at least a small number of these customers from W_1 (while keeping his own customers). Therefore, none of W_1's customers can lose money, and so, by the symmetry of the situation, nobody does.

The idea of the proof of Theorem C is similar; in place of each of the large traders W_i we now have a group of larger traders, the various groups being congruent to each other.

We shall start by proving the theorems for a subset of the core, namely, for allocations in the core in which similar traders receive the same commodity bundle. For this subset of the core we shall actually prove (in Lemma 6) the results for more general markets having some symmetry properties concerning their nonmonopolistic structure. Let $(A_1, A_2, \ldots)$ be a partition of the set T_1 of atoms

---

[15] In [11], it is proved that if in a finite market there are exactly n traders of each kind, $n \geqq 2$, then every x in the core assigns equivalent bundles to traders of the same kind. This phenomenon remains unchanged if a continuum of traders is added to such a market. The phenomenon also holds under other conditions; see [16].

[16] If the bundles are different, they must lie on the same indifference curve, and this indifference curve must be flat between them (it is assumed that the large traders have convex indifference curves). Furthermore, the efficiency budget line must coincide with the indifference curve on this flat part. Therefore, we may replace x by an allocation x' such that $x'(W_1) = x'(W_2) = (x(W_1) + x(W_2))/2$. Once we prove that x' is competitive, it follows that x is also competitive.

[17] We do not distinguish between a large trader and the set consisting of that large trader only.

such that A_k $(k \geqslant 1)$ is a coalition of traders of the same type, and

(6.1)   there is an α with $0 < \alpha < 1$ such that for each k $(k \geqslant 1)$ there is a coalition $B_k \subseteq A_k$ with $\mu(B_k) = \alpha\mu(A_k)$.

Note that under the assumptions of both Theorem B and Theorem C, there is a partition of T_1 with property (6.1). The common preference order of the members of A_k will be denoted $\succ_k$; recall that it is convex and is derived from a quasi-order, which we shall denote $\succsim_k$.

Let $A = \cup_k A_k$ and $B = \cup_k B_k$; the union is over all k such that $k \geqslant 1$, for which $\mu(A_k) > 0$. We assume that $\mu(A) > 0$ and denote $T \setminus A$ by A_0.

Given an allocation x such that $x(t) = x_k$ is the same for all $t \in A_k$, we define

(6.2) $$H(t) = \begin{cases} G(t) & \text{for} \quad t \in A, \\ G(t) \cup \{i(t) - x(t)\} \cup \{x(t) - i(t)\} & \text{for} \quad t \in A_0. \end{cases}$$

Denote the common value of all the $G(t)$ for $t \in A_k$ by G_k. Then G_k is convex, and it may be verified (see [9]) that $g \in G_k$ implies $\gamma g \in G_k$ for all γ with $0 < \gamma < 1$.

LEMMA 5: *Let C be a convex set in R^n, and let $a = \int g$ where g is integrable and $g(t) \in C$ for almost all $t \in T$. Then $a \in C$.*

PROOF: This lemma is well known; nevertheless we shall sketch its proof for the sake of completeness. The proof is by induction on the dimension of C. Suppose, contrary to the lemma, that $a \notin C$. By a separation theorem, there exists a p $(0 \neq p \in R^n)$ such that $p \cdot C \geqslant p \cdot a$. In particular, $p \cdot g(t) \geqslant p \cdot a$ for almost all $t \in T$; but[18] $\int p \cdot g = \int p \cdot a = p \cdot a$ (since $\mu(T) = 1$). Therefore, we have $p \cdot g(t) = p \cdot a$ for almost all $t \in T$, i.e., $g(t) \in C^*$ for almost all $t \in T$ where $C^* = \{x : x \in C$ and $p \cdot x = p \cdot a\}$. On the other hand, $a \notin C^*$, since $C^* \subseteq C$. Since the dimension of C^* is less than n, we can proceed by induction, till we obtain a contradiction. This proves the lemma.

By Lemma 5 and our definitions we have:

(6.3) $$\frac{1}{\alpha} \int_B G = \int_A G;$$

(6.4)   for any γ with $0 < \gamma < 1$, we have $\gamma \int_B G \subseteq \int_B G$; and

(6.5) $$\int_{B^*} (i - x) = \beta \int_A (i - x) = \beta \int_{A_0} (x - i) \text{ where } B^* = A \setminus B \text{ and}$$

$$\beta = 1 - \alpha.$$

Note that $G(t) = H(t)$ for all $t \in A$. Hence, we can replace G by H in the above assertions.

Now we are in a position to state and prove our main lemma.

---

[18] We denote $a\chi_T$ by a.

482   BENYAMIN SHITOVITZ

LEMMA 6: *Let x be an allocation in the core such that $x(t) = x_k$ is the same for all $t \in A_k$. Then $0 \notin \int H$.*

REMARK: This lemma holds whenever there exists a partition of T_1 that has property (6.1).

PROOF: Suppose, contrary to the lemma, that $0 \in \int H$. Let $0 < \gamma < \min(\alpha, \beta)$ where $\beta = 1 - \alpha$. Then (by (6.3) and (6.4)) we have

$$0 \in \gamma \int H = \gamma \int_{A_0} H + \gamma \int_A H = \gamma \int_{A_0} H + \frac{\gamma}{\alpha} \int_B H \subseteq \int_{A_0} H + \int_B H,$$

i.e.,

(6.6) $$0 = \gamma \int_{A_0} h + \int_B h$$

where h is integrable and $h(t) \in H(t)$ for almost all $t \in A_0 \cup B$. Let $D = \{t \in A_0 : h(t) = x(t) - i(t)\}$ and $C = A_0 \setminus D$. Define a non-atomic measure m by

$$m(S) = \left(\int_S i, \int_S x, \int_S h \right)$$

for any $S \subseteq A_0$. By Lyapunov's theorem, there exist coalitions C_1, C_2, D_1, and D_2 with the following properties (see Figure 3):

(6.7) $C_1 \subseteq C$ and $m(C_1) = \gamma m(C)$, hence $\int_{C_1} h = \gamma \int_C h$.

(6.8) $C_2 \subseteq C^* = C \setminus C_1$ and $m(C_2) = \dfrac{1 - \alpha}{1 - \gamma} m(C^*) = \beta m(C)$, hence

$$a_1 = \int_{C_2} (x - i) = \beta \int_C (x - i).$$

(6.9) $D_1 \subseteq D$ and $m(D_1) = \dfrac{\gamma}{\beta} m(D)$, hence

$$a_2 = \gamma \int_D h = \gamma \int_D (x - i) = \beta \int_{D_1} (x - i).$$

(6.10) $D_2 \subseteq D^* = D \setminus D_1$ and $m(D_2) = \beta m(D^*)$, hence

$$a_3 = \int_{D_2} (x - i) = \beta \int_{D \setminus D_1} (x - i).$$

Combining (6.8), (6.9), (6.10), and (6.5) above, we obtain

(6.11) $$\int_{B^*} (i - x) = \beta \int_{A_0} (x - i) = a_1 + a_2 + a_3.$$

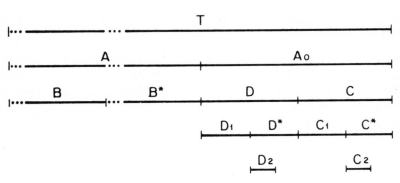

FIGURE 3

Now define

$$z = x + (i - x)\chi_{B^* \cup C_2 \cup D_2} + h\chi_{B \cup C_1}.$$

Then (by (6.6)–(6.11)),

$$\int (z - x) = a_1 + a_2 + a_3 - a_1 - a_3 + \int_B h + \int_{C_1} h,$$

$$= \gamma \int_D h + \int_B h + \gamma \int_C h,$$

$$= \gamma \int_{A_0} h + \int_B h = 0.$$

Since $\int x = \int i$, it follows that $\int z = \int i$, i.e., that z is an allocation.

From the definition of z it follows that for almost all t, either $z(t) = x(t)$ or $z(t) \succ_t x(t)$ or $z(t) = i(t)$. Let S be the set of those t such that one of the first two possibilities holds.

Then

$$\int_S z = \int_T z - \int_{T \setminus S} z = \int_T z - \int_{T \setminus S} i$$

$$= \int_T i - \int_{T \setminus S} i = \int_S i,$$

so that S is effective for z. Furthermore, if $R = \{t \in S : z(t) \succ_t x(t)\}$, then $R \supseteq B$, and hence $\mu(R) > 0$. So from the definition of S it follows that z *dominates x via S; hence x is not in the core, contrary to assumption. This completes the proof of the lemma.

We proceed now with the proofs of Theorems B and C. We have that $\int H$ is convex (Theorem 1) and $0 \notin \int H$ (Lemma 6). By the supporting hyperplane theorem, there exists p ($\neq p \in R^n$) such that $p \cdot \int H \geqq 0$. Hence (Lemma 2), (p, x) is an efficiency equilibrium.

Let $z = (x - i)\chi_{A_0} + e\chi_A$ and $y = (i - x)\chi_{A_0} + e\chi_A$. Since z and y are in $\mathscr{L}_H$ it follows from Lemma 2 that $p \cdot z(t) \geqq 0$ and $p \cdot y(t) \geqq 0$ for almost all $t \in T$. Hence $p \cdot x(t) \geqq p \cdot i(t)$ and $p \cdot i(t) \geqq p \cdot x(t)$ for almost all $t \in A_0$, i.e., (p, x) is an e.e. with $p \cdot i(t) = p \cdot x(t)$ for almost all $t \in A_0$. This proves Theorem C for the subset of the core mentioned above.

In the situation considered in Theorem B, since x is an allocation, we have $\int x = \int i$. Hence

$$p \cdot x_1 \mu(A_1) + \int_{A_0} p \cdot x = p \cdot i_1 \mu(A_1) + \int_{A_0} p \cdot i.$$

But $p \cdot x(t) = p \cdot i(t)$ for almost all $t \in A_0$. Therefore $p \cdot i_1 = p \cdot x_1$, i.e., (p, x) is a competitive equilibrium.

This completes the proofs of Theorems B and C for allocations in the core in which traders of the same type receive the same commodity bundle. Let us now treat the general case.

We describe now two models, named Model B and Model C, which represent the situations considered in Theorems B and C respectively.

Model B: $\mu(A_k) = 0$ for all $k \geqq 2$. A_1 is not an atom.

Model C: Each A_k ($k \geqq 1$) contains exactly m atoms of the same kind, where m is the g.c.d. mentioned in Theorem C.

Let x be an allocation in the core. For each k ($k \geqq 1$) define

$$(6.12) \qquad z_k = \frac{1}{\mu(A_k)} \int_{A_k} x.$$

LEMMA 7: $x(t) \sim_k z_k$ for all $t \in A_k$.

PROOF: First, we show that

$$(6.13) \qquad x(t) \succsim_k z_k \quad \text{for all } t \in A_k.$$

We shall prove this separately for the two models.

For Model B: Suppose (6.13) is not true; then $W = \{t \in A_1 : z_1 \succ_t x(t)\}$ has positive measure. Let $\alpha = \mu(W)/\mu(A_1)$. Define a non-atomic vector measure on A_0 by

$$m(S) = \left(\int_S i, \int_S x \right)$$

for any coalition $S \subseteq A_0$. By Lyapunov's theorem, there exists a coalition $S_0 \subseteq A_0$ such that $m(S_0) = \alpha m(A_0)$. Let $R = W \cup S_0$ and $y = x\chi_{S_0} + z_1\chi_W$.

It is obvious that $y(t) \succ_t x(t)$ for $t \in W$ and $y(t) = x(t)$ for $t \in S_0$. Hence $W \subseteq D = \{t \in R : y(t) \succ_t x(t)\}$, and therefore $\mu(D) > 0$. Hence, y *dominates x via R, since effectiveness holds because R is an α-reduction of the market (i.e., $\int_R y = \alpha \int x$

and $\int_R i = \alpha \int i$; compare [**11**, **16**]). Thus x is not in the core, contrary to assumption. This proves (6.13) for Model B.

For Model C: Suppose (6.13) is not true; then for at least one $k \geqslant 1$, $\mu(C_k) > 0$, where $C_k = \{t \in A_k : z_k \succ_k x(t)\}$. For those k with $\mu(C_k) > 0$, let $W_k \subseteq C_k$ be an atom. For the others, let $W_k \subseteq C_k$ be an atom for which $z_k \succsim_k x(W_k)$. (We have that $x(t) \succ_k z_k$ for all $t \in A_k$ is impossible by convexity and irreflexivity of the preference $\succ_k$.) Define $W = \cup_k W_k$, and let

$$\alpha = \frac{\mu(W_k)}{\mu(A_k)} = \frac{\mu(W)}{\mu(T_1)} = \frac{1}{m}.$$

In a similar way to that used for Model B, we get a coalition $S_0 \subseteq A_0$ with $m(S_0) = \alpha m(A_0)$ where $m(S) = (\int_S i, \int_S x)$ is defined for all coalitions $S \subseteq A_0$. Define $y = x\chi_{S_0} + \Sigma_k z_k \chi_{W_k}$, and let $R = W \cup S_0$. Then by an argument similar to that used for Model B, we get that y *dominates x via R. Hence x is not in the core, contrary to assumption. This proves (6.13) for Model C.

Now, it is well known that (6.13) implies the lemma; i.e., $x(t) \succsim_k z_k$ for all $t \in A_k$ implies that $x(t) \sim_k z_k$ for all $t \in A_k$. For the sake of completeness, we sketch the proof. Let $C_k = \{t \in A_k : x(t) \succ_k z_k\}$ and $B_k = A_k \backslash C_k$. Suppose, contrary to the lemma, that $\mu(C_k) > 0$ for some k. Let $\alpha = \mu(C_k)/\mu(A_k)$, and define $H = \{y : y \succ_k z_k\}$ and $E = \{y : y \succsim_k z_k\}$. Then by Lemma 5

$$a = \frac{1}{\mu(C_k)} \int_{C_k} x \in H,$$

and

$$b = \frac{1}{\mu(B_k)} \int_{B_k} x \in E.$$

Therefore $z_k = \alpha a + (1 - \alpha)b \succ_k z_k$, a contradiction. This completes the proof of the lemma.

We now proceed in the proofs of Theorems B and C. Let x be in the core, and define:

$$z = x\chi_{A_0} + \sum_k z_k \chi_{A_k}.$$

Then z is in the core (by Lemma 7) and moreover z is in the subset of the core for which we have proved Theorems B and C. Let p be an efficiency price with respect to z that satisfies the conclusions of Theorems B and C. We shall complete the proofs of the theorems by proving the following lemma.

LEMMA 8: $p \cdot x(t) = p \cdot z(t)$ *for almost all* $t \in T$.

PROOF: For each $t \in A_k$ and $\varepsilon > 0$, we have $x(t) + \varepsilon e \succ_k z_k$. Hence $p \cdot x(t) + \varepsilon p \cdot e > p \cdot z_k$. Letting $\varepsilon \to 0$, we get $p \cdot x(t) \geqslant p \cdot z_k$ for all $t \in A_k$. But by (6.12) $\int_{A_k} p \cdot x = \int_{A_k} p \cdot z_k$, and therefore $p \cdot x(t) = p \cdot z_k$ for all $t \in A_k$. This proves the lemma and completes the proofs of Theorems B and C.

PROOF OF THEOREM D: Finally, we come to Theorem D. Since the market M^* (the market after some of the large traders have been split) obeys the conditions of Theorem C, it follows that the small traders end up with zero profit, i.e., for almost all small traders t, $x(t)$ is maximal in t's budget set. In particular, it follows that almost all small traders of the same type must get equivalent bundle densities $x(t)$, and we may assume that they actually get the same $x(t)$. In particular this holds for the traders in each "split atom" W^*. Now since x is in the core of M^*, it cannot be blocked by any coalition, and in particular, it cannot be blocked by any coalition in which the traders of each split atom W^* appear en bloc (i.e., for each W^*, either all the traders in it appear or none of them appear). But since almost all traders in each W^* get the same $x(t)$, this may be interpreted to mean that $x(t)$ is, essentially, in the core of the "unsplit" market M. But this market, too, satisfies the conditions of Theorem C, so here all corresponding large traders get the same amount.[19] It follows that large traders of the same kind as large traders who get split end up with zero profit. So everybody ends up with zero profit, except possibly the large traders of the one kind of which no representative gets split. But then these large traders, too, can neither gain nor lose money, because otherwise the whole market would do so, i.e., the value of the total initial bundle would differ from that of the final bundle. It follows that everybody ends up with zero profit, i.e., we have a competitive equilibrium. We gave a verbal description of the proof and the mathematical proof can easily be achieved from our description.

7. EXAMPLES AND OPEN PROBLEMS

We begin with an example showing that Theorem B cannot be extended to the monopoly case; i.e., we will exhibit a monopolistic[20] market in which the equivalence theorem is false.

EXAMPLE 1: Here $T = [0, 1] \cup \{2\}$ where $T_0 = [0, 1]$ is taken with Lebesgue measure; $T_1 = \{2\}$ is an atom with $\mu(T_1) = 1$; and the number n of commodities is 2.

The initial assignment is $i = 4e_1\chi_{T_0} + 4e_2\chi_{T_1}$. All traders t have the same preference relation $>_t$, namely the relation derived from the utility function $u(x, y) = \sqrt{x} + \sqrt{y}$ (throughout this section we write (x, y) instead of (x_1, x_2)).

There is a unique competitive equilibrium, namely the allocation that assigns $(2, 2)$ to all traders. On the other hand, the core consists of all allocations x of the form

$$x(t) = \alpha(t)e \qquad \text{for almost all } t,$$

where $1 \leqslant \alpha(t) \leqslant 2$ for almost all $t \in [0, 1]$, $2 \leqslant \alpha(2) \leqslant 3$, and $\int \alpha = 4$. In particular, the allocation x_0 that assigns $(1, 1)$ to the small traders and $(3, 3)$ to the large trader

---

[19] Not as a consequence of Theorem C itself, but as a consequence of the fact that under the conditions of Theorem C, large traders of the same kind get the same bundles.

[20] A market is "monopolistic" if it has precisely one large trader.

is in the core, and it obviously differs from the competitive equilibrium. At x_0, the small traders are "monetarily exploited," i.e., we have

$$p \cdot x_0(t) = p \cdot (1, 1) < p \cdot (4, 0) = p \cdot i(t)$$

(the unique[21] efficiency price at all points in the core is $(1, 1)$). Moreover, the utility of every small trader at x_0 is exactly the same as that of his initial bundle. Note that the allocation in which the "tables are turned," i.e., the allocation that assigns $(3, 3)$ to the small traders and $(1, 1)$ to the large trader, is not in the core; the large trader must receive at least $(2, 2)$ in the core, i.e., at least as much as at the competitive equilibrium (see Figure 4, in which the heavy line indicates the set of possible bundles assigned to the large trader by core allocations).

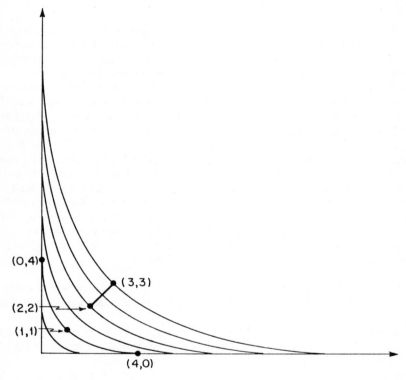

FIGURE 4

The next two examples deal with the idea of "exploitation" of the small traders, which is fundamental in our treatment of oligopoly in markets with a continuum of traders. We have expressed this idea in terms of value or monetary profit. Actually, however, each trader is concerned with his preferences rather than with

---

[21] I.e., up to multiplication by a positive constant.

488   BENYAMIN SHITOVITZ

any monetary criterion. There does exist a class of markets in which the monetary profit expresses the relative situation of some traders, in terms of preferences, namely the homogeneous markets (Example 2). But in general this is not the case, and there exist markets (even monopolistic ones) in which some small traders are monetarily exploited in the sense of Theorem A, i.e., "lose money;" but nevertheless, these traders are actually better off than at any competitive equilibrium (Example 3).

These examples raise the following open problem:

Open Problem: In a market with exactly one large trader, is it true that at every allocation in the core, the large trader is not worse off in terms of utility than at the competitive equilibrium which is worst for him?

EXAMPLE 2 (Homogeneous Markets): A homogeneous market is a market in which all traders t have the same homogeneous preference relation $\succ_t$, namely a relation derived from a concave utility function $u(x)$ that is homogeneous of degree 1 and has continuous partial derivatives in the neighborhood of $\int i$.

Let us assume that the indifference curves (or surfaces) of u are strictly convex.[22] It is easy to see that each Pareto optimal allocation x has the form $x(t) = \alpha(t) \int i$. Hence, the efficiency prices p are the same for all Pareto optimal allocations, namely p is the vector whose components are the partial derivatives of the utility function $u(x)$ at $\int i$.

Let x^* be the unique competitive allocation. Given a Pareto optimal allocation x, let $p(t) = p \cdot x(t) - p \cdot i(t)$ be the monetary profit of trader t. Then we have (i) $p(t) \leqslant 0$ if and only if $u(x(t)) \leqslant u(x^*(t))$ and (ii) $p(t) \geqslant 0$ if and only if $u(x(t)) \geqslant u(x^*(t))$. For x in the core, therefore, it follows from Theorem A that small traders are at most as "satisfied" (in the sense of preference) as they are at the competitive equilibrium; and from Theorem C it follows that in symmetric markets (i.e., markets in which the g.c.d. is $\geqslant 2$), the small traders receive in the core the same bundle that they receive at the competitive equilibrium.

EXAMPLE 3: Here $T = [0, 1] \cup \{2\}$ where $T_0 = [0, 1]$ is taken with Lebesgue measure; $T_1 = \{2\}$ is an atom with $\mu(T_1) = 1$; and the number n of commodities is 2.

The initial assignment is $i = 14e_1\chi_{T_0} + 14e_2\chi_{T_1}$. All traders t have the same preference relation $\succ_t$, namely the relation derived from the utility function $u(x)$ defined in the following way:

Let $g(s)$ be a continuous monotonic function on $[0, \infty)$ such that $g(s) = 1$ for $s \leqslant 4$ and $g(5) = 8$. Define

$$u(x, y) = \begin{cases} g(s)x + y, & x \leqslant y, \\ x + g(s)y, & x \geqslant y, \end{cases}$$

where s is the unique value for which $u(x, y) = u(s, s)$ (see **Figure 5**).

---

[22] Similar results can be obtained without this assumption; it simply makes the exposition less clumsy.

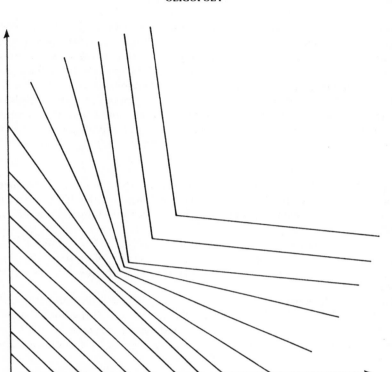

FIGURE 5

Let $x = 7e\chi_{T_1} + 12e\chi_A + 11e\chi_B + 5e\chi_C$, where $A = [0, 2)$, $B = [.2, .3)$, and $C = [.3, 1]$. We shall show that x is in the core, and therefore, by Theorem A, there are efficiency prices p at which almost all the small traders "do not gain," i.e., $p \cdot x(t) \leqq p \cdot i(t)$. In particular, the traders in A "do not gain," and therefore the traders in B actually "lose," i.e., $p \cdot x(t) < p \cdot i(t)$. But the traders in B are better off than they would be at any competitive equilibrium. Indeed, any competitive equilibrium (in fact any Pareto optimal allocation) must yield almost all traders a bundle on the diagonal. Hence, at a competitive equilibrium, *almost all* small traders get the same bundle. This bundle cannot be better than 10e, for otherwise the large trader will get less than 4e, whose utility is less than that of his initial bundle. Thus, the 11e that the traders in B get at x is much better than anything that they get at a competitive equilibrium.

To prove that x is in the core, apply the "if" half of Theorem A* (Section 5), using $p = (8, 1)$. It follows that x is not blocked by any non-null coalition containing the large trader, and so if it is not in the core, it must be blocked by a coalition consisting of small traders only. But this is impossible, since a coalition with only one commodity cannot block any i.r. allocation.

In connection with this example, it should be noted that Theorem A does *not* assert that the small traders are monetarily exploited at *all* the efficiency prices, but only that there exist such efficiency prices. Thus, at the x of this example, there are efficiency prices, e.g., $(1, 8)$, at which all the small traders "gain money" (i.e., such that $p \cdot x(t) > p \cdot i(t)$). The question therefore arises whether a similar example can be constructed in which the efficiency prices are unique; this would be the case, for example, if the indifference curves would be differentiable. The answer is positive; by "smoothing" the corners of the indifference curves in the preceding example, one can get an example similar to Example 3 in which there are unique efficiency prices.

Example 4 shows that it *is* possible for the small traders to lose by merging. Another way of saying this is that it is possible by splitting himself into a continuum of small traders, a large trader can make himself better off in terms of utility.

EXAMPLE 4: Here $T = \{1, 2, 3\}$ where $\mu(1) = \mu(2) = \mu(3) = 1$, and $n = 2$. The initial assignment is $i = 4e_1\chi_{\{1\}} + e_2\chi_{\{2,3\}}$; the utility of trader 1 is given by $u_1(x, y) = \sqrt{x} + \sqrt{y}$, and $u_i(x, y) = x + y$ $(i = 2, 3)$ are the utilities of traders 2 and 3.

The core of the market obtained by splitting trader 1 is the competitive allocation $x^* = 2e\chi_{\{1\}} + e_1\chi_{\{2,3\}}$ (Theorem B). But in the core of the finite market, this allocation is the best allocation for trader 1, and the core contains other allocations, namely, allocations of the form $x = x^* - 2\varepsilon e\chi_{\{1\}} + \varepsilon e\chi_{\{2,3\}}$ for sufficiently small positive ε.

The next four examples revolve around the idea of Theorem D. First we bring an example illustrating a typical application of Theorem D (Example 5). Next, we show that neither of the conditions $m \geqq 2$ and $m^* \geqq 2$ can be dispensed with. In Example 6, we exhibit a market in which M and M^* have profiles[23] $(2, 2)$ and $(2, 1)$ respectively, and the equivalence theorem fails in M^*; in Example 7, we exhibit a market in which M and M^* have profiles $(3, 2)$ and $(2, 2)$ respectively, and the equivalence theorem fails in M^*. Example 8 will be discussed later.

EXAMPLE 5: Suppose M has a profile of the form $(q(q + 1), q + 1, \ldots, q + 1)$, where q is a positive integer $\geqq 2$; then $m = q + 1 > 2$. If now exactly one large trader of each kind other than the first splits into a continuum, then the profile of the resulting market M^* is $(q(q + 1), q, \ldots, q)$; thus $m^* = q \geqq 2$. This is therefore an example of a market obeying Theorem D.

EXAMPLE 6: Here $T = [0, 1] \cup \{2, 3, 4\}$ where $T_0 = [0, 1]$ is taken with Lebesgue measure, $\mu(2) = \mu(3) = \mu(4) = 1$; and the number n of commodities is 2. The initial assignment is $i = 14e_1\chi_A + 14e_2\chi_B$, where $A = [0, 1] \cup \{2\}$ and $B = \{3, 4\}$. All traders t have the same utility function $u(x)$, namely that which was described in Example 3.

---

[23] The *profile* of a market $(T_0: A_1, A_2, \ldots)$ is $(|A_1|, |A_2|, \ldots)$.

Let $x = 7e\chi_{\{2,3,4\}} + 5e\chi_C + 9e\chi_D$, where $C = [0, .5)$ and $D = [.5, 1]$. Obviously x is not a competitive allocation, since the traders in C do not receive under x bundles equivalent to the bundles that the traders of D receive, though they are of the same type.

To prove that x is in the core, we need the following lemma, which holds in general.

LEMMA 9: *Let (p, x) be an efficiency equilibrium and let S be a non-null coalition such that*

$$\int_{S^*} p \cdot i \geqq \int_{S^*} p \cdot x, \qquad \text{where} \qquad S^* = T \setminus S.$$

Then S does not block x.

PROOF: See Appendix D.

Returning to the proof that x is in the core of our market, we use $p = (8, 1)$. It then follows from the lemma that x is not blocked by any non-null coalition S such that $|S \cap B| = 2$ or $|S \cap B| = 1$ and $2 \notin S$. On the other hand, using $p = (1, 8)$, it follows that x is not blocked by any non-null coalition such that $|S \cap B| = |S \cap \{2\}| = 1$ or $|S \cap B| = 0$. Therefore x is in the core.

EXAMPLE 7: Here $T = [0, 1] \cup \{2, 3, 4, 5\}$, where $T_0 = [0, 1]$ is taken with Lebesgue measure; $\mu(2) = \mu(3) = \mu(4) = \mu(5) = 1$; and the number n of commodities is 2. The initial assignment is $i = 4e_1\chi_A + 6e_2\chi_B$, where $A = [0, 1] \cup \{2, 3\}$ and $B = \{4, 5\}$. All traders t have the same utility

$$u(x, y) = (\sqrt{x} + \sqrt{y})^2.$$

The unique competitive allocation is $x^* = 2e\chi_A + 3e\chi_B$. Let δ be a sufficiently small positive number, and let

$$x = x^* - \delta e\chi_{\{2,3\}} + \delta e\chi_{\{4,5\}}.$$

Obviously x is not a competitive allocation, since the traders in $[0, 1]$ do not receive under x bundles equivalent to the bundles that traders 2 and 3 receive, though they are of the same type. Next, we prove that x is in the core. Suppose not, and let S be some blocking coalition. Since $p = e = (1, 1)$ is an efficiency price for x, therefore by Lemma 9 it follows that $|S \cap \{2, 3\}| \neq |S \cap \{4, 5\}|$. Now, since no coalition with only one commodity can block any i.r. allocation, therefore $|S \cap \{4, 5\}| \neq 0$. Next, if $|S \cap \{4, 5\}| = 2$ or $|S \cap \{2, 3\}| = 0$, then

$$\int_S p \cdot i \leqq \int_S p \cdot x,$$

and hence, by Lemma 9, we obtain a contradiction. Therefore $|S \cap \{4, 5\}| = 1$ and $|S \cap \{2, 3\}| = 2$. Denote $\alpha = \mu(S \cap T_0)$; then $\int_S i = (8 + 4\alpha, 6)$ and $\int_S x = (7 +$

$2\alpha - 2\delta)e$. Now, using concavity and homogeneity properties of u, one can obtain that

$$u(8 + 4\alpha, 6) = u\left(\int_S i\right) > u\left(\int_S x\right) = u(7 + 2\alpha - 2\delta, 7 + 2\alpha - 2\delta).$$

But this inequality cannot hold if δ is sufficiently small, since for each $0 \leqslant \alpha \leqslant 1$ we have[24]

$$u(8 + 4\alpha, 6) < u(7 + 2\alpha, 7 + 2\alpha).$$

We now turn to Example 8. This example deals with a market with profile of the form $(r, \ldots, r)$. If there are sufficiently many small traders of each type, it follows from Theorem D that the market obeys the equivalence theorem. For example, this would be the case if the set of small traders of each type has measure $\geqslant$ the measure of one large trader of that type. Thus Theorem D may apply even if there are relatively few small traders. The purpose of Example 8 is to show that they must not become *too* few. Specifically, we will demonstrate that if the set of small traders of each type has sufficiently small (but positive) measure, the equivalence theorem may fail.

EXAMPLE 8: For positive integers $(n; r)$ and for sufficiently small positive ε, the market $M_\varepsilon(r; n)$ will be defined as follows: The set of traders is $T = T_1 \cup T_0$, where T_1 is the union of n sets A_k, each of which contains r atoms of measure 1; T_0 is the union of n disjoint intervals B_k; and $\mu(B_k) = \varepsilon$ for $k = 1, \ldots, n$. The number n of commodities is also the number of different types of traders in the market. The initial assignment is

$$i = \sum_{k=1}^{n} e_k \chi_{A_k \cup B_k}$$

All traders t have the same preference relation $\succ_t$, namely the relation derived from the utility function

$$u(x_1, \ldots, x_n) = \left(\sum_{k=1}^{n} \sqrt{x_k}\right)^2.$$

Obviously $\int i = (r + \varepsilon)e$, and the unique competitive allocation is

$$x^* = \frac{e}{n}\chi_T.$$

For sufficiently small numbers $\delta_1, \ldots, \delta_n$ such that $\sum_{k=1}^{n} \delta_k = 0$, let

$$x = x^* + \sum_{k=1}^{n} \delta_k e \chi_{A_k}.$$

Then x is in the core.

[24] This inequality can be proved using Lagrange's multipliers.

To prove this, let S be some blocking coalition; let s_k be the number of atoms in S that are of the kth kind; and let $\alpha_k = \mu(S \cap B_k)$. If $s_1 = s_2 = \ldots = s_n$, then $p \cdot \int_S x = p \cdot \int_S i$ for $p = e$, and by Lemma 9, it follows that S does not block x. Therefore, if x is not in the core, then $(s_1, \ldots, s_n)$ is not on the diagonal. But

$$\int_S i = \sum_{k=1}^n s_k e_k + \varepsilon \sum_{k=1}^n \frac{\alpha_k}{\varepsilon} \cdot e_k,$$

and

$$\int_S x = \sum_{k=1}^n s_k \frac{e}{n} + \varepsilon \sum_{k=1}^n \frac{\alpha_k}{\varepsilon} \cdot \frac{e}{n} + \sum_{k=1}^n s_k \delta_k e.$$

Therefore, by the concavity and homogeneity of degree 1, it follows that

$$u\left(\int_S i \right) > u\left(\int_S x \right).$$

But this inequality cannot hold for sufficiently small ε and $\delta_1, \ldots, \delta_n$, because

$$u\left(\sum_{k=1}^n s_k e_k \right) < u\left(\sum_{k=1}^n s_k \frac{e}{n} \right);$$

the last inequality follows from an argument similar to that mentioned in Example 7.

The last group of examples deals with the extent to which traders of the same kind or type get, in the core, equivalent bundles (or bundle densities). We have seen that this property is of fundamental importance in the proofs of Theorems B and C, and therefore also of Theorem D (see Footnote 15). First we shall show that in case of monopoly, small traders of the same type need not get the same bundle densities (Example 9). By a slight modification of this example, we will obtain similar phenomena for various non-monopolistic markets, and we shall describe a market which exhibits this anomaly though it obeys the conditions of Theorem C. Specifically, the market has profile (2, 2, 2), and the first two kinds of traders are of the same type but get different bundle densities. This can be summed up as follows: Under the conditions of Theorem C, large traders of the same *kind* get the same bundle, as do small traders of the same *type*. But large traders of the same *type* need not get the same bundle density.

EXAMPLE 9: This example is based on Example 1. In that example, there are allocations in the core that assign inequivalent bundles to different small traders of the same type; for example, the allocation that assigns $(2\frac{1}{2}, 2\frac{1}{2})$ to the large trader, $(1, 1)$ to half the small traders, and $(2, 2)$ to the other half, is in the core. Alternatively, we could assign $(2\frac{1}{2}, 2\frac{1}{2})$ to the large trader and $(1 + t, 1 + t)$ to the small trader t; here any two small traders receive different bundles. This situation is well-known in the classical theory of monopoly under the name

494   BENYAMIN SHITOVITZ

"price discrimination."[25] We may modify Example 1 by having various groups of small traders merge. Above, we saw that in the core, half of the small traders could get (1, 1) and the other half (2, 2). If each of these halves merges into a single player, the resulting allocation is still in the core; thus, we have a three-traders market with two traders of the same kind who get different bundles. One can also merge some groups of small traders, leave others as a continuum, and still get the same phenomenon.

EXAMPLE 10: This example is based on Example 8. In that example, taking $(n; r) = (2; 2)$, one obtains allocations in the core that assign inequivalent bundles to the traders of the first kind A_1 and to the small traders in B_1 (which are of the same type as those of A_1). Now, divide the set B_1 into two halves with equal measures and consider the market obtained by merging the small traders in the two halves into two large traders. We obtain a market whose profile is (2, 2, 2), and an allocation in the core that assigns inequivalent bundles to traders of the same type.

8. DISCUSSION OF THE LITERATURE

The classical approach to oligopoly theory differs from ours in a number of basic respects. Treating monopolistic markets, Chamberlain and others [5, 14, 32, and 35] assume that the situation involves only one decision maker (or two decision makers in the case of a duopoly; see [6, 24, 33, and 35] whose strategies space embodies the monopolistic features of the market. Shubik made this clear; "In our brief discussion we did not treat the purchasers as though they were players in any strategic sense, i.e., we assumed that they acted independently, each in turn assuming that he had no effect on the market price" [35, p. 42]. Von Neumann and Morgenstern treat monopoly and monopsony in a different way, i.e., as an n-person game in which the many buyers and sellers are considered as players in the strategic sense of game theory (see [12, 34, and 38]). In our paper we follow this approach and treat an oligopolistic market as a game whose set of players is a measure space, i.e., the set of traders consists of a continuum of small traders and several large ones (compare [2, 16, 19, 20, 25, and 28]). The main point in our treatment is that the small and the large traders are not segregated into different groups a priori; they are treated on exactly the same basis. The distinctions we have found between them are an *outcome* of the analysis; they have not been artificially introduced in the beginning, as is the case in the classical approach.

In this section we will first compare our results with some of those obtained by the classical approach. Then we will discuss some of the recent literature that

---

[25] The meaning of the word "price" in this phrase is the amount that a small trader has to "pay" in terms of x for the amount of the y good that he buys. This is quite different from our "efficiency prices:" these are, of course, the same for all small traders, and indeed for all traders.

attacks the oligopoly problem from a point of view which is more similar to ours, i.e., one in which all participants are treated as decision making units. We begin with the case of monopolistic markets.

A market which consists of one seller and a very large number of buyers is a monopoly. The classical approach assumes that each buyer, acting independently, adapts himself to the market price, while the monopolist has the advantage of determining the price that maximizes his net revenue. The classical result obtained under these assumptions is that every buyer is in a position inferior to that in which he would be under the competitive equilibria. We obtain a similar result: monetary exploitation of every small trader (Theorem A). Nevertheless, the two approaches differ in their assumptions as well as in their conclusions. The classical approach claims that a monopolist can determine either the price or the quantity, since the aggregate demand function he faces is decreasing. Therefore, the solution will generally be unique. We attack the problem in a different way, and our results show that in most monopolies, the core has a large *range of indeterminateness*,[26] which is large enough to contain both the competitive equilibria on the one hand, and many allocations that express the exploitation of the small traders on the other hand.

We now pass to a discussion of duopolistic markets, in particular markets with two sellers and a very large number of buyers. In the classical approach the situation is treated as a two-person game between the sellers. Nevertheless, there is no commonly agreed upon solution in this case: "It has been held that competition between two sellers will result in a monopoly price, a competitive price, a determinate price intermediate between them, an indeterminate price intermediate between them, a perpetually oscillating price, and no price at all because the problem is impossible" [5, p. 30].

Perhaps Bertrand's solution to a duopoly is the one closest to ours (see [5, 35]). Bertrand suggested that each duopolist assumes that the other will keep his *price* unchanged, and on this assumption the two duopolists would keep on undercutting each other until they reach the competitive equilibrium. This is also our result (Theorem B), and it prevailed among Marshall, Pareto, and others (see [5, p. 37]).

Edgeworth [14] added to Bertrand's solution the ideas about the *contract curve*. He argued that there are no allocations in the core, and that in particular even the competitive equilibrium is not in the core; a conclusion which is obviously not consistent[27] with his general theory of contract curves. Nevertheless, the other part of his conclusion, the part that states that any noncompetitive allocation is outside the core, is similar to ours. The ideas of his argument are very similar to our proof of Theorem B (see Section 6).

Other approaches to duopoly in the classical vein have been discussed in [24, 33]. It turns out that most of them display the phenomenon of the exploitation of the small traders by the large traders, an outcome which is very far from ours.

---

[26] The core contains an infinite number of final settlements.
[27] This inconsistency was pointed out by Chamberlain, and it is thoroughly described in his book [5].

A very similar situation to ours occurs in [28], in which Shapley considers a proxy battle in a large corporation with a continuum of small stockholders and two large stockholders. His result is that at the *Shapley value* the small stockholders are generally not exploited by the large ones, a phenomenon that is the result of the "cutthroat competition" that emerges between the large stockholders.

We now pass to a discussion of some of the literature, most of it fairly recent, that attacks the oligopoly problem from a point of view more similar to ours.

Perhaps the first mention of such an attack is in [38, Section 4, pp. 13–14, and Section 64.2, p. 586], where a model is set up to deal with such situations. Beyond the setting up of the model, however, the results in [38] on this question are somewhat fragmentary. Probably the first author using this kind of model actually to establish a result of some economic content on the oligopoly problem was Shubik [34]. He considered a two-commodity market in which a single trader initially holds an amount a of the first commodity, and each of n traders initially hold an amount b of the second commodity; he then looked at what happens to the core when $n \to \infty$. His conclusion was that "in the limit," the single trader gets "all of the gain from trading," whereas each of the n traders only get as much utility as they initially held. This situation is not really similar to our situation; although there is "one trader against many," the many traders are not small[28]. Also, Shubik considers only a very special kind of market called a "market with side payments," and he assumes that both kinds of traders have the same utility.

Another paper in this area is that of Gabscewicz and Mertens [16]. Their model is essentially identical to ours, i.e., they work with a market containing a continuum of small traders and several large ones, as described in Section 2. Their theorem is as follows: Suppose that for each type A_k of large trader, there is a continuum of positive measure of small traders of the same type. Let $\mu(A_k)$ be the measure of the large traders of type A_k, and μ_k the measure of *all* traders of this type. Then if

$$(8.1) \qquad \sum_k \mu(A_k)/\mu_k \leqslant 1,$$

the equivalence theorem holds.

This result is not directly comparable to any of our results, in the sense that it neither implies nor is implied by any of our results. However, we note that as soon as it is proven that

(8.2)   traders of the same type get the same bundle density,

the theorem of [16] follows from our Theorem A. For by Theorem A, the small traders cannot lose in the core, and so no trader can lose; therefore no trader can gain either, i.e., we have a competitive equilibrium.

The chief difficulty in their paper is the proof of (8.2). To overcome this, Gabscewicz and Mertens use (8.1) and Lyapunov's theorem to divide the market into a

---

[28] L. S. Shapley has pointed out (in private correspondence) that the fact that the large trader gets all the benefit out of trading is a consequence of the scarcity of the good he is holding, and not of his monopoly status. If m traders (rather than just one) initially held the amount a between them (i.e., a/m each), the result would be no different; they would still get, in the limit as $n \to \infty$, "all of the gain from trading."

number of submarkets. They then use an argument that is reminiscent of that of Debreu and Scarf [11] to deduce (8.2).

The theorem of [16] is an equivalence theorem; it may therefore be contrasted with our Theorems B and D. On the one hand, unlike the theorem of [16], our Theorem B does not require that there be any small traders of the same type as the large traders; and our Theorem D does not require this for all types. Also, whereas the theorem of [16] requires a relatively large proportion of small traders (in the case of more than one type of large trader), our Theorem D holds even when there are relatively few small traders (see Example 5). On the other hand, the theorem of [16] does not require symmetry conditions such as those required in our theorems.

Finally, we come to the paper of Drèze, Gabscewicz, and Gepts [12]. Although chronologically it came before [16], it is perhaps most easily described by saying that it is an asymptotic analogue of [16]. Their paper [12] considers a sequence of markets, each containing finitely many traders, including a fixed number of "large" traders and a number of "small" traders that tends to infinity. The proportions and types of the large and the small traders are essentially as in [16], except that the number of types is fixed (i.e., the continuum can contain no heterogeneous part as in [16]). It is proved that as the number of small traders tends to infinity, the core tends to the set of competitive allocations. This result bears a relation to [16] that is similar to the relation of [11] to [2].

9. CONCLUDING REMARKS

The core of a market has been the subject of intense analysis since Edgeworth, and most especially in the last decade or so [13, 39, 40]. The economic significance of this concept is unquestionable, both for markets with many traders and for markets with few traders. The subject of this paper, namely the analysis of the core of markets with small and large traders, is therefore altogether fitting and appropriate.

Nevertheless, the core concept is not without its difficulties. Consider for example a monopolistic market, in which a single large trader has a corner on a certain good which he is selling to a continuum of small "customers" (see Example 1). For definiteness, think of a town with a single large hotel. We have seen that the core of such a market is fairly large, and that the monopolist can exploit the small traders to the maximum within the confines of the core; that is, the point at which the small traders get only the utility of their initial bundles is still in the core. This result is intuitively reasonable, because the small traders have no resource other than the monopolist; the travellers must go to the single hotel or sleep in the street. Suppose now that a small entrepreneur enters the scene with a small hotel or pension. If the pension is very small, one feels that the situation should not change by very much. But this is false; no matter how small the additional oligopolist is, it follows from Theorem B that the new core has shrunk to the competitive equilibrium. That is, the large hotel has suddenly lost all its power and must take competitive prices as if the town was full of all kinds of hotels.

It is not only the discontinuity that is disturbing here; one feels that intuitively the original monopolist has not, in fact, lost his power. He can continue to demand a high price for the rooms he is providing because he knows that his competitor can supply only a very small part of the market. The large hotel can, and probably will, simply ignore the new entrepreneur. It is true that he will thereby lose some of his customers, but this will hurt him much less than he would be hurt by descending to competitive prices. The prices that will presumably prevail in the end, far from being competitive, will presumably be near the original prices in the monopolistic market, with the pension taking somewhat less than the hotel in order to ensure itself of a "full house" regularly. This result, of course, is not in the core; the pension, together with some of the hotel's customers, can block it; but, in fact, it will not act to do so.

This kind of phenomenon can presumably be handled by an appropriate notion of ε-core (see [22, 31]); the blocking coalition mentioned above will not act because, in some sense, the small gain is not worth the trouble. The ε-cores are approximations to cores; the reason that the ε-core is far from the core in the above case is because the pension was chosen to be very small. For a fixed pension size, the ε-core will tend to the core, as $\varepsilon \to 0$, also in the above case.

The above discussion is not meant to discredit the idea of the core, but rather to indicate that it must be used with care. In some cases, it may be more useful to look at the core as a kind of limiting phenomenon, and to regard core analysis as giving qualitative insights rather than exact predictions of market behavior.

The Hebrew University, Jerusalem

Manuscript received November, 1970; revision received April, 1971.

APPENDIX A

Proof of Lemma 1

PROOF: If (p, x) is an e.e., then necessarily $p \cdot G(t) > 0$ for almost all traders t.

Conversely, let $0 \neq p \in R^n$ be such that $p \cdot G(t) \geqq 0$ for almost all t. By desirability, $G(t)$ contains a translate of Ω, and therefore $p \geqslant 0$.

Let[29] $z \succ_t x(t)$; we have to show that z is not in the efficiency budget set $B_p^*(t)$. Suppose not; then we have $p \cdot z \leqslant p \cdot x(t)$. By continuity, there is an $\alpha < 1$ sufficiently close to 1, such that $\alpha z \succ_t x(t)$. Therefore $p \cdot \alpha z \geqq p \cdot x(t) \geqq p \cdot z \geqq p \cdot \alpha z$. Since $\alpha < 1$ we have $p \cdot x(t) = p \cdot z = 0$, i.e., we have proved that $p \cdot x(t) > 0$ implies that $x(t)$ is maximal with respect to $\succ_t$ in $B_p^*(t)$.

Since $p \cdot \int x = p \cdot \int i > 0$, there is a coalition S with $\mu(S) > 0$ such that $p \cdot x(t) > 0$ for all $t \in S$. For all $i, 1 \leqslant i \leqslant n$, and all $t \in S$, we have by desirability that $x(t) + e_i \succ_t x(t)$. Since $p \cdot x(t) > 0$, $x(t)$ is maximal in $B_p^*(t)$, and therefore $p \cdot x(t) + p \cdot e_i > p \cdot x(t)$, which implies $p_i > 0$ for all i, i.e., $p > 0$. Therefore, $p \cdot x(t) = p \cdot z = 0$ implies $x(t) = z = 0$.

We conclude that if R is the set of all traders t for which $x(t)$ is not maximal with respect to $\succ_t$ in $B_p^*(t)$, then $R = \{t : x(t) = 0 \text{ and } 0 \succ_t 0\}$. But $x(t) = 0$ and $0 \succ_t 0$ imply $i(t) \succ_t x(t)$, and therefore $\mu(R) = 0$ by the individual rationality of x. This completes the proof of the Lemma.

[29] In the following, t is outside the exceptional set.

OLIGOPOLY   499

APPENDIX B

Proof of Lemma 2

PROOF: For each x in R^n, let $G^{-1}(x) = \{t : x \in G(t)\}$. From $G^{-1}(x) = \{t : x + x(t) \succ_t x(t)\}$ and measurability, it follows that $G^{-1}(x)$ is measurable for each x.

Let N be the set of all those rational points r in R^n for which $G^{-1}(r)$ is null. Obviously N is denumerable. Define $S = \bigcup_{r \in N} G^{-1}(r)$. Then S is null.

Suppose that for some $t \notin S$, there is an $x \in G(t)$ with $p \cdot x < 0$. By continuity, we may find a rational point $r \in G(t)$ sufficiently close to x, so that we still have $p \cdot r < 0$. Since $t \in S$, it follows that $\mu(A) > 0$, where $A = G^{-1}(r)$. By desirability, for each $\varepsilon > 0$, we have $f_\varepsilon = r\chi_A + \varepsilon e\chi_{A*} \in \mathcal{L}_G$ where $A^* = T \setminus A$. Hence, $f_\varepsilon \in \mathcal{L}_F$. Therefore

$$0 \leqslant p \cdot \int f_\varepsilon = p \cdot r\mu(A) + \varepsilon p \cdot e\mu(A^*) \xrightarrow[\varepsilon \to 0]{} p \cdot r\mu(A) < 0.$$

a contradiction. Therefore $p \cdot G(t) \geqslant 0$ for almost all traders t, and by Lemma 1, (p, x) is an efficiency equilibrium. Thus we have proved (i) of the Lemma.

Let $f \in \mathcal{L}_F$. Define $A = \{t : p \cdot f(t) < 0\}$ and $A^* = T \setminus A$. Then, for each $\varepsilon > 0$, the function $f_\varepsilon = f\chi_A + \varepsilon e\chi_{A*} \in \mathcal{L}_F$. Therefore

$$0 \leqslant p \cdot \int f_\varepsilon = \int_A p \cdot f + \varepsilon p \cdot e\mu(A^*) \xrightarrow[\varepsilon \to 0]{} \int_A p \cdot f.$$

Therefore, $\int_A p \cdot f \geqslant 0$, which implies by the definition of A that $\mu(A) = 0$. This completes the proof of the Lemma.

APPENDIX C

Proof of Lemma 4

PROOF: Obviously, the core contains the *core. Next, let an allocation x be in the core and suppose that x is not in the *core. Then x is *dominated via a coalition S by an assignment y. Let $R = \{t \in S : y(t) \succ_t x(t)\}$. Since x is in the core, we have $\mu(S \setminus R) > 0$. For each rational α in the interval $(0, 1)$, define:

$$R_\alpha = \{t \in R : \alpha y(t) \succ_t x(t)\}.$$

By continuity (2.3), for each $t \in R$ there exists some rational α in $(0, 1)$ such that $t \in R_\alpha$. Hence R is the countable union of all the R_α, where α in $(0, 1)$ is rational. Therefore, from $\mu(R) > 0$ it follows that there exists an α_0 in $(0, 1)$ such that $\mu(R_{\alpha_0}) > 0$.

For each $t \in R_{\alpha_0}, y(t) \succ_t x(t)$. Hence by Theorem A we have, for each $t \in R_{\alpha_0}, p \cdot y(t) > p \cdot x(t) \geqslant 0$ where p is the efficiency price with respect to x. In particular, $y(t) \geqslant 0$ for almost all $t \in R_{\alpha_0}$. Hence $a = \int_{R_{\alpha_0}} y \geqslant 0$.

Let $a = a\chi_T$ and define

$$z = y\chi_{R \setminus R_{\alpha_0}} + \alpha_0 y\chi_{R_{\alpha_0}} + \left(y + \frac{1 - \alpha_0}{\mu(S \setminus R)} a \right) \chi_{S \setminus R}.$$

Then z dominates x via S, contrary to assumption. This completes the proof of the Lemma.

APPENDIX D

Proof of Lemma 9

PROOF: Suppose, contrary to the Lemma, that some allocation y dominates x via S; let

$$z = y\chi_S + i\chi_{S*}.$$

By the definition of efficiency equilibrium we have

$$p \cdot z(t) = p \cdot y(t) > p \cdot x(t) \quad \text{for almost all} \quad t \in S.$$

500   BENYAMIN SHITOVITZ

Hence, from $\mu(S) > 0$ it follows that $\int_S p \cdot z > \int_S p \cdot x$. Therefore, we obtain

(A1) $$p \cdot \int z = \int_S p \cdot z + \int_{S^*} p \cdot i > \int_S p \cdot x + \int_{S^*} p \cdot x = p \cdot \int x.$$

But by the effectiveness of y,

$$\int z = \int_S y + \int_{S^*} i = \int_S i + \int_{S^*} i = \int i = \int x,$$

and this contradicts the strict inequality in (A1). This completes the proof of the Lemma.

REFERENCES

[1] ARROW, K. J.: "An Extension of the Basic Theorems of Classical Welfare Economics," *Proceedings of the Second Berkeley Symposium on Math. Statist. and Probab.* Berkeley: University of California Press, 1951, pp. 507–532.

[2] AUMANN, R. J.: "Markets with a Continuum of Traders," *Econometrica*, 32 (1964), 39–50.

[3] ———: "Integrals of Set-Valued Functions," *Journal of Mathematical Analysis and Application*, 12 (1965), 1–12.

[4] ———: "Existence of Competitive Equilibria in Markets with a Continuum of Traders," *Econometrica*, 34 (1966), 1–17.

[5] CHAMBERLAIN, E. H.: *The Theory of Monopolistic Competition*, 6th ed. Cambridge, Mass.: Harvard University Press, 1950.

[6] COURNOT, A. A.: *Researches into the Mathematical Principles of the Theory of Wealth*. New York: Macmillan and Co., 1897.

[7] DEBREU, G.: "Valuation Equilibrium and Pareto Optimum," *Proceedings of the National Academy of Science of the U.S.A.*, 40 (1954), 588–592.

[8] ———: "Integration of Correspondences," *Proceedings of the Fifth Berkeley Symposium on Math. Statist. and Probab.* Berkeley: University of California Press, 1951, pp. 351–372.

[9] ———: *Theory of Value*. New York: John Wiley, 1959.

[10] ———: "On a Theorem of Scarf," *Review of Economic Studies*, 30 (1963), 178–180.

[11] DEBREU, G., AND H. SCARF: "A Limit Theorem on the Core of an Economy," *International Economic Review*, 4 (1963), 235–246.

[12] DRÈZE, J., J. GABSZEWICZ, AND S. GEPTS: "On Cores and Competitive Equilibria," *Aggrégation et Dynamique des Ordres de Préférence, Colloques Internationaux du C.N.R.S.*, 171 (1969), 91–114.

[13] EDGEWORTH, F. Y.: *Mathematical Psychics*, London: Paul Kegan, 1881.

[14] ———: *Papers Relating to Political Economy*. London: Macmillan, 1925.

[15] FARRELL, N. J.: "Edgeworth Bounds for Oligopoly Prices," *Econometrica*, 37 (1970), 341–361.

[16] GABSZEWICZ, J., AND J. F. MERTENS: "An Equivalence Theorem for the Core of an Economy Whose Atoms are not 'Too' Big," *Econometrica*, 39 (1971), 713–722.

[17] HALMOS, P. R.: "The Range of a Vector Measure," *Bulletin of the American Mathematical Society*, 54 (1948), 416–421.

[18] HILDENBRAND, W.: "The Core of an Economy with a Measure Space of Economic Agents," *Review of Economic Studies*, 35 (1968), 443–452.

[19] ———: "Pareto Optimality for a Measure Space of Economic Agents," *International Economic Review*, 10 (1969), 363–372.

[20] ———: "Existence of a Quasi-Equilibrium for an Economy with Production and a Measure Space of Consumers," *Econometrica*, 38 (1970), 608–623.

[21] ———: "On Economies with Many Agents," *Journal of Economic Theory*, 2 (1970), 161–188.

[22] KANNAI, Y.: "Continuity Properties of the Core of a Market," *Econometrica*, 38 (1970), 791–815.

[23] LYAPUNOV, A.: "Sur les Fonctions-Vecteurs Complètement Additives," *Bulletin of the Academy of Sciences URSS. Series Math.*, 4 (1940), 465–478.

[24] MAYBERRY, J., J. F. NASH, AND M. SHUBIK: "A Comparison of Treatments of a Duopoly Situation," *Econometrica*, 21 (1953), 141–154.

[25] MILNOR, J., AND L. S. SHAPLEY: "Values of Large Games II: Oceanic Games," Research Memorandum RM2649, RAND Corp., Santa Monica, Calif., 1961.

[26] RICHTER, H.: "Verallgemeinerung eines in der Statistik benotigten Satses der Masstheorie," *Math. Annalen*, 150 (1963), 85–90.

[27] SCARF, H.: "An Analysis of Markets with a Large Number of Participants," in *Recent Advances in Game Theory*. Princeton University Conference, Princeton, 1962, pp. 127–155.

[28] SHAPLEY, L. S.: "Values of Large Games III: A Corporation with Two Large Stockholders," Research Memorandum RM 2650 PR, RAND Corp., Santa Monica, Calif., 1961.

[29] ———: "Values of Large Market Games: Status of the Problem," Research Memorandum RM 3957, RAND Corp., Santa Monica, Calif., 1964.

[30] ———: "Values of Large Games VII: A General Exchange Economy with Money," Research Memorandum RM 4248, RAND Corp., Santa Monica, Calif., 1964.

[31] SHAPLEY, L. S., AND M. SHUBIK: "Quasi-Cores in a Monetary Economy with Nonconvex Preferences," *Econometrica*, 34 (1966), 805–827.

[32] ———: "Concepts and Theories of Pure Competition," in *Essays in Mathematical Economics: In Honor of Oskar Morgenstern*, ed. by Martin Shubik. Princeton: Princeton University Press, 1967, pp. 63–79.

[33] SHUBIK, M.: "A Comparison of Treatment of a Duopoly Situation," *Econometrica*, 23 (1955), 417–431.

[34] ———: "Edgeworth Market Games," *Annals of Mathematical Studies, No. 40*, ed. by A. W. Tucker and R. D. Luce. Princeton: Princeton University Press, 1959, pp. 267–278.

[35] ———: *Strategy and Market Structure*. New York: John Wiley, 1959.

[36] VIND, K.: "Edgeworth Allocations in an Exchange Economy with Many Traders," *International Economic Review*, 5 (1964), 165–177.

[37] ———: "A Theorem on the Core of an Economy," *Review of Economic Studies*, 32 (1965), 47–48.

[38] VON NEUMANN, J. AND O. MORGENSTERN: *Theory of Games and Economic Behavior*. Princeton: Princeton University Press, 1944.

[39] WALD, A.: "On Some Systems of Equations of Mathematical Economics," *Econometrica*, 19 (1951), 368–403.

[40] WALRAS, L.: *Mathematische Theorie der Preisbestimmung der Wirtschaftlichen Guter*. Stuttgard: Ferdinand Enke, 1881.

[40]

Econometrica, Vol. 39, No. 5 (September, 1971)

AN EQUIVALENCE THEOREM FOR THE CORE OF AN ECONOMY WHOSE ATOMS ARE NOT "TOO" BIG

By Jean Jaskold Gabszewicz and Jean-François Mertens

This paper is a natural outgrowth of recent studies in markets with a "continuum" of traders. An equivalence theorem for the core of such economies was obtained, under the assumption that the measure space of economic agents is atomless. We introduce a sufficient condition under which the preceding result can be extended to economies containing "atomic" traders. The condition bears on the measure of the atoms.

In 1964, R. Aumann proved that in an atomless economy, the core coincides with the set of competitive allocations [1]. We prove here an extension of this theorem to the case of a general economy, with a constraint on the size of its atoms. In the limit approach, a very similar situation has been examined in [2]. More recently, B. Shitovitz has obtained interesting results for an atomic measure space of economic agents [4].

1. THE MODEL

The set of *agents* is the finite measure space $(T, \mathcal{T}, \theta)$. The *commodity space* is the positive cone Ω of R^m, where m denotes the number of commodities. An *assignment* is an integrable function from T to Ω. Let $\underline{w}$ be the *initial* assignment. We assume $\int_T \underline{w}(t)\, d\theta > 0$. An *allocation* $\underline{x}$ is an assignment such that

$$\int_T \underline{x}(t)\, d\theta = \int_T \underline{w}(t)\, d\theta.$$

For each agent t, a complete, reflexive, and transitive *preference ordering* $\succsim_t$ is defined on Ω; it satisfies the following assumptions: (i) *desirability*; (ii) *continuity*; (iii) *measurability* in the sense of Aumann;[1] and (iv) *convexity*: for all x and $y \in \Omega$, $\alpha \in\,]0, 1[,\, x \succsim_t y$ implies $\alpha x + (1 - \alpha)y \succsim_t y$. A *coalition* is a nonnull element of $\mathcal{T}$; an allocation y *dominates* an allocation $\underline{x}$ *via* a coalition C if, (i) for all $t \in C$, $y(t) \succsim_t \underline{x}(t)$, (ii) for a nonnull subset of traders t in C, $y(t) \succ_t \underline{x}(t)$, and (iii) $\int_C y(t)\, d\theta = \int_C \underline{w}(t)\, d\theta$. The *core* is the set of all allocations that are not dominated via any non-null coalition. A *price system* p is a nonnull element of Ω. A *competitive equilibrium* is a pair $(p, \underline{x})$, consisting of a price system p and an allocation $\underline{x}$, such that, for almost every trader t in T, $x(t)$ is a maximal element in the budget set. A *competitive allocation* is an allocation $\underline{x}$ for which there exists a price system p such that $(p, \underline{x})$ is a competitive equilibrium.

The measure space $(T, \mathcal{T}, \theta)$ contains at most countably many atoms. For each atom $\tau \in \mathcal{T}$, consider the class

$$\{t|\underline{w}(t) = \underline{w}(\tau);\, \forall(x, y) \in \Omega x \Omega : x \succsim_t y \Leftrightarrow x \succsim_\tau y\}.$$

This class is the set of all traders who have the same preferences and the same initial

---

[1] For these definitions, see [1, p. 43].

J. GABSZEWICZ AND J. MERTENS

resources as the atom τ; we shall further refer to these classes as the *types*. So we obtain a partition of the set of agents into at most countably many types, say $T_i, i \in N^*$, and an atomless part $D, D = T \setminus \bigcup_i T_i$. It is easily seen that this partition is measurable. We will denote by $\succsim_i$ the common preferences of agents in T_i. The restriction of the σ-algebra $\mathscr{T}$ to the parts T_i and D will be denoted by $\mathscr{T}_i$ and $\mathscr{T}_D$; μ_D will designate the restriction of θ to $\mathscr{T}_D$. Finally, the atoms of type i will be denoted by $\tau_k^i, k \in N^*$.

2. THE EQUIVALENCE THEOREM

THEOREM: *If* $\Sigma_i (\Sigma_k \theta(\tau_k^i)/\theta(T_i)) \leqslant 1$—*or, in case there is a single type, if* $\Sigma_k (\theta(\tau_k^1)/\theta(T_1)) < 1$—*the core coincides with the set of competitive allocations.*

REMARKS: (1) The inequality says the sum over all types of the atomic proportions of the types should be less than one. (2) We shall not prove again the well known fact that the set of competitive allocations is contained in the core.

3. PROOF OF THE THEOREM

A. Introduction to the Proof

In the proof of the theorem, it will be shown that, if x is in the core, and if all agents of the same type receive a vector $x(t)$ which is in the same indifference class with respect to the preference relation of that type, then we may rely on Aumann's proof to demonstrate the equivalence theorem. Consequently, it is sufficient to show that, if x is in the core, all agents of the same type are, in fact, in the same indifference class. This is the object of the main lemma. The idea of the proof of this lemma can be stated in the following way.[2] Let x be in the core. Suppose that traders in each type are represented on the unit interval, with Lebesgue measure λ, atoms of that type being subintervals. Figure 1 provides a representation of the economy where, for all pairs of traders in a given type, one trader is "below" another if, and only if, he prefers under x the other's situation to his own.

If, contrary to the lemma, all traders in some type are not in the same indifference class, then the condition of our theorem implies that there exists a number $\alpha \in]0, 1[$ such that if a horizontal straight line is drawn in Figure 1 at level α through the types, no atom is "split" by this line. Then the agents below this line are worse off in all types and they will, supplemented by some subcoalition P in D, form a blocking coalition. The idea is to choose, by Lyapounov's Theorem, a subset P of D such that the agents below α together with this subset define an α-reduction of the initial economy. Of course, the agents of a given type are not originally defined in this way, so we have to build a correspondence Γ from each type of trader to the $[0, 1]$-interval in such a way that the previous argument can be used. Unfortunately, the construction of this correspondence and the proof of its

---

[2] This idea was already explicit in [2, Lemma 4].

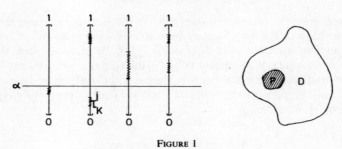

FIGURE 1

properties are rather tedious. Therefore, they are gathered together under the heading "the rearrangement of traders of type T_i." The reader is advised to begin immediately at the main lemma, at least in a first reading, going afterwards to the rearrangement.

B. The Rearrangement of Traders of Type T_i

LEMMA 1 : *Let (S, Σ, μ) be a finite atomless measure space. Then there exists a map $f : S \to \,]0, \mu(S)[$, where f is measurable and f induces Lebesgue measure.*

REMARK : This fact is surely well known, but the reference is unknown to us.

PROOF : We can of course suppose $\mu(S) = 1$, and it is sufficient to prove the existence of $f : S \to [0, \mu(S)]$, inducing Lebesgue measure. By non-atomicity, we can define a sequence of partitions of S, say $P_1, \ldots, P_n, \ldots, P_n = \{P_n^0, P_n^1\}$, such that, $\forall n \in N^*, \forall \psi : \underline{N} \to [0, 1], \mu(\bigcap_{i=1}^n P_i^{\psi(i)}) = 1/2^n$. Let χ_i be the characteristic function of P_i^1. Let $x \in S$ and define

$$f(x) = \sum_{i=1}^{\infty} \frac{1}{2^i} \chi_i(x).$$

Trivially, f is measurable. By the uniqueness of Caratheodory's extension, in order to show that f induces Lebesgue measure, it is sufficient to show that

$$\mu\left(f^{-1}\left(\left[\frac{k}{2^n}, \frac{k+1}{2^n}\right[\right)\right) = \frac{1}{2^n};$$

that is,

$$\mu\left(\bigcap_{i=1}^n P_i^{\psi(i)}\right) = \frac{1}{2^n}.$$

Q.E.D.

Definition of the Correspondence Γ

Let $\underline{x}$ be in the core. For any measurable set B in $\mathcal{T}_i$, define $\mu(B) = \theta(B)/\theta(T_i)$. Define further, for all $t \in T_i$, $\Phi(t) = \mu(\{s | \underline{x}(s) \prec_i \underline{x}(t)\})$; it is easily seen that Φ is measurable. Clearly $\mu(\Phi^{-1}(\alpha)) > 0$ at most for a countable set $\{\alpha_1, \ldots, \alpha_h, \ldots, \alpha_n, \ldots\}$. Furthermore, for all h, the interval

$$]\alpha_h, \alpha_h + \mu(\Phi^{-1}(\alpha_h))[$$

does not intersect the range of Φ. Let $t_1, \ldots, t_n, \ldots$ be the atoms of $\Phi^{-1}(\alpha_h)$ and define $\Gamma(t_k) =]\alpha_h + \Sigma_{j<k}\mu(t_k), \alpha_h + \Sigma_{j\leqslant k}\mu(t_k)[$. It remains a segment $[\alpha_h + \Sigma_k \mu(t_k), \alpha_h + \mu(\Phi^{-1}(\alpha_h))[$, the length of which is equal to the measure of the atomless part of $\Phi^{-1}(\alpha_h)$. By Lemma 1, we can thus define on this atomless part a function $\Gamma(t)$ with values in that segment and which induces Lebesgue measure on that segment. Define finally $\Gamma(t) = \Phi(t)$ for t outside $\bigcup_h \Phi^{-1}(\alpha_h)$: the correspondence Γ is defined and measurable on the whole of T_i.

Properties of the Correspondence Γ

Let $\mathscr{B}$ be the σ-algebra of the Borel subsets of $[0, 1]$ which do not split $\Gamma(t)$ in two non-void parts for any atom t of T_i. We first prove the following lemma.

LEMMA 2: $\forall B \in \mathscr{B}, \mu(\Gamma^{-1}(B)) = \lambda(B)$, where λ is Lebesgue measure.

PROOF: By the uniqueness of the Caratheodory's extension, it is sufficient to check this for subsets of the form $[0, \gamma[$, where $\gamma \notin \bigcup_k \Gamma(\tau_k^i)$.

We first consider the case: $\gamma \in]\alpha_h, \alpha_h + \mu(\Phi^{-1}(\alpha_h))[$ for some h. The index j will refer here to atoms in $\Phi^{-1}(\alpha_h)$. Then

$$\mu(\Gamma^{-1}([0, \gamma[)) = \mu(\Gamma^{-1}([0, \alpha_h[)) + \mu(\Gamma^{-1}(\{\alpha_h\})) + \sum_j \mu(\Gamma^{-1}([0, \gamma[\cap\Gamma(t_j)))$$

$$+ \mu(\Gamma^{-1}([\alpha_h + \sum_j \mu(t_j), \gamma[)).$$

Since $\Gamma^{-1}(\{\alpha_h\}) = \varnothing, \mu(\Gamma^{-1}(\{\alpha_h\})) = 0$. Trivially, $\mu(\Gamma^{-1}([0, \gamma[\cap\Gamma(t_j))) = \lambda([0, \gamma[\cap\Gamma(t_j))$. Then, by Lemma 1, $\mu(\Gamma^{-1}([\alpha_h + \Sigma_j\mu(t_j), \gamma[)) = \lambda([\alpha_h + \Sigma_j\mu(t_j), \gamma[)$. It follows that

$$\mu(\Gamma^{-1}([0, \gamma[)) = \mu(\Gamma^{-1}([0, \alpha_h[)) + \sum_j \lambda([0, \gamma[\cap\Gamma(t_j))$$

$$+ \lambda\left(\left[\alpha_h + \sum_j \mu(t_j), \gamma\right[\right)$$

$$= \mu(\Gamma^{-1}([0, \alpha_h[)) + \lambda([\alpha_h, \gamma[).$$

Consequently, if we prove $\mu(\Gamma^{-1}([0, \alpha_h[)) = \lambda([0, \alpha_h[)$, our statement is proved. But $a_h \notin \bigcup_n]\alpha_n, \alpha_n + \mu(\Phi^{-1}(\alpha_n))[$; so it is finally sufficient to prove that if $\gamma \notin \bigcup_n]\alpha_n, \alpha_n + \mu(\Phi^{-1}(\alpha_n))[$, then $\mu(\Gamma^{-1}([0, \gamma[)) = \lambda([0, \gamma[)$.

In this case, let us first prove $\Gamma^{-1}([0, \gamma[) = \Phi^{-1}([0, \gamma[)$. Since $\forall t \in T_i, \Phi(t) \leqslant \Gamma(t)$ we have of course $\Gamma^{-1}([0, \gamma[) \subseteq \Phi^{-1}([0, \gamma[)$. So it is sufficient to prove that $\forall t : \Phi(t) \in [0, \gamma[\Rightarrow \Gamma(t) \subseteq [0, \gamma[$. But either $t \notin \bigcup_h \Phi^{-1}(\alpha_h)$ and then $\Gamma(t) = \Phi(t) \subseteq [0, \gamma[$, or there exists h such that $t \in \Phi^{-1}(\alpha_h)$; but then $\Gamma(t) \subseteq]\alpha_h, \alpha_h + \mu(\Phi^{-1}(\alpha_h))[$ and

$\alpha_h = \Phi(t) \in [0, \gamma[$ by assumption, so that $]\alpha_h, \alpha_h + \mu(\Phi^{-1}(\alpha_h))[\cap [0, \gamma[\neq \varnothing$. Then, by assumption on γ, $]\alpha_h, \alpha_h + \mu(\Phi^{-1}(\alpha_h))[\subseteq [0, \gamma[$. Since now $\Gamma(t) \subseteq]\alpha_h, \alpha_h + \mu(\Phi^{-1}(\alpha_h))[$, it follows that $\Gamma(t) \subseteq [0, \gamma[$.

By definition of Φ, $\Phi^{-1}([0, \gamma[) = \{r | \mu(\{s | \underline{x}(s) \prec_i \underline{x}(r)\}) < \gamma\}$. Let u be a continuous utility index representing the preordering $\gtrsim_i$ (the assumptions on $\gtrsim_i$ imply the existence of such an index) and v the measure on $\underline{R}$ induced by the measurable map $u(\underline{x}(t))$. Define $F(x) = v(]-\infty, x[)$. Then $\Phi = F \circ u \circ \underline{x}$ so that $\mu(\Phi^{-1}([0, \gamma[)) = v(F^{-1}([0, \gamma[))$ with $F^{-1}([0, \gamma[) = \{x | v(]-\infty, x[) < \gamma\}$. It is trivial that $x \in F^{-1}([0, \gamma[) \Rightarrow]-\infty, x] \subseteq F^{-1}([0, \gamma[)$. Thus there exists a number ρ such that either $F^{-1}([0, \gamma[) =]-\infty, \rho[$ or $F^{-1}([0, \gamma[) =]-\infty, \rho]$. Suppose first $F^{-1}([0, \gamma[) =]-\infty, \rho[$. Then

$$v(F^{-1}([0, \gamma[)) = v(]-\infty, \rho[) = \sup_{x \in F^{-1}([0, \gamma[)} v(]-\infty, x[) \leqslant \gamma.$$

$$\rho \notin F^{-1}([0, \gamma[) \Rightarrow v(]-\infty, \rho[) \geqslant \gamma.$$

So

$$\mu(\Phi^{-1}([0, \gamma[)) = v(F^{-1}([0, \gamma[)) = v(]-\infty, \rho[) = \gamma = \lambda([0, \gamma[).$$

Suppose then $F^{-1}([0, \gamma[) =]-\infty, \rho]$. Then $\rho \in F^{-1}([0, \gamma[) \Rightarrow v(]-\infty, \rho[) < \gamma$; furthermore $\rho + 1/n \notin F^{-1}([0, \gamma[) \Rightarrow v(]-\infty, \rho + 1/n[) \geqslant \gamma, \forall n \in N^* \Rightarrow v(]-\infty, \rho]) \geqslant \gamma$. It thus follows that $v(\{\rho\}) > 0$, and thus $\mu(\Phi^{-1}(F(\rho))) > 0$; so $F(\rho) = \alpha_h$ for some h. But $\alpha_h = F(\rho) = v(]-\infty, \rho[) < \gamma$. Moreover,

$$\alpha_h + \mu(\Phi^{-1}(\alpha_h)) \geqslant \alpha_h + \mu((u \circ \underline{x})^{-1}(\{\rho\})) = \alpha_h + v(\{\rho\})$$

$$= F(\rho) + v(\{\rho\})$$

$$= v(]-\infty, \rho[) + v(\{\rho\})$$

$$= v(]-\infty, \rho]) \geqslant \gamma.$$

Consequently, $\alpha_h < \gamma \leqslant \alpha_h + \mu(\Phi^{-1}(\alpha_h))$. Since, by assumption on γ, $\gamma \notin]\alpha_h, \alpha_h + \mu(\Phi^{-1}(\alpha_h))[$, we must have $\gamma = \alpha_h + \mu(\Phi^{-1}(\alpha_h))$. So $\gamma = \alpha_h + \mu(\Phi^{-1}(\alpha_h)) \geqslant v(]-\infty, \rho]) \geqslant \gamma$ and thus

$$\mu(\Phi^{-1}([0, \gamma[)) = v(F^{-1}([0, \gamma[)) = v(]-\infty, \rho]) = \gamma = \lambda([0, \gamma[).$$

It follows that the correspondence Γ induces Lebesgue measure on $\mathscr{B}$.   Q.E.D.

The two following lemmas show that the correspondence Γ induces the natural ordering of $[0, 1]$.

LEMMA 3: *There exists a set $M, M \subset T_i$, $\mu(M) = 0$, such that, $\forall t \in T_i \backslash M$, $\forall s \in T_i$,*

$$\Gamma(s) \leqslant \Gamma(t) \Rightarrow \underline{x}(s) \precsim_i \underline{x}(t).$$

PROOF: First it is clear that, for all $(s, t) \in T_i \times T_i$, $\Gamma(s) \leqslant \Gamma(t) \Rightarrow \Phi(s) \leqslant \Phi(t)$ and that $\Phi(s) \leqslant \Phi(t) \Rightarrow \mu(\{r | \underline{x}(t) \precsim_i \underline{x}(r) \precsim_i \underline{x}(s)\}) = 0$. Let $M_{s,t} = \{r | \underline{x}(t) \precsim_i \underline{x}(r) \precsim_i \underline{x}(s)\}$ and $M = \bigcup_{s,t} M_{s,t}$. If we can prove that there exists a sequence $\{(s_i, t_i)\}_{i \in N^*}$ such that $M = \bigcup_i M_{s_i,t_i}$, it will follow that $\mu(M) = 0$ and $\Gamma(s) \leqslant \Gamma(t)$, $\underline{x}(s) \succ_i \underline{x}(t) \Rightarrow t \in M_{s,t} \Rightarrow t \in M$, from which the lemma follows. In fact we will extract a sequence such that $\forall(s, t): \Gamma(s) \leqslant \Gamma(t)$, $\underline{x}(t) \prec_i \underline{x}(s) \Rightarrow \exists i: \underline{x}(t_i) \precsim_i \underline{x}(t) \prec_i \underline{x}(s) \precsim_i x(s_i)$; this is trivially sufficient. Assume thus $F(u(\underline{x}(s))) \leqslant F(u(\underline{x}(t)))$ and $u(\underline{x}(s)) > u(\underline{x}(t))$, where u and F are defined as in Lemma 2. Since F is increasing, it follows that $F(u(\underline{x}(s))) = F(u(\underline{x}(t)))$, and thus F is constant on $[u(\underline{x}(t)), u(\underline{x}(s))]$. There is a maximal interval $]\rho, \rho']$ or $[\rho, \rho']$ (with $\rho < \rho'$) containing the interval $[u(\underline{x}(t)), u(\underline{x}(s))]$ on which F is constant (this maximal interval is closed on the right because F is left-continuous). It is easily seen that there can exist only a countable family of such maximal intervals I_i. Consider an interval I_i. Define $\sigma_i = \inf\{u(\underline{x}(r)) \in I_i\}$ and $\sigma'_i = \sup\{u(\underline{x}(r)) \in I_i\}$. If there exists r such that $u(\underline{x}(r)) = \sigma_i$, define $\forall k$, $k \in \underline{N}$, $t_{i,k} = r$. If there exists r such that $u(\underline{x}(r)) = \sigma'_i$, define $\forall k$, $k \in \underline{N}$, $s_{i,k} = r$. Otherwise there exists a sequence $\{(s_{i,k}, t_{i,k})\}$ such that $\sigma_i < u(\underline{x}(t_{i,k})) < u(\underline{x}(s_{i,k})) < \sigma'_i$ and such that $\lim_{k \to \infty} u(\underline{x}(t_{i,k})) = \sigma_i$, $\lim_{k \to \infty} u(\underline{x}(s_{i,k})) = \sigma'_i$.

Consider now an $M_{s,t}$ such that $\Gamma(s) \leqslant \Gamma(t)$. Either $M_{s,t} = \varnothing$, in which case there is no problem, or $u(\underline{x}(s)) > u(\underline{x}(t))$, in which case we know that $[u(\underline{x}(t)), u(\underline{x}(s))][$ is in some I_i. From the construction of the sequence $\{(s_{i,k}, t_{i,k})\}$, it follows that there exists k such that $[u(\underline{x}(t)), u(\underline{x}(s))][\subseteq [u(\underline{x}(t_{i,k}), u(\underline{x}(s_{i,k}))[$. Thus

$$M_{s,t} = (u \circ \underline{x})^{-1}([u(\underline{x}(t)), u(\underline{x}(s))][) \subseteq (u \circ \underline{x})^{-1}([u(\underline{x}(t_{i,k})), u(\underline{x}(s_{i,k}))][)$$

$$= M_{s_{i,k},t_{i,k}}.$$

Since,

$$\forall i, \forall k, \mu(M_{s_{i,k},t_{i,k}}) = 0,$$

we have

$$\mu\left(\bigcup_{(i,k) \in \underline{N} \times \underline{N}} M_{s_{i,k},t_{i,k}}\right) = 0;$$

consequently, if

$$M = \bigcup_{(i,k) \in \underline{N} \times \underline{N}} M_{s_{i,k},t_{i,k}},$$

then $\mu(M) = 0$ and $\forall(s, t)$ such that $\Gamma(s) \leqslant \Gamma(t)$, $M_{s,t} \subseteq M$, which completes the proof of Lemma 3.   Q.E.D.

LEMMA 4: *If $\underline{x}(t)$ is not a.e. on T_i in the same indifference class, then, for each α, $\alpha \in]0, 1[, \alpha \notin \bigcup_k \Gamma(\tau_k^i)$, there exist two disjoint nonnull coalitions B and C such that $B \subseteq \Gamma^{-1}([0, \alpha[)$ and $C \subseteq \Gamma^{-1}(]\alpha, 1])$, and, for each (s, t), $s \in B$, $t \in C$, $\underline{x}(t) \succ_i \underline{x}(s)$.*

PROOF: If $\alpha \notin \bigcup_n]\alpha_n, \alpha_n + \mu(\Phi^{-1}(\alpha_n))[$, define $B = \Gamma^{-1}([0, \alpha[)$ and $C = \Gamma^{-1}(]\alpha, 1])$. B and C are evidently disjoint and nonnull coalitions. Suppose $u(\underline{x}(s)) \geqslant u(\underline{x}(t))$, for $s \in B$, $t \in C$. Then $\Phi(s) \geqslant \Phi(t)$. We know that $\alpha > \Gamma(s) \geqslant \Phi(s)$. Since $\Gamma(t) > \alpha$, $\Phi(t) \geqslant \alpha$ (since otherwise $\alpha \in]\Phi(t)$, $\Phi(t) + \mu(\Phi^{-1}(\Phi(t)))[$). Consequently,

$\Phi(t) \geqslant \alpha > \Phi(s)$, which contradicts $\Phi(s) \geqslant \Phi(t)$. If, for some h, $\alpha \in]\alpha_h$, $\alpha_h + \mu(\Phi^{-1}(\alpha_h))[$, let first $\alpha_h > 0$. Define $B = \Gamma^{-1}([0, \alpha_h[)$ and $C = \Gamma^{-1}(]\alpha, 1])$. A similar argument applies. Finally, if $\alpha_h = 0$, then, since $\underline{x}(t)$ is not a.e. in the same indifference class, $\alpha_h + \mu(\Phi^{-1}(\alpha_h)) < 1$. Define then $B = \Gamma^{-1}([0, \alpha[)$ and $C = \Gamma^{-1}(]\alpha_h + \mu(\Phi^{-1}(\alpha_h)), 1])$. Again a similar argument applies.

Q.E.D.

C. The Main Lemma

LEMMA: *For all types T_i and almost all $t \in T_i$, $\underline{x}(t)$ is in the same indifference class relative to the common preference of traders in T_i.*

PROOF: Clearly, by Lemma 2, for all types T_i,

$$\sum_k \mu(\tau_k^i) = \sum_k \frac{\theta(\tau_k^i)}{\theta(T_i)} = \sum_k \lambda(\Gamma(\tau_k^i)).$$

So $\Sigma_{i,k} \lambda(\Gamma(\tau_k^i)) = \Sigma_{i,k} (\theta(\tau_k^i)/\theta(T_i)) \leqslant 1$, with strict inequality in case of a single type. If $\lambda(\bigcup_{i,k} \Gamma(\tau_k^i)) < 1$, then clearly there exists α, $\alpha \in]0, 1[$, such that $\alpha \notin \bigcup_{i,k} \Gamma(\tau_k^i)$. If $\lambda(\bigcup_{i,k} \Gamma(\tau_k^i)) = 1$, then $1 \geqslant \Sigma_{i,k} \lambda(\Gamma(\tau_k^i)) \geqslant \lambda(\bigcup_{i,k} \Gamma(\tau_k^i)) = 1$, so that $\Sigma_{i,k} \lambda(\Gamma(\tau_k^i)) = \lambda(\bigcup_{i,k} \Gamma(\tau_k^i))$. This implies that for all $(i, k), (i', k'), (i, k) \neq (i', k'), \Gamma(\tau_k^i) \cap \Gamma(\tau_{k'}^{i'}) = \varnothing$; otherwise, the intersection would be an open interval and thus of positive measure, so that $\Sigma_{i,k} \lambda(\Gamma(\tau_k^i)) > \lambda(\bigcup_{i,k} \Gamma(\tau_k^i))$, which is impossible. Consider then for some (i, k) the corresponding $\Gamma(\tau_k^i) =]\alpha, \beta[$. We know that either α or β is in $]0, 1[$; otherwise, we would be in the case of a single atom τ_1^1 of type T_1 such that $\theta(\tau_1^1)/\theta(T_1) = 1$, which is impossible. Suppose $\alpha \in]0, 1[$. If α were in $\Gamma(\tau_{k'}^{i'})$ for some (i', k'), then $\Gamma(\tau_{k'}^{i'})$ would intersect $]\alpha, \beta[= \Gamma(\tau_k^i)$, which is impossible. Consequently, in any alternative, there exists a number α, $\alpha \in]0, 1[$, such that $\alpha \notin \bigcup_{i,k} \Gamma(\tau_k^i)$. Define $\underline{B}_i = \Gamma^{-1}([0, \alpha[) \cap T_i$, $\bar{B}_i = \Gamma^{-1}([\alpha, 1]) \cap T_i$, $\underline{B} = \bigcup_i \underline{B}_i$ and $\bar{B} = \bigcup_i \bar{B}_i$. Define further, for $t \in \underline{B}_i$,

$$y(t) = \alpha \underline{x}(t) + (1 - \alpha) \frac{\int_{\bar{B}_i} \underline{x}(t)\, d\theta}{\theta(\bar{B}_i)}.$$

Since $\theta(\bar{B}_i) = (1 - \alpha)\theta(T_i)$, $y(t) = \alpha \underline{x}(t) + (1/\theta(T_i)) \int_{\bar{B}_i} \underline{x}(t)\, d\theta$. If the lemma were false, there would exist a type T_i, all the agents of which are not in the same indifference class. From Lemma 4, it follows then that for nonnull coalitions E and F, $E \subseteq \underline{B}_i$, $F \subseteq \bar{B}_i$, we have, $\forall(s, t)$, $s \in E$, $t \in F$, $\underline{x}(s) \prec_i \underline{x}(t)$. From Lemma 3, it follows that, $\forall i$, $\forall(s, t)$, $s \in \underline{B}_i$, $t \in \bar{B}_i$, $\underline{x}(s) \precsim_i \underline{x}(t)$. By convexity, it follows then that, $\forall t \in \underline{B}$, $y(t) \succsim_t \underline{x}(t)$ and that, $\forall t \in E$, $y(t) \succ_t \underline{x}(t)$, where E is a nonnull subcoalition of $\underline{B}$. Further we have that $\int_{\underline{B}_i} y(t)\, d\theta = \alpha \int_{\underline{B}_i} \underline{x}(t)\, d\theta + (\theta(\underline{B}_i)/\theta(T_i)) \int_{\bar{B}_i} \underline{x}(t)\, d\theta$. But $\theta(\underline{B}_i)/\theta(T_i) = \alpha$, so that $\int_{\underline{B}_i} y(t)\, d\theta = \alpha \int_{\underline{B}_i} \underline{x}(t)\, d\theta + \alpha \int_{\bar{B}_i} \underline{x}(t)\, d\theta = \alpha \int_{T_i} \underline{x}(t)\, d\theta$. Finally, by summation, we have $\int_{\underline{B}} y(t)\, d\theta = \alpha \int_{D^c} \underline{x}(t)\, d\theta$, where D^c denotes the complement of D in T (remember that $D^c = \bigcup_i T_i$). Also, it is trivial that, for each type T_i, $\int_{\underline{B}_i} \underline{w}(t)\, d\theta = \alpha \int_{T_i} \underline{w}(t)\, d\theta$, since $\underline{w}$ is constant on the type T_i. $(D, \mathcal{T}_D, \theta_D)$ is a finite atomless measure space. Define, for $t \in D$, $y(t) = \underline{x}(t)$ and let $P \in \mathcal{T}_D$, $C = P \cup \underline{B}$.

J. GABSZEWICZ AND J. MERTENS

Clearly

$$\int_C (y(t) - w(t))\, d\theta = \int_B (y(t) - w(t))\, d\theta + \int_P (x(t) - w(t))\, d\theta$$

$$= \alpha \int_{D^c} x(t)\, d\theta - \alpha \int_{D^c} w(t)\, d\theta + \int_P (x(t) - w(t))\, d\theta.$$

Since x is an allocation, $\int_{D^c} (x(t) - w(t))\, d\theta = -\int_D (x(t) - w(t))\, d\theta$. So, $\int_C (y(t) - w(t))\, d\theta = -\alpha \int_D (x(t) - w(t))\, d\theta + \int_P (x(t) - w(t))\, d\theta$. By Lyapounov's theorem, we can choose P such that $\int_P (x(t) - w(t))\, d\theta = \alpha \int_D (x(t) - w(t))\, d\theta + (1 - \alpha)0$; the corresponding C will then satisfy $\int_C (y(t) - w(t))\, d\theta = 0$. Thus the allocation y is feasible for the coalition C. Moreover, $\forall t, t \in C, y(t) \succsim_t x(t)$ and, for t in the nonnull subcoalition E, we have $y(t) \succ_t x(t)$. The coalition C blocks x, contrary to the assumption that x is in the core.   Q.E.D.

D. *Proof of the Theorem*

The assumption of non-atomicity of $(T, \mathscr{T}, \theta)$ is used at only one point of Aumann's equivalence theorem, namely, in Lemma 4.1 [1, p. 45], in order to prove that the so-called $G^{-1}(r_i)$ sets contain subsets of arbitrary small measure. But $G^{-1}(r_i)$ being nonnull is either non-atomic (in which case there is no difficulty), or it contains some atom τ_k^j (in which case, by our lemma, it contains the whole type T_j). It follows from the condition of the theorem that for all types j, T_j contains an atomless and nonnull set of traders. In that case also, the proof goes through. This completes the proof of the equivalence theorem for an economy whose atoms are not too big.   Q.E.D.

4. CONCLUSION

In [1], Aumann writes: "In many real markets the competition is far from perfect; such markets are probably best represented by a mixed model, in which some of the traders are points in a continuum, and others are individually significant." The present paper is a first attempt to study these more real situations. It shows that these markets fall into two main categories: the easy one, in which the condition of the theorem is satisfied, and the interesting one, in which the condition is not satisfied. The fact that a given economy falls in the first or the second category could thus depend on this extravagant condition; this does not satisfy the authors at all. At least we want an economic interpretation of this condition, which is the first open question of this paper.

The second open question concerns the economic significance of an atom. The classical interpretation considers a significant trader as an atom and an insignificant trader as a drop in an ocean (see [1] and [3]). For instance, on the world wheat market, the individual farmers of Western countries appear as insignificant traders, while the Soviet Union is a big atom. Of course, we should not limit ourselves to this interpretation; its interpretation is another open question to enrich our analysis.

The third and most interesting open question concerns the economies for which the condition of the theorem is not verified. Then, how does the core bear on the set of competitive allocations? What could be said about allocations that are in the core, but are not competitive? The following interesting property could pave the way for further research in this area. Consider an economy with two types T_1 and T_2, each being of measure 1, and two atoms τ_1^1 and τ_2^1, falling, respectively, in T_1 and T_2. Assume that $1 < \theta(\tau_1^1) + \theta(\tau_2^1) < 2$ and let y be an allocation in the core which is not competitive. Then it can be shown that, for some type i, and for almost all t in $T_i \setminus \tau_i^1$, $y(\tau_i^1) \succ_i y(t)$, while, for the other type j, $j \neq i$, and almost all t in $T_j \setminus \tau_j^1$, $y(t) \succ_j y(\tau_j^1)$.

A final open question concerns the determination of the extent to which the recent results obtained by B. Shitovitz will bear on the present analysis, and vice versa [4].

Center for Operations Research and Econometrics, Universite Catholique de Louvain.

Manuscript received July, 1969; revision received November, 1969.

REFERENCES

[1] AUMANN, R. J.: "Markets with a Continuum of Traders," *Econometrica*, 32 (January, 1964), 39–50.
[2] DRÈZE, J., S. GEPTS, AND J. JASKOLD GABSZEWICZ: "On Cores and Competitive Equilibria," in *La Décision. Agrigation et Dynamique des Ordres de Préférence*. Paris, C.N.R.S., 1969.
[3] MILNOR, J. W., AND L. S. SHAPLEY: "Values of Large Games II: Oceanic Games," *RAND Memo* 2649, February, 1961.
[4] SHITOVITZ, B: "Oligopoly in Markets with a Continuum of Traders," Research Memorandum 47, Department of Mathematics, The Hebrew University of Jerusalem, July, 1969.

[41]
Monopolistic Competition and General Equilibrium[*]

1. It has been suggested that the partial equilibrium analysis in the theory of mono-polistic competition (Chamberlin [3], Robinson [9]) must be extended to general equi-librium analysis (Triflin [13]). On the other hand, from the point of view of realism, the general economic equilibrium model (Walras [15], Arrow and Debreu [2], Arrow, Block and Hurwicz [1]) should contain some imperfections of competition. This paper deals with the foundation of this problem. The existence and the stability of an equilibrium for the economy with some monopolistic competition will be discussed.

We assume that monopolistically competitive firms have subjective inverse demand (supply) functions for their outputs (inputs) in which prices are linear and decreasing (increasing) functions of their outputs (inputs), being consistent with the given information of the present state of the market. We further assume the convexity of possible production sets—the sets of possible input–output combinations—of firms. Then it will be proved that there is an equilibrium for a mixed economic system of perfect and monopolistic competitions. A similar result can be obtained in the case in which there is some kinkiness in the demand or supply functions.

With further assumptions such that all goods are gross substitutes, demands (supplies) for the outputs (inputs) of monopolistically competitive firms are functions of prices only, and these firms adjust their prices with some feedback process, etc., the stability of an equi-librium can be proved by using recently developed techniques in the study of the stability of a perfectly competitive equilibrium.

2. In this section there will be given a proof of the existence of an equilibrium for an economy which contains some imperfections of competition among firms.

Let us construct our static economic model. Let their be m goods, n consumers, and r firms (r' perfectly competitive, and $r - r'$ monopolistically competitive). Let x_i be a consumption vector of consumer i (whose element is $x_{ij} \geqslant 0$), $\bar{x}_i$ be an initial holding vector (whose element is $\bar{x}_{ij} > 0$), and $U_i(x_i)$ be a utility function. Let y_k be a production vector of firm k whose element $y_{kj} > 0$ (< 0) is output (input) of the j-th good, and Y_k be the possible set of y_k. Let P (whose element $P_j \geqslant 0$) be the price vector. Let x_i^*, y_k^*, P^* be the expected values of x_i, y_k, P respectively. Let λ_{ik} be the proportion of profit of the k-th firm distributed to the i-th consumer. Without loss of generality, let $R^1 = (1, \ldots, r')$ be the set of competitive firms, and $R^2 = (r' + 1, \ldots, r)$ be the set of monopolistically competitive firms, and let $j \in J^k$ mean the j-th good's market is dominated by the k-th firm, $k \in R^2$, and $j \in J^0$ mean $j \notin J^k$ for any $k \in R^2$.

Our assumptions are:

Assumption I. Utility functions $U_i(x_i)$ are continuous, non-decreasing, unsaturated, and quasi-concave.

* I am indebted to Professors K. J. Arrow, R. W. Clower, L. Hurwicz, and H. Uzawa for discussions. This work was supported by the Office of Naval Research under Task NR 047 004.

MONOPOLISTIC COMPETITION AND GENERAL EQUILIBRIUM   197

Assumption II.   (1) $o \in Y_k$; (2) Possible production sets Y_k are convex; (3) possible production sets are compact.

These assumptions are familiar ones in the theory of the equilibrium for a competitive economy.   Assumption II (3) is not necessary but we assume it for the sake of simplicity. See Arrow and Debreu [2].

Assumption III.   Every monopolistically competitive firm is separated from every other such firm; that is $J^k \cap J^{k'} = \Phi$, for any k, $k' \in R^2$. Φ denotes null set.
The aim of this assumption is to exclude from our model such situations as the bilateral monopoly, oligopoly etc., and confine ourselves to the study of monopolistic competition.

Assumption IV.   The k-th firm ($k \in R^2$) has subjective inverse demand or supply functions for its outputs or inputs:

$$P_j^{\bullet} = P_j^{\bullet}(\dot{y}_{kj}, P, \Sigma_i x_{ij} - \Sigma_{k' \neq k} y_{k'j})$$

which are single valued, continuous, and

$$P_j = P_j^{\bullet}(\dot{y}_{kj}, P, \Sigma_i x_{ij} - \Sigma_{k' \neq k} y_{k'j}), \text{ if } \dot{y}_{kj} = \Sigma_i x_{ij} - \Sigma_{k' \neq k} y_{k'j} - \Sigma_i \bar{x}_{ij}.$$

This assumption implies that (with the information on the present state of the market P, $\Sigma_i x_{ij} - \Sigma_{k' \neq k} y_{k'j}$ given,) the firm can have an expectation of the market condition, the expected relation between $P_j^{\bullet}$ and $\dot{y}_{kj}$, which is consistent with the given information.[1]

Assumption V.   Functions $P_j^{\bullet}(\dot{y}_{kj}, P, \Sigma_i x_{ij} - \Sigma_{k' \neq k} y'_{k'j})$ are linear and decreasing with respect to $\dot{y}_{kj}$.

$$P_j^{\bullet} = P_j^{\bullet}(\dot{y}_{kj}, P, \Sigma_i x_{ij} - \Sigma_{k \neq ki} y r_{\cdot j}) = a_j(P, \Sigma_i x_{ij} - \Sigma_{k' k \neq} y_{k'j}) \, \dot{y}_{kj}$$
$$+ b_j(P, \Sigma_i x_{ij} - \Sigma_{k \neq k'} y_{k'j}), \quad a_j(P, \Sigma_i x_{ij} - \Sigma_{k \neq k'} y_{k'j}) < 0.$$

This is a simplifying assumption.   A more interesting assumption is to be introduced later.

The definition of an equilibrium is

Definition I.   A set of vectors (P, x_i, y_k) is an equilibrium if (1) x_i is the maximum point of $U_i(x_i)$ ffnder the restriction

$$\Sigma_j P_j x_{ij} \leqslant \Sigma_j P_j \bar{x}_{ij} + \Sigma_k \lambda_{ki} \Sigma_j P_j y_{kj} = M_i > 0$$

(2) y_k, $k \in R^1$, is the maximum point of $\Sigma_j P_j y_{kj}$ subject to the restriction $y_k \in Y_k$;

(3) y_k, $k \in R^2$, $(P_j = a_j y_{kj} + b_j, j \in J_k)$ is the maximum point of quadratic function $\Sigma_{j \notin J^k} P_j y_{kj} + \Sigma_{j \in J^k} (a_j y_{kj} + b_j) y_{kj}$ under the restriction $y_k \in Y_k$

(4) $\Sigma_i x_{ij} \leqslant \Sigma_i \bar{x}_{ij} + \Sigma_k y_{kj}$, $P_j(\Sigma_i x_{ij} - \Sigma_i \bar{x}_{ij} - \Sigma_k y_{kj}) = 0.$

Then we have an existence theorem of an equilibrium as follows:

Theorem I.   Under Assumptions I-V, we have an equilibrium defined in Definition I.

Proof: Because of the zero degree of the homogeneity of the system with respect to prices, we can normalize price vector P such that $P \in S_m$ (m-dimensional simplex).

---

[1] See D. W. Bushaw and R. W. Clower; *Introduction to Mathematical Economics*, 1957, p. 181.

From the conditions (1) and (4) of Definition I, and condition (3) of Assumption II, the domain of x_t can be restricted to $x_t \in \Gamma_t$, Γ_t being a suitably large convex compact set, without causing any change in the definition of an equilibrium (see Arrow and Debreu [2]).

With $P \in S_m$, $y_k \in Y_k$, given, we can get from condition (1) of Definition I a consumption vector x^0, setting temporarily

$$M_t = \Sigma_j P_j \bar{x}_{tj} + \max \ [0, \ \Sigma_k \lambda_{tk} \Sigma_j P_j y_{kj}] > 0.$$

As is well-known, x_{ij}^0 is an upper semi-continuous function of P, y_k, whose image is non-void and convex.

From condition (2) of Definition I, we can have y_k^0, $k \in R^1$, when $P \in S^m$ is given. This is also an upper semi-continuous function of P, whose image is non-void and convex.

With $P \in S^m$, $x_t \in \Gamma_t$, $y_k \in Y_k$, given, we have y_k^0, $k \in R^2$, from condition (3) of Definition I. This is the maximum of the concave quadratic function $\Sigma_{j \in J} k(a_j y_{kj} + b_j) y_{kj} + \Sigma_{j \notin J} k P_j y_{kj}$, a_j and b_j being functions of given P, x_t, y_k, on the domain of the compact, convex set Y_k, from the above assumptions. Therefore, y^0 is a function of P, x_t, y_k, which is upper semi-continuous, of non-void and convex image.

If $P \in S^m$, $x_t \in \Sigma_t$, $y_k \in Y_k$ are given, we have the following mapping suggested by Uzawa [14]:

$$P_j^0 = \frac{1}{\lambda} \max[0, \ P_j + \mu(\Sigma_t x_{tj} - \Sigma_k y_{kj} - \Sigma_t \bar{x}_{tj})]; \ \mu > 0;$$

$$\lambda = \Sigma_j \max[0, \ P_j + \mu(\Sigma_t x_{tj} - \Sigma_k y_{kj} - \Sigma_t \bar{x}_{tj})] > 0 \text{ for sufficiently small } \mu.$$

Combining all these, we have a mapping from $S^m \times \Pi_t X_t \times \Pi_k Y_k$ into itself, (P, x_t, y_k) $\longrightarrow (P^0, x_t^0, y_k^0)$. Because this is an upper semi-continuous mapping from a compact convex set into itself, and its image is non-void and convex, there is a fixed point $(\bar{P}, \bar{x}_t, \bar{y}_k)$, which maps itself into itself, from the fixed point theorem of Kakutani [6].

Now we will show this fixed point $(\bar{P}, \bar{x}_t, \bar{y}_k)$ is an equilibrium defined in Definition I. From condition (1) of Assumption II, $0 \in Y_k$, we have $\Sigma_j \bar{P}_j y_{kj} \geqslant 0$. Therefore, we have Walras' law,

$$\Sigma_t \bar{P} \ \bar{x}_t - \Sigma_k \bar{P} \ \bar{y}_k - \Sigma_t \bar{P} \ \bar{x}_t = 0,$$

from condition (1) of Definition I and from Assumption I. Using Walras' law, we see from $(\lambda - 1)\Sigma_j \bar{P}_j^2 = \mu(\Sigma_j \bar{P}_j \Sigma_t \bar{x}_{tj} - \Sigma_j \bar{P}_j \Sigma_k \bar{y}_{kj} - \Sigma_j \bar{P}_j \Sigma_t \bar{x}_{tj}) = 0$, that $\lambda = 1$ at the fixed point. Therefore, we have

$$\Sigma_t \bar{x}_{tj} - \Sigma_k \bar{y}_{kj} - \Sigma_t \bar{x}_{tj} \leqslant 0, \text{ and } \bar{P}_j(\Sigma_t \bar{x}_{tj} - \Sigma_k \bar{y}_{kj} - \Sigma_t \bar{x}_{tj}) = 0,$$

which is condition (4) of Definition I. From the construction of x_t^0, y_i^0, and Assumption IV, we see conditions (1)-(3) of Definition I are satisfied at $(\bar{P}, \bar{x}_t, \bar{y}_k)$.   (Q. E. D.)

If, in Assumption V, we assume P_j^* is constant with respect to y_{jk}^* then we have the case of the perfect competition, considering Assumption IV. In this limiting case, our proof coincides with usual proofs of the existence of a perfectly competitive equilibrium.

Assumption V is not necessary. What is needed is to make the profit function $\Sigma_j P_j y_{kj}$ a concave function of y_{kj}. Therefore, a possible extension is the introduction of the kinky demand or supply function (see Stigler [12]), i.e.,

MONOPOLISTIC COMPETITION AND GENERAL EQUILIBRIUM   199

Assumption V*

$$P_j{}^* = P_j{}^*(y_{kj}{}^*, P, \Sigma_i x_{ij} - \Sigma_{k' \neq k} y_{k'j}) = a_j y_{kj}{}^* + b_j, \; y_{kj}{}^* > \Sigma_i x_{ij} - \Sigma_{k' \neq k} y_{k'j} - \Sigma_i \bar{x}_{ij}$$
$$= a_j' y_{kj}{}^* + b_j', \; y_{kj}{}^* < \Sigma_i x_{ij} - \Sigma_{k' \neq k} y_{k'j} - \Sigma_i \bar{x}_{ij}$$

and $a_j(P_j, \Sigma_i x_{ij} - \Sigma_{k' \neq k} y'_{kj}) < a'_j(P, \Sigma_i x_{ij} - \Sigma_{k \neq k'} y_{k'j}) < 0.$

Together with Assumption IV, we have $a_j y_{kj}{}^* + b_j = a_j' y_{kj}{}^* + b_j'$ at $y_{kj}{}^* = \Sigma_i x_{ij} - \Sigma_{k \neq k'} y_{k'j} - \Sigma_i \bar{x}_{ij}$. Under Assumptions I-IV, V*, we can prove the existence of an equilibrium;

> *Theorem II.* Under Assumption I-IV, V*, we have an equilibrium defined in Definition I.

In the proof of Theorem I, an essential role is played by the assumption of the convexity of production sets or non-decreasing returns. Considering that the equilibrium we are discussing is temporary equilibrium, there is some plausibility of this assumption (Hicks [5], p. 83). But with the introduction of some imperfections of competition, we may not assume convex production sets, considering the fact that monopolistic competition has much to do with so-called increasing returns. (Sraffa [11]). If we assume that production sets are contractible, but not necessarily convex, we can prove the existence of an equilibrium imposing some conditions on the forms of the subjective demand and supply functions, so as to assure that the set which satisfies condition (3) of Definition I is also contractible. The formal proof of this possibility was given by the theorem in Debreu [4]. Therefore, the work left to be done is to find such conditions as are economically meaningful.

3. In this section we will give a proof of the stability of an economy which contains some imperfections of competition. As is well-known, in the perfectly competitive market the price goes up and down according to the excess demand. But in the monopolistically competitive market, the excess demand is always zero by definition (see Lange [7]) and what makes the price go up and down is the profit of the firm which dictates the market.

Let us make a dynamic economic model. Let $P \geqslant 0$ be the price vector whose element is P_i, x_i, $i \in I'$ be the excess demand of the i-th good whose market is perfectly competitive, $\bar{P}_i$, $i \in I^2$ be the price of the i-th good which assures the maximum profit for the dominating firm in its monopolistically competitive market. The excess demand of the monopolistically competitive good is always zero, $x_i = 0$, $i \in I^2$.

Our dynamic process is

$$\dot{P}_i = v_i F_i = \begin{cases} v_i x_i & i \in I^1 \quad (1) \\ v_i(\bar{P}_i - P_i), & i \in I^2 \quad (2) \end{cases}$$

This is an extension of the dynamic price adjustment process discussed by Walras [15], Samuelson [10], Arrow, Block, and Hurwicz [1] to the case with some imperfection of the competition. The first half (1) is the usual process of price adjustment according to the excess demand while the second half (2) implies a kind of the feed-back adjustment process of the monopolistically competitive firm to get to the maximum profit.

A similar extension of the price adjustment to the case with monopoly is also given in Lange [7]. But there we find Walras' law $\Sigma_{i \in I}{}^1 P_i x_i \equiv 0$ which we cannot assume because monopolistically competitive firms distribute their profit but not their loss. We can only say that at the equilibrium $E_{i \in I}{}^1 P_i x_i = 0$. See Section 2 above.

Let us make the following assumption:

Assumption VI. Both x_i, $i \in I^1$ and $\bar{P}_i$, $i \in I^2$ are functions of prices P only. Further $x_i(p)$ is homogeneous of degree zero while $\bar{P}_i(p)$ is homogeneous of degree one.

This assumption is satisfied if we assume that participants in a monopolistically competitive market other than the monopolistic firm consist of perfectly competitive firms and consumers who get their income from their initial holding and from the profit of perfectly competitive firms, but not from the profit of monopolistically competitive firms.

Assumption VII. $\dfrac{\partial x_i}{\partial P_j} > 0, i \neq j, i \in I^1$ and $\dfrac{\partial \bar{P}_i}{\partial P_j} > 0 \; i \neq j, i \in I^2$.

The first half of this assumption is so-called gross substitutability. The second half of the assumption is quite plausible once we assume gross substitutability. We can see this in the following analysis of a very simplified case. Let there be only one output whose market is monopolistic while markets of other outputs and all inputs are perfectly competitive. The monopolistic firm determines $\bar{P}_i$, the price of the monopolistic good, which assures the maximum profit. With P given, it estimates the demand function as $P_i^* = a_i y_i^* + b_i$, where y_i^* is the amount of output and a_i, b_i are functions of price vector P such that $P_i = a_i D_i(p) + b_i$, $D_i(p)$ being the demand for it. See Assumptions IV, V in Section 2. Let us assume a_i is constant while b_i is a function of P. Then gross substitutability $\dfrac{\partial D_i}{\partial P_j} > 0$ implies $\dfrac{\partial b_i}{\partial P_j} >$ which in turn implies $\dfrac{\partial \bar{P}_i}{\partial P_i} > 0$, when the marginal cost of producing the i-th good is increasing.

Now we are in the position to state the following theorem.

Theorem III. Under Assumptions VI-VII, the dynamic process is stable.

Proof: The local stability of an equilibrium price vector, which is assumed positive, in the dynamic process, normalized with some appropriate numéraire, can be proved as in Negishi [8], because at the equilibrium Euler's identity is reduced to the same thing regardless of the degree of the homogeneity of the function. We have a linear approximation of the dynamic process;

$$\dot{P}_i = v_i \sum_{j \neq 1} \frac{\partial x_i}{\partial P_j} (P_j - \bar{P}_j), i \in I^1, i \neq 1$$

$$\dot{P}_i = v_i \sum_{j \neq 1} \left(\frac{\partial \bar{P}_i}{\partial P_j} - \delta_{ij} \right) (P_j - \bar{P}_j), i \in I^2, i \neq 1$$

with $\sum\limits_{j \neq 1} \dfrac{\partial x_i}{\partial P_j} P_j = - \dfrac{\partial x_i}{\partial P_1}$, $i \in I^1$, and $\sum\limits_{j \neq 1} \left(\dfrac{\partial \bar{P}_i}{\partial P_1} - \delta_{ij} \right) P_j = - \dfrac{\partial \bar{P}_i}{\partial P_1}$, $i \in I^2$,

the first good being numeraire and δ_{ij} being Kronecker's δ. Then the matrix

$$\left[\frac{\partial F_i}{\partial P_j} \right] = \begin{vmatrix} \dfrac{\partial x_i}{\partial P_j} \\[2ex] \hline \dfrac{\partial P_i}{\partial P_j} - \delta_{ij} \end{vmatrix}$$

has characteristic roots with negative real parts.

MONOPOLISTIC COMPETITION AND GENERAL EQUILIBRIUM   201

The global stability is proved by using the lemma 3 in Arrow, Block and Hurwicz [1] that under assumption of gross substitutability, if $F(p) = [F_1(p), \ldots, F_m(p)] \neq 0$, $F(\bar{P}) = 0$, $P_{k'}/\bar{P}_{k'} = \max\left(\dfrac{P_k}{\bar{P}_k}\right)$, $\dfrac{P_{k''}}{\bar{P}_{k''}} = \min\left(\dfrac{P_k}{\bar{P}_k}\right)$ then $F_{k'}(p) < 0$, $F_{k''}(p) < 0$.

In this case, the proof of the lemma is modified on account of the homogeneity of the degree one of F_i, $i \in I^2$ as follows.   Let us define $P^* = \left(\dfrac{P_{k'}}{\bar{P}_{k'}}\right) \bar{P}$ and $P^{**} = \left(\dfrac{P_{k''}}{\bar{P}_{k''}}\right) \bar{P}$. Then we have $F_{k'}(p) < F_{k'}(p^*) = F_{k'}(\bar{P}) = 0$ and $F_{k''}(p) > F_{k''}(p^{**}) = F_{k''}(\bar{P}) = 0$, With this lemma established we can prove the global stability in the same way as in Theorem I in Arrow, Block and Hurwicz [1].   Q. E. D.

Stanford, California.   TAKASHI NEGISHI.

REFERENCES

[1] Arrow, Kenneth J., H. D. Block and Leonid Hurwicz, " On the stability of the equilibrium, II," *Econometrica*, 27: 82-109.

[2] Arrow, Kenneth J., and Gerard Debreu, " Existence of an equilibrium for a competitive economy," *Econometrica*, 22: 256-290.

[3] Chamberlin, E. H., *The Theory of Monopolistic Competition*: *A Re-Orientation of the Theory of Value*.   Cambridge; Harvard University Press, 1953.

[4] Debreu, Gerard, " A social equilibrium existence theorem," *Proceedings of the National Academy of Sciences*, 38: 886-893.

[5] Hicks, J. R., *Value and Capital*.   Cambridge: Oxford University Press, 1939.

[6] Kakutani, S., " A generalization of Brouwer's fixed point theorem," *Duke Mathematical Journal*, 8: 457-459.

[7] Lange, Oscar, *Price Flexibility and Employment*, Cowles Commission Monograph 8, Bloomington, Indiana, 1944.

[8] Negishi, Takashi, " A note on the stability of an economy where all goods are gross substitutes," *Econometrica*, 26: 454-447.

[9] Robinson, Joan, *The Economics of Imperfect Competition*.   London: Macmillan and Company, 1933.

[10] Samuelson, P. A., *Foundations of Economic Analysis*, Cambridge: Harvard University Press, 1947.

[11] Sraffa, Piero, " The laws of returns under competitive conditions," *Economic Journal*, 36: 535-550.

[12] Stigler, George J., " The kinky oligopoly demand curve and rigid prices," *The Journal of Political Economy*, 55: 432-449.

[13] Triffin, R., *Monopolistic Competition and General Equilibrium Theory*.   Cambridge: Harvard University Press, 1940.

[14] Uzawa, Hirofumi, " A note on the stability of equilibrium," *Technical Report* 61, Department of Economics, Stanford University, 1958.

[15] Walras, Leon, *Elements of Pure Economics*, trans. by W. Jaffe, Homewood, Illinois: Richard D. Irwin, Inc., 1954.

[42]

JOURNAL OF ECONOMIC THEORY **4**, 381–400 (1972)

Oligopoly "A la Cournot" in a General Equilibrium Analysis

JEAN JASKOLD GABSZEWICZ AND JEAN-PHILIPPE VIAL

CORE, de Croylaan 54, 3030 Heverlee, Belgium

Received April 7, 1971

I. INTRODUCTION

A common justification of the concept of competitive equilibrium is that the number of economic agents being "large", none of them could (and/or hope to) exert any influence on the prices and each of them has to behave as a price-taker. This statement seems to be relevant for the exchange side of the economy; by contrast, on the production side, the number of firms might not be "large enough" to support as well this justification. In this paper, we consider an economy in which the behavior of the economic agents is asymmetric; namely, on the exchange side the agents are price-takers; on the production side—by analogy with the Cournot solution in partial analysis—the firms behave as the players of a noncooperative game.

The institutional organization of this economy can be described as follows. The consumers provide firms with labor and other nonconsumable resources, like primary factors. With these resources, the firms choose production plans which consist only of bundles of consumption goods. The various forms of labor and other primary factors are not "marketable"; rather, the firms distribute "real wages" to the consumers —who have provided them with these factors and labor—in terms of preassigned shares of their output.[1] At the end of the production process, each consumer is thus endowed with the sum of his shares in the various firms, namely, with some bundle of consumption goods. Exchange markets are then organized, where the consumers aim at improving their consumption through trade. The institutional rule of exchange consists in using a price mechanism. The prices on the exchange markets then serve as an

---

[1] One can imagine that the "preassigned shares" distributed by the firms to the factor owners have been established through collective conventions; it would explain why labor and other primary factors are not "marketable."

381

382   JASKOLD GABSZEWICZ AND VIAL

information for the firms, to adjust eventually their production plans according to some preassigned rule.[2]

Let us assume that in our economy, there are relatively few firms, compared with the large number of consumers. We would like to adapt the decision criteria of the economic agents so as to reflect their relative importance in the collective decision process. For instance, it would be unnatural to assume that the firms would adapt to the price system observed on the exchange markets, *taking these prices as given*. It is clear, indeed, that these firms should be aware that they may—at least, partially—control the price system that will emerge on the exchange markets. As far as these prices react to changes in the relative aggregate supplies of the commodities, each firm has partial control over them, via the choice it makes of its production plan. Indeed, if a firm decides to perturb its initial supply, the initial endowments of all the consumers who have a share in its production are simultaneously perturbed. The final impact will then be registered on the relative prices for the consumption goods, through the displacement in the endowments of these consumers.

So, we shall first assume that each firm is fully aware of this impact. We shall then assume that each firm adjusts its production plans so as to increase the real wages of its shareholders, evaluated with the prices of the exchange markets. But since these prices depend themselves on the particular production plan that the firm will choose, it is not true that this behavior is equivalent to profit maximization adjustment at *given* prices. Under normalization, each firm typically faces a price function, one argument of which is its own supply. Let us now recall that there is only a small number of firms. If all of them act according to the above-mentioned criterion, their strategies are interrelated through the price function just described, the arguments of which are precisely the production plans of the firms. Typically, the firms are in a game situation, in which the players of the game have conflicting interests and partial control on the payoffs.

The solution which is adopted here consists in assuming that the firms behave as the players of a *noncooperative n*-person game; namely, that their equilibrium supplies will form a Nash equilibrium point, the profit-payoffs being defined in terms of the corresponding price system on the exchange markets. The formation of prices on these markets remains

---

[2] A typical example of such an economy is provided by a "kibboutzim" economic organization. Individual farmers provide the kibboutzim with their labor force and land. They receive in exchange some combination of the agricultural products resulting from the productive activities of the kibboutzim. The exchange of these products among the farmers supplies the kibboutzims with a price system which serves to them to adjust eventually their production plan.

OLIGOPOLY, GENERAL EQUILIBRIUM ANALYSIS 383

to be defined. We have assumed from the beginning that the economy involves a large number of consumers. It is then reasonable to assume that the exchange side of the economy will behave in a competitive way. Namely, we assume that, whatever may be the particular production plans chosen by the firms, the exchange markets will lead to a competitive allocation of the goods among the consumers and, consequently, to a competitive price system. Through this competitive mechanism, and given an *a priori* normalization rule, the prices on the exchange markets are functions of the firm's production plans. But, conversely, the choices of the production plans by the firms are functions of the prices on the exchange markets.

Our objectives in the present paper are (1) to study, in a general equilibrium model, the compatibility conditions of this asymmetric behavior of the production and consumption sides of the economy; (2) to analyze to what extent this asymmetric behavior keeps the state of the economy away from a general competitive equilibrium, both on the production and consumption sides.

The mathematical model is introduced in Section II and an example is discussed in Section III; the statements of the results and their proofs are presented in Sections IV and V. The conclusion reviews briefly the significance of the results and assumptions, and defines some directions for further research.

II. THE MODEL

We consider a productive economy with m *firms* j, $j = 1,..., m$, and n *consumers* i, $i = 1,..., n$. The consumers provide the firms with labor and other types of nonconsumable initial resources. Each consumer receives in exchange a fixed (given) share of the various consumption goods produced by the firms. Let us assume that there are l such consumption goods and let $\theta_j{}^i$ be the *share* of the i-th consumer in the production of the j-th firm, $i = 1,..., n$; $j = 1,..., m$; of course, for all j, $\sum_{i=1}^{n} \theta_j{}^i = 1$. A bundle of consumption goods or a *commodity bundle* is a point of $R_+{}^l$, the positive orthant of R^l. The consumption set of each consumer is $R_+{}^l$. For each consumer i, a *preference relation* $\succsim_i$ is defined on $R_+{}^l$ which satisfies the following assumptions:

   (i)   the relation is *complete, reflexive* and *transitive*;

   (ii) *desirability*: $x \geqslant y \Rightarrow x \succ_i y$;[3]

---

[3] For two vectors x and y in $R_+{}^l$, the notation $x \geqslant y$ means: $x^k \geqslant y^k$, $k = 1,..., l$, and $x^h > y^h$ for some h; the notation $x \gg y$ means: $x^k > y^k$, $k = 1,..., l$.

384   JASKOLD GABSZEWICZ AND VIAL

(iii)   *continuity*: for all $y \in R_+^l$, the sets $\{x \mid x \succsim_i y\}$ and $\{x \mid y \succsim_i x\}$ are closed;

(iv)   *strict convexity*: for all x and y with $x \succsim_i y$ and $\alpha \in \,]0, 1[$, $\alpha x + (1 - \alpha) y \succ_i y$.

(v)   Each consumer is assumed to hold initially a commodity bundle w_i, with $w_i \gg 0$.

The production possibilities for the j-th firm are defined by a compact convex subset G_j of R_+^l: namely, the *production set* of the firm j. A *feasible production plan* of firm j is a point y of G_j. After each firm has chosen a production plan in its production set, the resulting outputs are distributed to the consumers according to their preassigned shares. An exchange economy is generated, which is described now. Given feasible production plans $(y_1 ,..., y_m)$, the *intermediate endowment* of consumer i is the vector $w_i + \sum_{j=1}^m \theta_j{}^i y_j$. An *equilibrium allocation* is a n-tuple $(x_1 ,..., x_n)$ of commodity bundles, one for each consumer, such that $\sum_{j=1}^m y_j + \sum_{i=1}^n w_i = \sum_{i=1}^n x_i$. A *price system p* is a nonnull element of R_+^l. For a set $(y_1 ,..., y_m)$ of feasible production plans, a *competitive equilibrium relative to* $(y_1 ,..., y_m)$ is a pair $[p; (x_1 ,..., x_n)]$ consisting of a price system p and an equilibrium allocation $(x_1 ,..., x_n)$ such that, for all i, $p \cdot x_i \leqslant p \cdot w_i + p \cdot \sum_{j=1}^m \theta_j{}^i y_j$ and $\{y \mid p \cdot y \leqslant p \cdot w_i + p \cdot \sum_{j=1}^m \theta_j{}^i y_j \,; y \succ_i x_i\} = \varnothing$.[4] A *price function π* is a function defined on $\prod_{j=1}^m G_j$ with values in R_+^l such that, for any $(y_1 ,..., y_m)$, $[\pi(y_1 ,..., y_m); (x_1 ,..., x_n)]$ is a competitive equilibrium relative to $(y_1 ,..., y_m)$ for some equilibrium allocation $(x_1 ,..., x_n)$. It is well known that under assumptions (i–v) the set of competitive equilibria relative to $(y_1 ,..., y_m)$ contains at least one element (cf., for instance, [4]). If, furthermore, we assume the uniqueness of this element, any normalization rule will yield the existence of a price function. So we will assume

A₁ :   For any m-tuple of production plans $(y_1 ,..., y_m)$, the set of competitive equilibria relative to $(y_1 ,..., y_m)$ contains a unique element $[\pi(y_1 ,..., y_m); (x_1 ,..., x_n)]$.

In the following definitions, the price function π refers to an implicit normalization rule. The behavior of the firms remains to be formally defined. This will be done by considering the firms as the players of a noncooperative m-person game. A *pure strategy* for firm j is a feasible production plan for firm j. Given a price function π, an m-tuple $(y_1{}^* ,..., y_m{}^*)$ of pure strategies is an *equilibrium point* for π, if and only if, for all j and all $y_j \in G_j$,

$$\pi(y_1{}^* ,..., y_j ,..., y_m{}^*) \cdot y_j \leqslant \pi(y_1{}^* ,..., y_j{}^* ,..., y_m{}^*) \cdot y_j{}^*.$$

[4] The notation $x \cdot y$ denotes the scalar product in R_+^l.

A *Cournot–Walras equilibrium* is a triplet $[\pi; (x_1^*,..., x_n^*); (y_1^*,..., y_m^*)]$ consisting of a price function π, an equilibrium allocation $(x_1^*,..., x_n^*)$ and an m-tuple $(y_1^*,..., y_m^*)$ of pure strategies such that (i) the pair $[\pi(y_1^*,..., y_m^*); (x_1^*,..., x_n^*)]$ is a competitive equilibrium relative to $(y_1^*,..., y_m^*)$ and (ii) $(y_1^*,..., y_m^*)$ is an equilibrium point for π. A *global competitive equilibrium* is a triplet $[\pi, (x_1^*,..., x_n^*); (y_1^*,..., y_m^*)]$ consisting of a price function π, an equilibrium allocation $(x_1^*,..., x_n^*)$, and an m-tuple of pure strategies such that (i) the pair $[\pi(y_1^*,..., y_m^*); (x_1^*,..., x_n^*)]$ is a competitive equilibrium relative to $(y_1^*,..., y_n^*)$; (ii) $\pi(y_1^*,..., y_j^*,..., y_m^*) \cdot y$ achieves its maximum on G_j at y_j^*, $j = 1,..., m$. Given the assumptions on the economy, there exists a global competitive equilibrium.

III. An Example

In order to illustrate the concepts and the definitions of the preceding section, we shall consider a two-commodity economy with two firms and two consumers. The production sets of firm I and firm II are, respectively,

$$G_1 = \{y^1 = (y_1^1, y_2^1) \mid 0 \leqslant y_1^1 \leqslant 2, 0 \leqslant y_2^1 \leqslant 8, 2y_1^1 + y_2^1 \leqslant 10\}$$

and

$$G_2 = \{y^2 = (y_1^2, y_2^2) \mid 0 \leqslant y_1^2 \leqslant 8, 0 \leqslant y_2^2 \leqslant 2, y_1^2 + 2y_2^2 \leqslant 10\}$$

(cf. figure 1).

The utility functions of consumer I and consumer II are, respectively, $u_1(x_1^1, x_2^1) = (x_1^1)^{1/4} (x_2^1)^{3/4}$ and $u_2(x_1^2, x_2^2) = (x_1^2)^{3/4} (x_2^2)^{1/4}$, whereas their intermediate endowments are, respectively, (y_1^1, y_2^1) and (y_1^2, y_2^2).

The price system π of the competitive equilibrium relative to (y^1, y^2) is constrained by the following set of equations:

$$\pi_1 x_1^1 + \pi_2 x_2^1 = \pi_1 y_1^1 + \pi_2 y_2^1,$$

$$\pi_1 x_1^2 + \pi_2 x_2^2 = \pi_1 y_1^2 + \pi_2 y_2^2,$$

$$3\pi_1 x_1^1 - \pi_2 x_2^1 = 0,$$

$$\pi_1 x_1^2 - 3\pi_2 x_2^2 = 0,$$

$$x_1^1 + x_1^2 = y_1^1 + y_1^2,$$

$$x_2^1 + x_2^2 = y_2^1 + y_2^2,$$

to which we add the arbitrary normalization rule

$$\pi_1(y_1{}^1 + y_1{}^2) + \pi_2(y_2{}^1 + y_2{}^2) = 1.$$

Provided $y_1{}^1$ and $y_1{}^2$ or $y_2{}^1$ and $y_2{}^2$ are not simultaneously equal to zero[5], routine calculations yield the following price function:

$$\pi_1(y^1, y^2) = \frac{1}{D}(y_2{}^1 + 3y_2{}^2), \;\; \pi_2(y^1, y^2) = \frac{1}{D}(3y_1{}^1 + y_1{}^2),$$

with

$$D = (y_2{}^1 + 3y_2{}^2)(y_1{}^1 + y_1{}^2) + (3y_1{}^1 + y_1{}^2)(y_2{}^1 + y_2{}^2).$$

We prove that the triplet $(\pi; \bar{x}^1, \bar{x}^2; \bar{y}^1, \bar{y}^2)$ with $\bar{x}^1 = \bar{y}^1 = (2, 6)$ and $\bar{x}^2 = \bar{y}^2 = (6, 2)$ is a Cournot–Walras equilibrium. First it is easy to verify that $\pi(\bar{y}^1, \bar{y}^2) \underset{\text{Def}}{=} \bar{\pi} = (1/16, 1/16)$ and that $(\bar{\pi}; \bar{x}^1, \bar{x}^2)$ is a competitive equilibrium relative to $(\bar{y}^1, \bar{y}^2)$. Consider the profit function of firm I when firm II's production plan is $\bar{y}_2$:

$$f_1(y^1, \bar{y}^2) = \pi(y^1, \bar{y}^2) \cdot y^1$$

$$= \frac{2y_1{}^1 y_2{}^1 + 3y_1{}^1 + 3y_2{}^1}{2y_1{}^1 y_2{}^1 + 6y_1{}^1 + 6y_2{}^1 + 24}.$$

The isoprofit curves, $f_1(y^1, \bar{y}^2) = k$ with $0 < k < 1$, defined on the nonnegative orthant are branches of hyperbolas which are convex. Moreover, $f_1(y^1, \bar{y}^2)$ is strictly increasing along the ray $y_1{}^1 = y_2{}^1$. Hence $f_1(y^1, \bar{y}^2)$ is strictly quasi-concave and achieves its maximum on the convex set G_1 at a unique point. The Kuhn–Tucker conditions are:

$$\frac{\partial f_1}{\partial y_1{}^1} - \lambda_1 - 2\lambda_3 \leqslant 0, \;\;\;\; \frac{\partial f_1}{\partial y_2{}^1} - \lambda_2 - \lambda_3 \leqslant 0,$$

$$y_1{}^1\left(\frac{\partial f_1}{\partial y_1{}^1} - \lambda_1 - 2\lambda_3\right) = 0, \;\; y_2{}^1\left(\frac{\partial f_1}{\partial y_2{}^1} - \lambda_2 - \lambda_3\right) = 0.$$

At $y^1 = \bar{y}^1$ these conditions are satisfied with $\partial f_1/\partial y_1{}^1 = 3\alpha$, $\partial f_1/\partial y_2{}^1 = \alpha$, $\lambda_1 = \lambda_3 = \alpha$, $\lambda_2 = 0$ and $\alpha = 29/384$. It is easily verified that, for this problem, the $K - T$ conditions are sufficient to guarantee that $f_1(y^1, \bar{y}^2)$ attains its maximum at $y^1 = \bar{y}^1$.

Similarly the profit function of firm II, $f_2(\bar{y}^1, y^2) = \pi(\bar{y}^1, y^2) \cdot y^2$, attains its maximum value on G_2 at $y^2 = \bar{y}^2$. Hence $(\pi; \bar{x}^1, \bar{x}^2; \bar{y}^1, \bar{y}^2)$ is

---

[5] There exist production plans (y^1, y^2) for which the equilibrium price system is not defined. This difficulty can be discarded by restricting the set of strategies of each firm to the intersection of their respective production set with the strictly positive orthant.

a Cournot–Walras equilibrium. A direct inspection on Fig. 1 shows that it is not a global competitive equilibrium. In this economy the global competitive equilibrium is unique and corresponds to the triplet $(\bar{\pi}; \bar{x}^1, \bar{x}^2; \bar{y}^1, \bar{y}^2)$ with $\bar{\pi} = (1/18, 1/18)$, $\bar{x}^1 = (11/4, 33/4)$, $\bar{x}^2 = (33/4, 11/4)$, $\bar{y}^1 = (1, 8)$ and $\bar{y}^2 = (8, 1)$. Furthermore, one can check that the global competitive equilibrium is not a Cournot–Walras equilibrium.

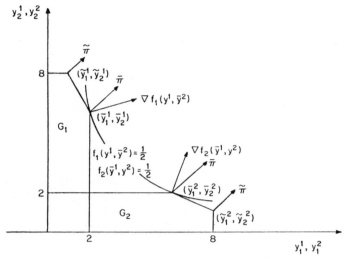

FIGURE 1

IV. EXISTENCE THEOREM

This section is devoted to the proof of an existence theorem for Cournot–Walras equilibria. The proof of our existence theorem rests crucially on the following result, which is a simplified version of a result due to Hildenbrand and Mertens.[6]

THEOREM 4.1. *The price function π is continuous.*

Proof. For the proof of the theorem, we normalize the price systems $\pi(y_1, ..., y_m)$ in a compact set P of R_+^l. We denote by Ω the set of intermediate endowment vectors

$$\{\sum_{j=1}^{m} \theta_j^1 y_j + w_1, ..., \sum_{j=1}^{m} \theta_j^i y_j + w_i, ..., \sum_{j=1}^{m} \theta_j^n y_j + w_n\}.$$

[6] Compare [3].

Let $\{[\pi(\bar{y}_1{}^k,..., \bar{y}_m{}^k); (\bar{x}_1{}^k,..., \bar{x}_n{}^k)]\}$ be a sequence of competitive equilibria relative to $(\bar{y}_1{}^k,..., \bar{y}_m{}^k)$, $k = 1, 2,...$, with $\bar{y}_j{}^k \to \bar{y}_j$ in G_j for all $j, j = 1,..., m$. Let also $[\pi(\bar{y}_1,..., \bar{y}_m); (\bar{x}_1,..., \bar{x}_n)]$ be the competitive equilibrium relative to $(\bar{y}_1,..., \bar{y}_m)$. We have to show that $\pi(\bar{y}_1,..., \bar{y}_m) = \lim_{k\to\infty} \pi(\bar{y}_1{}^k,..., \bar{y}_m{}^k)$. Since for all j, $\bar{y}_j{}^k \to \bar{y}_j$, it follows that, for all i,

$$\sum_{j=1}^{m} \theta_j{}^i \bar{y}_j{}^k + w_i \to \sum_{j=1}^{m} \theta_j{}^i \bar{y}_j + w_i .$$

Consequently, the sequence of intermediate endowment vectors

$$\{v^k\} \underset{Def}{=} \left\{ \left(\sum_{j=1}^{m} \theta_j{}^1 \bar{y}_j{}^k + w_1 ,..., \sum_{j=1}^{m} \theta_j{}^i \bar{y}_j{}^k + w_i ,..., \sum_{j=1}^{m} \theta_j{}^n \bar{y}_j{}^k + w_n \right) \right\}$$

converges, in Ω, to the intermediate endowment vector

$$\bar{v} = \left(\sum_{j=1}^{m} \theta_j{}^1 \bar{y}_j + w_1 ,..., \sum_{j=1}^{m} \theta_j{}^i \bar{y}_j + w_i ,..., \sum_{j=1}^{m} \theta_j{}^n \bar{y}_j + w_n \right).$$

Given the assumptions on the economy, it follows from standard arguments that, for each consumer i, his individual demand function $\xi_i(p, w_i + \sum_{j=1}^{m} \theta_j{}^i y_j{}^k)$ is continuous both in prices and endowment; consequently, the excess demand function ξ defined by

$$\xi(p, v) = \sum_{i=1}^{n} \left[\xi_i \left(p, w_i + \sum_{j=1}^{n} \theta_j{}^i y_j{}^k \right) \right] - \left(\sum_{i=1}^{n} w_i + \sum_{j=1}^{m} y_j \right)$$

is continuous both in prices and intermediate endowments.

Assume then that $\pi(\bar{y}_1,..., \bar{y}_m) \neq \lim_{k\to\infty} \pi(\bar{y}_1{}^k,..., \bar{y}_m{}^k)$. Since P is compact, the sequence $\{\pi(\bar{y}_1{}^k,..., \bar{y}_m{}^k)\}$ has a converging subsequence $\{\pi(\bar{y}_1^{k_n},..., \bar{y}_m^{k_n})\}$ with $\lim_{k_n\to\infty} \pi(\bar{y}_1^{k_n},..., \bar{y}_m^{k_n}) =_{Def} \hat{\pi} \neq \pi(\bar{y}_1,..., \bar{y}_m)$. By assumption we have $\xi(\pi(\bar{y}_1^{k_n},..., \bar{y}_m^{k_n}); \bar{v}_k) = 0$ for all k_n. Then, by continuity of ξ and the fact that $\bar{v}_k \to \bar{v}$ in Ω,

$$\xi(\hat{\pi}; \bar{v}) = 0,$$

which contradicts that $\pi(\bar{y}_1,..., \bar{y}_m)$ is the unique price system for which $\xi(p, \bar{v}) = 0$.   Q.E.D.

We need also:

A_2 :   For all j and all fixed z_k, $z_k \in G_k$, $k \neq j$, the real-valued function f_j defined on G_j by $f_j(z_1,..., y_j,..., z_m) = \pi(z_1,..., y_j,..., z_m) \cdot y_j$ is strictly quasi-concave, under the normalization rule adopted for π.

OLIGOPOLY, GENERAL EQUILIBRIUM ANALYSIS 389

EXISTENCE THEOREM. *Under assumptions* (A_1) *and* (A_2), *there exists a Cournot–Walras equilibrium.*

Proof. Let f_j be defined as under assumption (A_2) and π be defined as under assumption (A_1), with $\pi(y_1,...,y_m)$ in some compact set P of R_+^l. Since by Theorem 4.1, π is continuous on G_j, for all j and all fixed z_k, $z_k \in G_k$, $k \neq j$, the function f_j is continuous on G_j. Furthermore, by strict concavity of f_j, it follows that for all j and all fixed z_k, $z_k \in G_k$, $k \neq j$, there is a unique point $\bar{y}_j$ in G_j which satisfies: for all $y_j \in G_j$, $f_j(z_1,...,\bar{y}_j,...,z_m) \geqslant f_j(z_1,...,y_j,...,z_m)$. Let ϕ be the function on $\prod_{j=1}^m G_j$ with values in $\prod_{j=1}^m G_j$ defined by

$$\phi(z_1,...,z_m) = (\bar{y}_1,...,\bar{y}_j,...,\bar{y}_m)$$

with, for all j, $\bar{y}_j$ such that $f_j(z_1,...,\bar{y}_j,...,z_m) \geqslant f_j(z_1,...,y_j,...,z_m)$; $\bar{y}_j \in G_j$, $y_j \in G_j$. We prove that the function ϕ is continuous on $\prod_{j=1}^m G_j$. Let $\{(\bar{z}_1^k,...,\bar{y}_j^k,...,\bar{z}_m^k)\}$ be a sequence of points in $\prod_{j=1}^m G_j$ converging to a point $(\bar{z}_1,...,\bar{y}_j,...,\bar{z}_m)$ and assume that, for all k, $k = 1, 2,...,$ and $y_j \in G_j$,

$$f_j(\bar{z}_1^k,...,\bar{y}_j^k,...,\bar{z}_m^k) \geqslant f_j(\bar{z}_1^k,...,y_j,...,\bar{z}_m^k).$$

We have to prove that $f_j(\bar{z}_1,...,\bar{y}_j,...,\bar{z}_m) \geqslant f_j(\bar{z}_1,...,y_j,...,\bar{z}_m)$ for all $y_j \in G_j$. Assume on the contrary that for some $y_0 \in G_j$, the converse inequality is verified. Since for all k we have that

$$f_j(\bar{z}_1^k,...,\bar{y}_j^k,...,\bar{z}_m^k) \geqslant f_j(\bar{z}_1^k,...,y_0,...,\bar{z}_m^k)$$

we have also by continuity of f_j,

$$\lim_{k \to \infty} f_j(\bar{z}_1^k,...,\bar{y}_j^k,...,\bar{z}_m^k) = f_j(\bar{z}_1,...,\bar{y}_j,...,\bar{z}_m)$$
$$\geqslant f_j(\bar{z}_1,...,y_0,...,\bar{z}_m) = \lim_{k \to \infty} f_j(\bar{z}_1^k,...,y_0,...,\bar{z}_m^k),$$

which contradicts $f_j(\bar{z}_1,...,\bar{y}_j,...,\bar{z}_m) < f_j(\bar{z}_1,...,y_0,...,\bar{z}_m)$. So, the function ϕ is continuous on $\prod_{j=1}^m G_j$. By Tychonoff's theorem, the compactness of each G_j implies that $\prod_{j=1}^m G_j$ is compact. Since $\prod_{j=1}^m G_j$ is also convex, it follows from Brouwer's fixed point theorem that there exists $(y_1^*,...,y_m^*)$ in $\prod_{j=1}^m G_j$ such that $\phi(y_1^*,...,y_m^*) = (y_1^*,...,y_m^*)$, i.e., for all j, $y_j \in G_j$,

$$f_j(y_1^*,...,y_j^*,...,y_m^*) \geqslant f_j(y_1^*,...,y_j,...,y_m^*)$$

or, for all j, and all $y_j \in G_j$,

$$y_j^* \cdot \pi(y_1^*,...,y_j^*,...,y_m^*) \geqslant y_j \cdot \pi(y_1^*,...,y_j,...,y_m^*),$$

so that $(y_1^*,..., y_m^*)$ is an equilibrium point for π. On the other hand, it follows from the definition of π that $[\pi(y_1^*,..., y_m^*); (x_1^*,..., x_n^*)]$ is a competitive equilibrium relative to $(y_1^*,..., y_m^*)$ for some equilibrium allocation $(x_1^*,..., x_n^*)$. This completes the proof of the existence theorem.   Q.E.D.

V. A LIMIT THEOREM

In this section, we shall follow a well-known procedure introduced by Edgeworth for enlarging the economy; this procedure consists in replicating the "basic" economy E_1, described in Section II, in the following way. Let k be some integer. The economy E_k contains mk firms and nk consumers. There are k firms of type $j, j = 1,..., m$ and k consumers of type i, $i = 1,..., n$; i.e., there are k firms with the same production set G_j and k consumers with the same preference relation $\succsim_i$, the same initial endowment w_i and the same share θ_{jk}^i defined by $\theta_{jk}^i = (1/k)\,\theta_j^i$.[7] It follows that all consumers of type i have the same intermediate endowment defined by $w_i + \sum_{j=1}^m \theta_j^i(1/k \sum_{h=1}^k y_{jh}^k)$, with y_{jh}^k denoting the production plan of the h-th firm of type j in the economy E_k.

LEMMA 1. *For any fixed k, and any mk-tuple $(y_{11}^k ,..., y_{1h}^k ,..., y_{1k}^k ;...;$ $y_{m1}^k ,..., y_{mh}^k ,..., y_{mk}^k)$ of feasible production plans, all the consumers of type i receive the same commodity bundle at the competitive equilibrium relative to $(y_{11}^k ,..., y_{1k}^k ;...; y_{m1}^k ,..., y_{mk}^k)$.*

Proof.   All the consumers of type i in E_k have the same strictly convex preferences and the same intermediate endowment.   Q.E.D.

It follows that a competitive equilibrium relative to $(y_{11}^k ,..., y_{1k}^k ;...;$ $y_{m1}^k ,..., y_{mk}^k)$ in the economy E_k is fully described (1) by the vector of *average* supply of the firms of the same type, i.e., $(y_1^k,..., y_j^k,..., y_m^k)$ with $y_j^k =_{\text{Def}} 1/k \sum_{h=1}^k y_{jh}^k$; (2) by the vector of demands $(x_1^k,..., x_n^k)$ of the n types of consumers, and (3) by a price system $\pi = \pi(y_1^k,..., y_j^k,..., y_m^k)$, which only depends on the average supplies of the firms in each type. Further, according to Theorem 4.1, the price function π is continuous on $\prod_{j=1}^m G_j$. On the other hand, an equilibrium point in the economy E_k is an mk-tuple $(y_{11}^k ,..., y_{1h}^k ,..., y_{1k}^k ;...; y_{j1}^k ,..., y_{jh}^k ,..., y_{jk}^k ;...; y_{m1}^k ,..., y_{mh}^k ,..., y_{mk}^k)$

---

[7] This definition of the shares aims at endowing each consumer of type i with the same intermediate endowment whatever may be the production plans of the firms.

of feasible production plans such that, for each firm h of type j, $h = 1,..., k, j = 1,..., m$, the function

$$f_{jh}^k(y) = \pi\left(y_1^k,..., \frac{1}{k}\sum_{\substack{l=1\\l\neq h}}^{k} y_{jl}^k + \frac{1}{k} y,..., y_m^k\right) \cdot y$$

achieves its maximum on G_j at y_{jh}^k. So the concept of a Cournot–Walras equilibrium of the economy E_k is well-defined by an evident extension of the corresponding definition in E_1.

A sequence of Cournot–Walras equilibria of the economies E_k is said to converge if (i) $\lim_{k\to\infty} \pi(y_1^k,..., y_j^k,..., y_m^k)$ exists; (ii) $\lim_{k\to\infty} x_k^i$ exists and (iii) $\lim_{k\to\infty} y_{jh}^k$, $(h \leq k)$ exists and is in G_j. We add now the three following assumptions:

(A$_3$) For all k, the functions f_{jh}^k are strictly quasi-concave on G_j, $j = 1,..., m, h = 1,..., k$;

(A$_4$) The global competitive equilibrium of the economy E_1 is unique;

(A$_5$) The production sets G_j are strictly convex, $j = 1,..., m.$, i.e., for all $a \in \,]0, 1[$ and $y, y' \in G_j$, $\alpha y + (1 - \alpha) y'$ is in the interior of G_j.

THE LIMIT THEOREM. *Let* $\{[\pi(y_1^k,..., y_j^k,..., y_m^k); (x_1^k,..., x_n^k); (y_{11}^k,..., y_{1k}^k ;...; y_{j1}^k,..., y_{jk}^k ;...; y_{m1}^k,..., y_{mk}^k)]\}$ *be any sequence of Cournot–Walras equilibria of the successive economies* E_k; *under assumptions* $(A_1), (A_3)$–(A_5), *this sequence converges to the global competitive equilibrium of the economy* E_1.

We shall first prove the following

LEMMA 2. *Let* $\{(y_{11}^k,..., y_{1k}^k ;...; y_{j1}^k,..., y_{jk}^k ;...; y_{m1}^k,..., y_{mk}^k)\}$ *be the sequence of equilibrium points corresponding to a sequence of Cournot–Walras equilibria in the successive economies* E_k; *let* $\{(y_1^k,..., y_j^k,..., y_m^k)\}$ *be the sequence defined in* $\prod_{j=1}^{m} G_j$ *by*

$$(y_1^k,..., y_j^k,..., y_m^k) \underset{\text{Def}}{=} \left(\frac{1}{k}\sum_{h=1}^{k} y_{1h}^k ,..., \frac{1}{k}\sum_{h=1}^{k} y_{jh}^k ,..., \frac{1}{k}\sum_{h=1}^{k} y_{mh}^k\right)$$

and assume that $\{(y_1^k,..., y_j^k,..., y_m^k)\}$ *converges in* $\prod_{j=1}^{m} G_j$ *to some point* $(\bar{y}_1 ,..., \bar{y}_j ,..., \bar{y}_m)$. *Then any sequence* $\{y_{jh_k}^k\}$, $1 \leq h_k \leq k$, $k = 1, 2,...$ *converges to* $\bar{y}_j$, *for any* $j, j = 1,..., m$. *Moreover,* $\bar{y}_1 ,..., \bar{y}_j ,..., \bar{y}_m$ *are the production plans of the firms in the global competitive equilibrium of the economy* E_1.

Proof. Let $\{y^k_{jh_k}\}$ be a given sequence of production plans of firms of type j in the corresponding equilibrium points of the economies E_k. First notice that, by continuity of π, we have

$$\lim_{k \to \infty} \pi(y_1^k,..., y_j^k,..., y_m^k) = \pi(\bar{y}_1,..., \bar{y}_j,..., \bar{y}_m).$$

Then it is clear that, by compacity of G_j, for all y in G_j,

$$\lim_{k \to \infty} \left(\frac{1}{k} \sum_{\substack{l=1 \\ l \neq h_k}}^{k} y_{jl}^k + \frac{1}{k} y \right) = \bar{y}_j,$$

so that, by continuity of π again,

$$\lim_{k \to \infty} \pi \left(y_1^k,..., \frac{1}{k} \sum_{\substack{l=1 \\ l \neq h_k}}^{k} y_{jl}^k + \frac{1}{k} y,..., y_m^k \right) = \pi(\bar{y}_1,..., \bar{y}_j,..., \bar{y}_m).$$

So, by compacity of G_j again, for all y in G_j,

$$\lim_{k \to \infty} f^k_{jh_k}(y) = \pi(\bar{y}_1,..., \bar{y}_j,..., \bar{y}_m) \cdot y.$$

Consequently, the sequence of functions $\{f^k_{jh_k}(\cdot)\}$ converges uniformly to the limit function $f_j(\cdot) =_{\text{Def}} \pi(\bar{y}_1,..., \bar{y}_m) \cdot (\cdot)$. For all k the function $f^k_{jh_k}(\cdot)$ is strictly quasi-concave in the convex domain G_j: it achieves its maximum at a unique point which, by definition of an equilibrium point, is precisely $y^k_{jh_k}$; so $f^k_{jh_k}(y^k_{jh_k}) = \max_{y \in G_j} f^k_{jh_k}(y)$, $k = 1, 2,...$. Since, for all k, $y^k_{jh_k}$ is in the compact set G_j, the sequence $\{y^k_{jh_k}\}$ has a converging subsequence $\{y^{k_s}_{jh_{k_s}}\}$, $s = 1, 2,...$; let y_0 be its limit point. Then, by continuity of $f^{k_s}_{jh_{k_s}}(\cdot)$ for all k_s and uniform convergence of $f^k_{jh_k}(\cdot)$ to $f_j(\cdot)$, we have that

$$\lim_{s \to \infty}[f^{k_s}_{jh_{k_s}}(y^{k_s}_{jh_{k_s}})] = \lim_{s \to \infty} [\max_{y \in G_j} f^{k_s}_{jh_{k_s}}(y)]$$

$$= \max_{y \in G_j} [\lim_{s \to \infty}(f^{k_s}_{jh_{k_s}}(y))]$$

$$= \max_{y \in G_j} f_j(y)$$

$$= \max_{y \in G_j} \pi(\bar{y}_1,..., \bar{y}_m) \cdot y.$$

OLIGOPOLY, GENERAL EQUILIBRIUM ANALYSIS 393

On the other hand, since $\{f_{jh_{k_s}}^{k_s}(\cdot)\} \to f_j$ uniformly and $\{y_{jh_{k_s}}^{k_s}\} \to y_0$, the difference $|f_{jh_{k_s}}^{k_s}(y_{jh_{k_s}}^{k_s}) - f_j(y_0)|$ tends to zero when $s \to \infty$. So

$$f_j(y_0) = \lim_{s \to \infty}[f_{jh_{k_s}}^{k_s}(y_{jh_{k_s}}^{k_s})] = \max_{y \in G_j} \pi(\bar{y}_1, ..., \bar{y}_m) \cdot y.$$

But strict convexity of G_j implies that the point $\hat{y}_j$ where f_j achieves its maximum on G_j is unique. Consequently, $\lim_{s \to \infty} \{y_{jh_{k_s}}^{k_s}\} = \hat{y}_j$. By unicity of this limit point, any other converging subsequence of $\{y_{jh_k}^k\}$ must also converge to $\hat{y}_j$. Consequently, the whole sequence $\{y_{jh_k}^k\}$ converges to this point. A straightforward implication of the last conclusion is that the production plans y_{jh}^k of any firm h of type j converges to $\hat{y}_j$ and similarly for the average supply $y_j{}^k = 1/k \sum_{h=1}^{k} y_{jh}^k$ of type j. So

$$\hat{y}_j = \lim_{k \to \infty} \{y_{jh_k}^k\} = \lim_{k \to \infty} \{y_j{}^k\} = \bar{y}_j.$$

This completes the proof of the first statement in the lemma. The second statement follows directly from the fact that $\bar{y}_j$ maximizes the function $\pi(\bar{y}_1, ..., \bar{y}_j, ..., \bar{y}_m) \cdot y$ on G_j, $j = 1, ..., m$. Consequently, $\bar{y}_1, ..., \bar{y}_j, ..., \bar{y}_m$ are the production plans of the firms in the global competitive equilibrium of the economy E_1. Q.E.D.

Proof of the Limit Theorem. Let $\{[\pi(y_1{}^k, ..., y_j{}^k, ..., y_m{}^k); (x_1{}^k, ..., x_n{}^k); (y_{11}^k, ..., y_{1k}^k; ...; y_{j1}^k, ..., y_{jk}^k; ...; y_{m1}^k, ..., y_{mk}^k)]\}$ be any sequence of Cournot–Walras equilibria in the successive replicas E_k. Its corresponding sequence of average supplies $(y_1{}^k, ..., y_j{}^k, ..., y_m{}^k)$ is defined on the compact set $\prod_{j=1}^{m} G_j$. By Lemma 2, any converging subsequence generated from this sequence necessarily converges to the m-tuple $(\bar{y}_1, ..., \bar{y}_j, ..., \bar{y}_m)$ of production plans of the m firms in the global competitive equilibrium of the economy E_1. Since $\prod_{j=1}^{m} G_j$ is compact, there exists at least one subsequence which converges to $(\bar{y}_1, ..., \bar{y}_j, ..., \bar{y}_m)$. Since this limit point is unique in $\prod_{j=1}^{m} G_j$, the whole sequence must also converge to this point. Let $[\pi(\bar{y}_1, ..., \bar{y}_m); (\bar{x}_1, ..., \bar{x}_n)]$ be the competitive equilibrium relative to $(\bar{y}_1, ..., \bar{y}_m)$. Finally, we have to show that $\lim_{k \to \infty} \pi(y_1{}^k, ..., y_j{}^k, ..., y_m{}^k) = \pi(\bar{y}_1, ..., \bar{y}_j, ..., \bar{y}_m)$ and that, for all i, $\lim_{k \to \infty} x_i{}^k = \bar{x}_i$. The first assertion follows from the continuity of π; the second follows from the fact that the sequence of intermediate endowments $\{w_i + \sum_{j=1}^{m} \theta_j{}^i(1/k \sum_{h=1}^{k} y_{jh}^k)\}$ of any consumer of type i converges to $w_i + \sum_{j=1}^{m} \theta_j{}^i \bar{y}_j$, which is the intermediate endowment of consumer i at the global competitive equilibrium of E_1. Q.E.D.

VI. Conclusion

The results of this paper are twofold. First a new type of general equilibrium concept has been introduced, namely, the Cournot–Walras equilibrium. It integrates two well-known solution concepts, the first due to Cournot (and generalized by Nash) in a partial equilibrium context, the second defined by Walras in a general equilibrium framework. This integration may be viewed as an attempt to represent imperfect competition on the production side of the economy, together with perfect competition on the exchange markets. Assumptions (A_1) and (A_2) are sufficient conditions for the existence of a Cournot–Walras equilibrium. Second, the impact of an increase in the number of firms is studied through a replicating device "à la Debreu–Scarf."[8] In the expanding economy resulting from these replicas, the production possibilities of a particular firm become less and less significant when compared to the total production of the remaining firms. Consequently, one would expect that the prices prevailing on the exchange markets become less and less sensitive to the supply of any one of these firms; this, in turn, implies that each firm tends to choose its equilibrium strategy closer and closer to the competitive supply. The limit theorem is a mere formalization of these statements.

1. *Discussion of the Model*

The model we have considered is of course an oversimplified representation of the observable processes of production and exchange. Particularly odd is the fact that the allocation problem of inputs among the firms is ignored. On the other hand, the existence of intermediary goods produced by some firms for other firms is excluded from the formal structure of the model: the consumers are the only buyers and sellers of the products on the exchange markets. Should these simplifications be dropped then the consumers would get an inspection hole on the production decisions of the firms "via" the markets on which the inputs would be allocated among the firms; on the other hand, the firms would be in a position to influence the *mechanism* of price formation on the exchange markets since they would be active parties on these markets. The increased complexity that would result from this more realistic proposal would destroy the relative simplicity of the mechanism we analyze here. In regard of the strong assumptions we are already compelled to introduce, this more general treatment seems prematurate to us.

Another point of the model that could be questioned is the use of monetary profits as a decision criterion for the firms. A referee has

[8] See [2].

pointed out to us a situation in which the maximization of monetary profits could be hardly regarded as a rational decision criterion. "Consider a firm owned by many consumers, all of whom are identical. Given the strategies of the other firms in the economy, this firm chooses an output vector so as to maximize the wealth of each of its consumers. However, it is possible that this firm could choose a different strategy which would result in slightly lower wealth, but in a much lower price of some particular commodity which is greatly 'desired' by the owners of the firm. Thus this alternative strategy might yield greater 'real income' to the firms owners."[9] We acknowledge that in such a situation profit maximization cannot appear as a rational objective for this firm. We notice, however, that the kind of inconsistency inherent to the preceding example may well happen *even in a pure competitive context.* To show this consider, in a two-commodity economy, a firm owned by one individual and let G be, on Fig. 2, its production set.

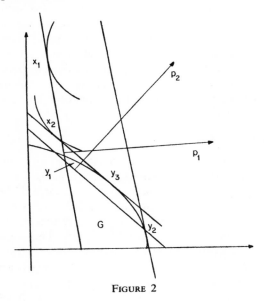

FIGURE 2

If, as a producer, the individual chooses the point y_1 in G, let p_1 be the corresponding equilibrium price system on the exchange market between the two commodities, i.e., the value of the price function if y_1 is supplied. As a "price-taking" consumer, our individual could move from y_1 to x_1. But as a "price-taking" producer, he should first move

[9] Referee's report.

its production choice from y_1 to y_2 (profit maximization at given prices p_1). Let p_2 be the resulting equilibrium price system on the exchange market *after the move*, i.e., the value of the price function if y_2 is supplied in lieu of y_1. Assume further that the equilibrium price system is still y_2 if, as a price-taking producer, the individual moves again from y_2 to y_3 (profit maximization at given prices p_2). The point y_3 is then an equilibrium position for the firm and the corresponding equilibrium consumption is now x_2, which is less prefered than x_1 ! It follows that profit maximization at given prices appears here as an "irrational" pattern of behavior.

Of course, under the assumption of pure competition, this kind of difficulty can always be discarded by arguing that the competitive behavior is "myopic": our individual does not know, *by assumption*, that he will influence the relative prices when he changes its relative supplies. Thus, the apparent inconsistency of this behavior does not follow from irrationality, but ignorance. We do not have in our case such an argument at hand, since our firms are assumed to know the influence of their supply on the prices. The only way for us to discard the difficulty is thus to recognize that our analysis may not apply if some firms are "owned" by "similar" consumers who have agreed beforehand on some unanimous preference ordering. By contrast, if all firms are owned by many "different" consumers, the impossibility of aggregating their various preferences justifies, by default and as a first approximation, the use of monetary profits as an objective for these firms.

2. *Discussion of the Assumptions*

These results have been obtained at the cost of four assumptions, namely, assumptions (A_1), (A_3)–(A_5), $[(A_2)$ being implied by $(A_3)]$. Assumption (A_1)— which states, for any intermediate endowments vector, the unicity of the corresponding price system on the exchange markets—is a minimal requirement to guarantee that the payoff of a firm is a well-defined function on its production set. This makes possible to apply to the production side of our economy the abstract concept of a Nash equilibrium point. However, under the usual assumptions on consumers' preferences, little can be said, in effect, about the cardinality of the values of the equilibrium-set correspondence. A recent result of Debreu [1] asserts that, except on a null subset of the space of intermediate endowments vectors, this equilibrium set correspondence takes on each point a finite set of values only. If we would accept that the intermediate endowments in our exchange economy never intersect this "exceptional" set, the payoff functions of the firms would be multivalued, but only with a finite number of values. Furthermore, Debreu [1, p. 6] has shown that, for any given intermediate endowments vector, except for a null set again, there exists an open neighborhood in the space of intermediate endowments such that, if the intermediate endowments vector varies in this neighborhood, there exists a continuous selection of the values of the equilibrium-set correspondence in this neighborhood. So, there seems to be two alternatives to overcome the major difficulty raised by our unicity assumption. On the one hand, one could try to devise a new solution concept, economically significant, for a non-cooperative n-person game with multivalued payoff functions. On the other hand—and this seems to be more promising—one could take advantage of Debreu's result; namely, that to any intermediate endowments vector, other than the exceptional ones, is associated a neighborhood with a continuous selection of price systems. Then the payoffs of the firms are well-defined in this neighborhood. By restricting adequately the range of the strategies of the firms, in such a way that intermediate endowments remain in this neighborhood, one could introduce a concept of local Nash equilibrium point. This equilibrium would be defined as a set of supplies and an associated price system such that, in a neighborhood of its current supply, each firm maximizes its (continuous) payoff function at the equilibrium point. This is an open field for further research. Since higher mathematics would be involved, it is felt that, by contrast, the simplicity of the proofs carried under assumption A_1 justifies our present analysis.

Assumption A_3 deals with the strict quasi-concavity of the payoff function of each firm. Strict quasi-concavity has been introduced to guarantee the continuity property of the maximizing strategy of a firm as a function of the strategies of the $(m - 1)$ other firms. This, in turn, implies our existence theorem. Quasi-concavity, and not strict quasi-concavity, would yield upper-hemi continuity of the maximizing strategy defined as a correspondence. By a more general fixed point argument, one would get a comparable existence theorem. Thus, this part of the assumption is not crucial. How restrictive the assumption of quasi-concavity is remains an open problem. Its difficulty is inherent to our ignorance about the behavior of the price function. A way to avoid this difficulty would consist to dispose off the assumption by means of mixed strategies. Then we would obtain our existence theorem stated in terms of mixed strategies, without assumption A_3 : in spite of the apparent generality of this alternative result, it looks like an artifice which might not be very meaningful for our purpose.

Assumption A_4 on the uniqueness of the *global* competitive equilibrium must not be confused with assumption A_1, which only bears on the *exchange* economy generated by a given set of production plans $y_1, ..., y_m$. We could have dispensed with assumption A_4 and then yield a different form of the limit theorem, namely, that any *convergent* sequence of Cournot–Walras equilibria converges to *some* global competitive equilibrium.

3. *The Role of Normalization*

In the course of this paper it has been pointed out several times that a normalization rule for the price system should be introduced and should be considered as a specification of the model. By means of a simple example we may illustrate the dependency of the Cournot–Walras equilibria of an economy on the normalization rule which is selected.

Let us consider a two-commodity economy with two firms and one consumer. The production sets of firm I and firm II are, respectively,

$$G_1 = \{y^1 = (y_1^1, y_2^1) \mid 0 \leqslant y_1^1 \leqslant 1, 0 \leqslant y_2^1 \leqslant 1\},$$

and

$$G_2 = \{y^2 = (y_1^2, y_2^2) \mid y_1^2 = 0, 0 \leqslant y_2^2 \leqslant 6\}.$$

The utility function of the consumer is

$$u(x_1, x_2) = e^{x_1} \log(1 + x_2),$$

whereas his intermediate endowment is $(y_1^1 + y_1^2, y_2^1 + y_2^2)$.

Thus, the price system π of the competitive equilibrium relative to (y^1, y^2) must satisfy

$$\frac{\pi_1}{\pi_2} = (1 + y_2^1 + y_2^2) \log(1 + y_2^1 + y_2^2)$$

and is fully determined once the normalization rule is given. We shall successively consider the following normalization rules

$$\pi_1 \cdot (y_1^1 + y_1^2) + \pi_2 \cdot (y_2^1 + y_2^2) = 1, \tag{1}$$

and

$$\pi_2 = 1. \tag{2}$$

Normalization rule (1) yields the following price function[10]:

$$\pi_1(y^1, y^2) = \frac{1}{D} (1 + y_2^1 + y_2^2) \log(1 + y_2^1 + y_2^2),$$

$$\pi_2(y^1, y^2) = \frac{1}{D},$$

[10] Compare footnote 5, p. 386.

OLIGOPOLY, GENERAL EQUILIBRIUM ANALYSIS 399

with

$$D = y_1^1 (1 + y_2^1 + y_2^2) \log(1 + y_2^1 + y_2^2) + y_2^1 + y_2^2.$$

The payoff function of firm I,

$$f_1(y^1, \bar{y}^2) = \pi_1(y^1, \bar{y}^2) \cdot y_1^1 + \pi_2(y^1, \bar{y}^2) \cdot y_2^1,$$

corresponding to a production plan $\bar{y}_2$ of firm II, can be checked to be monotonically increasing in both arguments. Hence $f_1(y^1, \bar{y}^2)$ achieves its maximum on G_1 at $\bar{y}^1 = (1, 1)$.

The payoff function of firm II,

$$f_2(\bar{y}^1, y^2) = \pi_2(\bar{y}^1, \bar{y}^2) \cdot y_2^2,$$

corresponding to a production plan $\bar{y}^1 = (1, 1)$ of firm I, reduces to

$$f_2(\bar{y}^1, y^2) = \frac{y_2^2}{(2 + y_2^2) \log(2 + y_2^2) + 1 + y_2^2}.$$

Since

$$\frac{df_2}{dy_2^2} = \frac{2 \log(2 + y_2^2) + 1 - y_2^2}{[(2 + y_2^2) \log(2 + y_2^2) + 1 + y_2^2]^2},$$

$f_2(\bar{y}^1, y^2)$ achieves a unique maximum on G_2. The root of the equation $df_2/dy_2^2 = 0$ is $\bar{y}^2 \simeq 4.85$ and $\bar{y}^2$ is the maximizing strategy on G_2.

Hence, for normalization rule (1), $(\bar{\pi}; \bar{x}; \bar{y}^1, \bar{y}^2)$, with $\bar{y}^1 = (1, 1)$, $\bar{y}^2 = (0, 1)$; $\bar{x} = (1, 2)$; $\bar{\pi} = (0.69, 0.05)$ is a Cournot–Walras equilibrium, but not a global competitive equilibrium.[11]

Normalization rule (2) yields the price function:

$$\pi_1(y^1, y^2) = (1 + y_2^1 + y_2^2) \log(1 + y_2^1 + y_2^2),$$

$$\pi_2(y^1, y^2) = 1.$$

A direct inspection shows that the payoff function of firm I is monotonically increasing in both arguments and that the payoff function of firm II is monotonically increasing in its argument y_2^2. Hence the payoff functions achieve their maximum, respectively, at $\hat{y}^1 = (1, 1)$ on G_1 and at $\hat{y}^2 = (0, 6)$ on G_2. So $(\hat{\pi}; \hat{x}; \hat{y}^1, \hat{y}^2)$ with $\hat{y}^1 = (1, 1)$, $\hat{y}^2 = (0, 6)$; $\hat{x} = (1, 7)$; $\hat{\pi} = (16.6, 1)$ is a Cournot–Walras equilibrium and coincides with the global competitive equilibrium.

The preceding example shows that our concepts and assumptions cannot be unambiguously defined without a formal reference to some

---

[11] Note that $\bar{y}^2$ is in the relative interior of G_2. This Cournot–Walras equilibrium thus displays some technological inefficiency.

normalization rule on the prices (even if this rule can be chosen arbitrarly). This rule is an intrinsic element of our model since both the set of Cournot–Walras equilibria and the quasi-concavity of π can depend on it. Thus, this particular feature of our theory breaks with the long-standing theory according to which no "monetary illusion" should be introduced in "real" economies. It is a well-known virtue of the concept of competitive equilibrium that it remains invariant over the set of normalization rules. The loss of this invariance in our case is the prize we pay to enrich the behavioral assumptions on the firms. Any attempt to depict in a general equilibrium model the behavior of profit maximizing firms which are not price-takers but—totally or partially—price-setters, will meet, indeed, this difficulty. This is not surprising since the price system only defines a *direction* in the commodity space: this information is not sufficient to specify how the influence that the firms exert on this direction can affect their monetary profits.[12] Such a specification is needed, however, if the profit criterion is incorporated into the model. On this basis, some readers could accordingly be tempted to reject our theory as a whole; but they should be aware that they would simultaneously reject the whole theory of imperfect competition in partial analysis. By a similar argument, it can be shown indeed, that the graph of the classical demand function in the price-quantity coordinates is not invariant on the set of normalization rules of the whole price system on the economy!

ACKNOWLEDGMENTS

The authors are grateful to Jacques H. Drèze, Louis Gevers, and B. Martinet for stimulating discussions of the issues raised in this paper. They owe to an anonymous referee many interesting suggestions which have improved the final version of this paper.

REFERENCES

1. G. DEBREU, Economies with a finite set of equilibria, *Econometrica* **38** (3), (1970), 387–392.
2. G. DEBREU AND H. SCARF, A limit theorem on the core of an economy, *Int. Econ. Rev.* **4** (3), (1963), 235–246.
3. W. HILDENBRAND AND J.-F. MERTENS, Upperhemi continuity of the Walras correspondence, *Econometrica* to appear.
4. H. NIKAIDO, On the classical multilateral exchange problem, *Metroeconomica*, **8** (1956), 135–145.

[12] For the competitive equilibrium concept, one has not to worry about this specification since, *by assumption*, the firms do not exert any influence on the direction of prices.

[43]

The Economic Journal, **98** (*Conference* 1988), 37–49
Printed in Great Britain

THE OBJECTIVE DEMAND CURVE IN GENERAL EQUILIBRIUM WITH PRICE MAKERS*

Jean-Pascal Benassy

The purpose of this paper is to do for models of competition by prices what was done in the seminal paper of Gabszewicz-Vial (1972) for the Cournot–Nash model of competition by quantities.[1] Namely we want to construct, in a framework of general equilibrium with actual price makers, a concept of an objective demand curve which contains all the feedback effects of the price decisions of the various competitors, and study the associated general equilibrium concept.

The theory of general equilibrium with explicit price-making behaviour was first elegantly developed by Negishi (1961) in a framework of subjective demand curve: each price maker has a subjective perception of the demand curves, which is correct at the equilibrium point but which may be different elsewhere. By contrast the idea of an objective demand curve is that it should be correct everywhere, and not only at the equilibrium point.

The first concepts of equilibrium with objective demand curves were built in the pioneering works of Marschak and Selten (1974) and Nikaido (1975). As we shall see below these concepts were developed in particular cases where price makers do not sell to each other (Marschak and Selten) or for a Leontief economy (Nikaido), and the definitions of objective demand curves are valid only in a subset of the price space. Though a number of later writers have used the idea of equilibrium with objective demand curves for various applied purposes,[2] at this stage there is no definition of an objective demand curve or of the associated general equilibrium concept which matches the generality of that found in Cournotian analysis.[3]

So what we shall do in this paper is first, address the problem of the proper definition of an objective demand curve in a general equilibrium model where prices are strategic variables. As might be expected, this definition will involve an equilibrium concept, and we shall thus be concerned with the problem of existence of such an objective demand curve. We shall find out that it exists for the whole domain of strictly positive prices under traditional assumptions. Then we shall show how agents set prices with such objective demand curves, and define an associated concept of general equilibrium. Finally simple, sufficient existence conditions will be given.

* I wish to thank C. d'Aspremont, C. Bean, M. Quinzii, R. Selten, the referees and the editors of this supplement for their useful comments on earlier versions of this paper.

[1] This Cournot-Nash model has spanned a very abundant literature. For a survey, see for example Mas-Colell (1982).

[2] See for example the applications to unemployment theory in d'Aspremont *et al.* (1986), Dehez (1985), Silvestre (1986), Snower (1983), Weitzman (1985), or in Benassy (1987) which uses the framework of this article.

[3] For example the quite recent survey by Hart (1985) basically uses the Marschak and Selten definition.

I. THE GENERAL FRAMEWORK

We shall thus consider a general equilibrium setting, with a set of l goods $h \in H$, and an additional good, called money for convenience, which serves both as a numeraire and medium of exchange. The price of good h in terms of this numéraire is p_h. The vector of these prices is denoted by $\mathbf{p}$.

The agents in the economy are firms and households. Firms are indexed by $j \in J$. Households are indexed by $i \in I$. We shall denote by $A = I \cup J$ the set of all agents, firms and households together, indexed by $a = 1 \dots n$.

Firm j has a production vector $\mathbf{y}_j$ which must belong to a production set $Y_j \subset R^l$. Its objective is to maximise profits $\pi_j = \mathbf{p}\mathbf{y}_j = -\mathbf{p}\mathbf{z}_j$, where $\mathbf{z}_j$, the net trade vector of firm j, will be equal to $-\mathbf{y}_j$ since we assume the firm carries no inventories.

Household i has an initial endowment of goods and money ω_i and $\bar{m}_i$, and owns shares θ_{ij} of firms j (households' total shares of each firm of course sum to one). Household i carries a vector of net trades $\mathbf{z}_i$ and maximises a utility function $U_i(\mathbf{x}_i, m_i)$ where $\mathbf{x}_i = \omega_i + \mathbf{z}_i$ is the vector of final holdings of goods and the final quantity of money m_i is given by the budget constraint:

$$\mathbf{p}\mathbf{z}_i + m_i = \bar{m}_i + \sum_{j \in J} \theta_{ij} \pi_j.$$

As for price making, the basic institutional setting, as is usual in most models with explicit price makers, is that on each market one side consists of price makers, the other of price takers.[4] We shall moreover identify goods by their physical characteristics *and* the agent who sets their price. In that way each good has its price controlled by one and only one of the agents, and each price maker is alone on his side of the market. Call H_a the (possibly empty) subset of the goods whose price is controlled by agent a. Subdivide H_a into H_a^d (goods demanded by a) and H_a^s (goods supplied by a). Agent a appears, at least formally, as a monopolist on markets $h \in H_a^s$, as a monopsonist on markets $h \in H_a^d$, and we have

$$H_a \cap H_b = \{\varnothing\} \quad \text{if} \quad b \neq a.$$

We shall denote by p_a the set of prices controlled by agent a and by p_{-a} the set of prices controlled by the other agents (i.e. the rest of prices)

$$p_a = \{p_h \mid h \in H_a\}$$

$$p_{-a} = \{p_b \mid b \neq a\}.$$

II. A QUICK REVIEW

We shall now very quickly review the previous literature, concentrating especially on the model by Marschak and Selten (1974), which is the most suited for a general equilibrium framework.

---

[4] This formalisation thus applies to markets in which buyers and sellers are well identified, and not to markets, such as securities markets, where people regularly shift from buying to selling, etc. For these markets a more symmetric formulation is called for. See, for example Benassy (1986 a), and references therein, for a formalisation of symmetric Nash equilibria with strategic price quoting.

The Marschak and Selten Model[5]

In that model, goods are subdivided into non-produced goods, sold by households to firms, and produced goods, sold by firms to households. There are no intermediary products. Furthermore it is assumed that firms are the sole price setters, so that H_i is empty for all i.

A main import of these assumptions is that no price maker buys from or sells to other price makers. This will allow us to base the concept of objective demand curve directly on the Walrasian demand of the household sector, as we shall see below. A further important assumption is made: All price makers serve whatever demand or supply is addressed to them. Under this assumption, each household i can satisfy his Walrasian demand, given by the solution in z_i to the following programme:

$$\text{Maximise } U_i(\omega_i + z_i, m_i) \quad \text{s.t.}$$

$$m_i + p z_i = \bar{m}_i + \sum_{j \in J} \theta_{ij} \pi_j.$$

The Walrasian demand of household i is denoted functionally as $\xi_i(\mathbf{p}, \pi)$, where π is the vector of all firms' profits. Consider now a good $h \in H_j$ controlled by firm j. This good is only sold to, or purchased from households. Moreover by the assumption that households are never rationed, they will be able to achieve their Walrasian demands and supplies on all markets. Consequently the objective demand (or supply) on market h is simply the sum of the Walrasian net demands of the household sector, i.e.

$$\sum_{i \in I} \xi_{ih}(\mathbf{p}, \pi).$$

With this definition of objective demand, we can now give the definition of an equilibrium.

DEFINITION 1. *An equilibrium with price-making firms consists of a set of* $\mathbf{p}_j^*$, $\mathbf{y}_j^*$, π_j^* *and* z_i^* *such that*
  (a) $z_i^* = \xi_i^*(\mathbf{p}^*, \pi^*)$ $(i \in I)$,
  (b) $\mathbf{p}_j^*$ *and* $\mathbf{y}_j^*$ *are solutions of*:
    Maximise $\mathbf{p} y_j$ s.t.
    $$\begin{cases} y_j \in Y_j, \\ y_{jh} = \sum_{i \in I} \xi_{ih}(\mathbf{p}, \pi^*) & (h \in H_j), \\ p_h = p_h^* & (h \notin H_j), \end{cases}$$
  (c) $\pi_j^* = \mathbf{p}^* \mathbf{y}_j^*$ $(j \in J)$.

Conditions (a) and (c) are self-evident. Condition (b) says that the firm j chooses its price p_j and production plan y_j to maximise profits, assuming that it serves all demand and supply on markets $h \in H_j$, and taking all profits as given.

---

[5] We actually give here a slightly simplified version of the Marschak and Selten model, as presented by Hart (1985). In their original contribution Marschak and Selten considered the feedback of a firm's own profits on its objective demand.

40   THE ECONOMIC JOURNAL   [CONFERENCE

A Few Problems

As we just saw, the definition of the objective demand curve is fundamentally based on the Walrasian demands of the household sector. We shall now see that such a definition, and therefore the associated equilibrium concept, have serious limitations.

The first problem of the above definition is the absence of 'quantity feedback' effects. As we underlined above, a very important feature of the model is that no price maker sells to another price maker. If such was not the case, then the various demand functions would have as arguments some quantities, which themselves would be functions of other quantities, etc. This problem, which was noted by Marschak and Selten (1974), has never been solved, except in the case of a Leontief economy by Nikaido (1975). In such a case the quantity feedback effects could be resolved simply by matrix inversion, but of course that method is very particular to the Leontief economy, and does not generalise readily to other cases.

The second problem one encounters with this definition is that of the domain of definition of the objective demand curve. This curve was constructed under the maintained assumption that all price makers will serve all demands and supplies addressed to them. But this is feasible only if the demands and supplies given by the objective demand and supply curves correspond to feasible production vectors. In mathematical terms the domain of definition of the objective demand curve is at the very most the set

$$\{(\mathbf{p}, \pi) \mid \sum_{i \in I} \xi_i(\mathbf{p}, \pi) \in \sum_{j \in J} Y_j\}.$$

Obviously if the price-profits vector falls outside this set, not all demands and supplies can be satisfied, and some rationing must occur. We may further note that the actual domain of validity of the objective demand curve is actually quite smaller than the above set. Indeed the production plan implied by the condition of satisfying demands and supplies may very well be feasible, but imply negative profits, in which case a firm will not want to satisfy demand even though the corresponding production is physically possible. The consequence of such a limited domain of validity is that the optimal price strategies derived under the above definition will be at best local optima, and that taking instead into account the 'true' objective demand curve may have a substantial impact on the existence and characteristics of an equilibrium.[6]

Of course what we would like, and shall work on in the following sections, is a definition of an objective demand curve which is valid on the whole price domain, and moreover can handle a larger set of quantity feedback effects.

---

[6] See Benassy (1986 b) for a further elaboration in a more partial equilibrium framework.

III. THE QUESTION AND SOME BASIC CONCEPTS

The Question

The concept of equilibrium we shall work with is that of a general imperfectly competitive equilibrium where agents use prices as strategic variables, thus some kind of 'Bertrand–Nash' equilibrium (as opposed to a 'Cournot–Nash' equilibrium where agents would use quantities as strategic variables). In such a model an objective demand curve is a function (or a correspondence) which indicates for each price choice of his competitors p_{-a} and for each of his own price choices p_a the total demand forthcoming to an agent a on all markets.

Our analysis will proceed in a manner quite symmetrical to that used by Gabszewicz-Vial (1972) for the Cournotian case. In the same way as the Cournotian analysis of an objective demand curve involves the study of a Walrasian equilibrium concept for given quantities, the definition of an objective demand curve with price makers will involve an equilibrium concept with given prices. At this stage the reader might be surprised that concepts where rationing and quantity signals play an important role should be an important building block for a theory where prices are endogenous. But we should note that the 'traditional' approach is also based, though much more implicitly, on a 'rationing scheme' whereby each price maker, whatever his own preferred transactions, is forced to purchase and sell whatever is supplied to or demanded from him on the market he controls. We saw, however, that such a rationing scheme led to internal contradictions, and we shall thus now make these features more explicit, and consistent, at a general equilibrium level.

Some Basic Concepts

A basic idea of fixprice (or more generally non Walrasian) analysis is that not all agents may be able to trade what they want on all markets, and that accordingly they receive quantity signals which tell them the maximum quantity they can trade. This is expressed by the following transaction rules:

$$d^*_{ah} = \min(\tilde{d}_{ah}, \bar{d}_{ah}),$$
$$s^*_{ah} = \min(\tilde{s}_{ah}, \bar{s}_{ah}),$$
(1)

where $\tilde{d}_{ah}$ and $\tilde{s}_{ah}$ are agent a's demand and supply on market h, d^*_{ah} and s^*_{ah} his purchase and sale (i.e. his actual transactions), and $\bar{d}_{ah}$ and $\bar{s}_{ah}$ quantity signals representing the maximum quantities agent a can respectively buy or sell on market h. We may note already that such quantity signals very naturally relate to the idea of an objective demand curve, since objective demand for a given price vector precisely represents the maximum quantity a price maker can sell at that price. As we shall see below, these quantity signals depend on all demands and supplies expressed on the market. They have, however, a particularly simple and natural form for price makers on the markets they control: indeed, since they are alone on their side of these markets, their quantity constraints have the simple form

$$\bar{s}_{ah} = \sum_{b \neq a} \tilde{d}_{bh} \quad (h \in H^s_a),$$
$$\bar{d}_{ah} = \sum_{b \neq a} \tilde{s}_{bh} \quad (h \in H^d_a),$$

(2)

i.e. the maximum quantity that price setter a can sell is the total demand of the others, and conversely if he is a buyer. Now our ultimate purpose is to find out how these constraints can be 'manipulated' by prices, once all feedback effects have been taken into account. For that we need to describe in more detail the interrelations of the various quantities in a fixprice equilibrium.

Fixprice Equilibrium[7]

To shorten notation, we shall work in what follows with net demands and transactions:
$$\tilde{z}_{ah} = \tilde{d}_{ah} - \tilde{s}_{ah}; \quad z^*_{ah} = d^*_{ah} - s^*_{ah}.$$

Now call $\tilde{\mathbf{z}}_a$, $\mathbf{z}^*_a$, $\bar{\mathbf{d}}_a$, $\bar{\mathbf{s}}_a$ the vectors of effective demands, transactions and quantity constraints for agent a. The transactions realised will be given by a rationing scheme:
$$\mathbf{z}^*_a = F_a(\tilde{\mathbf{z}}_1, ..., \tilde{\mathbf{z}}_n) \quad (a \in A = \{1, ..., n\}).$$

(3)

and quantity signals will also be functions of demands and supplies:

$$\bar{\mathbf{d}}_a = G^d_a(\tilde{\mathbf{z}}_1, ..., \tilde{\mathbf{z}}_n) \quad (a \in A),$$
$$\bar{\mathbf{s}}_a = G^s_a(\tilde{\mathbf{z}}_1, ..., \tilde{\mathbf{z}}_n) \quad (a \in A).$$

(4)

Each agent a is thus faced with a vector of price signals $\mathbf{p}$ (part of which, $\mathbf{p}_a$, is determined by himself) *and* quantity signals $\bar{\mathbf{d}}_a$, $\bar{\mathbf{s}}_a$. As a function of these signals he expresses net demands $\tilde{\mathbf{z}}_a$, which are given by:

$$\tilde{\mathbf{z}}_j = \tilde{\xi}_j(\mathbf{p}, \bar{\mathbf{d}}_j, \bar{\mathbf{s}}_j) \quad (j \in J),$$

(5)

$$\tilde{\mathbf{z}}_i = \tilde{\xi}_i(\mathbf{p}, \bar{\mathbf{d}}_i, \bar{\mathbf{s}}_i, \boldsymbol{\pi}) \quad (i \in I),$$

(6)

where $\boldsymbol{\pi} = \{\pi_j | j \in J\}$ is the vector of all firm's profits, which enter households' budget sets. We can now give the definition of a fixprice equilibrium:

A *fixprice equilibrium* associated to $\mathbf{p}$ is a set of $\tilde{\mathbf{z}}_a$, $\mathbf{z}^*_a$, $\bar{\mathbf{d}}_a$, $\bar{\mathbf{s}}_a$, π_j such that (3), (4), and (5) and (6) hold for all agents and moreover $\pi_j = -\mathbf{p}\mathbf{z}^*_j$ for all $j \in J$.

A fixprice equilibrium exists for all strictly positive prices, provided the household's utility functions are strictly concave and the firms' production sets strictly convex, which we shall assume in all that follows (Benassy 1975; 1976; 1982). A fixprice equilibrium is globally unique under fairly reasonable assumptions (Schulz, 1983).

We shall denote by $\tilde{Z}_a(\mathbf{p})$, $\tilde{D}_a(\mathbf{p})$, $\tilde{S}_a(\mathbf{p})$, $Z^*_a(\mathbf{p})$, $D^*_a(\mathbf{p})$, $S^*_a(\mathbf{p})$, $\bar{D}_a(\mathbf{p})$, $\bar{S}_a(\mathbf{p})$ respectively the values of $\tilde{\mathbf{z}}_a$, $\bar{\mathbf{d}}_a$, $\bar{\mathbf{s}}_a$, $\mathbf{z}^*_a$, $\mathbf{d}^*_a$, $\mathbf{s}^*_a$, $\bar{\mathbf{d}}_a$, $\bar{\mathbf{s}}_a$ at a fixprice equilibrium associated to $\mathbf{p}$.

[7] What follows is borrowed from Benassy (1975; 1976; 1982), to which the reader is referred for further developments. An alternative concept of equilibrium with rigid prices is found in Drèze (1975).

IV. THE OBJECTIVE DEMAND CURVE, PRICE MAKING AND EQUILIBRIUM

Definition of the Objective Demand Curve

Consider a vector $\mathbf{p} = (\mathbf{p}_a, \mathbf{p}_{-a})$. As indicated above the objective demand curve should give the total demand forthcoming once all feedback effects have been taken into account. This objective demand (or supply if the price maker is a demander) is thus on the markets controlled by a:

$$\sum_{b \neq a} \tilde{D}_{bh}(\mathbf{p}) \quad (h \in H_a^s),$$

$$\sum_{b \neq a} \tilde{S}_{bh}(\mathbf{p}) \quad (h \in H_a^d).$$

In view of equation (2) the objective demand curve is alternatively written

$$\bar{D}_{ah}(\mathbf{p}) \quad (h \in H_a^d),$$

$$\bar{S}_{ah}(\mathbf{p}) \quad (h \in H_a^s).$$

This form shows quite well how the price allows to 'manipulate' the demand or supply constraints faced by price maker a on the markets $h \in H_a$ he controls. We may also note that agent a perceives as well constraints $\bar{D}_{ah}(\mathbf{p})$ and $\bar{S}_{ah}(\mathbf{p})$ on markets $h \notin H_a$ (even though these constraints are not binding whenever the other price makers satisfy demand or supply). Therefore the objective demand and supply curves will consist of the whole vectors $\bar{S}_a(\mathbf{p})$ and $\bar{D}_a(\mathbf{p})$ respectively (note that the objective demand curve is a constraint on a's supply, and symmetrically).

Existence and Uniqueness

We see immediately that the objective demand curve exists for all prices for which a fixprice equilibrium exists. Standard results (Benassy, 1975, 1982) show that a fixprice equilibrium as defined above exists for all strictly positive prices and all continuous non-manipulable rationing schemes. The objective demand curve thus exists on the *whole* domain of strictly positive prices.

Similarly the objective demand curve will be unique (i.e. a function) if the fixprice equilibrium is globally unique. Schulz (1983) has given some sufficient conditions for global uniqueness. Intuitively the basic condition is that changes in quantity constraints 'spill over' onto the other markets by less than 100% in value terms. A traditional example is that the marginal propensity to consume should be less than 100%. We shall assume in all that follows that the Schulz conditions hold, and thus that the objective demand curve is actually a function.

Price Making

With the above definition of the objective demand curve, it is now easy to describe the price-making behaviour of firms and households.

The optimal price of firm j is obtained by maximising profits subject to technological constraints, and to the fact that trades are limited by the objective demand and supply curves $\bar{S}_j(\mathbf{p})$ and $\bar{D}_j(\mathbf{p})$. This optimal price is thus the solution in $\mathbf{p}_j$ of the following programme $\hat{P}_j$ (in both $\mathbf{p}_j$ and $\mathbf{z}_j$):

$$\text{Maximise} \ -\mathbf{pz}_j \qquad \text{s.t.,}$$

$$\begin{cases} -\mathbf{z}_j \in Y_j \\ -\bar{S}_j(\mathbf{p}) \leqslant \mathbf{z}_j \leqslant \bar{D}_j(\mathbf{p}) \end{cases} \qquad (P_j),$$

which yields

$$\mathbf{p}_j = \psi_j(\mathbf{p}_{-j}).$$

We should note that at most one of the constraints will be binding for each market. Consider now household i. He receives profits in the amount

$$\pi_i(\mathbf{p}) = -\sum_{j \in J} \theta_{ij}\,\mathbf{p}Z_j^*(\mathbf{p}).$$

The programme P_i yielding the optimum price $\mathbf{p}_i$ (and $\mathbf{z}_i$) is

$$\text{Maximise} \ U_i(\boldsymbol{\omega}_i + \mathbf{z}_i, m_i) \quad \text{s.t.,}$$

$$\begin{cases} m_i = \bar{m}_i - \mathbf{pz}_i + \pi_i(\mathbf{p}) \\ -\bar{S}_i(\mathbf{p}) \leqslant \mathbf{z}_i \leqslant \bar{D}_i(\mathbf{p}) \end{cases} \qquad (P_i),$$

which yields

$$\mathbf{p}_i = \psi_i(\mathbf{p}_{-i}).$$

Equilibrium with Price Makers

It is now easy to define an equilibrium with price makers.

DEFINITION 2. *An equilibrium with price makers is characterised by a set of* $\mathbf{p}_i^*$, $i \in I$ *and* $\mathbf{p}_j^*$, $j \in J$ *(and of course the associated* $\bar{\mathbf{z}}_a$, $\bar{\mathbf{z}}_a^*$, $\bar{\mathbf{d}}_a$, $\bar{\mathbf{s}}_a$, $a \in A$) *such that*

$$\mathbf{p}_i^* \in \psi_i(\mathbf{p}_{-i}^*) \quad (\forall i \in I),$$

$$\mathbf{p}_j^* \in \psi_j(\mathbf{p}_{-j}^*) \quad (\forall j \in J).$$

Before giving an existence theorem for such an equilibrium in the next section, we shall make a few comments indicating how our concept of objective demand curve and equilibrium allows us to lift the two main objections to previous definitions, concerning the absence of feedback effects and the incomplete domain of definition.

First the previous definitions, using Walrasian demand as a basic building block, had to eliminate any kind of quantity feedback, notably by not allowing situations where a price maker sells to another, and also by treating profit incomes as parametric (whereas they should be endogenous in a full general equilibrium treatment). Contrary to this our concept of objective demand curve, being based on a concept of fixprice equilibrium where all quantity feedbacks are by definition taken into account, places no such restrictions as to who sells to whom and fully takes into account these feedbacks. As a result, in the equilibrium concept each price maker only treats as parametric the prices set by others, as should be in a Nash equilibrium in prices.

The second problem is that of the domain of definition. The traditional definitions of the objective demand curve were based on the assumption that price makers would satisfy all demand and supply addressed to them. Ignoring for the moment the above mentioned feedback effects, this means that the traditional definition would be valid only in the subregion of all prices where price makers are actually willing to satisfy demands and supplies, which corresponds to

excess supply for goods h belonging to $\bigcup_a H_a^s$;

excess demand for goods h belonging to $\bigcup_a H_a^d$.

For example if the suppliers set prices, the definition based on the traditional assumption would be valid only in the zone of excess supply on all markets, a fairly restricted domain. We already mentioned above the problems related to such a limited domain.

Instead, our definition of objective demand is valid even in that part of the price domain where some demands and supplies cannot be fulfilled, because the corresponding rationing is fully taken into account.

V. AN EXISTENCE THEOREM

As an illustration we shall give here an existence theorem for the case, most often considered in the literature, with produced and nonproduced goods, and no intermediary products, as this will substantially lighten notation.[8] The set of produced goods will be denoted as H_p, the set of non-produced goods, i.e. factors of production owned by the households, by H_f. Of course:

$$H = H_f \cup H_p.$$

We shall first need a natural continuity assumption:

ASSUMPTION A1. *For all agents* $a \in A$, $Z_a^*(\mathbf{p})$ *is a continuous function.*

In order to obtain boundedness of produced goods prices, we shall make the fairly traditional assumption that for all produced goods, the households have a 'reservation price' bounded above, which is expressed as:

ASSUMPTION A2. *If good* h *is a produced good* $(h \in H_p)$, *there exists* $\beta_h > 0$ *such that*

$$\frac{\partial U_i / \partial x_{ih}}{\partial U_i / \partial m_i} \leqslant \beta_h \quad (\forall i \in I).$$

We shall make the symmetric assumption that suppliers of factors of production have a 'reservation price' bounded below, which is expressed as:

---

[8] Note that this framework does not preclude the main conceptual difficulty, price makers selling to price makers. One may think for example of the case (Benassy, 1987) where workers set wages and firms set product prices. Then every price maker sells to other price makers.

ASSUMPTION A3. *If good h is a factor of production $(h \in H_f)$ there exists an $\alpha_h > 0$ such that*

$$\frac{\partial U_i / \partial x_{ih}}{\partial U_i / \partial m_i} \geqslant \alpha_h \quad (\forall i \text{ such that } \omega_{ih} > 0).$$

We shall also assume that all factor productivities are bounded.

ASSUMPTION A4. *If good h is a factor of production $(h \in H_f)$ and good k a produced good $(k \in H_p)$, then there exists a $\gamma_{hk} > 0$ such that*

$$\frac{\partial y_{jk}}{\partial z_{jh}} \leqslant \gamma_{hk} \quad (\forall j \in J),$$

where y_{jk} is firm j's output of good k and z_{jh} is firm j's input of factor h. The partial derivative must of course be taken at an efficient point, all other inputs and outputs being maintained constant.

We shall finally make the usual assumption that the optimal prices chosen by each firm, given the others' prices, form a convex valued set.[9]

ASSUMPTION A5. *For all a, $\psi_a(\mathbf{p}_{-a})$ is convex valued.*

We can now state and prove the existence theorem.

THEOREM. *Under Assumptions A1, A2, A3, A4 and A5 an equilibrium with price makers exists.*

Proof. The equilibrium will be constructed as a fixed point of a mapping $\psi(\mathbf{p})$ from the set of prices into itself, consisting of the following submappings:

$$\mathbf{p}_i \to \psi_i(\mathbf{p}_{-i}) \quad (i \in I),$$

$$\mathbf{p}_j \to \psi_j(\mathbf{p}_{-j}) \quad (j \in J).$$

In order to reduce the domain of this mapping to a bounded set, we want to show boundedness of prices. Consider first a produced good $h \in H_p$. In view of Assumption A2, the effective demand of households for this good is zero if $p_h > \beta_h$. Therefore the price of that good is bounded above by β_h. Symmetrically, in view of A3, the price p_h of a factor of production $h \in H_f$, will be bounded below by α_h.

We shall now look for an upper bound for the price p_h of a factor of production $h \in H_f$. Consider the number β_h defined as

$$\beta_h = \max_{k \in H_p} \gamma_{hk} \beta_k > 0.$$

Clearly if $p_h > \beta_h$ the demand for that factor will be zero. Indeed by Assumption A4, it would be profitable for every firm j to decrease its input of factor h in the production of any produced good $k \in H_p$ to zero, and factor h would not be demanded. Therefore p_h is bounded above by the β_h just defined.

[9] Actually the most usual form of this assumption is that the relevant payoff functions, for example the firms' profit functions, are quasi-concave in the choice variables, which immediately leads to a convex valued best response.

Symmetrically the price p_h of a produced good $h \in H_p$ is bounded below by the number α_h defined by:

$$\alpha_h = \min_{k \in H_f}(\alpha_k/\gamma_{kh}) > 0.$$

We shall now take as the domain of the above mapping ψ the product of the closed intervals $[\alpha_h, \beta_h]$, $h \in H$, which is a convex compact set. Note that if for some h this interval is empty because $\alpha_h > \beta_h$, then the price p_h can be fixed arbitrarily at any value between β_h and α_h. The corresponding market will be inactive.

We want now to show the continuity of the mapping ψ, and for that purpose we shall characterise optimal prices $\psi_i(\mathbf{p}_{-i})$ and $\psi_j(\mathbf{p}_{-j})$ in a slightly different way as above. We may note indeed that the above maximisation programmes P_i and P_j are programmes in $(\mathbf{p}_i, \mathbf{z}_i)$ and $(\mathbf{p}_j, \mathbf{z}_j)$ respectively. We know from the theory of non-Walrasian equilibria that the solutions in $\mathbf{z}_i$ and $\mathbf{z}_j$ for a given $\mathbf{p}$ are $Z_i^*(\mathbf{p})$ and $Z_j^*(\mathbf{p})$ respectively. Since what we are directly interested in are $\mathbf{p}_i$ and $\mathbf{p}_j$, we can replace $\mathbf{z}_i$ and $\mathbf{z}_j$ by these values (unique by virtue of A1) and rewrite programmes P_i and P_j more compactly as P_i' and P_j':

$$\text{Maximise } -\mathbf{p}Z_j^*(\mathbf{p}) \qquad\qquad (P_j'),$$

$$\text{Maximise } U_i[\mathbf{\omega}_i + Z_i^*(\mathbf{p}), m_i - \mathbf{p}Z_i^*(\mathbf{p}) + \pi_i(\mathbf{p})] \quad (P_i'),$$

yielding respectively $\mathbf{p}_j = \psi_j(\mathbf{p}_{-j})$ and $\mathbf{p}_i = \psi_i(\mathbf{p}_{-i})$.

Because of the continuity of $Z_a^*(\mathbf{p})$ for all a (by A1), the maximands of programmes P_i' and P_j' are continuous functions, and therefore by the theorem of the maximum $\psi_i(\mathbf{p}_{-i})$ and $\psi_j(\mathbf{p}_{-j})$ are upper semi-continuous correspondences. The mapping ψ is thus an upper semi continuous correspondence with convex values from a compact convex set into itself. By Kakutani's theorem it has a fixed point and an equilibrium exists. Q.E.D.

Comments

At this point it may be useful to comment a little on the theorem and assumptions, and further avenues for research.

The most delicate assumption in our theorem is evidently A5, which is not derived from households' tastes or firms' technologies. Though such an assumption is always used under one form or the other in the literature, it would be worthwhile to investigate more basic conditions for existence, as it is known that this assumption may not hold for non-pathological demand functions (see for example Roberts and Sonnenschein, 1977). A few steps have already been taken in this direction: Dierker (1986), working in the traditional framework, investigated the role of the distribution of consumers' preferences. Benassy (1986 b), in a framework closer to the one of this article, showed that both the number of competitors and the degree of substituability between goods, obviously two fundamental parameters in imperfect competition, played a crucial role in existence of an equilibrium of this sort. All this should be a worthwhile topic for future research.

Another fruitful area of research would be to investigate different forms of strategic price interaction between price makers. In the 'Chamberlinian' tradition of monopolistic competition, we adopted here the so-called 'Bertrand–Nash' conjectures that each price maker expects the other price makers not to change their prices as a response to his own moves. While this may be a good assumption in markets with many competitors, there may be some oligopolistic situations where strategies allowing more feedback effects on prices could be a more suitable representation.[10] This too should be the subject of future research.

VI. CONCLUSIONS

We have given in this paper a definition of an objective demand curve in the context of a general equilibrium with price makers. This definition is valid on the full price domain and takes into account all the general equilibrium feedback effects of price decisions. Both features represent a clearcut progress over previous definitions, and accordingly the associated general equilibrium concept has also a wider applicability.

We may note that an instrumental element of this progress was the use of the methods of non-Walrasian theory. This, which had already been used earlier in the framework of subjective demand curves,[11] appears thus as a powerful tool to analyse price making by decentralised agents in the absence of an auctioneer.

CNRS and CEPREMAP, Paris

REFERENCES

d'Aspremont, C., dos Santos, R. and Gerard-Varet, L. A. (1986). 'On monopolistic competition and involuntary unemployment.' CORE Discussion paper, Louvain.

Benassy, J. P. (1975). 'Neo-Keynesian disequilibrium theory in a monetary economy.' *Review of Economic Studies* vol. 42, pp. 503–23.

—— (1976). 'The disequilibrium approach to monopolistic price setting and general monopolistic equilibrium.' *Review of Economic Studies*, vol. 43, pp. 69–81.

—— (1977). 'A neoKeynesian model of price and quantity determination in disequilibrium.' In *Equilibrium and Disequilibrium in Economic Theory* (ed. G. Schwödiauer). Boston: Reidel Publishing Company.

—— (1982). *The Economics of Market Disequilibrium.* New York: Academic Press.

—— (1986a). 'On competitive market mechanisms.' *Econometrica*, vol. 54, pp. 95–108.

—— (1986b). 'On the role of market size in imperfect competition: a Bertrand–Edgeworth–Chamberlin model.' Working paper, CEPREMAP.

—— (1987). 'Imperfect competition, unemployment and policy.' *European Economic Review*, vol. 31, pp. 417–26.

Dehez, P. (1985). 'Monopolistic equilibrium and involuntary unemployment.' *Journal of Economic Theory*, vol. 36, pp. 160–5.

Dierker, H. (1986). 'Existence of Nash equilibrium in pure strategies in an oligopoly with price setting firms.' Working Paper, University of Bonn.

Dreze, J. (1975). 'Existence of an equilibrium under price rigidities.' *International Economic Review*, vol. 16, pp. 301–20.

Gabszewicz, J. J. and Vial, J. P. (1972). 'Oligopoly "à la Cournot" in a general equilibrium analysis.' *Journal of Economic Theory*, vol. 4, pp. 381–400.

Hahn, F. H. (1978). 'On non-Walrasian equilibria.' *Review of Economic Studies*, vol. 45, pp. 1–17.

Hart, O. D. (1985). 'Imperfect competition in general equilibrium: an overview of recent work' in *Frontiers of Economics*, (ed. K. J. Arrow and S. Honkapohja). Basil Blackwell.

[10] For early attempts in this direction, see notably Marschak and Selten (1974), or Hahn's (1978) idea of rational conjectures.

[11] See Benassy (1976; 1977; 1982).

Laffont, J. J. and Laroque, G. (1976). 'Existence d'un équilibre général de concurrence imparfaite: une introduction.' *Econometrica*, vol. 44, pp. 283–94.

Marschak, T. and Selten, R. (1974). *General Equilibrium with Price Making Firms*. Lecture Notes in Economics and Mathematical Systems, Berlin: Springer-Verlag.

Mas-Colell, A. (1982). 'The Cournotian foundations of Walrasian equilibrium theory: an exposition of recent theory' in *Advances in Economic Theory*, (ed. W. Hildenbrand). Cambridge: Cambridge University Press.

Negishi, T. (1961). 'Monopolistic competition and general equilibrium.' *Review of Economic Studies*, vol. 28, pp. 196–201.

Nikaido, H. (1975). *Monopolistic Competition and Effective Demand*. Princeton: Princeton University Press.

Roberts, J. and Sonnenschein, H. (1977). 'On the foundations of the theory of monopolistic competition.' *Econometrica*, vol. 45, pp. 101–13.

Schulz, N. (1983). 'On the global uniqueness of fixprice equilibria.' *Econometrica*, vol. 51, pp. 47–68.

Silvestre, J. (1986). 'Undominated prices in the three good model.' Forthcoming. *European Economic Review*.

Snower, D. (1983). 'Imperfect competition, unemployment and crowding out.' *Oxford Economic Papers*, vol. 35, pp. 569–84.

Weitzman, M. L. (1985). 'The simple macroeconomics of profit sharing.' *American Economic Review*, vol. 75, pp. 937–52.

[44]

Monopolistic Competition in a Large Economy with Differentiated Commodities

OLIVER D. HART

Churchill College, Cambridge

1. INTRODUCTION

Since the publication of Chamberlin's (1933) famous book " The Theory of Monopolistic Competition ", it has become customary to regard the theory of the perfectly competitive firm and the theory of the monopolistically competitive firm as two distinct pieces of economic analysis. Perfect competition, it is argued, will rule in a market where there are many small firms producing a homogeneous product. Under these conditions, each firm will be too insignificant relative to the market as a whole to exert any influence on the market price. Thus individual firms will face horizontal demand curves and will set price equal to marginal cost.

In contrast, monopolistically competitive behaviour arises when the outputs of different firms are heterogeneous. Under these conditions, by varying the quality of its output, a firm can differentiate its product from the products of other firms. As a result, each firm will, in general, produce a unique commodity and will face a downward-sloping demand curve. Hence, even in the long-run, the equilibrium of the economy will involve firms setting price in excess of marginal cost and producing at a point to the left of the minimum point on their U-shaped average cost curves.

Much of the controversy which followed the publication of Chamberlin's book concerned the exact nature of the conditions under which firms possess monopoly power. Kaldor (1935) and Robinson (1934) maintained that monopoly power would disappear, both in the homogeneous product case and in the differentiated product case, if there was a sufficiently large number of very small firms in the industry. They put forward the following argument (see also Samuelson (1967)). A firm maximizes profits by setting marginal revenue equal to marginal cost, where $MR = P + QdP/dQ$, P is output price and Q is quantity. If Q is very small for each firm, then the QdP/dQ term will be insignificant and MR will be approximately equal to P. Hence price will be approximately equal to marginal cost (MC) and each firm will behave almost like a perfect competitor.

In fact, even in the homogeneous product case, this argument only clinches the matter if firms face constant or decreasing returns to scale.[1] For letting the number of firms tend to infinity and Q tend to zero for each of them, we obtain from the above argument that $P = MC$, where the latter is evaluated at $Q = 0$. If marginal costs are non-decreasing, we may deduce that each firm, by choosing $Q = 0$, is behaving like a profit maximizing perfect competitor at the price P. But, if, as is more usually assumed, marginal cost is initially falling, then $Q = 0$ is not consistent with competitive behaviour; in particular, while the first-order conditions for profit maximization are satisfied, the second-order conditions are violated since d^2C/dQ^2 is negative.[2,3]

Actually, the assumption that the number of firms in the industry is very large and that each firm is very small turns out to be something of a red herring.[4] What is important for perfect competition is not that each firm produce a small amount in absolute terms but that the output of every firm be small relative to the economy as a whole (more precisely, that any amount that a firm might *wish* to produce be small relative to the economy as a whole). To see this, consider a firm which operates in a market where there are many consumers and assume for simplicity that these consumers are identical. Let the firm increase its output by 1 per cent. In order to sell this extra output, the firm will have to lower its price. But, if there are many consumers, then the extra amount of the firm's product that each consumer consumes after the one per cent increase will be very small since the output is divided equally among all the consumers. Hence, the marginal rate of substitution between the firm's output and other goods will hardly change for each consumer, and the reduction in output price which is necessary to induce the consumers to consume the extra output is close to zero. Thus, the elasticity of demand for the firm's product will be nearly infinite and marginal revenue will be approximately equal to price; however, this is not because Q is small, but rather because dP/dQ is small.[5]

The idea that a firm (or consumer) will face a high elasticity of demand if it is small relative to the aggregate economy is not new. The same principle, for example, underlies the results of Gabszewicz and Vial (1972) and Roberts and Postlewaite (1976) on the nature of equilibrium in large homogeneous product economies, and much of the work on the equivalence of the core and the set of competitive equilibria (on the latter, see in particular the equivalence proof of Hansen (1969)). What seems to have received little emphasis, however, is the fact that this idea applies to a world of differentiated commodities just as much as to a world of homogeneous goods. In other words, whether a firm is the sole supplier of a particular commodity or whether it is supplying a commodity for which there are many close substitutes, the firm's elasticity of demand will be close to infinity if the firm is small relative to the aggregate economy, and will in general be bounded away from infinity if the firm is large relative to the aggregate economy.[6] Thus, contrary to the Chamberlinian point of view, what ensures that a firm behaves like a perfect competitor is not the presence of other firms producing close substitutes, but rather the fact that the firm is a negligible part of the aggregate economy (here negligibility must be carefully defined; see the remarks in Section 7).[7]

The purpose of this paper is to clarify and develop these ideas in a general equilibrium model with differentiated commodities. Our main concern is to show that when firms are small relative to the aggregate economy, a monopolistically competitive equilibrium is approximately Pareto optimal. This result is, of course, closely related to the proposition that firms' elasticities of demand are almost infinite under these conditions. In order to establish the result, we will consider an economy in which there is a given, possibly infinite, set F of potential firms. Corresponding to each element f in F, there is a technology which describes which types of goods firm f can produce and in what quantities. We will assume that firms' production sets are bounded and that there is a set-up cost for each firm, so that, in an economy with finite resources, only a finite number of firms can actually operate. There will be assumed to be a finite number of types of consumers. We will make the size of individual firms small relative to the aggregate economy by increasing the number of consumers of each type and at the same time the aggregate endowment vector of the economy. Among other things, this has the effect of permitting more firms to set up and of making it possible (although not necessarily desirable) for a wider range of commodities to be produced.

The assumption that firms' production sets are bounded is important. For if the assumption does not hold, it is possible for the size of individual firms to remain significant relative to the aggregate economy as the aggregate economy becomes large. Under these conditions, firms will generally retain monopoly power since although dP/dQ tends to zero, QdP/dQ will not tend to zero and hence marginal revenue will be bounded away from price.

Our treatment of the consumption side of the economy is based on the recent work of

Mas-Colell (1975) on the relationship between the core and set of competitive equilibria in economies with differentiated commodities. We will assume that the set of differentiated commodities, A, is a compact metric space (A will be infinite in most applications). In addition to the differentiated commodities, there will be one homogeneous good which will be regarded as the numeraire. A consumer's consumption of differentiated commodities will be represented by a measure x_1 on the set A, with the interpretation that if B is a (Borel) measurable subset of A, then $x_1(B)$ is the total quantity of commodities consumed whose characteristics lie in B.

Firms will be assumed to produce those commodities which maximize profits, subject to the demand curves facing them. In order to make this assumption operational, it will be assumed that each firm knows the complete demand curve for all its products, where this demand curve is based on Cournot–Nash quantity conjectures. That is, each firm will be assumed to believe that, if it changes its output, other firms will respond by keeping their own outputs fixed (we will assume that there are no intermediate products; thus firms do not purchase each other's outputs). This assumption is not particularly realistic in small economies, but becomes much more reasonable when the number of consumers is large.

Consumers, acting as price-takers, will be assumed to purchase those goods which maximize utility subject to their budget constraints. It is assumed that there are markets for the homogeneous good and for the differentiated commodities which firms decide to produce, and that prices adjust to clear these markets. Markets for all differentiated commodities which are not produced are closed.

A measure of the welfare loss implied by monopolistically competitive behaviour is introduced. In rough terms, this measure represents the per-capita increase in utility that consumers could achieve if an omniscient central planner took over and moved the economy from a monopolistically competitive equilibrium to a Pareto optimal allocation. Our main result is that this welfare measure tends to zero as the number of consumers of each type tends to infinity. The result is proved by showing that the monopolistically competitive equilibrium converges to a competitive equilibrium of a well-defined limit economy.

The paper is organized as follows. In Section 2, we present a simple example which illustrates the fact that an agent's monopoly power is insignificant if the agent is sufficiently small relative to the aggregate economy. In Sections 3–4, we study a general model of monopolistic competition. In Section 5, we discuss the interpretation of our main result and consider some extensions. In Section 6, we show that our results have implications for the recent literature on firms' investment decisions in stock market economies. It turns out that the one good–two period model which has been studied in most of the stock market literature is isomorphic to the differentiated commodities economy studied in this paper. In particular, the differentiated commodities produced by firms may be thought of as random variables representing firms' profits in different states of the world, and the purchasers of differentiated commodities as the final shareholders of the firms producing these commodities. Our main welfare result, when restated in these terms, says that, in large stock market economies, net market value maximization by firms leads to allocations which are approximately constrained Pareto optimal.

In Section 7, we will discuss the relationship between our work and some of the literature on monopolistic competition. Section 8 contains our conclusions and the proofs of theorems are to be found in the Appendix.

2. AN EXAMPLE

In this section we will present a simple example which shows that an agent's monopoly power becomes negligible as the agent's size relative to the aggregate economy tends to zero. In order to simplify matters, we will consider an exchange economy.

We assume that there are two types of agents. The economy will be made large by increasing the number of type 1 agents, but there will always be only one type 2 agent. There

4   REVIEW OF ECONOMIC STUDIES

are two goods 1 and 2. Each type 1 consumer has an endowment $\alpha > 0$ of good 1 and a zero endowment of good 2. The single type 2 consumer (whom we shall call consumer 2) has an endowment $\beta > 0$ of good 2 and a zero endowment of good 1.

We will assume for simplicity that consumer 2 likes only good 1, so that we can write her/his utility function as $V(y)$, where y is consumption of good 1 and V is continuous and strictly increasing. Consumers of type 1 will be assumed to like both goods and their utility functions will be written $U(x_1, x_2)$, where x_i is consumption of good i and U is assumed to be strictly quasiconcave and to have strictly positive, finite, continuous partial derivatives.

We consider the economy ^rE, $r = 1, 2, ...$, consisting of r consumers of type 1 and one consumer of type 2. Since the type 2 consumer is the sole owner of good 2, we might expect this consumer to have some monopoly power. This is indeed the case when r is finite, but we will see that the type 2 consumer's monopoly power tends to zero as r tends to infinity.

We may obtain an upper limit for consumer 2's monopoly power by considering the polar case where consumer 2 can discriminate perfectly between the type 1 consumers. Perfect discrimination permits consumer 2 to enjoy all the gains from trade while the type 1 consumers are left no better off than they would be without trade with consumer 2. Thus, in the post-trade situation we have

$$U(\alpha - t_1, \beta/r) = U(\alpha, 0), \qquad \qquad ...(2.1)$$

$$V = V(rt_1), \qquad \qquad ...(2.2)$$

where t_1 is the amount of good 1 each type 1 consumer gives up and β, the amount of good 2 that consumer 2 gives up, is divided equally between all the type 1 consumers (this is an optimal strategy for consumer 2 if U is strictly quasiconcave). Given r, let t_1^* be the unique solution of (2.1). Then consumer 2's utility from perfect discrimination is $V_r^* = V(rt_1^*)$.

In contrast to perfect discrimination, let us consider the perfectly competitive outcome. Normalize so that the price of good 1 is unity. Then, denoting the price of good 2 by p_2, we must have in a competitive equilibrium

$$\frac{\frac{\partial U}{\partial x_2}(\alpha - t_1, \beta/r)}{\frac{\partial U}{\partial x_1}(\alpha - t_1, \beta/r)} = p_2, \qquad \qquad ...(2.3)$$

$$t_1 = p_2 \beta/r, \qquad \qquad ...(2.4)$$

and we may write consumer 2's utility in the competitive equilibrium as

$$V_r = V(rt_1) = V(p_2\beta).$$

Now it is clear that $V_r^* \geq V_r$ for all r since consumer 2 cannot do worse by discriminating than by behaving competitively. We will show that $\lim_{r\to\infty} (V_r^* - V_r) = 0$. To establish this, note first that the competitive equilibrium allocation must satisfy

$$U(\alpha - t_1, \beta/r) \geq U(\alpha, 0) \qquad \qquad ...(2.5)$$

since type 1 consumers cannot become worse off as a result of trade. Since $\beta/r \to 0$ as $r \to \infty$, we may conclude that $t_1 \to 0$. Therefore, taking limits in (2.3), we get

$$\lim_{r\to\infty} p_2 = \frac{\frac{\partial U}{\partial x_2}(\alpha, 0)}{\frac{\partial U}{\partial x_1}(\alpha, 0)}, \qquad \qquad ...(2.6)$$

HART   MONOPOLISTIC COMPETITION   5

from which it follows that

$$\lim_{r \to \infty} V_r = \lim_{r \to \infty} V(p_2 \beta) = V \left(\frac{\frac{\partial U}{\partial x_2}(\alpha, 0)\beta}{\frac{\partial U}{\partial x_1}(\alpha, 0)} \right).$$

Consider now $\lim_{r \to \infty} V_r^*$. We may use (2.1) to write $t_1^* = f(\beta/r)$. Furthermore, since $\beta/r \to 0$ as $r \to \infty$, t_1^* also tends to zero. Hence,

$$\lim_{r \to \infty} \frac{t_1^*}{\beta/r} = \frac{df(0)}{d(\beta/r)} = \frac{\frac{\partial U}{\partial x_2}(\alpha, 0)}{\frac{\partial U}{\partial x_1}(\alpha, 0)}. \qquad \qquad ...(2.7)$$

But this means that

$$\lim_{r \to \infty} V_r^* = \lim_{r \to \infty} V(rt_1^*) = V \left(\frac{\frac{\partial U}{\partial x_2}(\alpha, 0)\beta}{\frac{\partial U}{\partial x_1}(\alpha, 0)} \right), \text{ by (2.7).}$$

We see that $\lim_{r \to \infty} V_r^* = \lim_{r \to \infty} V_r$, i.e. while consumer 2 may benefit from exploiting her/his monopoly power when r is finite, the *gains* from behaving as a monopolist tend to zero as $r \to \infty$.

This result at first seems paradoxical. The reason perhaps is that one feels intuitively that consumer 2, being the only supplier of a scarce commodity, should have a large amount of power in the market and that this power should be even greater when r is large than when r is small. This is, in fact, quite correct since V_r^* is an increasing function of r. The mistake is to confuse this sort of power with monopoly power. The point is that V_r is also increasing in r and that consumer 2 can, in the limit, obtain as large a utility by behaving as a competitor as by behaving as a discriminating monopolist.

It may be useful to look at this another way. Consider equation (2.3). This equation relates p_2 to β. Now suppose that consumer 2 reduces her/his supply of good 2 by 50 per cent, say, to $\beta/2$ units. Then (2.6) implies that the limiting price p_2 will be unchanged. In other words, the elasticity of demand for consumer 2's product $\to \infty$ as $r \to \infty$. In view of this, it is hardly surprising that consumer 2 has little to gain from adopting non-competitive behaviour.

This last argument makes it clear that the assumption that consumer 2's endowment of good 2 does not grow as r increases is absolutely crucial. For suppose that consumer 2's endowment of good 2 in the economy $'E$ is βr. Then, replacing β by βr in (2.3) and taking limits as $r \to \infty$, we get

$$\frac{\frac{\partial U}{\partial x_2}(\alpha - \bar{t}_1, \beta)}{\frac{\partial U}{\partial x_1}(\alpha - \bar{t}_1, \beta)} = \lim_{r \to \infty} p_2, \qquad \qquad ...(2.8)$$

where $\bar{t}_1 = \lim_{r \to \infty} t_1$. Obviously, if consumer 2 withdraws 50 per cent of her/his endowment of good 2 from the market, $\lim p_2$ will change and hence consumer 2's monopoly power does not disappear when r is large.

So far we have assumed that both goods 1 and 2 are divisible. It is easy to see, however, that the argument can be generalized to the indivisible case. Suppose, for example, that good 2 is available only in k unit lots and that $\beta = nk$. Consider a competitive equilibrium (assuming one exists). Then, if $r > n$, there must be at least one type 1 consumer who does

6   REVIEW OF ECONOMIC STUDIES

not consume good 2. Since type 1 consumers are treated equally in a competitive allocation, it follows that no type 1 consumer can gain from trade with consumer 2. Hence the competitive outcome and the discriminating monopoly outcome are the same; moreover, this is true not just in the limit $r \to \infty$ but for all $r > n$.

Returning to the divisible case, we may note that the above example can be used to illustrate the recent work of Joseph Ostroy on the no surplus characterization of a competitive equilibrium (see Ostroy (1976), Makowski (1976)). Ostroy has argued that competitive behaviour by agents is plausible only if, in a competitive equilibrium, each agent contributes a zero surplus to the rest of the economy, i.e. if it is the case that, for each agent a, all of the other agents excluding a can do just as well for themselves without agent a as in the competitive equilibrium with agent a.

It is easy to check that this no surplus condition is satisfied in the limit in our example. For the *aggregate* increase in utility that type 1 consumers enjoy as a result of trading with consumer 2 in the competitive equilibrium is given by

$$W_r = r[U(\alpha - ({}^r p_2 \beta / r), \beta / r) - U(\alpha, 0)], \qquad \qquad ...(2.9)$$

where ${}^r p_2$ is the competitive equilibrium price of good 2 in the economy ${}^r E$. But, since U has continuous partial derivatives, we may write

$$U(\alpha - {}^r p_2 \beta / r, \beta / r) - U(\alpha, 0) = -{}^r p_2 \beta / r \left(\frac{\partial U}{\partial x_1} (\alpha, 0) + \varepsilon_1 \right) + \beta / r \left(\frac{\partial U}{\partial x_2} (\alpha, 0) + \varepsilon_2 \right), \quad ...(2.10)$$

where $\varepsilon_1, \varepsilon_2 \to 0$ as $r \to \infty$ (recall that $t_1 \to 0$ as $r \to \infty$ and hence, by (2.4), ${}^r p_2 \beta / r \to 0$). Therefore,

$$\lim_{r \to \infty} W_r = -\frac{\partial U}{\partial x_1} (\alpha, 0) [\beta \lim_{r \to \infty} {}^r p_2] + \frac{\partial U}{\partial x_2} (\alpha, 0) \beta$$

$$= 0 \text{ by } (2.6). \qquad \qquad ...(2.11)$$

Before leaving this example, we should mention an important caveat. We have assumed that the utility function U has finite, continuous partial derivatives. These assumptions rule out the Cobb–Douglas utility function $U = x_1^k x_2^{1-k}$, $0 < k < 1$, and the C.E.S. utility function $U = x_1^k + x_2^k$, $0 < k < 1$, since these utility functions have infinite partial derivatives when $x_1 = 0$ or $x_2 = 0$ (the Cobb–Douglas utility function also has discontinuous derivatives at $x_1 = x_2 = 0$). Once the derivatives of U are permitted to be infinite, consumer 2's monopoly power does not necessarily disappear as $r \to \infty$. Suppose, for example, that $U = x_1^{\frac{1}{2}} x_2^{\frac{1}{2}}$. Then, by acting as a discriminating monopolist, consumer 2 can obtain all of the type 1 consumers' endowment of good 1, i.e. $rt_1 = r\alpha$ and $V_r^* = V(r\alpha)$. On the other hand, in the unique competitive equilibrium, $x_1 = \alpha / 2$, $x_2 = \beta / r$, $p_2 = \alpha r / 2\beta$ and $V_r = V(r\alpha / 2)$. Hence, although $\lim_{r \to \infty} V_r = \lim_{r \to \infty} V_r^* = V(\infty)$, $(V_r^* - V_r)$ will not generally tend to zero unless V is bounded, and so it may continue to pay consumer 2 to act as a monopolist even when r is large.

Despite the difficulties caused by utility functions with infinite derivatives for our example, we will not need to rule out such utility functions in order to obtain our main welfare result, Theorem 1. However, utility functions whose partial derivatives are sometimes *discontinuous*, such as the Cobb–Douglas, will be ruled out throughout the paper.

3. THE MODEL

Our treatment of commodities is based on the work of Mas-Colell (1975).

Commodities

We will denote by A the set of all differentiated commodities which could conceivably be consumed or produced in the economy. An element of A is to be understood as a complete

HART   MONOPOLISTIC COMPETITION   7

description of a commodity. Thus, for example, one element of A might stand for "King Edward Potatoes" while another might stand for "Idaho Potatoes". (A is best thought of as the set of commodity names.)

We will assume that A is a compact metric space with metric d. This structure seems sufficiently general for most purposes. For example, if there is a finite number of commodities, L, then $A = \{1, 2, ..., L\}$ and we may use the metric $d(i, j) = (i-j)^2$. On the other hand, in the Lancastrian model (see Lancaster (1971) and Rosen (1974)) with a finite number of characteristics, C, we may write $A = \{x \in R_+^C \mid \sum_{i=1}^{C} x_i^2 = 1\}$, where $x \in A$ represents the commodity consisting of x_i units of characteristic $i(i = 1, ..., C)$; and we may use the metric $d(x, y) = (\sum_{i=1}^{C} (x_i - y_i)^2)^{\frac{1}{2}}$. As a third example, if there are n goods each of whose qualities can be represented by a parameter in the interval $[0, 1]$, then $A = \{(i, s) \mid i = 1, ..., n \text{ and } 0 \leq s \leq 1\}$ and $d((i, s), (j, t)) = (i-j)^2 + (s-t)^2$.

Commodities which are close in terms of the metric d will be regarded as having similar economic properties—in particular such commodities will be assumed to have similar impacts on consumers' utilities (see (3.1) below).

In addition to the differentiated commodities, there will be assumed to be a single homogeneous good, good 0.[8]

Consumption Bundles

We will represent a consumption bundle by a pair (x_0, x_1). The first component $x_0 \in R_+$ denotes consumption of good 0 and the second component x_1, a finite, non-negative Borel measure on A, describes consumption of commodities in A. If $B \subset A$, then $x_1(B)$ refers to the total number of units consumed of commodities lying in B. Thus, if $a, b \in A$, then $x_1(\{a\})$ is the number of units of commodity a consumed; while $x_1(\{a, b\})$ is the number of units of commodity a consumed plus the number of units of commodity b consumed (note that we are here adding together quantities of quite different commodities, e.g., apples and oranges). Once the measure x_1 is given, $x_1(B)$ is determined for each Borel subset B of A, and so the quantity consumed of every differentiated commodity is specified. Let M denote the set of all finite, non-negative Borel measures on A. Note that, in contrast to Mas-Colell (1975), we assume that all commodities are *divisible*.

Consumers

There are assumed to be I types of consumers.[9] The preferences of a type i consumer will be represented by a utility function $U^i: R_+ \times M \to R$, where $U^i(x)$ is the utility derived from the consumption bundle $x = (x_0, x_1)$. We endow R_+ with the usual Euclidean topology, M with the topology of weak convergence (see Parthasarathy (1967)), and $R_+ \times M$ with the product topology.[10] We assume that, for all i:

U^i is continuous   ...(3.1)

U^i is strictly increasing in x_0.   ...(3.2)

If $x_1' \geq x_1$, then $U^i(x_0, x_1') \geq U^i(x_0, x_1)$.[11]   ...(3.3)

U^i is semi-strictly quasiconcave, i.e. $U^i(x_0', x_1') > U^i(x_0, x_1) \Rightarrow U^i(\lambda x_0' + (1-\lambda)x_0,$

$\lambda x_1' + (1-\lambda)x_1) > U^i(x_0, x_1)$ if $0 < \lambda < 1$.[12]   ...(3.4)

$U^i(x) > U^i(0) \Rightarrow x_0 > 0$.   ...(3.5)

If $x_0 > 0$, then the partial derivative of U^i with respect to x_0, $\partial U^i / \partial x_0$, exists, and is finite and strictly positive.   ...(3.6)

If $x_0 > 0$, $\partial U^i / \partial x_0$ is continuous in x.   ...(3.7)

These assumptions are fairly standard. Note that while we assume that good 0 is desirable, we assume only that other commodities are not undesirable. Also, we assume

8   REVIEW OF ECONOMIC STUDIES

that consumers require positive consumption of good 0 in order to obtain "positive" utility.

As well as making the differentiability assumption (3.6), we will also wish to assume that U^i is differentiable with respect to the consumption of commodities in A. Given $a \in A$, let the measure $\mathscr{X}(a) \in M$ be defined as follows: for each Borel subset B of A, $\mathscr{X}(a)[B] = 1$ if $a \in B$ and $\mathscr{X}(a)[B] = 0$ if $a \notin B$. Define

$$\partial U^{i+}(x)/\partial \mathscr{X}(a) = \lim_{k \to 0, \, k>0} \{U^i(x_0, x_1 + k\mathscr{X}(a)) - U^i(x_0, x_1)\}/k.$$

We assume that, for all i:

$\partial U^{i+}(x)/\partial \mathscr{X}(a)$ exists (but is possibly infinite) for all $x \in R_+ \times M$, $a \in A$.   ...(3.8)

$\partial U^{i+}(x)/\partial \mathscr{X}(a)$ is finite if $a \in \text{supp } x_1$.[13]   ...(3.9)

$\partial U^{i+}(x)/\partial \mathscr{X}(a)$ is jointly continuous in (x, a) for all $x \in R_+ \times M$ and $a \in A$.   ...(3.10)

Assumption (3.9) embodies the idea that $\partial U^{i+}(x)/\partial \mathscr{X}(a)$ will only be infinite if commodity a contains a special characteristic that is not presently in consumer i's bundle x. For if $a \in \text{supp } x_1$, then i consumes positive amounts of commodities arbitrarily close to a and so all the characteristics of a are already contained in x.[14]

Firms

We will assume that there is a set of "potential" firms, denoted by F (F may be infinite). A firm $f \in F$ is represented by a technology which describes which commodities in A the firm can produce and how much input is required to produce these commodities. We will assume that, for all firms, good 0 is the sole input and some commodity in A is the sole output. It will also be assumed that it is technologically infeasible for any firm to produce more than one commodity in A at the same time (but see Section 5, Remark 7). Thus, although a firm might be able to produce either apples or oranges, it cannot produce both. This means that one of the most important decisions facing any firm is which commodity in A to produce.

The technological possibilities of firms are represented by a correspondence $Y: F \times A \Rightarrow R_- \times R_+$. Here $Y(f, \cdot)$ is the production set of firm f and $y = (y_0, y_1) \in Y(f, a)$ means that it is feasible for firm f to use $(-y_0)$ units of good 0 to produce y_1 units of commodity a. (Inputs are treated as non-positive numbers.) We will assume:

$0 \in Y(f, a)$ for all $f \in F$, $a \in A$.   ...(3.11)

There exists a number $\bar{y}_0 < 0$ such that: for every $f \in F$, $a \in A$ and $y \in Y(f, a)$,

$$y_1 \neq 0 \Rightarrow y_0 \leq \bar{y}_0.$$ ...(3.12)

Condition (3.12) states that any firm which wishes to produce a positive amount of output must pay a set-up cost, and that the set-up costs for different firms are uniformly bounded below by $(-\bar{y}_0)$. The existence of set-up costs implies that, in any finite economy, it is feasible for only a finite number of firms to operate, i.e. to produce positive amounts of output.

Note that under our assumptions it is quite possible for some firm in F to be the sole potential supplier of a particular commodity in A.

We will make two further assumptions about firms' production sets. First, we assume that firms' production sets are uniformly bounded.

Assumption A: There exists $b > 0$ such that, for all $f \in F$, $a \in A$,

$$y \in Y(f, a) \Rightarrow y_0^2 + y_1^2 < b^2.$$

Secondly, we assume:

There is a number $k > 0$ such that for all $f \in F$, $a \in A$: $y \in Y(f, a)$ and $y_1 > 0 \Rightarrow$ there exists $y' \in Y(f, a)$ with $y_1' \geq k$.   ...(3.13)

Assumption A ensures that each firm becomes small relative to the aggregate economy when the aggregate economy is made large. As noted in the introduction, without this assumption there is no guarantee that a firm's monopoly power will disappear in a large economy.[15]

Condition (3.13) says that if it is possible for firm f to produce commodity a at all, then it is possible for firm f to produce at least k units of commodity a, where $k > 0$ can be chosen independently of f, a.

The Economy ${}'E$

We consider an economy ${}'E$ in which there are r consumers of each type $i = 1, ..., I$. Each consumer of type i is assumed to have an initial endowment of good 0 given by $w^i \in R_{++}$, and an initial shareholding in firm f given by $\bar{\theta}^{if}/r$, where $\bar{\theta}^{if} \in R_+$ for all $i \in I$, $f \in F$ and $\sum_{i \in I} \bar{\theta}^{if} = 1$ for each $f \in F$. We are assuming that, as r increases, the aggregate shareholding of the consumers of type i in firm f remains the same, so that each consumer of type i gets a smaller shareholding in firm f. This assumption ensures that all type i consumers will have the same wealth in the economy ${}'E$.

We define an exchange equilibrium in ${}'E$ relative to a particular set of production decisions by firms. Let the array $((a^f, y^f))_{f \in F}$ represent the production decisions of firms in F, where the pair (a^f, y^f) indicates that firm f produces y_1^f units of commodity a^f using $-y_0^f$ units of good 0 as input. *In the following definition, it is assumed that $y_0^f = y_1^f = 0$ except for a finite number of $f \in F$; i.e. only a finite number of firms actually operate.* R_+^* denotes the set $R_+ U\{\infty\}$.

Definition. An exchange equilibrium in ${}'E$ relative to $((a^f, y^f))_{f \in F}$ is an array $((x_0^i, q^i)_{i \in I}, p)$ such that

$$p: A \rightarrow R_+^*. \qquad \qquad ...(3.14)$$

$$p(a) = \infty \Leftrightarrow y_1^f = 0 \text{ for all } f \text{ such that } a^f = a. \qquad ...(3.15)$$

For all $i \in I$, $x_0^i \in R_+$ and $q^i: F \rightarrow R_+$.[16]   ...(3.16)

For all $i \in I$, (x_0^i, q^i) is a solution of: max $U^i(\tilde{x}_0^i, \tilde{x}_1^i)$ subject to
$$\tilde{x}_0^i + \sum_{f \in F} p(a^f) \tilde{q}^{if} \le w^i + \sum_{f \in F} (\bar{\theta}^{if}/r)(p(a^f)y_1^f + y_0^f), \text{ where}$$
$$\tilde{x}_1^i = \sum_{f \in F} \tilde{q}^{if} \mathscr{X}(a^f), \tilde{x}_0^i \in R_+ \text{ and } \tilde{q}^i: F \rightarrow R_+. \qquad ...(3.17)$$

$$r\sum_{i \in I} q^{if} = y_1^f \text{ for all } f \in F. \qquad \qquad ...(3.18)$$

$$r\sum_{i \in I} x_0^i - \sum_{f \in F} y_0^f - r\sum_{i \in I} w^i = 0. \qquad \qquad ...(3.19)$$

In the above definition, we use q^{if} to denote the value of the function q^i at $f \in F$. The number $p(a)$ refers to the price of one unit of commodity a and q^{if} refers to the number of units of firm f's product (i.e. a^f) consumed by a type i consumer. As a result of the quasiconcavity of U^i, all type i consumers can be assumed to consume the same bundle of goods and so we do not have to distinguish between different members of the same type.

The price of good 0 is normalized to be 1. If $y_1^f = 0$ for all f such that $a^f = a$, we set $p(a) = \infty$ to indicate that the market for commodity a is closed. The convention $\infty.0 = 0$ and $\infty.k = \infty$ if $k > 0$ is adopted, so that the budget constraint in (3.17) implies that $q^{if} = 0$ if $p(a^f) = \infty$. Condition (3.17) says that each consumer is maximizing utility subject to her/his budget constraint. The equation $x_1^i = \sum_{f \in F} q^{if} \mathscr{X}(a^f)$ relates the measure x_1^i on A to the quantities of the commodities purchased. All consumers are assumed to act as price-takers. Condition (3.19) states that demand equals supply for good 0, while condition (3.18) states that demand equals supply for produced commodities in A.

Note that all summations over the set F are well-defined since, by assumption, $y_0^f = y_1^f = 0$ except for a finite number of f.

We turn now to the determination of firms' production plans. We will assume that each firm, subject to the demand conditions facing it, chooses a production plan to maximize profits in terms of the numeraire, good 0.[17] In order to make this assumption operational, we will assume that each firm can calculate the complete demand curve for its products. By this we mean that firms can work out not only how the demand for the product they are producing at present varies with price, but also how the demands for products they could conceivably produce depend on price. Each firm's demand curve is computed under the assumption that a change in the firm's production plan will not lead to any changes in the *quantity* decisions of other firms.[18] This assumption does not seem particularly plausible in small economies, but it becomes much more reasonable when the number of consumers of each type, r, is large.

The assumption that firms know their complete demand curves is, of course, a very strong one. The acquisition of this information would in practice be very difficult, particularly for firms that have not yet set up. Implicitly we are assuming that firms obtain the information either (1) by trying out new production plans and observing the results; (2) by engaging in market research; or (3) by constructing a general equilibrium model of the economy and calculating the relationship between the general equilibrium and their production plan.

Definition. A monopolistically competitive equilibrium in ^rE is an array $((a^f, y^f)_{f \in F}$, $(x_0^i, q^i)_{i \in I}, p)$ such that

$$y_0^f = y_1^f = 0 \text{ except for a finite number of } f \text{ in } F. \qquad \text{...(3.20)}$$

$$y^f \in Y(f, a^f) \text{ for all } f \in F. \qquad \text{...(3.21)}$$

$$((x_0^i, q^i)_{i \in I}, p) \text{ is an exchange equilibrium relative to } (a^f, y^f)_{f \in F}. \qquad \text{...(3.22)}$$

There does not exist $f \in F$, $\tilde{a}^f \in A$, $\tilde{y}^f \in Y(f, \tilde{a}^f)$ and an exchange equilibrium $((\tilde{x}_0^i, \tilde{q}^i)_{i \in I}, \tilde{p})$ relative to $(\tilde{a}^f, \tilde{y}^f)_{f \in F}$, such that $\tilde{p}(\tilde{a}^f)\tilde{y}_1^f + \tilde{y}_0^f > p(a^f)y_1^f + y_0^f$, where $\tilde{a}^{\tilde{f}} = a^{\tilde{f}}$ and $\tilde{y}^{\tilde{f}} = y^{\tilde{f}}$ for all $\tilde{f} \in F, \tilde{f} \neq f$. $\qquad \text{...(3.23)}$

$$p(a^f)y_1^f + y_0^f \geqq 0 \text{ for all } f \in F. \qquad \text{...(3.24)}$$

This definition requires some comment. First, condition (3.22) says that any monopolistically competitive equilibrium must be an exchange equilibrium relative to firms' production plans. Secondly, condition (3.23) states that it pays no firm, either one that is already operating or one that is not, to change its production plan. In particular, it is impossible for any single firm to change its production plan, while other firms keep their production plans fixed, in such a way as to increase its profits in some new exchange equilibrium. Thirdly, condition (3.24) says that each operating firm is making a non-negative profit.

Note that (3.20) must hold in equilibrium as a result of the existence of set-up costs (conditions (3.12) and (3.13)) and the fact that the aggregate resources in the economy ^rE are finite.

At first sight it might seem that (3.23) would make (3.24) redundant since a firm can always choose to close down. We include (3.24) in order to allow for pathological cases where a firm's closing down might result in the non-existence of an exchange equilibrium.

It should be noted that (3.23) is a very strong condition in the case of multiple exchange equilibria: in particular it is based on the idea that firms are optimistic and assume that the most favourable new exchange equilibrium will be selected after they change their production plan (this is despite the fact that the most favourable exchange equilibrium need not be chosen relative to their status-quo production plan). This assumption almost implies that the exchange equilibrium relative to the monopolistically competitive equilibrium production plans $(a^f, y^f)_{f \in F}$ is unique. For if there were two exchange equilibria, then it is almost certain that one firm would have a higher profit in one of the exchange equilibria and another firm would have a higher profit in the other, thus violating (3.23) (here, of course, a firm which is not operating has zero profits). Fortunately, condition (3.23) can be substantially weakened without destroying our results; see Section 5, Remark 8.

Obviously, a monopolistically competitive equilibrium is a strong notion of equilibrium and there are several reasons for thinking that such an equilibrium will not generally exist (in addition to the multiple exchange equilibrium problem just discussed). First, as Roberts and Sonnenschein (1977) have recently observed, the reaction functions of firms may not be convex-valued even if firms' production sets are convex. Secondly, because of the existence of set-up costs, firms' production sets in our model are not in fact convex. Thirdly, another sort of non-convexity is introduced by our assumption that firms can produce only one commodity in A at a time. (The convex combination of the output " 1 apple " and the output " 1 orange " is the joint output " λ apples and $(1-\lambda)$ oranges ", which is by assumption infeasible.) Finally, one runs into serious difficulties in applying the usual fixed point theorems as a result of the fact that several exchange equilibria may exist relative to some production plans and no exchange equilibria may exist relative to other production plans.

These considerations suggest that it may be impossible to find general conditions under which a monopolistically competitive equilibrium exists. At the same time, when r is large, several of the non-convexities mentioned above disappear, and so the problem of proving existence may be more tractable under these conditions. In any case, in the remainder of this paper, we will in cavalier fashion ignore the existence problem and simply assume that a monopolistically competitive equilibrium exists in the economy $'E$.

4. MONOPOLISTICALLY COMPETITIVE EQUILIBRIA IN LARGE ECONOMIES

We now consider the properties of a monopolistically competitive equilibrium as r becomes large. In particular, we wish to show that a monopolistically competitive equilibrium is approximately Pareto optimal when r is large. In order to make this idea precise, we must introduce a measure of how far an allocation is from being a Pareto optimum.

Let $'H = \{(x^i)_{i \in I} \mid$ there exist $(a^f, y^f)_{f \in F}$ and $(q^i)_{i \in I}$ such that $x_1^i = \sum_{f \in F} q^{if} \mathcal{X}(a^f)$, and (3.16), (3.18), (3.19), (3.20) and (3.21) are satisfied}. $'H$ is the set of feasible consumption allocations for the economy $'E$. Note that this feasible set will depend on r since, when r is large, a greater variety of commodities can be produced.

Given an allocation $(x^i)_{i \in I} \in 'H$, define $\alpha = \sup \{U^1(\tilde{x}^1) - U^1(x^1) \mid (\tilde{x}^i)_{i \in I} \in 'H$ and $U^i(\tilde{x}^i) \geq U^i(x^i)$ for $i = 2, ..., I\}$. The number α represents the maximum increase in the per-capita utility of consumers of type 1 which is possible starting from the allocation $(x^i)_{i \in I}$, given that consumers of type $i > 1$ are not made worse off. (It is easy to show that α is finite under our assumptions about the technology.) Clearly $\alpha \geq 0$ and $\alpha = 0$ if and only if $(x_i)_{i \in I}$ is a Pareto optimum.

We will use the measure α to represent how far an allocation is from being a Pareto optimum. Obviously, this measure suffers from certain drawbacks. First, it depends on the particular way in which we have normalized consumers' utility functions. Secondly, we have singled out the type 1 consumers in calculating α. However, from our point of view, neither of these drawbacks is important. In particular, it can easily be shown that our results would be unchanged if a more neutral measure of Pareto inefficiency were adopted, say along the lines of Debreu (1951).

We now present our main result which states that, with respect to a monopolistically competitive equilibrium, $\alpha \to 0$ as $r \to \infty$. The result requires Assumption B, which has yet to be stated.

Theorem 1. *Assume that firms' production sets are uniformly bounded; i.e. that Assumption A holds. Let $(((^ra^f, ^ry^f)_{f \in F}, (^rx_0^i, ^rq^i)_{i \in I}, ^rp))$ be a sequence of monopolistically competitive equilibria in the economies $'E, r = 1, 2, \ldots$. For each monopolistically competitive equilibrium,* *let $^r\alpha$ be defined as above. Then, if the sequence $((^ra^f, \, ^ry^f)_{f \in F})$ satisfies Assumption B,* $\lim_{r \to \infty} {}^r\alpha = 0$.

In order to state Assumption B, we will need to introduce the idea of a limit economy $^\infty E$ towards which the economies $^r E$ converge. In particular we will wish to define an exchange equilibrium for $^\infty E$.

Definition. An exchange equilibrium in $^\infty E$ relative to the " artificial " endowments $(\bar{x})^i_{i \in I} = (\bar{x}^i_0, \, \bar{x}^i_1)_{i \in I}$, where $\bar{x}^i_0 \in R$ and $\bar{x}^i_1 \in M$ for all i, is an array $((x^i)_{i \in I}, \, p)$ such that

$p \colon \bar{X}_1 \to R_+$ is a continuous function, where $\bar{X}_1 = \operatorname{supp} \sum_{i \in I} \bar{x}^i_1$.   ...(4.1)

$x^i \in R_+ \times M$ for all $i \in I$.   ...(4.2)

For all $i \in I$, x^i is a solution of: max $U^i(x)$ subject to

$$x_0 + \int_{X_1} p(a) dx_1(a) \le \bar{x}^i_0 + \int_{X_1} p(a) d\bar{x}^i_1(a).$$ ...(4.3)

$$\sum_{i \in I} x^i_0 - \sum_{i \in I} \bar{x}^i_0 = 0.$$ ...(4.4)

$$\sum_{i \in I} x^i_1 - \sum_{i \in I} \bar{x}^i_1 = 0.$$ ...(4.5)

This exchange equilibrium differs from that defined previously for ^rE in several important respects. First, we now insist that p be a continuous function with finite values for all $a \in \operatorname{supp} \sum_{i \in I} \bar{x}^i_1$. Secondly, the quantities q^i of firms' outputs purchased by consumers no longer appear in the definition; instead we imagine consumers purchasing the measure x^i_1 directly. Thirdly, the summations in the budget constraint (3.17) are replaced by integrals in (4.3). Fourthly, we have expressed the quantity variables in per-capita terms by including only one representative consumer of each type.

Finally, we have defined the exchange equilibrium relative to the " artificial " endowments $(\bar{x}^i_0, \, \bar{x}^i_1)$. In order to interpret these artificial endowments, consider the exchange equilibrium defined for ^rE. The budget constraint (3.17) can be rewritten as

$$x_0 + \Sigma p(a^f) q^f \le (w^i + \Sigma(\theta^{if}/r) y^f_0) + \Sigma p(a^f)(\theta^{if}/r) y^f_1.$$ ...(4.6)

We may interpret the right-hand side of (4.6) as follows. The first term $(w^i + \sum (\theta^{if}/r) y^f_0)$ represents a type i consumer's endowment of good 0 *after* firms have determined their production plans, while the term $(\theta^{if}/r) y^f_1$ represents a type i consumer's endowment of commodity a^f again *after* firms' production plans have been determined; we can imagine that each firm calls for inputs from consumers and distributes outputs to consumers according to consumers' shareholdings in the firm.

Once we know the " artificial " endowments $(w_i + \sum (\theta^{if}/r) y^f_0), \, (\theta^{if}/r) y^f_1$, the exchange equilibrium for ^rE can be defined without any further reference to the production plans $(a^f, \, y^f)$. This is the approach which we have chosen to follow with respect to the definition of an exchange equilibrium in $^\infty E$. The artificial endowments $(\bar{x}^i_0, \, \bar{x}^i_1)$ are to be interpreted as the endowments after firms have made their production decisions. By specifying these artificial endowments directly, we have avoided any reference to production plans in the economy $^\infty E$.

We can now introduce Assumption B.

Definition. We will say that the sequence $((^ra^f, \, ^ry^f)_{f \in F})$ satisfies *Assumption B* if the following is true for each limit point $(\bar{x}_i)_{i \in I}$ of the corresponding sequence of " artificial " endowments $((w^i + \sum_{f \in F} (\theta^{if}/r)^r y^f_0, \, \sum_{f \in F} (\theta^{if}/r)^r y^f_1 \mathscr{X}(^ra^f))_{i \in I}$:

Given an exchange equilibrium $((x^i)_{i \in I}, \, p)$ in $^\infty E$ relative to the " artificial " endowments $(\bar{x}^i)_{i \in I}$ and a sequence $(^r\bar{x}^i)_{i \in I}$ satisfying $^r\bar{x}^i \in R \times M$ and $\lim_{r \to \infty} {}^r\bar{x}^i = \bar{x}^i$ for each i, we can find r^* such that, for all $r \ge r^*$, there is an exchange equilibrium $((^rx^i)_{i \in I}, \, ^rp)$ in $^\infty E$ relative to the " artificial " endowments $(^r\bar{x}^i)_{i \in I}$ and $\lim_{r \to \infty} {}^rx^i = x^i$ for each r.

In other words, the equilibrium correspondence which maps endowments into final allocations in the economy $^\infty E$ is lower hemicontinuous at every limit point corresponding to the sequence of production plans $(({}^r a^f, {}^r y^f)_{f \in F})$.

Theorem 1 is proved by showing that the monopolistically competitive equilibria in the economies ${}^r E$ converge to an exchange equilibrium in $^\infty E$ in which firms maximize profits, taking as given the limiting prices p. The proof is given in the Appendix.

5. GENERAL REMARKS

In this section, we will make some general remarks about the analysis of previous sections.

1. In general, there is no reason to expect the profits of individual firms in a mono-polistically competitive equilibrium to tend to zero as $r \to \infty$. If, however, we assume that firms have " similar " technologies, then zero profits are guaranteed in the limit.

Assumption C. Given $f \in F$, $a \in A$, $y \in Y(f, a)$ and $\varepsilon > 0$, then, for infinitely many $f' \in F$, there exist $a' \in A$ and $y' \in Y(f', a')$ such that $d(a', a) < \varepsilon$ and $(y_0' - y_0)^2 + (y_1' - y_1)^2 < \varepsilon$.

Assumption C states that, if we pick a feasible production plan for any firm f, then we can find infinitely many other firms with feasible production plans arbitrarily close to this production plan. Here " close " refers both to the characteristics of the commodity produced and to the quantities of output produced and input used (recall that d is the metric on A).

Proposition 2. *Assume Assumptions A and C. Let* $((({}^r a^f, {}^r y^f)_{f \in F}, ({}^r x_0^i, {}^r q^i)_{i \in I}, {}^r p))$ *be a sequence of monopolistically competitive equilibria in the economies* ${}^r E$, $r = 1, 2, \ldots$ *Then, if the sequence* $(({}^r a^f, {}^r y^f)_{f \in F})$ *satisfies Assumption B,* $\sup_{f \in F} [{}^r p({}^r a^f)^r y_1^f + {}^r y_0^f] \to 0$ *as* $r \to \infty$.

Proof. See Appendix.

In other words, under Assumption C, the famous Chamberlinian tangency between firms' demand curves and average cost curves is achieved in the limit as $r \to \infty$ (however, it is achieved at the minimum average cost point rather than to the left of this point!).

2. It is interesting to compare the consequences of profit maximizing behaviour in large economies and in small economies. In small economies, profit maximization does not lead to Pareto optimal outcomes because, roughly speaking, the price a firm's product fetches on the market depends on the marginal utility of the commodity to consumers rather than on the average or total utility. For this reason, if the intramarginal contri-butions to utility are significant, it may be the case that production of a commodity is socially desirable and yet unprofitable. As $r \to \infty$, however, the supply of any firm's output is divided between so many consumers of each type that, as long as the firm is small relative to the aggregate economy, each consumer's marginal utility of consumption and average utility of consumption are almost the same. Hence, the intramarginal effects become negligible and there is no divergence between what is profitable and what is socially desirable (in the Pareto sense).

3. It has been noted by Drèze (1974) and Drèze and Hagen (1975) that, even in the absence of set-up costs, there is a non-convexity in the feasible set of the model of Section 3 arising from the assumption that each firm can produce only one commodity at a time (or, more generally, that there is an upper limit on the number of different commodities that a firm can produce at one time). This non-convexity has the implication that, in general, it is impossible for Pareto optimal allocations to be achieved unless firms' actions are co-ordinated; that is, situations may arise in which a Pareto improvement is possible only if several firms change their production plans simultaneously (see the examples in Drèze

(1974)). In contrast, Theorem 1 of Section 4 states that unco-ordinated profit maximizing behaviour by firms leads to Pareto optimal outcomes. How can these two apparently conflicting conclusions be reconciled?

The answer is that, while replicating the consumer sector in order to obtain competitive conditions, we have at the same time got rid of the troublesome non-convexity. This can be seen from the fact that the limiting aggregate production set of the economy (in per-capita terms), defined by $^\infty G$ in the Appendix, is convex (this fact is established in the Appendix). Since $^\infty G$ is convex, it follows that the set of feasible allocations for the economy $^\infty E$ is also convex. Hence, as in classical Arrow–Debreu economies, a Pareto optimum can be achieved in a decentralized manner with prices guiding firms in their production decisions.

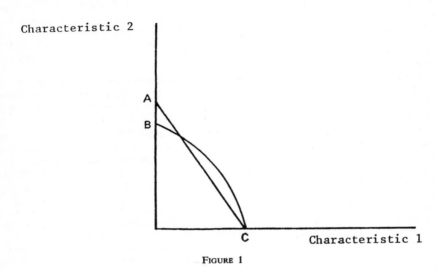

FIGURE 1

In spite of the convexifying effect of replication, some non-convexities remain even in the limit $r \to \infty$. Consider, for example, a Lancastrian economy with two characteristics. In Figure 1, a line AC represents the production frontier of a firm in this economy in characteristics space (imagine that the firm has already decided to set up and has made its input decision).

The curved line BC represents an isoprofit line, i.e. in terms of the limiting economy $^\infty E$, a line whose equation is $p(a)y_1(a) = $ constant.

Now it is clear from the diagram that point A is more profitable for the firm than point C. Since the intramarginal contributions to utility are negligible when r is large (see Remark 2), it follows that the production plan A is Pareto superior to the production plan C. But, by the same argument, points close to C on the line AC are less profitable than C and so are Pareto inferior to C. Hence, if in either the planned economy or the market economy a procedure for reaching equilibrium allocations is adopted which considers only *local* changes, the economy can get stuck at the non-Pareto optimal position C. We see then that a non-convexity remains even when $r = \infty$.

4. In the Introduction, we emphasized that it is the fact that each firm is small relative to the economy, rather than the existence of close substitutes for firms' products, which ensures that firms behave competitively in the model of Section 3 when $r \to \infty$. However,

it is easy to see that, under our assumption that the set of commodities is compact, for each commodity a lying in the support of the limiting aggregate production plan (denoted by Y_1 in the Appendix), there must exist an infinite number of firms producing commodities arbitrarily close to a. So the reader may wonder whether it is not after all substitutability which is responsible for competitive behaviour.

The point is, however, that although a theory based on substitutability can explain why competitive conditions exist for commodities which are produced in equilibrium, it cannot explain why these conditions also exist for commodities which are not produced. Suppose, for example, that there are infinitely many identical firms which can produce either apples or oranges. Suppose that consumers' tastes are such that it is Pareto optimal for every firm to produce apples. Then we know from Theorem 1 that, in the limit, only apples will be produced in the monopolistically competitive equilibrium. Since so many firms are producing apples, we would expect, according to the substitutability theory, that the apple market will be competitive. But the substitutability theory does not explain why the orange market is also competitive, i.e. it does not explain why it does not pay one firm to become the only orange producer, and thereby make monopoly profits (remember each firm makes the Nash assumption that other firms will not follow it). In contrast, the smallness theory does explain this: since each firm is small relative to the (potential) orange market, it will have no monopoly power and so a switch to orange production is profitable if and only if it is socially desirable. By assumption it is Pareto optimal for all firms to produce apples and so such a switch is not socially desirable.

5. Although we have argued throughout that substitutability is not a factor in determining whether conditions are competitive, it should be recognized that this view may be partly a result of our Cournot–Nash assumption about the way other firms react to a change in a particular firm's production plan. Suppose, for example, that in the exchange equilibrium of ^rE there are many firms producing the same good. Consider the consequences of one firm doubling its supply of this good. In order to induce consumers to purchase the extra output, the price of the good will in general have to fall. However, as the price begins to fall, we might expect, contrary to the Cournot–Nash assumption, that other firms will reduce their supplies, thus making the decrease in price necessary to restore equilibrium smaller than it would otherwise be. For this reason the elasticity of demand for a particular firm's output may be greater if there are other firms producing close substitutes than if the firm is producing a unique commodity.

It should be noted that the above (very impressionistic) argument does not affect our conclusion that, both in the homogeneous and in the differentiated cases, a firm's elasticity of demand will be close to infinity only when r is large. What it does suggest, however, is that the *rate* at which a firm's elasticity of demand tends to infinity as r tends to infinity might be influenced by the number of other firms producing close substitutes.

6. Throughout our analysis, we have assumed that the set of commodities A is compact. This assumption is important in ensuring that there is a well-defined limit economy $^\infty E$ towards which the economies ^rE converge. Without such a limit economy, there may be no valid sense in which one can talk about convergence of a monopolistically competitive equilibrium to a Pareto optimum. For a discussion of some of the problems which can arise when the set of commodities is not compact (although in a somewhat different context), see Ostroy (1973).[19]

7. Throughout Sections 3 and 4, we have assumed that firms cannot produce more than one commodity at a time. It is easy to show that all our results generalize to the case where firms can produce at most k commodities where $k \geq 1$ is a given number. In this case we may represent the technological possibilities of firms by a correspondence $Y: F \times A^k \Rightarrow R_- \times R_+^k$, where A^k is the k-fold Cartesian product of A. Now

$$(y_0, y_1, ..., y_k) \in Y(f, a_1, ..., a_k)$$

means that it is feasible for firm f to use $(-y_0)$ units of good 0 to produce y_1 units of commodity a_1, y_2 units of commodity a_2, ..., y_k units of commodity a_k. The proof of Theorem 1 is unchanged (Assumption A must be modified in an obvious way).

8. We noted in Section 3 that condition (3.23), which is based on the idea that a firm changes its production plan whenever its profits go up in the most favourable new exchange equilibrium, is very strong. It is easy to show, however, that Theorem 1 still holds if (3.23) is replaced by the condition that a firm changes its production plan as long as its profits go up in some new exchange equilibrium whose consumption allocation $(x^i)_{i \in I}$ lies in an ε-neighbourhood of the original exchange equilibrium consumption allocation. Here ε is some positive number which is fixed *a priori*, and we metrize M in a way which is consistent with the topology of weak convergence (see Parthasarathy (1967)). The proof of Theorem 1 is unchanged (note that the only place where (3.23) is used is in Step 2).

6. RELATIONSHIP TO LITERATURE ON PRODUCTION UNDER UNCERTAINTY

Theorem 1 of Section 4 may be shown to have a bearing on the recent literature on firms' production decisions in stock market economies (see, e.g. Diamond (1967), Jensen and Long (1972), Stiglitz (1972), Drèze (1974), Ekern and Wilson (1974), Leland (1974) and Merton and Subrahmanyam (1974)). Most of this literature has been concerned with a two period economy where the state of the world is unknown in period 0, but is revealed in period 1. In period 0, resources are allocated to firms for investment purposes, the returns from investment being realized in period 1. There is assumed to be a single good in each period. In period 0, markets open for the current good and for firms' shares (for the moment we ignore other sorts of finance). There are assumed to be no markets for contingent commodities. In period 1 consumers receive outputs from firms in proportion to the shares purchased in period 0. There is no trading in period 1 (see Drèze (1974) for a detailed description of the model).

It has been observed by several authors (see, e.g. Drèze and Hagen (1975)) that the above stock market model is isomorphic to the model of differentiated commodities that we have studied in this paper. (Note, however, that as soon as the assumptions that the stock market economy contains only one good and lasts for just two periods are relaxed, the structure of the stock market model becomes considerably more complicated and this isomorphism disappears. See Grossman and Hart (1976).) To see this, let S be the set of states of the world and let $\mathscr{S}$ be a σ-field of subsets of S representing possible events. Then the uncertain return of a firm in period 1 can be represented by a measurable function (random variable) g from S into R_+, where $g(s)$ is the number of units of output that the firm produces in state s. Let $A' = \{a \mid a \text{ is a measurable function from } S \text{ to } R_+ \text{ and } \sup_{s \in S} a(s) = 1\}$ be the set of all such functions suitably normalized. Then it is easy to see that A' is a metric space with metric $d(a, b) = \sup_{s \in S} |a(s) - b(s)|$. Unfortunately, if S is infinite, A' may not be compact. We will therefore assume that all the normalized random variables which it is feasible for firms to produce can be restricted to some compact subset A of A'.

As in the model of Section 3, A can be regarded as the commodity space. When a firm selects a production plan, it is essentially choosing a normalized random variable (i.e. a point in A), a scale at which to produce this random variable (i.e. $y_1 \in R_+$) and a level of input (i.e. $y_0 \in R_-$). As before, we can represent firms' technological possibilities by a correspondence $Y: F \times A \Rightarrow R_- \times R_+$.

Consumers' preferences can also be represented as in the model of Section 3. Let (x_0, x_1) be a consumption bundle for consumer i, where $x_0 \in R_+$ and x_1 is a finite, non-negative Borel measure on A. Given $s \in S$, let i_s be the function from A to R defined by $i_s(a) = a(s)$. Then the number of units of output consumed by i in state s is

$$\int_{a \in A} i_s(a) dx_1(a).$$

Thus, if consumer i has a von Neumann–Morgenstern utility function V^i whose arguments are consumption in periods 0 and 1, $U^i(x_0', x_1') \geqq U^i(x_0, x_1)$ if and only if

$$EV^i\left(x_0', \int_{a \in A} i_s(a) dx_1'(a)\right) \geqq EV^i\left(x_0, \int_{a \in A} i_s(a) dx_1(a)\right).$$

(E is the expectations operator.) It is easy to see that U^i is continuous with respect to the topology of weak convergence of probability measures as long as V^i is continuous.

The transformation from the stock market model to the differentiated commodities model is now complete once it is understood that the shareholders in firm f after the stock market has closed are simply the purchasers of the differentiated commodity produced by firm f (q^{if}/y_1^f in the definition of an exchange equilibrium in Section 3 represents the proportion of firm f's shares purchased by a type i consumer (note that we rule out short-sales)). The market value of firm f, i.e. the value of 100 per cent of its shares, is $p(a^f)y_1^f$ and $p(a^f)y_1^f + y_0^f$ is firm f's *net* market value. Thus net market value maximization in the stock market model corresponds to profit maximization in the differentiated commodities model.

Having demonstrated the equivalence between the stock market model and the differentiated commodities model, we may apply Theorem 1 to the stock market model. The theorem tells us that, if firms are small relative to the aggregate economy, then net market value maximizing behaviour by firms leads to outcomes which are approximately *constrained* Pareto optimal. Note the use of the word constrained here. It refers to the fact that we are comparing net market value maximizing allocations with other allocations which can be achieved through the stock market, not with those allocations which could be achieved through the opening up of Arrow–Debreu contingent commodity markets. There is, of course, no reason to expect convergence to Pareto optimality in the unconstrained sense as $r \to \infty$.

Let us return to the question of how firms raise finance.[20] So far we have assumed that the only assets available are firms' shares. Implicitly, therefore, we have assumed that firms raise the finance for investment by floating new equity. Suppose, however, that firms can also float (possibly risky) bonds, where a bond is a promise to pay one unit of output in each state in period 1.[21] Then, if firm f floats $b^f \geqq 0$ units of bonds, the firm's payment to shareholders in state s, period 1 is given by max $[y_1^f a^f(s) - b^f, 0]$, while its payment to bondholders is given by min $[y_1^f a^f(s), b^f]$. Note that we are allowing for the possibility that the firm goes bankrupt in some states of the world.

Obviously, in the language of the differentiated commodities model, the random variables which represent payments to shareholders and bondholders are two different commodities. Thus, by permitting bond finance, we are allowing the firm to produce two commodities instead of one. Applying Remark 7 of Section 5, we see that the production correspondence of the economy must now be written as $\tilde{Y}: F \times A \times A \dashrightarrow R_- \times R_+ \times R_+$, where $(y_0, y_1, y_2) \in \tilde{Y}(f, a_1, a_2) \Leftrightarrow$ there exists $a^* \in A$, $y_1^* \in R_+$ and $b^f \in R_+$ such that

(1) $(y_0, y_1^*) \in Y(f, a^*)$;

(2) $y_1 a_1(s) = $ max $[y_1^* a^*(s) - b^f, 0]$ for all $s \in S$;

(3) $y_2 a_2(s) = $ min $[y_1^* a^*(s), b^f]$ for all $s \in S$.

Here $Y(f, a)$ is the "basic" production set of firm f, representing its technological possibilities, and $\tilde{Y}(f, a_1, a_2)$ is the derived production set which takes into account the effect of financial decisions on the firm's output.

In view of Remark 7 of Section 5, we see that the extended version of Theorem 1 tells us that net market value maximization again leads in large economies to outcomes which are approximately constrained Pareto optimal (a firm's market value includes now the value of both its outstanding shares and bonds). Note that the definition of constrained Pareto optimality is now different because, as a result of the introduction of a new financial instrument, the feasible set in the economy $'E$ is larger for each r.

Thus, we see that the result that net market value maximization leads to approximately constrained Pareto optimal outcomes in large stock market economies generalizes to the case where firms can finance inputs by floating risky bonds as well as shares.[22]

Let us note finally that " large " stock market economies have also been studied by Jensen and Long (1972) and Merton and Subrahmanyam (1974). These authors obtain similar results to ours using the mean–variance framework. However, despite the similarity in conclusions, the approach adopted by Jensen and Long and Merton and Subrahmanyam is quite different from ours. Jensen and Long and Merton and Subrahmanyam make the economy large by increasing the number of consumers, but they do not increase the number of consumers. They assume that firms have zero set-up costs and face constant returns to scale. We have remarked in the introduction that, while increasing the number of firms does lead to competitive behaviour under these conditions, it does not as soon as we allow for set-up costs or any other type of increasing returns to scale. To deal with these more general cases, it is necessary to increase the number of consumers as well as the number of firms.

7. RELATIONSHIP TO THE LITERATURE ON MONOPOLISTIC COMPETITION

In this section we will attempt to relate our work to some of the other literature on monopolistic competition. We have already noted in the introduction that there have been previous attempts to analyse the properties of monopolistically competitive equilibria in large economies. The first of these appears in the paper by Gabszewicz and Vial (1972). Gabszewicz and Vial consider an economy with a finite number of (undifferentiated) goods, a finite number of consumers and a finite number of firms. Consumers behave as price-takers while firms maximize profits subject to correct conjectures about the demand curves facing them. The economy is made large by replicating both consumers and firms. Gabszewicz and Vial show that the monopolistically competitive equilibrium converges to a competitive equilibrium in the limit.

Our analysis is close in spirit to that of Gabszewicz and Vial. The main difference is that we have incorporated commodity differentiation into the model by permitting an infinite commodity space. Also, we have made the number of operating firms an endogenous variable of the model and we have allowed the supply side of the economy to become large in a more general way than by the replication of firms' technologies.

The convergence of monopolistically competitive outcomes to competitive outcomes as the size of the economy becomes infinite has also been established by Roberts and Postlewaite (1976) in a somewhat different context. Roberts and Postlewaite are concerned with the incentives that exist for economic agents to adopt non-price-taking behaviour in finite economies. They show that, under quite general conditions, these incentives become negligible as the size of the economy tends to infinity. However, Roberts and Postlewaite confine their attention to economies with homogeneous goods and they also ignore production.

A rather different approach to the study of monopoly power is to be found in the extensive literature on the relationship between the core and the set of competitive equilibria of an economy. It is argued that the famous equivalence theorems of Debreu and Scarf, Aumann, Hildenbrand and others (see Hildenbrand (1974)) provide a general demonstration of the fact that small agents possess no monopoly power in (non-atomic) infinite economies. From our point of view, the most relevant of these equivalence theorems is that of Mas-Colell (1975). Mas-Colell establishes the equivalence of the core and the set of competitive equilibria in an exchange economy with an infinite number of differentiated commodities and an infinite number of consumers. The consumption side of our model has been based closely on that of Mas-Colell's model. The main differences are that (i) Mas-Colell assumes that differentiated commodities are indivisible; (ii) Mas-Colell does not require any differentiability assumptions on utility functions; (iii) Mas-Colell allows there to be an infinite number of different types of consumers, although the preferences and endowments of these consumers are restricted to lie in a compact set.

In introducing his model, Mas-Colell (1975, p. 263) argues that " . . . it is a common contention of imperfect competition theory that in a large economy with a large number of mutually substitutive commodities and no ' big ' trader, every commodity will be substitutable in the market with infinite elasticity and a perfectly competitive outcome will prevail ". Our results are quite consistent with Mas-Colell's, but they do suggest that the crucial factor responsible for the realization of a perfectly competitive outcome is that all traders are small, not that there exists a large number of substitutable commodities.

An equivalence theorem has been established by Shitovitz (1974) under rather different assumptions from those of the above authors. Shitovitz shows that the core and the set of competitive equilibria are equal in an exchange economy where there are two or more " big " traders with the same tastes and endowments (but of possibly different sizes). In Shitovitz's model, substitutability of the goods supplied by the different " big " traders *is* the factor responsible for the realization of the competitive outcome. However, it is easy to check that the set of Cournot (or Nash-quantity) equilibria is not equal to the set of competitive equilibria in the Shitovitz model. In other words, " big " traders do not face flat demand curves and so, in the terms of this paper, they possess monopoly power. Thus there is no difficulty in reconciling Shitovtiz's result and our conclusion that demand curves are flat only when traders are small.

In addition to the literature on monopolistic competition in large economies, there is a growing literature on the properties of monopolistically competitive equilibria in " small " economies. Ever since the publication of Chamberlin's book, there has been a debate over whether monopolistic competition leads to too much product diversification. However, only recently has this question been examined in a rigorous manner (see, for example, Dixit–Stiglitz (1977), Spence (1976)). The main conclusion of this recent work is that in many cases a monopolistically competitive equilibrium will involve too few commodities being produced relative to the social optimum. Thus, there is no presumption that monopolistic competition leads to excessive diversity.

The work on the optimal amount of product differentiation has been concerned with economies of fixed size, i.e. economies like ^rE of Section 3 for fixed r. Our results say nothing about the relationship between the actual number of goods provided under monopolistic competition in such economies and the optimal number. What our results do indicate, however, is that the welfare loss due to the wrong number of goods being produced tends to zero in per-capita terms as r tends to infinity.

Finally, let us mention briefly the relationship between our model and the location models of Hotelling, Lösch and others. In the simplest location models, it is assumed that there is a population distributed uniformly along an infinite straight line. Shops selling a homogeneous product set up at points along the line, subject to the payment of a fixed cost. Each consumer visits that shop which charges the lowest price, where the price includes the cost of getting to and from the shop. Each shop sets price to maximize profits, taking as given the prices charged by other shops. It is shown that the density of shops under monopolistic competition will in general differ from the socially optimal density (see Stern (1972) for a formal analysis).

At first sight, the conclusions of the location model appear to contradict the results which we have established. For in the location model, each shop is of negligible size relative to the infinite population of consumers. According to our arguments, this should result in a perfectly elastic demand curve for shops' products and no divergence between the monopolistically competitive and socially optimal outcomes.

In fact, it is quite easy to reconcile our results with the results of the location model. For while it is true that each shop is negligible relative to the aggregate economy, each shop is not negligible relative to the market for its good. The consumers who actually purchase from a particular shop are contained in a finite interval of the infinite line and therefore form a finite, not an infinite, set. Thus it is hardly surprising that the shops retain some monopoly power.[23]

Another way of putting this is that, starting off with a finite line instead of an infinite line, one can think of making the location economy large by increasing the length of the line and adding new consumers at the extremities. These consumers are not of the same type as the previous consumers, however, since they are located in new positions. Thus the economy is being made large, but not by replication. Furthermore, representing consumers by their distance from the origin, we see that the set of consumers is not *compact*.

Of course, if we increased the *density* of consumers along the line, then we would essentially be replicating the economy. According to our results, the monopoly power of each shop ought to disappear under these conditions as the density tends to infinity. However, since the location model and the model of this paper are not exactly comparable, this question requires further investigation before any definite conclusions are reached.

8. CONCLUSIONS

The conclusions of this paper can be summarized as follows. If firms are " large " relative to the aggregate economy, they will possess monopoly power and a monopolistically competitive equilibrium will not be Pareto optimal. On the other hand, if firms are " small " relative to the aggregate economy, their monopoly power disappears and a monopolistically competitive equilibrium is Pareto optimal. In both cases, this is true whether firms are producing homogeneous or differentiated products.[24]

APPENDIX

Theorem 1. *Assume Assumption A. Let* $(((^r a^f, {}^r y^f)_{f \in F}, (^r x_0^i, {}^r q^i)_{i \in I}, {}^r p))$ *be a sequence of monopolistically competitive equilibria in the economies* ${}^r E, r = 1, 2, \ldots$ *For each monopolistically competitive equilibrium, let* ${}^r \alpha$ *be defined as above. Then, if the sequence* $((^r a^f, {}^r y^f)_{f \in F})$ *satisfies Assumption B*, $\lim_{r \to \infty} {}^r \alpha = 0$.

Before proving Theorem 1, we need to introduce the production side of the economy ${}^\infty E$. Consider the finite economy ${}^r E$ and let firms' production plans be $(^r a^f, {}^r y^f)_{f \in F}$. Then we may represent the supply side of the economy ${}^r E$ in per-capita terms by the variable ${}^r Y = ({}^r Y_0, {}^r Y_1)$ where ${}^r Y_0 = \sum_{f \in F} {}^r y_0^f / r$ and ${}^r Y_1$ is a measure defined by

$$^r Y_1 = \sum_{f \in F} ({}^r y_1^f / r) \mathscr{X}({}^r a^f).$$

Here ${}^r Y_0$ is the total amount of input used by firms and ${}^r Y_1(B)$ is the total supply of commodities lying in B, where both quantities are normalized by dividing by r. The variable ${}^r Y$ provides us with a macroscopic description of the supply side of the economy ${}^r E$, but it does not tell us which firms are producing which goods. Thus ${}^r Y$ provides us with less information than the array $(^r a^f, {}^r y^f)_{f \in F}$.[25]

Let ${}^r G = \{{}^r Y \mid {}^r Y_0 = \sum_{f \in F} {}^r y_0^f / r, \; {}^r Y_1 = \sum_{f \in F} ({}^r y_1^f / r) \mathscr{X}({}^r a^f)$ for some $(^r a^f, {}^r y^f)_{f \in F}$ satisfying (3.20) and (3.21)\} Then we define ${}^\infty G$, the set of feasible aggregate production plans for the economy ${}^\infty E$, as follows:

Definition. ${}^\infty G = \{Y \mid Y \text{ is a limit point of some sequence } ({}^r Y) \text{ of elements of } {}^r G\}$.

In the above definition, convergence of $'Y_0$ is defined with respect to the Euclidean topology and convergence of $'Y_1$ with respect to the topology of weak convergence.

In Section 4 we defined an exchange equilibrium for the economy $^\infty E$, taking firms' production plans as given. We now define a competitive equilibrium for $^\infty E$ under the assumption that firms maximize profits *in the aggregate*, taking prices to be fixed.

Definition. A competitive equilibrium in $^\infty E$ relative to the " artificial " endowments $(\bar{x}^i)_{i \in I}$ is an array $((x^i)_{i \in I}, Y, p)$ satisfying

$$Y \in {}^\infty G. \qquad\qquad \text{...(A.1)}$$

$$p: A \to R_+^* \text{ is a continuous function, taking finite values on supp } Y_1. \qquad \text{...(A.2)}$$

$$x^i \in R_+ \times M \text{ for all } i \in I. \qquad\qquad \text{...(A.3)}$$

For all $i \in I$, x^i is a solution of: max $U^i(x)$ subject to

$$x_0 + \int_A p(a)dx_1(a) \leq \bar{x}_0^i + \int_A p(a)d\bar{x}_1^i(a). \qquad \text{...(A.4)}$$

$$\int_A p(a)dY_1(a) + Y_0 \geq \int_A p(a)d\tilde{Y}_1(a) + \tilde{Y}_0 \text{ for all } \tilde{Y} \in {}^\infty G. \qquad \text{...(A.5)}$$

$$\sum_{i \in I} x_0^i = Y_0 + \sum_{i \in I} w^i = \sum_{i \in I} \bar{x}_0^i. \qquad \text{...(A.6)}$$

$$\sum_{i \in I} x_1^i = Y_1 = \sum_{i \in I} \bar{x}_1^i. \qquad \text{...(A.7)}$$

In (A4) and (A5),

$$\int_A p(a)d\mu(a)$$

is defined to be $+\infty$ if $\mu(\{a \in A \mid p(a) = \infty\}) > 0$, and to be

$$\int_S p(a)d\mu(a)$$

otherwise, where $S = \{a \in A \mid p(a) \text{ is finite}\}$. As a result of (A2) and (A7), both

$$\int_A p(a)dY_1(a) \quad \text{and} \quad \int_A p(a)dx_1^i(a)$$

are finite, and so the inequalities in (A4) and (A5) are meaningful.

The last two equalities in (A6) and (A7) simply say that the artificial endowments $\bar{x}^i$ are consistent with the endowments w^i and the production plans Y.

Proof of Theorem 1.[26] Suppose the theorem is false. Then, choosing subsequences if necessary, we can find a sequence of monopolistically competitive equilibria

$$(((^ra^f, {}^ry^f)_{f \in F}, (^rx_0^i, {}^rq^i), {}^rp))$$

such that $\lim_{r \to \infty} {}^r\alpha > 0$. Let the production side of the monopolistically competitive equilibrium in $'E$ be represented in macroscopic terms by $'Y \in 'G$.

Lemma 1. *The sequence* $('Y_0, 'Y_1(A))$ *is bounded.*

Proof. The boundedness of $'Y_0$ follows from (3.19), while the boundedness of $'Y_1(A)$ follows from Assumption A and (3.12).

By Lemma 1, we can assume without loss of generality that $'Y \to Y$ (see Parthasarathy (1967, Theorem 6.4, p. 45)). Clearly $Y \in {}^\infty G$. The sequence of " artificial " endowments $(^r\bar{x}^i) = ((w^i + \sum_f (\bar{\theta}^{if}/r)^r y_0^f, \sum_f (\bar{\theta}^{if}/r)^r y_1^f \mathcal{X}(^ra^f)))$ is also bounded and so we may assume that it converges to $\bar{x}^i$ for each i. Similarly the sequence of consumption plans $(({}^r x_0^i, \sum_f {}^r q^{if} \mathcal{X}({}^r a^f)))$ is bounded and we may assume that it converges to x^i for each i. Taking limits in (3.18) and (3.19), we get (A6) and (A7). Clearly, by (3.5), (3.24) and the fact that $w^i \in R_{++}$, $x_0^i > 0$.

Given $a \in A$, define

$$p(a) = \max_{i \in I} \left(\frac{\partial U^{i+}(x^i)}{\partial \mathcal{X}(a)} \middle/ \frac{\partial U^i(x^i)}{\partial x_0} \right). \qquad \qquad ...(A.8)$$

We will prove that $((x^i)_{i \in I}, Y, p)$ is a competitive equilibrium in $^\infty E$ relative to the artificial endowments $(\bar{x}^i)_{i \in I}$.

Step 1: *To show that* x^i *satisfies* (A4) *for all* i

Consider the monopolistically competitive equilibrium $(({}^r a^f, {}^r y^f), ({}^r x_0^i, {}^r q^i), {}^r p)$ in $^r E$. From the first order conditions for utility maximization, we know that, if commodity a is produced,

$${}^r p(a) \geq \frac{\partial U^{i+}({}^r x^i)}{\partial \mathcal{X}(a)} \middle/ \frac{\partial U^i({}^r x^i)}{\partial x_0} \qquad \qquad ...(A.9)$$

for each i with equality if type i consumers consume a in positive amounts. Hence

$${}^r p(a) = \max_{i \in I} \left[\frac{\partial U^{i+}({}^r x^i)}{\partial \mathcal{X}(a)} \middle/ \frac{\partial U^i({}^r x^i)}{\partial x_0} \right]. \qquad \qquad ...(A.10)$$

We use (A10) to redefine ${}^r p(a)$ for all $a \in A$.

Lemma 2. $p(a)$ *is finite if* $a \in$ supp Y_1.

Proof. If $a \in$ supp Y_1, then $a \in$ supp x_1^i for some i by (A7). Hence type i consumers must, in the monopolistically competitive equilibrium in $^r E$, purchase commodities in A which are close to a. From the first order conditions, we therefore have

$${}^r p(\tilde{a}) = \frac{\partial U^{i+}({}^r x^i)}{\partial \mathcal{X}(\tilde{a})} \middle/ \frac{\partial U^i({}^r x^i)}{\partial x_0} = \max_{j \in I} \left[\frac{\partial U^{j+}({}^r x^j)}{\partial \mathcal{X}(\tilde{a})} \middle/ \frac{\partial U^j({}^r x^j)}{\partial x_0} \right],$$

where $\tilde{a}$ is close to a. Taking limits as $r \to \infty$ and letting $\tilde{a}$ converge to a, we get, by (3.10),

$$p(a) = \max_{j \in I} \left[\frac{\partial U^{j+}(x^j)}{\partial \mathcal{X}(a)} \middle/ \frac{\partial U^j(x^j)}{\partial x_0} \right] = \frac{\partial U^{i+}(x^i)}{\partial \mathcal{X}(a)} \middle/ \frac{\partial U^i(x^i)}{\partial x_0}.$$

The result now follows from (3.9).
Let C^* be any compact set on which $p(a)$ is finite. Then,

Lemma 3. ${}^r p(a)$ *converges to* $p(a)$ *uniformly on* C^* *as* $r \to \infty$.

Proof. Suppose not. Then, by choosing subsequences, we can find $\varepsilon > 0$ and a sequence $({}^r a)$ of points in C^* such that $|{}^r p({}^r a) - p({}^r a)| \geq \varepsilon$ for all $r = 1, 2, ...$ Therefore, from (A10) we obtain

$$\left| \max_{i \in I} \left[\frac{\partial U^{i+}({}^r x^i)}{\partial \mathcal{X}({}^r a)} \middle/ \frac{\partial U^i({}^r x^i)}{\partial x_0} \right] - \max_{i \in I} \left[\frac{\partial U^{i+}(x^i)}{\partial \mathcal{X}({}^r a)} \middle/ \frac{\partial U^i(x^i)}{\partial x_0} \right] \right| \geq \varepsilon \qquad ...(A.11)$$

for all r. Since C^* is compact, we may assume that ${}^r a \to a \in C^*$. But taking limits in (A11) and using (3.10) and the fact that ${}^r x^i \to x^i$, we get $0 \geq \varepsilon$, which is a contradiction. This proves Lemma 3.

Corollary 4. *There exists* $\varepsilon > 0$ *such that* $p(a)$ *and* ${}^r p(a)$ *take finite values on the set* $C = \{a \in A \mid d(a, a') \leq \varepsilon$ *for some* $a' \in$ supp $Y_1\}$ *for all* $r \geq$ *some* r^*.

Proof. If not, we can find a sequence $({}^r a)$ converging to $a \in$ supp Y_1 such that either $p({}^r a)$ or ${}^r p({}^r a) = \infty$ for all r. But this contradicts (3.10) and Lemma 3 since, by Lemma 2, $p(a)$ is finite.

We now establish that

$$x_0^i + \int_A p(a)dx_1^i(a) \leq \bar{x}_0^i + \int_A p(a)d\bar{x}_1^i(a) \qquad \text{...(A.12)}$$

for all i. Suppose not. Then from the market clearing conditions (A6), (A7), it follows that (A12) must hold with *strict inequality* for some consumer i. Hence for this consumer we can find a bundle $\tilde{x}^i$ satisfying

$$\tilde{x}_0^i + \int_A p(a)d\tilde{x}_1^i(a) < \bar{x}_0^i + \int_A p(a)d\bar{x}_1^i(a) \qquad \text{...(A.13)}$$

and $U^i(\tilde{x}^i) > U^i(x^i)$. Moreover, using the fact that the set of measures with finite supports is dense (Parthasarathy (1967, p. 44)), we can choose $\tilde{x}^i$ so that supp $\tilde{x}_1^i$ is finite.

Since $U^i(\tilde{x}^i) > U^i(x^i)$, it follows from (3.1) that $U^i(\tilde{x}^i) > U^{i(r}x^i)$ for large r. Hence, since $^rx^i$ is chosen rather than $\tilde{x}^i$ in the monopolistically competitive equilibrium of ^rE, we may conclude that $\tilde{x}^i$ must violate i's budget constraint in ^rE, i.e.

$$\tilde{x}_0^i + \int_A {}^rp(a)d\tilde{x}_1^i(a) > {}^r\bar{x}_0^i + \int_A {}^rp(a)d^r\bar{x}_1^i(a). \qquad \text{...(A.14)}$$

Now since $^rp(a) \to p(a)$ and $\tilde{x}_1^i$ has finite support it follows that

$$\lim_{r\to\infty} \int_A {}^rp(a)d\tilde{x}_1^i(a) = \int_A p(a)d\tilde{x}_1^i(a). \qquad \text{...(A.15)}$$

Also, by Lemma 2, $p(a)$ is finite on supp $\bar{x}_1^i$ and so, applying Corollary 4, we see that we can find $\varepsilon > 0$ such that $^rp(a)$ is finite on $B = \{a \in A \mid d(a, a') \leq \varepsilon \text{ for some } a' \in \text{supp } \bar{x}_1^i\}$ for large r. Hence, by Parthasarathy (1967, Theorem 6.1, p. 40) and Lemma 3,

$$\liminf_{r\to\infty} \int_A {}^rp(a)d^r\bar{x}_1^i(a) \geq \lim_{r\to\infty} \int_B {}^rp(a)d^r\bar{x}_1^i(a)$$

$$= \int_B p(a)d\bar{x}_1^i(a)$$

$$= \int_A p(a)d\bar{x}_1^i(a) \qquad \text{...(A.16)}$$

since supp $\bar{x}_1^i \subset B$.

Combining (A14)–(A16), we obtain

$$\tilde{x}_0^i + \int_A p(a)d\tilde{x}_1^i(a) \geq \bar{x}_0^i + \int_A p(a)d\bar{x}_1^i(a),$$

which contradicts (A13).

This establishes that (A12) holds with equality for all i. The same argument shows that there does not exist $\tilde{x}^i$ such that $U^i(\tilde{x}^i) > U^i(x^i)$ and

$$\tilde{x}_0^i + \int_A p(a)d\tilde{x}_1^i \leq \bar{x}_0^i + \int_A p(a)d\bar{x}_1^i(a).$$

This completes Step 1.

Step 2: *To establish that Y satisfies (A5) with respect to the prices p*

For each $f \in F$, let $^r\pi^f = {}^rp(^ra^f)^ry_1^f + {}^ry_0^f$ be firm f's profits in the monopolistically competitive equilibrium of ^rE. Also let $\hat{\pi}^f = \sup\{(p(a)y_1 + y_0) \mid y \in Y(f, a)\}$ be firm f's maximum profits *if it could act as a price-taker with respect to the limit prices p(a)*, where the supremum is taken over a and y.

Lemma 5. (1) *Given $\eta>0$ and $h>0$, there exists r^* such that $\hat{\pi}^f <{}^r\pi^f +\eta$ for all $r \geq r^*$ and for all f with $\hat{\pi}^f <h$.*

(2) *Given $h>0$, there exists r^* such that ${}^r\pi^f >(h/2)$ for all $r \geq r^*$ and for all f with $\hat{\pi}^f >h$.*

Proof. Suppose (1) does not hold. Then we can find a sequence (f_r) such that $\hat{\pi}^{f_r} -{}^r\pi^{f_r} \to k>0$ as $r\to\infty$ and $\hat{\pi}^{f_r} <h$. Therefore, for sufficiently large r,

$$p({}^ra)^ry_1 +{}^ry_0 -({}^rp({}^ra^{f_r})^ry_1^{f_r} +{}^ry_0^{f_r})>k/2 \qquad \text{...(A.17)}$$

for some ${}^ry \in Y(f_r, {}^ra)$. Since A is compact we may assume that ${}^ra\to a$ and ${}^ra^{f_r}\to a'$. By Assumption A, we may also assume that ${}^ry\to y$, ${}^ry^{f_r}\to y'$.

Consider now the consequences of firm f_r choosing the production plan $({}^ra, {}^ry)$ instead of $({}^ra^{f_r}, {}^ry^{f_r})$ in the economy ${}^rE$. It is clear from Assumption A that the limiting " artificial " endowments $\bar{x}^i = \lim_{r\to\infty} {}^r\bar{x}^i$ will not be affected by the change in firm f_r's production plan. Hence, Assumption B tells us that, for sufficiently large r, there exists a new exchange equilibrium in ${}^\infty E$, and hence in ${}^rE$, such that the new equilibrium consumption allocation $({}^r\tilde{x}^i)$ converges to (x^i) as $r\to\infty$. Denote the new exchange prices, defined as in (A10), by ${}^r\tilde{p}$. Clearly, by (3.10), $\lim_{r\to\infty} {}^r\tilde{p}(a) = p(a)$ for all a.

Now since firm f_r does not in fact choose the plan $({}^ra, {}^ry)$ we know that

$${}^r\tilde{p}({}^ra)^ry_1 +{}^ry_0 \leq {}^rp({}^ra^{f_r})^ry_1^{f_r} +{}^ry_0^{f_r}. \qquad \text{...(A.18)}$$

Also (3.13) and the facts that $\hat{\pi}^{f_r}<h$, ${}^ra\to a$, ${}^ra^{f_r}\to a'$ imply that $p(a)$ and $p(a')$ are finite. Taking limits in (A18), we get

$$p(a)y_1 + y_0 \leq p(a')y_1' + y_0'. \qquad \text{...(A.19)}$$

But, taking limits in (A17), we get

$$(p(a)y_1 + y_0)-(p(a')y_1' + y_0') \geq k/2, \qquad \text{...(A.20)}$$

which contradicts (A.19).

This proves Lemma 5(1). Part (2) is proved similarly.

Corollary 6. *For each $h>0$, the number of firms f in F satisfying $\hat{\pi}^f >h$ is finite.*

Proof. If not, Lemma 5(2) implies that ${}^r\pi^f >(h/2)>0$ for infinitely many firms when r is large. But this is impossible since, by feasibility, only a finite number of firms can be operating in the equilibrium of the economy ${}^rE$.

We show that Lemma 5 and Corollary 6 imply that Y satisfies (A5) with respect to the prices p. Suppose that there exists $\tilde{Y} \in {}^\infty G$ such that

$$\int_A p(a)d\tilde{Y}_1(a)+ \tilde{Y}_0 > \int_A p(a)dY_1(a)+ Y_0. \qquad \text{...(A.21)}$$

Let $({}^r\tilde{Y})$ be a sequence of points of ${}^rG$ converging to $\tilde{Y}$. Applying Lemma 5(1) with h set equal to 1, we obtain

$$p({}^r\tilde{a}^f)^r\tilde{y}_1^f +{}^r\tilde{y}_0^f \leq \hat{\pi}^f <{}^rp({}^ra^f)^ry_1^f +{}^ry_0^f +\eta \qquad \text{...(A.22)}$$

for large r and all f with $\hat{\pi}^f <1$, where η is some positive number and $({}^r\tilde{a}^f, {}^r\tilde{y}^f)$ are the individual production plans corresponding to ${}^r\tilde{Y}$.

Summing (A22) over firms with $\hat{\pi}^f <1$ and dividing by r, we get

$$\int_A p(a)d^r\tilde{Y}_1'(a)+{}^r\tilde{Y}_0' < \int_A {}^rp(a)d^rY_1'(a)+{}^rY_0' +\eta^rN/r, \qquad \text{...(A.23)}$$

where ${}^r\tilde{Y}'$ (resp. ${}^rY'$) differs from ${}^r\tilde{Y}$ (resp. ${}^rY$) in that firms f with $\hat{\pi}^f \geq 1$ have been left out when computing the aggregate production plan, and where ${}^rN$ is the number of firms such that $\hat{\pi}^f <1$ and ${}^r\tilde{y}_1^f>0$. (Note that if ${}^r\tilde{y}_1^f = 0$, (A.22) can be replaced by $p({}^r\tilde{a}^f)^r\tilde{y}_1^f +{}^r\tilde{y}_0^f \leq {}^rp({}^ra^f)^ry_1^f +{}^ry_0^f$.)

Now, by Corollary 6, the number of firms satisfying $\hat{\pi}^f \geq 1$ is finite. Therefore, by Assumption A, ignoring these firms cannot affect the limiting aggregate production plan, i.e. $^r\tilde{Y}' \to \tilde{Y}$, $^rY' \to Y$. Consider the left-hand side of (A.23). We have

$$\int_A p(a)d^r\tilde{Y}'_1(a) = \int_S p(a)d^r\tilde{Y}'_1(a) + \int_{A\backslash S} p(a)d^r\tilde{Y}'_1(a), \qquad \text{...(A.24)}$$

where $S = \{a \in A \mid p(a) \text{ is finite}\}$. Now let $h(a)$ be any bounded measurable function satisfying $h(a) \leq p(a)$ on S. Since S is open and $^r\tilde{Y}'_1 \to \tilde{Y}_1$, we may apply the argument of Parthasarathy (1967, Theorem 6.8, p. 51) and the Bounded Convergence Theorem (Royden (1968, p. 81)) to show that

$$\lim_{r\to\infty} \int_S h(a)d^r\tilde{Y}'_1(a) = \int_S h(a)d\tilde{Y}_1(a). \qquad \text{...(A.25)}$$

Hence for each bounded measurable $h \leq p$, we have

$$\lim \inf_{r\to\infty} \int_S p(a)d^r\tilde{Y}'_1(a) \geq \lim_{r\to\infty} \int_S h(a)d^r\tilde{Y}'_1(a)$$

$$= \int_S h(a)d\tilde{Y}_1(a). \qquad \text{...(A.26)}$$

But

$$\int_S p = \sup_{h \leq p} \int_S h$$

(see Royden (1968, p. 81)), and so (A.26) implies that

$$\lim \inf_{r\to\infty} \int_S p(a)d^r\tilde{Y}'_1(a) \geq \int_S p(a)d\tilde{Y}_1(a). \qquad \text{...(A.27)}$$

Since the second term on the right-hand side of (A.24) is non-negative, it follows that

$$\lim \inf_{r\to\infty} \int_A p(a)d^r\tilde{Y}'_1(a) \geq \int_S p(a)d\tilde{Y}_1(a). \qquad \text{...(A.28)}$$

Finally, since the left-hand side of (A.28) must be infinite if $\tilde{Y}_1(A\backslash S) > 0$, we obtain

$$\lim \inf_{r\to\infty} \int_A p(a)d^r\tilde{Y}'_1(a) \geq \int_A p(a)d\tilde{Y}_1(a). \qquad \text{...(A.29)}$$

Consider now the right-hand side of (A.23). We have

$$\int_A {}^rp(a)d^rY'_1(a) = \int_C {}^rp(a)d^rY'_1(a) + \int_{A\backslash C} {}^rp(a)d^rY'_1(a), \qquad \text{...(A.30)}$$

where $C = \{a \in A \mid d(a, a') \leq \varepsilon \text{ for some } a' \in \text{supp } Y_1\}$ and ε is chosen as in Corollary 4. Clearly $\lim_{r\to\infty} {}^rY'_1(A\backslash C) = Y_1(A\backslash C) = 0$. Hence, by (A.7),

$$\lim_{r\to\infty} {}^rx^i_1(A\backslash C) = x^i_1(A\backslash C) = 0$$

for all i. In other words a type i consumer's consumption of commodities in $A\backslash C$ tends to zero. But, by (3.1), (3.2) and utility maximization, this means that a type i consumer's expenditure on commodities in $A\backslash C$ also tends to zero (otherwise a type i consumer could do better when r is large by setting $^rx^i_1(A\backslash C) = 0$). In other words,

$$\lim_{r\to\infty} \int_{A\backslash C} {}^rp(a)d^rx^i_1(a) = 0,$$

and so,

$$\lim_{r\to\infty} \int_{A\setminus C} {}^r p(a)d^r Y_1'(a) \leqq \lim_{r\to\infty} \int_{A\setminus C} {}^r p(a)d^r Y_1(a)$$

$$= \lim_{r\to\infty} \sum_{i\in I} \int_{A\setminus C} {}^r p(a)d^r x_1^i(a) \qquad \ldots(\text{A.31})$$

$$= 0.$$

Hence, by (A.30),

$$\lim_{r\to\infty} \int_A {}^r p(a)d^r Y_1'(a) = \lim_{r\to\infty} \int_C {}^r p(a)d^r Y_1'(a)$$

$$= \int_C p(a)dY_1(a) = \int_A p(a)dY_1(a) \qquad \ldots(\text{A.32})$$

by Lemma 3 and Corollary 4.

Finally, from (3.12) we know that

$${}^r\tilde{Y}_0 \leqq ({}^rN/r)\bar{y}_0. \qquad \ldots(\text{A.33})$$

Hence, since ${}^r\tilde{Y}_0 \to Y_0$, the sequence $({}^rN/r)$ is bounded. Therefore, choosing η small enough in (A.23), letting $r\to\infty$, and using (A.29) and (A.32), we find that (A.21) is contradicted.

This completes Step 2.

Step 3: To show that $\lim_{r\to\infty} {}^r\alpha > 0$ *yields a contradiction*

If $\lim_{r\to\infty} {}^r\alpha > 0$, then it is easy to see that there must exist $((\tilde{x}^i)_{i\in I}, \tilde{Y})$ satisfying (A.1), (A.6), (A.7) and $U^i(\tilde{x}^i) \geqq U^i(x^i)$ for all i, $U^1(\tilde{x}^1) > U^1(x^1)$. However, the usual argument showing that a competitive equilibrium is Pareto optimal demonstrates that this contradicts the fact that $((x^i), Y, p)$ is a competitive equilibrium in ${}^\infty E$.

We have now established a contradiction and thus proved Theorem 1. ‖

Proof of Proposition 2 in Remark 1 of Section 5

Suppose the proposition is false. Then it is straightforward to show that $\hat{\pi}^f > 0$ for some $f \in F$ (see, for example, the proof of Lemma 5). By Assumption C, this implies that $\hat{\pi}^f > h > 0$ for infinitely many f and some h, which contradicts Corollary 6. ‖

Finally, we prove that ${}^\infty G$ is convex (see Section 5, Remark 3).

Proof that ${}^\infty G$ *is convex under Assumption A*[27]

Suppose $Y, \tilde{Y} \in {}^\infty G$. We show that $\lambda Y + (1-\lambda)\tilde{Y} \in {}^\infty G$ if $0 \leqq \lambda \leqq 1$. Choosing subsequences if necessary, we can find $({}^rY)$, $({}^r\tilde{Y})$ such that ${}^rY \to Y$, ${}^r\tilde{Y} \to \tilde{Y}$ and ${}^rY$, ${}^r\tilde{Y} \in {}^rG$ for all r. Let $({}^ra^f, {}^ry^f)$, $({}^r\tilde{a}^f, {}^r\tilde{y}^f)$ be production plans corresponding to the macroscopic descriptions ${}^rY$, ${}^r\tilde{Y}$ respectively, and let ${}^rF = \{f \in F \mid \text{either } {}^ry_0^f > 0 \text{ or } {}^r\tilde{y}_0^f > 0\}$ be the set of firms which set up under either ${}^rY$ or ${}^r\tilde{Y}$.

Since A is a compact metric space, we can, for each integer n, write $A = \bigcup_{j=1}^{K_n} B_{n_j}$, $B_{n_j} \cap B_{n_k} = \varnothing$ if $j \neq k$, where K_n is finite, each B_{n_j} is a Borel set and the diameter of $B_{n_j} \leqq 1/n$ for all j. Let $a_{n_j} \in B_{n_j}$. Given a measure μ on A, we will define μ' to be the measure with masses $\mu(B_{n_j})$ at the points a_{n_j} respectively.

Consider the production plan $({}^ra^f, {}^ry^f)$ of firm f. An alternative way of representing this plan is by the pair $({}^ry_0^f, {}^ry_1^f \mathscr{X}({}^ra^f)) \in R_- \times M$, indicating that the firm uses ${}^ry_0^f$ units of input to produce the output measure ${}^ry_1^f \mathscr{X}({}^ra^f)$. Let ${}^rS^f$ be the set containing the two points $({}^ry_0^f, {}^ry_1^f \mathscr{X}({}^ra^f))$, $({}^r\tilde{y}_0^f, {}^r\tilde{y}_1^f \mathscr{X}({}^r\tilde{a}^f))$, and let ${}^rS'^f$ be the set containing the two points

$(^ry_0^f, {}^ry_1^f \mathcal{X}'(^ra^f))$, $(^r\tilde{y}_0^f, {}^r\tilde{y}_1^f \mathcal{X}'(^r\tilde{a}^f))$ where the measure $\mathcal{X}'(^ra^f)$ is obtained from $\mathcal{X}(^ra^f)$ in the manner described in the paragraph above. Then, from the definition of ^rY, $^r\tilde{Y}$,

$$r^rY', r^r\tilde{Y}' \in \sum_{f \, e^rF} {}^rS'^f,$$

where $^rY' = (^rY_0, {}^rY_1')$, $^r\tilde{Y}' = (^r\tilde{Y}_0, {}^r\tilde{Y}_1')$.

Since, for each μ, the measure μ' is defined by the K_n values $\mu(B_{n1}), \ldots, \mu(B_{nK_n})$, we may regard μ as a point in K_n-dimensional Euclidean space. In this way, $^rY' = (^rY_0, {}^rY_1')$ can be regarded as a point in (K_n+1)-dimensional Euclidean space. Hence, for fixed r, we may apply the Shapley–Folkman theorem (see Arrow and Hahn (1971, p. 396)) to the family of sets $^rS'^f$, $f \in {}^rF$. This theorem tells us that, given $0 \leq \lambda \leq 1$, there exists $\tilde{Z} \in \sum_{f \, e^rF} {}^rS'^f$ such that

$$\| \tilde{Z} - \lambda r^r Y' - (1-\lambda) r^r \tilde{Y}' \| \leq b\sqrt{(K_n+1)}, \qquad \ldots(A.34)$$

where $\| \ \ \|$ is the Euclidean norm and b is defined in Assumption A in Section 3.

Let $\tilde{Z} = \sum_{f \, e^rF} {}^r\alpha'^f$ where $^r\alpha'^f \in {}^rS'^f$. Define $Z = \sum_{f \, e^rF} {}^r\alpha^f$. Then (A.34) implies that $Z' \in \sum_{f \, e^rF} {}^rS^f$ satisfies

$$\| Z' - \lambda r^r Y' - (1-\lambda) r^r \tilde{Y}' \| \leq b\sqrt{(K_n+1)}. \qquad \ldots(A.35)$$

Define $z = Z/r$. Then $z \in {}^rG$ and, by (A.35),

$$\| z' - \lambda^r Y' - (1-\lambda)^r \tilde{Y}' \| \leq b\sqrt{(K_n+1)}/r. \qquad \ldots(A.36)$$

For each $x \in R^{K_n+1}$, let $| x | = \sum_i | x_i |$. Then, using the fact that $| x | \leq \sqrt{(K_n+1)} \| x \|$, we see that (A.36) implies that

$$| z' - \lambda^r Y' - (1-\lambda)^r \tilde{Y}' | \leq b(K_n+1)/r. \qquad \ldots(A.37)$$

We have shown that, for each n and r, there exists $z \in {}^rG$ satisfying (A.37). To make it clear that z will in general depend on n and r, we write z as $z(n, r)$. We now set $r = \max((K_n+1)^2, n)$ for each n, and let $n \to \infty$. By Parthasarathy (1967, Theorem 6.4, p. 64), we may assume without loss of generality that $z(n, r) \to$ some $\hat{z}$, where we return now to thinking of $z(n, r)$ as an element of $R_- \times M$ and convergence of $z_1(n, r)$ is defined with respect to the weak convergence topology. Clearly $\hat{z} \in {}^\infty G$. Also it is easy to see that $\lim_{n \to \infty} z'(n, r) = \hat{z}$, $\lim_{n \to \infty} {}^rY' = Y$, $\lim_{n \to \infty} {}^r\tilde{Y}' = \tilde{Y}$ (see, for example, the proof of Parthasarathy (1967, Theorem 6.3, p. 45)).

Let f be any continuous function from $A \to R$. Then

$$\left| \int_A fd\hat{z} - \int_A fd(\lambda Y + (1-\lambda)\tilde{Y}) \right| = \lim_{n \to \infty} \left| \int_A fdz'(n, r) - \int_A fd(\lambda^r Y' + (1-\lambda)^r \tilde{Y}') \right|$$

$$\leq \lim_{n \to \infty} | \sum_{j=1}^{K_n} f(a_{nj})(z(n, r)(B_{nj})$$

$$- (\lambda^r Y + (1-\lambda)^r \tilde{Y})(B_{nj})) |$$

$$\leq \lim_{n \to \infty} \max_{a \in A} | f(a) | \ \ | z'(n, r) - \lambda^r Y' - (1-\lambda)^r \tilde{Y}' |$$

$$\leq \lim_{n \to \infty} \max_{a \in A} | f(a) | \ b(K_n+1)/r \qquad \ldots(A.38)$$

by (A.37). But since $r = \max((K_n+1)^2, n)$, the right-hand side of (A.38) $\to 0$ as $n \to \infty$. Therefore

$$\int_A fd\hat{z} = \int_A fd(\lambda Y + (1-\lambda)\tilde{Y}) \qquad \ldots(A.39)$$

for all continuous functions f and so, by Parthasarathy (1967, Theorem 6.1, p. 40), $\hat{z} = \lambda Y + (1-\lambda)\tilde{Y}$. Since $\hat{z} \in {}^\infty G$, it follows that $\lambda Y + (1-\lambda)\tilde{Y} \in {}^\infty G$. $\|$

First version received February 1977; *final version accepted December* 1977 *(Eds.)*.

Part of this work was done while the author was at the Institute for Mathematical Studies in the Social Sciences, Stanford University, July–August 1976. Support from NSF grants SOC73-05510-A02 and SOC76-18771 is gratefully acknowledged.

I am greatly indebted to Andreu Mas-Colell, William Novshek, Joseph Ostroy and Hugo Sonnenschein for very helpful comments. All errors are my own, however.

NOTES

1. It should be noted that Kaldor was well aware of this fact (see Kaldor (1935)).

2. See Ruffin (1971).

3. It should be noted that we are implicitly adopting the Cournot assumption that each firm takes the *quantity* decisions of other firms as given. If, on the other hand, we adopt the Bertrand assumption that *price* decisions of other firms are taken as given, then in the homogeneous case the only possible equilibrium is the perfectly competitive solution. We reject the Bertrand approach because it has the implausible implication that perfect competition is established even under duopoly.

4. In fact, in a complete model of the economy, the number of operating firms is an endogenous variable not an exogenous one. Thus any *assumption* about the number of operating firms should be treated with some suspicion.

5. The above argument relies on the assumption that the firm's output is divisible, so that it can be divided equally among consumers. A similar argument applies in the indivisible case, however. Under these conditions, the firm will generally have to lower its price in order to induce any one consumer to consume an extra unit of output; but at this lower price the firm will then be able to sell as many additional units of output as there are (identical) consumers.

6. This statement must be qualified somewhat if consumers' marginal rates of substitution are discontinuous or infinite when consumption of certain goods is zero. See Section 2.

7. Our conclusion can be regarded as general support for the Kaldor–Robinson–Samuelson position. The difference is that whereas Kaldor, Robinson and Samuelson emphasized the absolute smallness of firms, we emphasize smallness relative to the economy.

8. The analysis generalizes easily to the case where there are several homogeneous goods.

9. We have not attempted to generalize the model to the case where there are infinitely many consumers whose preferences and endowments lie in a compact set in the space of consumers' characteristics (see Hildenbrand (1974)). However, we suspect that such a generalization is possible.

10. R^n denotes n-dimensional Euclidean space. R_+^n denotes the non-negative orthant of R^n and R_{++}^n the interior of R_+^n. R_-^n denotes the non-positive orthant of R^n. If $x \in R_+^n$, we write $x \geqq 0$.

11. We use $x_1' \geqq x_1$ to mean $x_1'(B) \geqq x_1(B)$ for all Borel subsets B of A.

12. Addition of measures and multiplication of measures by scalars are defined in the usual way.

13. supp x_1 is the support of the measure x_1, i.e. the smallest closed set B satisfying $x_1(B) = x_1(A)$. It is easy to see that if $a \in$ supp x_1, then $x_1(N) > 0$ for every neighbourhood N of a. See Parthasarathy (1967).

14. Note that (3.10) rules out utility functions which are of the C.E.S. type when expressed in terms of Lancastrian characteristics. Suppose, for example, that there are C characteristics and that $U^i = \sum_{k=1}^{C} y_k^{\frac{1}{2}}$. Let a be a commodity which contains a zero amount of characteristic 1. Then, if the bundle x also contains no characteristic 1, $\partial U^{i+}(x)/\partial \mathscr{X}(\bar{a})$ is discontinuous in $\bar{a}$ at $\bar{a} = a$.

15. For the case where $\partial U^{i+}(x)/\partial \mathscr{X}(a)$ is finite for all x, a, i, it is not difficult to show that Assumption A can be replaced by the assumption that firms have U-shaped average cost curves with eventually infinite slope.

16. When there is no ambiguity, we will use I to denote the set of consumers as well as the number of consumers.

17. We disregard the fact that profit maximization may not be in the interests of firms' shareholders. See, for example, Gabszewicz and Vial (1972) and Drèze (1974).

18. We are thus ignoring the problems raised in Hahn (1977).

19. Dixit and Stiglitz (1977), in their study of monopolistic competition, use the commodity space $A = \{1, 2, 3, \dots,\}$ which, under the usual topology, is not compact. From their point of view, this non-compactness is unimportant since they are concerned with economies of fixed size and do not consider asymptotic results. However, the non-compactness of A does explain why in some of Dixit's and Stiglitz's examples own elasticities of demand for goods remain finite as the size of the economy tends to infinity.

20. I am grateful to Douglas Gale for useful discussions on this question.

21. The argument generalizes to the case where firms can raise finance by issuing other financial instruments, such as preferred shares, warrants, etc.

22. It should be noted that, because of the possibility of bankruptcy, the Modigliani–Miller theorem does not hold in this model when $r \to \infty$. Consider a firm which initially chooses the plan

$$(y_0, y_1, y_2) \in \bar{Y}(f, a_1, a_2).$$

Its market value in the limit economy $^{\infty}E$ will be given by

$$v = p(a_1)y_1 + p(a_2)y_2.$$

Now suppose that the firm decides to issue only shares. Then its new market value is given by

$$v' = p(a)y'_1$$

where $y'_1 a = y_1 a_1 + y_2 a_2$ (it is shown in the Appendix that, in the limit $r = \infty$, the price function $p(\cdot)$ will not be affected by a change in one firm's production plan). Now it is easy to show from the first order conditions for utility maximization (see (A.8), (A.11) and Lemma 3) that $v \geqq v'$, i.e. a levered firm is worth at least as much as an unlevered firm. However, since p may be non-linear, we can have $v > v'$.

23. In other words, in general there is a distinction between the size of the market for a firm's product and the size of the aggregate economy. It is the former that determines the extent of a firm's monopoly power. If, however, as we have assumed, the economy is made large by replication, the two concepts coincide.

24. It should perhaps be noted that our results do not deny the existence of any relationship between the amount of product differentiation and the degree of monopoly power. For example, one might expect that, *ceteris paribus*, the more products that are available in the economy, the smaller will be the potential market for each one, and hence the more monopoly power the producer of each product will have. Our point is simply that it is the size of the market rather than the amount of differentiation which is the casual influence here.

25. For a discussion of macroscopic descriptions of economies, see Hildenbrand (1974).

26. I am grateful to William Novshek and Hugo Sonnenschein for pointing out an error in the original proof of Theorem 1.

27. I am grateful to Andreu Mas-Colell for suggesting the use of the Shapley–Folkman theorem in this proof.

REFERENCES

ARROW, K. J. and HAHN, F. H. (1971) *General Competitive Analysis* (San Francisco: Holden-Day, Inc.)
CHAMBERLIN, E. H. (1933) *The Theory of Monopolistic Competition* (Massachusetts: Harvard University Press).
DEBREU, G. (1951), " The Coefficient of Resource Utilization ", *Econometrica*, 19, 273-292.
DIAMOND, P. A. (1967), " The Role of a Stock Market in a General Equilibrium Model with Technological Uncertainty ", *American Economic Review*, 57, 759-776.
DIXIT, A. K. and STIGLITZ, J. E. (1977), " Monopolistic Competition and Optimum Product Diversity ", *American Economic Review*, 67, 297-308.
DRÈZE, J. (1974), " Investment under Private Ownership: Optimality, Equilibrium and Stability ", Chapter 9 in Drèze, J., ed., *Allocation under Uncertainty: Equilibrium and Optimality* (Macmillan).
DRÈZE, J. and HAGEN, K. (1975), " Choice of Product Quality: Equilibrium and Efficiency ", *Econometrica*, Forthcoming.
EKERN, S. and WILSON, R. (1974), " On the Theory of the Firm in an Economy with Incomplete Markets ", *The Bell Journal of Economics and Management Science*, 5 (1), 171-180.
GABSZEWICZ, J. and VIAL, J. (1972), " Oligopoly 'a la Cournot' in General Equilibrium Analysis ", *Journal of Economic Theory*, 4, 381-400.
GROSSMAN, S. J. and HART, O. D. (1976), " A Theory of Competitive Equilibrium in Stock Market Economies ", *Econometrica*, Forthcoming.
HAHN, F. H. (1977), " Exercises in Conjectural Equilibria ", *Scandinavian Journal of Economics*, 79 (2), 210-224.
HANSEN, T. (1969), " A Note on the Limit of the Core of an Exchange Economy ", *International Economic Review*, 10, 479-483.
HILDENBRAND, W. (1974) *Core and Equilibria of a Large Economy* (Princeton University Press).
JENSEN, M. C. and LONG, J. B. (1972), " Corporate Investment under Uncertainty and Pareto Optimality in the Capital Markets ", *The Bell Journal of Economics and Management Science*, 3 (1), 151-174.
KALDOR, N. (1935), " Market Imperfection and Excess Capacity ", *Economica*, 33-50.
LANCASTER, K. (1971) *Consumer Demand, A New Approach* (New York: Columbia University Press).
LELAND, H. (1974), " Production Theory and the Stock Market ", *The Bell Journal of Economics and Management Science*, 5 (1), 125-144.
MAKOWSKI, L. (1976), " A Characterization of Perfectly Competitive Economies with Firms " (mimeo).
MAS-COLELL, A. (1975), " A Model of Equilibrium with Differentiated Commodities ", *Journal of Mathematical Economics*, 2 (2), 263-296.
MERTON, R. and SUBRAHMANYAM, M. (1974), " The Optimality of a Competitive Stock Market ", *The Bell Journal of Economics and Management Science*, 5 (1), 145-170.
OSTROY, J. (1973), " Representation of Large Economies: the Equivalence Theorem " (mimeo).
OSTROY, J. (1976), " The No-Surplus Condition as a Characterization of Perfectly Competitive Equilibrium " (mimeo).

PARTHASARATHY, K. (1967) *Probability Measures on Metric Spaces* (Academic Press).

ROBERTS, D. J. and POSTLEWAITE, A. (1976), " The Incentives for Price-Taking Behavior in Large Exchange Economies ", *Econometrica*, **44**, 115-128.

ROBERTS, J. and SONNENSCHEIN, H. (1977), " On the Foundations of the Theory of Monopolistic Competition ", *Econometrica*, **45**, 101-114.

ROBINSON, J. (1934), " What is Perfect Competition? ", *Quarterly Journal of Economics*, **49**, 104-120.

ROSEN, S. (1974), " Hedonic Prices and Implicit Markets: Product Differentiation in Pure Competition ", *Journal of Political Economy*, 34-55.

ROYDEN, H. L. (1968) *Real Analysis* (London: Macmillan).

RUFFIN, R. J. (1971), " Cournot Oligopoly and Competitive Behaviour ", *Review of Economic Studies*, 493-502.

SAMUELSON, P. (1967), " The Monopolistic Competition Revolution ", in Kuenne, R. E. (ed.) *Monopolistic Competition Theory: Studies in Impact* (New York: Wiley).

SHITOVITZ, B. (1974), " Oligopoly in Markets with a Continuum of Traders ", *Econometrica*, **41**, 467-501.

SPENCE, M. (1976), " Product Selection, Fixed Costs and Monopolistic Competition ", *Review of Economic Studies*, 217-236.

STERN, N. (1972), " The Optimal Size of Market Areas ", *Journal of Economic Theory*, 4(2), 154-173.

STIGLITZ, J. E. (1972), " On the Optimality of the Stock Market Allocation of Investment ", *Quarterly Journal of Economics*, **86**, 25-60.

Name Index

The International Library of Critical Writings in Economics

The Economics of Unemployment
P.N. Junankar

The Economics of Energy
Paul Stevens

The Economics of Science and Innovation
Paula E. Stephan and David B. Audretsch

International Finance
Robert Z. Aliber

Welfare Economics
William J. Baumol and Janusz A. Ordover

The Economics of Crime
Isaac Ehrlich

The Economics of Integration
Willem Molle

The Rhetoric of Economics
Deirdre McCloskey

The Economics of Defence
Keith Hartley and Nicholas Hooper

The Economics of Business Policy
John Kay

The Economics of Increasing Returns
Geoffrey Heal

The Balance of Payments
Michael J. Artis

Cost-Benefit Analysis
Arnold Harberger and Glenn P. Jenkins

Privatization in Developing and Transitional Economies
Colin Kirkpatrick and Paul Cook

The Economics of Intellectual Property
Ruth Towse

The Economics of Tourism
Clem Tisdell

The Economics of Organization and Bureaucracy
Peter Jackson

Realism and Economics: Studies in Ontology
Tony Lawson

The Economics of the Welfare State
Nicholas Barr

Path Dependence
Paul David

Alternative Theories of the Firm
Richard Langlois, Paul Robertson and Tony F. Yu

The Economics of the Mass Media
Glenn Withers

The Economics of Budget Deficits
Charles Rowley

Economic Forecasting
Terence C. Mills

The Economic Theory of Auctions
Paul Klemperer

Corporate Governance
Kevin Keasey, Steve Thompson and Mike Wright

Welfare Measurement
John Creedy

The Economics of Regional Policy
Harvey W. Armstrong and Jim Taylor

Forms of Capitalism: Comparative Institutional Analyses
Ugo Pagano and Ernesto Screpanti